Dictionary of Psychology

Dictionary of Psychology

Howard C. Warren

Routledge
Taylor & Francis Group

First published in 1935 by George Allen & Unwin Ltd.

This edition first published in 2018 by Routledge
2 Park Square, Milton Park, Abingdon, Oxon, OX14 4RN
and by Routledge
711 Third Avenue, New York, NY 10017

Routledge is an imprint of the Taylor & Francis Group, an informa business

Publisher's Note

The publisher has gone to great lengths to ensure the quality of this reprint but points out that some imperfections in the original copies may be apparent.

Disclaimer

The publisher has made every effort to trace copyright holders and welcomes correspondence from those they have been unable to contact.

A Library of Congress record exists under ISBN: 34042807

ISBN 13: 978-1-138-61628-8 (hbk)

ISBN 13: 978-1-138-61634-9 (pbk)

ISBN 13: 978-0-429-46222-1 (ebk)

DICTIONARY OF PSYCHOLOGY

EDITED BY

HOWARD C. WARREN

Princeton University

LONDON

GEORGE ALLEN & UNWIN LTD

MUSEUM STREET

FIRST PUBLISHED IN GREAT BRITAIN 1935

COLLABORATORS

Arthur I. Gates, *Columbia University*
Henry Herbert Goddard, *The Ohio State University*
Samuel P. Hayes, *Mt. Holyoke College*
Harry Helson, *Bryn Mawr College*
H. L. Hollingworth, *Barnard College, Columbia University*
S. J. Holmes, *University of California*
James Quinter Holsopple, *New Jersey State Hospital*
Edwin B. Holt, *Princeton University*
Wilbur S. Hulin, *Princeton University*
Clark L. Hull, *Yale University*
George Humphrey, *Queen's University*
Walter S. Hunter, *Clark University*
Joseph Jastrow, *New School of Social Research, N.Y.*
Arthur Jenness, *University of Nebraska*
H. M. Johnson, *American University*
Truman Lee Kelley, *Harvard University*
Heinrich Klüver, *Institute for Juvenile Research, Chicago*
K. Koffka, *Smith College*
Carney Landis, *Medical Center, Columbia University*
Herbert S. Langfeld, *Princeton University*
K. S. Lashley, *University of Chicago*
James H. Leuba, *formerly of Bryn Mawr College*
Howard Scott Liddell, *Cornell University*
William Line, *University of Toronto*
D. I. Macht, *Johns Hopkins University*
S. O. Mast, *Johns Hopkins University*
William McDougall, *Duke University*
Milton Metfessel, *University of Southern California*
Adolf Meyer, *Johns Hopkins University*
Walter R. Miles, *Yale University*
John J. B. Morgan, *Northwestern University*
Carl Murchison, *Clark University*
Gardner Murphy, *Columbia University*
Elsie Murray, *Cornell University*
John P. Nafe, *Washington University*
Sidney M. Newhall, *Yale University*
Robert M. Ogden, *Cornell University*
James W. Papez, *Cornell University*
Joseph Peterson, *George Peabody College*
Henri Piéron, *Université de Paris*
Walter B. Pillsbury, *University of Michigan*
Rudolf Pintner, *Columbia University*
A. T. Poffenberger, *Columbia University*
Carroll C. Pratt, *Harvard University*
A. A. Roback, *University Extension, Boston, Mass.*
Edward Stevens Robinson, *Yale University*
Christian A. Ruckmick, *University of Iowa*
Herbert Charles Sanborn, *Vanderbilt University*
H. C. Stevens, *Western Reserve University*
George M. Stratton, *University of California*
Lewis M. Terman, *Stanford University*
Miles A. Tinker, *University of Minnesota*
Edward Chace Tolman, *University of California*

COLLABORATORS

Alfred M. Tozzer, *Harvard University*
Lee Edward Travis, *University of Iowa*
Roland C. Travis, *Western Reserve University*
†Leonard T. Troland, *Harvard University*
Carl John Warden, *Columbia University*
Margaret F. Washburn, *Vassar College*
John B. Watson, *formerly of Johns Hopkins University*
†Albert P. Weiss, *The Ohio State University*
H. P. Weld, *Cornell University*
F. L. Wells, *Boston Psychopathic Hospital*
George R. Wells, *Hartford Seminary Foundation*
Ernest Glen Wever, *Princeton University*
Raymond Holder Wheeler, *University of Kansas*
Guy M. Whipple, *formerly of Cornell University*
Raymond Royce Willoughby, *Clark University*
Clark Wissler, *Yale University*
Herbert Woodrow, *University of Illinois*
R. S. Woodworth, *Columbia University*
Kimball Young, *University of Wisconsin*
Paul Campbell Young, *Louisiana State University*
Paul Thomas Young, *University of Illinois*
Michael J. Zigler, *Wellesley College*

† Deceased.

INTRODUCTORY

Scope. — This book is designed to explain the meaning of technical terms which the reader will meet in psychological literature or which the psychologist may wish to use in his writings. It is not a cyclopedia of facts except as these facts help to explain the meaning and bearing of the terms defined.

Contemporary psychology touches upon a variety of neighboring fields — neurology, physiology, anatomy, physics, sociology, education, art, folk-lore, religion, psychiatry, industry, and others. Terms in these subjects have been included so far as they seem relevant to the psychologist's interests. Mathematical and logical terms are also included, since the proper treatment of all scientific data depends upon exact reasoning. Philosophical terms and meanings have been excluded, except where they bear directly upon psychological problems — as for instance the mind-body relation. Psychological terms belonging to earlier literature, and no longer in use, are marked *hist.* (historical). Many terms which the psychologist of today will regard as *pseudoscientific* are inserted for the benefit of readers who may find these subjects discussed in psychological writings.

Vocabulary. — While the function of a dictionary is to record actual (or historic) usage, in a few cases we have found it advisable to suggest slight amendments, either because a term has been misformed or misused, or because such modification would do away with present ambiguity or confusion. Certain psychologists have shown a tendency to coin new terms. Some of these words have come into general use; others have not. In general we have not included terms used only by a single writer. We have also declined (with regret) the suggestions of brand-new terms offered by friendly counselors. Granted that such terms are badly needed in psychology; who would ever discover them, hidden in the bypaths of an alphabetic maze?

In certain cases technical terms coined from Greek or Latin have been misspelled by certain writers, e.g. *ambystoma* for *amblystoma*, *enteroceptor* for *interoceptor*, *scotophilia* or *scoptophilia* for *scopophilia*, *palmesthesia* for *pallesthesia*, *diad* for *dyad*. In such cases we have preferred the correct etymological form.

We have omitted certain terms which seem self-explanatory — whose general, popular meaning is adequate. And it has seemed unnecessary to include negative terms which begin with *un-*, *in-*, or *non-*, if they have no distinctive value in themselves.

English Usage; Foreign Terms. — The prevailing tendency in the sciences is to translate or anglicize foreign technical terms. When there is doubt as to the proper English equivalent, the foreign term is used in the original form for a time, but in the end it is generally modified or replaced. French terms can usually be easily changed into similar English forms, e.g. *questionnaire* into *questionary*; *rôle* into *role*. In constructing new terms, Greek or Latin roots are most acceptable. Linguistic purity requires that both parts of a new word be derived from the same language. A few violations of this rule have persisted, e.g. *monocular*, instead of *uniocular*.

In this volume foreign terms still frequently used are inserted in the proper alphabetic place, and the most suitable translation is given.

French and German technical terms not used in English literature are given under the appropriate English terms when they differ substantially from the latter. It seemed inadvisable to include French or German equivalents which are substantially similar in form to the English term, nor was it feasible to include terms in other foreign languages. The reader's attention is called to the **French Glossary** and

German Glossary at the end of the volume, which will assist him in finding the English equivalent for terms encountered in reading French and German psychological literature.

Principles of Definition. — A fundamental principle in the present work is that a technical definition should be somewhat of the nature of the mathematical equation. It should not be fragmentary, or tautological, or a mere synonym of the term defined. The use of the symbol = is intended to emphasize this ideal, which we realize has not always been successfully attained.

It has also been our aim to separate the definition proper from explanatory matter. The latter is placed separately, in brackets, except for illustrative examples which are sometimes more conveniently annexed (with e.g.) to the definitions.

Pronunciation; Related Terms; Spelling. — It will be noticed that pronunciation is not indicated, except in a few cases. This for two reasons: (1) The technical reader rarely consults his dictionary to find out the pronunciation of a word. (2) If he looks up a word he is apt to ignore the phonetic re-spelling. On the other hand, the statement "Accent **cer-**" is apt to "strike his attention." Only words which we have heard frequently mispronounced, or which are likely to be mispronounced, are so indicated — and that in plain, common English syllables.

For much the same reason, ordinary plural and participial forms are not indicated. It may be assumed that students of psychology will add the -s (or -es), -ing, and -ed, without instruction. Other plural and adjectival forms are given. Cognate verbs or nouns are also indicated, and occasionally adverbs. It has been found convenient to indicate *personal* nouns by the superscript *np*; thus, **psychologist**^{np} means "one who is concerned with psychology."

Where variant spellings are in use today, both (or all) forms are indicated in the *definiendum*, the preferred spelling being given first. We give preference to the standard American spelling (e.g. behavior, fiber) rather than the British (e.g. behaviour, fibre), both because this volume was prepared in America, and because there are more workers and readers in the field of psychology on the American continent than in Britain. In conformity with the prevailing tendency to anglicize foreign words, we give preference to such forms as *repertory*, *questionary*, *program*. Historical variants in spelling are not included.

Special Conventions Adopted. — We have deliberately violated one accepted grammatical rule: *whose* is used for *of which*, in order to simplify certain definitions. We have also ignored the pedantic ban on split infinitives where this construction brings out the meaning more clearly. The word *individual* as used in definitions always means *human* individual, unless specifically qualified. Commas are inserted plentifully, in order to mark off new phases of the definition.

There is no uniform practice in our literature for hyphenation, consolidation without hyphen, or separation of certain terms into two words. We have followed so far as possible the rules adopted in other sciences and the forms given in the Standard Dictionary.

Technical Difficulties. — In preparing our definitions we have been struck by the extreme difficulty of finding a good technical meaning for many of the terms in common psychological use. This is particularly true in the field of emotion. There are hosts of these terms in popular use, which presumably have distinguishable shades of meaning — and which would seem to be fair grist for the psychologist's mill. Yet in many cases the attempt to define them in technical language has proved a failure, and they have been discarded as "merely popular" or "self-explanatory." The fault lies not altogether with the Editor and his associates. In many cases it means that psychology has not yet reached a stage sufficiently advanced to give a technical meaning to these terms. We have cited the field of emotion merely as an example. The same criticism applies to terms in other fields as well. It is our hope that these omissions and the obvious imperfection of many of the definitions may direct research toward widening our knowledge of the processes and phenomena which these terms imply.

There are other omissions from this volume which have not the same justification. We can only plead the rapid advance of psychology in so many directions, which has made the task of collecting terms extremely difficult. Each definition has been passed upon by at least two Collaborators, selected as experts in the topic. In case of irreconcilable disagreement alternative definitions are given. The Editor himself is responsible in every case for the final form.

Acknowledgments.* — The Editor wishes to express his gratitude to the Collaborators, who have spent much time and labor in carefully weighing the meaning of terms in their several fields and in formulating or revising the definitions; to Madison Bentley (Cornell) who for three years served as a member of the Advisory Board; and to the members of the Advisory Board for valuable counsel. He acknowledges also the assistance given by C. F. W. McClure (Princeton) in connection with the Table of Topographical Reference Terms, by Edmund Y. Robbins (Princeton) in preparing the Table of Prefixes and Suffixes, by D. M. Purdy (University of Kansas) in connection with the Table of Spectral Lines and Range of Colors, by Parrish Little Jette, who furnished a large number of statistical and other terms, and by Herbert C. Sanborn, who read the entire preliminary copy and offered many valuable suggestions. E. M. K. Geiling assisted with the proprietary terms; Raymond Willoughby was most helpful in reading the entire galley proof. Incidental suggestions offered by various persons from time to time have proved very useful.

Thanks are due especially to Dorothy J. Brown, Marion N. Hulin, and Anna A. Weelans, not only for their care in transcribing the material, but also for many helpful suggestions which have improved both form and content.

Howard C. Warren

September, 1933.

* Appreciation and gratitude are due Leonard Carmichael of Brown University, editorial advisor in psychology for Houghton Mifflin Company, and Marion N. Hulin, both of whom assisted after Professor Warren's death in preparing the completed manuscript for publication.

ABBREVIATIONS

a = adjective
abbrev. = abbreviation
adv = adverb
advert. = advertising
affect. = affection
ambig. = ambiguous
anal. psychol. = analytical psychology
anat. = anatomy
anthrop. = anthropology
approx. = approximately
A.S. = Anglo-Saxon
arith. = arithmetic
assoc. = association
aud. = audition
beh. = behaviorism
biol. = biology
bot. = botany
cf. = compare
chem. = chemistry
comp. = comparative
contr. w. = contrasted with
corresp. = corresponds, -ing
crim. = criminology
cutan. = cutaneous (sense)
distg. fr. = distinguished from
econ. = economics
educ. = education
e.g. = for example
elect. = electricity
embryol. = embryology
emot. = emotion
epistem. = epistemology
esp. = especially
esth. = esthetics
etymol. = etymology, -gically
exper. = experimental
fem. = feminine
fig. = figuratively
fr. = from
Fr. = French
galv. = galvanic, -ism
geom. = geometry
Ger. = German
Grk. = Greek
hist. = historic(al)
histol. = histology
hypnot. = hypnotism
i.e. = that is
immunol. = immunology
indiv. psychol. = individual psychology
introsp. = introspectionism
kin. = kinesthesia
lang. = language
Lat. = Latin
liter. = literally
math. = mathematics
med. = medicine
metaph. = metaphysics
morphol. = morphology
musc. = muscular
mus. = music
n = noun
neurol. = neurology
np = personal noun
obstet. = obstetrics
ophthal. = ophthalmology
opt. = optics
pathol. = pathology
pharmacol. = pharmacology
phenomen. = phenomenology
philol. = philology
philos. = philosophy
photog. = photography
photom. = photometry
physiol. = physiology
phys. = physics
pl = plural
pop. = popular (usage)
prefd. = preferred
prep = preposition
pron. = pronounced
psychiat. = psychiatry
psychoan. = psychoanalysis
psychol. = psychology
psychophys. = psychophysics
psychophysiol. = psychophysiology
psych. res. = psychic(al) research
relig. = religion
resp. = respectively
rhet. = rhetoric
sens. = sensation, sensory
sing = singular
soc. = social
sociol. = sociology
specif. = specific(ally)
statist. = statistics, -ical
syll. = syllable(s)
syn. = synonym, -ous
tech. = technical
teleol. = teleology
theor. = theoretical(ly)
trans. = translation, -ted
typog. = typography
v = verb
vi = intransitive verb
vis. = vision
viz. = namely
vt = transitive verb
vs. = versus
w. = with
zool. = zoology

DICTIONARY OF PSYCHOLOGY

A

a fortiori = argument in which the conclusion is held to be established by the proof of an analogous or more inclusive proposition of apparently greater improbability. [Lat.]

a posteriori = designating a mode of reasoning or of reaching conclusions in which the final judgment is based upon experience, i.e. is inductive. [Contr. w. **a priori,** in which the judgment is based upon general assumptions. In epistemology **a posteriori** knowledge is contr. w. **a priori** = knowledge existing prior to sensation.]

a priori = (*logic*) designating a mode of reasoning in which conclusions are deduced from definitions or from previously known or assumed premises. [Contr. w. **a posteriori,** in which judgment is based upon former experiences rather than upon accepted generalizations. In epistemology, **a priori knowledge** = knowledge which exists in the mind logically prior to sensory experience; contr. w. **empirical knowledge.**]

AQ = abbrev. for **accomplishment** (or **achievement) quotient.**

'A' test = a test for speed of discrimination, in which the testee is required to cancel every **A** in a long series of capital letters set in page form, in random order, often without spacing between the letters. [Cf. **cancellation test.**]

abdomen = the part of the body between the thorax and the pelvis. (Accent **-doe-.**) **abdominal**[a] (accent **-dom-**). — Ger. *Unterleib, Bauch.*

abdominal reflex = contraction of the muscles of the ventral abdominal wall on sudden stroking of the skin lateral to the rectus abdominis. [Mediated by 8th to 12th thoracic segments.]

abdominocardiac reflex = slowing of the heart after mechanical irritation of the abdominal aortic plexus. [Mediated by 1st to 10th thoracic segments. Syn. **Livierato's sign.**]

abducens, abducent nerve = the VIth cranial nerve, which innervates exclusively the external rectus muscle of the eyeball.

aberration/mental = mental unsoundness, as evidenced by the individual's abnormal behavior. [The term is used pop. to denote episodic abnormality, and more technically to denote mental disorder without defining its character.] — Ger. *Geistesstörung.*

aberration of light = (*opt., vis.*) the passage of light by paths other than those making for the efficiency of an optical system (including that of the eye), and exclusive of the effect of poor adjustment of focus. [Cf. **defect/optical, chromatic aberration, spherical aberration, diffusion circle** (2).] — Fr. *aberration de la lumière*; Ger. *Abweichung des Lichtes.*

abient = tending to remove the organism from the source of stimulation. [Syn. **negative, avoiding, avoidant.** Contr. w. **adient.**]

ability = power to perform responsive acts, including complex coordinated movements and solution of mental problems. [An organism's degree of ability is usually measured by the complexity of the acts of behavior which it performs and the rapidity and precision of performance. In general, a distinction is made between **ability** (= what can be done with present training and development), **capability** (= what can be accomplished in the present stage of development with additional training), and **capacity** (= the potentiality of the organism as provided and limited by native constitution). **special abilities,** peculiar to certain types of performance, are distinguished from **general ability,** conceived as a factor present in different degrees in different individuals and operating in all or many types of performance. Cf. **differentiable abilities, factor theories.**] — Fr. *capacité, habileté*; Ger. *Fähigkeit, Eignung, Begabung.*

ability distribution = a frequency distribution of measures indicative of some ability. [Cf. **frequency distribution.**] — Fr. *distribution de capacité.*

ability/initial,—/final = the ability which a learner possesses at the beginning (**initial**) and at the end (**final**) of a period of systematic practice.

ability/special, see **special abilities.**

ability/specific, see **specific ability.**

abiogenesis, see **spontaneous generation.**

Abklingen = the fading out of a tone or other sensation, involving either an intensive or a qualitative change or both. [Ger.]

abnormal = widely divergent from the norm or type. [Characterizing actions, mentality, modes of behavior, etc. of an organism, which differ so much from the average, sane, healthy, or typical that they are not readily treated as belonging to the same group or series. Frequently confused with **pathological,** which designates one ground of abnormality; abnormal phenomena or individuals may be either **subnormal, supernormal,** or qualitatively deranged or disorderly, i.e. **extranormal.**] **abnormality**[n].

abnormal mental processes = mental processes which diverge strikingly from those typical of the species. [Usually restricted to pathological cases. Cf. **abnormal psychology.**]

abnormal psychology = the investigation of abnormal behavior, mental processes, and phenomena. [It includes (*a*) pathological psychology, (*b*) psychology of superior individuals, (*c*) special mental conditions such as dreams, hypnosis, etc.] — Ger. *pathologische Psychologie.*

aboral = (in lower animals) pert. to or located in the region farthest from the mouth. [Syn. **anal.**] (Accent **-o-.**)

aboulia, see **abulia.**

abreaction = (*psychoan.*) the process of working off or discharging a pent-up emotion or a disagreeable experience by living it through again in speech, action, or feeling, usually (but not always) in the presence of the psychoanalyst. [Syn. **cathartic method.**] — Fr. *abréaction*; Ger. *Abreagierung.*

abridgment of response = a shortening of the processes of executing an act of behavior, following practice. — Fr. *abréviation de réaction.*

abscess of the brain = a localized collection of pus, often originating in the brain envelopes. — Fr. *abcès cérébral.*

abscissa = the horizontal axis of reference in a two-dimensional chart. [Syn. **base line**; contr. w. **ordinate.**]

absent-mindedness = the tendency to be absorbed in trains of thought or in special features of a situation, and to be inattentive to surrounding conditions. [**absent-mindedness** denotes a general characteristic; **abstraction** or absence of mind (*pop.*) applies to a particular instance, whether characteristic of the individual or incidental.] — Fr. *distraction*; Ger. *Geistesabwesenheit.*

Absicht = purpose, intention; a certain relation between *Zielvorstellung* and *Bezugsvorstellung* (Ach). [Ger.]

absolute = characteristic of an object or phenomenon by itself, as distg. fr. its relations to other objects or phenomena (except the standard). [Cf. **absolute impression, pitch/absolute.** Contr. w. **relative.**]

absolute accommodation, see **accommodation/absolute.**

absolute impression = a judgment of the intensity, brightness, etc. of a stimulus in isolation from any other stimulus. [Distg. fr. **comparative judgment.**] — Ger. *absoluter Eindruck.*

absolute judgment = a comparative judgment in which, as a result of previous experience with the presented series of stimuli as a whole, the first member of a pair is evaluated with respect to the second before the latter is actually presented.

absolute judgment/method of = a psychophysical method in which no standard stimulus is used, and each member of the series of variables is judged by absolute impression, being related to a subjective impression of the range of the series as a whole which had been built up by experience. [Syn. **method of single stimuli.** Contr. w. **method of constant stimuli** (DL form) in which the observer is required to compare each stimulus with a given standard stimulus that is presented in conjunction with it.]

absolute pitch, see **pitch/absolute.**

absolute sensitivity = degree of sensory acuity, as measured by (*a*) magnitude of the stimulus required to evoke a minimal sensory response, or by (*b*) amount of sensation in terms of the appropriate standard unit. [Contr. w. **relative sensitivity** = degree of acuity as measured by amount of change in stimulation required to make a minimal discriminative response.]

absolute threshold (or **limen**), see **threshold.** — Fr. *seuil absolu.*

absolute value = (*math.*) the value of a magnitude without regard to sign. [E.g. the absolute value of $+7$ or of -7 is 7, written $|+7|=|-7|=7$.]

absorption = a high degree of attention to one thought, object, or activity, with inattention to others. [Syn. **abstraction,** which emphasizes the ineffectiveness of the external situation. Cf. **concentration.**] — Ger. *Vertiefung* (Herbart).

abstract = 1. characterizing that which cannot be directly perceived through the senses; 2. characterizing an item, aspect, or unit viewed apart from the organized whole to which it belongs. [E.g. (1) meanness; (2) man considered in isolation from society, or society in isolation from the universe; all general terms are abstract. Contr. w. **concrete.**]

abstract idea = an idea which means an aspect or quality of an object or group of experiences rather than the object or experiences themselves. [Since it implies or derives from several experiences rather than one, an abstract idea may be said to involve generalization as well as abstraction. Cf. **general idea, concept.**]

abstract intelligence = 1. the effective use of abstract concepts and symbols in dealing with novel situations; 2. such intelligence as is measured by tests requiring the use of abstract concepts, and of verbal, numerical, and other symbols. [Distg. fr. **mechanical** or **concrete intelligence,** and fr. **social intelligence.**]

abstract reasoning = reasoning or working out conclusions concerning abstract rather than concrete subject-matter. [Cf. **abstraction.**] — Fr. *raisonnement abstrait.*

abstract thought, abstract thinking = a train of thought whose subject-matter is general rather than concrete, as in dealing with geometry or philosophy. — Fr. *pensée abstraite.*

abstraction = 1. absorption in thought, with inattention to external events (syn. **absent-mindedness**); 2. the mental process in which some attribute or characteristic is observed independently of other characteristics or of an experience as a whole. [(2) may be either logical, as in a conscious analysis, or the result of an instruction (Aufgabe) or of other prior determination.] (1) **abstracted**[a]; (2) **abstractive**[a] (pert. to the process); (2) **abstract**[a] (pert. to the result). — Ger. (1) *Geistesabwesenheit,* (2) *Abstraktion.*

abstraction experiment = 1. an experiment in which the observer is limited by the **Aufgabe,** or instructions, to a partial aspect of a perceptual situation, so that he cannot later report upon other aspects of it; 2. an experiment in which **situations** or perceptual **wholes** are presented successively to a subject until he can recognize or respond to the common features which he has thus abstracted from the total entities. [(1) is a specialized but common use that has been derived from the **abstraction experiment** of Külpe (1904); (2) applies in general to experimental research on **abstraction.**]

absurdity = an irreconcilable contradiction between a given conclusion and certain known or accepted general truths. [It is generally implied that the contradiction is easily recognizable.] **absurd**[a]. — Ger. *Sinnwidrigkeit.*

absurdities test = a kind of test in which the task is to point out an incongruity or absurdity in a given verbal statement or picture. [Most commonly applied to absurd or self-contradictory statements. E.g. "I have three brothers, Paul, Ernest, and myself." Included by Binet in his 1908 Intelligence Scale.]

abulia, aboulia = inability to arrive at decisions and volitions and their activation. — Ger. *Willenslosigkeit, Willensschwäche, Abulie.*

acatamathesis = 1. inability to comprehend language; 2. defective perception.

acataphasia, akataphasia = a disorder of vocal language, characterized by inability to connect words properly in sentences.

acceleration = 1. (broadly) rate of change (either positive or negative) in the velocity of a moving body; 2. (more narrowly) rate of increase in velocity (rate of decrease being denoted by **deceleration**). [**acceleration** is uniform when the change in velocity per unit time dv/dt remains constant.] — Ger. *Beschleunigung*.

acceleration/zero = a constant rate of growth or a constant rate of improvement in function due to practice. [Distg. fr. **growth** or **improvement,** in which the rate increases (= **positive acceleration**) or decreases (= **negative acceleration**).]

accelerator nerve = 1. any nerve which hastens or promotes the performance of a function; 2. (specifically) the cardiac sympathetic nerve, which quickens the heart-beat; it is opposed to the inhibitory N. vagus of the parasympathetic nervous system. [Contr. w. **depressor nerve.**]

accent, see **ictus.**

acceptance = an experience, or feature of experience or behavior, characterized by a positive (approaching) attitude toward some concept, or judgment. [Syn. **belief.** Contr. w. **rejection** = **disbelief.**]

accessory nerve/spinal = the XIth cranial nerve, a nerve which partly unites with the vagus nerve, sending fibers to the heart and to other viscera, and by a separate branch to the sternomastoid and the trapezius muscles.

accessory sense-apparatus = all cells and tissues of a sense organ which contribute to the effective functioning of the organ, but which are not themselves part of the afferent nerves or special receptor cells of the organ in question. — Fr. *appareil sensoriel, accessoire*; Ger. *Hilfsapparat*.

accidental = characterizing that which is held to have no cause or which occurs without anyone's intent and hence is unpredictable. [Cf. **chance, random.**] — Ger. *zufällig*.

accidental error = the relatively small, variable, unpredictable amount by which a single observation or measurement differs from the mean of a series of similar observations after all controllable sources of error have been eliminated. [Such observations usually tend to distribute themselves normally about a mean value; consequently the positive and negative errors tend to balance. If there is no source of constant error effective, the accidental error of each observation should be, theoretically, the measure of its departure from the true value, because the true value should then coincide with the mean. Accidental errors in psychological experimentation are due to varying factors within the individual observer and in the external environment, including apparatus and experimenter.]

accommodation = (*vis.*) change in shape of the eye-lens as the individual focuses for a different distance. [The curvature increases for a nearer focus; cf. **accommodation sensation.**]

accommodation/absolute = the accommodation of either eye separately, i.e. with binocular vision excluded, e.g. by covering the other eye. [Cf. **accommodation/relative.**]

accommodation muscle, see **ciliary muscle.**

accommodation of attention, see **attention/accommodation of.**

accommodation/relative = an alteration of accommodation, or a change in the focusing of the crystalline lenses, relative to that which is normal for a given state of convergence of the two eyes. [**relative accommodation** involves a certain deviation from normal coordination of convergence and accommodation.]

accommodation sensation = a sensation which accompanies changes of visual accommodation, attributed to changes in tension of the ciliary muscle that controls the shape of the lens.

accommodation time = (*vis.*) temporal duration from the moment a visual stimulus is presented in the line of regard until the lenses of the eyes have become adjusted for clear vision of the object. — Fr. *temps d'accommodation*.

accompanying movement = any movement of other parts of the body which occurs simultaneously with a given response, but is not treated as an integral part of that response. [E.g. scowling or winking in performing a new and difficult act; symmetrical movements of the left side in connection with actions involving the right side. Syn. **synkinesis.**] — Fr. *mouvement associé*.

accomplishment quotient = 1. the ratio of actual achievement (of an individual or group) to a standard or expected accomplishment; 2. the ratio between achievement age (however determined) and mental age (however determined). [Abbrev. **AQ.** Cf. **achievement quotient.**]

accord[v] = (*mus.*) to agree or harmonize, as in the tuning of musical instruments.

acculturation = the process of acquiring a culture through contact of one tribe with another, or with a more advanced people, by borrowing or by diffusion.

accuracy = absence (or relative absence) of error. [In a report, and in testimony, the degree of accuracy is measured by the correspondence between the statement and the objective facts or occurrences; in behavior it is measured by the degree in which the action conforms to the given conditions of the problem or to the requirements of the task. Progress in learning is measured sometimes in terms of increasing accuracy, sometimes in terms of decreasing time. Cf. **precision, error, speed.**] **accurate**[a]. — Fr. *précision*; Ger. *Genauigkeit*.

accuracy score = the number of items in a test to which the testee responds correctly. [Contr. w. **speed score.**] — Fr. *note de précision*.

acephalia, acephalism, acephaly = the state of being congenitally without a head. **acephalous**[a].

acephalous[a] = 1. headless; 2. pert. to the Acephala, or bivalve mollusks.

achievement = 1. proficiency of performance, generally measured by a standardized task or test; 2. the act of attaining an end, or of carrying out a purpose. [**achievement** (1) is more commonly applied to performance in educational than in psychological tests, i.e. it implies demonstration of acquired ability rather than inherent capacity. Syn. (1) **accomplishment, performance, attainment.** Cf. **achievement test.**] — Fr. *rendement*; Ger. *Leistung*.

achievement age = the chronological age at which, on the average, a given score is found to be attained on an achievement test. [In effect, it is an empirically determined norm, or standard, expressed in terms of life age, which corresponds to a given score on an educational test, as distinguished from an intelligence test. Syn. **educational age.** The achievement age divided by the chronological age gives the educational quotient or **achievement quotient;** divided by the mental age it gives the **accomplishment quotient,** or **AQ.** Cf. **mental age.**] — Fr. *âge de rendement.*

achievement quotient, AQ = the ratio between achievement age and chronological age. [Cf. **accomplishment quotient.**]

achievement test = a test designed to measure the progress which a testee has made in the mastery of anything to be learned, such as arithmetic, reading, spelling, writing, typing, etc. [Distg. fr. a test designed to measure intelligence, aptitude, or capacity to achieve.] — Fr. *épreuve (test) de rendement.*

Achilles' tendon reflex = contraction of the gastrocnemius complex of the calf of the leg, producing plantar flexion of the foot when the calcaneal tendon is sharply tapped or the anterior tibial muscles are percussed. [Mediated by 2d sacral segment of the cord. Syn. **ankle r., tendo calcaneus r., tendo Achillis r.**] — Fr. *réflexe Achilléen*; Ger. *Achillessehnenreflex.*

achondroplasia, achondroplasty = developmental absence of the cartilage at the epiphyses of the long bones, resulting in a characteristic form of dwarfism.

achromatic = 1. (*psychol.*) lacking in chroma (i.e. hue and saturation), so as to fall in the series of colors which vary only in brilliance, from black to white; 2. (*phys.*) characterizing any optical system in which the final distribution of rays is wholly or substantially independent of their wave-lengths, for the range of wave-lengths considered, i.e. which is corrected for **chromatic aberration.** — Ger. (1) *farblos, tonfrei.*

achromatic color = a visual quality which belongs to the white-gray-black series, i.e. one which exhibits no hue or saturation and hence is characterized solely by its brilliance.

achromatism, achromasy, achromatic vision = defective color vision, hereditary or acquired, in which all colors appear as grays. [Syn. **total color-blindness, monochromatism, achromatopsia.** Ordinarily accompanied by photophobia, amblyopia, presence (independent of illumination) of the Purkinje phenomenon, and often by central scotoma and nystagmus. Cf. **color-blindness.**] **achromatope**[np], **achromate**[np].

achromatopsia, see **achromatism.**

acid, acidulous, see **sour.**

acmesthesia, acmaesthesia = tactual perception of pointedness devoid of pain, resulting from contact with sharp objects. [Syn. **acuesthesis.**]

acoasma = an auditory hallucination in which indefinite sounds are heard.

aconative = not involving conation, i.e. volition or desire (Baldwin). (Accent **-ko-.**)

acoumeter, see **audiometer.**

acoumetry = the quantitative determination of auditory intensive sensitivity. [Syn. **audiometric measurement.**]

acousma = a form of auditory hallucination with a sensory defect.

acousimeter, see **audiometer.**

acoustic nerve, see **auditory nerve.**

acoustic ossicle, see **ossicle/auditory.**

acoustic shadow = (*phys.*) a region of reduced pressure beyond some rigid body in the path of an advancing sound-wave. — Fr. *ombre acoustique.*

acoustics = 1. the investigation of sound; 2. the branch of physics which deals with sound reflection and transmission, with special reference to the conditions for distinct hearing (e.g. in auditoriums); 3. the conditions characteristic of a given room or building relevant to distinctness of hearing, such as the nature of the sound reflecting and absorbing surfaces, their form, size, and mutual relations. [Improperly used also as syn. for **audition** = the branch which investigates the physiological and psychological effects of sound vibrations.] **acoustic**[a]. — Ger. *Akustik.*

acquaintance with = experience with. [Denotes the direct perception of objects, as distg. fr. **comprehension** = indirect knowledge about them.] — Fr. *la connaissance*; Ger. *Bekanntschaft.*

acquired character = a modification, either structural or functional, which occurs in an organism as a result of its own activities or through the influence of the environment. [It is generally held that such modifications are not heritable.] — Fr. *caractère acquis*; Ger. *erworbene Eigenschaft.*

acquired responses (or **reactions**) = modes of response which are not inherited but are built up during the individual's life-time. [Contr. w. **inherited** (or **congenital**) **reactions or responses.**]

acquisition = 1. the formation of a new mode of behavior; 2. the obtaining of new ideas; 3. (*econ.*) the appropriation or obtaining possession of objects. [The result of such processes is called **an acquisition.** Cf. **learning.**] **acquire**[v]. — Ger. *Aneignung.*

acquisitiveness = behavior in certain species which results in the possession of nutritive or other objects and in the hoarding of them. [Sometimes regarded as an instinct or an inherited tendency.]

acro-agnosis = inability to appreciate kinesthetic configurations.

acro-anesthesia = loss of sensitivity in the extremities of the human limbs.

acro-esthesia, acro-aesthesia, acro-a(e)sthesis = 1. increased sensitiveness; 2. pain in the extremities.

acromegaly = a disease characterized by non-congenital hypertrophic changes in the skeleton and other connective tissues, the face, head, hands, and feet being especially involved. [Syn. **Marie's disease. acromegaly** is caused by a pituitary hyperfunction produced by an adenoma composed of the acidophilic cells of the anterior hypophysis; it is sometimes accompanied by genital atrophy, polyuria, glycosuria, and other symptoms which are of separate etiology. Distg. fr. **pituitary gigantism** = a disease of identical etiology, in which the hyperpituitarism commences while the cartilages are still unossified, resulting in abnormal length of the long bones.] **acromegalic**[a].

acromial reflex = partial pronation or flexion (or both) of the forearm when the region of the acromial process in the shoulder is tapped. [Mediated by 4th cervical to 1st thoracic segments of the cord.]

acromion = the point or bony process of the shoulder. **acromial**[a] (accent **-cro-**).

acroparesthesia = recurrent numbness, usually of the hands or finger-tips.

acrophobia = morbid fear of being on high places.

act^n = a mental process, or psychical phenomenon, which is characterized by the intentional inherence of an object. [There are, according to Brentano, three general classes: (1) ideating = seeing, hearing, imagining, etc.; (2) loving-hating = feeling, wishing, etc.; (3) judging = acknowledging, recalling, willing, etc.] — Ger. *Akt.*

act^v = 1. to operate, work, perform a function; 2. to do something with desire for the outcome of the performance and with a feeling that one is the performer. (1) **activity**^{n}, **actively**^{a}; (2) **action**^{n}, **act**^{n} (a completed or total action), **actively**^{a}. — Fr. *agir.*

act psychology = 1. a system of psychology which holds that every psychical phenomenon is characterized by the intentional inherence of an object; 2. a system of psychology in which the data are psychic activities, usually of a subject upon an object. [(1) generally implies (2) and comes directly from Aristotle through the Scholastics. Brentano (1874) is the modern representative of (1). (2) does not always imply (1), as in Külpe's later views. Syn. (1) **intentionalism**; (2) **functional psychology** (1).] — Ger. *Aktpsychologie.*

actinia = a genus of non-colonial sea-anemones belonging to the order Actiniaria, coelenterate animals with no free-swimming stage.

actinic rays = radiant energy of the short-waved visible and of the ultraviolet region of the spectrum, formerly thought to be the only rays capable of producing chemical effects.

action = 1. a general term for all movements or patterns of movements with which certain conscious patterns are or have been correlated; 2. syn. for **behavior.** [Cf. **impulsive action, selective action, automatic action.**] — Ger. *Handlung, Tätigkeit, Wirkung.*

action current = an electric current which accompanies a wave of excitation in a nerve, muscle, or gland. [It is observed on a galvanometer as a negative deflection. May be recorded by means of an oscillograph with amplifying circuits.] — Ger. *Aktionsstrom.*

action/stream of = the succession of activities on the part of an organism. [Suggested as a complementary or substitutive concept for stream of consciousness.]

action system = 1. (*morphol.*) the structural basis of movements in an organism; 2. (*physiol.*) the total possible movements of an organism as determined by its structure.

active (or **activity**) **experience** = an experience derived mainly from the kinesthetic senses.

active powers = (*hist.*) the mental faculties concerned in action and emotion. [Reid and his followers divided the mind into (*a*) intellectual or cognitive powers, and (*b*) active or motive powers.] — Fr. *facultés actives.*

active therapy = (*psychoan.*) a method of treatment sometimes resorted to in analysis in which the analyst, assuming a more active role than in the usual procedure, imposes certain prohibitions or artificial situations, in order to elicit more unconscious material and thus break down resistances that were retarding the analysis.

activity = 1. (*pop.*) change or motion in general; 2. any mental or biological process dependent on the life of the organism and on the utilization of energy stored within the organism; 3. any mental or motor process conceived as dependent on the initiative of the individual; 4. organized motion. **active**^{a}. — Ger. *Aktivität, Tätigkeit.*

activity cage = a cage equipped with a recording device for registering some phase of the motor activity of an animal placed within; a common type is a cylindrical cage which the animal can rotate about its (horizontal) axis by walking or running, or which the experimenter can rotate by hand or motor; usually provided with a mechanical revolution counter. [Cf. **cyclostat.**]

activity/feeling of = according to Wundt, an essential qualitative part of the experience during a volitional act, which follows a parallel course, increasing and decreasing with volitional experience. [In external volitional acts it has a sensational substratum of tension.] — Ger. *Tätigkeitsgefühl.*

actual = actively present or manifesting itself dynamically at the given moment, in contrast with potential or latent possibilities. [Often used syn. w. **real;** the latter is a broader term, including all existing facts and relations, whether actual or potential; **real** is often restricted to objective existence, while **actual** includes subjective phenomena as well. Thus also opposed to **real** as meaning the phenomenally given in experience, whereas **real** applies to objects or constructs which are derived from but are not in experience (Külpe).] — Ger. *wirklich.*

actual neurosis = (*psychoan.*) a neurosis of physical origin representing the direct somatic consequence of sexual disturbances. [The individual symptoms are in themselves purely physical processes, which arise without any of the complicated mental mechanisms characteristic of the psychoneuroses. E.g. **neurasthenia, anxiety neurosis.**]

acuity = ability to distinguish sensory impressions in space or direction, esp. in the visual and tactual modalities. [**auditory acuity** refers to the ability to hear sounds of low intensity. Cf. **visual acuity.**] **acute**^{a}. — Ger. *Sinnesschärfe.*

acute = 1. able to discriminate or differentiate to a high degree, either in general discernment (e.g. acute thinking), or in regard to spatial details (e.g. acute sensitivity); 2. intense or severe (e.g. acute pain); 3. applied to certain disorders, characterizing their sudden appearance and rapid culmination as contr. w. **chronic;** 4. characterizing an angle of less than 90°. **acuity, acuteness**^{n}. — Fr. *aigu*; Ger. (1) *scharfsinnig,* (2) *heftig,* (3) *akut,* (4) *spitz.*

acute hallucinosis = a state akin to delirium but without clouding of consciousness, usually a panic, toxic or emotional (often over sexual arousal), with hallucinations (usually auditory) of comment, threat, or accusation. [Usually lasting a number of weeks and sometimes associated with other psychoses.] — Fr. *hallucinose aiguë.*

adaptability = the ability of an individual to make more or less successful adjustments in behavior in response to social situations or to the general environment. [Nearly syn. w. **docility.**] **adaptable**^{a}. — Ger. *Anpassungsfähigkeit.*

adaptation = 1. (*biol.*) any change in an organism, either in form or in function, which renders it better able to maintain its life or to perpetuate its kind. [The result of the adaptation process is **adjustment.**] **adapt**^{v}, **adaptive**^{a} (pert. to the result), **adaptational**^{a} (pert. to the process). — Ger. *Anpassung.*

adaptation = 2. (*psychol.*) the change in quality, intensity, or clearness of a sensory experience, which occurs with continuous, unchanged stimulation. [E.g. in vision, olfaction, touch, pain, gustation.]

adaptation = 3. (*vis.*) a set of processes which occur in the retina after change of exposure from light to dark (or vice versa), whereby the eye is better fitted to receive stimuli under the new conditions. [It includes (1) **scotopic (dark) adaptation** = increase of brilliance of fixed stimuli, due to decrease of general illumination; (2) **photopic (light) adaptation** = decrease of brilliance of fixed stimuli, due to increased intensity of general illumination; (3) **chromatic adaptation** = alteration of hue or saturation (or both) due to preëxposure to light of a certain other wave-length; syn. **chromatic** (or **color**) **fatigue.** Cf. **Purkinje phenomenon.**]

adaptation in learning = a change in an organism's mode of behavior which results in more effective or more satisfactory adjustment to the situation. [Not to be confused with **negative adaptation,** the gradual *loss* of effectiveness of a stimulating situation.] — Fr. *adaptation d'apprentissage.*

adaptation/social, see **social adaptation.**

adaptation time = 1. the time which elapses from the onset of a continuous stimulation until a point is reached beyond which (the stimulation remaining constant) there is no further change in the sense organ or its responsiveness; 2. (*attention*) the length of the period during which there is a diminution in clearness of response to a given kind or intensity of stimulation; 3. (loosely) the time taken to adjust oneself to efficient performance of a task. — Fr. *temps d'adaptation*; Ger. *Adaptationszeit.*

adaptive = 1. promoting improvement; 2. pert. to **adaptation.** [N.B. **adaptive** is used as a generic term to characterize both inherited and acquired modes of behavior; inherited behavior is said to be *racially* adaptive, and acquired (or intelligent) behavior to be *individually* adaptive.]

adaptive adaptation, see **economy of effort.**

adaptive response = any response which is appropriate to the situation, i.e. which promotes the organism's life processes. [Used to characterize both **instinctive responses** (= adaptive by racial evolution) and **intelligent responses** (= adaptive by individual learning).]

adaptometer = any device for measuring the course or degree of sensory adaptation, in terms of fall or rise of threshold or sensitivity. [**dark adaptation** is commonly measured in terms of the simple light threshold, the **adaptometer** consisting of a variable, measured light stimulus of low brightness.]

addict = a person pathologically habituated to alcohol or narcotic drugs and unable to desist from their use. (Accent **ad-**.) — Fr. *toxicomane.*

Addison's disease = a disease characterized by asthenia, prostration, progressive anemia, low arterial pressure, digestive disturbance, and a bronzelike pigmentation of the skin, due to hypofunction of the adrenal cortex.

addition test = a test in which the task is arithmetical addition, performance being scored in terms of speed or accuracy or both.

adendritic = without dendrites. [Characterizing a certain type of neuron.]

adenoids = 1. overgrowths of lymphatic tissue; 2. (more specifically) overgrowths of lymphatic tissue in the nasopharynx, resulting in mouth-breathing.

adequate stimulus = the type of stimulus which normally serves to excite a given receptor. [E.g. light is the adequate stimulus of the eye. Contr. w. **inadequate stimulus** = some unusual type of stimulus which operates upon a receptor; e.g. an electric current passed through the head may be an inadequate stimulus of vision; electrolysis is an inadequate stimulus of taste, etc. The terms are awkward in English and might well be replaced by **normal** and **abnormal,** or **appropriate** and **inappropriate.**] — Fr. *stimulus adéquat*; Ger. *adäquater Reiz.*

adient = tending to expose the organism to the continued action of a stimulus. [Used to describe the orienting effects of a response with reference to a stimulus. Syn. **positive.** Contr. w. **abient.**]

adjustment = any operation whereby an organism or organ becomes more favorably related to the environment, or to the entire situation, environmental and internal. [Often used syn. w. **adaptation** and **accommodation.** Strictly, **accommodation** denotes the change itself, **adjustment** the bringing about of a new relation, **adaptation** the improvement resulting from the change.] — Ger. *Anpassung.*

adjustment levels = degrees in complexity of behavior integration in the human individual. — Fr. *niveaux d'ajustement.*

adjustment/method of, see **average error/method of.**

adjustment/neural = the action of the central nervous system whereby the incoming impulses are transformed into outgoing impulses.

adjustment of observations, adjustment of measurements = 1. (*tech.*) the process of determining by the principle of least squares the best or most probable value to represent a series of independent and differing measurements of the same magnitude; 2. any correction, weighting, or reinterpretation of observed values aiming to offset the effects of disturbing conditions. [According to the theory of least squares, the arithmetic mean is the best value for representing a simple series of direct measurements.]

adjustment/physical = the harmonizing of the human organism with its physical environment.

adjustment/social, see **social adjustment.**

adjustor = (*biol.*) the central or ganglionic part of a reflex arc (Parker). [Syn. **connectors** (pfd.).]

admiration = an attitude characterized by approval of a certain act or course of action, together with a feeling of sympathy towards the performer. — Ger. *Bewunderung.*

adolescence = the period in human life during which the reproductive functions mature, i.e. the period between the onset of puberty and adulthood. [Cf. **puberty.** Contr. w. **senescence.**] **adolescent**[a]. — Ger. *Jünglingsalter, Jugend(zeit).*

adoration = a social or religious attitude involving intense esteem for one who is held to be in a position higher than oneself. — Ger. *Anbetung.*

adrenal = located near the kidneys. [Cf. **adrenal glands.**]

adrenal glands = paired compound endocrine glands situate in the retroperitoneal tissue adjacent to the kidneys. [They vary in shape, size, and position among different species. Each gland consists of two distinct parts: (*a*) an internal **medulla** (developed from the same neuroblast-masses that give rise to the cells of the sympathetic ganglia) which yields adrenalin, a sympathicomimetic autacoid; (*b*) an external **cortex** of mesodermal origin which yields an autacoid (or autacoids) necessary for life but of unknown nature and action. Syn. **adrenals, adrenal capsules, atrabiliary capsules, suprarenals, suprarenal capsules, suprarenal glands.** Cf. **epinephrin.**] **adrenal**[a]. — Fr. *capsules surrénales*; Ger. *Nebennieren.*

adrenalin(e) (accent **-ren-**), see **epinephrin.**

adrenals, see **adrenal glands.**

adrenin (accent **-ree-**), see **epinephrin.**

adult = 1. an individual who has completed his growth; 2. (*legal*) in the U.S., a person over 21 years of age. **adult**[a]. — Ger. *Erwachsener.*

advantage/law of = one of four laws of response formulated by Woodworth, which states that, "Of two or more inconsistent responses to the same situation, one has an advantage over the others, and is more dependable than the others." — Fr. *loi d'avantage.*

advertising = the process of notifying or persuading people without personal solicitation. — Fr. *réclame*; Ger. *Reklame* (= advertisement).

ae-, æ- = alternative spelling for **e-**. [E.g. aesthesiometer, aesthetics, etc.; see **esthesiometer, esthetics,** etc.]

affect = 1. a stimulus or motive which arouses feeling rather than perception or thought; 2. the diffusely regulative reaction thus aroused, with evidence of a visceral component; 3. (*psychoan.*) the dynamic and essential constituent of emotion. [(2) is an inclusive term, used to denote any variety of emotional experience or emotional concomitants, esp. a strong emotion, and also moods. **pleasantness** and **unpleasantness** denote specific feeling qualities; **affect** denotes feeling qualities in general. Not to be confused with **affection.**] — Fr. *affect, état affectif*; Ger. *Gemütsbewegung, Affekt.*

affect/displacement of = (*psychoan.*) movement of affect from one idea to another, in which the second idea may be a representative of the first (Freud).

affect/fixation of = (*psychoan.*) a condition of mental development in which the individual remains attached to feelings which are characteristic of (or dominant in) an earlier phase of development.

affect psychoses, affective psychoses = psychoses which are especially characterized by disturbances in the emotional life. [Largely used as syn. for **manic-depressive psychosis.**]

affection = 1. feeling and emotion generally, as distg. fr. (*a*) **cognition** and (*b*) **volition;** 2. any elementary or simple feeling, e.g. pleasantness, unpleasantness, distg. fr. **sensation** and **idea;** 3. (*pop.*) **love,** esp. in its milder and (often) nonsexual forms. **affective**[a] (1); **affectionate**[a] (2).

affective = a generic adjective used to connote any variety of feeling, emotional experience, or emotional concomitant. [Distg. fr. **affectionate** = manifesting affection or love.]

affective experience = an experience or mental state which is characterized by feeling tone.

affective failure = extreme deficiency or complete inadequacy of the individual's emotional adjustment. [Applied to either a sporadic or a permanent condition.] — Fr. *défaillance affective.*

affective state = 1. a generic term used to denote any variety of emotional experience or emotional concomitant; 2. pleasantness or unpleasantness.

affective tone, see **feeling tone.** — Fr. *tonalité affective.*

affectivity = 1. susceptibility to affective stimuli or disposed to affective experiences and affective responses; 2. a generalized emotional reaction which has definite effects upon the body and mind (Bleuler). [Contr. (1) w. **sensitivity.**]

afferent = leading toward; conducting or conveying from the periphery toward a more central region of the body, i.e. distal-proximally. [As applied to nerves, conducting from receptor organs toward the central nervous system; syn. **sensory.** Contr. w. **efferent** (or **motor**) = conducting from a central region toward the periphery (or toward muscles).] — Ger. *zentripetal.*

after-brain, see **myelencephalon.**

after-care = the care or nursing of convalescents; specifically, the treatment of patients discharged from hospitals or from the physician's supervision. — Fr. *soins de convalescence.*

after-discharge = the discharge of neural impulses from a strongly excited nerve center, continued after the exciting stimulus has ceased to act. — Fr. *décharge consécutive.*

after-effect = 1. the experience which under certain conditions follows the removal of a stimulus; it may be continuous with the primary experience or may follow after an interval of time; 2. an after-image or after-sensation. [(2) used to avoid the implication of central or peripheral origin; syn. **after-experience.**] — Fr. *effet consécutif*; Ger. *Nachwirkung.*

after-image = a prolongation or renewal of a sensory experience after the external stimulus has ceased to operate. [The term implies a central origin. Where a peripheral origin is implied the proper term is **after-sensation.**] — Fr. *image consécutive*; Ger. *Nachbild.*

after-image/memory = a perceptual or sensory experience which follows another in the absence of direct stimulation (Fechner). [It is a sort of instantaneous photograph of the preceding sensation or perception.]

after-image (or **after-sensation**)/**negative** = an experience which follows another and is dependent upon the prior stimulation, but which is of a quality antagonistic or complementary to the preceding experience. [E.g. a visual after-image in which black and white relations are reversed and the colors are usually approximately complementary to those of the original sensation. Contr. w. **positive after-image.**]

after-image (or **after-sensation**)/**positive** = an experience which follows another in the absence of direct stimulation, and reproduces the qualities of the preceding experience. [Syn. **positive after-sensation** (prefd.). Contr. w. **negative after-image** (or **after-sensation**), in which the qualities are reversed, or complementary. But the **after-effect** following a light pulse is sometimes termed a **positive after-image** if it appears brighter than the surrounding field, and a **negative after-image** if it appears less bright. In this use, the terms **positive** and **negative** refer to *brightness* only, and not to the *hue* of the image. Cf. **Purkinje after-image,** which is positive in brightness and complementary in hue to the primary image.]

after-nystagmus, see **nystagmus.**

after-sensation = a prolongation or renewal of a sensory experience after the external stimulus has ceased to operate, but while the receptor is presumably still active. [Commonly but incorrectly called **after-image;** the latter term implies a central rather than peripheral origin. Syn. **after-effect.**] — Fr. *sensation consécutive*; Ger. *Nachempfindung*.

age = the period elapsed from birth to a given date or time. [When expressed in units of one year, human age is sometimes reckoned to the nearest birthday and sometimes to the last preceding birthday.] — Ger. *Lebensalter*.

age/basal = the highest age level at which all of the tests are passed, in a scale of individual mental tests in which a number of items are assigned to each age level. [E.g. if all tests up to and including the fifth year are passed, and one test for the sixth year is not passed, the **basal age** is five years.]

age calibration = any process of standardization with reference to chronological age, e.g. the arrangement of tests by chronological ages, and the adoption of a system of scoring these so that attainment may be expressed in terms of mental age.

age/chronological, see **chronological age.**

age-grade table = statistical tabulation showing the number of children of each age to be found in each school grade.

age/mental, see **mental age.**

age-norm = the average score made by a large unselected group of children of a given age on a standard set of tests; i.e. the score which is normal or typical for a child of a given age. — Fr. *norme d'âge*.

age-scale = a series of tests (or a single test) for which satisfactory age norms have been determined. [Cf. **age-norm.**] — Fr. *échelle d'âge*.

age score = a score of an individual in terms of a scale of **age-norms.** — Fr. *note d'âge*.

agent = (*psych. res.*) the person in the position of the "sender" in a telepathic situation. [His agency may be voluntary or unconscious, and the suspected telepathy may be spontaneous (as in a dream) or experimental. Contr. w. **percipient.**]

ageusia = lack or impairment of sensitivity to taste-stimuli. **ageusic**[a], [np]. — Ger. *Geschmackslähmung*.

aggregate = 1. a total; applied esp. where the units or groups are somewhat distinct; 2. the totality of individuals in an unorganized group. [Syn. (2) **aggregation** (prefd.). Contr. (2) w. **organization.**]

aggregate idea = a general idea of a group or class, taken collectively rather than discretely.

aggregation = an unorganized or loosely organized group of individuals in physical proximity.

aggression = (*indiv. psychol.*) that aspect of the will to power which involves treatment of other individuals as if they were simply objects to be used in the attainment of the superiority goal. [Contr. w. **social feeling.**]

aggressiveness = a type of behavior characterized by attacking or pushing forward rather than shunning danger or difficulties. — Fr. *agressivité*; Ger. *Angriffslust*.

agitated melancholia = depression with anxious anticipations, especially frequent in the later decades of life and less apt to be of the retarded type than the manic-depressive.

agitation = 1. (*psychiat.*) exaggerated restlessness or mental disturbance; 2. (*soc.*) continued and excited appeal and discussion in society, e.g. labor agitation; 3. (*pop.*) an emotional condition in the individual, often intense and usually unpleasant, with conflicting ideas and impulses. **agitator**[np] (2).

agitolalia = a condition of excessive rapidity or cluttering of speech with sounds or syllables slurred, omitted, or distorted. [A form of **dyslalia.** Syn. **agitophasia.**]

agnosia = an inadequacy of perception, in which a sensory cue or impression fails to be understood or ceases to have meaning. [Sometimes used as a general term for **sensory aphasia.**]

agnosticism = 1. (*epistem.*) the doctrine that neither the nature nor the ultimate character of the universe is knowable; 2. the doctrine which limits knowledge to experience, but also affirms the existence of something non-experiential or unknowable. [A term coined by T. H. Huxley; the most prominent representative of the doctrine was Herbert Spencer. Distg. fr. **positivism.**] **agnostic**[a], [np].

agoraphobia = morbid fear of any open or public place. [Sometimes experienced by otherwise normal individuals.] — Ger. *Platzangst*.

agrammatologia, agrammatism, agrammatica = inability to utter words in their correct form and sequence; i.e. incoherent speech. [A form of **dyslogia.** Cf. **acataphasia.**]

agraphia = a cerebral disorder characterized by inability (total or partial) to write or to form letters. [The corresponding disability in reading is called **alexia.**] **agraphic**[a].

agreeableness = the characteristic of being attractive or causing pleasure. [Syn. **pleasantness.** Contr. w. **disagreeableness** = causing pain or displeasure.] — Fr. *plaisir, agrément*; Ger. *Annehmlichkeit*.

agreement/canon (or **method**) **of** = a general working principle or canon of induction, which consists in finding many instances of a given phenomenon which all agree in one detail though differing in other respects, the point of agreement being regarded as the probable cause or effect (or as an indispensable part of cause or effect) of the given phenomenon. [Formulated by J. S. Mill; cf. **difference/canon of, Mill's canons, probability.**] — Fr. *canon d'accord*.

agricultural stage = the state of human culture in which agriculture furnishes occupation to the larger part of the group, and is usually associated with sedentary customs, weaving, pottery, and the domestication of animals. [Contr. in part w. the **nomadic stage.**] — Fr. *stade agricole*.

aim = a relatively remote situation to be attained by voluntary activity. [Syn. **goal, purpose** (1), used more formally.] **aim**[v], e.g. to aim to accomplish (or at accomplishing) a certain thing. — Fr. *but*; Ger. *Ziel*.

aiming test = any of several devices for measuring precision of movement or perfection of motor coordination by recording the extent of error made by the testee when he tries (in a series of discrete voluntary movements of hand or arm) to hit, with a pencil, wand, marble, ball, etc., some form of mark or target. [Terms used for some aiming tests are **probing test, thrusting test, accuracy of movement test, precision of movement test.**]

air conduction = the normal manner of transmission of sound energy to the auditory receptors, by way of the auricle and external auditory meatus. [Contr. w. **bone-conduction** = transmission by the mechanical vibrations of the bones of the head.] — Fr. *conduction aérienne*; Ger. *Luftleitung*.

akat-, see **acat-**.

akinesia, akinesis = loss or weakness of motor function; usually a loss of movements in a not really paralyzed part.

ala = any wing-like lobe or process of an organ.

alalia = mutism, due to paralysis or defect of the vocal organs. [A form of **dyslalia. alalia** includes: **alalia cophica** = deaf mutism; **organica** = mutism due to organic pathology; **physiologica** = physiologic mutism; **prolongata** = delayed speech.]

albedo = the *whiteness* of a surface, or (photometrically) its diffuse reflecting power.

albedo perception = the discrimination of surfaces according to their diffuse reflecting power or **albedo,** regardless of the illumination under which they are seen. [So far as the constancy of appearance of visual objects holds under different levels and colors of illumination, the diffuse reflecting power will correspond closely to the brilliance of the surface or its position in the white-gray-black series.]

albinism = (*biol.*) a condition characterized by the absence of pigment in the skin, hair, feathers, or eyes. [Contr. w. **melanism.**] **albino**^{np}.

alcheringa = in Australian ethnology, the mythological period in which lived the supernatural ancestors of the present clans and gentes. [These ancestors were half human and half animal.]

alcoholic dementia = (*pathol.*) deterioration of memory and judgment in chronic alcoholism (often due to complicating arteriosclerosis and senility). [Cf. **Korsakow's psychosis.**]

alcoholic hallucinosis = the (usually auditory) hallucinations of threat and reproach directed toward the patient, which arise while he is clear but frightened. [It is a delirium with preserved orientation, apt to last a number of weeks and sometimes difficult to distinguish from **schizophrenia.**]

alcoholic psychosis = a generic term embracing the following types of psychosis, depending upon constitution: (*a*) simple alcoholic intoxication, various types, including the pathological intoxications with epileptiform reactions; (*b*) **alcoholic delirium,** the result of alcohol, gastritis, and lack of food and sleep, with clouding, fearful dream states, tremulous excitement with visual and tactile hallucinations and occupation delirium, visions of small animals, etc. (lasting 3–5 days); (*c*) **alcoholic hallucinosis,** with clearness but largely auditory hallucinations of threatening, defamatory, and accusatory content (duration longer); (*d*) **polyneuritic reaction** with **Korsakow psychosis** (loss of retention, compensated by confabulations), protracted, often with lasting defect; (*e*) **alcoholic paranoic** developments (esp. of jealousy); (*f*) **alcoholic deterioration of character** (non-dependability, lying, etc.); (*g*) **alcoholic-senile** disorders; (*h*) **alcoholic coloring** of affective psychoses, etc.

alcoholism = constitutionally or socially determined habitual excesses and abuses, with cravings and cumulative demand for alcohol, for its stimulating and soothing and social effects (removal of inhibitions at the expense of lowering of efficiency, neglect of responsibility, etc.). [Cf. **alcoholic psychoses.**]

alcoholism/acute = acute intoxication, a mixture of stimulation and paralysis of inhibition, judgment, and motor control. — Fr. *alcoolisme aigu*.

alertness = 1. the transition from a state of relative passivity to an active one (Aveling); i.e. the self as alert; 2. preference for speed, showing itself as an individual difference, significant in tasks which offer little intellectual difficulty but are performed under speed conditions. [(1) almost syn. w. **consciousness of action** (Michotte).]

alexia = a cerebral disorder characterized by inability to read, i.e. to understand written language. [A form of **dysphasia.** Syn. **word-blindness, text-blindness, strephosymbolia.** Distg. fr. **agraphia** = inability to write; **aphasia** = inability to speak or inability to understand spoken language. Cf. **asymbolia.**]

algebraic summation = (*neurol.*) the summation, with regard to positive and negative influence, of exciting and inhibiting impulses coming from different sources which impinge upon a center and give rise to a response modified in the direction of preponderating or prepotent excitation.

algedonic = pert. to pleasantness and unpleasantness.

algedonic esthetics = the view that the value, or lack of value, of a work of art is directly proportional to the degree of pleasure or displeasure which it affords. [Syn. **hedonistic esthetics.**]

algesia = the capacity of experiencing pain. [Sometimes used as syn. of **hyperesthesia;** contr. w. **analgesia** = inability to feel pain.] **algetic**^{a}, **algesic**^{a} (prefd.). — Ger. *Schmerzempfindlichkeit*.

algesimeter, algesiometer = an instrument for measuring the degree of pricking-pain sensitivity, according to the extent to which a needle is inserted into the skin. [Cf. **algometer.**]

algesthesia = specific pain sensation.

algesthesis = pain sensibility; i.e. the pain sense.

algolagnia = pleasure, particularly of a sexual character, which is aroused either by causing or by experiencing pain. [It may be either active = **sadism,** or passive = **masochism** (rare.)]

algometer = an instrument for measuring the sensitiveness to pain in terms of amount of pressure exerted upon the skin by a blunt instrument. [Sometimes called **algesimeter.** Cf. **Cattell algometer.**]

algophobia = morbid fear of pain.

alienation coefficient, alienation/coefficient of = a term applied to the expression $(1 - r^2)^{1/2}$ (wherein r is a product moment correlation coefficient) which measures the lack of relation between two correlated variables (T. L. Kelley).

alienation/mental = a generic term for those forms of mental disorder which estrange the personality and character so as to constitute insanity.

alienist = a specialist in the study and treatment of mental disorders. [Not used technically except in medical jurisprudence. Syn. **psychiatrist** (prefd.).] — Ger. *Irrenarzt.*

alimentary canal = the tubular system of the organism, whose primary function is nutrition.

alimentive instinct, see **food response.**

alkaline = a quality of sensation of which the taste of mingled solutions of sugar and salt is a typical example. [Not considered elementary by most authorities. Cf. **gustatory qualities.**] — Ger. *laugig.*

all-or-none law = the principle according to which the intensity of the response evoked by a stimulus in a single nerve or muscle cell is always maximal or zero, dependent only on the condition of the cell at that moment and not on the intensity of the stimulus. [Discovered by Bowditch, in cardiac muscle.] — Fr. *loi du tout ou rien*; Ger. *alles oder nichts Gesetz.*

allachesthesia, allachaesthesia = a condition in which a tactual sensation is localized at a place remote from that stimulated. [Syn. **allesthesia.**]

allelomorph = (*biol.*) one of a pair of contrasted Mendelian characters.

allergy = a condition characterized by an unusual specific susceptibility to a substance which produces no such specific effect in the majority of members of the same species. [Cf. **hypersensitiveness.**] **allergic**[a].

allesthesia, allaesthesia, see **allachesthesia.**

alliaceous = a quality of olfactory sensation of which garlic and the fishy smells are typical examples. [A class of Zwaardemaker's. Henning puts garlic between his **putrid** and **resinous** classes. Cf. **odor, odor-prism.**] — Ger. *Allyl-Cacodylgerüche.*

allied reflexes = 1. two or more simultaneous or closely successive reflexes which reinforce one another or combine into a harmonious movement; i.e. reflexes whose intraspinal mechanisms are united into a more or less harmonious whole; 2. the phenomenon that one and the same reflex response can be stimulated from a number of different receptor organs (Sherrington). [An area of the skin from any point of which a certain reflex response can be elicited, is the receptive field of that response; such **allied reflexes** (2) illustrate Sherrington's principle of the final common path. Syn. **synergic r.**]

allochiral[a] = characterizing a reversal of manual relations.

allochiria, allocheiria = a pathological condition in which the location of touch or pain sensations is transferred to a corresponding place in the member opposite to that stimulated. (Accent **-ky-**.)

allo-eroticism, allo-erotism = erotic tendencies toward other individuals. [Contr. w. **auto-eroticism.**]

allopsychic delusion, allopsychosis = delusions (and hallucinations) assigning to others intentions or actual influences, due to one's projection of his personal malice or maladjustment. [Cf. **persecution/delusion of.**]

alogia = inability to speak, due to disturbances of the central nervous system. [A form of **aphasia.** Distg. fr. **alalia,** due to local defect of vocal organs.]

alpha movement, see **apparent (motion** or) **movement.**

alpha tests = a set of mental tests first used in the United States army in 1917–8 to determine the relative mental ability of recruits; they include 8 different types of test: directions, arithmetical problems, practical judgment, synonyms and antonyms, disarranged sentences, number series completion, analogies, and information, and are designed especially for testing large groups of individuals simultaneously, and for rapid mechanical scoring. [Distg. fr. **beta tests,** in which the instructions are given in signs and the material is pictorial.]

alter[n] = the individual's conception of other beings as distinct from himself. [Contr. w. **ego.**] (Pron. **al-**, not **all-**.)

alteration current, see **injury/current of.**

alternating current = an electric current which regularly and rapidly reverses its direction of flow.

alternating psychoses = the succession of contrasted mental conditions of affective, depressive-excited, or hibernation-like (vegetative) attacks, applied esp. to the successive conditions in manic-depressive psychoses, but also occurring in paresis, in dementia praecox. [Syn. **alternating insanity** (rare).] **psychosis**[sing]. — Fr. *psychose circulaire, folie à double forme*; Ger. *zirkuläres Irresein.*

alternating reflex = a reflex succeeding another, usually its antagonist, in a series in which these two follow each other. [E.g. flexion following extension in stepping.]

altruism = the type of conduct based on consideration of the welfare of other beings, rather than of one's own advantage. [Contr. w. **egoism.**] (Pron. **al-**, not **all-**.)

altruistic instincts = instincts or innate tendencies conceived as issuing in forms of behavior that promote the welfare of others, without regard to the welfare of the individual himself, and often to his detriment. [Now generally replaced by the term **altruistic habits** (or **attitudes**).]

alveolar = 1. pert. to the gums or other spongy tissue of the body; 2. containing alveoli or open spaces, as in alveolar connective tissue. (Accent **-ve-**.)

Alzheimer's disease = a relatively rare presenile deterioration of the brain with disorganization of speech and premature senility. — Fr. *maladie d'Alzh.*

amaurosis = loss of sight due to defect of the optic nerve, which is not accompanied by any perceptible change in the eye itself.

amaurotic family idiocy = a peculiar type of defect characterized by amaurosis and early death.

ambidextrality = ability to perform motor acts equally well with right or left hand (or side), and to perform bimanual acts with either hand leading or guiding. [Cf. **dextrality.**] **ambidextral**[a]. — Ger. *Doppelhändigkeit.*

ambidextrous = 1. equally expert with each hand; 2. exhibiting no preference between right and left sides in motor function. [Used rather loosely and popularly; **ambidextral** implies a more precise scientific characterization.]

ambiguous = admitting of two interpretations. [In common practice syn. for **equivocal** = admitting of two or more interpretations.] — Ger. *mehrdeutig.*

ambiguous figure = an outline picture in which

certain parts are open to two interpretations. [Either part may be seen as figure and the other as ground, or one element may be seen as either nearer the observer or farther away than the parts adjacent, giving different perspective effects in the two cases. Cf. **ambiguous perspective.**]

ambiguous perspective = the alternating perspective effects observed in an **ambiguous figure.**

ambivalence = simultaneous existence of contradictory and contrasting emotions towards the same person. [In psychoanalysis it is held that any object or person may have (according to some writers must have) both of two opposite affective values, e.g. love and hate (Bleuler).] **ambivalent.**[a] (Accent **-vay-.**)

ambiversion = a type of personality which is balanced between the extremes of introversion and extraversion. **ambivert**[np].

amblyopia = dimness of vision for which no organic defect in the refractive system of the eye has been discovered. [Found in total color-blindness, in albinism, in toxic conditions, and associated with excessive use of tobacco and various drugs.]

amblyscope = (*vis.*) an instrument consisting of two tubes with accompanying prisms at the ocular end, used to test the fusion-set, either dormant or active, of individuals having various degrees of strabismus or squinting; the subject views two stereoscopic images and reports the point at which they fuse into a single object. [The apparatus can be adjusted to any angle of strabismus up to 90°.]

Amblystoma = a genus of salamander (Urodela). [Sometimes improperly spelled **Ambystoma.**]

amboceptor = (*immunol.*) a class of hypothetical substances figuring in Ehrlich's side-chain theory of immunity as the agency which serves to destroy the invading pathogenic organism by linking it with a second hypothetical substance, the **complement,** which exists normally in the body fluids. [Syn. **immune body.** Distg. fr. **uniceptors** = hypothetical bodies which fix and inactivate toxins independently of complement. Both **amboceptors,** represented by the bacteriolysins, and **uniceptors,** represented by the antitoxins, are formed by body cells in response to invasion by micro-organisms or toxins.]

ambrosiac = a quality of olfactory sensation of which the odor of musk is a typical example. [A class of Zwaardemaker's. Cf. **odor.**] — Ger. *Amber-Moschusgerüche.*

Ameba, Amoeba = a unicellular animal which lacks mouth and locomotor organs; it moves about by sending out temporary projections called **pseudopodia** and feeds by enveloping the nutritive substances. [Distg. fr. other Rhizopoda by the shortness and bluntness of its pseudopodia and by the absence of a shell.]

amebic, amoebic = relating to or caused by Amebas. [E.g. amebic dysentery.]

ameboid, amoeboid = like an Ameba. [E.g. ameboid movement.]

amentia = 1. (*English writers*) subnormal development of mind; 2. (*Viennese school*) conditions of protracted delirium-like disorders on ground of toxic-infectious-exhaustive etiology. [Syn. (1) **oligophrenia, oligergasia, feeblemindedness, hypophrenia, mental deficiency.**] — Fr. *faiblesse mentale*; Ger. *Verrücktheit.*

ametrometer = an instrument for measuring the kind and degree of ametropia or refractive error of the eyes; it consists essentially of a complete set of trial-lenses, mounted in several rotating disks, so that the lenses may be rapidly changed while the patient is looking through them. (Accent **-trom-.**)

ametropia = a general term embracing any sort of regular refractive defect in the eye. [Cf. **myopia, hyperopia, presbyopia, astigmatism, defect/optical** (2).]

amimia = a disorder of language, characterized by inability to use expressive or significant gestures. [The equivalent in gesture language to **motor aphasia** in vocal language.]

amitosis = cell division in which the nucleus divides by constriction without the formation and splitting of chromosomes or other operations involved in mitosis, or karyokinesis. **amitotic**[a].

amixia = restriction of general intercrossing in a species, resulting in inbreeding. [Contr. w. **panmixia** = unrestricted crossing between members of the same species.]

ammeter = an instrument for measuring the magnitude of an electric current, in standard units of amperes. — Fr. *ampèremètre*; Ger. *Amperemeter.*

Ammon/horn of, see **horn of Ammon.**

amnesia = a functional disorder characterized by partial or total inability to recall or to identify past experiences. [Cf. **aphasia.**] **amnesic**[a].

amnesia/localized = amnesia restricted to events connected with a certain time, place, or some other special incident. [Practically syn. w. **systematized amnesia.**]

amnesia/retroactive = 1. inability to recall or remember any event which occurred during a certain period of time prior to a shock or functional disturbance, with relatively unimpaired memory for earlier events; 2. general impairment of memories previously acquired, due to disease or other pathological process. [Syn. **retrograde amnesia.** Distg. fr. **inhibition/retroactive.**] (Accent **ret-.**)

Amoeba, see **Ameba.**

amok, see **amuck.**

amoral = characterizing actions, etc. which do not involve distinctions of morality and immorality. [Cf. **morality, moral.**]

ampere = the practical unit of electric current, defined as a rate of flow of one coulomb of electricity per second.

Amphibia = a class of cold-blooded vertebrates, intermediate between fishes and reptiles. [With few exceptions, they are hatched as larvae and develop in the water until the gills are replaced by lungs.]

amphimixis = (*hist.*) the mingling of germ plasm from the two parents in sexual reproduction (Weismann).

Amphioxus = a small animal, segmented and elongated, lacking in appendages and with only the most rudimentary sense cells, which belongs to the chordates or animals with a spinal cord, but not to the craniates or true vertebrates, which have brains.

Amphipod = a sessile-eyed, malacostracous crustacean with thoracic gills and usually laterally compressed body.

amplification/sound = 1. an increase or decrease in the amplitude of a sound wave (produced, e.g. by the auricle of the ear or by an ear-trumpet) designed to concentrate sound energy in an advancing wave-front; 2. an increase in the effectiveness of a sound by first changing it into electrical vibrations, amplifying these, and then transmuting the energy again into sound. — Ger. *Schallverstärkung*.

amplitude = 1. the value of a fluctuating magnitude at any specified moment of time; 2. the maximum value of a vibration or other fluctuating quantity, measured from the zero position. [Syn. (2) **maximum amplitude.** The root-mean-square (rms) or **effective amplitude** of a periodic quantity is the square root of the average of the squares of all values assumed by the quantity during one period.] — Ger. *Amplitude, Schwingungsweite*.

ampulla = an enlargement at one end of each of the semicircular canals of the internal ear. [Applied both to the enlargement of the bony canal and to the corresponding dilation of the inner membranous canal. Within the ampulla of the membranous canal is a sensory structure bearing hair-cells, which are ramified by filaments of the VIIIth cranial nerve; the hair-cells are supposedly stimulated by movements of the endolymph of the canal resulting from movements of the head or body. Cf. **semicircular canal.**]

amuck, amok = 1. specifically, a state of frenzy among Malay peoples under the influence of which a man dashes into the village killing people until he himself is cut down; 2. any emotional state influencing a person to kill until he is slain; e.g. running amuck. — Fr. *furieux*.

amulet = an ornament, relic, or packet of magic powder which is worn as a charm or preventive against evils, such as diseases or witchcraft. [Syn. **charm, talisman.**]

amusia = a mental disorder, or unusual condition, characterized by inability to recognize tunes or by inability to reproduce them. [Strictly, applied to a disorder, but often used to denote a mere departure from the typical musical ability of mankind. There are two types of **amusia,** sensory and motor, corresponding to the two types of aphasia. Cf. **tone-deafness.**]

anabolism = a synthesis of organic structures within the living tissues of the body. [Contr. w. **catabolism** = the destruction or tearing down of tissue; the two are opposite forms of **metabolism** = any change in intimate condition of cells whereby the complexity of their structure is increased or decreased.] **anabolic**[a].

anaclitic object-choice = (*psychoan.*) taking one's earliest attachments (to mother or nurse) as a model for the selection of the first love object. [Contr. w. **narcissistic object-choice.**] — Ger. *Anlehnungstypus*.

anacrotic pulse = a pulse having a notched ascending wave, the principal expansion being preceded by a lesser one.

anaglyptoscope, anaglyphoscope = an instrument which brings the light upon an object in relief from the direction opposite to that from which it would seem to come; the result is to produce an apparent reversal of perspective. [Used to demonstrate the importance of shadows in the interpretation of perspective.]

anagogic = a term applied by Silberer and Jung to the moral, spiritual, allegorical, or uplifting trends of the unconscious.

anal = pert. to or located on the anus. (Accent **ay-**.)

anal character, see **character trait.**

anal erotism = (*psychoan.*) the stage of pregenital libido referring to pleasurable gratification in the anal region. — Ger. *Analerotik*.

anal reflex = contraction of the sphincter ani muscles upon stimulation of the skin and mucosa of the anus. [Mediated by 3d to 5th sacral segments of spinal cord.]

anal-sadistic stage = (*psychoan.*) one of the early stages of pregenital (infantile) libido development, in which the sadistic and anal component-instincts are most prominent, and in which the contrast between masculine and feminine as yet plays no part. — Fr. *stade anal-sadistique*.

analgesia, analgia, analgesthesia = inability to experience pain sensations. [**partial** = diminished sensitivity to pain; **local** = insensitivity to pain stimuli in some region of the body, due either to local application of some (analgesic) drug, or to impairment of the afferent nerves connected with that region, or to disorder in some brain area.] **analgesic**[a], **analgetic**[a]. — Ger. *Schmerzlosigkeit*.

analgesic[n] = a drug or pharmacological agent producing analgesia. [Syn. **anodyne.**]

analgesic[a] = 1. relieving pain, producing analgesia; 2. affected with analgesia.

analogical thinking = 1. the use of analogies, esp. verbal analogies, to prove conclusions; 2. the use of analogies to suggest hypotheses. [Both (1) and (2) are common in childhood. (1) is generally an illegitimate procedure; (2) is frequently of great value in discovery and invention.]

analogies test = a type of mental test in which there is presented to the testee a series of items, usually verbal, in each one of which three stimuli (*a*, *b*, and *c*) are given and a response (*d*) is requested such that *d* will be related to *c* as *b* is related to *a*, i.e. in which *c-d* will be analogous to *a-b*. [E.g. (*a*) face, (*b*) mouth, (*c*) house — (*d*) door. The relations are varied from item to item, e.g. cause-effect, part-whole, genus-species, etc.]

analogous organs, analogues = organs which are superficially similar, but differ in fundamental plan of structure. [Contr. w. **homologous organs** (or **homologues**), which are fundamentally similar in structure but superficially different.]

analogy = 1. (*logic*) an assumed or poetical similarity between two things, events, etc., which are recognized as belonging to separate regions of discourse; e.g. camel = ship by analogy; 2. (*biol.*) incidental similarity in function or structure of an organ in two distantly related organisms. [Distg. fr. **homology** = similarity in fundamental plan of structure, indicative of an evolutionary connection between living forms.]

analyser, analysator, analysor = a term used by I. Pavlov to designate a receptor together with its central nervous connections, by which differential sensitivity to stimulation is produced.

analysis = 1. (*psychol.*) attention directed to parts of a total experience in the effort to discover its constituents and their modes of arrangement; 2. the division or resolution of a compound or complex datum into simpler parts or elements; 3. syn. for **psychoanalysis.** [Contr.

(1, 2) w. **synthesis.**] **analyses**^{pl}, **analyze**^{v}, **analytic**^{a}. — Ger. *Analyse.*

analysis/functional = the process of modifying the conditions under which an event occurs, or an object exists, for the purpose of ascertaining those conditions necessary for the occurrence of the event or for the existence of the object.

analytic method = the method of investigation which starts with and emphasizes analysis, i.e. which seeks to separate compounds into more elementary units.

analytical psychology = 1. the systematic attempt, by means of introspection, to reduce mental phenomena to their elements; 2. the method of psychical analysis used by C. G. Jung, and the systematic psychology associated with this method. [Contr. (1) w. **genetic psychology,** which studies developmental changes.]

analytical situation = (*psychoan.*) the affective relation between analyst and patient as instanced by either positive or negative transference, through resistance or through an ambivalent attitude.

analyzer, see **analyser.**

anamnesis = 1. (*psychol.*) recollection, recalling to mind; 2. (*med.*) the history of an illness up to a critical time, e.g. admission to a hospital.

anaphia = lack or loss of the sense of touch.

anarthria = 1. defect of articulation and formation of words due to lesion of the motor speech area; 2. P. Marie's term for **motor aphasia,** as the only effect of lesion in the Wernicke zone or actual speech area.

anastomosis = 1. a connecting passage opened between two organs, e.g. between two arteries; 2. the joining of two nerves by means of small branches or fibers. **anastomose**^{v}.

anatomical age = a rating of the individual's anatomical development, usually as shown by x-rays of bones, in terms of **age norms** (the average anatomical development of unselected sample groups of successive chronological ages).

anatomy = 1. the structure of plants and animals; 2. the branch which deals with the structure of organisms; 3. the art of dissection. [Syn. (2) **morphology** (prefd.).]

ancestor worship = 1. a form of religion in which the spirits of ancestors are the objects of worship; 2. any extreme respect for the beliefs, customs, and methods of former generations. — Fr. *culte des ancêtres.*

ancestral inheritance/law of = a principle formulated by Francis Galton, which states that on the average 1/4 of the individual's characters are derived from each parent, 1/16 from each grandparent, etc. [The law has been practically superseded by Mendel's formulas, though many writers regard Galton's law as reducible to Mendelian terms.] — Fr. *l. d'héritage ancestral.*

androgyny = 1. tendency of the body, esp. of the male, to approach in form that of the opposite sex; 2. syn. for **hermaphroditism. androgynous**^{a}, **androgyne**^{np}.

andromania, see **nymphomania.**

anecdotal method, anecdote/method of = an attempt to appraise behavior, esp. of animals or young children, by the report of isolated incidents of a striking nature. [The name has usually a derogatory connotation, but is used by recognized authorities to distinguish the method of **selected incidents** from (*a*) the method of **systematic observation** = study of the behavior of animals or children in ordinary life and surroundings, and from (*b*) the method of **experiment** = study of behavior under artificially arranged and significant conditions.]

anelectrotonus = decreased nerve or muscle irritability in the neighborhood of the anode. [Cf. **catelectrotonus.**]

anemia = a decrease in the volume of blood or some of the normal constituents of the blood. [Usually referring to number, morphology, and color of the red corpuscles and measured by the per cent of hemoglobin present. **acute anemia** is distinguished from **chronic,** and **primary** from **secondary.**]

anemotropism = a simple orienting response, either positive or negative, to air currents. [Cf. **tropism.**] (Accent **-mot-.**) **anemotropic**^{a}.

anencephalia, anencephaly = absence of the brain. **anencephalic**^{a}.

anesthesia, anaesthesia, an(a)esthesis = total or partial loss of sensitivity, esp. loss of the tactual sense, but applied also to other sense modes. [Pop. used instead of **analgesia** = loss of pain sensitivity. **central anesthesia** = due to condition within the central nervous system; **muscular** = loss of sensitivity in muscles; **surgical** = produced by the administration of drugs; **tactile** = loss or impairment of sensitivity to contact and pressure; **thermal** = loss or impairment of sensitivity to warm and cold; **total** = loss of all sensitivity in the affected part; **visceral** = loss or impairment of sensitivity in the viscera.] **anesthetic**^{a}.

anesthetic^{n} = a substance which produces loss of some form of sensitivity or entire loss of sensibility. [**general anesthetic** produces a condition of unconsciousness with relaxation of skeletal muscles; **local anesthetic** = a substance which, when applied to some part of the body, renders that locality insensitive to pain, to pressure, to cold, etc.; **regional anesthetic** = a substance which when injected into nerves causes a loss of all sense qualities in the region innervated by the nerves so treated; **spinal anesthetic** = a substance which when injected into the subdural space of the spine causes a total loss of sensation in those parts of the body innervated from the segments of the cord affected.]

anesthetic glove (or **shoe,** or **stocking**) = sharply bounded areas of anesthesia which are confined within arbitrary limits, such as those covered by a glove, shoe, or stocking. [The boundaries do not correspond to distributions of sensory nerves, therefore such anesthesias are considered hysterical.] — Fr. *anesthésie en gant.*

angakok = the Eskimo shaman or magician-priest.

anger = a fairly well-defined group of reactions usually evoked by actual or imaginary injury or restraint, characterized by mixed hedonic qualities with unpleasantness predominating, often marked by a rather consistent discharge over the autonomic nervous system, and often accompanied by somatic activity of the attack or offense type. [Sometimes grouped with fear and love as the three primary emotions.] — Fr. *colère*; Ger. *Zorn, Wut, Ärger.*

angioneurosis = a disorder of the vasomotor system.

angle of incidence = the angle between the path of an oncoming ray of light, projectile, or other body, and the normal to the surface on which it impinges. — Ger. *Einfallswinkel.*

angle of reflection = the angle formed between the path of a ray of light, projectile, or other body, and the normal to the surface from which it is reflected.

angle/visual, see **visual angle.**

angles of displacement = the angles by which the respective eyes deviate from the direction occupied in the primary position. [The **vertical displacement** is the angle of the eye upward or downward from the primary position; the **lateral displacement** is the angle to right or left.]

Ångström unit, Å U. = a unit of length originally and principally used in designating the wavelengths of radiant energy, esp. those of the visible spectrum and shorter waves. [An **Ångström unit** is one ten-millionth of a millimeter; or 10 millimicrons (mμ).]

angular gyrus = a convolution of the cerebral cortex which lies caudad to the sulcus interparietalis, surrounding the posterior end of the sulcus temporalis superior. [In the left hemisphere a probable locus for some functions of speech.]

angular velocity = the number of radians per second passed over by a rotating body. For sinusoidal quantities, such as alternating electric currents, which are considered as analogous to uniformly rotating vectors, the **angular velocity** is equal to 2π times the frequency.

anhedonia = absence of feeling of pleasantness or unpleasantness in the acts or experiences which are usually characterized by affective quality.

anima = the inner attitude, character, or personality that is turned towards the unconscious (Jung). [Contr. w. **persona.**]

animal = a member of one of the two great divisions or kingdoms of living organisms distinguished from members of the other kingdom (plants) chiefly by inability to compose protoplasm out of inorganic substances. Generally characterized also by greater capacity of locomotion, and much greater variety of responses.] — Ger. *Tier.*

animal behavior = 1. the muscular or glandular responses of animals to stimuli; 2. the general activity and performance of animals without regard to their origin or initiation. [Contr. w. **human behavior.** Often used to designate the systematic study of such behavior. Cf. **behavior.**] — Fr. *comportement animal.*

animal hypnosis, see **tonic immobility.**

animal magnetism = (*hist.*) a term used by Mesmer and his followers to designate hypnosis, under the belief that the state was in some way connected with magnetism.

animal psychology = the branch of psychology which investigates animal mind or behavior. [It may include **phylogenetic psychology,** and also **comparative psychology.**] — Ger. *Tierpsychologie.*

animalcule = 1. a minute animal; 2. (*hist.*) the preformed germ-semblance of man. [Applied by earlier scientists to microscopic animals, such as protozoa; pop. applied to small creatures, such as rotifers and water fleas.] (4 syll. accent **-mal-.**)

animatism = 1. (*anthrop.*) a feeling of awe or fear in the presence of nature; 2. (*biol.*) the ascription of psychic qualities to inanimate as well as animate beings. [(1) is usually considered as preceding **animism** which endows nature with spirits or souls.]

animism = (*anthrop.*) a theory which holds that all objects in nature, both animate and inanimate, may be the abode of spirits or souls.

anion = a negatively charged ion. (3 syll.)

anisometropia = an inequality of the refractive condition of the two eyes. [Contr. w. **isometropia.**] (Accent **-eye-** and **-tro-.**)

ankle clonus = an abnormal rhythmical contraction of the calf muscles obtained when the toes are quickly flexed dorsally toward the leg. [It indicates involvement of the cerebrospinal tracts, most commonly by organic disease of the cord. Cf. **pseudo-clonus.**] — Fr. *clonus de la cheville.*

ankle reflex, see **Achilles' tendon reflex.**

Anklingen = the initial rise of sensation. [Ger.]

Anlage = the inherited (biological or mental) organization of an individual or an organ, esp. in early development, which forms the basis or general set of bodily or mental development. [Ger. There is no recognized Eng. equivalent; **disposition, fundament,** or **rudiment** are used for the biological meaning. Cf. **primordium.** (3 syll. accent **An-.**)

annelida, annelids = a phylum of invertebrates having elongated bodies divided into a series of rings or segments, but without segmented appendages such as feet. [Their nervous system consists of a cephalic ganglion, esophageal connectives, and a ventral nerve cord. E.g. earthworm.]

annoyer = a stimulus which gives rise to an unpleasant feeling tone and which leads to activity directed toward the removal of the stimulus (Thorndike). [Contr. w. **satisfier.**] — Fr. *irritant.*

anoci-association = the combination of procedures whereby a patient is protected from surgical shock by the use of both general and local anesthetics (Crile).

anode = a conductor by which a positive current flows from a circuit into an electrolyte, or to which negatively charged ions (anions) are attracted in the electrolytic process. [Syn. **positive electrode.**]

anode block = failure of conduction of impulses through a section of nerve or muscle, due to extreme anelectrotonus in that region.

anodyne = a remedy which diminishes pain. [Usually refers to such an effect operating through the nervous centers but may be applied to locally acting drugs. Syn. **analgesic**[n].]

anoegenetic, anoetic = neither self-evident nor generative of items in the field of cognition (Spearman). [Contr. w. **noegenetic;** cf. **noetic.**]

anomaloscope = a spectral apparatus for the precise determination of color deficiency by the use of the Rayleigh equation (Nagel). [Syn. **chromatoptometer.**]

anomalous dichromasy = defective color vision which is ordinarily reduced to blues, yellows, and grays, but in which reds or greens may be distinguished under especially favorable conditions. [Syn. **incomplete color-blindness.**]

anomalous differences = (*psychophys.*) differences in the proportion of correct responses when pairs of stimuli are presented to an observer in various time and space orders. [They are principally of two kinds: (*a*) more correct reports are obtained when the variable is presented second than when presented first; (*b*) some observers give more correct reports with standard > variable, others with standard < variable.]

anomalous trichromasy = defective color vision in which no hue is lost but a lowered or heightened sensitivity to red or green is indicated in testing for the Rayleigh equation (red + green = yellow). [Cf. **Rayleigh equation.**]

anomaly = any striking deviation from the typical or normal. [Applied in psychology to deviations from normal development, experiences, or modes of behavior. The term emphasizes the irregularity of the manifestation, without definitely classing it as abnormal or pathological.

anomia = an occasional characteristic of aphasia, in which there is difficulty in recalling the names of things.

anorexia = loss of appetite, marked or extreme. [Contr. w. **bulimia.**]

anorthopia = a defect of vision in which objects are seen distorted, straight lines do not appear straight, etc. [Sometimes syn. for **strabismus.**]

anorthoscope = an apparatus devised by Plateau, consisting of two disks rotating at different speeds on concentric vanes; one disk carries a distorted drawing, which is viewed through a slit in the other disk; when the apparatus is in motion, the drawing is seen in undistorted form.

anosmia = lack or impairment of sensitivity to odor stimuli. [A condition analogous to blindness or deafness; it may be congenital or acquired, lasting or temporary.] **anosmic**$^{a, np}$.

Anregung = incentive, incitation, impulsion, instigation, or stimulation. [Ger.] (Accent **An-.**)

Anschauung = immediate apprehension, as in sense perception; intuition. [Ger.] (Accent **An-.**)

ant communities = relatively permanent groups of ants, consisting of fully developed males and females and imperfectly developed females or workers; these last are usually sterile, but perform the work of the community. — Fr. *communautés de fourmis.*

antagonism = action of two forces, things, individuals, or groups, in opposite directions or against each other. [Applied technically to certain pairs of muscles or pairs of colors; cf. **antagonists.**] **antagonize**^{v}; **antagonistic**^{a}.

antagonistic colors, see **Hering theory of vision.** — Ger. *Gegenfarben.*

antagonistic process theory, see **Hering theory.**

antagonistic reflexes = a pair of reflexes whose paths terminate in antagonistic muscles.

antagonists, antagonistic muscles = a pair of muscles (or muscle groups) which counteract each other by pulling a given member in opposite directions. [E.g. the flexor and extensor of the arm.]

antecedent/necessary = a condition which always precedes the appearance of a given phenomenon and in the absence of which the phenomenon never occurs. [Syn. **cause.**]

antenna = a jointed appendage found on the head of some insects and other arthropods. [It contains various receptors, notably those associated with touch and smell.] **antennae**^{pl}. — Ger. *Fühler, Fühlhorn.*

antergic = exerting force in opposition. [Applied chiefly to pairs of muscles or muscle-groups which oppose each other in flexing or extending a joint. Syn. **antagonistic.** Cf. **synergic.**]

anterior = 1. preceding in time; 2. in front. [In human anatomy syn. w. **ventral** = toward the belly (contr. w. **dorsal**); in the lower animals syn. w. **cephalic** = toward the head (contr. w. **caudal**). Contr. w. **posterior.**] — Ger. (1) *früher,* (2) *Vorder-.*

anterior-posterior axis = syn. for dorsoventral axis in man or for cephalocaudal axis in quadrupeds.

anterograde amnesia = a memory defect in which the individual is incapable of reporting recent events because of shock, physical or mental, before the moment of experiencing them. [Syn. **amnesia of fixation.** Contr. w. **retrograde amnesia.**]

anthropocentrism = the view that man is the measure of all things, i.e. that the universe centers about man.

anthropoid = manlike; commonly used to designate the highest apes, i.e. gibbon, gorilla, orang, and chimpanzee.

anthropoidea, anthropoids = one of the two suborders of primates (the other being the **Lemuroidea**); the highest mammals, including monkeys, apes, and man. — Ger. *Menschenaffen.*

anthropology = the science which investigates the human species. [It may include the appropriate portions of anatomy (= **morphological anthropology**), of bodily form (= **anthropometry**), of mental traits (= **human psychology**), of racial distribution (= **ethnography**), of varietal similarities and differences and of the origin and evolution of races (= **ethnology**), or social relations (= **sociology, criminology,** etc.).] **anthropologist**^{np}, **anthropological**^{a}.

anthropometry = the branch of biology which deals with the measurements, proportions, shape, and relative characteristics of the human body in different individuals, races, peoples, and communities.

anthropomorphism = the attribution of human characteristics, particularly mental, to other beings besides man, i.e. to the Deity or other supernatural beings, or to animals, or even non-living objects. [Often applied (by way of criticism) to the assumption that animals share the higher mental traits of man; extended sometimes to the animistic interpretation of inorganic objects. Organismically, the anthropomorphic error applies to content, not function. Contr. w. **theriomorphism** = the attribution of distinctively subhuman characteristics to human beings. The (suggested) term **enelicomorphism** would denote the attribution of adult (human) characteristics to children.] **anthropomorphic**^{a}, **anthropomorphize**^{v}.

anthroponomy = 1. the science which investigates the development of man and the functions of the human organism; 2. the investigation of human behavior (Hunter).

anthropopathy = the ascription of human feelings and passions to non-human beings, especially to a deity. **anthropopathetic**^{a}.

antibody = (*immunol.*) a constituent of the body fluids of animals rendered immune by inoculation, which is formed in response to the presence of an antigen, and which exerts a specific antagonistic influence on the inciting antigen. [The antibodies include agglutinins, antitoxins, bacteriolysins, hemolysins, opsonins, and precipitins. Syn. **antitoxin.**] — Fr. *anticorps*.

antibrachium = the forearm. (Accent **-brake-.**) **antibrachial**[a].

anticipation = 1. adjustment to a coming stimulus or situation; 2. a mental attitude of readiness for a coming event. [Syn. (2) **foresight, expectation.** Cf. **anticipatory response.**] — Ger. *Erwartung*.

anticipation image, see **image/anticipation.**

anticipatory movements = slight movements or muscular contractions which occur when the corresponding full movements are either inhibited or have not yet appeared.

anticipatory reaction (or **response**) = an inadvertent response to some stimulus that precedes the stimulus to which the individual is instructed to react. [Identified by the extremely short response time, or by response preceding the appropriate stimulus. It is due to various causes: e.g. extreme preparedness to react, a tendency to react at the end of a certain interval after preparatory signal, nervousness, occurrence of an unexpected stimulus preceding the proper one, lack of expectant attention to the proper stimulus.]

antidromic nerve impulses = nerve impulses which pass in a direction opposite to normal. [Cf. **conduction/antidromic.**]

antigen = (*immunol.*) a substance which has the power of inducing, within the organism, the formation of antibodies. [The **antigens** include such substances as toxins, ferments, precipitogens, agglutinins, opsogens, lysogens, etc.]

antimodal, see **mode.**

antineuritic vitamin = syn. for Vitamin B, a food principle essential in prevention of polyneuritis and beriberi.

antinode, see **crest.**

antipathy = 1. a social attitude characterized by antagonism toward some other individual; 2. an attitude of intense aversion, usually directed toward other human beings. [The term as pop. used implies an intensity of feeling greater than the situation or circumstances seem to warrant.] — Ger. *Abneigung*.

antiperistalsis, see **peristalsis.**

antirrheoscope = a device for producing the **waterfall illusion;** it consists of an upright board with a window 5 or 6 inches wide and of any convenient height, behind which passes, as a crank is turned, an endless roll of cloth; the cloth is figured (usually horizontally striped) and the front of the board is covered with a similar cloth; as the actual motion stops, motion in the opposite direction is observed.

antisocial = 1. opposed to society or to existing social organization and moral codes; 2. averse to social intercourse. [Applied both to individuals and to forces, tendencies, etc. (2) often confused with **unsociable** = not inclined to seek company, or, not agreeable in company.]

antitoxin, see **antibody.**

antonym test, see **opposites test.**

Antrieb = 1. impulse, inducement, drive, motive; 2. a spurt of effort during continued work (Kraepelin). [Ger.] (Accent **An-.**)

anus = the distal end and outlet of the rectum. **anal**[a]. — Ger. *After*.

anvil bone, see **incus.**

anxiety = an emotional attitude or sentiment concerning the future, characterized by an unpleasant alternation or mingling of dread and hope. [In Freudian usage the term represents a combination of apprehensions, uncertainty, and fear, with special reference to their bodily manifestations; **anxiety** may be of the neurotic type or the reaction to the presence of an actual external situation; in both cases it is the reaction of the ego to danger.] — Fr. *anxiété, angoisse*; Ger. *Angst, Besorgnis*.

anxiety-hysteria, see **hysteria/anxiety.**

anxiety-melancholia = depression with predominance of anxiety and apprehension, either more or less continuous or in paroxysms. [Probably related to excitements in response to unrelieved tensions esp. in the sexual field.] — Fr. *mélancolie anxieuse*.

anxiety neurosis = a neurosis whose most prominent symptom is a marked degree of morbid and objectively unfounded dread, either essentially actual neurosis or of psychogenic origin. — Fr. *névrose d'angoisse*; Ger. *Angstneurose*.

apathy = 1. a condition marked by absence of feeling and emotion in situations which usually call forth such reactions; 2. pathological indifference, considered as a major symptom in psychopathological conditions. **apathetic**[a].

apes = a group of the order primates, closely related to the human species. [Pop. used to designate all the larger anthropoid species below man.] — Fr. *anthropoïdes*; Ger. *Affen*.

aphakia = absence of the crystalline lens of the eye, as the result of defect, injury, or the removal of cataract.

aphanisis = (*psychoan.*) the fear of losing the capacity to obtain sexual gratification (Jones).

aphasia = 1. a cerebral disorder consisting essentially of an inability to use articulated speech and to comprehend spoken words; 2. disorder of symbolic formulation and expression (Head). [Several different types are commonly distinguished: (*a*) **motor aphasia** or **aphemia** or **anarthria** = a condition in which the patient knows what he wishes to say, but cannot utter the words; (*b*) **sensory aphasia** = inability to understand the meaning of written or spoken words; syn. **word-blindness, word-deafness;** (*c*) **mixed aphasia** = combinations of several varieties of aphasia, such as **agrammataphasia, syntactical aphasia, bradyphasia** (groping speech), **cataphasia** (repetitious speech), and **paraphasia** (substitution of one word for another). Head gives four varieties of aphasia: (*a*) **verbal** = defective power of forming or pronouncing words; (*b*) **syntactical** = characterized by faulty grammatical structure of the phrase; (*c*) **nominal** = inability to find the word or expression desired; (*d*) **semantic** = inability to comprehend the significance of words and phrases as a whole. Cf. **dyslogia.**] **aphasic**[a, np].

aphasia zone = the left lateral surface of the cerebrum (in right-handed individuals) surrounding the Sylvian fissure, concerned with the integrative functions of language. [The auditory-visual, kinesthetic, and motor elements of language and thought processes may be involved.]

aphemia = a condition in which the patient knows what he wishes to say, but cannot utter the words, due to a psychoneurotic state. [A form of **dysphemia.** **aphemia** includes: **aphemia hysterica** = hysterical mutism; **a. pathematica** = due to fright or passion; **a. plastica** = voluntary mutism; and **a. spasmodica** = spasmodic dumbness. Cf. **aphasia.**]

aphonia, aphony = inability to utter vocal sounds, due to some structural or functional defect in the vocal cords. [Syn. **voicelessness.**]

aphrasia = 1. a disorder of language, in which the individual is unable to speak connected phrases, though able to utter detached words; 2. inability to utter phrases, due to the individual's general mental inferiority; or refusal to speak, incident to the obstinacy of insanity. [Not to be confused w. **aphasia.**]

aphrodisiac = an agent or drug which excites sexual activity.

aphthongia = inability to utter words due to spasm of the speech muscles, esp. of the tongue.

apicobasal axis = a vertical line used as axis of reference in sessile animals.

aplasia, aplasy = failure of an organ or tissue to develop. [Contr. w. **atrophy** = degeneration of an organ or tissue after it has developed.]

apnea, apnoea = temporary cessation of respiration due to excess oxygen in the blood.

apolar cell = a nerve cell which lacks processes, i.e. projections. [Distg. fr. **unipolar, bipolar, multipolar cell.**] — Fr. *cellule apolaire.*

apopathetic behavior = behavior characterized by the individual's adapting his actions to the presence of others, but without making them the object of his actions. [E.g. the child's "playing up" to the crowd.] — Fr. *comportement apopathétique.*

apoplectiform seizures = convulsive states akin to *status epilepticus,* occurring esp. in paresis.

apoplexy = a sudden loss of consciousness and muscular control, due to cerebral hemorrhage or thrombosis. — Ger. *Schlaganfall.*

aposematic = (*biol.*) warning. [Applied to colors of animals and plants which serve to advertise the harmful qualities of their possessors.]

apparatus = any instrument, device, or related group of devices, designed or used to help control or measure stimulus, response, or psychological function. [Syn. **instrument.**] (Accent **-ray-** or **-rah-.**) **apparatus**^{pl} (used also as a generalized term). — Fr. *appareil, dispositif;* Ger. *Apparat, Vorrichtung.*

apparatus/mental, see **topography/mental.** — Fr. *appareil mental.*

apparent = 1. obvious, i.e. noticed at a glance; 2. seeming, i.e. phenomenal, but not actual or objectively real. [Cf. **appearance.**] **apparently**^{adv} (2). — Ger. *scheinbar.*

apparent magnitude = the perceived size of an object as projected at a set distance from the subject in the field of vision. — Ger. *scheinbare Grösse, Sehgrösse.*

apparent (motion or) **movement** = the perception of motion when stationary stimuli are exposed in brief succession. [Syn. **illusory movement** (ambig.). Cf. **phi phenomenon.** These movements are classed as (1) **alpha** = motion when parts of figures exposed successively change in size due to "illusory" differences in size, as in varieties of the Müller-Lyer figure (Kenkel); (2) **beta** = motion in successive exposures of stimuli which actually differ in size or position (Kenkel); (3) **gamma** = expansion or contraction within a single figure when the figure is suddenly exposed or withdrawn or when the illumination is suddenly increased or decreased (Kenkel); (4) **delta** = motion perceived when the second stimulus exposed is more intense than the first; the motion beginning between the stimuli, goes toward the stimulus first exposed and then returns to the position occupied by the second (Korte); (5) **epsilon** = motion seen when a white line on a black ground is changed into a black line on a white ground with change in position (Linke); also called **positive-negative movement.** N.B. the word **motion** is more appropriate to these phenomena than **movement,** which is more commonly used.] — Ger. *Scheinbewegung.*

apparent resistance, see **ohmic resistance.**

apparition = a sudden and unexpected appearance of some being or object, usually implying a supernatural manifestation. [E.g. a ghost, a "sign" in the heavens. The term is pop. rather than scientific, but is used technically in descriptions of visual hallucinations.] — Ger. *Erscheinung.*

appeal = (*industry*) the incentive used in advertising or selling, in order to induce the individual to buy. [Usually divided into **short-circuit appeal** = by suggestion, instinct, etc., and **long-circuit appeal** = by reasoning or giving information.] — Ger. *Aufforderungscharakter.*

appearance = 1. the onset of an experience, usually visual; 2. the general features or distinctive marks of an object or being, as noted in visual observation; 3. a misleading visual or other impression. [The verbal forms distinguish these meanings; e.g. 1. the light appeared; 2. the man appeared like (or as); 3. it appeared to be.] **appear**^{v}, **apparent**^{a}. — Fr. *apparence;* Ger. (1) *Erscheinung,* (2) *Anschein,* (3) *Schein.*

appendicular = pert. to or located in the limbs or other appendages. [Contr. w. **axial** when applied to skeleton.] (Accent **-dick-.**)

apperception = 1. focused perception, as exhibited in the relative clearness or prominence of certain of the data in perception; 2. the mental function or operation which brings about such focusing. [Plato originated the distinction between merely having an idea and being actively aware of it; i.e. the difference between being unaware and being aware, or between inattention and attention. Later Greek writers and the Latin Stoics evolved a faculty of attention and the Christian Fathers also distinguished unintentional (unconscious) acts from intentional. This led to the view that assent (or the will to know) is essential for actual comprehension. The empirical psychology of Locke was met by opposition from Platonists (Cudworth) who insisted on the need for inner activity. Leibnitz elaborated the theory on a mathematical analogy to include the imperceptible elements of conscious states, degrees of intensification, and final conscious realization (= **apperception**). Kant made apperception the equivalent of persistent identity. Herbart reverted, in part, to the empirical value of attention and the reinforcement of a new content by previously existing contents (**apperception-mass**). Wundt regarded **apperception** as "the one elementary process indispensable to any sort of manifestation of intelligence," with a hypothetical physiological substrate in the brain. Later writers have disputed this view and in some cases consider association a sufficient principle.] **apperceptive**[a] = pert. to the data or process; **apperceptional**[a] = pert. to the study. — Ger. *Apperzeption, Auffassung.*

apperception/tendentious = (*indiv. psychol.*) the shaping of the perceived world in a pattern dictated by the will to power.

apperceptive mass = the group of ideas present in mind and influential in determining what new ideas shall gain admission and in what way new objects shall be perceived (Herbart).

appetence = 1. (*psychol.*) motor tendencies leading to responses which are characterized by pleasure or satisfaction; 2. (*hist.*) a vague term used by older philosophers to include motive, desire, volition, inclination, etc.

appetite = 1. lust or desire for anything, but more especially for food. [If hunger be regarded as the specific sensory experience localized in the region of the stomach and presumably aroused by slow rhythmical contractions of the stomach walls, then appetite for food can exist without hunger, and in civilized man ordinarily does occur, especially as habituated behavior dependent upon past experience with food.]

appetite = 2. a tendency (instinctive) originating in inner conditions (Drever); 3. the welling up of the energy of an instinct (McDougall). [Distg. (2) fr. **reactive tendency** (instinctive). In its broader usage, it would include **aversion,** in cases where the precipitating cause is internal. **appetites** (3) and **instincts** are not regarded as two distinct kinds of innate organizations.]

appetition = the direction of desire towards an object or purpose.

application = 1. employment of an item in the way suggested by its relations; e.g. employment of a theory to the discovery of fact, or of facts to suggest a theory; 2. the items referred to by a term or proposition; 3. (*educ.*) careful attention and study; 4. employment of principles in meeting practical problems. **apply**[v].

applied psychology = 1. that branch of psychological investigation which is devoted to practical rather than theoretical ends; 2. the application of psychological principles to any data outside the field of theoretical psychology. [(1) is a broader term than **psychotechnics.** It ordinarily refers to industrial, medical, and legal psychology, but includes also educational psychology, and the psychological explanation of data in history, etc. (2) includes applications to the explanation of data in historical fields, literature, etc., as well as psychotechnics. Distg. fr. **application of psychology,** in which the problem and procedure fall outside the psychological field, but psychology is applied to the problem.] — Ger. *angewandte Psychologie.*

apport = (*psych. res.*) an object said to be brought by supernormal means from a distance into an inclosed or guarded space; it presumes the passage of matter through matter.

appreciation = judgment or report regarding the value or significance of some situation, event, relation, etc. [As applied to introspective data, distg. fr. **description.**] **appreciative**[a], **appreciate**[v].

apprehend, see **apprehension** and **apprehensiveness.**

apprehension = 1. the act or process of becoming aware of presented facts or objects; 2. the formation of a judgment or conclusion; 3. knowing immediately the characters of experience. [Often used (ambig.) as syn. for **apprehensiveness,** an attitude of anxiety.] **apprehend**[v]. — Ger. *Erfassung.*

apprehension of experience/law of = the principle that any lived experience tends to evoke immediately a knowing of its characters and experiences (Spearman).

apprehension-span test, see **attention-span test.** — Fr. *test de la capacité limite d'appréhension.*

apprehensiveness = an attitude marked by anxiety or anticipation of some undesired or unfavorable event, with a preponderance of belief that the undesired event will occur. **apprehend**[v], **apprehensive**[a]. — Ger. *Ängstlichkeit.*

apprentice = a worker in process of learning a trade, who has not reached the stage where he is competent to work without supervision. [Distg. fr. **novice, journeyman, expert.**]

approaching response = a response in which the individual extends a member or moves toward the stimulus or situation that induced the activity. [Syn. **adient response.** Contr. w. **avoiding response.**] — Fr. *réaction de rapprochement.*

approbation = a judgment or attitude toward some act of behavior, which classes the act as morally good.

Appunn reed, see **lamella.**

Appunn tonometer, see **tonometer.**

apraxia = a cerebral disorder characterized by loss of ability to manipulate and use common objects and to execute planned movements. [Distg. fr. **abulia** = inability to decide and act.]

apraxia/zone of = the dorsal and mesial region of the surface of the cerebrum, concerned with the integrative functions of locomotion and manipulation. [Visual guidance, kinesthetic and motor functions may be involved. A lesion causing **apraxia** may be at either end of (or may directly involve) the superior occipito-frontal association bundle or the corpus callosum.]

aprosexia = inability to maintain fixed attention.

apselaphesia, apselaphesis = derangement of the sense of touch.

apsychical = non-mental.

aptitude = a condition or set of characteristics regarded as symptomatic of an individual's ability to acquire with training some (usually specified) knowledge, skill, or set of responses, such as the ability to speak a language, to produce music, etc. [Cf. **aptitude test.**] — Ger. *Begabung.*

aptitude test = a test designed to indicate the intrinsic, constitutional, or dispositional fitness of a testee for undertaking successfully a specific kind of activity, e.g. a test of musical, of mechanical, or of linguistic aptitude. [Distg. fr. tests of general ability and also from tests of skill or efficiency after training or experience, e.g. trade tests. Includes both specific tests designed for special aptitudes and also blanket (or battery) tests designed to discover and define any of a number of aptitudes. Syn. **special aptitude test, capacity test.**]

aqueduct of Sylvius = the ventricle of the midbrain, which connects the third and fourth ventricles.

aqueous, aqueous humor = a transparent, watery fluid, which fills the space between the cornea and the lens in the anterior part of the eye. — Ger. *Kammerwasser.*

arabesque = 1. grotesque decoration derived from the debased style of the Roman classical period and consisting of fanciful grouping of animal- and plant-forms, etc., as in Roman and Renaissance ornamentation; 2. flat ornamentation of interlaced lines and convoluted curves, developed by the Byzantine Greeks for their Arabian masters. [(1) is the usual use of the term. (2) is the historical usage for which now the specific terms **Saracenic, Moorish,** and **Alhambresque** are employed.]

arachnitis = inflammation of the arachnoid membrane of the brain. [Cf. **arachnoid.**]

arachnoid = a very delicate membrane which overlies the pia mater, situate intermediate between the **pia mater** (next the brain) and the **dura mater** (next the skull).

arbitrary = involving choice between alternative possibilities. [The choice may be capricious or based on reasons, but in the latter case the objective grounds are held to be inadequate to compel decision.]

arbor vitae = a term applied to the internal white substance of the cerebellum as seen in median section, due to its resemblance (in form) to the branching of a tree. [Lat. "tree of life."] — Ger. *Stammbaum.*

arborization = the ramification of fibrils which characterize the terminations of the axon or other projecting fiber ("processes") in neurons, e.g. the end-brush of one neuron with the dendrites of another. [Cf. **synapse.**]

arc = (*neur.*) a short designation for **neural arc.**

archeology, archaeology = a division of anthropology and history which investigates the culture and anatomy of extinct tribes and peoples who possessed no written documents, as indicated by their remains. [Cf. **anthropology.**]

arches of Corti = arch-like structures in the organ of Corti of the internal ear, formed by the fusion of the inner and outer rods of Corti at their upper ends. [Cf. **Corti/organ of.**] — Ger. *Cortische Bogen.*

archetype = (*anal. psychol.*) the content of the racial unconscious.

architectonic = orderly or systematic, as applied to the arrangement of evidence, etc. in treating a science, or to the hierarchy of principles in some specific branch of science or in nature itself.

arcuate fibers = association fibers which connect the neighboring regions in gyri of the cerebrum or in the folia of the cerebellum.

arcus senilis = an arc of opacity, grayish or yellowish-white in color, about 1 to 1.5 mm. wide, just within the boundary of the cornea, sometimes encircling it completely. [Due to degenerative changes in the superficial corneal tissue, chiefly in old persons.]

area = 1. a definite extent of surface; 2. a region of the brain in which some specific function is localized or centered; 3. a region which has a uniform or distinctive cytoarchitectural structure. [In frequency polygons, histograms, and mathematical curves of distribution, the **area** (1) bounded by a segment of the abscissa, verticals at the ends of a segment, and the plotted curve, bears a one-to-one relation with the number of cases represented. Thus **area** (1) is not uncommonly used as synonymous with number of cases. Syn. (2) **center.**] — Fr. *aire;* Ger. (1, 2) *Fläche,* (2) *Sphäre.*

area olfactoria, see **olfactory area.**

argument = 1. any specific use of reasoning in which the grounds or supporting evidence for the conclusion are explicitly stated; 2. a debate between opponents maintaining different standpoints, in which each opponent endeavors to mass his evidence so as to refute the other; 3. (*math.*) a value used in entering a table by means of which a related value, the **consequent,** is drawn out from the table; 4. (*math.*) a value assigned to an independent variable in an equation, as a consequence of which a specific value is determined for the dependent variable; 5. (*literary*) a summary statement of what is elsewhere expounded at greater length, i.e. an abstract. [**argument** (2) is contr. w. **discussion,** in which attempt is made to reconcile two clashing positions by impartial weighing of each item of evidence.] **argue**^{v}. — Ger. *Erörterung.*

argumentation = the art of reasoning in a systematic and explicit manner from conclusion to supporting premises. [Contr. w. **exposition** = reasoning from premises to conclusion. Cf. **argument.**]

Argyll-Robertson pupil = (*vis.*) a pupil which fails to contract with light, but responds synergically with the shift of accommodation to near-by objects and with convergence of the optic axes. [A characteristic symptom of locomotor ataxia and general paresis.]

aridity = 1. barrenness, i.e. inaptitude to produce fruit; 2. dullness of mind, tedium; 3. (*relig.*) a state of painful dullness and depression. [(3) is regarded by the mystics as an indication of the withdrawal of God from the soul. In some persons it appears repeatedly at irregular intervals.] — Ger. *Trockenheit.*

Aristotelian method = the method which employs purely deductive reasoning, and depends upon deduction as a means of discovering facts. [So called because it was the aspect of Aristotle's thinking stressed by the Scholastics.]

Aristotle's dictum, see **dictum de omni et nullo.**

Aristotle's experiment = a phenomenon noted by Aristotle, namely, that if the middle fingers of one hand are crossed and a ball or marble is placed by another between the crossed fingers, the individual without looking perceives the object as double. [One of the tactual illusions.] — Fr. *expérience d'Aristote.*

arithmetic(al) mean = the average obtained by dividing the sum of a given set of numbers by the number of items in the set. (Accent **-met-.**)

arithmomania = an obsessive tendency to count objects on every favorable occasion or to think persistently and unduly on numerical and other mathematical relations. [Sometimes applied to an exaggerated but not pathological tendency to count.]

arm-chair psychology = a general term (usually derogatory) for psychological doctrine not founded upon experimental or other factual grounds (Scripture, 1895).

arm-rest = a device to hold the arm in a fixed and comfortable position for observation and experiment, e.g. with the sphygmograph, ergograph, and instruments for testing sensory responses. [Made in a variety of forms to meet specific needs.]

army tests, see **alpha test, beta test, trade test.**

aromatic = a quality of olfactory sensation, of which the odor of nutmeg and anise are typical examples. [A class of Zwaardemaker's, with five subclasses, exemplified respectively by camphor, nutmeg, anise, lemon, and almond. Not equivalent to Henning's **spicy** class. Cf. **odor.**] — Ger. *aromatisch.*

arpeggio = (*mus.*) production of the tones of a chord in rapid succession rather than simultaneously.

array = the distribution of the measures or scores within any one row or column of a correlation table. — Fr. *rangée, alignement.*

arrectores pilorum = ribbon-like bundles of smooth muscles connected with the sheaths of hair follicles. [Contraction of the muscles causes erection of the hair, "goose-flesh," and a slight discharge of the sebaceous glands.]

arrest of development, see **development/arrest of.**

arson = the malicious burning of an inhabited house or other property for fraudulent gain. [Distg. fr. **pyromania,** a psychopathic manifestation.] — Fr. *incendie par malveillance*; Ger. *Brandstiftung.*

art = 1. a generic term denoting productions of any sort which appeal to the esthetic feelings in man; 2. a human creation, contr. w. the products of nature; 3. skill or skillfulness; 4. cunning. **artistic**[a], **artful**[a] (4), **artist**[np] (1). — Ger. *Kunst.*

art impulse = a tendency in certain individuals which manifests itself in the production of works of art. — Fr. *instinct artistique.*

arteriosclerosis = a pathological alteration in the thickness of the wall of an artery, due to fibrosis or other degenerative change, usually in the intima.

artery = a member of that portion of the circulatory system which conveys blood away from the heart. — Ger. *Pulsader.*

articular = pert. to a joint.

articular sensation = a sensation due to excitation of the receptors in or near the joint surfaces by the rubbing or pressure of one bony surface upon another. [Difficult to isolate introspectively from the general mass of kinesthetic sensations. Cf. **tendon sensation.**]

articulate language, articulate speech, see **speech.**

articulation = the act of producing consonants. **articulate**[v].

artifact = 1. a product of human activity, as distg. fr. the objects produced by natural means without human intervention; 2. (by extension) a product of voluntary human activity as distg. fr. a natural, non-voluntary process. **artifactual**[a] (technically prefd.), **factitious**[a] (more common, but confusing), **artificial**[a] (often implies deception or superficiality).

artificial selection = selection by man of plants or animals which have certain desired characters, and crossing or breeding them, with the aim of changing or enhancing these characters in their offspring. [Syn. **methodical selection.** Distg. fr. **natural selection** = independent of human agency.]

artistic activities = organized actions which are directed toward the production of works of art, or which spontaneously exemplify the principles of art.

artistic appreciation = the mental characteristic of passing discriminative judgment on works of art or of discovering the esthetic quality in products of nature. — Ger. *Kunstgenuss.*

arytenoid cartilages = pyramidal-shaped cartilages of the back of the larynx situate at the upper border of the cricoid cartilage.

ascendence, ascendance = a mode of behavior in face-to-face relations with others, characterized by the tendency to dominate or take the leading role. [Contr. w. **submission** = yielding or adjusting one's behavior to the control of another.] **ascendent (ascendant)**[a], characterizing attitudes, individuals, or behavior. — Fr. *autorité, ascendant.*

ascendent- (or **ascendant-**) **submissive relation** = interaction of a dominant person with one who is in a position of subordination or submission. [Cf. **ascendence, submission.**] — Fr. *relation de dominance-soumission.*

ascetic = an individual whose mode of living is marked by the absence of sensuous pleasure. [Applied to those in whom the internal drives are feeble, as well as to those who repress these impulses because of moralistic considerations.] **ascetic**[a] = characterized by repression of sensuous enjoyment. **asceticism**[n].

asceticism = 1. the practice (or theory) of severe self-denial and discipline; 2. (*relig.*) self-denial and mortification for the purpose of attaining holiness. **ascetic**[np].

asemia, asemasia = a pathological condition characterized by total loss of ability to understand or use language. [A generic term including **aphasia,** together with **agraphia** and **alexia.**] **asemic**[a, np].

asexual reproduction = any mode of reproduction not involving the union of sex cells or of conjugating organisms. [The usual forms are **parthenogenesis, fission,** and **budding.**] — Ger. *geschlechtslose Zeugung.*

asexualization = the act of rendering an animal or human being sterile, esp. by vasectomy.

asonia, see **tone-deafness.**

asphyxia = suspended animation due to deprivation of oxygen.

assault/criminal = an attack upon a human being with illegal violence. [Pop. syn. for **sexual assault.**]

assemblage = an unorganized group of contiguous individuals. [Applied also to objects. Syn. **assembly** = of persons.]

assent = acceptance by one individual of a statement or conclusion put forward by another. [Usually implies reluctant acceptance, but sometimes syn. for **belief** or for affirmation of a **judgment.**] — Fr. *consentement*; Ger. *Zustimmung, Einwilligung.*

assertion = a statement, judgment, or conclusion given forth without indication of its basis. [Often implying that such statement is open to reasonable challenge.] — Ger. *Behauptung.*

assiduity = prolonged and careful attention to a vocation or to a task. [Syn. **diligence.**] **assiduous**[a].

assimilation = 1. a form of simultaneous association which accounts for the combination into a unitary whole, either of direct and reproduced elements of immediate experience (Wundt), or of new and old ideas (Herbart); 2. a physiological process of the anabolic type initiated by stimulation (as in Hering's theories of vision and temperature); 3. (*biol.*) the process of converting substances into protoplasm; 4. (*soc.*) the process of accommodating one's behavior to group life by adopting the attitudes and habits common to the members of the group (Chicago school). [Distg. (1) fr. **apperception** as passive rather than active; contr. (1) w. **complication**; distg. (4) fr. **differentiation,** which is another aspect of characterization.] — Ger. *Assimilation, Angleichung.*

assimilation (or **analogy)/law of** = the principle that an organism responds to a new or unfamiliar situation in somewhat the same manner as to a familiar situation which has similar elements. [Cf. **transfer of training, identical elements.**]

assimilative illusion = a perception which is uniformly distorted on the basis of associative material suggested by the context, by nearby objects in the visual field, or by the observer's attitude. [To a degree almost all illusions may be explained on the basis of assimilation or association; but **assimilative illusions** are sometimes distg. fr. **contrast illusions.**]

associate points = points in the field of perception which are referred to a single point in external space. [Syn. **congruent points.**]

associated movements (*vis.*), see **conjugate movements.**

associates/paired, see **paired associates.**

association = 1. (*psychol.*) the establishment of functional relations among psychological activities and states in the course of individual experience. [Used more broadly by Hartley to denote succession of an idea or movement after a perception, idea, or movement. Sometimes used to include the union of simultaneous experiences = **simultaneous association,** for which **assimilation** or **composition** is a preferable term. The principle of the conditioned reflex is regarded by some writers as an objective statement of the law of association.] **associate**[v], **associative**[a].

association = 2. (*soc.*) the bringing into relation of two or more individuals, human or animal, with interaction or communication of some sort between them; 3. (*soc.*) a relatively permanent co-acting group, e.g. corporation, society, or partnership.

association area = any region of the cerebral cortex occupied mainly by neurons which connect one projection area with another in the same hemisphere. [Cf. **association fibers, commissural fibers.**]

association/controlled = a series of verbal ideas or responses (usually given in pairs) which follows some restriction previously announced by the experimenter. — Ger. *gebundene Assoziation.*

association fibers = axons (or nerve fibers) which connect different regions in the same hemisphere of the brain. [Contr. w. **commissural fibers,** which connect equivalent regions in the two hemispheres.] — Ger. *Assoziationsfasern.*

association of ideas = a term used by Locke and later British associationists to denote mental association. [Limited by Locke to adventitious connections in thought of material not "naturally" connected.]

association/neural = 1. the process by which separate nerve impulses are brought together to form a complex resultant; 2. a functional connection between nerve centers or reaction systems; 3. the process of forming such connections. [Cf. **convergence** (5), **conditioned reflex, neurobiotaxis.**]

association test = 1. a term applied generically and somewhat loosely to a variety of tests (e.g. in the fields of memory, learning, habit-forming, imagination) which are designed to determine the nature of the connections between mental elements; 2. (more specifically) a test designed to determine the nature, or measure the speed, of the connection made by the testee between a verbal stimulus and a verbal response. [(2) includes: (*a*) **controlled association,** in which the instructions restrict the response to a specified logical relation to the stimulus, e.g. cause-effect, part-whole, genus-species; and (*b*) **uncontrolled** (or **free**) **association,** in which the response is unrestricted. The Kent-Rosanoff test illustrates the latter. Syn. **associative reaction.**]

association time = 1. (*hist.*) the time required to form an association, i.e. for the passage from one idea to another suggested by it; 2. the time measured in **association test** (2). [(1) is measured by determining the total time required for a response which includes an association (i.e. **association reaction time**) and deducting therefrom the time required for a simple response of the same sensory sort. Many contemporary psychologists do not consider this method of determination valid.] — Fr. *temps d'association*; Ger. *Assoziationszeit.*

associationism = a theory, allied with **sensationism,** which emphasizes the role of **association** in mental life and traces all constructions of experiences to the operation of association. [The rigid adherents of this view assume **sensation, reproduction** (= memory), and **association** as the sole mental processes, and attribute to these processes all the data (simple and complex) of experience; the theory dates from Aristotle, who formulated the laws of **similarity** and **contiguity** as explaining remembrance: this was restated by Hobbes and mentioned by Locke; the most explicit statements are found in Hume, Hartley (who gives association a physiological mechanism), James Mill, and Bain. The theory was usually the mark of an empirical standpoint and as such was opposed by the doctrine of **apperception.** Contr. (*hist.*) w. **faculty psychology,** and recently w. **Gestalt psychology.**] **associational**[a] = pert. to the process, **associationistic**[a] = pert. to the school, **associationist**[np].

associative facilitation = 1. the strengthening of one associative connection through the operation of another; 2. the increased ease in the formation of an association, A–B, due to the prior formation of an association, A–X or X–B.

associative illusion = a class of visual illusions in which areas and extent of lines are over- or under-estimated, due to the presence of adjacent areas, lines, distances, etc., which are perceptually connected with the figure whose extent is being judged, usually by way of contrast. [Cf. **assimilative illusion, contrast illusion.**] — Ger. *Assoziationstäuschung.*

associative inhibition = 1. the weakening of one associative connection through the operation of another; 2. the increased difficulty in the formation of an association, A–B, due to the prior formation of an association, A–X or X–B. — Ger. *assoziative. Hemmung.*

associative learning = a term used to emphasize the bringing into relation of elements in learning. [The elements may be (e.g.) ideas, or verbal or other stimuli. There is often the implication that one idea may arouse the other, or that one stimulus may call forth the response originally called forth by the other. Cf. **association, conditioned reflex, redintegration.**] — Fr. *acquisition associative.*

associative memory = 1. the process of recalling past experiences through association, or of responding in a manner learned through similar past behavior, when a similar stimulus is given; 2. the function or ability on the part of an organism to recall or respond through association.

associative reaction, see **association test.**

associative tendency = the characteristic of the organism or its nervous system that is the ground of **association** (1). [Measured experimentally by the frequency with which the association follows its sensory antecedent. Cf. **tendency**.]

assonance = similarity or correspondence of vowel sounds.

assumption = an underlying principle, the truth of which is taken for granted in treating or testing some theory, but which has not been proved. [A generic term covering both **hypothesis** = a principle to be tested, and **postulate** = a principle adopted without testing. A **tacit assumption** is one which is unwittingly or surreptitiously introduced.] **assume**[v]. — Ger. *Annahme.*

assurance = 1. an attitude of confidence in one's own beliefs or conduct; 2. the personal vouching for a fact or for the truth of a statement by an individual. — Ger. (1) *Selbstvertrauen,* (2) *Versicherung.*

astasia = unsteadiness or tremor of muscular contraction or of posture. [A form of **ataxia.**]

astasia-abasia = hysterical inability to stand or walk, without evidence of reflex disorders or paralysis for other uses of the limbs.

astereognosis = a pathological condition characterized by inability to recognize the form of objects by the sense of touch. [Syn. **stereoagnosis.**[

asteroides, see **starfish.**

asthenia = lack of general strength, or impairment of vitality. [Used in compounds to denote impairment; e.g. **neurasthenia** = impaired neural vigor.] **asthenic**[a], **asthenics**[n].

asthenic = a type of human bodily structure characterized by long extremities and a comparatively small trunk, largely associated with schizophrenic mental traits (Kretschmer). [Syn. **leptosome.**]

asthenic feelings = those feelings (such as grief, depression, or despondency) in which activity is repressed or inhibited. [Contr. w. **sthenic feelings.**]

asthenopia = weakness of vision, resulting in rapid fatigue and signs of eye-strain after moderate use.

asthma = paroxysmal expiratory as well as inspiratory difficulty of breathing. [It may be either of allergic or of emotional origin.]

astigmatism = in an optical system, the failure of light-rays from a point to come to a focus at a point, generally excluding the effect of spherical and chromatic errors of the system. [In the eye, two types are recognized: **regular,** in which the error is attributable to a maximum curvature of a refractive surface (chiefly the cornea) in one meridian, and which may be corrected with a cylindrical lens; and **irregular,** in which the refraction is irregularly unequal within the pupillary area and which is not corrigible.]

astral body = (*psych. res.*) a dual or shadow self supposed to be visible to **sensitives** who have **cryptesthesia,** and when not dissociated from the body (as in the traveling **clairvoyance** of the hypnotic subject or a dreamer) believed to take the form of an **aura** surrounding the body. [Syn. **aura.**] — Fr. *corps astral.*

astraphobia = morbid fear of thunder and lightning. [Syn. **brontephobia.**]

astrology = an ancient system, frequently revived, by which the fate of a man is read from the position occupied by the heavenly bodies at the time of birth. [Part of the equipment of the ancient priest, or magician, to be applied to all human affairs.]

asylum = an institution for mental defectives, for the insane, or for minors. [The term is falling into disuse, and is generally replaced by **hospital** if the institution is designed for treatment, or by **home** if it is merely custodial.] — Fr. *asile.*

asymbolia = a cerebral disorder characterized by inability to understand or use language, i.e symbolic communication.

asymmetry = lack of correspondence in structure or function between opposite sides of a body. [In biol. used to characterize marked difference in structure of paired members or organs; in psychol. applied esp. to dextrality of function; in esthetics applied to works of art which deviate somewhat from absolute mathematical symmetry for the sake of artistic effect; in logic to a relation that is not simply reversible.]

asymmetry/visual = a peculiarity of convergence in certain individuals, in which one eye operates more than the other, so that the median plane of fixation is at one side of the point of regard; e.g. at the left if the right eye muscles overoperate.

asynergia = a term introduced in 1899 by J. Babinski to describe the underlying symptom of cerebellar deficit, i.e. an inability to carry out complex motor acts involving harmonious cooperation of separate muscle groups.

atavism = the reappearance after one or more generations of a character which has not manifested itself meanwhile. [The Mendelian view of inheritance has somewhat modified the use of this term. It is preferably used to denote the reappearance of a character or group of characters long absent or dormant, while **reversion** denotes reappearance of a latent character, after any period, long or short.] **atavistic**[a].

atavistic heredity = those inherited traits which are found, not in the parents but in more remote ancestors.

ataxia = a disorder characterized by marked disturbance in the coordination of voluntary movements. [E.g. **locomotor ataxia** = impairment of the locomotor functions.]

ataxia/locomotor, see **tabes dorsalis.**

ataxia/static = defective muscular coordination of the individual while attempting to maintain a fixed position of body or limbs.

ataxiagraph, see **steadiness apparatus.**

ataxiameter = an apparatus which automatically totalizes all the dorsoventral and lateral movements (at the vertex) of a subject who is endeavoring to stand motionless. [Syn. **station test.**]

ataxic writing = writing with irregularities of form due to inability to coordinate writing movements. [It ranges from defects produced by lack of skill to pathological incoordinations caused by lesions in the cerebrospinal nervous system. May be associated with **writing tremor.**] — Fr. *écriture ataxique.*

athletic = characterizing a type of human bodily structure in which the relation of limbs to trunk is well-balanced (Kretschmer).

atomism/logical = the assumption that any whole can be derived from, or explained in terms of, pre-existing parts.

atomism/psychological = the theory of mind which assumes that experiences are composed of elementary psychic units or atoms. [Syn. **composition theory.** Cf. **mind-dust theory.**] **atomistic**[a].

atonicity, atony = (strictly) a condition of muscular relaxation characterized by complete absence of postural contraction. [E.g. in the hind limbs of primates following complete transection of the spinal cord; relative atonicity is common in disturbances of the cerebellum and vestibular nuclei.]

atrabiliary capsule, see **adrenal gland.**

atrophy, atrophia = reduction in the size and structural complexity of an organ, with decrease in its functional efficiency.

atropin = the chief active principle of *atropa belladonna,* or deadly nightshade, a crystalline alkaloid, possessing powerful antispasmodic and delirifacient properties. [It causes dilatation of the pupil, relaxation of the smooth muscle of the intestine, bladder, uterus, and spleen; it diminishes or checks the secretions of the salivary, sweat, pancreatic, gastric, and mammary glands. The locus of its action on smooth muscle is the myoneural junction.]

attachment = 1. the connection or bond between stimulus and response; 2. (loosely) a mild form of the emotion of love, accompanying the attitude of **attraction**; 3. (*anat.*) that by which one part is bound to another, e.g. attachment of muscles. — Fr. (1) *rapport,* (2) *affection*; Ger. (1) *Verknüpfung,* (2) *Anhänglichkeit.*

attack = (*pathol.*) a sudden, usually temporary manifestation of some disorder, characterized either by loss of consciousness or of motor ability, or by a notable excess of motor discharge. — Ger. *Anfall.*

attack psychosis = a mental disorder which appears in circumscribed periods, e.g. in the manic-depressive conditions.

attainment/final, /initial, see **ability/final, /initial.** — Fr. *acquisition finale, a. initiale.*

attensity = syn. for **sensory clearness.** [Term coined by Titchener to avoid confusion between sensory and cognitive clearness. Cf. **clearness.**] **attense**[a], **attensive**[a].

attention = 1. (*existential*) a state of consciousness characterized by the existence of two or more levels of sensory or imaginal clearness; 2. (*functional*) the process of focusing certain portions of an experience so that they become relatively more vivid; or, conation so far as it requires for its satisfaction fuller cognizance of its object (Stout); or, the application of intellectual energy (Maher); 3. (*behavioral*) an adjustment of the sensory apparatus which facilitates optimal excitation by a specific stimulus or complex of stimuli, and which inhibits the action of all others; 4. (*pop.*) a concentration of the mind. [Two kinds of **attention** are usually distinguished: (*a*) **primary** = passive, involuntary, spontaneous, automatic, instinctive, or reflexive; and (*b*) **secondary** = active, or voluntary. Some writers distinguish a third kind: (*c*) **derived primary** = habitual, derived passive, or non-voluntary.] **attentive**[a] = pert. to the individual, **attentional**[a] = pert. to the state or process. — Ger. *Aufmerksamkeit.*

attention/accommodation of = the adjustment or readjustment of the individual which is essential to the maximal clearness (**attensity**) of an impression. [The normal accommodation time is about 1.5 sec., with a range of 0.2–3.0 sec.]

attention/duration of = 1. the length of time that an attentive conscious experience is maintained without change in degree; 2. the length of time that an attentive conscious experience may be maintained without change in content. [(2) not recommended. Cf. **attention/fluctuation of.**] — Fr. *durée de l'attention.*

attention/fluctuation of = 1. the periodic variation in the sensory clearness of the upper level of attention, regardless of change in content; 2. the alternate appearance and disappearance of a minimally intense experience. [In both senses the phenomenon is closely related to **oscillation.**] — Fr. *oscillations de l'a.*; Ger. *Aufmerksamkeitsschwankung.*

attention/focus of = the upper level of attention; i.e. the clearest portion of a perceptual or ideational experience. — Fr. *foyer d'a.*; Ger. *Brennpunkt der A.*

attention/inertia of = 1. the lag of attention involved in a shift or change of content; 2. the time required for unclear processes (low attensity) to become clear (high attensity).

attention-level, level of attention = any one of the several degrees of clarity into which the subject matter of experience (content of consciousness) may be classed. [Certain writers distinguish as many as five degrees or levels: **unconsciousness, subconsciousness, marginal consciousness, general consciousness,** and **focal consciousness (apperception).** Two simultaneously appearing levels have been definitely established experimentally.] — Fr. *niveau d'a.*

attention/range (or **span**) **of** = the number of objects that can be perceived or correctly apprehended during an exposure so short as to exclude eye-movements and counting. [Usually regarded, on the principle of the psychophysical limen, as the number that can be correctly apprehended in 50 per cent of the trials. Syn. **span of apprehension.**] — Fr. *champ d'a.*; — Ger. *Aufmerksamkeitsumfang.*

attention reflex = a change in the size of the pupil upon sudden fixing of the attention. [Probably associated with accommodation. Syn. **Piltz's reflex.**]

attention/rhythm of = the recurrent shift of focal experiences.

attention-span test = a test designed to measure the amount or complexity of perceptual material which a testee is able to grasp at a single brief presentation. [The presentation is most often visual (e.g. of digits, syllables, drawings, or objects), and is commonly made by tachistoscopic exposure. Syn. **range of attention test; apprehension-span test.**] — Fr. *test (épreuve) du champ d'attention.*

attenuation = 1. (*statist.*) reduction in the product moment correlation coefficient due to the unreliability of the measures employed (Spearman); 2. a change in statistical constants other than correlation coefficients, due to unreliability of the measures employed. [Spearman (1904) gives formulas for correction of **attenuation** (1) which furnish an estimate of the correlation which might be expected if the measures were perfectly reliable.]

attenuator = (*phys.*) an instrument for reducing an electric current (or other physical quantity) by a determined amount.

attitude = 1. a stabilized set or disposition; 2. an abbreviated but comprehensive experience; 3. the specific mental disposition toward an incoming (or arising) experience, whereby that experience is modified, or, a condition of readiness for a certain type of activity; 4. the established tendency to renew neural functions, esp. those within the brain (G. E. Müller). [Cf. **attitude/social.**] — Ger. (1) *Haltung*, (2) *Bewusstseinslage*, (3) *Einstellung*.

attitude/esthetic = the mental state which conduces to the production and appreciation of beauty. [Cf. **artistic appreciation.**]

attitude scale = a scale for measuring degrees of attitude upon a particular question, as distg. fr. a scale for measuring general dispositions in traits of personality.

attitude/social = 1. a set, or readiness to respond in a definite way to social stimuli of a general or specific character; 2. an attitude upon a question of social or public importance or upon the social relations of individuals.

attitudinal (or **attitude**) **test** = a phrase applied somewhat broadly to numerous tests of non-intellectual mental traits, esp. of those dispositional tendencies loosely referred to as **temperament** and **personality.** [E.g. tests of moral attitude (Voelker, Raubenheimer), of emotional disposition and will-temperament (Downey, Pressey), of social attitude (Hart), and of esthetic appreciation (Meier).]

attitudinizing = 1. the tendency to assume postures for their effect upon others; 2. in psychiatry, sometimes used in connection with the cataleptoid positions assumed by catatonic dementia praecox patients. [Cf. **stereotypy, mannerisms.**]

attraction = a term applied figuratively to an attitude of approach taken by one individual toward another. [Contr. w. **repulsion** = an attitude of avoidance.] — Ger. *Anziehung*.

attribute = (*psychol.*) a fundamental, intrinsic characteristic or property of mental elements. [In structural psychology the attributes generally recognized are **quality, intensity, duration,** and **extensity;** other attributes, such as **clearness** or **attensity,** are recognized by certain writers. Syn. **character.** Cf. **dimension/psychological.**] **attributive**[a] = pert. to or characterizing an attribute.—Ger. *Attribut, Eigenschaft*.

attrition = 1. (*phys.*) the wearing down or wearing away of bodies; 2. (*logic*) a method of disposing of hypotheses by disposing of each argument or each item of evidence separately.

atypical = a loose term used to indicate marked deviation in pattern, number, or amount from the sum total of characteristics regarded as defining a class or category, e.g. the class "normal children."

Aubert phenomenon = the apparent displacement suffered by a vertical line in a direction opposite to that in which the head is tilted, when it is viewed without the presence of other objects in the visual field. [Owing to great individual differences, several "types" have been proposed; an A-type, for whom the effect is strong; an E-type, for whom the opposite effect appears under identical conditions; and an E-A-type, who experience the effect normally up to a certain angle of inclination of the head, after which the opposite effect appears.]

Aubert-Förster law = a generalization regarding visual acuity based upon the **Aubert-Förster phenomenon:** objectively small objects can be distinguished as two at greater distances from the fovea than objectively larger objects subtending the same visual angle.

Aubert-Förster phenomenon = small near objects can be recognized over a larger portion of the retina than larger, farther off objects that subtend the same visual angle. [Not to be confused with the **Aubert phenomenon.**]

Aubert's diaphragm = a device used in apparatus for visual work to control the amount of light passing into the eye; it is composed of two leaves each with a right-angled notch cut into it, so overlapping that the two notches form a square opening; the size of the opening may be varied within wide limits by moving the leaves one upon the other.

audibility limits = the lowest and highest vibration frequencies which evoke tonal sensation. [The lower limit corresponds to 16–20 cycles per sec., and the upper limit to 18,000–20,000, varying with the individual and with experimental conditions. The tonal distance between these limits is called the **range of audibility.** There are also intensity limits of hearing; cf. **auditory absolute threshold.**] — Fr. *limites d'audibilité*.

audibility range = the extent or distance between the lower and upper boundaries of a tonal continuum. [Syn. **range of hearing.** Cf. **audibility limits.**] — Fr. *champ auditif, c. des tons audibles*.

audience = an assembly of hearers or beholders, generally a co-acting group, who react in a direct manner to a speaker or performer. [In an **audience** the individual to whom the members of the group are responding is also addressing or responding directly and primarily to them, a two-way situation; contr. w. the relation between **spectators** and the object watched, e.g. in a motion picture performance or a football game. A facilitation of response between speaker and hearers, and between the hearers themselves, usually characterizes the audience situation.]

audile, auditory type = a class of individuals who rely mainly upon audition (hearing) or whose imagery is mainly auditory. [Cf. **type/mental.**]

audio-frequency = a frequency of oscillation, whether mechanical or electrical, which lies approximately between the limits of 20 and 20,000 cycles per second, i.e. within the range of audibility for sound waves.

audiogram = a graphic record of the auditory sensitivity of an individual. [The threshold of intensity is usually plotted for a number of tones extending throughout the audible range. Such a graph indicates the presence and limits of any **tonal gaps** or **tonal islands.**]

audiometer = an instrument for the study of hearing, esp. for measuring the intensive threshold (i.e. the least perceptible intensity) for sound. [Various types of audiometer have been devised, older forms of which were called **acoumeters, acousimeters,** or **phonometers. Politzer's acoumeter** consisted of a hammer which fell from a constant distance to give a standard sound; the distance of the instrument from the ear was varied to measure the threshold. **Schafhäntl's phonometer, Lehmann's acoumeter,** and **Zoth's acoumeter** produced sounds of varying intensities by adjusting the height of fall of a pellet. **McCallie's audiometer** gave a standard click after the fashion of Politzer's, but varied the intensity by adjusting the size of an aperture in the box in which the hammer mechanism was enclosed. **Seashore's audiometer,** which is newer, uses a buzzer or electrically maintained tuning fork operating into a telephone receiver, and varies the intensity by means of a potentiometer. More recent instruments, such as the **Western Electric 1 A** and **2 A audiometers,** employ vacuum-tube circuits to deliver tones throughout the frequency range at definitely calibrated intensities. Cf. **audio-oscillator.**] — Ger. *Hörschärfe(n)messer.*

audiometric measurement, audiometry = the determination of auditory sensitivity, esp. of the lower intensive thresholds for several tones throughout the audible range. [See **audiometer.**]

audio-oscillator = an apparatus which generates alternating electric currents within the frequency range of audition, i.e. roughly between 20 and 20,000 cycles per second. [Devices of this sort utilizing vacuum tubes are capable of producing in a telephone receiver sound-waves of a high degree of purity, and of any desired frequency and intensity. Cf. **audiometer.**]

audition = a sense whose receptor is in the ear, and which is stimulated by sound waves. [Syn. **hearing** (preferably limited to the function).] **auditory**[a], **hear**[v]. — Fr. *audition, ouïe*; Ger. *Gehör.*

audito-oculogyric reflex= turning of eyes in the direction of a sudden sound. [Mediated by the auditory and oculomotor arcs.]

auditory = pert. to the ear, or to the sense of audition, or hearing. [Syn. **aural, otic. auditory** is the general term; it is used to designate the sense as a whole, e.g. auditory acuity, auditory theory. **aural** is commonly restricted to anatomical use, and has a topographical connotation, e.g. aural surgery, the aural region. **otic** pertains more specifically to the sensory endings proper, their nerve connections, or (esp.) the Anlagen of these in the embryo, as otic vesicle, otic ganglion. Distg. fr. **acoustic** = pert. to (*physical*) sound vibrations.]

auditory absolute threshold = 1. (*stimulus threshold*) the stimulus-energy necessary to excite the receptor cells of hearing in 50% of the trials; 2. (*upper intensive limit,* improperly called *upper threshold*) the stimulus-energy necessary to excite the pressure or pain receptor cells of the ear in 50% of the trials. [Syn. **limen, stimulus limen, intensive threshold.** In the case of periodic vibrations both the upper limit and the threshold vary with the frequency. Cf. **audibility limits.**] — Fr. *seuil auditif absolu.*

auditory acuity = the sensitivity of hearing measured by the stimulus-energy which gives an audible sound in 50% of the trials. [For tonal stimuli the intensive threshold varies with the frequency. Cf. **audiometer.**] — Ger. *Hörschärfe.*

auditory fatigue, see **fatigue/auditory.**

auditory flicker, see **flicker/auditory.**

auditory lobe, see **temporal lobe.**

auditory localization, see **localization/auditory.**

auditory masking, see **masking.**

auditory nerve, acoustic nerve = the portion of the VIII cranial nerve which mediates the sensation of sound. [Syn. **cochlear nerve.**]

auditory oculomotor associated reflex = turning of the eyes toward a source of sound above or below the level of the eyes. [Mediated by the lateral lemniscus, inferior colliculus, and the III and VIII cranial nerves.]

auditory ossicles, see **ossicles/auditory.**

auditory sensation = a sensation dependent upon structures in the inner ear and normally upon stimulation by sound waves. [Syn. **sensation of hearing.**] — Ger. *Gehörsempfindung.*

auditory space = the extent which is perceptible by means of the ear. [Cf. **localization of sound.**]

auditory stimulus = a form of physical energy which acts upon the auditory receptor so as to produce sensations of hearing. [The proper or adequate stimuli for tonal hearing are sound-waves within the frequency limits of approximately 20 and 20,000 cycles per second.]

auditory tube, see **Eustachian tube.**

auditory vesicle, see **vesicle/auditory.**

Aufgabe = 1. a task or purpose offered by the experimenter to the observer who, if he accepts it, is prepared or set for the experiment; 2. an individual's attitude or mental set toward a task or problem as determined by instruction or other influence. [Ger.: frequently used in English lit. Syn. (1) **task** or **problem,** which may refer to an objective state of affairs; (2) is a loose but wide usage springing from the original meaning (1) given by Watt of the Würzburg school. Cf. **Einstellung; Bereitschaft.**]

augmentor nerve = any (afferent or efferent) nerve whose action is to increase the force and amplitude of contractions in muscles of the heart.

augury = 1. (*hist.*) the art of foretelling the future by means of natural signs, such as the position of the stars, the flight of birds, the entrails of animals, etc.; 2. syn. for **omen.** [Officially recognized in ancient Rome. Cf. **divination.**] **augur**[np].

aura = 1. (*pathol.*) a subjective sensory phenomenon which marks the onset of a nervous attack, such as epilepsy; 2. an event in consciousness which exhibits the character of being *tied* to the thoughts evoking it; 3. (*psych. res.*) syn. for **astral body. aural**[a].

aura/epileptic = various experiences, felt as the initial stage of an epileptic attack, more or less typically recurring as warning according to the individual case (gastric aura, visual aura, etc).

aural, see **auditory.**

auricle = 1. a shell-like cartilaginous body which opens into the external auditory meatus, and acts as a collector of sound; 2. a cavity in the heart (or compartment of the heart) into which the blood flows directly from the blood vessels. [Syn. (1) **pinna;** the two terms are interchangeable, but **auricle** is used more often for the organ in man, and **pinna** in the lower mammals.] — Fr. (1) *pavillon,* (2) *oreillette du coeur;* Ger. (1) *Ohrmuschel,* (2) *Herzvorhof.*

auricular = pert. to or located on or in the ear.

aurist = syn. for **otologist.**

auscultation = listening, with or without a stethoscope, to the sounds of internal bodily activity.

Ausfragemethode = 1. the method of examination (Külpe); 2. the method of questioning the subject about the conscious processes which occur during the solution of **Aufgaben** or problems; 3. the questionary (questionnaire) method. [Ger.]

Aussage test = a test of the fidelity with which certain past events are reported by a testee. [Ger. Performance depends upon perceptual and observational accuracy as well as upon memory, honesty, and verbal ability.]

autacoid = 1. "a specific organic substance formed by the cells of one organ and passed from them into the circulatory fluid to produce effects upon other organs similar to those produced by drugs" (Sharpey-Schafer, 1913); 2. the secretion of an endocrine organ. [Syn. **internal secretion, incretion.** The name **autacoid substances** was suggested by Sharpey-Schafer as a generic name embracing (*a*) excitatory autacoids = **hormones,** and (*b*) inhibitory autacoids = **chalones,** e.g. adrenalin, which constricts most arterioles, but inhibits the muscular coat of the intestine. Hence no absolute distinction can be drawn between **autacoid, hormone,** and **chalone. hormone** is often used as the generic term.]

authority = the credibility claimed for a statement of fact or theory on the basis of the original promulgator's general credibility. [Loosely used also for what should be distinguished as **second-hand authority,** where the basis is the credibility of persons assenting to a statement. As a basis for belief or action **authority** is distg. fr. **reasoning** or **reason,** and fr. **empirical demonstration.**] **authoritative**[a]. — Ger. *Autorität.*

autism = a type of thinking dominated by subjective trends, the material being uncorrected in its essential features by objective standards, e.g. day-dreams.

autistic = 1. directed toward oneself; 2. inordinately subjective. [Cf. **autistic thinking.**]

autistic personality, see **introversion.**

autistic thinking = 1. a tendency to represent desires (or wishes) which originate in deep, personal strivings as already fulfilled, ignoring any contradictions with reality; 2. pleasure or fantasy thinking which serves directly or obscurely the imaginary gratification of unfulfilled wishes or longings. [Normal forms in fantasy-life, poetry, dreams, wit; pathologically most developed in schizophrenia or paranoid states. Syn. (Bleuler) **dereistic thinking.**] — Fr. *pensée autistique.*

autochthonous ideas = ideas which arise independently of trains of thought and are interpreted as foreign to the individual's normal mode of thinking. [E.g. obsessive thinking in the obsessional neuroses; also a schizophrenic symptom. Syn. **sejunctive ideas** (Wernicke).]

autocompetition = the attempt of an individual to surpass a previous record of his performance, e.g. in a test or laboratory task.

auto-eroticism, auto-erotism = sexual activity which is self-generated and directed toward oneself, characteristic of the sexual life of children and certain neurotics. [E.g. masturbation, rhythmical thumb-sucking, pleasure sucking on skin, mucous membrane, or other erogenous zones. A term proposed by Havelock Ellis and later utilized by Freud, but in a more restricted sense. Contr. w. **allo-eroticism.**]

autogenic reinforcement = a condition of self arousal and subjective strengthening of a reaction tendency, such that the response to a certain stimulus is more prompt or more intense than that otherwise exhibited by the same subject to the same stimulus, or than would be expected from the total external situation.

auto-intoxication = poisoning by some uneliminated endogenous toxin. [Usually refers to the disordered state due to absorption of toxins formed in the intestine as a result of intestinal stasis (constipation). Commonly distg. fr. toxic conditions resulting from general or focal infection.]

autokinesis = movement initiated by stimuli within the organism itself, i.e. proprioceptive stimuli (Sherrington). [Contr. w. **heterokinesis** = movements which result from external stimulation.] **autokineses**[pl].

autokinetic illusion = an apparent motion of a single point of light or small object presented on a dark field and observed continuously. [The point may seem to move 20° or more. Syn. **Charpentier's illusion.**]

automatic = 1. (*beh.*) precise and machine-like; 2. generated within the body; 3. varying but little in duration and in character. [Applied to movements and organic activity.]

automatic action = 1. movements generated within the body and not due to obvious external stimulation; 2. precise and machine-like movements; 3. responses which vary little in duration and in character on successive arousals. [(1) generally used in plural; (2) in singular; (3) in either.]

automatic drawing = delineation in which there is little or no conscious control on the part of the producer. [Cf. **automatic writing.**] — Fr. *dessin automatique.*

automatic response = a response which takes place without delay or deliberation. [Also syn. for **automatic action.**]

automatic speaking = speaking which is performed without voluntary control. [Common with the aged, with normal persons in a state of excitement or sleep, but esp. with persons in a hypnotic or a mediumistic trance. Syn. **automatic voice.**] — Fr. *langage (parole) automatique.*

automatic writing = 1. the act of writing with attention concentrated entirely on the content of the composition rather than on the technical details of the writing act; 2. a type of graphic expression produced with diminished or with no conscious control. [(2) ranges from loss of feeling of agency on the part of the writer, to complete unawareness of what is being written; in the latter case it indicates considerable psychic dissociation which may, however, be experimentally produced; in certain cases (2) is performed by an otherwise paralyzed member of the body. Syn. (2) **mediumistic writing.**] — Fr. *écriture automatique.*

automatism = the performance of more or less complicated actions of a non-reflex type without conscious guidance on the part of the performer.

automatism/sensory = (*psych. res.*) the automatic functioning of the senses resulting in **illusions** and **hallucinations.** [In the field of vision it is responsible for **clairvoyance,** and may be incited by gazing into a crystal or any translucent or reflecting medium; in the field of audition it produces **clairaudience,** for which the sea-shell is an appropriate aid; a process in the functioning of **cryptesthesia.**]

automatist = (*psych. res.*) 1. syn. for **medium;** 2. any person who presents through automatic writing or speaking messages purporting to come from extraneous personalities. [The personalities so evoked are considered by many investigators to be secondary personalities induced by autosuggestion.]

automatization = that stage in a repeated motor performance at which it comes to operate without continuous extrinsic stimulation, whether exteroceptive or ideational. **automatize**[v].

automatograph = an instrument used to record the automatic or undirected movements of an individual. [The **Jastrow automatograph** consists of two smooth plates of glass, separated by three spherical balls and adjusted horizontally; the subject places the finger tips of one hand on the upper plate where it moves freely and noiselessly; a projecting piece attached to the upper plate carries a marker which records every slight movement of the hand.]

automaton = a mechanism which performs human-like activities. [For Descartes, animals were **automatons.**]

autonomic = 1. having independent functions; 2. pert. to the autonomic nervous system. [Sometimes confused with **automatic** = precise and machine-like, or internally generated.]

autonomic function = 1. a specific physiological process, either part of or governed by the autonomic nervous system; 2. any self-governed or autonomous process.

autonomic nervous system = an efferent system of widely distributed peripheral nerves, ganglia, and plexuses, which innervates smooth muscle and gland cells, and which consists of a chain of ganglia, of motor fibers running from the spinal cord to this ganglionic chain (the preganglionic fibers), and of fibers (postganglionic) running from the ganglionic chain to the tissue innervated. [Syn. **autonomic system, sympathetic n.s.** (*hist.*), **involuntary n.s.** (*hist.*), **vegetative n.s.** The **autonomic n.s.** is connected with the **central n.s.** by preganglionic fibers whose cell bodies are centrally located and subject to central excitation and inhibition; it is divided into (*a*) the **sympathetic system** or thoracicolumbar autonomic, and (*b*) the **parasympathetic** or craniosacral autonomic, on the basis of level of outflow of preganglionic fibers from the **central n.s.,** the distribution of peripheral ganglia, and the antagonism of physiological effects in visceral tissues, which in general receive innervation from both divisions. By Langley and others the **autonomic n.s.** was regarded as a purely peripheral system.]

autonomic reflex = a reflex response which involves in whole or in part the autonomic nervous system. [E.g. breathing, heart action. Many writers restrict **reflex** to cerebrospinal activity; strictly, **autonomic reflex** should be limited to activity involving merely the autonomic system; where both systems are involved the proper term is **cerebro-autonomic** or **autonomic-cerebral reflex.**]

autonomy = guidance or control by oneself of one's own actions or conduct. [Used in discussions of the ethical bearings of behavior, in opposition to the rigid stimulus-response view, or as opposed to **determination;** the usual phrase is **autonomy of the will.**]

autopsychic orientation = the state of a person's orientation concerning himself (Wernicke).

autopsychoses = mental disorders characterized by ideas relating to the individual's own personality, rather than to his environment (Wernicke). **autopsychosis**[sing].

autorivalry = the endeavor to equal or surpass one's own previous attainment. [Used in connection with experiments in which the individual tries to improve his record in some type of activity, or in a test measuring progress in some special ability. Syn. **autocompetition** (more accurate).]

autoscope = an instrument by means of which imperceptible, involuntary and non-conscious muscular movements are converted into visible and significant motion or movements. [Typical forms are (1) the **dousing** and **divining rods,** (2) a ring or bob suspended by a thread (**pendule explorateur**), (3) a poised index or pointer traversing letters of the alphabet, (4) the **planchette** or **ouija board,** (5) a light table (for **table-tipping, table-turning**). Cf. **automatograph.**]

autosomes = the chromosomes other than the sex chromosomes.

autosuggestion = suggestion which emanates from the individual himself, as distg. fr. **hetero-suggestion,** which emanates from another. [Cf. **suggestion.**]

auxesis/visual = the process of increase in any specific visual sensibility under the influence of the stimulus which arouses the visual process.

avalanche conduction = conduction in which nerve impulses spread from few to many neurons, producing an effect which is apparently disproportionate to the stimulation.

average = (*statist.*) a measure of central tendency. [The most common averages are the **arithmetic mean** (frequently called the **mean** or the **average**), the **median,** the **geometric mean,** the **harmonic mean,** the **quadratic mean,** and the **mode.**] — Fr. *moyenne*; Ger. *Durchschnitt.*

average deviation = the average amount by which the individual values in a statistical series differ from the arithmetic mean of that group, obtained by finding the difference between the group-average and each individual value, regardless of sign, and averaging these differences. [Syn. **mean deviation.** In a normal distribution the average deviation = .7978846 × standard deviation.] — Fr. *écart moyen.*

average error = a term used in psychophysics to denote the average amount by which the separate values in a series of observations differ from the standard. [Distg. fr. **average deviation.**] — Fr. *erreur moyenne.*

average error/method of = a procedure devised by G. T. Fechner for psychophysical measurement, in which a constant (standard) stimulus is presented and the observer is required to adjust a variable stimulus until the two are subjectively equal. [Syn. **method of mean error.**] — Fr. *m. des erreurs moyennes*; Ger. *M. der mittleren Fehler.*

average score = 1. (*statist.*) any measure of central tendency; 2. the arithmetic mean score. — Fr. *note* (*notation*) *moyenne.*

averages/law of = a statement of the fact that the average or arithmetic mean of a group of observations has a probability of occurrence which is greater than that of any single observation.

aversion = a pronounced unpleasant feeling or attitude toward an object, person, person's actions, or situation perceived or imagined, together with a conative impulse of avoiding it. — Ger. *Abneigung.*

avocation = a form of activity which an individual pursues in addition to his regular occupation or vocation, either as an individual recreation or as a social (national, religious) obligation, self-imposed.

avoiding response, see **negative response.** — Ger. *Vermeidungsreaktion.*

awake[a] = characterizing the normal condition of the organism, in which it responds effectively to stimuli and exhibits signs of consciousness. [Contr. w. **asleep;** distg. fr. special conditions of **coma, hypnosis,** etc.] **waking state**[n], **wake**[v]. — Fr. *éveillé.*

awake[v] = to pass from sleep to the normal condition of consciousness. [Distg. fr. **awaken** = to cause another to awake (i.e. to rouse him from sleep) and fr. **wake**[v] = to remain in the waking state.] — Fr. *se réveiller.*

awareness = 1. the mere apprehension of an object, ideal, conceptual existence, or bodily condition; 2. the experience by an individual of items corresponding to external objects or to conditions within his own body; 3. syn. for **Bewusstheit** (Ach).

awe = 1. a complex compound of fear and admiration which differs from reverence by absence of the element of goodness (Shand); 2. reverential fear. — Fr. *crainte révérencieuse*; Ger. *Ehrfurcht.*

axes of reference = (*anat.*) the (three) lines of reference used in describing the location of parts, organs, etc. of the body. [Various terms have been used, some of which are confusing as between man and quadrupeds (e.g. vertical, anterior-posterior). The following are unambiguous: **cephalocaudal, dextrosinistral, dorsoventral.** See Table XVI.]

axial = pert. to the spinal axis or region of the body. [Contr. w. **appendicular** = pert. to the limbs, etc.]

axial gradient = a gradual change in metabolism in the direction of any of the axes of an organism or any of its organs. [In bilaterally symmetrical forms, the major axis connects head or apex (high end of gradient) with tail or basis (low end of gradient); from this central axis extend minor axes downward toward each side. Gradients are revealed in various ways, the high or dominant end being (1) more susceptible to noxious agents (chemicals, x-rays), (2) more easily penetrated by vital stains, (3) more readily oxidized or reduced, (4) electro-negative to lower end, etc.]

axillary = pert. to or located in the armpit, or the axils of leaves or axillary buds.

axiom = any proposition which is susceptible of neither logical proof nor logical disproof but which is presumed to be accepted as true by every human being who is capable of comprehending its meaning. [In any system or field of mathematics, the underlying body of axioms consists of the minimal number of mutually consistent propositions upon which the whole system can be logically constructed, whether or not these axioms accord with empirical facts.]

axis = 1. (*math.*) one of two or more straight lines which are taken as coordinates of reference in a figure or in space in order to define the position of a given point or to plot a figure in two or more dimensions; 2. a straight line in a figure or plot, etc., or in an organism, with respect to which the two sides are symmetrical; 3. a line which constitutes the center of rotation of a revolving body. [Cf. **axes of reference.**] **axes**[pl], **axial**[a].

axis cylinder = the conducting or central part of a nerve fiber. [Cf. **axon.**]

axis/optical, see **optical axis.**

axis/visual, see **visual axis.**

axon, axone = the fiber projecting from the cell-body of a neuron, which conducts the nerve impulse away from the cell-body toward the dendrites of the next neuron in the chain. [Cf. **dendrite.**] — Fr. *cylindraxe, axone*; Ger. *Achsenfortsatz, Achsenzylinder.*

axon reflex = a peripheral reflex response, the efferent part of which is supposed to be mediated by a collateral branch of an afferent nerve fiber without passing through a reflex arc (Bayliss).

B

B-type = in eidetic theory, a type of individual who manifests certain Basedow symptoms (exophthalmic goiter) and a tendency to eidetic imagery that is flexible, imaginative, natural in coloring, and relatively under voluntary control. [Cf. **T-type.**]

Babinski reflex (or **phenomenon,** or **sign**) = extension of the toes (in place of flexion) upon stroking the sole of the foot with a pointed instrument. [Mediated by the 5th lumbar to 2d sacral segments of the cord; it occurs in infancy and in cerebrospinal tract involvements.]

bacillary layer, see **rods and cones/layer of.** — Fr. *couche bacillaire.*

background = in visual perception, the neutral surroundings and interstices of a figure or solid, attributed to an unpatterned surface lying beyond and not perceived as belonging to the figure or object. [Lack of pattern is more characteristic than distance, (e.g.) the background in paintings, etc. Syn. **ground.** In certain reversible perceptions the interwoven black-white pattern (e.g.) appears either as a white figure on a black background, or vice versa. Cf. **figure-ground.**]

backhand, backhanded writing = handwriting in which the downward strokes of the letters incline to the right. [Cf. **writing angle.**] — Fr. *écriture renversée.*

backward associations = associative connections formed between any item of experience and some other item earlier presented or experienced. [These associations probably occur only when the various items constitute related items in a larger experiential unity. There is little, if any, evidence to support the older interpretation of **retrogressive association** implied by the term.] — Fr. *associations rétrogrades (à rebours)*.

backwardness = a condition of mild mental inferiority due to a slowing up of mental development. [Syn. **mental retardation**; the two terms are used interchangeably; strictly, **retardation** denotes the process, **backwardness** the resulting condition.] **backward**[a] applied to individuals. — Fr. *arriération*.

Baconian method = the method of inductive investigation. [Named after Francis Bacon, the earliest systematic proponent of the method. The term is sometimes applied to the special inductive procedure developed by Bacon. Contr. w. **Aristotelian method** = deductive procedure.]

bad = 1. characterizing a judgment applied to actions, attitudes, or conditions which contravene standards of conduct generally considered desirable, or which unjustifiably hamper the well-being, happiness, or self-realization of individuals in terms of social standards; 2. inadequate, unsuitable, defective, or unreliable. [(2) is used loosely to express an unfavorable judgment, e.g. bad scientific procedure or results. Contr. w. **good.** Cf. **evil.**] — Fr. *mauvais*.

Baer's law, von Baer's law = the doctrine that the embryos of different kinds of organisms are at first similar and develop for a time along similar lines, those of organisms least closely related diverging first, the others diverging at later periods in proportion to the closeness of relationship. [Often confused with the theory of **recapitulation,** or the **biogenetic law.**]

balance = 1. the maintenance of an assumed posture or a succession of postures by the harmonious adjustment of sensorimotor components, involving particularly the kinesthetic and labyrinthine receptors; 2. (*esth.*) equivalence of value between right and left sides or upper and lower halves of a picture, etc., or between first and last halves of a succession, as in music. [Syn. (1) **equilibration;** (2) **symmetry,** rather than **equivalence** (a point to point correspondence being usually absent). Cf. **equilibrium.**] — Fr. *équilibre*.

balance/Mosso = a device for measuring changes in blood supply; it consists of a large platform balance (tilting board), movable in a vertical plane; the reactor lies flat on the balance, any disturbance of which, due to increased blood supply in legs or head, is recorded directly on a kymograph.

balance of mind, mental balance = integration of the mental processes, indicated by absence of eccentricity or of maladjustments of behavior. [Contr. w. **unbalanced mentality,** mental lack of balance, etc.] — Fr. *équilibre mental*.

balancing response (or **reaction**) = a type of response which enables an organism to maintain or reestablish an assumed posture with respect to gravity. — Fr. *réaction d'équilibre*.

ball-and-field test = a test of practical intelligence, in which the testee is asked to indicate how he would go about searching for a ball or other object lost in a field of a given shape (Stanford Revision of Binet Scale). — Fr. *test de la balle et du champ*.

balsamic = 1. a quality of olfactory sensation of which frankincense is a fair example (Henning); 2. a quality of olfactory sensation of which the odor of jasmine, tuberose and vanilla are examples (Zwaardemaker). [For Zwaardemaker the class includes the *odores fragrantes* of Linnaeus, and is practically identical with Henning's **fragrant** (*blumig*), not with his **resinous** (*harzig*) class. Cf. **odor, fragrant resinous, odor prism.**]

band chart = a curve wherein the abscissa represents time and the ordinate represents amount (either absolute amount or percentage of a total) of a number of classes, each taken separately, which together make up some total (total output, total expenditures, etc.). [The ordinates for class 2 are added to those of class 1; those of class 3 are added to the total of classes 1 and 2 combined, etc. When each class is shaded in a distinctive manner the chart shows a number of bands.] — Fr. *courbe cumulative de progrès*.

bar, barye = (*phys.*) a pressure of one dyne per sq. cm.

bar diagram = a statistical chart in which a series of magnitudes are represented by separate bars or rectangles of the same width, but of different lengths. [If the bars are not separated from one another, the figure is called a **histogram.**]

baragnosis = inability to recognize or compare the weights of objects.

Bárány chair, see **rotation chair.**

barbaralalia = an individual's use of articulate speech in a foreign language, characterized by difficulties with certain consonants, habitual use of rising inflection, accenting wrong syllable, and false vowel quality. [Syn. **foreign accent.** The term includes also dialectical speech.]

barotropism, barotaxis = a simple response involving a reaction against a pressure stimulus, such as a water current, etc.

barylalia = indistinct and thick utterance.

baryphonia = a form of **dysphasia** characterized by a thickness of voice.

basal age, see **age/basal.**

basal ganglia, basal masses = several ganglionic masses which lie within the white matter of each cerebral hemisphere. [Of these the **optic thalamus** and the **corpus striatum** are the most massive.]

basal metabolism, basal metabolic rate = the minimal heat produced by an individual, measured from 14 to 18 hours after eating, and when the individual has been completely resting for at least 30 minutes, but not sleeping. [It represents the energy expended in the vital and vegetative functions of the body. It is expressed in calories per hour per sq. meter of body surface.]

base = the lowest part of an object, presumably the part on which it stands. [Distg. fr. **basis,** commonly applied to logical and other nonphysical foundations.] **bases**[pl] **(-sez,** not **-seez), basal**[a].

base line, see **abscissa.**

Basedow's disease, see **exophthalmic goiter.**

bashfulness = an attitude characterized by partial inhibition of social responses, usually confined to children. [**bashfulness** and **shyness** are practically syn., but **bashfulness** may imply blushing and other autonomic indications, while **shyness** lacks these characteristics; **timidity** is a broader term, including inhibition of responses toward lower species and inanimate objects as well as of social responses.] — Fr. *timidité spontanée, t. instinctive*; Ger. *Schüchternheit.*

basilar membrane = a membrane of the internal ear, which extends from the osseous spiral lamina to the spiral ligament on the outer wall of the osseous cochlea, and separates the scala tympani from the scala vestibuli and cochlear duct. [The membrane bears on its upper surface, within the cochlear duct (or membranous cochlea), an epithelial structure called the organ of Corti, whose hair-cells are believed by many to be stimulated by movements of the basilar membrane in response to pressure-changes in the perilymph set up by sound and to constitute the actual auditory receptor.] (Accent **bass-.**) — Ger. *Basilarmembran.*

basis = a general designation for whatever underlies and supports a theory, law, procedure, or statement. [Cf. **base,** applied to physical bodies or geometrical figures.] **bases**[pl] **(-seez,** not **-sez)**; **basic**[a]. — Fr. *fondement.*

bathmism = growth force or energy (Cope).

bathophobia = morbid fear of depths.

battery = 1. a combination of tests, carefully selected empirically so as to elicit a variety of pertinent responses, and yet so balanced with respect to the total score as to provide maximal efficiency as a measuring instrument. [E.g. modern intelligence tests; tests of clerical ability.] — Fr. *batterie de tests.*

battery = 2. (*elect.*) a set or series of cells in which chemical changes set up a galvanic electrical current.

beat = 1. (*phys.*) a fluctuation in sound intensity dependent upon the combination of two sound-waves of slightly different periodicity; 2. (*psychol.*) the experience produced by such fluctuation; 3. (*music*) the arbitrary subdivision of the measure giving the formal temporal pattern. [The rate or periodicity of the **beat** (1) is equal to the difference in rate or periodicity of the two waves. Cf. **beat-tone, pulsation, beat/binaural.**] — Fr. *battement*; Ger. *Schwebung,* (3) *Takt.*

beat/binaural = a periodic change of position heard when two tones which are slightly out of tune are conducted separately to each ear; the rate of fluctuation corresponds to the frequency-difference of the primary tones. [The fundamental difference between **binaural beats** and **true beats** is that the former consist of fluctuations of position while the latter consist of fluctuations of loudness; the perceived sound, or phantom, may lie outside or inside the head, observers differing as to its spatial course. The phenomenon is better called **binaural shift.**] — Fr. *battement binaural.*

beat-tone = a tone of characteristically rough quality, produced by applying simultaneously to the same ear two sound-frequencies which differ by more than 16 to 20 cycles. [The pitch of the beat-tone is equal to the frequency difference of the generating tones, and for this reason **beat-tone** and **difference tone** are often used as syn. Koenig believed the two phenomena to be distinct, but the main difference between Koenig's **beat-tone** and Helmholtz's **difference tone** lay in the theoretical origin and interpretation of the tones. Cf. **beat, difference tone, combination tone.**] — Fr. *ton de battement*; Ger. *Stosston.*

beautiful/the = an abstract designation of whatever manifests the characteristic of beauty. — Fr. *le beau.*

beauty = any characteristic in objects which appeals to the esthetic sense in its purest form. **beautiful**[a]. — Fr. *beauté*; Ger. *Schönheit.*

behave[v] = to respond. [Applied to organic responses of any sort.] — Fr. *agir.*

behavior, behaviour = 1. a generic name for all modes of muscular or glandular response of the organism to stimulation; 2. such portions of the organism's responses as are open for observation; 3. (*hist.*) syn. for **conduct.** [Used also in the physical sciences to designate the mode of activity of any substance, and in introspective psychology to denote modes of mental activity; these uses are confusing and are not favored.] **behavioral**[a]. — Fr. *comportement, conduite*; Ger. *Verhalten.*

behavior/adaptive, see **adaptive response.**

behavior/emotional = 1. total behavior which is characterized by marked affective aspects; 2. those aspects or segments of total behavior which are ascribable to the functioning of visceral or vegetative effectors (esp. smooth muscles and glands but also striped muscles), and which importantly influence the activity of the organism, whether of overt or of implicit thinking type, with reenforcing or inhibiting effects.

behavior/extrinsic = behavior which to a large extent is dependent for its manifestation neither upon any single organ nor upon any fixed mode of response of any organ. [E.g. language behavior; maze solution. Contr. w. **intrinsic behavior.**]

behavior/intrinsic = functions which depend upon certain specific organs for their manifestation. [E.g. reflexes, glandular secretions, and the functions of the receptors in relation to their proper stimuli. Contr. w. **extrinsic behavior.**]

behavior/language, see **verbal behavior.**

behavior method = the systematic observation and description of motor and glandular responses of the organism. [Applied to a fundamental method of psychological research, distg. fr. **introspective** and **neurological.**]

behavior pattern = the temporal or spatial grouping of responses, as in rhythmical tapping or perfected maze running. [The pattern need not be absolutely stereotyped nor invariable in all details. Cf. **pattern.**] — Fr. *système de comportement.*

behavior patterns/integration of = 1. the process or result of combining behavior elements into a more stable combination or complex act, e.g. the development of a writing habit out of previously uncoordinated finger, hand, and arm flexions and extensions; 2. the individuation of finer movements from mass-action.

behavior/prenatal = behavior of the fetus, i.e. responsive movements prior to birth.

behavior/primitive = the responses peculiar to primitive peoples, i.e. to races or groups in the initial stages of cultural development. [The types of behavior out of which the behavior of modern man has evolved. **primitive** is here used both in its true sense of *first* and in its derived sense of *crude, uncultured.*]

behavior psychology = the systematic investigation of responsive activity in organisms without reference to consciousness. [As applied to man it deals only with the phenomena of psychology which are observable objectively, i.e. by another individual than the subject himself, thus excluding any treatment of his conscious experiences.] — Fr. *psychol. de la conduite, psychol. du comportement.*

behavior segment = 1. the smallest descriptive unit of the responses of an organism to a stimulus; 2. (*soc.*) an aspect of the behavior of an individual, usually consisting of institutionalized habits, taken as a unit, e.g., the economic segment, the religious segment.

behavior/social, see **social behavior.**

behaviorism = 1. behavior psychology; 2. the theoretical standpoint that all psychological phenomena can be adequately treated by the behavior method. [The view (2) is old, but the formal school began with Watson (1913).] **behaviorist**[np].

being/a = an organism. — Fr. *être*; Ger. *Wesen.*

Bekanntsqualität = quality of contents as known or quality of knownness. [Ger.]

bel = a logarithmic unit denoting difference in levels of intensity. [The **bel** is defined as N (in bels) = $\log_{10} I_2/I_1$, where I_1, I_2 are the two intensities in question. A more convenient unit is the **decibel** = 1/10 of a bel.]

belief = 1. acceptance of a principle, doctrine, statement, etc. on the basis of evidence which is assumed to be adequate; 2. a primary, undefinable type of experience; 3. a generic term embracing acceptance (belief) and rejection (disbelief). [Contr. (1) w. **disbelief** (= rejection); distg. (2) fr. **faith** (= acceptance without adequate evidence); contr. (3) w. **doubt.**] **believe**[v]. — Fr. *croyance*; Ger. *Glaube.*

belladonna = a perennial plant of the order of Solanaceae, indigenous to Southern Europe and Asia; also cultivated in the United States. [It is a cerebral excitant and also affects the medulla oblongata; mildly anodyne and powerfully mydriatic; also antispasmodic and in proper dosage a cardiac and respiratory stimulant. Its properties are due to two principal alkaloids, atropin (the racemic variety of hyoscyamin) and hyoscin. Both leaves and roots are employed.]

Bell-Magendie law = the principle that stimulation of the ventral spinal roots gives rise directly to muscular contraction but not to sensory response, and that stimulation of the dorsal roots produces sensory responses but does not directly excite muscular contractions. [Elaborated by later workers into the law that conduction from cell to cell within the central nervous system occurs only in the direction from receptor to effector.]

belongingness = the property of one item of a unit-response, in terms of which it is originally an integral part of another item in the same unit.

beneceptor = a receptor or sense organ whose stimuli are beneficial and produce pleasantness. [Cf. **nociceptor.**]

beneficial = characterizing any stimulus or response which promotes the operation of the life processes of an organism. [Contr. w. **detrimental** (or **harmful**) = which hampers the life processes. Cf. **optimal** = the most favorable situation, stimulus, or response.] — Fr. *avantageux.*

benign = 1. (*pharmacol.*) a term applied to medicines characterized by mildness; 2. (*pathol.*) a term used chiefly of tumors that are not malignant.

benign stupor = a term used to denote stuporous states of affective or manic-depressive origin, as contr. w. those of dementia praecox (schizophrenia) in which the outlook is less favorable.

benign trend = the tendency toward recovery in any illness.

berdache = a male who adopts the dress and occupations of a woman, according to the conventions of certain American Indian tribes. [While probably pathological in origin, the culture of these tribes provides a social pattern for the conduct of the individual.] (Accent **-dash.**)

bestiality = 1. any type of behavior which resembles that of beasts, in that it is irrational and disgusting; 2. sexual intercourse between a human being and an animal.

Bereitschaft = in psychological laboratory experiments, syn. for preparedness or **readiness.** [Ger. Except for a flavor of anticipation the term is practically the equivalent of **Einstellung, mental set.**]

beta movement, see **apparent (motion** or) **movement.**

beta tests = a set of mental tests first used in the United States Army in 1917–8 to determine the relative mental ability of recruits; they are designed especially for illiterates and those deficient in knowledge of English, the instructions being given in signs and the material being pictorial in character. [Distg. fr. **alpha tests,** in which instructions and material are verbal.]

Betz cells = large pyramidal ganglion-cells present in the fifth layer of the motor cortex. — Fr. *cellules de B.*

bewilderment = 1. a pathological condition characterized by inhibition of response to significant stimuli and by certain diffuse responses; 2. an emotional condition involving a high degree of cognitive confusion, sometimes with rapidly alternating and conflicting impulses. **bewilder**[v], **bewildered**[a]. — Fr. *étourdissement*; Ger. *Bestürzung.*

Bewusstheit = awareness devoid of sensory or imaginal features, including awareness of meaning and awareness of relation (Ach). [Ger. Cf. **Bewusstseinslage** (a special form of **Bewusstheit**).]

Bewusstseinslage = a type of experience reported as not appearing obviously sensory or affective; e.g., doubt, ease, bafflement, sense of approaching the goal (Mayer and Orth). [Ger. Translated **conscious attitude.** Cf. **Bewusstheit.**]

Bezold-Brücke phenomenon = a change in the hues evoked by chromatic visual stimuli, due to variation in intensity or illumination level of the stimuli in question; with increasing intensity the hues shrink away from red and green, towards either yellow or blue, in the chromatic cycle.

Bezugsvorstellung = idea of objects (Ach). [Ger.]

bhang, see **Cannabis indica.**

bias = an attitude either for or against a certain unproved hypothesis, which prevents the individual from evaluating the evidence correctly. [The term often carries an emotional implication; it is preferable to restrict **bias** to intellectual prepossession, and use **prejudice** for the emotional attitude.] — Fr. *biais, penchant.*

bias/error of = a distorting factor in the report or performance of an observer or subject, which is based on prior experience and not on the present experimental situation. — Fr. *erreur de préjugé.*

biceps reflex = contraction of the biceps brachii muscle upon tapping its distal tendon. [Mediated by 5th to 7th segments of the cord.]

Bidwell's ghost, see **Purkinje after-image.**

bigamy = the situation of having two wives or two husbands at once. [Usually a legal term. Cf. **polygamy.**]

bile = the external secretion of the liver; a brownish or yellowish fluid of bitter taste, which aids digestion both by producing an alkaline reaction in the small intestine and by promoting the emulsification and absorption of fat, and which acts as a vehicle for the elimination of a variety of excretory products. [In ancient times considered as fundamental to one of the temperaments.] **biliary**[a].

bilious = 1. a temperament characterized by querulousness; 2. indisposition or peevishness attributed to excess of bile. [A mild form of the **choleric** temperament, attributed to indigestion.]

bimodal = characterizing a frequency curve in which there are two peaks, or two intervals containing a relatively large number of cases, separated by an interval or intervals with fewer cases. [Cf. **mode.** Distg. fr. **normal probability curve,** which is **unimodal.**]

binaural = pert. to the two ears acting conjointly. [Contr. w. **uniaural (monaural).**] (Pron. **bin-** or **buy-.**) — Fr. *binauriculaire (binaural).*

binaural beats, see **beat/binaural.**

binaural fusion, see **fusion/binaural.**

binaural hearing (or **audition**) = hearing with the two ears conjointly. [Syn. **dichotic hearing, diotic hearing.** Contr. w. **uniaural hearing** = with one ear alone.] — Fr. *audition (ouïe) binaurale.*

Binet-Simon scale = a series of graded tests devised by Alfred Binet and Th. Simon in 1905, to rate the relative mental development of children. [Often called the **Binet scale,** or **Binet tests;** the tests measure the average child between the ages of 3 and 12, and are used to fix the **mental age** of normal, subnormal, and supernormal individuals within these limits.] — Fr. *échelle de B.-S.*

Binet tests, see **Binet-Simon scale.**

binocular = pert. to the two eyes acting conjointly. [E.g., binocular field = the total visual field as seen by the two eyes. Contr. w. **uniocular (monocular).**] (Pron. **bin-** or **buy-.**)

binocular color mixture, see **color mixture/binocular.**

binocular flicker = flicker evoked by the rapidly alternating presentation of stimuli to the right and left eyes, usually in such a manner that the gaps in the stimulus presented to one eye are filled by the stimulus presented to the other. — Fr. *papillotement binoculaire.*

binocular fusion, see **fusion/binocular.**

binocular parallax, see **parallax/binocular.**

binocular rivalry, see **retinal rivalry.** — Fr. *lutte b.*

binocular vision = vision with the two eyes operating conjointly, usually with fixation of both on the same objective point. [In general, characterized by a single perception of the objects fixated, but in certain conditions by doubling or by rivalry. An important factor in perception of space, giving **projection and relief.** Contr. w. **uniocular** (or **monocular**) **vision.**]

binomial = (*math.*) an algebraic expression consisting of the sum or difference of two terms. (Pron. **buy-.**)

binomial expansion = (*math.*) the form which a binomial raised to any power, n, takes when expanded by means of the binomial theorem:

$$(x + y)^n = x^n + nx^{n-1}y + \frac{n(n-1)}{1 \times 2}x^{n-2}y^2 + \frac{n(n-1)(n-2)}{1 \times 2 \times 3}x^{n-3}y^3 + \ldots$$

[When convergent (y small with reference to x), a limited number of terms of the expansion yields a close approximation to the exact value.]

biocenosis, biocoenosis = the relation subsisting between organisms which live in association. **biocenoses**[pl].

biochemistry = the investigation of the chemical aspects of vital processes. **biochemical**[a].

biogen = a hypothetical unit of living matter postulated by Verworn as the basis of vital activities.

biogenesis = the origin and evolution of living forms. **biogenetic**[a].

biogenesis/law of = the principle that all living organisms are derived from a parent or parents. [Syn. **theory of continuity,** contr. w. **spontaneous generation** or **abiogenesis** = the view that certain organisms arise directly from inorganic matter. — Fr. *l. de la biogenèse.*

biogenetic law = a principle according to which an organism in its individual development passes through stages similar to those that occurred in the course of its evolution. [Syn. **doctrine of recapitulation.**] — Fr. *l. biogenétique.*

biological analogy = (*soc.*) the description or explanation of society and social relations in biological terms, i.e. the transfer of biological concepts to sociology. [According to this view the individual organism is regarded as analogous to the biological cell, and society as analogous to the biological organism; the term **social organism** is used in connection with this theory.]

biological fallacy, see **historical fallacy.** — Fr. *sophisme biologique.*

biologism = the application of biological method to the whole field of experience, with the implication that knowledge so gained is preeminently valid. [**biologism** includes certain forms of **pragmatism** in so far as, for these, truth is a matter of biological utility.]

biology = the branch of science which deals with organisms, i.e. plants and animals. [It includes **morphology, physiology, embryology, paleontology, psychology** (as a study of behavior), etc.]

biometry = the application of statistics and measurement generally to the structures and functions of living organisms. **biometric**[a].

bionomic factors = factors which control or limit the evolution or development of living forms apart from the processes within the organism itself. [These include the chemical, mechanical, and other conditions of the environment in which the organism is situated.]

bionomics = the branch of biology which deals

with the relations of organisms to their environment. [Syn. **ecology.**]

biophore = an elementary unit postulated by Weismann as the basis of the structural composition of organisms. [Cf. **determiner.**]

biopsychic = pert. to mental phenomena in their relation to the living organism.

biopsychology, see **psychobiology.**

biosocial = 1. pert. to those social relations which are determined largely by biological factors; 2. pert. to organisms which have social uses or significance for man, e.g. animals used as pets, human beings serving as slaves. [Distg. fr. **physicosocial, psychosocial.**]

biotype = a group of organisms of common descent having the same complex of hereditary factors.

biparental inheritance = inheritance from two parents.

bipolar cell = a neuron or nerve-cell which has two projecting fibers, one conducting toward the cell-body, the other away from it. — Fr. *cellule bipolaire.*

bipolar cells/layer of, see **nuclear layer/inner.**

birth control = regulation of the birth rate by controlling conception. [Applied either to artificial prevention of conception (contraception), or, contrariwise, to the removal of factors which prevent conception.] — Fr. *contrôle de la procréation.*

birth-mark = any minor congenital disfigurement of the human body. [Cf. **nevi**[pl], the most common type.] — Fr. *marque de naissance.*

birth symbolism = 1. (*psychoan.*) a symbolic representation which reproduces the first separation from the first libido object, namely that of the new-born child from its mother; 2. (*psychoan.*) a symbolic metaphor which tends to ignore the libidinal aspect (Jung and Silberer). [Cf. **birth trauma.**]

birth trauma = 1. a physical injury received at birth.

birth trauma = 2. (*psychoan.*) the child's original anxiety at the time of birth which, if not completely mastered, may reproduce itself in later life in the form of neurotic anxiety or fear (Freud, Rank). — Fr. *trauma de la naissance.*

biserial r. = the relation between two variables, one of which has only two values.

bisexuality = 1. possession by an individual of the psychological or anatomical characteristics of both sexes; 2. (*pathol.*) a sexual abnormality in which the individual is more or less equally attracted to members of both sexes. [Syn. (1) **hermaphroditism.** Contr. (2) w. **heterosexuality, homosexuality.**] **bisexual**[a], **bisexualism**[n] (rare).

bitter = a quality of gustatory sensation of which the taste of sulphate of quinine is a typical example. [Cf. **gustatory qualities.**] — Fr. *amer.*

black = a visual sensation of minimum brilliance and achromatic in character, evoked on unstimulated or minimally stimulated portions of the retina under certain conditions. [Its arousal depends upon either simultaneous or successive achromatic contrast. It constitutes the lower limit of the **gray** or achromatic series. The complement, or antagonist of **white.**] — Fr. *noir;* Ger. *schwarz.*

black art = (*hist.*) the art practiced by sorcerers and witches, usually for evil designs. [Syn. **necromancy, conjuration, magic.**] — Fr. *magie noire.*

black body radiation = radiant energy emitted from a theoretically non-selective incandescent radiator, and having the spectral distribution given by Planck's law, i.e. a distribution determined solely by the temperature of the radiating body. [Cf. **color temperature.**] — Fr. *radiation du corps noir.*

bladder reflex, see **vesical reflex.**

blank experiment = an experiment occasionally introduced into a series of experiments, which does not conform to the given conditions, and whose results are not reckoned with the other results, being inserted to prevent automatic response or guessing in the general experiment. [Syn. **puzzle experiment.** Contr. w. **control experiment,** or **control series** = trials systematically arranged with a view to valid comparison with the experimental series.] — Fr. *expérience de contrôle;* Ger. *Vexierversuch.*

blastoderm = a layer of cells on the surface of the yolk from which the embryo develops.

blastogenic = originating in the germ cell.

blastomere = any one of the cells produced by the first few cleavages of the fertilized egg.

blastopore = (*biol.*) the mouth of the gastrula.

blastula = a stage of embryonic development in which the embryo usually contains a mass of cells arranged (roughly) in the form of a hollow sphere. [It precedes the **gastrula** stage.]

blend = an experience or datum which is not analyzed, but is due to the fusion of elements. [The term applies either to composition of the effect of two or more stimuli from the *same* sense, or to the composite effect of stimuli from *various* senses, including sometimes memory and other elements; it is most frequently applied to perceptual integrations of taste and touch. Cf. **fusion, colligation.**] — Fr. *fusion.*

blending = 1. a gradual or imperceptible change from one color to another in the landscape, etc.; 2. syn. for **fusion** — Fr. *fusion;* Ger. *Verschmelzung.*

blind spot = a small area in the retinal field which is not sensitive to light-stimulation. [In man the **blind spot** is situated near the horizontal plane and about 12° to 15° to the nasal side of the center of the retina, corresponding to the place of exit of the optic nerve from the eyeball; it contains no rods nor cones. Syn. **Mariotte's spot,** from its discoverer.] — Fr. *tache aveugle;* Ger. *blinder Fleck.*

blind writing = 1. writing produced by individuals who have lost their eyesight; 2. writing produced in the dark or under artificial deprivation of eyesight, e.g. by bandaging. — Fr. *écriture d'aveugle.*

blindness = a generic term denoting inability to see, whether the cause of the abnormality be peripheral, central, or intermediate. — Fr. *aveuglement, cécité;* Ger. *Blindheit.*

blindness/functional = lack of vision, with eyes and nervous mechanism intact, e.g. in hysteria or under hypnotic suggestion. — Fr. *cécité fonctionnelle.*

blinking = a reflex of the eyelids, slower than winking, induced either by sudden bright illumination or by a change in the direction of attention. — Fr. *clignement;* Ger. *Blinzeln.*

Blix's temperature experiment = the first report of warm and cold spots minutely localized on the skin by the application of cooled or warmed metal points, or droplets of oil.

block = a barrier to the transmission of a wave or excitation in muscle or nerve.

block-design test = a test of intelligence, in which the task is to assemble a set of blocks, each of which has a painted or figured surface, so that the assembled set matches a single more or less elaborate given design. [Standardized by S. C. Kohs.] — Fr. *test de cubes colorés, t. de dessins de Kohs.*

blocking = 1. (*neurol.*) establishing (e.g. by regional anesthesia) an obstruction to the passage of neural or muscular impulses; 2. (*psychoan.*) the repression of an idea from consciousness, or the cutting off of an association, owing to mental conflict; 3. **(of thought)** a mental state in which the patient feels that his thinking or speech is unaccountably impeded. [Cf. (2) **repression.**] — Fr. (1) *arrêt, blocage,* (2) *refoulement,* (3) *sentiment d'obstruction mentale.*

blood groups = types of blood distinguished by the effect of the serum on the red corpuscles. [In man four groups are commonly recognized, the serum of any one group causing agglutination of the red corpuscles in the other groups.] — Fr. *groupes sanguins.*

blood tests = examination of blood specimens by microscopic, chemical, physical, physiological, pharmacological, or other methods, for diagnostic and other medical or biological purposes. [Used e.g. for determining the type and therefore the compatibility of bloods for blood transfusion and as indicating the relationship between child and parents. Cf. **blood groups.**] — Fr. *tests sanguins.*

blood vessel = any artery, vein, or capillary. — Ger. *Blutgefäss.*

blue = 1. a visual sensation typically evoked by stimulation of the normal retina with radiation of wave-length approximately 478.5 millimicrons (mμ.); 2. any color manifesting a hue predominantly similar to that of blue (1). [The complement of **yellow.**]

blue-arc phenomenon = an effect produced by a stimulus at the center of the visual field against a dark background; it consists of a pair of bluish, luminous arcs seen as connecting the stimulus with the locus of the blind spot. [The effect is seen best when a long-wave (red) stimulus is employed, and is attributed to secondary excitation of the retinal receptors along the course of the nerve-fibers originally excited.]

blue-blindness, see **tritanopia.** — Fr. *cécité au bleu;* Ger. *Blaublindheit.*

blue-sighted = displaying a heightened color sensitivity (congenital or acquired) for blue. — Fr. *hypersensible au bleu.*

blue-yellow blindness = a rare type of partial color-blindness, or dichromatic vision, usually acquired, in which the visual system is reduced to reds, greens, and grays. [Cf. **tritanopia.**] — Fr. *cécité au bleu-jaune;* Ger. *Blaugelbblindheit.*

blues = (*pop.*) a mood characterized by low spirits, melancholy, gloom, emotional depression, i.e. a condition in which the predominating feeling-tone is sometimes a pleasurable melancholy. **blue**[a].

blur = lack of clear outline in an optical image, or in any visual conscious experience. — Fr. *flou.*

blush, blushing = an involuntary vasodilation, manifested by a reddening of the skin of face, ears, and neck, sometimes spreading to the chest and indicative of bashfulness or shame. [Syn. **flushing** (when associated with anger).] — Fr. *rougeur.*

boasting = a mode of behavior characterized by insistent attempts to force others to accept an exaggerated valuation of one's own accomplishments or abilities. [Often an attempt to conceal some deficiency or inferiority; cf. **inferiority complex, compensation.**] — Fr. *vantardise;* Ger. *Prahlerei.*

body = 1. (*biol.*) the central part of an organism, i.e. the trunk or part which bears the appendages; 2. the material organism; 3. (*physiol.*) a coherent unitary object, or organ, e.g. the suprarenal body, the pineal body, etc. [In psychol. (2) is contr. w. **mind.**] — Fr. *corps,* Ger. *Körper, Leib.*

bolometer = 1. an instrument for measuring minute differences in radiant heat in terms of the changes of resistance of a metallic strip exposed to the radiations; 2. a device for measuring the force of the heart beat.

bond = whatever in the organization of the individual is responsible for his making, more or less regularly, a certain response to a given stimulus or situation, the concept of **bond** being noncommittal as to the anatomy or physiology of the connection between stimulus and response. — Fr. *lien.*

bone conduction = (*aud.*) the transmission of sound waves to the auditory receptors by way of the bones of the skull. [It occurs, e.g. when the base of a vibrating tuning fork is applied to the teeth, or against the head. Contr. w. **air conduction** = the usual mode of transmission.] — Fr. *transmission osseuse;* Ger. *Knochenleitung.*

bone-conduction test = a test of auditory acuity for sounds conducted to the inner ear through the bones of the head, as compared with acuity by conduction through the meatus; it is made by placing a vibrating body, such as the stem of a tuning fork, in contact with the skull. [Greater acuity for sounds by bone conduction than by air conduction indicates impairment of the conductive mechanism (meatus, drum, ossicles) of the ear. Cf. **conduction deafness.**]

bone reflex, see **periosteal reflex.** — Fr. *réflexe osseux.*

bone sensibility, see **pallesthesia.**

borderline cases = phenomena which fall between two distinguishable classes and are not readily assigned to either. [Applied to cases falling between sanity and insanity, sensation and imagination, low normal and subnormal intelligence, normal and supernormal (*psych. res.*), etc.] — Fr. *cas marginaux.*

Bordet-Gengou phenomenon = (*immunol.*) fixation of a complement, or inactivation of complement when antigen combines with its specific antibody. [This phenomenon is the basis of the Wassermann test for syphilis and other similar complement-fixation tests. Cf. **complement.**]

boredom = a condition of diffused attention, unpleasant in quality, resulting from the automatization of the activity in which the subject is engaged and the concurrent presence of obstacles to changing that activity. — Fr. *ennui.*

botany, see **zoology.**

boulimia, see **bulimia.**

brachial paralysis = a state of paralysis of the

upper extremity which occurs, e.g. after injuries involving rupture of the brachial nerve trunks.

brachium = the arm, esp. the part above the elbow. (Accent **brake-**.) **brachial**[a].

brachycephaly = a form of (human) skull which is relatively short in the sagittal direction, i.e. from front to back, i.e. a broad skull. [Contr. w. **dolichocephaly** = a relatively long skull. Cf. **cephalic index**.] (Pron. **brack-**.) **brachycephalic**[a].

brachydactyly = a condition characterized by abnormally short fingers, usually with a reduced number of phalanges. (Pron. **brack-**.) **brachydactylic**[a].

bradyarthria, bradylalia, bradyglossia = a speech disorder due to brain lesions, characterized by abnormal slowness in articulation. [A form of **dysarthria**. Distg. fr. **bradylogia**, which occurs without demonstrable brain lesions.] (Pron. **brad-**.)

bradycardia = an abnormally slow rate of heartbeat.

bradylogia = sluggish speech due to some functional defect. [A form of **dyslogia**. Distg. fr. **bradyarthria**, due to brain lesions.]

Braidism = (*hist.*) the theory of hypnosis and (esp.) method of James Braid (1843), one of the first to attempt a psychological explanation of the phenomena previously designated as mesmerism.

Braille = a form of reading material in which letters are replaced by groups of raised points (point writing), enabling blind individuals to read through tactual perception. (Pron. **Brayl**.) — Ger. *Punktschrift*.

brain = the mass of neural tissue within the skull. [Syn. **encephalon**. The chief parts are the cerebrum, mid-brain, cerebellum, pons, and medulla oblongata. The term is sometimes applied also to the supra-esophageal ganglia of invertebrates.] — Fr. *cerveau*; Ger. *Gehirn, Hirn*.

brain fag = (*pop.*) a term applied to a condition of nervous irritability and fatiguability, induced by overwork. [Cf. **neurasthenia**.] — Fr. *fatigue cérébrale*.

brain-spot hypothesis = (*hist.*) a term applied by E. E. Southard to theories which emphasize organic factors in the etiology of mental disease. [Contr. w. **mind-twist hypothesis**.] — Fr. *hypothèse de la tache cérébrale*.

brain stem = the portion of the brain which remains after removal of the cerebellum and of the cerebral hemispheres, down to their junction with the basal ganglia. — Fr. *tronc cérébral*.

brain-storm = (*pop.*) any form of emotional excitement or uncontrolled behavior. — Fr. *crise émotionnelle*.

brain weight = the weight of the entire brain when removed from the surrounding tissue. [Used as a measure of the quantity of neurons in an individual brain, and regarded by some investigators as an index of mental capacity.] — Fr. *poids du cerveau*.

branchial = pert. to or located in the gills. (Accent **brank-**.)

Braun tube, see **cathode-ray oscillograph**.

break phenomenon = a point where the prepotent of two or more rival stimuli suddenly loses its power to call forth response and there is a correspondingly rapid modification in behavior. [E.g. in athletic contests and fatigue experiments.]

breathing spots = the spots left by the condensation of the cloud of moisture upon any cold smooth surface which intercepts the current of air exhaled through the nose. [If the nasal passages are in a normal condition, the cloud first divides into a right and a left half. Then each half divides into an anteromedial and a posterolateral portion. The former represents that part of the current which passes nearer the smell receptors.] — Fr. *taches d'empreinte respiratoire*.

breed[n] = a group of closely related animals within a species. [Syn. **variety, strain**.] — Fr. *race*.

breed[v] = 1. to propagate organisms; 2. to mate. [Sometimes limited to animal propagation. Contr. w. **crossing**, which denotes the propagation of plants.] — Fr. *engendrer, propager*.

breeding behavior, see **mating behavior**.

Breton's law = a formula proposed by P. Breton as a substitute for Weber's law; it states that there is a parabolic relation between stimulus and just noticeable difference, expressed by the formula $S = (R/C)^{1/2}$.

bright = characterized by high illumination, intense light-emitting power, or by a high degree of brilliance. [Cf. **brilliance, brightness**.] — Fr. *lumineux*; Ger. *hell*.

bright adaptation, see **adaptation**. — Fr. *adaptation lumineuse*.

brightness = 1. a photometric measure of light emission per unit area of a luminous body or of a translucent or reflecting surface, i.e. candle-power per unit area; 2. a qualitative attribute frequently ascribed to visual, auditory, cutaneous, and kinesthetic sensations; in this sense, **dull** is its qualitative opposite, but the difference is relative. [**brightness** (1) determines the stimulus value of a given surface as a visual object, and in this sense is conveniently expressed in **candles per square meter** or in **millilamberts**. Cf. **brilliance**.] **bright**[a]. — Fr. *brillance, éclat*; Ger. *Helligkeit*.

brightness = 3. that quality of mind which determines the rate at which a child's "general intelligence" will grow. [Distg. fr. **mental age**.] **bright**[a] (limited to superior degrees).

brightness/specific = the degree to which any of the several elementary color processes, according to the Hering theory of color vision, contributes to the brilliance of the total sensation. [Cf. **valence/chromatic, chroma-brilliance coefficient**.]

brilliance = that attribute of any color or visual sense-quality in respect to which it may be classed as equivalent to some member of a series of grays ranging from black to white. [Distg. fr. **brightness**, which has reference solely to stimulus-magnitude.] — Fr. *luminosité, clarté*; Ger. *Helligkeit*.

brilliance contrast = a change in brilliance in a given area of the visual field, due to very recent stimulation (in respect to brightness) of an adjoining or neighboring area, or of the given area. [Syn. **brightness contrast**.] — Fr. *contraste lumineux*; Ger. *Helligkeitskontrast*.

brilliance threshold (or **limen**) / **absolute** = the intensity of the least visual stimulus (of any specified wave-length composition) sufficient to evoke a brilliance noticeably in excess of that of the adjacent unstimulated visual field. [The value is determined after complete dark adaptation, but does not exclude the effect of processes normally active in the sense-organ.] — Fr. *seuil absolu lumineux*; Ger. *Lichtschwelle*.

bringing up = the care and education of human offspring during the years of immaturity. [Usually emphasizes the development of moral character.] **bring up**ᵛ. — Fr. *élevage de la progéniture*.

Broca/area of = an area of gray matter on the base of the brain, situate behind the gyrus rectus and in front of the tractus opticus. — Fr. *aire de B*.

Broca/convolution of = the inferior frontal gyrus in the left hemisphere of right-handed persons. [This gyrus was identified by Broca (1861) as the cortical center for articulation, or spoken language.]

bronchus = either of the two branches of the trachea or windpipe. [Sometimes applied to the trachea as a whole.] (Pron. **bronk-**.) **bronchi**^{pl}, **bronchial**^{a}.

brontephobia, see **astraphobia.**

Brown-Séquard syndrome = "paralysis and hyperesthesia of one side and anesthesia of the opposite side of the body" (Gould). [Due to a lesion on one lateral half of the spinal cord.]

Brown-Spearman formula = a formula for estimating the **reliability** (2) of a test, when the test has been increased in length, either by addition of extra items, or by averaging several forms of the original test. [Usually written, $r_{nn} = nr_{II}/[1 + (n - 1)r_{II}]$, in which n = degree to which the test has been increased; r_{II} = reliability coefficient of the original test; and r_{nn} = the estimated reliability coefficient of the lengthened test.]

Bruch's membrane = the transparent, nearly structureless inner layer of the choroid coat of the eye, which lies next to the outermost, or pigmented layer of the retina.

buccal = pert. to or located in the cheek. (Accent **buck-**.)

budding = 1. asexual reproduction in which a new organism starts as a bud which protrudes from the parental body and later separates and becomes independent; 2. the formation of new parts of an organism by the outgrowth and differentiation of primordia, as in the formation of leaves and flowers in plants. [Syn. **gemmation.**] — Fr. *gemmation*.

bulb = syn. for **medulla oblongata,** or posterior hind-brain segment.

bulb/olfactory = an oval mass of gray matter which lies on the cribriform plate of the ethmoid bone just above each nasal cavity; each bulb is the extension of a cerebral hemisphere and constitutes a primary center of olfaction.

bulbar retraction reflex = retraction of eye with closing of the nictitating membrane (in animals), when conjunctiva or cornea is touched.

bulbocavernous reflex, see **virile reflex.**

bulbopontine region = that portion of the brain consisting of the pons plus the portion of the medulla oblongata lying dorsad of it.

bulimia, boulimia = morbidly exaggerated hunger. [Contr. w. **anorexia.**]

bulky color = a transparent, three-dimensional color experience, as observed e.g. in looking at a colored liquid. [Distg. fr. **film-color** (*Flächenfarbe*) and **surface color** (*Oberflächenfarbe*).] — Fr. *couleur volumineuse*; Ger. *Raumfarbe*.

Bunsen-Roscoe law, see **reciprocity law.**

Burdach/columns of = the spinobulbar tracts situate between the columns of Goll and the dorsal cerebellar tracts.

burnt, see **empyreumatic.**

C

CA = abbrev. for **chronological age.**

CAVD test = a battery of four tests (completions, arithmetical problems, vocabulary, and directions) developed by E. L. Thorndike and first exhaustively described in 1926. [**Intellect CAVD,** which these tests measure, is reported to be nearly the same thing as the aspects of general intelligence measured by most standard tests of intelligence.]

c factor, cleverness factor = a general factor in human abilities, constituting an important individual difference, functionally interpreted as the facility with which an individual can change rapidly from one mental task to another that is quite different. [Postulated by Garnett and adopted by Spearman as an important aspect of quickness, originality, humor, etc., the common basis of which would be freedom from inertia. The **c factor** shows itself statistically to be independent of **the g factor.** It is the obverse of the **p factor.** Cf. **p factor, factor theories.**] — Fr. *facteur d'habileté*.

C.G.S. system = a system of mensuration which employs the **centimeter** (**centimetre**) as unit of length, the **gram** (**gramme**) as unit of mass, and the **second** as unit of time. [The gram is also used as unit of weight; but whereas the mass of a body is considered constant, its weight depends upon its distance from the center of the earth, its latitude (centrifugal effect of earth's rotation), the medium surrounding it, and other conditions.]

cachexia = a morbid or depraved condition of general nutrition and impoverishment of blood, present in grave diseases such as carcinoma, pernicious anemia, etc., and characterized by emaciation, anemia, and a peculiar sallow complexion. (Pron. **cack-**.) **cachectic**^{a}.

cadence = 1. a fall of the voice in reading or speaking; 2. a sequence of chords at the end of a musical phrase or composition, expressing finality, conclusion, or repose.

calamus scriptorius = a groove on the dorsal surface of the medulla oblongata at its caudal end. [Lat. writer's pen. So called from its shape.]

calcarine cortex = the cerebral cortex surrounding the calcarine fissure in the occipital lobe of the human brain. [The locus for visual sensations.] — Fr. *écorce c*.

calcarine fissure = a fissure on the mesial surface of the cerebral hemisphere, which runs forward from the extreme rear, below the cuneus, to join the parieto-occipital fissure. — Fr. *scissure c*.

calc-spar prism, see **Nicol prism.**

calibration = the process or result of translating the values given by a certain instrument into terms of a known standard. [The relations determined are made permanently available, either by marking the standard values on the instrument itself, or by means of a formula, table, or graph indicating the standard values as related to the corresponding values given by the instrument.] **calibrate**ᵛ.

calligraphy = 1. beautiful or artistic handwriting without irregularity of form; 2. handwriting or graphic style. [(1) carries frequently the implication of professional skill, proceeds by a slow drawing movement rather than an automatic writing movement.] **calligraphic**[a].

callosum, corpus callosum = a thick band of commissural nerve fibers which lie immediately above the third ventricle and unite the two cerebral hemispheres. — Fr. *corps calleux.*; Ger. *Balken.*

caloric nystagmus, see **nystagmus.**

calorimeter = a device for directly measuring heat production in the organism; it consists of a well-insulated box, equipped inside with a coiled pipe through which a measured amount of water flows; the heat radiated and conducted away from the organism inclosed in the box is absorbed by the water and its amount is calculated from the difference of temperature of the water entering and leaving the chamber. [Used in experiments on metabolism and the nutritive value of foods.]

calorization = 1. the application of heat; 2. specifically, the application of heat to the region of the semicircular canals of the inner ear.

campimeter = a flat chart used to map out the visual field. [In the **campimeter,** equal visual angles are represented by greater lengths as the distance from the fixation point increases, in accordance with the tangent function; contr. w. **perimeter,** in which the instrumental measures are proportional to the visual angles.] **campimetry**[n], **campimetric**[a].

canal/central, canalis centralis = a small tube filled with cerebrospinal fluid, situate within the gray matter of the spinal cord, and extending throughout its entire length. [The **central canal** is the vestige of the cavity of the embryonic neural tube.] — Fr. *c. de l'épendyme.*

canal/tympanic, see **scala tympani.**

canal/vestibular, see **scala vestibuli.**

canals/semicircular, see **semicircular canals.**

canalization = the formation in the central nervous system, through the repeated passage of nerve-impulses, of pathways of permanently lowered resistance (**engrams**). [This phenomenon is attributed by some writers to a growth of dendrites stimulated by the nerve-impulses. Cf. **neurobiotaxis.**]

cancellation test = a test of speed in the discrimination of forms; in the simplest case the subject is required to cancel a single letter (e.g. A) wherever it appears in a long series of letters randomly arranged; this may be complicated by requiring the cancellation of two or more letters. [Cf. **"A" test.**]

candle = the unit of **luminous intensity** of a source of light. [The **international candle,** agreed upon in 1909, is reproduced from any one of a number of carefully intercompared standard incandescent lamps, operated and used under specified conditions; the German **Hefnerkerze** (Hefner candle) is about 0.9 **international candle.**] — Fr. *bougie*; Ger. *Kerze.*

candlepower = luminous intensity expressed in candles. [Syn. **candle.** E.g. "the intensity of a source is 60 candles," "the candlepower of a source is 60."]

Cannabis indica = Indian hemp, the flowering tops of *C. sativa,* of which there are two varieties, *C. indica* and *C. americana,* the first being much more potent. [The active principle is a cannabin oil from which a light hydro-carbon $C_{18}H_{20}$ known as cannabene is obtained. It is an antispasmodic and a narcotic producing peculiar psychological effects. In large doses, it produces mental exaltation and intoxication, a sensation of double consciousness, perverted conception of time, illusions of sight, hearing, and other senses. Used as a mild hypnotic in delirium tremens, in spasm of bladder, and as an aphrodisiac in impotence. Syn. **hashish, bhang, Ganjah,** and **Churras** (all Indian names).] — Fr. *chanvre indien.*

canon = a normative formula or working rule which is recommended for use in scientific procedure, as likely to lead to the discovery of truth. [Cf. **Mill's canons, Morgan's canon, economy/principle of.** Contr. w. **law** = a formula which embodies a discovered principle of nature, and **hypothesis** = an unproved principle of nature, assumed provisionally and to be proved or disproved later.]

capability = the upper limit of an organism's functional ability at a given stage of its development, with optimal training. [Cf. **ability, capacity.**]

capacity = 1. the full potentiality of an individual for any function, as limited by his native constitution and as measured, theoretically, by the extent to which that function would develop under optimal conditions. [Cf. **ability, capability.**] — Ger. *Fähigkeit.*

capacity = 2. (*elect.*) the quantity of electricity per volt of pressure which a condenser will hold; capacity = charge/voltage. [Syn. **capacitance.** The commonly used unit of **capacity** (2) is the **microfarad,** μf.]

capacity/cranial = the volume contents of the (human) skull.

capacity/mental = potential mental ability. [Believed to be determined largely but not exclusively by native endowment. Distg. fr. **aptitude,** which implies also a taste or liking for the activity in question, and fr. **proficiency** = actual ability at the present time.]

capacity test, see **aptitude test.**

capillary = a member of that portion of the circulatory system which connects the arterial and venous systems; it consists of very fine ducts or tubes. — Ger. *Haargefäss.*

capillary electrometer = a device for indicating minute electric currents; it consists of a thread of mercury in contact with dilute acid in a vertical capillary tube; the normal balance between the upward and downward forces of gravity and surface tension is disturbed when a current to be measured is passed through the tube, and the junctional meniscus moves up or down the tube to a new point of balance. [Commonly in the study of nerve impulses the current is amplified and the meniscus movement is optically magnified and photographically recorded on a moving plate.]

capital punishment = the official putting to death of an offender. — Fr. *punition capitale.*

caprice = abrupt changes in an individual's mode of behavior on the basis of fleeting and unpredictable ideas and feelings.

capricious = characterizing motions or movements which are free, i.e. which lack complete determination.

cardiac = pert. to or located in the heart.

cardinal point = (*psychol.*) the point in a quantitative series of sensations at which the difference limen begins to increase according to Weber's law, i.e. in proportion to the stimulus. [The term denotes a specific sensation; distg. fr. **cardinal value** = the corresponding stimulus value.]

cardinal value = the value at which the difference limen of a quantitative series of sensations begins to increase according to Weber's law, i.e. in porportion to the stimulus (Fechner). [Cf. **cardinal point.**]

cardinal virtues = (*hist.*) the leading social virtues, on which all others depend or hinge. [Enumerated by Plato as *prudence, temperance, fortitude, justice.*]

cardiograph = an instrument which mechanically measures the heart action and records the rate and intensity of the beats.

cardiotachometer = an instrument which indicates, by means of the action currents, the rate of the heart-beat.

card sorting, card sorting test = a type of continuous discrimination response experiment, in which the subject takes a pack of shuffled cards, turns them over one at a time, and makes the responses by throwing them into the appropriate trays or bins; usually the total time for sorting the entire pack is taken and errors are counted. [A variation of technique is sorting to previous card, in which the suit of the last card thrown face up into the tray determines the compartment for the next card.] — Fr. *test de rapidité du classement de cartes.*

career = the social life of an individual taken as a whole (i.e. as studied from the genetic approach), with emphasis on his accomplishments, the range of his social influence, and the attitudes of other persons toward him. — Fr. *carrière*; Ger. *Karriere.*

caressing = an expression of affection, characterized by patting and gentle rubbing of the object with the hands.

carpal = pert. to or located in the wrist.

carrier bracket = a device consisting essentially of two wooden carriers which turn on vertical axes and which are so interconnected that one can be swung into the position previously occupied by the other; it is used in lifted-weight experiments to eliminate the space error. — Fr. *crochet-support rotatif.*

cartridge weights = a set of weights extending, in more or less uniform steps, over a certain range of intensities and used to determine accuracy of judgment to intensive differences of touch, hefting, etc. [Usually made by loading cartridge cases with shot, packing with cotton and closing with a wad.] — Fr. *cartouches de soupèsement.*

case = a specific type or example. [Used in experimental work to designate one of a series of observations or trials, or one set of conditions among many that are included in the research.]

case history method = the technique for studying an individual, which attempts to gather all relevant material and to arrange it in such a manner as to give it genetic significance. [Applies to both normal and pathological individuals. Syn. **case method, case study.**]

case study = study of individuals by the **clinical** as contr. w. the **experimental method.** [Usually assembles various items of information in order to arrive at an understanding of the individual, generally with the practical purpose of planning measures for his welfare.]

caste = a class of individuals distinguished from others by racial difference or by social barriers. [The *racial* significance of the term is now generally limited to half-caste or other intermediates; the *social* application is generally based on religious grounds, marking off social classes within the same race, e.g. priestly caste, warrior caste, etc.]

castration = the removal of gonads, or sex glands, from either sex. **castrate**[v], **spay**[v] (female).

castration anxiety = (*psychoan.*) the mental state associated with fear of castration.

castration complex = 1. (*psychoan.*) those unconscious excitations and affects which are bound up with the loss of the genital organs or their analogues, e.g. withdrawal from mother's breast in nursing; 2. (*psychoan.*) a reaction to intimidation regarding loss of the genital organs or the restraint of early infantile sexual activity. [Syn. (1) **castration anxiety.**]

casual = characterizing events that are unexpected or random. [Applied generally to the conjunction of two events belonging to different (unrelated) sequences; **random** includes this and also the conjunction of a large number of independent factors.] — Fr. *accidentel, fortuit*; Ger. *zufällig.*

catabolism, katabolism = the tearing down of tissue, i.e. the resolution of chemical compounds in the living organism into their elements, or into other chemical compounds which are not part of the organic tissue and are known as waste products. [Contr. w. **anabolism.**] **catabolic**[a], pert. to catabolism or to its products.

catacrotic = designating the secondary rise in the descending pulse curve which is due to two or more expansions of the artery in the same beat.

catalepsy = a state of *flexibilitas cerea* or involuntary retention of position, or of limbs or parts in positions where placed, with varying resistance to the placing. [Observed esp. in schizophrenia and in hysterical and hypnotic states.] **cataleptic**[a, np].

catalogia, cataphasia, see **verbigeration.**

catalysis = an alteration of the velocity of a chemical reaction produced by a substance which may not itself enter into the reaction, or which may combine with a reactant only during some intermediate phase of the reaction. [Two important types of catalysis are recognized: (*a*) **negative cat.** = in which the rate of reaction is slowed; and (*b*) **positive cat.** = in which the rate of reaction is accelerated.] **-ses**[pl], **catalytic**[a].

catalyst = a substance producing catalysis. [Syn. **catalyzer, catalyzator.**]

cataplexy = a state of fear or shock characterized by immobility, found in some animals particularly when they have been held firmly in certain positions for some time. [Considered by some writers analogous to human catalepsy induced by hypnotic suggestion.]

cataract = any opacity of the crystalline lens of the eye.

cataract/morgagnian = a mature or overripe cataract, in which a nucleus is left floating in the dissolved outer layers of the lens.

catatonia = 1. a supposed disease entity of the motor system (as an analogy or counterpart of paresis, Kahlbaum); 2. a state of profound mental automatism akin to somnambulism, in which the skeletal musculature remains in any position in which it is passively placed. [(1) includes both **catalepsy** and **negativism.** Cf. (1) **catatonic dementia praecox;** (2) **catalepsy.**]

catatonic deme tia praecox = a psychosis with specially marked involvement of motor tension, catalepsy, automatic resistance, and contrary action (negativism, mutism, refusal of food from special persons or echolalia, echopraxia — in general, reactions of the order of submission, passivity, and withdrawal).

catatonic stupor = a mental state associated with catatonia, and accompanied by almost total inaccessibility.

catch muscle = a muscle found in some mollusks which holds or locks the valves of the shell in any position to which they are drawn by the action of contractile muscle fibers. [Syn. **lock mechanism, ratchet mechanism.**] — Fr. *muscle-verrou.*

catechetical method = a method of instruction or of inducing conviction by means of a skillfully devised series of questions, whose answers lead gradually to acknowledgment of the conclusions desired by the questioner. [Syn. **Socratic method.** Used by Socrates as a principal method of instruction and debate, according to Plato.]

categorical = without conditions or qualifications. [Contr. w. **hypothetical.**]

categorical imperative = a moral duty which is held to be binding regardless of conditions. [Generally used in the abstract, i.e. to denote the unconditioned nature of the moral sense. It forms the basis of the Kantian ethics.]

category = 1. a fundamental or principal class; 2. a class of psychophysical judgments, e.g. the categories *greater, equal,* and *less.* [Hist. the name used by Aristotle for the ten fundamental classes into which all predicates of reality can be grouped; later, one of the fundamental classes of judgments concerning phenomena according to Kant. In scientific work often used as a syn. for **class.**]

catelectrotonus = enhanced excitability and conductivity of a nerve or muscle in the region of the cathode during the passage of a steady direct current. [Cf. **electrotonus.**]

catharsis, katharsis = 1. (*esth.*) the alleviation of unpleasant emotions by witnessing their representation in an artistic production, such as the drama; 2. (*pathol.*) the relief of abnormal excitement by reestablishing the connection between the emotion and the object which originally excited it; 3. (*psychoan.*) a term applied by Breuer to the technique of unburdening disturbing complexes, which was subsequently developed as psychoanalysis. [Cf. (3) **abreaction.**]

cathartic method, see **abreaction.**

cathexis = (*psychoan.*) a concentration or accumulation of mental energy on some particular idea or object or along some particular channel. [By analogy w. electrical charge.] **cathectic**[a]. — Fr. *investissement*; Ger. *Besetzung.*

cathode = a conductor by which a positive current leaves an electrolyte to pass into a circuit, or to which positively charged ions (**cations**) are attracted in the electrolytic process. (Syn. **negative electrode.**]

cathode-ray oscillograph = an instrument in which a beam of electrons is deflected by a magnetic or electrostatic field. [Syn. **Braun tube.**]

cation = a positively charged ion. (Pron. **cat-eye-on.**)

catoptrics = that branch of optics which deals with the reflection of light. [Contr. w. **dioptrics,** which deals with the refraction of light. Cf. **optrics.**]

Cattell algometer = an apparatus devised by J. McK. Cattell for the measurement of pain sensitivity; it consists of a plunger (working against a coiled spring) whose tip is pressed against the skin until pain is felt; the pressure exerted is indicated on a scale.

caudal = pert. to or located in the tail, or rear portion of the body of an animal. **caudad**[adv] = toward the tail.

caudate nucleus = a pyriform mass having its greatest enlargement at the cephalic end, which forms part of the outer wall of the lateral ventricle. [It is the largest component of the corpus striatum and lies in contact with the cephalic extremity of the thalamus. It has relation to the production of voluntary activity, but its relation to the cortical motor areas and to the spinal motor cells has not been discovered. Syn. **nucleus caudatus.** Cf. **lenticular nucleus.** — Fr. *noyau caudé.*

causal = (*anal. psychol.*) pert. to physical or logical necessity. [Contr. w. **final,** pert. to struggle towards a goal.]

causal chain = a sequence of events regarded as a case of repeated **causation.** — Fr. *enchaînement causal.*

causal nexus = the relation between two successive phases of an event, or between two successive phenomena. [In certain philosophical schools this relation is pictured as an actual bond, whence the term *nexus* (Lat. for bond). Cf. **cause, causality.**] — Fr. *lien causal.*

causal theory, see **interactionism.** — Fr. *doctrine de l'action causale, d. de l'influence naturelle.*

causalgia, see **thermalgia.**

causality = 1. the relation of uniform coexistence and sequence between phenomena; 2. (*psychol.*) the feeling of expectation, or tendency to anticipate a consequent when an antecedent is given; 3. (*phys.*) the methodological use of the concept of force. [Syn. (1) **causal relation, cause and effect.**] **causal**[a]. — Ger. (2) *Kausalität.*

causation = 1. the process of transition or transformation of phenomena, objects, events, etc., when the earlier stages are regarded as the conditions of the later stages; i.e. if in the absence of the earlier phenomena, or their equivalents, the later phenomena never occur; 2. the conditioning of a present event by factors which surround that event both in space and in time. [In certain systems, notably in nineteenth-century natural philosophy, **causation** is regarded as a force or agency which produces transition or transformation (cf. **causal nexus**); in scientific work (1) is treated as merely a phenomenal (2) as a dynamic process.

cause = a phenomenon, object, or group of phenomena or objects so related to a simultaneous or succeeding phenomenon, etc., that in the absence of the former or of some equivalent the latter never appears. [Contr. w. **effect** = the succeeding or conditioned phenomenon involved in the relation. Syn. **necessary antecedent.** Cf. **causality.**] **causal**[a] (used also w. **causality**). — Ger. *Ursache.*

cause and effect, see **causality.**

caution = an attitude (either emotional, or intellectual, or both) characterized by partial inhibition of the typical responses to a given situation. [**caution** emphasizes retardation of motor response; **timidity** emphasizes an emotional state which is one of several causes of motor retardation.]

cave art = the art of the cave man or of the upper paleolithic period in western Europe, in which perspective is usually lacking and group composition is rare. [The conspicuous feature of this art is the fidelity with which the large game animals of the time are depicted in line drawing, carving, and modeling. Sometimes contr. w. **geometric art.**]

cecum, caecum = the pouch which extends downward from the beginning of the large intestine. (Accent **see-.**) **cecal (caecal)**[a].

cell = the fundamental unit of structure in the living organism, which consists of a nucleus surrounded by cytoplasm and is usually enclosed by a cell wall. [The simpler organisms (protozoa and protophyta) consist of a single cell; higher organisms consist of many cells of various specialized types joined together. The individual cell is complex, containing many special parts, each part consisting of many molecules.] — Fr. *cellule*; Ger. *Zelle*.

cell-body = (*neurol.*) the central, cellular portion of a neuron or nerve-cell, exclusive of the projecting fibers. [The term is used in describing nerve-cells to avoid confusion between the cell with its projections and the cell proper; in other types of cell there are no significant projections.] — Fr. *corps cellulaire*.

cell division = the processes involved in the separation of a cell into parts, each of which usually develops into a cell similar to the original one.

cell theory = the theory that all organisms are composed of one or more cells and of substances produced by these cells.

cellulifugal, cellifugal = as applied to nerve fibers or impulses, directed away from the cell-body. [Contr. w. **cellulipetal** = directed toward the cell-body.] (Accent **-if-.**)

cellulipetal, cellipetal = as applied to nerve fibers or impulses, directed toward the cell-body. [Contr. w. **cellulifugal** = directed away from the cell-body.] (Accent **-ip-.**)

censorship = 1. (*soc.*) the exercise by an individual, or individuals, of restraint, through institutional channels, upon the public dissemination of views on political, religious, moral, or related questions, or upon esthetic, literary, or other presentations offered for public consumption or enjoyment; 2. (*psychoan.*) a selective agency, inhibitive mechanism, or force assumed to be at work within the mind, whereby a displeasing or painful memory, thought, or impulse is prevented from rising into consciousness from the unconscious. [The main censorship (2) is imposed between unconscious and preconscious; a weaker one occurs between preconscious and consciousness itself. The agency effecting censorship is practically identical with **repression.** Cf. **dream censorship.**] — Ger. *Zensur*.

cent = (*mus.*) the one hundredth part of an equal semitone. [The **cent** has been used esp. in England and Germany in comparing natural with tempered intervals and in describing unusual musical intervals; there are 1200 cents in an octave. Cf. **centioctave.**]

center, centre = 1. a focal point, e.g. center of attention; 2. any portion of the nervous system which marks the transition from afferent to efferent paths; 3. a region of the cortex, in which some specific function is supposedly localized, e.g. the visual area. [Cf. **area.**] **central**[a], **centrad**[adv] = toward the center.

center/cortical = any group of nerve-cells in the cortex which act as an integrated unit in the performance of some more or less specific function.

center of rotation = the theoretical intersecting-point of all possible axes about which the eyeball may rotate in performing its normal movements. [The center of rotation of the human eyeball is said to lie 13.5 mm. back of the extreme front of the cornea and 10 mm. in front of the extreme back surface of the sclera. Cf. **Listing's law.**] — Ger. *Drehpunkt*.

center/spinal = any group of nerve-cells in the spinal cord which act as an integrated unit in the performance of some relatively specific sensorimotor function.

centile rank = (*statist.*) a value which, for a given score, gives the percentage of the entire distribution below the given score. [E.g. a score with a centile rank of 30 exceeds 30% of the scores in the distribution. Cf. **percentile.**] (Pron. **-ill** or **-ile.**)

centioctave = one hundredth part of an octave, i.e. 12 **cents.**

centrad[n] = (*vis.*) a unit of angular measurement represented by the arc of a circle equal in length to 1/100 of the radius, i.e. 1/100 of a **radian.** [Used in ophthalmology to designate the deviating power of prisms.]

central = 1. pert. to center; 2. situate farthest away from the periphery. [In neurol. applied either to the cord and brain, or to the brain alone, this organ being farthest away from the periphery as the nerve impulse travels. Contr. w. **peripheral.**] **centrad**[adv] = toward the center.

central canal, see **canal/central.**

central fissure, see **Rolandic fissure.** — Fr. *scissure centrale*; Ger. *Zentralwindung*.

central interval, CI = in the method of single stimuli, the difference between the upper and lower limens. [Cf. **interval of uncertainty.**]

central lobe, see **Island of Reil.**

central nervous system = the brain and cord, exclusive of afferent and efferent nerves. [Contr. w. **peripheral nervous system** and distg. fr. **autonomic system.**]

central neuron = any neuron belonging entirely to the central nervous system. [Distg. fr. **sensory neuron** = belonging to the afferent nerves, and **motor neuron** = belonging to the efferent nerves.]

central tendency = any typical or representative value (e.g. arithmetical mean, median, mode, etc.) of a set of data. — Ger. *Hauptwert*.

central tendency of judgment = a general tendency for the judgments of a given individual, with respect to a given quality, to gravitate toward the middle portion of the judgment or rating scale which he is using. [This tendency, first described by Hollingworth, has the effect of decreasing the effective or working length of rating scales, and hence their reliability.]

centralis/sulcus, see **Rolandic fissure.**

centrifugal = (*neurol.*) conducting or moving away from the central portion of the nervous system. [Syn. **efferent, exodic.** Contr. w. **centripetal.**] (Accent -**rif**-.)

centripetal = (*neurol.*) conducting or moving toward the central portion of the nervous system. [Syn. **afferent, esodic.** Contr. w. **centrifugal.**] (Accent -**rip**-.)

centrosome = a specialized part of the cell, regarded as the active center of the operation of mitotic cell division.

cephalad, see **cephalic.**

cephalagra = pain in the head. [Syn. **headache.**]

cephalalgia, see **headache.**

cephalic = pert. to or located in the head or head-end of an animal. [Contr. w. **caudal** = pert. to or located in the tail or tail-end.] **cephalad**[adv] = towards the head.

cephalic index = a measure of the (human) skull or head, found by dividing the maximum breadth (i.e. distance in direction of the frontal axis) by the maximum length (i.e. distance in direction of the sagittal axis), and multiplying by 100. [Cf. **brachycephalic, dolichocephalic.**]

cephalization = the concentration of parts toward the head, or their modification so as to become organs of the head.

cephalocaudal axis = (*anat.*) the axis of reference passing from head to tail. [Syn. in man **vertical axis**; in sessile animals **apicobasal axis.**]

cephalometry, see **craniometry.**

cephalothorax = the anterior part of the body of a crustacean, a fusion of head and thorax. **cephalothoracic**[a].

cerebellum = a main division of the vertebrate brain, situate dorsad to the medulla and believed to be an organ for muscular coordination. [In man the cerebellum is large and ovoid.] **cerebella** (or **cerebellums**)[pl], **cerebellar**[a]. — Fr. *cervelet*; Ger. *Kleinhirn.*

cerebral (accent **cer**-.) see **cerebrum.**

cerebral cortex, see **neopallium.**

cerebral dominance = a condition apparently brought about largely through maturation and formation of transcortical gradients, wherein one cerebral hemisphere dominates or leads the other in the initiation and control of bodily movement, e.g. in handedness.

cerebral dominance theory = the theory that cortical activity relating to higher functions, speech, etc., is dominated normally by the cerebral hemisphere which controls the most used hand. [Lacking this dominance, incoordination of neural control results, according to the theory, in speech defects, reading difficulties, emotional and personality disturbances.]

cerebral layer = a term applied to the 5th–9th layers in the retina of the human eye. [See Table XI.] — Fr. *couche cérébrale.*

cerebral vesicles = expansions of the medullary tube in the embryo, which later develop into the several main divisions of the brain. [There are 3 primary vesicles, later transformed into 5 secondary vesicles.]

cerebration = 1. activity of the cerebral hemispheres; 2. (*pop.*) thinking; mentation.

cerebrospinal fibers = fibers in the internal capsule which pass from the motor region of the cortex to the pyramids of the medulla.

cerebrospinal fluid = a lymph contained in the ventricles of the brain and in the central canal of the spinal cord and also diffused between the arachnoid membrane and pia mater throughout the entire central nervous system. — Fr. *liquide céphalo-rachidien.*

cerebrospinal system = that part of the nervous system which includes the brain and cord, and the peripheral nerves immediately connected with these. [Contr. w. **autonomic system** = the system of ganglia situate outside the cord, whose connecting nerves control the internal bodily processes. Cf. **nervous system.**] — Fr. *s. cérébro-spinal.*

cerebrum = a main division of the vertebrate brain, including all the structures cephalad to the thalamus; divisible into three portions: (1) the olfactory brain or **rhinencephalon**; (2) the **corpus striatum**; and (3) the **cerebral cortex** proper or **neopallium.** [The term **cerebrum** is most often used to denote portion (3). It is the division which has undergone the greatest phylogenetic differentiation. Syn. **forebrain, telencephalon.**] (Accent **cer**-.) **cerebra** (or **cerebrums**)[pl], **cerebral**[a] (accent **cer**-). — Fr. *cerveau*; Ger. *Grosshirn.*

ceremonial = a system of rites and practices, often symbolic in nature, established by law or custom. **ceremonial**[a].

certainty = the highest degree of belief. [**certainty** and **certitude** are fairly synonymous, but **certitude** is more abstract; **certainty** is often ascribed to phenomena, to indicate that their future is actual, i.e. without condition; **certitude** remains subjective, i.e. it is not objectified. Cf. **probability.**] **certain**[a] (may take an objective reference). — Ger. *Gewissheit.*

certitude = the highest degree of belief. [Cf. **certainty, probability.**]

cervical = pert. to the region of the neck. [Applied to the vertebrae nearest the head and to the nerves distributed in this region. There are 8 (double) pairs of cervical nerves.]

chain reflex = a group of closely related reflexes which initiate one another in succession; e.g. swallowing. — Fr. *chaîne d'actes réflexes.*

chalone = a specific chemical substance formed by one organ and passed into the circulatory fluid to produce an inhibitory effect upon other organs; i.e. an inhibitory **autacoid.** [Syn. **colyone.** Distg. fr. **hormone** = excitatory autacoid, but cf. **autacoid.**] (Accent **kal**-.) **chalonic**[a].

chalonic autacoid, see **autacoid.**

chance = 1. syn. for **randomness**; 2. the theoretical probability of some occurrence, calculated mathematically, in the light of a knowledge of certain basal events; 3. (*pop.*) a supposed agency which unpredictably governs the course of events. [Cf. **random.**] (1) **random**[a], (1, 2) **chance**[a]. — Fr. *hasard*; Ger. *Zufall.*

chance occurrence = an occurrence brought about by the conjunction of two or more independent trains of antecedents, this conjunction being usually unpredictable. [Cf. **random.**] — Fr. *événement fortuit.*

chance variation = (*biol.*) a variation in characters in organisms, which has no discoverable antecedents, or which is due to the conjunction of two or more independently variable factors. [More properly **random variation.**] — Fr. *variation fortuite.*

change = the advent of a specific difference in the character of a phenomenon in the course of time. [E.g. change in position, in form, in ownership.

A certain identity or continuity is always assumed.] **change**[v]. — Fr. *modification*; Ger. *Veränderung*.

character = 1. (*ethics*) the moral nature of an individual; 2. (*psychol.*) a phase of personality comprising esp. the more enduring traits which are of ethical and social significance; 3. (*biol.*) any distinguishable feature of an organism, by which it can be compared with another; 4. (*logic*) any mark by which individuals or groups differ from other individuals or groups. [Also used to denote (*a*) the synthesizing subject manifested in the synthesis (Ward); (*b*) the system of directed conative tendencies (McDougall); (*c*) the expression of a Person in the process of self-training, self-expression, and self-development (Aveling). Cf. **characteristic.**]

character analysis, see **characterology.**

character/tonal, see **timbre.**

character trait = (*psychoan.*) the original pregenital tendency, either as persisting, or as sublimated, or as changed into a reaction-formation. [Classed as **oral** (generally optimistic), **urethral** (assuming the form of ambition), and **anal** (combining orderliness, stinginess, and obstinacy), frequently associated with pessimism, hate, and excessive neatness. Cf. **trait.**]

characteristic[a] = peculiar to an individual or prominent among his distinctive features. **characterize**[v].

characteristic[n] = 1. a character or distinguishing mark; 2. (*math.*) the integral part of a logarithm. [Cf. **character** (4).] — Ger. *Merkmal*.

characterization = (*soc.*) the processes by which personality and character are developed in an individual through interaction with other members of a group. [Chief among these processes are **differentiation** and **assimilation** (Chicago school).]

characterize[v] = 1. (*passive*) to be a notable or distinctive feature of an individual, species, disease, etc.; 2. (*active*) to point out such a feature or features in an individual, etc. [Cf. **character** (4). Distg. (2) fr. **define.**] **characteristic**[a].

characterology = the field in psychology which deals with the study of human character in the broad sense, including personality. [A term appropriated till recently by pseudopsychologists, but now, following German usage, adopted by technical psychology. Syn. **character analysis** (a pseudopsychological term).]

charlatan = an individual who claims to have an expert knowledge and practical skill in some specific branch (e.g. medicine), but is actually lacking in such knowledge or skill. [Syn. **faker, quack.**] **charlatanism**[n], **charlatanry**[n].

charm[n] = 1. an ornament or other object, worn for its supposed efficacy either to ward off evil or to secure good fortune; 2. a magical word or combination of words or characters (e.g. the swastika). [Syn. (2) **amulet, talisman, spell, conjuration. enchantment, incantation.** Cf. **conjure** (2).]

Charpentier's bands = a series of alternating light and dark bands which follow a moving slit-shaped stimulus presented against a dark visual field and which are due to fluctuations of visual excitation similar to those which give rise to after-images.

Charpentier's illusion, see **autokinetic illusion.**

Charpentier's law = (*hist.*) the principle that in the fovea of the retina, the product of the area of the image and the intensity of the light is constant for threshold stimuli.

chart = a diagram upon paper or other two-dimensional surface, showing the relations between two or more classes, rubrics, or variable quantities. — Fr. *graphique, tableau*.

chartometer = a device for measuring the length of a curved or meandering line; it consists of a small disk which is wheeled along the given line, and is connected by gears to dials reading in standard units of length. [Syn. **rotameter.** Cf. **planimeter.**]

check[v] = 1. to inhibit a movement of one's own, or to oppose some action in another individual; 2. to test the correctness of an observation or result. [Syn. (2) **control, verify, check up.**] **check**[n]. — Fr. (1) *arrêter*, (2) *contrôler*.

chemical reflex = 1. any reflex in which the stimulation is chemical in nature; 2. a vital process caused by hormone action; e.g. action of CO_2 on the respiratory center. [Syn. (1) **chemoreflex.**]

chemical sense = 1. a sense in which the afferent nerve-current is produced by a chemical reaction between the stimulus-substance and some substance in the receptor; 2. in protozoa and other low animal species, a sense or stimulus mechanism which brings about tropistic response to chemical stimulation. [The senses classed as **chemical** (1) in higher species include smell, taste, and the common chemical sense, which in man is best represented by the sensitivity of the respiratory membrane of the nose to pungent substances, such as ammonia.]

chemical stimulation = the excitation or effective irritation of a living cell or cells through application of substances in solution or gaseous form where simple mechanical irritation is presumably not involved.

chemical synthesis = the formation of new chemical compounds by combination of two or more known constituents. [The term **mental synthesis** has been used by analogy to denote the assumption that compound mental phenomena exhibit certain new characteristics.]

chemoreceptor = a generic name applied to all receptors of the organism which are adequately stimulated by the chemical environment of the organism; e.g. the common chemical sense receptors, taste receptors, smell receptors.

chemotropism, chemotaxis = a simple orienting response, either positive or negative, to external chemical stimulation. [Cf. **tropism.**] (Accent **-mot-, -tax-.**) **chemotropic**[a], **-tactic**[a].

chess-board illusion = a checkered figure in a circle, with the black and white quadrangles shown progressively larger toward the periphery to compensate for the distortion upon the peripheral portion of the retina, and seen as if in perspective; an illusion of depth results. [When viewed close to the retina, the checkers seem square. The figure was designed by Helmholtz to demonstrate the compensation in perception for the distortion of figures by the spherical shape of the retina.] — Fr. *illusion de l'échiquier*.

Cheyne-Stokes respiration = a pathological condition, characterized by a rapidly decreasing, followed by a rapidly increasing, rate of respiration.

chiaroscuro = the production of apparent differences of distance in the items of a bidimensional pattern by appropriate distribution of light and shade.

chiasm, optic chiasm = the junction point of the optic nerves, from which they again diverge and pass to the respective cerebral hemispheres. [In the human eye the fibers from the nasal half of each retina cross at this point, the remainder passing to the hemisphere on the same side.] — Ger. *Chiasma, Sehnervenkreuzung.*

child = an immature human being. [Pop. applied to any age up to 15 or even later. In psychology used (*a*) generically for individuals from birth to sexual maturity, (*b*) specifically for the ages above infancy, (i.e. 2 years) to adolescence. Cf. **adolescence.**] **childhood**[n], **child**[a]. — Fr. *enfant*; Ger. *Kind.*

child-bearing age = the period during which the human female is capable of pregnancy and reproduction. — Fr. *âge de procréation.*

child-parent fixation = (*psychoan.*) an attitude of the child toward one parent characterized by either love or hate. [A generic term embracing both **Edipus complex** and **Electra complex.**] — Fr. *fixation de l'enfant à ses parents.*

child psychology = the branch of psychology which investigates the development of mental life and behavior in immature human beings from birth, or earlier, to maturity. — Fr. *psychol. de l'enfant*; Ger. *Kinderpsychologie.*

chin reflex, see **mandibular reflex.**

chirognomy = (*hist.*) the art or practice of attempting to read the mental character of a person from the form and markings or lines of the hand. [Syn. **palmistry.** Cf. **chiromancy.**] (Accent **-rog-.**)

chirography = 1. syn. for **handwriting**; 2. graphic style. (Accent **-rog-.**) **chirographic**[a].

chirology, see **dactylology.**

chiromancy = (*hist.*) the art or practice of attempting to foretell the future of a person by inspecting the lines and lineaments of his hand; i.e. divination by the hand. [Distg. fr. **chirognomy** = character reading from the hand; both are included in **palmistry** and **chirosophy.** (Accent **ky-.**)

chirosophy = (*hist.*) ostensible knowledge of a person's character and probable future, derived from the inspection of lines and other features of the hand. [Syn. **chiromancy.**]

chlorophyl, chlorophyll = green coloring matter in plants.

choc = poorly coordinated responses elicited by sudden stimuli which have not been responded to in the immediate past.

choice = (*psychol.*) the initiation of a voluntary act, or the attainment of a verdict, after a period of deliberation during which alternative acts have been experienced in thought. [Some writers (e.g. Ach, Michotte, Aveling) regard **choice** as the *condition* only of the release of energy, the choice itself being effortless. This emphasizes the distinction between volition and conation. Syn. **conscious selection.** Cf. **selection.**] — Fr. *choix*; Ger. *Wahl.*

choice experiment = a series of motivated trials, in each of which some one of two or more specific stimuli is presented to the human or animal subject, who is required to *exercise choice* by making a different prescribed response to each stimulus as it occurs. [An elaborated form of the **signal experiment.** The aim may be to determine the speed attainable, as in early choice reaction-time experiments, or it may simply be to determine whether the animal can learn to make the correct responses to the stimuli. In either case the stimuli are presumed to be definitely supraliminal and to differ appreciably in quality or intensity. Cf. **discrimination experiment.**] — Fr. *expérience de choix.*

choked disk, see **papilledema.** — Fr. *distension papillaire, élargissement de la tache aveugle.*

choleric = a type of temperament characterized by the rapidity and intensity of the emotional course, particularly in the direction of anger or rage. [Cf. **temperament.**]

chord = 1. (*mus.*) a combination of tones, sounded simultaneously, which have a definite harmonic relation; 2. (*hist.*) syn. for (spinal) **cord.** [Cf. (1) **harmony, consonance, dissonance.**] (Pron. **cord.**) — Fr. (1) *accord*; Ger. (1) *Akkord, Mehrklang* (like *Zweiklang, Dreiklang,* etc.).

chorda tympani = a branch of the VIIth cranial (facial) nerve which crosses the tympanic cavity of the ear and joins the lingual branch of the trigeminal nerve. [Most of its fibers are sensory from taste endings on the anterior two-thirds of the tongue; a few are motor to submaxillary and sublingual salivary glands.]

chordotonal organ = a structure found at various places in the bodies of insects, supposed to constitute a receptor for hearing.

chorea = a pathological disorder of the motor control centers, characterized by irregular jerky or spasmodic involuntary movements, either as an acute illness of several weeks' duration, often related to the infections of acute rheumatism (**Sydenham's chorea**) or a progressive, often familial, disease (**Huntington's chorea**), or symptomatic of striatal and brain-stem lesions. [Syn. **St. Vitus' dance.**] — Fr. *chorée, danse de St. Guy*; Ger. *Veitstanz.*

choreiform movements = spasmodic movements similar to those occurring in chorea, whether due to that disorder or to other conditions.

choreoid = resembling chorea.

chorioid, see **choroid.**

choroid (or **chorioid**), **choroid coat** = the intermediate of the three coats of the eyeball, situate between the (outer) sclerotic and the (inner) retina. [It is composed chiefly of blood-vessels.] Fr. *couche choroïde*; Ger. *Aderhaut.*

choroid plexus = a network of blood-vessels in the roof-membrane of the hind-brain and the fore-brain with ependyma secreting the cerebrospinal fluid.

choromania, see **dancing mania.**

Christian Science = a system of morals and religion founded by Mary Baker Glover Eddy, in 1866, according to which pain and disease, as illusions of the mind, are forms of erroneous interpretations of reality and are to be treated by denial and assertion.

chroma = 1. (*vis.*) syn. for **saturation**; 2. syn. for **chromatic color. chromatic**[a] (1).

chroma = 3. (*mus. hist.*) a semitone whether large or small, or the sign (♯, ♭) which indicates that a note is changed by a semitone. **chromatic**[a].

chroma-brilliance coefficient = the chromatic valence of a visual stimulus per unit of photometric intensity, or the ratio of color-producing power to brilliance-producing power. [This coefficient varies radically with the wave-length of the stimulus, being very high in the short-wave (violet) end of the spectrum compared with the long-wave (red) end, with a minimum in the yellow.] — Fr. *coéfficient du rapport chroma-brilliance.*

chromatic aberration, chromatic error = (*opt., vis.*) in an optical system, the failure of rays of light from a given point to come to a focus at a point, owing to the fact that light from different parts of the spectrum is refracted unequally. [Cf. **aberration, achromatic** (2), **defect/optical.**]

chromatic adaptation, see **adaptation.**

chromatic color = a color, or visual quality, which manifests hue and saturation, and therefore cannot be placed in the white-gray-black series.

chromatic dimming phenomenon = an effect observed when a chromatic stimulus, after some seconds of fixation, is suddenly diminished in intensity: owing to **successive contrast** the saturation of the hue is greatly diminished, or the hue may even become complementary to that of the stimulus. — Fr. *phénomène d'affaiblissement chromatique.*

chromatic scale = a succession of tones, each differing by one semitone from the preceding, extending through an entire octave. [Cf. **scale.** — Fr. *gamme chromatique.*

chromatics = 1. (*vis.*) the science of color or of color sensations; 2. (*aud.*) syn. for **chromatic scales.** — Ger. (1) *Farbenlehre.*

chromatin = that portion of the substance of the nucleus which is readily stained.

chromatism, see **photism.**

chromatophore = 1. a small protoplasmic body containing pigment, such as the plastids (containing chlorophyll) in the cells of plants; 2. a cell containing pigment. [In many animals the **chromatophores** contain branching processes into which and out of which the pigment granules move in such a way as to change the color of the animal.]

chromatopseudopsia, see **color-blindness.**

chromatopsia = an abnormal state of vision in which colorless objects appear colored. [E.g. yellow after santonin, red in snow-blindness. Syn. **colored vision.**]

chromesthesia, chromaesthesia, chrom(a)esthesis = a vivid and persistent association of specific colors with sounds, with spoken or written words or letters, or with any non-visual sensations. [A variety of **synesthesia; colored hearing** is the more common type of **chromesthesia.**]

chromatotropism = a simple orienting response, either positive or negative, to a given color, or hue. (Accent **-tot-.**)

chromatoptometer, see **anomaloscope.**

chromosome = a small body containing chromatin, found in the nucleus during mitotic cell division. [The chromosomes are believed to contain minute bodies (**genes**) which are responsible for hereditary traits.]

chromosomes X and Y = the **sex chromosomes.** [In most species the female has two X chromosomes while the male has one X and in place of the other either a Y chromosome (often small) or no chromosome at all.]

chromotropism, chromotaxis = a type of tropism characterized by differential response to different wave-lengths of light. [Cf. **tropism.**] (Accent **-mot-, -tax-.**) **chromotropic**[a], **-tactic**[a].

chronaxy, chronaxia, chronaxie = an index of excitability of a tissue, expressed as the minimal effective duration of a constant current of double the liminal (or rheobasic) intensity necessary for excitation (Lapicque). [Lapicque distinguishes between *chronaxie de constitution* and *chronaxie de subordination,* depending on whether the nerve and muscle are connected with the central nervous system or are severed from it. Cf. **rheobase** and **strength-duration curve.**]

chronic = a term applied to certain disorders, denoting their slow onset and persistent duration. [Contr. w. **acute** = sudden, and with rapid culmination.]

chronic conflict = (*psychoan.*) the struggle of opposed id, ego, and superego trends over a considerable period, characteristic of the psychoneuroses.

chronic mania = protracted excitements of any sort or continued and unyielding, usually hypomanic states.

chronograph = an instrument for measuring time intervals by marking the beginning and end of the period on a record sheet, in parallel with a time record made by registering the beats of a seconds pendulum, the vibrations of a tuning fork, or other standard timing device. [Cf. **chronometer.**]

chronographic method = the measurement of response time or other duration by some self-registering device, which produces a permanent record. [Cf. **graphic method, graph.** A typical example is the use of a pointer resting on smoked paper covering a rotating cylinder, the pointer marking the beginning and end of a reaction, etc. with a tuning fork record in parallel to mark the time intervals.]

chronological age, CA = the duration of an individual's life from birth to the date under consideration. [Contr. w. **mental age** = the degree of a given individual's mental development, measured in terms of the average chronological age at which this mental development is reached.] — Ger. *Lebensalter.*

chronometer = a carefully constructed mechanism for measuring time, with one or more dials and pointers, which indicate the lapse of time at any instant. [Strictly, a **chronometer** runs continuously, a **chronoscope** is stopped at end of period to be measured, a **chronograph** traces a permanent record. The **d'Arsonval chronometer** is actually a form of **chronoscope.** Cf. **Jacquet chronometer, fall chronometer.**]

chronometry = the measurement of time intervals. — Ger. *Zeitmesskunst.*

chronometry/mental = the systematic investigation of the duration of mental processes and phenomena. [In practice the term is broadened to mean the total time within the stimulation-to-response interval, which includes transmission of neural impulses to and from periphery as well as the strictly central processes. Cf. **compound reaction, psychometry** (1), **response time.**]

chronoscope = an instrument for measuring duration, which consists essentially of a graduated arc or dial, over which moves a pointer (or clock-hand), and a device for starting and stopping the pointer, so that the time interval between start and stop may be calculated from the difference between the two readings of the scale. [Used for the determination of reaction time, rate of muscular contractions, etc. Distg.

fr. **chronometer,** which runs continuously, and **chronograph,** which provides a permanent graphic record of each period measured. Cf. **Hipp chr., pendulum chr., Dunlap chr., spark chr., vernier** (pendular) **chr.**]

churinga = in Australian ethnology, certain ceremonial stone and wooden slabs, two for each individual, kept in secret places, which are supposed to represent a soul or second body of the owner.

cilia[pl] = 1. hair-like processes on the surface of cells or of unicellular organisms. [They serve extensively as organs of locomotion and in creating currents in the adjacent medium, thereby assisting the organism in procuring food, in excretion, respiration, reproduction, etc.] **cilium**[sing], **ciliary**[a].

cilia = 2. the eyelashes. **ciliary**[a].

ciliary muscle, ciliary body = an annular mass of unstriped muscle fibers, which surrounds the eye-lens and regulates its curvature, thereby accommodating or focusing the eye for vision at various distances.

ciliary processes = a series of about 70 folds or projections extending inward from the ciliary muscle of the human eye, composed largely of connective tissue and blood-vessels, which afford attachment for the radial bands of the *zonule of Zinn* or supporting ligament of the lens. [The **ciliary processes** are believed also to play a part in the secretion of the aqueous humor of the eye.]

ciliospinal reflex, see **cutaneous pupillary reflex.**

cinematograph = 1. (*technical*) an apparatus which records, by means of a succession of discrete impressions, usually photographically, the motion of objects; 2. (*pop.*) the apparatus which projects these records on the wall or on a specially prepared background (*screen*), as with the motion-picture machine. [Syn. **kinetograph, kinetoscope,** (briefly) **cinema** (applied chiefly to the picture on the screen). In the best usage the **cinematograph** and the **kinetograph** record photographically the motion, while the **kinetoscope** projects the developed record on the screen.] — Ger. *Kinematograph.*

circular definition, circular reasoning = a pair of definitions or conclusions, each of which in turn is based upon the other, or a series which rest one upon another, having no common, accepted basis.

circular psychosis = a type of psychosis or mental disorder characterized by alternate phases of exaltation and depression. [Includes **cyclothymia, manic-depressive** or **alternating psychoses.**]

circular reflex = a reflex in which the response serves to renew the original stimulus, leading to a repetition of the same response.

circular response = 1. a type of **chain reflex** in which the afferent impulse originating from an effector response passes to the central nervous system and out again through the efferent pathway previously excited, resulting in the repetition of the same motor activity; 2. (*soc.*) a type of social behavior in which the responses of each person are re-voked or increased by the reactions which his own activity has called forth from the other or others, e.g. when the smile of one person stimulates a second person to smile, thus facilitating the smile of the first person.

circumstances = the concomitant external conditions which affect an organism or an event. [Usually limited to a narrow range of external conditions; distg. fr. **environment** = the total external conditions which affect an organism.] — Ger. *Begleitumstände.*

circumstantial evidence = a mass of facts which, taken together, establish by inference a certain situation, phenomenon, law, etc., that is not directly open to substantiation. — Fr. *preuve tirée des circonstances par induction.*

circumvallate papilla, see **papilla.**

circus movements = a type of forced movement in which the organism tends to move in a circle, or a spiral, due either to one-sided brain injury or to unequal stimulation of the two sides of the organism. — Fr. *mouvements de manège.*

clairaudience = a hypothetical power of hearing and understanding sounds and voices without the use of the ears, by which knowledge of distant events is said to be obtained. [A form of **cryptesthesia.**]

clairvoyance = 1. an assumed ability to see without the use of the eyes; 2. an assumed awareness of the past, present, and future events without the use of the special senses. [Distg. fr. **telepathy,** which refers to a process between two minds; both are forms of **cryptesthesia** (= supernormal sensibility); **clairvoyance** should be limited to the visual modality; general sensibility for distant events is **telesthesia.**] **clairvoyant**[a, np]. — Ger. *Hellsichtigkeit.*

clamminess = a complex tactual perception which arises from stimulation by a cool and damp (moist) object. — Ger. *Nasskälte.*

clan = 1. (*anthrop.*) a line of human descent through the mother; 2. (*anthrop.*) a social group, the individual's place in which is inherited through the mother. [Contr. (1) w. **gens** = descent through the father.]

clang = any musical tone, whether simple or compound, considered from the standpoint of its timbre or character. [Helmholtz used *Klang* for *musical tone,* which generally but not always meant *compound tone.* Ellis, in translating Helmholtz, objected to using the English term **clang,** on the ground that the word means a harsh, metallic noise or tone, and hence is not suitable for **musical tone** in general. Titchener uses **clang** as here defined and notes as its aspects the timbre due to upper partials, incidental noises, its pitch, intensity, temporal changes, etc.] — Fr. *son*; Ger. *Klang.*

clang-color, clang-quality, clang-tint, see **timbre.** — Fr. *timbre, couleur du son*; Ger. *Klangfarbe.*

Clarke's column = a column, or central group of cell-bodies, in the dorsal horn of gray matter in the spinal cord, whose axons pass up to the cerebellum.

class = the totality of objects, individuals, events, etc., distinguished from others by some selected mark or marks. [In scientific procedure, when certain marks have been selected to identify a **class,** all other similarities and differences among the members are irrelevant to the grouping. The term is used in logic in a very wide sense; in biology it is applied specifically to a group of organisms less inclusive than a **phylum,** more inclusive than an **order;** in sociology it may be applied to various social groupings, esp. to those based on economic status and the correlated distinction in social intercourse; in statistics it denotes the group of values or items which fall within any one of the equal parts into which a scale or range of values is arbitrarily divided.]

class interval = (*statist.*) in quantitative data arranged in order of magnitude and divided into a number of natural or arbitrary classes, (1) the number of units within a given class, or (2) the range of values covered by a given class. [(1) is designated by a single number, (2) by two numbers. Syn. **step interval.**]

class system = 1. a type of social organization in which certain co-acting groups of individuals having common interests are distinguished from other co-acting groups of individuals having different common interests, e.g. the intelligensia, working class, leisure class, military class; 2. syn. for **caste system.** [The essence of class distinctions is in the attitudes of individuals toward one another.]

classes/special = 1. classes organized for the instruction of children who, because of mental or physical peculiarities, do not fit into the regular school classes; e.g. the classes for hard of hearing, crippled, dull, blind, feebleminded, cardiac, very bright, neurotic, etc.; 2. sometimes used to denote specifically classes for dull and feebleminded.

classification = the sorting of data (i.e. objects, individuals, qualities, events, etc.) into separate groups based on certain selected differentiating marks, whether this sorting be actual or theoretical. [Cf. **class.**]

classification test = 1. a form of test in which the task is to select from a number of elements, such as words or objects, those elements that logically belong in the same category; 2. a designation given by Otis to a test designed by him, which comprises an omnibus achievement test and an omnibus intelligence test, from the performances in which inference is to be drawn concerning the proper classification of the pupil in a school system. [E.g. (1) in Test 9 of the Terman Group Test of Mental Ability, the task is to cross out one word which does not belong in a group of five words.]

classification/zoological = a designation for the hierarchy of animal types arranged from most to least inclusive as follows: kingdom, phylum, class, order, family, genus, species, and variety.

Claudius' cells = columnar epithelial cells located at the outer border of the organ of Corti in the internal ear.

claustrophobia = morbid dread of being in a closed or confined place. [Contr. w. **agoraphobia.**]

claustrum = a thin layer of gray matter in the white matter of the cerebrum, between the lentiform nucleus and the island of Reil.

clavicle = the collar-bone. **clavicular**[a].

clavus hystericus = a pain localized near the sagittal suture of the skull, such as would result if a nail were being driven into the skull. [One of the symptoms of hysteria.] — Fr. *clou hystérique.*

clearness = 1. (*sens.* or *attributive*) one of the quantitative attributes of sensation and imagery, corresponding closely to the salience of an experienced item from its background; 2. (*cognitive*) a characteristic of apprehension or cognition such that the meanings of the items of experience are understood or grasped; 3. degree of differentiation of phenomenal structure. [Syn. (1) **attensity, vividness;** distg. fr. **indistinctness.** Syn. (2) **definiteness** or **comprehensibility**; distg. fr. **ambiguity** or **obscurity.** Distg. (3) fr. **awareness;** cf. **attention.**] **clear**[a]. — Fr. *clarté, vivacité;* Ger. *Klarheit.*

cleavage = the process of cell-division. [Usually employed to designate the divisions of the ovum in early development.] — Fr. *segmentation.*

Clever Hans, der kluge H. = a trained horse, exhibited at Berlin by von Osten and later at Elberfeld by Krall, who claimed for the animal the ability to perform intricate mathematical operations and other processes indicating high reasoning powers. [Krall later trained several other horses; the group was known collectively as the **Elberfeld horses.**]

cleverness, see **c factor.**

click = a sharp, metallic noise of complex nature. — Fr. *déclic.*

climacteric, climacterium = 1. period of the menopause; 2. (rare) any critical period occurring in health or constitution during life, as puberty, menopause, etc. — Fr. *âge critique.*

climacteric psychoses = types of mental disorder which occur at certain transitional periods of life, notably adolescence and menopause. [Syn. **epochal psychoses.** Cf. **paraphrenia.**]

clinic = a place and organization for the examination, diagnosis, and treatment of physical and mental disorders. [E.g. heart clinic, chest clinic, endocrinology clinic, behavior clinic, mental retardation clinic.] **clinical**[a].

clinical = pert. to demonstration or diagnosis in the living, as contr. w. *necropsy* or *autopsy.* [E.g. clinical picture = portrayal of symptoms, etc., clinical history = record of events relevant to the patient's condition. Originally limited to bedside observations. Cf. **clinic.**]

clinical crib = a crib in which an infant is placed for observation, so constructed as to permit placing him in a variety of positions. — Fr. *crèche clinique.*

cloaca = the passage through which, in some lower animals, intestinal waste products are discharged. (Accent **-ake-.**) **cloacal**[a]. — Fr. *cloaque.*

cloaca theory = (*psychoan.*) a theory of birth, frequently held by children, according to which the baby is born through the anal opening.

clonic contraction, see **clonus.**

clonus = a series of rapid contractions and relaxations of antagonistic pairs of extensor and flexor muscles of an extremity, which are myotatic in origin, i.e. due to rhythmic stretching of the muscles at one or other points of the attachments. [Cf. **convulsion, spasm.**] **clonic**[a].

closed pipe, see **pipe.**

closure = (*Gestalt*) one of the principles of psychophysical organization, whereby the course of behavior and its segregated wholes (actions, perceptions, memories) tend to become complete or *closed* forms; also, the process whereby changing, incomplete systems attain a final stability. — Fr. *prégnance;* Ger. *Schliessung, Geschlossenheit.*

cloud experiment/Fechner's = an experimental demonstration of Weber's law: if two adjacent cloud areas are just noticeably different in brilliance to the naked eye, and a gray glass be placed before the eyes (thus proportionately reducing the brightness) there will still be a liminal difference in brilliance between the two clouds (Fechner, 1860).— Fr. *expérience des nuages de F.*

clouding of consciousness = a partial loss of orientation in the present situation, which occurs in certain psychotic conditions. — Fr. *confusion mentale.*

clue, see **cue.**

coats of eyeball = the three principal layers which compose the wall of the eyeball. [They are termed the **sclera** or **sclerotic coat** (outermost); **choroid** or **choroid coat,** and **retina.**] — Fr. *couches de la paupière.*

cocain = the chief alkaloid of Erythroxylon coca. (3 syll.)

cocain delirium, cocainism = a condition of excitement and mental confusion induced by the use of cocain.

coccygeal nerve = the lowest (most caudad) spinal nerve in the human body. (Pron. **cock-sidg-i-al**; accent **sidg-.**)

coccyx = the caudal end of the spine or back-bone. (Pron. **kok-six.**) **coccygeal**[a] (accent **-sij-**).

cochlea = a spiral conical structure which forms the cranial portion of the labyrinth of the internal ear of mammals, and contains the receptors for hearing. [The central core, the **modiolus,** is broad at the base and terminates in a rounded peak, the *apex*; around this core are wound spirally the turns of the **cochlear canal.** Projecting from the modiolus, and following the turns of the canal and partly dividing the cochlea in two, is the **bony spiral lamina.** Stretching from the spiral lamina to the **spiral ligament** on the outer wall of the canal is the **basilar membrane,** which separates the cochlea into two main tubular portions, called the **scala tympani** and **scala vestibuli;** a second membrane of delicate structure, **Reissner's membrane,** divides off a third tubular portion, called the **cochlear duct.** The cochlear duct contains the **organ of Corti,** in which the fibers of the cochlear nerve terminate. The scala tympani and scala vestibuli come together at the apex in an opening called the **helicotrema.**] (Accent **kok-.**) **cochlear**[a]. — Fr. *limaçon*; Ger. *Schnecke.*

cochlear duct = the central canal of the **cochlea,** which contains the organ of Corti. [Cf. **cochlea.**]

cochlear nerve, see **auditory nerve.**

cochleo-orbicular (or **cochleopalpebral**) **reflex** = contraction of the orbicularis palpebrarum following a sudden loud sound.

co-consciousness = a term proposed by Morton Prince to designate mental states which coexist in the individual's personal consciousness, but are dissociated from it, i.e. states of which the individual is not aware, yet which are dynamically active and may account for various mental phenomena, both normal (e.g. lapses of the pen) and abnormal (e.g. crystal gazing, visions, hallucinations, dual or multiple personality). **co-conscious**[a]. — Fr. *co-conscience.*

code = 1. (*soc.*) a system of social rules and canons; 2. (*lang.*) a system of secret signs, representing letters, words, or phrases.

code test = a test of mental ability in which the testee is required to translate as quickly as possible a series of code signs. [Cf. **substitution test; code.**]

coefficient = 1. (*psychol.*) a constituent in any experience, or state of consciousness, which marks its relation to some special type of experience, e.g. the feeling coefficient of a sensation; 2. (*math.*) a number which expresses the degree to which some characteristic or attribute appears in a given case; e.g. the **coefficient of correlation** is a numerical index of relation; the **coefficient of variability** gives a quantitative estimate of variability.

coefficient law = (*vis.*) the principle that the alteration in the state of the organ of vision which is produced by stimulation has approximately the same effect on excitation due to a subsequent stimulus as if the intensity of the latter were diminished by a definite fraction of its amount. [Syn. **Fechner-Helmholtz law.**]

coefficient of alienation, see **alienation coefficient.**

coefficient of correlation = 1. any numerical measure which indicates the closeness of the tendency of two series of paired measures to vary concomitantly; 2. (specifically) the product-moment coefficient of correlation. [Cf. **correlation.**]

coefficient of regression, see **regression coefficient.**

coefficient of validity, see **validity coefficient.**

coefficient of variation = (*statist.*) the ratio of the standard deviation of a distribution to the arithmetic mean of that distribution (Pearson, 1895).

coefficient of visibility, see **visibility coefficient.**

Coelenterata, Coelenterates = the lowest phylum of metazoa or many-celled animals, characterized by soft body-structure, a body cavity, and in general by radial symmetry. [The lowest coelenterates possess scattered neurons; the higher species possess a nervous system of the **nerve-ring** type.]

coenaesthesis, coenesthesia, cenesthesia = 1. diffused internal or organic sensibility; i.e. common or undifferentiated sensibility; 2. the mass of undifferentiated internal impressions which forms the basis of our sense of body and of bodily condition, e.g. the feeling of health, comfort, well-being, lassitude, languor, illness, etc.

co-existence = the presence of two phenomena, objects, etc., at the same instant or during the same period of time.

co-existence/law of = a law of mental association, which states that if two mental events occur at the same time, the recurrence of one tends to call forth the idea corresponding to the other. [Cf. **contiguity/law of.**]

cogitation = (*pop.*) reflection, meditation. [Not used in precise, scientific discussion.] **cogitate**[v].

cognition = a generic term used to designate all processes involved in knowing. [It begins with immediate awareness of objects in perception and extends to all forms of reasoning. Contr. w. **affective** and **conative processes,** or w. **orexis.** Cf. **knowledge, intellect.**] **cognize**[v] (often limited to perception and the relations implied in perception; **know** has not this limitation). — Fr. *connaissance*; Ger. *Erkenntnis.*

cognitive = 1. pert. to the processes concerned in cognition; 2. pert. to the intellect.

cognitive clearness, see **clearness** (2).

cognitive faculty (or **function**) = (*hist.*) a major division or aspect of the mind, usually coordinated with **affective** and **volitional** faculties. [As a faculty (*vis cogitativa*) this was regarded as a power of the **common sense** to combine impressions; more generally it was taken to be equivalent to the organ of reason (*nous, noetic faculty*) and is now used only in a wide sense as capacity to understand, reason, etc. Cf. **noetic, faculty psychology.**]

cognitive-intensity = degree of consciousness. [Distg. fr. **determinateness.** Cf. **clearness.**]

coherence = (*eidetic*) the tendency of images to accommodate themselves to perceptual data that are simultaneously present; e.g. the blending of the color of an image with the color of the projection ground.

cohesion = a term used to describe the tendency of successive or simultaneous acts to become connected in learning; i.e. the principle of association by contiguity (or succession) as applied to action. [Cf. **contiguity/law of.**]

cohesion/law of = a principle of learning according to which acts that occur simultaneously or in close succession tend to become combined or unified, thus forming an integrated act of more complex character. [Syn. **law of combination** (Woodworth) and **law of association.** Cf. **redintegration.**]

coincidence = 1. a pair of events which belong to two independent causal series, but which bear such a resemblance as to appear attributable to a common cause; 2. a conjunction of two events belonging to independent causal series, which conjunction results in some unexpected event or situation; 3. (*math.*) a point-to-point correspondence of two geometrical figures or certain portions thereof. **coincidental**[a] (1, 2); **coincident**[a] (3).

coincidence point = that point in a range of brightness variation, at which two adjacent field parts of different color have the same brightness (Ackermann). [Used in English by Koffka and Harrower.] — Ger. *Koinzidenzpunkt.*

coincidence variations = (*biol.*) congenital variations which are similar in character to certain acquired modifications, so that the latter seem to be inherited in succeeding generations. [A term suggested by C. Lloyd Morgan in connection with the theory of **organic selection.**]

coition, coitus = sexual intercourse or copulation. [**coition** applies to the process in general, **coitus** to specific acts.] (Accent (1) **-ish-**, (2) **co-**.) — Fr. *coït.*

cold sensation = a quality of sensation due normally to stimulation by some object whose temperature is lower than the temperature of the skin or other part stimulated. [The normal or adequate stimulus is a temperature of 1/8° C or more lower than the skin temperature.] — Fr. *s. de froid*; Ger. *Kälteempfindung.*

cold sense = a specific sense which gives experiences termed **cold sensations.** [The proper or adequate stimulus of the cold sense is a body or air current of lower temperature than that of the skin.] — Fr. *sens du froid.*

cold spot = a point or minute area on the skin which is peculiarly sensitive to stimuli normally below the body temperature. [Cf. **cold-stimulus, paradoxical cold.**] — Fr. *point de froid*: Ger. *Kältepunkt.*

cold-stimulus = a stimulus which gives rise to a cold sensation. [Besides the proper or adequate cold-stimulus, certain substances such as menthol give rise to cold sensations regardless of their temperature. Cf. **cold sense.**] — Fr. *stim. froid.*

collapse = an acute pathological condition characterized by a weak, rapid heart, low blood-pressure, flaccid muscles, rapid, shallow respiration, cold, perspiring extremities, and extreme prostration. [Related to traumatic and surgical **shock.**] — Fr. *collapsus, choc.*

collateral[n] = a fiber which branches off from the axon or main fiber of the neuron. [Collaterals serve to form alternative connections between neurons, and are assumed to be the basis for alternative nerve pathways.]

collateral heredity = descent along different lines, from a common ancestry. [A term used in discussing common traits in two or more branches derived from common ancestry.]

collecting instinct = a congenital tendency to acquire and hoard certain classes of objects, without regard to their usefulness. [Syn. **acquisitive instinct** (generic).]

collection = the gathering together of separate nerve impulses to form a composite neural response. [Syn. **convergence.**]

collective = characterizing a term, judgment, mind, consciousness, etc., which applies to a group as a whole and not to individuals separately; e.g. army, committee.

collective consciousness = (*soc.*) a hypothetical aggregation or summation of the conscious processes of the individuals in a given group. [Used particularly with respect to groups in which the individuals are characterized by a similarity of ideas, beliefs, or behavior segments. Cf. **collective mind.**]

collective mind = 1. the mental activity of the individuals in a group, regarded hypothetically as a unitary process; 2. the consensus within a group of individuals regarding a given question. [Cf. (1) **crowd mind**; (2) **public opinion.**] — Fr. *esprit collectif.*

collective psychology = that phase of sociology, anthropology, or social psychology which treats of the activities of groups as units, without reference to the specific individuals who compose the groups. [Cf. **social psychology.**]

collective unconscious = (*anal. psychol.*) that part of the individual unconscious which derives from ancestral experience.

colligation = 1. a species of mental composition in which the elementary units remain relatively distinct, e.g. a printed word; 2. the union of similar elements in a composite experience. [Contr. (1) w. **fusion,** in which the units partly merge and lose their identity; contr. (2) w. **complication** = simultaneous union of disparate elements, and w. **association** = succession of disparate elements.] — Ger. *Verknüpfung.*

colloid = a substance of gelatinous nature which exhibits certain properties, such as permeability by crystalloid solutions and indiffusability through animal or vegetable membranes. [An important condition in living tissues.]

colon = the longest portion of the large intestine. **colonic**[a] (accent **-lon-**).

colony = 1. a group of unicellular organisms bound together structurally so that they live and act as a unitary organism, e.g. the Hydromedusae; 2. any permanent association of animals, e.g. a hive of bees.

color, colour = 1. a qualitative component of visual experience characterized by the attributes of brilliance, hue, and saturation, but in certain cases having zero saturation and (consequently) no hue; 2. the same as (1), but limited to those experiences which exhibit **hue,** as distg. fr. the members of the white-gray-black series; 3. the **color** (1) or (2), referable to radiant energy of specified wave-length or of definite wave-length composition; or to a substance (as stimulus) under usual conditions of illumination and dependent upon its selective (or non-selective) reflection, absorption, etc. of light; e.g. the **color** of a fabric, of a solution, of the sky, **colors** of the spectrum (seen in a spectroscope); 4. the stimulus for **color** (1) or (2), i.e. **radiant energy** of specified wave-length or of definite wave-length composition, or a particular surface or substance as in (3). [Hist. (2) has been more generally used; (1) is recommended by the Opt. Soc. of America. (4) applies to physical phenomena, and its use in psychology causes confusion. Syn. (2) **hue** (prefd.); (4) **color-stimulus** (prefd.), or **radiant energy, pigment,** etc. according to connotation. Cf. **color/invariable, /fundamental, /primal, /primary.**] — Ger. *Farbe*.

color-blindness = a defect of color vision, usually congenital, marked by a reduction in the number of discriminable hues. [Syn. **chromatopseudopsia.** It includes **achromatism** or achromatic vision = total color-blindness, and **dichromatism,** dichromatic vision = partial color-blindness. Normal human vision is called **trichromatism** under the influence of the Young-Helmholtz three-color theory.] — Fr. *cécité aux couleurs, c. chromatique;* Ger. *Farbenblindheit.*

color-blindness/acquired = partial or complete loss of color sensitivity in a part or the whole of the retina in pathological conditions of the eyes. [E.g. in diseases of the retina, choroid, or optic tract, in toxic conditions, etc.]

color-blindness/hereditary, see **Horner's law.**

color-blindness tests = devices used to discover abnormalities of color vision in the individual or to determine their extent. [The tests used fall into four groups: (1) *matching tests,* in which the subject is required to select from a large assortment those which are of the same color as a given sample (e.g. Holmgren wool sorting test); (2) *confusion tests,* in which numbers, letters, etc., are printed in colors which the color-blind cannot distinguish from the colors of the background (e.g. Stilling pseudo-isochromatische Tafeln); (3) *practical tests,* in which the conditions under which the subject will be expected to distinguish colors in his work are simulated artificially (e.g. Edridge-Green lantern test, in which colored lights appear in various sizes to simulate distance, are covered to appear as if through fog, rain, etc.); (4) *laboratory tests* for the exact measurement of color efficiency (e.g. Nagel anomaloscope, in which spectral red and green can be mixed to match yellows of different brightnesses). See Table I.]

color circle = 1. a device designed by Newton to illustrate color mixing, which consists of a disk with sectors of the colors in his system in such proportion that when the disk is rotated they yield a gray; 2. the **color cycle,** when the hues are thought of as being arranged in a circle. [Cf. **color triangle.**] — Fr. *cercle chromatique, table des couleurs*; Ger. (1) *Farbenkreis,* (2) *Farbentafel.*

color cycle = the closed, finite system of chromatic colors or hues (including the purples), which is characteristic of trichromatic vision.

color disk (or **disc**) = a circular piece of cardboard or paper, uniformly colored on one side, with a small hole in the center for application to a rotating device, and a slit from center to periphery for fitting together two or more different-colored disks of this kind, so that a section of each disk is exposed. [Used in the study of the laws of color mixture.]

color excitations = hypothetical elementary physiological visual processes which are quantitatively derived from the results of numerous color-mixing experiments, each using a limited number of spectral stimuli, properly selected. [For trichromatic vision it is not necessary to assume more than three elementary excitations, and the degrees of their arousal by the spectral stimuli are represented as three overlapping functions of wave-length. The representation of the color-mixture relations of dichromatic vision requires the assumption of only two color excitations. Cf. **Young-Helmholtz theory, three-component theories.**]

color/fundamental = a general term used to designate certain hues assumed to be original or of more importance than other hues. [The significance of the term differs according to the color theory adopted; cf. **color/primal, color/primary.**] — Ger. *Prinzipalfarbe* (Aubert), *Grundfarbe* (Mach).

color induction, see **induction** (3), **induced color, inducing color.**

color/invariable = a term applied to certain specific color sensations characterized by the fact that they do not change in hue as the intensity of the stimulus increases (Bezold-Brücke phenomenon), or as the stimulus moves from the center to the periphery of the retina. [Sometimes identified with **Urfarbe,** or **primal color.**]

color mixer = any apparatus for combining two or more chromatically different visual stimuli upon the same area of the retina. [Cf. **color mixture; color wheel.**] — Fr. *mélangeur de couleurs.*

color mixture = an experimental procedure by which two or more lights of different spectral distribution are made to fall on the same area of the retina effectively at the same time, for the purpose of eliciting their combined effect. [**color mixture** is used to determine the laws of color vision and to differentiate types of color-blindness or partial color defect; mixture is brought about by rapid alternation of the two component stimuli with the **color wheel,** or by reflection from a common surface, with an unsilvered mirror by combined partial reflection and transmission, or with nearly homogeneous components by specially devised spectral apparatus; it is usually *uniocular*; usually the effect of the mixture is equated subjectively to that of a homogeneous light, or one approximately so; the mixture of color stimuli by such means as these is quite simply *additive.* In the mixture of pigments or by the superposition of transparent filters the case is more complex and the result is (inexactly) said to be *subtractive.* Cf. **color mixer, color wheel, color mixture/binocular.**] — Fr. *mélange de couleurs*; Ger. *Farbenmischung.*

color mixture/binocular = the presentation of different color stimuli to corresponding areas of the two retinas, resulting in a single fused impression. [This effect occurs only under special conditions; often the effect is **rivalry,** esp. when the two stimuli are very different in their separate effects.] — Fr. *mélange binoculaire des couleurs.*

color mixture/Newton's law of, see **Newton's law.**

color of tones, see **timbre.**

color/primal = any one of four specific color sensations in the series of hues, characterized by the fact that it does not partake of the specific nature of any one of the other three. [Primal blue, green, and yellow are stimulated respectively by a certain blue, green, and yellow wave-length of the spectrum, the stimulus for primal red being a certain mixture of red and violet waves. The term (and syn. **psychological primary color**) is used in connection with four-color theories of color vision, and is identified by some writers with **invariable color.** Syn. **fundamental color** (ambig.). Values are given by Westphal as 478.5 mμ (blue), 505.5 (green), and 575.5 (yellow).] — Ger. *Urfarbe.*

color/primary = any one of three colors (i.e. hues) whose stimuli, when mixed additively with the other two in proper proportions, are capable of yielding colors of all hues (within a wide range of saturations) and the gray series. [The **primary colors** are those stimulated by certain red, green, and blue (or violet) wave-lengths of the spectrum. This term (and syn. **fundamental color**) is used esp. in the Young-Helmholtz theory, as distg. fr. **primal color** (**Urfarbe**) and **invariable color,** used in connection with other theories.] — Ger. *Hauptfarbe, Prinzipalfarbe, Grundfarbe.*

color pyramid, see **color solid.**

color sensation = 1. any visual experience which results from stimulation of the retina, as distg. fr. the physical considerations descriptive of the stimulus; 2. (more narrowly) those visual experiences which exhibit **hue.** — Ger. *Farbenempfindung.*

color shades = a series of colors of any fixed hue and saturation which vary only in brilliance. — Fr. *teintes.*

color solid/psychological = a symbolic figure in three dimensions, which represents the relations of all possible visible colors with respect to their fundamental attributes of brilliance, hue, and saturation. [Brilliance appears as the vertical axis of the figure, with hue and saturation represented in polar coordinates about the brilliance axis, saturation being radial. The boundaries of the solid are actually indeterminate, but it is usually represented as a cylinder, a sphere, a spindle, or a double pyramid with a common (square) base. Syn. **color pyramid.**]

color spindle, see **color solid.**

color/surface, see **surface color.**

color surface = a plane section of the solid schematic figure that represents all possible color experiences, usually taken perpendicular to the axis of brilliance variation, and representing all possible hues and saturations at a single brilliance level. [Cf. **color triangle.**]

color temperature = the temperature of a so-called black body or non-selective incandescent radiator, at which it yields a color matching that of a given sample of radiant energy. [The **black body** colors form a single series of relatively unsaturated visual qualities, ranging from red, through orange, white, pale blues, and violets, as the temperature is increased. The temperature is usually measured on the *absolute* or **Kelvin scale,** and **white** is evoked by a temperature of approximately 5200–5600 degrees absolute, corresponding to the composition of radiant energy as received from the sun.] — Fr. *couleur de température.*

color tint, see **tint.**

color tone, see **hue.**

color triangle = a schematic representation of the mutual relations of all hues and degrees of color saturation (of approximately spectral brilliance) upon a surface, in which each color effect that may be obtained from the additive mixture of two or more color stimuli, is assigned to a point between the position of these components as determined by their relative proportions, the three Young-Helmholtz primary colors being represented at the apices of the schematic triangular figure. [E.g. a mixture of 3/4 blue with 1/4 red, is represented at a point 1/4 the distance from blue on the line joining the position of the blue and the red components. Cf. **color solid,** of which the **color triangle** is a cross-section.] — Ger. *Farbendreieck.*

color value, see **brilliance.**

color vision/theory of = a hypothesis as to the physiological mechanism underlying color phenomena, which is used to explain or coordinate the phenomena in question. [Cf. **Young-Helmholtz theory, Hering theory, Ladd-Franklin theory, duplicity theory, trireceptor theory.**]

color-weakness = a defect in color vision marked by diminished color sensitivity rather than actual loss of any hue. [Any of the four primal hues may be affected.] — Fr. *faiblesse chromatique*; Ger. *Farbenschwäche.*

color wheel = an instrument used for **color mixture,** in which the color stimuli to be mixed are sectors of a rotating disk. [Cf. **color-mixer, color disk.**] — Fr. *disque rotatif*; Ger. *Farbenkreisel.*

color zone, see **zone/color.**

colored hearing = a phenomenon characterizing the experience of certain individuals, in which certain auditory sensations (tones, vowels, syllables, or words) are tinged with certain specific colors. [A variety of **synesthesia.**] — Fr. *audition colorée*; Ger. *Farbenhören, Phonopsie.*

colored shadow experiment (phenomenon or **principle)** = an accentuated type of simultaneous contrast observed when two shadows are cast upon the same surface near each other by two lights of different color; when the shadows are made about equal in brilliance, each one tends strongly to appear of a color complementary to that of the light which casts it, the general surface appearing of an indifferent color. [In case one of the lights is white, or achromatic, the shadow it casts is strongly of the color of the other light; a very moderate color-difference between the lights is usually sufficient.] — Fr. *expérience de l'ombre colorée, phénomène de l'ombre colorée*; Ger. *Versuch der farbigen Schatten.*

colorimeter = an instrument for measuring colors in order that they may be specified in numerical or definite symbolic terms. [In one type the sample color is matched with a mixture of monochromatic and white lights; in another type by a mixture of three standard primaries.] **colorimetry**[n], **-metric**[a].

colors/complementary, see **complements.**

columella = a cartilaginous or partly ossified rod in the middle ear of birds, reptiles, and amphibians, which performs the same function as the auditory ossicles in higher species, i.e. the communication to the internal ear of vibrations transmitted by the tympanic membrane.

column = (*neurol.*) a tract (i.e. a group of nerve fibers or cells) which extends for some distance longitudinally in the spinal cord or lower brain, and preserves substantially the same position and structure throughout its course. [E.g. Clarke's column in the cord, the columnæ fornicis in the brain stem.]

column diagram, see **bar diagram.**

colyone, colyonic, see **chalone.**

coma = a state of unconsciousness with abolition of even the reflexes, reduction of function to mere vegetative persistence (circulation and respiration), and loss of nearly all defense adjustments (non-responsiveness to pricks, and even to obstruction of breathing). [It passes with or without a delirious phase to consciousness. Due to toxic or circulatory disorders. Distg. fr. **sleep** by pathological conditioning and by impossibility of arousal.] **comatose**[a] (accent **co-**).

combination = (*psychol.*) a generic term applied to any union of elements or components in conscious experience. [It includes **integration, colligation, fusion, juxtaposition.**] — Ger. *Vereinigung.*

combination/chemical, see **chemical synthesis.**

combination/law of = a hypothesis employed in explaining **learning,** which assumes that responses made simultaneously or successively tend to appear together whenever the stimulus for either is present, and similarly that two or more stimuli may jointly elicit a single response. — Fr. *l. de combinaison.*

combination test = a type of test in which the essential task is to assemble fragments or isolated sections into a meaningful whole, as by putting together a formboard or arranging jumbled words to form a sentence. [The term has arisen as a rough translation of the *Kombinationsmethode* urged by Ebbinghaus as a valuable test of intelligence, but his arrangement of sentences with missing words or letters is now more commonly termed a **completion test.**]

combination tone = an additional tone which may arise when two tones are sounded simultaneously. [There are two types, the **difference tone** (sometimes called **grave harmonic**), whose frequency is the difference in the frequencies of the generating tones, and the **summation tone,** whose frequency is the sum of the frequencies of the generating tones. Syn. **resultant tone.**] — Fr. *ton résultant, ton de combinaison*; Ger. *Kombinationston.*

combined sclerosis = involvement of both the afferent and efferent systems of the cord, as in pernicious anemia.

comic[n] = a situation or episode which induces laughter or a strong tendency to mirth in the average observer, provided the event lacks any pronounced element of cruelty or pain to those concerned in the action. **comic(al)**[a].

comma = (*mus.*) a very small interval, usually found as the difference between two different derivations, by tuning, of what musically is regarded as the same note. [There are several commas, for different scales and methods of tuning; the most common is the **comma of Didymus:** e.g. by tuning upward four perfect fifths from C and then downward one major third, we obtain a note which is ostensibly c′, but is higher than the perfect double-octave of C by a comma. The **Pythagorean comma** is the difference between a Pythagorean whole-tone and two Pythagorean hemitones. Cf. **interval,** Table VII.]

commensalism = a type of association in which members of one animal species live in a community of another species without dominating the latter or preying upon them, and without serving as slaves. [Cf. **symbiosis.**]

commensurable = (*math.*) characterizing two or more quantities which are capable of being measured in terms of a common unit. [Syn. **commensurate.** Cf. **incommensurable.**]

commissural fibers = fibers which connect regions in one cerebral hemisphere with corresponding regions in the other. [Cf. **commissure.**]

commissure = a tract of nerve fibers which connect approximately corresponding regions in the two hemispheres or other divisions of the brain or in the spinal cord. [Distg. fr. **association tracts,** which connect regions in the same hemisphere.] **commissural**[a] (accent **-mish-**).

commitment = 1. (*crim.*) the legal deprivation of liberty, e.g. of a criminal, defective, or mentally unsound individual; 2. formal agreement by a normal individual to carry out some specific undertaking. — Fr. (1) *mandat de dépôt,* (2) *engagement.*

common sensation = (*hist.*) a sensation not derived from the senses that are provided with specialized receptors. [Applied sometimes to internal organic sensations (**coenesthesia**), sometimes to sensations from the cutaneous receptors and sometimes to pain.] — Fr. *sensation générale, sens du corps*; Ger. *Gemeinempfindung, Organempfindung.*

common sense = 1. judgments and conclusions based upon the individual's past experience in general rather than on a critical evaluation of data; 2. (*hist.*) a term used in Aristotle's doctrine to denote the capacity to unite the separate senses, also capacity to apprehend qualities common to all experiences (space, time, number, etc.), which are called **common sensibles.** [Transmitted (2) by medieval writers and used in the 18th century (esp. by Thomas Reid) to denote the source of mental acts such as intuitions, axiomatic truths. Cf. **critical common sense.**]

common sensibility = 1. a diffuse synthetic or integrated experience derived from tactual, organic, and kinesthetic sensations; 2. (a specific) sense experience, such as pain, aroused through receptors of various modalities. [Syn. **coenesthesia.** The scope of the term varies with different authors; sometimes contr. w. **special senses** yet derived from them; sometimes embracing visceral experience, affective states, and tactual-kinesthetic complexes such as shudder. Cf. **common sensation.**] — Ger. *Gemeingefühl, Gemeinempfindungen.*

common sensibles = perceptual experience, e.g. form and motion, derived from two or more senses (Aristotle). [Cf. **common sense** (2).]

communication = 1. the transmission of an impression or effect from one location to another without actual transportation of material; 2. the transmission of impressions from environment to organism or vice versa or from one individual to another. [Mostly used in the latter sense, as the basal phenomenon of social psychology, e.g. speech is a means of communication. Applied also to the general stimulus-response phenomenon, e.g. the stimulus is communicated to the organism.] **communicate**[v].

communicative tendency = a tendency on the part of an individual toward social intercourse, esp. as regards talking.

community = 1. a group of individuals of the same species dwelling in close proximity; 2. the fact that two or more individuals possess the same or similar things or possess a common characteristic; e.g. community of interest, community of property. — Ger. *Gemeinschaft.*

comparative judgment = an expression by an observer of the relative intensity or quality of two stimuli presented either simultaneously or in succession.

comparative method = the method of investigation which proceeds by examining individuals or classes that possess certain common characteristics and noting their similarities and differences. [Distg. fr. **descriptive method,** which studies a typical specimen, and **genetic method,** which studies origin and growth. Cf. **comparative psychology.**] — Ger. *vergleichende Methode.*

comparative psychology = that branch of psychology which investigates the relations between different species as regards their behavior and mental processes. [Strictly, limited to study by the **comparative method,** but often extended to phylogenetic investigation; **animal psychology** includes investigation by comparative, genetic, and descriptive methods; the term might also be applied to the comparative study of human races (**race psychology**) but is seldom so used.] — Ger. *vergleichende Psychologie.*

comparison = the process of discovering and examining the similarities and differences between two or more phenomena, etc. — Ger. *Vergleich.*

comparison/method of paired = 1. a procedure used in experimental investigation, in which two stimuli which differ in but one noticeable character are presented simultaneously or in close succession, and judgment is made upon that one character; e.g. "longer," "brighter"; 2. syn. for **comparative method.** — Ger. *Methode der paarweisen Vergleichung.*

comparison stimulus = (*psychophys.*) a stimulus which is compared with a normal or standard stimulus. [Cf. **standard stimulus.**] — Ger. *Vergleichsreiz.*

compatibility = 1. the fact that two or more characteristics may continue to coexist harmoniously in the same individual, organism, or mind; 2. (*logic*) the relation between two judgments such that both may be true at the same time; 3. (*soc.*) the fact that the general nature or temperament of two individuals is such that they may live together in harmony. [(1) contr. w. **incompatibility** = that the characteristics are such that they never coexist harmoniously in the same individual, etc.] **compatible**[a].

compensation = a psychic mechanism by which an individual covers up or disguises an undesirable trait by calling into play a desirable one, and exaggerating its manifestations. [According to Freud, the purpose of this process is to conceal from the individual's own consciousness the opposite undesirable tendency in the unconscious, thereby developing an exaggerated aim or character trait; according to Adler, the basis is always a sense of inferiority and the purpose is the attainment of the superiority goal.]

compensatory movements = movements of a member or part of the body which tend to restore that part or the whole body to normal position, when equilibrium is disturbed through the movements of another member in an opposite direction, or through movement imparted from without. [E.g. when the head is turned to the left, the eyes tend to make compensatory movements to the right, whether the head movement be imparted by muscular activity or by passive rotation of the body; when a leg swings forward in walking the homonymous arm tends to swing backward. Applied specifically to the reflexes initiated by stimulation of the semicircular canals and vestibule and to similar movements obtained by visual stimulation.]

compensatory reflex = a reflex which brings a moving part of the body back to the original position of equilibrium.

competency, competence = 1. ability to compete with normal persons; 2. the state or degree of mentality which is sufficient to render one legally responsible for his actions. **competent**[a, np]. — Ger. (2) *Zurechnungsfähigkeit.*

competition = contention of two or more individuals for the same object or for superiority. [Syn. **rivalry;** but **competition** involves essentially the mutual opposition of two or more individuals, whereas **rivalry** involves no personal opposition as such, but only that necessary to the constitution of the challenging task, as in many sports. Distg. fr. **conflict,** which involves personal contact or relations, while **competition** may or may not. Cf. **competition/biological, competition/mental.**] **compete**[v], **competitive**[a].

competition/biological = rivalry in securing the means of maintaining or perpetuating life, such as food, shelter, mates, etc. [Syn. **struggle for existence.**] **compete**[v].

competition/mental = rivalry between the various contents of an individual's mind. [It implies some such conception of span as that formulated by Spearman.]

complacence, complacency = a pleasantly toned condition of calm, marked by satisfaction, esp. self-satisfaction. **complacent**[a]. — Fr. *satisfaction.*

complement = (*immunol.*) a ferment-like substance normally present in body fluids and cell protoplasm, which acts to destroy an invading organism when linked to the latter by means of an amboceptor or immune body. [Cf. **amboceptor, uniceptors.**]

complements, complementaries, complementary colors = any pair of chromatic colors whose stimuli, when mixed additively, give rise to the sensation of gray or white. [All three terms are in common use. The singular is used for one member of the pair; e.g. yellow is the **complement** of blue.] **complementary**[a]. — Ger. *Komplementärfarben.*

complete learning (or **memorizing**) **method** = a technique of testing rote learning, in which the individual reviews repeatedly, in a prescribed manner, the material presented, until he can reproduce the whole without error. [It is the earliest of the formal memory methods, and was devised by Ebbinghaus (1885).] — Fr. *m. d'acquisition complète*; Ger. *Erlernungsmethode.*

completeness of response = a theory proposed by J. Peterson to explain selection in learning; it denies the adequacy of mere serial associations and assumes the selection of that movement which, on account of its general conformity with the totality of intra-organic and objective conditions, leads through less impeded activity to adjustments and release of tensions.

completion test = a type of mental test in which material is presented that has been mutilated by the omission of some of its parts, the testee being asked to supply the missing parts. [There are many kinds of completion tests, the first and best known being the sentence **completion test** devised by Ebbinghaus (1897). Other forms of the test employ mutilated words, paragraphs, pictures, geometrical forms, number series, etc.] — Fr. *épreuve de complètement de dessins (phrases) inachevés*; Ger. *Lückenergänzungstest*.

complex[a] = composed of different elements arranged in some relation of subordination or interdependence of parts. [Distg. fr. **compound,** in which the parts are coordinate. Contr. w. **simple, elementary.**] (Accent **-plex.**) **complexity**[n].

complex[n] = 1. an experience in which a number of different simple elements are united together; 2. (*psychoan., anal. psychol.*) a group of emotionally invested ideas which have unconscious activities, i.e. are partly or entirely repressed. [Some writers treat the **complex** (2) as a pathological condition. See Table II.] (Accent **com-.**)

complex (or **complexion**) = 3. a term used by Meinong and his followers to denote those wholes (*fundierte Inhalte*) which arise from the consolidation of part-contents (*fundierende Inhalte*).

complex reaction (or **response**) = a general term applied to reaction time experiments in which the subject or observer is instructed to make some recognition, discrimination, choice, or association after the presentation of the stimulus and before responding. [Contr. w. **simple reaction** or **response.**]

complication = 1. a combination of elementary sensations from different senses; 2. any combination of elements into a single complex experience. [Contr. (1) w. **assimilation** (1).] — Ger. *Komplikation*.

complication experiment = the investigation of the temporal displacement of simultaneous impressions derived from different senses, due to variations in the instructions given to the subject. [In the classic experiment the observer judges the location of a revolving pointer on a dial at the instant when a bell is sounded. The position indicated may differ in either direction from the true position. Syn. **prior entry experiment.**]

complication pendulum, complication clock = a pendulum pointer which swings along a graduated arc and presents, at a variable moment of its swing, an auditory or other stimulus; it is used for investigating prior entry or personal equation (Wundt, 1861). [According as attention is directed to the pointer or the sound, the scale position of the pointer when the sound occurs tends to be overestimated or underestimated.]

component instinct = (*psychoan.*) one of the elements of the libido which make up a total instinct. [E.g. **sadism** and **exhibitionism** are component parts of the sexual instinct.]

composite = a generic adjective denoting any sort of non-simplicity. [It includes **compound, complex, manifold,** etc.] — Ger. *zusammengesetzt*.

composite image, see **image/composite.**

composite person = (*psychoan.*) a figure in a dream which is constituted by the fusion of traits belonging to more than one actual person.

composition = the elements which comprise a construction, usually including the form of construction. [Syn. **synthesis.**]

composition theory, see **atomism/psychological.**

compound[n] = that which is formed by a mixture or union of elements. [Used by certain followers of Wundt to denote a relatively independent unit, which is composed of psychical elements but whose attributes are not limited to the attributes of these elements. Cf. **colligation, fusion.**] **compound**[a] (structural); **compounded**[a] (functional). — Fr. *composé*.

compound eye = an eye which contains more than one focusing or receptor system (ommatidium). [The longitudinal axis of the ommatidia diverge slightly, so that adjoining ones receive light reflected from adjoining areas in the field, resulting in a group of small images (one in each ommatidium) which in the higher invertebrates form an image of the entire field and produce mosaic vision. Found extensively in arthropods.] — Fr. *oeil composé*.

compound/mental = any composite experience, e.g. a complication, integration, fusion, blend. [Cf. **composite.**] — Fr. *composé mental*.

compound (or **complex**) **reaction** = (*hist.*) a response involving the **higher mental processes,** which was supposed to yield by the **subtraction method** the time of the higher processes. [Mental **chronometry** of this sort flourished in Wundt's laboratory at Leipzig in 1880–1900. **cognition time** was found by requiring the subject to cognize the stimulus before reacting to it, and then subtracting the **sensory response time** from the total time; **discrimination time** required the discrimination of two or more stimuli and then a single response, with the **muscular response time** subtracted from the total time; **choice** or **will** was timed by having several stimuli with a different response (usually a different finger movement) for each stimulus, with **discrimination time** subtracted from this; **association time** was the time of a verbal response less the **cognition time.** The technique failed to be accepted as valid because of confusion between sensory and muscular times, cognition and discrimination times, and discrimination and choice times, and because of the general disfavor into which the **subtraction method** fell.]

compound reflex = a group of associated reflexes which operate together in a single action, the role of the constituent elementary reflexes being coordinate. [E.g. the grasping reflex. Contr. w. **complex reflex,** in which some of the constituents are subordinate to others, e.g. vocal reflexes.] — Fr. *réflexe composé*.

compound tone, see **tone/compound.**

comprehension = 1. (*psychol.*) knowledge about an object, situation, event, etc.; 2. (*logic*) the marks which characterize a class. [Syn. (1) **understanding;** (2) **connotation.** (1) applies to the completed experience of external objects, general principles, etc., in which a thought of their composition, relations, origin, meaning, etc., is added to the direct experience of (**acquaintance with**) the datum concerned; the distinction between **acquaintance with** and **comprehension** is imperfectly recognized in the English vocabulary; Lat. *sapere, scire* vs. *cognoscere*; Fr. *savoir* vs. *connaître*; Ger. *wissen* vs. *kennen*.] **comprehend**[v]. — Ger. (1) *Verständnis*.

comprehension test = 1. a type of mental test designed by Binet, in which the testee is asked to state what one should do in a given practical situation, e.g. if the house is on fire, or if it is raining when one starts for school; 2. a type of educational test designed to measure degree of understanding of material read. [(2) is commonly used together with a speed test of reading; or the same test may be scored for speed and for comprehension, e.g. in Monroe's Standardized Silent Reading Tests.]

compromise-formation = 1. (*psychoan.*) a mental activity in which both the repressed sexual impulses and the repressing forces of the ego or superego are fused; 2. a compromise between the opposing tendencies of a conscious intention and an unconscious one (wishes), producing neurotic symptoms. — Ger. *Kompromissbildung*.

compulsion = the performance of an act at the suggestion of some other individual or individuals, the suggestion being irresistible, though contrary to the inclination or will of the performer. [Applied also to the feeling of powerlessness and inevitability when so acting.] **compulsive**[a] (performance), **compulsion**[a] (suggestion). — Fr. *contrainte*; Ger. *Zwang*.

compulsion/internal = the performance of an act in spite of the performer's conscious intention to refrain from such action.

compulsion neurosis, see **obsessional neurosis.**

compulsive repetition, see **repetition-compulsion.**

compulsive type = (*psychoan.*) a psychological type mastered by the fear of conscience instead of by the fear of losing love (Freud). — Fr. *type coercitif*.

compunction = an emotional attitude characterized by displeasure or distaste regarding a given act or procedure, which is nevertheless performed or seriously contemplated.

conarium, see **pineal body.**

conation = 1. purposive activity in its inception; i.e. the active phase of volition, desire, aversion, conscious impulse; 2. the mental state accompanying an impulse, desire, or voluntary act, in which kinesthetic components predominate; 3. the conscious tendency to act. (Accent **co-**, not **con-**.) **conative**[a] (not to be confused with **connate, connative** = native, inborn, inherited). — Ger. *Streben*.

conative channels = (*hist.*) the pathways through which the nerve impulses concerned in conation discharge. [Syn. **volitional channels.**] — Fr. *voies volitionnelles*.

concatenation = 1. a connected series; 2. (*neurol.*) a series of neurons or neural elements functionally united to form a conductive pattern; 3. (*physiol.*) a series of reflexes in which the action of one generates the stimulus-cue which excites the next, and so on; i.e. a chain of reflexes.

conceit = an emotional disposition marked by an exaggerated valuation of oneself or of certain aspects of oneself, the valuation being usually excessive, and often without observable foundation. [Cf. **pride.**] — Fr. *vanité, orgueil*; Ger. *Einbildung, Eitelkeit*.

conceivable = 1. characterizing a judgment which may be believed to be true; 2. characterizing an idea or other representative experience which may be believed to have some objective counterpart. [Cf. **conception.**] **conceivability**[n].

concentration = 1. the centering of attention on certain parts of an experience; 2. increased attensity or vividness of certain elements or items of experience. [Syn. (1) **mental focusing.**] **concentrate**[v].

concept = a mental state or process which means or refers to more than one object or experience, or to one object in relation to others. [When it represents different individuals or items, it is called a **class concept** or **general concept.** When it represents a common aspect or attribute of the class it is an **abstract idea.** Syn. **conception,** which strictly denotes the process, while **concept** denotes the product. The formulation of a concept in words is called a **term.**] **conceptual**[a]. — Ger. *Begriff*.

conception = 1. (*psychol.*) the formation or experiencing of a concept or general idea; 2. (*biol.*) the fecundation of an ovum. [Cf. **concept.**] **conceive**[v] (1, 2); **conceptional**[a]. — Ger. (2) *Empfängnis*.

concha = the central, cavernous portion of the auricle, or outer ear, which opens inward into the external auditory meatus. [Cf. **auricle.**] (Accent **conk-.**) — Fr. *cavité de la conque*; Ger. *Ohrmuschel*.

conclusion = a judgment which is formed as a result of reasoning. [In scientific procedure the endeavor is made to distinguish conclusions from the results of experimentation or data upon which the conclusions are based.] **conclude**[v]. — Ger. *Schluss, Folgerung*.

concomitance = the presence together and absence together of two phenomena, or their simultaneous occurrence and disappearance. [Cf. **concomitant variations.**]

concomitant sensation = a sensation which accompanies another sensation, upon the proper stimulation of the latter and in the absence of its own proper stimulus. [Syn. **synesthesia.** In colored hearing (e.g.) the colors (visual experiences) are aroused concomitantly with auditory stimulation in the absence of visual stimuli.] — Fr. *s. associée*; Ger. *Mitempfindung*.

concomitant variations/method (or **canon**) **of** = a general working principle or canon used in reaching inductive conclusions, according to which if two phenomena increase together or decrease together, or otherwise vary together, they are causally related. [Cf. **Mill's canons.**] — Fr. *m. des variations concomitantes*.

concord = a consonant chord. [Cf. **consonance, chord.** Contr. w. **discord.**] — Fr. *accord consonant*; Ger. *Zusammenklang*.

concrete[a] = characterizing an object, creature, thing, phenomenon, class, or any complete whole, as distg. fr. a quality or other attribute of an object, etc. [Contr. w. **abstract** = characterizing a quality or attribute considered apart from the thing, etc. to which it belongs.]

concrete intelligence = 1. the effective management of concrete objects in dealing with novel situations; 2. such intelligence as is measured by tests calling for the effective management of concrete objects.

concussion = traumatic impact on the head or spine, leading to circulatory and tissue disorders or to more transitory shock, with unconsciousness and varying after-effects. — Fr. *secousse, ébranlement*; Ger. *Erschütterung*.

condensation = (*psychoan.*) a fusion of ideational elements. [Particularly marked in dreams, where a given idea or representation may frequently be found to be derived from several others. This fusion is regarded as an unconscious process; in dreams, e.g. every element of the manifest content represents several latent dream thoughts; in proper names neologisms may be formed through fusion.] — Ger. *Verdichtung*.

condenser = (*elect.*) a system of conductors separated by dialectrics, capable of storing electric charges. [Cf. **capacity, farad.**]

condition[n] = 1. a phenomenon, force, situation, etc., without which a given event never occurs; 2. one of the antecedents or concomitants of a given event; 3. the state of anything, esp. whether good or bad. [In (1, 2), the phenomenon, antecedent, etc. is termed a **condition of** the given event; the event is **conditioned by** the phenomenon, antecedent, etc. in question. Cf. **cause.**] — Fr. (1, 2) *condition*, (3) *état*; Ger. (1, 2) *Bedingung*, (3) *Umstand*.

condition[v] = 1. to establish a **conditioned response;** 2. to occasion the organism to **learn.** [The second meaning has developed rapidly from the first and is now widespread. As loosely used it is almost syn. w. **teach,** with the added implications of individual **reflexes** or **bonds** to be established as the basis of **learning.**] **to become conditioned to** = to learn. **conditioning**[a].

conditioned emotion = responses of an affective character elicited by a stimulus or situation which was originally inadequate to evoke such responses but which became linked thereto through a process of **conditioning.** [Cf. **conditioned reflex.**]

conditioned reflex = an acquired simple response which was originally initiated by a certain stimulus A, and is now initiated by another stimulus B, that has occurred earlier in connection with A. [The term, originated by Pavlov, is generally adopted, though technically confusing; such terms as **substitute reflex, acquired reflex, conditional reflex,** or **associative reflex** would be more exact. Cf. **condition**[v], **conditioned response.**] — Fr. *réflexe conditionnel, r. conditionné*; Ger. *bedingter Reflex*.

conditioned response = a response, whether simple or elaborated, which, though originally not arousable by a given stimulus, has come to be arousable by it as a result of the simultaneous or nearly simultaneous presentation of the latter along with some stimulus that had been potent to arouse the response in question. [Syn. **substitute response.** Cf. **condition**[v], **conditioned reflex.**]

conditioned stimulus = an originally ineffective stimulus which, after presentation simultaneously or nearly simultaneously with an adequate or original stimulus to a given response, becomes capable of arousing this response when presented alone. [E.g. sound of bell, originally incapable of eliciting salivary reflex, after being presented along with food in mouth, becomes potent to elicit that response when presented alone. Syn. **substitute stimulus.** Cf. **conditioned response.**]

conduct[n] = 1. the behavior of an individual in its ethical bearings; 2. behavior of an individual so far as determined by foresight. (Accent **con-.**) — Fr. *conduite*; Ger. (1) *Betragen, Verhalten*.

conduct[v] = (*tech.*) to direct the course of a moving material or energy; e.g. the nerves conduct impulses to the brain. (Accent **-duct.**) **conduction**[n]. — Fr. *conduire*; Ger. *leiten*[v], *Leitung*[n].

conduction/antidromic = conduction of nerve impulses in a direction which is contrary to the normal direction of passage in a given nerve. — Fr. *transmission antidromique*.

conduction/avalanche, see **avalanche conduction.**

conduction/bone, see **bone conduction.**

conduction deafness = a type of auditory defect due to impairment of the conductive mechanism of the ear. [Frequent causes are partial or total destruction of the tympanic membrane, blocking of the air passages by foreign substances or secretions, and interferences with the normal movements of the ossicles through ossification or loosening of their joints. In such cases the internal ear may be normal, as demonstrated by tests. Cf. **bone-conduction test.**] — Fr. *surdité de transmission*.

conduction/membrane theory of, see **membrane theory** and **Nernst-Lillie theory of excitation.** — Fr. *théorie de conduction membraneuse*.

conduction/neural = the transmission of a wave of excitation along nerve fibers.

conduction path, see **path.**

conduction/synaptic = conduction of the nerve impulse from neuron to neuron, i.e. across the surfaces of contact termed **synapses.**

conduction time = the time required for the transmission of a wave of excitation between two determined points. — Fr. *temps de conduction*.

conduction-unit = an organized system of connections or bonds adapted to a given situation (Thorndike).

conduction with decrement = the transmission of a wave of excitation in tissue with a gradual loss of the energy of the wave. [It is now generally believed that **conduction with decrement** does not take place in nerve fiber.] — Fr. *conduction avec decrément*.

conductivity = 1. the capacity of a tissue to transmit a wave of excitation; 2. the capacity of a substance to transmit energy. **conductive**[a]. — Fr. *pouvoir de conduction*; Ger. *Leitfähigkeit*.

cone/retinal = a type of structure found in the retina of the eye which constitutes a specific receptor for vision. [The cones of the human eye are 0.022 to 0.085 mm. in length and 0.0025 to 0.0075 mm. in diameter. Distg. fr. **retinal rods,** another visual receptor; the cones are without visual purple and are believed to operate for both chromatic and achromatic (gray) visual qualities at higher levels of stimulation-intensity, the rods for achromatic only at low (twilight) levels; the rods and cones form the 2nd layer of the retina from the surface of the eyeball, lying just within the layer of pigmented cells; at the center of the retina the cones are long and slender and closely packed to the exclusion of rods; farther out they are shorter and thicker and interspersed among the more numerous rods, and their outer portion has become small and cone-shaped, whence their name; it is estimated that there are 7,000,000 cones in the human retina.] — Ger. *Zapfen*.

configuration = 1. (*geom.*) the arrangement of parts in an object or body, with special reference to the resulting form; 2. (*Gestalt*) any organized whole in which each member influences every other and is in turn influenced by it, so that the totality contains more than a mere sum of what analysis would call its *parts* and their relations. [Syn. (2) **system, organic whole, structure.** Cf. **Gestalt.**] **configurational**[a].

configuration theory, see **Gestalt theory.**

conflict^{n} = (*psychoan.*) a painful emotional state which results from a tension between opposed and contradictory wishes, and is due to the fact that an unconscious (repressed) wish is forcibly prevented from entering the conscious system. (Accent **con-**.)

conflict/intergroup = (*soc.*) the friction due to contrasting customs and social habits when a subject people is forced to adjust itself to the group life of the dominant people. [Cf. **culture conflict.**]

conflict/major = (*psychoan.*) the more dominant emotional state in a current conflict between opposed and contradictory wishes.

conflicting associations/law of = a principle of mental association, according to which a thought similar to the desired association tends to inhibit that association. [Cf. **inhibition.**] — Fr. *l. d'associations opposées.*

confluence = a secondary flowing together of what has just previously been apprehended apart. [The **illusion of confluence** is illustrated by the **Müller-Lyer figure.**]

conform = to agree in pattern with some standard type. [Applied to social behavior, biological species, statistical results, and less frequently to objects, etc.] **conformity**^{n}.

confusion = 1. the mingling of items of any sort, but particularly of ideas or concepts, so that clear discrimination is impossible; or the result of such mingling; 2. the mixing of ideas which have no logical association, so that the conclusion reached does not follow from the premises; 3. a state of mind characterized by lack of clear thinking, emotional disturbance, and sometimes by disturbed perception. — Ger. (1) *Verwechselung,* (3) *Verworrenheit.*

confusion/mental = bewilderment and difficulty of orientation, with tendency to hallucination and general clouding of consciousness. [Cf. **amentia.**]

congenital = actually or potentially present in the individual at birth, whether as a consequence of heredity or of environmental factors. [Syn. **connate;** the latter term is occasionally applied to characters appearing at birth, whether inherited or not.] — Ger. *angeboren.*

congenital alexia and **agraphia,** see **strephosymbolia.**

congenital character = a character present at birth, or one which develops later owing to hereditary factors. [Often contr. w. a character due to the environment or to experience.]

congestion = an abnormal accumulation of blood or lymph in some organ or region of the body. [Syn. **hyperemia.**]

congruent^{a} = (*vis.*) pert. to the same external source. [Applied to points and figures in the field of vision. Cf. **congruent figures, congruent points.**] — Fr. *congruent.*

congruent figures = (*vis.*) a pair of figures seen with the two eyes and referred to a single object in external space. — Fr. *images congruentes.*

congruent points = (*vis.*) a pair of points in the two retinas which are referred to the same point in the external source of stimulation. [Distg. fr. **identical points.**]

congruous^{a} = harmonious, capable of existing together or of being thought of together. [Distg. fr. **congruent,** which applies to objective agreement. Contr. w. **incongruous.**] **congruity**^{n}. — Fr. *congru.*

conjugal paresis = paresis in both husband and wife (infection with the same strain of syphilis).

conjugate movements = coordinated movements of the two eyes about their respective centers of rotation, such as to shift binocular fixation from one point to another in space. [These movements are normally accompanied by appropriate accommodation, or distance focusing, of both eyes. Syn. **associated movements.**]

conjugation = 1. temporary or permanent union of two unicellular organisms, usually followed by reproduction by fission; 2. the union of sex cell nuclei, or chromosomes, in higher organisms. — Fr. *conjugaison.*

conjunction = (*psychol.*) the occurring together of two events, e.g. of two stimuli. [Distg. fr. **connection:** "We only learn by experience the frequent **Conjunction** of objects, without ever being able to comprehend anything like **Connexion** between them" (Hume).]

conjunctiva = the mucous membrane which covers the anterior portion of the eyeball and the inside of the lids.

conjunctival reflex, see **corneal reflex.**

conjuncture of events = a combination of apparently disconnected circumstances which brings about some important result. [E.g. a revolution in one country and an earthquake in another leading to the collapse of the stock exchange in a third country.]

conjure = 1. to produce phenomena that appear to violate physical or mental laws, by means of sleight of hand, skillfully arranged or concealed devices, and the misdirection of the observer's attention. [Syn. **juggle (jugglery, legerdemain**^{n}**, prestidigitation**^{n}, and **natural magic**^{n}). (Accent **kun-**.) Distg. fr. **conjure** 2 (accent **-jure**).] **conjuring**^{n}, **conjury**^{n}, **conjurer**^{np}.

conjure = 2. (*hist.*) to call forth or send away demons, spirits, etc. by magic arts or by invoking supernatural aid. [Cf. **enchant, incantation.**] (Accent **-jure.**) **conjuration**^{n}.

connate = appearing at birth or shortly after. [Applied to characters of an organism. Syn. **congenital.** Strictly, congenital (or inherited) characters are either **embryonic, connate,** or **deferred,** as to epoch of manifestation.] — Fr. *inné, congénital;* Ger. *angeboren.*

connection = 1. the establishment of any sort of relation between two separate mental elements or phenomena; 2. the relation so established; i.e. the dynamic relation or neural linkage between stimulus and response by means of which the stimulus arouses the response. [A generic term, including various sorts of union or conjunction, both simultaneous and successive; cf. **association, integration, colligation, fusion, complication.**] — Ger. (1) *Verbindung,* (2) *Zusammenhang.*

connectionism = the doctrine that all mental processes consist of the functioning of native and acquired connections between situations and responses (Thorndike).

connectors = the portion of the neural arc between the receptors and the effectors. [Syn. **adjustor.**]

connotation = the qualities, attributes, and characters in general which are designated by a given term, i.e. which constitute one aspect of its meaning. [Syn. **extension.** Contr. w. **denotation** = the objects or class of phenomena which the term designates.] **connote**^{v}.

consanguinity = blood relationship, or degree of relationship through heredity.

conscience = the attitude of an individual toward the moral or social implications of his own behavior, involving a judgment of value. [**conscience** is experienced (e.g.) when one is presented with an incentive or stimulus to violate an ethical principle which he has previously recognized; it is characterized in such cases by an emotion of shame or remorse. Cf. superego.] **conscientious**[a].—Fr. *conscience*; Ger. *Gewissen*.

conscious = 1. in possession of awareness or mental life, i.e. having sensations and feelings; 2. characterizing the condition of an organic creature who is receiving impressions or having experiences; 3. characterizing a response of which the organism is aware; 4. pert. to consciousness or subjective experience. [Syn. (1, 2) **sentient,** (2) **aware**; sometimes used as syn. of **reflective.**]

conscious illusion theory = (*esth.*) the theory advanced by Konrad Lange which interprets art-experience as a process of illusion or esthetic play, resulting in a pleasurable "free and conscious oscillation between semblance and reality." — Ger. *Th. d. bewussten Selbsttäuschung*.

consciousness = 1. the distinguishing feature of mental life, variously characterized as (*a*) awareness, (*b*) the central effect of neural reception, (*c*) the capacity of having experiences, (*d*) the subjective aspect of brain activity, (*e*) the relation of self to environment; 2. the sum-total of an individual's experiences at any given moment; 3. the capacity of the individual to know external objects and to influence them. [Originally, consciousness signified the mind's immediate cognition of its own experiences (thus Occam, Locke), but later, the experiences themselves (e.g. Ladd). Often used as syn. for **experience** (a source of confusion). Cf. **subject of consciousness, object of consciousness, content of consciousness, conscious.**] — Fr. *conscience*; Ger. *Bewusstsein*.

consciousness/field of = 1. the totality of experiences at a given instant; 2. the field (arena) in which these experiences take place. — Fr. *champ de conscience*; Ger. *Bewusstseinsfeld, Blickfeld des Bewusstseins*.

consciousness/marginal = 1. the faint experiences which are present along with the vivid or focal experience at any given moment; 2. any faint, vague, unclear experience. [Syn. **margin of consciousness.** Cf. **subconscious.**] — Fr. *zone marginale de la conscience*.

consciousness of action (or **of act**) = the experience of self-activity (Michotte). [Distg. fr. **consciousness of effort.** It implies distinction between volition and conation. Cf. **determining tendency** (Ach); **alertness** (Aveling).]

consciousness of effort = the experience of striving, derived from kinesthetic and organic sensations. [Distg. fr. **consciousness of action.**]

consciousness of kind = awareness of characteristics in other individuals that are similar to one's own characteristics, esp. in respect to race, nationality, caste, class, religion, etc. [Sometimes extended to an analogous phenomenon in subhuman species.] — Fr. *conscience de classe, c. de similitude*.

consciousness/social, see **social consciousness.**

consciousness/stream of, see **stream of consciousness.**

consciousness/subliminal = an effect of stimulation which is not directly experienced, but which has some indirect effect upon experience.

consensual actions = (*hist.*) involuntary actions or movements which are accompanied by sensations or direct awareness of the act.

consent = a decision to perform an act or to allow it to be performed, the action having been proposed by some other individual. [Distg. fr. **decision** (proper), in which the individual selects a course of action irrespective of suggestion; and fr. **assent** = acceptance of a judgment suggested or proposed by another.] — Fr. *assentiment*; Ger. *Einwilligung, Zustimmung*.

consentience = (*hist.*) sensuous impressions apart from all intellectual processes. — Fr. *sentiment du moi primitif* (*organique*).

consequence = 1. the later phenomena in a sequence, considered as directly related to certain earlier phenomena in the series; 2. (*logic*) a thought or proposition which is so related to another thought or proposition, that the latter determines the validity of the former. [Syn. (1) **consequent**[n], applied to particular items; **effect,** which commonly implies a dynamic relation.] **consequent**[a].

consequent = (*math.*) the second term in a ratio. [Cf. **argument** (4).]

conservation = (*hist.*) retention of the effects of experience. [The basis of memory or recollection.]

conservation of energy (or **of force**) = the general principle that in any closed system (i.e. one not receiving energy from outside or sending energy outside itself) the total energy remains constant despite any transformation from one form of energy into another; i.e. the doctrine that no energy or force in nature is destroyed or created. — Ger. *Erhaltung der Energie*.

consistency = the relation of one proposition to another, such that the situations described by the two may both occur together. [Contr. w. **inconsistency** = a relation such that the two situations never occur together. Cf. **self-consistency.**] **consistent**[a].

consonance = an effect produced by two or more tones which blend or fuse, characterized by smoothness or unitariness, and (usually) pleasantness. [Cf. **dissonance, harmony.**] **consonant**[a].

consonant = 1. a conventional vocal sound produced by some obstruction to the breath by certain positions of the vocal organs, forming a triple (or more complex) resonating system above the larynx; 2. the letter representing such a sound. [Distg. fr. **vowel.**]

constancy = the fact that perceptual objects retain to a greater or lesser degree normal appearance in relative (though not in absolute) independence of the local stimulus conditions. [Applied to the following properties: **color** = preservation of normal hue and brightness under different illuminations; **form** = persistence of the shape of an object when, from geometrical optics, a change might be expected; **magnitude** = preservation of apparent size in spite of differences in the retinal image; **weight** = equal weights still appear equal when one is lifted with the free hand, the other with a hand carrying an extra load, etc.] **constant**[a].

constancy hypothesis = the theory that stimulation is correlated directly with sensation; i.e.

that the relation between local stimulus and sensation observed under one set of conditions holds equally well under all sets of conditions, provided that the condition of the sense-organ remains unchanged. [Also applied to other hypotheses involving unaltered persistence of relations, e.g. of stimuli to unit reflexes. Cf. **constancy.**] — Ger. *Konstanzannahme.*

constant^n = in equations, statistical tables, etc., a factor (additive, multiplicative, or exponential) which remains the same for all values of the other factors or constituents concerned. [Contr. w. **variable** = a factor which changes as some other factor changes.]

constant error = a deviation of experimental results from the true value, or from an established standard, due to some factor which remains unchanged during the entire series of observations. [Attributable either to instrumental limitations, to observational bias, or to some outside disturbing factor. Syn. **constant deviation.** Distg. fr. **variable error,** due to factors which affect each observation separately.] — Ger. *konstanter Fehler.*

constant orientation/law of (*vis.*), see **Donders' law.**

constant R = abbrev. for **constant stimulus.**

constant stimuli/method of = a psychophysical method in which the occurrence of a sensation or other experience is determined as a function of the variation of the stimulus. [The method yields a **psychometric function** which shows the frequency of occurrence of an experience or judgment as a function of the value of the stimulus, and which determines such statistical constants as the **threshold,** the **measure of precision,** and the **point of subjective equality.** The method was devised by Fechner as the method of **right and wrong cases,** and developed by G. E. Müller and F. M. Urban.]

constant stimulus differences/method of = a special form of the method of constant stimuli, in which a standard stimulus and a comparison stimulus are presented, and the judgment, whose frequency is to be determined, represents a comparison between the two experiences, as in the categories *greater, equal,* and *less.*

constellation = 1. a grouping or arrangement of ideas resulting from the operation of the laws of association; 2. the sum of all reproductive or other tendencies which operate, in accordance with the laws of association, to determine (by mutual reinforcement and inhibition) the actual course of ideas; 3. (*psychoan.*) a group of emotionally invested ideas which have not become repressed.

constitution = the totality of interrelated factors and elements which enter characteristically into the make-up of a given thing or datum of any sort. [Applied specifically to organisms, to denote the totality of hereditary factors as determining the individual's future development, or these factors plus his past acquisitions as determining his behavior.] **constitutional**^{a}.

constitutional disorders = disorders inherent in the make-up of the individual, inherited or at least ingrained, and not situationally or accidentally determined.

constitutional type = one aspect of typology, according to which individuals are classified as to bodily build. [According to Kretschmer, there are four types correlated with specific mental states: (*a*) **pyknic** or corpulent; (*b*) **leptosome** or slender; (*c*) **athletic**; and (*d*) **dysplastic,** i.e. deviating in parts from a regular type, disproportionate. Sigaud's earlier classification consists of (*a*) **digestive**; (*b*) **respiratory**; (*c*) **muscular**; and (*d*) **cerebral,** in accordance with the dominance of the particular system in the organism of the individual.]

constitutive relation = the relation between the constituents and the entity constituted thereby.

constrain = to compel another individual to adopt a certain course of action. [Contr. w. **restrain** = to prevent another from performing some action.] **constraint**^{n} = **compulsion** by another individual. — Fr. *contraindre*; Ger. *zwingen.*

construct^n = (*hist.*) a term used to denote the production of a synthesis of impressions. [Proposed as an empirical equivalent for **concept.** The term owes its significance to Karl Pearson, following Mach.] (Accent **con-.**)

construction/instinct of = an inherited tendency in certain individuals or species to put material objects together with the result of meeting the needs of life. [E.g. the building of shelters, devising of weapons, etc. The fact that human beings generally manifest a propensity toward such constructive work is ascribed by many to an inherited tendency or instinct. Syn. **constructiveness.**]

constructive imagination, see **creative imagination.**

constructive thinking = that form of the thinking process which results in the production of practically new judgments or conclusions, and which underlies invention, scientific discoveries, etc. — Fr. *pensée constructive.*

constructiveness = the behavior in certain individuals or species of putting materials together with the result of meeting vital needs. — Ger. *Bausinn.*

consulting psychologist = a psychologist who gives professional advice or services for a fee. [Distg. fr. **psychometrist** = a technical assistant who administers standard tests in a psychological clinic.] — Fr. *psychologue consultant.*

consummatory response = a final response, made possible by preparatory responses, which brings the organism into adjustment to the situation which has elicited the whole series of responses.

contact sensation = a touch sensation stimulated by an impact of low intensity which involves practically no dermal deformation. [Distg. fr. **pressure sensation,** in which deformation occurs. Cf. **touch sensation,** a generic term which includes both.] — Ger. *Berührungsempfindung.*

contagion = 1. (*soc.*) the spreading of suggestion throughout a given social group, which results in a more or less general imitation of some pattern of action; or the spread of some emotional display throughout the group; 2. (*pathol.*) the spreading of some delusion or functional mental disturbance throughout a social group; 3. the communication of disease from one individual to another. [(1) is classed as a special case of **social facilitation.**] **contagious**^{a}.

contemplate = 1. to consider or plan a course of action; 2. to view a phenomenon attentively. (Accent **con-** or **-tem-.**) **contemplation**^{n} (2).

contemplation = 1. the act of looking steadily at an external object or of giving sustained attention to an idea before the mind; 2. (*relig.*) an attitude, cultivated by mystics, characterized by withdrawal of thought from external events and interests, and by sustained consideration of something supposedly profitable to the soul; 3. (*esth.*) the act of absorption in a work of art or in nature which is conducive to an appreciation of its beauty. [Distg. (2) fr. **meditation,** which involves a greater activity of the mind; in Roman Catholicism, **contemplation** is regarded as a state of prayer between meditation and the lowest mystic state, or as the first mystic state.]

content[a] = syn. for **satisfied.** [Cf. **contentment.**] (Accent **-tent.**)

content[n] = the constituents of any composite totality, whether of experience or of material phenomena. [Used collectively in singular; distributively in plural.] (Accent **con-.**) — Fr. *contenu*; Ger. *Inhalt.*

content/dream, see **dream-content.**

content/founded = mental processes that have passed through the stage of organization and are thereby established on a higher synthetic level (Meinong). — Ger. *fundierter Inhalt.*

content of consciousness = the totality of an individual's experiences at a given time, i.e. the constituents of experience. [Often contr. w. **object of consciousness** = the source of these experiences, and **mental function** or **act.** The expression **mental content** is preferable, since consciousness is strictly an abstract term.] — Fr. *contenu de la conscience*; Ger. *Bewusstseinsinhalt.*

content psychology, see **structural psychology.**

contentment = an attitude characterized by a mild degree of pleasantness, induced by the total situation which confronts the individual. **content**[a].

context = the totality of conditions which affect an individual at a given time, and form the setting of some particular fact or partial experience.

contiguity = nearness of two or more objects, experiences, etc. in time, or space, usually without the interposition of anything else between them. **contiguous**[a]. — Ger. *Kontiguität.*

contiguity/law of = a principle of mental association, according to which, if two experiences have occurred close together in time or space, the recurrence of one leads to the reinstatement of the other. — Fr. *l. d'association par contiguité*; Ger. *Gesetz der Berührungsassoziation.*

contiguous receptor = a type of receptor or sense organ which is stimulated only by an energy the immediate source of which is in direct contact with the receptor or its accessory apparatus. [Syn. **proximoceptor** (prefd.). Contr. w. **distant** (or **distance) receptor** (distoceptor) in which the source may remain at a distance and transmit the stimuli proper to the receptor.]

contiguous sense = a sense whose receptor organ is adequately stimulated only by energies the source of which is in direct contact with the receptor or its accessory apparatus. [Distg. fr. **distance** (or **distant) sense,** in which the object remains at a distance from the receptor and operates upon it by means of projected waves or emanations.]

contingency method = (*statist.*) a method of determining the degree of association between two characters or two sets of data (usually classified in qualitative terms), in which the actual frequency of association is compared with the frequency to be expected, the complete independence of the characters compared being assumed. [**contingency coefficient** = the numerical value or ratio which measures the departure of the characters from complete independence, i.e. their degree of association. The **mean square contingency** (ϕ^2) is related to the **contingency coefficient** (C) according to the equation $C = [\phi^2/(1 + \phi^2)]^{\frac{1}{2}}$.

contingent[a] = depending upon the presence of some other phenomenon, event, etc. [Syn. **conditioned; contingent** emphasizes the hypothetical nature of the phenomenon under consideration; **conditioned** is used generally in relation to actual phenomena and their dependence upon others. Contr. w. **necessary.**] **contingency**[n].

continuity = 1. the absence of any break or gap in a series; 2. (*math.*) syn. for a **continuum.** [Contr. w. **discontinuity** = the existence of breaks or gaps in a series.] **continuous**[a].

continuity of the germ plasm = a doctrine developed esp. by Weismann, according to which the germ plasm of an organism is derived, not from differentiated organic material (somatoplasm), but from antecedent germ plasm. [The doctrine was employed as an explanation of hereditary transmission. Cf. **pangenesis, use and disuse theory.**]

continuous action theory = a theory of the operation of tropisms, according to which the orienting responses of animals (e.g. to light) depends upon the continuous application of the stimulus and not upon mere changes in intensity (Loeb).

continuous discrimination response (or **reaction**) = a technique for the reaction time experiment consisting of an apparatus which provides two or more stimuli in an order unknown to the observer, and which is so arranged that when the correct response is made to one stimulus the next stimulus is automatically presented, so that one stimulus-response pair immediately succeeds another. [Syn. **serial reaction.**]

continuous series, see **series.**

continuous variations = variations connected by numerous intergradations. [Contr. w. **discontinuous variations** or **mutations.**]

continuum = an aggregate without breaches or intervals between the elements which compose it. [In passing from any one element of a continuum to any other, one encounters nothing but additional elements. Syn. a **continuity.**] **continua**[pl].

contour = the outline or boundary of a plane figure.

contractility = a fundamental property of living tissue, whereby it contracts, or draws together, as a result of stimulation. [**irritability** or **excitability,** the generic property of responding to stimulation, includes **contractility,** and **glandular** or **chemical activity.**]

contraction = 1. the effect of activating a muscle, whether by neural or direct excitation, characterized by a shortening in the longitudinal dimension, i.e. a bringing of the two ends nearer together; 2. (*phys.*) decrease in volume. [**contraction** (1) occurs without change in total volume of the muscle. Contr. (1) w. **relaxation;** when a muscle remains contracted it is said to be in a state of **tension.** Contr. (2) w. **expansion.**] **contract**[v] (accent **-tract**). — Fr. *contraction*; Ger. *Kontraktion, Zusammenziehung.*

contracture = 1. a condition of muscle in which it fails to return to its normal length after contraction; 2. a state of permanent contraction causing anatomical deformity of the part. [Cf. **rigidity/muscular.**]

contradiction = 1. a statement made by one individual in direct opposition to a statement previously made by another; 2. (*logic*) the relation between two propositions such that if one is true the other is false. [Distg. (1) fr. **self-contradiction** = a statement in direct opposition to a previous statement made or implied by the speaker or writer himself.] **contradict**^{v}, **contradictory**^{a}. — Ger. *Widerspruch.*

contradiction/law of, see **non-contradiction/law of.**

contradictory representation = the relation between two images, ideas, or thoughts, such that the presence of the one by very nature inhibits the presence of the other; e.g. the representation of an object as cold inhibits its representation as warm. [Syn. **inconsistent representation,** prefd. as avoiding a confusion between logical and psychological relations.]

contralateral = on the opposite side of the body.

contrariety, see **negativism.**

contrary = opposed to or contrasted with. [Applied to two data of any sort which are mutually exclusive; syn. **contradictory,** but **contrary** implies a less sharp opposition, with opportunity for intermediation between the two; e.g. warm and cold are contrary, with neutral temperature between. In the logical use, two contrary propositions may both be false, but if one of two contradictory propositions is false, the other is true, and vice versa.]

contrast^n = the juxtaposition of two contrary or opposing sensations or other mental data, which results in intensifying or emphasizing their contrary characteristics. [Classed as (1) **simultaneous contrast** = between data experienced at the same time, and (2) **successive contrast** = between one experience and another which follows immediately or soon after. The phenomenon appears prominently in vision. Cf. **after-sensation, after-image.**] (Accent **con-**.) **contrast**^{v} (accent **-trast**).

contrast/binocular = a special type of contrast which may occur when the two eyes are simultaneously affected by stimuli that differ in color. [Cf. **side-window experiment.**]

contrast/brilliance, see **brilliance contrast.**

contrast/chromatic = a change in hue or saturation (or both) in a given area of the visual field, due to the concomitant state of chromatic stimulation of an adjoining or neighboring area, or of the given area or its neighborhood at a closely preceding time.

contrast illusion = a term applied to certain optical illusions in which the value of an angle, curve, distance, etc., is altered by the presence of some adjacent angle, curve, etc. through the (contrasting) effect of size, direction, or position of the adjacent figure.

contrast/law of = a principle of mental association formulated by Aristotle, according to which the idea of a specific quality, etc. tends to recall the idea of its opposite. [Often regarded as a form of **association by similarity.**] — Fr. *l. de contraste.*

contrasuggestibility = the tendency of certain individuals to act in a manner opposite to that suggested. [Syn. **negative suggestibility.**]

contrasuggestion = a suggestion presented by one individual to another, in order to take advantage of his known negativistic attitude. [It is presented with the expectation that the second person will do the opposite of what is suggested. Cf. **negativism.** Distg. fr. **counter-suggestion** = presented in order to inhibit the effect of some earlier suggestion.]

contravolitional = characterizing movements or thoughts which occur in opposition to the individual's voluntary attempts to suppress or direct them.

contributing cause = one of two or more antecedents which condition an effect.

control^n = 1. the coordination of behavior effected by adjustments at the nerve centers; 2. an experiment, or a subject used in an experiment, which is designed to check or verify the results obtained in another experiment of the same type but involving some additional factor; 3. the regulation of the activity of anything; 4. the direction of one's own behavior by volition or mental set; 5. (*soc.*) the deliberate evoking or inhibition (through suggestion, social institutions, etc.) of certain actions by an individual or by individuals or social groups, generally directed toward the real or assumed promotion of social order or betterment; 6. (*hypnot.*) the direction of the activity of a hypnotized person by the hypnotizer; 7. (*psych. res.*) a discarnate or other spirit, which purports to manifest itself through a **medium,** usually in a séance. **control**^{v} (1–6).

control analysis = (*psychoan.*) a trained analyst's technical supervision of another analyst's work.

control center, see **projection center.**

control experiment = an experiment in which the stated conditions are altered, or a different subject or group of subjects employed, or the experiment is carried out at a different time and place, for the purpose of comparison with former results. — Ger. *Kontrollversuch.*

control group = a group of subjects (human or animal) employed in a **control experiment** or **control series,** for the purpose of testing the adherence of the regular experimental group to certain prescribed conditions, or the effect of certain conditions upon them. [Ideally, both groups are the same in nature, and receive the same treatment except for those conditions the influence of which it is the object of the investigation to discover. Under certain circumstances the control group may be composed of the same individuals as the experimental group.]

control/physiological = that control which is exerted on local and specialized activities, in the organism, by a field exhibiting physiological gradients and polarization. [Syn. **physiological dominance.**]

control series = a set of observations or measurements designed to check up the conditions of the experiment proper. [This may include calibration of apparatus as well as altering the experimental conditions in order to note effect on subject's responses. The latter is equivalent to **control experiment.**]

controlled association = an association of responses or ideas which is influenced by specific limiting instructions. [In experimental investigations which employ controlled associations the subject is generally asked to respond to a verbal stimulus by giving as quickly as possible a word or phrase within a stipulated category, such as an opposite or synonym of the stimulus word, or a word having part-whole, genus-species, or cause-effect relation to it. Used extensively in studying mental make-up, appraising personality traits, and for detecting specific information, guilt, emotional complexes, etc. Contr. w. **free association,** in which the response is unrestricted.] — Fr. *association dirigée.*

convention = a custom which is tacitly recognized by the members of a social group, but is not regarded as rigidly binding. [Cf. **folkways, mores.**] **conventional**^{a} emphasizes adherence to stereotyped lines of social procedure.

conventionality = 1. the character in an individual of adhering closely to convention, i.e. to recognized social usage; 2. the character of a course of action in that it follows stereotyped lines of social procedure; 3. (in plural) used to designate the entire body of conventions or recognized social usages. **conventional**^{a}.

convergence = 1. (*math.*) the gradual approach of the sum of an infinite series to a fixed limit, as more terms are included in the addition; 2. (*geom.*) the mutual relation of certain lines, such that when extended they approach one another; 3. (*vis.*) the turning of the two eyes toward each other, so that their visual axes meet at a common point in space, and an object at that point may be imaged alike on the two foveas; or the extent to which this movement can be forced by placing prisms before the eyes; 4. (*biol.*) the evolution of similar organs, parts, etc. in phylogenetically diverse organisms; 5. (*neurol.*) the coming together of nerve impulses from different sensory sources, and meeting on one neuron; esp. such a meeting at the central end of a motor neuron or final common path (Sherrington). **converge**^{v}, **convergent**^{a}.

convergent evolution = the development of similarities, not based on community of descent, in two or more groups of organisms.

convergent series = (*math.*) a series of terms whose sum, as the number of terms added is increased, approaches more and more closely to a fixed value.

conversation = a loose term denoting the informal exchange of verbal communication between two or more individuals. [Generally implying a rather lengthy interchange. Contr. w. **correspondence** = written communication.] **converse**^{v} = to engage in conversation. — Ger. *Gespräch.*

converse^n = (*logic*) a proposition as transformed by conversion, i.e. by interchange of subject and predicate in the original proposition. (Accent **con-**.)

conversion = 1. (*psychol.*) a radical change in view or standpoint, esp. a change from an attitude of opposition toward a given hypothesis or world-view to an attitude of adherence thereto, or the reverse; 2. (*logic*) the transformation of a proposition by interchange of subject and predicate; 3. (*relig.*) a radical change of belief from one system of religious doctrines to another; 4. (*relig.*) a radical change of an individual's character and conduct, accompanying changes of religious belief, which is regarded as brought about by divine intervention; 5. (*psychoan.*) the transformation of a repressed mental state, or affect, into a physical manifestation, as in hysterical paralysis, hysterical blindness, etc. (**conversion hysteria**), such manifestation constituting a **conversion symptom.** — Ger. (3) *Bekehrung.*

conviction = complete conscious belief, with absence of disbelief or doubt. [It may be accompanied by an admitted lack of demonstrative evidence. Cf. **belief**^{n}.] **convince**^{v}. — Ger. *überzeugung.*

convince = to induce belief in another individual by suggestion, argument, etc. [**to convince oneself** = to bring oneself to believe some fact or principle by argument, perception, or auto-suggestion.] — Fr. *convaincre*; Ger. *überzeugen.*

convolution = a transversely rounded fold of the cortical surface of the cerebrum or cerebellum, bounded at the sides by sulci or fissures. [Syn. **gyrus, gyre**; a convolution of the cerebellum is called a **folium.**] — Fr. *circonvolution*; Ger. *Windung.*

convulsion = a violent contraction of an extensive group of muscles, brought about by action of the central nervous system. [Contr. w. **spasm,** involving a more localized group of muscles, **trembling** = a moderate or slight contraction repeated indefinitely, and **clonus** = contractions slower and more pronounced than in trembling; **fit** = a succession of convulsions.] — Ger. *Zuckung.*

cooperation = the working together of two or more units of a group in such manner as to produce jointly some effect. [The term applies to many spheres, e.g. the conjoint operation of several muscles in producing a complex movement; the united effort of individuals in a social group; the role of independent forces or factors operating together in some event.] **cooperative**^{a}, **cooperate**^{v}. — Ger. *Mitwerkung.*

coordinate^n = (*math.*) one of two or more bases of reference whereby a point is located. [The plural, **coordinates,** is used to indicate the entire system of reference. The most common systems for two dimensional figures are (1) **rectangular** and (2) **polar.** In rectangular coordinates a point is located with respect to its distance from two rectangular axes, termed **abscissa** (horizontal) and **ordinate** (vertical). In polar coordinates a point is located in terms of its distance from a center and its angular distance from a given line of reference.]

coordination = the relation between two or more data or classes such that both bear the same relation to a certain genus, or higher class. **coordinate**^{a} = having the character of coordination (applied to the subject matter); **coordinate**^{v} = to bring data into the relation of coordination. — Ger. *Koordination, Nebenordnung.*

coordination/muscular = the harmonious coalescence of activity of individual muscles in given groups (e.g. the hind limb) essential to orderly movement or locomotion. [The adjustments are brought about through regulation of the temporal sequence and intensity of action of the separate muscles. Cf. **synergy.**]

coprolalia = the obsessive-compulsive, uncontrollable utterance of obscene words.

coprophagy = the eating of excrement. (Accent **-prof-**.)

coprophilia = a tendency, characteristic of infancy, to be attracted by the excreta, particularly the feces. [When not repressed or changed into a **reaction-formation,** it may persist in adult life as a perversion. Contr. w. **coprophobia.**]

coprophobia = an abnormal repugnance to the excreta.

copy^n = 1. a reproduction of some figure, act, or other datum; 2. the pattern or model from which a reproduction is made. [These two opposite meanings have given rise to some confusion; it is preferable to use **copy** in the first sense only and substitute **model** for the second; but the printer's use of **copy** (= MS to be set in type) is too firmly established to be abolished, though it signifies the pattern, not the reproduction.] — Fr. *reproduction*; Ger. (1) *Kopie*, (2) *Modell*.

coquetry, see **coyness.**

cord = a short designation for **spinal cord.** [Formerly spelled **chord.**] — Fr. *moelle*; Ger. *Rückenmark*.

corium = the outer portion of the derma, or connective tissue division of the skin. [Sometimes syn. w. **derma**; cf. **skin.** The **corium** consists of two main layers (*a*) the **papillary stratum** (outer part), which is folded into ridges consisting of papillae (which underlie the superficial ridges of the epidermis that form the finger-print patterns), and (*b*) the **reticular stratum** (deeper part), composed of fibrous and elastic tissue.] — Fr. *chorium*; Ger. *Lederhaut*.

cornea = the transparent portion of the outer coat of the eyeball (anatomically continuous with the **sclerotic**), situate in front of the iris and constituting the first of the refractive media of the eye. [Cf. **sclerotic.**] — Ger. *Hornhaut*.

cornea/conic = a pathological condition in which the cornea becomes cone-shaped, owing to the bulging forward of its center.

corneal reflection method = a technique for the observation or photographic recording of eye movements in reading, etc.; the cornea is used as a mirror to reflect a beam of light to an enlarging camera; owing to the difference in radius of curvature of the cornea and the eyeball, the apparent position of the corneal reflection changes with each eye movement and in the same direction as the eye movement.

corneal reflex = closure of the eyelids, elicited by touching the cornea (or conjunctiva). [Mediated by the trigeminofacial arc. Syn. **lid** (or **eyelid**) **closure r., conjunctival r.**]

corniculate cartilages = horn-shaped cartilaginous nodules on the tips of the arytenoid cartilages at back of the larynx. [Syn. **Santorini's cartilages.**]

cornu ammonis, see **horn of Ammon.**

coronal plane = any plane in the (human) head at right angles to the cephalocaudal (vertical) axis. **coronal**[a], **coronad**[adv] = toward this plane.

corpora quadrigemina, see **quadrigemina.** — Fr. *tubercules quadrijumeaux*.

corporal[a] = pert. to the body. [Syn. **bodily.** Distg. fr. **corporeal** = having a body.] (Accent **corp-.**) — Fr. *corporel*; Ger. *körperlich*.

corporeal = having a body. [E.g. a corporeal being. Distg. fr. **corporal** = pert. to the body.] (Accent **-po-.**) — Fr. *corporel*.

corpus = a body or distinct organ. [Used with qualifying adjectives as an anatomical designation; e.g. corpus callosum; there is a growing tendency to shorten terms by dropping the word **corpus.**] **corpora**[pl].

corpus callosum, see **callosum.**

corpus geniculatum, see **geniculate bodies.**

corpus striatum = a division of the forebrain situate at the base of each cerebral hemisphere, laterad and dorsad to the thalamus, and composed of the **caudate nucleus** and **lenticular nucleus,** separated from each other by the **internal capsule.** [Often shortened to **striatum** and **striata** and sometimes called **striate body.**] **corpora striata**[pl], **striatal**[a].

corpuscle = 1. (*phys.*) a minute particle (e.g. the corpuscular theory of light); 2. (*anat.*) a protoplasmic cell, free-floating in blood, lymph, etc. or embedded in tissue; 3. a distinct multicellular body (e.g. **touch corpuscles** in the skin). **corpuscular**[a]. — Ger. *Körperchen*.

correct associates/method of, see **paired associates.**

correlates/eduction of = the immediate knowing of the correlative character, when a character and a relation are mentally presented together (Spearman).

correlation = 1. (*biol.*) a relation discovered between two organs or two structures, such that in the course of evolution any change in the one is accompanied by definite changes in the other; 2. (*psychol.*) a term applied historically to the generalized statement of the laws of mental association; also to the formation of relations between the elementary components of an experience by apperception.

correlation = 3. (*statist.*) the tendency of certain paired measures to vary concomitantly, so that knowledge of the value of one gives information as to the mean value of all measures paired with this one. [The degree of relation or association, as expressed numerically or as a ratio, is called **coefficient of correlation.** The **correlation ratio** is an index used to indicate the degree of relation when regression is non-linear or curvilinear. **correlations** are classed as (*a*) **rectilinear** = when the regression is linear; (*b*) **curvilinear** = when it forms a curve. **multiple correlation** = the extension of correlation methods to more than two variables. The concept of "co-relation" was originated by Galton (1886) in connection with his theory of **regression** (2). The coefficient of correlation was named by Edgeworth (1892) and its statistical treatment was developed by K. Pearson's biometric school.] **correlational**[a] = pert. to the process.

correlation center = a region or area in the nervous system where two or more afferent pathways unite to exercise a combined influence on neural (esp. efferent) functions.

correlation machine = (*statist.*) a type of computing machine which, when original scores (usually grouped) are entered, yields the various summations comprised in a correlation formula.

correlation/partial = the net relation between two variables, when the influence of one or more other variables, which might increase or diminish the true correlation, has been eliminated or held constant.

correlation/spurious, see **spurious correlation.**

correspondence = the interchange of written communication between two or more individuals. [Contr. w. **conversation** = oral or gestural communication.] **correspond**[v].

corresponding retinal points = 1. syn. for **identical points;** 2. syn. **for congruent points.** [Since these two meanings may be confused, the term is best avoided.]

cortex = 1. a shortened form for **cortex cerebri,** or **cerebral cortex;** 2. the outer layer or layers of any organ. [Lat. = rind or bark. When used in sense (2) the organ involved should be mentioned in the context.] **cortical**[a]. — Fr. *écorce*, *cortex*; Ger. *Hirnrinde, Rinde*.

cortex cerebelli = the layer of gray neural substance which forms the outer coating of the cerebellum. [Syn. **cerebellar cortex.**] — Fr. *écorce cérébelleuse*; Ger. *Kleinhirnrinde.*

cortex cerebri = the layer of gray neural substance which forms the outer coating of the cerebral hemispheres. [Commonly shortened to **cortex.** Syn. **cerebral cortex, cortex of the cerebrum** or **neopallium.**] — Fr. *écorce cérébrale*; Ger. *Grosshirnrinde.*

Corti/organ of = a spiral structure in the internal ear of higher animals, lying on the basilar membrane and within the cochlear canal. [It consists mainly of (1) the **arches of Corti,** formed by the union of the inner and outer **rods of Corti,** (2) **inner and outer hair cells** on either side of the arches, and (3) three types of supporting cells, the **cells of Deiters,** of **Hensen,** and of **Claudius.** The nerve fibers issuing from foramina in the **spiral lamina** divide near the **arch of Corti,** some going directly to the inner hair cells, while others traverse the tunnel space within the arch of Corti to end in the outer hair cells. Cf. **acoustic papilla.**] — Ger. *Cortisches Organ.*

Corti/pillars of, /rods of, see **rods of Corti.**

cortical, see **cortex.**

cortical blindness, see **mind-blindness.**

cortical gray (or **grey**) = (*vis.*) a term applied to a median gray, in the theory that gray is a primary color-process due to activity in the cerebral cortex, which appears in the absence of retinal stimulation. — Fr. *gris cortical*; Ger. *Rindengrau.*

cortical point = a point or small area of the cerebral cortex having some demonstrably specialized function. [Applied esp. to points in the motor cortex which on stimulation elicit isolated movements.]

cortical set, see **mental set, predisposition** (2).

cortin = the hormonal principle of the adrenal cortex.

cosine law, see **Lambert's law.** — Fr. *l. de cosinus.*

cosmogony = a theory of the origin and early history of the world or universe. [Generally restricted to the mythological accounts of creation; a special phase of the generic term **world-view.**] — Ger. *Weltanschauung.*

cosmos = the universe regarded as an orderly system. [Contr. w. **chaos.**] **cosmic**[a].

costal = pert. to or located in the ribs.

co-twin control/method of = a method of control (or checking results) in which one member of a pair or pairs of identical twins is subjected to a certain experimental condition which is lacking in the other, the second twin serving as a control or standard. — Fr. *m. de contrôle sur des jumeaux.*

cough = sudden expiratory movements produced by irritation of the larynx, trachea, bronchi, or pleura. [Cf. **laryngeal reflex.**] — Fr. *toux*; Ger. *Husten.*

coulomb = the practical unit of quantity of electricity, defined as the amount of electricity required to deposit 0.001118 grams of silver.

counter-irritant = a physical or chemical stimulus applied to some part of the body in order to diminish inflammation or pain.

counter-suggestion = a suggestion presented to an individual in order to inhibit the effect of some previous suggestion or to counteract the influence of some fixed idea. [Cf. **suggestion.**]

courage = an attitude or mode of response characterized by comparatively calm, intentionally directed, aggressive behavior in a situation which the individual knows is likely to result in danger, pain, or other unpleasant experience. — Ger. *Mut.*

couvade = the custom, present among certain primitive peoples, according to which, when a child is born, the father takes to bed as if he himself had suffered the pangs of childbirth.

covariance = (*statist.*) a measure of mutual tendency to vary. [If paired variables as deviations from their respective means are designated x and y, then their covariance = $\Sigma xy/N$, i.e. the average product of the paired deviation measures.] **covariant**[a].

covert response, see **implicit response.**

coyness = an attitude akin to shyness, restricted to the female sex, and characterized by semi-serious withdrawing responses from the amorous advances of males, this attitude being unaccompanied by fear, and generally including an expectation that the advances will be continued and intensified. [Distg. fr. **coquetry,** which includes more active forms of response calculated to provoke the sexual advances of males.] **coy**[a]. — Fr. *coquetterie*; Ger. *Sprödigkeit.*

coxa = the hip or hip-joint. **coxal**[a].

craft = 1. skill or dexterity in planning or executing (esp. a manual performance); 2. a trade or occupation involving such dexterity; 3. the workers (collectively) in a particular occupation. [Syn. (2) **handicraft;** distg. (2) fr. **art.**] Fr. (1) *habileté,* (2) *métier,* (3) *corps de métier.*

cramp = a violent contraction of some group or groups of muscles maintained for a considerable period without relaxation. [Cf. **convulsion, spasm.**] — Ger. *Krampf.*

cranial[a] = pert. to the cranium.

cranial capacity = the cubic contents of the cranium of a given individual. [Used as an anthropological measure to distinguish racial types.]

cranial conduction of sound, see **bone conduction.**

cranial index = a measure of the (human) skull. [Cf. **cephalic index.**]

cranial nerve = a nerve which has its origin or termination within the encephalon, i.e. within the cranium. [There are thirteen pairs — the **nervus terminalis** and twelve pairs, numbered I–XII. Syn. **cerebral nerve.** Distg. fr. **spinal nerve.** See Table XVIII.]

cranial reflex = any reflex whose path is mediated by cranial nerves and the brain stem. [Distg. fr. **spinal reflex** and **cerebrospinal reflex.**]

craniata, see **vertebrata.**

craniography = the investigation of the (human) skull by means of photographs, charts, etc. (Accent **-og-.**)

craniology = the branch of biology which investigates the various properties of the human skull, including its shape, dimensions, contents, pathology, etc. [A generic term including **craniography, craniometry, cranioscopy,** and in a historical sense **phrenology.**]

craniometry = systematic measurement of the (human) skull. [Syn. **cephalometry.**]

cranioscopy = a systematic description of the structural and functional characteristics of the (human) skull and its contents. [Hist. also syn. for **phrenology.**]

crank = (*pop.*) an individual with insistent fixed and obtrusive ideas and oddities. **cranky**[a]. — Fr. *toqué.*

cranium = the bony structure situate at the anterior or cephalic end of the vertebrate body and enclosing the brain. [Syn. **skull.**] **cranial**[a]. — Ger. *Hirnschädel.*

craving = an intense desire or longing. **crave**[v]. — Fr. *désir ardent.*

craze = the rapid adoption of some new mode of behavior, style of dress, sport, etc. by a given community, usually in an uncritical manner or to an exaggerated degree. [Not connected in meaning with **crazy. craze** and **fad** represent the more superficial aspects of **fashion, craze** denoting less rational and more emotional behavior than **fad**; the latter frequently refers to minor aspects of dress or ornamentation.] — Fr. *engouement.*

creation = 1. the act of bringing into existence something essentially or absolutely new; 2. an essentially new product. [In metaphysics often implies the production of something out of nothing; in biol. and psychol. there is no such implication, the distinctive feature being the newness in form of the product, and in some cases the appearance of new characters or properties; e.g. the products of **noetic** activity. Distg. fr. **transformation** = change from one form, mode, etc. into another. Cf. **achievement** (2).] **create**[v] (1), **creative**[a] (1). — Ger. *Schöpfung; Erschaffung.*

creationism = the doctrine which maintains that species of organisms were created or formed separately and immediately and are immutable. [Syn. **special creation theory.** Contr. w. **evolutionism,** which maintains that species are formed by modification of earlier species.]

creative imagination = the sequence of images, ideas, or constructs which proceeds under the guidance of a predetermination and according to a plan or goal. [Syn. **constructive imagination.** As used by some writers, syn. w. **creative thought.** Contr. w. **fancy,** which is lacking in plan or goal, and w. **reproductive imagination.**]

creative synthesis = a mental process in which results emerge that are not given through a mere summation of the elements involved. [Syn. **principle of creative resultants.** The significance of the term (or principle) is due to an implication of mental activity, based upon Kant's doctrine of apperception (*synthetic unity*) through J. S. Mill (*mental chemistry*) and Wundt.] — Ger. *schöpferische Synthese.*

creativity = the capacity of certain individuals to produce compositions of any sort (works of art, mechanical devices, etc.) which are essentially novel, or which were previously unknown to the producer. **create**[v], **creative**[a].

credibility = such compatibility of a statement or of extended testimony with known facts, or such a degree of reliance upon the reputation of an individual giving testimony, that belief is induced in the hearer or reader. [Contr. w. **incredibility** = such that disbelief is induced. Cf. **probability.**] **credible**[a]. — Ger. *Glaubwürdigkeit.*

credit[n] = acknowledgment or honor accorded to merit.

credulity = a tendency on the part of certain individuals to accept statements or hypotheses on very slight grounds. [Contr. w. **incredulity** = tendency to require overmuch evidence before accepting. Not to be confused w. **credibility,** a judgment attaching to evidence.] **credulous**[a]. — Ger. *Leichtgläubigkeit.*

cremasteric reflex = contraction of the dartos tunic and of the cremasteric muscle with elevation of the testicle and rugosity of the scrotum, when the skin over the femoral triangle or the inner side of the thigh is sharply stroked. [Mediated by 1st and 2d lumbar cord segments.]

crest = a point in a wave system at which the wave amplitude is a maximum. [Syn. **antinode.** Contr. w. **node.**] — Fr. *crête*; Ger. *Kamm.*

cretinism = a condition which appears in early childhood, due to thyroid insufficiency and characterized by a retardation in anatomical and mental development.

cricoid cartilage = a ring-like cartilage forming the lower and back part of the cavity of the larynx. (Accent **cry-.**)

crime = 1. a major contravention or infraction of civic law; 2. the performance of some act which is forbidden by statute and which is accompanied by social condemnation. [Contr. w. **misdemeanor** = a minor infraction of the law. Distg. fr. **sin** = a contravention of religious precepts, and **offense** = a contravention of social standards.] **criminal**[np, a]. — Ger. *Verbrechen.*

criminal psychology = that branch of psychology which investigates the mentality and social behavior of convicted criminals, more esp. of those who habitually violate statute law and social standards.

criminal responsibility = the legal liability of an individual to punishment for commission of crime. [This includes the determination of (*a*) whether the individual has actually performed or voluntarily participated in a criminal act, and (*b*) whether he was aware of the nature and consequences of his act; a marked degree of insanity or mental backwardness of the individual is generally recognized as freeing him from **criminal responsibility.**]

criminality = the characteristic of being a criminal act or a criminal individual. [The extent of the prevalence of crime in a community is termed the **criminality** of that community.]

criminology = the science which investigates crime and criminals, including the study of the bodily characters as well as of the mentality of offenders. **criminologist**[np].

crisis = 1. an unanticipated or novel combination of stimuli; 2. a turning point in the course of events, followed either by marked improvement or by marked deterioration. [Applied to many situations, e.g. the turning point in certain types of disease; in economic affairs; in war; in the progress of science, etc. Not to be confused w. **crux**[n], **crucial**[a].] **crises**[pl], **critical**[a].

crista acustica, crista ampullaris = a thickening of the membrane of the ampulla of the semicircular canals, covered with neuro-epithelium.

criterion = 1. a standard or model adopted for qualitative comparison; 2. a test of truth or a basis for judgment. [Distg. fr. **standard** (or **unit) of measurement** = a pattern adopted for quantitative comparison.] **criteria**[pl]. — Ger. *Kriterium.*

critical = 1. characterizing a judgment which involves careful and unbiased examination of a literary, artistic, or scientific work; 2. characterizing data, arguments, or changes which are decisive for a judgment; 3. (*math., nat. sci.*) marking transition from one condition to another; 4. characterizing conditions which involve suspense or danger. [**to be critical,** in technical use, involves finding worth as well as fault. Contr. w. **non-critical** = not passing judgment, or deliberately avoiding judgment; and **uncritical** = not giving the attention requisite for passing a considered judgment. Syn. (2) **crucial** (prefd.); cf. (4) **crisis.**] (1) **criticism**ⁿ.

critical common sense = 1. the understanding and formulation of the experience of the unbiased intelligent person, who lacks technical knowledge or use of terms and concepts except those familiar to the reasonably informed and inquiring individual; 2. the generally accessible background of technical and scientific experience.

critical flicker frequency = the minimum number of alternations per second of two different visual stimuli (or the frequency of any periodically variable stimulus) upon the same retinal area which will permit a constant effect in visual experience, as if from an invariable stimulus, i.e. which will result in the elimination of flicker. [Cf. **flicker.**] — Fr. *fréquence critique de papillotement*; Ger. *Flimmergrenze.*

critical ratio = (*statist.*) the ratio of a magnitude (a difference) to its standard error. [The designation of the ratio of a difference to its probable error as a **critical ratio** is not preferred usage.]

criticism = careful examination of the meaning, implications, or merit of anything. [**criticism** and **critical** do not imply censure, but in pop. use are generally so taken.] **critical**[a], **criticize**[v], **critic**[np]. — Fr. *critique*; Ger. *kritische Beurteilung.*

critique = the systematic statement of a detailed criticism, i.e. of an impartial examination of some theory.

Crô-magnon man = a type of primitive man represented by skulls found in various parts of western Europe, assigned to Aurignacian time and regarded as one of the earliest representatives of *Homo sapiens* as contr. w. **Neanderthal man.** — Fr. *homme de Crô-Magnon.*

cross-conditioning = the case of reflex conditioning in which an afferent path acquires secondary or collateral paths of motor discharge which excite movements that are not intrinsically related to the action primarily excited by this afferent path; impulses on these collateral paths will then reinforce intrinsically irrelevant movements. [E.g. the school-child's posture at his study-desk comes, by cross-conditioning, to be reinforced by any stimuli (intero-, proprio-, or exteroceptive) which habitually reach him while he is studying in the schoolroom. Employed by Holt to designate a process of significance in integration. It is one source of *Bahnung* (Exner) or subinnervation. Syn. **dynamogeny, dynamogenesis.**]

cross-education, cross training = the improvement of a motor adjustment made on one side of the body which results from practice in a similar movement on the other side. [Cf. **transfer of training.**] — Fr. *transfert d'apprentissage*; Ger. *Übertragung.*

cross-out tests = a method of test construction in which the testee responds by crossing out an extra, wrong, irrelevant, or undesirable element in a series of elements (S. L. and L. C. Pressey, 1919). [Cf. **X–O tests.**]

cross-section = 1. a view or diagrammatic presentation of a plane surface in the interior of any solid object, cross-wise in relation to its length; 2. (*fig.*) a sampling of attitudes, behavior patterns, etc., considered as representative of the individual. — Ger. *Querschnitt.*

crossed reflex = a response which occurs on the opposite side of the body from that on which the stimulus is applied. — Fr. *réflexe croisé.*

crossing over = an interchange of linkage relations of hereditary characters, commonly explained by assuming an interchange of parts between two homologous chromosomes, involving a corresponding interchange of genes. — Fr. *enjambement*; Ger. *Kreuzung.*

crossing-point, see **cycle.**

crowd = a temporary aggregation of individuals who are all attending and responding in a similar manner to some object of common attraction, their responses being simple, prepotent, and (usually) emotional in nature. [Distg. fr. **mob** = an aggregation whose members act violently under highly emotional conditions, usually in an attempt to control the actions of those who oppose them. Distg. fr. **audience,** whose responses are not usually so mobile, or outwardly expressive, or emotional in character.] — Fr. *foule*; Ger. *Gedränge, Gewimmel, Menge.*

crowd mind = 1. the mental characteristics brought into prominence by the aggregation of individuals into a **crowd,** and sometimes regarded uncritically as typifying the mentality of the aggregation as distg. fr. that of the individuals who compose the aggregation; 2. the mental activity of an individual in a crowd situation. — Fr. *mentalité de la foule.*

crowd psychology = 1. that branch of social psychology or sociology which treats of crowds or mobs as agents, behaving units, or phenomena; 2. the psychology of individuals acting in crowd situations. [Contr. w. **psychology** proper, which investigates the behavior or consciousness of individuals.] — Fr. *psych. de la foule*; Ger. *Massenpsychologie.*

crucial test, crucial experiment = an empirical observation or experiment of such character that it definitely establishes (or should establish) the truth or falsity of a given hypothesis. [Lat. *experimentum crucis.* Cf. **crux.**] — Fr. *épreuve cruciale.*

crude score, see **raw score.**

cruelty = an act (or the disposition to perform an act) which causes suffering in others, with satisfaction or pleasure on the part of the performer at the suffering. [The central feature of the experience is the pleasure-feeling which accompanies awareness of suffering in another; the active causing of this suffering is not essential to the experience. The term is complicated in that it represents the judgment of a third person.] **cruel**[a], applied to both the act and the performer. — Fr. *cruauté*; Ger. *Grausamkeit.*

crura cerebri = a pair of nerve tracts, right and left, which constitute the ventral portion of the midbrain; they lie below the corpora quadrigemina and extend from the medulla beneath the pons to the hemispheres. [Syn. **pedunculi cerebri.**] **crus cerebri**[sing].

crural = 1. pert. to or located in or on the thigh; 2. pert. to the **crura cerebri.**

crural monoplegia = a state of motor paralysis involving chiefly the sensory and motor supply of the quadriceps femoris muscle.

crus, see **crura cerebri.**

crustacea = a class of the invertebrate phylum of arthropods, characterized by having more than six legs and frequently by having the head and thorax fused. [E.g. lobsters, crabs.] **crustacean**^{n} = an individual, **crustacean**^{a}.

crux = in scientific theory and methodology, a factual situation whereby competing hypotheses may be so brought into opposition that a decision between them may be reached. [Cf. **crucial test.**] **cruces**^{pl}, **crucial**^{a}. — Fr. *point crucial.*

cryptesthesia, cryptaesthesia = (*psych. res.*) an assumed supernormal mode of sensibility which is said to reveal certain facts (past, present, or future) that lie beyond the range of the sensory receptors. [A generic term, embracing **telepathy, clairaudience, clairvoyance, prevision, monitions, premonitions,** and all other forms of hypothetical supernormal acquisition of knowledge. Syn. **lucidity.** Cf. **metagnomy, clairvoyance.**] **cryptopsychism** = the resulting mental process.

cryptic = (*biol.*) concealing. [Applied to the protective coloration of animals.] — Fr. *caché*; Ger. *verborgen.*

cryptomnesia = a condition of memory in which the original experiences are forgotten because of unconscious motives and consequently appear as apparently new creations lacking the attributes of memory.

crystal gazing, see **scrying.** — Fr. *vision au cristal, v. cristalloscopie*; Ger. *Kristallsehen.*

crystalline lens, see **lens.**

cubital = pert. to or located in the region inside the elbow. (Accent **cue-.**)

cue = 1. a secondary stimulus, usually of faint intensity, which serves to guide, usually subconsciously, the organism's movements or responses; 2. the stimulus which controls human behavior in such serial responses as maze running. [Used to designate, e.g. an obscure identifying mark, which enables one to select the larger of two nearly equal magnitudes, or the brightness factor which enables a color-blind individual to respond correctly to color distinctions, or a faint odor which may guide an animal in solving a maze. Distg. (strictly) fr. **clue,** which involves higher mental processes.] — Fr. *point de repère*; Ger. *Anhaltspunkt.*

culpability = a judgment of moral delinquency formulated with respect to one individual by another or by the social group. [Distg. fr. **legal responsibility** = the judicial judgment that the individual has voluntarily violated a legal ordinance.] — Ger. *Strafbarkeit.*

cult, cultus = 1. (*anthrop.*) a complex of beliefs, rites, etc. associated with a specific god, power, or object; 2. the manifestation of the religious consciousness in ceremonies, rites, and popular customs. [Contr. w. **dogma** = religious belief or doctrine.]

cultural area = a geographical region of similar environment, all the tribes within which have similar patterns of culture or possess in common a number of important culture complexes peculiar to the area. [Syn. **diffusion area.**]

cultural lag = 1. slowness in adapting institutions or cultural habits to new or changing conditions or situations; 2. the condition which ensues when certain elements of culture change more slowly than other elements.

culture = 1. the stage or degree of advance of the individual or of the social group in general knowledge and coordinated social behavior, due to the continued progress of social organization, attended by growth of knowledge and evolution of customs; 2. (*anthrop.*) the integrated customs, acts, beliefs, and social forms practiced by a given group or tribe; e.g. culture of the Iroquois Indians. — Ger. *Kultur, Bildung.*

culture borrowing, see **diffusion.**

culture change = the observed tendency of culture traits to alter their form in the course of time. [A substitute for the term **culture evolution,** which seems to involve a one-to-one type of origin theory for culture forms; the observed data indicate that culture is not static. Contr. w. **culture set, culture constants.**]

culture complex = a group of closely associated culture traits which stand in obvious structural and functional relations. [E.g. the bow and arrow, including the appliances, techniques, and social attitudes immediately related to the manufacture, functioning, and possession of this instrument.]

culture conflict = a condition arising when two or more peoples of different cultures live in close contact, in which the solidarity of the group is weakened by inhibitions due to contrasting beliefs and customs; e.g. economic individualism vs. tribal communism.

culture determination = (*anthrop.*) the process by which culture is supposed to fix or limit the development of behavior patterns in the individual. [Actually the process is one of learning through social contacts. Distg. fr. **biological determination,** which refers to the part played by genes in fixing or limiting the characteristics of organisms. Cf. **social transmission, self-determination.**]

culture epoch theory = the theory that, due to universal causes, all groups of mankind tend to pass through the same type of culture (i.e. organized social behavior) in the same order, such as hunting, pastoral, and agricultural; or stone, bronze, and iron, etc. [Also called the **monotypic evolution theory,** or the **unilineal** or **unilinear theory of cultural evolution.** Contr. w. the **fortuitous theory.**]

culture epochs = the successive stages in the growth of culture in the history of a given human group. [Cf. **culture.**]

culture hero = a legendary superhuman being, revered for his deeds while living on earth among mankind, the subject of hero-worship. [If such a hero when on earth sometimes engaged in deceit, theft, rape, etc. he may be designated as a trickster, yet still be revered for the good accomplished.]

culture set = (*soc.*) a relatively permanent attitude or condition in a human organism, which predisposes it toward a particular form of cultural behavior. [Cf. **set.**]

culture trait = a relatively indivisible unit of tribal culture, such as fire-making, forms of marriage, specific customs, taboos, etc.; i.e. an element of culture.

cumulative = pert. to progressive increase by successive additions of new data, more terms, etc.

cumulative frequencies, see **frequency.**

cuneiform cartilages = two small, elongated pieces of yellow elastic cartilage, situate one on either side, in the aryepiglottic fold, where they give rise to small whitish elevations on the surface of the mucous membrane, immediately in front of the arytenoid cartilages in the region of the larynx. [Syn. **cartilages of Wrisberg.**]

cuneiform writing = a variety of graphic language consisting of wedge-shaped or arrow-headed characters, used in ancient times in Persia, Assyria, etc. (4 syll., accent **-nee-**.)

cuneus = the triangular lobe on the inner surface of the cerebral hemisphere (at extreme back of head) behind the parieto-occipital and above the calcarine fissure.

cunnilingus = a form of sexual perversion performed by apposition of the mouth or tongue to the clitoris or vulva.

curare, curara = a vegetable extract obtained from Paullinia curare and certain members of the Strychnos family. [It is a powerful paralyzant of the motor nerve endings. The active principle is curare $C_{10}H_{15}N$. Large doses cause death by asphyxia through paralysis of respiratory chest muscle. According to Lapicque the **curare** effect is due to a change in the chronaxy of the muscle, which renders the muscle non-excitable when the nerve impulse arrives. The term is a corruption of Woorara.]

curiosity = a tendency, regarded by many as congenital, to seek information or knowledge, esp. to acquire information regarding a partly known event or situation. [**curiosity** may be general or it may be restricted to certain specific fields, e.g. scientific, historical, or with regard to the affairs of another individual.] **curious**[a]. — Ger. *Neugier.*

current = 1. a body of fluid or of discrete particles (corpuscles, grains) which moves continuously in a given direction; 2. by extension, applied to phenomena which seem to have the characteristics of a current, even though it is impossible to determine just what is flowing. [(1) is not applicable to independent movements of the several particles (e.g. molecules in a stationary gas), but only to progression of the constituent units in the same direction at a given instant.] — Fr. *courant*; Ger. *Strom.*

current of rest = a difference of electrical potential assumed to exist between points on the surface, esp. between the middle (+) and the ends (−), of a resting muscle or strip of nerve. [The phenomenon observed and so named by du Bois-Reymond is now, being differently interpreted, called **current of injury** or **demarcation current** (L. Hermann).] — Fr. *courant de repos.*

cursive writing = writing in which the letters are connected by running strokes formed without raising the pen. [Originated in ancient times for correspondence and other purposes demanding rapid writing. Distg. fr. **uncial writing,** in which each character is separate.] — Fr. *écriture cursive, é. courante.*

curve = 1. the boundary between two contiguous surfaces; 2. the path of a point defined by a given equation or principle. [In analytic geometry a straight line is one special form of curve. In statistics both a **line** whose curvature changes gradually from point to point, and a **figure** composed of a succession of straight line segments are called **curves.** Cf. **coordinate, graph.**] — Fr. *courbe.*

curve of learning, see **learning curve.**

curve of rest = in the galvanic skin reflex, the gradual change (either increase or decrease) in apparent skin resistance during a period of no stimulation. [Syn. **curve of adaptation, skin gain curve, polarization curve.**] — Fr. *courbe de repos.*

custodial case = an individual who, through mental defect, mental disorder, or criminality, requires organized supervision or exclusion from society. [Distg. fr. **educative case,** which requires training to attain fitness for social and economic intercourse.]

custom = a complex mode of behavior prevalent in any given social group over a comparatively long period of time, due not to biological inheritance but to the formation of habits by training early in the lives of the individuals concerned. [Cf. **tradition** = the social transmission of customs. Distg. fr. **habit** = pert. to an individual.] — Fr. *coutume, usage*; Ger. *Sitte.*

cutaneous = pert. to the skin.

cutaneous-pupillary reflex = a dilation of the pupil caused by scratching the skin on cheek or chin. [Mediated by V cranial (sensory) to 1st thoracic nerves and sympathetic efferent to eye. Syn. **ciliospinal r., pupillary skin r., platysma r.**]

cutaneous-secretory reflex = activity of the sweat glands elicited by any stimulation of the skin. [Mediated by cutaneous sensory nerve and sympathetic fibers.]

cutaneous sense = any one of the senses whose receptors lie in the skin or immediately beneath it. [These include pressure, warmth, cold, pain, and possibly others. Any specific sensation arising through these senses is called a **cutaneous sensation.** Syn. **dermal** or **skin sense.**] — Ger. *Hautsinn, Hautempfindung.*

cuticle = the outer layer of skin. [Syn. **epidermis.** Cf. **skin.**]

cutis, see **skin.**

cyan, see **peacock.**

cycle = 1. any series of events which is itself recurrent, but within which there is no recurrence; 2. (*phys.*) one complete series of changes of a periodic quantity. [Symbol $\sim$. In an alternating electric current of pendular form, a cycle is a complete positive and negative alternation, expressed as 360° or 2π radians in circular measure. In sound waves, a cycle is a complete vibration, i.e. the whole series of pressure changes from zero through maximum condensation, back to zero, through maximum rarefaction, and back to zero again. The **peak,** or **crest,** of the wave is the maximum positive value (or maximum condensation for sound waves); the **trough** is the maximum negative value (maximum rarefaction for sound waves); the **crossing-points** are the points of zero value. The term **cycle** is often used as an abbrev. of "cycle per second." Syn. **double vibration.**] — Fr. *cycle, période.*

cycloid = designating a type of personality tending toward **cyclothymia,** oscillating between exaltation and depression, due to faulty character development (Kretschmer).

cyclopean eye = a theoretical single eye which combines certain functions of both eyes and is used in discussions of coordinate eye movement and space perception. — Fr. *oeil cyclopéen*; Ger. *Zyklopenauge.*

cyclophoria = a tendency of one eye to deviate from its normal position of binocular fixation with respect to the other, in the sense of torsion or rotation about its sagittal or anteroposterior axis, which is normally overcome, but produces actual displacement when the stimulus to fusion is removed. [Cf. **imbalance/muscular.**]

cycloplegia = paralysis of the ciliary muscle of the eye, as the result of injury or disease, or of the use of a drug such as atropin. **cycloplegic**[a].

cyclorama/illusion of = the effect produced on an observer in a room or other confined place in which a foreground of solid objects on all sides melts into a painted background, so that he seems to be in the midst of a great open area. [Objects of natural history are often mounted in glass cases in such a way that they occupy the foreground on all four sides of the room with an almost imperceptible transition to painted scenery in the background, yielding this illusion.]

cyclostat = an apparatus consisting of a glass cylinder in which an animal is rotated uniformly at various speeds about its vertical axis. [Usually provided with a dial from which the number of rotations per unit of time can be read. Cf. **activity cage.**]

cyclothymia = a condition of alternating circumscribed periods of lack and excess of vim, or of actual depression and exuberance, or more outstanding manic-depressive attacks. [A segregation of normally blending affective contrasts. Cf. **cycloid.**] **cyclothymic**[a].

cylindrical lens = a lens whose surface is cylindrical, or which contains such a surface as one of its optical components. [**cylindrical lenses** are used in ophthalmology for the correction of regular astigmatism; in modern practice a **toric** rather than a **cylindrical** surface is generally used, but the optical effect is identical. Cf. **toric lens.**]—Fr. *lentille cylindrique*; Ger. *Zylinderlinse*.

cynic = an individual who questions the actuality of ideals and therefore depreciates the motives underlying every beneficent act. [From name of a Greek sect of philosophers (e.g. Diogenes) who affected contempt for sophistication and luxury and practised extreme bluntness of speech.] **cynical**[a], **cynicism**[n].

Cyon's nerve = depressor nerve of the heart, arising from the pneumogastric nerve.

cytology = the science which investigates the cells in organisms.

cytoplasm = the protoplasmic substance of the cell, exclusive of the nucleus. [Distg. fr. **karyoplasm** = the protoplasm of the nucleus.]

D

dactylology = the art of communication by means of signs made with the fingers and hands. [Syn. **chirology.**]

dadeleum, see **stroboscope.**

Daltonism = (*hist.*) syn. for color-blindness. [So called from John Dalton, 1766–1844, who was himself color-blind for red and green (probably scoterythrous) and published a description of his case. Cf. **color-blindness.**]

damping[n] = (*acoustics*) the opposition to vibratory movement imposed by frictional forces, both internal and external to the vibrating body, whereby such movement is reduced in amplitude or is brought to an end. [The vibration of a struck tuning fork dies away and finally ceases because of (*a*) *external damping* through air-resistance, and (*b*) *internal damping* through friction between the molecules comprising the fork.] — Fr. *amortissement*.

damping constant = a value expressing the rate of decrease in amplitude of a vibratory body. [It is usually expressed as the ratio of the logarithmic decrement to the period, δ/T.] — Fr. *constante d'amortissement du son*.

dancing = a prolonged series of rhythmic bodily movements, usually in time to music, and generally governed by movements of the feet, with subsidiary activities of other parts of the body. — Ger. *Tanz-*.

dancing mania = a mental disorder, characterized by a tendency to dance-like activities. [Syn. **choromania, epidemic chorea.**]

dancing mouse = a variety of mouse bred largely in Japan, characterized by continuous rotating movements. — Ger. *Tanzmaus*.

danger situation = (*psychoan.*) a situation which elicits typical fear in the psychoneuroses.

dangerous tendencies = (*crim.*) mental traits which are judged likely to result in acts entailing injury to others or to the individual himself.

daring[n] = a type of suggestion characteristic of childhood, in which one individual challenges another to undertake some dangerous or discountenanced performance. to **dare**[v] (a person).

dark = characterized by low brilliance, low illumination, or low brightness. [Contr. w. **light** or **bright.**] — Fr. *sombre*; Ger. *dunkel*.

dark adaptation, darkness adaptation = the progressive increase in retinal sensitivity, or the constant state finally reached, in the absence of general stimulation of the eyes by light. [Syn. **scotopic adaptation.** Cf. **adaptation.**] — Fr. *adaptation à l'obscurité*; Ger. *Dunkeladaptation*.

dark-adapted eye = an eye whose condition has been so modified by the withdrawal of general light stimulation that faint stimuli have become more effective. [Contr. w. **light-adapted.** Cf. **adaptation.**]—Fr. *oeil adapté à l'obscurité*; Ger. *Dunkelauge*.

dark-field illumination = a type of illumination in optical instruments (esp. the microscope), in which objects are seen by reflected or diffracted light (usually derived from a laterally directed beam) against an unilluminated background. — Fr. *éclairage du champ sombre*; Ger. *Dunkelfeldbeleuchtung*.

Darwinism = the theory of evolution formulated by Charles Darwin, esp. the use of the principle of **natural selection,** to explain the origin of species. [Cf. **natural selection.**]

Darwin's principles of emotional expression = three explanatory principles of expression formulated by Darwin (1872): (1) principle of serviceable associated habits; (2) principle of antithesis; and (3) principle of the direct action of the nervous system. [Cf. **Wundt's principles.**]

data[pl] = the group of known or "given" facts on which a scientific discussion is based. [Often misused as a singular. One may say "the mass (or body) of data is"; not "the data is."] (Pron. **day-** or **dat-**.) **datum**[sing]. — Fr. *données*; Ger. *Angaben, Gegebenheiten*.

day-blindness = a special condition, usually due to impairment (scotoma) of the central area of the retina, in which the individual sees better in dim light. [Syn. **nyctalopia** or **hemeralopia,** which are confused in usage and had best be avoided. Contr. w. **night-blindness.**] — Fr. *cécité diurne, héméralopie*; Ger. *Tagblindheit.*

day-dreaming = wishful or purposeless thinking during waking life, which takes the form of long trains of uncontrolled and fanciful imagery or of imaginary adventures. [Syn. **reverie.**] — Fr. *rêve de jour.*

daylight vision, see **photopic vision.**

daymare = an anxiety seizure during waking. [Cf. **nightmare.**] — Fr. *cauchemar éveillé.*

day residues = (*psychoan.*) experiences from the preceding day, or latent thoughts of the nature of preconscious ideas, which may excite or precipitate a dream. [Syn. **dream instigator.**] — Fr. *résidus de jour*; Ger. *Tagesreste.*

deaf-mute[np] = a person unable to hear or to produce intelligible speech. [Syn. **deaf-and-dumb.** Pop. applied also to those who have normal vocal organs, and may be taught to speak by proper training methods, despite their auditory defect.] **deaf-mutism**[n], **deaf-mute**[a]. — Fr. *sourd-muet*; Ger. *Taubstumm.*

deafness = the inability, or limited capacity, to perceive sounds by means of the ear. [Cf. **hearing. complete deafness** is insensitivity to all sounds however intense. **partial deafness** (much more common) may take various forms: (1) a condition of general insensitivity to all tones except when unusually intense (**hard of hearing**); (2) a condition in which sensitivity is normal to certain tones and is absent or defective to others (**tonal gap, tonal island**). **nerve deafness** = a type of deafness in which the defect is believed to lie in the sensory nerve cells or ganglion cells of the ear or of their central projections. **conduction deafness** = a type in which the defect is attributed to the conduction mechanism (meatus, ear drum, ossicles). **deafness** is further classed as **organic** = due to some structural defect in the ear, auditory nerve, or cortical centers for audition, and **functional** = due to malfunctioning of these structures. It may be **congenital** = due to heredity or to prenatal causes, or **acquired** = arising after birth, due to some environmental cause. Syn. **surdity.** Cf. **bone conduction.**] **deaf**[a], **the deaf**[np]. — Fr. *surdité*; Ger. *Taubheit.*

deafness/cortical = inability to hear, supposedly due to disturbance of the cortical center for audition. [Syn. **mental deafness.**] — Fr. *surdité corticale.*

death = the definite cessation of coordination in organisms, resulting in the termination of vital (i.e. of the specific organic) processes. — Fr. *mort*; Ger. *Tod.*

death-feigning (or **feint**), see **tonic immobility.** — Fr. *mort simulée*; Ger. *Scheintod.*

death instinct = 1. (*psychoan.*) a *primary impulse* (based on the bipolarity of instinctual tendencies) whose object it is to destroy organic units and reinstate them into their former inorganic state, the destructive-masochistic drive turned outward, and assuming the form of aggression (Freud); 2. a *secondary impulse*, a variant of **sadism,** but directed inwardly. [Syn. **destructive instinct.**] — Fr. *instinct de mort*; Ger. *Todestrieb.*

debauchery = a loose term denoting the propensity of an individual to indulge excessively in drink or sexual intercourse. **debauched**[a], used to characterize moral degradation of almost any sort. — Ger. *Schwelgerei.*

debility = abnormal lack of force or vigor in the vital functions. — Ger. *Schwäche.*

decadence = retrogression in social life and organization. [Denotes not a return to simplicity, but an ultra refinement of individual manners with disregard for social welfare.] **decadent**[a]. — Ger. *Verfall.*

decadent[np] = one who has regressed morally, or whose personality has become disintegrated. **decadent**[a].

decay = the disintegration of organic compounds after death, esp. through oxidation. — Fr. *désagrégation, décomposition.*

deceleration, see **acceleration.**

decency = conformity of an individual's conduct to the standards of behavior publicly or openly justified by the social standards of individuals in the community in which he lives. [Used esp. with regard to conformity to the social taboos. Contr. w. **indecency** = the violation of some social taboo. Cf. **decorum.**] **decent**[a], applied to conduct and to the individual. — Fr. *décence, convenance*; Ger. *Anstand, Schicklichkeit.*

deception = 1. intentional misrepresentation of data, such that another individual will be led to a false conclusion or into injudicious action; 2. the fact of being misled either intentionally by another or by an ambiguity in the elements in the situation. **deceive**[v], **deceptive**[a]. — Fr. *duperie*; Ger. *Betrug.*

decerebrate = deprived of the cerebrum. [Denoting the condition of an animal whose cerebrum has been removed for experimental purposes.]

decerebrate rigidity = a condition of marked exaggeration of the postural reflexes which appears in the extensor muscles of the limbs (esp. in the anti-gravity muscles of the limbs and trunk) after decerebration. [It is probably due to the release from cortical inhibition of postural reflexes which are mediated by the midbrain and medulla (Sherrington).]

decerebration = the process of removing the cerebrum. [Often loosely used for removal of *portions* of the cerebrum.]

decibel = a logarithmic unit, equal to 1/10 bel, expressing relative levels of intensity of sounds, electric currents, or the like. [Two sounds differ in intensity by N decibels when $N = 10 \log_{10} I_1/I_0$, where I_1 = intensity (in microwatts or similar power units) of the one sound, and I_0 = intensity of the other which serves in the measurement as a reference level. If the measurements are of sound pressure, or electric current or voltage, whose squares are proportional to power, the formula becomes $N = 20 \log_{10} P_1/P_2$, etc. The decibel was chosen so as to be equal to one just-noticeable difference of loudness under certain (limited) conditions.]

decision = 1. the formulation of a course of action with a firm intention of carrying it out; 2. an attitude characterized by firm adherence to some line of conduct. [In (1) the formulation is **determination,** the idea of putting it into practice is the **decision;** in (2) **decision** and **determination** are synonymous and may best be replaced by **resoluteness** to avoid ambiguity.] **decide**[v]. — Ger. *Entscheidung, Entschluss.*

decoration = a covering applied to some part of the body for esthetic purposes. [Used also to designate the application of esthetic covering to utensils, walls, buildings, etc.] **decorate**[v], **decorative**[a]. — Ger. *Verzierung.*

decortication = the removal of the cerebral cortex from an animal for experimental purposes.

decorum = conformity to social standards of conduct, esp. as regards dignity of manner in public gatherings. [Distg. fr. **good taste,** a more general term for that which is pleasing and appropriate in conduct, language, manners, or dress. Cf. **decency.**]—Ger. *Wohlanständigkeit.*

decrement = (*phys.*) a measure of the rate of decrease in amplitude of a partially damped vibration, obtained as the ratio of the (maximum) amplitudes in two successive periods. [**logarithmic decrement** = natural logarithm of the above ratio. Cf. **conduction with decrement.**] (Accent **dek-.**) — Ger. *Abnahme.*

decrement/work = decrease of efficiency of any activity as a result of its continuous exercise.

decussation = the crossing of nerve tracts from left to right (or vice versa) in their course to or from the lower centers of the central nervous system. Contr. w. **commissure** = a nerve tract connecting homologous centers in right and left sides of the central nervous system.] **decussate**[v]. — Ger. *Faserkreuzung, Kreuzung.*

decussation of pyramids = the oblique crossing of the motor fibers from each side of the medulla to the other, over the anterior median fissure. — Ger. *Pyramidenbahn.*

deduction = a type of inference or reasoning from premises or propositions to more concrete and specific truth. [Syn. **synthesis.** Contr. w. **induction** or **analytical method,** in which the conclusion possesses more generality than the individual items (taken singly) upon which it is collectively based.] **deduce**[v], **deductive**[a]. — Ger. *Schlussfolgerung.*

deep = 1. (*biol.*) underlying. [Contr. w. **superficial;** often applied to **muscular** as distg. fr. **skin sensibility.**] — Fr. *profond.*

deep = 2. (*aud.*) applied to tones of relatively slow rate of vibration. [Syn. **low,** which is confusable with faint intensity.] — Fr. *grave;* Ger. *tief.*

deep pressure sensibility = a system of subcutaneous sensitivity by which intense pressure stimulations are appreciated, often with an accompaniment of dull pain. [H. Head (1905) distinguished between deep pressure and deep pain.] — Fr. *sensibilité de pression profonde.*

deep reflex = contraction of an underlying muscle elicited by tapping a tendon, the origin or insertion of a muscle, or an adjacent bone. [Tests the condition of myotatic irritability. Common deep reflexes: ankle, biceps, chin, jaw, oculocardiac, patellar, pronator, scapulohumeral, supinator, triceps reflexes, etc. Cf. **tendon r., periosteal r., muscular r., monomuscular r., myotatic r., and proprioceptive r.**] — Fr. *réflexe profond.*

deep sensibility = a system of sensibility depending on deep-lying cutaneous and subcutaneous receptors. [It is experienced in isolation when stimulation is applied to an anesthetized cutaneous surface.] — Fr. *sensibilité profonde.*

defecation = discharge of (fecal) substances from the intestines. **defecate**[v].

defect = failure to conform to a given standard, either through some lack, or by misarrangement of parts. [Applied in many fields, e.g. anatomy, personality, experimentation, statistics, etc. Syn. **deficiency,** which always implies lack.] — Fr. *défaut;* Ger *Mangel.*

defect/optical = 1. any circumstance within an optical system which prevents the passage of light-rays to a clear focus or interferes with the passage of the rays as contemplated in the design; 2. (*ophthal.*) those defects in the refracting surfaces and media of the eye, or disproportions in its dimensions, which tend to prevent an accurate formation of the optical image upon the retina. [(1) Blemishes in lenses, prisms, or reflectors would constitute an optical defect if sufficient to interfere materially with the passage of the light; the design of an optical system to correct chromatic error and to secure sharp focusing over an adequate field is a matter of compromise in which absolute accuracy can only be approximated. (2) In the **emmetropic** or normal eye the ciliary muscle is at rest when the eye is focused or accommodated for the parallel rays from distant objects; in **myopia** the parallel rays cross before reaching the retina, distant objects are always out of focus, and less accommodation than normal is required; in **hyperopia (hypermetropia)** the rays cross behind the retina and effort of accommodation is required even for distant objects; in **presbyopia** the eye-lens has become inelastic from age and the power of accommodation is restricted or lost; in **regular astigmatism** the rays are focused unequally in two perpendicular meridians of the optical system. There are other optical defects of the eye which are not practically correctable: **chromatic error** = changes of hue, due to the fact that different wave-lengths focus unequally; **spherical error** = the unequal focusing by the zones of the optical system brought successively into play as the pupil enlarges; **irregular astigmatism,** not referable to any particular meridians; developmental blemishes in the vitreous, seen by the subject as **muscae volitantes;** etc.] — Fr. *défaut optique;* Ger. *optische Unvollkommenheit.*

defective[a] = lacking or inadequate in some particular. [E.g. defective organs, defective procedure, defective data; as noun, used only of a person, nearly always of a person *mentally* deficient. Cf. **degenerate.**] — Fr. *déficient;* Ger. *mangelhaft.*

defective delinquent = an individual who is at once a criminal and a mental defective, esp. one who is predisposed to commit crime owing to some mental deficiency.

defective/mental, see **deficiency/mental.**

defense, defence = a type of behavior which tends to protect an organism from injury. [Contr. w. **offense,** which tends to secure food or to injure the enemy.] **defensive**[a]. — Ger. *Abwehr.*

defense (or **defence**) **mechanism** = (*psychoan.*) an unconscious device or adjustment by which ideas become divested of the affect, or emotional coefficient, belonging to them.

defense (or **defence**) **reaction** = 1. (*psychoan.*) a force or resistance which keeps from consciousness mental processes that are unacceptable to the ego or to the superego; 2. behavior which tends (whether intentionally or unconsciously) to guard some aspect of the individual's personality or life history from scrutiny by others or by oneself, often by calling into play a disguised act; 3. defensive or self-protective behavior of any sort. [Syn. (3) **defensive response** (prefd.).] — Ger. *Abwehr.*

defense reflex = a sudden body or limb movement (usually flexion, and interpreted as primitive) elicited by an unexpected stimulus. [E.g. withdrawal of foot or hand from an irritating or painful object, raising of arm or closure of eyes against a menacing object.]

deferred character, deferred instinct = a character or instinct which is derived from one's ancestry by inheritance, but is not manifested till some time after birth (or hatching).

deficiency = lack of something, or inadequacy, as compared with some accepted standard. [Cf. **defect,** which is somewhat broader.] **deficient**[a]. — Fr. *déficience, défaut*; Ger. *Unvollständigkeit.*

deficiency/mental = lack of some mental function which is present in the normal individual. [Syn. **feeblemindedness, mental defectiveness;** strictly, the term **defect** applies to a misarrangement or incoordination, which may or may not be based on lack or **deficiency.**] — Fr. *déficience (insuffisance) mentale.*

definiendum = a term which is to be defined or is in need of definition. **definienda**[pl].

definite = precisely demarcated or distinguished from the environment or from other classes of phenomena. [Contr. w. **indefinite** = vague, i.e. not precisely marked off from other phenomena.] — Ger. *bestimmt.*

definition = the characterization of a given word or phrase in terms of its meaning, i.e. a description in simpler or more comprehensible terms. [Applies both to the act of formulation and to the resulting formula. A canon of definition prescribes that neither the word to be defined nor any direct synonym is to be included in the formula itself; violation of this canon is called **tautological definition;** a pair of definitions which are each based upon the other are called **circular definitions.** The use of contraries or opposites in a definition is likely to result in circular definition; e.g. black, the opposite of white; white, the opposite of black. A definition should not include terms less familiar than the term to be defined. An admissible but incomplete definition is called **delimitation.**] **define**[v].

deflection = (*psychoan.*) the process, usually unconscious, whereby thoughts are diverted from conscious attention.

deformity = a marked deviation from the standard. [Applied esp. to lack of normal proportions of the body or certain members, due to abnormal development, disease, or accident; applied also figuratively to abnormal mental character.]

defusion/instinctual = (*psychoan.*) a separation of the mixture of the death instincts and the life instincts, which are normally mobilized in the unconscious.

degeneracy = a condition of an individual characterized by striking deviation in conduct from the standards of the society in which he has been reared, this deviation tending in the direction of a lack of socialized modification of the native tendencies of human behavior. [Frequently (but figuratively) conceived as a deterioration of the germ plasm in the family tree or as a failure to attain the level of social evolution characteristic of the race. Cf. **social degeneracy.**] **degenerate**[a,np,v]. — Ger. *Entartung.*

degeneracy/social, see **social degeneracy.**

degeneration = 1. organic retrogression, as contr. w. **development,** applied particularly to changes in tissue or organs; 2. racial retrogression, as contr. w. progressive **evolution.** [Syn. (2) **degeneracy.**] **degenerate**[v], **degenerative**[a]. — Ger. *Entartung.*

deglutition = 1. the act of swallowing; 2. the group of chained reflexes involved in swallowing.

degradation/law of = a formula devised by J. R. L. Delboeuf as a partial substitute for Weber's law; it states that a sensation is always strongest as it enters consciousness and from then on becomes less intense. [Cf. **progression/law of, tension/law of.**] — Fr. *l. de dégradation.*

degree = 1. relative amount or quantity (e.g. degree of temperature, degree of information, etc.); 2. (*math.*) 1/360 of the angular distance of complete rotation. [(2) is symbolized by a superscript circle, e.g. $15° = 15$ degrees.] — Ger. *Grad.*

degree of an equation = the sum of the exponents of the variables found in that term of the given equation which yields the greatest sum.

deification = the attribution (usually by primitive races) of supernatural characteristics to animate or inanimate objects.

Deiters' cells = elongated cells which support the outer hair cells of the organ of Corti in the internal ear. — Fr. *cellules de D.*

déjà vu = an illusion of recognition in which a new situation is incorrectly regarded as a repetition of a previous experience. [Fr. = already seen. Cf. **paramnesia, error of recognition** (1), **pseudomemory.**]

dejection = a mood characterized by melancholy, tendencies to motor inhibition, unpleasantness, and attention to certain unfavorable features of one's experience. [Syn. **melancholy, sadness, depression.** Contr. w. **elation, joy.**] — Ger. *Niedergeschlagenheit.*

delamination = the splitting off of one cell-layer from another in the embryo.

delay/initial, see **initial delay.**

delay-path = a neurological entity assumed to take part in the prolongation of a response, e.g. in both excitatory and inhibitory after-discharge. — Fr. *voie supplémentaire, v. d'élan.*

delayed instinct = unlearned forms of behavior which, owing to immaturity of the organism, cannot be elicited in the period just after birth. [E.g. in the child, smiling and sex behavior.] — Fr. *instinct différé.*

delayed reaction = a response which does not occur immediately when the stimulus or situation is presented, but only after a certain interval. [The **delayed reaction** is regarded as made possible by ideational processes, i.e. by central nervous activity.] — Fr. *réaction différée.*

delayed reaction experiment = a complication of the **signal experiment,** in which the subject, a child or animal, is not allowed to react until a given time has elapsed after the signal, the typical aim of the experiment being to determine how long the response can be delayed without failing to occur altogether. [A common procedure is first to teach the subject to make appropriate response to the signal without delay, and then in a series of trials to increase the delay progressively until the response fails to occur.]

delayed reflex = a reflex response which occurs after an abnormal interval following stimulation. [Occurs in induction or summation of inadequate stimuli or in pathological conditions.] — Fr. *réflexe différé.*

Delboeuf disk = an apparatus devised by J. R. L. Delboeuf for the determination of difference thresholds for brilliance by the method of equal sense distances; it consists, typically, of a disk which, when properly rotated, presents to the observer three concentric rings of gray: the inner and outer rings, which are made to differ in luminosity by any desired amount, are separated by an intermediate ring whose brilliance or grayness is varied until it is judged to be midway between the other two.

deliberation = a type of thinking in which two or more alternative courses of action are compared. **deliberative**[a] = pert. to the process (or an instance); **deliberate**[a] = pert. to behavior which follows deliberation; **deliberational**[a] = pert. to the abstract function (rare). — Ger. *Überlegung*.

delinquent[np] = a criminal or social offender, viewed as a social type. [Usually limited to minors.] **delinquency**[n], **delinquent**[a].

délire du toucher = the obsessive-compulsive urge to touch objects. [Fr. = touching mania.]

delirium = a state of more or less clouding of consciousness, dreamlike incoherent notions, illusions and hallucinations, and restlessness or stupor, most common with fever or on a toxic basis, usually with poor memory for the experience. [Fr. term *délire* usually signifies **delusion,** not **delirium.**]

delirium tremens = an acute alcoholic psychosis characterized by a state of clouded consciousness and usually of threatening illusions and hallucinations of sight and touch, related to the patient's occupations, or fears of snakes and small animals, and tremor of the hands and tongue; usually lasting 3–5 days, in a setting of drinking without eating or sleeping.

delta movement, see **apparent (motion** or) **movement.**

deltoid = pert. to or located in the muscle or region just below the acromial region and forming the uppermost outer part of the arm.

delusion = a morbidly conditioned false belief or conviction which is more or less unshakable in the face of reason. [Distg. fr. **hallucination** = a subjective perceptual experience without obvious sensory stimulus, and fr. **illusion** = a perceptual distortion or a misinterpretation of a sensory experience.] **delusional**[a] = pert. to the condition; **delusive**[a] = characteristic of delusion. — Fr. *illusion*; Ger. *Wahnidee, Wahnvorstellung*.

delusional state = a condition in which delusions play a distinct or leading role.

demarcation current, see **injury/current of.**

dementia = a lasting deterioration of memory and judgment, either organic (i.e. with visible, usually diffuse) atrophy or destruction of the cerebral cortex or the brain in general (in the senile, in cerebral syphilis, or paresis, etc.), or more functional, with merely incidental (if any) structural disorder (in **dementia praecox**). [Cf. **amentia.**] **dement**[np]. — Fr. *démence*; Ger. *Schwachsinn*.

dementia praecox = a term used (principally under Kraepelin's influence) to denote a group of deteriorating mental disorders commencing mainly between the ages of fifteen and thirty. [The following subgroups have been distinguished: **hebephrenic** (Hecker) = with dilapidation of interests, and scattered, fantastic hallucinatory symptoms; **catatonic** = **with motor** symptoms, essentially with fixed postures, resistiveness, impulsive acts; **paranoid (dementia praecox** proper) = delusion formation with hallucinosis and tendency to dilapidation; **paraphrenia** (Kraepelin) = grandiose delusion formation with hallucinosis (Magnan's *délire chronique à évolution systématique*). Syn. **schizophrenia,** which now tends to replace the **dementia praecox** concept.]

dementia/senile, see **senile dementia.**

demography = (*hist.*) the statistical investigation of human populations in respect to their geographical situation and physical situation, as distg. fr. their social status.

demonology = (*hist.*) the body of folk-lore which deals with demons and evil spirits and their manifestations, including beliefs concerning Satan (or other devil) worship.

demonomania, demon possession = (*pop.* and *hist.*) a persistent delusion on the patient's part that he is controlled by a malignant spirit or demon. **demoniac**[a] = subject to demonomania; **demoniac**[np].

demonstration = an attempt to induce belief or understanding in another individual, either by a careful train of reasoning or by presenting empirical evidence, whether experimental or observational. [Cf. **proof.** In the laboratory a **demonstration** consists in presenting an experiment in outline, or operating apparatus in order to acquaint the student with some phenomenon, law, apparatus, or procedure.] — Ger. *Beweisführung*.

demophobia = morbid fear of crowds.

demorphinization = the gradual diminution of the doses of morphin in the treatment of morphin habit.

dendrite = a branch of a neuron, which conducts the nerve impulse toward the cell-body. [The **dendrite** of a neuron receives the impulse from a receptor organ or the axon of a preceding neuron in the chain. In the latter case there is an intervening space called the synapse. A **dendrite** may have the structure of a peripheral nerve fiber, though by definition a dendrite.

denotation = the objects or phenomena to which a given term is applied and which are included in its meaning. [Distg. fr. **connotation** = the qualities and characters which are designated by the term.] **denote**[v], **denotative**[a]. — Ger. *Bezeichnung*.

density = 1. the degree of concentration of matter, measured by the mass per unit volume (grams per cubic centimeter); 2. the logarithm, to the base 10, of the opacity of any medium used to transmit light or radiant energy, the opacity being the reciprocal of the fractional transmission. — Ger. *Dichtigkeit*.

dentate nucleus = a large group of nerve cells in the interior of the cerebellar hemispheres. — Fr. *noyau dentelé*.

dependence = a causal relation between two data or situations. [Cf. **cause**; contr. w. **independence** = absence of any direct causal relation between two data.] **dependent**[a], **depend**[v]. — Ger. *Abhängigkeit*.

dependency = a social relation of one individual to another or to society, such that the individual in question, termed the *dependent*, receives aid of some sort or is under the control of the other or of others. — Ger. *Abhängigkeit*.

dependent part = a part which derives its properties from the whole of which it forms a part.

depersonalization = 1. (*path.*) a term covering a wide range of loss of the sense of reality of oneself or one's body or the reality of others, or feelings of being dead; 2. (*anthrop.*) a change in the world-view occurring at some stage of culture evolution, in which the various operations of nature cease to be regarded as manifestations of activity on the part of supernatural personalities such as wind-gods, dryads, etc.

depolarization = 1. (*biol.*) discharge and rebalance of ionic layers on either side of a membrane; 2. (*galv. skin reflex*) changes in the apparent resistance of the skin, probably due to changes in permeability of sweat gland membranes caused by nerve impulses; 3. freeing electrodes of gas accumulation by a negatively flowing current. [Contr. w. **polarization.**]

depression = an emotional condition of lowered and unpleasant psychophysical activity, either normal or pathological. [The normal manifestation is preferably termed **dejection,** referring to discouraged or dispirited mood; the pathological usage refers to a mood of pronounced hopelessness and overwhelming feeling of inadequacy or unworthiness. Contr. w. **mania** = extreme emotional activity; the two conditions frequently alternate in the **manic-depressive psychoses.**] — Ger. *Niedergeschlagenheit.*

depressor nerve = 1. an afferent branch of the vagus nerve to the cardiac plexus which, when stimulated, causes peripheral vasodilatation; 2. any afferent nerve which when stimulated depresses a motor center or function; more esp. one which acts to lower the blood pressure or the activity of a visceral organ. [Syn. (1) **Cyon's nerve.** Contr. (2) w. **pressor nerve.**] — Fr. *nerf dépresseur.*

deprivation = 1. an involuntary lack of something desired, as of food or human associates; 2. the unpleasant conscious experience of such lack.

depth = (*vis.*) distance away from the observer's eye. [In the case of solid objects, and of bas-reliefs and intaglios, it includes the (relative) distance from front to back or from foreground to background. In physics **depth** is usually restricted to distance in the downward direction, i.e. toward the center of the earth.] — Fr. *profondeur, distance*; Ger. *Tiefe.*

depth criteria = the (visual) means by which the individual judges the distance of objects from him. [They are either uniocular (monocular) or binocular. (1) **uniocular:** awareness of contraction in the ciliary muscle during accommodation of the lens; apparent size of the object; its apparent rate of motion; its height in the field of vision (if on the ground plane); its clearness; distance as compared with other objects as indicated by shadows and by superposition. (2) **binocular** (in addition to the above): the strains of convergence of the two eyes; the relative displacement in the two retinal images of objects nearer and more remote.]

depth perception = direct appreciation of the distance of a given object or objects from the observer, or of the relative distance from front to back in the perception of solid objects, bas-reliefs, and intaglios. [Applied usually to visual data; the depth experience is determined by a number of factors; cf. **depth criteria.** Syn. **distance perception,** and (in part) **perspective.** Contr. w. **perception of surface.** Calculation of stellar distances by indirect means is not included under depth perception.] — Fr. *perception (visuelle) de la profondeur*; Ger. *Tiefenwahrnehmung.*

depth-psychology = (*psychoan.*) the psychology of the unconscious. [Syn. **topographical psychology.**] — Ger. *Tiefenpsychologie.*

derangement/mental, see **aberration/mental.** — Ger. *Geisteskrankheit.*

dereistic thinking = a term substituted by Bleuler for his earlier term **autistic thinking,** in which the individual totally ignores any contradictions with reality. [Cf. **autistic thinking.**]

derivative = (*math.*) the algebraic expression resulting from differentiation. [Cf. **differential.**]

derived primary attention, see **attention.**

derma, dermis = the skin; specifically, the true skin, which lies beneath the superficial epidermis. [Cf. **skin.**] **dermal**[a]. — Fr. *derme*; Ger. *Haut.*

dermal sensation = a sensation due to stimulation of one of the receptors situated in the skin. [Syn. **cutaneous sensation, skin sensation.**] — Fr. *s. dermique*; Ger. *Hautempfindung.*

dermal sense, see **cutaneous sense.**

dermatographia, dermatography = a vascular phenomenon due to unusual irritability of the capillaries in the skin, characterized by the appearance of words or pictures on the skin after they have been lightly traced. [The **stigmata** of mystics are regarded as a form of **dermatographia.** Also (improperly) spelled **dermographia.**]

dermis, see **derma.**

description = a report of observed phenomena and their relations. [Contr. w. **appreciation, evaluation,** and **theorizing,** in each of which the phenomena are reorganized to bring out what seems to be their meaning, value, or significance. Introspectionists emphasize the importance of confining the observer's report to description.] — Ger. *Beschreibung* (contr. w. *Kundgabe* = interpretation or evaluation).

design/pictorial = a sketch or graphic representation intended as a pattern to be copied, or as the plan of a tridimensional object to be constructed. — Fr. *dessin*; Ger. *Zeichnung.*

design/purposive = 1. a forethought or representation of some complex action to be performed by the individual himself; 2. the abstract characteristic of some event or of the course of nature as a whole, signifying that it is believed to have been planned or thought of beforehand. [Syn. **design** (ambiguous).] — Fr. *dessein*; Ger. *Absicht.*

desire = an experience or attitude concerned (*a*) with something lacking in the individual's present situation together with the idea or its attainment, or (*b*) with something present, together with the idea of its removal; including in either case a strong feeling tone. [The two forms of desire are sometimes distinguished as **appetite** (or **want**) and **aversion;** the classification depends on questions of fact as well as on definition.] — Ger. *Wunsch*; *Begehren.*

despair = an emotional attitude directed toward the future, characterized by quiescence and by the acceptance of the idea of an unfavorable outcome, and having an intensely unpleasant hedonic tone. [Contr. w. **hope,** characterized by the idea of a favorable outcome.] **despair**[v]. — Fr. *désespoir*; Ger. *Verzweiflung.*

despondency = a complex emotional attitude constituted of sorrow and sense of failure.

detachment = a generic term expressive of the fact that a response ceases to be elicited by a stimulus which was formerly capable of eliciting it. — Ger. *Absonderung, Trennung.*

detector/lie, see **lie detector.**

deterioration = the qualitative impairment of a physiological or mental function or of personality in general. [Certain psychoses, marked by progressive impairment, are grouped together as **deteriorative.**] — Fr. *affaiblissement, dégradation*; Ger. *Verschlimmerung.*

determinant = an organic self-perpetuating unit composed of simpler units, the biophores, postulated by Weismann to explain independently variable parts of the organism. [Not to be confused with **determiners** = the elementary units of individual development according to post-Mendelian writers.]

determinate, see **determinateness, indeterminate.**

determinate evolution = a theory according to which the direction taken by organic variations is not random, but that variations of the same sort tend to appear preponderantly and cumulatively. [The basis of this determinateness is variously explained as: *vital force, internal factors, persistent effects* of the environment. Syn. **orthogenesis.**]

determinateness = the character of mental objects denoting the definiteness of their apprehension. [Cf. **cognitive-intensity, clearness.**]

determination = a mental attitude characterized by thought of some course of action and a vivid idea of accomplishing that action. [Syn. **resoluteness** (prefd.). **determination** is used also as abstract noun corresponding w. verb **determine** = (1) to discover and (2) to cause (ambiguous).] — Ger. *Bestimmung.*

determine = 1. to cause or to limit in scope, or to produce the characteristic form of an object, the characteristic activity of an event, etc.; 2. to discover, establish, or formulate. [The two meanings are often confused; it is preferable to use **discover, ascertain,** or **define** for (2).] **determination**^{n}. — Ger. *bestimmen, feststellen.*

determiner = substance in the cell which controls the development of characters in organisms. [Syn. **gene,** or **factor.** Various terms were proposed by pre-Mendelian authors; e.g. **biophore** (Weismann), **gemmule** (Darwin), **pangen** (DeVries), **biogen** (Verworn), **nucella** (Nägeli), **idioblast** (Hertwig), **idiosome** (Whitman). By modern geneticists **determiners** are supposed to be located in the chromosomes.]

determining tendency = that effect of volition by virtue of which the appropriate activity is performed or the appropriate idea is aroused (Ach). [Implied here is the distinction between **volition** and **conation.** Cf. **consciousness of action** (Michotte), **alertness** (Aveling), **directive tendency.**]

determinism = the theory or working principle according to which all phenomena are considered as necessary consequents of antecedent conditions. [Distg. fr. **mechanism,** which asserts that the causal connection is in all cases ultimately a matter of the displacement of masses. Contr. w. **finalism.**] **deterministic**^{a}, **determinist**^{np}.

determinism/mental = 1. the theory which assumes that the course of thought and voluntary decision is conditioned by certain general principles; 2. (*psychoan.*) one of the fundamental bases of the psychoanalytic theory and method, which states that psychical processes are never isolated or accidental phenomena, but are precisely related to preceding and succeeding processes. [Syn. **mental** (or **psychic**) **determination**; cf. (2) **free association.** Contr. (1) w. **indeterminism** or **libertarianism** (mental freedom, free-will), which assumes that the course of thought and volition is or may be directed by the individual himself, regardless of external or internal influences.]

detraction = lessening the degree of attention without shift of the focal content; i.e. reduction of attensity or vividness. — Fr. *distraction.*

detrimental = characterizing any stimulus or response which injures the structure of an organism, or interferes with the operation of its life processes. [Syn. **harmful.** Contr. w. **beneficial.**]

detumescence = subsidence of swelling. [Applied technically to the condition of the penis or female genitalia. Cf. **tumid.**] **detumescent**^{a}.

deuteranomalous = characterizing color vision which differs from the normal chiefly in the relatively diminished effectiveness of medium frequency radiations (i.e. green), as indicated by the altered proportions in the Rayleigh equation. [An inadequately investigated type, described in terms of 3-color theory concepts. Cf. **protanomalous.**]

deuteranopia = a type of partial color-blindness, or **dichromatism,** in which the red end of the spectrum is not shortened. [von Kries's term, signifying loss of the "second" (*deuter*) color process of the **three-component theory,** hence **green blindness.** Now generally identified with the commoner form of red-green blindness. Distg. fr. **protanopia** and **tritanopia.**] **deuteranopic**^{a}, **deuteranope**^{np}.

deutoplasm = the yolk or nutritive material contained in the egg.

development = the changes in structure and form which occur during the transition of an individual organism from its origin to maturity. [The term is applied to the form changes involved in the production of an organ or tissue together with the resulting functional changes, and also to changes in a group of individuals such as a society, species, genus, class, etc. Cf. **growth.**] **develop**^{v}, **developmental**^{a}. — Ger. *Entwicklung.*

development/arrest of = a checking or slowing up of the normal course of development, which occurs in the life history of certain individuals, whether due to environmental inhibitions or to factors within the organism itself. [Applied to mental development as well as to general bodily growth.] — Ger. *Entwicklungshemmung.*

development/mental, see **mental development.**

developmental insanities = a non-technical term applied to mental disorders related to the period of development and its difficulties and disturbances, in contr. w. extraneous disorders and those of later life. — Fr. *folies de développement.*

developmental mechanics = a study of the mechanical principles involved in the development of organisms, undertaken experimentally by removing parts, by transplanting parts, and by controlling the environmental factors.

developmental unit = the unit in a scale for measurement of development, the scale being so constructed that successive units represent equal amounts of development, or equal amounts of time as in an age scale.

developmental zero = the hypothetical point which is taken as the origin in reckoning development.

deviation = 1. a movement out of the straight path; e.g. deviation of light by refraction; 2. a variation from standard procedure or standard results; 3. (*vis.*) the failure of one eye to assume its coordinate position with respect to the other when binocular fixation is attempted, due to defect of the extrinsic eye-muscles or their innervation; or (sometimes) a similar displacement induced by a prism placed before the eye for diagnostic purposes; 4. the amount by which a measure differs or departs from a given point of reference. — Ger. *Abweichung*.

deviation/mean (or/average) = (*statist.*) the mean of the amounts by which the scores or other measures of a group differ in absolute value from their arithmetical average or mean. [Syn. **average deviation,** A.D.] — Fr. *écart moyen*.

deviation of the retinal meridians = the irregularity in functional pairing of identical retinal points, which occurs in the normal human eye and is most marked in the vertical meridian. — Fr. *déviations des méridiens verticaux apparents*.

deviation/quartile = (*statist.*) one-half the difference between the 75th and the 25th percentiles in a frequency distribution of measures. [Twice the quartile deviation (Q) gives the range of the middle 50% of the measures of a series.] — Fr. *écart quartile*.

deviation/standard = (*statist.*) a measure of variability represented by the square root of the mean of the squared deviations of the separate scores or measures from their mean. [The formula for the standard deviation (S.D.), usually called sigma (σ), is $\sigma = [\Sigma x^2/N]^{\frac{1}{2}}$ in which Σ indicates a process of summation; x represents the deviation of a score from the mean, and N = the total number of scores. σ is the most frequently used measure of variability and enters into many statistical formulas.] — Fr. *écart étalon*.

device = a means planned to obtain some desired result. [Denotes either a physical instrument or a plan of procedure.] — Ger. *Einrichtung*.

devise = to construct mentally a plan or an instrument. [Cf. **device.**]

dexterity = skillfulness. [Sometimes confused with **dextrality.**] **dextrous**[a]. — Ger. *Geschicklichkeit*.

dextrad writing = writing in which the line of progress is from left to right. [Individual letters are usually formed by movements in harmony with the general direction of the writing. Contr. w. **sinistrad writing,** which progresses from right to left.] — Fr. *écriture dextre*.

dextral = pert. to or located on the right side of the body. [Contr. w. **sinistral.**] **dextrad**[adv] = toward the right.

dextrality = 1. preference in a given individual for using the right hand (or side) rather than the left in motor activity, and the right hand (or side) for directing bimanual (or bilateral) movements; 2. a generic term for **sidedness.** [Syn. (1) **right-handedness** (more specific), (2) **handedness.** Contr. (1) w. **sinistrality** = preference for the left hand or side; and w. **ambidextrality** = without preference as to hand or side. In (2) the distinction is between **dextrodextrality, sinistrodextrality,** and **ambidextrality.** See Table III.] **dextral**[a]. — Fr. *dextralité, droitier*.

dextrosinistral = naturally left-handed, but trained to use the right hand in skilled performances, esp. in writing.

dextrosinistral axis = (*anat.*) a reference line which extends from the right to the left side of the body. [Syn. **lateral axis.**]

diacoustics = the branch of physics which investigates the principles governing the transmission of sounds through media of varying densities. [Syn. **diaphonics.**]

diad, see **dyad.**

diagnosis = 1. the precedure by which the nature of a disease or disorder is determined by study of its origin, its evolution, and the signs and symptoms manifested by it; 2. the determination or identification of a disease by such procedure. **diagnoses**[pl], **diagnose**[v], **diagnostic**[a], **diagnostician**[np].

diagnostic test = a type of test, esp. of educational subject matter, in which the selection, arrangement, and scoring of items is planned so as to measure the ability of the testee in the several part-functions or unit-skills comprised in the total activity, and thus to facilitate individual remedial instruction to meet the weaknesses discovered.

diagram = a schematic drawing, used to show the logical relations of certain subject matter, or the spatial or temporal relations of a complicated instrument, situation, or procedure of any sort. [Distg. fr. **graph,** a curve showing a relation between two variables.] **diagrammatic**[a] = pert. to a diagram, resembling a diagram. — Fr. *diagramme*; Ger. *Figur*.

dialectic = a systematic course of reasoning or a system of logic. [Used esp. of reasoning that depends upon the elucidation of the meaning of concepts; it is deductive and does not deal with matters of fact. Cf. **psittacism.**]

dialogic method, see **Socratic method.**

diameter = the length of a straight line from one point on the boundary of a surface or solid through its center to a point on the opposite boundary. — Ger. *Durchmesser*.

diameter/cranial = a measure of the maximal distance across the skull. [In mensuration of the human skull, several such measures are used, being the maximal distance in each of the several planes; transverse, frontal, occipital, vertical, and anterior-posterior.]

dianoetic = pert. to the intellectual functions in general, esp. reasoning.

diaphonics, see **diacoustics.**

diaphoretic[n] = a drug which induces or increases the specific secretory activity of the sweat glands. **diaphoretic**[a].

diaphragm = 1. the muscular and tendinous wall which separates the thorax from the abdomen; 2. a membrane; 3. (*opt.*) a disk with adjustable opening, used to control the amount of illumination from a given source. [(1) is the chief muscle of respiration.] — Ger. *Scheidewand, Zwerchfell*.

diaschisis = the temporary lowering of excitability of a nerve center, due to the withdrawal of normally exciting impulses from other centers. [The mechanism postulated by von Monakow to account for shock.] (Accent **-sky-.**)

diastole = the period of dilatation of the heart. [Unless otherwise specified it signifies diastole of the *ventricles*. Contr. w. **systole.**] (4 syll., accent **-ass-.**) **diastolic**[a].

diathermy = the forcing of heat through tissue; specifically, (1) the ablation of tissues by the concentration of high-frequency electric currents upon them (**surgical diathermy**) and (2) the induction of high blood temperatures by diffuse high-frequency currents, used in the therapy of general paralysis of the insane.

diathesis = an inherited predisposition of the organism, such that it is liable to a certain disease or defect. [Distg. fr. direct inheritance of the disease, in that some environmental factor is needed in order to develop the disorder. Applied also to favorable dispositions.] (Accent **-ath-.**)

diatonic scale, see **scale** (2). — Fr. *gamme diatonique.*

dichoglottic = a term used by Henning to characterize gustatory stimulation by two different substances applied simultaneously to two separate small areas of the tongue. [Cf. **monoglottic, diglottic.**]

dichorhinic = a term used by Henning to characterize olfactory stimulation of both nostrils simultaneously but with a different stimulus for each nostril. [Cf. **dirhinic, monorhinic.**]

dichotic = pert. to the stimulation of the two ears simultaneously but with a different stimulus for each ear; e.g. *c* to the right and *e* to the left. [Contr. w. **diotic** = with like sounds. Cf. **fusion/binaural.**] (Accent **-kot-.**)

dichotomy = the separation of a group of items into two classes, one marked by the presence of a certain character, the other by its absence. [Distg. fr. **classification** = separation of a group into two or more natural classes, each of which has its own mark; in a **dichotomy** one subdivision is characterized only negatively.] (Accent **-kot-.**) **dichotomize**[v], **dichotomous**[a]. — Ger. *Zweiteilung.*

dichromatism, dichromasy, dichromatic vision = defective color vision, hereditary or acquired, in which the colors seen are reducible to two hues and their variants. [Syn. **Daltonism, partial color-blindness.** The hues retained are usually blue and yellow, more rarely red and green. Distg. fr. **trichromatism** = normal color vision, involving the three independent color factors of the Young-Helmholtz theory, and **achromatism** = total color-blindness or gray vision.] **dichromatic**[a], **dichromate**[np].

dicrotic pulse = a pulse curve which shows a notch in the descending wave.

dictum de omni et nullo = an axiom of reasoning, first formulated by Aristotle, according to which "whatever is asserted (or denied) distributively about a term may be asserted (or denied) of all instances falling under that term taken distributively"; e.g. whatever is true of *dog* is true of *all dogs.*

diencephalon = the brain region situate between the **mesencephalon** and the **prosencephalon,** properly divded into **thalamus, epithalamus,** and **hypothalamus.** [Syn. **interbrain, thalamencephalon.**] — Ger. *Zwischenhirn.*

diet = 1. the type or types of food habitually taken in by an organism; 2. the restriction of one's nutrition to certain specified types of food. **diet**[v] (2). — Fr. *diète, régime.*

difference/canon (or **/method**) **of** = a general working principle or canon used in reaching inductive conclusions, according to which any difference among effects that are otherwise similar is to be attributed to the differences in their antecedents. [Formulated by J. S. Mill and declared by him to be the most valid of his 5 canons. Cf. **Mill's canons.**]

difference judgment = a judgment based on the perception that two stimuli are not equal, but that one is louder, brighter, heavier, etc. than the other. — Ger. *Differenzurteil.*

difference/least noticeable = the objective measure of difference between two sensory data, such that if this difference be decreased the two can no longer be distinguished. [Syn. **just noticeable difference, least** (or **just**) **observable difference, just perceptible difference.**] — Fr. *la plus petite différence perceptible, différence juste perceptible*; Ger. *ebenmerklicher Unterschied.*

difference limen, difference threshold = the amount by which two supraliminal stimuli must differ if their difference is to be perceived in an exactly specified proportion (usually 50 or 75%) of trials. [Cf. **threshold.**] — Fr. *seuil différentiel*; Ger. *Unterschiedsschwelle.*

difference/method of least (or **just**) **noticeable** = 1. an experimental procedure, which consists in gradually decreasing the quantitative difference between two stimuli until the two resulting sensations are not distinguished, or of gradually increasing the difference, starting with equality, until the two resulting sensations are just distinguished; 2. a variation devised by G. E. Müller, by which many judgments are obtained from a series of stimuli which remain constant, the results being then treated statistically to determine the least (or just) noticeable difference. — Fr. *m. des différences juste perceptibles.*

difference tone = an additional tone heard when two generating tones are sounding simultaneously, which has for its frequency the difference between the frequencies of the generators. [**difference tones** may themselves produce other difference tones of the second, third, and higher orders. Difference tones are sometimes classified as **subjective** and **objective,** the former being dependent entirely upon the mechanisms of hearing and the latter having an origin outside the organism. Syn. **Tartini's tone** (from reputed discoverer, 1770), **grave harmonic.** Cf. **summation tone, combination tone, beattone.**] — Fr. *son résultant différentiel*; Ger. *Differenzton.*

differences/individual, see **individual differences.**

differentia = 1. (*logic*) a character selected as basis of classification, its presence in certain specimens marking them off from others in which it is absent; 2. (*psychophys.*) a term proposed by E. H. Weber to characterize the objective difference (in cm., grams, seconds) between perceived objects. [(1) is used to distinguish two coordinate classes or species belonging to the same higher class or genus. (2) distg. fr. **discrimen.**] **differentiae**[pl].

differentiable abilities = 1. distinct abilities in a given individual for performance of different specific activities; 2. comparison of such abilities among different individuals. [Cf. **ability, capacity, individual differences.**] — Fr. *capacités différenciées.*

differential[n] = (*math.*) the change which takes place in the first of two functionally related variables when a designated change, also called a **differential,** takes place in the second. [As the designated change in the second variable becomes indefinitely small, the ratio of the first change to the second becomes the **differential coefficient,** the **differential quotient,** or the **derivative,** of the first variable with respect to the second.]

differential diagnosis = the method of distinguishing between kindred diseases or disorders by certain significant symptoms or manifestations or test-data peculiar to one and not to the other.

differential psychology = the branch of psychology which investigates the differences or variations in certain fundamental characters as manifested in different races, or in social groups or individuals of the same group. [It deals with differences between different individuals or groups, such as age, sex, social, or racial groups, and with differences in the same individuals at different times. In *dynamic* psychology it consists largely in tracing out the effects of various instincts, complexes, drives, or other motivating factors in the life history of the individual, and may be either psychoanalytical or biographical, or both. In *experimental* psychology it deals with differences in the data obtained from different individuals in laboratory experiments (e.g. reaction time, visual imagery, associations, etc.), and has led to the classification of individuals by some writers into types (e.g. motor and sensory response-types), or to the analysis of abilities into underlying factors whose functional relations are thus sought. Syn. **variational psychology.**]

differential response (or **reaction**) = 1. a general term used to indicate a variation in adjustment or response to a given situation; 2. a quantitatively altered response time which indicates a change in the attitude of the observer due to direction of attention, unpreparedness, change in the stimulus situation, or some other factor.

differential sensibility = responsiveness to differences in the intensity or quality of stimuli. — Ger. *Unterschiedsempfindlichkeit.*

differential threshold (or **limen**), see **threshold.** — Fr. *seuil différentiel*; Ger. *Unterschiedsschwelle.*

differentiation = 1. (*biol.*) progressive change in the structure of the body, usually during the development of the individual or evolution of the race; 2. (*math.*) the process of obtaining a differential quotient; 3. (*phys.*) that process in terms of which a relatively homogeneously structured field of energy becomes heterogeneously structured; 4. (*soc.*) the process of accommodating one's behavior to group life by developing characteristics which give one a particular role or function in the group (Chicago School). [Distg. (4) fr. **assimilation,** which is another aspect of **characterization.** Cf. (2) **differential.**] — Ger. *Differenzierung.*

difficulty scale = an arrangement of problems or other items in serial order with respect to difficulty. [The relative difficulty of items is usually determined experimentally by finding the number of individuals in a large group who are able to solve each problem correctly, and comparing these numbers, reduced to percents.] — Fr. *échelon d'épreuves de sévérité croissante.*

diffraction = (*phys.*) a phenomenon connected with the propagation of waves (sound, light, etc.), which consists in the bending of a portion of the wave-front behind the edge of an obstacle. [The amount of bending increases with the wave-length; hence the diffusion of energy into what otherwise would be the shadow of the obstacle is particularly noticeable with the long waves of sound and much less noticeable with the short waves of light. Cf. **diffraction figure.**] — Ger. *Beugung.*

diffraction figure (or **pattern**) = the figure formed by the departure of light-rays from the paths indicated by geometrical optics, owing to the diffraction at the edge of any object obstructing the rays. [The image of a point-source of light which is formed by a lens-system consists of a very small spot of light surrounded by concentric dark and light rings of diminishing intensity; the dimensions of the pattern vary directly as the wave-length of the light, and inversely as the diameter of the aperture. Syn. **diffraction circle.**]

diffraction grating = a highly polished surface ruled with a large number of parallel finely-cut lines, used instead of a prism to produce a spectrum. [The wave-length of any part of the spectrum may be calculated from the spacing of the rulings, and the position of any wave-length in the spectrum is a linear function of the wave-length itself, producing a so-called normal spectrum. Gratings are often ruled with 14,000 to 25,000 lines per inch, and are sometimes several inches wide.] — Fr. *réseau de diffraction*; Ger. *Gitter.*

diffused expression, diffused response = responsive activity which is not definite and specific as in the reflex, but which involves widespread and uncoordinated responsive reactions in the organism. [The term emphasizes the *spread* of such responses. Cf. **random movements.**]

diffusion = the spread of culture traits among populations. [Syn. **culture borrowing.** Contr. w. **independent invention.**]

diffusion circle = 1. (*cutan.*) a cutaneous area in which an extensive pressure sensation is aroused by a stimulus applied to a point within the boundaries. [Sometimes explained as sympathetic excitation (Meissner's *Irradiationskreise*); sometimes explained as the area of skin deformation.]

diffusion circle = 2. (*opt., vis.*) in a lens-system, a circle of light or of color due to rays emanating from a point source, which have not been brought adequately to a focus and which therefore delineate the pupil or aperture of the optical system. [Cf. **aberration of light.**] — Ger. *Zerstreuungskreis.*

digestion = the motor and chemical processes by which nutritive substances are ingested, carried along the alimentary tract, and rendered capable of absorption into the blood and lymph. [In man the process starts with the insalivation of food in the mouth and includes a chain of operations in the esophagus, stomach, and intestines.] **digest**[v], **digestive**[a]. — Ger. *Verdauung.*

digestive (or **digestion**) **sensations** = a group of organic sensations resulting at least in part from stimulation of receptors in the alimentary canal. [The most specific digestive sensations are **hunger** and **thirst,** but the experiences of **repletion** and **nausea,** and perhaps of **appetite,** may also be included.]

digit-span test = a mental test in which a series of one-place numbers, or digits, is presented to the testee, who is asked to recall them in proper order; the length of the longest series correctly recalled measures the testee's memory span for digits. [The presentation may be either auditory or visual, and the latter may be either simultaneous or successive. Cf. **word-span test, syllable-span test.**] — Fr. *test de capacité d'appréhension de chiffres, t. de mémoire immédiate des chiffres.*

digital = pert. to or located in the fingers or toes. (Accent **dij-.**)

digitalgraph, see **steadiness apparatus.**

diglottic = a term used by Henning to characterize gustatory stimulation by the same substance applied simultaneously to two small areas of the tongue. [Cf. **dichoglottic, monoglottic.**]

dilator muscles (and **nerves**) = mechanisms for causing active enlargement of various bodily structures (e.g. iris, gut, blood vessels). **dilate**[v], **dilation** or **dilatation**[n].

dilemma = a situation presented to the individual offering two alternative explanations neither of which appears to fulfill the conditions completely, or offering two alternative courses of action which are mutually exclusive. [Strictly, a type of **syllogism** in formal logic; now generally applied in science to empirical situations and their treatment. The term **trilemma** is used when there are three alternatives, but **dilemma** may be extended to include any complex situation.]

dimension = 1. (*math.*) measurable extent of any kind; 2. (more narrowly) a particular mode of spatial extent; 3. each one of two or more quantitative or numerical systems which characterize some specific datum or set of data, each system being independent of the other or others; e.g. the dimensions of space.

dimension/psychological = a mode with respect to which conscious data may vary (Titchener). [The dimensions assigned are **quality, intensity, extensity, duration** (**protensity**), and **clearness** (**attensity**), and are thus modern equivalents of the older attributes of the mental elements.]

diminishing returns/law of = 1. (*learning*) the principle that, in memorizing a series of items, each successive repetition increases the amount recalled less than does the one preceding it; 2. (*theory of intelligence*) the principle that the more of an ability (e.g. "intelligence") a person has already available the less advantage accrues to his ability from further increments of it (Spearman). [This law (1) seems to hold for memorizing corrected and uncorrected items, and applies to successive practices of many (but not with certainty to all) acts of skill. Cf. **Jost's law.**] — Fr. *l. de diminution du progrès.*

dimming effect = an enhancement or rejuvenation of either a chromatic or an achromatic adaptation effect (i.e. an after-image) due to reduction in the intensity of the stimulating field upon which it is seen. [The colors evoked in this way usually differ from simple after-image colors, and depend upon the degree of dimming.] — Fr. *effet d'affaiblissement lumineux.*

dimorphism = 1. the capacity of an organism to produce two different forms, such as male and female (**sexual dimorphism**) or forms differing in other respects (e.g. dimorphic flowers); 2. the production of different types by an organism at different times (**seasonal dimorphism**); 3. the assumption by an organism of radically different forms during development (e.g. caterpillar and moth). (Pron. **die-.**) **dimorphic**[a].

dioecious = having the sexes represented by different individuals. [Contr. w. **monoecious; hermaphroditic.**] (3 syll. accent **-ee-.**)

diopter = a unit of convergence power applied to spectacle lenses, represented by a convex lens whose focal distance is 1 meter. [The measure of any lens in diopters is the reciprocal of its focal distance in meters, *plus* for convex and *minus* for concave lenses. Two lenses superimposed have, in this system, the same effect as a single lens whose power is the algebraic sum of their two powers.]

dioptrical defects, see **defect/optical.**

dioptrics = that branch of optics which deals with the refraction of light, esp. in the study of lenses, prisms, and optical systems. [Contr. w. **catoptrics,** which deals with the *reflection* of light. Cf. **optrics.**]

diotic = pert. to the stimulation of the two ears by like sounds. [Contr. w. **dichotic** = by unlike sounds.]

diplacusis = an auditory disorder in which a given sound produces different pitch-effects in the two ears. [In some cases a given frequency gives rise to a simple tone in each ear, but these tones vary slightly in pitch; more often there is also a timbre difference, the effect in one ear being distorted and noisy. Syn. **double disharmonic hearing.**]

diplogenesis = (*hist.*) a theory which assumes that an influence which modifies the bodily tissues or somaplasm, impresses (or may in some cases impress) a corresponding change on the germplasm, thus giving the appearance of inheritance of acquired characters. [Cf. **Lamarckism.**]

diploid = having parts in twos. [Applied commonly to organisms which have two sets of chromosomes. Cf. **haploid, triploid, tetraploid.**]

diplopia = any condition of the ocular mechanism in which a single external object is seen double. [The usual form of **binocular diplopia** is due to imperfect coordination of the two sets of extrinsic eye-muscles; **monocular diplopia** occurs when a double image is formed on the retina of one eye.] **diplopic**[a]. — Ger. *Doppelsehen.*

dipsomania = a mental disorder or symptom characterized by uncontrollable craving for alcoholic beverages. [Technically limited to cases with periodic attacks of not otherwise accountable drunkenness; often compared or identified with an epileptoid constitution.]

direct[a] = straight, immediate. [Contr. w. **indirect** = by a longer route or through intermediaries.] — Ger. *unmittelbar.*

direct apprehension = a form of partial recognition in which objects are identified without being fully recognized.

direct association = connections between items of a series which are related by immediate succession; e.g. in the alphabet, a–b, b–c, c–d, etc.

direct reflex = an effector response on the same side as the stimulation. [Contr. w. **crossed reflex** = a response on the opposite side.]

directed movements = those movements of an organism which are observed to be definitely related to a specific stimulus. [Contr. w. **random movements** = which occur in various members or in various directions, and which cannot be identified as the result of specific stimuli.]

directed thinking = a train of thought which is guided or controlled by suggestion by another individual, or which proceeds with reference to some goal. — Fr. *pensée dirigée.*

direction = 1. the characteristic which differentiates two or more straight lines that have only one point in common; 2. the attribute of behavior indicative of specific function. [(2) is variously expressed in terms of urge, drive, purpose, goal, content, or other concepts descriptive of particular acts.] — Ger. *Richtung.*

direction/line of = any line which passes through the nodal point of the eye or of an optical system and determines for the observer the direction of any object which intercepts its course. [It coincides with the **ray of direction** exterior to the first refracting surface. Syn. (loosely used) **line of sight, line of vision, visual line.** Distg. fr. **visual axis.**]

direction/sense of = 1. that element in spatial experience which allocates the various points in external space each to some definite point in the visual field, or to some point on the surface of one's body; 2. ability of an organism to orient itself to points of the compass (e.g. in homing and migration) without the use of known receptors.

direction theory of tropisms = the theory which assumes that the tropic orientation of an organism is determined by the direction or point in space from which the stimulus acts, rather than by its duration and intensity. [Contr. w. **intensity theory.**]

directions test = a test of ability to follow instructions. [The directions or instructions may be given orally, in print, or by pantomime; e.g. test 1 of Army Alpha tests.]

directive tendency, determining tendency = 1. a set of subjective conditions which serve to guide the course of ideas or other experiences: these conditions in their more explicit form being identifiable as goal-idea, but often being not directly experienced by the subject; 2. a set of organic conditions which, in conjunction with external stimuli, influence the course of behavior. [The **determining tendency** (1) (Ach, 1905) was introduced in the **Würzburg school** as the consequence of an **Aufgabe** and is somewhat more specific than **Einstellung.** (2) applies to thinking or to behavior under both natural and experimental conditions. Cf. (1) **determining tendency, Einstellung.**] — Ger. *determinierende Tendenz.*

dirhinic = a term used by Henning to characterize olfactory stimulation of both nostrils simultaneously by the same scent. [A procedure demanded when qualitative judgments are required. Cf. **dichorhinic, monorhinic.**]

disability = a structural impairment of some organ or member of the body, which results in impairment of certain functions. **disabled**[a]. — Fr. *déficience*; Ger. *Unfähigkeit.*

disaggregation = the dissolution of a social group or aggregation into its individual units. — Fr. *désagrégation.*

disagreeableness = 1. the characteristic of a stimulus or situation such that pain or displeasure results; 2. the feeling or attitude in an individual induced by (1). [Syn. **unpleasantness** (Angell). Contr. w. **agreeableness** = causing pleasure or attraction.] **disagreeable**[a]. — Fr. *désagrément*; Ger. *Unlust.*

disappearing differences/method of = a psychophysical method devised by P. Bouguer, in which two sensibly different stimuli are presented to the observer, and the lesser is gradually increased or the greater diminished until the original difference becomes unnoticeable. [Cf. **limits/method of.**] — Fr. *m. de limites.*

disappointment = an emotional attitude, characterized by a feeling of unpleasantness, which attaches to the perception of a situation that is contrasted with an earlier imagining of a similar situation containing certain different and more favorable elements. [Contr. w. **gratification.**] — Ger. *Enttäuschung.*

disarranged sentence test = a test of intelligence in which the task is to rearrange correctly or to comprehend the meaning of a sentence, the words of which are presented in random order. [Syn. **dissected sentences.**] — Fr. *test de phrases en désordre.*

disassociation, see **dissociation.** [Longer form is frequently redundant.]

disbelief = the sentiment or conviction that certain ideas do not represent real facts or relations. [Distg. fr. **unbelief** = absence of conviction (used chiefly in a religious sense). Contr. w. **belief; belief** is also used generically to include the two forms, positive and negative, of this type of experience; cf. **doubt.**] — Fr. *incrédulité*; Ger. *Unglaube.*

disc, see **disk.**

discarnate = (*psych. res.*) characterizing a person conceived to continue to subsist after bodily death. [Syn. **disembodied.** Contr. w. **incarnate.**] — Fr. *désincarné.*

discernible = (*psychophys.*) syn. for **noticeable.** [Distg. fr. **discriminable** = noticeably different.] — Fr. *discernable.*

discernment = 1. the perception of the characteristics of an object or situation, including observation of differences; 2. the characteristic of an individual such that he tends to note social processes and values.

discharge/neural (or **nervous**), see **neural discharge.**

discipline = 1. training by means of specific rules and exercises; 2. oversight or control of the conduct of pupils or subordinates; 3. control of conduct through reward and punishment; 4. the entire program of adapting the child to social life; 5. a branch of learning arranged for systematic study. **discipline**[v] = to punish or to train. — Ger. *Zucht.*

discipline/formal = the study of some branch or topic, not so much for its own sake as for the practice which it indirectly affords in other branches of learning. [The doctrine of formal discipline holds that certain branches of study develop concomitant intellectual and moral values, such as accuracy, ability to reason, fairness, strength of character, etc.]

discontinuity = a break or gap in a series of any sort. [Contr. w. **continuity** = the absence of any break or gap in a series.] **discontinuous**[a].

discontinuous series, see **series.** — Ger. *Lücke.*

discord = 1. (*mus.*) a combination of tones of complex or incommensurable ratio, which produces a jarring and usually unpleasant auditory effect; 2. syn. for dissonant chord. [Both **discord** and **dissonance** apply to combinations of tones of complex ratio, as contr. w. **consonance,** in which the ratio is simple; but in **dissonance** the departure from simplicity is only moderate, being represented by relatively large integers, while in **discord** the ratio is represented by very large or by non-integral numbers. Contr. w. **concord.**] — Fr. *dissonance*; Ger. *Missklang*.

discouragement = an emotional attitude toward some program of personal activity, characterized by a thought or thoughts of difficulties or failure, and by a feeling tone of unpleasantness or apathy.

discover = to ascertain hitherto unknown facts or to formulate hitherto unknown laws. [Syn. **determine** (ambig.), also means to cause.] **discovery**[n]. — Fr. *découvrir*; Ger. *entdecken*.

discrepancy = 1. a divergence between some theory, hypothesis, or statement, and the facts which it attempts to describe or explain; 2. an unaccounted for divergence between certain parts of a theory or statement, such that doubt arises regarding the truth or validity of the theory or statement. — Fr. *inconsistance*.

discrete series, see **series.**

discrete stimulus = a stimulus which is separate, distinct, or disjunct in space or time from other stimuli that are acting concomitantly or in temporal sequence with it.

discrete units, discrete measures = the values which a variable may take when characterized by the fact that a gradual and continuous change from one value to another is impossible. [E.g. the number of children in a family.]

discreteness = a characteristic of magnitudes of any sort, such that they are separate or discontinuous, i.e. that they do not grade imperceptibly into other values. **discrete**[a], not to be confused with **discreet** (cf. **discretion**).

discretion = a characteristic of certain individuals such that they tend to avoid unsolicited intervention in the affairs of others and to refrain from action in a given issue until its merits have been carefully examined. **discreet**[a]. — Ger. *Diskretion, Besonnenheit*.

discrimen = a term proposed by E. H. Weber to indicate a sensory difference which may or may not be noticed or perceived. [Distg. fr. **differentia** (2) = the objective difference.] **discrimina**[pl].

discrimination = 1. perception of difference between two or more objects in respect to certain characteristics (applied usually to quantitative differences); 2. a differential response to two stimuli which differ qualitatively or quantitatively. **discriminate**[v] (used in both senses). — Ger. *Unterscheidung*.

discrimination experiment = a series of trials in which the human or animal subject is presented, simultaneously or successively, with more or less differing stimuli, and is motivated to discriminate between the stimuli, and to give proof of this discrimination by a prescribed differential response. [In the simplest case there are two stimuli, the difference between which can be varied in successive trials with the aim of determining a threshold difference. It is a special form of the **signal experiment** and is much the same as the **choice experiment,** except for its emphasis on discrimination.] — Ger. *Unterscheidungsversuch*.

discrimination reaction (or **response**) = 1. a response to one of two or more stimuli that may be presented; 2. a specific response for each of two or more stimuli that may be presented. [E.g. (1) the human subject may be instructed to press a key when a blue light appears and not to respond when a red light appears; (2) five keys may be arranged, and the subject instructed to press with the thumb when a red stimulus light appears, with the index finger when a blue light appears, etc. Cf. **compound reaction.**] — Ger. *Unterscheidungsreaktion*.

discrimination/threshold of, see **threshold.**

discrimination time = the period of time required to **discriminate,** assumed by early investigators to be the difference between (*a*) the total response time when the response involves discrimination, and (*b*) the time of a simple response or reaction to the same sort of stimulus. [More recent psychologists consider that the longer response time for response involving discrimination denotes merely an increased complexity of the total process. Cf. **reaction time.**] — Fr. *temps de discernement*; Ger. *Unterscheidungszeit*.

discussion = 1. the examination of a problem or situation by two or more persons, either vocally or in writing, each or all of whom endeavor to contribute to the general understanding of the issue; 2. the examination by an author of a problematic issue. [Contr. (1) w. **argument** = an attempt to convince others.] **discuss**[v].

disease = an abnormal condition of mind or body involving a derangement of one or more functions. — Ger. *Krankheit*.

disesthesia, disaesthesia = a sensation of discomfort, such as "pins and needles," located in cutaneous and subcutaneous areas.

disgust = a feeling or attitude characterized by unpleasantness, together with an incipient tendency to nausea, induced by a stimulus or situation which when presented in greater intensity may lead to actual nausea. — Fr. *dégoût, répugnance*; Ger. *Ekel*.

dishonesty = a type of behavior through which one individual carries out his wishes, or gains some economic return or other advantage, through deception or false pretenses practiced upon another. [Contr. w. **honesty.**] **dishonest**[a]. — Fr. *malhonnêteté*; Ger. *Unredlichkeit*.

dishonesty/intellectual = the refusal to allow one's reasoning to be influenced by relevant facts which run counter to one's own adopted conclusions.

disintegration = the process by which organized material of any sort gradually loses its organization and is resolved into separate (or more segregated) parts or units. [A generic term, including **decomposition** = resolution of molecules, **decay** = disintegration of organisms or organic compounds, **demoralization** = social disintegration. Contr. w. **integration** = the process of organizing material of any sort.] **disintegrate**[v].

disjunctive = consisting of two antithetical parts. [E.g. a disjunctive sentence or proposition.]

disk, disc = 1. a surface which is approximately flat and has a circular outline; 2. a thin object of paper, cardboard, tin, etc. having a flat surface of circular form. [Cf. **color disk.**] — Ger. *Scheibe*.

dislike = an attitude characterized by unpleasant feeling tone, which is aroused by social situations or objects. [Used vaguely to designate one's attitude toward stimuli of any degree of intensity and covering various experiences, from slight feeling to violent emotion. It is advisable not to use the term or its opposite in any rigid technical sense. Contr. w. **like**[n], **liking**[n] = characterized by pleasant feeling tone.] — Fr. *antipathie*; Ger. *Abneigung*.

disorder = 1. a situation involving a group of phenomena which exhibit no intelligible relations with one another; 2. syn. for **disease.**— Ger. (1) *Unordnung*, (2) *Krankheit.*

disorganization/social = 1. a reversal of the process of systematic social organization; 2. the condition of a social group after such disintegration; 3. change or modification of the institutional habits of individuals, as when the children of a family become adults and no longer obey the father, or the members of a church cease to attend services. [Does not imply a lack of all organization; e.g. the disorganization of the family may be correlated to the process of urbanization. Cf. **organization.**]

disorientation = a temporary or a pathological condition, in which the individual loses the usual perception of spatial relations between himself and the environment, esp. the sense of direction. [Also used to characterize cases in which a patient has lost awareness of the passage of time.]

disparate = dissimilar in kind. [Distg. fr. **incommensurable** = quantitatively incomparable.]

disparate retinal points = points on the two retinas whose sensory representations fail to yield identical space impressions. [Contr. w. **congruent points, identical points.**]

disparate sensations = sensations which belong to different senses, or which lack mediating (i.e. transitional) forms though belonging to the same sensory field.

disparation = an effect of distance, which results in double images of all objects nearer or farther than the point of fixation. [Nearer images are crossed, since they are referred to the horopter circle beyond the object that gives the image. This is known as **crossed disparation or disparateness.** More remote objects are uncrossed, and might be said to have an **uncrossed disparateness.** Syn. **(retinal) disparity,** which refers to the fact that the images on the respective retinas coming from the solid object or from two stereograms are slightly different.]

disparition = the disappearance of items from the cognitive field.

disparity = (*vis.*) the difference which exists between the two retinal images when a solid object is viewed in binocular vision or when a stereogram is viewed. [The retinal images are not identical but differ slightly because of the difference in the visual angle.]

dispersion = (*statist.*) the extent to which the scores or measures obtained from a given group (*a*) differ from one another, or (*b*) vary from some designated point such as the **mean.** [Syn. **scatter.** The **average** (or **mean**) **variation,** the **standard deviation,** and the **quartile deviation** are measures of **dispersion.**] — Ger. *Zerstreuung.*

dispersion circle = a circle of light or of color due to rays emanating from a point source, which have not been brought adequately to a focus because of chromatic aberration in the optical system. [Ordinarily, a **dispersion circle** will show different hues at different distances from its center.]

displacement = 1. the transfer of an object, etc. from one position in space to another; 2. (*eidetic*) the spatial distortion of an image, usually the inversion of the image as a whole or rearrangement of its parts (confusion of up and down, vertical and horizontal, left and right); 3. (*psychoan.*) the transference of affect from one idea to another, usually to a logically inappropriate idea, but quite logical and appropriate for unconscious thinking. [(3) first observed in dreams, but later discovered to operate generally, particularly in obsessions and perversions. In psychoan. use, extended to include omission, modification, and regrouping of latent dream material through activity of the censorship.] — Ger. *Verlagerung, Verschiebung.*

disposition = 1. any arrangement of data which is due to prior conditions, emphasizing the dependence of the present on the past; 2. any organized mental tendency resulting from past experiences or from ancestral conditions; 3. (*biol.*) an organic tendency to a specific line of growth or development, due to ancestral conditions assumed to be present in an organism before the specific organ or part concerned has appeared; 4. (*emot.*) an organized emotional attitude or tendency; 5. the sum of all the innate dispositions or instincts with their specific impulses or tendencies (McDougall). [In sense (5) contr. w. **temperament** and w. **character.**] — Ger. (1) *Anordnung*, (2, 3, 5) *Anlage*, (4) *Gemütsstimmung.*

disposition/neural = (*psychophysiol.*) the tendency, whether innate or resulting from use, of a neural element, center, or system, to operate in a certain manner. — Ger. *Veranlagung.*

disruption = the sudden splitting apart or sundering of an organized unit of any sort, whether an artifact, a chemical compound, a cell, an organ of the body, or an organized social group. [Distg. fr. **disintegration** = a gradual and progressive reversal of the process of organization.] **disruptive**[a], **disrupt**[v]. — Ger. *Zerbrechung, Bruch.*

dissatisfaction = an attitude characterized by unrest and a feeling of unpleasantness. [Contr. w. **satisfaction** = characterized by pleasantness and quiescence.] — Ger. *Unzufriedenheit.*

dissent = refusal by one individual to accept a statement or conclusion put forward by another or adopted by the social group to which he belongs. [Contr. w. **assent.**] **dissent**[v]. — Fr. *dissentiment*; Ger. *Abweichung.*

dissimilarity = absence of correspondence between two or more data in various respects. [Contr. w. **similarity, likeness** = correspondence between the two in some respect. Distg. fr. **unlikeness,** which stresses absence of correspondence in certain respects only, while **dissimilarity** implies differences in all relevant respects; the latter term covers a wider territory.] **dissimilar**[a], **unlike**[a]. — Fr. *dissemblance*; Ger. *Ungleichheit.*

dissimulation = an act, or more generally a plan of conduct, which conceals from others the individual's actual aims and leads them to infer that he is working for some quite different outcome. [Cf. **hypocrisy.**] — Ger. *Verstellung.*

dissipation = 1. (*phys.*) the spreading of a definite group or mass of units into a larger area or space, which results in their becoming a less prominent portion of the total contents of the given locality (e.g. dissipation of gases, of energy, of a social group); 2. (*pop.*) a mode of life characterized by persistent overindulgence in intoxicants or drugs or other excesses which undermine the individual's constitution. — Ger. *Verschwendung.*

dissociation = 1. the breaking up of a combination of any sort into its constituents; 2. (*specif.*) the escape of certain activities from the control of the individual. [A generic term, including **dissolution** = gradual, and **disruption** = sudden disintegration or disorganization of a system; redundant syn. **disassociation.** Contr. w. **association.**] **dissociate**[v], **dissociative**[a].

dissolution = the reversal of the process of evolution. [A term introduced by H. Spencer and applied by J. H. Jackson in his work on the evolution and dissolution of the nervous system.]

dissonance = an effect produced by two or more tones within the same octave, which do not blend or fuse, characterized by roughness or lack of unity, and usually by unpleasantness. [Contr. w. **consonance.** Cf. **discord.**] **dissonant**[a].

distal = in the direction away from the point of reference or point of attachment of an appendage. [Contr. w. **proximal** = toward or nearer the point of reference or attachment.] **distad**[adv].

distance = 1. (*psychol.*) the amount of linear space between a given source of stimulation and the stimulated organism; 2. (*math.*) the amount of linear space between two given points. [(1) is used in discussions of space perception, in which distance away from the observer constitutes a different problem from linear or areal extent on the surface of the skin or retina. The two meanings occasionally cause confusion. It is preferable in psychology to limit **distance** to the first meaning and use **linear distance** or **apartness** for the second.] **distant**[a]. — Ger. (1) *Entfernung*, (2) *Abstand*.

distance perception, see **depth perception.**

distance/psychic, see **psychic distance.**

distant point = a point in the visual field more than 10 m. away from the observer's eye. — Ger. *Fernpunkt*.

distant (or **distance**) **receptor** = a type of receptor or sense organ which is stimulated by energies the immediate source of which may be at a distance from the organism. [The term **distance receptor** avoids the implication that the receptor itself is distant. Syn. **distoceptor** (prefd.), **tele(o)ceptor.** Contr. w. **contiguous receptor** or **proximoceptor,** in which the source of stimulation operates directly upon the receptor.]

distant (or **distance**) **sense** = a sense whose receptor is stimulated by energies the immediate source of which may be at a distance from the organism. [Contr. w. **contiguous sense.**] — Ger. *Fernsinn*.

distinct, see **distinctness** and **distinction.** [It is preferable to use **distinguished** as adj. for **distinction.**]

distinction = the basis of discrimination between two data of any sort. [Often confused with **distinctness.**] **distinguish**[v], **distinguished**[a], **distinct**[a] (ambiguous).

distinctness = the character of a perception such that its outlines and constituent parts are sharply defined or marked off. [Syn. **clearness.** Often confused with **distinction.** Contr. w. **indistinctness.**] **distinct**[a]. — Ger. *Ausgeprägtheit, Klarheit, Deutlichkeit*.

distinguish = to discriminate perceptually. **distinguished** [a] (pop. applied to individuals as syn. for **prominent**), **distinguishable**[a].

distoceptor, see **distant receptor.**

distortion/barrel = (*vis.*) a departure of optical images from truthful representation of their objects, such that a square is represented in the image with bulging sides. — Fr. *d. en barillet*.

distortion of form, see **form distortion.**

distortion/pincushion = (*vis.*) a departure of optical images from truthful representation of their objects, such that a square is represented in the image with its sides bent inwards. — Fr. *d. en croissant*.

distractibility = the ease with which an individual's attention is drawn away from a given content by extraneous (distracting) stimuli.

distraction = 1. withdrawal of attention from a given focus, either perceptual or imaginal, by irrelevant stimuli; 2. a condition in which the attention is not concentrated, but is divided among various parts of the experience. [In response experiments irrelevant stimuli are sometimes introduced to withdraw the observer's attention in order to discover the effect of inattention on the speed or accuracy of the response; these are termed **distractions.** Contr. (2) w. **concentration.** Often confused with **abstraction** or **absentmindedness** = concentration on a train of thought with inattention to external stimuli.] **distracted**[a], **distract**[v]. — Ger. (1) *Ablenkung*, (2) *Zerstreutheit*.

distributed repetitions/principle of = a principle of the learning process, according to which an ability is acquired with a smaller number of repetitions if these repetitions are distributed over a longer period of time than if they are crowded together. [In practice these repetitions are often spaced gradually farther and farther apart (progressively distributed practice). Cf. **spaced repetition.**]

distribution = (*statist.*) a table or graph which shows the frequency of occurrence of each successive value (or range of values) in a collection of data of any sort. [Applied to various statistical material, e.g. height of human beings, scores of tests, errors in experimental data, etc.] — Ger. *Verteilung*.

distributive law = the principle that an operation performed upon a complex whole affects each part of this complex in the same way as if performed upon that part separately. — Ger. *Streuungsgesetz*.

distrust = a mental attitude akin to suspicion, but more intense and more permanent, characterized by a tendency to doubt the statements, sincerity, or friendliness of another individual. **distrust**[v], **distrustful**[a]. — Fr. *méfiance*; Ger. *Misstrauen, Verdacht*.

disturbance = any interruption of the orderly progress of a process, or disarrangement of an orderly array. [Applied alike to physical, organic, and social phenomena.] **disturb**[v] = (in psychol.) to interrupt a train of thought, or to arouse fear or uneasiness. — Fr. *trouble, tumulte, déranger*[v]; Ger. *Störung*.

disturbance/propagated = a chemical or electrochemical change in the state of a tissue, induced locally by stimulation and transmitted through the tissue. [The term applies esp. to the normal physiological process of **conduction,** which is specific to nerves. It does not apply to a merely physical, i.e. non-physiological, current of electricity. Syn. **nerve impulse; wave of excitation.**] — Fr. *trouble propagé*.

disuse/ law of = a law of learning, which states that if a neural connection between a stimulus and a response is not exercised for a time, it becomes more difficult for that stimulus to bring about that response. [Cf. **use/law of.**] — Fr. *l. de la desuétude*.

diuretic = an agent which increases the formation of urine.

divergence = the turning of the two eyeballs outward with respect to each other, or their movement from a position of greater **convergence** to one of less; or the degree to which such a movement can be forced by placing prisms before the eyes.

diversion = 1. the changing of the course or direction of a progressive event; 2. a temporary change in activity engaged in for rest; i.e. recreation in a wide sense. **divert**[v] (in both senses). — Ger. (1) *Ablenkung*, (2) *Zeitvertreib*.

diversion hypothesis, see **drainage hypothesis.**

diversion of sex energy, see **sublimation.**

diversity = unlikeness or dissimilarity among three or more data. [Generally applied to a number of objects, classes, etc. no one of which resembles any of the others.] **diverse**[a], **diversify**[v] = to give variety.

divination = (*hist.*) the art of foreseeing or foretelling future events by (*a*) mystical or (*b*) magical means. [(*a*) implies divine guidance, (*b*) makes use of rites, omens, or auguries.]

divining rod = 1. (*hist.*) a magic wand, staff, or rod (*virgula divina*) used for divination (*virgula divinationis*); 2. a dousing rod, a forked rod (*virgula furcata*), used for indicating the location of objects or substances, usually under ground. [Divination by the *virgula divina* was called **rhabdomancy;** its efficacy was supposed to depend on ceremonies and cabalistic words accompanying its use. The *virgula furcata* was used originally for locating ores and later for locating water, properly called the **dousing rod;** its efficacy was assumed to depend on some influence of the object sought, or of knowledge about it that resulted in an indicative movement of the rod as by striking or dipping downward.] — Fr. *baguette divinatoire*; Ger. *Schlagrute, Wünschelrute*.

divisibility = the property of certain magnitudes, bodies, processes, or acts, such that they can be broken up into parts. **divisible**[a]. — Ger. *Teilbarkeit*.

dizygotic twins, see **twins.**

dizziness = a sensation of falling or whirling (often associated with optic or vestibular nystagmus, and sometimes accompanied by nausea), induced by prolonged or abnormal stimulation of the labyrinthine receptors, or by a rapidly moving visual field. [Cf. **nystagmus, vertigo.**] — Fr. *vertige, étourdissement*.

DL = abbrev. for **difference limen.** [Cf. **threshold.**]

docility = 1. the quality of being easily taught; 2. characterizing an animal which is easily managed. [Syn. (2) **tractable.**] — Ger. *Gelehrigkeit*.

document = a written or printed report, statement, etc., which is admissible as evidence in a scientific research, due to its being an original or a precise copy of the original. [Cf. **protocol.**]

doctrine = 1. a theory affirmed (or taught) dogmatically, i.e. without presentation of evidence; 2. a thesis put forward by a person of authority upon a controversial issue. [Cf. **theory, dogma, hypothesis.**] — Ger. *Lehre*.

Dogiel corpuscle = a transitional type of nerve end-organ located in the mucous membranes of mouth, nose, eyes, and genitals. [Sometimes described as a modification of Krause bulbs and sometimes as Meissner corpuscles.]

dogma = a theory or tenet promulgated or asserted by authority, and in the absence of conclusive evidence.

dogmatic = characterizing an attitude such that the individual seeks to impose his ideas upon others by reason of his authority and not by adducing evidence. **dogmatism**[n].

dolichocephaly = a form of (human) skull or head whose maximum length in median plane is relatively great, or which gives a cephalic index under 75 for skulls and 77 for heads. [Contr. w. **brachycephaly.**] **dolichocephalic**[a].

dolor, dolour = 1. syn. for **grief;** 2. syn. for **pain.**

domesticated = reared by man for his own use or enjoyment. [Applied to both animals and plants. Contr. w. **wild** = living and growing without human supervision. In evolution the propagation of domesticated organisms is important, since the action of natural selection is modified by artificial selection. The term is sometimes extended to species reared by infrahuman social types, e.g. aphids reared in an ant colony.]

dominance = 1. the trait or tendency of an individual to seek control over the actions of others; 2. (*biol.*) the power of one member of a Mendelian pair of factors to suppress the manifestation of its corresponding recessive member when both are present in the same organism; 3. (*esth.*) the characteristic of works of art in which elements or aspects are subordinate to some typical representative of the idea or theme. [Syn. (1) **ascendence.** Contr. (2) w. **recessiveness** = the inability of a character to appear when the corresponding dominant is present. Contr. (3) w. **equilibrium,** in which the elements are balanced over against each other.] **dominant**[a] (2). — Ger. (1) *Herrschaft*.

dominance/cerebral, see **cerebral dominance.**

dominance/physiological, see **control/physiological.**

dominant[n] = (*mus.*) the fifth tone of the diatonic scale, or a chord of which this tone is the root (e.g. if the tonic is *c*, the dominant is *g* and the dominant triad is *g-b-d'*).

dominant character = (*biol.*) a character which suppresses or prevents the appearance of the corresponding recessive character, when the factors of the two are associated. [Contr. w. **recessive character.**]

dominant complexes = complexes or emotional disturbances which dominate or control the individual's conduct.

dominant wave-length = the wave-length of that homogeneous spectral light which, when mixed with white light in suitable amounts, will match a given sample color. — Fr. *longueur d'onde dominante*.

domination = the act or state of controlling the lives or behavior of others, esp. by an ascendent person. **dominant**[a].

Donatism = hypnotic fascination, usually of the form found in early stages of hypnosis. [Syn. **cataplexy.**]

Donders' law = a principle of visual fixation, according to which every position of the lines of regard in relation to the head corresponds to a definite, invariable angle of torsion of the eyes, regardless of the path by which that position has been reached. [Formulated by F. C. Donders in 1846.]

dorsal = 1. pert. to or located on the back of an animal; 2. more exactly, in human anatomy, pert. to or located in the middle part of the back, just below the neck. [Contr. w. **ventral,** pert. to or located on the belly.] **dorsad**[adv] toward the back.

dorsal reflex, see **sacrospinal reflex.**

dorsoventral axis = a straight line connecting the back with the belly. [Syn. (in man) **sagittal** (or **anterior-posterior**) **axis.**]

dot figure = a figure consisting of a number of dots, arranged either regularly or irregularly, used to illustrate visual geometrical illusions. [The illusion consists in the fact that during an extended period of observation the patterns into which the dots are grouped change frequently.] — Fr. *figure de points*; Ger. *Punktfigur.*

dotting test = a form of psychophysical test of speed and accuracy of voluntary movement, in which the testee is directed to make a series of dots as rapidly as possible. [As developed it had two phases: (1) placing a dot in each of 100 small squares (speed test, akin to **tapping test**); (2) striking a series of 100 printed dots (speed and accuracy test, akin to **aiming test**); (3) placing dots in small circles at various lateral positions on a belt passing a window, (akin to pursuit test).] — Fr. *test de "tapping" à points.*

double alternation problem = an experimental situation in which the subject must respond twice in one way followed by twice in another, etc., in the absence of external stimuli which would cause the shift from one response to the other. [Used in the study of symbolic processes and in the **temporal maze.**]

double-aspect theory = a theory of the relation between mind and body which assumes that conscious experiences and brain processes are fundamentally identical, the two groups of phenomena being two manifestations or aspects of a single set of events. [Syn. **identity hypothesis.** Cf. **interactionism, parallelism/psychophysical;** the double-aspect theory is often confused with the latter.] — Fr. *théorie de l'unité à double face.*

double images = duplicate representations in experience of a single object in the field of vision, due (1) to non-congruent location of the optical images on the two retinas, or (2) to the formation of duplicate images upon one retina. [Cf. **diplopia.**]

double interpretation illusion = an illusion of visual perception, in which one and the same figure may appear successively as two quite different patterns or objects. [Cf. **reversible perspective;** a more complicated type includes the rabbit-duck and other ambiguous figures, also the reversible **figure and ground** effects of Gestalt psychology. Cf. **ambiguous figure.**]

double personality, see **personality/dual.**

double vibration, d.v., see **vibration.**

doubt = alternation of belief with disbelief, or the experience of both at once with absence of complete conviction. [Contr. w. **belief,** in its generic sense, which includes **belief** and **disbelief,** and w. **supposal.**] — Ger. *Zweifel.*

doubt/obsessive, see **psychasthenia.**

doubt/psychology of = a study of the conditions and nature of the attitude of uncertainty toward ideas, propositions or acts. [According to Bain and others, the state is due to alternatively accepting and rejecting a proposition, or decision.]

doubtful judgments = (*psychophys.*) judgments given by the observer or subject during an experiment, of the correctness of which judgments he is not fully convinced. [Historically there has been much discussion as to whether this class of judgments should be admitted in connection with the method of right and wrong cases.]

dousing (or **dowsing**) **rod,** see **divining rod.**

drainage = the drawing off of nerve impulses or nerve energy from a neural arc by some external agency, such as an adjacent activated arc. [Distg. fr. **irradiation,** in which the spread of energy is not dependent upon external agencies.]

drainage hypothesis = the theory that facilitation of neural conduction over certain neurons and its inhibition over others is due to a drainage of energy (on analogy with principles of hydraulics) from paths of higher resistance into those of lower. [This theory has been used to account for the varying direction of attention, for learning and habit, and for the formation of conditioned reflexes. Syn. **diversion hypothesis.**] — Fr. *hypothèse du drainage.*

dramatic = 1. (*pop.*) sudden, striking, impressive, theatrical; 2. (*esth.*) characterizing action in a play which portrays, often suddenly and unexpectedly, an appropriate resolution of a conflict.

dramatization = (*psychoan.*) a function of the dream-process in which the manifest content depicts a situation or action. — Ger. *Darstellung.*

drawing = a two-dimensional representation, by means of lines, shading, or color, of some natural or imagined object. [It may be realistic, schematic, or conventionalized.] **draw**[v]. — Fr. *dessin, image*; Ger. *Zeichnung.*

drawing scale = a device for measuring a child's achievement in drawing. [The earliest scale, constructed by Thorndike, consisted of fourteen samples of drawing varying in merit by approximately equal steps.] — Fr. *échelle de dessin.*

dread = an emotional attitude characterized by unpleasant hedonic tone, and by the idea of an unfortunate outcome of future events. [Contr. w. **hope** = pleasant anticipation of the future. Distg. fr. **fear,** a more general term, which may be directed toward present situations.] — Fr. *crainte*; Ger. *Furcht.*

dream = a more or less coherent imagery sequence, which (ordinarily) occurs during sleep. [Cf. **dream imagery.**] **dream**[v], **dreamy**[a] = dreamlike. — Fr. *rêve*; Ger. *Traum.*

dream censorship = (*psychoan.*) that form of dream activity or dream work which omits, modifies, distorts, or regroups elements of the latent dream material, so as to conceal the latent content from consciousness. [Amnesia for the dream is attributable in part to this censorship, so that the dreamer may be kept unaware of his deeper motivation.] — Fr. *censure de rêve.*

dream/clairvoyant = (*psych. res.*) a dream which is believed to reveal a real scene or an event to the sleeper. [Akin to a **veridical dream,** which depicts or refers to objective events, of which knowledge has not been obtained in any natural or normal way.] — Fr. *rêve clairvoyant.*

dream content = the experiences which occur during a single dream. [Psychoanalysts distinguish between **manifest dream content** = the images or items experienced during the dream (the dream story), and **latent dream content** = the hidden, unconscious meaning which may be discovered by following out the free associations which the individual makes with the dream material in the course of the analytic procedure. Cf. **dream material.**] — Fr. *contenu de rêve*; Ger. *Trauminhalt*.

dream imagery = the sequence of presentations, usually visual, which make up a dream story, or a cross-section (i.e. a momentary scene) from this.

dream instigator, see **day residues.** — Ger. *Traumerreger*.

dream interpretation = the analysis of a dream by means of free association of ideas, in order to discover the underlying motives, strivings, wishes, etc. of the dreamer. [The interpretation rests upon a distinction between *manifest content* and *latent content* (cf. **dream material**) and is the direct opposite of the folklore and pop. interpretation of dreams, which seeks to reveal the future rather than the past. In anal. psychol. the discovery of the *whole self*, esp. its highest strivings, is emphasized. In indiv. psychol. the dream is always interpreted as a reflection of the dreamer's attitudes toward the future, esp. his aim toward superiority.] — Fr. *interprétation des rêves*; Ger. *Traumdeutung*.

dream material = (*psychoan.*) the succession of experiences which occur during a single dream, together with the underlying meaning or significance of the dream. [Cf. **dream content.**] — Fr. *matière de rêve*; Ger. *Traumstoff*.

dream wish = (*psychoan.*) representation of the fulfillment of an egocentric and ungratified wish in a dream. [According to psychoanalytic theory, this wish fulfillment is so repressed and disguised in the adult, that it is unrecognizable until submitted to analysis; in children the ungratified wish is plainly represented as fulfilled, because there is neither repression nor disguise. Syn. **dream wish-fulfillment.**]

dream work = the formation of a dream, through a process by means of which the **latent content** of the dream transforms itself into the **manifest content.** — Fr. *travail de rêve*; Ger. *Traumarbeit*.

drill = practice or exercise by systematic repetition of an act or a performance, usually under the control or guidance of some other individual. [The effectiveness of mere repetitive drill, if certain precautions are neglected, has been questioned on experimental evidence.] — Fr. *exercer*.

drive = 1. any intra-organic activity or condition which supplies stimulation for a particular type of behavior; 2. an aroused reaction tendency characterized by the fact that activity of the organism is directed towards or away from some specific incentive, such as food, water, or animal of the opposite sex. [A **drive** is conceived after the analogy of the drive of a machine, and is intended as a concept broad enough to cover both organic activating conditions (such as hunger) and cerebral conditions (such as mental set or desire for a particular object). Syn. **urge.**] — Ger. *Trieb*.

dropping out of movements = an aspect of the learning process, in which certain elements included at the start in a complex act are gradually eliminated with successive repetitions, the elements so eliminated being those which are irrelevant, i.e. which do not constitute an integral part of the act in question. — Fr. *élimination de mouvements*.

drowsiness = a special condition of the organism, which often intervenes between sleep and waking, and which is characterized by partial disintegration and degradation of specific responses; so that the adaptive movements may be unusually retarded, feeble, clumsy, slow, and without regard to significant external stimuli. [**hypnagogic imagery** occurs frequently in **drowsiness.**] **drowsy**[a]. — Fr. *assoupissement*.

drug = a substance, in a state of minute division, introduced into the body for the purpose of counteracting the effect of disease, or of restoring normal function to tissues which have been pathologically altered. [Narcotic drugs, by reason of their depressant action on the nervous system, diminish or abolish nervous and mental activity.] — Ger. *Droge*.

drug addiction = the pathological use of narcotic drugs. [Cf. **addict.**]

drunkard = an individual addicted to the use of alcoholic stimulants to such an extent as to manifest symptoms of alcoholic intoxication continually or periodically. — Fr. *ivrogne*; Ger. *Säufer*.

dual division = (*anthrop.*) one of two approximately equal divisions of a tribe. [Syn. **moiety.**]

dual impression = two experiences from a single stimulus.

dual personality, see **personality/dual.**

dualism = the theory that reality consists of two different, relatively independent substances; more specifically, the assumption that psychic and physical phenomena are both real but are fundamentally different in nature. [Contr. w. **monism.**] **dualistic**[a], **dualist**[np].

du Bois Reymond/law of = the principle that the excitatory efficiency of an electric current which passes through neural or muscular tissue is dependent upon the rate of change of the current density (i.e. is not dependent upon the latter's *absolute* value).

duct = (*anat.*) a tube which provides means for the flow of some specialized secretion or liquid (e.g. tears or saliva), or for the restricted circulation of lymph in the body. — Ger. *Gang*.

duct of Steno (or **Stensen**) = the tube which connects the parotid gland with the mouth.

ductless glands = a class of multicellular glands not provided with ducts for discharging the products of their activity onto an external or internal body surface. [A generic term under which are comprised not only the internally secreting or **endocrine** glands, but also such gland-like organs as the lymph nodes, tonsils, thymus gland, and spleen, which have no demonstrated endocrine function. Distg. **fr. duct glands,** which discharge their secretion onto an internal or external body surface.] — Fr. *glandes endocrines*; Ger. *Drüsen der inneren Sekretion, endokrine Drüsen*.

dull = 1. (*literally*) blunt; not sharp; 2. used metaphorically in a variety of significations, including: lacking in brilliance, e.g. a dull color; spreading diffusely, e.g. a dull pain; lacking in high partials, e.g. a dull sound; stupid, not clever, e.g. a dull child. — Fr. (1) *émoussé*.

dumb = 1. unable to utter articulate sounds; 2. (*pop.*) not responding verbally on a given occasion; 3. (*pop.*) stupid. — Fr. *muet*; Ger. *stumm*.

dumbness, see **mutism.**

dumbness/mental = a type of aphasia characterized by inability to utter appropriate words or sentences.

Dunlap chronoscope = a chronoscope which employs a ten-pole synchronous motor as a constant speed rotator, and a double magnetic clutch for starting and stopping the dial hand. [Syn. **Johns Hopkins chronoscope.** Cf. **psychodometer.**]

duodenum = the upper part of the intestine, directly connected with the stomach. (Accent **-dee-.**) **duodenal**[a]. — Ger. *Zwölffingerdarm*.

duodenum/autacoid of, see **secretin.**

duplex inheritance = the inheritance by an organism of characters from its two parents. [According to the Mendelian view, one of each of the pairs of characters inherited from the two parents develops in the offspring, the other remaining latent but capable of transmission to the next generation. [Syn. **biparental inheritance.**]

duplex marker = an instrument which makes, in a single line with a single recording point, an unconfused graphic record of two variables, such as time and response; it consists of a jointed writing lever, either segment of which may be activated independently by electromagnets connected with the respective variables. [Devised by R. Dodge.] — Fr. *signal duplex*.

duplicity theory = the doctrine that visual sensation rests upon two distinct receptoral mechanisms present in the retina, the rod and cone systems, respectively; the rod-system is supposed to be responsible for vision at low or *twilight* illumination levels and to yield an achromatic result in consciousness; the cone system is supposed to mediate *daylight* and complete color vision, but to be inactive under twilight conditions. [The theory was formulated by von Kries in 1894. Cf. **rod/retinal, cone/retinal.**]

dura, dura mater = a fibrous membrane which covers the brain and spinal cord, lying next to the surrounding bones and enclosing the two other coverings, the arachnoid and pia mater. [Lat. "hard mother."]

duration = 1. the measured or estimated time of the occurrence of an event; 2. the temporal characteristic or attribute of mental phenomena; 3. the rise, poise, and fall as process in consciousness. [Syn. (2) **protensity.**] — Ger. *Dauer*.

duration/least perceptible (or **just noticeable**) = the least or shortest elapse of time between two successive events that can be distinguished from simultaneity. — Fr. *durée minimale perceptible*.

dust figure, see **Kundt tube.**

duty = 1. a term applied to actions prescribed as the customary behavior in social institutions such as the family, state, church, etc. upon the basis of which prescription some being (e.g. a father, a creditor, a ruler, or the Deity) expects or is said to expect performance of the act in question; 2. an individual's interpretation of suitable conduct as determined by his conscience or conception of moral relations. [Contr. w. **right** = (*legal*) the reciprocal expectancy or privilege conferred by institutional practice upon the person to whom the duty is owed.] — Fr. *devoir, obligation*; Ger. *Pflicht*.

dwarfism, see **nanism.**

dyad = a chord composed of two tones; e.g. *c–e*. [Also spelled **diad.**]

dynamic = 1. (*psychol.*) pert. to the causes and effects of behavior and mental activities, often with special emphasis on motivation; 2. syn. for **forceful** or **potent,** or for **moving, changing;** 3. pert. to the behavior of unified energy fields in accordance with the principles of balance, wherein activities occur in consequence of differentials; 4. (*psychoan.*) unconscious mental processes conceived as active or charged with energy (*libido*). [In psychol. generally contr. w. **static** = pert. to the mental structure or to the description of a given stage of mental organization.]

dynamic psychology = a systematic interpretation of mental phenomena, regarded as a succession of causes and effects, with emphasis upon internal drives and motives. [Sometimes used as syn. for **functional psychology.**]

dynamic theory, dynamism/psychic = the theory (propounded by W. Köhler) according to which physiological processes are determined by dynamic conditions (e.g. by forces involved in the central nervous field as a whole) rather than by structural conditions (e.g. neural structures and connections). [Contr. w. **machine theory.**]

dynamics/social, see **social dynamics.**

dynamogenesis, dynamogeny = initiation or increase of muscular activity or tension, due to sensory activity. [Cf. **dynamogenesis/principle of.**] **dynamogenic**[a], **dynamogenetic**[a] (prefd. but seldom used).

dynamogenesis/principle (or **law**) **of** = the principle according to which any change in sensory stimulation has a corresponding effect in altering muscular activity or tension. [This quantitative *law* is often confused with the *fact*, both being termed **dynamogenesis;** the distinction should be made between **dynamogeny** and law of **dynamogenesis,** or between **dynamogenesis** and **principle of dynamogenesis.**]

dynamograph = a recording **dynamometer;** commonly a dynamometer equipped either with a direct mechanical marker or with an air piston connected with a tambour marker, which makes a continuous record on a kymographic drum or other moving surface.

dynamometer = a type of instrument used to register the strength of muscular exertion. [In the **squeeze dynamometer** pressure is exerted by the fingers, etc. against (e.g.) a fairly rigid steel oval, which is gradually closed, the strength exerted being registered on a scale by a pointer. This type is more properly termed a **dynamoscope;** where the strength is permanently recorded on a moving drum or ribbon, the instrument is properly called a **dynamograph.**]

dynamometric test = a form of test of physical strength or endurance, in which the testee is required to exert a maximal muscular effort against a stiff coiled spring, commonly of a hand dynamometer (strength of grip test) or of a back-and-leg dynamometer. [If the testee is required to exert effort continuously or in a series of successive efforts, the dynamometer is, in effect, used as an **ergograph** for testing endurance and fatigue.]

dyne = the c.g.s. unit of force, defined as the force which, acting on a gram for a second, imparts to it a velocity of 1 cm. per sec.

dysarthria = defective speech due to lesions in the nervous system. [Includes 3 types: **anarthria, bradyarthria,** and **mogiarthria.**]

dysgenic = pert. to the deterioration of hereditary qualities. [Contr. w. **eugenic.**]

dysgraphia = a cerebral disorder characterized by inability to write. [Cf. **agraphia.**]

dyslalia = defective speech without demonstrable lesions in the nervous system and with or without abnormality in the peripheral speech mechanism. [There are 6 forms: **agitolalia, alalia, barbaralalia, idiolalia, paralalia,** and **uraniscolalia.** Distg. fr. **dysarthria** = due to central lesions.]

dyslogia = impairment of speech due to mental disorders. [There are 6 forms: **agrammatologia, alogia, bradylogia, catalogia** (= **verbigeration**) **paralogia,** and **polylogia.** Distg. fr. **dysarthria,** due to local lesions in the nervous system.]

dysparathyroidism = any disorder of the function of the parathyroid glands.

dysphasia = impairment of the power of language in any of its forms, due to injury or diseases of the brain, the vocal organs remaining intact. [There are 5 forms: **alexia, articulatory aphasia, auditory aphasia, mixed aphasia,** and **total aphasia.**]

dysphemia = variable nervous disorders of speech due to psychoneuroses. [There are 4 forms: **aphemia, paraphemia, spasmophemia,** and **tachyphemia.**]

dysphonia = any defect of phonation. [Includes the following forms: **aphonia, baryphonia, gutterophonia, hypophonia, idiophonia, megaphonia, metallophonia, microphonia, paraphonia, pneumophonia, rhinophonia, tanyphonia, trachyphonia,** and **tromophonia.**]

dysplastic = characterizing a type of human bodily build which does not fit into the three main classes: *pyknic, athletic, asthenic* (Kretschmer).

dyspnea, dyspnoea = difficult or labored breathing. (Accent **-nee-**.)

dysrhythmia = abnormality in the rhythm of speech. [There are 3 types: **dysrhythmia pneumophrasia** = defects of breath grouping; **dysrhythmia prosodia** = defects of stress placement; and **dysrhythmia tonia** = defects of inflection.]

dysteleology = the lack of purposiveness sometimes exhibited in the structure of organisms, esp. the possession of useless rudimentary organs (Haeckel).

dystimbria = defect of vocal quality or resonance.

dystrophia, distrophy = defective or faulty nutrition.

E

E = abbrev. for **experimenter.** [Prefd. italics without period; plural *E*s, possessive *E*'s, *E*s'.]

ear = the receptor for sound-wave stimuli; i.e. the organ of hearing. [In mammals, birds, and some reptiles the ear is composed of external (outer) ear, middle ear, and internal (inner) ear; in other reptiles and in amphibians the external ear is lacking, while in fishes the inner ear only is present. The **external ear** in mammals is made up of *auricle,* or *pinna,* an expanded cartilaginous body projecting from the side of the head, and the *external auditory meatus,* a tube leading inward through the temporal bone to the middle ear. The **middle ear** is made up of the *tympanic* (or *ear-drum*) *membrane,* and the *auditory ossicles* with their ligaments and muscles, situate within the *tympanic cavity* of the temporal bone. The drum membrane responds to sound, and transmits mechanical vibrations through the ossicles to the inner ear. (In lower forms there is a single ossicle, called the *columella.*) The **internal ear, or auditory labyrinth,** consists of a complex arrangement of passages within the petrous bone, called the *bony labyrinth,* partly filled with a fluid, the *perilymph,* and partly occupied by the *membranous labyrinth,* which is a greatly modified membranous tube. The membranous labyrinth is filled with fluid, the *endolymph.* The **internal ear** is divided into *cochlea, vestibule,* and *semicircular canals,* together with the *endolymphatic duct* and *sac.* The cochlear portion contains the sensory receptors for hearing and the terminations of the cochlear nerve. (In lower vertebrates it is simpler in structure and is not coiled as in the mammals; it is then called the *lagena.*) The vestibular portion consists mainly of *utricle* and *saccule,* which, together with the *semicircular canals,* are believed to have no auditory function, but to serve the sense of equilibrium. Also, in the vestibular region are the *oval* and *round windows* (the paths of entrance and exit of pressure-changes communicated to the endolymph by movements of the ossicles), and the origin of the *endolymphatic duct,* a slender tube terminating in a *sac.*] **aural**[a], **otic**[a]. — Fr. *oreille;* Ger. *Ohr* (*Paukenhöhle* = middle ear).

ear bones, see **ossicles/auditory.** — Fr. *os auriculaires.*

ear-drum membrane, see **tympanic membrane.**

ear/external (or **outer**) = a part of the auditory apparatus which serves for the collection of sound-waves and their conduction through the temporal bone. [In mammals, it consists of an expanded body, roughly funnel-like in form, called the **auricle** or **pinna,** and of a conducting tube, called the **external auditory meatus.** In birds and certain reptiles the **meatus** only is **present.** Cf. **ear.**]

ear/internal = an organ of complex form, contained within the petrous portion of the temporal bone, which consists of (1) a cranial portion, the **cochlea** (in lower forms the **lagena**), which contains the specific receptors for hearing, (2) a central portion, the **vestibule,** which contains the **utricle** and **saccule,** believed to have some role in the perception of movement, and (3) a caudal portion, the three **semicircular canals,** also believed to serve for the perception of movement and for equilibration. [Syn. **inner ear, auditory labyrinth.** Cf. **lagena.**]

ear reflex, see **pinna reflex.**

ecbatic = denoting a mere result or consequence (without aim or intention). [Contr. w. **telic,** which denotes a final end or purpose.]

eccentric projection = 1. the theory that experiences localized at the periphery of the body or outside it owe their spatial position to a projection of their constituent sensations either from within the body or from within the mind; 2. the localization of sensory experiences at the position in space occupied by the object responsible for their arousal, rather than at the point of stimulation (e.g. localization of contact at the point of a cane, of odor at a flower). [Cf. **referred sensation.**] — Fr. *extériorisation des sensations*.

eccentricity = notable oddness in an individual's habitual behavior. [Pop. implies a presumption of insanity, but technically denotes only unusual freedom from conventional types of response.] **eccentric**[a].

echinodermata, echinoderms = a major group or phylum of marine invertebrates, characterized by a radial arrangement of parts and an outer calcareous covering. [E.g. starfish. The second characteristic distinguishes this phylum from **coelenterata.**] (Accent **-ky-.**)

echo = a sound which is received by the ear after reflection and reaches the ear at an appreciably later time than the unreflected sound. — Ger. *Widerhall*.

echolalia = (*path.*) relatively automatic reiteration of words or phrases, often of what is spoken to the patient. [Esp. characteristic of catatonic conditions. Syn. **echophrasia.** Cf. **echopraxia.**]

echopathy = a nervous disease marked by a senseless repetition of words or actions. (Accent **-kop-.**)

echophrasia, see **echolalia.**

echopraxia = the automatic imitation by a patient of expressive movements made by others. [A part of the frequent contradictory positive and negative suggestibility and passivity of the catatonic reaction-type.]

eclampsia = a convulsion, esp. a type of recurrent convulsion which occurs during the later stages of pregnancy. [Usually associated with deficient renal function.] **eclamptic**[a].

eclecticism = the selection and organization into a comprehensive system of compatible features drawn from otherwise incompatible theories or world-views. [Distg. fr. **syncretism** = an uncritical attempt to combine incompatible systems.] **eclectic**[a, np].

ecology = the subdivision of biology which deals with the relation of organisms to their environment. [Syn. **bionomics.**] (Pron. **eek-.**)

ecology/human = that branch of sociology which studies society in its distributive aspect, i.e. the migrations of human beings and the relocations of their institutions.

economic = (*psychoan.*) pert. to the production, distribution, and consumption of psychical energy, according to the principle of the greatest advantage with the least effort.

economic motive = a motive of behavior or social conduct which is concerned with the gaining of livelihood, or with increasing wealth or potentiality for gaining wealth. [A term used for convenience to cover many diverse motives satisfied by the acquisition of wealth, rather than as representing a fundamental psychological process. Cf. **motive.**]

economics[sing] = 1. the science which deals with wealth and its relations to the individual and the community; 2. the study of the efforts of man to provide himself with the means of satisfying his material wants. (Pron. **eek-** or **ek-.**) **economic**[a], distg. fr. **economical,** which refers rather to the elimination of waste in the use of wealth.

economy = 1. the arrangement of any system whereby waste is avoided or eliminated; 2. the body of rules or relations according to which any system or organism operates or is arranged. (Pron. **eek-** or **ek-.**) **economical**[a] (1), **economic**[a] (2).

economy of effort = the tendency of an organism in repeated performances to minimize the expenditure of energy by eliminating useless movements. [Cf. **negative adaptation.** The principle is called **adaptive adaptation** by Borovski, who distinguishes this law from that of **least effort.**] — Fr. *économie dans l'effort*.

economy/principle (or **canon**) **of** = a working rule for treatment of scientific data, according to which the simplest available explanation is to be preferred, i.e. the explanation which involves the fewest or least complexly related concepts that are adequate. [Known by various names: **law of simplicity, law of parsimony;** originally proposed by William of Occam and (*hist.*) called **Occam's razor.** Its specific application in psychology is formulated in **(Lloyd) Morgan's canon.**]

ecphory, ecphoria, ekphorie = a term applied by R. Semon to the revival, by restimulation, of a memory-trace or engram.

ecstasy = 1. excessive and overmastering joy or rapture; 2. a state of suspension of voluntary activity and partial suspension of sensory and other mental functions incident upon prolonged contemplation of a limited group of ideas, noted frequently in religious mystics. [Syn. (1) **frenzy.**] — Fr. *extase*; Ger. *Ekstase*.

ectoderm = the outer germ layer of the embryo. [Syn. **epiblast.** Contr. w. **entoderm.**]

ectoplasm = 1. (*biol.*) the outer layer of cytoplasm in cells; 2. (*psych. res.*) a tenuous substance assumed by some observers to emanate from the human body during a mediumistic trance (Richet). [Syn. (2) **teleplasm.**]

ectosarc = the outer layer of cytoplasm of unicellular organisms.

Edipus (or **Oedipus**) **complex** = 1. (*psychoan.*) the desire (usually unconscious) of the son to possess the mother and to be hostile to the father or destroy him; 2. (*psychoan.*) an excessive erotic attachment of the son to the mother. [According to psychoanalysts this complex is the normal family situation in early childhood, later disappearing from consciousness, but continuing unconsciously to play a large role in the lives of normal, neurotic, and psychopathic individuals. Syn. (2) **mother fixation, mother complex.** Correlative (2) of **Electra complex.**]

education = 1. the development of abilities, attitudes, or forms of behavior, and the acquisition of knowledge, as a result of teaching or training; 2. the procedures or instrumentalities which are used to promote this development. [Usually restricted to training devised and directed by others, but may also include **self-education** = training carried out by the individual himself. For sub-human species the term **training** is prefd.] **educational**[a], pert. to the science or art or to the results of education; **educative**[a], pert. to that which educates. — Ger. (1) *Erziehung*, (2) *Unterricht*.

educational age = the grade of a child as measured by achievement tests (or other standards of educational attainment) expressed in terms of the average performance of children of the various ages tested. [Analogous to **mental age,**

except that **achievement tests** rather than **intelligence tests** are used.]

educational measurements = that branch of education which is concerned with the testing of the scholastic attainments of pupils by means of standardized tests and scales. [It does not include unstandardized examinations, but it may include standardized essay questions or methods of standardizing them.]

educational psychology = the investigation of the psychological problems involved in education, together with the practical application of psychological principles to education. [Syn. **pedagogical psychology.**] — Fr. *psych. éducative.*

educational quotient = the ratio between the score (expressed as a raw score, an educational age score, or in some other manner) and the standard (expressed in the same manner) for the chronological age in question. [Abbrev. **EQ.**]

educational tests = the instruments used in **educational measurements.**

eduction = the process of generating new cognitive items (relations or correlative characters) on the basis of apprehended characters or relations (Spearman). [Contr. w. **apprehension** (3).]

effect[n] = a phenomenon, object, or group of phenomena or objects so related to certain preceding or simultaneous phenomena, etc., that in the absence of these phenomena or of their equivalents the phenomenon in question (i.e. the **effect**) never appears. [Contr. w. **cause** = the preceding or simultaneous phenomena involved in the relation. Cf. **causation.**] **effect**[v] = to bring about an effect. — Ger. *Wirkung.*

effect/law of = the principle that a successful or satisfying outcome of a response tends to strengthen its association with the antecedent stimuli, and that an unsuccessful outcome tends to weaken such association. — Fr. *l. de l'effet.*

effector = an organ which receives excitations from the nervous system and as a result of such excitations performs activity of some sort; i.e. any organ which yields a response to stimuli. [The chief sorts of effectors are **muscles** and **glands;** in certain animals **electric organs, luminescent organs,** etc., serve as effectors also.]

effeminacy = the presence of feminine structural characters, or the manifestation of characteristically feminine modes of behavior, in the male of any species. [Cf. **masculinity.**] **effeminate**[a]. — Ger. *Unmännlichkeit.*

effemination = 1. extreme femininity in a man; 2. a form of homosexuality in which the sexual feelings and mental characteristics of a man resemble those of a normal woman. [Syn. (1) **effeminacy, androgyny.** Cf. **feminism** (2).]

efferent = 1. leading out from; 2. conducting or conveying from a central region of the body toward a more peripheral region, i.e. proximal-distally; 3. (specifically, of nerves) conducting from the central nervous system toward muscles or glands. [Syn. (3) **motor.** Contr. w. **afferent** = conducting from a peripheral toward a more central region.] — Ger. *zentrifugal.*

efficiency = the ratio of the work obtained from a mechanism, to the energy consumed by that mechanism. [E.g. the efficiency of a muscle, efficiency of a social organization.] — Fr. *productivité;* Ger. *Wirkungsgrad.*

efficiency/industrial = the ratio of output to effort. [**output** is measured in terms of both quantity and quality of production; **effort** is **usually measured only roughly, in terms of man-**hours of work. The term is pop. used to denote a *high degree* of efficiency.] — Fr. *productivité industrielle.*

efficiency/zero = inability to perform any scorable amount of a given task or test graded according to various difficulty levels. — Fr. *zéro de productivité.*

efficient cause = the sum total of direct antecedents to a given effect or event. — Fr. *cause efficace.*

effluvium = (*psych. res.*) emanation from bodies, assumed to be of spirit or occult origin.

effort = 1. voluntary activity in the presence of some hindrance; 2. a subjective experience of strain, which accompanies voluntary action, esp. impeded action. — Ger. (2) *Anstrengung.*

effort experience = the kinesthetic sensations which accompany the contraction or tension of muscles against resistance. — Fr. *sensation d'effort.*

effort/mental = the intensification of mental activity in order to overcome resistance to the flow of ideas or thoughts. — Fr. *sentiment de l'effort mental.*

egg = the female germ cell. [In some forms, e.g. birds, the term egg includes not only the germ cell (in this case the yolk), but a surrounding layer of nutritive substance, the white, the whole being enclosed by the shell.] — Fr. *oeuf;* Ger. *Ei.*

ego = 1. the individual's conception of himself; 2. (*psychoan.*) the superficial part of the **id** which has been modified by the direct influence of the external world through the senses, which has become imbued with consciousness, and whose functions are the testing of reality and the acceptance (through selection and control) of part of the demands or wishes made by impulses emanating from the **id.** [Contr. (1) w. **alter** = the individual's conception of other beings. Cf. (2) **id.**] (Accent **eg-.**) — Fr. *le moi;* Ger. *das Ich.*

ego-alter theory = 1. a theory which seeks to account for the origin or existence of social organization or institutions in terms of innate egoism or altruism; e.g. organized cooperation as due to self-interest, self-preservation as developed out of an instinct of race-preservation; 2. an explanation of social interaction in terms of the relation of the ego to the alter. [Cf. **ego, alter.**] — Fr. *th. du moi et d'autrui.*

ego-ideal = (*psychoan.*) a standard of perfection formed in childhood through self-identification with persons admired (i.e. love objects). [Syn. **superego.** Cf. **identification.**] — Fr. *idéal du moi.*

ego-instinct = (*psychoan.*) a general term covering all non-sexual instincts. — Fr. *instinct du moi;* Ger. *Ichtrieb.*

ego-libido = (*psychoan.*) attachment of libido to the ego. [Cf. **narcissism.**]

ego-syntonic[a] = (*psychoan.*) in harmony with the ego or consistent with its standards.

egocentric = disposed to dwell on oneself and to view every situation from a personal angle. [Syn. **self-centered.** Inward manifestation of egocentricity is characteristic rather of introverts than of extraverts, who usually express their egocentricity outwardly.]

egocentric predicament = a term signifying that the human observer is always tied to his own personality and is unable to share directly the experiences of others, or to experience a stimulus directly.

egocentric response = a type of response in association tests, characterized by a tendency toward responses which are distinctly personal to the reactor.

egoism = the type of conduct which is based on the motive of self-advantage rather than on the welfare of others. [The term is used either as characterizing the traits of individuals or as applying to a type of social philosophy. Syn. **selfishness.** Contr. w. **altruism.** Cf. **egotism.**] — Ger. *Selbstsucht.*

egoistic theory of dreams = a fundamental hypothesis of psychoanalysis, which assumes that dreams are absolutely egoistic, in that any person who plays the chief part in a dream is the dreamer himself, and can always be recognized as such when the dream is subjected to analysis. — Fr. *th. égoiste du rêve.*

egotism = the tendency to overvalue, in a rather obvious manner, one's own actions, qualities, possessions, or achievements. [Cf. **egoism.**] — Ger. *Eigenliebe.*

eidetic = characterizing such psychic phenomena as depend upon (or are otherwise related to) the capacity for clear projected images (*Anschauungsbilder*). [Term devised by E. R. Jaensch.] — Ger. *eidetisch.*

eidetic disposition = the ability of certain individuals (esp. children) to project images of an unusually lively, pseudoperceptual character. [Cf. **eidetic image.**] — Ger. *eidetische Anlage.*

eidetic image = a clear image (usually visual) which possesses an external or perceptual character, though generally recognized as subjective. [Commonly found among children; rarely after adolescence. Distg. fr. **imagination** by its strong sensory character, and fr. **hallucination** by its non-illusory character.] — Ger. *Anschauungsbild.*

Eidetiker, eidetic individual = an individual who possesses the ability to project unusually lifelike (eidetic) images.

Einstellung = 1. the set which immediately predisposes the organism toward one type of motor or conscious activity; 2. the established tendency to renew neural functions, esp. those within the brain (G. E. Müller); 3. specific readiness to prolong monotonous activities. [The **Einstellung** may be unconscious in contr. w. the **Aufgabe,** which is conscious and which may be the cause of the **Einstellung.** Syn. **Bereitschaft, mental set.** Cf. **directive tendency.**]

eject = the existence of another's mind or consciousness naively conceived after the analogy of one's own. [Cf. **projection** (2).]

ejective stage = the stage of mental development in the child in which he projects personal traits like his own into other persons and things. [Applied also to the corresponding stage in the mental evolution of the human race. Baldwin assumes 3 stages: the **objective, subjective,** and **ejective.**] — Fr. *stade éjectif.*

elaboration = (*hist.*) the process or function of thinking or reasoning. [Syn. **discursive thinking.**] — Ger. *Ausarbeitung.*

elaboration/secondary = (*psychoan.*) a dream mechanism, the object of which is to combine the dream into a fairly coherent whole. — Ger. *sekundäre Bearbeitung.*

elaborative faculty = (*hist.*) the mental faculty or power to which the process of thinking out problems is ascribed. [Used chiefly by the faculty psychologists. Cf. **elaboration.**] — Ger. *Denkvermögen.*

elasticity = the capacity of a body to recover its original shape or position after deformation by a force.

elation = a condition of emotional excitement marked by intense pleasure and a feeling of buoyancy, together with increased motor activity. [Contr. w. **depression, dejection.**] — Fr. *excitation*; Ger. *Übermut.*

Elberfeld horses = a group of trained horses in Elberfeld, Germany, which (it was claimed) were able to solve difficult arithmetical problems, including extractions of square roots. [The training of the first, called Clever Hans, was begun in 1901 by von Osten, and several other horses received a similar education later from Krall, their owner.] — Fr. *chevaux d'E.*

elbow-jerk, elbow reflex, see **triceps reflex.** — Fr. *réflexe du coude.*

Electra complex = (*psychoan.*) an excessive erotic attachment of the daughter to the father, combined with an antagonistic attitude toward the mother. [Syn. **father-fixation, father complex,** female **Edipus complex.** Correlative of **Edipus complex.**]

electric organ = modified muscle tissue of such nature that it forms an electric generator, which, on excitation through its nerve supply, produces an electric shock. [Found chiefly in primitive fishes.]

electric sense = a modality of experience assumed by some writers to exist in certain animal species, which depends upon the reception of electric stimuli by a specific sensory end-organ.

electric shock method = a variety of the method of punishment in animal training, whereby a habit is broken or a new habit formed by applying an electric shock at some point in the behavior series. [E.g. in teaching an animal to solve a maze, an electric shock may be used when the subject enters a blind alley.]

electrical stimulation = the application of electric current to excite a receptor. [It constitutes an inadequate or abnormal mode of stimulation.]

electrocardiogram = an oscillographic record of the electrical effects produced in the action of the heart muscles.

electrode = a device used to join an electric circuit to some substance or object which is usually regarded as non-electrical in nature. [The positive pole is termed **anode,** the negative **cathode.** **non-polarizable electrode** = one so constructed that the passage of an electric current sets up little or no polarization within the electrode itself.]

electrodiagnosis = 1. the determination of pathologically altered states of the body by means of electrical instruments; 2. specifically, the examination of the muscles and nerves by the galvanic and faradic currents. [Diseased muscles and nerves give the reaction of degeneration (abbrev. R.D.). Cf. **chronaxy,** an electrodiagnostic method.] **electrodiagnostic**[a].

electro-esthesiometer, electro-aesthesiometer = a device for tactual stimulation, in which a fine stimulus-point is brought down upon the skin by an electromagnet.

electrolysis = a process of chemical decomposition

produced by passing an electric current through a solution of ionizable substance.

electrolyte = a compound which in solution dissociates into positively and negatively charged particles called **ions.**

electrolytic stimulus = an inadequate or abnormal stimulus by means of which sensory experiences are aroused by electrochemical action. [Noted esp. in the sense of taste. On placing a nickel coin above the tongue and a bronze coin beneath, each coin touching the tongue and each other, a taste is aroused, although neither coin applied alone produces taste.]

electrometer = an instrument for measuring electrical potentials. [Cf. **capillary electrometer.**]

electromotive force = a force due to difference of electrical potential.

electron = a particle of matter equal to about 1/1800 the mass of the hydrogen atom, which carries, or is equivalent to, a unit charge of negative electricity. [**electrons** constitute the cathode rays emitted within a Crookes tube, and the beta rays thrown off by radioactive substances. Cf. **proton** (2).]

electrostimulator = any special apparatus devised or used for the purpose of delivering a current for shock stimulation.

electrotaxis, -tactic, electrotropism, -ic, see **galvanotaxis, galvanotropism.**

electrotonus = the altered physiological condition of a nerve or muscle during the passage of a (steady direct) galvanic current, as exhibited in altered excitability in the neighborhood of the electrodes.

element = a constituent part of any phenomenon, event, or system; usually, the most simple sort of constituent. [Contr. w. **factor** = an active force or agency cooperating with other forces to bring about a situation.] **elementary**[a] = simple; **elemental**[a] = pert. to an element or to elements. — Ger. *Grundstoff*.

element/mental, see **mental element.**

element(ar)ism = a system of psychology such as Wundt's, which describes the mind in terms of **mental elements** and their compounds. [Cf. **mental chemistry.**]

elimination = 1. in natural selection, the gradual disappearance of unfavorable traits by destruction of those organisms which possess them; 2. the gradual disappearance of useless movements; 3. the ejection of waste substances from the body. [Contr. (1) w. **survival** = the greater productiveness of those organisms which possess favorable traits, with consequent preponderance of such traits in the population.]

Ellis harmonical = a specially-tuned harmonium, similar to the American reed-organ, used to demonstrate certain exact pitches and intervals not found on the ordinary harmonium. [Described by A. J. Ellis in trans. of Helmholtz' Sensations of tone, 1885.]

embarrassment = an emotional condition marked by unpleasant self-consciousness, and by some degree of confusion and impulsional conflict. [Cf. **bewilderment.**] — Fr. *embarras, gêne*; Ger. *Verlegenheit*.

embolus = an obstruction in a blood vessel formed by a clot, air bubble, or other foreign body. **embolism**[n] = the forming of such an obstruction.

embryo = an organism in an early stage of development. [In mammals, esp. man, sometimes restricted to the early period of intra-uterine life, the term **fetus** being applied to the later stages. In many insects the term embryo is limited to the earlier and relatively inactive period of development before the production of the larva.] (Accent **em-.**) **embryonic**[a].

embryology = the branch of biology which deals with eggs and their development into adult organisms.

emergent = 1. characterizing a property, substance, or phenomenon which cannot be *predicted* (*a*) from the properties of its (chemical) constituents, or (*b*) from the properties of the antecedent phylogenetic or ontogenetic events; 2. characterizing a property of any Gestalt, or configuration, which *modifies* the constituents of which it is composed; 3. characterizing *descriptively* the gross or *molar* properties of a higher unit of any sort, as distinct from the specific or *molecular* properties of its constituents, apart from any question of predictability or of modification; e.g. the properties of animal behavior regarded as a total phenomenon, as distg. fr. the properties of the receptor, conductor, and effector processes.

emergent evolution = the doctrine that the successive steps in evolution result in the production of something essentially new and theoretically unpredictable, instead of involving merely recombinations or resultants of preexisting factors.

emetic = an agent which produces vomiting. — Ger. *Brechmittel*.

emission = the excretion of semen, esp. that which occurs involuntarily during sleep.

emissive functions (or **centers**) = those functions (or centers) which deal with efferent nerve impulses resulting in movement or other effector response.

Emmert's law = the tendency of a projected image (usually an after-image or eidetic image) to increase in size in proportion to the distance of the projection ground from the eye. [Contr. w. **invariance.**]

emmetropia, emmetropism = the normal condition of the ocular refractive system, in which rays from distant objects are focused sharply on the retina of the eye, while the accommodation muscle is relaxed. [Distg. fr. **myopia, hyperopia (hypermetropia), astigmatism.**] (Accent (1) **-trop-,** (2) **-met-.**) **emmetropic**[a].

emmetropic eye = (*ophth.*) an eye which is normally perfect in its refractive system. — Fr. *oeil emmétrope*.

emotion = 1. an experience or mental state characterized by a strong degree of feeling and usually accompanied by motor expression, often quite intense; 2. a total state of consciousness involving a distinctive feeling tone and a characteristic trend of activity; 3. non-discriminating or mass activity aroused by social situations, either perceived or represented by ideas; i.e. total responses of an organism in which a large proportion of the experience is made up of visceral or somatic elements; 4. the totality of experience during any period in which marked bodily changes of feeling, surprise, or upset take place; 5. (*psychoan.*) the dynamic expression of the instincts which may emanate from conscious or unconscious sources; 6. the conscious concomitant of instinctive impulses at work

(McDougall); 7. a highly complex innate disposition, within which instincts are organized as so many sensori-motor dispositions to particular bodily movements (Shand); 8. affective accompaniments of obstruction of instinctive behavior (Drever). [**emotion** and **instinct** are frequently used interchangeably, but **emotion** is preferably used as descriptive of responses involving *feeling-tone*, while **instinct** applies to serial responses without regard to any affective quality.] **emotional**[a]. — Ger. *Affekt, Gemütsbewegung, Emotion.*

emotion/esthetic = the emotion which is experienced during the perception of a work of art, or of a natural object or scene comparable to a work of art.

emotional bias = a tendency to assume and be guided by an emotional attitude in considering or discussing objective facts. — Fr. *préjugé émotionnel.*

emotional disposition (or **attitude**) = an attitude in which emotional factors, distinctive feeling-tones, or affective reactions predominate.

emotional expression = the entire group of motor activities, including bodily movements, facial expression, inhibitions, and glandular activity, which characterize emotional attitudes or experiences.

emotional pattern = a more or less definite grouping of bodily changes of any sort which occur either simultaneously or in a fixed temporal sequence, and which are characteristic of some emotion. — Fr. *complexus émotionnel.*

empathy = 1. (*esth.*) the imaginal or mental projection of oneself into the elements of a work of art or into a natural object; 2. (*psychoan.*) a mental state in which one identifies or feels himself in the same state of mind as another person or a group. **empath(et)ic**[a]. — Ger. *Einfühlung.*

empirical = 1. pert. to experience; 2. pert. to methods or conclusions based on observation or experiment. [Syn. (1) **experiential.** Contr. (2) w. **deductive** and **rational,** whether as a term of reproach (i.e. lacking necessary theorizing), or as a term of praise (i.e. avoiding rigorously all hypothesis except working hypotheses).]

empirical method = the scientific method which proceeds by observation and experiment. [Contr. w. **a priori method.**]

empirical psychology = 1. the investigation of mental phenomena by observation and experiment, as contr. w. **rational psychology,** which proceeds by deduction; 2. the investigation of what the mind does, as contr. w. what it is (Titchener). [Contr. (2) w. **existential psychology.**]

empiricism = 1. (*psychol.*) the theory that certain elements or factors in human knowledge (e.g. the perception of space) are derived by learning from other, more fundamental elements (e.g. sensations); 2. (*epistem.*) the theory that all knowledge is derived from experience. [British **empiricism** (2) begins with Locke (1690) and finally becomes British **associationism.** Contr. (1) w. **nativism;** (2) w. **rationalism** and **criticism.**] **empir(ic)ist**[np], **empiristic**[a].

employment psychology = the psychological principles and techniques used in selecting from applicants for a job those who show the greatest probability of success. [Cf. **selection/vocational.**]

empyreumatic = a quality of olfactory sensation, of which tar and tobacco smoke are typical examples. [Syn. **smoky, burnt.** Cf. **odor.**] — Fr. *defumée*; Ger. *brenzlich, empyreumatisch.*

emulation = 1. imitative rivalry; 2. ambition to excel in achievement. **emulate**[v], **emulative**[a]. — Ger. *Wetteifer.*

encephalitis = a pathological condition characterized by inflammation of the brain substance or of its envelopes. [Cf. **meningitis, arachnitis.**]

encephalization = the various phylogenetic processes which have resulted in the formation of the encephalon, or brain. [Not properly applied to the ontogenetic process in the individual.]

encephalon = the brain in its entirety.

enchant[v], see **incantation.**

end = 1. (the idea of) a result desired and made the object of conation; 2. an *emergent* resultant of purposive striving superior to or more universal than the goal consciously aimed at. [Syn. (1) **purpose.** Cf. **goal, aim, creative synthesis, emergent evolution.**] — Fr. *fin*; Ger. (1) *Zielvorstellung,* (2) *Ziel.*

endbrush = the fine branching of fibrils at the end of the axon of a neuron. [Syn. **telodendron.**] — Fr. *fibrilles terminales*; Ger. *Nervenendplatte.*

end-organ = 1. a sensory receptor; 2. any peripheral terminal, whether receptive or effective, functionally connected with a neuron or nerve-fiber. [Syn. (1) **receptor.** Cf. **end-plate.**] — Fr. *appareil terminal.*

end-path = the final neuron (or nerve) of a reflex path. [It is an efferent (motor) unit whose proximal origin is regularly within the central nervous system, and whose distal termination connects with an effector organ. Cf. **final common path.**] — Fr. *voie terminale.*

end-plate = the ultimate termination of a motor nerve, generally embedded beneath the hypolemma in a muscle fiber. — Fr. *plaque motrice.*

end-pleasure/sexual = the sensation complex aroused by or associated with the climax of sexual intercourse, i.e. with the orgasm. — Fr. *plaisir terminal sexuel.*

end spurt = a rise of activity in voluntary muscular (or other) work, which immediately precedes complete exhaustion of the exercised muscles, or the termination of the task. — Fr. *effort terminal.*

endocardiac = within the heart.

endocrine, endocrine gland = a ductless gland, or organ of secretion, which forms a specific chemical substance and passes this directly or indirectly into the circulating fluid to produce physiological effects upon other organs. [**ductless gland** is a generic name embracing both endocrine glands and certain gland-like organs (e.g. lymph nodes, spleen, tonsils, thymus gland) which lack ducts and (so far as known) do not produce internal secretions. Cf. **hormone.**] **endocrine**[a]. — Ger. *endokrine Drüse.*

endocrinology = the branch of science which deals with the morphology, physiology, chemistry, and pathology of the endocrine glands. [Cf. **endocrine.**]

endoderm = the inner germ layer of the embryo. [Contr. w. **ectoderm,** the outer layer.]

endogamy = the custom of confining marriage to individuals within the same community, caste, phratry, or sib. [Contr. w. **exogamy.**] **endogamous**[a]. — Ger. *Verwandtenehe.*

endolymph = fluid contained in the **membranous labyrinth** of the internal ear.

endolymphatic duct = a canal which leads from the posterior wall of the saccule of the internal ear, and ends in a blind pouch, the **endolymphatic sac.** — Fr. *conduit endolymphatique.*

endolymphatic sac = an expanded body at or near the termination of the **endolymphatic duct.**

endomusia = the implicit or silent reproduction of a song.

endophasia = the implicit or silent reproduction of a word or of phrases and sentences.

endoplasm = the central portion of a cell.

endosarc = the interior protoplasm of unicellular organisms. [Cf. **ectosarc.**]

endosomatic currents = electric currents or potentials set up within a living organism.

endothelium = the cellular lining of cavities which do not open to the exterior of the body. [Applied esp. to blood and lymph vessels.]

endowment = natural capacity for development and activity, both mental and physical, so far as determined by heredity. — Fr. *don*; Ger. *Begabung.*

endurance = the capacity of an individual to bear pain or hardship or to put forth effort in the face of difficulties. — Ger. *Ausdauer.*

endyma, see **ependyma.**

enelecomorphism, see **anthropomorphism.**

energy = 1. (*phys.*) the capacity for doing work; 2. degree of activity displayed in behavior. **energize**^{v} (1); **energic**^{a} (1) **energetic**^{a} (2). — Ger. (1) *Kraft*, (2) *Energie.*

energy/conservation of, see **conservation of energy.**

enervate^{v} = 1. to deprive of energy, or of mental or physical vigor; 2. (*neurol.*) to remove or detach, by surgical means, the nerves (sensory or motor) which supply any organ or tissue. [Not to be confused w. **innervate.** Syn. (2) **denervate.**] **enervation**^{n}. — Ger. *entnerven.*

engram = 1. a term applied originally by R. Semon to a permanently altered state of living tissue, resulting from a temporary process of excitation (the basis of **physiological memory** and of inheritance, according to Semon); 2. sometimes used as syn. for **neurogram.** [Cf. **organic memory.**]

engraphia = 1. the formation of records of experience, or **engrams**; 2. the property of organisms whereby they may become impressed with **engrams. engraphic**^{a}.

ennui = an experience characterized by an unpleasant hedonic tone, induced by prolongation of an uninteresting situation. [Syn. **boredom.**] (Pron. **on-wee.**) — Ger. *Langweile.*

entelechy = 1. activity of self-realization (Aristotle); 2. the autonomous, non-mechanical, natural activity which is essential for the processes of life (Driesch).

enteroceptor, see **interoceptor.**

entity = a portion of reality which maintains its identity. — Ger. *Wesenheit.*

entoderm = (*biol.*) the inner layer of cells in the embryo. [Syn. **hypoblast, endoderm.** Contr. w. **ectoderm.**]

entomology = the branch of biology which deals with insects.

entoperipheral feelings = (*hist.*) any experience whose source of stimulation is localized within the body (H. Spencer). — Fr. *sensibilité entopériphérique.*

entoptic phenomena = visual experiences due to stimuli or conditions within the eye itself. [Where these phenomena are due to activity within the eyeball, the stimuli are called **entoptic processes.** Cf. **muscae volitantes.** Modifications of vision due to films, etc. on the surface of the cornea are called **pseudentoptic phenomena.**]

enumeration = a method of classification or induction which consists in examining in turn every member of the class under consideration. [Cf. **induction/complete.**] — Ger. *Aufzählung.*

enuresis/nocturnal = involuntary discharge of urine during sleep.

envelopes/Sanford, see **Sanford envelopes.**

environment = a term covering all physicochemical, biological, and social phenomena which act from without upon organisms. [Distg. (properly) fr. **milieu,** which includes both the organism and its environment. Contr. w. (*a*) **organism** and (*b*) **heredity.**] **environ**^{v}, **environmental**^{a}. — Fr. *milieu, entourage, conditions ambiantes, ambiance*; Ger. *Umgebung.*

environmental factors = those factors which act upon the organism from without and influence its structure or its behavior. [Contr. w. **internal factors,** due to the constitution and heredity of the organism.] — Fr. *facteurs ambiants.*

envy = a social feeling or attitude, unpleasant in character, aroused in the individual by the possession or attainment of something on the part of another, which the individual himself lacks and which he desires. — Ger. *Neid.*

enzyme = a catalytic agent found in living organisms, which promotes chemical reactions, such as the diastase of germinating grain which converts starch into sugar. [Syn. **ferment**^{n}.]

Eoanthropus = the generic name for Piltdown or Sussex man, represented by the species Dawsoni. [Literally, "dawn man."]

epencephalon = the segment of the brain which lies next behind (i.e. caudad to) the midbrain, and consists of the cerebellum and pons, or of these plus the medulla. [Syn. **after-brain, hindbrain.**]

ependyma = the lining of the neural canal or tube, made up of (ciliated) cells of the glial order and secretory cells. [Syn. **endyma.**]

epiblast = the outer of the two primitive layers of the embryo. [Syn. **ectoderm.**]

epicritic sensibility = a system of cutaneous sensibility by which faint pressure, cool, and warm stimulations are appreciated, finely discriminated, and localized. [Contr. w. **protopathic sensibility** and **deep sensibility.**]

epidemic chorea, see **dancing mania.**

epidermis = 1. (*anat.*) the outer or epithelial layer of the vertebrate skin; 2. (*zool.*) a thin outer layer, e.g. the epidermis of molluscan shells; 3. (*bot.*) the thin outermost cellular layer in higher plants.

epigamic = tending to attract the other sex. [Applied to colors or other possibly alluring characteristics exhibited as a preliminary to mating.]

epigastric = pert. to or located in the region over the stomach.

epigastric reflex = drawing in of the abdominal wall, elicited by stroking the skin from nipple downward. [Mediated by the 7th to 9th thoracic segments of spinal cord.]

epigenesis = the hypothesis that embryonic development starts from a relatively simple structure and that differentiation results from the influence of the environment and the interaction of the parts of the embryo itself. [Contr. w. **preformism,** which assumes that the basis of all characters are already present in the germ.]

epiglottis = the structure (shaped like a bicycle saddle) which covers the entrance to the larynx. — Ger. *Kehldeckel.*

epilepsy = a nervous disorder, usually chronic, with characteristic convulsions of sudden onset, a tonic spasm often with crying and arrest of breathing followed by clonic twitching, biting of tongue, frothing at the mouth, relaxation of sphincters. [Duration 1–3 minutes. Usually complete unconsciousness. Occasionally with mere aura or petit mal absences or epileptic equivalents.] **epileptic**[a, np].

epileptic furor = one of the equivalents or accompaniments of epileptic fits, consisting of acts of blind, often brutal violence, for which the patient has no memory.

epileptic stupor = a state of near unconsciousness and difficulty of arousal, usually following the epileptic convulsion, in which the patient remains inert and unresponsive.

epileptiform seizure = a convulsion or fit resembling those which occur in epilepsy, but due to some specific cause such as irritation by a scar or residual of an injury or other brain disease such as tumor, paresis, etc. — Fr. *accès épileptiforme.*

epinephrin(e) = levo-methylamino-ethanol-catechol, a white or light brownish powder, very slightly soluble in water, obtained as an extract of the **adrenal glands** or formed synthetically, and having a sympathico-mimetic action when introduced into the blood stream or applied locally. [It is the autacoid of the adrenal medulla. Special proprietary products are termed **adrenalin, adrenin, suprarenalin, suprarenin.**] (Accent **-nef-.**)

epinosic = (*psychoan.*) pert. to the secondary gain or advantage through illness.

epiperipheral feeling = (*hist.*) any experience whose source of stimulation is localized outside the body (H. Spencer). — Fr. *sensibilité épipériphérique.*

epiphenomenalism = a theory of the mind-body relation, or a corollary to certain such theories, according to which conscious processes are not in any sense causal agents, even with respect to one another, but are merely correlated with certain causally effective physiological processes. **epiphenomenalistic**[a], **epiphenomenalist**[np].

epiphenomenon = an occurrence, process, or manifestation which accompanies some other process or phenomenon, but is devoid of causal efficacy. **epiphenomenal**[a]. — Fr. *épiphénomène.*

epiphora = a pathological overflow of tears, usually due to obstruction of the lacrimal duct or deformation of an eyelid. (Accent **-piff.**)

epiphysis, epiphysis cerebri = syn. for **pineal body** (or **gland**).

episcotister = a disk with adjustable open and closed sectors together with a mechanism for rotating it. [Used for the equating of luminosities and for the short exposure of visual material, esp. in the study of flicker.]

episode = (*pathol.*) any transitory phase in a disorder or disease. **episodic**[a].

epistemology = the branch of philosophy which deals with the nature and validity of knowledge. [Syn. **theory of knowledge.** Distg. fr. **metaphysics,** which deals with the nature of existence and reality.] **epistemological**[a]. — Ger. *Erkenntnistheorie.*

epithalamus = the dorsal portion of the **diencephalon,** which contains the **pineal body** and the **habenula.**

epithelium = the cellular covering of surfaces of the body exposed externally, or the lining of any of its natural cavities. **epithelial**[a].

epochal psychoses, see **climacteric psychoses.**

epsilon movement, see **apparent (motion** or) **movement.**

equal, see **equality.**

equal and unequal cases/method of = a modified form of the method of **right and wrong cases** devised by J. Merkel, in which a difference limen between two stimuli is first determined by the method of **minimal changes** and then these two stimuli are presented to the observer, who is required to judge whether the two are equal or unequal. [Cf. **right and wrong cases/method of.**] — Fr. *m. de cas égaux et inégaux.*

equal-appearing intervals/method of, see **mean gradations/method of.** — Fr. *m. des intervalles jugés égaux.*

equal distribution of ignorance = the principle that, when the relative probabilities of two or more events are unknown, the chances of their occurrences are equal (G. Boole, 1854). [The principle is applied incorrectly to the *a priori* establishment of chances without empirical grounds for the application. Syn. **law of insufficient reason.** Contr. w. **law of sufficient reason.**]

equal judgment = the judgment or report, upon comparison of two given stimuli, (1) that no difference is observed between them, or (2) that they are subjectively equal. [Cf. **constant stimuli/method of.**]

equal sense distances/method of = a psychophysical measurement method in which the observer is required to adjust a stimulus R_3, so that the difference between R_3 and a stimulus R_2 will appear to be the same as the difference between R_2 and a third stimulus R_1. [Syn. **method of mean gradations, method of supraliminal differences, method of equal-appearing intervals.**] — Fr. *m. des équidistances sensorielles.*

equal steps = a series of stimuli which differ in intensity or other quantitative character, such that the difference between any contiguous pair is judged equal to the difference between any other contiguous pair. — Fr. *échelons égaux;* Ger. *gleichmässige Stufen.*

equal-tempered scale, see **scale** (2). — Fr. *gamme tempérée.*

equality = (*psychol.*) the absence of discernible or discoverable difference in magnitude between two or more data. [Designated by symbol =.] **equal**[a]. — Fr. *égalité;* Ger. *Gleichheit.*

equally noticeable = syn. for **just noticeable** in psychophysics, according to the theory that all just noticeable differences are (relatively or absolutely) equal sense differences.

equation = an algebraic statement or formulation, in which one member (preceding the sign =) is asserted to be equal to another member (following the sign =). [Cf. **equality.**] **equate**[v]. — Ger. *Gleichung.*

equilibration, see **balance.**

equilibrium = 1. (*phys.*) a condition of stability in a body, due to balance of opposing forces, or a condition of instability which does not tend to depart from a fixed region of activity; 2. (*psychol.*) maintenance of an upright posture; 3. (*esth.*) equivalence in suggested weight or force of the right and left sides, the upper and lower parts, etc. of a picture or other artistic production; 4. (*biol.*) an evolutionary condition in which a given species manifests no tendency to develop into another type. [Cf. **balance.**] — Ger. *Gleichgewicht.*

equilibrium/illusion of = 1. a false perception of one's bodily position or orientation produced (*a*) through continuous rotation in any one direction with the head held in various positions, leading to such phenomena as **past pointing** and **nystagmus,** which are the reflex responses arising from the *semicircular canals,* or (*b*) through rotation in various directions and with reference to several axes under the blindfold conditions in the **Mach rotation frame** with the instruction to state at the end of the series which way the body is orientated or inclined; 2. the false perception of one's bodily position when, under blindfold conditions, objects on which the body is supported are moved in such a manner as to give the individual the erroneous impression that he has been lifted; e.g. when he is then asked to jump, the effort will be out of all proportion to the actual distance.

equilibrium/perception of = a type of experience which affords data with respect to the center of gravity of the organism, and enables the individual to establish and maintain an upright posture. [Syn. **static sensation.**]

equipotentiality = 1. the capacity of any part of the egg or embryonic tissue (at an early stage) to produce any or all parts of the developed organism; 2. the capacity of any intact part of a functional nerve center to carry out the functions lost by destruction of other parts. **equipotential**[a].

equiproportional table = a table of correlation coefficients satisfying the tetrad criterion (Spearman). [Cf. **hierarchical table.**]

equivalence = the relation between two terms or phenomena such that in a given context one may be substituted for the other without altering the result of the reasoning or the practical situation. **equivalent**[a]. — Ger. *Äquivalenz.*

equivalents/method of = a procedure devised by E. H. Weber as a form of the **method of average error,** in which the observer is required to adjust a variable stimulus to the point of subjective equality with a constant stimulus. — Ger. *Methode der Äquivalente.*

equivocal = susceptible of two or more different interpretations. [Syn. **ambiguous.** Contr. w. **univocal.**] **equivocality**[n]. — Ger. *zweideutig, mehrdeutig.*

erection = swelling of the genital organs from congestion, i.e. accumulation of blood. [Syn. **tumescence.** Cf. **virile reflex.**]

erector spinae reflex, see **sacrospinal reflex.**

erethism = an exaggerated degree of irritability or sensitivity in any part of the body. **erethismic**[a].

erg = the work done by a force of 1 dyne acting (i.e. displacing its point of application) through a distance of 1 centimeter. [If 1 gram is brought in 1 second from rest to a velocity of 1 cm. per second, 1 **erg** of work has been done. In lifting 1 gram vertically at sea-level through 1 cm., approximately 981 ergs are done. 1 **joule** = 10,000,000 ergs.]

ergasia = a comprehensive term for **psychobiological functioning** or behavior (A. Meyer). [Used esp. in compound forms to denote various disturbances of functioning: **anergasia, dysergasia, kakergasia** (= **merergasia**), **oligergasia, parergasia, pathergasia, thymergasia.**] **ergastic**[a].

ergograph = an instrument for measuring changes in the amount of muscular contraction, usually in experiments on work or fatigue; it ordinarily consists of some device for immobilizing all parts of a member except the part to be measured, and for recording the latter's movements. [E.g. forearm and all but middle finger strapped on horizontal board; the free finger by flexion and extension operates against resistance, such as is afforded by a hanging weight, records of its excursions being made typically on a **kymograph.**]

erogenous (or **erotogenic**) **zones** = 1. certain sensitive regions of the body where stimuli (esp. tactile and temperature) under certain conditions initiate sexual feelings and reactions; 2. (*psychoan.*) certain areas of the body which replace the genital organ, or act as a substitute for it. [These regions are primarily a zone surrounding the external genitalia, the mouth, and (in the female) the breasts and nipples. Nursing may be slightly erotogenic even in normal women; general mechanical manipulation of breasts and nipples, as with the breast pump, is not.]

erotic = pert. to sex sensations or their stimuli.

erotic type = (*psychoan.*) a type of individual whose main interest is applied to the libido or the love life (Freud).

eroticism, erotism = 1. (*pathol.*) an exaggerated development and display of sex sensations and reactions; 2. (*psychoan.*) a generic term for sexual excitement or craving, which is inherent in the mucous membranes, the skin, and organs of special sense; 3. a tendency in certain schools of literature, art, or medicine to magnify the sex factors in man and nature. [Syn. (2) **erotism.** In addition to **eroticism** arising from stimulation of the genital regions psychoanalysts distinguish **oral, urethral, anal, dermal,** and **muscle eroticism,** associated with stimulation of these parts (or tissues) respectively.] **erotic**[a].

erotogenic = arousing sex sensations. [Syn. **erogenous.**] **erotogenicity**[n].

erotomania = a pathological exaggeration of sex behavior (sensations, emotions, reactions). [Cf. **nymphomania** (in the female), **satyriasis** (in the male).]

error = 1. a divergence between an individual's statements or belief, and real or objective facts or relations; 2. (*beh.*) failure of an act of behavior to conform to the conditions of the problem, or to attain the desired or desirable result; 3. (*statist.*) deviation of a measure from the true value of that which is measured. [In certain types of experimentation individuals are compared or improvement measured by the relative *number* of errors; in other cases the *amount* of error or divergence is an essential factor and is calculated. Syn. (3) **deviation.** See Table IV.] — Ger. (1, 3) *Fehler,* (2) *Fehlhandlung.*

error/constant, variable, etc., see **constant error,** etc.

error judgment = a judgment which does not truly represent the stimulus conditions, e.g. a judgment of *two*, given in the two-point limen experiment when only one point is stimulated.

error methods = a term commonly applied, since Fechner, to two psychophysical methods, **average error** and **right and wrong cases;** contr. w. the **method of just noticeable differences** (Fechner) and w. **gradation methods** (Külpe). [Many writers (Wundt, G. E. Müller) prefer other designations. The term is misleading in that every psychophysical method involves both variable and constant errors; it was originally applied to those procedures whose results seemed to demand *statistical* treatment (law of errors).] — Ger. *Fehlermethoden.*

error/motivated = (*psychoan.*) the interference with an intended act by a so-called *accidental* and apparently purposeless act, resulting from the deeper mechanisms of an unconscious wish whose primary purpose it is to carry out this *accidental* performance. [Cf. **symptomatic act.**] — Ger. *Fehlhandlung.*

error of recognition = 1. the recognition, as familiar, of an item not previously experienced; 2. a term proposed by Foucault for the difference limens in the method of average error. [Syn. (1) **déjà vu.** Cf. **paramnesia.**]

errors of observation, observational errors = deviations of the reported results from the actual values, due either to the observer or to the recording apparatus. [Errors in the apparatus may be due to faulty design, construction, operation, or methods of use; they are called **instrumental errors. errors of observation** may be either **accidental** or **constant.**] — Ger. *Beobachtungsfehler.*

errors of reference = a term applied by Fechner to errors or deviations which occur (*a*) in the **method of limits,** according as the variable approaches the standard stimulus from above or below; and (*b*) in the **method of average error** due to the fact that only the variable (and not the standard) is subject to change. [Designated by symbol **S,** distg. fr. **P** (= time error) and **Q** (= space error).]

erythrogenic radiations = long-wave light stimuli which normally give rise to the experience of red. [Suggested by Ladd-Franklin to replace the physicists' equivocal term *red.*]

erythropsia = a type of chromatopsia or colored vision (usually following over-exposure to intense light) in which all objects appear tinged with red. [Cf. **snow-blindness.**]

escape tendency = an attitude looking toward flight or avoidance, which an individual may assume with respect to certain situations. — Fr. *tendance à s'échapper.*

eserin, see **physostigmin.**

esodic, see **centripetal.**

esophagus, oesophagus = the tube leading from the mouth to the stomach. (Accent **-soff-.**) **esophageal**[a]. (Accent **-fay-.**)

esophoria, see **imbalance/muscular.**

esoteric = pert. to the inner, hidden, or mystical meaning of a theory or system. [Applied to cults and adepts claiming to possess exclusive knowledge through reaching higher stages of control. Contr. w. **exoteric** = the superficial meaning.]

esprit de corps = the common or identical feelings of the members of an organization (accompanied by the awareness that these feelings are common to all), looking toward the interests of that organization and the maintaining of its prestige, esp. enthusiasm, and confidence in the ability and loyalty of other members. [In social psychology the term emphasizes the cumulative effect of this attitude on the efficiency of the organization. Syn. **morale.**]

esthesodic, aesthesodic, esthesiodic = afferent. [A rare term, denoting the course of nerve impulses from receptor to center.]

esthesiogenic, aesthesiogenic = producing sensation. [Applied particularly to stimuli or suggestions which arouse peculiar sensory effects in hypnotic subjects.]

esthesiometer, aesthesiometer = a device for measuring tactual acuity by determining the two-point threshold; there are several forms, the essential feature being a pair of slightly rounded points which may be adjusted at various distances from each other and applied simultaneously to the subject's skin. [Cf. **von Frey esthesiometer, electro-esthesiometer.**] — Ger. *Tast(er)zirkel.*

esthesiometry, aesthesiometry = the branch of psychophysics which deals with the measure of touch and pressure sensations and thresholds.

esthete, aesthete = one who attaches much or overmuch importance to the place of beauty in human experience.

esthetics, aesthetics, aesthetic = the scientific investigation of beauty and ugliness, or (more precisely) of the pleasant-unpleasant feelings aroused for their own sake by various composite (or simple) stimuli. [E.g. a visual "picture," an auditory "tune."] **esthetic**[a].

estimation difference = a term proposed by W. Wundt to designate half the difference between the upper and lower limens. [Syn. **estimation error.**] — Ger. *Schätzungsdifferenz, Schätzungsfehler.*

estral (or **estrous**) **cycle** = the period of recurrent estrum, or heat, in animals.

estrus, estrum, oestrus, oestrum = periodic sex desire, or heat, in female animals. [Syn. **rut.**] **estral**[a], **estrous**[a].

ethereal = a quality of olfactory sensation of which beeswax and sulphuric ether are typical examples. [A class of Zwaardemaker's. Not exactly equivalent to Henning's **fruity** quality. Cf. **odor.**] — Ger. *ätherisch.*

ethical judgment = the appraisal which an individual gives to acts of conduct as regards their conformity or non-conformity to some implied standard of fairness, justice, or kindness to his fellow-men.

ethical sense = the capacity to discriminate between human actions upon the basis of their conformity to a standard of fairness, justice, or kindness to those affected.

ethics = the branch of science which investigates the activity of individuals, not as events, but as judged with respect to moral values. **ethical**[a]. — Fr. *éthique, morale*; Ger. *Sittenlehre.*

ethmoidal = pert. to or located near the ethmoid bone, behind the nose. (Accent **-moy-.**)

ethnic = pert. to racial groups. [The term embraces both social and individual characteristics of races.]

ethnocentrism = the tendency to hold the characteristics of one's own group superior to the characteristics of those not in the group, and to judge outsiders by the standards of one's own group. **ethnocentric**[a].

ethnography = the branch which investigates, comparatively, the customs, occupations, culture, etc. of various races, more especially with regard to their geographic environment. [Cf. **ethnology.**] (Accent **-nog-.**) **ethnographic(al)**[a], **ethnographer**[np].

ethnology = the branch which investigates human culture, customs, and social relations from the genetic standpoint. [Cf. **ethnography.**] **ethnologic(al)**[a], **ethnologist**[np].

ethnopsychology = 1. the branch of psychology which studies the mental interactions of a natural human group, a community, or a tribe; 2. sometimes restricted to the psychology of primitive peoples.

ethology = 1. the branch of science which investigates the evolution of ethics and comparative systems of ethics in various races; 2. the science or empirical study of human character. **ethological**[a].

ethos = the predominant characteristic of a racial or ethnic culture considered as a whole.

etiology = 1. the investigation of the causes or significant antecedents of a given phenomenon; 2. (in a broader sense) the study of causal relations. [Most frequently used in medical and biological science.] **etiological**[a].

etiquette = the prescribed ceremonial procedure in any given racial group, with regard to definite events in social intercourse; e.g. meeting, eating, etc. [Contr. w. **ritual** = an extended ceremonial procedure, prescribed for some general community occasion.] (Pron. **-kett.**) — Ger. *Etikette.*

eugenics = the branch of biology which deals with changes in the hereditary endowments of human beings, whether these changes are in the direction of improvement or of degeneracy. [A term coined by Galton (1883). Practical (i.e. applied) **eugenics** is concerned with measures for race improvement by promoting either the perpetuation of good heredity or the curtailment of bad. The scientific treatment is now generally called **genetics.**] **eugenic**[a], **eugenist**[np].

euglena = a flagellate protozoan. [The species *euglena viridis* is particularly of interest on account of its pigment spot, a very primitive type of visual receptor.]

eunuchism = the condition of a castrated male where castration has been effected mechanically by removal of the testicles. **eunuch**[np].

eunuchoidism = a condition resembling **eunuchism** but produced by atrophy of the testes without removal of the testes themselves. [Cf. **eunuchism.**] **eunuchoid**[a, np].

euphoria = 1. bodily comfort or well-being; 2. a pathological mental state characterized by unfounded feelings of well-being, optimism, and bodily health or strength. **euphoric**[a].

Eustachian tube = a tube which connects the tympanic cavity of the ear with the nasal pharynx. [It opens during the act of swallowing and permits adjustment of the air-pressure within the tympanic cavity in relation to that outside. Syn. **auditory tube** (prefd.).] (Accent **-take-.**) — Fr. *trompe d'Eustache*; Ger. *Eustachische Röhre, Ohrtrompete.*

euthenics = a branch of applied science which aims at the improvement of man by regulating his environment. [Contr. w. **eugenics,** which aims at the improvement of man by selective breeding.] **euthenic**[a].

evaluate[v] = (*math.*) to find the value of a dependent variable by assignment of a specific value or specific values to the independent variable or variables. **evaluative**[a].

evaluation = (*psychol.*) determination of the relative significance of phenomena of the same sort in terms of some standard. [Syn. **appreciation,** which implies a report as well as conscious reorganization of the data, and is a better contrast term to **description** (= a report of the data as actually observed.)] **evaluate**[v]. — Ger. *Auswertung.*

event = 1. an occurrence which involves a certain elapse of time during which some change occurs in the data; 2. any psychic *process*, as contr. w. so-called *states* or elements of consciousness. [Contr. w. **phenomenon** = a relatively static grouping of data.] — Fr. *événement*; Ger. *Ereignis, Geschehen.*

evidence = facts or principles cited, which point toward a given conclusion or which tend to settle the conflict between two or more opposing conclusions. [A method of utilizing the data so as to induce belief. Strictly, **evidence** includes both the data and the proof.] **evidential**[a] = pert. to evidence. — Ger. *Beweis.*

evidence/relation of = the relation mediating between two statements, the second of which is an inference from the first. [Sometimes confused with likeness, in that both **likeness** and **evidence** have been equated to agreement (as by Locke, Bain).]

evident = producing unhesitating belief, or acceptance of a conclusion. [Syn. **apparent;** ambiguous, being used also to characterize deceptive evidence and phenomena.] — Ger. *offenbar.*

evil[a] = characterizing actions which are contrary to accepted moral norms. [Contr. w. **righteous, good. righteous** and **evil** are now generally limited to theological literature; **good** and **bad** are used in both an ethical sense, and also (loosely) in judgments regarding the value of scientific work.] **evil**[n]. — Fr. *mal, mauvais*[a]; Ger. *übel.*

evil eye = a popular superstition, according to which certain individuals work harm to those upon whom they fix their gaze. — Fr. *mauvais oeil*; Ger. *böser Blick.*

evisceration = 1. removal of the viscera; 2. (*ophthal.*) removal of the contents of the eyeball, as distg. fr. **enucleation,** or removal of the eyeball in toto; 3. (*obstet.*) removal of the viscera of a fetus in embryotomy. **eviscerate**[v].

evolution = the series of phylogenetic changes in the structure or behavior of organisms. [In the broadest sense it includes consideration of all factors which may be involved, and embraces all changes whether in the direction of decrease or of increase in complexity. Distg. fr. **development** = the series of ontogenetic changes. Cf. **Darwinism, Lamarckism, evolution/mental, social evolution.**] **evolve**[v], **evolutionary**[a], **evolutional**[a]. — Ger. *Entwicklung.*

evolution/mental = the origin and growth in a given phylum of responsive behavior, including any indication of subjective experiences.

evolutionism = a type of theory which maintains that existing organic species have arisen by variation from earlier species. [Contr. w. **creationism,** which maintains that each species was created or formed separately and immediately.] **evolutionist**[np], **evolutionistic**[a]. — Ger. *Entwicklungslehre.*

exacerbation = (*pathol.*) an increasing degree of violence in the symptoms or manifestations of a disorder.

exaltation = 1. an abnormal increase in mental function or excitement, e.g. an exaltation of memory; 2. intense elation. [Cf. **elation.** Contr. w. **depression.**] — Ger. *Erregungszustand.*

examination = 1. an appraisal by means of tests and other data of an individual's status with respect to one or more specific fields of ability, achievement, or skill; or with respect to other psychological traits; 2. (*statist.*) systematic inspection of collected data with a view to judging their value. **examine**[v]. — Ger. (1) *Examen, Prüfung,* (2) *Untersuchung.*

example = a typical instance cited to illustrate a given principle. **exemplify**[v]. — Ger. *Beispiel.*

excitability = 1. the property of living tissue whereby it responds to stimulation, the response being either physical (e.g. movement of protoplasm, contraction) or chemical (e.g. change in metabolism, transmission of a nerve impulse); 2. an attitude marked by a low threshold to irritating stimuli of an affective nature, with resulting reactions in which there is an excessive emotional display. [Syn. (1) **irritability** (ambig.), **sensitivity** (to be avoided on account of its theoretical implications).] — Ger. *Erregbarkeit, Reizbarkeit.*

excitation = an active metabolic (or other) vital process in living tissue; e.g. the process initiated in nerve by a stimulus. [Distg. fr. **stimulation.** Contr. w. **inhibition.**] **excitatory**[a], **excite**[v]. — Ger. *Erregung.*

excitatory agent, see **stimulus.**

excitement = 1. the state of being excited or aroused to activity, i.e. the subjective counterpart of an **excitation;** 2. in Wundt's tridimensional theory of the feelings, an elementary feeling, contr. w. **depression** or **calm.** — Ger. (1) *Aufregung,* (2) *Erregung.*

excitement-inhibition/feeling of = one of the three dimensions or attributes of affective experience (Wundt). — Ger. *Erregungs-Beruhigungsgefühl.*

exciting cause = 1. the specific stimulus which, taken in conjunction with existing conditions, produces a given effect; 2. (*pathol.*) the stimuli or conditions which directly produce the outbreak of a psychosis, as contr. w. **predisposing cause.**

exclusion/method of = the systematic elimination of non-essential material in the process of inductive reasoning. [A stage in the Baconian method of **induction.**]

exercise[n] = 1. the frequent repetition of an act for the purpose of learning or of acquiring skill in performance; 2. a task or problem set for the purpose of training an individual; 3. the performance of a motor act which has already been learned. [Only (1) and (2) are used in a technical sense; these uses are distg. as **exercise** and **an exercise** resp.] **exercise**[v]. — Ger. *Übung.*

exercise/law of = a principle explanatory of **learning,** which states that the repetition of a connection between stimulus and response tends to strengthen that connection. [This law, more clearly than the closely related **law of frequency,** assumes that exercise, or repetition, causes a neural change, e.g. reduction of synaptic resistance. Syn. **law of use.**] — Fr. *l. de l'exercice.*

exhaustion = the limiting case of muscular fatigue, in which the stimulus or excitation ceases to elicit any overt motor response whatever. [Cf. **fatigue.**] — Fr. *épuisement*; Ger. *Erschöpfung.*

exhaustion psychosis = delirium-like reactions related to the hallucinoses which occur in endurance races. [Syn. **exhaustion delirium, collapse delirium.**]

exhibitionism = a tendency (usually compulsive) to display an erogenous part of the body, esp. the sex organs, for the purpose of inducing sex excitement. [According to psychoanalytic theory **exhibitionism** appears as a normal part of the libido in childhood and may, in some cases, fail to be repressed. Contr. w. **inspectionism.**] — Fr. *exhibitionnisme*; Ger. *Zeigelust.*

existence = 1. the actual presence of a given datum or condition in the physical universe at some specific time; 2. (*biol.*) the persistence of an organism as a living unit. **exist**[v]. — Ger. *Dasein, Existenz.*

existence/struggle for, see **struggle for existence.**

existential judgment = a judgment which implies the actual existence of the subject. [It is a generally recognized canon of modern logic that an existential judgment, to be valid, must depend upon empirical evidence — that it cannot be deduced from any set of mere assumptions or definitions.]

existential psychology = a systematic point of view which in effect limits the subject matter of psychology to the purely sensory or palpable aspects of experience. [The term has been coined to designate the systematic position of Titchener and other closely related positions. Cf. **structural psychology.**]

exodic, see **centrifugal.**

exogamy = a folk-custom, prevalent in certain tribes or races, whereby an individual must marry outside the limits of his own clan, phratry, or village. [Contr. w. **endogamy,** in which one must marry within his clan, etc.] **exogamous**[a].

exophoria, see **imbalance/muscular.**

exophthalmic goiter (or **goitre**) = a disease marked by prominence of the eyeballs, enlargement of the thyroid gland, muscular tremors, and rapid heart action, accompanied by more or less profound mental disturbance. [Believed to be due to overactivity of the thyroid gland. Syn. **Basedow's, Graves', Parry's disease.**]

exorcism = (*hist.*) the attempt to expel demons from the body of a possessed individual by pronouncing magic formulas or by a prescribed ritual. **exorcize**[v]. — Ger. *Beschwörung.*

exosomatic current = electrical current or potentials set up by agencies outside the living organism. [In galvanic skin measurements this term is used to describe the current used in Wheatstone bridge or Féré methods.]

exoteric = pert. to the superficial or apparent meaning of a system or theory, as opposed to the hidden or mystical meaning. [Contr. w. **esoteric.**]

expansion, expansiveness = a personality trait characterized by marked loquacity with reference to oneself. [In pathol. cases, a symptom of manic-depressive insanity. Cf. **euphoria.**] **expansive**[a].

expectancy = 1. (*psychol.*) the prospective chance of an occurrence based on experience. as contr. w. **expectancy** based on logical grounds; 2. (*statist.*) the mean value in the sample or population. [(2) ordinarily indicated by E preceding the variable or variables in question.]

expectation = a mental attitude characterized by tension and characteristic of attention. [**anticipation** emphasizes the motor preparation, **expectation** the emotional attitude, **foresight** or **forethought** the intellectual attitude toward future occurrences.] — Fr. *expectation, attente*; Ger. *Erwartung*.

expectation/error of = in psychological experiments, an error in (*a*) perception or (*b*) response. due to the observer's preconceived idea of what is to be presented or of when the presentation will occur. [In (*a*) the observer may report images as being actual perceptions, in (*b*) he may react to the wrong stimulus. Cf. **anticipatory response.** In psychophysics, applied esp. to the difference of judgment between ascending and descending series of stimuli.]

expectation/statistical = probability based upon mathematical calculation.

expedient[n] = an experimental device used to overcome some difficulty in either the apparatus, the general conditions, or the make-up of the observer.

experience[n] = 1. the integration of an individual's mental phenomena at a given moment, or during a given period; 2. a specific item, or phase, or aspect of (1); 3. the totality of mental phenomena occurring at a given moment which are received by the individual directly, i.e. excluding inferences (Titchener); 4. something lived, undergone, enjoyed, or the like (Spearman); 5. (*pop.*) knowledge derived from proof furnished by one's own senses. [Cf. **mental phenomena.**] (Accent -pee-.) **experience**[v] = to have **experience**[n], **experienced**[a] = pert. to the data, **experiential**[a] = pert. to the process. — Ger. (1, 2) *Erfahrung*, (3) *Erlebnis*.

experiencer = the individual (or self) in whose life the experiences under consideration occur.

experiential apprehension, see **apprehension, apprehension of experience.**

experiment = an observation or series of observations undertaken for scientific purposes, in which certain of the conditions are carefully prearranged, in order that certain specific relations or principles may be discovered. [Syn. **artificial observation.** Contr. w. **observation,** which in its narrower use implies absence of prearrangement on the part of the inquirer. Distg. fr. **investigation** = systematic examination of either sort.] (Accent **-per-**, not **-pee-**.) **experiment**[v], **experimental**[a]. — Fr. *expérience, essai*; Ger. *Experiment, Versuch*.

experiment/crucial, experimentum crucis = an experiment so planned that its result is relatively conclusive in respect to the affirmation or negation of some theory or question of fact. [It not infrequently follows a number of related preliminary experiments or investigations which narrow the issue to a single point, viz. the point to be settled in the crucial experiment.]

experiment of nature = any event or development which occurs without human prearrangement, but is analogous to an experiment, in that it bears directly upon the discovery of certain principles or relations of natural phenomena. [Often applied to diseases, particularly mental diseases, where intentional experimentation is not practicable.]

experimental psychology = the investigation of mental phenomena and the behavior of organisms by experimental methods.

experimental series = a temporal succession of observations, measurements, or trials designed to reveal the effect of one or more experimental variables. [It is sometimes called the **experiment proper,** in contr. w. the **control experiment** or **control series,** in which the crucial factor is absent or modified.]

experimentation = (*psychol.*) the art of arranging and conducting systematic attempts to measure psychological impressions, expressions, **functions,** or influences.

experimenter = (*psychol.*) one who attempts systematically to control, repeat, or vary conditions or stimuli, in order to produce or modify psychological responses. [Distg. fr. **subject** or **observer** (sometimes called **experimentee**), who undergoes the experiment and reports his experiences or otherwise reacts. In experimental researches, often abbrev. to **E** = experimenter (**S** = subject, and **O** = observer).] — Ger. *Versuchsleiter* (*Vl*).

expert[n] = an individual who has had special training in any given branch of science, art, or industry, such that his statements or judgments or activities in that field are entitled to special consideration. [In industry, denotes a tradesman of high competence, capable of working without supervision, i.e. superior to the **journeyman.** As adjective (accent **ex-**) used in connection with various fields, e.g. expert testimony, witness, psychologist; distg. fr. **expert**[a] (accent **-pert**) which denotes proficiency in a vague way.] (Accent **ex-**.) — Ger. *Sachverständiger, Fachmann*.

explanation = 1. the setting forth of a principle or the description of an event or procedure in such terms that the average hearer or reader will understand the operation; 2. (*tech.*) the description of a complex event plus evaluation of the factors involved, with the aim of showing how or by what processes the antecedent situation was transformed into the later situation. [(2) is distg. fr. **description,** which omits evaluation.] **explain**[v], **explanatory**[a]. — Ger. *Erklärung*.

explicit = directly stated or included in the data. [Contr. w. **implicit** or **tacit.**] — Ger. *ausdrücklich*.

explicit response, see **overt response.**

exploratory movements = those movements made by an organism in a relatively new situation, which serve to orient him and which yield data regarding the elements and spatial relations of the situation. [Applies esp. to behavior of children in connection with the learning process. The entire process is termed **exploration.**]

exponent = 1. (*math.*) a number denoting the power to which a given number or expression is to be raised; 2. (*psychol.*) an individual who exemplifies or teaches authoritatively a specific doctrine. [E.g. (1) in the expression $(x + y)^2$ the exponent 2 signifies that $x + y$ is to be squared, i.e. raised to the second power. Syn. (1) **index.**] — Fr. (1) *exposant*, (2) *exemple, exemplaire*; Ger. (1) *Exponent*, (2) *Vertreter*.

expression = 1. any response, simple or complex, of an organism; 2. the subsidiary accompaniments of a response (e.g. trembling, blushing, adjustment of facial muscles, etc.) which serve to indicate the effect of the situation upon an individual when the gross responses are inhibited or distorted; 3. modulations of the voice in speaking or singing, which accentuate the meaning or emotional value of the words or music; 4. (*rhet.*) a word, phrase, or formula, considered as a unit. — Ger. *Ausdruck, Äusserung, Ausdrucksbewegung.*

expression/esthetic = 1. the manifestation of any esthetic emotion or sentiment in any one of the fine arts; 2. the associated ideas which are aroused by, and suffuse the formal structure of a work of art. [Syn. **content** (of the work of art), contr. w. **form.**]

expression/facial, see **facial expression.**

expressive functions = the motor and glandular capacities of an organism in the broadest sense, including the autonomic functions as well as those of the striped muscles. [Syn. **motor functions,** properly limited to muscular response.]

extension = 1. the spatial characteristic of physical phenomena; 2. (*physiol.*) the straightening of a jointed member of the body, brought about by rotation of the portion which lies beyond the joint; 3. (*logic*) the objects, etc. denoted by a given concept. [Cf. (1) **extensity.** Contr. (2) w. **flexion** = the folding-in of the member by a reverse rotary movement.] **extend**[v]. — Ger. (1) *Ausdehnung.*

extensity = (*psychol.*) the spatial characteristic or attribute of mental phenomena. [**extensity, intensity, duration** (or **protensity**) and **attensity** are often grouped together as quantitative characteristics or attributes, and distg. fr. **quality** of sensations, etc.] **extensity**[a] (or **extensive**[a]) = pert. to **extensity; extensive**[a] = pert. to great extent.

extensor muscle, extensor = a muscle which serves to straighten out a member, generally counteracting the normal action of gravity. [Contr. w. **flexor,** which bends or folds the member. Cf. **antagonists.**]

extensor thrust reflex = a reflex extension of the leg elicited by pressure on the sole of the foot. [Mediated by 2d lumbar to 3d sacral segments of the cord. This reflex is a component of standing, walking, etc.] — Fr. *réflexe d'extension en poussée.*

extent = (*psychol.*) the one or two dimensional aspect of experience found in the visual and tactual sensory modalities. [A generic term, including **length** and **surface** or **area.**] — Fr. *étendue, étalement*; Ger. *Ausdehnung.*

external = 1. (*psychol.*) outside the body of an organism; 2. on the limbs, the side farthest from the median plane. [Contr. (1) w. **internal** = within the body.] **externality**[n]. — Ger. *äusserlich.*

external objects = objects outside the body of an organism. [Usually applied to objects as stimuli; contr. w. **sensations** or experiences resulting from stimulation. Cf. **external world.**]

external rectus, see **eye-muscles.**

external sense = any sense or receptor system so located as to be adequately stimulated only by energies which originate from sources outside the body of the organism. [Contr. w. **internal sense.** Cf. **sense, exteroceptor.**]

external world = 1. the totality of physical phenomena outside the body of a given organism; 2. the totality of spatio-temporal phenomena, distg. fr. the **ego** or **self,** but including the body of the percipient. [In psychol. usually limited to stimuli or possible stimuli.] — Fr. (1) *monde externe,* (2) *connaissance du monde extérieur*; Ger. *Aussenwelt.*

exteroceptor = a receptor or sense organ normally activated by energies which originate outside the organism. [In general, **exteroceptors** are associated with supporting tissues of ectodermal origin. Distg. fr. **interoceptor** and **proprioceptor.** Cf. **receptor; nociceptor.**] **exteroceptive**[a].

extinction/experimental = the weakening or abolition of a conditioned reflex by repeated excitation without reinforcement by the primary or unconditioned reflex. [Originally described as *fatigue* of the conditioned reflex, it is now ascribed by Pavlov to the development of a conditioned inhibition.]

extirpation = the removal of some organ or part of the body for experimental purposes. [The **extirpation method** consists in removing some part of the brain, some receptor organ, etc. in order to observe the effect on an animal's behavior or to trace the connecting nerve tracts by means of the ensuing degeneration. Distg. fr. **excision** = the surgical act.] — Ger. *Abtragung.*

extramural = outside the walls of a given institution. [E.g. extramural psychiatry = investigations conducted outside the hospital.]

extraneous = outside or beyond the proper limits of the subject, etc. under consideration.

extraspectral hue = a hue which is not found within the series of spectral colors. [Such hues range from the extreme spectral violet to the extreme spectral red, through a series of hues generically termed **purple,** and include the psychologically primary red itself.] — Fr. *nuance extra-spectrale.*

extraversion, extroversion = 1. an attitude or type of personality in which one's interests are directed mainly toward external nature and social phenomena, rather than toward himself and his own experiences (Jung); 2. an outward turning of the libido (Freud). [Contr. w. **introversion.**] **extravert (extrovert)**[np].

extrinsic = characterizing a value which attaches to a given object or datum due to its relation with other data or to its general setting. [Contr. w. **intrinsic** = value attaching to the object or datum itself. These terms are distg. fr. **external** and **inherent,** which apply to qualities rather than values, but are often used as syn.]

extrinsic eye-muscles, see **eye-muscles.** — Fr. *m. extrinsèques oculaires.*

extroversion, see **extraversion.**

eye = the receptor for the visual sense, i.e. for the reception of stimulation by radiant energy of wave-lengths approximately 400 to 760 millimicrons. [The human eye consists of the **eyeball** and **optic nerve,** together with several accessory structures. The **eyeball** is shielded in front by the **eyelids,** and behind by the bony walls of the **orbit.** It is moved by six ocular muscles (cf. **eye-muscles**) which are supplied by the **oculomotor, trochlear,** and **abducent nerves.** The **eyeball** is a spheroidal vesicle formed by three layers of tissue. The outermost layer consists of the **sclerotic coat (sclera),** which is replaced anteriorly by the transparent **cornea.** The middle layer consists of the **choroid coat,** the **ciliary body,** and the **iris.** The **ciliary body** contains the **ciliary muscles,** which serve for accommodation. The **iris** is attached to the ciliary body, and is reflected inward as a partition separating the space between the cornea and the lens into anterior and posterior chambers; the **iris** is perforated by a variable circular aperture, the **pupil.** The innermost layer of the eyeball is a nerve structure, the **retina,** which connects with the **optic nerve.** The retina consists of a number of layers (see Table XI); the **rods** and **cones** which comprise the 9th layer are the photosensitive cells. Within the eyeball toward the front is the **aqueous humor** in the anterior and posterior chambers; behind these the **vitreous body** in the posterior and largest portion of the eyeball, and between the aqueous humor and the vitreous body is the **lens.** Other accessory optical structures are the **lacrimal apparatus, conjunctiva,** and **vascular supply.** Several types of eye occur in animals. Cf. **simple eye, compound eye, ocellus.**] — Fr. *oeil*; Ger. *Auge.*

eyeball = the round movable organ which forms the external eye in the higher vertebrate forms. [Cf. **eye.**] — Fr. *globe de l'oeil*; Ger. *Augapfel.*

eyeground = the inner aspect of the back of the eyeball, esp. as seen through the pupil by means of the **ophthalmoscope.** [Syn. **fundus oculi, fundus,** which carries a more directly anatomical reference, **eyeground** referring rather to the picture presented to the examiner.] — Fr. *fond de l'oeil.*

eyelid closure reflex, see **corneal reflex** and **winking.**

eye-movements = rotary changes in the position of the eyeball due to contraction of the extrinsic eye-muscles. [The term does not ordinarily include changes in the lens or iris muscle.] — Fr. *mouvements oculaires*; Ger. *Augenbewegungen.*

eye-muscles = 1. (usually) the six *extrinsic* muscles which rotate the eyeball in various directions; 2. sometimes including also the *intrinsic* muscles, i.e. the **ciliary body,** and the muscle of the **iris.** [The **extrinsic muscles** in the human eye consist of 3 pairs (6 muscles) for each eye: (1) **internal rectus** and **external rectus,** which rotate the eyeball inward and outward respectively, (b) **superior rectus** and **inferior rectus,** which rotate the eyeball upward and downward respectively, and also inward, and (c) the **superior oblique** and **inferior oblique,** which rotate the eyeball downward and upward respectively, and also outward.]

eye reaction (or **response**), see **fixation response.** — Fr. *réaction de l'oeil.*

eye/reduced, /schematic, see **reduced eye.**

eye-wink reflex, see **winking.** — Fr. *r. du clignement palpébral.*

F

fables test = a test in which the testee is asked to tell what lesson a fable, which is read to him or by him, is intended to teach. [A test in the Stanford Revision of the Binet-Simon Scale].

face = the anterior aspect of the head, from the forehead to the chin. **facial**[a]. — Fr. *visage, face*; Ger. *Gesicht.*

face-to-face group, see **group/face-to-face.**

facet = the cornea which covers one of the elements, or ommatidia, of a compound eye.

facial angle = (*anthrop.*) the angle of projection of the forehead from the basal or horizontal plane of the skull, measuring the amount of prognathism or projection of the upper jaw. [In practice the measure differs according to the points of reference used. The **facial angle** is supposed to indicate the relative cerebral development of different races or individuals.] — Ger. *Gesichtswinkel.*

facial expression, facies = 1. the pattern of shape, form, shade, and color based on the anatomical structure of the face and the functional activity of facial, head, and neck muscles, regarded as indicative of the individual's emotional experiences, mental attitudes, etc.; 2. certain acquired patterns of facial activity used as social and language mechanisms. [(1) pop. believed to be indicative of character and personality; (2) an important factor in pantomime.]

facial nerve = the VII cranial nerve, efferent to the facial muscles and (through the chorda tympani) afferent from the taste organs, supplying the anterior 2/3 of the tongue. [It arises from the brain at the lower border of the pons between the olive and the inferior cerebellar peduncle.]

facilitation = 1. increased ease of performance, measured by decrease in time of accomplishing an act and decrease in tensions and irregularities in its performance, or by increase of output; 2. (*neurol.*) summation, whether of nerve impulses, of synaptic charges, or of tonal or contractional effects in muscles; the stimuli of which the effects are thus summed may be applied either simultaneously or successively. [Syn. **summation, induction, reinforcement.**] — Fr. *frayage*; Ger. *Bahnung.*

facilitation/retroactive = the tendency of a later formed association to strengthen a previously formed association. [Cf. **retroaction.**]

facilitation/social, see **social facilitation.**

fact = an actual occurrence, or state of things, whether objective or subjective, as distg. fr. a statement, opinion, belief, or theory. [**questions of fact** = undiscovered phenomena, or reported phenomena whose reality or details are disputed, distg. fr. **questions of theory,** concerned with interpretation or explanation of phenomena; and fr. **questions of definition,** concerned with the distinguishing and characterization of concepts, whether representing reality or not.] **factuality**[n] (abstract), **factual**[a]. — Fr. *fait*; Ger. *Tatsache.*

factor = 1. a force or condition which cooperates with other forces or conditions to bring about a given situation or result; 2. (*math.*) one of the two or more quantities which enter into a product. [Contr. (1) w. **element** = a constituent part of the situation itself.] **factorial**[a] (rarely used for (2), but admissible).

factor theories of intelligence = theories, based on empirical and statistical findings, which seek to explain intelligence, as a measurable phenomenon, in terms of relations among capacities which vary in number, extensity, and organization. [Several (conflicting) theories have been proposed, which may be classed as (1) central or **g** factor theories; (2) group factor theories; (3) multimodal theories, i.e. theories based on many specific factors. Cf. **c factor, g factor, s factor, w factor.**]

factitious = pert. to an artifact or human production. [Syn. **artifactual** (prefd.); see **artifact.**]

factual, see **fact.**

faculty = 1. (*hist.*) a power or agency of the mind (e.g. intellect, feeling, will) through the action and interaction of which all mental phenomena were at one time supposed to be explained; 2. ability in any given performance. [(1) was the basis of a historic school or system of psychology known as the **faculty psychology,** and in this sense is still in popular use; it is now generally avoided by psychologists; (2) is frequently used in a non-technical way.] — Ger. *Vermögen, Seelenvermögen.*

faculty psychology = a historic school or system of psychology, based upon the classification of mental processes and performances under a small number of generic powers, called *faculties*, which are treated as entities, causes, or principles of explanation for the facts themselves. [Chr. Wolff and Th. Reid are typical exponents of this system.]

fad = 1. a line of activity, pursued by an individual with undue zeal, and not directly connected with his economic or vital interests; 2. anything new, temporarily adopted by the general public, usually as a result of publicity. — Fr. *caprice*; Ger. *Liebhaberei* (*Steckenpferd* = hobby).

failure = 1. the absence of results or usable data in an experiment; 2. (*soc.*) an individual whose social adjustment is inadequate. — Fr. (1) *échec,* (2) *manque*; Ger. (1) *Misserfolg.*

faint[a] = weak, lacking intensity, or hardly perceptible. **faintness**[n]. — Fr. *faible*[a], *languissant*[a]; Ger. *schwach.*

faint[n] = a state characterized by loss of consciousness due to circulatory disturbances. [Syn. **swoon.**] **faint**[v]. — Fr. *évanouissement*; Ger. *Ohnmacht.*

faintness = 1. a relatively low degree of intensity; 2. an organic condition characterized by dizziness or muscular weakness; 3. a partial loss of conscious integration. **faint**[a]. — Fr. *faiblesse*; Ger. *Schwäche.*

faith = acceptance (of a doctrine, principle, etc., or of an individual's moral integrity, etc.) which goes beyond perceptual or logical evidence, and is usually accompanied by some feeling or emotion. [Distg. fr. **belief,** in which the intellectual factor is emphasized. E.g. belief in the truth of a scientific law; faith in immortality. Little used in psychol. today as a technical term, except in connection with religion.] — Fr. *foi*; Ger. *Glaube.*

faith cure = the healing of disease by the patient's mental attitude alone, without resort to drugs or surgery. [The term covers a number of pop. and partly scientific theories of healing, historic and modern, variously known as **mind cure, mental healing, metaphysical healing, Christian science, Couéism,** etc., some of which assign the power to the healer, others to the patient; the scientific investigation of the modes and limits of this method of treatment is properly called **psychotherapy,** or **psychotherapeutics.**] — Fr. *guérison par la foi.*

fall chronometer = an instrument for measuring time intervals by means of the fall of a heavy weight. [Usually limited to instruments in which the weight falls vertically with a minimum of friction. Syn. **gravity chronometer.**] — Fr. *chronomètre de chute.*

fallacy = an error in reasoning which makes the conclusion seem valid when it is not, or which leads to an improper conclusion. [A fallacy may be detected by more attentive consideration of the reasoning without adducing any further data. Distg. fr. **error of procedure,** in gathering data, for which we have only the untechnical term **mistake. material fallacies** are those in which the conclusion follows from the premises but the conclusion is not the one required, or the premises are improperly assumed. See Table VI.] **fallacious**[a]. — Fr. *sophisme*; Ger. *Trugschluss.*

false reaction, see **anticipatory response.**

false vocal cords, see **vocal cords.**

falsity = a general term for what is characterized by lack of correspondence between a report, a conclusion, etc. and the objective facts or situation on which these are based. [Distg. fr. **inaccuracy,** in which the degree of lack is emphasized.] **false**[a]. — Fr. *fausseté, faux*; Ger. *Falschheit, Unrichtigkeit.*

fame = 1. the estimate on the part of a large number of individuals regarding the actions and characteristics of a given person; 2. a widely disseminated opinion or rumor. [Distg. (1) fr. **reputation** and **prestige,** which designate the estimation of a limited number of contemporary individuals; **fame** (1) is widely disseminated, is usually favorable, and may be posthumous.] **famous**[a] (applied to the object of fame). — Fr. *renom*; Ger. *Ruhm.*

familial = pert. to the family.

familiar[n], **familiar spirit** = (*hist.*) a spirit or demon supposed to attend on an individual, or to come at his call; the invisible agent of a sorcerer or witch. [Often identified in the form of a cat or dog seen with a witch.]

familiarity = acquaintance with an object or with an act to be performed, resulting in ease and quickness of recognition or of performance. **familiar**[a].

familiarity feeling = a specific feeling or experiential datum attaching to certain experiences, which serves as a cue to their identification with earlier experiences, i.e. as basis for **recognition.** — Fr. *sentiment de familiarité*; Ger. *Bekanntheitsgefühl.*

family = 1. a group of individuals typically represented by father, mother, and children, but including also groups lacking one parent, or groups embracing other relatives, adopted children, and in some cultures, slaves, and servants; 2. (*biol.*) a group of closely related genera constituting an element of the larger group above it, known as **order.** [(1) is extended to include the patterns of behavior or attitudes which characterize the institution of the family. **familial**[a].

family constellation = (*indiv. psychol.*) the number, age, and personality-traits of all persons in the family, conceived as influencing the style of life of a given child.

fanaticism = an attitude of excessive devotion to a given theory or practice (usually involving zeal for its propagation) which eventuates in activities and emotions of an extreme order. [The term generally carries a derogatory implication.] **fanatic**[np]. — Fr. *fanatisme.*

fancy = 1. the mental representation of a scene or occurrence which is recognized as unreal but is either expected or hoped for; 2. (*pop.*) moderately intense liking. [(1) is often used loosely as a syn. for **imagination** or for **day-dreaming.** Cf. **fantasy,** an older form of the same word.] **fanciful**[a] (1), **fancied**[a] (1, 2), **fancy**[v]. — Fr. (1) *fantaisie*; Ger. *Phantasie.*

fantasm, phantasm = a vivid subjective visual representation of a form or a person or of what is assumed to be a disembodied spirit. [When the representation is regarded as the product of subjective processes, it is called a **fantasm** or **phantasm;** when regarded as the product of perception, an **apparition.**]

fantastic = weird, whimsical, or distorted in shape. [Improperly used as adj. for **fancy** and **fantasy.**]

fantasy, phantasy = (*hist.*) syn. for **imagination.** [Gk. **phantasia** = capacity to form images (Lat. **imaginatio**). The process terminates in (*a*) images derived from sense perception, memory images; or (*b*) abnormal images, called **phantasms** or **fantasms** (hallucinations). The popular term **fancy** confuses these two meanings. Cf. **autistic thinking.**]

farad = a unit of electrical capacity; the capacity of a condenser which retains one coulomb of charge with one volt difference of potential. [The **microfarad** (= 0.000,001 farad) is the most frequently used unit.]

faradic current = the alternating electrical current produced by the secondary winding of an induction coil.

far-sight, farsightedness = a condition of the organ of vision, characterized by ability to see distant objects clearly, and inability to obtain clear and distinct pictures of nearby objects. [The condition may be either **hyperopic** or **presbyopic;** distg. fr. **near-sight** or **myopia.**] **farsighted**[a] (used more often in a figurative sense, to characterize individuals who foresee the probable course of distant events). — Ger. *Weitsichtigkeit.*

fashion = a phase of custom or convention which develops rather quickly and disappears after a time. [**fashion** applies esp. to the display or use of material objects, rather than to acts; **fad** and **craze** are temporary variants of **fashion.** Distg. fr. **custom** (in the broader sense), which is more stable and persistent.] — Fr. *mode, vogue*; Ger. *Mode.*

fatalism = the doctrine which holds that all the acts of man are inevitably predestined. [Strictly, syn. w. **determinism,** but commonly used with the connotation that environmental influence is negligible. Contr. w. free-will doctrine (**libertarianism**).]

father complex, see **Electra complex.**

fatigue = 1. decreased ability of performance on the part of an organism, or of some member or muscle, resulting from prolonged work; 2. a specific feeling or sensation, experienced after prolonged work. [**fatigue** (1) is classed as (*a*) **mental,** resulting from prolonged fixation of attention or work upon a problem, etc.; (*b*) **muscular,** resulting from prolonged exercise of some group of the larger skeletal muscles; (*c*) **sensory;** or (*d*) **reflex. fatigue** (2) is often differentiated into corresponding classes. Syn. (2) **weariness.**] **fatigue**[v], **fatigued**[a]. — Ger. *Ermüdung.*

fatigue/auditory = decrease in the sensitivity of the ear due to prolonged acoustic stimulation.

fatigue/nerve = 1. reduced capacity of the neuron for conduction, as a result of repeated stimulation; 2. (*pop.*) **neurasthenia.** [Fatigued nerve shows a more or less prolonged refractory phase.]

fatigue/retinal (or **visual**) = depletion of the capacity of the retina to respond to light and color stimuli. [Postulated to explain negative after-images, successive contrast, etc.]

fatiguability = the relative rate at which fatigue increases in an organ, or in an individual, as compared with other organs or individuals. [Cf. **fatigue.**] — Ger. *Ermüdbarkeit.*

faucial reflex = contraction of the fauces, gagging, or vomiting, elicited by irritation of the fauces, or passage from mouth to pharynx. [Mediated by IX and X cranial nerves and oblongata.]

fault = 1. a defect in apparatus, method, or procedure, which interferes with the reliability or validity of the results; 2. a minor moral defect. [Distg. (1) fr. **fallacy** = a defect in reasoning.] **faulty**[a] (1). — Ger. *Fehler.*

Faxensyndrom = a term used by Bleuler to denote a prison psychosis characterized by irrelevant ("clownish") behavior. [It suggests malingering, but is actually dissociated from the remainder of the personality.]

fear = emotional behavior characterized by a feeling-tone of unpleasantness, and accompanied by activity of the sympathetic nervous system together with various types of postural and motor reactions, e.g. trembling, prostration, flight, convulsive seizures. [Often grouped with **anger** and **love** as the three primitive emotions.] — Fr. *peur, frayeur*; Ger. *Furcht.*

feature profile test = a type of combination test in which the task is to assemble seven pieces to complete the profile (three pieces) and the ear (four pieces) of a man's head. [Cf. **formboard test.**]

febrile delirium, febrile psychosis = mental symptoms, usually of a delirious character, especially associated with a rise in body temperature.

feces[pl], **faeces** = the solid or relatively solid unassimilable material excreted from the body after the process of digestion. **fecal**[a].

Fechner-Helmholtz law, see **coefficient law.**

Fechner weight holders = an apparatus devised by G. T. Fechner for the presentation of stimuli in his lifted weight experiments; each holder was a square-bottomed receptacle covered with a lid and lifted by a handle in the act of comparison; holders for standard- and comparison-weights were identical except for a small differential weight fastened to the lid of the latter. — Fr. *soutiens de poids de F.*

Fechner's law = a formulation of the relation between changes of stimulus intensity and changes in sensation, proposed by G. T. Fechner as an extension of **Weber's law** and expressed as follows: "A change in sensation occurs when the stimulus is increased or decreased by a given proportion of itself, this proportion being constant for any given sense." [The law may be expressed in other ways: "A sensation varies as the logarithm of the stimulus"; "Sensation varies arithmetically as the stimulus varies in geometrical ratio." The formula is $S = K \log R$, where S is the magnitude of sensory intensity measured from the **absolute threshold** as zero; R is the magnitude of the stimulus measured with the **absolute threshold** as a unit; and K is an appropriate constant. It is the principal experimental result in Fechner's Elemente der

Psychophysik (1860), a book which established the methods for the measurement of sensation and thus contributed greatly to the founding of experimental psychology. **Fechner's law** is frequently incorrectly called **Weber's law,** and is now often referred to as the **Weber-Fechner law.** The law has provoked much controversy and is now conceded to be only an approximation to the truth.]

Fechner's paradox = in binocularly viewing, e.g. a landscape, while one eye is covered with a moderately light smoked glass, the total impression becomes *brighter* the instant that eye is completely occluded. [The paradox consists in the fact that a brighter impression is thus received when part of the light is withdrawn.]

Fechner's shadow experiment = an experimental demonstration of Weber's law: a pole casts two separate shadows on a screen; these shadows are caused to vary independently by altering the intensity of the lights or their distance from the screen; the difference thresholds between the two shadows are thus determined at various levels of screen brightness. (Fechner, 1860).

fecundity = physiological capacity of a given organism to participate in reproduction. [Often used as syn. for **fertility,** = (strictly) the number of actual offspring attributable to the given organism. Contr. w. **sterility** (or **infecundity**).] **fecund**[a].

feeblemindedness = 1. a generic term covering all grades of mental inferiority or backwardness; 2. (British usage) the type of mental deficiency nearest to the normal, known in America as **moron.** [Cf. **idiot, imbecile, moron.**] **feebleminded**[a, np]. — Fr. *faiblesse mentale*; Ger. *Schwachsinn*.

feel[vt] = to explore actively through the sense of touch. [Syn. **palp**[v], **palpete.**] **feel**[n]. Fr. *palper, tâter*.

feel[vi], see **feeling.**

feeling[n] = 1. an affective experience, esp. of pleasantness or of unpleasantness; 2. emotional or interoceptive experience (w. qualifying adj.); 3. (*hist.*) sensation; an indefinite sensation, or any conscious state; 4. (*hist.* and *pop.*) cutaneous experience, esp. touch; 5. (*pop.*) an opinion based on admittedly indefinite grounds. [In the earlier psychology, often used as (4) syn. for *touch*, one of the 5 senses, including also (1) the indefinite bodily states (pleasure, pain, etc.). James used the term to denote any immediate experience or conscious phenomenon. Ward made the distinction between **feeling** and **sensation** on the basis that the former is known as pert. to the knowing subject, the latter to the object known. At present the term and its associate forms are confined by most writers to uses (1) and (2), except **to feel**[v], which retains the tactual meaning. Syn. (1, 2) **affection, affective experience**; for **feeling**[a], the syns. **affective** and **hedonic** are much used. Syn. (4) **feel**[n]. Cf. **feeling tone.**] **feel**[v] (in all meanings), **feeling**[a] = pert. to **feeling, felt**[a] = pert. to the arousing of **feeling.** — Fr. (1) *affection*, (2, 3) *sentiment*; Ger. *Gefühl*.

feeling/esthetic = the affective tone of pleasantness or unpleasantness which is the core of esthetic experience. — Fr. *sentiment esthétique*.

feeling of activity, see **activity/feeling of.**

feeling of reality, of unreality, see **reality/feeling of, unreality/feeling of.** — Fr. *sentiment de réalité*.

feeling tone = 1. a sensation or affective datum which accompanies other sensations; 2. an affective attribute of sensation. [Opinion differs as to whether it is an attribute or an independent datum; in either view, feeling tones are distinguished as **pleasant** and **unpleasant.**] — Fr. *ton affectif*; Ger. *Gefühlston*.

feigning = a behavior attitude which reproduces the characteristic posture and signs of a totally different organic condition. [E.g. death-feigning, fear-feigning. Cf. **tonic immobility.**] — Fr. *feinte, simulation*.

fellatio = the performance of the sex act by the introduction of the penis into the oral cavity.

felt, see **feeling.**

female[n] = an organism which produces ova or egg-cells. [Biol. symbol ♀. Contr. w. **male,** which produces sperm cells. Cf. **sex.**] **female**[a] = intrinsically characteristic of females or of the female sex (e.g. female voice); **feminine**[a] = associated with the female sex (e.g. feminine attire). — Fr. *femelle, féminin*[a]; Ger. *Weibchen*[a].

feminine, see **female.**

feminism = 1. a social movement for the advancement of the female sex, esp. in the economic and political spheres; 2. (*biol.*) the possession by certain male individuals of feminine traits to a marked degree. [Cf. **effemination.**] **feminist**[np] (1).

feminization = the structural, functional, and behavioristic changes which follow successful implantation of ovarian tissue into a castrate male animal, involving regression of male characteristics together with the development of female qualities. [In psychology sometimes used to characterize personality change from so-called masculine attitudes to so-called feminine attitudes as a result of social or other factors.]

femur = the thigh bone. (Accent **fee-**.) **femora**[pl], **femoral**[a] (accent **fem-**). — Ger. *Schenkel*.

fenestra cochleae (or **rotunda**) see **window/round.**

fenestra vestibuli (or **ovalis**) see **window/oval.**

Féré phenomenon, see **galvanic skin response.**

ferment, see **enzyme.**

Ferree rotary campimeter = an apparatus operated on the principle of a fixed field of stimulation and a movable fixation point, used to explore the sensitivity of the retina in the entire visual field up to an angle of 92° from the center; the fixated stimulus is attached to a special radial arm which ends in a branch at right angles to the plane of the campimeter screen; an electric color-mixer is attached to this radial arm to determine the color seen in peripheral vision; eight radial arms, including the special stimulus arm, are attached to a collar that may be rotated about an opening through which the peripheral stimulus is seen, and serve as guides for the adjustment of the stimulus. [A modification permits the use of spectroscopic colors.]

Ferrier's experiment = an experiment devised by David Ferrier to demonstrate that sensations do not arise from efferent nerve impulses; it consisted in resting a finger upon a trigger and imagining vividly the act of pressing it without actually moving the finger; the result showed that the sensations attributed to the efferent impulses are actually kinesthetic sensations from neighboring muscles, from breathing, etc. [Cf. **innervation feelings.**]

fertility = 1. the characteristic of an organism of having produced offspring; 2. the characteristic of having produced numerous offspring. [Degrees of **fertility** of different species or members of a given species admit of numerical treatment. Syn. **fecundity,** which (strictly) means capacity for reproduction. Contr. w. **infertility,** or (in man) **childlessness.**] **fertile**[a]. — Ger. *Fruchtbarkeit.*

fertilization = the process whereby an ovum, or egg, is caused to begin its development into an independent organism. [The process consists normally in the union of a **sperm** and an **ovum** cell; but artificially certain ova may be fertilized without such union.] **fertilize**[v].

fetish, fetich = (*anthrop.*) an object to which some magical potency or *mana* is attributed, usually by way of protecting the owner or wearer. [No exact opposite in use.] — Fr. *fétiche.*

fetishism = (*pathol.*) a pathological condition characterized by an erotic attachment to certain parts of the body, or (more generally) to certain articles of clothing worn by the object of attachment, usually resulting in sexual gratification. **fetish**[n] = the object of attachment.

fetus, foetus = an embryo in its more advanced stages of development. [Used both loosely and technically — the latter for the human embryo after the second month.] **fetal (foetal)**[a].

fiat = a distinctive determinative experience which sometimes attends an act of volition or choice between alternatives (James).

fiber, fibre = a single nerve axon with its collaterals. [A **nerve** consists of a collection (or bundles) of nerve **fibers.**] **fibered (fibral)**[a]. — Ger. *Faser.*

fibril = one of the threads or filaments sometimes present within a neuron. **fibrils (fibrillae)**[pl], **fibrillar**[a].

fibrous layer = the 9th stratum of the retina from without inward, which consists of the axons of the ganglion cells of the 8th layer passing across the surface of the retina to collect and form the **optic nerve.** [Syn. **layer of nerve fibers.** See Table XI.] — Fr. *couche fibreuse*; Ger. *Faserschicht.*

fiction = 1. an imagined condition of affairs proved or believed to be contrary to reality; 2. (*indiv. psychol.*) an imaginary social situation conceived by an individual as a means of gratifying the will to power, and accepted as a reality; in particular, the make-believe of a neurotic by which a simulated illness is utilized to command the world about him. [Improperly used for **artifact** = a human construction or device.] **fictitious**[a]. — Ger. (1) *Erdichtung.*

field investigation = (*soc.*) the investigation of social conditions, heredity, etc. by interviews and observations. — Fr. *investigation relative au milieu.*

field of consciousness, see **consciousness/field of.**

field observation, field studies = the observation of animal behavior in the natural habitat. [Contr. w. **experimentation** = observation of behavior under set laboratory conditions.] — Fr. *observations éthologiques.*

field of touch, see **touch/field of.** — Fr. *champ tactile.*

field of vision, see **visual field.** — Fr. *champ visuel.*

field/tubular = constriction of the visual field, either hysterical or structural. — Fr. *champ tubulaire.*

fifth (*mus.*), see **interval** and Table VII.

fighting instinct, see **pugnacity.**

figure = (*psychol.*) a group of impressions derived from a single sense, which are perceived as a unit or object. [Contr. w. **ground** = the unfocused or unattended to impressions surrounding the figure; **figure is** used non-technically to denote a numeral, a drawing, a symbolic example; **figurative**[a] in latter sense only.] **figured**[a].

figure-ground = a general characteristic of perception in accordance with which segregation of the total field results in such a way that different parts are endowed with different degrees of shape and articulation, the highly-shaped parts being the **figures,** the less shaped ones the **ground.** [As a rule the organization does not possess such a simple duality of characters (viz. one ground with one or several figures upon it), but what is ground for one figure will be a figure on another ground.] — Fr. *figure et fond.*

filial = pert. to the offspring. [Contr. w. **parental.**]

filial generations = the successive generations from a given parent or pair. [The immediate offspring are called **first filial generation** (F_1), the offspring of the latter, **second filial generation** (F_2), etc.]

filial regression/law of = a principle formulated by Francis Galton, which states that the quantitative value of characters in the offspring tend, as a whole, to regress or revert toward the average value represented by the general group to which the parents belong. [Thus the offspring of two very tall or two very short parents would be more nearly of average height than the parents themselves.] — Fr. *l. de régression filiale*; Ger. *Rückschlagsgesetz.*

filiform script = a term applied to written words which end in a sinuous dash with no recognizable letters. [Literally, *threadlike.*]

filiform papilla, see **papilla.**

fillet = 1. (*neurol.*) a band of afferent fibers which arise in the cuneate and gracilis nuclei, ascend in the medulla just behind the pyramidal tracts, and cross in the sensory decussation; 2. (*esth.*) a narrow moulding, usually on a column, having the appearance of a narrow band like that used to confine the hair. — Ger. *Schleife.*

film color = a color which presents a filmy or non-substantial **mode of appearance** to visual introspection, e.g. the colors seen in the field of a spectroscope. — Fr. *couleur pelliculaire*; Ger. *Flächenfarbe.*

filum terminale = a thread-like tubular extension of the pia mater at the caudal end of the spinal cord; it contains remnants of the cord substance.

final = 1. pert. to the last term of a series; 2. syn. for **purposive, telic.**

final cause = that state of affairs for the sake of attaining which, action is undertaken.

final common path = motor neurons, or neurons at a higher level upon which nerve impulses from several other neurons converge (Sherrington). [Cf. **end-path.**] — Fr. *voie terminale commune.*

finalism = 1. the doctrine of purposiveness; 2. (*psychoan., indiv. psychol.*) the interpretation of life processes in terms of their goals. [Syn. (1) **teleology.**]

finality, see **purpose, finalism.**

finger spelling = a method of language communication whereby words are spelled on the fingers, a given position of the fingers indicating one letter of the alphabet. [There are two commonly-used manual alphabets, one making use of both hands and the other of one hand only.] — Fr. *épellation (langage) digitale*; Ger. *Fingersprache*.

finite = having measurable limits. [Two orders which are not finite are the infinitely small and the infinitely great. Contr. w. **infinite** = unlimited or possessing a value too great to be measured. Cf. **infinity.**]

fire-worship = a historic type of religion whose central object of adoration is fire. [Directed either toward fire itself, or toward a deity representing the principle of fire.] — Fr. *culte du feu*; Ger. *Feuerverehrung, Feueranbetung*.

fission = a method of reproduction found in nearly all unicellular and in a few lower multicellular species, in which the parent divides into two parts, each of which grows into a full-sized organism resembling it. [Cf. **reproduction.**] — Fr. *scissiparité*.

fissure = a deep depression or furrow in the surface of the brain, due to overgrowth of the surrounding gyri. [E.g. Rolandic fissure; Sylvian fissure. Syn. **sulcus.**] — Fr. *scissure, sillon*; Ger. *Furche, Spalt*.

fit^n = a succession of convulsions. — Fr. *attaque*.

fitness = (*biol.*) adaptation to the conditions of the environment; i.e. capability of an organism, due to its structural organization, to meet the general conditions of life. [Cf. **fittest/survival of the.**] **fit**^{a}, **fitted**^{a}, **the fit**^{np}. — Fr. *apte*^{a}.

fitness/feeling of = a feeling or judgment (*a*) of the ethical worth of a certain course of conduct, or (*b*) of the harmony of a given object or composition with esthetic standards. — Fr. *sentiment de la congruence*.

fittest/survival of the = a phrase originated by Herbert Spencer to designate the principle that those individual organisms or species whose structural organization is such as to best meet the general conditions of life will, on the average, live or endure longest and propagate most extensively. [Cf. **natural selection, struggle for existence.**] — Fr. *survivance des plus aptes*.

fix^v, **fixate**^{v}, see **fixation** (1), (2).

fixation = 1. (*learning*) the process of establishing or automatizing a motor habit, or of memorizing some given material; usually measured by the decrease (*a*) in time of performance, or (*b*) in number of accessory movements or errors; 2. (*vis.*) the directing and focusing of the eye, or both eyes, upon a certain point in space in such a way that an image of this point falls upon the fovea or foveas; extended also to the focusing of the eye or eyes upon a moving point in pursuit movement; 3. (*psychoan.*) an arrest or attachment of one of the component impulses of the libido to an early stage of psychosexual development, usually pregenital. [Contr. (1) w. **acquisition.**] **fixate**^{v} (2), **fix**^{v} (1, 2).

fixation/binocular = the focusing of both eyes upon the same point in space. [Syn. **binocular focusing** (ambig.).]

fixation-line, line of fixation = the straight line which joins the object of fixation and the center of rotation of the eyeball. — Ger. *Fixationslinie*.

fixation pause = a momentary cessation of eye-movement, in which the image of the object is at rest and in focus upon corresponding points of the retinas. [In reading and in other rapid eye-work, these pauses ordinarily endure only a fraction of a second.]

fixation-point, point of fixation = 1. the point in space upon which one or both eyes are fixated; 2. the point on the retina upon which the image of the fixated point or object falls; 3. (*psychoan.*) an emotional attachment to one of the pregenital stages of libido development. [Cf. **fixation.**] — Ger. (1, 2) *Blickpunkt, Fixationspunkt*.

fixation response (or **reflex**) = the response of the eye in turning to fixate an extrafoveal light stimulus. [Mediated by the optic tracts and oculomotor nerves. Syn. **eye reaction** (ambig.).]

fixation response time = the interval between the onset of an extrafoveal stimulus and the beginning of movement of the eye to fixate that stimulus. [Photographic records by the Dodge corneal reflection method show an approximate mean of 180 σ. The time is modified through practice under specific conditions. Syn. **eye reaction time** (ambig.).] — Fr. *temps de réaction de fixation de l'oeil*.

fixation time, fixation pause duration = the time which elapses in visual fixation, from the completion of one saccadic eye-movement to the beginning of the next, in reading and other quick visual work. [Contr. w. **saccadic time.** Cf. **fixation pause.**]

fixed idea = an idea or trend of thought which tends to recur and dominate the mental life of a given individual. [It may be symptomatic of certain psychoneuroses, e.g. **obsessional neuroses.**] — Fr. *idée fixe*.

flagellata, flagellates = an order of unicellular organisms which move by the intermittent lashing of one or more whip-like projections, or flagella; e.g. euglena.

flagellation = the practice of whipping, esp. in order to arouse emotional experience and induce attitudes of penitence, remorse, exaltation, mysticism, or sex excitement. [Often practiced at the instigation of the individual himself and sometimes practiced on himself.] — Ger. *Geisselung*.

flagellum = a lash-like structure projecting from certain unicellular organisms and from certain cells in multicellular organisms. [Cf. **flagellate.**]

flat^n = (*mus.*) 1. a tone whose pitch is slightly lower than a given standard; 2. a tone which is a semitone lower than some natural tone, or the sign (♭) used to indicate this lowering of pitch. [Contr. w. **sharp.**] **flat**^{a}. — Fr. (1) *ton grave(bas)*, (2) *bémol*.

flatworms, platyhelminthes = an invertebrate phylum of soft-bodied, bilaterally symmetrical, usually flattened animals, such as **planarians, flukes,** and **tapeworms.** [Formerly grouped with **annulata** and others as a single phylum of **vermes,** or worms. **planaria** form a typical genus of flatworms.] — Fr. *ver plat*.

flavor = a mingled but unitary experience which includes sensations of taste, smell, and pressure, and often sensations of warmth or cold or mild pain. [Best used technically to denote the olfactory experiences conditioned by food in the mouth or pharynx.] — Fr. *saveur, goût*.

flexibilitas cerea = a symptom of schizophrenia and occasionally of hysteria, in which an impressed attitude or posture of the patient is abnormally retained.

flexibility = 1. capacity (of a bodily member, etc.) to bend; 2. (*fig.*) the fact that a given term, theory, etc. may be extended to any one of a group of related meanings; 3. the capacity of an individual to alter his mental attitude or adjust himself readily to changing situations. [Syn. (3) **adaptability** (prefd.).] **flexible**[a].

flexion = the bending in of a jointed member of the body. [Contr. w. **extension** = the straightening of the member by a reverse movement.] **flex**[v]. — Fr. *flexion*.

flexion reflex = withdrawal of the lower limb at knee, hip, and ankle, usually upon nociceptive stimulation. [Mediated by 2d lumbar to 3d sacral segments of the cord. Cf. **nociceptive reflex, mass reflex.**] — Fr. *phénomène des raccourcisseurs*.

flexor muscle, flexor = a muscle whose function is to withdraw or flex some member of the body. [They are largely the protective muscles of the body, being prepotent over extensors when nociceptive stimuli are operating. Cf. **flexion.** Contr. w. **extensor.** Cf. **antagonists.**] — Fr. *muscle fléchisseur*.

flexure = the bending of an organ or of the body, esp. of the medullary tube, during embryonic growth. [The specific regions of bending are identified by local names; e.g. cervical flexure, sigmoid flexure, etc.] — Fr. *courbure*.

flicker, flicker phenomenon = (*vis.*) a rapid periodic change perceived in a visual impression, due to a corresponding rapid periodic change in the intensity or some other character of the stimulus. [**flicker** disappears when the frequency of the stimulus-change exceeds a rate called the **critical flicker frequency,** which is about 25 to 30 cycles per second when each cycle consists of a moderately bright and a wholly dark half-period; the critical rate is somewhat higher at higher intensity-levels and lower for lower intensities; the rate is lowered with decrease in the intensity-difference between parts of the period.] — Fr. *papillotement*; Ger. *Flimmern*.

flicker/auditory = an auditory experience caused by intermittent stimulation, the beginning and end of each stimulus being sharply defined. [The phenomenon may be produced by a method similar to that for **visual flicker,** by rotating a sector between the ear and the sound source. Syn. **tonal intermittence.** Distg. fr. **pulsation,** in which the intensity of stimulation varies gradually.]

flicker/chromatic = a pulsating or flicker phenomenon in the visual field due to differences in either hue or saturation, or both, between stimuli of equal brilliance which are alternately applied to the same retinal area. [Distg. fr. **flicker** in general, which may involve also pulsations in brilliance.]

flicker photometry = a method of photometry in which two different-colored and congruent light-fields are alternately presented to the eye at a suitable rate; the fields are considered equal in brightness when the appearance of flicker is at a minimum. — Fr. *photométrie de papillotement*; Ger. *Flimmerphotometrie*.

flight = a mode of response characterized by rapid locomotion away from the source of stimulation. [Often accompanied by **fear.**] — Fr. *fuite*; Ger. *Flucht*.

flight of colors = the succession of colors which occurs in the visual after-image. — Fr. *fuite des couleurs*.

flight of ideas = a rapid succession of superficially related or unrelated ideas, either in thought, or more esp. in speech. — Fr. *fuite des idées*; Ger. *Ideenflucht*.

flirtation = (*pop.*) incipient or superficially conditioned love-making, engaged in for the enjoyment of the experience itself, without serious intention. [Cf. **coquetry.**] — Fr. *flirt*; Ger. *Liebelei*.

flowery, see **fragrant.** — Fr. *floral*; Ger. *blumig*.

fluctuation of attention, see **attention/fluctuation of.**

fluctuations = (*biol.*) variations, or differences in some character exhibited by the members of a species, whose values are distributed uniformly about the mean value of the group. [Often applied to purely somatic, non-hereditary variations, contr. w. true **mutations,** which are due to discrete, transmissible changes in the germ plasm. By some writers, **fluctuations** is used to designate continuous variations which are assumed to be to a certain extent hereditary.] — Ger. *Schwankungen*.

fluctuations of sampling = the changes in value which a statistical constant takes when determined from successive (but otherwise similar) samples. [Cf. **sampling.**] — Fr. *f. d'échantillonnage*.

fluid/cerebrospinal, see **cerebrospinal fluid.** — Fr. *liquide céphalo-rachidien*.

fluttering hearts = an illusion observed with colored figures (e.g. of red, heart-shaped components against a blue background), which are moved to and fro, the illusion consisting in the apparent springing of the figures suddenly from side to side. — Fr. *illusion des coeurs flottants*.

flux (*vis.*), see **radiant flux, luminous flux.**

flux/sound energy, see **sound energy flux.**

focal, see **focus.**

focal distance = in a lens or any focusing optical system, the distance between a focus and the nodal point corresponding to the last optical surface left by the rays.

focal length = a characteristic of a lens or other focusing optical system, being the focal distance for parallel entering rays. — Fr. *longueur focale*; Ger. *Brennweite*.

focal symptoms = symptoms which pertain to the focus or principal seat of a disease. [Contr. w. **general symptoms,** which are not localized.]

focus = the point to which rays of light from a given point or point-source are made to converge, or from which they are made to diverge by means of a lens or optical system. **foci**[pl], **focal**[a]. — Fr. *foyer*; Ger. *Brennpunkt*.

focus of attention, see **attention/focus of.**

focusing, focussing = 1. (*opt.*) adjustment of an optical system by moving the parts lengthwise along the axis, in order that the light-rays may be brought to convergence and an image formed at a desired place; 2. (*vis.*) the regulation of curvature of the eye-lens by the action of the ciliary muscle so that a clear image falls upon the retina. [Syn. (2) **accommodation** (prefd.).]

focusing/binocular, see **fixation/binocular.**

foetus, see **fetus.**

foliate papilla, see **papilla.**

folie = insanity; mental disorder; psychosis. [A French term used with qualifying words to denote certain types of mental disorder, e.g. *folie à deux, folie du doute.*]

folium = a folding or convolution of the surface of the cerebellum. [Cf. **convolution.**] **folia**^{pl}.

folk psychology = the investigation of the mental processes peculiar to any race or people, esp. the study of primitive races. [Applied either to the study of single races or to the comparative study of races. Sometimes confused with **social psychology** = the study of group phenomena.] — Fr. *psych. des peuples*; Ger. *Völkerpsychologie.*

folklore = primitive and traditional customs, rites, legends, etc. originating in an early stage of culture, which survive in the more advanced stages of social evolution of any given race or folk. — Ger. *Volkskunde.*

folkways = the conventional or traditional patterns of behavior common to the members of a particular group. [Syn. **conventions.** Distg. (first by Sumner) fr. **mores** = those standards of conduct which have received the conscious approval of the members of the group. Departure from the mores is disapproved and frequently punished; departure from the folkways merely denotes lack of sophistication.]

fontanel, fontanelle = an unossified area of the cranium of the fetus of the young infant.

food-response, food-getting behavior = the complex behavior of an organism in the presence of food stimuli, which normally results in the ingestion of the food substance. [Syn. **alimentive instinct.**] — Fr. *comportement envers l'aliment.*

foot-candle = a unit of **illumination,** equal to the density of luminous flux upon a surface placed at right angles to the light-rays at a distance of 1 foot from a light-source of 1 candlepower. [It is the unit of illumination commonly used by engineers in the United States and England.]

foot-lambert = a unit of **brightness,** equal to the uniform brightness of a perfectly diffusing surface which emits or reflects 1 **lumen** per square foot.

footrule/Spearman, see **Spearman footrule.**

foot-writing (foot-drawing) = writing (drawing) in which the writing (drawing) implement is held between the toes. [The implement is held in place either by muscular contractions or by mechanical devices. Cf. **mouth-writing.**] — Fr. *écriture au pied.*

force = 1. (*phys.*) that which produces a change of motion or a change from the state of rest in masses or elements; 2. (*psychol.*) any condition or set of conditions which are effective in bringing about changes or maintaining equilibrium among mental or social phenomena; 3. (*biol.*) any condition, whether of heredity or of environment, which enters as a factor in the development of the organism, or in the evolution of species. [The c.g.s. unit of **force** (1) is the **dyne,** i.e. the force which, acting on a gram for a second, imparts to it a velocity of 1 cm. per sec. Cf. **energy.**] — Ger. *Kraft.*

forced movements = 1. (*physiol.*) asymmetrical movements of an organism induced by injury to one hemisphere of the brain or analogous controlling organ; 2. (*comp. psy.*) asymmetrical movements induced by unequal stimulation of the two sides of an organism. [(2) is regarded by Loeb as a general explanation of tropistic behavior.] — Fr. *mouvements forcés.*

forced resonance (or **vibration**), see **resonance.**

forebrain = the extreme (cephalad) division of the brain, consisting of the end-brain or telencephalon, and the interbrain or diencephalon. [Syn. **prosencephalon;** cf. **brain.**] — Fr. *cerveau antérieur*; Ger. *Vorderhirn.*

foreconscious, see **preconscious.**

fore-exercise = 1. in work-experiments, repeated reaction of the subject to the experimental situation prior to introduction of the experimental variable, the purpose being to establish a base line against which to measure the effect of the variable, or to discover variations in the base line from one experimental session to another; 2. in tests, a brief preliminary period of practice upon material similar to that in the test, interpolated between the instructions and the test proper, in order to prevent misunderstanding, excitement, or timidity. [Syn. (1, 2) **practice exercise,** (1) **preliminary period,** (2) **sample exercise.**] — Fr. *pré-exercice.*

foreperiod = 1. the initial period in an experience, esp. in connection with psychological experiments; 2. in reaction time experiments the interval between the *ready* signal and the stimulus. [Cf. **midperiod.**] — Fr. *période préliminaire*; Ger. *Vorperiode.*

forepleasure = (*psychoan.*) sexual pleasure experienced through excitation of an erogenous zone. [Contr. w. **end-pleasure.**] — Ger. *Vorlust.*

foresight = mental picturing of events as likely to occur, particularly of situations which may affect the individual himself. [Syn. **forethought.** Cf. **expectation, anticipation.**] — Fr. *prévision, prévoyance*; Ger. *Voraussicht.*

forethought = a thought (or thinking) of some event as one that will probably occur. [Usually applied to the more developed forms of anticipatory thinking. Syn. **foresight.**] — Fr. *prescience.*

forget = loss of capacity to recall an event on appropriate occasion.

forgetfulness = a tendency to forget readily. [Syn. **obliviscence,** used more technically to denote a low degree of amnesia.] — Ger. *Vergesslichkeit.*

forgetting^{n} = the loss, temporary or permanent, of an earlier acquisition. [Applies to (*a*) failure to recall an item once known, or (*b*) loss of ability to perform an act formerly learned. Cf. **forgetting rate, obliviscence.**] **forget**^{v}.

forgetting rate = the speed with which material, once learned, is forgotten during a period of no recall or review. [The rate is usually measured by the **saving method** in relearning or by the **recall method,** and is displayed graphically in certain of its aspects by means of a **curve of forgetting** (or **of retention**). First investigated by Ebbinghaus and published in 1885.] — Fr. *rapidité de l'évanouissement du souvenir, rapidité de l'oubli.*

fork, see **tuning fork.**

form = 1. the colligation or organization of data or elements into a unitary whole or system, such that definite relations (spatial, temporal, logical, etc.) subsist between them; 2. (*math.*) the algebraic or geometric mold or pattern wherein the variables in a given problem are permitted to find expression. [Syn. **shape** (*geom.*), **structure** (*biol.*), **configuration** or **Gestalt** (*psychol.*); **form** is regarded by Gestalt psychologists as a fundamental property of organized wholes; it depends not only upon the structure of the object or event under consideration, but also upon its ground or setting. It is defined by points of reference in both, but not by reduction to elements and subsistent relations. In older logic contr. w. **matter** or **material** = the constituent elements; also contr. w. **content** = the qualitative character of the system.] **formal**[a]. — Ger. *Gestalt, Anordnung, Form, Struktur.*

form distortion = any change in the image of an object, due to the spherical nature of the retina or to imperfections of the eye, which gives the image a character different from that of the object itself.

form psychology, see **Gestalt theory.**

form-quality = a positive content of consciousness which appears, according to von Ehrenfels, in complexes over and above their separable elements (sensations), and is responsible for the peculiar properties attaching to such complexes as wholes. [Distg. fr. **Gestalt.**] — Ger. *Gestaltqualität.*

form/visual = the total impression produced by the arrangement of the contour lines of an object or drawing. [Cf. **Gestalt.**]

formal = pert. to form; i.e. not concerned with the character of the subject matter. [**formal logic** (e.g.) concerns itself with the forms of the given propositions and of their relations to each other, without considering whether these propositions are true.] **formally**[a] (= logically).

formal cause = 1. (*hist.*) those properties or arrangements of parts in the antecedents to which the specific properties or form of the consequent are traceable; 2. the idea or plan which guides activity. [Cf. **cause.**] — Fr. *cause formelle.*

formal discipline, see **discipline/formal.**

formal exercises = (*learning*) drills based on one type of material or situation, used with a view to develop some general mental process or faculty or a character trait. [E.g. specific exercises in memorizing series of digits as a means of improving memory in general; specific exercises in tolerating fatigue or standing on tiptoes as a means of cultivating will-power. Cf. **formal discipline.**]

formalism = (*esth.*) theories of art which view beauty as a matter of form rather than of content. [Contr. w. **expression.**]

formant = a contribution to the timbre of vowel sounds made by the buccal resonance cavities. [According to L. Hermann **formants** correspond to a tonal region rather than to a fixed frequency, and they remain relatively constant whether the fundamental be spoken or sung; **formants** may also contribute to the timbre of certain wind instruments.]

formboard = a board with depressions of various shapes, into which solid blocks of corresponding shapes are to be inserted. [Used to test perception of form or shape, esp. in mentally deficient individuals. Originally devised by Seguin. Standardized by Norsworthy and later by Goddard. Various other patterns of formboard have since been devised.]

formboard test = a type of test in which the task is to place blocks of different shapes, sizes, colors, or designs in appropriate insets in a board or other background, the score being expressed in terms of time, errors, or both.

formication = a diffuse organic or tactual sensation as of ants or other insects crawling on the skin. [Sometimes considered as a form of **paresthesia.**] **formicate**[v].

formula = a concise (generally abstract) statement of fact, whether of principle, structure, method, or relationship, conventionally accepted or intended for acceptance as a fixed statement. [E.g. laws, principles, mathematical equations, prescribed legal procedures, articles of faith or dogma, fixed ceremonial statements (ritual). Scientific formulations are often expressed in mathematical or analogous symbols.] **formulas**[pl] (verbal), **formulae**[pl] (symbolic). — Ger. *Formel.*

formulation = the expression of a principle in words or symbols, whether mathematical or not.

fornix = a system of nerve fibers, which arise in the basal region of the brain, and form topographically a cephalocaudal tract between the optic thalamus and hippocampus major, and the uncinate gyrus. — Ger. *Gewölbe.*

fortuitous = pert. to chance. [Usually implies absence of known or intended antecedents. Applied in statistics to extreme values; improperly used as syn. for **random.**]

forward reference = the directional character of growth processes whereby the growth of organisms is accounted for in terms of a remote future stage or a remote end.

fortuitous variation, see **chance variation.**

fossa Sylvii, see **Sylvian fissure.**

fossae/nasal, see **nasal cavity.**

foul, see **putrid.**

founding process = (*Gestalt*) a term used by Meinong to denote an intellectual activity by which conscious contents are consolidated to form objects of higher order termed **complexes.** [Cf. **complex** (1).] — Fr. *processus constitutif*; Ger. *Produktionsvorgang* (*Benussi*).

Fourier's law = a mathematical principle developed by Fourier, according to which any complex periodic vibration may be resolved into a harmonic series of sine (or cosine) functions. [For acoustics, any complex sound may be represented as the sum of a series of pure tones, whose frequencies increase in the ratio of the natural numbers 1, 2, 3, 4, etc. Such resolution of a complex vibration into single components is called **Fourier analysis,** and the components obtained comprise a **Fourier series.**]

fourth (*mus.*), see **interval** and Table VII. — Fr. *quart*; Ger. *Quart.*

fovea, fovea centralis = a small depression in the **macula lutea** or yellow spot, in the central region of the retina. [In the human eye the receptors in the fovea are exclusively cones very closely packed together; the other layers of the retina are as if pushed aside, hence the depression; the fovea is a horizontal ellipse of about $52' \times 35'$; it is the area of sharpest vision and the center of fixation.] — Ger. *Netzhautgrube.*

fractionation = 1. (*introsp.*) a piecemeal method of describing a conscious experience, in which the situation is repeated exactly (or approximately so) a number of times with varied instructions, so that the observer may confine himself to a limited section each time and thus finally produce a relatively complete description; 2. (*statist.*) division of the entire group of experimental data into small groups, for separate mathematical treatment. [Watt of the Würzburg school was responsible for meaning (1).]

fragrant = 1. a quality of olfactory sensation of which violet, hyacinth, and heliotrope are typical examples; 2. all odors which are distinctly pleasant. [Syn. (1) **flowery.** Cf. **odor.**] — Ger. *duftig.*

frankness = the personal characteristic or trait of dealing with others openly and without reserve or inhibition, esp. in speech. **frank**[a]. — Fr. *franchise*; Ger. *Aufrichtigkeit, Offenheit.*

Fraunhofer's lines = certain dark lines seen in the solar spectrum, due to the absorption of light from the denser central portion of the sun while passing through its atmosphere of gases and vapors. [The position of the most prominent lines was determined by Fraunhofer in 1814. Over 14,000 lines have been noted in the solar spectrum but only 10 are prominent; the latter are designated by letters. Cf. **spectral line** and Table XIII.]

freak, see **sport.**

free association = 1. an association of ideas formed in the absence of limiting instruction or predisposing conditions; 2. one of the fundamental methods used in psychoanalytic technique, in which associations of ideas are allowed to arise spontaneously without conscious restraint or selective criticism. [Applied (1) generally to association experiments or tests in which the subject is not limited by previous instructions to some specific kind of relation; applicable also to trains of thought not guided by their relation to a problem. Contr. (1) w. **controlled association.**] — Fr. *a. libre.*

free nerve endings = afferent neurons which terminate in non-medullated arborizations in the skin. [They have been assumed to be pain receptors.] — Fr. *terminaisons nerveuses libres intra-épidermiques.*

free-will doctrine = the theory that the course of thought and volition is or may be directed by the individual himself, regardless of external influences and (according to some) regardless of internal or mental constitution. [A form of **indeterminism.** Syn. **libertarianism.** Contr. w. **mental determinism,** which assumes that thought and volition are conditioned by universal principles.] **libertarian**[a]. — Fr. *doctrine de la volonté libre*; Ger. *Willensfreiheitslehre.*

freedom/consciousness of = the conscious experience that our decisions are or may be made by ourselves, regardless of external influences and mental predisposition. — Fr. *conscience de liberté*; Ger. *Bewusstsein der Freiheit.*

freedom/ethical = the ability of an individual to make decisions and to act according to standards of value in conduct or principles of justice and fairness accepted by him. [Cf. **free-will doctrine.**] — Fr. *liberté morale.*

Freeman time-unit, F. T. U., F. U. = a standard unit of time between exposures in the cinematography of the writing movement equal to 0.04 sec. [Term suggested by R. Saudek, and named for F. N. Freeman, the pioneer in this field.] — Fr. *unité temporelle de F.*

frenzy = a violent emotional disturbance approaching utter disorganization. [Syn. **delirious rage.**] — Ger. *Raserei.*

frequency = 1. (*phys.*) the number of cycles per second of a wave or other periodic phenomenon, or more generally, the reciprocal of the period; 2. (*statist.*) the number of cases in which a given value or score occurs in a class (i.e. class frequency), or in a sample (i.e. frequency of sample or population of sample). [**cumulative frequencies** = a succession of sums of **frequencies** (2) in a series of data arranged in order of magnitude. Cf. **frequency curve, frequency surface.**]

frequency curve, frequency distribution, see **frequency polygon.** — Ger. *Häufigkeitskurve.*

frequency/law of = a principle advanced as explanatory of learning, according to which those responses which have been repeated many times will tend to be further repeated, rather than those which have occurred less often. [This law is formulated in more general terms than the **law of exercise** and lacks the neurological assumptions of the latter. Syn. **law of repetition.**] — Fr. *l. de fréquence, l. de répétition.*

frequency polygon = (*statist.*) the graphic representation of a frequency distribution by means of a closed figure formed by a series of straight lines. [In constructing a frequency polygon, equal distances are laid off on the base line (X axis) to represent the various class intervals. A point is located midway in each interval at a height which represents (on the Y axis) the number of cases lying within this interval. These points are joined to give the graph.] — Fr. *polygone de fréquence.*

frequency surface = (*statist.*) the surface of the three-dimensional solid which is formed when the heights (frequencies) in the cells (or compartments) of a scatter diagram, or correlation table, are joined. [Cf. **frequency polygon.**]

frequency table = (*statist.*) a tabulation of data showing the number of cases found at each successive score, grade, age, or other class interval. — Fr. *barème de fréquence.*

Freudism, Freudianism, see **psychoanalysis.**

friendship = a social relation between two individuals, characterized by mutual attraction and cooperation, in which the factor of sexual attraction is not present or is not emphasized. — Fr. *amitié*; Ger. *Freundschaft.*

fright = an acute manifestation of fear, which usually develops suddenly, is not restrained, and is short lived. [Syn. **terror,** which emphasizes the emotional rather than the motor characteristics.] — Fr. *épouvante, terreur*; Ger. *Schreck.*

frigidity = 1. decrease or absence of normal sexual desire; 2. decrease or absence of the normal sensation complex in coitus. [Used esp. with reference to women.]

frigorific nerve = any nerve-fiber whose excitation is accompanied by either a conscious experience of cold or a reaction typical for cold stimuli. [The normal or adequate stimulus is a temperature of 1/8° C (or more) lower than the body or skin temperature at the place of stimulation, with some apparent exceptions.]

fringe = (*psychol.*) the unobtrusive but functionally important feelings of meaning and relationship which accompany the perception or image of an object; e.g. the suggestion of meaning carried by a heard or seen word (James). [Often used as syn. for **margin** (of consciousness) or **marginal consciousness.**] — Fr. *frange*; Ger. *Franse.*

front tap reflex = contraction of the gastrocnemius muscle when skin above the muscles on the anterior part of the leg is struck, while the leg is in extension and the foot extended by pressure upon the sole. [Mediated by 3d lumbar to 2d sacral segments of the cord. An indication of increased postural reflexes.] — Fr. *réflexe du choc sur la face antérieure de la jambe.*

frontal = pert. to the forehead; or parallel to the forehead.

frontal lobe = that part of either cerebral hemisphere which in man lies above the Sylvian and in front of the central or Rolandic fissure; i.e. which is nearest the forehead. — Ger. *Stirnlappen.*

frontal plane = in bilaterally symmetrical animals any plane which is perpendicular to the dorsoventral axis.

frotteur = one who practices masturbatory rubbing.

fruity = a quality of olfactory sensations of which pineapple is a typical example. [A class of Henning's. Cf. **odor, aromatic, ethereal.**] — Ger. *fruchtig.*

fugue = 1. (*pathol.*) a term applied to episodes of non-remembered activity of considerable duration, usually involving disappearance from accustomed haunts. [A hysterical symptom.]

fugue = 2. (*mus.*) a form of musical composition in which several voices combine in stating and developing the theme; the theme is announced by one voice, instrumental or vocal, and then answered by a contrasting voice. [Lat. **fuga,** a flight.]

Fullerton-Cattell law = a formulation devised by G. S. Fullerton and J. McK. Cattell as a substitute for Weber's law; it states that the error of observation and least noticeable difference are proportional to the square root of the stimulus.

function[n] = 1. (*biol. psychol.*) a process in operation; e.g. the function of the thyroid gland, of locomotion, of growth, etc.; 2. operation or activity in general; 3. the use of a structure or activity, i.e. its rôle in biological and social adjustments; 4. (*math.*) a variable quantity, whose value in any case is determined by the value of one or more other variables; 5. (*hist.*) syn. for **faculty.** [Where a mathematical function (4) is expressed as an equation, y = f (x), x is the independent and y the dependent variable. Contr. (1, 3) w. **structure.** The confusion of (3) with (2) and (4) has caused misunderstandings. Cf. **operate.**] **function**[v], **operate**[v], **functionate**[v] (not recommended), **functional**[a].

functional analysis, see **analysis/functional.**

functional deafness, see **deafness.**

functional disorders = 1. disorders without known alteration of structure; 2. disorders of function by or through other functions. [Distg. fr. **organic disorders,** in which structural changes are found.]

functional psychology = 1. a systematic interpretation of mental phenomena which regards them as activities or processes rather than experiences; 2. the standpoint which emphasizes the biological role of mental phenomena, i.e. their utility to the organism in its adjustment to the environment. [The German psychology of *Funktion* (e.g. Stumpf) represents (1); American functional psychology (e.g. J. R. Angell) represents (2); and (2) is apt to imply (1). Syn. (1) **act psychology** (2); (2) sometimes **dynamic psychology.**]

functional psychosis = mental disorder formulated essentially in behavior terms, without reference to structural or physiological factors, e.g. **paranoia.**

functional selection = a mode of biological selection, whose distinctive feature is the survival of certain functions or motor capacities which are more useful to the individual or social group, and the disappearance of other functions that are not so useful.

functional unity = the degree of correlation between various pairs of measures necessary to the postulation of a power or ability common to the efficiencies measured. [Syn. **unitary function.**]

functionalism = the doctrine that an essential feature of all psychological processes is the part which they play in the adaptive functions of the organism. [Developed under J. Dewey at Chicago; most clearly and forcefully advocated by J. R. Angell in 1903–06.]

fundament, see **Anlage.**

fundaments = the mental elements between which a relation mediates.

fundamental formula = the simplest mathematical expression of Weber's law, viz. dS = c(dR/R). — Ger. *Fundamentalformel.*

fundamental tone, fundamental = the lowest tone in a compound tone or simple clang. — Ger. *Grundton.*

funding process, see **founding process.**

fundus oculi, see **eyeground.**

fungiform papilla, see **papilla.**

furor = an acute excitement of the nature of anger and violence. — Ger. *Wutanfall.*

fusiform gyrus = the convolution on the mesial surface of the cerebral hemisphere near the base, between the collateral and inferior temporal gyri.

fusion = 1. the combination of the effects of two or more stimuli in any given sense-mode, so as to yield a single, unanalyzed sensation; 2. an unanalyzed sensation, perception, or other datum, due to a combination of stimulations from various senses, with or without memory and other elements; 3. that sensory experience which is the undifferentiated product of contiguous multiple stimulation. [This term is preferable to **blending** as applied to the operation; the product of fusion is **a blend.** Contr. w. **colligation.**] — Ger. *Verschmelzung.*

fusion/binaural = the combination of the effect of stimuli presented to the two ears into a single auditory impression. [When two stimuli are presented separately to the ears, as *c* to the right and *e* to the left, there is **dichotic** fusion. When both ears receive the double stimulus (as under normal conditions) there is **diotic** fusion.]

fusion/binocular = the combination of two images, falling upon the two retinas, into a single visual impression. [The images may be alike, or may differ to some degree in form and color.]

fusion/tonal = (*psychol.*) the effect produced when two or more tones are sounding simultaneously. [Certain combinations are unitary, smooth, agreeable; other combinations are lacking in unity, rough, disagreeable; the former are said to have a relatively *higher degree* of fusion than the latter. Cf. **interval.**]

G

g factor, general factor = a psychoneural element, or determiner, according to the two-factor theory of intelligence, which is fundamental to all correlated abilities for the same individual, as distg. fr. the (specific) **s factors** which vary in different activities (Spearman). [Cf. **s factor, two-factor theory.**]

Galton bar = an instrument devised by F. Galton, for determining the threshold of difference for visual linear distance; the typical model consists of a wooden stick one meter long, with four flat sides about 25 mm. wide, the side nearest the observer being plain, and the rear side marked in mm.; there are 3 movable slides, of which the central one shows a thin vertical black wire, the two lateral slides being also black but broader; the slides are adjusted to give two apparently equal linear distances on the bar, or to determine just noticeable differences.

Galton's laws, see **ancestral inheritance,** and **filial regression.**

Galton whistle = an apparatus devised by F. Galton for the production of tones of very high frequency; it consists of a very small single pipe whose length may be varied by means of a screw piston; the tone is made by pressing a hand bulb or by compressed air. [Commonly used for determining the highest audible pitch. The width of the pipe makes necessary a correction in the theoretic pitch as determined by the length.] — Fr. *sifflet de G.*; Ger. *Galtonpfeife.*

galvanic current = a steady direct current. [Originally applied to currents obtained from galvanic batteries. Contr. w. **faradic current.**] — Ger. *galvanischer Strom.*

galvanic nystagmus, see **nystagmus.**

galvanic skin response (or **reflex**) = 1. decreased apparent resistance of the skin due to physiological activity under control of the autonomic nervous system, following sensory or ideational stimulation; 2. increase in the apparent electromotive force of the skin similar to (1). [Abbrev. G.S.R. (or P.G.R.) (1) often called *Féré phenomenon*; (2) also called **Tarchanoff phenomenon.** Both (1) and (2) are believed to be essentially sweat-gland phenomena associated with the mechanism of body temperature control. Under certain conditions circulatory and trophic influences are also important factors. Either (1) or (2) may be demonstrated by means of a **galvanometer** and recorded by a **photokymograph.** The record is a wave-like curve having a latent period of 3–7 seconds and a duration of 3–15 seconds. Syn. **psychogalvanic reflex, galvanic reaction, galvanic reflex, orectic reflex, general autonomic reflex.**] — Fr. *réaction galvanique de la peau, réflexe psychogalvanique.*

galvanism = 1. (*med.*) the use of a direct, unidirectional continuous electric current for therapeutic purposes; 2. (*phys.*) the investigation of electricity produced by chemical action, i.e. galvanic electricity, or direct current.

galvanometer = a class of instruments designed to measure the strength of electric currents. [The principal types used in psychological experimentation are (1) **string galvanometer** (Einthoven), consisting essentially of an extremely fine metallic thread supported between the poles of a powerful electromagnet; (2) **moving coil,** (*a*) **pointer type** consisting of a pointer placed over a scale attached to a coil of very fine wire which is supported in an electromagnetic field; (*b*) **mirror type,** consisting of a reflecting mirror attached to a moving coil in an electromagnetic field; (*c*) **ballistic type,** any undamped moving coil galvanometer.] **galvanometric**[a].

galvanotropism, galvanotaxis = a simple orienting response, either positive or negative, to electrical stimulation. [Cf. **tropism, taxis.**] (Accent **-not-; -tax-.**) **galvanotropic**[a], **(-tactic**[a]).

game = a form of **play** which is governed by definite rules, and usually involves a competition between individuals or groups, with some definite objective. [The success of one individual or group, measured by attainment of a goal or in some numerical score, is called *winning the game.* Distg. fr. **play,** in which one or more individuals may be involved and competition may be absent.] — Fr. *jeu*; Ger. *Spiel.*

gamete = a cell which combines with another cell to form a **zygote,** which latter is capable of developing into a complete organism. [**gametes** are usually (but not always) sexually differentiated. Cf. **zygote.**]

gametogenesis = the cytologic processes involved in the development of the male and female sex-cells or gametes. [Cf. **spermatogenesis, oögenesis.**]

gamma movement, see **apparent (motion or) movement.**

gamogenesis = reproduction which involves the union of two gametes. [Distg. fr. **fission, budding,** and **sporulation.** Cf. **reproduction.**]

gang = a group of individuals banded together for a common interest, more esp. for illegal or socially disapproved purposes. — Fr. *bande*; Ger. *Bande.*

gangliated nerve = a nerve on some part of which there is an enlargement containing cell bodies, the axons of which run in the nerve.

ganglioblast = a neuron of the spinal or extra-axial ganglia in the embryo. [Cf. **gangliocyte.**]

gangliocyte = a neuron of the spinal or extra-axial ganglia.

ganglion = 1. a cluster of nerve cells lying outside the brain and spinal cord; e.g. in the sympathetic system; 2. a mass of cells within the brain; e.g. basal ganglia. [The latter usage has been criticized.] **ganglionic**[a]. — Ger. *Nervenknoten, Nervenhügel.*

ganglion cells/layer of = the 8th stratum of the retina from without inward; it contains the cell-bodies of the third set of neurons in the visual path or the ganglion cells whose axons eventually form the **optic nerve.** [Syn. **vesicular layer.** See Table XI.] — Fr. *couche de cellules ganglionnaires.*

ganglioplexus = a loosely aggregated ganglion embedded in a meshwork of nerve fibers.

ganjah, see **Cannabis indica.**

Ganser's syndrome = a symptom of hysteria and simulation which consists in the patient's giving absurd random answers, usually of the nature of simulation. [E.g. "snow is green," "a horse has 5 legs."]

gap/tonal, see **tonal gap.** — Fr. *lacune tonale.*

Gasserian ganglion = the ganglion of the sensory root of the Vth cranial nerve.

gastraea theory = the theory, advanced by Haeckel, that the multicellular animals are descended from an ancestor, the gastraea, resembling the gastrula stage which occurs in early embryonic development.

gastric = pert. to or located in the stomach.

gastrin = a hormone produced in the pyloric mucous membrane of the stomach and probably acting most prominently upon the glands of the fundus. [There remains some doubt as to whether this is a specific hormone of the gastric mucosa; extracts of many tissues produce the same effect.]

gastrocolic reflex = a peristaltic wave in the colon caused by introduction of food into the empty stomach. [Mediated by autonomic arcs through thoracic segments of the spinal cord.]

gastro-ileac reflex = relaxation of the ileocecal valve, caused by pressure of food in stomach. [Mediated by autonomic arcs through thoracic segments of the spinal cord.]

gastrula = a two-layered stage of early embryonic development which follows the blastula stage. [In typical cases it resembles a hollow cup. Cf. **blastula.**]

Gaussian curve, see **normal curve of distribution.**

Gegenstandstheorie = a branch of science originated by Meinong, designed to investigate the properties and relations of objects as such, which the other sciences, particularly psychology, have neglected; it postulates that objects are divided into real, not-real, ideal, and other types, depending upon the kind of mental activity by which they are mediated. [Lit. *theory of objects.*]

gemmation = a mode of nonsexual reproduction in which the new organism starts as a **gemma** or bud protruding from the body of the parent organism and later breaks off. [Syn. **budding.**]

gemmule = 1. (*hist.*) an ultramicroscopic particle assumed by Darwin to be given off at times by each cell in the body and to serve as the basis for the reproduction of similar cells in the offspring; 2. a **gemma** or bud. [Cf. **gemmation.**]

Gemüt, Gemütsbewegung = a German term covering the affective or affective-conative processes or their underlying and accompanying conditions.

gender = a grammatical classification of nouns based primarily on sex distinctions, but extended to objects, etc. not sexually characterized. [The adjectives **masculine** and **feminine** apply to gender, rather than sex.]

gene = a factor in the germ cells which is involved in the production of a hereditary character. [Commonly supposed to be located in a chromosome.] (1 syll.)

gene mutation = a discrete change in a gene, or hereditary factor, which causes a stable germinal variation.

genealogy = the investigation of lines of ancestral ascent. [Used technically to denote a branch of **genetics.**]

general = pert. or applying to all or most members of a given class of beings, things, actions, etc.; or pervading an entire organism, etc. [E.g. **general term, general activity.** Distg. fr. **universal,** which implies entire absence of exceptions.] — Ger. *allgemein.*

general ability = 1. the capacity of an individual to cope successfully with a variety of problems in different fields of endeavor; 2. an average of a very large and inclusive range of abilities; 3. in Spearman's factor theory, syn. w. the **g factor.** [Distg. (3) fr. **general factor** in that it is one particular general factor. Cf. **ability, general factor.**] — Fr. *habileté (capacité) générale.*

general ability tests = mental tests designed to measure all-round intellectual capacity, as distg. **fr. special ability tests.** [E.g. the Binet-Simon scale, the Army Alpha tests, and other general intelligence tests.]

general concept, see **concept.** — Ger. *Allgemeinbegriff.*

general consciousness = the experiences which are common to two or more individuals, usually to all members of a given social group. — Ger. *Gesamtbewusstsein.*

general factor, see **g factor.**

general idea = an idea or concept which includes the likenesses and excludes the differences common to a number of individual or particular ideas. [A special form of abstract idea.] — Ger. *Allgemeinbegriff, Allgemeinvorstellung.*

general image, see **image/general.**

general intelligence = 1. the capacity and ability of a human or subhuman organism to respond adaptively to new situations on the basis of past experience; 2. ability to select the good from the bad, the true from the false, independently, in a wide variety of endeavors (Roback). [Cf. **general ability.**]

general norms = average scores according to age or grade, which are obtained by means of **mental** or **educational tests** based upon a supposedly random sampling of school children, and which presumably represent the attainment of the entire population.

general paralysis = a special (parenchymatous) invasion of the brain by syphilitic disease. [Syn. **general paresis.**]

general psychology = the branch of psychology which seeks to discover what is true of individuals in general rather than of one individual or class of individuals (e.g. animals, children, abnormal persons) in distinction from others. [Contr. w. **individual psychology.**]

general will = 1. the course of action determined upon by a given social group, and representing the decisions of most of its members; 2. an assumed entity or group phenomenon distinct from the individual wills of the community, but of similar tenets. [Usually restricted to human psychology. Syn. **social will.**] — Fr. *volonté générale.*

generalization = the mental process of forming a general idea or a judgment applicable to an entire class of data, on the basis of a limited number of specific instances. [Cf. **general idea.**]

generalizing = 1. (*introsp.*) the process of perceiving or conceiving a general characteristic or fact or meaning in single or in complex situations or things; 2. (*beh.*) responding to the common aspects (from any point of view) of the specific elements in a complex situation. [Cf. **perception, conception, insight, meaning.**] **generalize**[v].

generation = 1. the act of procreating or the production of a new individual; 2. the offspring of a pair of parents; 3. the average length of life between birth and the beginning of reproduction in a given species. **generate**[v] (1), **generative**[a] (1), **generational**[a] (2, 3). — Ger. (1) *Zeugung.*

generation/spontaneous = the production of organisms from non-living matter, i.e. their production without parents.

generative function = 1. the entire series of operations involved in the bringing into being of a new organism, in so far as these operations are activities of the parent organism or organisms; 2. any simple sort of operation included in this series (e.g. impregnation, ovulation, parturition). [Syn. **reproductive function, reproduction** (prefd.); **sexual functions** should be used only in reference to the distinctive role of either sex in reproduction.]

generative sensations, see **genital sensations.**

generator, generating tone = one of the two or more tones which when sounded together produce a **combination tone.**

generic = pert. to a **genus.** [Contr. w. **specific.**]

generic image, see **image/general.** — Fr. *image composée.*

genesis = the origin or first steps in the formation of any thing. [Cf. **ontogenesis, phylogenesis.** The combining form **-genetic** (= of origins) should be distg. fr. **-genic** (= of classes or species), but the two are used interchangeably.] **genetic**[a]. — Ger. *Entstehung.*

genetic method = the method of investigation which seeks to trace the historic course of changes, esp. in **development** and **evolution.**

genetic psychology = the systematic study of mental phenomena and behavior by the genetic method, i.e. in terms of the origin and historic unfolding of mental life and responsive activity in the individual, or in the organic series. [Contr. w. **analytic psychology.**] — Ger. *Entwicklungspsychologie.*

genetic theory = the theory of organic (and mental) evolution.

genetic theory of vision, see **Ladd-Franklin theory.**

genetics = the branch of biology which investigates heredity, variation, and evolution. — Ger. *Vererbungswissenschaft.*

geniculate body/lateral = a swelling on the rear of the **thalamus** toward the outer (right or left) side. [Syn. **external g.b.**] — Fr. *corps genouillé latéral*; Ger. *äusserer Kniehöcker.*

geniculate body/medial = a swelling on the rear end of the **thalamus** between the **lateral geniculate** and **pulvinar bodies.** [Syn. **internal g.b.**] — Fr. *corps genouillé médial*; Ger. *innerer Kniehöcker.*

genital = pert. to the reproductive organs of an animal.

genital character = the relatively adult type of character, conceived (as an inference from psychoanalytic observations) to result from the fusion of the partial erotic drives (oral, anal, urethral) under the primacy of the genital-erotic impulses.

genital primacy = (*psychoan.*) the final stage of genital organization, in which the component instincts have developed to the function of reproduction. — Fr. *primauté génitale*; Ger. *Genitalprimat.*

genital sensations = the sensations which ensue upon stimulation of the reproductive organs. [Syn. **generative sensations** (indefinite); **sex** (or **sexual**) **sensations,** which applies strictly to the distinctive genital sensations in each sex.]

genital zones = the external genitalia and adjacent areas of the skin which are susceptible to erogenous stimulation.

genius = 1. very superior mental ability; esp. superior power of invention or origination of any kind, or of execution of some special form, such as music, painting, or mathematics; 2. a person endowed with these characteristics. [Usually implies hereditary derivation. It has no special technical meaning, but has occasionally been defined as equivalent to an intelligence quotient (IQ) of 140 or above.] — Fr. *génie*; Ger. (1) *Genie.*

gens = (*anthrop.*) a line of human descent through the father. [Contr. w. **clan** = through the mother; cf. **sib.**]

genus = 1. (*logic*) a class considered as embracing certain subclasses or species; 2. (*biol.*) a group of closely related species constituting the elements of the larger group above it known as family. [Contr. (1) w. **species** = any one of the subordinated classes. In logic the genus-species relation is applied to any class and immediately subordinate class. In biology the two terms have a fixed position in the hierarchical grouping. Cf. **classification/zoological.**] **genera**[pl]; **generic**[a], **-genic.** — Fr. *genre*; Ger. (2) *Gattung.*

geometrical illusions = misinterpretation of simple straight and curve-line figures. [Cf. **illusion.** See Table XII.]

geometric(al) mean = (*math.*) the nth root of the product of n numbers. [E.g. $g = \sqrt{ab}$, is the geometrical mean of *a* and *b*. Distg. fr. **arithmetic (al) mean.**] — Fr. *moyenne géométrique*; Ger. *geometrisches Mittel.*

geotropism, geotaxis = a simple orienting response, either positive or negative, to the lines of force of gravity. [In *positive* geotropism (positive geotaxis) the head of the organism turns downward, in *negative* geotropism (negative geotaxis) the head turns upward, or away from the center of the earth. Cf. **tropism.**] (Accent **-ot-, -tax-.**) **geotropic**[a], **-tactic**[a].

germ = 1. a structure which develops into an organ or an organism; 2. a micro-organism which causes disease, i.e. a pathogenic micro-organism. — Ger. *Keim.*

germ-cell = a reproductive cell in all stages of its development. [Distg. fr. **gamete,** a mature germ-cell.] — Fr. *cellule germinale*; Ger. *Keimzelle.*

germ layer = a layer of cells which is formed early in embryonic development and gives rise to the fundamental organ systems of the body. — Fr. *couche germinale.*

germ-plasm = the substance which carries the hereditary factors of a new organism. [It contains the **genes.** Contr. w. **somaplasm.**]

germinal factors = the structures and their interrelations in the reproductive cell, which determine the inheritance of characters.

germinal selection = a phrase devised by Weismann to designate the hypothetical elimination of the weaker or less adapted vital units in the struggle which he assumed to occur between these units in the germ plasm. [The theory of germinal selection, which is essentially an extension of the doctrine of natural selection to the components of the germ plasm, was put forward as a means of accounting for the production of new germinal variations and for the assumed tendency of such variations to continue further in the direction in which they had started.]

germinal vesicle = the nucleus of the ovum before the polar bodies are formed.

gerontology = the investigation of the characteristics of old age.

Gestalt = a term applied to those organized units, both experiential and behavioral, which possess specific properties not derivable from parts and their relations; as contr. w. sensation, reflex, and certain other concepts which imply that complexes can be treated as sums of simple units. [A German word, frequently used in English literature; sometimes translated **configuration,** pattern, or structure. In its wider sense Gestalt means an *integration* of members, as contr. w. a *summation* of parts. Gestalten are classed as (1) *static* or non-temporal = a form or pattern of distribution which does not change in time and whose internal changes leave the whole unchanged, and (2) *dynamic* or temporal = processes which are patterned both in space and time; they are also distinguished with regard to the degree in which their parts are interdependent, as *strong* and *weak.* A Gestalt may be either (1) *phenomenal* = a perceptual, imaginal, or thought structure behaving as a unity, i.e. directly experienced units; (2) *physical* = any physical magnitude or any physical parameter in extension; (3) *physiological* = a functional system within a living organism, i.e. neural structure, functionally regarded; (4) *logical* = a thought or logical unity having logical necessity. Syn. **configuration** (liable to confusion).] **Gestalten**^{pl}. — Fr. *structure, forme.*

Gestalt theory = the theory which denies that psychic processes are (or can advantageously be regarded *as if*) composed of elements found in them by analysis, and which affirms that experience presents itself phenomenally in the form of organized structures which, when relatively incomplete, reveal an immanent tendency toward their own completion. [As applied to behavior, the theory denies that the response to a situation is compounded of elementary responses to elements of the situation, and regards situation and response as an incomplete structure tending toward an end — state of equilibrium. As applied to the brain, the theory renounces the conception of separate paths or arcs, whether native or acquired, and speaks in terms of stress — patterns resolving themselves into states of equilibrium. Von Ehrenfels (1890) formulated the doctrine of *Gestaltqualität* (**form-quality**) which approximates Gestalt theory applied to the perception of spatial and temporal **form.** The broad use of the term **Gestalt** derives by extension from this original usage. The modern school of Gestalt psychology (Köhler, Koffka, Lewin) comes from Wertheimer (1912); it expressly denies the existence of specific **form-quality.**] — Fr. *théorie de la forme.*

Gestalt(s)**qualität** = form-quality; the attribute of having a pattern or configuration.

gestation = the process of carrying the embryo in the uterus. [Used loosely to denote embryonic development; the period of gestation is the time elapsing between fertilization and birth, whose length differs widely in different species but is fairly constant within a given species, e.g. elephant 593 days, man 280 days, cat 56 days. Syn. **pregnancy.**] **gestational**^{a}.

gesture = a movement or position of the hands or other members of the body used in communicating with other beings. [Distg. fr. **manipulation** of objects or other uses of the hands or other members as direct means for altering the environment.] — Ger. *Gebärde.*

gesture language = a system of communication, generally among human beings, through conventional visual symbols which consist in movements or position of the hands or other members of the body. [Syn. **sign language.**] — Ger. *Gebärdensprache.*

ghost = 1. (*anthrop.*) a visual appearance attributed to the presence of a disembodied personality; 2. a shadowy semblance of some person or thing. [Syn. **apparition,** a more technical term.] — Fr. *fantôme, spectre*; Ger. *Gespenst.*

ghost theory = a non-technical designation for the theory that religion originated in primitive man's belief in ghosts, or disembodied spirits. — Fr. *t. des fantômes* (*t. animiste*).

giant cells/Betz, see **Betz cells.**

giddiness, see **dizziness.**

gifted = 1. possessing one or more special talents or abilities of a high order, e.g. in music, painting, mathematics; 2. possessing a very high degree of intellectual brightness. [Sometimes stated as an IQ (intelligence quotient) of 140 or above.] — Fr. *bien doué*; Ger. *begabt.*

gigantism = an abnormal increase in stature due to hyperactivity of the anterior lobe of the pituitary gland. [The term is used technically, while **giant** and **gigantic** are non-technical. Syn. **acromegaly, Marie's disease, hyperpituitarism.** Cf. **nanism.**]

girdle sensation = a painful sensation resembling that produced by a tightly drawn belt, which occurs in certain diseases, e.g. tabes dorsalis. [Cf. **Hitzig's girdle.**] — Fr. *douleur en ceinture.*

given^{n} = the material available to the investigator, upon which his generalizations and explanations are based. [Syn. **datum, data**^{pl} (more commonly used).] — Fr. *donnée*; Ger. (*das*) *Gegebene.*

given^{a} = an indefinite qualifier; e.g. a given individual = a sample individual.

gland = any one of a large and heterogeneous class of organs whose function is usually the formation of a specific product which may be (*a*) chemical substances in solution or suspension, or (*b*) cells. [**glands** are divided into (*a*) epithelial glands with persistent ducts, producing external secretions (e.g. sweat glands, pancreas); (*b*) epithelial glands with obliterated ducts, producing internal secretions = endocrine glands (e.g. anterior pituitary, thyroid); (*c*) epithelioid glands, never having duct or lumen, producing internal secretions (e.g. adrenal medulla, corpus luteum); (*d*) cytogenic glands, producing cells (e.g. gonads, lymph nodes, red bone marrow, spleen); (*e*) several gland-like organs without ducts and of lymphoid character (e.g. thymus gland, tonsils); (*f*) mixed types. Cf. *ductless glands.*] **glandular**^{a}. — Ger. *Drüse.*

glandular response = a type of response to stimulation, usually mediated by autonomic nerve fibers or chemicals in the blood stream, and characterized by increased or decreased activity of one or more glands. [Contr. w. **muscular response,** in which one or more muscles respond by an increase or decrease in tension.]

glass sensation = a subjective visual effect, noted by F. Schumann, according to which transparent solids appear different from empty space, i.e. as if filled by a colorless substance. — Fr. *s. de verre*; Ger. *Glasempfindung.*

glaucoma = a disease characterized by abnormally high pressure of the fluids within the eyeball, with consequent pain and impairment or loss of vision. [It may follow injury to the eye or be due to other local or systemic causes.]

glia, see **neuroglia.**

glioma = a mass of **gliosis** which, in its pathoclinical aspects, resembles a tumor.

gliosis = a diseased condition of the cerebrum, characterized by a localized increase of neuroglia.

globus hystericus = (*pathol.*) a sensation of contraction of throat or a globular mass rising from the stomach into the esophagus.

glossal = pert. to or located in the tongue.

glossolalia = speech in unknown tongues or in fabricated languages, which occurs in religious ecstasy, psychopathic states, and hypnotic and mediumistic trance. [Cf. **xenoglossis.**]

glossopharyngeal nerve = the 9th cranial nerve, which terminates in the back of the tongue and throat and serves the taste receptors in this region, and also motor functions in the throat.

glossophobia, see **lalophobia.**

glossosynthesis = the formation of nonsense-words. — Ger. *Sprachverwirrtheit.*

glottis = the opening between the arytenoid cartilages and the vocal bands. [Syn. **rima glottidis.** The opening between the cartilages is known as the *respiratory portion* and that between the cords as the *vocal portion.*] — Ger. *Stimmritze.*

glove anesthesia, see **anesthetic glove.**

glow = a mode of appearance (*Erscheinungsweise*) which is characteristically seen in self-luminous bodies, e.g. the appearance of an incandescent lamp filament or a flame. [It is usually to be referred to a comparatively small area which presents very high brightness or chromatic purity, at least relatively to the rest of the visual field.] — Fr. *incandescence*; Ger. *Glühen.*

glowing color = a color which presents a luminous or glowing *mode of appearance* to visual observation, e.g. the colors seen in flames, incandescent solids, the enclosing glassware of light-fixtures, mercury vapor lamps, etc. — Ger. *Leuchtfarbe.*

gluteal = pert. to or located in the buttocks. (Accent **glu-.**)

gluteal reflex = contraction of the gluteal muscles following irritation of the overlying skin. [Mediated chiefly by 4th to 5th lumbar segments of the cord.]

glycogen = a polysaccharid which forms the reserve or storage carbohydrate of the animal body and is found principally in the liver and muscles. [Syn. **animal starch.**]

glycosuria = the presence of glucose in the urine, esp. when due to hyperglycemia. [Distg. fr. **glycuresis** = an abnormal increase of sugar in the urine (S. R. Benedict), esp. the presence of minute amounts of reducing carbohydrates in urine without hyperglycemia. **alimentary glycosuria** = normal presence of sugar in urine after ingestion of carbohydrates; **emotional glycosuria** = a transitory condition due to hyperglycemia accompanying one of the major emotions; **renal glycosuria** = condition due to a low threshold of the kidneys for blood glucose.]

goal = 1. the end-result of any activity of an organism, whether muscular or ideational, individual, or social, as specified or formulated by an observer in advance of the actual attainment; 2. an end-result which an organism strives to attain; 3. (*indiv. psychol.*) an object or condition towards which an organism strives, referred by the organism to the immediate or remote future but acting in the present time. [Syn. (2, 3) **end** (less precise). Distg. (2, 3) fr. **purpose,** which properly denotes the determinant (conscious or unconscious) that guides the organism's activities toward the goal.] — Fr. *but*; Ger. *Ziel.*

goblet-profile figure, see **Rubin's goblet-profile figure.**

god = (*anthrop.*) a personified object of worship. [Prefd. to syn. **deity, divinity.**] — Fr. *dieu*; Ger. *Gott.*

golden section = the division of a line or area into two parts, or the relations of the sides of a rectangle, such that the ratio of the smaller to the larger equals the ratio of the larger to the whole. [A term used by Adolph Zeising, who called attention to the esthetic value of this division; tested experimentally by Fechner. Syn. **Zeising's principle.**] — Fr. *section dorée*; Ger. *goldener Schnitt.*

Golgi apparatus = an intracellular structure, highly variable in appearance. [First described by Golgi in the spinal ganglia cells of vertebrates. It ranges from a reticular form to discrete particles.]

Golgi-Mazzoni corpuscles = a type of capsulated nerve end-organ located in various layers of the dermis. [The term originally referred to *tendon spindles*, but was later also applied to bulbs in the *papillary layers*, believed to arouse pressure or cold sensations.] (Pron. **Matz-.**)

Goll/columns of = the spinobulbar tracts on either side of the posterior median fissure in the spinal cord.

gonad = a gland which produces gametes, or sex-cells. [A generic name embracing (*a*) **ovary,** which forms female gametes; (*b*) **testis,** which forms male gametes.] **gonadal**[a], **gonadial**[a].

goniometer = 1. a platform balance for measuring the tendency to sway in a given direction; the reactor stands upright on the platform as steadily as possible, the deflection when he sways being measured on a scale; 2. a physical instrument for measuring angles.

good = 1. characterizing actions which follow moral norms; 2. characterizing actions, means, devices, etc. as adapted to the end designed or proposed; 3. adapted to give pleasure, satisfaction, or benefit; 4. valid, effectual, or reliable. [(4) is used loosely to express a favorable judgment regarding the value of scientific work or results. Contr. w. **bad.**] — Fr. *bon*; Ger. *gut.*

grace = 1. (*esth.*) beauty as manifested in certain pleasing postures or movements, or in representations of the human body or natural objects whose contours suggest such postures or movements; 2. (*ethics*) an act of forbearance. **graceful**[a] (1); **gracious**[a] (2) — Ger. 1. *Anmut*, 2. *Gnade.*

gradation methods = a term commonly applied since Fechner to two psychophysical methods of **just noticeable differences:** the method of **minimal changes** and method of **mean gradations.** [Contr. w. the **error methods: right and wrong cases** and **average error.**]

grade = the position of a given individual, organism, or datum of any sort in a series or scale, in which values, determined on the basis of some character or group of characters are assigned to all the individuals, etc. included in the series. **grade**[v]. — Fr. *degré, rang*; Ger. *Stufe.*

grade norm = a numerical standard of performance, empirically determined, which represents the central tendency of pupils of a given school grade. — Fr. *norme de valeur scolaire.*

graded approach = the approach to the limen or threshold by a succession of small steps or by continuous change. [Syn. **gradual approach** (prefd., since it denotes both continuous and discrete succession).] — Fr. *rapprochement par degrés.*

gradient[n] = 1. any magnitude which slopes from a high to a low value by steps or degrees, instead of maintaining a uniform value or varying irregularly (e.g. pressure gradient, thermal gradient); 2. the rate at which the magnitude rises or falls (e.g. a gradient of 1 in 100). [Cf. **axial gradient.**] — Fr. (1) *variation graduelle,* (2) *gradient*; Ger. (1) *Gradient,* (2) *Steigung.*

gradient/physiological, /pressure, see **physiological gradient,** etc.

grand mal = the major epileptic attack, with unconsciousness, biting of tongue, incontinence, and amnesia.

grandeur/delusions (or **ideas**) **of** = exaggerated conceptions of one's own importance; e.g. the notion that one is of exalted station or has supernatural power. [Cf. **megalomania.**] — Ger. *Grössenwahn.*

granular layer/inner = the 7th layer in the retina of the human eye. [Syn. **inner molecular** (or **plexiform** or **reticular**) **layer.** See Table XI.] — Fr. *couche granulaire interne.*

granular layer/outer = the 5th layer in the retina of the human eye. [Syn. **outer molecular** (or **plexiform,** or **reticular**) **layer.** See Table XI.] — Fr. *couche granulaire externe.*

granular pressure = a specific pressure quality which results from moderately intense, blunt stimulation (Goldscheider).

graph = the representation of the relation between two variables by means of a curved or broken line. [Cf. **diagram.**] **graphic**[a] = by means of a graph. — Ger. *graphische Darstellung.*

graphic alinement (or **alignment**) = the relative distance of the successive elements of a word or of a line of writing to an actual or imaginary base line. [Largely a function of the mechanics of writing; it is frequently claimed in graphological and graphopathological investigations that specific variations in alinement have differential diagnostic value.]

graphic analysis = any analysis (e.g. of character, etc.) which is dependent upon the relations revealed in a graphic presentation.

graphic individuality = a pattern or combination of many specific writing characteristics, which by its uniqueness furnishes the basis for handwriting identification.

graphic language = communication or permanent recording of ideas by means of symbols perceived by the visual sense, being either cut into the background or overlaid on the background. [The term covers chiseled records, ink and brush writing and printing, pictorial writing, symbolic ideograms, syllabic and single-sound alphabets. It may be applied also to phonograph records, etc.; but such auditory records should be distg. fr. the visual, e.g. as **phonographic** languages or auditory graphic language, vs. **opticographic.** A graphic language for the blind has been devised which is apprehended through the tactile sense (**haptographic**).]

graphic method = 1. a method of recording responses by means of some device which registers the response or successive responses on a moving sheet of paper or other material; 2. the representation of a result or a series of results by means of a **graph.** [The method (1) may be used to measure time intervals, by registering a time line on the record sheet, or by arranging for the record sheet to move at a perfectly even and known rate, or to measure changes in extent of movement, intensity, speed, etc. as indicated by transverse motions of the recorder.]

graphic product = the visible, natural record of a writing movement. [Distg. fr. **graphomotor process,** which is analyzable by instrumental registration of the movements of the writing act.]

graphic rating scale = a method for securing and recording a judgment concerning the degree to which an individual possesses a specified trait, by placing a mark at an appropriate position between the two extremes of a line that represents the possible range of degrees of the trait, e.g. very lazy to very industrious. [Distg. fr. the method of checking an appropriate answer, e.g. "Is he industrious? Yes, No"; and from **man-to-man rating scale.**] — Fr. *échelon graphique d'appréciation.*

graphic size = height of the short or one-space letters in handwriting, as measured or estimated. [More than 3 mm. in height is held to be large; less than 2 mm., small.] — Fr. *hauteur des lettres dans l'écriture.*

graphic variability = 1. the range of variation in the handwriting characteristics of any individual penman (intra-individual variability); 2. range of variation in handwriting characteristics within groups (inter-individual variability).

graphokinesthetic = pert. to the muscular and other allied sensations aroused in writing.

graphological elements = the phases of handwriting upon which graphologists largely rely, in their characterological analyses. [They include graphic dimensions, slant, alinement, line-quality and pressure, continuity, proportions, and spacing.]

graphological portrait = the interpretation of graphic signs in their relation to one another and to the totality which comprises them. [A synthetic as contr. w. an **analytic process.**] — Ger. *Handschriftendeutung.*

graphology = 1. any scientific investigation of handwriting, either of graphic process or graphic product; 2. personality diagnosis from graphic signs. [(2) includes **medical graphology** = the attempt to find in handwriting indications of specific diseases; **forensic graphology** = study by the handwriting expert of graphic signs which are of service in the identification of handwriting.]

graphomania = an obsessive desire to write, typically resulting in uncriticized, repetitive, and irrationally valued compositions. [It tends to degenerate into **graphorrhea,** i.e. a meaningless flow of words.]

graphopathology = the investigation of changes in handwriting which accompany the incidence of mental or physical abnormality.

graphorrhea = a meaningless flow of written words. [Cf. **graphomania.**]

graphospasm, see **writer's cramp.**

grasping reflex = a coordinated response with the fingers (or toes, etc.), whereby an object is held fast. [In certain animals this reflex may be made with the lips or teeth, with the nasal proboscis, etc. Psychological interest lies in its early human manifestations in infancy. [Mediated in man by 7th to 8th cervical segments of spinal cord.] — Fr. *réflexe d'agrippement.*

gratification = a pleasant emotional attitude attached to the perception of a situation, which perception corresponds to a previous imagination, when the imagery was associated with a feeling of desire. [A narrower term than **satisfaction,** which need have no reference to past imagination. Contr. w. **disappointment.**] — Ger. *Befriedigung.*

grating/diffraction, see **diffraction grating.**

gratitude = (*pop.*) a pleasant and favorable attitude of one person toward another on account of some benefit received from him. **grateful**[a]. — Fr. *gratitude, reconnaissance*; Ger. *Dankbarkeit.*

grave harmonic, see **difference tone.**

Graves' disease, see **exophthalmic goiter.**

gravitation = the force which attracts one body toward another directly as to mass and inversely as the square of the distance separating their centroids. [Syn. **gravity** (3).] **gravitational**[a].

gravity = 1. an enduring disposition, marked by dignity or seriousness; 2. a transient posture or attitude marked by dignity or seriousness; 3. (*phys.*) syn. for **gravitation. grave**[a] (1, 2). — Fr. *pesanteur*; Ger. (1) *Ernst,* (3) *Schwerkraft.*

gravity chronometer, see **fall chronometer.**

gravity phonometer/Wundt, see **Wundt gravity phonometer.**

gray, grey = a type of visual sensation which possesses zero saturation, and (hence) no hue. [Syn. **achromatic color.** The stimuli for the grays may consist of a general mixture of radiant energies of many different wave-lengths (in sunlight), or of complementary pairs of wave-lengths, etc. The grays form a series, graded according to degree of brilliance or light-intensity; the high intensity end of the series is called **white,** the low-intensity limit **black.** According to some views white and black are distinct visual qualities.] — Fr. *gris*; Ger. *grau.*

gray/cortical, see **cortical gray.**

gray matter = the masses of neural substance in the brain or cord, which contain cell bodies. [So called from its grayish appearance in contrast to the whitish appearance of the substance which consists of myelinated nerve fibers. **gray matter** forms the outer layer or cortex of the cerebrum and cerebellum; it appears also in the deep-lying ganglionic masses; in the cord it lies only within the white matter.] — Fr. *substance grise*; Ger. *graue Substanz.*

green = 1. a visual sensation typically evoked by stimulation of the normal retina with radiation of wave-length approximately 505.5 millimicrons (mμ); 2. any color manifesting a hue predominantly similar to that of the typical green. [The complement of **purple.**] — Fr. *vert*; Ger. *grün.*

gregariousness = the tendency, manifested within certain species, to congregate or to live in groups. [Syn. **gregarious instinct,** which implies that the behavior is an inherited trait, while **gregariousness** merely describes the observed tendency.] **gregarious**[a]. — Fr. *instinct grégaire*; Ger. *Herdeninstinkt.*

grey, see **gray.**

grief = an emotional attitude characterized by intense unpleasantness, usually manifested in violent motor and glandular expressions, e.g. sobbing, weeping, etc. [Contr. w. **joy.**] — Fr. *chagrin, abattement, peine*; Ger. *Kummer.*

grimace = a distortion of the features, occasioned either by muscular paralysis or imbalance, or by momentary or habitual feelings, such as pain, disgust, contempt, vindictiveness, affectation, or the like. — Ger. *Grimasse.*

grotesque/the = a scene, figure, or occurrence which contains some of the elements of beauty, but owing to certain marked incongruities induces a tendency to laughter.

ground = 1. a rational basis of belief or action; 2. syn. for **background,** in treating of configurations. — Fr. (1) *raison, fondement,* (2) *fond*; Ger. (1, 2) *Grund.*

group = 1. any collection of objects, beings, or data, which may be treated as a unitary whole; 2. (*soc.*) a collection of organisms which associate or live together or which respond to one another or to a common stimulus; 3. (*Gestalt*) a pattern or configuration of items, the existence and properties of each of which depend upon the nature of the pattern or configuration as a whole. [Syn. (1) **class;** syn. (2) **social group.** Social groups are classed as **primary** (e.g. the family) and **secondary** (e.g. a labor union; the state).]

group behavior = 1. the activities of a social collection of individuals treated as a whole; 2. the general activities of group members along similar lines, after eliminating conflicting or individual tendencies; 3. behavior which is characteristic of individuals in a group, but not of the same individuals in solitary situations. — Fr. *comportement collectif.*

group/co-acting = (*soc.*) an aggregation of individuals who have a common interest or a like segment of behavior, i.e. who are responding primarily to a stimulus other than one another. [E.g. a company of soldiers, the Republican party. Often coincident with the **secondary group** of sociology, though the latter is considered from the point of view of structure, rather than behavior.]

group consciousness = 1. the consciousness, or mind, sometimes attributed to a collection of individuals or community, and regarded as something different and distinct, from the consciousness of any individual; 2. the consciousness which an individual has of other members of the group or of their common activities, attitudes, or sentiments. [Distg. fr. **general consciousness** = the experiences which are common to the individuals of a group. Cf. **collective psychology.**] — Fr. *conscience collective.*

group differences = deviations, in respect to any characteristics, between whole groups in a given population, as determined by some statistical measure, e.g. the average, or the variability. [It is assumed on the basis of probability that there will be corresponding differences between individual members of the group. When differences between such individuals are found, there is often the illicit inference that group differences exist. Contr. w. **individual differences,** and w. **sex differences.**]

group/face-to-face = (*soc.*) a group in which the individuals react mainly to one another. [E.g. a family, a committee. Often coincident with the **primary group** of sociology, though not necessarily so permanent in nature.] — Fr. *groupe de vis-à-vis.*

group factors in intelligence = factors (or determiners) which underlie efficiencies, and occur in more than one but less than all of any given set of abilities (Spearman). [The kinship of the specific factors in such performances, i.e. their eligibility to be considered group factors, may be detected by correlating these performances with two reference abilities. Cf. **factor theory.**]

group fallacy = 1. the assumption, generally regarded as erroneous, of a collective mind, or unitary group consciousness; 2. any postulation concerning group action which is of such a character that, when the supposed *group* activity is reduced to the activity of *individuals*, it will be shown to be either meaningless or false. [Cf. **biological analogy, crowd psychology** (1), **group consciousness.**] — Fr. *illusion de l'âme collective.*

group marriage = a form of marriage in which a few men, often brothers, marry in common with an equal number of women, often sisters. [The husbands may also be related to the wives. Esp. developed among Australian tribes.]

group mind, see **group consciousness.**

group selection = a process of selection in which the group, instead of the individual as such, operates as a unit in the struggle for existence. [Cf. **natural selection.**]

group test = an examination, or test, so arranged that it can be applied to a number of individuals at once. [Distg. fr. **individual test,** which is given to each testee separately; the U.S. Army **Alpha tests** are typical group tests; the **Binet-Simon tests** are individual.] — Fr. *test collectif.*

growth = 1. enlargement of the individual organism or its parts; 2. any kind of increase, e.g. growth in complexity, efficiency, value, etc. [(2) is applied to species and societies, as well as to individuals.] — Fr. (1) *croissance,* (2) *agrandissement*; Ger. (1) *Wachsen,* (2) *Wachstum.*

growth curve = a graphic representation of the changes which take place in a given mental or physical character or function with increasing maturity of the individual or group. [The usual **growth curve** is a rising curve, which represents progressive changes in the function with increasing maturity.]

guidance/educational = the process of assisting a person, by the use of standardized procedures and ascertained facts, to plan and pursue his education, in the light of his past achievements, difficulties, abilities, and interests. [The standardized procedures are called **educational guidance tests.**] — Fr. *orientation pédagogique.*

guidance/vocational = the process of assisting a person, by certain systematized procedures, to choose a vocation, prepare for it, enter it, and make progress in it. [Includes class instruction in occupational opportunities and requirements; provision of opportunities for vocational trial; assistance in self-appraisal, through systematic personal interview; and evaluation of record of past educational and occupational accomplishments. Scientific vocational guidance uses also standardized measures of general and specific abilities, interests, and vocationally significant traits of character and personality.] — Fr. *orientation professionnelle*; Ger. *Berufsberatung.*

guiding idea = an idea which constantly recurs or persists, and determines the course and direction of associated trains of thought. [The **guiding idea** may be general (e.g. an **ideal**); or specific problem or **task;** the pathological type is called a **fixed idea.** Cf. **determining tendency.**] — Fr. *idée directrice.*

guilt/sense of = an emotional state, in which the individual is dominated by the belief or knowledge that he has contravened some social custom, ethical principle, or legal regulation. — Fr. *sentiment de culpabilité*; Ger. *Schuldgefühl.*

gustation = a sense whose receptors lie in the mucous membrane covering the tongue and soft palate, and whose stimuli consist of certain soluble chemicals, e.g. salts, acids, etc. [Syn. **taste** (preferably limited to the function); cf. **taste tetrahedron, gustatory qualities.**] **gustatory**[a]. — Fr. *sensation du goût*; Ger. *Geschmacksempfindung.*

gustatory nerves = those portions of the 7th, 9th, and 10th pairs of cranial nerves which terminate in the taste receptors in the front and back of the tongue, respectively, and the epiglottis.

gustatory qualities = the several qualities of taste sensation. [Contemporary investigators usually limit gustatory qualities to four: *saline, sweet, sour,* and *bitter.* Henning lists these as **primary tastes** (like primary colors) with simple intermediate tastes connecting them. Cf. **taste tetrahedron, alkaline.**] — Ger. *Geschmacksqualitäten.*

gustatory stimulus = an aqueous solution of a substance which acts chemically upon some material in the receptor-cells of the lingual papillae. [The chemical constitution essential to the substances which serve as stimuli for the several tastes is not yet certain. The threshold concentration of a sapid substance is high in comparison with that of an odorous substance. Cf. **gustation.**]

guttural = pert. to or located in the throat.

gutturophonia = a form of **dysphonia** characterized by a guttural or throaty voice.

gynandromorphism = the union of both male and female characters in the same organism. **gynandromorph**[np], **gynandromorphous**[a].

gynandry = tendency of the female body to approach in form that of the male. **gynander**[np] = a masculine woman. **gynandrous**[a].

gynephobia = morbid fear of women.

gyrus, gyre = an arched ridge on the surface of the cerebrum bounded on each side by sulci or fissures. [Syn. **convolution.** The cerebral gyri are named according to their location or from the discoverer of their function; several **gyri** combine to form a **lobe.**] **gyri**[pl], **gyres**[pl]. — Fr. *circonvolution*; Ger. *Hirnwindung.*

H

h = (*psychophys.*) a value derived from the fundamental formula of the phi-gamma hypothesis, which reads $P = 1/2\ [1 - \phi\ (hx - 2)]$. [It is the measure of precision in a normal **psychometric function,** and bears an inverse relation to the **probable error,** $h = 0.4769/\text{p.e.}$]

Haab's pupil reflex = contraction of both pupils when attention is directed to a bright object in a darkened room. [Mediated by the optic tracts and oculomotor nerves. Cf. **pupillary reflex.**]

habenula = an area of fibers overlying the ganglion habenulae, and located in the **epithalamus,** which functions as an olfactory correlation center.

habit = a form of acquired response which is relatively invariable and is readily elicited. [Usually restricted to coordinated muscular movements, but sometimes more generally applied; e.g. habit of thought. **habit** is one of the end-products of learning and is therefore often contr. w. **instinct;** being nearly automatic it is often contr. w. **purposeful action.** On the experiential side, **habit** is usually characterized by decreased attention. In pop. psychology the term is improperly used with an explanatory connotation; e.g. force of habit. The neural correlate of habit is believed by many to be decreased synaptic resistance. According to Aristotle, habit (ἕξις) is of basic importance in morality. Distg. fr. **habituation,** which in psychological usage generally connotes a falling away of overt response, and fr. **custom,** which denotes racial habit. Cf. **fixation** (1).] **habitual**[a] (of the act), **habituated**[a] (of the organism). — Fr. *habitude*; Ger. *Gewohnheit.*

habit-deterioration, habit-disorganization = a noncommittal formulation of the essential nature of the deterioration in dementia praecox.

habit formation = the process, usually assumed to come about through repetition, whereby a response becomes gradually fixed in a relatively invariable and automatic form. [Syn. **learning,** a broader term.]

habit-forming drug = a drug, usually a narcotic, which produces a craving for continuing its use. [E. g. morphin. The resulting condition is called **drug addiction;** the user is a **drug addict,** or **addict.**]

habit interference = conflict of two or more contrary acts which are practiced in the same situation and hence likely to be elicited by the same stimulus. [E.g. if one has formed the habit of opening a door outward, this would interfere with later acts, necessitated by a change in the door, to open it inward.]

habits/hierarchy of = a phrase employed to describe the organization of simpler habits into progressively higher systematizations. [Such organization may be (e.g.) from letters to words, phrases, etc. The conception has been used to explain the occurrence of **plateaus** in the learning of such complex functions as the telegraphic code and typewriting.]

habitat = the usual environment of individuals, groups, varieties, or species of plants and animals.

habitual image, see **image/habitual.**

habituation = the process of becoming adapted to a given stimulus, situation, or general environment. [A pop. and rather loose term.] **habituate**[v]. — Fr. *accoutumance*; Ger. *Gewöhnung.*

hair = a fine filamentary structure which projects from the surface of organisms. — Fr. *poil.*

hair-bulb, see **hair-follicle.**

hair cells = a series of columnar cells found in the organ of Corti in the cochlea of the ear; they extend serially throughout the length of the cochlear canal in two groups, the inner and the outer hair cells; they vary in length according to their location in the canal, and have therefore been assumed to play a role in selecting stimuli of different frequency; the cells at the base are shortest. [Cf. **Corti/organ of.**] — Fr. *cellules ciliées*; Ger. *Haarzellen.*

hair cells of ampullae = the flask-shaped cells lying between the supporting cells in the membranous lining in the dilatations at the ends of the semicircular ducts. [The hair-like filaments of the hair cells project into the cavity where they are supposedly stimulated by the shifting of the otoconia due to changes in position of the head, in turn stimulating the vestibular branch of the 8th cranial nerve.] — Fr. *crêtes ciliés des ampoules.*

hair esthesiometer (or **aesthesiometer**) = an instrument, devised by M. von Frey, for measuring pressure sensitivity; it consists of a horsehair or human hair projecting from a handle; when pressed vertically on the skin the hair exerts its maximum intensity just as it bends and the point of inflection leaves the perpendicular; the bending point varies (inversely) with the diameter of the hair and (directly) with the length of projection from the handle. [Cf. **von Frey hairs.**] — Fr. *esthésiomètre à crin.*

hair-follicle = a sac-like structure in the skin, consisting of the hair root, the root sheaths, and the connective tissue envelope. [It is supplied with an afferent nerve termination which is considered to be a receptor for pressure sensibility; it is also connected with the arrector pili muscle. Syn. **hair-bulb.**] — Fr. *follicule pileux.*

hair sensibility = specific sensations, similar to touch sensations (or identical with them), which are aroused at the base of the follicle of a hair when it is bent or pulled. — Fr. *sensibilité pilaire.*

hair-strokes = upstrokes, downstrokes, or lateral strokes of the pen, which are written with slight pressure. [Contr. w. **shadow strokes.**]

half-center/motor = in a motor center concerned with reciprocal innervation, that part which controls one of the pair of antagonistic muscles.

Haller's tunica vasculosa = the vascular layer of the choroid coat of the eye. [Syn. **Haller's layer.**]

hallucination = abnormal misinterpretation of ideational experiences as perceptions. [Frequently, but not always, indicative of mental derangement. Syn. **pseudoperception.** Cf. **illusion, delusion.** In **illusion** there is erroneous perception of present sense data; in **hallucination** the error of perception goes so far as to suppose facts present to a sense which is actually receiving no relevant stimulation; in **delusion** (an error of judgment rather than of sense perception) there is misinterpretation of the state of affairs but not of the facts immediately present to sense.] **hallucinational**[a] = pert. to the process; **hallucinatory**[a] = pert. to data.

hallucinatory image, see **image/hallucinatory.**

hallucinosis = a disorder in which the patient is subject to hallucinations, without any disorder of consciousness or other setting. [Cf. **alcoholic hallucinosis.**]

halo = a narrow bright band which is observed surrounding the dark after-image of a bright stimulus. — Fr. *auréole, halo*; Ger. *Hof.*

halo effect = a tendency, when one is estimating or rating a person with respect to a certain trait, to be influenced by an estimate of some other trait or by one's general impression of the person. [An important source of error in rating-scale procedure; it may be obviated somewhat by rating one trait for the entire group of persons before rating the second trait.] — Fr. *effet d'auréole.*

hammer-bone, see **malleus.**

Hampton Court maze = a pattern of maze used in testing, which reproduces in miniature the historic out-door maze found in the gardens of Hampton Court, England.

hand = the terminal part of the forelimb of primates, consisting of carpus, metacarpus, and fingers, which is structurally adapted to the function of grasping. — Fr. *main.*

handedness, see **dextrality** and Table III.

handicraft, see **craft** (2).

handwriting = symbolic tracings or marks, made on paper or other material by the human hand or its equivalent, as a record of thought or as a means of communication. [Loosely used for **script,** a more general term; both terms exclude **chiseling** and **artistic representations;** but **script** would include **foot-writing** and **mouth-writing.** A more inclusive and exact term is **graphic language.**] — Fr. *écriture*; Ger. *Handschrift.*

handwriting scale = any device for measurement of excellence in writing by comparison with a standardized series of samples. [The two best known scales are the **Thorndike scale,** based on *general merit* as a criterion, and the **Ayres scale,** based on *legibility.*] — Fr. *échelle d'écriture.*

handwriting system = any conventionalized style of writing which involves standardization of design of letters, slant, size and proportion of parts (such as relative height and width of letters), and organization of one, two, and three space letters into a scale of thirds, fourths, or fifths. [Well-known American systems include round-hand, Spencerian, and vertical writing.] Fr. *système d'écriture.*

Hans/Clever, see **Clever Hans.**

haploid = having a reduced number (i.e. a single set) of chromosomes. [Cf. **diploid.**]

haploscope = an instrument, essentially the same as the **stereoscope,** with which figures may be presented separately to the two eyes in such a way as to force compensatory displacement or rolling movements of the eyes in order to maintain binocular fusion (Hering).

happen = syn. for **to occur.** [The term implies randomness or unexpectedness.] **happening**[n].

happiness = a general pleasurable condition, marked by satisfaction with life as a whole. [Contr. w. **unhappiness.**] **happy**[a]. — Fr. *bonheur, heureux*[a]; Ger. *Glück.*

haptic = pert. to the skin or to the sense of **touch** in its broadest sense.

haptics = the branch which investigates cutaneous sensations.

haptometer = a device for measuring differential sensitivity to touch; it consists of a system of levers, by means of which a standard weight is applied to a definite area of the skin and the pressure increased or decreased without jar by removal or addition of counterbalancing weights.

hard of hearing, see **hypacousia.**

hard palate, see **palate.**

Harder's gland = a rudimentary lacrymal gland situate at the inner canthus of the eye.

harmful, see **detrimental.**

harmonic = a partial tone or overtone, whose frequency is an integral multiple of the fundamental frequency. [Often used to denote an emphasized overtone.] **harmonic**[a].

harmonic analyzer = a mechanical device which resolves a complex curve into its theoretical sine and cosine components, in accordance with the assumptions of Fourier's law. [Cf. **Fourier's law.**]

harmonic mean = the reciprocal of the arithmetic mean of the reciprocals of a series of quantities. [The formula for H, the harmonic mean, is $1/H = (1/N)\,\Sigma\,(1/x)$ where N = number of cases, and x = any score or other quantity.] — Fr. *moyenne harmonique.*

harmonical/Ellis, see **Ellis harmonical.**

harmonium = a type of reed organ, esp. the type in which the air is forced through the reeds by a compression bellows, as contr. w. the American organ, in which the air is sucked through. [**harmoniums** are often given a special tuning for use in demonstrating unusual intervals and scales, and in experimental work. Cf. **Ellis harmonical.**]

harmony = 1. the branch of musical science which considers the combination of tones into chords (or discords) and the progression of these chords in musical composition; 2. a simultaneous combination of tones which produces a musical effect, usually consonant; 3. (*esth.*) any arrangement of forms, combination of colors, or other qualities, which induces a pleasurable feeling tone in the observer. [Contr. w. **disharmony; harmony** (1, 2) includes both **consonances** (= pleasing combinations) and **dissonances** (= displeasing effects), many of the latter being admissible provided they are resolved into a consonant chord.] **harmonize**[v], **harmonious**[a].

harp theory, see **hearing/theories of.**

harshness = a qualitative characteristic of sounds which are of particularly irregular wave form or which present frequent and abrupt variations in amplitude. [Syn. **roughness.**] — Ger. *Rauhigkeit.*

hashish = syn. for **Cannabis indica.** [Term derived from **hashishin,** a sect of malefactors addicted to habitual intoxication with **C. indica;** this word is believed to be the source of the term *assassin.*]

hate, hatred = an emotional attitude characterized by anger and an extreme aversion, enmity, or ill-will, together with a desire to inflict injury upon some individual or object. [Contr. w. **love.**] — F . *haine*; Ger. *Hass.*

haunted swing illusion = an illusion experienced when the individual is placed in a swing which apparently oscillates in the usual manner, whereas in reality it is motionless and the room with its entire contents is in motion. — Fr. *illusion de la balançoire.*

haunting = (*pop.*) the supposed return of the *spirit* or *ghost* of one who met his death by foul play, for the purpose of tormenting the guilty. [The ghost is said to frequent either the environs of the guilty person or the scene of the tragedy.] **haunt**[v]. — Fr. *hanter*; Ger. *spuken.*

hazard[n] = 1. randomness or chance; 2. a dangerous venture. [Too vague and equivocal a term for technical use. Cf. **randomness.**] **hazard**[v] = to put forward a hypothesis upon admittedly inadequate grounds. — Ger. *Zufall.*

head nystagmus = the oscillatory movement of the head which occurs when an animal is rotated; the head is slowly turned in the opposite direction to that of the rotation and then brought quickly back; this is repeated, with the rapid component of the action always in the direction of rotation. — Fr. *n. céphalique.*

head retraction = a reflex withdrawal of the head when the nares are sharply irritated. [Mediated by the trigeminocervical arcs.]

headache = pain or ache localized in the head. [**organic h.** = due to disease of the brain or its membrane; **reflex h., symptomatic h.** = due to disease of some part external to the brain, e.g. stomach, eyes, etc. Syn. **cephalalgia.** Cf. **cephalagra, migraine.**] — Fr. *mal à la tête, céphalée*; Ger. *Kopfweh, Kopfschmerz.*

Healy completion test = 1. a colored picture of an outdoor scene depicting ten simple activities; it is provided with ten inch-square openings so placed as to omit ten significant objects; the testee is to select from fifty one-inch blocks the ten which depict objects appropriate for insertion in the openings, thus supplying a non-language form of **completion test;** 2. a similar test showing ten successive scenes in the daily activity of a boy, having sixty blocks for ten openings, and provided with a more refined method of scoring. [(1) is technically known as **Healy PC–I;** (2) as **Healy PC–II.**]

hearing = the act or function of perceiving sounds by means of the ear. [Syn. **audition,** preferably applied to the sense or general field of sound perception.] — Ger. *Hören.*

hearing/double disharmonic, see **diplacusis.**

hearing loss = the proportion or percent of normally audible tones that cannot be heard by a given person of defective hearing. [Cf. **audiogram.**] — Fr. *taux de déficience auditive.*

hearing mute = a pop. term applied to certain individuals who from birth or from an early age have been unable to speak and who behave like deaf children, but who nevertheless possess considerable ability to hear. — Fr. *entendant-muet.*

hearing range, see **audibility range.**

hearing/theories of = theories which seek to explain the essential operations of the auditory mechanism through which physical stimuli give rise to the phenomena of hearing. [There are many such theories; the most prominent types are (1) **resonance** (Helmholtz) **theory,** according to which complex sounds are analyzed within the cochlea through specific response (i.e. through sympathetic vibration, or resonance) to the simple sine-form components of the sound by separate segments of the basilar membrane (or other structures); (2) **telephone** (Rutherford) **theory,** according to which the auditory mechanism plays a role like that of the telephone transmitter, relaying to the brain impulses similar in frequency and wave-form to the sounds striking the ear; according to this theory, analysis does not occur in the cochlea, but in the brain; (3) **hydraulic** (Max F. Meyer) **theory,** according to which (as in the telephone theory) sound frequencies are represented in the frequency of impulses relayed to the brain, but in which (unlike that theory) analysis in the cochlea is accounted for by postulating that different tonal components involve different lengths of the basilar membrane as measured from the oval window; (4) **sound-pattern** (Ewald) **theory,** which holds that sounds cause the basilar membrane to vibrate in segments, with a complex of nodes and antinodes, much like Chladni's plates, and that pitch and analysis occur by the appreciation of differences in the patterns set up by different frequencies. Syn. (1) **harp theory, piano theory.**] — Fr. *t. de l'audition*; Ger. *T. der Gehörsempfindungen.*

heart = a tubular muscular organ, usually divided into chambers, whose function is to force into the arteries blood received from the veins, thereby maintaining the circulation of blood through the body. [The **heart** (or **cardiac**) **muscles** are striate in type, but resemble the non-striate or smooth muscles in being regulated by the autonomic nervous system.] **cardiac**[a], — Fr. *coeur*; Ger. *Herz.*

heat = 1. (*phys.*) a form of vibration belonging to the same series as light, but with much greater wave-length; 2. (*psychol.*) a sensory experience due to the simultaneous stimulation of warmth and cold receptors; 3. (*biol.*) a state of sexual receptivity in female mammals. [(2) is often used as syn. for **warmth,** but is technically distg. fr. the latter as a different quality with a stinging character, and is attributed to a combination of warmth and cold sensations. Cf. **temperature.**] **hot**[a]. — Fr. (1) *chaleur,* (2) *sensation ardente*; Ger. *Hitze.*

heat grill = a device for simultaneously arousing warmth and cold sensations in adjacent skin areas; it consists of glass or metal tubes filled with warm water, alternated with tubes of cold water, in parallel series which can be simultaneously applied to an area of the skin. [The experience so aroused is, or resembles, the experience of heat as aroused by high temperatures.]

heat sensation, see **heat** (2).

heat spot, see **warm spot.**

hebephrenia = Kahlbaum and Kraepelin's term for a silly manneristic dilapidating form of dementia praecox. **hebephrenic**[a].

hebetic = pert. to youth or adolescence.

hederiform terminations = a type of sensory end-organ, described by Ranvier, and classed as free nerve endings. [They occur in the pig's snout with Merkel cells, but in the human without the latter. They are disk-shaped and are found in the interpapillary regions of the Malpighian layer of the skin.]

hedonic = pert. to feeling or feeling tone.

hedonic tone = the pleasurable or unpleasurable accompaniment or characteristic of conscious experiences. [Syn. **feeling tone; affective tone** (prefd.).] — Fr. *tonalité de plaisir ou peine, élément hédonique.*

hedonics = the branch of psychology which investigates pleasurable and unpleasurable feelings. — Fr. *théorie de la sensibilité.*

hedonism = 1. the ethical theory which is based on the assumption that personal pleasure is the standard for human behavior and conduct; 2. the psychological theory that men act so as to attain pleasant and avoid unpleasant feeling. [Cf. **utilitarianism.**] **hedonistic**[a], **hedonist**[np].

hedonistic esthetics, see **algedonic esthetics.**

heft[n] = syn. for sensation of **weight.**

heft[v] = 1. to lift; 2. to experience the weight of an object as judged by the kinesthetic sensations aroused by holding or lifting it. — Fr. (1) *soulever,* (2) *sentir la pesanteur*; Ger. *heben.*

Heidelberg man = an extinct human race represented by a fossil jaw found at Mauer near Heidelberg, Germany, regarded as a very early type of man. [Syn. **Homo heidelbergensis.**]

helicoid = resembling in shape the form of a snail, coil, or screw. — Ger. *spiralförmig.*

helicotrema = a small opening in the basilar membrane at the apex of the cochlear canal, through which the scala vestibuli communicates with the scala tympani. (Accent **-tree-**.)

heliotropism, heliotaxis = a simple orienting response, either positive or negative, to stimulation by the sun's rays, or by light in general. [Syn. **phototropism**, a broader term including response to any light source. Cf. **tropism.**] (Accent **-ot-**.) **heliotropic**[a].

helix = the curved border of the auricle, or outer ear. — Ger. *Ohrschnecke.*

Helmholtz theory of hearing, see **hearing/theories of.**

Helmholtz theory of vision, see **Young-Helmholtz theory.**

helplessness = 1. an emotional state attributed to the human infant, manifested in crying; 2. a general term denoting the inability of the human infant to cope with the environment without the assistance of other individuals. — Fr. *faiblesse*; Ger. *Hilflosigkeit.*

hematachometer, see **tachometer.**

hematophobia = morbid fear connected with the sight of blood.

hemeralopia = 1. (etymol.) day-blindness; 2. (commonly) night-blindness. [Contr. w. **nyctalopia.** Both terms have been used in two opposite senses. To avoid confusion, their use should be avoided. Cf. **night-blindness, day-blindness.**]

hemianalgesia = insensitivity to pain on one side of the body.

hemianesthesia, hemianaesthesia = insensibility to touch stimuli on one side of the body.

hemianopia, hemianopsia, see **hemiopia.**

hemiopia = restriction of vision to one lateral half or sector of the binocular visual field, consequent upon loss of sensitivity in corresponding areas of both retinas. [Most commonly due to a lesion in their neural connections centrad to the optic chiasm. Syn. **hemianopia, hemianopsia,** which emphasize the impaired half.]

hemiparesis = paralysis of one side of the body.

hemiplegia = paralysis (i.e. loss of ability to make voluntary movements) which affects one side of the body. [Due generally to interruption of the pyramidal pathways, e.g. after rupture of a blood-vessel in the internal capsule.] **hemiplegic**[a].

hemisphere = either of the two lateral halves of the cerebrum, or of the cerebellum. [Without qualifying adj. refers always to the cerebrum.]

hemispheres/cerebellar = expanded portions of the cerebellum at either side of the median plane.

hemitone = syn. for **semitone** in ancient Greek music.

hemorrhage (or **haemorrhage**)**/cerebral** = a dispersion of blood due to rupture of a blood vessel in the brain. [The pressure of the escaping blood affects the functions of the brain, causing temporary loss of sensation or motility, according to the region affected, and waste products from the absorption of the clot may cause permanent destruction of tissue.] — Ger. *Blutung.*

Hensen's cells = supporting cells of triangular shape, which form the outer rounded border of the organ of Corti in the internal ear.

hepatic = pert. to or located in the liver. (Accent **-pat-**.)

Herbartian psychology = the system of intellectualistic psychology and educational psychology developed by J. F. Herbart (1824–25) and his followers, which is based upon the presumption that various presentations are struggling to rise into consciousness, and that they inhibit one another, or interact and affect one another, in accordance with certain dynamic principles which can be expressed in mathematical formulae. [The standpoint was developed from the doctrine of Leibnitz, which emphasized activity in opposition to the empirical doctrine of passive reception: Herbartianism employed the concepts of threshold, inhibition, and degrees of clearness, rising to apperception; it thus became the opponent of pure associationism in Germany and gave psychology an idealistic character which influenced many later writers. Cf. **intellectualism.**]

herd = a group of animals, human or infra-human, which manifest a low degree of social organization. [Cf. **horde.**] — Fr. *horde*; Ger. *Herde.*

herd instinct, see **gregariousness.**

heredity = 1. the transmission through the germ plasm of factors or genes, which determine the resemblances of offspring to parents or other ancestors; 2. the sum total of characters derived from factors transmitted through the germ plasm or genes; e.g. a child's heredity. [Syn. (1) **heritage,** (2) **inheritance.** Contr. w. (*a*) **acquired characters,** (*b*) **environmental influences, environment.**] **hereditary**[a]; **inherit**[v]. — Ger. (1) *Vererbung,* (2) *Erblichkeit.*

Hering after-image = the first positive after-image, or after-sensation, which occurs following a brief light-stimulus. [It is bright and of the same hue as the primary sensation.]

Hering grays = a set of 50 neutral gray papers, graded from extreme white to extreme black in steps which are subjectively equal. [The set represents the **achromatic** series of colors.] — Fr. *papiers gris de H.*

Hering illusion = an illusion, or distorted perception of visual form, observed when a number of lines radiating from a point are crossed by two parallel lines on opposite sides of the point and equidistant from it; the parallel lines appear to bow outward, i.e. away from the central point. [Distg. fr. **Wundt illusion,** in which lines radiating from two points meet at the center and the parallel lines crossing them appear to bow inward at the center.]

Hering theory of vision = the theory proposed by E. Hering and modified by later writers, according to which visual sensations are due to three pairs of antagonistic processes in the optic system, one member of each pair being catabolic, the other anabolic, the pairs yielding respectively the sensations of white and black, of yellow and blue, and of red and green. [The two members of any one pair of colors are said to be **antagonistic colors.** Cf. **vision/theory of.**]

Hering window = a device arranged by Hering to demonstrate color contrast, the essential features of which are a black shutter with 2 oblong openings, placed over the window of a darkened room; one opening is filled with a ground glass, the other with a colored glass; the shadows of a black rod are thrown from the two openings upon a screen of white-glass and are compared. [Cf. **colored shadow experiment.**] — Fr. *fenêtre de H.*

heritage = the sum total of traits and characters derived by hereditary transmission. [Cf. **heredity.**] — Ger. *Erbschaft.*

hermaphroditic dreams = dreams which are bisexual in their blurrings or blendings, indicating the bipolarity of the sexual impulse (Coriat). [They occur most frequently in homosexuality.] — Fr. *rêves hermaphroditiques.*

hermaphroditism = presence of both the male and female reproductive organs in a single organism. [Cf. **somatic hermaphroditism.**] (Accent **-maff-.**) **hermaphroditic**[a], **hermaphrodite**[np] (4 syll.). — Ger. *Zwitterbildung.*

hermetics = (*hist.*) any system of secret lore. [E.g. the Cabalas and the doctrines of the Rosicrucians.]

hero = 1. a human being, real or legendary, distinguished for valor, fortitude, or bold enterprises, and revered by his contemporaries or by posterity; 2. a human being, real or imagined, whose behavior typifies the ideals of another person or persons. [Cf. **culture hero.**] **heroine (heroin)**[n fem]. (accent **her-), heroism**[n], **heroic**[a], — Ger. *Held.*

herpes zoster = an eruption of pustules on the skin, following the path of some nerve and symptomatic of an inflammation of the spinal or cranial ganglia of the sensory nerves. [Syn. **posterior poliomyelitis, shingles** (pop.).]

Herring-Binet test = a modification of the **Binet-Simon scale** published in 1922 by J. P. Herring, containing thirty-eight tests, taken mainly from Binet. [The test differs from the original Binet chiefly in scoring as a **point scale** and in being assembled in five groups, so arranged that the first group alone forms a brief test and that the remaining groups can be used as supplements to the first, as desired.]

heterochronia, heterochrony, heterochronism = a difference between two processes in respect to their time or rate of occurrence. [Applied esp. to the chronaxia of nerves and muscles. Contr. w. **isochronia.**] (Accent (1) **het-** and **-chro-**; accent (2, 3) **-rock-.**) **heterochronic**[a], **-ous**[a].

heterodox = (in science) characterizing fundamental beliefs which are contrary to the generally accepted scientific principles of the time; or, characterizing the individual who holds such beliefs. [Contr. w. **orthodox;** the terms are borrowed from theology, but are used in science without the emotional coloring.] **heterodoxy**[n]. — Ger. *irrgläubig.*

heterogeneity = difference in quality, kind, or sort among the constituents of any group. [Contr. w. **homogeneity.**] (Accent **-nee-.**) **heterogeneous**[a] (accent **-jee-.**). — Ger. *Verschiedenartigkeit.*

heteromorphic = (*biol.*) deviating from the normal type.

heteromorphosis = the development of an organ in a position in which it does not normally occur, e.g. the formation of an antenna in place of an eye in the crayfish.

heteronomy = the subjection of an individual to the authority or guidance of another, as in hypnosis. [Cf. **heterosuggestion.**] (Accent **-ron-.**)

heterophoria, see **imbalance/muscular.**

heterosexuality = 1. attraction on the part of an individual for or toward individuals of the opposite sex; 2. sexual intercourse between individuals of opposite sex. [Contr. w. **homosexuality** and **bisexuality.**] **heterosexual**[a].

heterosuggestion = the inducing of an idea or action in one individual by another. [Contr. w. **autosuggestion.** Cf. **suggestion.**]

heterotropia, see **strabismus.**

heterozygote = an organism of mixed heredity, i.e. which possesses two contrasted Mendelian characters, derived respectively from the two parents. [Contr. w. **homozygote.** Cf. **zygote.**]

hexagonal cells/layer of, see **pigment layer.**

Heyman's law = a law pert. to the threshold value of visual stimuli, to the effect that the threshold value of a given stimulus is increased, proportionately to the intensity of the inhibitory stimulus, when an inhibitory stimulus is offered.

hibernation = a condition of torpor and inactivity which persists in animals of certain species usually during the winter season. **hibernate**[v]. — Ger. *Winterschlaf.*

hiccup, hiccough = spasmodic contraction of the diaphragm causing inspiration, followed by closure of the glottis. — Fr. *hoquet;* Ger. *Schlucken.*

hierarchical table = a table of correlation coefficients which satisfy the **inter-columnar correlation** criterion. [This term is now replaced by the less equivocal one, **equiproportional table.**]

hierarchy of habits = a complex organization of habits, whereby habits of a higher order include as components those of the next lower order. [E.g. in learning telegraphy, letter habits are combined into word habits, and these in turn into phrase habits.]

hieroglyphic writing = a graphic system in which pictures are used to represent objects, words, syllables, or occasionally phonetic elements. [The best example is the ancient Egyptian system. Grk. "sacred carving."] — Fr. *écriture hiéroglyphique;* Ger. *Bilderschrift.*

high = (*aud.*) characterizing the pitch of tones which are of relatively rapid rates of vibration. [Syn. **acute, shrill.**] — Fr. *élevé;* Ger. *hoch.*

higher mental processes = a term used to distinguish roughly certain complex cognitive processes or functions (e.g. thought, constructive imagination, etc.) from the more elementary (e.g. sensation and simple apprehension). [Probably based upon a distinction between human and animal experience or upon genetic considerations.] — Fr. *processus mentaux supérieurs.*

higher units of response = complex unitary responses (e.g. a word in typewriting) which are integrations of simpler acts. [They may in turn function as integral parts of still higher units. Cf. **hierarchy of habits.**] — Fr. *unités réactionnelles supérieures.*

highest audible tone = the upper limit of the tonal continuum, corresponding to the relatively high stimulus-frequencies. [For the normal human ear, the limit is 18,000–22,000 cycles. Early determinations placed the limit too high, and there was also confusion through the use of single vibrations (s.v.) rather than double or complete vibrations (d.v.) i.e. cycles ($\sim$).] — Fr. *limite auditive supérieure.*

hind-brain = that division of the brain which is derived from the most caudad of the three primary cerebral vesicles, and which lies nearest the spinal cord. [It includes the **cerebellum,**

pons, and **medulla.** Cf. **epencephalon.**] — Fr. *cerveau postérieur, arrière-cerveau*; Ger. *Hinterhirn.*

Hipp chronoscope = a chronoscope driven by clock-work, whose movement is regulated by a vibrating tongue; it is provided with two dials of 100 divisions each, one recording seconds and 10ths, the other 100ths and 1000ths (sigma); the movement of the pointers is started and stopped by means of a clutch actuated by electromagnets, and there are connections whereby the record may either be started by making the circuit and stopped by breaking it, or vice versa. [First made by Mathias Hipp, a watchmaker, in 1843. It had been preceded by Wheatstone's chronoscope (1840), and was later greatly improved (1849). It was used about this time by astronomers for measuring the **personal equation** (response or reaction lag) in astronomical observation, and was later introduced into psychological laboratories for the measurement of reaction times.]

hippocampus = a term applied to two protuberances, consisting of nerve tracts, situate on the floor of the lateral ventricles of the brain. [The **hippocampus major,** or **horn of ammon,** lies in the inferior horn of the lateral ventricle, the **hippocampus minor** in the posterior horn.] **hippocampi**[pl], **hippocampal**[a]. — Ger. *Ammonswindung.*

hircine = a quality of olfactory sensation, of which cheese is a typical example. [A class of Zwaardemaker's. Cf. **odor.**] — Ger. *Kaprylgeruch.*

histogenesis = the origin, differentiation, and growth of tissues in the body.

histogram = (*statist.*) a graph of a frequency distribution, in which the number of cases within each class is represented by the height of a horizontal line drawn above the base or x-axis; these horizontals are each the length of a class interval, and are connected by verticals erected at successive class limits. [Cf. **bar diagram.**]

histology = the branch of biology which deals with the structure of the tissues. [Contr. w. **cytology,** which deals with the internal structure of cells.]

histonal selection = a variety of natural selection resulting from competition between the various kinds of tissue in the body. [Rarely used. Syn. **intraselection.**]

historical fallacy = the assumption that the study of the history of a species, race, etc., enables one to understand its entire nature. [Syn. **biological fallacy.**] — Fr. *sophisme historique.*

historical method = the investigation of biological evolution by comparison of the temporal succession of forms.

history = 1. (*phenomenal* and *pop.*) the temporal or chronological succession of events in the development of an organism, social group, disease, etc.; 2. the causal connection of events presented phenomenally as a mere chronology; 3. the purposive interpretation of the data of chronology. [The causal connection under (2) may be merely the record of uniformities of coexistence and sequence, or it may refer these uniformities to underlying efficient causation.] **historical**[a] = pert. to history, **historic**[a] = important in history. — Ger. *Geschichte.*

Hitzig's girdle = analgesia (i.e. insensibility to pain) at the level of the breast, which occurs in tabes dorsalis. [Cf. **girdle sensation.**] — Fr. *ceinture de H.*

Holmgren test = a test of color-blindness which involves the matching of skeins of different-colored yarn with three standard skeins.

holograph = a document, the whole of which is in the handwriting of its purported author.

homatropin = (*chem.*) a synthetic compound of tropein and mandelic acid; it resembles atropin in its physiological effects, but is much milder. [Chiefly used as a mydriatic in ophthalmologic practice.]

homicidal tendency = a pathological attitude characterized by a propensity to kill other human beings.

homicide = the illegal killing of one human being by another.

homing = behavior observed in certain animal species, characterized by an ability and tendency to return to their former habitat when removed to a distance. — Fr. *orientation lointaine dans le retour au gîte*; Ger. *Heimkehrvermögen.*

homo = the genus to which man belongs, the only existing species of which is **homo sapiens.**

homo-erotic = syn. for **homosexual** (Ferenczi). **homo-eroticism**[n].

homogamy = interbreeding between organisms which contain similar characters or are themselves similar. (Accent **-mog-.**)

homogeneity = similarity of the constituents of any group in respect to quality, kind, or sort. [Contr. w. **heterogeneity.**] (Accent **-nee-.**) **homogeneous**[a] (accent **-jee-**). — Ger. *Gleichartigkeit, Gleichförmigkeit.*

homogenesis, homogeny = similarity of organs in different species, due to inheritance from a common ancestry; i.e. the characteristic of being homologous organs or homologues. [Distg. fr. **homoplasy** = having analogous organs.] **homogenetic**[a], **homogenic**[a].

homolateral = on or pert. to the same side.

homologous organs, homologues = organs which are fundamentally alike in development and structure, but which may differ in function, e.g. the wing of a bat and the front leg of a mouse. [Distg. fr. **analogous organs** (or **analogues**), which are only grossly similar.]

homology = (*biol.*) similarity in the fundamental plan of structure of organs, which is indicative of a common evolutionary origin. [Distg. fr. **analogy** = superficial similarity in structure or in function, as between two distant species.] **homologous**[a].

homophony = music which consists of one part or melody. [Believed to be the original form with all peoples. In modern music the term applies to music with simple harmony in which all parts sound together, as contr. w. **polyphony,** in which the parts move independently.] (Accent **-moph-.**) **homophonic**[a].

homoplasy = similarity of corresponding organs in different species which is not due to inheritance from a common ancestry; i.e. the characteristic of being **analogous organs,** or **analogues.** [Distg. fr. **homogenesis** = similarity due to inheritance.] **homoplastic**[a].

homosexual neurosis = 1. (*psychoan.*) a term applied to the paranoid group of psychoses which are the result of repressed homosexual trends; 2. sometimes (more loosely) applied to that form of sexual inversion known as **homosexuality.**

homosexuality = 1. sexual intercourse between individuals of the same sex; 2. sexual attraction on the part of an individual for or toward individuals of the same sex. [Gr. **homo-**, same; Lat. **sexus;** not derived fr. Lat. **homo,** man. **androgyny, effemination, gynandry, inversion, viraginity** are usually considered as forms of homosexuality. Contr. w. **heterosexuality** and **bisexuality.**] **homosexual**[a].

homotaxis = the similarity of succession of organic forms in the geological strata in different regions.

homozygote = an organism of pure heredity, which (therefore) produces only gametes containing identical hereditary factors. [Contr. w. **heterozygote.** Cf. **zygote.**]

honesty = a type of behavior characterized by careful regard for the rights of others, esp. with respect to freedom from fraud and untruthfulness in gaining economic or other advantage. [Contr. w. **dishonesty.**] **honest**[a]. — Fr. *honnêteté*; Ger. *Ehrlichkeit.*

honor, honour[n] = the fact of being regarded by others, and of regarding oneself, as conforming to commonly accepted standards of honesty, truthfulness, rectitude, etc.; a condition accompanied by a feeling of self-esteem. [As referring to women, purity and chastity have been traditionally associated with the term **honor.**] **honorable**[a]. — Ger. *Ehre.*

hope = an attitude or sentiment having a mixed hedonic quality, characterized by an idea of a favorable outcome of future events. [Contr. w. **despair,** which accepts the idea of an unfavorable outcome.] **hopeful**[a], **hope**[v]. — Fr. *espérance*; Ger. *Hoffnung.*

horde = a small social group having a low degree of organization. [A degree higher than the **herd,** but less organized than the **clan.**]

horizontal = level, i.e. parallel to the horizon; i.e. at right angles to the direction of gravity. [Cf. **horizontal plane; horizontal axis** is ambig., since it applies to two axial directions.]

horizontal plane = any plane of the body parallel to the plane of the horizon. [In man, syn. for **transverse plane;** in quadrupeds, syn. for **mesial** or **medial plane.**]

horizontal-vertical illusion = a visual phenomenon, in which a vertical line or dimension appears longer than the horizontal line or dimension of the same length; e.g. the figure of the opera hat.

hormic theory = the view that organic phenomena are largely determined by purposive factors (e.g. native dispositions, tendencies, urges), which transcend the realm of physics and chemistry (W. McDougall). [Grk. **horme,** an urge to action.]

hormone = 1. a specific chemical substance formed by one organ, which, on passing into the circulatory fluid, evokes functional changes in other organs; 2. an excitatory autacoid. [(1) syn. for **autacoid;** (2) contr. w. **chalone** = inhibitory autacoid; but cf. **autacoid.**] **hormonic**[a].

hormonic autacoids, see **autacoid,** and **hormone.**

horn of Ammon = a portion of the cerebral cortex having a characteristic coiled form and unusual structure, which lies along the medial portion of the temporal lobe and bounds the inferior horn of the lateral ventricle. [Syn. **cornu Ammonis, hippocampus major.**] — Fr. *corne d'Ammon.*

Horner's law = a principle of the inheritance of color-blindness, according to which the common type of color-blindness is transmitted from males to males through unaffected females. [Cf. **color-blindness.**]

horopter = the locus of all points in the binocular field of vision, the images of which fall upon **identical points** of the two retinas. [With the fixation point in the median plane, at a definite distance, and in the same horizontal plane as the nodal points of the two eyes, the horopter becomes substantially a circle passing through the fixation-point and the two nodal points, together with a vertical straight line through the fixation point (**Müllerian horopter**). Cf. **Müller's circle.**]

horoscope = (*hist.*) the positions of the stars and planets at the time of a person's birth, on the basis of which astrologers attempt to read his character and to predict his fate. [Cf. **astrology.**]

horse-power, see **power.**

hostility = an attitude characterized by unpleasantness, and by activity detrimental to the welfare of the individual or group toward whom the attitude is directed. [Distg. fr. **pugnacity** = tendency to fight or to resist violently any hampering of one's actions.] **hostile**[a]. — Ger. *Feindschaft.*

hot, see **heat.** — Fr. *brûlant.*

hot spot, see **warm spot.**

hue = the character of a visual impression as typically determined by the predominant wave-length or wave-lengths of the stimulus. [Syn. **color tone**; cf. **color.**] — Fr. *tonalité chromatique, nuance*; Ger. *Farbenton, Farbton.*

hue/extraspectral, see **extraspectral hue.**

humerus = the bone of the upper arm. (Accent **hue-.**) **humeral**[a]. — Ger. *Oberarmknochen.*

humility = an attitude in which the individual behaves toward others as if he were inferior to them. [A term used esp. in ethics and religion. Cf. **inferiority complex, inferiority feeling.**] **humble**[a]. — Ger. *Demut.*

humor, humour = 1. (*esth.*) a complex situation which combines an element of the comic and a sympathetic appeal; or, a linguistic or mixed expression on the part of an individual which intentionally portrays such a situation; 2. an emotional attitude which is characteristically pleasant or unpleasant (e.g. good humor); 3. a liquid secretion (e.g. aqueous humor). (1) **humorous**[a]. — Ger. (1) *Humor,* (2) *Laune.*

humoral reflex = a vital response caused by a hormone.

humoral theory = (*hist.*) the theory that the body contains four humors, a mixing of which, in right proportion, constitutes health; while an improper proportion or irregular distribution constitutes disease. [According to tradition, black bile gives rise to the **melancholic** temperament, yellow bile to the **choleric,** blood bile to the **sanguine,** and phlegm to the **phlegmatic.**]

hunger = 1. desire for food, the drive or motive in food-seeking behavior, often measured (in animal experiments) by the duration of food-deprivation, a term used without connotation of any particular sensory conscious experience; 2. (more specifically) the dull, aching, gnawing sensation, referred to the region of the stomach and presumably aroused by slow rhythmic contractions of the stomach walls and adjacent parts of the esophagus and small intestine. [Distg. (2) fr. **appetite,** for which there is no specific sensory quality.] **hungry**[a]. — Fr. *faim.*

hunger contraction = contraction of the empty stomach, elicited by hormone stimulation and resulting in hunger pains. [Mediated by the musculature and nerve plexuses of the stomach.] — Fr. *contraction de faim.*

hunger pain = a sensation resulting from the hunger contractions. [Mediated through the X cranial nerve and bulbocortical tracts.]

hunting, hunting behavior = behavior on the part of certain animal species, including man, directed toward the discovery of animal food. [The characteristic of hunting is the wandering of the object as well as of the searcher; distg. fr. **search for fruit,** and fr. **fishing,** where the object is relatively fixed.] — Fr. *chasse*; Ger. *Jagd, Hetzjagd.*

hunting stage = the stage of human culture in which hunting provides most of the food, clothing, and technological materials. [It is assumed by many investigators that the earliest form of human society was of this character.] — Fr. *stade de la chasse.*

hybrid[n] = the offspring of two parents which belong to different varieties or species. [Hist. limited to the progeny of two different species; in Mendelian heredity, any progeny one of whose parents alone possesses a given unit character is **hybrid** with respect to that character.] **hybrid**[a]. — Ger. *Bastard.*

hybridization = the production of hybrids.

Hydra = a genus of fresh water polyps (Coelenterata).

hydrocephalus, hydrocephaly = an abnormal accumulation of fluid within the cranium, either in the cerebral ventricles (internal h.) or outside the cavities of the brain (external h.). [It results in abnormal enlargement of the head, often with limited brain development.] **hydrocephalous**[a]. — Ger. *Wasserkopf.*

hydroid = a Hydra-like Coelenterate, usually attached and branching, and frequently forming the asexual stage, which alternates with a medusa, or sexual stage.

hydrotherapy = (*med.*) treatment by means of hot or cold water in form of bottles, packs, douches, syringes, compresses, baths, etc.

hydrotropism, hydrotaxis = a simple orienting response of an organism or of certain organs to stimulation by water or moisture. [Cf. **rheotropism.**] (Accent **-rot-, -tax-.**) **hydrotropic**[a], **-tactic**[a].

hygiene = the science or systematic practice which is concerned with the maintenance of health in the individual or community. (Accent **hy-.**) **hygienic**[a] (4 syll.).

hyoid = pert. to or located in the region on the front of the throat between the submental (i.e. beneath the chin) and the laryngeal regions.

hyoid bone = a bone situate between the root of the tongue and the larynx, which supports the tongue and gives attachment to its muscles. — Fr. *os hyoïde*; Ger. *Zungenbein.*

hypacousia, hypacousis = the state or condition of being slightly deaf, making it difficult for the individual to follow ordinary conversation. [Differentiated from **deafness** by the fact that hearing has been sufficient in early life to permit the individual to acquire language in the ordinary way. Syn. **hard of hearing**[a].] **hypacousic**[a] **hypacousic**[np].

hyperacusis = exceptionally good auditory acuity. [Contr. w. **hypacusis.**]

hyperalgesia = pathologically excessive sensitiveness to pain. [**auditory h.** = a condition in which slight sounds cause pain; **muscular h.** = a condition in which slight exertion causes great weariness or feelings of strain or aches. Syn. **hyperalgia**; contr. w. **hypalgesia, hypalgia.**] **hyperalgesic**[a] (prefd.), **hyperalgetic**[a].

hypercritical = indulging in too much or too minute criticism. [Applied to one who, in examining a theory, report, etc., emphasizes minor objections or flaws without due weight to its merits. Not to be confused with **hypocritical** = addicted to **hypocrisy.**] **hypercriticism**[n] (rare).

hyperdactylism, see **polydactylism.**

hyperesthesia, hyper(a)esthesis, hyperaesthesia = an excessive or unusual degree of sensitivity, esp. to tactual stimuli. [Contr. w. **hypesthesia** = blunted sensitivity.] **hyperesthetic**[a].

hyperfeminization = exaggerated feminization of structure and behavior which is reported as appearing in certain cases of castrated male animals in which female sex gland elements have been implanted. [Cf. **feminization.**]

hyperfunction = the functioning of an organ or system at more than its normal level.

hyperkinesis = a condition characterized by excessively vigorous responses, or motor restlessness. [Contr. w. **hypokinesis.**] **hyperkinesic**[a].

hypermasculinization = exaggerated masculinization of structure and behavior which is reported as appearing in certain cases of castrated female animals in which male sex gland elements have been implanted (Steinach). [Cf. **masculinization.**]

hypermetropia, see **hyperopia.**

hypermnesia = an exaggerated degree of retentiveness or recall, usually pathological. **hypermnesic**[a].

hypernormal phase, see **supernormal recovery phase.**

hyperopia = a defect of the eye structure or lens mechanism, such that, with accommodation muscles relaxed, parallel rays of light focus behind the retina. [Syn. **far-sightedness** (ambig.), **hypermetropia;** distg. fr. **presbyopia.** Contr. w. **myopia. hyperopia** is classed as **manifest** (= revealed by trial-lenses), **latent** (= revealed by use of a mydriatic), or **total** (manifest + latent); also as **absolute** (= degree of failure to bring about clear vision at a distance by accommodation) or **relative** (in which excessive convergence accompanies effort of accommodation); and as **facultative** (= the range of clear vision by accommodation).] **hyperopic**[a].

hyperopic blur = indistinctness of vision due to **hyperopia.** — Fr. *flou hypéropique.*

hyperphoria, see **imbalance/muscular.**

hyperpituitarism, see **acromegaly.**

hyperplasia, hyperplasy = excessive multiplication of elements in an organism. [Distg. fr. **hypertrophy** = abnormal growth of an organ in part.] **hyperplastic**[a].

hyperpnea = panting or exaggerated respiration.

hyperprosexia = exaggerated arousal of attention and inability to ignore the stimulus. [Cf. **distractibility.**]

hyperthymia = (*rare*) exaggeration of emotional response, or state of excitement.

hyperthyroidism = a pathological or experimental condition which results from excessive production of the internal secretion of the thyroid gland or from excessive administration of thyroid gland or its active principle. [Psychologically, marked hyperthyroidism seems to involve no impairment of the general intelligence of the individual; but it is often accompanied by emotional hyperexcitability and occasionally by hallucinations. A tendency to insomnia is noted; also an increase in reflex excitability and general activity. Exophthalmic and adenomatous goiter are conditions of pathological hyperthyroidism. Syn. **hyperthyreosis.** Contr. w. **hypothyroidism** = a condition resulting from insufficient production of thyroid secretion.] **hyperthyroid**[a] = marked by or due to hyperthyroidism.

hypertonia, hypertonicity = a state of increased resting contraction (tonus) due to an exaggeration of normal postural reflexes, generally most pronounced in antigravity muscles (Sherrington).

hypertrophy = excessive growth of an organ by enlargement of its tissue elements. [Distg. fr. **hyperplasia** = excessive multiplication of the elements.] (Accent **-pert-.**) **hypertrophic**[a].

hypesthesia, hyp(a)esthesis, hypaesthesia = a blunting of sensitivity or raising of the threshold, esp. in the case of tactual stimuli. [Syn. **undersensitivity.** Contr. w. **hyperesthesia** = excessive sensitivity.] **hypesthetic**[a].

hypnagogic = pert. to drowsiness. [E.g. hypnagogic illusions and hallucinations.]

hypnagogic image = imagery of any sense modality, frequently of almost hallucinatory character, which is experienced in the drowsy state preceding deep sleep. [Cf. **hypnopompic.**]

hypno-analysis = psychoanalysis carried out in the hypnotic state, as in the early work of Breuer and Freud, instead of by their later method of free association in the waking condition.

hypnogenic, hypnogenetic = 1. producing hypnosis; 2. producing sleep.

hypnoidal = characterizing a state which resembles to a certain extent the milder hypnotic conditions but is usually brought about by means other than those used in hypnosis.

hypnology = 1. the systematic investigation of sleep; 2. (*hist.*) the study and art of **hypnosis** (James Braid, 1843). [Syn. (1) **somnology** (rare, but less ambiguous), (2) **hypnotism** (more common).]

hypnopompic = characterizing the drowsy state following deep sleep and preceding awaking. [Usually applied to imagery experienced in that state. Cf. **hypnagogic image.**]

hypnosis = 1. an artificially induced state, usually (though not always) resembling sleep, but physiologically distinct from it, which is characterized by heightened suggestibility, as a result of which certain sensory, motor, and memory abnormalities may be induced more readily than in the normal state; 2. (*psychoan.*) the capacity to be influenced by suggestion, dependent on the possibility of transference. [Cf. **hypnotism.**] **hypnotic**[a].

hypnotic[n] = 1. a drug used to induce sleep; 2. a hypnotized person. [Syn. (1) **soporific.**]

hypnotism = the scientific investigation of hypnosis and hypnotic phenomena. [Pop. confused with **hypnosis** = the condition itself.] **hypnotist**[np].

hypnotize = to induce hypnosis in an individual. **hypnotizer**[np].

hypoblast, see **entoderm.**

hypochondria, hypochondriasis = a pathological condition characterized by exaggerated anxiety about one's health, and pessimistic interpretation of various discomforts about some organ or function. **hypochondriac**[np], **hypochondriacal**[a].

hypochondriac[a] = pert. to or located on the body surface over the liver and on the region symmetrical to this on the left side. (Accent **-kon-.**)

hypochondriacal reflex = sudden inspiration elicited by quick pressure below the inferior border of the ribs. [Mediated by the 8th thoracic to 4th cervical segments of the cord.]

hypocrisy = the simulation by an individual, through his behavior and general line of conduct, of certain ideals or moral characteristics which are foreign to his nature. **hypocritical**[a], **hypocrit (e)**[np]. — Ger. *Heuchelei.*

hypodermic[n], **hypodermatic** = a drug or other solution introduced into subcutaneous tissues by injection or infusion through a needle, usually by means of a syringe; or the administration of such a drug, etc. **hypodermic**[a].

hypoesthesia, see **hypesthesia.**

hypofunction = the functioning or operation of an organ or system at less than its normal intensity.

hypoglossal nerve = the 12th cranial nerve efferent to the tongue, which leaves the brain from the anterolateral sulcus between the pyramid and olive, below the cranial accessory nerve.

hypognathous = having the under jaws protruding beyond the upper. [Cf. **prognathous, orthognathous.**]

hypokinesis = a condition characterized by subnormal vigor of motor response. [Contr. w. **hyperkinesis.**] **hypokinesic**[a].

hypomania = the mild forms of manic excitement (elation and unmotivated excess of well-being, over-activity, and flight of ideas and enterprise). [Syn. **hyperthymergasia.**]

hypophonia = a form of **dysphonia** characterized by a whispered voice.

hypophoria, see **imbalance/muscular.**

hypophrenia = lack of (or deficiency in) mental or intellectual ability. **hypophrenic**[a].

hypophysin, see **pituitary/solution of.**

hypophysis, see **pituitary gland.** (Accent **-poff-.**)

hypothalamus = the region of the forebrain which includes the subthalamic tegmental region, the mammillary bodies, the tuber cinereum, the infundibulum, the hypophysis, and the optic chiasm.

hypothenar reflex = flexion of the little finger produced by pressure on the pisiform bone of the wrist. [Mediated by the 8th cervical to 1st thoracic segments of the cord.] (Accent **-poth-.**)

hypothesis = a preliminary assumption, presupposition, or principle adopted for the explanation of observed facts. [The terms **speculation, hypothesis, theory, law,** form a progressive series, according to the increasing adequacy of the evidence.] **hypotheses**[pl], **hypothetical**[a], **hypothesize**[v] (*not* **hypothecate**) = to formulate a hypothesis. — Ger. *Hypothese.*

hypothetical = unproved; advanced as an assumption. [In a **hypothetical statement,** one clause (the *protasis*), introduced by *if* or some equivalent expression, formulates the hypothesis, the other clause (the *apodosis*) formulates a logical deduction which is valid if the former is found to be true; e.g. if all men are born equal, slavery is unjust. Syllogisms in which one of the premises is hypothetical are called **hypothetical syllogisms.**]

hypothymia = (*rare*) lowering of emotional response, or depression.

hypothyroidism = a pathological or experimental condition which results from insufficient production of the internal secretion of the thyroid gland. [**cretinism, myxedema,** and **endemic goiter** are conditions of pathological hypothyroidism. Syn. **hypothyreosis.** Contr. w. **hyperthyroidism** = resulting from excessive production.] **hypothyroid**[a] = marked by or due to hypothyroidism.

hysteria = 1. a psychogenic instability and disorder characterized by dissociations, i.e. a dispelling from clear consciousness of desired but tabooed preoccupations and an autosuggestive production of various substitutions intelligible only in the light of the pathogenic experiences: fits, spastic states, palsies, anesthesias, and other involvements of parts and functions which have played a role in the *repressed* and *dissociated* experiences; 2. (*psychoan.*) a psychoneurosis, resulting from a conflict between the ego and the primitive tendencies of the id, in which the latter tendencies are repressed, and are thus excluded from direct conscious expression, it being assumed that the unconscious, repressed material finds an indirect physical outlet through conversion, producing the hysterical symptoms. [Formerly looked upon as the simulation of diseases through pressure of a wandering womb against various organs. The attacks or episodes are usually remembered only under hypnosis or prolonged use of free association. Grk. ὑστέρα, womb.] **hysteric(al)**[a], **hysteric**[np].

hysteria/anxiety = (*psychoan.*) a psychoneurosis in which the symptoms consist of one or several varieties of phobias, accompanied by the usual manifestations of fear. [Cf. **anxiety.**] — Fr. *syndrome anxieuse*; Ger. *Angsthysterie*.

hysteria/conversion, see **conversion.**

hysteria/fixation = (*psychoan.*) a form of hysteria in which the symptoms are related to an organic disease, making use of the latter through a conversion process.

hysterical mutism = a state in which a person, because of his hysterical condition, cannot utter words.

hysterical twilight states, see **twilight states/hysterical.**

hysteriform seizures = convulsions or other episodic motor disturbances which appear to be of hysterical origin, usually with only partial unconsciousness and partial amnesia. — Fr. *crises hystériformes*.

hystero-epilepsy = a disorder which manifests symptoms of hysteria and of epilepsy and suggests the mechanism of hysteria. [A disorder suggested or determined by emotionally charged experiences; contr. w. the crudely automatic epileptic attack.]

hysteroneurasthenia = neurasthenia with evidences of the mechanism of hysteria.

I

iconolatry = the worship of images; or more specifically, the worship of pictures. [Sometimes distg. fr. **idolatry** = worship of statues or other solid objects.]

ictus = 1. the characteristic of some particular tone (or syllable) in a series, whereby it is more prominent than those preceding and succeeding it. [Syn. **accent.** In music, an **ictus** is generally attached to one tone or chord in every three, four, or six, depending upon the nature of the composition. It is made in various ways: by greater intensity, by prolongation, by diversity of bass accompaniment, or by mere differences in attention. Cf. **rhythm.**] **ictual**[a].

ictus = 2. (*pathol.*) a seizure or stroke.

id = 1. (*biol.*) a term proposed by Weismann for a postulated complex vital unit composed of an organized group of hypothetical determinants; 2. (*psychoan.*) the impersonality of the mind apart from its ego, the true unconscious or deepest part of the mind, the reservoir of instinctive impulses, dominated by the pleasure-principle and blind impulsive wishing; i.e. the dynamic equivalent of the descriptive unconscious. [Cf. (1) **idant, determinant;** (2) **ego, super-ego.**] — Fr. (2) *le ça*; Ger. (2) *Es*.

idant = a term proposed by Weismann for a postulated complex unit of germ plasm composed of simple postulated units (**ids**), composed of still simpler postulated units (**determinants**), composed of the simplest vital units (**biophores**). [All these structures were postulated to account for observed vital phenomena.]

idea = 1. an experience or thought not directly due to sensory stimulation; 2. a mental complex consisting wholly or in major part of images; 3. a psychological process having a symbolic or representative rather than a direct function; 4. (*hist.*) any cognitive experience, whether due to direct stimulation or not; 5. (*hist.*) the objective eternal archetypes or laws of natural things (Plato). [Locke (1690) established the term as (4), but Hume (1739) distinguished between **impression** and (2).] **ideational**[a] (prefd. to **ideal**[a], which is ambiguous). — Fr. *idée*; Ger. *Vorstellung*.

idea/fixed, see **fixed idea.**

ideal[n] = an emotionally colored representation of some future line of behavior or situation as desirable, though scarcely attainable. **ideal**[a].

idealism = 1. a term applied to several types of world-view, which insist (*a*) that the world (or reality as a whole) is most adequately conceived of in terms of ideas or thought, interpreted in various ways, rather than in terms of matter and purposeless motion in space, (*b*) that values have a cosmic significance and are discovered, not invented, by man; 2. (*esth.*) the theory which emphasizes the subjective aspect of beauty. [**idealism** (1) includes the following types: (*a*) *subjective* i. = that the world exists only as an order of ideas in a society of minds (Berkeley, Ward); (*b*) *objective*, or *absolute* i. (Hegel) = that it consists (not only as known to us, but in itself) of *ideas* belonging to universal Mind (an impersonal rational order); and that logical structure and values (moral, esthetic, and religious) possess in it objective reality; (*c*) *transcendental*, or *critical* i. (Kant) = that *a priori* conditions of experience determine the possibility of objects of experience. Contr.

(1, 2) w. **realism.**] (Accent **-dee-.**) **idealistic**[a], **idealist**[np].

idealization = the conceiving of an object in accordance with one's desires or ideals. **idealize**[v].

ideation = the process or mental operation of forming ideas.

ideational[a] = pert. to ideation or to ideas. [Not to be confused with **ideal**[a] = pert. to an ideal.]

ideational learning = learning, or acquisition, which proceeds largely in terms of inner analysis and reflection, and with a minimum of overt movement [Distg. for practical purposes fr. **motor learning,** though the two types are identified by some investigators.] — Fr. *acquisition mentale, apprentissage mental.*

ideational stimuli = stimuli which produce a reaction through the mediation of associated ideas. [Syn. **ideal stimuli** (ambig.).]

idée-force = a term proposed by A. Fouillée to denote an idea as possessing dynamic properties and acting as a force. [French term.] — Ger. *Kraftidee.*

identical = 1. similar in every respect; 2. asserted to be the same; 3. interchangeable in every (essential) respect under all conditions. [(1) applies to two separate figures (e.g. triangles), (2) is used where an item discerned at different times or in different circumstances is asserted to be not two items but one. Cf. **identity, equality.**] — Ger. *identisch,* (3) *gleichbedeutend.*

identical elements = components of two or more situations, or organic sets to such situations, which are the same or similar. [The term is incorporated in the educational theory that the effects of practice in one situation are transferred to another situation to the extent that the two situations contain identical elements. Cf. **transfer of training.**]

identical points = any pair of retinal points in the two eyes which, when the eyes are in the primary position, receive stimuli from the same objective point at infinite distance. [Distg. fr. **congruent points.**] — Ger. *korrespondierende Netzhautpunkte, Deckpunkte* (Hering).

identical proposition = a statement in which the predicate repeats the subject so completely that the assertion does not promote thought.

identical series/method of = a **recognition method,** in which the test materials are identical with the learned materials and in which there are no **blank experiments.** [Introduced by Reuther (1906) and espoused by Wundt.]

identical twins, see **twins.**

identical visual direction/law of = in binocular vision, any pair of corresponding lines of direction in actual (objective) space are represented by a single line of direction in visual space in such a way that everything which actually lies upon either line of the pair appears to be on this single line, regardless of the location in actual space which these external objects may occupy.

identification = 1. the assertion, or demonstration by evidence, that two or more separate characterizations of individuals, classes, etc., actually denote the same individual, class, etc.; 2. (*psychoan.*) an unconscious mental process which expresses itself in the form of an emotional tie with other persons or situations in which the subject behaves as if he were the person with whom he has this tie; 3. (*biol.*) subsumption under a named class, e.g. the identification of an organism. [(2) plays an important part in the development of the Edipus-complex.] **identify**[v].

identity = 1. the characteristic of an organism, sense datum, etc. such that it persists without essential change; 2. (*math.*) an equation which is satisfied for all values of the constants and variables entering into it; 3. (*logic*) consistency in the use of a term within a given realm of discourse. [Designated (2) by symbol ≡. Cf. (1) **sameness.**]

identity hypothesis, see **double-aspect theory.**

identity/personal, see **personal identity.**

ideograph, ideogram = 1. the graphic representation of an object or idea by a single symbol, as distg. fr. representation by the use of letters or syllabic signs; 2. syn. for **pictogram;** 3. a curve or tracing giving a direct record of muscular movements due to changes of thought. **ideographic**[a].

ideology = 1. the theory of the nature of ideas and of intellectual operations; 2. syn. for **psychology** (Destutt de Tracy); 3. syn. for **Weltanschauung,** or **world-view. ideologist**[np] (applied usually to members of the French school (latter 18th and early 19th centuries) which followed the teachings of Condillac and Locke).

ideomotor[a] = pert. to the sequence of movements upon ideas. [Contr. w. **sensorimotor** = pert. to the direct sequence of movements upon sensory stimuli.] (Accent **i-** not **id-.**)

ideomotor activity = responses which follow upon thought processes, even though of a fleeting character, as contr. w. those which follow directly upon sensory stimulation. [Contr. w. **sensorimotor activity.**]

ideoplasy = the operation of ideas upon physiological processes. **ideoplastic**[a].

idiocy, see **idiot.**

idiogamy = (*psychoan.*) the restriction of male potency to cohabitation with one woman.

idiogenetic theory = the theory proposed by F. Brentano which assumes that the function of judgment is an original or primordial mental fact.

idioglossia = speech which is unintelligible because of many sound omissions, substitutions, and transpositions.

idiographic = pert. to the study of particular cases or individual instances. [Contr. w. **nomothetic.**]

idiolalia = invented language, characteristic of individuals of low mentality. [A form of **dyslalia.**]

idiopathic = characterizing a disorder or pathological condition as primary, i.e. not the effect of some other disorder nor the result of accident or injury.

idiophonia = a form of **dysphonia** characterized by unpleasant voice quality.

idioplasm = a word coined by Nägeli to designate that portion of living substance concerned in reproduction, as distg. fr. **trophoplasm,** which has to do with nutrition. [Nägeli maintained that idioplasm occurs in the form of a network pervading the organism. Later the term came to be identified with the **chromatin** of the nucleus.]

idioretinal light = visual sensations of light which occur in the absence of stimulation of any sort, and are attributed to physiological processes within the retina itself or in the brain. — Fr. *lumière rétinienne*; Ger. *Eigenlicht der Netzhaut.*

idiosyncrasy = any item of behavior peculiar to a given individual, which is not readily assignable to general or well-known psychological processes. **idiosyncratic**[a].

idiot = a feebleminded individual who manifests the lowest grade of mentality. [Generally limited to those who maintain throughout adult life a mental age of from 0 to approximately 2 years (Goddard), or an intelligence quotient ranging approximately from 0 to 25 (Terman). Cf. **feeblemindedness.**] **idiocy**[n], **idiotic**[a].

idiot-savant = a feebleminded individual of any grade who has a special talent in one or more directions, such as music, checker playing, rapid calculating, or handicraft. [French term; a possible English equivalent is **simpleton-prodigy.**] **idiots-savants**[pl].

idol = (*logic*) a prejudice, usually due to social tradition, which hampers the discovery of truth. [Bacon, in the Novum Organum, distinguished four kinds of idols, the *idola tribus, idola specus, idola fori,* and *idola teatri.* The first are common human prejudices, such as anthropomorphisms of various kinds; the second are prejudices due to special development and occupations of the individual, such as the tendency of a biologist toward biologism, a mathematician toward mathematicism, etc.; the third are those due to social intercourse, such as the tendency to repeat current appreciations uncritically and mechanically; the fourth is the tendency to systematic dogmatism, scepticism, or mysticism.]

idolatry = the worship of statues or other inanimate objects. [Cf. **iconolatry.**]

iletin, see **insulin.**

ileum = the lowest part of the small intestine. **ileac**[a].

illegitimate = 1. (*logic*) characterizing inferences or other reasoning processes which violate the accepted principles of logic; 2. (*soc.*) born out of wedlock. [Syn. (1) **illicit.**] **illegitimacy**[n].

illicit = contrary to law or to logic. [Applies to faulty reasoning; also to sexual relations forbidden or not approved by law or custom. Syn. **illegitimate,** applied to faulty reasoning or to children born of illicit relations.]

illiteracy = inability to read, due to lack of education rather than to mental deficiency. **illiterate**[a] (applied only to mature individuals). — Fr. *analphabetisme*; Ger. *Analphabetismus.*

illumination = (*photom.*) the density of light-flux incident upon a surface. — Fr. *éclairement*; Ger. *Beleuchtung.*

illumination/law of = the principle that the illumination upon a surface varies directly as the luminous intensity of the light-source, inversely as the square of its distance, and directly as the cosine of the angle made by the light-rays with the perpendicular to the surface.

illusion = a misinterpretation of certain elements in a given experience, such that the experience does not represent the objective situation, present or recalled. [Broadly divided into **illusions of memory,** in which the memory is mislocated in time, or includes elements not in the original perception, and **illusions of perception,** which are of many sorts, such as **of motion** = apparent motion of an immobile object or field; **of movement** = apparent movement of a rigid member or of one's entire body: **of orientation** = misinterpretation of the position of one's body in space; **visual space illusion** = misinterpretation of the spatial relations of objects or figures seen. The most striking spatial illusions have been named after their discoverers; e.g. **Hering, Müller-Lyer, Poggendorff, Zöllner** (cf. these terms); **illusions of reversible perspective** occur in flat or solid figures when certain parts appear sometimes nearer, sometimes farther from the eye (e.g. **staircase illusion**). Distg. fr. **hallucination,** which mistakes a central construction for a real object, while **illusion** merely distorts perception. See Table XII.] — Ger. *Täuschung, Sinnestäuschung.*

illusion/correction of = the reduction or entire elimination of illusory effects in geometric or spatial illusions, (*a*) through the addition of counteracting lines and spaces, (*b*) by the gradual effect of practice, or (*c*) through the sudden suggestion of a new idea or meaning associated with the figure.

illusion/optical, see **optical illusion.**

illusory movement, see **movement/theory of,** and **apparent** (**motion** or) **movement.**

image = 1. an element of experience which is centrally aroused and which possesses all the attributes of sensation; 2. an experience which reproduces or copies in part and with some degree of sensory realism a previous perceptual experience in the absence of the original sensory stimulation; 3. (*opt.*) the picture or reproduction of an object produced by a lens, reflector, or optical system, as a result of the focusing of the light emanating from each point in the object. **imaginal**[a], not to be confused w. **imaginary** = pert. to imagination, or fictitious.

image/anticipation = an image which is accompanied by reference to a future time when a corresponding sensory experience is expected.

image/composite = an image which is derived from a plurality of previous sensory experiences and does not copy any single such experience.

image/eidetic, see **eidetic image.**

image/general = an image regarded by the subject as referring to any one of a class of objects.

image/habitual = an image which regularly or frequently recurs as a representation of a certain meaning.

image/hallucinatory = an image which seems at the moment to be a perceptual experience.

image/hypnagogic, see **hypnagogic image.**

image/imagination = an image, usually built up from several previous sensory experiences and accompanied by reference to an object that has never been perceived by the subject.

image/retinal = 1. the optical image of external objects formed upon the retina by the refracting surfaces of the eye; 2. the consequent pattern of physiological activity excited in the retina and corresponding to the distribution of energy in the optical image. [Syn. **retinal picture** (*prefd.*), **retinal impression.**] — Ger. *Netzhautbild.*

image/tied = imaginal content attached to a present perception.

imageless thought = an idea, thought, or train of thinking which is wholly lacking in sensory contents. [The theory of **imageless thought,**

originated by Külpe and the Würzburg school (1901–9), maintains that such experiences actually occur; critics of the theory have asserted the existence, in all cases, of vague sensory components or aspects.] — Fr. *pensée sans images*; Ger. *unanschauliches Denken.*

imagery = images taken collectively, or the imaging operation in general.

imaginary, imaginary quantity = (*math.*) a magnitude containing the factor $\sqrt{-1}$. [Designated by symbol i, e.g. $\sqrt{-9}$ or i $\sqrt{9}$.]

imagination = the reorganization of data derived from past experiences, with new relations, into a present ideational experience. **imaginative**[a] = pert. to the data or process; **imaginational**[a] = pert. to the study; **imaginary**[a] = fictitious. — Ger. *Phantasie, Einbildungskraft.*

imaging = forming an image, i.e. picturing, reproducing. [Applied esp. to an image-forming optical system, including that of the eye. Cf. **image/retinal.**] — Fr. *représentation optique*; Ger. *abbildend.*

imago = 1. (*biol.*) the final state of an insect after it has undergone metamorphosis and become sexually mature; 2. (*psychoan.*) a memory, phantasy, or idealization of a beloved person, formed in childhood and remaining uncorrected in adult life. (Accent **-may-**.)

imbalance/muscular = the tendency of either eye (owing to abnormalities in the extrinsic muscles or in their innervation) to deviate abnormally from its position of fixation when fusion of the two images is prevented, e.g. by the use of a **Maddox rod** or an opaque screen before that eye alone. [In a pair of normal eyes fixated on a point at 20 feet distance the covered eye usually retains its position of fixation; at 13 inches it deviates outward 2 or 3 prism degrees. Syn. **heterophoria, muscular insufficiency.** Cf. **muscle balance.** If there is no deviation of the covered eye the condition is called **orthophoria;** if the deviation of the latter is inward, **esophoria;** outward, **exophoria;** upward **hyperphoria;** and downward, **hypophoria; cyclophoria** has also been observed.] — Fr. *hétérophorie, déséquilibre de convergence.*

imbecile = an individual who manifests a medium grade of feeblemindedness. [Generally limited to those who maintain throughout adult life a mental age of approximately from 3 to 7 years (Goddard), or an intelligence quotient ranging approximately from 26 to 50 (Terman). Cf. **feeblemindedness.**] **imbecility**[n], **imbecile**[a].

imitation = 1. the process of performing an act which act is stimulated by the observation of similar behavior in another person or animal; 2. (*esth.*) characterizing, according to mimetic theories of art, the art-process. [Syn. (2) **mimesis.** Cf. **copy, mimetism, protective coloring, mimicry.**] **imitate**[v], **imitative**[a], **imitativeness**[n] (the trait). — Ger. *Nachahmung.*

immaterialism = (*epistem.*) the view that the existence of matter cannot be confidently affirmed, inasmuch as all perceptual experiences are items of consciousness. [Contr. w. **materialism.** Cf. **spiritualism.**]

immediate = 1. without intervening phenomena; 2. without any considerable intervening time. [Contr. (1) w. **mediate** = involving some intervening event.] — Ger. *unmittelbar.*

immediate association = a thought which arises directly as a result of suggestion, and not through some interpolated thought. [Distg. fr. **mediate** (or **mediated**) **association,** where some interpolated thought or train of thought occurs between the suggestion and the thought in question.]

immediate experience = the type of experience dealt with by psychology, as contr. w. the **mediate experiences** with which the physical sciences deal (Wundt).

immobility = the condition of being temporarily incapable of movement, as in paralysis, death-feigning, hypnosis, etc.

immobility/tonic, see **tonic immobility.**

immoral = a term characterizing acts which violate social standards with respect to what is considered right or wrong, frequently connoting a sanction from some superhuman source such as society, an absolute Right, or a deity. [Syn. **unethical.** Cf. **bad, evil.** Distg. fr. **unconventional,** which implies merely lack of conformity without serious disapproval by social or divine sanction; and distg. fr. **illegal** which implies a violation of social usage punishable by legal methods, and fr. **unmoral** and **non-moral.**] **immorality**[n].

immortality = the endless survival of the personality of an organism after biological death. **immortal**[a]. — Ger. *Ansterblichkeit.*

immunization = the protection of an organism, through inoculation, against some specific germ disease. [Includes **active im.** in which protective substances are elaborated in cells of the organism having the disease; and **passive im.** in which protection is conferred by the injection of immune bodies produced actively in the blood of other animal species.] **immune**[a], **immunize**[v].

impedance = (*elect.*) that property of an electric circuit which limits the current set up by a given electromotive force. [When the electromotive force is a varying one, e.g. an alternating voltage, the impedance will be of two kinds, resistive and reactive. **resistive impedance** is manifested as an immediate transfer of electrical energy into heat by reason of the resistance of the conductors. **reactive impedance** (**reactance**) is either inductive or capacitative. **inductive reactance** for a sinusoidal current is the angular velocity multiplied by the inductance. **capacitative reactance** for a sinusoidal current is the reciprocal of the product of angular velocity and capacitance.]

impediment/speech = a loose term applied to stuttering and other slight disturbances of the free flow of speech. — Fr. *embarras de parole.*

imperative[a] = characterizing actions which are obligatory, i.e. compelled by command, by circumstances, or by recognized principles of ethics, logic, etc.

imperative/categorical = an ethical principle, recognized by any given individual, which is considered as a kind of compulsion, obliging him to adopt certain courses of conduct and to refrain altogether from others.

imperative idea, imperative conception = a dominant or persistent idea which is correlated with the behavior of an individual in certain pathological conditions.

imperceptible = characterizing a stimulus which is too weak to give rise to any conscious experience.

imperceptible difference = characterizing a difference between two stimuli which is too small (in respect to intensity, extent, or duration) to be distinguished. [The two resulting experiences, in such cases, are reported as **equal** or **similar.**] — Ger. *unmerklicher Unterschied.*

impersonation = the (active) representation of one person by another, either legitimately, as on the stage, or illegally, so as to obtain certain advantages by the misrepresentation.

implicit = not directly stated or given, but deducible from the data or proposition. [Contr. w. **explicit.** Cf. **implicit response.**]

implicit response = any response involving muscles or glands or both, which is not easily observable by another person without instrumental or experimental aid. [It includes deep-seated changes within the body (e.g. contractions or secretions of the stomach) as well as skeletal changes of minimal degree (e.g. changed tonus in biceps muscle or subvocal speech movement). The term was coined by J. B. Watson (1913). Syn. **covert response.** Contr. w. **overt** or **explicit response;** this distinction is one of convenience and not thoroughgoing.]

import[n] = the meaning of a judgment or statement; or the implications of a proposition. [Cf. **meaning.**] — Fr. *portée, signification.*

impossible = characterizing a proposition which violates the accepted principles of logic or of empirical science and thus represents a condition or situation which is never found in nature. [Often applied improperly, in rebuttal, to preclude re-examination of the underlying premises or principles. Distg. fr. **untrue,** which fails to represent actual facts, but is not obviously contrary to logic or science, and fr. **inconceivable,** which characterizes limitation of human intellect. Contr. w. **possible,** characterizing a proposition, etc., which may represent reality.] **impossibility**[n]. — Ger. *unmöglich.*

impotence = the inability (usually in a male) to perform normal coitus. [Cf. **sterility.**] **impotent**[a].

impression = 1. (*psychol.*) the neural results of stimulation, 2. (*esth.*) the effect produced by the intrinsic characters of an object, as distg. fr. its meaning; 3. (*pop.*) a vague judgment or conclusion. [Distg. (1) fr. **sensation,** which refers to the subjective effect; Hume used the term in contr. w. **idea,** or revived impression.] — Ger. *Eindruck.*

impression/method of = any approach to the investigation of feeling (emotion), in which the subject reports (or describes from introspection) his affective experiences that arise in connection with a given stimulus. [**paired comparisons** is the method most frequently employed. Distg. fr. **method of expression** = any one of the methods of recording bodily changes involved in feeling or emotion.] — Ger. ***Eindrucksmethode.***

impressionability = a characteristic of certain individuals such that they are extremely susceptible to new situations and readily absorb elements from a new environment. **impressionable**[a].

impressional tendency = the tendency of certain ideas or conscious contents to recur in mind because of the strength or vividness of their original impression. [Cf. **associative tendency.**]

impropriety = the quality of an act, such that it is not in accordance with conventional patterns of behavior common to the members of the given social group. [Cf. **propriety.**] **improper**[a].

improvement = (*beh.*) progressive approximation to some standard as a result of training. [Applied either to a single response or to an organized series of responses; **improvement** may be measured in various ways; e.g. by increased *simplification* (i.e. dropping out of non-essential movements, or by *decrease in time* required for the entire act.] **improve**[v]. — Fr. *progrès;* Ger. *Verbesserung.*

improvement/zero = failure of an individual organism to gain in rate, accuracy, or other measure of performance as a result of practice. — Fr. *zéro de progrès.*

impulse = a tendency to action which is involuntary and is not directly traceable to stimulation. **impulsive**[a] (characterizing both the action and an individual who is specially subject to impulse). — Fr. *impulsion;* Ger. *Regung, Impuls, Anstoss.*

impulse/nerve (**neural,** or **nervous**) = the specific activity which is propagated along neurons, and esp. along their fibers. [Syn. **propagated disturbance.**] — Fr. *influx nerveux.*

impulsion = a state of the organism which predisposes it for some specific type of activity. — Ger. *Drang.*

impulsive act = a response made without reflection or delay.

impulsive action = (*introsp.*) an action (e.g. in the reaction experiment) which includes in course (1) a knowledge of the end, together with an awareness of the determination to move; (2) a perception which releases the movement; and (3) a knowledge that the movement has occurred and that the end has been attained or not attained. [Cf. **action, selective action, automatic action.**] — Ger. *Triebhandlung.*

impulsive obsession = an irresistible urge to do things which one recognizes as foolish or undesirable. [Syn. **compulsion neurosis.**]

impulsiveness = a tendency to act without deliberation or to respond immediately, although not reflexly, to a situation. **impulsive**[a]. — Fr. *impulsiveté.*

inaccessibility = a general condition of the individual in certain mental disorders, characterized by extreme irresponsiveness to suggestion and failure to respond to questions. [Specially characteristic of schizophrenia.]

inaccuracy = 1. lack of correspondence, in any significant respect, between a given report or formula and that which it represents; 2. the presence of some error in a report or formula. [Contr. w. **accuracy** = close correspondence or absence of error.] **inaccurate**[a]. — Fr. *inexactitude;* Ger. *Ungenauigkeit.*

inadequacy, inadequate personality = behavior characterized by slight mental inferiority, specifically observed in an inability to cope with complex social and economic situations. — Fr. *personnalité insuffisante (incomplète).*

inadequate stimulus = a type of stimulus which is unusual to a given receptor, but operates effectively upon it. [E.g. an electric current producing visual sensations. Contr. w. **adequate stimulus.** The terms are awkward in English and might well be replaced by **abnormal** and **normal,** or **inappropriate** and **appropriate.**]

inattention = a state of consciousness in which there is no well-defined focus of attention, i.e. no part of which is characterized by a high degree of clearness. [Often used pop. to mean lack of attention to some particular content.]

Inbegriff = a German term denoting an inclusive concept or totality of varied contents, united by some common interest.

inborn = present in the individual at birth. [Often syn. w. **innate, connate, inherited,** or **congenital** = potentially present in the fertilized germ-cell.] — Fr. *inné*; Ger. *angeboren*.

incantation = a formula or ritual used in applied magic, either to injure an enemy or to obtain some possession or attribute for oneself or for another. **enchant**[v].

incapable = totally lacking in ability. — Ger. *unfähig*.

incapacity = (*legal*) inability to manage one's own affairs, due to mental disorder. **incapable**[a].

incendiarism = (*criminol.*) a tendency to set fire to dwellings or other buildings. [Distg. fr. **pyromania,** a pathological tendency. Cf. **arson.**]

incentive = 1. an interoceptive stimulus, or a central neural activity combining with some external stimulus, which leads to a response; 2. an extra-organic stimulus or situation which serves to maintain or to direct motivated conduct. [(1) generally denotes a **drive,** or an idea or any motor tendency not the direct **result** of exteroceptive stimulation, which leads to responses toward an objective such as food, property, matrimony, etc. (2) is a counterpart to the intra-organic drive or urge, though not always necessary to the latter. If the motivation of conduct be conceived as originating in some maladjustment between organism and environment, the organism's efforts are said to be the immediate result of inner **drive** while the critical environmental conditions are called the **incentive;** i.e. food is an *incentive* to a *hunger driven* animal or person; a badge of honor is an *incentive* to one under the urge of ambition. Contr. w. **deterrent** = which leads to inhibition or movement away from.] — Ger. (1) *Motiv,* (2) *Anregung*.

incest = sexual intercourse between two closely related individuals of opposite sex. [Now generally restricted to parent-child, grandparent-grandchild, brother-sister, and (in many races) avuncular-nepotistic intercourse; hist. used also in a broader and a narrower sense; in exogamous tribes any intercourse within the clan is incest.] **incestuous**[a].

incest barrier = (*psychoan.*) the barrier in the development of the libido in which the individual seeks to pass from objects unsuited to sexual wish-gratification, to those other persons with whom genuine sexual life may be carried on without feelings of guilt. — Fr. *obstacle à l'inceste*.

incest dream = (*psychoan.*) a dream having an incest motive or reference, either literal or symbolic. — Fr. *rêve d'inceste*.

incidental = occurring occasionally, but not properly a part of a given situation or sequence. — Fr. *occasionnel*; Ger. *zufällig*.

incidental cause = an antecedent which occurs occasionally in a given process, but which is disregarded as being not an essential element or factor in the process itself.

incidental cues = stimuli which occur occasionally in connection with a given stimulus and assist in determining the character of the response to that stimulus. — Fr. *points de repères occasionnels*.

incidental errors of observation = errors entering into the report of an observer which have no relation to the controlled conditions of an experimental situation.

incidental learning = the learning in a casual manner of items in one's environment, i.e. without special effort or specific attention to them, or without special intent to learn them. [Cf. **incidental memory.**] — Fr. *apprentissage (acquisition) occasionnel*.

incidental memory = memory of experiences in the absence of any set intention to retain the impression. [Applied esp. to the learning process. Syn. **unintentional memory.**] — Fr. *mémoire occasionnelle*.

incipient = pert. to the beginning of a process. [E.g. incipient movement; often applied to a rudimentary activity which does not progress beyond the initial stage.] — Fr. *commençant, naissant, débutant*.

incitogram = the neural conditions which underlie the organization of efferent impulses.

incoherence = lack of orderly or systematic connection of parts. [Applied to speech, to presentation of a theory, etc. Used also to designate a symptom of mental disorder.] **incoherent**[a].

incommensurable = 1. (*math.*) characterizing magnitudes which have no common measure, e.g. the circumference and diameter of a circle, the side and diagonal of a square; 2. (*arithmetic*) characterizing numbers which have no common divisor except unity.

incompatibility = 1. the fact that two characteristics are such that they can never coexist in any given individual organism or mind; 2. the relation between two judgments such that if one be true the other is false; 3. the characteristic or quality of two persons such that they do not associate freely or harmoniously with each other. [Syn. (2) **contrariety.** Contr. w. **compatibility** in all three senses.] **incompatible**[a].

incompetency = a lack, on the part of an individual, of the qualifications essential for the normal performance of certain tasks. [Used technically in law, and loosely in social science. Syn. **incapability,** prefd. in psychol. Cf. **non compos mentis.**] **incompetent**[a].

incomprehensible = characterizing a statement or attitude on the part of an individual which the reader or critic, after careful consideration, finds self-contradictory or confused. [The term usually implies a characteristic *inherent* in the statement or attitude.] — Ger. *unverständlich*.

inconceivability, inconceivableness = the character of a statement, theory, etc., such that the critic is unable to represent it in terms corresponding to any actual situation. [Spencer's ultimate criterion of truth is the **inconceivability of the opposite.** Cf. **conceivable.**] **inconceivable**[a].

incongruous = 1. out of keeping with a prior thought or pattern; 2. esthetically discordant. [Contr. w. **congruous.**] **incongruity**[n].

inconsistency = the relation between two properties or sets of data, not formally contradictory or contrary, such that if they were fully understood they would seem to be mutually incompatible or to involve contradiction. **inconsistent**[a].

incontinence = 1. inability to restrain a natural discharge, esp. of urine; 2. lack of self-control, esp. of sexual indulgence.

incoordination/motor (or **muscular**) = lack of balance or harmony in the simultaneous action of different muscle groups which normally co-operate in the performance of a complex act. [Syn. **ataxia.** Contr. w. **coordination.**]

incredibility = the incompatibility of a statement (or of extended testimony) with known facts, such that the hearer or reader is led to an attitude of intense disbelief. [Contr. w. **credibility** = such that an attitude of belief is induced.] **incredible**[a].

increment = the amount of change in a magnitude. [Literally, the amount of *increase*, but usually generalized to include decrease (i.e. negative increment, or **decrement**) also. In psychophysics, the increment of stimulation is that fractional increase of the stimulus which yields a just noticeably greater sensation.]

incremental reflex = increase of a reflex on sudden intensification of the provoking stimulus.

incubus = 1. (*hist.*) a demon; 2. syn. for **nightmare.**

incus = one of the **auditory ossicles** intermediate between **malleus** and **stapes.** [Syn. **anvil, anvil bone.**] — Ger. *Amboss.*

indecency = conduct which contravenes the standards of the community in which it occurs, particularly in violation of certain social taboos. [Applied most commonly to violation of intersex or intercaste conventions and to disapproved modes of dress, language, and (in primitive races) eating. Contr. w. **decency** = conformity of conduct to standard, in these respects. Cf. **obscenity.**] **indecent**[a]. — Ger. *Unanständigkeit.*

indecision = an attitude, either normal or pathological, characterized by inability to select a course of action, with consequent inhibition of movements.

indefensible = pert. to conduct which, even when fully explained, is subject to social disapproval. [Contr. w. **defensible.**]

indefinite = not precisely specified or demarcated. [Contr. w. **definite.**] — Ger. *unbestimmt.*

independence = 1. absence of (known) causal relations between two data or sets of data; 2. an attitude of self-reliance or refusal to be dominated by others. [(1) implies that the two data are not both due to the same cause, and that neither is caused by the other. Cf. **cause, condition.** Contr. w. **dependence** (in both senses).] **independent**[a]. — Ger. (1) *Unabhängigkeit.*

independent invention = the independent origination of similar culture traits by two or more peoples. [Contr. w. **diffusion, culture borrowing.**]

independent phenomena = (*psych. res.*) any phenomena expressive of intelligence which occur independently of the physical agency of the **medium** or any other person. [Typical forms are (*a*) voices through a trumpet, etc.; (*b*) **psychography** = writing on paper, slates, etc.; (*c*) **telekinesis,** or **levitation.**]

indeterminate = 1. (*math.*) characterizing (*a*) values which are not fixed, owing to lack of sufficient equations, or (*b*) expressions which are not amenable to specific evaluation, e.g. $\infty \times 0$ or $0/0$; 2. (*psychol.*) ambiguous syn. for **undetermined** or **undeterminable.** [Contr. w. **determinate.**]

indeterminism = 1. (*psychol.*) the theory that man can act or choose reflectively in relative independence of given stimuli; 2. (*biol.*) the theory that some or all organic events are not necessary consequents of antecedent conditions. [Syn. (1) **libertarianism** (prefd.), **free-will doctrine.** Contr. w. **determinism.**]

index = 1. any value which is deemed significant of class differences in biology or general science; 2. (*anthrop.*) abbrev. for **cephalic index;** 3. (*math.*) syn. for **exponent** or **root;** 4. (*anat.*) the finger next to the thumb. **indices**[pl] (2, 3), **indexes** (1, 4). — Ger. (4) *Zeigefinger.*

index of change = the blur of a perceptual experience, which occurs when one distinct impression changes continuously into another and serves as a basis for the judgment that a change has occurred (W. Stern).

index of precision = a term proposed by F. M. Urban to denote the value of h of the **phi gamma hypothesis** for the method of constant stimuli; this value determines the steepness of the curves of the psychometric functions and hence indicates the homogeneity or precision of the several judgments. [Cf. **h, method of constant stimuli.**]

indifference = 1. neutrality or balance between two opposing characteristics, such as pleasure and pain; 2. failure to appreciate an appeal; e.g. moral indifference, political indifference.

indifference point = the zero or transition value between two opposing continua of experiences. [In temperature sensations, measured by the range of values in centigrade units of stimuli which yield neither warmth nor cold sensations; cf. **zero/psychological.** In feeling, measured by the stimulus values intermediate between pleasantness and unpleasantness.] — Ger. *Indifferenzpunkt.*

indirect = 1. by a longer path than the shortest possible; 2. through intermediaries. [Contr. (1) w. **direct** = by a straight path; (2) w. **immediate.**]

indirect reflex = a crossed reflex, or a reflex induced by other than the usual source of stimulation.

indirect selection, see **organic selection.**

indirect vision = visual experiences evoked by stimuli which fall upon peripheral (as contr. w. central) regions of the retina.

individual = a single organism. [Distg. fr. (*a*) the **social group,** (*b*) the **general type** of a species, (*c*) the **cells** which compose the organism. N.B. In this dictionary used as syn. w. **human being,** unless specifically qualified.] **individual**[a].

individual differences = deviations or variations in respect to certain characteristics which occur among the members of a group or in the same individual at different times. [Contr. w. **group differences.** Cf. **differential psychology.**]

individual psychology = 1. the branch of psychology which investigates differences between individuals; 2. the investigation of individual differences in the mode of striving toward the superiority goal (Adler). [Contr. w. **general psychology,** which investigates the average or type of the species. Cf. **differential psychology,** which embraces individual, group, and race psychology.]

individual response = a type of response in association tests which is peculiar to an individual, as distinct from the nodal or community response, and yet is not of a personal nature. [Cf. **egocentric response.**]

individual selection = the application of natural selection to competition between individual organisms, as distg. fr. competition between organs or parts or social groups. — Fr. *sélection entre individus*.

individuality = 1. the organized sum-total of characteristics in any organism which distinguish it from any other; 2. that which distinguishes one person or thing from another. [Distg. fr. **personality:** (*a*) **individuality** may refer to any organism of a sufficiently complex structure; **personality** is strictly applicable to human organisms; (*b*) **individuality** attaches itself to any trait, quality, or manifestation of behavior (gait, voice, drinking, playing); **personality** relates to the whole complex of characteristics which make up the individual; (*c*) **individuality** is a differentiating concept with little or no implication of a standard; **personality** implies a positive standard and therefore allows of evaluation.]

individuation = the differentiation or emergence of a specific and local activity out of general mass activity. [Contr. w. **integration.**]

individuation/law of = 1. the principle that parts come into existence from wholes through a process of individuation (Wheeler); 2. the principle that the behavior-pattern from the beginning expands throughout the growing normal animal as a perfectly integrated unit, whereas partial patterns arise within the total pattern and by a process of individuation acquire secondarily varying degrees of independence (Coghill).

induced color = a color or change in color which appears in a given portion of the subjective visual field, due not to direct stimulation of the corresponding portion of the retina, but to concomitant stimulation of other portions. [Cf. inducing color.] — Fr. *couleur induite*.

induced emotion/theory of = 1. the theory that the perception of emotional behavior or expression is sufficient to excite the same emotion in the person who perceives it; 2. the theory that the stimulations to action by individuals in a crowd augment the activities of the entire group and vice versa. [Cf. (1) **sympathetic induction;** (2) is advanced to account for mob action.] — Fr. *t. d'émotion induite*.

induced hallucination = hallucination aroused in one individual by the suggestion of someone else. [The phenomenon can be induced in the deeper stages of hypnosis, and is also frequently a symptom in certain toxic conditions.] — Fr. *h. induite*.

inducing color = (*vis.*) a color-stimulus which induces a contrast effect. [Distg. fr. **induced color,** the color that constitutes the effect.] — Fr. *couleur inductive*.

inductance = a property of an electric conductor or circuit which determines the extent to which electrical energy may be transferred between the conductor and the magnetic field surrounding the conductor. [The unit is the **henry.**]

induction = 1. (*logic*) the act or process of reasoning from particular to general; 2. the end result of such reasoning; 3. (*physiol.*) the indirect arousal of some condition in an organism, e.g. color induction; 4. (*neurol.*) a term applied to certain cases of facilitation between neural paths, usually where the regions showing facilitation are close together. [Syn. (4) **facilitation.** Contr. (1, 2) w. **deduction.**]

induction coil = an electrical device consisting typically of two concentric coils of wire wound about an iron core; one coil (the primary) usually contains a small number of turns of heavy wire, while the other (the secondary) is made up of a large number of turns of fine wire. [A change of current in the primary induces in the secondary a current whose voltage is dependent upon the ratio of turns in primary and secondary coils. By opening and closing the primary circuit with an automatic vibrator, an alternating current of high potential may be set up in the secondary circuit.] — Fr. *bobine d'induction*.

induction/complete (or **formal**) = the affirmation in a single proposition, with respect to a class or group of phenomena, of what has previously been affirmed separately of each member of the group. [Cf. **enumeration, deduction.**]

induction/cortical = an alteration in the functional activity of a point on the cerebral cortex as a result of excitation of some adjacent point. [E.g. the influence of the cerebellum upon the precentral cortex.]

induction/immediate spinal (or **direct spinal**) = the principle that if the dermal area from any point of which a certain reflex can be elicited, is stimulated at two points simultaneously, the response will be evoked even though both of the stimuli are subliminal (Sherrington). [This is summation on the final common path. Cf. **allied reflexes.**]

induction shock = (*beh.*) an induced electric shock given to an animal while in the performance of some task, in order to inhibit him from pursuing a certain line of action. [One of the methods of punishment used in experiments on learning.]

induction/successive spinal, /successive, /indirect spinal, see **rebound.**

induction/sympathetic = the setting up of emotions, ideas, or acts in an individual, which are similar to those manifested in his presence by another. [Cf. **imitation, contagion, social facilitation, induced emotion.**]

induction test = a type of test in which the task is to derive a rule or principle from a number of particular instances given. [Most commonly applied to a test devised by Terman and included in the 14-year tests of the Stanford-Binet scale.]

industrial group = a collection of individuals pursuing the same economic occupation. [Cf. **industry** (2).]

industrial psychology = the branch of applied psychology which investigates the problems and situations found in the **industries** (2). — Ger. *Wirtschaftspsychologie*.

industry = 1. the characteristic or habit of steady and continued attention or devotion to any useful or productive occupation or task, either manual or mental; 2. a generic term applied to any or all systematic economic occupations (i.e. occupations concerned in furnishing means of livelihood, protection, social communication, etc.) but exclusive of purely biological functions. **industrious**[a] (1), **industrial**[a] (2). — Ger. (1) *Geschäftigkeit*, (2) *Wirtschaft*.

inebriety = habitual alcoholic intoxication. [Syn. **alcoholism** (prefd.).]

ineffability = (*relig.*) an experience, or a quality of experience, which is incapable of being expressed in words; specifically, the mystical ecstasy.

inertia = 1. (*phys.*) the resistance offered by a body to a change of its state of rest or of motion; 2. (*neurol.*) a property of reflex conduction whereby a stimulus does not at once produce its full physiological effect, and whereby this effect to some extent persists after the stimulation ceases; 3. (*esth.*) the principle according to which art perpetuates forms and structures which have under changed conditions lost their *raison d'être*, e.g. the *abacus* of a marble column; 4. (*psychol.*) the tendency for mental processes to have a certain lag, to perseverate; 5. (*pop.*) mental or bodily sluggishness, apathy, torpidity. [Cf. (2) **latency.**] **inert**[a].

inertia/sensory = the lag or tardiness of a sensory mechanism (i.e. receptor) in beginning to respond on the application of the specific kind of physical energy which is its adequate stimulus.

inexistence = existing within, not actually, but by implication. [Used in the phrase **intentional inexistence.**]

infancy = 1. the earliest period of postnatal life in human beings (or other animals), during which the individual is wholly or almost wholly dependent upon parental care; usually applied only to the first two years, e.g. infant in arms; sometimes extended to include the whole period from birth to maturity; 2. (*anat.*) the period from birth to assumption of erect posture; 3. (*legal*) the period from birth to legal majority. **infant**[np]; **infanthood**[n] = the condition (rare); **infantile**[a]. — Fr. (1, 2) *enfance*, (3) *mineur*; Ger. *Kindesalter*.

infant psychology = the study of the mental life and behavior of infants. [Cf. **infancy.**]

infantile[a] = 1. pert. to an infant or resembling the stage of infancy; 2. characterizing behavior on the part of an older child or adult which is like that shown by an infant or young child in similar situations. (Last syll. **-il** or **-ile.**)

infantile amnesia = (*psychoan.*) lapsed memory of certain early childhood experiences, due to ater repression. [They are 'requently recalled under adequate analys s.]

infantile birth theories = the notions of young children concerning birth. [E.g. that babies come out of the breast, are cut out of the body, that the navel opens itself, the begetting of children through eating, or birth through the anal opening. Cf. **cloaca theory.**] — Fr. *t. enfantines de naissance*.

infantile complex = (*psychoan.*) an emotional condition which occurs pathologically in adult life, when the usual outlet for libido is blocked, and as a result, has regressed to modes of behavior that are characteristic of childhood.

infantilism = a condition of partly arrested development in man, characterized by mental retardation and usually by a stunting of bodily growth. **infantile**[a].

infection = invasion of the tissues of an animal or plant by a pathogenic organism, whose growth and toxins tend to injure the bodily tissues, thereby causing the symptoms of disease. **infectious**[a]. — Ger. *Ansteckung*.

inference = 1. a judgment or conclusion which is reached from previously accepted judgments or premises and not from direct observation of data; 2. the mental process of reaching a conclusion indirectly. **infer**[v], **inferential**[a]. — Ger. *Folgerung, Schluss*.

inferior oblique, -rectus, see **eye-muscles.**

inferiority complex = (*psychoan.*) a narcissistic wound or the psychical scars left on a wounded narcissism (Freud). [Syn. **castration complex.** Cf. **inferiority feeling.**]

inferiority feeling = 1. a dominant affective attitude due to the inadequacy of some organ and often coordinated with an accompanying defect in the sexual apparatus and leading to neurotic behavior in varying degrees, according to environmental complications (upbringing, social relations, etc.) and insufficient compensation (Adler); 2. the feeling of weakness and helplessness present in all infants, and characteristically reinforced through their repeated failures to command their environment as well as by their recognition of their physical limitations or blemishes. [This *primary* inferiority feeling (2) is later complicated by the *secondary* inferiority feeling, the use of pretended weakness to achieve control of others through pity.] — Fr. *sentiment d'infériorité*; Ger. *Minderwertigkeitsgefühl*.

infinitesimal[n] = a quantity which becomes and remains less than any defined value, however small, that may be assigned. [Contr. w. **infinity.**] **infinitesimal**[a].

infinity = the limit which finite magnitudes approach as they grow greater and greater. [Other characteristics than the magnitude which approaches the infinite limit may remain finite as the limit is approached. Designated by ∞ or by ω. Contr. w. **infinitesimal.**] **infinite**[a].

inflection = 1. a bending, as of the head or of a curve; 2. any modification in the form of a word which indicates grammatical modification; e.g. gender, possession, tense, number, etc.; 3. (*vocal*) the rise and fall of pitch during speaking.

influence[n] = any prior condition which, in explaining the temporal succession of events, is considered as a factor in determining or leading to the later conditions. **influence**[v] = to play a part in determining an event. **influential**[a] (used only to characterize major factors).

information = 1. facts or ideas acquired by an individual in any manner, such as observation, experiment, reading, oral instruction; 2. (*hist.*) implications concerning the content of consciousness (trans. of Ger. *Kundgabe*) as contr. w. the accurate introspective description of consciousness (*Beschreibung*). **inform**[v] = to give information to another individual, **informatory**[a] = yielding information, **informational**[a] = pert. to information.

information test = a type of test designed to determine the testee's knowledge of facts, commonly of facts drawn from a variety of fields of information. [E.g. Test 8 in Army Alpha Examination. Syn. **range of information test.** Distg. fr. (1) tests of knowledge of specific subject matter (e.g. literature); (2) tests of capacity to learn (e.g. general intelligence tests); and (3) vocabulary tests, in which the test items are commonly selected by chance.]

infraclavicular = pert. to or located in the regions just below the collar-bone.

infraconscious = characterizing the primordial psychic states from which consciousness has been evolved and which in the individual underlie consciousness in its marginal aspects (C. L. Morgan).

inframammary = pert. to or located in the regions on the front of the body lying below the breast or nipple and above the hypochondriac regions.

infraspinatus reflex = simultaneous outward rotation of the arm and straightening of the elbow, elicited by tapping a point on the shoulder-blade on a line bisecting the angle formed by the spine of the bone and its inner margin. [Mediated by the 5th to 7th cervical segments of the cord.]

infundibulum = (*anat.*) a stalk arising from the forebrain under the cerebral hemispheres, by which the pituitary body is attached to the tuber cinereum. — Ger. *Hirntrichter.*

ingestion = the process of taking substances into the body in mass.

inguinal = pert. to or located in the groin. (Accent **in-**.)

inherent = belonging to or existing in an object or person. [Contr. w. **external,** which may be associated w. the object but does not constitute an integral part of it; **intrinsic,** often used as syn., refers rather to *values,* while **inherent** refers to *qualities.*] **inhere**[v]; **inherence**[n] = the fact of inhering; **inherency**[n] = the characteristic.

inherit = 1. (*biol.*) to receive from a parent the capacity to develop characters similar to those found in this parent or in an earlier ancestor; 2. (*econ.*) to receive property from the estate of a deceased person; 3. (*soc.*) to acquire by imitation or instruction certain traditions, customs, etc., prevalent in the community. [(1) and (3) are likely to be confused; it is advisable not to use (3) in psychol. unless carefully denoted. Cf. **heritage.**] — Fr. *hériter*; Ger. *erben.*

inheritance = 1. (*biol.*) the characters received by an organism from its ancestors; 2. (*econ.*) property of any sort received by an individual from the estate of a deceased person. [Syn. **heritage** (applied generally to the total inheritance).] **inherit**[v]. — Fr. (1) *hérédité,* (2) *héritage*; Ger. (1) *Erbschaft, Vererbung.*

inheritance/alternative = (*biol.*) inheritance in which one of two corresponding characters possessed by the parents appears in the offspring to the exclusion of the other.

inheritance/blending = inheritance in which two characters of the parents combine in the offspring to produce a relatively stable character, usually of a more or less intermediate type, which is capable of being passed on to subsequent generations without segregation into its parental components.

inherited[a] = derived from one's ancestors. [Prefd. to **innate, inborn, connate, congenital,** which signify existence at birth (or earlier) but do not clearly designate derivation from ancestors; an **inherited trait** may not develop till long after birth (e.g. the reproductive functions) and would then strictly not be innate or inborn.] — — Fr. *hérité*; Ger. *vererbt, angeboren.*

inherited tendency, see **tendency/inherited.**

inhibition = 1. (*physiol.*) the partial or complete arrest of an already active function (esp. of a muscular contraction); 2. that condition of a tissue or organ in which a function cannot be excited by the usual stimulus; 3. (*psychoan.*) a mental condition which, through an opposing force, tends to check or prevent certain modes of expression, esp. such as would expose to others the individual's thoughts or character. [Syn. (3) **repression, suppression.**] **inhibit**[v], **inhibitory**[a]. — Fr. *inhibition, arrêt*; Ger. *Hemmung.*

inhibition/central = inhibition of nerve impulses at centers within the central nervous system. [Attributed either (1) to Wedensky interference between the nerve impulses, or (2) to the presence in the centers of an active inhibitory substance. Cf. **habit interference.**]

inhibition/reflex, see **reflex inhibition.**

inhibition/retroactive = the tendency of a later formed association to impair a previously formed association. [Distg. fr. **amnesia/retroactive.**]

inhibitionism = the view that character is a function of the inhibition of instinctive tendencies.

inhibitory nerve = a nerve, afferent or efferent, whose specific function is to arrest existent excitation in a nerve center or in any effector. [There is some uncertainty as to whether the mechanism of this function lies wholly and specifically in the nerve.]

inhibitory reflex = a reflex in which the previous activity of the effector organ is diminished or suppressed. [E.g. decrease of tonus in the extensor muscles when the flexor muscles of a limb are thrown into reflex contraction.]

initial delay = the pause or slowing down process immediately prior to the execution of a patterned movement.

initial reflex = the earliest reflex evoked by a series of stimuli of increasing strength when the first stimulus is below the threshold value.

initial spurt = a notably great expenditure of energy, or speeding up, observed at the beginning of certain muscular or other performances, which is followed by a slowing down to a level maintained with little fluctuation for some time. — Fr. *effort initial.*

initiation = the setting of a movement or process into actual operation.

initiative = 1. the action of an individual in starting a chain of events, e.g. a social movement; 2. ability or capacity for original conception and independent action.

injury = 1. any damage inflicted upon an organism; 2. an impairment of structure or function not due to the ordinary biological processes. [An **injury** may either affect the *structure* or may result in impairing some *function.*] — Fr. (1) *atteinte, blessure,* (2) *lésion*; Ger. *Verletzung.*

injury/current of = an electric current in tissue, which follows the rupture of cell membranes and is due to the difference in potential on opposite sides of the membranes. [The point of injury is electronegative to other parts of the surface of the tissue. Syn. **demarcation current.**] — Fr. *courant de lésion.*

ink-blot test = a test in which the testee examines a series of irregular figures, usually black on a white ground, and reports what objects or scenes he can imagine in the figures. [The material commonly used consists of ink-blots. Variety or speed of response is commonly the basis of scoring. Cf. **Rorschach test.**] — Fr. *t. des taches d'encre.*

innate = present in the individual at birth. [Used as syn. for **congenital** = present in the fertilized germ-cell; both terms usually imply inheritance, but not always. Cf. **connate.**] — Ger. *angeboren.*

innate (or **connate**) **ideas** = certain fundamental or general ideas assumed to be present in the individual anterior to experience. [The doctrine had its origin in the distinction between the data of sensation and the activity of the intellect. The Stoics recognized some ideas as common to all minds (κοιναὶ ἔννοιαι: notiones communes) and these were ultimately described as **innate ideas.** The specific term seems due to Henry More and refers to religious concepts. Descartes and others rejected this doctrine but claimed that intellectual faculties (not ideas) are innate. After Leibnitz ("the mind is innate") the distinction of *a priori* and *a posteriori* (Kant) takes its place.]

inner = 1. within the organism or body; 2. subjective. [The antithesis **inner-outer** or **internal-external** is often confused by these two meanings; it is preferable to use (1) **intra-organic** vs. **extra-organic** (or **environmental**) and (2) **subjective** vs. **objective.**] — Fr. *interne.*

inner ear, see **ear/internal.**

inner psychophysics = the relation of sensory experience to the neural events upon which it is dependent. [A concept proposed by Fechner (1860), and contr. w. **outer psychophysics,** which is concerned with the relation between stimuli and the consequent sensory experience.] — Fr. *psychophysique interne.*

innervation = 1. the supply of efferent nerves which go to an organ (or to a single muscle, gland, or cell); 2. (less frequently) the nerves, both sensory and motor, which are supplied to any organ; 3. the excitation of an effector (muscle, gland). [Not to be confused w. **enervation.**] **innervate**[v]. — Fr. *innervation.*

innervation feeling = (*hist.*) a sensation formerly attributed to outgoing or efferent nerve impulses. [The experiences in question are now generally attributed to the **proprioceptive** system, i.e. to stimulation of receptors in some muscle which contracts as a result of the efferent impulse.]

inoculation = the introduction of disease virus, bacteria, or non-living proteins into an organism in order to produce disease or immune sera. **inoculate**[v].

inorganic = 1. (*biol.*) characterizing a body or substance which possesses no capacity for growth, or life; 2. (*chem.*) designating a compound not containing carbon. [Contr. w. **organic,** which is used also in other senses.]

insanity = any form of mental disorder which renders the individual incompetent to act in accordance with the legal and conventional standards of his social environment. [The term should not be used as syn. for **psychosis,** but only for a medico-legal condition.] **insane**[n]. — Fr. *aliénation mentale*; Ger. *Wahnsinn, Irrsinn.*

insecta, insects = a class of invertebrates belonging to the phylum *arthropoda* and distg. fr. other members of the phylum by the possession of only three pairs of legs when fully mature. [Generally regarded as the highest invertebrates from the psychological point of view; ants, bees, and wasps are the insects which have been most frequently observed and experimented upon.]

insensibility = 1. temporary or general absence of some given class or mode of sensation; 2. (*pop.*) a state of unconsciousness due to swooning or to a blow on the head. [Syn. (1) **anesthesia,** (2) **coma.** Not used, except in adjectival form, as antithesis of **sensibility.**] **insensible**[a].

insight = 1. (*introsp.*) the direct or immediate apprehension of form, meaning, or general truths; 2. (*Gestalt*) the sudden apprehension of meaning without reference to previous experience, as evidenced by the appropriateness of an organism's behavior (i.e. of its response to the given situation); 3. a peculiar characteristic, present in consciousness, which attaches to a belief that is based upon adequate evidence (Spearman). [**insight** (2) may be evidenced e.g. by a sudden drop in the learning curve. Contr. (2) w. **automatized response.**] — Fr. *connaissance intuitive*; Ger. *Einsicht.*

insistence = a concurrence of two or more attributes of a sensation resulting in an attribute of a higher order (Stumpf, Titchener), or of two or more psychophysical processes resulting in a forced attention. [A typical example is to be found in tones of high pitch (intensity and quality).] — Ger. *Eindringlichkeit.*

insistent idea = an idea which tends to recur persistently, even in connection with irrelevant circumstances. [Syn. **fixed idea** (prefd.), **persistent idea.** Usually symptomatic of insanity.]

insomnia = chronic inability to sleep. — Ger. *Schlaflosigkeit.*

inspectionism = the practice of examining the genitals, usually of a heterosexual object. [Syn. **scopophilia.** Cf. **exhibitionism.**]

inspiration = 1. an instantaneous grasping of the solution of a problem or of a proper method of procedure, or of the plan of a work of art, without the usual intermediate steps of association and reasoning; 2. drawing in of the breath. [(1) is a loose term, indicating one's inability to trace the mental processes involved.]

instability = 1. (*emotional*) liability to excessive, quickly changeable, and therefore inappropriate display of emotion; 2. (*nervous*) lack of effectiveness in those functions which involve organization, steadiness of aim, self-control. [Syn. (1) **emotionalism.**] **unstable**[a].

instance = a sample case, cited from among collected data for illustrative purposes. — Fr. *exemple*; Ger. *Beispiel.*

instant = an exceedingly brief period of time, less than the limit of the **psychological present.** [E.g. at the same instant = lying within the same psychological present.] **instantaneous**[a]. — Ger. *Augenblick.*

instinct = 1. an organized and relatively complex mode of response, characteristic of a given species, that has been phylogenetically adapted to a specific type of environmental situation; 2. (*hist.*) a faculty or endowment of living beings which enables them to act in an adaptive manner apart from experience and learning; 3. (*psychoan.*) the innate tendency to react to an emotional stimulus in a definite manner, thus bringing the stimulus under the influence of the three polarities which govern mental life. [Contemporary uses of the term vary in all degrees between the extreme mechanistic meaning of a *response pattern,* and the extreme purposivist meaning of an *inner spring* leading to accomplishment of a certain biological end. The term comes from Cicero through medieval Latin (instinctus = impulse) and originally implied that animals possess reason at the unconscious (i.e. unreflective) level.] **instinct**[a] (or **instinctual**[a]) = pert. to or characterizing instinct; **instinctive**[a] = pert. to the response. — Fr. (1, 2) *instinct,* (3) *pulsion*; Ger. *Trieb, Instinkt.*

instinct defusion, see **defusion/instinctual.**

instinct/delayed = an instinct which does not operate till some time after birth or hatching.

instinct maturation = the development of the bodily mechanisms which underlie certain forms of behavior characteristic of a given species, so far as this development is the outcome of growth rather than of learning.

instinct/transitory = an unlearned form of behavior which can be elicited only during certain portions of an animal's life. [Applied particularly to certain forms of infantile behavior which disappear with growth, e.g. sucking.]

instinctive = 1. pert. to instinct; 2. innate, i.e. not individually acquired. [Frequently used loosely as syn. for **automatic, unthinking, unconscious.**] **instinctively**[a].

instinctive behavior = any relatively complex response which is mainly determined (or so far as determined) by the creature's inherited constitution. — Fr. *comportement instinctif*.

instinctive stimulus = (*hist.*) a perception which arouses some normal, congenital mode of behavior. [Cf. James, Princ., i, 417.]

instinctive tendency = a tendency to act so as to produce some generic type of result (usually having some biological utility), this tendency being due to inherited conditions, while the specific mode of behavior may be acquired (James). [E.g. the food-getting behavior in animals.]

instinctual fusion = (*psychoan.*) the theory that every mental process is the result of a fusion of the life instinct and the death instinct.

institution = an organized mode of social behavior in some specific field or for some specific object, which has some degree of permanency or indefinite duration. [E.g. the state, the church; a university. Distg. fr. a **temporary organization,** such as a convention, parade, etc. Sometimes includes such types of cultural behavior as language, number systems, etc.]

instruction = 1. the systematic imparting of knowledge to others; 2. a command or advice given by one individual to another. [(1) contr. w. **education** = reception of knowledge; (2) used in psychol. to denote the experimenter's directions to the observer as to his mode of procedure.] **instruct**[v], **instructional**[a] = pert. to organized instruction, **instructive**[a] = inducing knowledge. — Ger. (1) *Unterricht, Instruktion,* (2) *Aufgabe*.

instrument = (*psychol.*) a self-contained device or mechanism which has some specific purpose and is used to assist in controlling or measuring stimulus or response. [Syn. **apparatus,** generally applied to more precise implements or to complex constructions.]

instrumental error = a constant error in experimental data, due to some fault or inadequacy in the measuring instrument; e.g. a chronoscope which records longer time intervals than actually occur; a measuring rod which is too short.

insufficient reason/principle of, see **equal distribution of ignorance.**

insula, see **island of Reil.**

insulin = the active product of the internal secretion of the islands or islets of Langerhans in the **pancreas.** [An autacoid which is necessary for the normal metabolism of carbohydrates and whose deficient production leads to the condition of pancreatic diabetes. A special proprietary product is termed **iletin.**]

integer = a whole number.

integral[a] = (*math.*) related to integers or to integration.

integral[n] = (*math.*) the result of integration.

integral/definite = (*math.*) the result of integration between definite limits.

integral part = an essential constituent of a complex whole, i.e. a part whose elimination would alter fundamentally the nature of the complex whole.

integration = 1. the process by which material of any sort becomes organized, or systematically arranged, into units of a higher order; 2. (*neurol.*) the combination and organization of neural excitations within nerve centers in such a way as to produce coordinated and adaptive activity; 3. (*math.*) the process of summing up an infinite number of infinitesimals; 4. (*psychoan.*) the orderly assemblage of psychophysical components into a harmonious and integrated structure. [(1) is applied chiefly to organic composition and social organization; distg. fr. **coordination** and **organization,** in that the parts appear to lose to some extent their identity after integration; contr. (1) w. **disintegration. integration** (3) is contr. w. **differentiation;** the two operations together are called **calculus.** Cf. (4) **primary integration** and **secondary integration.**] **integrate**[v], **integral**[n] = the product of integration (3).

integration/neural (or **nervous**) = the coordination of neural functions or of neural activity.

integration/primary = (*psychoan.*) the conscious recognition by the young child that his body is something apart from the environment.

integration/secondary = (*psychoan.*) the incorporation of pregenital components into a complete psychosexual unit.

intellect = 1. the group of cognitive processes, more esp. their higher forms, e.g. the discovery of relations; 2. the capacity to perform these mental processes. [Cf. **intelligence.**] **intellectual**[a] = possessing a high degree of intellect, or employing intellect; **intellective**[a] = pert. to intellect. — Fr. *intellect*; Ger. *Verstand*.

intellection = the process of forming concepts or judgments or the process of reasoning. **intellectional**[a] (rare).

intellectual, see **intellect.**

intellectual deficiency, see **feeblemindedness.**

intellectual type = an individual who is preoccupied with abstract and theoretical problems rather than with social, political, industrial, economic, or physical activities.

intellectualism = 1. (*metaphys.*) the theory that ultimate reality is of the nature of idea or intellect; 2. (*epistem.*) the theory that knowledge is derived or deduced from reason alone; 3. (*psychol.*) the theory which reduces all (other) phenomena to intellectual processes. [Syn. (1) **idealism,** (2) **rationalism,** (3) **associationism (associationalism).** Contr. (1) w. **voluntarism,** and **materialism;** (2) w. **sensationism (sensationalism)** and **empiricism;** (3) w. **hormic theory.**]

intelligence = 1. the capacity of certain organisms to meet a novel situation by improvising a novel adaptive response; 2. ability to meet new situations quickly and successfully; 3. measured success in performance at tasks commonly called **intellectual,** i.e. arithmetical computation, completing verbal relations, etc. [Hist. contr. w. **instinct,** which emphasizes stereotyped forms of response. At present, in animal study, motor criteria are generally sought; in human study, both motor and intellectual criteria are used. Cf. **mental test.**] **intelligent**[a] (not to be confused w. **intellectual**). — Ger. *Intelligenz; Klugheit.*

intelligence measurement, see **measurement of intelligence.**

intelligence quotient, I Q = the ratio of an individual's intelligence, as determined by some mental measure, to normal or average intelligence for his age. [Of various possible forms of such ratios, the most common is mental age divided by chronological age (MA/CA). In practice the CA above a certain limit is usually assigned to that limit; e.g. in the Stanford-Binet test a chronological age above 16.0 is credited as being 16.0, since intellectual maturation is practically complete by this age.]

intelligence scale = a series of graded mental tests, by which the grade of intelligence, or mental development, of an individual may be determined. [E.g. the Binet-Simon scale.] — Fr. *échelle d'intelligence.*

intelligence test = a problem or series of problems presented to an individual for solution, or a task or series of tasks assigned to be performed, with a view to determining the grade or level of the individual's mental ability. [Intended to measure intellectual capacity, or native ability, rather than achievement resulting from formal instruction. Contr. w. tests of non-intellectual traits, such as motor ability, attitudes, interests, etc. Cf. **mental test.**] — Ger. *Intelligenzprüfung.*

intelligible = characterizing a statement or theory which is capable of conveying explicit meaning to the hearer or reader, or to the informed hearer or reader, so that at once or upon reflection it is judged to be either free from self-contradiction, or else plainly self-contradictory.

intend[v] = 1. to set oneself toward an end or goal with clear consciousness of the end, and with purpose or desire to attain it; 2. to be consciously ready to strive for some defined goal as soon as favorable opportunity shall arise. **intention**[n] (not to be confused w. **intension** = in logic, the meaning of a term); **intentional**[a]. — Fr. *se proposer, prétendre, avoir l'intention de*; Ger. *beabsichtigen.*

intension, see **connotation.**

intensity = the magnitude or degree of quantity attributed to a phenomenon, apart from its spatial or temporal value, i.e. the quantitative value of a sensory unit. [Correlated in general with the force or intensity of the physical stimulus. Cf. **attribute.**] **intensity**[a] (or **intensitive**[a]) = pert. to the phenomenon; **intense**[a] = pert. to great intensity; **intensive**[a] = emphasizing completeness as, contr. w. extendedness. — Ger. *Intensität, Stärke.*

intensity/cognitive, see **cognitive intensity.**

intensity difference limen (or **threshold**) = (*psychophys.*) that value of the comparison stimulus which is judged greater or less than a standard stimulus, with a probability arbitrarily chosen and statistically determined from a set of observations. [Usually 0.75 when only two categories of response (greater, smaller) are employed; 0.50 when a third (equal or doubtful) is added.] — Fr. *seuil différentiel d'intensité.*

intensity discrimination = a judgment in intensity between a standard and comparison stimulus.

intensity theory of tropisms = the theory which assumes that the tropic orientation of an organism to a stimulus is due to unequal intensity of stimulation of symmetrical points on the body. [Contr. w. **direction theory.**]

intent = that which the giver of a suggestion or the performer of an act seeks or aims to accomplish indirectly by his suggestion or directly by his actions. [Cf. **aim, purpose.**] — Ger. *Absicht.*

intentional = 1. performed voluntarily, not by accident; 2. of the nature of an intention or reference. [For Brentano the distinguishing feature of psychical phenomena (e.g. acts of perception, acts of judgment, etc.) is their **intention** of an object, i.e. their reference to an object. Following scholastic terminology he expressed this view by stating that such phenomena involved the **intentional inexistence** of an object, i.e. the presence of an object, not as existent, but merely as intended; this is the theory of **intentionalism**; cf. **act psychology.**] — Fr. *intentionnel.*

intentional response = an explicit movement (e.g. closing eyelids, pressing key with finger, etc.) initiated voluntarily by a subject after the occurrence of an expected stimulus in a controlled laboratory situation. [Syn. **voluntary reaction.**]

intentionalism = a psychological theory (e.g. Brentano's) which defines the psychical as that which *intends*, or refers to an object. [Syn. **act psychology.**]

interaction = a relation between two units or systems of any sort, such that the activity of each is in part determined by the activity of the other. — Ger. *Wechselwirkung.*

interactionism = the theory which accounts for the factual concomitance of conscious and bodily processes by assuming a system of reciprocal causation.

interbrain, see **diencephalon.**

intercalation = (*speech*) verbal tic in which a given word is automatically and illogically interposed between syllables or phrases in speaking.

inter-columnar correlation = the correlation between columns of coefficients in a table of correlations. [Formerly used by Spearman as a technique for demonstrating equiproportionality in tables satisfying the conditions of **two-factor** division; now replaced by the **tetrad** criterion. Cf. **equiproportional table, hierarchical table.**]

intercostal = pert. to the region between the ribs. (Accent **-cost-**.)

intercourse = any reciprocal stimulation and response among individuals or groups. [A vague generic term, including two specific notions: **commerce** (= exchange of material), and **communication** (= exchange of ideas, etc.).] — Fr. *échange*; Ger. *Verkehr.*

intercourse/sexual, see **coitus.**

interest = 1. a feeling which accompanies special attention to some content; 2. an attitude characterized by focusing attention upon certain cognitive data.

interest-attitude tests, see **X-O tests.**

interest/doctrine of = 1. the theory that all education should begin by a direct appeal to the immediate, present interests of the individual; 2. the theory that the aim of education is to awaken in the individual a many-sided interest (Herbart).

interest measurement = the technique of measuring an individual's interests, esp. vocational. [E.g. detailed questionary as to his interest in previous activities, checking of items as liked or disliked, and cross-out tests with content known to be related to particular interests.]

interference = 1. a phenomenon which attends the combination of physical waves, visual or auditory, when two such waves in different phases reach the same point in space at the same time, the result being a diminution of the amplitude of vibration, and of the intensity of sensation; 2. in habit formation, the effect of learning two partly similar activities at once, such that the rate of improvement in each is diminished. [Cf. (2) **habit interference.**] **interfere**[v].

interference/method of = a memory method in which the memory of one learned task is measured by the degree with which it interferes with the learning of a second task that involves new relations of the material of the first task. [Contr. w. **method of savings.**]

interference/psychic = a pathological phenomenon characterized by the checking of the normal response to suggestion through an antagonistic attitude on the part of the patient. [Syn. **blocking.**] — Ger. *Sperrung*.

interference/sound = the mutual cancellation (partial or complete) of two or more sounds, which act simultaneously but in contrary directions on the same vibratory body or medium.

interference tube = an acoustic conduit with one or more side-branches whose length is so adjusted as to render the system selective in the transmission of particular sound-frequencies. [In the Quincke type the branch is re-entrant and has a length such that the difference between the lengths of main pathway and side-branch is one-half the wave-length of the sound-component to be eliminated. In general, the difference between these paths may be any odd multiple of one-half the wave-length, or the sum may be any multiple of the wave-length.] — Fr. *tuyau d'interférence*; Ger. *Interferenzröhre*.

interjectional theory = the theory that spoken language arose from the automatic utterance of exclamations or ejaculations.

intermediary nerve, see **Wrisberg/nerve of.**

intermediate category (or **categories**) = in the method of **single stimuli,** those reports which will decline in frequency as the upper category increases on one side, and as the lower category increases on the other.

intermediate tone, see **intertone.**

intermittence/tonal, see **flicker/auditory.**

intermittence tone = a tone produced by interrupting a tone of uniform pitch and renewing it; when such interruptions and renewals succeed one another at a very rapid rate, a secondary tone is produced whose pitch is determined by the rate of succession. [The phenomenon (discovered by Koenig and Dennert) is analogous to the beats and difference tones produced by two simultaneous tones. Syn. **interruption tone.**] — Ger. *Intermittenzton*.

internal = 1. (*psychol.*) within the body of the organism; 2. (*anat.*) as applied to the limbs, the side nearer the spine. [Contr. w. **external;** these terms are sometimes confused in psychol. with subjective and objective; in distinguishing sensory receptors, **internal** is sometimes contr. w. **peripheral.**]

internal capsule = a band of nerve fibers in the brain, which pass between the thalamus and caudate nucleus on the one side and the lenticular nucleus on the other. [The ventral part is efferent, the dorsal part is afferent.]

internal ear, see **ear/internal.**

internal rectus, see **eye-muscles.**

internal secretion = 1. a specific chemical substance formed by an endocrine gland and discharged into the circulatory fluid; 2. the process of forming and discharging an internal secretion (1). [Distg. fr. the secretion of a duct-gland, which is discharged onto an internal or external body surface. Syn. (1) **autacoid, incretion.** Cf. **hormone, chalone.**]

internal sense = any sense whose receptors are normally activated by stimuli arising within the body. [A generic term including both **interoceptors** and **proprioceptors.** Distg. fr. **external sense.**]

internal speech = the revival experience of vocal symbols whether actually uttered or not. [From the behavioristic standpoint the non-uttered revivals are termed **implicit speech responses.**]

international intelligence tests = a battery of tests devised by Brigham and Dodd, under the auspices of the National Research Council, and designed in such a way as to be as free as possible from the influence of linguistic and cultural inequalities. [The instructions are unspoken, and the testee makes all responses manually by rotating disks of cardboard so as to bring drawings into proper relations with one another.]

interoceptive system = the totality of nerves and receptors which lie and function in the internal organs of the body. [Sometimes written **enteroceptive.**]

interoceptor = a receptor or sense organ whose stimuli operate within the body of the organism. [In general, **interoceptors** are associated with supporting tissues of entodermal origin. Distg. fr. **exteroceptor** and **proprioceptor.** Cf. **receptor, nociceptor.** Sometimes written **enteroceptor.**] **interoceptive**[a].

interocular distance = the horizontal distance between the centers of the pupils of the two eyes.

interpolation = the process of estimating a value or values intermediate between two given values in a series. **interpolate**[v] (accent **-terp-.**)

interpretation = 1. the arrangement or organization of data into a system; 2. the addition of meaning to the primary data of experience. [**interpretation** = the act of organization, as its resulting expression; **appreciation** = the attitude which leads to the act; **signification** = the supplementary data. Cf. **Kundgabe.**]

interpretation of dreams, see **dream interpretation.**

interquartile range = the distance or range from the end of the 1st to the beginning of the 3rd quartile, i.e. the 75th percentile minus the 25th percentile. [It is twice the quartile deviation. Cf. **quartile.**] — Fr. *écart interquartile*.

interruption tone, see **intermittence tone.**

interscapular = pert. to or located in the middle of the back, between the shoulder-blades.

interscapular reflex, see **scapular reflex.**

intersex = an individual of a normally bisexual species which is intermediate between a male and a female. [Syn. **sex intergrade.**]

intersubjective = pert. to or characterizing a

mutual relation among a plurality of minds. [Applied esp. to intercourse by means of language.]

intertone = a tone which appears under certain conditions when two primary tones are producing beats. [The **intertone** has a pitch intermediate between the primaries, and its fluctuations of intensity constitute the beats. Syn. **intermediate tone.**] — Ger. *Zwischenton.*

interval = 1. the amount of time between two limiting instants or events; 2. the extent of space between two objects or boundaries; 3. (*mus.*) the difference in pitch between any two tones which are sounded together (harmonic interval) or successively (melodic interval), usually expressed as a ratio of two physical frequencies. [A *true* (or *perfect*) *interval* (3) is that formed by two tones whose frequency ratio follows exactly a standard set by musical theory (i.e. a simple numerical relation); a *tempered interval* (3) is one that closely approximates the value prescribed by the theory of true intervals. Cf. **just intonation, scale.** See Table VII.] — Ger. (1) *Zwischenzeit*; (2) *Zwischenraum*; (3) *Tonabstand, Intervall.*

interval of uncertainty = a term applied by F. M. Urban to the range between the upper and lower limens within which no part of the psychometric functions for the difference judgments will assume a value as great as their value at the limens.

interval/sense of = the ability of an individual to discriminate or to recognize differences of interval. [Keenness of discrimination is expressed as a differential limen for a given individual and a given interval.]

intestine = the membranous tube which extends from the stomach to the anus. **intestinal**[a] (accent **-tes-**). — Ger. *Darm.*

intoxication = an abnormal condition of the organism, due to drugs or poisons (esp. alcohol), having a great range of manifestations, both excitatory and stupefying. [Metaphorically applied to the exhilarating effects of personal success, etc.] **intoxicated**[a] = manifesting these symptoms; **intoxicant**[n] = a substance which produces intoxication.

intracranial = within the **cranium.** [Usually, within the brain; e.g. intracranial pressure.]

intra-ocular modification = any modification in a visual stimulus which results from the peculiar structure of the eye. [In addition to the formation of the retinal image, these modifications include such effects as scattering of light, selective absorption, fluorescence, and various refractive aberrations.]

intrapsychic conflicts = (*psychoan.*) the expression of an emotional tension between two opposing tendencies or wishes, which result from abnormally repressed mental processes.

intraselection = a form of natural selection which arises from the competition in growth between various elementary vital units, cells, tissues, or organs of the body, resulting in survival of the most viable. [Syn. **histonal selection.**]

intra-uterine = within the uterus or womb. [E.g. intra-uterine life, behavior, etc.]

intrinsic = characterizing the value (in any specific respect) of a given object or datum regardless of its relations to others. [Contr. w. **extrinsic** = value due to its relations or setting. Distg. fr. **inherent,** which applies to qualities rather than values, but often used as syn.]

intrinsic eye-muscles, see **eye-muscles.** — Fr. *m. intrinsèques de l'oeil.*

introception = the adoption by an individual of social standards (e.g. morals and conventions) into his own personal system of motives and desires. [Cf. **socialization,** which indicates conformity of behavior rather than of purpose or motive.]

introjection = 1. (*epistem.*) the theory of the relation between cognition and the external world which holds that the individual consciousness is localized within a given organism and that external things are represented in consciousness by internal replicas or images of them; 2. (*psychol.*) the ascription to inanimate objects of the characteristics of sentient or responding organisms; 3. (*psychoan.*) the tendency or act of absorbing the environment or the personality of others into one's own psyche to the extent of reacting to external events as though they were internal ones, thus producing identification of oneself with other persons or objects. [(1) originated with Avenarius, who combated the theory. Cf. **projection.**]

introspection = 1. the contemplation or reflection upon an experience, either while in course or in memory; 2. observation from a psychological standpoint, leading to description; 3. the description of immediate experience in terms of elements and attitudes. [(1) is the usual meaning of the term as employed by the Cartesians, Herbartians, English empiricists, and some recent psychologists; (2) is the equivalent of observation in the scientific sense, and is sometimes distg. fr. *Kundgabe* or comment. Syn. (2, 3) **observation, inspection.** Cf. **reflection** (2), **observation, introspective method.**] **introspect**[v], **introspective**[a]. — Ger. (1) *innere Wahrnehmung,* (2) *Selbstbeobachtung.*

introspectionism = the doctrine that the introspective method is the fundamental method of investigation in psychology. [Cf. **introspection, introspective method.**]

introspective method = a method of psychological research based upon introspection. [Cf. **introspection.**]

introspective psychology = 1. psychological investigation by the introspective method; 2. the body of knowledge whose facts are obtained by the introspective method; 3. syn. for **introspectionism.**

introversion = 1. (*anal. psychol.*) turning inwards of the libido and withdrawal of interest from the external world (Jung); 2. an attitude or type of personality in which one's psychic energy is directed toward oneself and one's own experiences. [Contr. w. **extraversion.**] **introvert**[np].

introversion-extraversion test = a test designed to measure the extent to which an individual tends, in his attitudes and behavior, toward the reflective, self-centered type, or the energetic, externally-minded type. [The Colgate mental hygiene test is a typical example.]

intuition = 1. immediate or innate apprehension of a complex group of data or of a general principle; 2. a judgment without known preliminary cogitation, the significant feature being the immediacy of the process; 3. (*psychol.*) the final stage in the act of perceptive synthesis (rare). **intuitive**[a] = by the process of intuition; **intuitional**[a] = pert. to the process; **intuit**[v]. — Ger. (1) *Anschauung,* (2) *Verstehen.*

intuitionism = 1. (*epistem.*) the theory that knowledge of reality in general or knowledge of certain truths is immediate; 2. (*esth.*) the theory that the beauty of a work of art is apprehended immediately in an attitude of contemplation; 3. (*ethics*) the theory that ethical law (i.e. the rightness or wrongness of given acts of conduct) is immediately known.

invagination = the process of inpushing or folding of a surface layer of cells, which results in the formation of a cavity partially or completely enclosed by the layer.

invalid[a] = characterizing an argument, conclusion, method, etc., as being not logically correct. [Contr. w. **valid.**] (Accent **-val-.**) **invalidity**[n]. — Ger. *ungültig.*

invalidate = to impair the force or logical value of an argument. (Accent **-val-.**)

invalidism = a condition of chronic ill-health. [Applied esp. to imaginary or exaggerated ailments.] (Accent **in-.**)

invariability = the quality or condition of occurring in the same manner in every case, i.e. of remaining ever the same. [Syn. **changelessness;** cf. **invariant.**] **invariable**[a].

invariable color, see **color/invariable.**

invariance = the tendency of an image to preserve its original size, however the distance of the projection ground may vary from the eye. [Contr. w. **Emmert's law.**]

invariant = 1. (*math.*) a relation or property of the data or figure under consideration which does not change as linear transformations are made; 2. (less commonly) a relation or property which does not change when other types of transformation are made.

invention = a new or original combination of material. [In psychol. applied to combinations of **imagery;** in technol. applied to devices which yield some useful result. Distg. fr. **discovery,** in which the material, or the combination, or some underlying principle already existing, is noted for the first time by some observer.] — Ger. *Erfindung.*

inverse square law = (*psychol.*) the principle that the intensity of a stimulus which reaches the receptor from a distant source, varies inversely as the square of the distance of the source from the receptor. [The law applies to light, sound, heat, odor, etc., and is an instance of the general physical law which applies to influences emanating in straight lines from a center; e.g. gravitation. Cf. **illumination/law of.**] — Fr. *l. de l'inverse du carré.*

inversion = transposition of the order of certain members of a series. [It is usually implied that the inverted is a departure from the true, normal, or usual order.] — Ger. *Umkehrung; Umstellung.*

inversion/sexual = 1. the assumption by members of one sex, of the characters or role of the other sex; 2. (*psychoan.*) a deviation in reference to the sexual object of the same sex, e.g. homosexuality. [Cf. **perversion, transvestism.**] **invert**[np] (accent **in-**).

invertebrata, invertebrates = a general division of animal organisms, embracing many phyla, characterized by the absence of backbone or notochord. [Contr. w. **vertebrata (vertebrates)** or more properly with **chordata,** which possess this character.] **vertebrate**[a]. — Ger. *Wirbellose.*

investigate = to examine a group of phenomena systematically, with intent to explain or understand them. [Also used loosely to denote the examination of a vaguely defined situation, in order to discover what phenomena are involved.] **investigation**[n]. — Fr. *rechercher, faire des investigations;* Ger. *erforschen, untersuchen.*

invisible = below the limen of vision or of visual discrimination, or incapable of being seen for any other reason.

involuntary = characterizing a movement, action, or direction of attention which takes place despite the individual's effort to inhibit it. [Often loosely used instead of **non-voluntary** = automatic or without volition.] — Ger. *unwillkürlich.*

involuntary reaction (or **response**) **time** = a time interval between stimulus and response such as exists and may be measured for reflexes, both unconditioned and conditioned, and for secondary automatic actions. [Cf. **reaction time.**]

involution = 1. (*pathol.*) retrograde development of a tissue or organ; 2. the return of an organ to its normal condition after a physiological increase in structure or size, e.g. the involution of the uterus after pregnancy. [Syn. (1) **degeneration.**] **involutional**[a].

ion = an electrically charged particle of atomic or molecular size. [Cf. **anion, cation.**] (Accent **eye-.**)

IQ = abbrev. for **intelligence quotient.**

iris = a flat, ring-shaped structure situate within the eyeball immediately in front of the lens, containing unstriped muscle-fibers whose contraction and relaxation regulate the amount of light admitted through the pupil or central opening which it encircles. — Ger. *Regenbogenhaut.*

iris reflex = the reflex action of the iris muscles in regulating the size of the pupil. [Mediated by the retina, optic tracts, oculomotor nerves for **constriction;** 1st thoracic, and cervical sympathetic for **dilation.** Syn. **pupillary reflex** (an obvious misnomer).]

irony = the use of language in the contrary sense to that which the speaker covertly implies, or the assertion of ignorance with a covert implication of superior knowledge. [Syn. **sarcasm,** generally a more offensive form.] **ironic(al)**[a] = characterized by irony. — Ger. *Ironie.*

irradiation = 1. (*vis.*) the apparent excess in size of a visual stimulus of relatively high intensity, e.g. of a white figure on a black ground compared with an equal black figure on white; 2. (*neurol.*) the diffusion or spread, from few to many neurons, of afferent nerve impulses as they travel through the central nervous system. [(1) is believed to be due to a spreading of the excitation, or of its effect, to adjacent retinal elements. (2) is probably accomplished by the branching of nerve fibers and by the stimulation, at synaptic regions, of new fibers.] **irradiate**[v].

irradiation of conditioned reflexes = the phenomenon that when a response is conditioned to a certain (e.g. a cutaneous) receptor organ, stimulation of other (cutaneous) receptors, and esp. those more immediately adjacent, may elicit the same (conditioned) response, although less vigorously (Pavlov). [Cf. **allied reflexes.**]

irradiation of reflexes = the spread of reflex activity over a larger and larger field from the focus of reflex discharge. [Cf. **induction** (4), **allied reflexes.**]

irradiation/reflex = the phenomenon that as the intensity of a stimulus which elicits a certain reflex is increased, not only is the intensity of that reflex response increased, but also a greater number of muscles and muscle groups become engaged in the response (Sherrington).

irradiation theory = a hypothesis, advanced in explaining **learning**, which assumes that excitation spreads into neighboring structures, such as nerves or muscles. [It is assumed, as a corollary, that desirable variations of action may thus come about (trial and error learning, conditioning, etc.) or that useless movements may result, which must later be eliminated.]

irrational = contrary to reason or to the principles of logic. [Syn. **illogical.** Sometimes, but improperly, used as syn. for **non-rational,** i.e. beyond the sphere of logic.] — Ger. *unvernünftig*.

irrational reaction (response, conduct) = an act of behavior on the part of an individual who is capable of reasoning, which to the observer appears to be illogical or based upon false premises.

irreciprocal conduction = the property possessed by reflex pathways (or more specifically by the synaptic membrane of these pathways) of transmitting impulses in one direction only, viz. from telodendron to dendrite. [This property presumably depends upon irreciprocal permeability of the synaptic membrane.]

irrelevant = not pertinent to the problem under consideration. [Applied to data or arguments used to support a conclusion when such data lie outside the sphere of discussion.] **irrelevancy**[n]. — Fr. *sans rapport à, inapplicable*; Ger. *belanglos*.

irreversibility of conduction = the property of the reflex arc, or more specifically of the synapses within the arc, to conduct impulses only in the direction from receptor to effector. [Syn. **irreciprocal conduction.** Contr. w. **reversibility of conduction** in nerve trunks.]

irritability = 1. susceptibility to stimulation; 2. (*pop.*) a mood characterized by anger or bad humor. [In technical use (1) is fairly syn. w. **sensitivity,** but with no implication of an ensuing sensation. Syn. (2) **excitability. irritability** is often listed as a fundamental characteristic of organic matter, or (in higher organisms) of nerve, receptor, muscle, and gland.] — Ger. *Reizbarkeit*.

irritant = 1. an agent, chemical or physical, which produces an irritation or inflammation of tissue; 2. an excitant of irritable tissues.

irritation = 1. the state of activity in living tissue when excited by stimulation; 2. the act of stimulation, esp. the act of exciting muscle contractions; 3. physiological activity which produces a morbid or abnormal tissue condition, such as swelling and blistering; 4. a morbid state of oversensitiveness, in which ordinary stimulation produces pain or exaggerated response; 5. an emotional state aroused by continued stimulation which cannot be adequately reacted to, with consequent ill-temper, impatience, vexation, etc. [Syn. (1) **irritability** (prefd.); **excitability;** (2) **excitation, stimulation. irritate**[v].

island of Reil, insula Reili = an infolding of the cerebral cortex consisting of a series of 3 to 5 gyri which lie laterad to the lenticular nucleus in the depth of the Sylvian fissure and are covered by surrounding opercula. [The **insula** is characteristic of the primate brain.] — Fr. *insula de Reil*; Ger. *Insel*.

islands of Langerhans = small cellular masses in the pancreas which elaborate the autacoid insulin (iletin). [Langerhans, E. R., German histologist, 1847–1888.]

island/tonal, see **tonal island.** — Fr. *îlot tonal*.

isochronia, isochronism = 1. correspondence between two or more processes with respect to their time, rate, or frequency of occurrence; 2. having the same chronaxie (L. Lapicque). [Contr. w. **heterochronia.**] (Accent (1) **-kro-,** (2) **-sock-.**) **isochronous**[a] (accent **-sock-**), **isochronic**[a] (accent **eye-** and **-kro-**).

isolation = (*biol.*) the separate existence of a group of organisms from others of the same variety or species. [Two distinct forms noted are **geographical isolation,** in which the group is kept apart by some geographical barrier, and **biological isolation,** in which differences in seasonal maturity or in some character of the reproductive system prevents interbreeding. Syn. **segregation** (2).] (Accent **iss-** or **eye-.**) **isolate**[v]. — Ger. *Isolierung*.

isolation mechanism = (*psychoan.*) a symptom peculiar to the compulsion neuroses, in which after an unpleasant event and also after any personal activity significant in the sense of a neurosis, a pause is interpolated in which nothing is to happen, and no action is carried out.

isomerism = the characteristic of certain pairs of chemical compounds in that they contain the same molecules but with different arrangements of their constituent atoms. (Accent **-som-.**) **isomeric**[a] (accent **eye-** and **-mer-**).

isometric twitch = a muscular contraction in response to a single volley of nerve impulses, in which the muscle, owing to previous rigid fixation, is incapable of much shortening. [Applied to a system of recording, in which the muscle pulls against a rigid spring, or torsion wire, as contr. w. **isotonic recording,** a mechanical system in which the muscle is made to lift a weight. Cf. **myograph.**] (Accent **eye-** and **-met-.**) — Fr. *contraction isométrique*.

isometropia = equality of the refractive condition of the two eyes. [Contr. w. **anisometropia.**] (Accent **eye-** and **-tro-.**)

isomorphism = the structural correspondence of excitatory fields in the brain with the experienced contents of consciousness. [The term and principle are used in *Gestalt* psychology.] — Ger. *Isomorphismus*.

isoscope = an instrument devised by Donders for testing the **law of rotation;** it consists essentially of a pair of parallel vertical wires presented to one eye, and a single wire presented to the other and seen binocularly superimposed upon the pair; the single wire may be inclined one way or the other until it appears parallel to the other two. (Accent **eye-.**)

isotonic recording, see **isometric twitch.**

isotropic = (*opt.*) singly refracting, as contr. w. doubly refracting media such as calcite, etc.

isthmus = the contracted part of the brain between the midbrain and hind-brain, marked dorsally by the decussation of the 4th cranial nerve and on the ventral aspect by the cephalic border of the pons. [The term has little value. Syn. **midbrain** in older literature.]

itch = 1. an irritating cutaneous and internal disorder; 2. a sensory experience which involves mild pricking-pain sensations, unpleasantness, and a persistent impulse to scratch. — Fr. *démangeaison*; Ger. *Jucken*.

item = a single fact or part of a group of data, isolated for purposes of separate examination.

item of experience, item of consciousness = any single fact or portion of experience. [A phrase used to avoid choice between structural and functional terminology.]

J

j.n.d. = abbrev. for **just noticeable difference.**

Jacksonian epilepsy = a form of epilepsy, usually without loss of consciousness, characterized by localized spasm, which is mainly limited to one side of the body or one limb or part. [Indicates usually irritation of motor area of cortex. First described by Hughlings Jackson.]

Jackson's law = the principle that when mental functions are impaired and lost through disease, the first to disappear are those which were the last to appear in the individual's development; i.e. that the order of degeneration is the reverse of the order of ontogenesis (J. Hughlings Jackson).

Jacob's membrane, see **rods and cones/layer of.**

Jacquet chronometer = an instrument designed to measure and record seconds and fifths of seconds; it consists of a clock-work mechanism which raises a recording stylus after each interval, at the same time indicating, by hands on two dials, the total period elapsed.

James-Lange theory = the theory that in emotional experiences the stimulus first arouses a motor response, and that the experiencing of these organic responses constitutes the feeling. [Formulated independently by Wm. James (1884) and C. G. Lange (1885) in opposition to the intellectualistic view that the feeling precedes and arouses the motor responses.]

Jastrow automatograph, see **automatograph.**

Jastrow cylinders = a series of weights for measuring the limen of intensity and limen of discrimination for pressure and kinesthesis; they consist of hollow, hard-rubber cylinders, the ends of which can be opened so as to insert shot, etc., thereby adjusting the series to any desired grade of difference in weight. [The cylinders are set on the palm for pressure experiments, and are grasped and lifted in experiments on kinesthesis.]

Java man, see **Pithecanthropus erectus.** — Fr. *homme de Java*.

jaw reflex, see **mandibular reflex.** — Fr. *réflexe mandibulaire, r. massétérin*.

jealousy = an emotional attitude, characterized by envy directed toward another individual, the specific ground of the emotion being the intimate relation of that individual to a third. [Cf. **envy.**] **jealous**[a]. — Fr. *jalousie*; Ger. *Eifersucht*.

Jehovah-complex = (*psychoan.*) a megalomanic fantasy of identification with God. [Syn. **God-complex.**]

jellyfish = a popular descriptive name applied to the free-swimming stage of certain coelenterates; i.e. a medusa. [The body is soft, umbrella-shaped, and semi-transparent.] — Fr. *méduse*, Ger. *Qualle*.

Jendrassik reinforcement (or **maneuver**) = a procedure for increasing the patellar reflex, in which the subject hooks his hands together by the flexed fingers and pulls vigorously. [A form of facilitation.]

job analysis = a systematic study of all the facts about a specific industrial occupation which have a bearing on selecting or training workers, or improving methods of work. [Includes analysis of the work elements and description of duties, responsibilities, difficulties, working conditions, pay, opportunity for advancement, requisite personal qualities, education and experience, and critical scores in employment tests. Results in a **job specification** or occupational description in which the findings are concisely formulated.] — Fr. *analyse de la profession*.

Johns Hopkins chronoscope, see **Dunlap chronoscope.**

joie de vivre = a loose term applied to the restless behavior which arises from surplus energy, when this behavior is accompanied by a pleasant feeling tone and general exuberance of motor expression. [French; "joy of living."]

joint sensation, see **articular sensation.**

joking relationship = the recognized right among some primitive peoples, of certain relatives by marriage to jocularize, defame, and deride one another in public with impunity, regardless of differences in age, sex, or rank.

Jost's law = the principle that when two associations are of the same strength but of unequal age, repetition increases the strength of the older more than of the younger association. [Cf. **diminishing returns/law of, distributed repetitions/principle of.**]

joule = a standard for measuring work, equal to 10,000,000 ergs. [Cf. **erg.**]

journeyman = a tradesman who has completed his apprenticeship and is capable of working without supervision but does not possess the highest degree of skill. [The trade hierarchy is **novice, apprentice, journeyman, expert.**] — Fr. *journalier*; Ger. *Geselle*.

joy = a sentiment or emotional attitude characterized by a pleasant feeling tone and related to events or experiences of the immediate present. [Contr. w. **grief;** distg. fr. **satisfaction** = directed toward the past, and **hope** = directed toward the future.] — Ger. *Freude*.

judgment = 1. the mental act of relating two concepts, accompanied by the belief or assertion of some objective or intrinsic relation between the two; 2. the application of a concept to a given situation or object. [(1) is the usual meaning in formal logic. (2) is more frequent in modern logic and psychology; the latter includes **appreciation** of a situation, **comparison** (in which the concept of greater or less is applied), and **evaluation** (in which reference is made to a series of standards of beauty, right, goodness, or economic worth). The formulation of a judgment in words is called a **proposition.**] — Fr. (1) *jugement*, (2) *appréciation*; Ger. *Urteil*.

jugglery, juggling, see **conjure** (1).

jugular = pert. to or located in the throat. (Accent **joo-** or **jug-**.)

Jukes = a fictitious name given by R. L. Dugdale (1877) to a degenerate family in New York State; the record, extended by A. H. Estabrook (1915), includes 2,820 persons, half of them feebleminded.

justice = 1. a situation in which a certain reward or deprivation is meted out to an individual as a fitting and equal exchange or exaction for the results of his own conduct toward another; 2. a subjective feeling or experience that fairness in reward or punishment has been accomplished; 3. a trait of an individual predisposing him to fairness in the bestowal of rewards or punishments upon others. [Contr. w. **injustice,** where the reward or punishment is manifestly disproportionate or unsuitable to the act.] **just**[a] (not to be confused with **just**[adv] = barely). — Ger. (1, 2, 3) *Gerechtigkeit.*

just intonation = the production of tones in their true or mathematically exact vibration ratios, as in the untempered scale. [Contr. w. **tempered intonation** = in the scale of equal temperament. Cf. **scale, temperament** (2).]

just noticeable difference = the least difference in value between two stimuli which, in a given individual, gives rise to two different sensations; or which gives rise (statistically) to a perceived difference as often as it does not. [Abbrev. **j.n.d.** Syn. **just perceptible difference, least noticeable** (or **perceptible**) **difference, threshold of difference, limen of difference, minimal change.** Strictly, **j.n.d.** applies to the experience, **threshold** or **limen** to the statistical value.] — Fr. *différence juste perceptible*; Ger. *ebenmerklicher Unterschied.*

juvenile = pert. to youth or young persons. [Last syll. **-il** or **-ile.**] — Ger. *jugendlich.*

K

k = symbol for coefficient of **alienation.**

kakon = the abnormal reaction in anxiety disorders (v. Monakow).

Kallikak = a fictitious name given by H. H. Goddard (1912) to a New Jersey family which showed two lines of descendants: a line of 496 persons, nearly all high-class citizens; and a line of 480, largely degenerate and feebleminded.

kalotropic = characterizing the influence exerted by the observer's esthetic tastes upon the content of his images (esp. eidetic images).

karyokinesis, see **mitosis.**

karyoplasm = the protoplasmic substance of the nucleus of a cell. [Syn. **nucleoplasm.** Distg. fr. **cytoplasm** = other protoplasmic substance of the cell.]

kata-, see **cata-.**

Kelvin scale = a temperature scale which is absolute in the sense of being independent of the properties of any particular substance. [Devised by Kelvin on the basis of the equation of Carnot's cycle, which shows the temperature difference between two bodies measured in terms of work per cycle done by a perfect (reversible) heat engine taking heat from one body and discharging heat into the other. The Kelvin scale starts from − 273° C as zero, and measures in centigrade units.] — Fr. *échelle de K.*

Kent-Rosanoff test = a standardized free association test, described by Grace Kent and A. J. Rosanoff in 1910, consisting of one hundred stimulus words, supplemented by tables showing the frequency of different verbal responses to each word, whereby may be determined the percentage of common, individual, and doubtful responses made by a testee. [Cf. **association test.**]

keratometer = 1. an instrument for measuring the curvature of the cornea of the eye; 2. an instrument used for measuring the diameter of the cornea, consisting of a small scale held before the observed eye and viewed through a system of lenses by which the error due to the difference in distances of the cornea and the scale is eliminated. [Cf. (1) **ophthalmometer.**]

keratoscope, see **Placido's disk.**

Kiesow's painless cheek-area = a small area on the inner surface of the cheek opposite the lower molars which has been found by some to be insensitive to pain while sensitive to cold, warmth, and contact. — Fr. *aire analgésique de la joue.*

kilowatt, see **watt.**

kindness = a type of behavior characterized by the promotion of another's welfare, without expectation of benefit to oneself. **kind**[a]. — Fr. *bonté, bienveillance.*

kinephantom = a subjective response of misinterpretation of the direction or pattern of motion exhibited by a moving visual object, esp. when seen in silhouette shadows. [E.g. the familiar windmill illusion where the observer reports the appearance of the vanes turning in a direction opposite to that of the actual motion.]

kinephantoscope = an instrument for projecting shadows or other stimuli which lend themselves to various movement pattern interpretations. [Cf. **kinephantom.**]

kinesimeter = an instrument used for measuring thresholds of sensations of movement. [The earliest form (1885) consisted of a small table, which could be placed over the forearm or other portion of the body, and which bore on a carriage driven by a **kymograph,** a stimulating point that moved over the skin at various controlled speeds.]

kinesis = (*psychol.*) movement of some member of the body resulting from muscular contraction. [Rarely used.]

kinesthesia, kinaesthesia = sensations attending movements of any members of the body which arise from stimulation of special receptors situate in the muscular tissue, joints, and tendons, the stimulus being some mechanical effect of the contracting muscle, or moving members. [Usually applied to the sense, the data being called **kinesthetic sensations.** Variant form, **kinesthesis,** which might be applied to the *sense*, using **kinesthesia** for the *sensation*. Syn. **weight sense.**] (Accent **kin-.**) **kinesthetic**[a].

kinesthetic memory = any memory which takes the form of **kinesthesis.**

kinetic = pert. to **motion.** [A term used in physics, not properly applicable to biological movement or response.]

kinetic energy = the capacity for doing work which a body possesses due to its motion. [Contr. w. **potential energy.**]

kinetogenesis = the production of evolutionary changes through activity or functioning (Cope).

kinetoscope = an apparatus which uses the projecting photographic record of motion in such a way as to produce perceived motion on a **screen.** [It mechanically presents to view the motion-picture film which has been originally exposed by the **cinematograph.**]

kinetoscotoscope = an instrument for projecting on a screen the movement of bones in the human body, as shown by x-ray photographs.

kinohapt = a type of esthesiometer used for presenting one or more tactual stimulations at precise temporal and spatial intervals; it consists essentially of small points set at various distances along a supporting rod, which are swiftly pressed upon the skin and released from it by magnets and springs. [Devised by Benussi, 1913, to study apparent movement.]

kinship = biological relationship between individual organisms, both consanguine and assumed, usually reckoned either in the maternal or paternal line, and including collateral relations. — Fr. *parenté, consanguinité*; Ger. *Verwandtschaft*.

Kirschmann's law of contrast = the principle that the saturation of a color induced by chromatic contrast is proportional to the logarithm of the saturation of the contrast-inducing color.

kleptomania, cleptomania = an irresistible, impulsive tendency to steal, usually the taking of unwanted objects.

knee-jerk, see **patellar reflex.**

knowledge = a type of experience which includes a vivid representation of a fact, formula, or complex condition, together with strong **belief** in its truth. [The simple form of knowledge is **acquaintance** with, or **apprehension;** when to this is added thoughts of relations, meaning, etc. the experience is called **comprehension** or **understanding.**] **known**[v]. — Fr. *connaissance, connaître*; Ger. *Kenntnis, Wissen*.

Knox Cube Test = a non-linguistic (performance) test, devised by H. A. Knox, in which the examiner places four small wooden cubes on a table and taps them with a fifth cube in various serial orders which increase in complexity, requiring the testee to repeat the same tapping. [Sometimes called **cube imitation test.** Used originally for testing immigrants to the U.S.A.]

Koenig cylinders = a series of short, solid, metal cylinders devised by A. Koenig for determining the upper limen for tone. [The tone is generated by striking the cylinder.]

Korsakow's psychosis, Korsakow syndrome = a mental disorder, usually accompanying alcoholic or other polyneuritis, marked by disturbance of orientation through loss of retention, and by confabulations.

Korte's laws = a set of statements which formulate the optimal conditions for apparent motion, where two (stationary) stimuli are given in succession.

Krause end-bulbs = sensory end-organs found in the conjunctiva, cornea, glans, and in connection with some blood vessels. [Considered by some investigators to be receptors for cold sensibility.]

Kundgabe = statement about a mental process or event, contr. w. a direct description of it. [Syn. **commentary.** Ger.]

Kundgabe error = a misleading report by an experimental subject or observer, in that he includes information or knowledge about a datum of experience instead of reporting the descriptive characteristics of the experience. [Logically the stimulus error is a special case of the **Kundgabe error.**]

Kundt's rule = 1. the principle that divided or graduated distances appear greater than physically equal non-graduated distances; 2. the principle that in attempting to bisect a horizontal line in uniocular vision, there is a tendency to place the middle point too far toward the median (nasal) side. — Fr. *règle de K.*

Kundt tube = an apparatus for determining the wave-length of sound from which the velocity of sound is calculated; it consists of a resonator tube containing a small amount of fine dust or powder; the tube is completely closed at one end and partially closed by a vibrating disk at the other end. [When the air within the tube is excited by sound, and the tube-length is adjusted for resonance, the dust, being agitated more at certain points within the tube, arranges itself in a series of piles representing nodes in the stationary waves of sound; the distance between two adjacent piles of dust is one-half the wave-length of the sound. The resulting arrangement is called a **dust figure.**]

kurtosis = (*statist.*) a property of a frequency distribution, mainly of significance with reference to unimodal distributions, not concerned with (*a*) its central tendency, (*b*) its variability, or (*c*) its skewness, but with the relative frequency of parts at intermediate distance from the mean (the hips), to the remaining parts (the mode and the tails) of the distribution. [If the frequency is relatively great at the hips the curve is **platykurtic,** if of average amount, as in a normal distribution, **mesokurtic,** and if small it is **leptokurtic.** Pearson's **coefficient of kurtosis** = $\mu_4/\mu_2{}^2$, the fourth moment divided by the square of the second moment.] — Fr. *voussure*.

kymograph = an instrument used to record the temporal variations of any physiological or muscular process; it consists essentially of a revolving drum, bearing a record sheet (usually of smoked paper) on which a stylus or penpoint travels to and fro at right angles to the motion of the cylinder; the drum is rotated by a mechanism at a presumably uniform rate, or the rate is indicated by a time marker which registers on the sheet. [In some types the record sheet surrounds the drum, which rotates spirally, to allow a continuous record at different levels of the sheet; in other cases the record sheet is a long roll.] (Accent **kime-** or **kee-.**)

L

LS = abbrev. for **liminal sensitivity.** [Cf. **DL, RL.**]

labia[pl], **lips** = the fleshy folds which surround the orifice of the mouth or other orifices (e.g. vagina). **labial**[a].

labor (or **labour**) **mobility** = 1. the rate of movement of labor into and out of an industry, including not only replacements (labor turnover) but also increases or decreases of working force; 2. the ease with which workers shift from one occupation to another. [Syn. (1) **labor flux.**]

laboratory = a room, building, or place designed or used for the pursuit of scientific research, esp. experimentation. [Distg. fr. **study (-room), class-room, lecture-room,** etc., which are designed for indirect research, through books, lectures, etc. The first formal psychological laboratory was founded at Leipzig by W. Wundt in 1879, and many other psychological laboratories in Germany and America were established in the last two decades of the nineteenth century.]

labyrinth, see **maze.**

labyrinth/auditory = an organ of complex form enclosed within the petrous portion of the temporal bone, and containing the sensory receptors for hearing and equilibrium. [It comprises two portions, the osseous or **bony labyrinth,** which consists of the ramified hollow spaces of the petrous bone, and the **membranous labyrinth,** a series of connected tubes and sacs situate within the bony labyrinth and roughly corresponding to it in form. Syn. **internal ear, inner ear.** Cf. **cochlea, semicircular canals, utricle, saccule.**]

labyrinthine perception = the mode of experience which includes those sensory data resulting from stimulation of the semicircular canals and the vestibule, i.e. vertigo, dizziness, perception of rectilinear and rotary motion, etc. [Often confused with data from other sensory fields, which modify labyrinthine stimulation. Cf. **static sense, vestibular system.**]

labyrinthine righting reflexes = reflexes which depend on the labyrinth (vestibular organ) for righting the position of the head, or (when the head is in the righted position) for righting the position of the body. [Mediated by the vestibular nerves, nuclei, vestibulospinal tracts, and nerves to neck and limbs, in cooperation with midbrain centers and medial longitudinal fasciculus.]

labyrinthine sense = the static or equilibrium sense, whose receptor organ is the semicircular canals and sacs in the labyrinth of the ear. [Cf. **static sense** (prefd.).]

labyrinthine system, see **vestibular system.**

lacrimal glands = glands secreting tears, located in depressions of the frontal bones. [Their activity is related to various physical and mental conditions.]

lacrimal reflex = an increased secretion of tears following irritation of the nasal mucous membrane. [Mediated by V (sensory) and VII cranial, great petrosal nerves, and sphenopalatine ganglion.]

lacrimation, lachrymation = the secretion and discharge of tears. **lacrimal**[a].

lactation = 1. the feeding of infants from the breast; 2. production of milk by mammary secretion. [Syn. **suckling.**] **period of lactation** = the period during which the infant is suckled.

lacuna = a gap. [Applied to certain data, elements, or parts, which are apparently needed to complete a report, an argument, a perceived object, etc.] **lacunae**[pl].

Ladd-Franklin theory of color vision = a theory which assumes that in the retinal nerve-endings the respective light-stimuli liberate red-, green-, and blue-stimulating substances from a complex photosensitive molecule, and that, of these, red and green, when present, unite to form a yellow-stimulating substance, which may in turn unite with blue to form a white-stimulating substance. [According to this schema blue and green, or blue and red, can not so unite, and so do not individually disappear in the respective blue-green and blue-red (or purple) mixtures; **dichromatic** vision is explained by the assumption of a less highly developed molecule, and for the **achromatic** or colorless vision of the rods the original molecule is still more primitive.]

lag = the continuation of the sensory impression after the stimulus excitation has ceased. — Ger. *Nachdauer.*

lagena = a portion of the auditory labyrinth of lower vertebrates, appearing as a more or less elongated diverticulum from the saccule; it contains an epithelial structure which is ramified by fibers from a division of the acoustic nerve, and which (in higher forms at least) is probably the specific receptor organ of hearing. [The corresponding organ in mammals is coiled, and is called the **cochlea.**]

lalling, lallation = reiteration of a sound or syllable, observed particularly in infants and idiots.

lalopathy = any form of speech disorder. [Speech defects have been divided into seven classes: **dysarthria, dyslalia, dyslogia, dysphasia, dysphemia, dysphonia,** and **dysrhythmia.**]

lalophobia = morbid fear or extreme dislike of speaking. [Syn. **glossophobia.**]

lalorrhea, see **logorrhea.**

Lamarckism, Lamarckianism = the theory of evolution propounded by J. B. Lamarck (1809), which assumes that some of the structural changes which occur in organisms through use or disuse of organs are potentially transmitted to the offspring. [Distg. fr. **Darwinism,** which attributes evolution mainly to random variations and the survival of the fittest among such variations.]

lambert = a unit of **brightness,** equal to the uniform brightness of a perfectly diffusing surface which emits or reflects 1 lumen per square centimeter. [The **millilambert** (= 0.001 lambert) is often a more convenient unit.]

Lambert's law = 1. (cosine law of *incidence*) the illumination on a surface varies directly as the cosine of the angle between the incident ray and the perpendicular to the surface; 2. (cosine law of *emission*) the intensity of the light emanating in a given direction from a perfectly diffusing surface is proportional to the cosine of the angle of emission measured between the perpendicular to the surface and the emitted ray. [(2) applies to reflected and transmitted light, as well as to emitted light, but only for the case of a perfectly diffusing surface, which, however, is never more than approximated in fact. Syn. **cosine law.**]

lamella = a thin, flexible plate or reed, used to produce deep tones. **[Appunn's lamella** (or **reed**) is tipped with a circular disk to reduce higher partials, and is clamped to a standard at varying lengths to alter the frequency; it is used to determine the lowest (deepest) audible tone.]

lamina terminalis = the anterior boundary of the 3d ventricle of the brain.

lancination = 1. a sharp, piercing pain; 2. a tearing away or laceration.

landmarks = a term applied to the sensory cues, of whatever sort, which assist an animal (human or subhuman) in orientation or in determining the location of its home or some other goal. [Usually limited to visual cues.] — Fr. *points de repère.*

Langerhans/cells of = a type of free nerve endings which terminate in the epithelium. [They represent the oldest phylogenetic form of nerve end in the vertebrate epidermis.]

language = any system of communication among beings, through conventional symbols. [The chief varieties of language in the human species are **vocal** (speech), **graphic,** and **gesture.**] **linguistic**[a]. — Fr. *langue*; Ger. *Sprache.*

language behavior = behavior involving the use of symbols, as in speaking, writing, and gesturing.

language center = a more or less circumscribed group of nerve-cells in the brain which is supposed to be essential to some phase of the language function. [The existence of any such center or centers (as also of Broca's and Wernicke's speech centers) is disputed. Cf. **language.**]

language function = the operation of the mechanism of communication in an organism, either as expression, or as reception, or both.

languid, see **listless.**

languor, languour = a complex of organic and general sensations accompanied by neuromuscular relaxation and disinclination to motor activity. [Syn. **lassitude,** which applies more properly to the neuromuscular condition.] — Fr. *langueur*; Ger. *Mattigkeit.*

larva = an immature but active stage of development in which the organism is radically different in form from the adult. [E.g. the free-swimming stage in the development of many worms, mollusks, and crustaceans; a caterpillar = the larva of a butterfly or moth.]

laryngeal reflex = coughing produced by irritation of the larynx or fauces. [Mediated by X cranial, 4th cervical, and thoracic nerves.]

laryngeal tones = tones uttered in singing which are varied by different adjustments of the larynx.

laryngograph = a device for recording movements of the larynx esp. in speech, usually by means of a tambour pressed against the larynx. [Several forms are in use, including Piltan's, Zund-Burguet's, Rousselot's, and Zwaardemaker's.] (Pron. **-go-,** not **-jo-.**)

laryngopharynx, see **pharynx.**

larynx = an organ situate in the upper part of the windpipe or trachea, consisting of a cartilaginous box across which are stretched the vocal cords, which are set in vibration by the passage of air from the lungs and produce vocal sounds. [It is the essential organ of speech and singing.] **laryngeal**[a] (accent **-rin-.**) — Ger. *Kehlkopf.*

lassitude = a state of neuromuscular relaxation, not due to fatigue from overexertion, accompanied by a disinclination to neuromuscular activity. [Syn. **languor,** which applies more properly to the accompanying sensation.]

latah, lattah = a mental disorder characterized by high suggestibility, intermittent course, sexual content, and hallucinations. [Esp. prevalent among Malay adult females.]

latency = 1. (*physiol.*) the condition of apparent inactivity between the moment of stimulation of any tissue or function, and the beginning of its response; 2. (*hist.*) subconsciousness. [More often used in adj. form, e.g. latent period (1), latent memory (2).] **latent**[a] = hidden. — Ger. *Latenz.*

latency period = (*psychoan.*) the period of life between the ages of 4 or 5 and ca. 12 years, which separates the infantile or pregenital sexuality from the beginning of puberty or genital sexuality and in which the sexual manifestations are as a rule less prominent. [Syn. **latent sexuality.**]

latent (dream) content, see **dream content.**

latent period = the time elapsing between the application of any stimulus and the beginning of a response. [Cf. **latency** (1).] — Ger. *Latenzzeit.*

latent process = a subliminal neural or mental process (*a*) intervening between two supraliminal events, or (*b*) preceding a supraliminal event. [E.g. (*a*) applies to the hidden changes between the futile voluntary effort to recall a name and the later intrusion of the name into consciousness when it is irrelevant, and (*b*) applies to the hidden associative process, following (e.g.) a subliminal odor of the smoke from Bohemian coal, that issued in an hallucinatory vision depicting a Bohemian scene. Syn. **unconscious cerebration.**]

latent time, see **latency** (1).

lateral[a] = pert. to or located on the side of the body. **laterad**[adv].

lateral axis, see **dextrosinistral axis.**

lateral line canal (or **organ**) = an organ present in fishes, situate in the lining of the groove which runs longitudinally along each side of the body, terminating in three head branches. [Some hold that it is stimulated by water vibrations intermediate in frequency between those required for contact and for audition; others hold that it is stimulated by streaming movements of the water.]

laughter = an emotional or social response consisting in violent convulsive movements of the diaphragm and noisy expulsion of air from the lungs. [Generally stimulated by situations which arouse an idea of incongruity, feeling of superiority, sudden relief of tension or expectation, etc., and a pleasant feeling tone. Also evoked as a social expression of approval, agreement, happiness, or as a means of deception. Usually accompanied by a facial response called **smiling.**] — Fr. *rire*; Ger. *Lachen.*

law = 1. the verbal statement of a more or less fundamental uniformity found in nature; 2. (*hist.* and *pop.*) an assumed active force or agency which brings natural phenomena to pass; 3. (*soc.*) a rule of action prescribed by duly constituted civil (or other) authority as a means of social control. [Cf. **principle;** for specific laws, see each particular title.] (3) **lawful, legal**[a]. — Fr. *loi*; Ger. *Gesetz.*

layer of rods and cones, see **rods and cones/layer of** and Table XI. — Fr. *couches des bâtonnets et des cônes*; Ger. *Stäbchen- und zapfenschicht.*

leadership = (*soc.*) the role of one individual as initiator, director, or organizer of group activities in a community or herd. [**leadership** depends on attitudes and habits of **dominance** in certain individuals and **submissive** behavior in others. Distg. fr. **headship,** a form of authority determined by caste, class, or other factors than popular selection or acceptance.] **leader**[np]. — Fr. *direction, qualité de chef,* Ger. *Führerschaft.*

leading tone = (*mus.*) the seventh note of a scale, which is said to lead or make a transition to the principal or tonic note immediately above it. — Fr. *la sensible, note sensible*; Ger. *Leitton.*

leakage = (*psychoan.*) any discussion by an individual of his own analysis with a person other than the analyst during the analysis. — Fr. *effluence.*

learning = 1. the process of acquiring the ability to respond adequately to a situation which may or may not have been previously encountered; 2. the favorable modification of response tendencies consequent upon previous experience, particularly the building up of a new series of complexly coordinated motor responses; 3. the fixation of items in memory so that they can be recalled or recognized; 4. (*Gestalt*) the process of acquiring insight into a situation. [In general, (1) and (2) are applied to the acquiring of combinations of responses which enable the individual to cope more economically with a complex or variable situation; in these senses **learning** is a more inclusive term than **habit formation.** Progress in learning is measured in terms of efficiency, i.e. by some criterion of performance, such as speed, freedom from error, complexity of coordination, economy of effort, or perfection of form.] — Fr. (1, 2) *apprentissage* (= motor), (3) *acquisition* (= mental); Ger. *Lernen.*

learning capacity = the efficiency of an individual in learning, relative to that of other individuals. [There is implied a maximal limit for the individual in question.] — Fr. *capacité d'acquisition* (*d'apprentissage*); Ger. *Lernfähigkeit.*

learning coefficient = the theoretically expected ratio of right to wrong choices at any given bifurcation, or pair of alternatives, in the maze. [The backward elimination of errors in the learning of a mental maze, which is free from disturbances by space factors, has been attributed to the gradual decrease of the **learning coefficients** from the final, backward to the first coefficient.] — Fr. *coefficient d'acquisition* (*d'apprentissage*).

learning curve = a graphic representation of certain aspects of progress in ability during successive periods of practice, in terms of equal time or of equal accomplishment units. [Syn. **curve of learning, practice curve.**] — Fr. *courbe d'apprentissage* (*d'acquisition*); Ger. *Lernkurve.*

learning/insight in = that stage in the learning process in which grasp of essential relations is evidenced by sudden improvement in the mode of response. [Cf. **insight.**] — Fr. *connaissance profonde dans l'acquisition.*

learning/laws of = various formulations of principles according to which the process of learning is explained or described. [Cf. **(law of) combination, effect, exercise, frequency, readiness, recency, assimilation.** A single law may be advanced to account for all learning, or several principles may be assumed to cooperate.] — Fr. *l. d'acquisition* (*d'apprentissage*).

learning/theories of = various attempts to account for learning or acquisition of habits in terms of certain processes, often of a physiological nature. [Cf. **drainage theory, irradiation theory, overlapping of responses.**] — Fr. *t. de l'acquisition* (*de l'apprentissage*).

learning types = types of individuals as distinguished by certain characteristics of their learning processes, such as the rate and course of learning, or the sense mode most effectively used in learning. — Fr. *types individuels dans la capacité d'apprendre.*

least noticeable (or **observable**), see **just noticeable** (prefd. as indicating the limen or threshold, rather than some value beyond it).

least resistance/line of = an expression taken from physics and applied metaphorically to the course of action, on the part of an individual, which meets with the fewest social objections or general environmental obstacles. — Fr. *ligne de moindre résistance.*

least squares/law of = (*math.*) the principle that for a series of unknown quantities, the most acceptable values are those which make the sum of the squared residual errors of the observations a minimum. [Residual errors are differences between observed values and calculated values, the latter being determined upon the assumption that the true relation between the variables is best expressed by a mathematical equation.] — Fr. *l. des moindres carrés.*

least squares/method of = a method of curve-fitting in which the sum of the squares of the differences between (*a*) the points to be fitted (observed values) and (*b*) the corresponding points on the fitted line (theoretical values) is a minimum. [In determining this sum, each point is weighted by the number of cases represented by it.] — Fr. *m. des moindres carrés.*

left = that side of any animal which, if the animal faces the rising sun, lies to the north. [Contr. w. **right.**] **left**[a], **sinistral**[a]. — Fr. *gauche*; Ger. *links.*

left-handedness, see **sinistrality.**

legend = 1. (*anthrop.*) a tradition concerning some noted historical personage, group, or place; 2. (*typog.*) the explanation appended to a cut or illustration in a volume. [Distg. (1) fr. *myth,* which lacks historical basis and usually deals with some fanciful personage or personification.] **legendary**[a] (1).

legerdemain, see **conjure** (1).

legibility = that characteristic of printed or written material which determines the speed and accuracy with which it may be read. [In typography it depends on such factors as type face, length of line, upper or lower case, lead (i.e. space between lines), and general arrangement.] **legible**[a]. — Fr. *lisibilité*; Ger. *Lesbarkeit.*

legitimate = 1. characterizing any reasoning which accords with the principles of logic, i.e. which yields valid or reliable conclusions; 2. characterizing offspring born to wedded parents. [Contr. w. **illegitimate.**] **legitimacy**[n]. — Ger. (1) *berechtigt,* (2) *ehelich.*

Lehman acoumeter, see **audiometer.**

lemmocytes, see **neurilemma cells.**

lemniscus, see **fillet.**

lens, crystalline lens = the transparent body, convex on its front and back surfaces, situate just behind the iris and pupil of the eye; it serves, through changes in its shape brought about by the action of the ciliary muscles, to focus the eye for different distances. — Fr. *cristallin*; Ger. *Linse.*

lenticular nucleus = the lateral portion or nucleus of the corpus striatum of the brain. [It is embedded in the white matter of the cerebral hemisphere. Cf. **caudate nucleus.**]

lenticular papilla, see **papilla.**

leptokurtic, see **kurtosis.**

leptosome = a person having a slender or asthenic physique.

Lesbian = a homosexual woman.

lesion = 1. (*pathol.*) any morbid change in living organs; 2. in general, any injury or wound in any part of the body. — Ger. *Verletzung.*

lethargy = (*hist.*) a condition held by Charcot to form a stage in **hypnosis** (others being **catalepsy** and **somnambulism**), characterized by neuromuscular hyperexcitability, some anesthesia, and muscular flaccidity.

letter square = a group of letters placed in rows and columns in the form of a square, and used as a memory test to determine the number of separate items reported (and correctly located) after a brief exposure. — Fr. *carré de lettres*.

leucocyte = a white blood-corpuscle.

levator = any muscle concerned in lifting a member. [E.g. **levator palpebrae superioris** = for lifting the upper eyelid.] (Accent **-vay-**.)

level = 1. the general field or background in which a quality appears; 2. (*psychophys.*) the state of sensitivity of a receptor as measured in relation to the threshold value; 3. (*physiol.*) a center for combining various impulses so that more complex reactions are possible; e.g. degrees of integration are often designated as first, second, and third (or spinal, brain-stem, and cortical) levels. [Cf. **attention levels.**] — Fr. (1, 2) *niveau*, (3) *étage*, *niveau*; Ger. (1) *Niveau*, *Lage*, (2) *Zustand*, (3) *Stufe*.

levitation = 1. the power of rising in the air without material support, as experienced in dreams or attributed to spirit mediums; 2. (*psych. res.*) movement of ponderable objects against either friction or gravity under conditions that are assumed to exclude known forces. [Syn. (2) **telekinesis.**]

libertarianism, see **free-will doctrine.**

libertinism = unrestrained and promiscuous indulgence, usually of a sexual nature. [Conventionally applied to males, but admitting of generalization.]

lid reflex, see **corneal reflex** and **winking.**

libido = 1. (*psychoan.*) sexual desire or energy; 2. the dynamic expression or aspect of the sexual instinct which may attach itself to the ego or to external objects or persons; 3. sexual desires and longings in their various aspects; 4. psychic energy irrespective of the object upon which it acts (Jung). [(1) corresponds to the popular concept **love,** and in this broad sense is akin to **psychic energy** (Jung); (2) includes several types e.g. ego libido, object libido, mother libido. (3) corresponds to hunger as applied to the nutritional instinct, and might be rendered as **craving** or **sexual hunger.**] (Pron. **lib-ee'do.**) **libidinal**[a] (accent **-bid-**).

libido/bisexual = (*psychoan.*) a fixation of the sexual impulse on both masculine and feminine, thus lacking, at least in its conscious aspect, the character of sexual exclusiveness. [Characteristic of childhood and also of certain cases of homosexuality. Cf. **psychosexual hermaphroditism.**]

libido damming = (*psychoan.*) the thwarting of the psychosexual element in the individual. — Ger. *Libidostauung*.

libido development = (*psychoan.*) the various stages through which the psychosexual development of man progresses from its earliest pregenital phases to that of complete genital organization. — Ger. *Libidoentwicklung*.

libido/object, see **object-choice.**

lie, see **lying.** — Ger. *Lüge*.

lie detector = a sensitive instrument for indicating, during the course of an examination, certain physiological changes correlated with marked changes in emotional tension of a person suspected of crime or deceit, for the purpose of revealing suppressed knowledge or incriminating facts and inducing, if possible, a frank confession; the instrument may be a **sphygmomanometer** for measuring changes in blood pressure, a **pneumograph** for use in determining the inspiration-expiration ratio, or a **galvanometer** for indicating changes in electrical potential of the body or bodily resistance to an electric current. — Fr. *machine à arracher des aveux*.

life = 1. the group of processes (metabolism, growth, response, reproduction, etc.) which take place in organisms and distinguish them from other material objects (or systems) and which, by their coordinated operation, serve to maintain the individual as an organism; 2. a specific factor or causal agent which is assumed (according to certain biological theories) to operate in every organism and thereby maintain the existence of the individual as an organism. [Cf. **organism.**] **live**[v], **living**[a] = possessing (1) life-processes or (2) **life; vital**[a] = pert. to life. — Fr. *vie*, *vivre*[v]; Ger. *Leben*.

life instinct = (*psychoan.*) the antithesis of the death instinct, in the sense of reproduction and the preservation of life. [Syn. **libido, sexual instinct.**] — Fr. *instinct de vie*.

light[a] = 1. having relatively high brilliance, as applied to a color, or high illumination, as applied to a room, etc.; 2. having a relatively slight degree of weight. [Contr. (1) w. **dark,** (2) w. **heavy.**] — Fr. (1) *clair*, (2) *léger*; Ger. (1) *hell*, (2) *leicht*.

light[n] = 1. (*phys.*) radiant energy of those wave-lengths which act as adequate stimuli to the visual sense, i.e. 390 to 760 mμ; by extension, radiant energy of the wave-lengths in adjoining regions of the spectrum, i.e. ultraviolet or infra-red light; 2. (*photom.*) syn. for **luminous flux.** [It is transmitted through space at the rate of ca. 300,000 km. per second. Cf. **radiant energy.**] — Fr. *lumière*; Ger. *Licht*.

light-adapted eye = an eye which has been exposed to light stimuli of relatively high intensity and has so become relatively insensitive to lower intensities. [Cf. **adaptation.**]

light dread, see **photophobia.**

light-induction/simultaneous = the effect of stimulation from one part of the visual field upon the conscious experience referred to another part. [**simultaneous contrast** is one such phenomenon, but **induction** covers the cases in which the effect is in the same sense as the direct effect of the stimulus.] — Fr. *induction simultanée de lumière*; Ger. *simultane Lichtinduktion*.

light sensation = a type of sensation whose proper stimuli consist of radiant energy of wave-lengths approximately 400 to 760 millimicrons, and whose receptor is the eye or some equivalent organ. [Usually applied without reference to **hue.** Sometimes used incorrectly for **achromatic sensations.** Cf. **vision.**] — Fr. *s. lumineuse*; Ger. *Lichtempfindung*.

light waves = luminous radiant energy, when regarded as an undulatory or wave-like phenomenon; i.e. the transverse electromagnetic disturbance (sometimes considered to involve a physical medium called the ether) which serves as a stimulus for the visual receptors. [Cf. **wave.**] — Fr. *ondes lumineuses*; Ger. *Lichtwellen*.

likelihood = the degree to which a given hypothesis is confirmed by sample values experimentally obtained. [The likelihood that any parameter (or set of parameters) should have any assigned value (or set of values) is proportional to the probability that if this were so, the totality of observations should be that observed; more precisely, the likelihood of a hypothesis is proportional to the probability on that hypothesis of obtaining a known sample. The factor of proportionality is arbitrary, but is the same for all hypotheses. Distg. fr. **probability** = the degree to which, under a given hypothesis, an empirical sampling may be expected to conform to the total distribution prescribed by that hypothesis.] **likely**[a, adv]. — Fr. *vraisemblance*; Ger. *Wahrscheinlichkeit*.

likeness, see **resemblance, similarity.**

liking = an attitude characterized by pleasant feeling tone, aroused by social situations or general stimuli. [Used vaguely to cover all degrees. Contr. w. **dislike.**] **like**[v]. — Fr. *aimant, aimer*[v]; Ger. *Zuneigung*.

limen, see **threshold.** (Accent **lie-.**) **liminal**[a] (accent **lim-.**) — Fr. *seuil*; Ger. *Schwelle*.

limen gauge = an instrument devised by M. von Frey for presenting pressure stimulation to the skin at regulated speeds of application; it consists essentially of a pressure point attached to a lever which is actuated by a clock spring; the intensity and speed of stimulation depend on the tension exerted upon the spring by a second lever which is displaced to different extents and at different rates by a revolving drum. — Fr. *appareil pour mesurer le seuil*.

liminal sensitivity = degree of sensory acuity, as expressed by the lowest value of a given stimulus which gives rise to sensation. [Abbrev. **LS**; the term is generally used in respect to intensity; contr. w. **terminal sensitivity** (**TS**) = the greatest value which gives rise to a more intense sensation; distg. fr. **differential sensitivity** (**DS**) = the ratio of difference between two stimuli which are just distinguishable in intensity.] — Fr. *sensibilité liminaire*.

limit = 1. the first or last value of a series of values, or the end value of a mathematical function; 2. the boundary of a sense-continuum or of a series of stimulus-magnitudes. [Receptive tissue responds to energy within certain bounds of frequency or intensity but not to energy outside those **limits.**] **limitative**[a] = pert. to the limit-value. — Ger. (1) *Grenze*, (2) *Grenzwert*.

limiting membrane/external = a part of the supporting tissue of the retina, the 3rd stratum from without inward. [See Table **XI.**]

limiting membrane/internal = a part of the supporting tissue of the retina, the **10th** or innermost stratum. [See Table XI.]

limits and differences/combined method of = a psychophysical method devised by Kraepelin, which combines the procedure of these two methods; it consists in first obtaining judgments in accordance with the method of limits, and then treating them statistically in accordance with the method of right and wrong cases. [The method enables a finer determination of the threshold value than is obtained by either method separately.]

limits/method of = a psychophysical method of investigation, which proceeds by gradually decreasing the value of a given stimulus (or the difference between two stimuli) till it is no longer noticeable; and also by increasing the stimulus value (or the difference between two stimuli) from zero until it becomes just noticeable. [The **limit,** or limiting value, lies between the two values thus determined. Syn. **method of minimal changes, of least differences, of just noticeable differences.**] — Ger. *Grenzmethode*.

limits of audibility (or **hearing**), see **audibility limits.**

limma = a musical interval. [The Pythagorean limma is the difference, or "defect" of two perfect major tones (408 cents) from a perfect fourth (498 cents) = 90 **cents,** or .90 tempered semitones. See Table VII.]

line = 1. the path of a moving point, characterized by length but not breadth or thickness; **2.** a one-dimensional, non-curved continuous series. [Syn. (2) **straight line.**] **linear**[a].

line of beauty = a serpentine line regarded by Hogarth as the most beautiful shape.

line of direction, see **direction/line of.**

line of fixation, see **fixation/line of.**

line of regard, see **regard/line of.**

line-quality/graphic = habitual minor variations in pen-pressure. [An individual characteristic, of importance in identification of handwriting.]

line/sighting, syn. for visual axis.

line/spectral, see **spectral line.**

line/visual (or **of vision,** or **of sight**) see **visual axis** and **direction/line of.**

linear correlation, see **correlation** (3).

linear transformation, see **transformation** (2).

lingual gland = a type of gland located on the tongue. [The posterior lingual glands secrete a serous liquid which is found in the moats of the circumvallate papillae and probably serves to wash out the taste buds. The anterior lingual glands, situate near the top of the tongue, are non-serous or mixed glands.]

linguistic, see **language.**

linkage = 1. (*biol.*) the tendency of characters to remain associated in hereditary transmission, as contr. w. independent or random assortment; **2.** (*psychol.*) the connection between stimulus and response. — Fr. (1) *enchaînement, association héréditaire* (2) *lien*; Ger. *Verkettung*.

linked characters = characters which are associated in inheritance. — Fr. *caractères enchaînés*.

lip-eroticism = 1. the complex of sex sensations induced by kissing; 2. excessive sex sensations induced by kissing or other forms of stimulation of the mouth region. — Fr. *érotisme labial*.

lip-key = a response key for reaction time, consisting of two plates separated by a spring, which are held together between the lips, making an electric circuit; when the lips open to pronounce the response word, the plates separate, breaking the circuit. — Fr. *clef labiale*; Ger. *Lippenschlüssel*.

lip-reading = the art of comprehending the speech of another person by interpreting his facial movements, particularly those of the lips. [Syn. **speech-reading.**] — Fr. *lecture sur les lèvres*; Ger. *Lesen von den Lippen*.

lisping, see **paralalia, dyslalia.**

Lissajou's figures = visible closed figures produced by the successive reflection of a narrow beam of light from two small mirrors, attached to two tuning forks which vibrate in perpendicular planes. [The figure-pattern is essentially a plot of the movement of one fork against that of the other; when the periods of the forks are very nearly in simple ratio the figure-pattern is seen to undergo slow changes.]

Listing's law = a principle of eye movement formulated by Listing, which states that if the eye moves from the primary position to any other, the torsional rotation of the eyeball in this new position is the same as it would be if the eye had turned about a fixed axis, lying at right angles to the initial and final directions of the line of regard.

Listing's reduced (or **schematic**) **eye,** see **reduced eye.**

listless = lacking desire or interest, with no tendency to action or activity. [Distg. fr. **languid,** which implies weakness, whereas **listless** implies indifference.] **listlessness**[n]. — Fr. *indolent*; Ger. *teilnahmlos*.

literature = (*tech.*) the published reports of observations, experiments, systematic treatment, etc. relating to some given problem or subject.

Lloyd Morgan's canon, see **Morgan's canon.**

loathing, see **disgust.**

lobe = a rounded or projecting part of any organ (e.g. ear lobe) or one of the parts into which a globular body may be divided (e.g. brain lobe). — Ger. *Lappen*.

lobe/cerebral = a main division of the human cerebral cortex. [There are 5 in each hemisphere; frontal, parietal, temporal, occipital, and central (island of Reil); the boundaries are in some cases not definite.]

lobe/olfactory, see **olfactory lobe.**

local = limited to a small region in the body. [Contr. w. **general** or **diffuse.**]

local galvanic reaction = regional change in apparent skin resistance due to local stimulation or irritation of the skin.

local sign, locality sign = a specific character assumed to be inherent in the sensory experience aroused by a single receptor, or by a single afferent neuron, and to differ for each receptor or for each afferent neuron. [So called because it furnishes a cue to the position of the receptor-unit stimulated, and hence to the location of the stimulus. The term is derived from Lotze (1852). **local signs** are required by most nativistic theories of space (e.g. Hering) and may be the material upon which genetic theories are grounded (e.g. Wundt). **locality sign** is prefd., but **local sign** (or **signature**) is generally used.] — Fr. *signes locaux*; Ger. *Lokalzeichen*.

locality memory = the ability of an organism to identify a given region or locality through memory of certain landmarks. — Ger. *Ortsgedächtnis*.

locality survey = the exploring behavior by an animal of a given locality or region, particularly its home. — Fr. *examen des lieux*.

localization = 1. the placing of a source of stimulation in a spatial or temporal manifold, esp. w. reference to or on the body of the observer; 2. the placing of a specific sensation or perception or memory, or their objective source, in space or time with relation to the totality of experience; 3. the identification of some specific structure of the body as concerned with some given function.

localization of sound, auditory localization = judgment of the position of a source of sound in terms of direction or distance, or both. [There are two kinds: (1) **monaural** = using a single ear; aside from mere judgments of right and left this depends upon knowledge of the source or upon head movement; (2) **binaural** = using both ears; this depends upon the stimulus-pattern, including R–L differences of time, energy, phase, and wave-form, as well as upon organic factors such as head movement, attentive set, etc. Cf. **phantom sound.**]

localization theory = the theory that all receptive and motor, and many associative (e.g. *language*) functions have their neural locus in some specific region or area of the brain. [Cf. **motor area.**]

localized amnesia, see **amnesia/localized.**

localized stimulus = a stimulus applied to a very small region of the body.

lock mechanism, see **catch muscle.**

locomotion = the movement of an organism from place to place by means of its organic mechanism. [Cf. **locomotor function.**] — Ger. *Ortsveränderung*.

locomotor = pert. to the act or organs of locomotion.

locomotor ataxia, see **tabes dorsalis.**

locomotor function = the operation of any organic mechanism which enables an organism to travel from place to place. [Classed as *swimming*, *flying*, and *walking*, the last including running, crawling, etc.]

logarithm = (*math.*) the exponent of that power of a fixed number (called the base) which equals a given number. [E.g. since $10^2 = 100$, the logarithm of 100 to the base $10 = 2$. The base of the system of **common** logarithms is 10; of the **natural** system 2.71828....]

logarithmic curve = (*math.*) a curve in which one rectangular coordinate of any given point (e.g. y) is the logarithm of the other (x). [The equation is $y = \log x$. Cf. **logarithm.**]

logarithmic decrement = for a partially damped sinusoidal wave, the natural logarithm of the ratio of the maximum amplitudes during two successive cycles. [Cf. **damping, damping constant.**]

logic = the science which investigates the theory and principles of reasoning, i.e. the principles that enable an individual to make judgments or conclusions which are consistent with the data at hand. **logical**[a] (usually restricted to conclusions reached by reasoning).

logic/affective = a term used to denote certain sequences of ideas which resemble logical processes but are controlled by the emotional factors that supply or suggest the connecting links. [Related to the theory of **affective memory,** the logic of the **unconscious mind,** and **rationalizing.**]

logic/formal = the body of formulated principles which describe the processes involved in thinking, with special reference to the validity of conclusions drawn from certain forms or types of premises regardless of the truth or falsity of these premises. [Sometimes emphasis is upon the form of the propositions as distinct from the meaning.]

logical = concerned with or following the principles of logic. [Applied to arguments, reasoning, or the arrangement and classification of data, not to the facts or data themselves. As applied to conclusions, **logical** may mean either those reached by sound reasoning (contr. w. **illogical**) or those reached by explicit reasoning (contr. w. **alogical** or **intuitive**). Cf. **logic.**]

logorrhea, logorrhoea = a mental disorder characterized by continual talking, usually incoherent. [Syn. **lalorrh(o)ea, polylogia.**]

Lombroso/theory of = the theory that overdevelopment of certain capacities or traits is accompanied by certain defects which indicate an instability of organization pointing toward degeneration. [Formulated by C. Lombroso (1888) as the degeneracy theory of genius.]

long-circuit appeal = a method of salesmanship which involves presenting information about the product, or reasons why one should purchase it. [Distg. fr. **short-circuit appeal** = to the emotions.]

longevity = a span of individual life which is notably above the average span in the species. [Applied loosely also to the average span of life in certain species which is above the average in man.] — Ger. *Langlebigkeit.*

longitudinal = in a lengthwise direction. [Vibrations are longitudinal when each vibrating particle oscillates to and fro parallel to the path of transmission; a longitudinal section is cut along the antero-posterior or cephalocaudal axis of the organism. Contr. w. **transverse.**] — Ger. *Längs-, Längen-.*

longing = an intense desire or craving. — Fr. *désir ardent*; Ger. *Sehnsucht.*

looking-glass self = a term denoting the impression or appraisal of himself which an individual receives from overt evidences of what other persons consider him to be. [The impression is not necessarily a correct representation of the opinions of others. Distg. fr. **social self,** a broader term, indicating the general behavior and attitudes of an individual when in a social group.]

loquacity, loquaciousness = a tendency on the part of an individual to speak frequently and at great length. [Distg. fr. **logorrhea,** a pathological and incoherent manifestation; contr. w. **taciturnity** = a tendency to vocal repression.] **loquacious**[a]. — Ger. *Schwatzhaftigkeit.*

loudness = the intensity character of sounds. [Sounds of high intensity are described as strong, loud, intense, etc. and those of low intensity as weak, faint, low, etc. **loudness** depends upon stimulus energy, which is measured by the formula $I = P^2/pc$, where P denotes sound wave pressure, c the wave velocity, and p the density of the medium. Distg. fr. **pitch** = the quality character.] **loud**[a]. — Fr. *sonorité du son*; Ger. *Lautheit, Stärke.*

loudness level = for a given sound, the absolute sensation level of a standard 1000-cycle pure tone adjusted so as to appear of the same loudness as the sound in question.

love = a feeling or sentiment of attachment toward some person, often growing out of sexual attraction, relations, or situations, and exhibiting a great diversity of psychological and physiological manifestations. [Often grouped with **anger** and **fear** as the three primitive emotions. Syn. **affection.** Contr. w. **antipathy, enmity, hatred.**] — Fr. *amour*; Ger. *Liebe.*

low = 1. characterizing the pitch of tones whose stimuli are vibrations of relatively small frequency; 2. characterizing the intensity of sounds with relatively small stimulus-energy. [To avoid confusion the syns. (1) **deep,** and (2) **faint** are prefd. Contr. (1) w. **high** and (2) w. **loud.**] — Fr. (1) *grave,* (2) *faible*; Ger. (1) *tief,* (2) *leise.*

lower category = in the method of single stimuli, those reports which will surpass the other reports in frequency if the stimulus-magnitude is sufficiently decreased. — Fr. *catégorie inférieure.*

lowest audible tone = the lower limit of the tonal continuum, corresponding to relatively low stimulus frequencies. [This is estimated as about 20 cycles in the normal human ear.] — Fr. *limite auditive inférieure.*

loyalty = an attitude of firm attachment or allegiance on the part of an individual to a single individual, a group, a symbol, or (figuratively) an ideal. **loyal**[a].

lucidity = 1. (*path.*) an interval of sanity in the midst of the incoherent manifestations of insanity; 2. (*psych. res.*) a power, supposed to transcend the limitations of sensory reception, by which distant or hidden objects are perceived. [(2) attributed esp. to magnetized or mesmerized subjects. Syn. (2) **clairvoyance.** Cf. **cryptesthesia, metagnomy.**] **lucid**[a]. — Ger. (1) *Klarheit.*

ludicrous[n] = a situation tending or fitted to excite mirth. [Syn. the **comic,** prefd.] **ludicrous**[a]. — Fr. *risible, comique.*

lumbar = pert. to or located on the loins, or (more exactly) the regions on either side of the median regions of the back between the infrascapular and coxal regions. — Ger. *Lenden-.*

lumbar nerve = any one of the nerves issuing from the spinal cord in the interstices between the lumbar vertebrae. [There are 5 pairs in man.]

lumbar puncture = the withdrawal of cerebrospinal fluid by the introduction of a needle into the subarachnoid space through the opening between the lumbar vertebrae. [A diagnostic and therapeutic procedure introduced by Quincke.]

lumbar reflex, see **sacrospinal reflex.**

lumen = the unit of luminous flux; it is equal to the flux emitted within a unit solid angle by a uniform point-source of light of 1 international candle. [E.g., a source of 1 candlepower placed at the center of a hollow sphere of 1 meter (or foot) radius sheds 1 lumen upon 1 square meter (or square foot) of the spherical surface.]

luminosity = a word somewhat variably and indefinitely used as syn. with **brightness** or **brilliance.** — Fr. *luminosité, éclat*; Ger. *Helligkeit.*

luminous = 1. (*phys.*) having the power of exciting the visual receptors, e.g. luminous radiant energy; 2. (*phys.*) emitting light, as a source; 3. (*pop.*) bright, having the appearance of emitting light.

luminous flux = the rate of passage of radiant energy evaluated by reference to the conscious experience of brilliance produced by it; i.e. the quantity of light emitted by a given source or incident upon a specified surface. [The unit of luminous flux is the **lumen.** Distg. fr. **luminous intensity** and fr. **radiant flux.**]

luminous intensity = the luminous flux per unit solid angle emitted in a given direction by a source of light. [**luminous intensity** is expressed in *candles* or as *candlepower* and is seldom if ever equal in all directions in any practical light-source. Any element of a surface from which light is scattered by emission, transmission, or reflection behaves as a light-source with a luminous intensity proportional to its area. Cf. **illumination/law of.**]

lunacy = (*pop., legal*) insanity. [A technically obsolete term, based upon supposed magical association between mental disorders and influence of the moon.] **lunatic**[np]. (Accent **lu-**.) — Fr. *folie*.

lust = sexual desire. [In loose usage it implies an excessive sex desire or indulgence. Not to be confused w. German *Lust* = pleasure.] — Fr. *convoitise*; Ger. *Wollust*.

luster, lustre = a visual phenomenon characteristically experienced when a somewhat irregular and more or less polished metal object is seen. [It is believed to be due to the fact that the distorted images of other objects, reflected therein, are differently presented to the two eyes, but it is not wholly due to this since it can be effectively reproduced in a flat picture.] **lustrous**[a]. — Fr. *lustre, luisance*; Ger. *Glanz*.

lux = a unit of illumination, equal to the density of luminous flux upon a surface placed at right angles to the light-rays at a distance of 1 meter from a light-source of 1 candlepower. [Cf. **luminous flux.**]

lycanthropy = 1. (*hist.*) the supposed power to change one's self, or another person, into the form of a wolf or other wild beast; 2. (*med.*) a symptom of mental disorder in which the patient has the delusion that he is a wolf or other wild animal. **lycanthrope**[n].

lying = making a statement or assertion which within the knowledge of the individual making it is contrary to fact and which is made with the intent of inducing others to believe the statement to be true. [The term **pathological lying** is applied to statements contrary to fact, but imagined to be true, made by an insane individual; children's lies belong also to the field of imagination.] **lie**[v,n]; **lying**[a]; **liar**[np]. — Fr. *mentir, mensonge*[n]; Ger. *lügen*[v].

lymph = a fluid concerned in the drainage of the tissues and filling the **lymphatics,** a system of vessels opening into a proximal part of the venous system. [The composition of lymph varies and depends on the nature and state of activity of the organ from which it arises. Lymph taken proximally to a distal lymph gland contains **lymphocytes. Chyle,** the milky fluid taken up by the lacteals or intestinal lymphatics after digestion, is lymph rich in emulsified fat.] **lymphatic**[a].

lymphatic temperament, see **phlegmatic.**

lypemania = (*hist.*) a depressive type of insanity. [Syn. **melancholia** (prefd.) Esquirol's term, replacing melancholia, which for him was syn. w. **monomania,** whether depressive or not.]

M

M = abbrev. for **mean.**

MA = abbrev. for **mental age, meter angle.**

Mach rotation frame = a large rectangular frame pivoted at the top and bottom so that it may be rotated on a vertical axis in order to investigate the perception of bodily movement; at one end of the frame the observer's chair is mounted in a smaller rectangular frame which is pivoted at the top and bottom and in which the chair may also be tilted. [Devised by E. Mach (1875).] — Fr. *châssis de rotation de M.*

machine = a contrivance for performing certain specific activities. [Usually limited to a human construction; syn. **mechanism,** which includes also equivalent structures found in nature.] **machine-like**[a] = acting in the manner of a machine.

machine theory = (*psychol.*) the theory that physiological processes are machine-like, i.e. are determined by constant conditions (e.g. by neural topography) rather than by dynamic conditions (e.g. **electrical stresses).** [A term devised by the Gestalt school; contr. w. **dynamic theory.**]

macrocephaly = a pathological condition characterized by an excessive enlargement of the head. **macrocephalic**[a], **macrocephalous**[a].

macrocosm = 1. the physical universe; 2. human society. [Contr. w. **microcosm,** applied to man as an organic unit.] **macrocosmic**[a].

macropsia, see **megalopsia.**

macroscopic = pert. to the gross, to masses as wholes, or to aggregations of interrelated parts.

macrosplanchnic = characterizing a physique in which the volume of the trunk is developed in excess of the limbs, showing a high morphological index. [Contr. w. **microsplanchnic.** Cf. **pyknic.**]

macula, macula lutea = a small, indefinite pigmented area about 2 mm. in diameter, situate centrally in the human retina, within which area is the *fovea centralis*. [So called from its yellowish color. Lat. *luteus* = yellow. Syn. **yellow spot.**] — Ger. *gelber Fleck*.

macula acustica = a structure found in both the utricle and the saccule which resembles the crista acustica but with shorter cells and with a denser mass of hairs.

Maddox rod = (*ophthal.*) a glass rod, mounted in a disk which can be inserted in a trial-frame, so that the patient looks through the rod at right angles to its axis; it has the effect of making a small light-spot appear as a streak, and is used in measuring the degree of **muscular imbalance.** [Sometimes two or more small rods are used, mounted side by side, sometimes a piece of ribbed glass called **Maddox prism.**] — Fr. *baguette de M.*

magic = 1. (*pop.*) the art of jugglery or sleight-of-hand; 2. (*hist.*) the art of producing phenomena with the assistance of secret forces, departed spirits, or supernatural beings; 3. a term applied, esp. by anthropologists, to explanations of physical forces and phenomena by means of supernatural concepts. [Under (1) fall the arts of natural **magic;** cf. **conjure** (1). Syn. **conjury, jugglery, legerdemain, prestidigitation.** Under (2), the occult arts of **conjuration, augury, divination, incantation, enchantment, witchcraft, rhabdomancy, sorcery, necromancy,** etc., which make use of charms, talismans, amulets, relics, mystic ceremonies, etc., to invoke the supernatural forces.] **magician**[np]; **magic(al)**[a].

magnetic force, magnetism = a force of attraction, positive or negative, exerted by certain metallic substances upon others in close proximity. **magnetic**[a]. — Fr. *force magnétique* (*d'aimantation*); Ger. *magnetische Kraft*.

magnetism/animal, see **animal magnetism.**

magnetotropism, magnetotaxis = a simple orienting response, either positive or negative, to magnetic stimulation. [Cf. **tropism.**] (Accent **-tot-; -tax-.**) **magnetotropic**[a], **-tactic**[a].

magnitude = that characteristic in respect to which one thing may be greater or less than another (commensurable) thing. — Fr. *grandeur*; Ger. *Grösse*.

maintenance level = a stage of development at which growth has practically ceased, and the organism is maintained in a relatively constant state. [Applied esp. to modes of response and the learning process.] — Fr. *niveau de soutien (d'entretien)*.

major = greater, larger. [Mostly used as a tech. designative; e.g. *major premise, scale*. Contr. w. **minor** = lesser, smaller.]

major premise (or **premiss**), see **premise.**

major scale, see **scale** and Table VII. — Ger. *Durtonleiter*.

major sixth, third, etc., (*mus.*), see **interval** and Table VII.

majuscule = a large letter or capital, as distg. fr. **minuscule,** or lower-case letter.

make-believe = an attitude or mode of behavior on the part of an organism, which reproduces the characteristics of a totally different situation or condition. [Applied esp. to the imagined situations in children's play (not games); syn. **feigning,** applied to animal behavior; e.g. death-feigning, etc.] — Fr. *feinte, faux semblant*. — Ger. *vormachen*[v].

maladjustment = the inability of an individual to adapt his behavior to the conditions of his environment, or the *fact* of such maladaptation. — Fr. *mésadaptation*.

maladjustment/vocational = a condition resulting from an attempt to pursue a vocation for which the individual lacks the requisite capacities for success. [Cf. **selection/vocational, guidance/vocational.**] — Fr. *mésadaptation professionnelle*.

malaise = 1. a slight indisposition; 2. the general feeling of unwellness which frequently ushers in serious disease, esp. the acute infections.

male = an organism which produces sperm cells. [Biol. symbol ♂. Contr. w. **female,** which produces ova or egg cells; cf. **sex.**] **male**[a] = intrinsically characteristic of males or of the male sex (e.g. male voice); **masculine**[a] = associated with the male sex (e.g. masculine attire). — Ger. *Männchen*.

malevolence = a general disposition on the part of an individual to cause pain or distress to others, or to derive satisfaction from such pain or distress. [Syn. **malice,** which implies action on the part of the individual in question.] — Fr. *malveillance*; Ger. *Böswilligkeit*.

malformation = structural defect or anomaly in an organism. — Ger. *Missbildung*.

malice, maliciousness = the disposition on the part of an individual to cause pain or distress to another. [Syn. **malevolence,** a broader term, including satisfaction derived from pain or distress in others, however caused. **malice** usually refers to motivation of specific acts with intent to do harm, while **malevolence** implies a more general trait in the one who possesses it.] **malicious**[a]; Ger. *Bosheit, Übelwollen*.

malign = to utter false statements concerning another individual, which tend to injure his reputation. — Fr. *diffamer*; Ger. *verleumden*.

malinger = to feign sickness or disability. [**malingering** is distg. fr. **hypochondria** in which the illness, though imaginary, is believed in by the patient.] **malingering**[n], **malingerer**[np]. — Fr. *simuler (une maladie)*; Ger. *simulieren*.

malleolar = pert. to or located over the ankle-bone. [From **malleolus,** one of two processes of the tibia.] (Accent **-lee-.**)

malleus = the first of the **auditory ossicles,** which joins the tympanic membrane and the second ossicle, the **incus.** [Syn. **hammer, hammer-bone.**] — Fr. *osselet du marteau*.

malobservation = 1. observation which misses at the moment of the event the essential elements of the phenomenon; 2. recorded observation which fails as a faithful description of the elements in the event that were observed. [It may consist in omission, transposition in temporal sequence, substitution of an absent for a present element, or interpolation of absent elements. The cause of (1) is frequently misdirected attention, esp. due to a preconceived hypothesis; of (2), the continued effect of the failure of memory, or confusion of description with inference.]

Malthus' law = a genetic-statistical principle, formulated by T. R. Malthus, according to which the population of any given region, in respect to any given species, tends to increase in geometrical progression, while the means of subsistence increases at a less rapid rate. **Malthusian**[a].

Malthusianism = the theory of population and of its limitation based on **Malthus' law.**

mammalia, mammals = a class of vertebrates, characterized by embryonic development in the uterus and nourishment after birth from the secretions of the mammary gland. **mammal** = an organism of the mammalian order; **mammalian**[a]. — Fr. *mammifères*; Ger. *Säugetiere*.

mammary = 1. pert. to or located near the mammary or milk-secreting glands; 2. applied to regions, in either male or female, surrounding the nipples. (Accent **mam-.**)

mammary gland = a gland with duct, which is laid down in the embryo of both sexes. [In males it involutes after birth; in females it develops through puberty and reaches final development at end of pregnancy, when milk is secreted, and remains in this fully functional condition until the end of lactation, when partial involution again takes place; in old age almost complete involution may occur.]

mammillary bodies = two small round bodies in the hypothalamus in the floor of the third ventricle between the cerebral peduncle and the tuber cinereum. [Syn. **corpora mammillaria, corpora albicantia.**]

man, mankind = 1. a genus of animals belonging to the class of primates, and distinguished in behavior by language, civilization, and the use of tools; 2. (*pop.*) a specimen of this species; 3. (*pop.*) a male of this species. [Syn. homo, of which genus homo sapiens is the sole existing species.] **human**[a] (cf. **subhuman**). — Fr. *les hommes, genre humain*; Ger. *Menschheit, Menschengeschlecht*.

man-to-man rating scale = a rating scale designed to facilitate ease and accuracy of estimating the degree to which a person possesses a given trait, by providing as standards of comparison a list of persons selected as possessing different degrees of the trait in question. [The rater compares the person to be rated with these individuals, decides which of them he most resembles in the given trait, and assigns him the rating that has previously been assigned to that individual on the master scale.] — Fr. *échelle de correspondance d'individu à individu*.

mana = a Polynesian religious concept of power, impersonal, not a spirit, but supernatural and supreme, which manifests itself in immaterial and living objects, including man, and can be used for good or evil.

management = 1. the function, in any enterprise, of directing men and manipulating facilities to accomplish a predetermined result, in contrast to **administration**, which is the determination of purpose and policies; 2. the group of executives exercising this function, i.e. supervisors, foremen, superintendents, managers, vice-presidents, and president. [(1) includes management of finance, production, personnel, and sales.] — Fr. *gestion*; Ger. (1) *Handhabung*, (2) *Verwaltung*.

mandibular reflex = elevation of the lower jaw caused by contraction of the masseter muscles, brought about by a blow on the chin or teeth. [Mediated by the V sensory and V motor cranial nerves and pons. Syn. **chin r., jaw r., masseteric r.**]

mandibuloconjunctival reflex = a drawing of the lower jaw toward the side of stimulation when the corneal conjunctiva is touched. [Mediated by the trigeminal nerve and masticator nucleus and nerve.]

mania = mental disorder characterized by excitement. [Mainly historical. Cf. **manic-depressive psychosis.**] **manic**[a], **maniacal**[a]; **manic**[np], **maniac**[np].—Fr. *excitation maniaque*; Ger. *Wahnsinn*.

mania/acute = (*hist.*) a non-technical or merely descriptive term for suddenly developing excitement. [Usually limited to the narrower concept of **mania.**]

mania/homicidal = a mental derangement characterized by a constant desire to kill others. [Cf. **amuck.**]

manic, see **mania.**

manic-depressive psychosis = a type of mental disorder characterized by alternating periods of exaltation (with excessive activity) and depression with inhibition. [Cf. **cyclothymia.**] — Fr. *folie périodique, psychose maniaque-dépressive*.

manifest = to disclose something to an observer by means of attitude or behavior. **manifestation**[n], **manifested**[a], **manifest**[a] (= obvious).

manifest (dream) content, see **dream content.**

manifold = an assemblage composed exclusively of elements which all possess one common feature or characteristic. — Ger. *Mannigfaltigkeit*.

manikin test = a type of **performance test** devised by Pintner in which the task is to piece together the parts (arms, legs, head, and trunk) of a small wooden man.

manipulation = a type of behavior in which the organism's activity is limited largely to local movements (i.e. of fingers, claws, or teeth) and the effect of which is to change the physical arrangement of the object or objects dealt with; e.g. unlocking a problem box, stacking blocks, arranging a bed, tying a knot, etc. [Distg. fr. activities involving more general musculature, as **locomotion;** it has usually indirect, and sometimes no observable, relation to the organism's biological responses of food-getting, sex, defense, etc.]

manitou, manito = an Algonkin concept of an all-pervading power in the universe which emanates from indefinite sources; but any such source upon the manifestation of this power acquires the attributes pertaining to the power. [Similar to **orenda, wakanda, tirawa,** etc. Cf. **mana.**]

mankind = syn. for **man** in treating the mental and social characters of the species, or in distinction from sub-human species. [Syn. **humanity.**] — Fr. *les hommes, l'humanité*; Ger. *Menschheit*.

mannerism = 1. a gesture or other expressive act peculiar to a given individual and performed so frequently that it becomes closely associated with him in the minds of others and may serve to identify him; 2. the semi-automatic gesturing in dementia praecox as more or less unintentional symbolic expressions of undercurrents of attitude and reaction. — Ger. *Manieriertheit*.

manometer = an instrument for measuring pressure in a liquid or gas.

manometric flame apparatus, manometric capsule = an apparatus for studying sound-waves; the sound-waves are conducted through a speaking-tube to one of the two compartments of a capsule, where they impinge upon a thin rubber membrane that separates this compartment from the other, which is a gas chamber connected with a small burning gas-jet; the pressure variations resulting from the sound are communicated through the rubber membrane to the gas stream, and cause observable variations in the height of the jet.

manoptoscope = a hollow truncated cone for testing ocular dominance on the principle of unilateral sighting; the subject may test himself by holding the base of the cone against his face and viewing some object through the small end; he then closes his eyes alternately and the object disappears (i.e. shifts out of the restricted field of view) when the dominant eye is closed. [The name implies a fixed or normal relation between eyedness and handedness.]

mantissa = the decimal (or fractional) part of a logarithm. [Contr. w. **characteristic** = the integer part.]

manual = 1. pert. to the hands; 2. pert. to bodily skill or its lack in contr. w. verbal or intellectual skill.

manual method = a method of instruction in the education of the deaf which makes use of the sign language and finger-spelling as the chief means of communication among the deaf and between the deaf and others.

manuscript writing = a form of handwriting which omits joinings of the letters and uses instead the plain letters of the (Roman) alphabet. [Distg. fr. **cursive writing,** and fr. **print-script.**] — Fr. *écriture manuscrite*.

Marey tambour = an instrument used for recording the time and degree of physiological motor processes; it consists essentially of a shallow chamber, one side of which is made of flexible rubber; a tube connects this chamber with the moving or pulsating part, so that the rubber surface is raised and lowered by the fluctuations of air in the tube; the short end of a lever rests on the rubber surface, and a pointer or marker on the long end records the movements on a moving record sheet.

margin = the periphery of a two-dimensional figure. **marginal**[a].

marginal consciousness, margin of consciousness, see **consciousness/marginal.**

marginal contrast = (*vis.*) an accentuated type of simultaneous contrast, which occurs in regions close to the boundary between two contrasting areas. — Ger. *Randkontrast.*

Marie's disease, see **acromegaly.** — Fr. *maladie de M.*

Mariotte's spot, see **blind spot.**

mark = any distinguishing character or characteristic of any datum.

marriage = an enduring relation, usually involving coitus, between two individuals of opposite sex, contracted according to any form prescribed or recognized by the community. [The types of relation are classed as **monogamy** and **polygamy,** the latter including **polygyny** and **polyandry.**] **marital**[a]. — Ger. *Ehe.*

marsupialia, marsupials = an order of the class Mammalia, containing animals such as the opossum and kangaroo, which, instead of nourishing the young through a placenta in the uterus, are provided with an external pouch for their reception and nourishment. — Ger. *Beuteltiere.*

Martius disk = an apparatus devised by G. Martius for determining the gray-value of colors; a ring of the color to be investigated is placed on the disk between a central and a peripheral gray (each variable from black to white); the grays are varied until they are neither darkened nor lightened by the contrast-inducing action of the interposed ring; the gray of the variables gives the gray-value of the color.

masculine, see **gender, male.**

masculine protest = 1. (*indiv. psychol.*) the desire for masculine superiority, resulting from the identification of inferiority with femininity; 2. the struggle to overcome inferiority feelings in the interest of domination. [A term proposed by Adler, embodying a central doctrine of his individual psychology.] — Fr. *revendication masculine.*

masculinity = 1. the state or condition of an individual organism which has male characters; 2. the state of a female which has certain male characters. [Syn. **masculinism.**]

masculinization = 1. the structural, functional, and behavioral changes which follow successful implantation of testicular tissue into a castrate female animal, involving regression of female characteristics together with the development of male qualities; 2. (*soc.*) a change in personality from a predominance of feminine traits or attitudes to a predominance of masculine attitudes as a result of response to social or other environmental stimulation.

masked epilepsy = a type of epilepsy in which the period of unconsciousness is brief and the epileptic attack or convulsion is replaced by more normally integrated (but nevertheless automatic and not remembered) activity. [Syn. **epilepsia larvata.**]

masking = the partial or complete obscuring of a given tone by the simultaneous presentation of a tone of a different frequency. [There are two types: (1) **monaural,** when the second tone is presented to the same ear; (2) **binaural,** when the second tone is presented to the other ear; the latter is apparently an interference with clear perception rather than an actual reduction of peripheral sensitivity. The term applies to other sense departments in similar meaning.]

masochism = 1. a type of sexual perversion characterized by pleasure, often culminating in sexual orgasm, in being whipped or otherwise physically maltreated; 2. (*psychoan.*) the destructive instinct turned inwards and erotically bound: three forms are distinguished, erotogenic, feminine, moral. [Syn. **passive algolagnia.** Contr. w. **sadism,** in which the individual takes pleasure in maltreating one of the opposite sex.] (Pron. **-oke-.**) **masochistic**[a].

mass = 1. (*phys.*) the quantity of matter in a material body; 2. (*soc.*) a group of individuals, regarded apart from its social organization. — Fr. (1) *masse,* (2) *foule*; Ger. *Masse, Menge.*

mass action = the doctrine that learning, or intelligence, depends upon the joint action of large segments of the central nervous system and not upon the formation of specific bonds between small segments. — Fr. *action globale.*

mass methods = the measurement of a considerable number of individuals by a particular test or experimental procedure, with the frequent result that more (but less precise) data are secured than when greater control is exercised over fewer subjects. [**mass methods** may be useful when greater control is either not feasible or not justified. Data secured by mass methods are generally amenable to elucidation by statistical methods.] — Fr. *m. globales.*

mass reflex = a reflex movement extending over the whole of an area innervated from a part of the spinal cord, especially when this has been injured. [An abnormal reflex usually affecting the lower limbs. Mediated by segments of the cord below level of injury.] — Fr. *réflexe de masse.*

massed learning = the memorizing of relatively long verbal series, or the formation of a complicated motor habit, by repetition without interruption. [Distg. fr. learning by **spaced repetition,** in which the repetitions are interrupted by periods of rest. Cf. **unspaced repetition.**] — Fr. *apprentissage* (*acquisition*) *massé.*

masseteric reflex, see **mandibular reflex.**

Masson disk = an apparatus devised by V. Masson for determining the difference limen in vision; it consists of a white disk upon which are drawn, from center to circumference, a radial series of concentric black rectangles; when properly rotated, the disk shows a series of concentric gray circles which are increasingly lighter toward the periphery. [The first ring (from within outward) which becomes indistinguishable from the white background measures the DL, by the ratio: degrees of black/degrees of white in that ring. Used also in experiments upon fluctuation of attention.]

mastery = 1. the condition of being able to control (or of being in control of) the actions of others; 2. an attitude which implies one's consciousness of ability to control the actions of others; 3. extreme proficiency in the knowledge and handling of any language, science, or other material which the individual has learned. [Contr. (1, 2) w. **subservience.**] — Fr. *maîtrise*; Ger. (1) *Herrschaft,* (2) *Meisterschaft.*

mastication = the act of crushing food with the teeth. **masticate**[v]. — Ger. *Zerkauen.*

mastoid = pert. to or located in the mastoid process lying just behind the ear.

masturbation = the inducing of tumescence and orgasm by manual or other artificial types of stimulation of the genitalia.

matched groups = groups of individuals which are equated or matched, pair by pair, for experimental purposes, each member of the control group being equated or matched with a member of the test-group in as many respects as are considered significant for the problem (e.g. in age, school-performance, I Q, or any measurable trait). [Any differences which then appear between test- and control-groups are presumably due to the experimental situation and *not* to inequalities between the two groups.]

mate[v] = 1. to copulate; 2. to enter into durable relation with one of the same species and of opposite sex. [Distg. (1) fr. **cross,** applied to plant fecundation.] **mating**[n], **mate**[np].

material world, see **physical world.**

materialism = 1. the theory that matter is the only ultimate reality; 2. the view which regards the body, more especially the brain, as the *substratum* of the psychic processes, which are ultimately material products.

materialization = (*psych. res.*) the forming of objects or parts (or the whole) of the human body by supernormal means. [Cf. **teleplasm.**]

maternal behavior = behavior (generally limited to the female sex) characterized by being directed toward care of the offspring or other helpless young. [Distg. fr. **paternal behavior** by the sex of the parent and (in mammals) by the act of suckling.] — Fr. *comportement maternel*; Ger. *mütterliches Verhalten.*

mathematics = "the science concerned with the logical deduction of consequences from the general premises of all reasoning" (Encyclop. Brit.). [Ordinarily limited to the investigation of numerical and quantitative values and relations, or of other data (e.g. positional) which can be quantitatively treated.] **mathematic(al)**[a].

mating[n], see **mate.** — Fr. *pariade*; Ger. *Paarung.*

mating behavior = the total group of responses involved in courtship and in sexual intercourse. — Fr. *pariade, comportement d'accouplement.*

matter = 1. (*phys.*) the totality (or any part) of the units of which the physical universe is composed, regarded either as mass, molecules, atoms, electrons, etc.; 2. (*psychol.*) the actual constituents of the universe which may serve as stimuli of any sort. **material**[a].

maturation = 1. (*biol.*) attainment of the state of complete development, or the process whereby this state is attained; 2. the reduction of the number of chromosomes in the sex cells preparatory to fertilization. [(1) applies to any organic growth, e.g. cells, organs, functions, organisms. Cf. **maturity.**] **maturing**[a]. — Ger. *Reifung.*

maturation hypothesis = the theory that certain modes of behavior are inherited, but are not capable of performance upon presentation of the proper stimulus until the appropriate organs (or specific innate neural pathways) have matured. [Sometimes applied to the development of instinctive dispositions without reference to any anatomical or physiological basis. Contr. w. the theory that all forms of behavior are the result of learning rather than of inheritance.]

maturation of instinct, see **instinct maturation.**

mature[v] = to advance toward a complete state of development. [Applied to animals and plants. Syn. **ripen,** applied to plants only.] **maturing**[a]. — Fr. *mûrir*; Ger. *reifen.*

maturity = the stage of complete development. [Applied to cells, organs, functions, and organisms. Cf. **maturation.**] **mature**[a].

maxillary = pert. or located in the jaws. (Accent **max-.**)

maxim = a practical guiding rule. [In scientific investigation a well-tested **maxim,** or one of wide-spread application, is called a **canon.**]

maximum = (*math.*) the greatest value reached by a variable quantity which first increases and then decreases. [Contr. w. **minimum.** At a maximum the first derivative of a function is zero, and the second derivative negative.] **maxima**[pl], **maximal** or **maximum**[a].

maximum (or **maximal**) **sensation** = that intensity of a given sensation which is not enhanced or augmented by any increase in the value of the stimulus. [Contr. w. **minimal sensation.**]

Maxwell's demons = minute beings assumed as a device for discussion of certain physical phenomena by Clerk Maxwell, and imagined to be endowed with various human characteristics adapted to their atomic order of existence. [One demon is conceived as sorting the molecules of a gas according to their velocity and so making one section of the gas hot, another cold. Another demon, endowed with unlimited visual acuity, is assumed to move away from the earth at a velocity exceeding the speed of light, and is thus able to view the panorama of history unfolding backwards to the earliest times.]

maze = a device consisting of a system of pathways, with turns, branches, and blind alleys, usually one path only leading from the starting-point to some goal. [Used to test human and animal learning ability or intelligence. The progress of learning is rated in terms of decrease in time, number of errors, or both, in a series of trials. In animal work the goal is usually a food-box. **mazes** vary in form and intricacy, from a simple path with a single blind alley to the historical **Hampton Court maze.** In human tests a pencil maze or high-relief finger maze is sometimes used. Syn. **labyrinth.**] — Fr. *labyrinthe*; Ger. *Irrgarten.*

McCarthy's reflex, see **supraorbital reflex.**

mdn. = abbrev. for **median.**

mean[n] = an intermediate value in a given series. [Most commonly applied to the **arithmetic mean** or average.] — Fr. *moyenne.*

mean[v], see **meaning.**

mean deviation, mean error, mean variation = syn. for **average deviation.**

mean gradations/method of = a psychophysical method, in which two appreciably different stimuli are presented, simultaneously or successively; the observer is instructed to bisect the sensory interval which separates them by adjusting a third, intermediate stimulus until it appears just midway between them; or, he is instructed to adjust a third stimulus which is greater (or less) than the two so that the two sense-distances appear equal. [Syn. **method of equal sense distances; of supra-liminal differences; of equal-appearing intervals,** of mean stimuli.] — Fr. *m. de gradations moyennes*; Ger. *M. der mittleren Abstufungen.*

meaning = 1. (*logic*) the phenomena, relations, etc. which a given term, phrase, etc. designates (denotes) or stands for (connotes); 2. (*assoc.*) the context or imaginal elements associated with the sensory data in a perceptual experience (or with a memory image or other revival) which serve to unify the experience and relate it to others; 3. (*introsp.*) that aspect of experience which constitutes its character as object, value, or reference, as distg. from the sensory aspect of experience which may be concomitant therewith; 4. (*beh.*) as applied to a stimulus or situation, the definite responses, whether overt or implicit, which it may call forth; 5. the significance of an experience. **mean**[v], **meaningful**[a]. — Fr. (1) *sens*, (2) *signification*, (3) *sens, signification*; Ger. (1) *Sinn*, (2) *Bedeutung, sinnvoll*[a].

means = the intermediate actions or activities of an organism involved in bringing about a final situation. [In human activities, generally used where the final situation has been pictured or purposed beforehand; in animal behavior used to designate the intermediate activities in a life-preserving or other unitary behavior process.] — Fr. *moyens*.

measure[n] = 1. (*mus.*) a short series of tones in a musical composition usually marked by a single ictus; 2. (*general*) a result obtained by measurement; 3. (*pop.*) a standard for measurement. [Cf. **measurement.**] — Fr. *mesure*; Ger. (1) *Takt*, (2, 3) *Mass*.

measure of precision = a quantity, denoted by the letter **h**, which varies directly with the precision of the measurements and is defined by the relation $h = 1/\sigma\sqrt{2}$, where σ denotes the standard deviation. [Syn. **index of precision.**]

measurement = the comparison of a quantitative datum of any sort with a fixed, enduring datum or standard of the same sort, in order to discover its numerical value. [**measurement** may be either **direct** = by immediate comparison, or **indirect** = comparison by means of some intermediary. Contr. w. **appraisal** = estimation of value by personal judgment. [Cf. **standard, scale** (1), **measure**[n].] **measure**[v]. — Fr. *mesure*; Ger. *Messung*.

measurement method = a term used to designate any specific procedure for finding the quantitative value, in some specified respect, of an object, event, or other datum. [In psychophysics, the recognized methods are the **method of limits,** of **average error,** of **equivalents,** of **equal sense differences,** of **right and wrong cases** (or **constant stimuli).** In determining individual differences, the term *method* is used less formally and rigidly; characteristic **methods** are seen in (1) the use of single tests of specific functions (e.g. auditory memory for digits); (2) the use of groups of tests of either (*a*) nonrelated traits (e.g. the profile method), or (*b*) related traits (e.g. general intelligence tests) which are scored and interpreted either by the point-scale method or the age-scale method; and (3) the method of rating.] — Ger. *Massmethode*.

measurement of intelligence = the comparison of individuals in respect to the quantitative value of their intelligence in terms of a standardized scale. [Cf. **standard, scale** (1).]

meatus/external auditory = the canal which leads from without through the temporal bone to the middle ear, and serves as the path for sound vibrations. [Often called **auditory meatus,** or the **meatus.**] (Accent **-ay-.**) — Fr. *conduit auditif externe*; Ger. *äusserer Gehörgang*.

meatus/internal auditory = a canal in the petrous portion of the temporal bone, which leads from the internal ear inward to the skull cavity, and contains, in man and other high forms, the acoustic and facial nerves and the internal auditory artery and vein. (Accent **-ay-.**) — Fr. *conduit auditif interne*; Ger. *innerer Gehörgang*.

mechanical = 1. (*beh.*) automatized, machine-like; 2. proceeding according to traditional principles of physics (and chemistry). [Syn. (2) **mechanistic** (prefd.).]

mechanical intelligence = general capacity on the part of an individual for dealing with mechanisms, as contr. w. capacity for dealing with ideas or with people. [Syn. **concrete intelligence.** Distg. fr. **abstract intelligence** and **social intelligence.**]

mechanical stimulation = the application of mechanical forces, such as traction or impact, to excite a receptor.

mechanics = the branch of physics which investigates the activity of masses or other material units or groups.

mechanics of ideas = a term devised by Herbart (1824) to denote the rise and subsidence of ideas in consciousness by a process in which force or energy (equivalent to attention) is transferred from one content of consciousness to another, the relative quantities having definite mathematical relations analogous to the general mechanics of physical force.

mechanism = 1. a machine or machine-like system, fitted to perform certain activities in a fairly precise manner; 2. the mode in which the system operates; 3. (*psychoan.*) the unconscious direction of a mental process in which feeling or emotion plays an important part; 4. syn. for **mechanistic theory.** [As applied to human behavior, the term refers to those activities which are machine-like in their constancy and regularity. Cf. **mental mechanism.**] **mechanical**[a] (1); **mechanistic**[a] (2).

mechanism/neutralizing = (*psychoan.*) a mental mechanism which enters into the structure of a dream and criticizes it, thus neutralizing the whole or a portion of its manifest content. [Cf. **mental mechanism.**]

mechanistic theory = 1. the dynamic interpretation of the universe as a system of bodies moved by resident forces; 2. the consistent application of (1) to any field of investigation, esp. biology and psychology. [Contr. (2) w. **vitalism** in biology and w. **teleology** in psychology. Cf. **mechanism.**]

mediacy = (*psychol.*) the genesis of an idea indirectly (i.e. through a two-fold or manifold association) from a stimulus. [The intermediate ideas are called **mediating ideas** or **associations.** Cf. **mediation.**] **mediating**[a].

mediad (or **mesad**)[adv] = toward the medial plane or axis.

medial (or **mesial**) **plane** = that plane in the body of a bilaterally symmetrical organism, which is at right angles to the dextrosinistral axis and divides the body into halves. [Distg. fr. **sagittal plane** = any plane parallel to the medial, lying either to right or to left of the center. Syn. **median plane.**]

median = the midpoint in a series of values, arranged in order of magnitude. [If the number of such values is odd, the median is the value of the mid-measure. If the number is even, the median may be taken as the arithmetic average of the two mid-measures. Distg. fr. **mean.**] — Ger. *Zentralwert*.

median deviation = the median value of the deviations of a set of measures (usually) from the median of the whole set. [In a symmetrical distribution (but not in general) the median deviation = the **quartile deviation.**] — Fr. *écart médian.*

median gray = a gray which is characterized as neither whitish nor blackish, or the color of a surface or stimulus which presents such an appearance. [As a conscious experience it is presumably identical with the **cortical gray** of Müller.]

median plane, see **medial plane.**

mediate[a] = interposed between two terms or data. [Applied to an idea or ideas intermediate between an initial idea and a later idea in the same series. Cf. **mediate association.** Distg. fr. **mediating,** which implies a relating function for the interposed item.] **mediate**[v], **mediation**[n] (these may also imply a relating function). — Fr. *interposé, médiat*; Ger. *mittelbar.*

mediate (or **mediated**) **association** = the linking or association of one idea with another indirectly through one or more intervening ideas. [Contr. w. **immediate association** = direct association or sequence between the two ideas.]

mediation = (*psychol.*) the interposition of one or more ideas or acts between an initial stimulus or idea and a given end result whose genesis is under investigation. — Fr. *médiation, entremise*; Ger. *Vermittelung.*

medical graphology = the utilization of handwriting in differential diagnosis of disease. [The term may be broadened to include analysis not only of graphomotor abnormalities but also of simultaneously occurring disorders in written content.]

medicine = 1. (*anthrop.*) as applied to American Indians, the belief in systems of magical practices for curing the sick, influencing others for good or ill, and enhancing the fortunes of the practitioner; 2. the objects employed in magical practices, e.g. medicine bundles; 3. the science and art of healing. [Also used as syn. w. **the supernatural.**]

medicine man, see **shaman.**

medicolegal = pert. to the legal implications of medicine, e.g. the legal status of those suffering from nervous disorder, the legal obligations of physicians, etc.

meditation = 1. sustained reflection; 2. (*relig.*) a chain of reflections referring to religious subjects or to conduct connected with one's duty to God or to man. [(2) is regarded by mystics as the form of prayer with which one may begin the attempt to realize union with God.]

medium = 1. the contents of any portion of space through which a wave or moving body passes; 2. (*psych. res.*) an individual who is said to be directed or controlled by a disembodied spirit and to transmit that spirit's thoughts to living beings by means of speech, writing, gestures, etc. **media**[pl] (1), **mediums**[pl] (2).

mediumistic writing, see **automatic writing.**

medulla = 1. the marrow or inner portion of an organ; 2. used to characterize neural substance (e.g. medulla spinalis, spinal cord); 3. abbrev. for **medulla oblongata.** (Accent **-dull-.**) **medullary**[a] (accent **med-**). — Fr. *moelle*; Ger. *Mark.*

medulla oblongata = the portion of the brain which adjoins the spinal cord and extends cephalad as far as the cephalic border of the pons. [It is virtually a continuation of the cord in which the cord structures are rearranged and new structures added. Abbrev. to **medulla.** Syn. **metencephalon.**] — Fr. *bulbe*; *myélencéphale*; Ger. *verlängertes Mark.*

medullary groove, see **neural groove.**

medullary sheath, see **myelin sheath.**

medullary substance = (*hist.*) **myelin**

medullary tube, see **neural tube.**

medullated = consisting of or covered with medullary substance (myelin). [E.g. **medullated nerve fiber** = covered with a myelin sheath. Syn. **myelinated.** Cf. **medullation.**]

medullation = the covering of a nerve fiber with a sheath of medullary substance, or myelin. [Syn. **myelinization, myelination.**] (Pron. **-dull-.**)

Medusa = a sexual and usually free-swimming stage in the life history of many Coelenterates. [Syn. **jelly-fish.**]

megalomania = morbid overvaluation of oneself. [Cf. **grandeur/delusions of.**] **megalomanic**[a, np]. — Ger. *Grössenwahn.*

megalopsia = an increase in the apparent size of visual objects, ascribed to changes in the retinal end-organs or to spasm of accommodation. [Syn. **macropsia.**]

megaphonia = a form of **dysphonia** characterized by a loud voice. **macrophonic**[a].

megrim, see **migraine.**

meibomian glands = small sebaceous glands situate between the cartilage and conjunctiva of the eyelids and opening on the edge of the lid. [An acute inflammation of one of these glands is called a **stye** or **hordeolum.**]

meiosis = the division of the germ cells during the process of maturation, in which the number of chromosomes is reduced by one half. [Cf. **mitosis.**]

Meissner corpuscles = nerve terminations located in the papillary stratum of the corium. [They occur most frequently in the soles and palms. Usually considered to be receptors for pressure sensibility. Syn. **Meissner-Wagner corpuscles.** A modification is called **Dogiel corpuscle.**] — Ger. *Meissnersche* or *Tastkörperchen.*

melancholia = a type of mental disorder characterized by emotional depression and motor inhibition or agitation. [Distg. fr. **melancholy,** a mood of sadness.] **melancholic**[a], **melancholiac**[np], **melancholic**[np] (prefd.).

melancholia/affective = a type of mental disorder corresponding to the depressive phase of manic-depressive insanity.

melancholic = a type of temperament given to frequent and protracted spells of depression. [Hist. attributed to the predominance of black bile in the bodily humors. Cf. **temperament.**]

melanism = (*biol.*) abnormal, but not morbid, development of pigment in the skin, eyes, hair, etc. [Contr. w. **albinism.**] **melanic**[a].

melody = a rhythmical succession of tones expressing some musical idea or motive. [Distg. fr. **harmony** = the simultaneous combination of tones into a chord. The essential elements of music are **melody, harmony, rhythm.**] — Ger. *Melodie.*

membership character = (*Gestalt*) the effect of dynamic participation whereby a part alters its individuality in becoming a constituent of the whole.

membrane = a thin layer of substance, usually covering or lining the cavity of an organ or interposing between two organs or parts. — Fr. *membrane, cloison.*

membrane of Bruch, see **Bruch's membrane.**

membrane theory of conduction = an explanation of the propagation of the nerve impulse in terms of the electrochemical properties of surface films or membranes. [Cf. **Nernst-Lillie theory of excitation and conduction.**]

memorize = to stamp in or perfect a memory, especially of a long verbal passage, by repetition of the sequence. **memorization**[n], **mnemonic**[a]. — Fr. *apprendre par coeur, mémorizer*; Ger. *auswendig lernen.*

memory = 1. a generic term for those experiences, movements, or functions which are conditioned upon earlier experiences, movements, or functions of the organism; 2. an experience which is conditioned upon earlier experiences, but which does not refer specifically to such experiences, e.g. the recall of a name, date, etc.; 3. a present experience which is conditioned upon some specific earlier experience and which refers definitely to that experience, i.e. the recollection of occurrences in their actual setting; 4. the process of responding to a partial repetition of an earlier stimulus-situation. [In **rote memory** original material is retained or recited verbatim with no required attention to its meaning; in **logical memory** the material is always meaningful, and the meaning is to be retained or reported with no requirement that the original terms or symbols be recited. The essential characteristic of (1) is **retention,** but it may also include **reproduction,** which characterizes (2) and (3). Syn. (1) **mneme,** (2) **recall** (prefd.), **remembrance,** (3) **recollection** (prefd.), **reminiscence** = an extended series of **memories.**] **memorial**[a], **memory**[a] = pert. to memory; **mnemonic**[a] = concerned w. memorizing. — Fr. (1) *mémoire,* (2, 3) *souvenir*; Ger. (1) *Gedächtnis,* (2, 3) *Erinnerung.*

memory after-image, see **after-image/memory.**

memory apparatus = a device, usually visual, for presenting successively, at a desired rate, a series of stimuli to be memorized; in typical form it consists of a motor-driven cylinder, disk, or strip bearing the nonsense syllables or other visual material, each item of which in turn is brought into temporary register with an exposure slot before which the memorizer sits.

memory color = modification of the color of a perceived object as the result of previous experience. [Syn. **memory tinge.**] — Ger. *Gedächtnisfarbe.*

memory curve = a graphic representation of the relative amounts of memorized material that can be recalled, or that are forgotten, after various intervals of time.

memory drawing = graph reproduction of an object or scene from recall of one or more previous views of it when no model is present for copy. — Fr. *dessin mnémonique.*

memory image = the revival of a former experience in the absence of the appropriate stimuli, the content of the revival being similar to the original experience, but not a copy of it.

memory levels = in eidetic theory, the hierarchy of memory images, eidetic images, after-images. — Fr. *niveaux mnémoniques*; Ger. *Gedächtnisstufen.*

memory-odor, see **object-odor.**

memory span = the number of items of a specified character that can be correctly reproduced or reported immediately after their first presentation. — Fr. *capacité d'appréhension, champ de mémoire immédiate.*

memory span test = a test devised by J. Jacobs (1887) to determine the maximal number of related or unrelated elements which a testee can reproduce exactly after (usually) a single presentation. [Materials most commonly used for this purpose include nonsense syllables, numerals, unrelated words, and sentences. Commonly distg. fr. **logical memory test** by insistence upon exact reproduction, but not usually distg. fr. **attention-span** (or **range of apprehension**) **test.**]

memory system = any general artificial device used to assist recollection. [Syn. **mnemonic system.**]

memory time = the time required to respond to a stimulus by recalling some appropriate memory. [Cf. **response time.**]

mendacity = a tendency on the part of an individual to deceive others by false statements. [Distg. fr. **fiction,** in which the false statements are not aimed to deceive. Syn. **lying.**]

Mendel's law = a principle of hereditary transmission, discovered by Gregor Mendel, according to which the characters of the parents are transmitted to the offspring in units without change, some becoming perceptible in individuals of the first generation, others in those of later generations, with a definite ratio for each generation. [Cf. **Mendelian ratio.**]

Mendelian ratio = in biparental offspring, the ratio between those which, according to Mendel's law, possess a given unit character or combination of unit characters (dominants) and those which do not (recessives). [For a single unit character the ratio in the first filial generation is 3 dominants to 1 recessive. Cf. **dominant character, recessive character.**]

Mendelism = the theory of inheritance, based on Mendel's law, according to which the constitution of the offspring is determined by a certain number of independent factors (called **unit-characters**), contributed by the parents. [Syn. **Mendelian theory,** a narrower term. Cf. **hybrid.**] **Mendelian**[a].

meninges = the membranes which cover the brain and cord, consisting (in the brain) of the pia mater, arachnoid, and dura mater. **meningeal**[a] (accent **-inj-.**) — Ger. *Hirnhaut.*

meningitis = inflammation of the meninges, and any one of several disorders resulting therefrom.

meniscus = a lens, one of whose refracting surfaces is convex and the other concave.

menopause = the time of life at which menstruation ceases.

menstrual function, menstruation = the periodic sanguineous discharge connected with the sexual function in the human female. [So called from its monthly occurrence; related to **estrus,** or heat-period, in females of other mammals.]

mental = 1. (*psychol.*) pert. to **mind.** [Used with various meanings and interpretations (cf. **mind**); sometimes syn. for **conscious,** sometimes a generic adj. embracing **conscious** and **unconscious** (or **subconscious**) and nearly equivalent to **responsive.** Occasional syn. **psychic.**] — Ger. *seelisch, geistig.*

mental = 2. (*anat.*) pert. to or located on the chin. [Lat. **mentum.**]

mental activity = 1. any performance which has a mental character; 2. rapidity and alertness of perception and thought.

mental age = the degree of mental development of an individual, measured in terms of the chronological age of the average individual of corresponding mental ability. [E.g. 10-year mental age = the degree of mental development attained by the average child of 10 years. In practice **mental age** is used in a limited sense as syn. with **intelligence age.**]

mental-age-grade table = in mental testing, a table similar to an **age-grade table,** showing the number of children of each mental age found in each grade. [Cf. **age-grade table.**]

mental alienation, see **alienation.**

mental apparatus, see **topography/mental.**

mental capacity, see **capacity.**

mental chemistry = a phrase devised to express the view that the mind does not passively receive and compound data but supplies from itself an activity which is to some degree creative. [Current in the time of J. S. Mill and indicative of dissatisfaction with a purely mechanical theory of association of ideas. An important link between **associationism** and doctrines of synthetic activity, apperception, etc. Sometimes incorrectly identified with compounding by mere mechanical addition of parts and thus opposed to **Gestalt** and **Gestalt theory.** Cf. **creative synthesis, mental synthesis.**]

mental chronometry, see **chronometry/mental.**

mental content = the experiences or constituents of experience of an individual at a given moment. [Cf. **content of consciousness.**]

mental deafness, see **deafness/cortical.**

mental defective, mental deficiency, see **deficiency /mental.**

mental deterioration = the progressive loss of mental abilities which takes place in certain types of psychoses.

mental development = the progressive unfolding or organization of mental life and behavior in the individual from embryonic life to maturity. [Distg. fr. **mental evolution,** the progressive organization of these functions in the animal scale. Contr. w. **mental decay** (or **degeneration**) = the loss of these functions in old age.]

mental discipline = the doctrine that specific training (e.g. the study of mathematics) results in a general improvement of ability in all or in several functions. [Nearly syn. w. **formal discipline.** Cf. **transfer of training.**]

mental disease (or **disorder**) = any disturbance of the mental organization. [The term has been largely replaced by **psychosis,** both minor and major.] — Fr. *maladie mentale.*

mental element = a mental fact which is apparently simple, i.e. which remains unanalyzed at the present stage of scientific knowledge. [Usually applied to an element of conscious content (e.g. a sensation), rather than an element of performance. Sensations (1), images (1), and feelings (1) have been the conventional elements. There have been attempts to find others (e.g. **imageless thoughts**) and also to reduce all to sensation. (Cf. **sensationism.**)]

mental evolution = the progressive unfolding or organization of mental functions and of behavior in the animal scale. [Distg. fr. **mental development** = the progressive organization of these functions in the individual.]

mental examination = the systematic application of mental tests to an individual, in order to determine his mental status in relation to others in a given population.

mental faculties = (*hist.*) certain powers supposed to be inherent in the mind at all times, whether active or not; e.g. memory. [As a doctrine this has been attacked by those who maintain the functional or dynamic view. Cf. **faculty psychol.**]

mental function = 1. an operation performed on mental content (Stumpf); 2. any type of performance which has the characteristics of mentality; 3. mental activity or operation, as distg. fr. content or structure.

mental healing = the healing of diseases and disorders by suggestion, supported by the faith of the patient in their cure. [Syn. **mind-cure, faith-cure, divine healing,** etc.; cf. **psychotherapy.**] — Fr. *guérison (cure) mentale.*

mental hygiene = the investigation and systematic practice of measures for the preservation of mental health; i.e. for the maintenance of mental functions in normal condition.

mental imagery/type of = the preponderance of a certain mode of sensory content (visual, auditory, etc.) in the imagery experiences of a given individual. [Used also to distg. one kind of sensory material from another in imagery.]

mental life = phenomena regarded as a continuing process in the individual. — Fr. *vie mentale*; Ger. *Seelenleben.*

mental maturity = the condition or attainment of complete general development of mental life and behavior in an individual.

mental measurement = the evaluation of mental phenomena, or of the observable responses which represent them, in terms of some standard or scale. [Applied esp. to psychophysical research and to investigation of individual differences by mental tests.]

mental mechanism = 1. the neural organization, or the functional organization which controls mental operations in an individual; 2. (*psychoan.*) an indirect and typically unconscious manner of gratifying a repressed desire.

mental organization = 1. the system of mental operations in an individual; 2. the systematized physiological mechanisms which, when operating as a result of stimulation, give rise to conscious experiences and responses.

mental pathology, see **psychopathology.**

mental phenomena = 1. phenomena of consciousness; 2. these phenomena, together with subconscious or unconscious phenomena akin to those of consciousness; 3. any of the phenomena investigated by psychology.

mental process (or **operation**) = 1. any responsive activity of the individual, esp. such as involve goal-seeking and the use of previously learned responses; 2. any such activity involving consciousness.

mental scale, see **scale/mental.**

mental science = (*hist.*) syn. for **psychology.**

mental set = the attitude or determination of an individual before receiving an expected stimulus or with reference to a problem or general situation. [Syn. **readiness.** Cf. **attitude; Aufgabe; Einstellung; Bereitschaft.**] — Fr. *ajustement mental, prédisposition m.*; Ger. *Einstellung, Bewusstseinslage.*

mental synthesis = a type of compounding elementary mental phenomena, in which the product manifests certain new characteristics, apparently not found in the elementary constituents. [Term introduced by J. S. Mill, by analogy with **chemical synthesis.** Cf. **mental chemistry, creative synthesis.**]

mental telepathy, see **telepathy.**

mental test = 1. a standardized device used for measuring a mental trait, or for studying the mental operations or attitudes of an individual; 2. the process of applying such device.

mental topography (or **apparatus**), see **topography/mental.**

mental type, see **type/mental.**

mentalism = the doctrine that psychology is concerned (wholly or in part) with the investigation of conscious phenomena. [Contr. w. **behaviorism.**] **mentalist**[np], **mentalistic**[a].

mentality = the distinctive characteristic included in the notion of **mind,** or the specific manifestation of mind in any organism. [Used also comparatively, to denote differences in degree of mental organization, either among individuals or between species. Cf. **mind.**]

meridian = (*ophthal.*) 1. in the surface representing the visual field of a single stationary eye, any *line* which passes through the fixation-point, horizontally, vertically, or at any oblique angle; 2. (more generally) a *plane* passing through the fixation-point and the nodal point of the eye.

merit[n] = an ethical concept denoting a positive evaluation or a belief in the worth of some act of an individual or of his general conduct. [Applied loosely in science to the positive evaluation of a hypothesis or theory.]

Merkel corpuscle = a type of cell located in the submucous tissue of the tongue and mouth. [Believed by some writers to be receptors for pressure sensations.]

Merkel's law = a theoretical principle formulated by J. Merkel, according to which equal differences between sensations correspond to equal differences between stimuli. [**Merkel's law** and **Weber's law** do not conflict, since Weber's law is based upon liminal differences, Merkel's upon larger (supraliminal) differences.]

mescal = a preparation of the cactus, Anhalonium Lewinii, possessing peculiar narcotic properties. It produces depression of the respiratory center, nausea, and a stimulation of the central nervous system, characterized by hallucinations of the higher senses, particularly that of sight.

mesencephalon = that part of the brain which develops from the middle cerebral vesicle; it is formed by the corpora quadrigemina, the tegmental region, and the crura cerebri, and is pierced by the aqueduct of Sylvius. [Syn. **midbrain.**]

mesenchyme = a mass of tissue in the embryo which consists of isolated, non-layered cells, proliferated usually from the mesoderm. [It gives rise to the connective tissues, skeleton, blood, and most of the muscular tissue in vertebrate animals.]

mesentery = a fold of the peritoneum which envelops the abdominal organs and suspends them from the abdominal walls. (Accent **mes-.**) **mesenteric**[a] (accent **-ter-**).

mesmerism = (*hist.*) hypnotism. [So-called from Franz Anton Mesmer, who first brought hypnosis to the attention of the scientific world (1775). Syn. **animal magnetism.**] **mesmeric**[a]; **mesmerize**[v].

mesoblast = the middle germ layer of the embryo. [Syn. **mesoderm.**] — Fr. *mésoblaste, feuillet moyen.*

mesoderm = the middle germ-layer, lying between the **ectoderm** and **entoderm.** [Syn. **mesoblast.**] — Fr. *mésoderme, feuillet moyen.*

mesial plane, see **medial plane.**

mesogastric = pert. to or located in the central region of the abdomen, below the epigastric region and above the pubic region.

mesognathous = designating a shape of skull which neither recedes greatly from the frontal plane of the jaw (prognathous) nor approaches to that plane (orthognathous). (Accent **-og-.**)

mesokurtic, see **kurtosis.**

metabolic gradients = gradations in the intensity of metabolic activity in organisms or their parts. [The rate of metabolic change often decreases in passing back from the head region in animals, and from the tip of the stem downward in plants.]

metabolism = 1. the energy exchanges in living organisms; 2. the sum of physical and chemical changes which take place in the body of a living organism. [Includes the constructive (anabolic) and destructive (catabolic) processes. Cf. **basal metabolism, catabolism; anabolism.**] (Accent **-tab-.**) **metabolic**[a]. — Ger. *Stoffwechsel.*

metacarpal = pert. to the bones of the hand above the fingers. — Ger. *Mittelhandknochen.*

metagenesis = the alternation of two distinct forms in successive generations of certain species. [Syn. **alternation of generations.**]

metagnomy = (*psych. res.*) the apparent acquisition of knowledge about things or thoughts which are normally inaccessible to the mind, the source of such knowledge being often ascribed to discarnate persons. [Distg. fr. **prosopopesis,** in which the discarnate personality is supposed to be merely personated by means of telepathy from the living. Syn. **clairvoyance, clairaudience,** but esp. **psychometrizing.**] **metagnomous**[a], **metagnome**[np], or **metagnomist**[np].

metakinesis = 1. a term suggested by Lloyd Morgan to designate the prototype of consciousness present in the lowest animal species; 2. (*cytol.*) the middle stage of mitosis, during which the chromosomes are grouped in the equatorial plate.

metallic = an assumed quality of gustatory sensation due to the contact of certain metals (especially brass) with the tongue. [Not regarded by recent authorities as an elementary taste quality.]

metallophonia = a form of **dysphonia** characterized by a metallic voice.

metamere = a segment of the animal body. [Syn. **somite.** Cf. **neuromere.**]

metamorphopsia = a mislocation of certain portions of the field of vision, due to a pathological displacement of the corresponding portions of the retina, and resulting in a distorted appearance of objects seen. [Rare term.]

metamorphosis = a radical and more or less abrupt change of form which occurs during the lifetime of certain animals and affects their general appearance, structure, behavior, and physiological processes. [E.g. the changes of an insect larva into the chrysalis and imago.]

metaphysics = 1. the branch of philosophy which treats of the ultimate nature of things; 2. philosophy in general. [Distg. (1) fr. **epistemology** or theory of knowledge, which treats of the nature and validity of knowledge.] **metaphysical**[a] (*pop.* syn. for **abstruse**).

metaplasm, see **teleplasm.**

metapsychics = the study of physical or psychical phenomena apparently dependent upon (*a*) an undetermined intelligence, (*b*) unknown but intelligent forces, (*c*) unknown powers latent in the human mind, or (*d*) subconscious or unconscious processes (Richet). [**objective metapsychics** deals with mechanical, physical, or chemical effects, such as **raps, levitation, apparitions; subjective metapsychics** deals with psychical or subjective phenomena, such as **telepathy, clairvoyance, presentiments,** which seem to manifest a mysterious faculty of **lucidity** or **cryptesthesia** or **metagnomy.** Syn., **cryptopsychism, parapsychics, parapsychology, psychic(al) research, psychic science.**] **metapsychic(al)**[a], **metapsychism** or **metapsychosis**[n] = the process, **metapsychist**[np].

metapsychology = a point of view in psychoanalysis which regards every mental process under three aspects, viz. the dynamic, topographical, and economic.

metapsychosis, see **metapsychics.**

metatarsal = pert. to the part of the foot between the heel and the toes.

metazoa = the general division which includes all many-celled animals. [A plural term; singular form **metazoön,** or more commonly **metazoan**[n].] **metazoan**[a].

metempirical = characterizing that which is not open to experimental or empirical verification; i.e. "whatever lies beyond the limits of possible experience" (Lewes). [Applied to concepts, etc. which are conceived as beyond, and yet related to, the knowledge gained by experience; syn. **transcendental.**]

metempsychosis = the theory of the transmigration of the soul after death into the body of some animal or of another person. (Accent **-emp-** and **-ko-.**)

metencephalon = 1. that part from which the medulla oblongata is developed (present usage); 2. that part of the embryonic brain from which the pons and cerebellum are developed (Huxley).

methectic = (*psych. res.*) characterizing communications between one stratum of a man's personality and another, as when he writes messages whose origin is the subconscious activity of his own mind. [Exhibited in **automatic writing** and the use of the **ouija board** and other **autoscopes.**]

method = 1. a systematic and general manner of working, especially in the endeavor to reach scientific truths; 2. a special manner of working in science. [Syn. (2) **procedure** (prefd.), restricting **method** to (1).]

methodeutic, see **methodology.**

methodical selection, see **artificial selection.**

methodology = the systematic investigation and formulation of the methods to be used in scientific research. [It may be regarded either as a branch of logic or as a technological counterpart of logic. Syn. **methodeutic.**]

metric[a] = 1. relating to measurement; 2. pert. to the standard of measurement based upon the meter.

metric[n] = a system or standard of measurement in terms of which the conclusions stated hold.

metric formula = the formulation, by Fechner, of **Weber's law,** in the equation $S = k \log R$, where S is sensation, R is stimulus, and k is constant for a given sense-modality. — Ger. *Maasformel.*

metric methods, see **psychophysical methods.**

metronome = an instrument for marking off short periods of time by sharp sounds; it consists of an inverted pendulum, which makes an audible stroke during each swing, and whose speed can be regulated within certain limits by raising or lowering a bob. [It is frequently equipped with electric contacts for graphic recording, and sometimes with a bell, which may be set to ring with every second, third, or other stroke.]

Meyer's experiment, Meyer's contrast pattern = a demonstration of visual contrast devised by H. Meyer, which consists in laying a small gray paper on a larger colored field and overlaying the whole with tissue paper; the complementary color is observed upon the gray area by contrast.

microcephaly = a pathological condition of human growth, characterized by exceptional smallness of the head and brain. **microcephalic**[a], **microcephalous**[a].

microcosm = 1. (*hist.*) a miniature universe, esp. a human being, regarded as an epitome or mirror of the universe; 2. the world of minute organisms revealed by the microscope. [Contr. (1) w. **macrocosm** = the **universe.**]

micromillimeter, see **micron.**

micron[n] = a unit of length largely used in microscopic measurements and in measurements of the wave-lengths of radiation, equal to one millionth of a meter, or one thousandth of a millimeter. [A **millimicron** ($m\mu$) or **micromillimeter** is one thousandth of a **micron.**]

micro-organism = a minute organism, either plant or animal. [A loose term, applied to protozoa, protophyta, etc., invisible (or nearly invisible) to the human eye.]

microphone = an instrument which transforms acoustic into electric power, with (ideally) no alteration in wave-form. [Two types are in common use. (*a*) **carbon-button** type: the air-vibrations, impinging on a thin metal diaphragm which bears on a cup filled with carbon granules, vary the resistance of the granules, and hence produce variations in an electric current that is passed through the granules; (*b*) **condenser** type: the diaphragm is placed very close to a back plate, and a high voltage is impressed on the condenser formed by the diaphragm and back plate; movements of the diaphragm produce alterations in the electrical system by varying the capacity of this condenser. Syn. **telephone transmitter.**]

microphonia = a form of **dysphonia** characterized by marked weakness of the voice.

micropsia = a decrease in the apparent size of objects seen, supposed to result from changes in the retinal end-organs.

microscope = an instrument with magnifying lenses, used for the observation of very small objects or details which are invisible or indistinct to the unaided human eye.

microscopic = that which is so small or fine as to be invisible to the naked eye.

microsplanchnic = characterizing a physique with low morphological index, so that the individual has a small trunk with long limbs (Naccarati). [Contr. w. **macrosplanchnic.** Cf. **asthenic** and **leptosome.**]

micturition = the discharge of urine from the bladder. [Syn. **urination.**] **micturate**[v].

midbrain = that part of the embryonic brain which lies beyond or cephalad to the cerebellum and behind the cerebrum, embracing the parts from which the crura, quadrigemina, and other middle ganglia develop. [Syn. **mesencephalon.**] — Fr. *cerveau moyen, mésencéphale*; Ger. *Mittelhirn.*

middle ear = the hollow section of the auditory receptor which lies between the external meatus and the labyrinth. [It is bounded peripherally by the ear-drum membrane or **membrana tympani,** and centrally by the walls of the **labyrinth** and the two membranous windows; it contains the three auditory bones (*hammer, anvil,* and *stirrup*), and is projected as the Eustachian tube into the mouth cavity.] — Fr. *oreille moyenne*; Ger. *Paukenhöhle, Mittelohr.*

midparent = the mean or average measure of the two parents in respect to any specific character. [Applied to man and subhuman species. In measuring human stature, a correction is made to allow for the different average height of males and females.] — Fr. *parent moyen.*

midperiod = the central period or portion of an experience, following the preparatory stage. [Cf. **foreperiod.**] — Fr. *période moyenne.*

midpoint = (*statist.*) the point half-way between the limits of a given interval or range.

midscore = the middle score in a series arranged in numerical order. — Fr. *point central, p. médian, note centrale, n. médiane.*

migraine, megrim = a pathological headache, often on only one side, characterized by nausea; 2. dullness, depression of spirits.

migration = 1. the seasonal displacement of certain animal species, stimulated by variations in climate or food supply, or by the mating impulse; 2. the permanent removal of a species to another habitat, due to scarcity of food, presence of enemies, etc. in their former environment. (1) **migratory**[a], (1, 2) **migrational**[a].

milieu = 1. the physical and social setting in which an organism is placed, including its surroundings and self; 2. the immediate social environment of an individual. [French. **setting** and **social setting** are available English equivalents.]

millilambert, see **lambert.**

millimicron, see **micron.**

Mill's canons = certain principles which aim to guide the use of induction, first explicitly formulated by J. S. Mill. [They consist of the principles of (1) **agreement,** (2) **difference,** (3) **joint agreement** and **difference,** (4) **residues,** and (5) **concomitant variation.**]

mimesis = (*esth.*) the theory that art is some sort of imitation.

mimetic response = a responsive act which is stimulated by some act of another creature, and which tends to resemble this act in character and form. [Syn. **mimicry;** cf. **mimetism.**]

mimetism = 1. the assumption by one creature of the color, shape, attitude, movements, etc. of another, serving as a protection against enemies or for concealment from prey; 2. the reproduction by one creature of some act by another, which serves as stimulus. [The term is preferably limited to (1), reproduction of a given stimulus being termed **mimicry** or **imitation.**] **mimetic**[a].

mimicry, see **mimetism** (2).

mind = 1. the sum total of those activities of an organism by means of which it responds as an integrated, dynamic system to external forces, (usually) in some relation to its own past and future; 2. the organized totality of conscious experience; 3. (*pop.*) syn. for **intellect.** [The term is used or interpreted by different writers with various shades of meaning. **mind** (1) is limited by some to responsive activity (behavior); for many others it includes conscious phenomena also; while for others it includes both conscious and unconscious or subconscious phenomena (e.g. in psychoanalysis, where mental processes are regarded as essentially unconscious, conscious processes being merely isolated parts of the entire psychic entity). **mind** (2) may be limited to conscious experiences and their assumed elements (introspective view), or it may include the intentional or telic implications of these experiences and their resulting motor activities.] **mental**[a], **psychic**[a] (sometimes used w. **mind** 2). — Fr. *esprit*; Ger. *Psyche, Geist, Seele.*

mind-blindness = inability to grasp the meaning of objects seen, attributed to separation of visual centers from the rest of the cortex. [Syn. **cortical blindness.**] — Fr. *cécité mentale, c. corticale*; Ger. *Seelenblindheit.*

mind-body problem = the problem of harmonizing or accounting for the relations of mind and body taken as entities. [Aristotle attempted to solve the problem as presented in Platonic dualism by a concrete functional view of organic life. In modern times the problem has presented difficulty because of the sharp dualism of the Cartesian system. Early solutions were the theories of **occasionalism** and **preestablished harmony.** More recent attempts are the **double-aspect theory, parallelism, epiphenomenalism, phenomenalism, immaterialism, interactionism.**] — Fr. *problème de l'esprit et du corps.*

mind-cure, see **mental healing.**

mind-dust theory = the view that atoms or particles of mind or mental substance exist extensively in the universe and are combined to form actual minds. [Syn. **composition theory.** Cf. **atomism/psychological.**] — Fr. *t. de l'atomisme mental.*

mind-reading = the interpretation by an individual or an animal of the ideas or unspoken commands of another individual from voluntary or involuntary signals given by the latter. [It is believed to depend upon the reception of slight motor indications through the special senses; when giver and receiver are in physical contact, it is sometimes called **muscle-reading;** when both the giving and the interpreting of the signals are unconscious, it is mistaken for **telepathy;** syn. **thought-reading.**] — Fr. *lecture de la pensée*; Ger. *Gedankenlesen.*

mind-set, see **mental set.**

mind-stuff theory = the view which interprets mind as formed by the combination of atoms or particles, which are held to be the same as those elements that appear to the observer as matter. [Syn. **monadism;** distg. fr. **composition theory,** which does not identify the mental and material elements.] — Fr. *t. de la matière mentale.*

mind-twist hypothesis = a functional (as distg. fr. a structural) interpretation of dementia praecox, schizophrenia, or parergastic reactions.

mind wandering = a loose term applied to states such as **reverie, day dreaming,** and **distraction.** — Fr. *rêverie*; Ger. *Phantasieren.*

miners' nystagmus, see **nystagmus.**

minimal, see **minimum.**

minimal change (or **changes)/method of** = a method of psychophysical investigation, in which the variable stimulus is varied, by a series of changes so minute as to be individually imperceptible to the observer, from a value definitely greater (or smaller) than the standard to a value definitely smaller (or greater). — Fr. *m. des moindres changements*; Ger. *M. der Minimaländerungen.*

minimal (or **minimum**) **essentials** = (*educ.*) those portions of the field covered by school topics which are considered absolutely essential, i.e. standards or requirements which are basic, and below which instruction or practice should not fall. — Fr. *minimum indispensable.*

minimum = (*math.*) the lowest value reached by a variable quantity which first decreases and then increases. [At a minimum the first derivative of the function is zero, and the second derivative positive.] **minima**^{pl}, **minimal**^{a} or **minimum**^{a}.

minimum (or **minimal**) **sensation** = a sensation which cannot be decreased in intensity without vanishing; i.e. the sensation evoked by a just perceptible stimulus. [Syn. **liminal sensation, threshold of sensation.**]

minor = lesser, smaller. [Lat. Mostly used as a technical designation; e.g. minor premise, scale. Contr. w. **major,** = greater.]

minor premise, see **premise.**

minor scale, see **scale** and Table VII. — Ger. *Molltonleiter.*

minor sixth, third, etc. (*mus.*), see **interval,** and Table VII.

minuscule = a small or lower-case letter, as distg. fr. **majuscule,** or capital.

minuthesis/visual = the process of reduction in any specific visual sensibility under the influence of the stimulus which arouses the visual process.

miosis, see **myosis.**

miotic^{n}, **myotic**^{n} = any drug or agent which causes contraction of the sphincter iridis muscle and diminution in size of the pupil. **miotic**^{a}, **myotic**^{a} = causing iris contraction. [Contr. w. **mydriatic.**]

miracle = (*hist.*) an event or effect contrary to the established constitution and sequence of events, believed to be performed by deities, or by men utilizing divine or magical powers.—Ger. *Wunder.*

mirror-drawing = a line drawing made by viewing a given design in a mirror and attempting to trace or reproduce it while the hand, pencil, and paper bearing the design are concealed from direct view. — Fr. *dessin en miroir*; Ger. *Spiegelzeichnung.*

mirror experiment = an experiment by Lambert (1760), in which two bits of color are observed, one through a pane of glass, the other by oblique reflection from the same glass, one appearing behind the other, or the two mixing, according to their relative distance from the pane.

mirror galvanometer, see **galvanometer.**

mirror-writing = 1. written or printed words in which the right-left relations are reversed, so that the writing appears in normal form when reflected in a mirror held at either side; 2. the act of writing in the reverse lateral direction, so that the script appears normal when reflected in a mirror held at the side. [Observed in children and in certain mental disorders; produced in normal adults most often by bimanual symmetrical writing movements. Syn. (1) **mirror-script.**] — Fr. *écriture en miroir*; Ger. *Spiegelschrift.*

miscegenation = the marriage or union of individuals belonging to different races (e.g. Caucasian and negro).

mischievousness = a disposition on the part of children to disarrange or destroy, with no anti-social aim. [Extended pop. to include various actions which cause discomfort to the adult.] **mischievous**^{a}, **mischief**^{n} = any specific instance.

misdemeanor = a minor infraction of legal enactments. — Fr. *délit, contravention*; Ger. *Vergehen.*

misogamy = a morbid dread of marriage.

misogynist = an individual who hates women.

mistuned forks = tuning forks which are intentionally tuned slightly above or below the pitch of a standard, for use in investigating pitch discrimination or differences of sensitivity between the ears. — Fr. *diapasons désaccordés.*

misunderstand = to interpret wrongly the meaning of spoken or written language or of any other sign, symbol, or act. **misunderstanding**^{a}. — Fr. *malentendu*^{n}, *méprise*; Ger. *missverstehen.*

mitosis = cell division which involves splitting of the chromosomes and various other preliminary transformations in the nucleus and the cytoplasm. [Syn. **karyokinesis, indirect cell division.**] — Fr. *mitose.*

mixed mode = a term used by Locke to characterize the combination of simple ideas of several kinds into one complex idea. [The **mixed mode** is a complex idea, such as a lie, which has existence for the mind but is not itself a substance: Locke's description makes it a combination of simple ideas.]

mixoscopia = excitement incident to the witnessing of a sexual act.

mixture = a mass of components in which every member retains its own individual characteristics. [Contr. w. **compound,** in which fusion occurs. Applied in psychology to certain combinations of sensations.] — Fr. *mélange*; Ger. *Mischung.*

mneme = the basis or basic principle of memory and habit. [Used by R. Semon to denote the general pervasiveness in nature of the stamping-in process or recording of the past.] **mnemic**^{a}.

mnemic, see **mneme,** and **memory.**

mnemic theory = the theory which interprets heredity as a form of memory.

mnemonic = pert. to memorizing.

mnemonics = the art of improving one's memory of certain facts or of facilitating recall by means of special devices, such as catch-words, formulas, etc.

mob = an incidental aggregation of individuals acting under high emotional conditions, often in an attempt to control the actions of those who oppose them, or to accomplish some illegal act. [Distg. fr. **crowd,** in which a common emotional element is lacking or is less violent.] — Ger. *Pöbelhaufen.*

mobile type = a type of temperament characterized by a flexibility in shifting from one type of task to another, and by a tendency to proceed rapidly in a task with less stress upon accuracy (Downey).

mobility = the capacity for movement or contraction. [Generally applied to muscles or systems of muscles. Distg. fr. **motility** = capacity to move about, as in locomotion.]

mobility/labor, see **stability/occupational.**

modal sensitivity, MS = 1. (*hist.*) the range of stimuli to which the organism is sensitive in respect to some sensory **modality,** e.g. 405 to 700 mμ in the case of visual line and light; 2. the number of sensations or **just noticeable differences** within this range, e.g. 128 hues.

modality = a separate sense or department of sense. [Helmholtz (1878) defined modality as a qualitative sensory continuum discrete from other sensory continua. Thus visual sensations form a single continuum or modality but warmth, cold, pressure, and pain, which are supposed to be discrete and without intermediate qualities, would form four distinct modalities. Cf. **mode/sensory.**]

mode = 1. (*psychol.*) any general class of characteristics or attributes of the data under investigation; 2. (*statist.*) the most common value in a given series; 3. (*soc.*) the manner of dress, living, or social intercourse prevalent in a given community. [Cf. (1) **mode/sensory.** A statistical curve is termed **multimodal** if there are several high points with troughs between, and **unimodal** if there is but a single maximum; if it is V-shaped, with a single minimum, it is termed antimodal. Syn. (3) **fashion.**] **modal**[a].

mode = 4. (*mus.*) the arrangement of tones and intervals within a given scale, which results when a certain note is taken as the tonic; e.g. the major and minor modes. [For discussion of the basic modes in Greek, ecclesiastical, and modern music, see Grove's Dictionary of Music and Musicians. Cf. **scale.**]

mode of appearance = (*vis.*) a class of properties of colors or other sensory phenomena, in addition to their primary attributes, which tend to have a spatial or temporal character. [The most common modes of appearance of color are: bulkiness, surface nature, film nature, luster, transparency and glow.] — Ger. *Erscheinungsweise.*

mode/sensory = a subdivision of the total group of sensory experiences, including those experiences which resemble one another more closely than they resemble experiences of other subdivisions. [The criteria for such resemblance are obscure; in general the term **sensory mode** is used as equivalent to a **sense;** e.g. vision, audition, etc. Cf. **modality.**] **modal**[a], **modality**[n].

model = an object or datum which is copied or may be copied. [Applied to static data, distg. fr. a movement or action to be imitated. Cf. **pattern.** Syn. **copy** (ambiguous).] **model**[a] = suitable for copying.

modesty = 1. an attitude or mild emotion characterized by self-effacement, or self-depreciation; 2. an attitude of conformity with social conventions as to concealment of the body or of bodily functions. [Contr. (1, 2) w. **immodesty.** Cf. **shame.**] **modest**[a]. — Ger. *Scham, Bescheidenheit.*

modifiable = subject to change. **modifiability**[n].

modification = 1. (*biol.*) a change in an organism due to environmental influences; 2. any alteration in the form of an action or scheme of procedure. [Contr. (1) w. **variation,** a change due to hereditary influences or occurring in the fertilized germ and heritable. (2) used technically in behavior and semitechnically in scientific procedure.] **modify**[v].

modiolus, see **cochlea.** [Accent **-dye-.**]

modulation = (*mus.*) the progression of a melody from one key to related keys.

modulus = a constant multiplier or parameter by means of which one set of numbers may be transformed into or related to another set. [E.g. the constant used for transforming logarithms to the base *e* into logs to the base 10; the constant (modulus of elasticity) which relates the tension applied to a wire and the resultant stretching. A **modulus** serves to convert a proportionality or equivalence (designated by $\propto$) into an equality (designated by =).

mogiarthria = defective speech in which the vocal muscles fail to coordinate properly due to lesions of the nervous system. [Syn. **ataxic speech.** A form of **dysarthria.**]

moiety, see **dual division.**

molar = 1. pert. to mass or masses; 2. of, pert. to, or containing a gram molecular weight or **mole.** [Contr. (1) w. **molecular, atomic,** etc. E.g. molar force.]

molecular layer, see **granular layer.**

molecule = a chemically unitary combination of atoms. [Cf. **mass, molar.**] **molecular**[a].

Mollusca, mollusks = a phylum of invertebrates characterized by unsegmented structure and as a rule by a hard shell; e.g. oyster, snail.

moment = 1. the measure of a force by its effect in producing rotary movement in a body; 2. an instant (or small interval) of time, in which some event occurs; 3. syn. for **importance.** — Ger. (2) *Augenblick.*

moment = 4. (*statist.*) the sum of the deviations from the mean (raised to some given power) in a distribution, divided by the size of the sample. Simple moments, i.e. $\Sigma x^m/N$ are those wherein N is the size of the sample, and *m* is the power to which deviations *x* are raised. [The order of the moment, 1st, 2d, etc. is indicated by the value of m, thus $\Sigma x/N$ = 1st moment, $\Sigma x^2/N$ = 2d moment, etc. When deviations are taken from the mean the common designation of the moments is that given in Table XV, C (Statistics). Product moments = $\Sigma x^m y^n \ldots\ldots z^p/N$. Herein two or more variables raised to the same or different powers are multiplied together before summation. The most common **product moment** is the **covariance.**]

moments/method of = a general method for fitting any desired theoretical curve to a particular observed distribution. [The curve-fitting consists in finding what parameter-values of the desired theoretical curve will yield the same **moments** (4) as the empirical distribution. The best fitting normal curve (e.g.) will have the same zero, first, and second moments as the observed distribution.]

momentum = the product of the mass of a moving body and its velocity. [The unit is one gram-centimeter per second.] — Fr. *moment*.

monad = 1. (*metaph.*) an individual, independent unit having the characteristics of both mind and matter. [A Pythagorean concept, revived by Giordano Bruno; adopted by Leibnitz as a means of overcoming both the dualism of Descartes and the monism of Spinoza. The world-view based on this conception is called **monadism;** distg. fr. **monism,** any world-view based upon a single type of unit.]

monad = 2. (*biol.*) a small flagellate protozoan which has a single flagellum.

monaural (or **uniaural**) **hearing** = hearing with one ear alone. [Contr. w. **binaural** = with the two ears conjointly; the form **monaural** is etymologically incorrect.] — Fr. *audition monauriculaire*; Ger. *einohriges Hören*.

mongolian = the name given by Langdon Down to certain aments because of the fancied presence of Mongolian facial characteristics. **mongolism**[n], **mongolian**[a].

monism = 1. the theory that ultimate reality is qualitatively of one sort; 2. syn. for **singularism;** 3. (*epist.*) the theory that absolute reality is presented immediately in conscious experience. [Contr. w. **dualism** and **pluralism.**] **monistic**[a], **monist**[np].

monition = (*psych. res.*) an alleged revelation of some past or present event by other than the normal senses. [A form of **cryptesthesia.** Cf. **metagnomy.**]

monkey = a term commonly used to designate the common smaller primates. — Fr. *singe*; Ger. *Affe*.

monochord = a one-stringed instrument, with a scale of division into parts, used for testing hearing and musical ability. [Cf. **sonometer.**]

monochorial twins, see **twins.**

monochromatism, monochromatic vision, see **achromatism.**

monocular (or **uniocular**) **vision** = vision with one eye alone. [Contr. w. **binocular vision** = w. both eyes acting conjointly. The form **monocular** is more frequently used, but is etymologically incorrect.] — Fr. *vision monoculaire*; Ger. *einäugiges Sehen*.

monoecious = 1. (*zool.*) having both sexes in one individual; 2. (*bot.*) having stamens and pistils on different flowers of the same plant. [Syn. (1) **hermaphroditic.**]

monogamy = the durable pairing or mating of two individuals of opposite sex. [Distg. fr. **polygamy** = durable mating with several members of opposite sex, and fr. **promiscuity** = absence of durable sex relations.] **monogamous**[a].

monogenism = the theory that the various human races developed from a single ancestral human stock. **monogenist**[np].

monoglottic = a term applied by Henning to gustatory stimulation acting upon a small area of the tongue. [Cf. **dichoglottic, diglottic.**]

monogony = asexual reproduction.

monograph = an exhaustive treatise or report on a single specific (i.e. subordinate) topic.

monoideism = (*hist.*) a pathological condition characterized by a tendency on the part of an individual to revert constantly, in thought and talk, to some one subject of action. [Cf. **fixed idea, monomania.**] — Fr. *idée fixe, monoidéisme*.

monomania = a mental disorder characterized by dominating or fixed ideas, in the presence of an otherwise integrated personality. [No longer used technically. Syn. **paranoia.**]

monomuscular reflex = motor response of a single muscle, elicited by stimulating its proprioceptors, or in some cases by a cutaneous stimulus.

monoplegia = paralysis confined to a single member of the body. [Cf. **hemiplegia.**] **monoplegic**[a].

monorhinic = a term used by Henning to characterize smelling with one nostril only. [Cf. **dirhinic, dichorhinic.**]

monotone = continuous sameness of pitch during speaking.

monotonic = (*math.*) descriptive of a curve which is continually rising or continually falling, so that each of two variables is a single-valued function of the other.

monotony = 1. lack of inflection or cadence in speaking or singing; 2. continuance of an uninteresting situation without change, resulting in boredom. **monotonous**[a].

monotreme = a primitive egg-laying mammal which has a single opening for the urogenital system and alimentary canal. [The best known representatives are the duckbilled platypus (Ornithorhynchus) and the spiny ant-eater (Echidna), both Australian.]

monotypic evolution = the development of a group in any direction without the formation of divergent lines of development. [Distg. fr. **polytypic evolution,** which involves the formation of diverging groups.]

monozygotic twins, see **twins.**

monster = an organism which diverges greatly from the normal of the species. [Distg. fr. **sport** = slight deviation, and fr. **malformation,** confined to a single part.] **teratological**[a].

mood = an enduring, but not permanent emotional attitude. [Distg. fr. **temperament,** a more permanent attitude.] — Fr. *humeur*; Ger. *Stimmung*.

moon-blindness = 1. syn. for **night-blindness;** 2. (*pop.*) **amblyopia,** said to result from sleeping in the moonlight in the tropics. — Fr. *cécité crépusculaire*.

moon-illusion = an illusion of visual magnitude, in which the moon appears larger on the horizon than at the zenith. — Fr. *illusion de la lune à l'horizon*.

moral = 1. pert. to morality; 2. characterizing conduct which is called good or right, i.e. which conforms to standards accepted throughout the group in which the individual lives, and which are usually believed to be based upon some sanction more absolute and authoritative than the will of individuals. [Originally corresponding to custom (mores). Contr. (2) w. **amoral** and w. **immoral.**]

moral faculty = (*hist.*) the mental power or capacity to distinguish between right and wrong, or to evaluate specific acts as right or wrong.

moral imbecile = a mentally defective individual with pronounced criminal tendencies. [Obsolescent.] **moral imbecility**[n].

moral insanity = (*hist.*) a term used to designate

a supposed symptom-complex marked by an impairment of moral values. — Fr. *folie morale.*

moral judgment = a judgment concerned with distinctions between right and wrong, or with evaluating specific acts as right or wrong.

moral science, see **ethics.**

moral sense = the capacity to distinguish between right and wrong conduct and to evaluate each.

morale = the individual (or more generally the group) attitude in respect to confidence, perseverance in work, and adherence to ideals. [Usually implying a high degree of perseverance. Syn. **esprit de corps** (as group attitude).] (Accent **-ral.**)

morality = conduct of the individual which conforms to the standards set by the community, particularly those standards which deal with right and wrong. [Often believed to rest upon a more absolute authority than mere convention, an authority such as the public conscience, the categorical imperative, natural or divine law, etc. Distg. fr. **ethics** = science of morality.] **moral**[a] (distg. fr. **ethical**[a] in the same way, though the two are often confused).

morals = 1. personal or social standards of behavior regarding the rightness or wrongness of acts of conduct; 2. the appraisal of the behavior of an individual as measured by standards of right and wrong commonly accepted in the group in which he lives. [Distg. fr. **morality,** the abstract character, and **ethics,** the systematic investigation of morality.]

morbid = pert. to or attending an abnormal or diseased condition. [In psychol. generally confined to tendencies suggestive or productive of disease, and characteristic ideas or behavior attending them; distg. fr. **pathological,** a more general term.] **morbidity**[n] = frequency of disease; **morbidness**[n] = the condition itself. — Ger. *krankhaft, ungesund.*

mores[pl] = customs which a social group regards as the only right ones and as vital to the welfare of the group (e.g. monogamy among Christians). [Cf. **folkways.**] (2 syll.) **mos**[sing] (rare).

Morgan's (or **Lloyd Morgan's**) **canon** = a canon or maxim for the evaluation of data in animal psychology, formulated by Lloyd Morgan, which states that an act of behavior may not be interpreted as due to the operation of a higher mental faculty or function if it can be interpreted as the outcome of one which stands lower in the psychological scale. [Cf. **economy/principle of.**]

moron = an individual who manifests the highest grade of feeblemindedness, i.e. who most nearly approaches the normal. [Generally limited to those who maintain throughout adult life a mental age of approximately from 8 to 12 years (Goddard), or an intelligence quotient ranging approximately from 51 to 70 (Terman). Cf. **feeblemindedness.**] **moronity** (or **morosis**)[n], **moronic**[a]. — Fr. *arriéré simple, débile simple.*

morphin = the principal alkaloid of opium, $C_{17}H_{19}NO_3$. [It is an analgesic, hypnotic in cases of pain, and narcotic.]

morphinism = addiction to the use of morphin.

morphogenesis = the development of form or structure in organs or organisms.

morphological index = (*anat.*) a quotient obtained by dividing the volume of the trunk by the length of the limbs (Naccarati).

morphology = the branch of biology concerned with the structure of organisms. [Syn. **anatomy.**] **morphologic(al)**[a].

mosaic eye = a compound eye which contains numerous ommatidia (distinct units) so arranged as to result in a mosaic pattern of vision. [Cf. **compound eye.**] — Fr. *oeil en mosaïque.*

Mosso balance, see **balance/Mosso.**

mother complex (or **fixation**), see **Edipus complex.**

mother instinct, see **maternal behavior.**

motile[a] = characterizing organisms which are capable of moving from place to place. [Contr. w. **sessile** = fixed in location; distg. fr. **mobile** = capable of axial movement (e.g. the arm, eye, etc.).]

motile[n], **motor type** = a class of individuals in whom kinesthetic experiences and ideas predominate. [Cf. **type/mental.**]

motility = 1. capacity to make complex and coordinated movements; 2. capacity to move from place to place; 3. (*ind. differences*) the style and speed which characterize an individual's habits of movement. [Cf. **mobility.**]

motion = continuous change of position. [Cf. **movement.**] — Fr. *mouvement*; Ger. *Bewegung.*

motion/illusion of = a mental experience in which a motionless object appears to move. [Often a question of relative motion, e.g. setting sun, moon among the clouds, one train as seen from another; sometimes due to the after-effect of continuously perceived motion, as in the **waterfall illusion,** apparent motion of the road in front when one's motor car stops, etc. Cf. **phi-phenomenon.**]

motion picture = a series of photographic (or other) views of a changing scene, presented in rapid succession, so that the objects, persons, etc. in the scene appear to be moving. [Cf. **cinematograph.** Syn. (*pop.*) **moving picture, movie.**] — Fr. *cinéma*; Ger. *Kinematograph.*

motion study = (*industrial*) the systematic observation of workers engaged in a repetitive task, to determine the nature and sequence of each element of the cycle of movements made, in order to eliminate unnecessary movements and establish the best sequence, thus reducing fatigue while increasing output. [The usual technique involves moving pictures or continuous photographs with a small lamp attached to the moving member under consideration.]

motivate = to serve as an incentive or to provide an incentive for an act. [E.g. hunger motivates the act of eating.] **motivation**[n].

motivation = 1. the application of incentives to individuals from whom activity is desired; 2. the investigation of motives and incentives.

motive = a conscious experience or subconscious condition which serves as a factor in determining an individual's behavior or social conduct in a given situation. — Fr. *motif*; Ger. *Triebfeder, Motiv.*

motive/ethical = 1. a situation in the behavior of an individual in which the choice of a given act is characteristically accompanied by considerations of right and wrong, so that the act performed is that which the individual judges to be right; 2. an inner force or principle assumed to determine the choice of an individual's conduct according to ethical standards or considerations of right and wrong.

motoneuron = a motor neuron; i.e. a nerve cell which is in direct connection with an effector and exercises an excitatory or inhibitory influence upon it.

motor = pert. to movement or to the mechanism or consciousness of movement. [Cf. **movement.**]

motor activity = 1. syn. for **movement;** 2. bodily activity involving muscular processes; 3. muscular and glandular activity. [(3) is not contr. w. vegetative or visceral processes, but includes these.]

motor amusia, — aphasia, see **amusia, aphasia.**

motor area = the ascending frontal or pre-rolandic convolution and (less directly) the ascending parietal or post-rolandic convolution of the cerebral cortex. [A projection area within which electrical stimulation of any point elicits contraction of some definite skeletal muscle or circumscribed group of muscles. This correlation between individual muscles and points of the motor area is the best attested evidence in support of the brain **localization theory.**] — Fr. *aire motrice*; Ger. *motorisches Zentrum.*

motor experience, motor consciousness = the organized information or data received by an individual concerning his own bodily movements or attitudes.

motor function = a generic term embracing centrifugal or efferent neural processes and the end-organ activities excited thereby. [Contr. w. **sensory function** = afferent processes and their excitation.]

motor habit = training of the response mechanism so as to develop many varieties of behavior and to increase the precision and speed of performance. [Contr. w. **sensory habit** = training of discrimination between stimuli; but the differentiation is usually not easy in practice, and appears superficial.] — Fr. *habitude motrice.*

motor incoordination, see **incoordination/motor.**

motor learning = learning in which bodily movements are conspicuous. [For practical purposes, this type of learning, which results in better execution, is distg. fr. **ideational learning** or **insight,** which may give a correct idea without facility of performance.] — Fr. *apprentissage moteur.*

motor nerve = a nerve which conveys impulses from any center toward the periphery. [Syn. **efferent nerve.** Contr. w. **sensory nerve,** which conveys impulses toward the centers.]

motor organ = 1. a muscle or contractile tissue which receives nerve impulses, and whose contractions or relaxations from these excitations constitute responses of the organism; 2. syn. for **effector.**

motor point, see **neuromuscular junction.**

motor reflex = 1. (*zool.*) a stereotyped mode of response found in primitive forms such as the Protozoa; 2. a direct muscular response to stimulation which occurs through the mediation of the central nervous system. [In Paramecium (1) consists in swimming backward by a reversal of the ciliary beat, and turning to the aboral side; (2) contr. w. **glandular** and other types.]

motor (or **muscular**) **response type,** see **response type.**

motor sense = a sense dependent on receptors embedded in the deeper tissues of movable parts, which is stimulated by tension or movement of the parts, and furnishes data concerning the creature's bodily movements and the positions of its members. [The receptors of these senses are termed *proprioceptors.* Sometimes extended to include the **static sense.** Cf. **kinesthesia.**]

motor skills, see **proficiencies.**

motorium = the cortical and subcortical centers directly concerned with the innervation, through efferent nerves, of striped muscle. [Contr. w. **sensorium.**]

mouth-writing = writing produced by holding the writing implement between the teeth and moving it with the help of the tongue. [Cf. **foot-writing.**] — Fr. *écriture buccale.*

movement = 1. change in position of some member of the body, usually through muscular contraction; 2. change in position of an object; i.e. physical motion. [**movement** (1) is classed as (*a*) **active** = bodily change resulting entirely from efferent innervation and contraction of muscles affecting the parts moved, and (*b*) **passive** = bodily change or resting of limp members resulting from external physical displacement; the kinesthesis of passive movement is more poorly discriminated than that of active movement. In psychol. it is preferable to confine the term to (1); distg. fr. **motion** = physical displacement.] **move**[v].

movement/illusion of = an experience involving motor sensations from a non-moving member. [Sometimes applied also to the apparent (illusory) motion of objects, etc.; cf. **apparent (motion** or) **movement.**]

movement/random, see **random movements.**

movements/spontaneous, see **spontaneous movements.**

moving average method = (*statist.*) a method of smoothing a series, in which the frequencies in successive classes of items are replaced by arithmetic averages of a number of neighboring classes. — Fr. *m. de polissage.*

mucous membrane = (*anat.*) a layer of soft tissue which secretes slimy substance. — Ger. *Schleimhaut.*

Müller's circle = a circle which passes through the fixation point and nodal points of the two eyes, and which lies in the plane of regard when the eyes are in the primary position of convergence. [Cf. **horopter,** of which this circle forms part.]

Müller-Lyer illusion = an illusion of visual space perception, in which two physically equal distances appear unequal, due to the partial enclosure of one distance and an apparent widening of the other by lines, arrow-heads, etc.

Müller-Lyer rectangles = an illusion of the comparative extent of two rectangular areas partially enclosed, in the one case by the neighboring sides of two squares, and in the other case by the neighboring sides of two rectangles of the same length as the dimensions of the square and separated by the same distance as are the squares.

multicellular = consisting of many cells. [Distg. fr. **unicellular** = one-celled.]

multicellular organisms, see **metazoa.**

multi-individual behavior = the approximately simultaneous (though not necessarily similar) reactions of a considerable number of individuals in the same situation or circumstances. [Cf. **pluralistic behavior.**]

multimodal theory of intelligence = the view that intelligence is a pattern of an indefinite number of specific capacities (Thorndike). [Contr. w. **two-factor theory** (Spearman).]

multimodality = (*statist.*) that characteristic of a frequency distribution which results from its having several modes or peaks. [Cf. **mode** (2).] **multimodal**[a].

multiple choice method = a procedure employed in investigations on motor learning, in which two or more alternative modes of response, equally available, are presented simultaneously, only one of which leads to the actual goal or end-result designed by the experimenter. [Distg. fr. **delayed reaction method,** in that no cue indicating the correct response is given by the experimenter. Sometimes used in investigations of reasoning capacity.]

multiple choice test = a type of test in which a test item or problem is presented to the testee, with two or more alternative responses, only one of which is correct, the task being to designate the correct response. [Includes yes-no, true-false, right-wrong types, but oftener applied to use of three to five (or more) responses. E.g. tests 7 and 8 of Army Alpha. Syn. **alternative response test.**]

multiple correlation, see **correlation.**

multiple personality, see **personality/multiple.**

multiple sclerosis = a disease marked by sclerosis or hardening of various spots in the brain and cord, and characterized by motor incoordination, hallucination, etc. — Fr. *sclérose en plaques.*

multiplicity = that which is made up of many diverse elements, or the characteristic of being so composed.

multipolar cell = a nerve cell which has several processes, i.e. projections. [Distg. fr. **unipolar** and **bipolar cell.**]

multivalence = the normal (freer) functioning of evaluations and interests concerning any object, as contr. w. conflicts. [Cf. **ambivalence.**]

Munsell colors = a group of samples of colored surfaces associated with symbols, according to a system of notation by which colors of every hue, saturation, and brilliance are systematically designated by appropriate combinations of letters and numerals. [So called from the designer of the system. Cf. **Ridgway colors,** similar in general character.]

muscae volitantes[pl] = a type of entoptic phenomenon, due to the presence of small foreign particles in the lymph between the vitreous humor and the retina of the eye. [They float about and change their form, being thereby distinguished from imperfections in the lens, which do not change, and from the darting blood corpuscles visible under certain conditions. Lat. "flying flies." Cf. **entoptic phenomena.**] — Fr. *mouches volantes.*

muscarin = the alkaloid of one of the poisonous mushrooms, amanita muscaria. [Closely related chemically to choline. It stimulates glandular secretions and contracts the pupil.]

muscle = a structure composed of many fibers of contractile tissue, the combined contraction of which, due normally to neural excitation, produces gross movement of the structure. [Cf. **antagonists, musculature/skeletal, smooth muscle, striate muscle.**] — Ger. *Muskel.*

muscle-balance = 1. the tendency of either eye to remain in the position of fixation, when fusion of the images is prevented, e.g. by covering this eye alone; 2. the degree to which the eyes fulfill or fail to fulfill this test. [Cf. **imbalance/muscular.**]

muscle erotism = (*psychoan.*) sexual excitation or pleasure produced by muscular activity.

muscle imbalance, see **imbalance/muscular.**

muscle-nerve junction, see **neuromuscular junction.**

muscle reading = the interpretation by one person (the percipient) of ideas or willed commands in the mind of another person (the agent) from involuntary muscular signals given by the latter and received by the former through physical contact. [A form of **mind-reading.**] — Fr. *lecture de la pensée par les muscles.*

muscle (or **muscular**) **sensation, muscle sense,** see **kinesthesia.** — Ger. *Muskelsinn.*

muscle spindles = a specialized end-organ in muscle consisting of a modified muscle fiber surrounded by an encapsulated sensory nerve ending of complex structure and lying in parallel with the active fibers. [They respond to passive stretch.] — Fr. *fuseaux musculaires*

muscle tonus = a state of partial contraction reflexly maintained which keeps the muscles taut and thus prevents slack, especially in the maintenance of the various postural reflexes. [Syn. **muscle tone, tonicity.**]

muscular = pert. to muscle.

muscular atonicity, atrophy, etc., see **atonicity, atrophy,** etc.

muscular incoordination, see **incoordination/motor.**

muscular reaction type, see **reaction type.**

muscular reflex = 1. the reflex contraction of a muscle when it is stretched; 2. the operation of a reflex arc which results in contraction of a muscle, as contr. w. glandular secretion, etc. [Syn. (1) **myotatic** or **stretch reflex.**]

muscular (or **motor**) **response** = a response in which the subject's attention during the foreperiod is directed toward making (or muscularly preparing for) the response, rather than toward the stimulus. [Syn. **muscular** (or **motor**) **reaction.** Distg. fr. **sensory** and fr. **natural response** (or **reaction**). Usually applied to the **reaction-time experiment.** Cf. **compound reaction.**]

muscular rigidity, see **tetanus, rigidity/muscular.**

muscular twitching = spasmodic involuntary contractions of muscle. — Fr. *contraction musculaire spasmodique.*

musculature/skeletal = those contractile tissues of the body innervated by somatic nerves which are under control of the central nervous system and are responsible for all external movements of the animal body in space. [The individual contractile fibers are characterized histologically by crossed striations. Cf. **smooth muscle, striate muscle.**]

musculature/smooth, see **smooth muscle.**

music = the branch of esthetics which investigates the principles of pleasing or expressive tonal combinations and sequences. [It includes **melody** and **harmony.**] **musical**[a] = pert. to music or characterizing pleasing tonal effects.

music deafness, see **tone-deafness.**

musical scale, see **scale/tonal.**

musical tone, see **tone** (1).

musk = the dried secretion from the preputial follicles of Moschus moschiferus, characterized by a strong and persistent odor. — Ger. *Moschus, Bisam.*

mutation = 1. (*biol.*) a suddenly appearing variation which is transmitted to the offspring; 2. the act of producing sudden heritable variations. [Formerly the term connoted a variation of considerable magnitude sufficient to produce a new variety or even species; it is now recognized that there is no essential difference between large hereditary variations and those which are barely detectible. Syn. **saltation;** cf. **variation.**] — Fr. *mutation, saut.*

mutilation = (*anthrop.*) the cutting, amputating, scarifying, and incising of the body common among primitive peoples, including incision, circumcision, and excision. [Usually distg. fr. (intentional) **deformation,** e.g. head-flattening.] — Ger. *Verstümmelung.*

mutism, mutitas = lack of development of the speech function. [Usually associated w. **deafness.** Syn. **dumbness.** Contr. w. **aphasis** = disturbance of speech function due to structural defect or injury.] **mute**[a]; **mute**[np]. — Ger. *Stummheit.*

m.v. = abbrev. for **mean variation.**

mydriasis = 1. extreme dilatation of the pupil of the eye; 2. abnormal dilatation of the pupil due to disease or to the effect of a drug such as atropin. [Contr. w. **myosis.**] (Accent **-rye-.**) **mydriatic**[a].

mydriatic[n] = a drug which causes enlargement of the pupil and also relaxation of the ciliary muscle. [Contr. w. **miotic.**] **mydriasis**[n] = the result.

myelencephalon = 1. the cerebrospinal system; 2. (*embryol.*) that portion of the medulla oblongata lying caudad to the pons and cerebellum. [Syn. (2) **after-brain.**] — Ger. *Nachhirn.*

myelin, myelin sheath = the white covering formed by the substance of Schwann, which envelops the medullated (or myelinated) nerve fibers. — Fr. *gaine myélinique, g. médullaire;* Ger. *Markscheide.*

myelinated, see **medullated.**

myelinization, myelination = the formation of the myelin sheath. [Syn. **medullation.**]

myelitis = an inflammatory condition of the spinal cord.

myelon, see **spinal cord.**

myenteric reflex = a contraction above and relaxation below a stimulated portion of the intestine. [Similar to **peristalsis.**]

myogenic, myogenetic = originating in the muscular tissue.

myograph = an instrument for measuring either the extent, force, and duration of isotonic muscular contraction, or the tension and duration of isometric contraction; commonly it consists of a pivoted recording lever of the third class, operated by the given muscle, and with its free pointed end making a kymographic or photographic amplified tracing of the muscle movement, i.e. a **myogram.** [Measurements of *isotonic* contraction are made by having the muscle contract against a relatively small constant resistance, such as that of a mass suspended from the lever; *isometric* measurements are made by making the muscle act against a strong spring which permits of but slight change in muscle length.]

myology = the branch of anatomy which deals with muscles.

myoneural junction, see **neuromuscular junction.**

myopia = a refractive defect of certain eyes, such that, with relaxed accommodation of the lens, parallel rays of light are brought to a focus before they reach the retina. [Syn. **near-sight (edness).** Contr. w. **hypermetropia (hyperopia),** in which the rays focus behind the retina.] **myopic**[a]. — Ger. *Kurzsichtigkeit.*

myosis, miosis = 1. (*ophthal.*) extreme contraction of the pupil; 2. abnormal contraction of the pupil due to disease or to the effect of drugs such as morphin or eserin. [Contr. w. **mydriasis.**] **myotic**[a], **miotic**[a].

myotatic reflex = reflex contraction of a muscle produced by suddenly stretching it longitudinally. [The proprioceptive organs stimulated by this tension, and responsible for the reflex contraction, are believed to lie in the muscle fibers themselves, not in the tendon. Syn. **stretch reflex, muscular reflex.**]

myotomy = experimental or operative separating of muscles one from another. [Syn. **dissection of muscles.**]

myrmecophily, myrmecophilism = relations to the ants of their numerous guests and parasites, and of the plants frequented by ants (W. M. Wheeler).

mysophobia = morbid fear of dirt or contamination. [Manifested by constant washing of hands, etc. It may be a symptom of the compulsion neurosis.]

mysterious = 1. unexplained and puzzling; 2. (*pop.*) secret and known only to the initiated. [The word has generally an emotional tinge, which is lacking in the synonyms **unknown, unexplained.** Cf. **magic.**] **mystery**[n]. — Ger. *geheimnisvoll.*

mysticism = 1. the doctrine that ultimate reality is revealed through a special mode of knowledge, which is distinct from perceptual and ideational cognition and is superior to them; 2. (*pop.*) the view that certain events are supernatural, i.e. that they occur in violation of the known or knowable principles of the workings of nature. [Syn. (2) **occultism.** Cf. **magic.**] **mystic(al)**[a], **mystic**[np].

myth = 1. (*anthrop.*) a tradition without actual historical basis; 2. an accepted theory, etc. in the realm of science, which is demonstrably false. [Cf. **magic.** Contr. (1) w. **legend,** which has a historical basis.] **mythical**[a]. — Ger. *Mythos, Heldensage.*

mythology = (*anthrop.*) a body of more or less fixed narratives embodying beliefs and accounts relative to the supernatural, including the exploits of gods, magicians, and culture heroes, as well as the assumed supernatural experiences of historical individuals. [It embraces a large part of the unwritten literature of a people. Cf. **folklore.**]

mythomania = 1. a tendency to exaggerate and report imaginary adventures; 2. (*psych. res.*) the process by which a subject in a state of trance or hypnosis personates a character as a result of suggestion; i.e. the utilization, in personation, of a vaster store of memories and of feelings than are available to the subject in ordinary conscious life. [Syn. (2) **induced prosopopesis.**]

myxedema, myxoedema = a disease characterized by a decreased functioning of the thyroid gland, possibly through atrophy of the gland, resulting in an increase in adipose tissue, with thickening and serous infiltration of the skin, and usually accompanied by mental deficiency.

N

nadir = 1. the point or location directly beneath the observer; 2. the lowest point in a given system of phenomena. [Contr. w. **zenith.**]

naive = 1. characterizing an unreflective, child-like attitude toward the problems of society and life; 2. indicating a fresh and unbiased approach to scientific problems. [The masc. form **naif** is not often used in English.] (Pron. **nah-eve.**) **naiveness**[n], **naiveté**[n], **naively**[adv].

name = a verbal expression associated symbolically with a person, object, event, or other phenomenon, or with a relation, etc. such that when used it suggests this datum. [Primarily a spoken word (auditory stimulus); transferred to written words (visual); applicable also to gestures, touch forms, etc. used by the deaf or others.] **nominal**[a] (used more broadly). — Fr. *nom.*

Nancy school = the school of hypnosis founded by H. Bernheim at Nancy, France, in 1882, which held in general that hypnosis is a normal phenomenon induced by suggestion. [Based on the views of J. Braid and A. A. Liébeault, and opposed to J. M. Charcot's school of La Salpêtrière, which associated hypnosis with the pathology of hysteria.]

nanism = abnormal smallness of size supposedly due in certain instances to disturbances of certain endocrine glands. [Syn. **dwarfism.** It is due to various causes. **pituitary nanism** = a type related to hypofunction of certain elements of the anterior lobe of the pituitary body. Cf. **gigantism.**]

napier, see **neper.**

narcissism = 1. syn. for **self-love;** 2. (*psychoan.*) the persistence of an early stage of psychosexual development, in which the sexual object, or love-object, remains the self. [From the myth of Narcissus. Syn. **narcism,** etymologically incorrect. An important factor in the psychoanalytic theory of homosexuality.] **narcissistic**[a].

narcissistic type = (*psychoan.*) a psychological type in which the chief interest is focused on self-preservation (Freud).

narcolepsy = an uncontrollable desire for sleep, manifested at intervals.

narcosis = 1. (in general) a physiological condition in which the normal responsiveness or automatic activity of a living system — organism, tissue, or cell — is temporarily decreased or obliterated; 2. (more specifically) a state of stupor produced by certain drugs or poisons in higher animals, which passes into insensibility and motor paralysis. **narcoses**[pl]. — Ger. *Narkose.*

narcotic[n] = a drug which induces narcosis, a condition of stupor, diminished sensitivity to pain, motor paralysis, and a tendency toward sleep.

nares[pl] = the nasal passages. [Syn. **nostrils.**] (2 syll.) **naris**[sing]. — Ger. *Nasenlöcher.*

narrative method = method of obtaining testimony (or an account of events) by allowing the observer to relate the facts in his own way without interrupting him with hints or suggestions.

nasal = pert. to or located on or in the nose. (Accent **nay-.**)

nasal cavities = the two chambers, right and left, above the roof of the mouth, which contain the olfactory receptors and through which the breathing current passes from the exterior nose to the pharynx. [Syn. **nasal fossae.**]

nasal reflex = sneezing elicited by irritation of the mucous membrane of the nose. [Mediated by V cranial (sensory) and 4th cervical nerves.]

nascent = in the earliest stages of development. [Applied to structural growth of cells and organs, to growth of functions, and to unfolding of ideas, movements, etc. Distg. fr. syn. **incipient,** which implies possibility of a check in development, and **implicit,** which applies to movements, and denotes an actual check.] **nascence**[n], **arise**[v]. — Fr. *naissant.*

nasomental reflex = contraction of the mentalis muscle with elevation of point of chin elicited by a blow on side of nose. [Mediated by the trigeminofacial arc.]

nasopharynx, see **pharynx.**

nation = a collection of people, usually large and occupying a common territory and possessing a fairly uniform culture, who, in their sentiments and behavior, express loyalty to a common national symbol.

National Intelligence Tests = two batteries of tests, Scale A and Scale B, each consisting of five sub-tests and made up in five comparable forms, devised in 1919 under the auspices of the National Research Council by Haggerty, Terman, Thorndike, Whipple, and Yerkes. [Scale A includes arithmetical reasoning, sentence completion, logical selection, same-opposite, and symbol-digit tests; Scale B includes computation, information, vocabulary, analogies, and comparison tests. Both scales are standardized for use in school grades III to VIII.]

native = present in the individual at birth. [Syn. **inborn.** Generally used to characterize inherited or congenital structure and functions; strictly it should include transmitted disease germs, etc. which are not part of the biological inheritance. Cf. **nativism.**] — Fr. *inné;* Ger. *angeboren.*

native endowment = the sum-total of an organism's inherited capacities for response and mental functioning. [Contr. w. **acquisition through experience.** Cf. **native trait.**]

native trait = 1. any capacity or structural characteristic which is inherited; 2. a characteristic conditioned in part by pre-natal environment, esp. by the organic environment of the embryo and of the germ plasm. [Contr. w. **acquired trait.** The sum-total of native traits is called **native endowment.**] — Fr. *don inné, trait inné.*

nativism = a term introduced by Helmholtz to designate the historical view that certain elements or factors in human knowledge are inherited and are consequently present in the individual independent of stimulation and experience. [Cf. **innate ideas.** Contr. w. **empiricism,** which attributes all knowledge to experience.]

natural[a] = a loose adjective, signifying formed by nature, pert. to nature (e.g. natural science), as found in nature, as would be expected apart from training, unconstrained, etc. [Technically contr. w. (*a*) **artificial** = produced by human agency, (*b*) **acquired,** (*c*) **constrained,** and (*d*) **unnatural** = (assumed to) violate the basic functions of the (human) species. Cf. **nature.**]

natural[n] = (*mus.*) a tone which has neither a flat nor a sharp for its signature. [Cf. **flat, sharp.**]

natural law = 1. a general statement of the principles according to which the phenomena of the universe proceed, with special reference to their interrelations; 2. any sanction of social behavior based on established custom, divine sanction, etc. rather than on legislative enactment. Syn. **law of nature.** Contr. (1) w. **human law,** (2) w. **positive law.**] — Fr. *l. naturelle*; Ger. *Naturgesetz.*

natural philosophy = (*hist.*) syn. for the **natural sciences,** more particularly physics, chemistry, and astronomy. [Distg. (*hist.*) fr. **mental philosophy** = psychology.]

natural or **mixed reaction** (or **response**) = a response in which the subject's attention is left undetermined in the fore-period, and which tends to vary between the **sensory reaction** and the **muscular reaction.**

natural scale = a scale of just intonation. [E.g. the major diatonic scale. Cf. **just intonation, scale.**]

natural sciences = the branches which investigate the phenomena of nature and formulate the principles according to which they occur. [Syn. **sciences of nature, nature sciences, science** (ambig.). Originally contr. w. **mental science** and w. **normative sciences** (logic, ethics) as well as w. **metaphysics.** Today contr. chiefly w. **social sciences.** A term of doubtful value, owing to its ambiguities.] — Ger. *Naturwissenschaften, Naturforschung.*

natural selection = the elimination of those individual organisms which are least well adapted to the environment, with the survival and greater proportionate increase of those which are better adapted. [On the basis of this process, Ch. Darwin formulated a theory of evolution. The operative factor, according to this theory, is **competition** (or **struggle**) **for existence**; the result is **survival of the fittest.**] — Ger. *natürliche Auslese.*

naturalism = (*metaph.*) the theory that nature as the totality of spatio-temporal objects is the only reality.

nature = 1. the sum total of phenomena in the universe together with all their modes of interrelation; 2. (*biol.*) the inherent constitution or make-up of an organism.

nature/law of = the verbal statement of a more or less fundamental uniformity found in nature. [Syn. **natural law** (also used abstractly). Cf. **law** (1).] — Fr. *l. de la nature.*

naturism = (*anthrop.*) the belief, probably antecedent to animism, that there is power or **mana** in nature.

nausea = a complex sensation of varying genesis and unpleasant affective tone, accompanied by a tendency to gastric contraction and (if intense) by vomiting. [Salivation, sweating, dizziness, dull epigastric pain, vasomotor disturbances may enter the complex in varying degrees.] — Ger. *Übelkeit.*

nauseous, see **putrid.**

Neanderthal man = the best known extinct species of man, first discovered in 1856 at Neanderthal, Germany; later skeletons were found in Belgium, Croatia, France, and elsewhere. [As now known, the geographical range of this species was from extreme western Europe to central China. In western Europe the species is identified with Middle Palæolithic cultures and possibly originated in the Lower Palæolithic.]

near-sight, near-sightedness, see **myopia.** — Ger. *Kurzsichtigkeit.*

necessary = 1. characterizing either (*a*) any factor, element, or condition without which a given result is unobtainable; or (*b*) the result as dependent upon such factors; 2. characterizing a conclusion which follows logically from the premises or the connection between subject and predicate in a judgment; 3. imposed upon an individual by force or by his recognition of a compelling moral principle. [Contr. (1, 2) w. **contingent,** and (3) w. **free.** Cf. **necessity.**]

necessary antecedent, see **antecedent/necessary.**

necessity = 1. an unavoidable sequence of events or of thought; 2. a very powerful need. (1) **necessary**[a], (2) **needful**[a]. — Ger. *Notwendigkeit.*

necromancy = the branch of magic which claims to reveal future events through communication with the dead. **necromancer**[np].

necrophilism, necrophilia, necrophily = morbid (sexual) attraction toward dead bodies.

need = 1. any factor or condition in the environment of an organism which assists to a marked extent in preserving its life and health or in furthering its usual modes of behavior; 2. the experience which is aroused by the lack of such factor or condition; 3. a condition of the tissues which determines seeking or adient behavior. [Syn. **want,** which emphasizes the idea of lack.] — Fr. *besoin*; Ger. *Bedürfnis.*

neëncephalon = the cerebral cortex and the parts of the brain developed in relation to it (Edinger). [Liter. **new brain.** Cf. **telencephalon.** Contr. w. **paleëncephalon.**]

negation = denial or disproof of a statement or refusal of a suggestion. [Cf. **negativism.**] **negative**[a].

negative[a] = (*math.*) characterizing a quantity less than zero, or extension in a direction opposite to that called **positive.**

negative[n] = a word or other expression which denotes dissent or negation. **negative**[a].

negative acceleration, see **acceleration.**

negative adaptation = gradual cessation of response to a continuous or repeated stimulus. [It occurs with stimuli when the response produces no biologically useful result.]

negative after-image, see **after-image/negative.**

negative magic, see **taboo.**

negative response (or **reaction**) = a response which is directed away from the source of stimulation. [Contr. w. **positive response** = toward the source.]

negative self-feeling = the feeling associated with whole-hearted submission of oneself to another's domination. — Fr. *sentiment négatif de soi.*

negative sensation = a term suggested by Fechner to designate a sensation whose stimulus is below the absolute limen or threshold.

negative supporting reaction = resolution of a positive supporting reaction (static reflex), thereby enabling the limb to be used for purposes other than support.

negative therapeutic reaction = (*psychoan.*) resistance to recovery from a neurosis produced by an unconscious sense of guilt (Freud).

negative transfer = the transfer of training effects from one act to another (somewhat conflicting) act, resulting in impeding the latter. [E.g. practice in proof-reading to note misspellings may develop techniques which interfere with rapid reading for the meaning. Cf. **transfer of training, interference** (2). Contr. w. **positive transfer.**]

negative transference (*psychoan.*), see **transference.**

negative tropism, negative taxis = a simple orienting response, in which the organism turns away from an external source of stimulation. [Contr. w. **positive tropism, positive taxis.**]

negative variation = the normal electrical response of active tissue. [In physiological experimentation, the negative potential change which results from stimulation of nerve or muscle. Cf. **action-current.**]

negativism = an attitude characterized by strong resistance to suggestions coming from others, to the extent of carrying out the opposite of what is suggested. [It may be general, or related only to specific kinds of acts, such as refusal to eat, to dress, to hear, to see, or to open the eyes. Frequent in children at early ages. Syn. **contrasuggestibility, contrariety.** Distg. fr. **non-suggestibility.** Cf. **mutism,** (a special case).] **negativistic**[a].

Negri bodies = rounded bodies present in the nerve cells of animals suffering from rabies. [The presence of these bodies is diagnostic of this disease. Named from their discoverer, A. Negri. Many consider them to be parasitic protozoa.]

nekton, see **plankton.**

neocatharsis = (*psychoan.*) a technical method, sometimes used in analysis, in which the analyst attempts to make conscious the childhood relations of the patient (Ferenczi).

neolalia = speech characterized by a multiplicity of neologisms, i.e. of words devised by the speaker.

neo-Lamarckism, neo-Lamarckianism = the theory of evolution by the inheritance of characters acquired through use or modified through disuse, as propounded by Lamarck and revised to accord with later biological discoveries. [Cf. **Lamarckism.**]

neologism = 1. (*path.*) construction of new words, as a characteristic of the insane, of the dream state, and of young children; 2. any newly coined word, or new use of a word or phrase, which is not sanctioned by literary or scientific canons. [(2) does not cover the meaning of new discoveries, inventions, etc.]

neonatal[a] = pert. to the new-born. **neonate**[np].

neopallium = the cerebral cortex, exclusive of the olfactory pallium. [So called because its phylogenetic origin is more recent than that of the olfactory pallium.]

neper, napier = a unit of sound-intensity of the same nature as the **bel** and **decibel,** one neper being equivalent to 8.686 decibels. [When used for expressing power ratios, the number of nepers N by which the power P exceeds the power P_0 is given by $N = 1/2 \log_e P/P_0$; if used for expressing the current, velocity, voltage, or force ratios when these are working into the same or equal impedances, $N = \log_e a_1/a_0$.]

Nernst-Lillie theory of excitation and conduction = the theory that excitation of a living cell results from a change in the electrical polarization of a protoplasmic membrane, following local change of ionic concentration at the membrane surface; the effect is automatically transmitted because of resulting secondary changes (e.g. of permeability) in the properties of the membrane itself.

nerve = 1. a collection or bundle of **neuraxons** or **nerve fibers;** 2. the substance of which neurons are composed. **neural**[a] = consisting of nerves, pert. to the functions of nerves, etc.; **nerve**[a] = pert. to the (neural) mechanism or its parts; **nervous**[a] = pert. to the pathology of nerve; but **nervous**[a] is frequently used instead of **neural**[a] and **nerve**[a], esp. in Britain; the present tendency is to limit this use to the two expressions **nervous system** and **nervous arc.**

nerve/accessory, —/auditory, etc., see **accessory nerve,** etc.

nerve block = 1. a local, temporary impairment or complete suspension of the property of a nerve to transmit a wave of excitation, produced by treating a section of the nerve chemically, faradically, etc.; 2. regional anesthesia produced by injecting a paralyzing drug in the vicinity of a nerve-trunk (and by other means). — Fr. *blocage du nerf.*

nerve-cell = 1. the compact mass of a neuron, i.e. a neuron considered apart from all its branches; 2. a neuron or unit cell of neural substance with all its branches. [To avoid ambiguity it is preferable to use syn. (1) **cell body** (or **nerve-cell body**), and (2) **neuron.**]

nerve center, see **center** (2).

nerve/centrifugal = a nerve which conducts impulses from the central nervous system toward the periphery. [Syn. **efferent nerve; motor nerve.**]

nerve/centripetal = a nerve which conducts impulses from the periphery or the lower centers toward the central nervous system or the higher centers, respectively. [Syn. **afferent nerve; sensory nerve.**]

nerve conduction, see **neural conduction.**

nerve deafness, see **deafness.** — Fr. *surdité nerveuse.*

nerve ending = a term applied to the several arrangements of cells among which the motor or sensory axons may terminate. [Sometimes the axon is directly applied to the cell innervated.] — Fr. *terminaison nerveuse*; Ger. *Nervenendigung.*

nerve fiber = the long, hair-like projection of neural substance which emanates from the cell body. [Syn. **axon.**] — Fr. *fibre nerveuse*; Ger. *Nervenfaser.*

nerve fibers/layer of, see **fibrous layer** and Table XI.

nerve-head, see **optic disk.**

nerve impulse, nervous impulse = 1. the current or disturbance which is propagated along the nerve fiber as a result of excitation; 2. one pulsation. [It typically consists, at least in the skeletal nerves of vertebrates, of a more or less rhythmic series of minute, all-or-none pulsations. Syn. **wave of excitation.**] — Fr. *influx nerveux.*

nerve/motor, peripheral, etc., see **motor nerve,** etc.

nerve-muscle preparation = an excised portion of the organism, consisting of muscular tissue with the nerves pertaining thereto, used in investigating the functions of nerve or muscle.

nerve-ring = the earliest example of a central nervous system: a double ring of nerve cells and fibers round the margins of the jellyfish, which carry the reproductive organs in certain genera of the Anthomedusae and Leptomedusae.

nerve root = a collection of axons connected directly with the cord or brain. [Cf. **spinal nerve, radix.**] — Fr. *racine médullaire, tronc nerveux*; Ger. *Nervenwurzel.*

nerve tract, see **tract.**

nerve trunk = a peripheral nerve or bundle of axons, excluding their terminations.

nervous = 1. pert. to neurons or nerves, or consisting of neurons or nerves; e.g. the nervous system; 2. pert. to disorders or diseases of the nervous system; 3. (*pop.*) exhibiting excessive but twitchy and unsustained activity. [Cf. **nerve, neural.**] — Ger. (1) *Nerven-*, (3) *nervös.*

nervous disease, nervous disorder = any kind of disorder of the nervous system and its functions. [Best limited to the structurally and structural-functionally definable disorders, in contrast to the psychodynamically determined disorders improperly called **neuroses,** properly **psychoneuroses.**] — Fr. *maladie nerveuse.*

nervous prostration, see **neurasthenia.**

nervous system = the totality of neurons in the body of any organism. [More properly, **nerve system;** a term not used in English. The human nervous system is divided into the **cerebrospinal** and **autonomic systems.**]

nervous system/autonomic,/cerebrospinal,/sympathetic, see **autonomic n.s.** etc.

nesting = the complex behavior of insects, birds, and certain other animals, which results in the building of nests. — Fr. *nidification*; Ger. *Nisten.*

neural = pert. to the structure or functions of nerves. [Cf. **nerve.**]

neural arc, nervous arc = any connected series of neurons which extends from receptor to effector and is capable of transmitting a wave of excitation, so that, given a stimulus, a response may follow. [A more inclusive term than **reflex arc.** Syn. **sensorimotor arc.**]

neural circuit, nervous circuit = a neural pathway capable of conducting impulses from one center to another or from a receptor to an effector.

neural conduction, nerve conduction, nervous conduction = the transmission of a wave of excitation along nerve fibers.

neural crest = a cellular band lying along the line where the neural folds meet to form the neural tube in the embryo. [The **neural crest** develops into the **spinal ganglia.**] — Fr. *crête neurale.*

neural discharge, nervous discharge = the excitation or propagated disturbance which results from stimulation of any point or center in the nervous system. [This regularly travels toward the musculature and spreads to a greater number of (motor) neurons than were at first stimulated.] — Fr. *décharge d'influx nerveux.*

neural groove = a groove formed in the neural plate of the embryo, which marks the site of the developing neural tube. [Syn. **medullary groove.**] — Fr. *gouttière neurale.*

neural pattern = the spatial or functional arrangement of the nerve cells excited by a given stimulus. — Fr. *complexus nerveux.*

neural plate = the thickened plate of ectoderm within the embryonic disk in which the neural groove is formed.

neural process = 1. (*physiol.*) any change of state in nerve cells, esp. such changes as pertain to the excitation and transmission of nerve impulses; 2. (*anat.*) any slender terminal branch, axonic or dendritic, of a neuron or of a nerve. [Syn. (1) **nerve process** (prefd).]

neural rivalry = a condition in which reflex and cortical control compete for dominance of some **final common path** to a muscle or muscle group.

neural tube = the epithelial tube which develops from the neural plate and forms the central nervous system of the embryo. [Syn. **medullary tube.**] — Ger. *Medullarrohr.*

neuralgia = a nervous disorder characterized by sharp intermittent pain, usually limited to a single nerve, and due to nutritive or functional conditions in the nerve or nerves concerned. **neuralgic**[a].

neurasthenia = a condition characterized by lack of physical and mental vigor, by abnormal fatiguability, and often by the presence of phobias. [Syn. **nervous prostration.** The state has no demonstrated relation to elementary nervous functions.] (Accent **-the-.**) **neurasthenic**[a, np] (accent **-then-**).

neuraxis = the brain and spinal cord; i.e. the central portion of the cerebrospinal nervous system, regarded as the axis of the neural mechanism.

neurilemma = the thin outer membranous covering of a nerve fiber. [In medullated fibers it lies outside the medullary sheath. Syn. **primitive sheath, sheath of Schwann.**]

neurilemma cells = cells which are associated with the neurilemmal sheath of the peripheral nerve fibers and are believed by some to be involved in the production of myelin. [Syn. **lemmocytes.**]

neurility, neuricity = the sum of the properties and functions of nerve tissue.

neurin = 1. the most important protein constituent of nerve tissue; 2. an extract of nerve tissue employed in therapy; 3. a special form of energy postulated in explanation of nervous action.

neurite = the axon and its branches, or collaterals. — Fr. *cylindraxe.*

neuritis = an inflamed condition of a peripheral nerve, accompanied by pain and other disturbances both of sensation and of motion. — Fr. *névrite.*

neuritis/central = a term used by A. Meyer to denote diffuse central fiber degenerations with axonal alteration of the cell bodies, in contrast to peripheral neuritis. [Present in pellagra and nutritional deficits.]

neurobiotaxis = the principle that the dendrites of nerve cells are stimulated to growth by electrical influences which reach them from other neurons, provided that both groups are simultaneously active. [The dendrites grow *toward* other active neurons (cathode pole), and their cell-bodies often migrate in the same direction. A form of **galvanotropism** (Ariëns Kappers).]

neuroblast = an embryonic neuron.

neurocyte = syn. for **neuron.** [Sometimes limited to the **nerve-cell body.**]

neuro-epithelial layer = the layer of rods and cones and the outer nuclear layer of the retina which, when taken together, contain the **neuro-epithelial** or **visual cells.** [Cf. **retinal layers** and Table XI.]

neuroepithelium, neurepithelium = 1. specialized epithelial cells (e.g. cells of Corti, rod and cones) in connection with which sensory fibers terminate; 2. the epiblastic cells from which the developing cerebrospinal axis arises.

neurofibril, neurofibrilla = one of the small threads or fibers at times observed in the axon of the nerve and assumed by some to be the actual conductors of the nerve impulse. **-brils**^{pl}, **-brillae**^{pl}.

neurogenic, neurogenetic = forming nerve tissue or stimulating neural energy.

neuroglia = supporting tissue of the cerebrospinal axis, which consists largely of a special type of branched cells, called glia cells.

neurogram = 1. a term employed by Morton Prince for the impressions or lasting effects produced in the central nervous system as a result of stimulation or of central activity, and constituting the basis of memory, personality, etc.; 2. any well canalized central (e.g. cortical) neural paths. [Cf. **engram.**]

neurohumoral = pert. to the physiological relation between nervous and chemical agencies, esp. the integration of bodily activities effected by the discharge of nerve impulses and of one or more hormones, e.g. the secretion of adrenin resulting from splanchnic discharge and acting to supplement and reinforce generalized sympathetic activity.

neurology = the branch of biology which investigates the structure and functions of the nervous system. **neurologic(al)**^{a}.

neuromere = a segment of the neural tube which stands in one-to-one relation with a metamere or segment of the body in the vertebrate embryo. [Cf. **metamere.**]

neuromuscular = pert. to the structure or functions of nerve and muscle, whether in the body or isolated. [Cf. **nerve-muscle preparation.**]

neuromotor apparatus = (*biol.*) a system of interconnected fibrils in a unicellular organism, which probably functions like the nervous system of higher animals in coordinating the movements of motor organs.

neuromuscular junction = the surface of contact (i.e. end-plate) between a motor nerve and the fibers of the muscle which it innervates. [It is believed to be a region of decrement, to be susceptible to certain drugs, etc. Syn. **myoneural junction, muscle-nerve junction, motor point.**]

neuromuscular spindles = nerve end-organs located in the muscles. [They contain afferent nerve ends which are supposed by some writers to arouse a special sensation of muscular activity (**proprioceptors**); also believed by some to contain efferent fibers.] — Fr. *fuseaux neuromusculaires.*

neuron, neurone = a neural element, consisting of a cell-body with its projections, including dendrites, axon, and collaterals. **neuronic**^{a}.

neuron (or **neurone**) **theory** = the theory that any sensorimotor neural pathway is not a continuous tissue, but consists of separate nerve cells (the **neurons**), which are merely contiguous end-to-end. The **neuron,** according to this view, is the histological and metabolic unit of the nervous system (W. v. Waldeyer, 1891).]

neuronymy = the (systematic) nomenclature of the nervous system and its parts. (Accent **-ron-**.)

neuropathy = a diseased condition of the nervous system or of its parts. [Cf. **neurosis.**] (Accent **-rop-**.) **neuropathic**^{a} (accent **-path-**). — Fr. *névropathie, maladie nerveuse*; Ger. *Nervenleiden.*

neurophysiology = that branch of physiology which deals with the functional activities of the nervous system; in particular, that part of the science which treats of the phenomena of conduction. **neurophysiological**^{a}.

neuropil, neuropile, neuropilem = a network of unmedullated nerve fibrils situate at the synapses between two neurons.

neuroplexus = a network of peripheral nerve fibers. [Cf. **plexus.**]

neuropore = the opening by which the embryonic medullary tube communicates with the exterior at its cephalic extremity.

neuropsychiatry = the branch of medicine which deals with both neurology and psychiatry.

neurosis = 1. a (functional) disorder of the nervous system for which no actual lesion is found; 2. (*hist.*) the specific and normal activity of the nervous system. [Current psychiatric usage tends to confine the term (1) to psychogenic disorders, and to employ **psychosis** for disorders in which some physical or chemical cause is discoverable. Some authorities substitute **psychoneurosis** or **neuropsychosis** for **neurosis.** Psychoanalysts attribute **neurosis** (1) to a conflict between the ego and the id. Etymologically, the suffix **-osis** denotes disease; but **neurosis** and **psychosis** were formerly used (as in sense 2) to designate normal phenomena.] **neurotic**^{a,np}. — Fr. *névrose*; Ger. *Nervenkrankheit.*

neurosis/actual = (*psychoan.*) a neurosis of physical origin where the individual symptoms cannot be further reduced or explained by psychological analysis. [E.g. **neurasthenia, anxiety neurosis.**]

neurosis/narcissistic = (*psychoan.*) a neurosis in which the ego is far more deeply involved than the libido, or in which the libido regresses to much earlier stages of pregenital development than those found in the transference neuroses. [E.g. schizophrenia, paranoid states, stammering.] — Fr. *névrose narcissique.*

neurosis/transference = (*psychoan.*) a neurosis in which the chief symptoms proceed from abnormal substitutions or satisfactions of the libido. [As a rule, the easiest type to treat psychoanalytically; e.g. anxiety hysteria, conversion hysteria, and the obsessional neuroses.] — Fr. *névrose de transfert.*

neurotendinous spindle, see **tendon spindle.**

neuroterminal = pert. to the nervous system together with its receptor and effector attachments.

neurotic^{n} = an individual constitutionally affected with a minor nervous disorder. [The term **psychopathic** probably comes closer to the facts. Cf. **neurosis.**] **neurotic**^{a}. — Fr. *névrosique.*

neurotic character = 1. (*indiv. psychol.*) a combination of traits resulting from an attempt at compensation for organ inferiority or from a striving for complete masculinity (Adler); 2. (*psychoan.*) an exaggerated character trait which lies midway between health and neurosis.

neurypnology, neurhypnology = (*hist.*) the study and art of **hypnosis** (James Braid, 1843).

neutral = characterizing an intermediate or zero region between two connected series, one of which is treated as positive, the other as negative. [E.g. neutral temperature, neutral gray.]

neutron = a hypothetical physical unit proposed as the genetic antecedent of the electron-proton complex and assumed by some to be an undifferentiated unit.

nevi[pl], **naevi**[pl] = permanent reddish patches of the skin, present at birth, which occur in certain individuals. [A species of **birth-mark.**] **nevus**[sing].

Newton's law of color mixture = the principle that if two color mixtures arouse the same sensation of light or color, then a mixture of these mixtures will also arouse that sensation.

nexus = the mutual dependence or interrelation of the elements in a series. [Applied usually to the relation between antecedents and consequents; e.g. causal nexus. Lat.]

Nicol prism = a crystal calcite (calc-spar, Iceland spar) especially cut so as to polarize completely the light passing through it. [The distinguishing feature is the fact that it is cut obliquely to the intended optical axis and recemented with Canada balsam; the ordinary ray, which obeys the ordinary laws of refraction, is reflected out of the optical path at this film of balsam and lost; the extraordinary ray, which does not obey the ordinary laws of refraction, passes through the prism; since both rays are completely polarized in planes perpendicular to each other, the emergent ray is completely polarized. Cf. **polariscope.**]

nicotin = the alkaloid of Nicotiana tabacum, a clear, colorless, volatile liquid, strongly alkaline in reaction. [It acts chiefly on the central nervous system, the sympathetic ganglia, and the myoneural junctions, first stimulating and then paralyzing them.]

nictitating reflex = a closing of the nictitating membrane of the eyelid caused by contact with cornea or conjunctiva. [Syn. **bulbar retraction reflex.**]

nidus (or **nidulus**) = a nucleus or group of cell bodies from which a nerve, or tract, originates, or which is the seat of some pathological process.

night-blindness = an imperfection of vision, congenital or acquired, which involves diminished powers of dark-adaptation, absence of the Purkinje phenomenon, and blue-weakness. [Syn. **hemeralopia;** this term and **nyctalopia** are confused by usage and had best be avoided. Contr. w. **day-blindness.**] — Fr. *cécité nocturne, c. crépusculaire*; Ger. *Nachtblindheit, Hühnerblindheit.*

night terrors = disturbing dreams from which the sleeper commonly awakes in a terror. — Fr. *terreurs nocturnes.*

nightmare = a dream in which the affect, or emotional toning, is intense anxiety. — Fr. *cauchemar*; Ger. *Alpdrücken.*

night-walker = syn. for **somnambulist.**

nigra/substantia = a pigmented layer of gray substance which separates the dorsal and ventral portions of the cerebral peduncle, containing many nerve cells, and extending from the upper surface of the pons to the subthalamic region.

nihil est in intellectu quod non prius fuerit in sensu = "there is naught in the intellect which was not first in the senses." [Lat. The watchword of historic sensationism. Leibnitz added **nisi intellectus ipse** (except the intellect itself).]

nihil ex nihilo fit = "nothing arises out of nothing." [Lat. A scholastic statement, in negative form, of the principle of universal causation.]

nirvana principle (Low) = syn. for **death instinct.**

Nissl corpuscles (or **bodies**) = certain large granules observed in the dendrites and cell-body of the neuron when specially treated with the methylene or toluidin blue stain. [Syn. **tigroid bodies.**]

nisus = 1. the tendency of any active organism to strive against obstacles; 2. conscious effort or endeavor. [Used by Leibnitz in a technical sense, nearly corresponding to the recent term **drive.** Used by Lloyd Morgan as the equivalent of **biological striving** = akin to **conation.**]

nociceptive reflex = a defense reflex evoked by a nocuous or painful stimulus. [E.g. in a spinal animal the brisk reflex flexion of the limb when its skin is pinched or pricked.]

nociceptor = a receptor or sense organ whose stimuli are harmful to the body. [The resulting sensations are always unpleasant.]

nocive = injurious or harmful to the organism.

noctambulism = a term occasionally used for **somnambulism.** [Inaccurate, since the condition has no necessary relation to time of day.]

nocturnal enuresis, see **enuresis.**

nodal point = the point in the eye through which all lines pass which join points in the visual field with their respective retinal images. [There are two nodal points located in the axis of any optical system; each line is conceived as leaving the second nodal point parallel to its course in reaching the first. In the human eye the two are close together and are about 7.2 mm. back of the surface of the cornea.] —Ger. *Knotenpunkt.*

node = a point in any wave system at which the wave has zero amplitude. [Contr. w. **crest,** or **antinode,** the point of maximum amplitude.] — Fr. *noeud*; Ger. *Schwingungsknoten.*

noegenesis = noesis with generation of new items (Spearman).

noesis = 1. the operation of the intellect alone; 2. the manifestations of the three basic processes of cognition, esp. as regards their property of being self-evident (Spearman).

noetic = 1. pert. to cognition or to the intellect; 2. syn. for **self-evident.** [Used with various shades of meaning by different writers, including the notion of direct, non-sensory apprehension or intuition; **noetic consciousness** = experiences which are chiefly cognitive; contr. w. **anoetic consciousness.** Cf. **cognitive faculty.**]

noise = an auditory experience dependent upon aperiodic sound-waves. [**noise** and **tone** are generally contrasted, but there is a continuous gradation from the purest tone to the purest noise.] — Fr. *bruit*; Ger. *Geräusch.*

nolition = the will or decision not to do a given act. [A rare term, contr. w. **volition.**]

nomadism = a propensity to wander from place to place. [A normal trait in certain individuals and social groups; found pathologically in certain cases of mental disorder.] **nomadic**[a], **nomad**[np].

nomenclature = the systematic naming of data, etc. in a given branch of investigation, or the resulting system of names. [Cf. **terminology.**] (Accent **no-.**)

nominal[a] = applied to distinctions based solely

upon the verbal characterization of objects or items, not upon their phenomenal or factual differences. **nominally**[a].

nominal aphasia, see **aphasia**.

nomograph (or **nomogram**) = 1. (*math.*) a graphic representation of mathematical relationships; 2. (*statist.*) a chart consisting of three (or more) scales, ordinarily parallel straight lines, which represent values of related variables; given the values of two of these variables, one can determine, by means of a supplementary straight edge, the value of the third related variable (e.g. given r and N one can determine the PE_r) from the chart.

nomology = the division of science, or of any particular branch, which investigates general principles and formulates laws. [Distg. fr. **classification**, and from **explanatory theory.**] **nomologic(al)**[a]. — Ger. *Gesetzeskunde*.

nomothetic = pert. to the study of general principles and laws. [Contr. w. **idiographic.**]

non compos mentis = not of sound mind. [Lat. A phrase characterizing an individual legally recognized as incompetent to manage or dispose of property.]

non sequitur = "it does not follow." [Lat. Used as a noun to designate attempts at reasoning in which the conclusion seems to follow from the premises, but does not actually do so.]

non-conscious = without consciousness. [Best confined to lifeless beings or substances, using **unconscious** to denote conditions in living beings.]

non-contradiction/law of = a canon of logic, or rational thinking, which states that if a certain proposition is true its exact opposite or contrary or contradictory is false. [E.g. if "sponges are animals" be true, then "sponges are not animals" is false. Syn. **law of contradiction.**]

non-critical, see **critical**.

non-ego = everything or anything which is not the subjective self. [Contr. w. **ego**, the self; a broader term than **alter**, the other, which is limited to other human beings.] — Fr. *non-moi*; Ger. *Nicht-Ich*.

nonius, see **vernier**.

non-language test, see **non-verbal test**.

non-moral = outside the province of morality, i.e. not capable of being characterized as either right or wrong, as moral or immoral. [E.g. non-moral behavior; distg. fr. **immoral** = (conduct) belonging within the sphere of ethics, but contravening its canons. Syn. **amoral.**]

non-polarizable electrode, see **electrode**.

non-rational = outside the province of reason; i.e. not characterized by reason. [E.g. non-rational behavior; distg. fr. **irrational** = lying inside the province of reason but violating its canons.]

nonsense[n] = a series of words or symbols which convey absurd meanings or no meaning whatever. **nonsense**[a] (applied also to single words or syllables). — Ger. *Unsinn*.

nonsense syllable = an artificially constructed combination of letters (commonly of three letters), which can be readily pronounced but which does not represent a meaningful word. [Series of nonsense syllables are used in investigations on memorization. Devised by Ebbinghaus (1885).] — Fr. *syllabe privée de sens*; Ger. *sinnlose Silbe*.

non-sensory = lacking sensory elements. [E.g. **non-sensory experience** = any component of experience which has no sensory aspect; **non-sensory recall** = recall of facts observed in an experience without recall of the sensory qualities of the experience. Not to be confused with **nonsense** = without meaning (a different use of the term sense).] — Fr. *asensoriel*.

non-social = 1. not possessing social characteristics; 2. not falling within the sphere of sociology. [E.g. (1) non-social animals, (2) non-social stimuli. Distg. fr. **unsocial, unsociable,** not entering readily into social relations; and fr. **anti-social,** actively opposing social relations. Cf. **social.**] — Fr. *asocial*.

non-specific response (or **reaction**) = a response which may be attributed equally well to any one of several stimuli. [In association-response experiments, applied to verbal responses which have no obvious association with the given stimulus word.]

non-suggestibility = (*hypn.*) a state of being non-responsive either positively or negatively to suggestions, while at the same time normally perceiving the stimulations. **non-suggestible**[a].

non-verbal test = a type of mental (generally intelligence) test, in which no words are used in the test content, but the directions for giving the tests may be either verbal or by pantomime.

non-voluntary = lying outside the sphere of voluntary activity; i.e. neither voluntary nor involuntary. [Distg. fr. **involuntary.**]

norm = 1. a pattern, standard, or representative value for a group or type; 2. the mean, median, or modal score (or group of scores) of the subjects employed in standardizing a given test or measure. [(1) used loosely to designate the usual or typical in any class of data, where precise mathematical formulation is lacking; in ethics, the term denotes a canon or principle of conduct which serves as pattern.] **normal**[a] = representing or copying the norm; **normative**[a] = pert. to the norm.

norm/occupational = a frequency distribution of scores of achievement in a test, or group of tests, made by workers in a particular occupation and used as a standard of reference in interpreting scores made by candidates for employment in that occupation.

normal = 1. representing or copying a norm, type, or standard; 2. (*statist.*) pert. to the form of the normal distribution. [Distg. fr. **abnormal,** markedly different from type.] **normality**[n].

normal curve of distribution = the curve which represents the frequency of occurrence of data for each successive value of a variable, when these variations arise from (or behave as though they arose from) the operation of a large number of independent random causes. [The normal curve is bell-shaped. Syn. **normal frequency distribution, normal probability distribution, Gaussian curve.**]

normal stimulus = a stimulus used as standard in a series of experiments, and compared with other stimuli called comparative stimuli. [Syn. **standard stimulus** (prefd.).] — Ger. *Normalreiz*.

normality = the characteristic of being a representative value or pattern for the members of a given class of data. [Distg. fr. **abnormality** = the condition of being markedly different from the norm.]

normative sciences = those branches which attempt to establish norms or correct patterns for conduct. [They include logic, ethics, esthetics, etc. Contr. w. **empirical sciences,** which investigate facts.]

normosplanchnic = characterizing a physique in which trunk and limbs show average or normal development, i.e. an average morphological index.

nose = the structure which serves as the peripheral organ of respiration and which contains the receptors of olfaction. [It comprises the **exterior nose,** the **nasal cavities,** and the **paranasal sinuses;** it is divided in the median plane by a partition-wall, the **septum.**] **nasal**[a]. — Fr. *nez*; Ger. *Nase*.

nosogenesis = (*psychoan.*) the classification of a neurosis according to the circumstances and character of its onset.

nosophobia = morbid fear of some specific disease. [Cf. **pathophobia.**]

nostrils = the apertures through which the breathing-current enters and leaves the nose. [Applied either (*a*) to both the external and the internal openings (syn. **nares**), or (*b*) to the external opening alone: not syn. w. **nasal cavity,** which denotes the internal chambers of the nose.] — Fr. *narines*; Ger. *Nasenlöcher*.

note = 1. (*mus.*) the written or printed symbol for a musical tone; 2. (*pop.*) a musical tone.

note-blindness = a rare variety of alexia, characterized by inability to read musical notes.

notice[v] = to perceive with sufficient attention to enable the observer to give a report afterwards. — Fr. *remarquer, observer*; Ger. *bemerken*.

noticeable = 1. characterizing a stimulus or situation which is sufficiently intense to give rise to a sensation that can be reported upon; 2. characterizing a sensation or other experience that can be reported introspectively. [The term **just noticeable difference** applies to experiences of difference in (2).] — Fr. *perceptible, notable*; Ger. *merklich*.

notion = 1. a concept or other symbolic idea; 2. (*hist.*) a form of knowledge which is not idea but rather immediate acquaintance (Berkeley).

notochord = a rod of specialized supporting tissue found in primitive vertebrates and in all vertebrate embryos; it is permanent in the former and forms the embryonic basis of the central part of the axial skeleton in the latter. [The **notochord** constitutes one of the most fundamental characteristics of vertebrate animals.] — Fr. *notochorde, corde dorsale*; Ger. *Rückenstrang*.

nous = (*hist.*) syn. for **intellect.** [Specially used as antithesis of **sense:** a Greek term in use from earliest times (Homer) and consistently used as the special name for the highest faculty: transmitted by Arabs (*nafs*) and in modern times used occasionally to revive historical relations. Root term of **noumenon, noetic.**]

novel impression = an impression which has never before been presented to the given individual or has not formed associations, and accordingly must initiate its own associations. [Treated as a factor in determining *attention,* and thus indirectly a factor in *recall.*] — Fr. *impression neuve*; Ger. *neuer Eindruck*.

novice = a person with practically no training or experience in a particular trade or profession. [Distg. fr. **apprentice, journeyman, expert.**] — Ger. *Anfänger*.

nuchal = pert. to or located on the back of the neck. (Pron. **new′-kal.**)

nuclear complex = (*psychoan.*) the child's earliest impulses, alike tender and hostile, toward various members of the family, after its curiosity has been awakened, which form the content of a later neurosis; e.g. Edipus complex. — Ger. *Kernkomplex*.

nuclear layer/inner = the 6th layer in the retina of the human eye from the outside. [Syn. **layer of bipolar cells.** See Table XI.]

nuclear layer/outer = the 4th layer in the retina of the human eye from the outside. [See Table XI.]

nucleolus = a small body within the nucleus of the cell, usually spherical in form. (Accent **-kle-.**)

nucleoplasm, see **karyoplasm.**

nucleus = 1. a core of specialized substance situate within every cell and rather sharply demarcated from the remainder (the *cytoplasm*), which is essential to the continuance of the cell as a living organism; 2. a cluster of cells within the cerebral nervous system. **nuclear**[a]. — Fr. *noyau*; Ger. *Kern*.

Nuel's space = a space within the organ of Corti, situate between the arch of Corti and the outer hair cells in the internal ear.

nulliplex inheritance = inheritance determined by two recessive factors. — Fr. *héritage nulliplexe*.

number = 1. any member of a series representing the scale of values of discrete data of any sort; 2. syn. for **numeral.** [Distg. (1) fr. **quantity** = position on a scale of continuous or non-discrete data.] **numeric(al)**[a]. — Ger. *Nummer*.

number completion test = a test in which the task is to complete or supply the omissions in a series of numbers arranged according to some plan or pattern; e.g. 1, 2, 4, 8, 16, —, —. [E.g. Test 6 in Army Alpha. Syn. **number sequence test, number series test.**] — Fr. *test de séquences de chiffres, t. de complètement de chiffres*.

number concept = the mental representation of abstract number, i.e. of a serial scale of discrete values.

number form = an ideational configuration of the number-series represented in some spatially arranged scheme. [Cf. **synesthesia.**] — Fr. *schème (diagramme) numérique*.

numerology = (*psych. res.*) a system of reading character and telling fortunes by assigning numbers to each letter in names or other words, adding together these numbers or the numerals in dates, etc., and attaching a mystical significance to the numerical results so obtained. [A recent form of **sciosophy,** said to have come down from Pythagoras.]

nutriment = substances taken into the body of an organism and transformed into living tissues. [Cf. **nutrition.**] **nutritive**[a]. — Fr. *aliment*; Ger. *Nahrungsstoff*.

nutrition = the processes by which substances are taken into the body of an organism and transformed into tissue. [Sometimes used as syn. for **nutriment** = that which nourishes.] **nutritional**[a]. — Ger. *Ernährung*.

nyctalopia = 1. (*etymologically*) night-blindness; 2. (commonly) day-blindness. [Contr. w. **hemeralopia.** Both terms have been used in two opposite senses; to avoid confusion their use should be avoided. Cf. the distinctive syns. **day-blindness, nightblindness.**]

nyctophobia = morbid fear of darkness, or of night.

nymphomania = an exaggerated degree of sexual desire in the human female. [Frequently (not always) a symptom of mental disorder. Syn. **andromania.** Contr. w. **satyriasis** = in the male. Cf. **erotomania.**]

nystagmic response, see **nystagmus.**

nystagmic time = the interval from the beginning of a nystagmic response until this ceases to be observable. [Cf. **nystagmus.**]

nystagmus = involuntary movements of the eyes (or head), composed of alternate slow and quick phases in opposite directions or rapid oscillatory movements. [Occurs frequently in the totally color-blind and in albinos; in normal individuals it is due to specific stimulations or conditions. The following types are distinguished: **caloric nyst.,** produced by irrigation of the ear with warm or cold liquid; **galvanic nyst.,** produced by passage of electric current through labyrinthine region of head; **miners' nyst.,** involuntary oscillatory movements of the eyes due to long-continued vision in relative darkness; **optic** (or **railroad**) **nyst.,** alternate slow and quick movements, each slow phase being the fixation of a moving object, and each quick phase the refixation of a new oncoming object; **post-rotation nyst.,** or **after-nyst.,** the continuation of alternate slow and quick phases after cessation (or slowing down) of rotation of the head; **pathological nyst.,** rapid oscillatory or alternate slow and quick phases due to vestibular, cerebellar, or intra-cranial involvements; **vestibular nyst.,** reflex alternate drifting and quick compensatory movements due to stimulation of labyrinthine end organs by positive or negative acceleration of the head in rotation.] **nystagmic**[a].

O

O = abbrev. for **observer.** [Prefd. italics without period; plural *O*s, possessive *O*'s, *O*s'.]

o factor, oscillation factor = a general factor in cognition, pert. to fluctuations of mental efficiency. [Cf. **general factor, g factor, c factor,** etc.]

obedience = social behavior characterized by conformity on the part of the individual to commands, general rules, or suggestions given by another or prescribed by tradition or by the community. [The term generally implies that the individual who gives the commands, etc. occupies a position of superiority (as parent, guardian, official superior, etc.) or exercises domination over the other.] — Fr. *obéissance*; Ger. *Gehorsam.*

object = 1. any group of material data, considered as a unit; 2. that portion of the environment which is related to the individual in a psychological experience; 3. whatever is present to the mind in a cognitive experience. [Cf. **subject.**] **objective**[a] = pert. to **object; objectivity**[n]. — Ger. *Objekt, Gegenstand.*

object attitude = the attitude in which the observer regards the stimulus as an object or gives attention to the stimulus rather than the experience. [Syn. **stimulus attitude;** contr. w. **process attitude.**]

object-blindness = a type of mental disorder in which the individual, though able to see, is unable to apprehend present visual experiences as objects. — Fr. *cécité psychique.*

object-cathexis = (*psychoan.*) a diversion of the love or sexual instinct from its primary sexual aim. — Fr. *investissement objectal*; Ger. *Objektbesetzung.*

object-choice = (*psychoan.*) selection of a love-object to produce gratification, determined by pregenital fixations. [It may be either **narcissistic** (taking oneself, or someone resembling oneself, as a model), or **anaclitic** (taking one's earliest love attachments or dependents as a model, e.g. mother or nurse).] — Fr. *choix objectal*; Ger. *Objektwahl.*

object of consciousness, object-consciousness = that of which the individual is aware; i.e. that part of the environment or of intra-organic conditions to which a given momentary experience refers. [Cf. **subject of consciousness, content of consciousness.**]

object-odor, object-smell = a term applied by Henning to the olfactory perception of a substance whose nature the observer knows. [Proposed syn. **memory-odor;** cf. **memory color.** Contr. w. **perception odor** (*Gegebenheitsgeruch*) = the pure olfactory perception of the scent itself.] — Ger. *Gegenstandsgeruch.*

objective[a] = 1. syn. for **physical;** 2. admitting of record by physical instruments; 3. open to verification by any investigator; 4. localized in psychological space outside the observer's body (e.g. most visual data, as contr. w. feelings); 5. not dependent on the special bias or judgment of the individual observer (e.g. objective tests and scoring methods); 6. pert. to an object. [In psychol. the term **objective data** and other phrases are used by different writers in senses (2), (3), (4), (5), often without precise discrimination. Contr. w. **subjective data,** etc. Cf. **subjective.**] — Ger. *gegenständlich.*

objective[n] = that towards which a purposive act is directed.

objective idealism, see **idealism.**

objective psychology = that division of psychology which is concerned with a study of the behavior of organisms, to the exclusion of introspective data. [A term used, esp. in Russia, prior to the inception of behavior psychology. It has a broader connotation than **behaviorism** as regards schools of thought; and in strictest sense it is more inclusive as to subject-matter since it includes both behavior and physiological data. Contr. w. **subjective psychology.** Distg. fr. **behaviorism** which rejects both consciousness and introspection.]

objective score = the score upon a test the grading (or marking) of which is arrived at according to a key, or is otherwise so clearly defined that the subjective judgment of the scorer does not enter in. — Fr. *notation objective.*

objective trait = a trait which may be measured through actual performance, or which is manifest in overt behavior, e.g. neatness, suggestibility. [Contr. w. **subjective trait.**]

obligation = 1. an act or course of conduct by one individual toward another, or toward others, which is regarded as a just equivalent for services rendered to him and as being more or less compulsory; 2. a feeling or experience, on the part of an individual, of compulsion to act in a certain manner toward society or toward some given individual. [The compulsory character is measured by the individual's ability to perform the act, etc.; distg. fr. **duty,** which assumes such ability.] **obligatory**[a]. — Ger. *Verpflichtung.*

oblige[v] = 1. to compel by suggestion; 2. (*pop.*) to perform some action in order to please another individual.

oblique muscles = a pair of muscles, the inferior and superior oblique, which are attached to each eyeball, and participate in the various movements of the eyeball. [Distg. fr. **rectus muscles.** Cf. **eye-muscles.**]

oblique reflex = 1. contraction of the obliquus externus muscle on irritation of skin below the inguinal ligament; 2. syn. for **cremasteric reflex** in the male. [Mediated by 1st and 2d lumbar nerves.]

obliviscence = 1. syn. for **forgetfulness;** 2. the tendency of ideas to disappear, as contr. w. **reminiscence,** the tendency to become more firmly fixed with time.

oblongata, abbrev. for **medulla oblongata.**

obscenity = gestures or spoken language which violate the social conventions of fitness in respect to sexual or other bodily functions. **obscene**[a].

obscurantism = opposition to enlightenment, investigation, and culture in general, esp. to the advancement of science and knowledge. [The term arose in the 16th century in connection with a satirical criticism of the conduct of the clergy in their opposition to humanism.] (Accent **-skew-.**) **obscurantic**[a], **obscurantist**[np].

obscure, obscurity, see **clearness.**

observation = 1. the attentive (analytical) examination of phenomena or events as part of the process of scientific investigation; 2. such examination when the conditions are not prescribed by the investigator. [(2) is shorthand for **ordinary** or **natural observation,** contr. w. **experimental observation.** The term is used also non-technically to signify the act of perceiving, and to characterize a casual remark.] **observe**[v]. — Ger. *Beobachtung*.

observation/mental, see **introspective method.**

observation of self, see **self-observation, introspective method.** — Fr. *observation de soi;* Ger. *Selbstbeobachtung*.

observational errors, see **errors of observation.**

observer = in a psychophysical or introspective experiment, the individual who reports a description of his conscious experience. [Distg. fr. **subject,** a broader (but ambig.) term, including also one who participates in an experiment merely by responsive activity without later reporting upon it. Contr. w. **experimenter** who conducts the investigation. The terms are often abbrev. to **O, S,** and **E.**] — Ger. *Versuchsperson* (*Vp*).

obsession = 1. the presence, pathologically, in an individual of a persistent and irresistible idea or emotion or urge; 2. (*hist.*) the presence in an individual of an evil spirit who controls his actions; 3. (*psych. res.*) the possession or control of a person by an intruding personality believed to be organized from dissociated elements of his own personality but often assumed to be a discarnate personality or other spirit. [Syn. (2) **possession.**] **obsessed**[a], **to be obsessed**[v]. — Ger. *Besessenheit*.

obsessional neurosis = a psychoneurosis characterized by obsessive ideas, doubts, and compulsive ceremonials of a complicated sort. [According to psychoanalysis, the symptoms and character traits result from an unconscious regression to the early anal-sadistic organization. Syn. **compulsion neurosis.**] — Fr. *névrose d'obsession, névrose de compulsion;* Ger. *Zwangsneurose*.

obsessional type = (*psychoan.*) a psychological type which is governed by anxiety of conscience instead of by the dread of losing love (Freud).

obsessive doubt, see **psychasthenia.**

obstruction = (*beh.*) anything which hinders the completion of a response.

Occam's razor, see **economy/principle of.**

occasion[n] = a specific situation in a specific temporal setting. **occasional**[a] (more generally used as syn. for **infrequent**). — Ger. *Gelegenheit*.

occasion[v] = to initiate, permit, or facilitate the production of an effect by a cause.

occasional cause = an antecedent of a given event which is regarded as not directly related to the event.

occasionalism = (*metaph.*) the view, propounded by Geulincx and Malebranche, that the concomitance between conscious and bodily processes is due to intervention of the Deity, who determines that a specific conscious process shall occur on the occasion or occurrence of a specific bodily process, and vice-versa.

occipital = pert. to or located in the back of the head. [Contr. w. **frontal.**] (Pron. **ok-sip-.**)

occipital lobe = that part of either cerebral hemisphere situate (in man) in the occiput or dorsal portion of the cerebrum and separated from the parietal lobe by the parieto-occipital fissure and from the temporal lobe by a conventional extension of that fissure. — Ger. *Hinterhauptslappen*.

occiput = the back part of the head, represented by the os occipitale. (Accent **ox-.**) **occipital**[a]. — Ger. *Hinterhaupt*.

occultism = 1. (*hist.*) the theory that insight into and control over nature is to be obtained by mysterious magical procedures and by long apprenticeship in secret lore (e.g. alchemy, astrology, theosophy, chiromancy, etc.); 2. (*pop.*) belief in mysterious or supernatural causes of physical phenomena. [Syn. (2) **mysticism** 2.] **occult**[a] = characterizing these procedures (1) or causes (2). (Accent **-cult-.**) **occultist**[np].

occupational hierarchy = the serial arrangement of occupational groups according to average intelligence, from unskilled labor up through the skilled trades and clerical occupations, business, and the professions. — Fr. *hiérarchie professionnelle*.

occupational level = the status or position of a person on a scale of occupations or vocations.

occupational therapy = treatment of mental and to some extent of physical disorders by occupational work, undertaken because of its remedial value. [E.g. shop work designed to exercise some defective muscle; simple weaving operations to arouse interest in creating something.]

ocellus = a small, simple eye, found chiefly in insects, in addition to compound eyes. **ocelli**[pl].

octave = (*mus.*) a pitch interval between two tones, one of which is produced by waves of twice the vibration rate of the other. [So called because the latter forms the eighth tone in the musical scale when the former is the first or tonic. The higher pitched tone is called the **octave** of the deeper. Cf. Table VII.]

octave quality, see **tonality.**

ocular = pert. to the eye. [Syn. **ophthalmic.** Cf. **optic.**]

ocular measurement = the measurement of visual space perception and visual space discrimination.

oculocardiac reflex = slowing of heart-beat, produced by pressing firmly on the ball of one or both eyes. [Mediated by V (sensory) and X (motor) cranial nerves. Usually absent in locomotor ataxia.]

oculomotor nerve = the III cranial nerve, which innervates all the extrinsic muscles of the eye except the external rectus and the superior oblique, and also sends fibers to the sphincter pupillae and the ciliary muscles within the eyeball.

od, odic (or **odylic**) **force** = (*hist.*) an undefined but peculiar energy assumed to be manifested to a sensitive person by emanations from all matter (Reichenbach). [These emanations are felt as heat and cold, and seen as luminous vapors and flames, often in colors. Syn. **Reichenbach phenomenon.** The hyperesthetic perception is now attributed to an illusion of sensory automatism induced by auto-suggestion.]

odor, odour = 1. a type of sensation due to the chemical stimulation of certain receptors which are embedded in two small brownish patches of mucous membrane, situate one in the roof of each nasal cavity; 2. a substance whose emanations stimulate these receptors. [Syn. **smell, scent** (prefd. for 2). Zwaardemaker gives nine classes of odor: ethereal (ätherisch), aromatic (aromatisch), fragrant (balsamisch), ambrosiac (Amber-Moschusgerüche), alliaceous (Allyl-Cacodylgerüche), empyreumatic (empyreumatisch), hircine (Kaprylgerüche), virulent (widerlich), and nauseous (ekelhaft). The first class he adopted from Lorry, the sixth from Haller, the rest from Linnaeus. Henning gives six classes: fruity (fruchtig), flowery (blumig), spicy (würzig), resinous (harzig), smoky or burnt (brenzlich), and foul or putrid (faulig). Cf. **olfaction, odor prism.**] **smell**[v], **odorous**[a]. — Fr. *odeur*; Ger. *Geruch*.

odor prism = a figure devised by Henning to show in schematic fashion the mutual relations of his six classes of odors and of the transitional odors between them. [Cf. **odor.**]

Oedipus complex, see **Edipus complex.**

oesophagus, see **esophagus.**

oestrum, see **estrum.**

offense, offence = 1. a type of behavior by which the organism endeavors to injure some enemy; 2. an act which contravenes some legal enactment or which is otherwise subject to social disapproval. [Contr. (1) w. **defense,** which tends to protect from injury.] **offensive**[a] (in both senses).

ogival (or **ogive**) **curve** = 1. an S-shaped or sigmoid curve with a point of inflexion in the middle and the slope positive (or negative) throughout its length; 2. (*esth.*) the diagonal rib of a Gothic vault. [If the cumulative frequencies of a unimodal distribution are plotted with the axes representing "score," and "percent falling short of designated score," an ogive curve (1) results.]

ohm = the unit of electrical resistance. [The international ohm is defined as the resistance at 0° C. of a mercury column of uniform cross-section, whose length is 106.3 cm. and whose mass is 14.4521 grams.]

Ohm's law = 1. (*aud.*) the principle that a complex sound is analyzed by the ear into a series of simple tones whose frequencies correspond to the members of the Fourier series; 2. (*phys.*) the current which flows in a non-reactive electric circuit is directly proportional to the electromotive force and inversely proportional to the resistance in the circuit. [Cf. (1) **harmonic analyzer, Fourier's law.**]

ohmic resistance = the measured resistance, expressed in ohms, of any substance (e.g. the human body) to the passage of an electric current. [When corrected for artifacts such as polarization, the figure is called **true resistance.** When not so corrected it is called **apparent resistance.**]

olecranal = pert. to or located on or around the point of the elbow. (Accent **-lek-.**)

olfactie = a unit of olfactory intensity; i.e. one olfactie is the strength of the threshold stimulus of a particular scent as measured by Zwaardemaker's olfactometer.

olfaction = a sense whose receptors are spindle-shaped bodies (nucleated nerve fibers) lying in a small patch of brownish mucous membrane situate in the roof of the nasal cavity on both sides of the septum, and whose stimuli consist of gaseous particles given off from the surface of certain organic and inorganic substances and producing a chemical effect upon the receptors. [Syn. **smell,** preferably limited to the function. Cf. **odor, odor prism, scent.**] **smell**[v], **olfactory**[a]. — Fr. *odorat*; Ger. *Geruch, Geruchsinn*.

olfactometer = an instrument, devised by Zwaardemaker, for measuring the stimulus limen, difference limen, and quantitative values of olfactory stimuli; it consists essentially of a glass inhaling tube, bent up at one end for insertion into the nostril, with a larger tube (lined with odorous substance) which can be pushed in over the straight portion of the inhaling tube to any desired extent, thus exposing various amounts of odorous surface to the current of air inhaled. [The amount of exposed surface is indicated on a scale marked on the inhaling tube. A double olfactometer consists essentially of two inhaling and two odor tubes arranged to stimulate each nostril separately.] **olfactometry**[n].

olfactory area = the region of the cerebrum containing the secondary olfactory centers, divided into anterior, medial, intermediate, and lateral olfactory nuclei. [It is the center for sensations of smell.] — Fr. *aire olfactive*; Ger. *Riechsphäre*.

olfactory bulb = (*anat.*) an outgrowth of the forebrain, to which it is joined by the olfactory tract. [Sometimes erroneously called the **olfactory nerve.** The olfactory nerves arise from the bipolar neurons in the olfactory epithelium of the nose and terminate among the cortical cells of the olfactory bulb.] — Ger. *Riechkolben*.

olfactory cell = a spindle-shaped neuron, whose ovoid and nucleated body and distal projection are embedded in the olfactory mucous membrane, and whose axon forms part of the olfactory nerve. [The distal extension is bristle-like and at the external surface of the membrane swells slightly and bears cilia, which extend into the covering of mucous and upon which the olfactory stimulus probably acts.] — Fr. *glomérule (bâtonnet) olfactif*.

olfactory lobe = the region directly beneath the frontal lobe, including the olfactory bulb, tract, and trigone, the parolfactory area, and the anterior perforated substance. — Ger. *Riechlappen.*

olfactory nerve, olfactory fila = the 1st cranial nerve; a group of nerve fila connecting the olfactory surfaces in the nose which serve as receptors for smell, with the gyrus fornicatus.

olfactory receptor = 1. the olfactory mucous membrane, a brownish patch of membrane situate at the top of each nasal cavity, about 500 mm. square in man; 2. (more exactly) the **olfactory cells** which are embedded in the olfactory mucous membrane.

olives, olivary bodies = elevated regions on the front of the medulla, situate one on either side of the pyramids. — Fr. *corps olivaires*; Ger. *Oliven des verlängerten Mark.*

omen = (*magic*) an occurrence supposed to portend or foreshadow a future event, but not causally connected with it. [Cf. **augury.**] — Fr. *présage*; Ger. *Vorzeichen.*

ommatidium = one of the parts or divisions of a compound eye. **ommatidia**[pl].

omnibus test = a psychological or educational test which consists of many items or tasks of two or more different kinds (e.g. arithmetical problems, opposites, analogies, and vocabulary questions) presented in apparently haphazard order. [If the items of each kind are arranged in order of increasing difficulty, it is called a **spiral omnibus test;** if not, and if the different types of items recur regularly, it is a **cycle omnibus test.**]

omnipotence of thought = (*psychoan.*) an exaggerated conviction that mere wishes are and must be followed by results or changes in the external world. [An over-estimation of **psychical processes** as contr. w. **reality;** characteristic of obsessional neuroses, the thinking of childhood, the beliefs of primitive people, and belief in magic.] — Ger. *Allmacht der Gedanken.*

onanism = masturbation. [From the Biblical character, Onan, who, however, practised coitus interruptus and not masturbation.]

oneirology, onirology = 1. the study of dreams; 2. (*hist.*) divination by means of dreams. [Syn. (2) **oneiromancy.**]

oneiromancy = divination by means of dreams. **oneiromantic**[a].

one-level attention = a conscious experience in which all the content-items are experiences at a single level or degree of clearness or attensity. — Fr. *attention à niveau unique.*

one-way vision screen = an observation screen made of wire netting or thin cloth brightly illuminated on one side and dark on the other, permitting vision from the dark side toward the light but not vice versa. [Used mainly in the observation of children and animals; it serves to conceal the observer from view.] — Fr. *écran pour la vision dans une seule direction.*

onomatomania = obsessive preoccupation with words and names, either by persistent efforts to recall certain words, or by attaching peculiar significance to certain words.

onomatopoeic (or **onomatopoetic**) **theory of language** = the theory which attributes the origin of language to the attempt to imitate certain sounds produced by natural forces, animal cries, etc. [E.g. crack, splash, ding dong.]

ontogenesis = the origin and development of the individual or of some organ or function in the individual. [Contr. w. **phylogenesis** = racial origin and growth. The term **ontogeny** usually denotes the general problem of individual development, contr. w. **phylogeny;** while **ontogenesis** denotes the same problem in reference to specific cases, especially of specific organs and functions.] **ontogenetic**[a].

ontogenetic psychology = the systematic study of the origin and growth of mental life and behavior in the individual. [Contr. w. **phylogenetic psychology** = of their origin and growth in the race.]

ontogeny = the origin and development of the individual. [Contr. w. **phylogeny.** Cf. **ontogenesis.**] (Accent **-toj-**.) **ontogenic**[a].

ontology = the branch of metaphysics which investigates the ultimate nature of being. [**metaphysics** is usually divided into **ontology** and **cosmology** (Paulsen); C. v. Wolff further included in it **natural theology** and **rational psychology.**]

ontotropic = characterizing the tendency of images (esp. eidetic images) to conform to nature in respect to content and coloration.

oögenesis = the cytologic processes involved in the development of the ovum, or female sex-cell. [Cf. **gametogenesis.** Contr. w. **spermatogenesis.**]

oögonium = the primordial germ cell which gives rise to the female germ cell, i.e. to the ovum or egg. **oögonia**[pl].

oösperm = a newly fertilized egg. [Cf. **zygote.**]

open pipe, see **pipe.**

operate = to act or to perform work. [Properly distg. fr. **function**[v], which implies activity that forms part of a systematic process or **function**[n]. E.g. a muscle, nerve, or receptor *operates* in a certain manner; a muscle *functions* to produce flexion of the member, etc. Similarly an **operation**[n] = a mode of activity; distg. fr. a **function**[n] = a systematic activity or a type of activity. E.g. uttering a sentence is an *operation*; speech is a *function.*] **operation**[n].

opercula of insula = overlapping folds of the cerebral cortex which bound dorsally the anterior part of the Sylvian fissure, and cover the insula, or island of Reil. **operculum**[sing].

ophthalmia = an inflammation of the superficial tissues of the eye, esp. of the conjunctiva.

ophthalmic = pert. to the eye. [Syn. **ocular.** Cf. **optic.**]

ophthalmic reflex, see **supraorbital reflex.**

ophthalmometer = (*vis.*) an instrument for measuring the curvature of the front surface of the cornea in various meridians by means of the images seen reflected in it. [Used to determine **astigmatism,** which is due almost wholly to inequality of the curvature of the corneal surface in different directions; the term is also sometimes used to designate certain instruments of less importance used for other measurements upon the eyeball.]

ophthalmometry = 1. mensuration of the eyeball, especially the determination of the constants of its optical system; 2. the use of the **ophthalmometer.**

opthalmoplegia = paralysis of the eye muscles.

ophthalmoscope = a diagnostic instrument consisting essentially of a perforated mirror, which reflects a beam of light through the pupil of the eye, whereby an observer looking through the hole in the mirror is enabled to see the retina, its blood-vessels, the nerve-head, etc. **ophthalmoscopy**[n], **ophthalmoscopic**[a].

ophthalmotrope = an apparatus for demonstrating the movements of both eyes; a series of strings, pulleys, and weights shows the action of the six eye-muscles in a model of the two eyes.

opinion = 1. a conclusion or judgment based on grounds admittedly insufficient to produce certainty; 2. an individual's own account or statement (frequently a rationalization) of his attitude. [Distg. fr. **attitude** = a fundamental tendency to act, or a particular set to respond to a given stimulus or situation; and fr. **belief,** a more certain judgment or attitude, usually emotional in nature. Cf. **public opinion.**] — Fr. *opinion, avis*; Ger. *Ansicht, Meinung*.

opisthotonus = a condition of tetanic contracture of the dorsal muscles of the vertebral column resulting in marked ventral convexity.

opium = a drug, the active principles of which are morphine, codeine, papaverine and other alkaloids, derived from the inspissated juice of the poppy, Papaver somniferum.

opiumism = addiction to the use of opium.

opposites test = a type of mental test in which the testee is instructed to respond with the opposite or contrary of a given stimulus word. [Syn. **antonym test;** often combined with a **synonym test.** Cf. **synonym-antonym test.**]

opposition = antithesis or antagonism, of whatever sort, between two concepts, individuals, etc. **oppose**[v], **opposite**[a]. — Ger. *Gegensatz*.

optic, optical = pert. to vision or its organ, or to the science of optics.

optic chiasm, see **chiasm.** — Ger. *Sehnervenkreuzung*.

optic disk (or **disc**) = a small, low eminence on the inner surface of the retina, within the eyeball, formed by the nerve-fibers of the retina, as they collect just before emerging from the eyeball to form the optic nerve. • [The term refers esp. to the disk-like appearance of this structure as seen by the **ophthalmoscope,** while **papilla** and **nerve-head** apply rather to the anatomical structure itself.]—Fr. *papille optique*; Ger. *Sehnervenscheibe*.

optic lobes = the superior pair of the **corpora quadrigemina.**

optic nerve = the II cranial nerve, a sensory nerve, which connects the retina of the eye with the visual centers. [It contains also some fibers which transmit impulses from the brain.] — Ger. *Sehnerv*.

optic nystagmus, see **nystagmus.**

optic thalamus, see **thalamus.**

optic tracts = fibers which pass from the optic chiasm to the lateral geniculate body, pulvinar, and superior colliculus. — Fr. *voies optiques*.

optical axis = 1. (*opt.*) a line drawn through the centers of curvature of the refracting (and reflecting) surfaces of an optical system; 2. the direction or directions in which light may pass through a doubly refracting crystal without undergoing double refraction. — Ger. *Augenachse*.

optical illusion = any visual perception of spatial relations (or other attributes) which views or interprets these relations differently from the physical relations among the objective stimuli that give rise to the perception. — Ger. *optische Täuschung*.

optical pendulum = a device for presenting visual stimuli; it consists of a moving pendulum bearing a screen with a slit, which passes before a similar slit in a fixed screen behind the pendulum.

optical surface = a surface at which reflection or refraction takes place, especially one designed for the purpose with accurate conformation and adequate polish, as part of an **optical system.**

optical system = those parts of an optical instrument, considered in their relations one to another, which have directly to do with the refraction or reflection of light. [In mathematical optics an **optical system** consists of two or more **optical surfaces,** the simplest being a single lens or prism.]

optics = that branch of physics which deals with the phenomena of light, or radiant energy, in its broadest sense.

optimism = that attitude of an individual toward the social organization or life in general, which emphasizes the good and is hopeful regarding the trend of social evolution. [Contr. w. **pessimism.**] **optimist**[np], **optimistic**[a].

optimum = the best value in a given series (generally not the maximum or minimum) for the purpose in hand. [Used adjectivally, e.g. **optimum** (or **optimal**) **temperature** = the temperature most favorable to the life functions of a given organism.] **optimal**[a].

optimum duration = a term used in reaction experiments to denote the most favorable duration between signal and stimulus for producing prompt response in a given situation. [Both shorter and longer stimulus durations would tend to produce slower response.]

optometry = 1. the science and practice of measurements upon the eye; 2. the fitting of glasses by non-medical practitioners.

optrics = an unsanctioned generic term, used to designate that branch of optics which deals with the refraction and reflection of light, esp. in the study of optical systems. [Cf. **catoptrics, dioptrics** (accepted terms).]

ora serrata = the jagged anterior border of the retina.

oracle = (*hist.*) 1. a prophet, sibyl, or other person who possesses the power of foreseeing the future; 2. a shrine where such persons answer inquiries respecting future events.

oral = pert. to the mouth or located on the region around it. — Ger. *mündlich*.

oral cavity = the cavity of the mouth extending from the lips to the oral pharynx. [Commonly treated in three parts: 1. the **rima,** between the lips; 2. the **vestibule,** between lips and teeth; 3. the **oral cavity proper.**]

oral character, see **character trait.**

oral erotism = (*psychoan.*) the stage of pregenital libido which refers specifically to the sexual activity in nursing.

oral method = a method of instruction in the education of the deaf, which makes use of speech and lip-reading as the chief means of communication among the deaf themselves and between the deaf and others.

oral neurosis = (*psychoan.*) a term applied to stammering as indicating more definitely its unconscious motivation from the oral libido and oral character traits, consciously manifested by the tic-like symptoms in the speech mechanism (Coriat). — Fr. *névrose orale*.

oral sadism = (*psychoan.*) the tendency on the part of infants to suck or bite or introduce into the mouth any external object. [Characteristic of the early pregenital stage. Syn. **cannibalistic stage.**]

oral stage, oral libido = (*psychoan.*) that stage of pregenital (infantile) libido development in which the sexual activity has not yet become separated from the taking of nourishment. [Usually divided into the earlier oral (sucking or nursing) and the later oral (cannibalistic or biting) stages. — Fr. *stade oral.*

orang-utan = an ape belonging to the family of simiidae and genus simia. [Distg. fr. the **gibbon, gorilla,** and **chimpanzee.**]

orbital = pert. to or located in the cavities containing the eyes. (Accent **or-.**)

order = 1. the type of relation found among data, or assigned to them, such that the investigator may proceed from item to item according to certain regular and determinate principles or in determinate directions without omission of any item; e.g. temporal order; 2. (*biol.*) a group in the classification of species, higher than **family** and lower than **class.** [Cf. (2) **genus, species.**] **orderly** (1)[a]. — Fr. (1) *suite, ordre,* (2) *ordre*; Ger. (1) *Reihenfolge,* (2) *Ordnung.*

order of merit/method of = a procedure used in investigating **judgment** (1), or **affection** (1) by presenting all the stimuli at one time, to be rated and cast into a one-dimensional order of relative preferences. [One of the **methods of impression.** Syn. **rank order method.**]

ordinate = (*math.*) the vertical axis of reference in a chart or curve. [Contr. w. the **abscissa,** the horizontal axis.]

orectic, see **orexis.**

orectic process = the organic events concerned in the initiation or increase of appetite or desire.

orenda = in Iroquoian religion a force, a magic power believed to pervade nature and man. [Cf. **manitou.**]

orexis = the affective and conative aspects of experience, as distg. fr. the cognitive. **orectic**[a].

organ = 1. (*anat.*) a structure in the body which performs some specific function or functions. **organic**[a].

organ = 2. (*mus.*) a wind instrument of many pipes, operated by directing air into one or more at a time by means of keys and a system of valves; 3. (*mus.*) an instrument differing from (2) in that the tones are produced by forcing air across vibrating reeds. [Syn. (2) **pipe organ,** (3) **reed organ.**] — Fr. (2) *orgue*; Ger. (2) *Orgel,* (3) *Harmonium.*

organ of Corti, see **Corti/organ of.**

organ (or **organic**) **inferiority** (Ger. *Minderwertigkeit von Organen*), see **inferiority complex** and **inferiority feeling.**

organelle = an organ within a cell. [It constitutes part of the cell in which it is found.]

organic = 1. pert. to structure; 2. pert. to the organism. [The second use is confusing; the ambiguity can be avoided by substituting syn. **organismic.**]

organic deafness, see **deafness.**

organic memory = any persistent alteration (with consequently altered capacity for response) of living tissue which results from a temporary process of excitation. [This *capacity to learn* inherent in all living tissue is the basis of theories of the inheritance of acquired characters proposed by E. Hering, S. Butler, R. Semon, and E. Rignano. Cf. **mneme.**]

organic psychosis = any mental disorder which is due to structural changes in the brain. [Distg. fr. **functional psychosis** = due to functional disturbances.]

organic selection = the operation of **natural selection** as supplemented by the effects of use or disuse in individuals during successive generations. [The theory of **organic selection** assumes that such individual accommodations may keep alive a slight variation which of itself is of no selective value; syn. **indirect selection.**]

organic sensation = a sensation arising from stimulation of receptors in any one of the internal organs. [Cf. **organic sense.**] — Ger. *Organempfindung.*

organic sense = the sense or senses whose receptors lie in the internal organs. [Broadly speaking it includes both visceral sensitivity and kinesthetic sensitivity, i.e. the sensitivity of the muscles and joints. More specifically the term is limited to the sensitivity of the viscera and can be used interchangeably with **visceral sense.** Cf. **sensitivity/visceral.**] — Fr. *sens interne.*

organic set, see **set/organic.**

organism = a highly specialized system of material substances, consisting mainly of carbon, hydrogen, oxygen, and nitrogen, integrated into a cell or system of cells, the entire complex being capable of maintaining its existence as a unitary system. [**organisms** are divided into **plants** and **animals.** The term is sometimes extended, by vague analogy, to other organizations; e.g. the social organism. Cf. **life.**] **organismic**[a], **organismal**[a] (not recommended), **organic**[a] (ambig.).

organismic, organismal = pert. to an organism, or to the organism as a unitary whole. [**organismic** is prefd. etymologically. The adjective **organic,** sometimes used, is ambiguous; it relates more properly to **organ.**]

organization = 1. a structure or grouping of any sort in which there is systematic differentiation of parts and functions, e.g. social organization; 2. (*Gestalt*) the process by which psychophysical excitations distribute themselves so as to form more or less articulated and stable fields; (or) the product of such process. [The term **organism** is properly limited to biological organization. Cf. **organize.**] — Ger. *Organization.*

organization/mental, see **mental organization.**

organize = 1. to arrange the parts of an aggregate or members of a group in such a way that a working, orderly, or integrated whole results; 2. to arrange data in such manner as to show their interrelations, or to arrange them in accordance with some plan or idea. [Cf. **organization.**] **organized**[a].

organogenic = attributable to a specific organ, such as the heart, or an endocrine secretion.

organon = a body of principles by means of which knowledge may be acquired or produced. [The classic or Aristotelian organon was purely logical, i.e. concerned with correct thinking and reasoning; the newer or Baconian organon attempted to bring reasoning into accord with objective reality.]

organotherapy = the treatment of disorders by administration of animal organs or extracts made from them.

orgasm = 1. the culmination of coitus, comprising viscero-motor and body motor components; 2. the intense sensation-complex accompanying the culmination of coitus. **orgastic**[a].

orientation = 1. the determination of the spatial relations of objects or data to one another; 2. the assumption in a cell, an organ, or an organism of a definite axial position in reference to the direction of an external stimulating agent. [Syn. **tropism.** For orienting terms used in anatomy, see Tables XVI, XVII.] **orient**[v]. — Ger. *Orientierung.*

orientation/illusion of = any misinterpretation of one's position with reference to space or time. — Fr. *renversement de l'orientation.*

orientation/mental = ability of an individual to recognize his surroundings and their temporal or spatial relations to himself, or to appreciate his relations to his social environment.

orientation/photic = the assumption by an organism of a definite position with reference to a light stimulus. [Syn. **phototropism.**]

orienting response, orienting = a response to gravity, light, or other type of stimulus which involves adjustment of the creature's entire body with reference to the location of the stimulus. [Syn. **tropism.**]

origin = (*math.*) the zero reference-point of the measures employed. [In plotting curves, etc. the point where the **abscissa** and **ordinate** axes intersect.]

origin versus nature = a phrase used to indicate the difference between a genetic account of organisms (or any other sort of data) and a complete description of their characteristics.

original[a] = not derived from or patterned after anything else. [Syn. **primordial, primitive, fundamental.**]

original[n] = a model. [Contr. w. **copy**[n] = the reproduction from an **original.**]

original nature = the sum-total of characters or traits inherited by an organism. [Contr. w. **acquired characters.**]

originality = the ability to conceive new ideas, to produce new devices or inventions or works of art or literature.

oropharynx, see **pharynx.**

orthocardiac reflex = dilation of the right side of the heart, which occurs when the upright position of the body is assumed.

orthodox = characterizing the principles officially accepted at any given period by a community, by a religious body, or by scientists as a coherent social group, or the individuals who accept such principles. [Contr. w. **heterodox.**] **orthodoxy**[n].

orthogenesis = the theory which assumes that the course of evolution is not random, but is in some way directed along specific lines, irrespective of the selective process. **orthogenetic**[a], **orthogenic**[a].

orthognathous = designating a skull which protrudes toward the vertical plane of the jaw. [Contr. w. **prognathous,** in which the jaw protrudes beyond the forehead.] (Accent **-thog-.**)

orthophoria, see **imbalance/muscular.**

orthoplasy = (*hist.*) determinate evolution as brought about by organic selection. [Distg. fr. **orthogenesis,** which attributes evolution to other causes.]

os = a Latin term signifying both **mouth** and **bone.** **oral**[a] = pert. to the mouth; **osseous**[a] = pert. to bone.

oscillation, see **o factor.**

oscillator, see **audio-oscillator.**

oscillograph = an instrument which produces a visual representation or record of the wave-form of electrical or other oscillations. [The **mechanical oscillograph** is essentially a galvanometer with a moving system of small inertia and high natural frequency; the **Duddell** type consists of a single loop of wire which is suspended under tension in a strong magnetic field, and which carries a small mirror to reflect a beam of light upon a moving photographic plate, thereby affording a record of the electrical current. Cf. **cathode-ray oscillograph, galvanometer, capillary electrometer.**] (Accent **-sill-.**) **oscillogram**[n] = the record produced.

oscillometer = an instrument for the measurement of vibratory motion, esp. the angle of pitching or rolling of a ship at sea. (Accent **-lom-.**)

oscilloscope = 1. (*hist.*) an arrangement on the principle of the **stroboscope,** which provides successive momentary illuminations of limited areas, the rate of succession being under the control of the observer; 2. a form of **oscillograph.** [Used (1) in the study of rapidly moving mechanisms.] (Accent **-sill-.**)

osmosis = the diffusion of substances through a membrane or porous wall.

osseous = pert. to bone. [Cf. **os.**]

ossicles/auditory = a chain of bones in the middle ear, which serve to communicate the movements of the tympanic membrane to the fluid of the internal ear. [In man these are three in number, called **malleus** (hammer), **incus** (anvil), and **stapes** (stirrup). The handle of the malleus is attached to the tympanic membrane, while the footplate of the stapes is fused to the oval window of the vestibule. The three bones form an articulated chain, fixed in the tympanic cavity by a number of ligaments. Syn. **ear bones.**] — Fr. *osselets auriculaires*; Ger. *Gehörknöchelchen.*

Ostwald colors = a system of pigment colors based upon the admixture of black and white pigments to a series of colored standards. [Cf. **Ridgway colors, Munsell colors,** generally similar in character.]

other/the = the social environment. [Syn. **alter.** Contr. w. **self** or **ego.**] — Fr. *l'autrui.*

otic = pert. to the ear. [Cf. **auditory.**]

otic vesicle, see **vesicle/auditory.**

otoconia, see **otoliths.**

otocyst = 1. the auditory vesicle of the mammalian embryo; 2. syn. for **statocyst.**

otoliths = small crystals of calcium carbonate contained in the endolymph of the inner ear, which, when the head moves, impinge on the nerve endings in the utricle and saccule, thus aiding in the maintenance of equilibrium. [Syn. **statoliths, otoconia**[pl].]

otology = the branch of science which treats of the ear and its disorders. **otologic(al)**[a], **otologist (aurist)**[np].

otosclerosis = an auditory disorder characterized by loss of sensitivity, usually gradual and progressive, caused by induration, or hardening, of the moving parts (particularly the ossicles) of the middle ear.

ouija board = a device used by mediums and others as a substitute for automatic writing, which consists of a board upon which are printed the alphabet, numerals, and the words *yes* and *no*, and a heart-shaped traveler which is involuntarily moved from letter to letter (by the hands of two persons resting upon it) so as to spell words. [Combined from French and German words, oui + ja, both meaning "yes." Syn. **autoscope.** Cf. **planchette.**] — Fr. *planchette d'ouija.*

outer = 1. beyond the organism or body; 2. towards the region surrounding the organism. [Contr. w. **inner.** Syn. **external, objective.**] — Fr. *externe*; Ger. *äusser.*

outer ear, see **ear/external.**

outrage[n] = a loose term, denoting an act exceedingly displeasing to the speaker and regarded as injurious and insulting. [The term has a highly emotional tinge.] **outrageous**[a].

ovary = the reproductive gland in the female, which functions in the production of ova and certain internal secretions. [Cf. **gonad.**] **ovarian**[a]. — Ger. *Eierstock.*

overblowing = the application to a wind-instrument (e.g. a whistle or organ-pipe) of a blast of air of such force as to produce a tone of a pitch higher than the tone normally produced by the instrument. [In properly constructed instruments the frequency of a tone produced by overblowing bears a simple integral relation to the fundamental.] — Fr. *emploi d'une surpression.*

overcompensate = to make more than the necessary amount of allowance or adjustment. [E.g. to **overcompensate** for an extra loading of one arm in comparing weights lifted by the two hands.] **overcompensation**[n]. — Fr. *excès de compensation.*

overdetermination = (*psychoan.*) an unconscious mechanism which brings about a symptom or dream element by convergence from several different directions. [E.g. every element of the **manifest content** of a dream is said to be **overdetermined** in that it represents several **latent dream thoughts** or day instigators, or a symptom may have many meanings.] — Fr. *surdétermination.*

overindividual = a term used by certain writers to imply the existence of social or group factors of behavior which do not rest upon purely individual mechanisms. [Often implies the assumption of a **group mind.**]

overlapping elements (or **factors**) = in mental or other types of testing, the elements (or factors) common to whatever tests are used. — Fr. *facteurs communs.*

overlapping of groups = (*statist.*) the extent to which the distributions of scores of two groups of individuals, etc. fall within the same limits. [Usually measured by the per cent of one group which exceeds the median of the other.] — Fr. *empiètement des groupes.*

overlapping of responses = the initiation of a second response or aspect of a response before the first is fully completed. [The principle of **overlapping** is a factor in learning and in complex responses. It is based on the fact that each response sets up stimuli of different kinds (esp. proprioceptive) to other acts or to continued activity, so that *a response* is not usually a discrete thing.] — Fr. *empiètement des réponses.*

overlearning = learning in which practice has proceeded beyond the point necessary for immediate recall or immediate use with a prescribed degree of skill. [**overlearning** is assumed to be necessary for superior retention during and after a period of disuse. The effects of **overlearning** are functions of many other factors, and indicate diminishing returns with continued repetitions of practice, possibly due in large part to a decrease in motivation.] — Fr. *surapprentissage.*

overproduction = 1. increase in the number of organisms in a given species to such an extent that the supply of food is insufficient for all; 2. movements made by an organism in excess of those necessary for its adequate adjustment to the (usually novel) environment. [Such overproduced movements are also largely ill-adaptive. Cf. **trial and error theory.** Syn. **excess movements.**] — Fr. *surproduction*; Ger. *Überproduktion.*

overstatement, see **understatement.**

overt response = any response which involves changes in muscles or glands (or both) that can be easily observed by another person. [Syn. **explicit response.** Contr. w. **implicit** or **covert response.**]

overtone = any partial in a compound tone, except the fundamental. [When the frequency of an overtone is an exact multiple of the fundamental frequency, it is called a **harmonic overtone** (or **harmonic**); if not a multiple, an **inharmonic overtone.** Cf. **partial tone.**] — Fr. *ton partiel* (*harmonique*) *supérieur*; Ger. *Oberton.*

ovum = the female germ cell. [Contr. w. **sperm-cell** = the male cell.] **ova**[pl], **ovic**[a]. — Fr. *oeuf*; Ger. *Ei.*

P

P = symbol for **probability ratio.**

p factor, perseveration factor = a unitarily functioning factor varying in degree from one individual to another, showing itself as a tendency for mental processes to have a certain lag or inertia, and, accordingly, to *perseverate* (Spearman). [Obverse of **c factor.** Cf. **c factor, inertia.**]

Pacinian (or **Vater-Pacinian**) **corpuscle** = a type of large capsulated nerve end-organ located in fatty subcutaneous tissue in hairless bodily regions (e.g. the tactile pads) and along the course of nerves, close to the joints, and in the intestines. [Believed by some writers to arouse a special articular sensation at the joints; also to arouse pressure sensations in the viscera.]

paidophilia, see **pedophilia.**

pain = 1. a specific sensation stimulated by powerful processes in various bodily tissues, the impulse being commonly assumed to be conveyed by a distinct set of nerves having a ready motor outlet; 2. syn. for **unpleasantness. painful**[a]. — Fr. *douleur, pénible*[a]; Ger. (1) *Schmerz.*

pain sense = a special sense found in every part of the periphery and in many internal regions. [Cf. **free nerve endings.**] — Fr. *sens de la douleur*; Ger. *Schmerzsinn.*

pain spot = a point on the skin which is peculiarly sensitive to pain stimuli, i.e. which has a much lower limen for pain stimuli than the adjacent regions. — Fr. *point de douleur*; Ger. *Schmerzpunkt.*

painless cheek area, see **Kiesow's painless cheek area.**

paired associates = a type of procedure in which impressions (usually words or nonsense syllables) are presented in pairs one or more times, and the testee is subsequently asked to respond with the second member of any pair when the first member is given. [Employed more often to study the nature of the associative connections than to measure the efficiency of the testee. Syn. **(method of) right** (or **correct**) **associates.**] — Fr. *test de comparaisons par paires*; Ger. *Treffermethode*.

paired comparison/method of = a method used in judgment of affective preference of colors, etc., in which each member of a series is compared in pairs with every other member in respect to a given quality, the individual indicating the member he prefers in each pair till a graded scale of the entire series is obtained. [This method may also be used in comparing weights, length of lines, etc. One of the methods of impression; also a method of psychophysics.]

pairing = arrangement of the stimulus items included in an experiment in groups of two, for purposes of comparison, association, etc., or of individuals in the making of comparable groups. — Fr. *accouplement*; Ger. *Paarung*.

palatal reflex = contraction of palatal and pharyngeal muscles, and the act of swallowing, elicited by touching the palate. [Mediated by IX and X cranial nerves through their bulbar centers and the pharyngeal plexus.]

palate = the roof of the mouth. [It is composed of the **hard palate,** formed by the palatal processes of the superior maxillary bones and the palatal bones, and the **soft palate,** consisting of an aggregation of muscles.] — Fr. *palais*; Ger. *Gaumen*.

paleëncephalon = the parts of the encephalon, or brain, that are phylogenetically the more primitive, i.e., those related to the sense of smell. [Syn. **archencephalon.** Contr. w. **neëncephalon.**]

paleontology = the branch of biology which investigates organisms that existed in the past. [Distg. fr. **archeology,** which investigates the remains of human productivity in prehistoric times.]

paleopsychology = the investigation of primitive features of mentality which persist from a previous evolutionary stage.

palingenesis = the development of an individual organism, in so far as it epitomizes the separate stages in the evolution of its race or species. **palingenetic**[a].

palingenetic characters = those characters in an organism which represent ancestral types.

pallesthesia = sensibility to vibrations, esp. in regions of bony prominences. [Sometimes written **palmesthesia.** Syn. **bone sensibility.**]

pallium = the vesicular wall of the forebrain covered by gray matter or cortex. [The cerebral cortex exclusive of the olfactory areas is called **neopallium;** the olfactory areas constitute the **archipallium.**]

pallor = any shading of a tissue lighter than normal, occasioned by reduction of blood supply or withdrawal of pigmentation or both. [In psychology usually limited to the paling of the human face, expressive of certain emotional attitudes.] — Fr. *pâleur*; Ger. *Blässe*.

palmar = pert. to or located in the palm of the hand. (Accent **pal-** or **pahm-.**)

palmar reflex = flexion of fingers elicited by irritation of the palm of hand. [Mediated by 8th cervical to 1st thoracic segments of the spinal cord.]

palmesthesia, see **pallesthesia.**

palmistry = (*hist.*) an attempt (*a*) to read character by interpretation of the shape, lines, prominences, and other characteristics of the hand (**chirognomy**); or (*b*) to reveal the past and predict the future of a person from these indications (**chiromancy**). [Syn. **chirosophy.** Cf. **chiromancy, sciosophy.**]

palp, palpate = 1. to touch with the fingers or other member; 2. to receive a touch sensation. [Syn. for **feel** (= **touch**) which is ambig.]

palpable = directly perceptible or observable. — Ger. *anschaulich*.

palpebral = pert. to or located on the eyelids. (Accent **pal-.**)

palpitation = excessively rapid action of the heart. [Cf. **tachycardia.**]

panasilinic telegraph = (*hist.*) a means of communication at a distance dependent upon the sympathy (rapport) of two snails, one at each station: the message is read from the letters on an alphabet board over which the **percipient** snail travels in exact correspondence to the movements the **agent** snail is made to make on a similar board. [A hoax perpetrated at the time of the success of the electric telegraph; still used to illustrate credulity stimulated by new scientific marvels.]

pancreas = a large, pinkish internal gland which consists functionally of two parts: (1) a portion which elaborates certain digestive juices, and (2) an endocrine portion, the internal secretion of which is important in the regulation of metabolism. [The portion of the pancreas known as the **islands of Langerhans** is important in the second function; these produce the hormone **insulin,** whose presence in the blood is essential for the normal combustion of carbohydrate.] **pancreatic**[a]. — Ger. *Bauchspeicheldrüse*.

pangen = a hypothetical organic unit having the power of self-perpetuation and supposed to afford the organic basis of heredity (de Vries). (Pron. **pan-jen.**) — Fr. *pangène*.

pangenesis = a theory proposed by Darwin to account for heredity, which assumes that each organ and type of cell in the body throws off minute particles, or *gemmules*, which reach the generative organs and serve to reproduce cells and organs in the offspring similar to those of the parent.

pangenesis/intracellular = a doctrine advanced by De Vries to explain reproduction, heredity, and other vital processes as a result of the activities of minute organic units called **pangens.**

panmixia = unrestricted intercrossing or interbreeding between members of a variety or a species. [The notion of **panmixia** was employed by Weismann to explain the degeneration of organs independently of the action of natural selection.]

panpsychism = the monistic theory which assumes that reality is ultimately psychic in nature. [Cf. **monism.**]

Panum phenomenon = if two lines near together are presented to one eye and a third line to the other eye, and either of the first two is combined stereoscopically with the third, then two lines will be seen of which the line lying nearer the median plane appears to be nearer than, or to stand in front of, the other. [Change of fixation can reverse the effect.]

papilla = (*biol.*) a small nipple-shaped elevation. (Accent **-ill-**.) **papillae**[pl], **papillar**[a].

papilla/acoustic = the epithelial organ of the internal ear, which bears the sensory endings and receives the terminations of the cochlear (or lagenar) branch of the acoustic nerve. [In higher vertebrates, it reaches an advanced stage of differentiation and is called the **organ of Corti.**]

papilla/lingual = a type of small projection or knob in the mucous membrane of the tongue. [There are four forms, three of which contain taste buds: (1) **circumvallate papillae,** each resembling a truncated cone and surrounded by a ring-shaped depression, few in number, situate in a V-shaped line across the back of the tongue, and richly supplied with taste buds; (2) **filiform p.,** small, thread-like, and very numerous, not containing taste buds but probably tactile in function; (3) **foliate p.,** leaf-like, situate along the edges toward the back of the tongue, and supplied with taste buds; (4) **fungiform** (or **lenticular) p.,** mushroom-shaped, occurring largely on the front of the tongue, esp. on the margins and apex and also supplied with taste buds.]

papilla/optic, see **optic disk.**

papillae/tactile = protuberances of tissue which occur in double rows, forming ridges in the outer surface of the corium, each protuberance, or papilla, containing a terminal capillary loop and certain touch receptors. [In man, most prominent on soles and palms.]

papillary stratum, see **corium.**

papilledema, papilloedema = a non-inflammatory swelling of the optic disk, generally due to brain tumor. [Syn. **choked disk.**]

papillitis = (*ophth.*) inflammation of the optic disk or papilla of the eye, due to pathological changes in the optic nerve.

parabiosis = 1. the partial fusion of two individuals, congenitally or by surgical operation, so that there is a mutual physiological influence; 2. temporary abolition of excitability and conductivity in a nerve. **parabiotic**[a].

paracentral gyrus = a convolution situate on the mesial surface of the cerebral hemisphere, lying above the caudal end of the sulcus cinguli and surrounding the upper (dorsal) end of the sulcus centralis.

paracentral vision = vision mediated by the zone of the retina immediately surrounding the fovea centralis.

paracusis, paracusia = an anomaly of hearing in which acuity (e.g. for conversation) is apparently increased by the presence of a noise. [It is generally agreed that the increased acuity is an illusion occurring only with persons selectively deaf to deep tones; such persons when conversing with normal individuals are relatively favored by most noises, since the normal individual speaks louder to overcome the masking effect of the noise.] **paracusic**[n,p].

paradox = a condition of affairs (or a statement thereof) which apparently includes some inherent incongruity. [It is usually implied that a fuller understanding shows the incongruity to be unreal.] **paradoxical**[a].

paradoxical cold = a sensation of cold whose stimulus is approximately 43° C. or over, i.e. a typical warmth stimulus. — Fr. *froid paradoxal*; Ger. *paradoxe Kälte.*

paradoxical patellar reflex = contraction of the adductor muscle but not of the quadriceps femoris complex when the patellar tendon is tapped. [Mediated by 3d lumbar segment of spinal cord.]

paradoxical pupillary reflex = dilation of the pupil upon stimulation of the retina by light. [Mediated by optic tract and oculomotor nerve.]

paradoxical warmth = a sensation of warmth whose stimulus is approximately 29°–31° C., i.e. a typical cold stimulus. — Fr. *chaleur paradoxale*; Ger. *paradoxe Wärme.*

parageusia = a distortion of a taste experience or a taste hallucination. **parageusic**[a].

paragraphia = a pathological condition in which the individual habitually inserts wrong and unintended words in what he is writing. **paragraphic**[a].

parakinesis = (*psych. res.*) levitation with contact, some or all of the power exercised being attributed to supernormal forces. [Cf. **telekinesis.**]

paralalia = impairment of the ability to utter certain speech sounds. [A form of **dyslalia.** Syn. **lisping,** a term often confined to the s or z sound defects.]

paralexia = a pathological condition in which the individual misreads words and phrases. **paralexic**[a].

parallax = the apparent relative shift of two unequally distant objects, observed when the point of view is shifted perpendicularly to the line of vision.

parallax/binocular = the inequality of separation, in the two eyes, of the retinal images of unequally distant objects. [It is due to the lateral difference in position of the two eyes, the more remote object appearing to the right eye relatively farther to the right in the visual field and *vice versa*; it is one of the stimulus conditions by which solidity and relative distance are mediated in binocular vision.]

parallel induction = (*biol.*) the production through the influence of the environment of the same kind of variation both in the body and in the germ cells.

parallel law = a psychophysical principle, formulated by Fechner as follows: if two stimuli of different intensity be applied to a receptor for a certain length of time, the absolute sensations aroused by the unchanged stimuli are diminished by fatigue; but the sensed ratio of difference remains unchanged. — Fr. *l. du parallélisme.*

parallel movements = movements of the two eyeballs in which the lines of sight remain parallel, as in looking at distant objects; or movements in which convergence and divergence play no part.

parallelism = (*anthrop.*) the development of culture traits in similar sequences and forms independently among distant tribes. [Distg. fr. **convergence.**]

parallelism/biological = the evolution of two or more groups of organisms along similar or parallel paths.

parallelism/psychophysical = a theory of mind-body relations, according to which, for every variation in conscious processes or experiences, there is a concomitant variation in neural processes. [The theory makes no assumption of a causal relation between the two. The theory of **parallelism** was formulated by Spinoza; the psychophysical interpretation was made by Fechner.]

paralogia = irrelevant expression of ideas by speech, due to difficulty in thinking logically. [A form of **dyslogia.**]

paralogism = an argument which involves some fallacy unnoticed by the proponent. [Contr. w. **sophism** = an argument intended to mislead by a concealed fallacy.] (Accent **-al-.**) **paralogistic**[a].

paralysis = 1. impairment or complete loss of motor function due to some disturbance of the neural or muscular mechanism; 2. impairment or destruction of sensory function (by analogy from 1.). **paralyses**[pl], **paralyze**[v], **paralytic**[a,np]. Ger. *Lähmung*.

paralysis agitans = a disease of late life, characterized by tremor of the muscles, delay of voluntary movement, and muscular contraction, causing peculiar position of limbs and head. [Syn. **Parkinson's disease.**]

paralytic dementia, see **paresis.**

paramecium, paramoecium = a genus of holotrichous ciliate protozoans. [The individuals are cigar-shaped, with an oblique oral groove.]

parameter = 1. (*math.*) a constant, in an equation containing two or more variables, for each value of which is given a particular curve of a system of curves; 2. (*psychol.*) any of the constants in learning or mental growth curves which define the form of the curve and which ordinarily differ when experimental conditions, subjects, material, etc. are changed.

paramnesia = a distortion of memory or of recognition either by inclusion of false details or by wrong temporal reference. [Cf. **déja vu.**] **paramnesic**[a].

paranoia = a psychosis characterized by fixed and systematized delusions. **paranoic**[a], **paranoic**[np] (*pop.* **paranoiac**[np]). — Fr. *folie lucide, paranoia.*

paranoid dementia = a type of more or less systematized delusion-formation, not purely paranoic (because of evidences of **additional** disorders), such as hallucinations, and deterioration or disorganization. [A branch of the dementia praecox (schizophrenic) group of psychoses. Syn. **délire chronique a évolution systématique** (Magnan).]

paranosic = (*psychoan.*) pert. to the primary gain or advantage arising from an illness. [Contr. w. **epinosic.**]

paraph = a terminal embellishment of a signature.

paraphasia = a pathological condition in which the individual habitually introduces wrong words in his speech. [Applied also to incidental substitutions of wrong words by normal individuals.] **paraphasic**[a].

paraphemia = the employment of wrong sounds or words in speaking, due to psychoneuroses. [Syn. **neurotic lisping;** a form of **dysphemia.**]

paraphonia = a form of **dysphonia** characterized by morbid alterations of the voice.

paraphrenia = a diagnostic term which includes both **paranoia** and **dementia praecox (schizophrenia).**

paraphysics = the theory of existence which deduces the nature of the psychical parallel of any given physical factor on the basis provided by general psychophysical laws.

paraphysis, see **pineal body.**

paraplegia = paralysis of the lower limbs or of the lower section of the body.

parapraxis = 1. (*pathol.*) a generic term for slips of the tongue and pen, forgetting, errors, faulty acts and similar mistakes, due to erroneous mental functioning; 2. a pathological condition in which the individual persistently commits errors in motor adjustments [(1) is attributed by psychoanalysts to unconscious wishes which counteract the desires in consciousness.] — Ger. *Fehlleistung.*

parapsychology, parapsychics, see **metapsychics.**

parasite = an organism which lives more or less continuously at the expense of another organism (the host) without compensation. **parasitic**[a], **parasitism**[n]. — Ger. *Schmarotzer.*

parasympathetic nervous system = the *cranial* and *sacral* parts of the autonomic system as distg. fr. the *thoracic* and *lumbar* portions.

parataxis = maladjustment, esp. of emotions and desires (T. V. Moore).

parathymia = (*rare*) a contrary or abnormal emotional reaction or state.

parathyroid glands = four small bodies situate one on the lateral and one on the mesial surface of each lateral lobe of the thyroid gland. [These bodies often occupy atypical positions. An extract of the parathyroids (Collip), containing the hormone or active principle of these endocrine organs, relieves parathyroid tetany and increases the blood calcium.]

parent = an organism which has produced offspring. **parental**[a].

parent-child relation = social behavior as between parent and child. [Particularly applicable to personality relations.] — Fr. *rapport entre parent et enfant.*

parental behavior = behavior concerned with the care and protection of the young. [It includes both maternal and paternal behavior.] — Fr. *comportement parental.*

paresis = 1. incomplete paralysis of a muscle or group of muscles central or peripheral in origin; 2. a brief term for the parenchymatous invasion of the cerebral cortex and brain, generally by the spirochaetes of syphilis, with grave memory and judgment defect, speech disorder, and tremor and reflex-alterations. [When occurring in early years, regularly through congenital syphilitic infection, it is termed **juvenile paresis.** If symptoms of spinal cord involvement are prominent, it is spoken of as the tabetic form, or **taboparesis.** Other categories (self-explanatory) are **conjugal** (in origin), and **cerebral, diffuse,** and **focal** forms. Syn. (hist.) **general paralysis of the insane, paralytic dementia.** (Accent **par-.**) **paretic**[a]. — Fr. *paralysie générale*; Ger. *Lähmung.*

paresis/juvenile = the parenchymatous syphilis of the brain of paresis in the child or adolescent, usually due to congenital infection.

paresthesia, paraesthesia = an abnormal or wrongly localized sensation, such as pricking, burning, etc. [Cf. **formication.**]

parietal = 1. pert. to or located on the middle region of the top of the skull, between the frontal and occipital regions and extending down on each side behind the temporal regions; 2. pert. to the outer wall of the body, as contr. w. the viscera. (Accent **-rye-.**) — Ger. (1) *Scheitel-.*

parietal lobe = a division of each cerebral hemisphere, bounded in man cephalad by the Rolandic fissure, caudad by the parieto-occipital fissure, and ventrad by the Sylvian fissure; the other boundaries are arbitrary. [The cortex on the convex surface of this lobe forms the **parietal area.**] — Ger. *Scheitellappen.*

parietal organ = a structure representing a third eye and arising as an outgrowth from the dorsal side of the third ventricle of the brain. [Cf. **pineal gland, epiphysis.**]

Parisian line = a linear measure = 2.25 mm. [Used by E. H. Weber and contemporaries.]

Parkinson's disease, see **paralysis agitans.**

parotid gland = a salivary gland situate in the side of the face in front and slightly below the external ear. [In man the largest salivary gland.] — Ger. *Ohrspeicheldrüse.*

paroxysm = a sudden, spasmodic onset or intensification of certain disease symptoms. — Ger. *krampfartiger Anfall.*

Parry's disease, see **exophthalmic goiter.**

parsimony/law of, see **economy/principle of.**

part = a loose term, applied to any result of division, whether actual or ideational. [E.g. part of body, of organ, etc. Contr. w. **whole.**] **partial**[a] (functional), **part**[a] (structural). — Ger. *Teil.*

part and whole learning, see **whole and part learning.**

parthenogenesis = the development of a new organism from an unfertilized ovum.

partial activity = 1. the prepotency of a part or aspect of a situation in the re-excitation of responses or the reviving of memories or images which were formerly constituents of the whole act or experience; 2. syn. for **piecemeal activity** (Thorndike). [Syn. (1) **focal recall,** as in association by similarity or in a conditioned reflex.]

partial activity/law of, see **piecemeal activity/law of.**

partial coefficient, partial correlation, see **correlation/partial,** and **correlation.**

partial color-blindness = a defect of color vision, congenital or acquired, characterized by absence or loss of one or more of the primal or fundamental components. [Usually two (sometimes one, or three) of the four Hering primaries, green, red, blue, and yellow, are missing, or disappear in sequence, with the progress of disease. Cf. **color-blindness; dichromatism.**]

partial impulse = (*psychoan.*) a sexual impulse which is not primary but can be subjected to further analysis (e.g. perversion).

partial tone, partial = any one of the simple constituents of a compound tone or simple clang. [The terms **fundamental tone** and **overtones** are also used; i.e. first partial = fundamental tone, second partial = first overtone, etc. Syn. **harmonic.**] — Ger. *Teilton.*

particular complex = (*psychoan.*) an emotional experience, or complex, based upon *incidental* circumstances in the individual's life history, rather than upon some fundamental instinct. [Contr. w. **universal complex** = based upon one of the fundamental instincts.]

particulate inheritance = a term proposed by Galton for inheritance in which the offspring present a mosaic of paternal and maternal characters which do not blend.

parturition = the act of giving birth to offspring.

part-whole test = a type of mental test in which the stimulus word represents some part of an object, and the required response is the naming of that object; i.e. naming the whole of which the given stimulus word denotes a part. [Distg. fr. **whole-part test,** in which the stimulus word is the name of the object, a part of which is to be named in the response.] — Fr. *test d'association de partie à tout.*

passion = strong, uncontrolled emotional expression. [In plural, often denotes any or all emotional experience.] **passionate**[a]. — Ger. *Leidenschaft.*

passive = characterizing a state of rest and inactivity, or a condition in which behavior is externally rather than internally initiated and controlled. [Contr. w. **active.**] **passiveness, passivity**[n].

passive forgetting = the fading away of certain memories due to lack of interest or exercise. [Contr. w. **active forgetting** = dismissal of memory data on account of unpleasant associations.] — Fr. *oubli passif.*

passivity = 1. a state of inactivity and of submission to external force or to another's will; 2. (*relig.*) the state of submissiveness and receptivity in which the soul stands before God without will of its own. [The mystics regard passivity (2) as a condition of attaining union with God.]

passivity feelings = (delusional) feelings of being influenced by various forces; e.g. religious, mystical, electrical, hypnotic. [A form of dissociation or projection phenomena, especially characteristic of schizophrenic symptom-complexes.] — Fr. *sentiments de passivité.*

past pointing = a procedure used to test the normal response to rotary movement; the subject, who has been rotated in a standard manner, normally points with his finger past the position indicated by the experimenter's finger. [If the subject has been rotated to the right, there is normally an illusion of motion to the left when he is brought to a stop. This he counteracts by pointing to the right of the indicated position.] — Fr. *pointage consécutif*; Ger. *Vorbeizeigen.*

pastoral stage = (*anthrop.*) that form of culture in which herds of sheep, cattle, etc. are maintained for livelihood. [It is often assumed that this stage succeeds the **hunting stage** and precedes the **agricultural stage.**] — Fr. *stade pastoral.*

patella = the knee-cap. **patellar**[a]. (Accent **-tell-.**)

patellar (or **patellar-tendon**) **reflex** = contraction of the quadriceps femoris upon tapping the patellar tendon when the leg is relaxed and flexed at the knee. [Mediated by 2d to 4th lumbar segments of spinal cord. Syn. **knee-jerk, quadriceps extensor r.**] — Fr. *réflexe patellaire, r. rotulien*; Ger. *Kniesehnenreflex.*

path, pathway = the line of conduction along which a nerve impulse proceeds through the chain of neurons which form a neural arc. — Fr. *voie*; Ger. *Leitungsbahn, Bahn.*

patheticus, see **trochlear nerve.**

pathic reflex = a response elicited by artificial stimulation of a sensory nerve at some point in its course.

pathogenesis = the development of disease or of morbid conditions.

pathography = the study of human personality in the light of an individual's ailments.

pathological lying = a tendency, present in certain types of mental disorder, to utter falsehoods or tell imaginary tales as true, even when no benefit accrues from concealing the truth. — Fr. *menteur constitutionnel*[np].

pathological nystagmus, see **nystagmus.**

pathology = 1. the branch of biology and medicine which investigates diseases, disorders, and abnormal conditions of the organism; 2. diseases and disorders, as distg. fr. normal conditions of the organism. [In medical circles often restricted to organic changes as distg. fr. functional (i.e. overt behavioral) disorders or *symptoms*.] **pathological**[a].

pathoneurosis = (*psychoan.*) a neurosis which supervenes upon an organic illness or injury and in which the libido that has withdrawn from the outer world is directed, not toward the whole ego, but chiefly to the diseased or injured organ, and evokes symptoms in this particular area (Ferenczi). — Fr. *pathonévrose.*

pathophobia = morbid fear of disease or of general suffering. [Syn. **nosophobia.**]

pathos = mental suffering, as distinguished from sensory pain. [Applied esp. to painful situations in life or dramatic literature which appeal to the sympathy of the onlooker.] **pathetic**[a].

pattern = 1. a sample or model which is to be copied or imitated; 2. (*neurol.* and *psychol.*) a functional integration of discriminable parts, which operates or responds as a unitary whole: e.g. neural pattern, thought pattern, social pattern. [Contr. (2) w. **blend** or **fusion.** Cf. **model.**] — Fr. (1) *modèle,* (2) *forme, complexus, schéma, ensemble structurel*; Ger. (1) *Muster,* (2) *Anordnung.*

pattern reaction = a reaction considered from the standpoint of its component parts and their relations to each other and to the whole reaction. [Usually the patterning is descriptive of responsive reactions (i.e. behavior), but it may carry neural or physiological implications also.] — Fr. *complexus de réaction.*

pause duration, see **fixation time.**

Pavlov's (or **Pawlow's**) **experiment** = a type of experiment devised by Pavlov, in which the saliva of a dog or other animal is diverted through an external fistula, and may be observed and measured. [Used to measure the formation and strengthening of conditioned food reflexes; e.g. when a light or the sound of a bell, presented before the food appears, serves as a signal (i.e. as a conditioned, or substitute, stimulus) for feeding.]

p.e. (or **P.E.**) = abbrev. for **probable error.**

peacock = a bluish green hue (Ladd-Franklin). [Syn. **cyan.**] — Fr. *bleu cyanique.*

peak, see **cycle.**

peccatophobia = morbid fear of sinning or of having committed (imagined) crimes.

pecking experiment = an experiment in which chicks (usually recently hatched), are permitted to peck at grains of food, the observed modification of behavior being correlated with increasing age and practice. — Fr. *expérience du picotement des poulets.*

pectoral = pert. to or located in the breast, i.e. the front of the thorax. (Accent **peck-.**) — Ger. *Brust-.*

pedagogical psychology, see **educational psychology.**

pedagogy, pedagogics = the theory and art of teaching.

pedal = pert. to or located in the foot. (Accent **ped-** or **pee-.**)

pederasty = sexual intercourse with youths through the anus.

pedogenesis = reproduction by animals in an immature (commonly larval) state.

pedophilia, paidophilia = love for immature children. [Generally used with pathological implications.]

peduncle = a superficial band of nerve fibers in the brain. [Applied to several diverse structures: callosal, cerebellar, cerebral, olfactory, of corpora mammillaria, pineal peduncle.] **peduncular**[a]. — Fr. *pédoncule.*

pedunculi cerebri, see **crura cerebri.** — Ger. *Hirnschenkel.*

Peking man = the name given to an extinct variety of man as evidenced by skeletal remains found near Peking, China. [Now generally regarded as a variety of **Neanderthal man.**]

pelagic = pert. to organisms living near the surface of the sea, as contr. w. **littoral** (i.e. coastal) forms and with forms living on the bottom (bathic).

pellagra = a deficiency disease of the skin and intestinal tract, due to inadequate variety of nutrition and climatic exposure, often with depressive and delirious mental involvement.

pelvis = the bony ring attached to the lower end of the vertebral column and supporting, in man, the abdominal organs. [The upper leg bones articulate with the pelvis.] **pelvic**[a].

penalty = the effect of punishment, considered in respect to the mental distress or material loss which it occasions to the individual. — Fr. *pénalité*; Ger. *Strafe.*

pendular vibration, see **pendulum.**

pendule explorateur = (*psych. res.*) a pendular form of **autoscope** consisting of a thread and a ring or bob; in use, the bob is suspended by a thread from the band of a free arm; its swing, actuated by involuntary movement, is assumed to indicate (*a*) the object of search or answer to a question, by taps on the inner side of a glass, or (*b*) by the direction of movement, the location of subterranean water or ore, the criminal in a line of suspects, etc. [Syn. **magic pendulum.**]

pendulum = a body suspended from a fixed point, and free to oscillate to and fro under the combined actions of gravity and momentum. [Often used for time measurements or the regulation of time-keeping instruments. The **seconds pendulum** (so-called) is one in which the time of a half cycle (movement from one extreme position to the other) is one second; its length is approximately 39.1 inches.] — Ger. *Pendel.*

pendulum chronoscope = an instrument for measuring response time, in which the stimulus releases a pendulum carrying a pointer controlled by an electromagnet (or mechanically); the response via the magnet checks the movement of the pointer, and the intervening time is read directly from a scale. [The commonest form is the Bergstrom, in which the pointer moves with the pendulum by means of a spring, which presses it against a disk clutch, and stops through the positive action of an electromagnet.]

penile (or **penis**) **reflex,** see **virile reflex.**

penis envy = (*psychoan.*) a repressed wish (encountered in the analysis of many neurotic women) to possess a penis. [This envy forms part of the feminine **castration complex.**] — Ger. *Penisneid.*

penitence = the attitude of an individual who acknowledges and deeply regrets some breach of the moral code or some injury which he has done to another, and who is anxious to renounce all conduct of this type in the future. **penitent**[a],[n,p]. — Ger. *Busse, Reue.*

penology = the scientific investigation of punishment for crime, both as a deterrent and as a means of reformation.

pentatonic scale, see **scale** (2). — Fr. *gamme pentatonique.*

percent = (*statist.*) the value of a certain part, if the whole to which it belongs is arbitrarily valued at 100. [Distg. fr. **proportion,** in which the whole is arbitrarily valued at unity. Written also **per cent.**] **percentage**[n] (abstract).

percentile = (*statist.*) in a group of data arranged serially in order of magnitude, that point or value in the series below which lies the percentage of the group indicated by a specific member. [E.g. the 10th percentile is that point, or value, below which fall 10% of the group and above which fall the remaining 90%. Applied commonly to the ranking of individuals in a test. **percentile score** = the percentile at which the score of a given individual in the group lies; **percentile rank** = the percentile at which the individual is rated, or scored, among the group; **percentile scale** = a set of equivalents, giving percentiles for each score, as distg. fr. **mental age scale,** or **point scale.** Cf. **quartile.**] (Pron. **-till** or **-tile.**) **percentile**[a]. — Fr. *centile.*

percentile curve = (*statist.*) a curve whose rectangular axes are (1) score, or measure, and (2) percent falling short of, or failing to attain, the score indicated upon the other axis. [Cf. **ogive.**]

percept = 1. the object of perception, i.e. the thing perceived; 2. a single perceptive act or response, i.e. what is known of an object in perceiving it. [Cf. **perception.**] — Ger. *Wahrnehmungsinhalt.*

perception = 1. the awareness of external objects, qualities, or relations, which ensues directly upon sensory processes, as distg. fr. **memory** or other central processes; 2. a mental complex or integration which has sensory experiences as its core; 3. awareness of present data, whether external or intraorganic; 4. awareness or belief of the truth of a proposition. [Cf. **percept.**] **perceive**[v], **perceptual**[a] = pert. to the data; **perceptive**[a] = pert. to some act of perceiving, **perceptional**[a] = pert. to the study. — Ger. *Wahrnehmung.*

perception/binocular = perception with the two eyes acting conjointly and presenting a single visual field, in which objects may stand out in relief, i.e. in the dimension of visual depth.

perception odor, see **object-odor.**

perception of difference, see **discrimination.**

perception of depth, see **depth perception.**

perception of space, see **space perception.**

perception time = 1. the time which elapses from the presentation of an object to its recognition by the observer less (*a*) the time spent in overcoming inertia of the receptor and (*b*) the time of transmission of the nerve impulse from receptor to brain centers; 2. (*reading*) the sum of the fixational pauses (of the eyes) which are the periods of relatively clear vision during reading. — Fr. *temps de perception.*

perceptual, see **perception.**

percipient = (*psych. res.*) the person in the position of *receiver* in a telepathic situation. [Contr. w. **agent.**]

performance = 1. any mental or motor process considered as producing a certain result; 2. (*beh.*) an activity which involves motor or manual rather than verbal responses. [(1) applies to animal and human behavior, (2) is applied esp. to **test** procedure.] **perform**[v]. — Fr. *accomplissement*; Ger. *Leistung.*

performance test = a type of mental test in which the role of language is greatly diminished, the test material consisting of concrete objects (or pictures or drawings) instead of words, and the responses consisting of manipulations of these objects, though the directions are often given verbally. [First devised as substitutes for the **Binet scale** when testing deaf, illiterate, or foreign-speaking persons. Distg. fr. **non-language test,** in which the instructions are given by pantomime, i.e. without use of words, and no words are required in solving the test. A **performance scale** = a series of performance tests in which the exercises are arranged in order of difficulty, beginning with the easiest.] — Fr. *test d'exécution.*

pericardial = pert. to or located in the region around the heart. (Accent-**car-**.)

perifibrillar substance = a plasma-like substance surrounding neurofibrils.

perilymph = a fluid which is contained within the bony labyrinth, and which in certain regions separates the membranous labyrinth from the bony walls.

perimeter = an instrument for mapping the retinal field; it consists typically of a quadrant rotating about one of its limiting radii as an axis so that on every point of this arm, and at every angle (corresponding to some point on the retina) a stimulus can be given and the visual impression recorded on a chart, the eye being placed at the center of the quadrant and fixated upon its center of rotation. [Sometimes a semicircular arm is used rotating about its middle radius. Cf. **campimeter** = for mapping the retinal field on a flat surface.]

perimetry = the operation of mapping the visual field, i.e. the retinal field projected outward on a spherical surface by means of a **perimeter.** [Cf. **campimetry,** in which the map is projected upon a flat surface, so that as the value of the angles increases, the distance from the center of fixation becomes relatively greater.]

perineum = the region at the base of the pelvis and surrounding the abdominal outlets. (Accent **-nee-**.) **perineal**[a].

period = (*phys.*) the time in seconds required for one complete cycle of a sine-wave or other regularly recurring phenomenon. [The **period** is the reciprocal of the **frequency.**]

periodic function = (*math.*) any function which repeats the same set of values at regular intervals when the variable increases or decreases uniformly.

periodic psychosis = a mental disorder which recurs at more or less uniform intervals. [Often used for any kind of recurrence.]

periodicity = the recurrence of an event or type of event at regular intervals.

periosteal reflex = sharp contraction of the muscle upon tapping a bone of forearm or leg. [An abnormal reflex. Mediated by 5th to 8th cervical (or) by 2d lumbar to 3d sacral segments. Syn. **bone reflex.**] — Fr. *réflexe périosté.*

peripheral = pert. to or located in the outermost part of the body or of an organ. [Contr. w. **central.**] **peripherad**[adv] = toward the outermost part.

peripheral hallucination = a hallucination which is suggested by a slight stimulation of some receptor, the effect of which is magnified and distorted. [E.g. a slight touch on the skin may be interpreted as an intense pain.]

peripheral nerve = any one of the nerves which connect receptor or effector organs with the cord or brain. [Includes both sensory and motor nerves.]

peripheral nervous system = the totality of nerves connecting the brain and spinal cord with the receptor and effector peripheral organs. [Usually, but not strictly, limited to the peripheral portion of the cerebrospinal system, excluding the **autonomic.** Contr. w. **central nervous system.**]

periphery = the outermost part of the body or an organ. **peripheral**[a]; **peripherad**[adv] = towards the periphery. — Ger. *Umfang, Umkreis.*

periphery of retina = the region of the retina remote from the center of vision, as distg. fr. the **central region.**

peristaltic contraction = a rhythmic wave of constriction which occurs normally in the digestive tract and other tubular hollow viscera, such as ducts.

peristalsis = wave-like contractions which pass along the alimentary canal or other similar structure, and serve to propel the contents. [Contr. w. **antiperistalsis** = contractions passing in the reverse direction.] **peristaltic**[a]. — Fr. *péristaltisme.*

peristomial = (in low animals) pert. to or located in the region about the mouth. (Accent **-stow-.**)

peritoneum = the smooth membrane which lines the abdominal cavity and covers many of the contained organs, such as the alimentary canal, liver, and other viscera. (Accent **-nee-.**) **peritoneal**[a]. (Accent **-nee-.**) — Ger. *Bauchfell.*

permanence = persistence in time without change. **permanent**[a].

permutation = any one of the possible arrangements of the items of a group, as contr. w. other possible arrangements. [Thus, the items *abc* have six permutations, *abc, acb, bac, bca, cab, cba.*]

pernicious trend = (*psychoan.*) the expression of ideas showing a deep regression from conventional thinking so that the pregenital interests are active and predominant, e.g. schizophrenia. [Syn. **malignant trend** (prefd.). Contr. w. **benign trend.**]

peroneal reflex = reflex muscle movements elicited by a stroke on the peroneus muscle of the fibula. [Mediated by 5th lumbar to 1st sacral segments of spinal cord.]

persecution/delusion of = morbid misinterpretation of feelings and experiences as due to machinations and malicious influences or intentions of inimical forces. [Syn. **persecution mania** (obsolete). Cf. **paranoia.**] — Fr. *folie (idées délirantes) de la persécution*; Ger. *Verfolgungswahn.*

perseveration, perseverative tendency = 1. the tendency of a feeling, idea, act, or disposition to recur with or without the aid of associative tendencies; 2. the tendency of any mental formation, once initiated, to remain and run a temporal course; 3. (*path.*) the persistent repetition or continuation of a word, sentence, or action after it has been once begun or recently completed. [Cf. **p factor.**]

persistence = 1. continued existence; 2. continuance of an effect after its cause is removed; e.g. persistence of a visual impression; 3. continuance of a line of behavior against opposing incentives or motives. — Ger. (1) *Beharren,* (2) *Nachdauer,* (3) *Beharrlichkeit.*

person = a human organism regarded as having distinctive characteristics and social relations. [Cf. **personality, self.**] **personal**[a].

persona = a function-complex which has come into existence for reasons of adaptation or necessary convenience in relation to an object, but not identical with individuality (Jung). [Contr. w. **anima.**]

personal equation = a time error in observing and recording the onset of an observation, which varies in value from observer to observer and to some extent in the same observer. [Variability of the personal equation is influenced by the nature and intensity of the stimulus, direction of the observer's attention (cf. **complication experiment**), age, maturation, and physiological condition of the observer, etc. Astronomers originated the term and concept to account for individual differences in recording stellar transits.] Pop. used to characterize any individual difference in the action of a person. — Ger. *persönliche Gleichung.*

personal identity = 1. the continuous existence of a given individual in spite of changes in structure and functions; 2. the subjective sense of such continuous existence.

personalism = the doctrine that in mental science and philosophy the person must be central. [E.g. Stern's system of philosophy and psychology.] — Ger. *Personalismus, Personalistik.*

personality = 1. the integrated organization of all the cognitive, affective, conative, and physical characteristics of an individual as it manifests itself in focal distinctness to others; 2. the general characterization, or pattern, of an individual's total behavior; 3. the field property or form of the individual's total behavior-pattern; 4. those characteristics of an individual most important in determining his social adjustments; 5. (*pop.*) the physical and affective qualities of an individual as they synthetically attract or impress others. [Cf. **personality type.**]

personality/dual = an abnormal organization of the individual, in which two distinct systems of personality are manifested at different times, or at the same time. [Cf. **personality/multiple** (the generic term), and **co-consciousness.**] — Fr. *dédoublement de la personnalité*; Ger. *Doppelbewusstsein, Doppelich, doppelte Persönlichkeit.*

personality/multiple = the personality of a single individual, dissociated functionally into partly independent systems of experiences, usually in alternation. [Sometimes used generically to include **dual personality** = personality dissociated into two systems.]

personality/primary = the fundamental or predominant phase of personality in cases of dissociated personality. [Cf. **personality/multiple.**]

personality/secondary = 1. an organized group of experiences split off from (i.e. unrelated to) the general mental organization; 2. in cases of dual or multiple personality, an organized group of experiences which is subordinate to the predominant or **primary personality.** [Cf. **personality/multiple.**]

personality type = the classification of an individual according to the pattern of his outstanding responses or behavior tendencies. [Classifications differ according to the aspect of personality under consideration; the most prominent are those based on (1) the direction of the psychic energy or libido: introvert vs. extravert (Jung); (2) the faculty psychology: thinking, feeling, willing; (3) temporal relation of the mental process: primary vs. secondary function (i.e. narrow-deep and shallow-wide types, Otto Gross); (4) clinical morphology: macrosplanchnic, microsplanchnic (DeGiovanni school); (5) constitutional system: digestive, respiratory, cerebral, and muscular types (Sigaud); (6) biotypes: cycloid vs. schizoid; (7) physique: leptosome (asthenic), dysplastic, pyknic, and athletic (Kretschmer); (8) values: economic, social, political, theoretical, artistic, religious (Spranger).]

personation = assuming the character and acting the part of another person; i.e. assuming the identity of another. [Cf. **impersonation, personification.**]

personification = the attribution to inanimate objects or natural forces of personal or human characteristics. **personify**[v].

personnel = the staff or employees of a business, army, or institution, as distg. fr. its **equipment** or **plant.**

personnel management = the selection, induction, and maintenance of the personnel of an industry or an institution. [Includes functions of hiring, placement, transfer, promotion, and discharge; training and supervision; maintenance of health, safety, satisfactory working conditions, and wholesome personal relations; supervision of employee insurance, pension and benefit funds; recreation and library facilities, etc.] — Fr. *organisation du personnel.*

personnel research = the study of man in relation to his occupations and his training therefor. [Generally undertaken with a view to improving the adjustment of employees or students to their work or to improve their attitude toward it. Cf. **personnel management.**]

personology = a term sometimes used to designate the study of personality as a distinct branch of psychology. [Cf. **characterology, psychography** (2).]

perspective = perception of the relative distance of various objects, or their parts, from the body of the observer, by means of the apparent size of the objects, relative size of parts, shading, etc. [Cf. **depth perception.**]

perspective/binocular = perception of depth or distance as effected by the use of both eyes. [Distg. fr. **monocular** (or **uniocular**) **perspective** = based on data furnished by a single eye.]

perspective/temporal = memory for the relative distance in time of various past experiences from the present moment.

perspicacity = a high degree of discernment or understanding. [Not to be confused with **perspicuity.**] — Ger. *Scharfsinn.*

perspicuity = clearness of expression in a narrative or report. [Distg. fr. **perspicacity** = exceptional ability in discerning relations.] **perspicuous**[a].

perspiration = secretion of the sweat (or sudoriferous) glands. [**sensible perspiration** = sweat in quantities sufficient to be visible; **insensible perspiration** = not detectable by the senses.]

persuasion = the act of convincing another individual, or the act of making effective suggestions. [Usually takes the form of an appeal to the intellect, but its effectiveness depends upon an appeal to (non-rational) prejudice, emotion, and suggestion.] **persuade**[v], **persuasive**[a]. — Ger. *Überredung.*

perturbation = an unpleasant emotional condition marked by confusion, unrest, worry, or inability to form conclusions leading to an acceptable line of action.

perversion = 1. degeneration or pathological alteration of any of the fundamental instincts or tendencies; 2. (*psychoan.*) = a deviation or aberration in reference to the sexual object; e.g. fetishism, sadism, masochism, etc.; 3. misrepresentation of facts, etc.

perversion/sexual = any pathological or abnormal sexual desire or manner of gratification. [The term includes **inversion,** but covers other forms as well.] **pervert**[np]. — Ger. (1) *Verschlechterung,* (2) *Verkehrtheit,* (3) *Verstellung.*

pessimism = that attitude toward the social organization, or toward life in general, which emphasizes the elements of discord therein, and despairs of the future of social evolution. [Contr. w. **optimism.**] **pessimist**[np], **pessimistic**[a].

petitio principii = a fallacy of reasoning, which consists in assuming covertly at the outset (i.e. in the premises) the very conclusion which the reasoning is designed to prove. [Lat. Syn. **begging the question.**]

petit mal = momentary suspense of consciousness with or without presence of full-fledged epilepsy. [Fr.]

petrous bone, see **temporal bone.**

phacoscope, phakoscope = an instrument for observing the accommodative changes of the eye-lens in another individual by means of the images reflected from its surfaces. [Cf. **Purkinje-Sanson images.**]

phagocyte = a variety of white blood-corpuscle, which engulfs and devours solid materials such as micro-organisms and broken-down fragments of disorganized tissues.

phagocyte theory = the doctrine developed by Metschnikoff, that immunity to disease is conferred through the destruction of invading micro-organisms by phagocytes.

phalanges[pl] = the bones of the fingers or toes.

phallic phase = (*psychoan.*) a belief occurring in the early period of childhood, according to which, only the male genital organ (**phallus**) is supposed to exist in both sexes. (Freud). [Syn. **phallic organization.**]

phallus = 1. (*anthrop.*) an artifact designed to represent any or all of the male sex organs; 2. (*psychoan.*) a symbolic representation of the male sex organs. **phallic**[a].

phantasm, see **fantasm.**

phantasy, see **fantasy, fancy.**

phantom sound, phantom = an auditory perception of a sound-source localized with reference to the head, either stationary or in motion. [The term is used specifically in reference to the effects produced in auditory localization experiments by unequal stimulation of the two ears. Syn. **sound image.** Cf. **localization of sound.**]

pharyngeal reflex = contraction of the pharyngeal constrictors elicited by touching the back of the pharynx. [Mediated by the glossopharyngeal and vagal arcs through the pharyngeal plexus.]

pharynx = the musculomembranous sac situate between the mouth and the nares and the esophagus. [Commonly divided into three parts: (1) **nasopharynx** = part above soft palate; (2) **oropharynx** = part which communicates with the mouth; (3) **laryngopharynx** = part which opens into larynx and esophagus.] **pharyngeal**[a] (accent **-rinj-**).

phase = the momentary value of a magnitude which is executing simple periodic variations, as measured in relation to one of its values chosen as a reference point. [Sound vibrations, alternating electric currents, and other periodically varying magnitudes which may be expressed in terms of simple circular or simple harmonic motion, undergo a phase change of 360°, or 2π radians, during each period, or cycle; any given point within the cycle may be expressed by the number of degrees (or radians) of phase from the reference point. Two simple harmonic motions are *in phase* when both attain their maximum values at the same time. When this is not so, they are *out of phase*. When one attains its maximum as the other reaches its minimum (i.e. when they are 180° out of phase) they are said to be at *contrary* or *opposite* phases. The *phase difference* of two simple harmonic motions is the time difference (expressed as a fraction of a period, or cycle) of their respective maxima. The motion attaining its maximum first within a given half-period is said to be *leading in phase* and the other motion to be *lagging in phase*.] **phasic**[a].

phenomenal field = the totality of objects or events which are directly experienced at any one moment. [Syn. **perceptual field, perceptual pattern;** contr. w. **sensation** (an elementary experiential process).] — Fr. *champ phénomenal*.

phenomenalism = the theory which holds that human knowledge is limited to phenomena (i.e. to possible experience), and does not reach the real nature of things. **phenomenalist**[np].

phenomenology = the systematic investigation of phenomena or conscious experiences, esp. as they occur immediately in experience, without implications. [Used technically for the philosophical method of Husserl, based on the concept that transcendental subjectivity is immediate experience. This method is a propaedeutic to all special sciences (Stumpf), including psychology; but as the method implies pure consciousness, it is closely allied to introspective psychology and owes much to Brentano's empirical (i.e. intentional) psychology. Husserl distinguishes phenomenological psychology as the study of the types and forms of intentional psychology.] **phenomenological**[a].

phenomenon = a datum of experience, or a group of such data, which occur at a given moment and are observed or are capable of observation. **phenomena**[pl], **phenomenal**[a]. — Ger. *Phänomen, Erscheinung*.

phi-gamma function = an **ogive** plotted from a normal probability curve, whose frequencies have been cumulated from the lower end upward; i.e. the $\phi(\gamma)$ function is the integral of a normal curve.

phi-gamma hypothesis = a hypothesis concerning the distribution of comparative judgments in the method of constant stimuli: if a series of comparison stimuli, separated by equal intervals and extending on each side of the standard, be compared with this standard under carefully controlled and strictly uniform conditions, it may be assumed that the proportion of greater (or smaller) reports will lie upon a curve known as phi function of gamma, $\phi(\gamma)$, an **ogive** or S-curve which is the cumulative or integral function of the **normal curve of error.**

phi-phenomenon = 1. (*hist.*) the specific movement-aspect of objects perceived in motion, as an experience not reducible to other sense qualities (Wertheimer); 2. the appearance of motion from stationary stimuli when they are presented successively in two neighboring positions. [Most often limited to visual perception of motion, but also applied to auditory and tactual phenomena. In the **pure phi-phenomenon** no trace of color, of an object, or of anything except motion can be discerned.]

philander = to perform some of the distinctive acts of courtship without serious intention. **philandering**[n], **philanderer**[np]. — Fr. *courtiser*.

philosophy = the branch of learning which investigates the ultimate nature of knowledge and of existence. [Applied historically to any systematic attempt at knowledge; e.g. natural philosophy = physics. Still often used to cover certain social sciences, such as ethics. The recognized branches are **epistemology** (= theory of knowledge) and **metaphysics** (= theory of the real nature of things).] **philosophical**[a] (used also loosely to characterize an optimistic or a stoical attitude).

phlegmatic = a type of temperament characterized by passivity and indifferent feeling tone. [Formerly attributed to the predominance of the phlegm in the bodily humors. Syn. **lymphatic.** Cf. **temperament.**]

phobia = exaggerated and usually pathological dread of some specific type of stimulus or situation. [A number of common types have been named (see Table VIII); other forms are named by more occasional observers. Used extensively as suffix in a non-technical way (e.g. Anglophobia), and contr. w. **-mania** or **-philia** = exaggerated predilection toward.]

phonation = the production of speech sounds by the human voice.

phonautograph = an instrument for the direct recording of sound-waves; a stylus is attached to a membrane placed at the focus of a sound collector, and writes on a revolving drum a record of the movements of the membrane in response to sound. [Cf. **phonelescope, phonoscope, phonodeik.**]

phoneidoscope = an instrument for the visual observation of sound-waves, consisting of a soap-film placed in the path of the sound so as to vibrate with the changes of pressure, and to reflect a beam of light cast upon it.

phoneloscope = an instrument for the observation and measurement of sound-waves by means of a mirror attached by a thread to the diaphragm of a telephone receiver so as to deflect a beam of light in accordance with movements of the diaphragm. [Cf. **phonoscope.**]

phonetic law = a generalization made from studies of common tendencies and changes among the sounds of speech. — Ger. *Lautgesetz.*

phonetics, phonology = the branch which investigates vocal sounds in all their manifestations, physiological, physical, and experiential. [The study includes various forms of vocalization, the positions of vocal organs for each form, principles of modification of sounds from one language to another, etc. **phonetics** is concerned with vocal sounds in general; **phonology** with a particular language.]

phonodeik = an instrument for recording or projecting sound-waves which resembles the **phonautograph** somewhat, but is of greater refinement and sensitivity; a diaphragm at the end of a resonator horn carries at its center a fine thread, which leads around the pulley of a minute spindle to a tension spring; the spindle bears a small mirror on which a beam of light is cast, and movements of the diaphragm in response to the pressure variations of sound are thus communicated to the light beam, and may be observed on a screen or recorded on a photographic plate.

phonogram = 1. a graphic representation of a word, syllable, or single speech sound; 2. a phonograph record, or a reproduction of sounds by means of it.

phonometer = 1. a type of instrument for measuring differences of auditory acuity; 2. also sometimes applied to an instrument for determining the lower intensive threshold for sound. [Cf. **Wundt's gravity phonometer, Rayleigh disk, phonoscope.**]

phonopathy = any disease or disorder of the organs of speech.

phonophobia = morbid dread of speaking aloud.

phonoscope = a generic term applied to various types of instrument for visual observation or recording of sound-waves or the movements of sounding bodies. [Syn. **phono-projectoscope.** Cf. **phonautograph, phoneidoscope, oscillograph, tonoscope, phoneloscope.**]

phoria = (*ophthal.*) a suffix sometimes used as a word, syn. with **muscle balance.** [Cf. **imbalance/muscular.**]

phorometry = the measurement of the degree of imbalance of the extrinsic eye-muscles.

phosphene = a bright area in the visual field produced by distortion of the eyeball, either by pressure of an external object or during the normal process of accommodation.

photerythrous = characterizing color vision in which the effectiveness of long wave-length stimuli is normal or heightened. [A peculiarity of **deuteranopia,** and certain forms of **anomalous trichromasy.** Distg. fr. **scoterythrous.**]

photism = 1. a false perception (hallucination) of bright light, either localized or widespread. [The brightness gives the impression of freshness or newness. It appears occasionally on recovering from intense fever, or as a sequel to violent emotion, e.g. in religious conversion and in other mystical experiences. A corresponding phenomenon appears, more rarely, in the field of taste and smell.]

photism = 2. a form of *synesthesia* in which a visual perception of color, tint, or form appears invariably and persistently attached to specific sensations of other modalities. [A common form is colored hearing.]

photochemical = pert. to photochemistry, which treats of chemical changes as produced or modified by light.

photochromatic interval = the range of visual stimulus-intensity, for a chromatic stimulus, between the absolute threshold or limen for light-perception, and the threshold for hue. [There is said to be no photochromatic interval for long-wave light, i.e. in the red end of the spectrum. Syn. **colorless interval.**]

photo-electric cell = an electrical device for detecting and measuring light; it depends upon the principle that radiant energy releases electrons from certain of the less heavy metals or their compounds (potassium or caesium are ordinarily used); such electron emission, within the exhausted glass globe of the cell, renders the space of the globe conductive, and permits an electric current to pass between electrodes sealed into the glass, this current being approximately proportional to the radiant intensity at any instant. — Fr. *cellule photo-électrique.*

photographic observation dome = an arched room or compartment for the observation of infants, which is provided with adjustable cameras and other recording instruments; the sides are made up in whole or in part of **one-way vision screens** permitting vision from the outside inward, but not from the inside outward.

photokinesis = the effect of light upon organisms in producing activity, apart from their specific responses to visual stimuli. [Applied to the relative general activity of certain lower species in bright light, as compared with their sluggishness or general inactivity in the dark.] **photokinetic**[a].

photokymograph = a camera having a narrow slit and cylindrical lens, and an arrangement by which photographic paper or film may be made to pass at a controlled rate across the opening; a beam of light projected upon the slit casts shadows of moving pointers, etc., or of the string of a string galvanometer, upon the sensitive surface, the movements of these shadows being photographically recorded. [Syn. **recording camera.**]

photoma = a simple type of visual hallucination, in which flashes of light, sparks, etc. are seen. **photomata**[pl].

photometer = any optical device which utilizes equations of brilliance to permit the measurement of a photometric quantity, such as candle-power, illumination, or brightness. [The **equality-of-brightness photometer** employs simultaneous comparison of juxtaposed visual areas; in the **flicker photometer** the stimuli which are to be compared are presented successively in the same visual area.]

photometric measure = a measure of luminous radiant energy in photometric terms, rather than in terms of (introspective) sensation-magnitude, on the one hand, or of physical energy, on the other.

photometry = the measurement of luminous radiation on the basis of its effect upon the visual receptors; under standard conditions, and usually involving an adjustment of two contiguous parts of the visual field, either to identity or to a minimal difference. [**heterochromatic photometry** involves the measurement of the relative intensity of differently colored radiations. Cf. **flicker photometry.** Distg. fr. **radiometry,** based on radiant energy measures only.] (Accent **-tom-**.) **photometric**[a].

photon = a unit of visual stimulation defined as that illumination upon the retina which results when a surface brightness of 1 candle per square meter is seen through a pupil of 1 square millimeter area.

photopharmacology = a systematic study of the effects of light and other radiations on the pharmacological properties of drugs and poisons.

photophobia = 1. reluctance to use the eyes in strong light; 2. morbid fear of strong light. [Syn. **light-dread.** Found (1) in the totally color-blind, and in albinos. Probably associated with pigmentary anomalies.]

photopic adaptation, see **adaptation.**

photopic vision = vision as it occurs under illumination sufficient to permit the discrimination of colors. [Believed to depend upon the functioning of the retinal cones instead of the rods alone. Syn. **daylight-vision;** contr. w. **twilight** or **scotopic vision.**]

photoreceptive (or **photoreceptor**) **process** = that specific process which is set in motion in a visual sensory end-organ or other photic receptor by the incidence of its adequate stimulus, i.e. light. [It is usually assumed to be a photochemical change of some sort, e.g. the decomposition by light of the visual purple of the retinal rods.]

photoreceptor = a receptor which is adequately stimulated by energy of the band of wave lengths that make up the visible spectrum.

photosynthesis = the production of carbohydrates from carbon dioxide and water through the agency of light. [This process occurs in the green parts of plants in the presence of a pigment, chlorophyll, which plays an essential part in the process.]

phototropism, phototaxis = an orienting response, either positive or negative, to light. [Cf. **tropism.**] (Accent **-tot-**; **-tax-**.) **phototropic**[a], **-tactic**[a].

phrenic nerve = the peripheral nerve through which the diaphragm is activated, and which sends branches to the pericardium and to the pleura.

phrenology = (*hist.*) the doctrine that specific mental faculties are localized in definite cerebral regions, the degree of development of the faculty correlating with the prominence of the region as indicated largely by the contour of the overlying skull. [Developed by F. J. Gall and J. G. Spurzheim (1810 ff.). The faculties assumed to be thus localized were complex and general, e.g. philoprogenitiveness, veneration, truthfulness, etc. The system was at first called **cranioscopy,** also **physiognomy.**]

phrictopathetic sensations = tingling sensations of a tactual character, irritating, and indefinitely localized.

phyletic = pert. to a **phylum.**

phylogenesis = the origin and evolution of races or species, or of any organ or function in a given species. [Applied usually to the general problem of evolution. Contr. w. **ontogenesis** = individual development.] **phylogenetic**[a].

phylogeny = the origin and evolution of races or species. [Cf. **phylogenesis.** Contr. w. **ontogeny** = the development of the individual.] **phylogenic**[a].

phylum = a term applied to the most general and comprehensive divisions of the animal or plant kingdom. [Cf. **classification/zoological.**] **phyla**[pl], **phyletic**[a].

physical = 1. pert. to physics; 2. pert. to the physicochemical world, as distg. fr. the realm of mental phenomena.

physical anthropology, see **somatology.**

physical (or **physicochemical**) **science** = the entire group of branches which investigate matter, its constitution, and its principles of interrelation and activity. [Cf. **physical world.**]

physical phenomena = (*psych. res.*) = the occurrence of raps, the movement of objects, the appearance of lights, the passage of matter through matter, etc. all associated with an undetermined intelligence, and under conditions assumed to exclude known physical causes. [Syn. **objective metapsychics.**]

physical world = the universe as investigated by physics and chemistry, consisting of units of matter (electrons, atoms, etc.) and their relations. [Syn. **physicochemical world, material world.** Contr. w. **psychical** (or **mental**) **world,** consisting of experiences or subjective phenomena, and of selves.] — Fr. *monde physique.*

physicochemical = pert. to the realm of physics and chemistry.

physicosocial = pert. to those social relations which are determined largely by the physical environment. [Distg. fr. **biosocial** and **psychosocial.**]

physics = the branch of science which investigates matter and the principles of its activity, excluding the compounding of elements (*chemistry*) and the special principles of organic life (*biology*). **physical**[a].

physiogenesis = the development of vital functions. [Contr. w. **morphogenesis** = the development of structure.]

physiognomy = 1. the interpretation of the structure or expressive movements of the body, esp. of the cast and expression of the face, as subject to emotional and other mental conditions; 2. (*pop.*) syn. for facial expression or the face itself; 3. (*hist.*) syn. for **phrenology.** [(1) applied chiefly to unscientific systems of interpreting human character from the form of the face and other outward appearances.] — Fr. (1) *physionomie.*

physiognomy systems = methods of determining mental characteristics or traits by observing or measuring aspects of the individual's outward appearance, esp. the face. [Usually applied to systems exploited commercially; empirical correlations of physiognomic and mental characteristics are uniformly insignificant.]

physiological age = a rating of an individual's physiological development in terms of the average physiological development of unselected samples of successive chronological age groups. [Physiological development is usually defined in terms of the functioning of the sex organs. Cf. **anatomical age; mental age.**]

physiological gradient = a line of decreasing intensity of the vital reaction which results from stimulation. [A physiological gradient lying along the longitudinal axis of the organism has the area of most intense activity cephalad.

Areas of high metabolic rate tend to dominate adjacent areas which have a lower rate.] — Fr. *gradient physiologique.*

physiological limit = 1. the limit of possible attainment of speed or efficiency in any given motor act, simple or complex, due to the limitations of speed or energy in the nerves and muscles; 2. that maximum of any physiological function which cannot be exceeded without permanent impairment of the function.

physiological process = a process which is specifically correlated with some vital phenomenon in an organism.

physiological psychology = the branch which investigates the functions of the nervous system, receptors, and effectors in their bearing on behavior and mental processes.

physiological selection = a form of selection which depends upon different degrees of sterility in the matings of different incipient varieties. [These differences were supposed by Romanes to lead to the sexual isolation of certain types and hence to create the possibility of their divergence from other members of the species with which they might otherwise be swamped by intercrossing.]

physiological state = the general metabolic condition of an organism at any given moment, regarded as modifying its responses to external stimuli. [E.g. the condition of the digestive organs modifies the response to food stimuli.] — Fr. *condition physiologique.*

physiological time = the time required for a new stimulus to overcome the inertia of the sense organ, plus the time required for the transmission of the aroused impulse from receptor to center and from center to effector. [This hist. use excludes the duration of central processes, although these are also physiological.] — Fr. *temps de latence physiologique.*

physiological zero, see **zero/physiological.**

physiology = the branch of biology which deals with the functions (or modes of operation) of an organism or any part of it. [Contr. w. **morphology** (or **anatomy**) = the structural arrangement.] **physiologic(al)**[a].

physique = a loose term denoting the general structural organization of an individual. — Ger. *Körperbau.*

physostigmin = the active principle of Calabar Bean or Ordeal Nut, a powerful alkaloid which stimulates the myoneural junctions of the sympathetic system and also (to some extent) striped muscle. [Its principal medicinal use is to produce myosis (contraction of the pupils) and to stimulate intestinal peristalsis. Syn. **eserin.**]

pia-arachnoid = the pia mater and arachnoid coverings of the cerebrum, considered as a single organ.

pia mater, pia = a membrane which immediately covers the brain and spinal cord, being itself covered in turn by the **arachnoid** and (outermost) the **dura mater.** [Lat. "fostering mother." The **pia** is highly vascular.] — Fr. *pie-mère.*

piano theory, see **hearing/theories of.**

pictograph, pictogram = the pictorial representation of an idea or event. [**pictogram** prefd. Cf. **ideogram.**] — Ger. *Bilderschrift.*

picture = 1. a representation on a surface by pen, chisel, etc.; 2. a verbal representation of some situation, e.g. disease picture. — Fr. (1) *image, représentation graphique,* (2) *description*; Ger. *Bild.*

picture completion test = a type of test in which the task is to supply or indicate the missing parts in an incomplete or mutilated picture. [E.g. the **mutilated pictures test** in Year VI of the Binet-Simon scale.] — Fr. *test de complètement de dessins.*

picture interpretation test = a type of test designed to measure ability to understand or explain the meaning of pictures. [As developed in the Binet-Simon scale, the simple *enumeration* of objects in specified standardized pictures is regarded as a three-year-old, the *description* of them as a seven-year-old, and the satisfactory explanation (*interpretation*) of them as a twelve-year-old performance.] — Fr. *test d'interprétation d'image.*

picture/retinal = the effect on the retina due to stimulation by some object. [Less ambiguous than **retinal image,** the accepted term.] — Fr. *image rétinienne.*

picturesque = any visual perception which seems to conform to the ordinary rules of artistic composition. **picturesque**[a].

piecemeal activity/law of = the principle that a part or element or aspect of a situation may be prepotent in causing response, and may have responses bound more or less exclusively to it, regardless of some or all of its accompaniments (Thorndike). [Syn. **law of partial activity.**] — Fr. *l. de l'activité fragmentaire.*

piecemeal learning, see **whole and part learning.**

pigment layer = the 1st or outermost stratum of the retina, consisting of a single layer of epithelial cells containing pigment. [Syn. **layer of hexagonal cells.** Cf. **retinal layers** and Table XI.]

pillars of Corti, see **rods of Corti.**

pilomotor nerves = nerves which control the muscles that erect the hairs.

Piltdown man = one of the earliest types of primitive man, represented by a skull found in 1912 near Piltdown, England. [Though in general the skull resembles modern man rather than Neanderthal man, the lower jaw is simian in form; other peculiarities suggested a new genus, as *Eoanthropus dawsoni,* distinct from *Homo neanderthalensis,* etc. Also called **Sussex man,** or Eoanthropus dawsoni.]

Piltz's reflex, see **attention reflex.**

pineal body (or **gland**) = a small oval glandular outgrowth of the epithalamus which projects from the dorsal wall of the third ventricle of the brain and is situated medially in the groove separating the lateral halves of the diencephalon, just anterior to the upper border of the tectum of the mesencephalon. [Syn. **conarium, corpus pineale, epiphysis cerebri.** Distg. fr. **paraphysis,** an evagination of the membranous roof of the telencephalon in front of the velum transversum in some vertebrate brains. In certain lower vertebrates the pineal body is modified to form a dorsal median eye; in higher forms it probably has an endocrine function, but in the child it undergoes an involution after the seventh year. Considered by Descartes to be the seat of the soul.] — Fr. *glande pinéale*; Ger. *Zirbeldrüse.*

pinna = a funnel-shaped cartilaginous body which opens into the external auditory meatus, and serves as a collector of sound. [It is supplied with muscles, which in many animals serve to turn the concave face of the organ toward the source of sound. Syn. **auricle,** applied more often to man.] — Fr. *pavillon*; Ger. *Ohrmuschel.*

pinna reflex = movements of the external ear of certain animals when that organ is pricked, squeezed, or tickled, or in some cases on stimulation by sound. [Syn. **Preyer's reflex, ear reflex.**] — Fr. *réflexe auriculaire.*

pipe = (*mus.*) a sound-producing instrument, consisting of a tube of calibrated length and an aperture for applying wind. [There are two sorts; the **closed pipe,** in which the farther end of the tube is sealed, and the **open pipe,** in which it is open. The pitch of a closed pipe is one octave lower than that of an open pipe of the same length.] — Fr. *tuyau sonore*; Ger. *Pfeife.*

pistonphone = an apparatus which produces alternating pressures (tones) directly by the movements of a piston against an air column.

piston recorder = a piston-cylinder combination for recording pulse or other volume changes.

pitch = 1. (*psychol.*) that attribute or characteristic of tonal sensation by means of which tones and noises may be differentiated as high and low, or acute and grave; 2. (*phys.*) the frequency of periodic sound-wave vibrations; 3. (*mus.*) the region of frequency in which a piece of music is executed. [In musical notation, **pitch** is designated by position on the staff or by a letter with or without accent. In designation of pitch by letter and accent, the successive octaves are represented as C_2, C_1, C, c, c^1, c^2, c^3 ... where c^1 represents middle C (= 256 ∼ on the scientific scale), c^2 the first octave above (= 512 ∼), c the first octave below (= 128 ∼), etc. Cf. (3) **pitch/standard.**] — Fr. (1) *hauteur tonale,* (2) *hauteur*; Ger. *Tonhöhe.*

pitch/absolute = the ability to recognize a tone and name it, or to reproduce a designated tone after a considerable interval of time. [Distg. fr. **relative pitch** = ability to recognize a given pitch *interval,* or to reproduce the second tone if the first be given.] — Fr. *hauteur absolue*; Ger. *absolutes Gehör.*

pitch fork = a small tuning fork of standard pitch used for tuning violins or other instruments or to give the initial tone in singing. — Fr. *diapason étalon.*

pitch pipe = a small pipe containing a reed, designed to produce a tone of standard pitch, used to tune musical instruments and to determine the key in singing. — Fr. *tuyau d'orgue étalon.*

pitch/relative = ability to recognize or reproduce pitch intervals, as in humming or singing a tune. [Contr. w. **pitch/absolute.**]

pitch/standard = a certain tone of fixed vibration rate, selected as a standard for the tuning of musical instruments. [In music, various standards have been used. *Classical pitch,* used in the late 18th century, gave *a'* a frequency between 415 and 438 cycles (∼) or double vibrations (d.v.). *Concert pitch,* or high pitch, giving *a'* a frequency of about 450∼, is still used in some English organs and bands. *Scheibler's pitch,* or *Stuttgart pitch,* is based on *a'* = 440∼. The prevailing pitch since 1859 is *international* or *low pitch,* with *a'* = 435∼. In scientific work *philosophical* or *scientific pitch* is used, with *c'* = 256∼, i.e. *a'* = 426.7∼. Cf. **scale** (2) and Table VII.] — Fr. *son étalon.* Ger. *Normalstimmung.*

pithecanthropus erectus = an extinct type of primate which resembles *homo sapiens,* identified from a skull found in Java by Dubois. [It is the earliest and lowest known type of man's immediate precursors. Syn. **Java man.**]

pithecoid = resembling or pert. to an ape or monkey.

pithiatism = 1. the cure of nervous and mental disorders by persuasion; 2. syn. for **hysteria** (Babinski).

pituitary gland = a small compound endocrine gland situate at the base of the brain in the *sella turcica* of the basisphenoid bone; it is united with the floor of the third ventricle by the pituitary stalk or infundibulum, and is composed of (*a*) an anterior lobe or *pars anterior,* which produces at least two important autacoids, (*b*) a posterior lobe consisting of *pars intermedia* and *pars nervosa,* extracts of which are physiologically potent, and (*c*) a *pars tuberalis,* surrounding the infundibulum and covering the tuber cinereum. [Syn. **hypophysis cerebri, pituitary body.**] **pituitary**[a] = pert. to this gland.

pituitary liquid, see **pituitary/solution of.**

pituitary/solution of = an extract of the posterior lobe of the pituitary gland, whose principal pharmacological actions are pressor, oxytocic, and antidiuretic in the mammal, and melanophore-expanding in the frog. [Its precise relation to the autacoid or autacoids of the **pituitary gland** is not yet established. Special proprietary products are termed **hypophysin, pituitary liquid, pituitin, pituitrin, posterior pituitary extract.**]

pituitin, see **pituitary/solution of.**

pituitrin, see **pituitary/solution of.**

pity = an emotional attitude in which the misfortunes or ills of another individual arouse a feeling of sadness or tender solicitude. [Distg. fr. **sympathy,** an attitude in which the emotional state or circumstances of another are felt for the time as one's own.] — Fr. *pitié*; Ger. *Mitleid.*

Placido's disk = a white disk with concentric black circles and a central sight-hole for observing its reflection in the cornea of an eye under examination; irregularity of the corneal surface is revealed by corresponding distortion of the reflected image. [Syn. **keratoscope.**]

plan = a complex scheme of action mentally elaborated in advance of the performance.

planaria, see **flatworms.**

planchette = a small heart-shaped traveling table supported by two legs and a pencil, manipulated by the hands of one person for the purpose of obtaining involuntary writing. [Syn. **autoscope.** Related to the **ouija board** and **dowsing rod.**]

plane = 1. (*geom.*) a two-dimensional figure (i.e. surface) such that the straight line joining any two points in it lies wholly in the surface.

plane = 2. any one of the three reference surfaces in the body which are used in describing location of parts of the body, etc. [They are known as the **transverse, frontal,** and **mesial** (or **medial**); planes parallel to the mesial are called **sagittal.** See Table XVI.]

planimeter = a device for measuring the area of plane figures, particularly those of irregular outline; it consists essentially of two levers pivoted together, one bearing a point which is traced by hand round the bounding line, while the resulting lever movements cause a contact wheel and connected dials to register cumulatively and thus supply the data for computing the area. [Syn. **platometer.** Cf. **chartometer.**]

plankton = the floating or slowly moving (usually small) forms of plant and animal life found in the sea or in bodies of fresh water. [Distg. fr. **nekton,** consisting of the larger, more active forms, such as fishes.]

plant = a member of one of the two kingdoms of living organisms, chiefly characterized by ability to transform inorganic matter into organic compounds. [Contr. w. **animal.**]

plantar reflex = flexion of the toes, caused by stroking of the sole. [Mediated by 1st and 2d sacral segments of the spinal cord. Syn. **sole r.** Cf. **Babinski reflex.**]

plasm, plasma = the substance in cells (except inanimate inclusions). [Generally used in compounds, e.g. germ-plasm, cytoplasm.] **plasmic**[a].

plastic art = those objects of art which are generally produced by molding, modeling, or carving, such as sculpture.

plastic response = any response of an organism which is subject to progressive variation (e.g. a conditioned response), thereby adapting behavior to changes in environment. [Chiefly of cortical origin in higher vertebrates, of origin in correlation centers in lower vertebrates.]

plastic tonus, see **tonus/plastic.**

plasticity = 1. (*biol.*) the ability of organisms to change (or vary) if the environment changes; 2. (*psychol.*) in eidetic theory, the tendency of an image to be influenced by conditions immediately preceding the experiment, esp. by a preceding experiment. [(1) applies to either structure or function. **Cf.** (2) **perseveration.**] **plastic**[a].

plateau = a temporary halt in the progress of learning, or in the aspect of learning shown in a particular curve, indicated by inability to increase speed or to decrease the number of errors. [So named from the level aspect of the curve or graph at this region.] **plateaus, plateaux**[pl].

platometer, see **planometer.**

Platonic friendship = a social relation between two individuals of opposite sex, in which sexual relations or sentiment are absent. [Not to be confused with **Platonism** = a general philosophical theory.] — Fr. *amour platonique.*

platyhelminthes, see **flatworms.**

platykurtic, see **kurtosis.**

platysma reflex, see **cutaneous-pupillary reflex.**

play = the exercise of any of the typical forms of behavior of a given species without specific reference to organic needs. [Characteristic of the young and also exhibited by adults as a means of relaxation; e.g. hunting as a sport.] — Fr. *jeu*; Ger. *Spiel.*

pleasantness = a characteristic of hedonic tone or feeling, whose motor correlate is movement toward the stimulus or a tendency to maintain the stimulus. [Syn. **agreeableness, pleasure.** Contr. w. **unpleasantness,** whose motor correlate is movement away from the stimulus.] — Fr. *plaisir*; Ger. *Lust, Annehmlichkeit.*

pleasantness-unpleasantness/feeling of = one of the three dimensions or attributes of affective experience (Wundt).

pleasure-pain = a term used to denote the two antithetical qualities which characterize the affective aspect of consciousness. [Syn. **pleasantness-unpleasantness.**] — Fr. *plaisir-douleur*; Ger. *Lust-Unlust.*

pleasure-principle = (*psychoan.*) the automatic regulation (or aspect) of mental activity, whose object is to avoid pain or procure pleasure. [It is regarded by many as characteristic of the earliest stages of human development, both in the individual and in the race. Contr. w. **reality-principle.**] — Fr. *principe de l'agréable*; Ger. *Lustprinzip.*

plethysmograph = an instrument for measuring and recording variations in the size of the finger, hand, or other bodily member due to fluctuations in the blood supply; it consists essentially of a rigid vessel filled with water, into which the member is inserted; a small tube leading from the vessel is connected with the recording device, which moves to and fro as the water in the tube advances or recedes according to the change in size of the member. **plethysmographic**[a].

pleura = the membrane that envelops the lungs. **pleurae**[pl], **pleural**[a].

plexiform layer, see **reticular layer/outer, /inner.**

plexus = a network of nerves outside the central nervous system. [E.g. **solar plexus** = in the region of the stomach, dorsad to this organ.] — Fr. *plexus, réseau*; Ger. *Geflecht.*

pluralism = the theory which assumes that ultimate reality consists of more than one sort of entity, such as electrons, monads, persons, etc. [Contr. w. **singularism** or **monism,** and w. **dualism.**] **pluralistic**[a], **pluralist**[np].

pluralistic behavior = any type of action, or any response to a specific stimulus, which is performed universally, or almost universally, by the individuals of a given group or region. [E.g. covering exposed parts of the body in cold weather. The concept as introduced by F. H. Giddings implied only the distributive behavior of individuals who all react alike; later construed by some sociologists to indicate behavior performed by a group as such. To avoid this ambiguity, Giddings later substituted the term **multi-individual behavior.**] — Fr. *comportement pluraliste.*

pluteus = a free-swimming larval stage of a sea urchin or ophiuran, characterized by having long ciliated arms and an internal skeleton of calcareous spicules.

pneumatograph, pneumograph = an instrument for measuring the rate, depth, and other characteristics of breathing, generally via chest movements, which are made to actuate a pneumatic recording system.

pneumodynamograph = a **dynamograph** with an air piston in which the air pressure is varied by oral breathing; a recording tambour is attached.

pneumogastric nerve = the X cranial nerve, which sends fibers to the breast, heart, lungs, larynx, trachea, esophagus, and abdominal viscera, and by small branches to the external ear. [While commonly called *inhibitory,* it is also *motor.* Syn. **vagus.**] — Ger. *Lungenmagennerv.*

pneumograph = a device for recording the rate and extent of respiratory movements by means of a double-headed tambour stretched across the individual's chest, with an attached rubber tube for communicating the movements to a recording tambour.

pneumophonia = a form of **dysphonia,** characterized by a breathy voice.

Poggendorff illusion = an illusion of visual space relations, in which a continuous straight line is broken by a super-imposed pair of parallel lines or a long-sided rectangle which crosses it at an acute angle; the two parts of the line do not appear to belong to the same straight line.

point = 1. (*math.*) that which has position but neither length, breadth, nor thickness; 2. the place of intersection of two lines; 3. a space location, disregarding the extensity of the object or stimulus there situate; e.g. warmth point or cold point on the skin, luminous point. — Ger. *Punkt.*

point of regard, see **regard/point of.**

point of subjective equality = 1. that value of the comparison stimulus which will be judged equal to the standard stimulus with a higher probability than any other comparison stimulus; 2. the point where the two psychometric functions of the greater and less judgments intersect, i.e. where the comparison stimulus is just as likely to be reported greater as less; 3. the point mid-way between the upper and lower **thresholds.** [In a symmetrical distribution of frequencies, these three points coincide. All these meanings were suggested by F. M. Urban (1908).]

point of symmetry, PS = (*psychophys.*) the point at which the psychometric functions of the upper category and the lower category intersect. [Cf. **point of subjective equality.**]

point-scale = a form of arranging the material and particularly the scoring of a test, so that credit for passing a test or a portion of a test is given in points, or units of score, as contr. w. credit in terms of ages. [The arrangement commonly permits partial credit, in distinction from the "all-or-none" method of scoring. Cf. the **Yerkes-Bridges scale,** the first point-scale published. Contr. w. **age-scale.**] — Fr. *échelle en points.*

pointer galvanometer, see **galvanometer.**

polar body = a small cell given off at the animal pole of the egg during one of the maturation or reduction divisions. [Commonly two polar bodies are given off during maturation.] — Fr. *corps polaire.*

polariscope = an instrument for observing the behavior of any substance toward polarized light; it consists essentially of a polarizer and an analyzer, mounted on a common axis, each consisting of a Nicol prism; when these are turned so that their planes of polarization coincide, the light polarized by the first is transmitted freely by the second; when the analyzer is turned at right angles to this, no light passes through; any substance placed between the two which rotates the plane of polarization of the light passing through it, will alter these settings of the analyzer by a corresponding angle.

polarity = 1. (*soc.*) a form of relation between two organisms, in which one is attracted towards the other, the attracted organism being figuratively conceived as a positive, the attracting as the negative pole; 2. (*soc.*) the tendency for individuals to assume either the active or the passive role in social relations. [(2) is extended to centers of attention in an audience. Syn. (2) **ascendence-submission relation.** Cf. **polarization.**]

polarization = 1. (*phys.*) the treatment of a beam of light or radiant energy in such a way that the waves oscillate parallel to a single axis transverse to the direction of propagation, e.g. by eliminating the wave-components parallel to a similar axis at right angles to the first; 2. (*biol.*) a phenomenon of living tissue attributed to the accumulation of differently charged ions on opposite sides of a membrane; 3. a change in potential of the skin, esp. during periods of no stimulation; 4. (*elect.*) an effect produced on the electrodes of a cell by the deposition of gas due to electrolytic dissociation. [Contr. w. **depolarization.**] **polarize**[v].

pollution = the discharge of seminal fluid without coition.

Poltergeist = (*pop.*) a reputed roistering spirit to whom is attributed the commission of miscellaneous petty mischief in the household. [Ger.]

polyandry = a marriage between one female and two or more males. [Contr. w. **polygyny;** in **fraternal polyandry** the husbands are brothers.]

polydactylism = the possession of supernumerary digits, such as six or more fingers or toes. [Syn. **hyperdactylism.**]

polygamy = marriage of one man to two or more women, or of one woman to two or more men. [Syn. **plural marriage.** Cf. **polygyny, polyandry.**]

polygraph = an apparatus for measuring simultaneously a number of physiological processes, such as heart-beat, breathing, and muscular contraction, and for recording them side by side (together with a time line) on a revolving drum.

polygyny = the marriage of one male to two or more females. [Contr. w. **polyandry.**]

polylogia = continual talking, usually incoherently, due to mental disorder. [A form of **dyslogia.** Syn. **logorrhea.**]

polymorphism = the occurrence of several types of individual animals in a colony or community of individuals derived from the same parent. **polymorphic (polymorphous)**[a].

polymorphous perverse = (*psychoan.*) a term characterizing the constitutional multiple sex predispositions of the child (oral, anal, etc.) from which, owing to the repression of certain components through education and social environment, the normal sex behavior of the adult develops. [If these predispositions remain unrepressed in the adult, the same behavior is regarded as perverted (Freud).]

polyneuritis = inflammation of many nerves simultaneously.

polyopia, polyopsia = a condition in which, owing to abnormal or pathological irregularities in the refractive apparatus, more than one image is formed on the retina of one eye. [Contr. w. **diplopia** which ordinarily applies to a doubling of images on the two retinas.]

polyphony = music in which two or more parts or melodies are rendered simultaneously. [In the middle ages two voices often proceeded simultaneously, separated by fifths or octaves. Cf. **homophony.**] (Accent **-liff-.**) **polyphonic**[a]. — Ger. *Mehrstimmigkeit.*

polyphyletism, see **convergent evolution. polyphyletic**[a].

polytypic evolution = evolution which results in the formation of several divergent types. [Contr. w. **monotypic.**]

pons Varolii = a large transverse band of decussating nerve fibers which form the middle cerebellar peduncle and encircle the medulla oblongata at this level. [Abbrev. to **pons.**] — Ger. *Brücke.*

popliteal = pert. to or located in the region behind the knee. (Accent **-te-** or **-lit-.**)

population = the totality of organisms, varieties, species, or groups of organisms which occupy a certain geographical region at a given time. [Applied in genetic studies to human beings or other animals or plants.] — Ger. *Bevölkerung.*

pornography = literature dealing with prostitution or sexual relations. [Usually designating an obscene as distinct from a scientific mode of treatment.] **pornographic**[a].

portamento = (*mus.*) passage from one note to another by a continuous glide.

Porter's law = the principle that the frequency of intermittence of a visual stimulus just necessary to abolish **flicker,** increases by equal amounts for equal increases in the logarithm of the intensity or brightness of the stimulus, and is independent of its wave-length composition or color.

posit = 1. to assume, i.e. to make an assumption; 2. to state an assumption or hypothesis. — Fr. *poser, affirmer*; Ger. *aufstellen, setzen.*

position = 1. the spatial location of an object or datum in relation to other objects and with reference to the body of the observer; 2. a bodily posture or attitude; 3. the general mental attitude assumed with respect to a given problem; 4. (*math.*) location within some frame of reference. — Ger. *Lage, Stellung.*

position habit = a stereotyped response of going toward a given locality. [E.g. persistence in entering certain culs-de-sac of a maze, or a certain side of a discrimination box.]

positive = 1. agreeing in some quality or character with a model or an original (e.g. positive after-image); 2. directed toward a stimulus or source of stimulation (e.g. positive tropism); 3. designating a real quantity greater than zero; 4. syn. for **affirmative,** with an emotional setting. [Contr. w. **negative.**]

positive acceleration = the change from a slower to a more rapid rate of progress, e.g. in the early stages of the learning process.

positive after-image, see **after-image/positive.**

positive and negative cases/method of, see **right and wrong cases.**

positive-negative movement, see **apparent (motion or) movement.**

positive self-feeling = the attitude of self-assertion. — Fr. *sentiment positif de soi.*

positive supporting reaction (or **reflex**) = a local static reflex, elicited by disturbance of equilibrium, which brings and holds the limb in position for a rigid support of the body. [Depends in part on cutaneous stimuli of the sole and stretching of the deeper muscles (Rademaker). Mediated by proprioceptive arc in spinal cord. Cf. **negative supporting reaction, postural reflexes.**] — Fr. *réflexe coordonné d'attitude, réaction de soutien.*

positive transference, see **transfer of training.**

positive tropism, positive taxis = a simple orienting response, in which the organism turns toward an external source of stimulation. [Contr. w. **negative tropism, negative taxis.**]

positivism = the doctrine developed by Comte which limits knowledge to experience, and holds that problems of ultimate reality do not fall within the scope of science.

possession = (*hist.*) a term applied to insanity generally or to special forms, on the assumption that the patient is under the control of an evil spirit.

possible = characterizing an assumption or hypothesis which is free from contradiction but for which there is, at the time, little affirmative evidence. [Distg. fr. **probable** = having a preponderance of favorable evidence, fr. the **improbable,** against which there is a preponderance of evidence, and fr. **impossible** = which the evidence absolutely refutes. All three are free from self-contradiction and are contr. w. **necessarily false. possible** is the most common and is often used for any degree of probability.] **possibility**[n]. — Ger. *möglich.*

post-epileptic stupor = a condition of coma or vague consciousness following epileptic crises.

posterior = pert. to or located in a rear or hind-part position. [Contr. w. **anterior;** the terms *dorsal* (contr. w. **ventral**) and *caudal* (contr. w. **cephalic**) are now generally prefd. in anatomy as eliminating ambiguity as between upright and horizontal postures.]

posterior pituitary extract, see **pituitary/solution of.**

post-hypnotic suggestion = a suggestion given to an individual during hypnosis of some act which is to be carried out by him later in the waking **state.** [During the carrying out of the post-hypnotic suggestion the subject may either apparently lapse back into the hypnotic state, with subsequent waking amnesia, or he may apparently remain fully awake, but be unconscious of the actual motive of his act, which he usually rationalizes.]

post-natal = pert. to the life of an organism after birth.

post-rotation nystagmus, see **nystagmus.**

postulate = a statement of some fundamental principle which is provisionally adopted, though crucial evidence of its truth is lacking. [Syn. **presupposition.** Distg. fr. **hypothesis,** which embodies a conclusion rather than an underlying principle, and which is assumed to be susceptible of empirical proof or refutation. Distg. also fr. **axiom** and **assumption.**] **postulate**[v], **postulated**[a].

postural = pert. to or tending to produce or maintain a **posture** (e.g. postural reflex). [Syn. **positional, tonic.** Contr. w. **kinetic, phasic.**]

postural contraction = the contraction of the skeletal musculature produced by the postural reflexes. [The state of contraction so produced was designated as **tonus** before the postural reflexes were discovered.]

postural reflexes = the totality of the proprioceptive and exteroceptive reflexes which give the body its attitudes. [Two groups are **static** (or stance) reflexes and **stato-kinetic** (or movement) reflexes.]

posture = a general bodily attitude or position of the entire body, or of a segment of the body. — Ger. *Haltung, Stellung.*

potency = 1. a latent or undeveloped power; 2. power of procreation, esp. in the male. **potential**[a], **potent**[a] (used rather as syn. for **powerful**). — Fr. *potentialité*; Ger. (1) *Wirkungsvermögen.*

potential[a] = pert. to characteristics which are not present or manifest in an organism at the given moment, but may develop or appear later. [Contr. w. **actual.**] **potentiality**[n] = contr. w. **actuality.**

potential[n] = degree of electrical charge. [Cf. **electromotive force.**]

potential energy = the capacity for doing work which a body possesses, due to its position. [Contr. w. **kinetic energy.**]

power = 1. (*phys.*) the rate of doing work. [Units (1), erg per second; watt (= 1 joule per second); horse-power (746 watts).] — Ger. (1) *Leistung.*

power = 2. muscular strength; 3. degree of an individual's ability in a given field, measured by the difficulty of tasks which he can perform without regard to time, as in a power test; 4. (*hist.*) syn. for (**mental**) **faculty.** [(3) is the opposite of the usage in physics, where power is rate of work.] — Fr. *pouvoir, puissance*; Ger. (2) *Kraft,* (3) *Vermögen.*

practical = 1. (*philos.*) pert. to social and ethical values and appreciative judgment, as contr. w. cognitive apprehension of facts and logical reasoning; 2. (*psychol.*) manifested in practice, i.e. workable (e.g. a practical example). [Distg. fr. **practicable** = capable of being performed.]

practice[n], **practise**[n] = 1. the repetition of an action as a means of improving the performance or as a means of habit formation; 2. a customary or habitual action. [The second use is non-technical; syn. **habit** prefd. for this.] — Fr. *entraînement, pratique*; Ger. *Übung.*

practice curve = a graphic representation of certain aspects of the progress made in acquiring information or skill, during equivalent periods of time or units of practice. [Syn. **learning curve.**] — Fr. *courbe d'entraînement*; Ger. *Übungskurve.*

practice effect = the progressive improvement which may occur in the speed, quality, or type of a response, either during continuous practice or at periods following active practice. — Fr. *effet d'entraînement*; Ger. *Übungswirkung.*

practice limit = the highest degree of skill or ability attainable by practice in a given field or task. [Syn. **physiological limit.** Cf. **plateau.**] — Fr. *limite d'entraînement*; Ger. *Übungsgrenze.*

practice period = 1. a period of time of uniform duration devoted to practice and separated from preceding and succeeding periods by determined intervals; 2. a period devoted to preliminary rehearsal of experimental procedure, the results of which are not as a rule included in the final data. — Fr. *période d'entraînement.*

practice theory = a theory of the nature of play, which assumes that its function is to train the human child or young animal in the performance of certain fundamental activities that are important for his development. — Fr. *t. d'entraînement*; Ger. *Übungstheorie.*

practise[v], **practice**[v] = to perform or attempt to perform a given act repeatedly, with a view to improvement. [Distg. fr. **exercise,** which refers to the motor organs rather than to the act.] — Fr. *entraîner*; Ger. *üben.*

praecox, see **dementia praecox.**

pragmatism = "the doctrine that the whole *meaning* of a conception expresses itself in practical consequences" (James). **pragmatic**[a].

Prägnanz = (*Gestalt*) a term proposed by Wertheimer to denote the most characteristic shape which a form or structure can assume, and towards which, according to Köhler, every form or structure tends. [Cf. **precision/law of.**]

prayer = 1. (prayer of petition) an earnest request or supplication addressed to someone in a position of power or authority, esp. to a deity; 2. (prayer of communion — *relig.*) an intimate intercourse with a deity, in which the intellectual activity is at a minimum and the feelings, particularly the tender feelings, are dominant; 3. (*relig.*) in a wider sense, petition, communion, together with thanksgiving and adoration. **pray**[v]. — Fr. *prière*; Ger. *Gebet.*

Pray's letters = a test for astigmatism, consisting of capital letters composed of strokes which run in a different direction for each letter.

praxinoscope, see **stroboscope.**

precipitate[n] = (*psychoan.*) a term applied to the material in the unconscious which is in readiness to act in determining any motivation process.

precision = the degree of approximation to uniformity of observations or measurements dependent upon the constancy or variability of the underlying conditions. [Syn. **reliability,** but its so-called measure, P.E., bears an inverse relation to the **measure of precision, h.**] **precise**[a]. — Ger. *Präzision, Genauigkeit.*

precision index, see **measure of precision.**

precision/instruments of = measuring or recording instruments which are carefully constructed, so as to eliminate as far as possible every sort of variable error. [Cf. **instrumental error.**]

precision/law of = (*Gestalt*) the most general law of organization, according to which organization occurs in such a way that its products, viz. the whole field (perceptual, ideational, and behavioral) becomes as well articulated as possible. [This law connects stability of organization with descriptive characteristics. These characteristics are of two kinds: *Nivellierung,* and *Präzisierung.* In many cases, *Präzisierung* of one part of the whole takes place together with *Nivellierung* of the rest.] — Fr. *l. de la précision*; Ger. *Gesetz der Prägnanz.*

precocity = a notably early development of mental or physical traits in a child. **precocious**[a]. — Ger. *Frühreife.*

preconception = a notion or theory formulated before sufficient data are at hand to render it in any degree probable. [Used generally to imply an initial bias which subsequent opposing evidence has failed to remove.] **preconceive**[v], **preconceived**[a].

preconscious[n] = (*psychoan.*) latent mental processes of which the individual is not aware at a given moment, but which it is possible for him to call to consciousness more or less readily. [They are unconscious only in the descriptive sense, i.e. on the basis of the structure of the mental apparatus, and not in the dynamic sense. Syn. **foreconscious.**] — Ger. (*das*) *Vorbewusste.*

precuneus, see **quadrate lobe.**

predetermine = to formulate a result in advance of its empirical observation, on the basis of other (cognate) data or of authoritative pronouncement. [Distg. fr. **predict,** which implies more conclusive evidence.] **predetermination**[n].

predication = the formal association of one concept with another. [The term is generally limited to formal logic but is admissible in psychology; the associated concept is termed the *predicate*.] **predicate**[v], **predicative**[a].

prediction = a description of the result or outcome of certain processes, formulated or stated in advance of the outcome (or without observation of the outcome), the advance statement being based upon knowledge of certain general principles of nature. [A **prediction** may be quantified according to its degree of probability. Not to be confused with **predication.**] **predict**[v]. — Ger. *Vorhersagung*.

predisposing cause = a factor which is not rigorously necessary to the occurrence of a given effect but which, when present, either renders the effect more intense or may replace some factor or part of the usual causal pattern.

predisposition = 1. a structure or condition in the body of an individual before birth, due to inheritance or pre-natal acquisition, which renders him likely to develop certain mental characteristics or certain diseases; 2. (*psychol.*) a preparation or set which facilitates the adoption of certain specific lines of behavior or the acceptance of certain theories, views, etc. rather than others. [One is said to be **predisposed** to an emotional temperament, etc. The term assumes that certain environmental conditions are needed to bring about the given result.] — Ger. (2) *Anlage*.

pre-Edipal (or **pre-Oedipal**) **phase** = (*psychoan.*) a phase of early development in which there is an exclusive attachment to the mother.

pre-established harmony = (*hist.*) a theory of the relation between mental and physical events, which assumes that they occur independently, i.e. without either affecting the other causally, but that they harmonize and constitute parallel series owing to some fundamental, original characteristic of reality. [A phase of the more general theory which was originated by Leibnitz.]

preference method = a method of research, used esp. with subhuman organisms, which consists in presenting two stimuli that differ only in one character (i.e. in quality, or intensity, etc.), and observing which one the animal responds to without previous training. [By repeating the experiment with other combinations, a **preference scale** may be mapped out for the given class of stimuli.]

preformation = the assumed existence of the various organs and parts of an organism, in rudimentary form, in the germ cell from which the organism is derived, development being regarded as a mere unfolding of what is already present in miniature. [Cf. **preformism.**]

preformism = the hypothesis that in the differentiation of structure in the embryo all characters are produced by the unfolding of characters already present in the germ. [Contr. w. **epigenesis,** which assumes that all differentiations are due to the action of the environment or to interaction of the parts of the embryo.]

pregenital phase (of **sexuality**) = (*psychoan.*) the organization of the sexual life of the child during the early infantile period, in which the genital zone has not yet assumed a dominating role. [During this phase, the genital component-instincts and the contrast between masculine and feminine have not yet developed. This sexual organization assumes the form of (1) the **oral stage,** in which the sexual activity is not yet separated from the taking of nourishment, and (2) the **anal-sadistic stage,** in which sadism and anal erotism play the leading parts.

pregnancy = the condition of a vertebrate female during the development of an embryo in the uterus. **pregnant**[a]. — Fr. *grossesse, enceinte*[a]; Ger. *Schwangerschaft*.

prehensile = adapted or fit to grasp objects; e.g. prehensile thumb. — Ger. *greifend, Greif-*.

prehension = 1. the act of taking hold of a thing or grasping it; 2. the simple noting of facts or objects. [**prehension** (1) implies a certain amount of adjustment, as in the human hand, the ape's foot, or the elephant's trunk; it is not used to describe biting with the teeth, etc. Cf. **prehensile.** The immediate memory span has been called a **test of prehension** (Jacobs).] — Ger. (1) *Ergreifen*.

prejudice = an attitude, either for or against a certain unproved hypothesis, which prevents one from evaluating new evidence correctly. [**prejudice** carries an emotional implication; the syn. **bias,** strictly, lacks this element.] — Ger. *Vorurteil*.

preliminary signal, see **warning signal.**

premeditation = (*crim.*) the planning of a crime beforehand. [In law distg. fr. **unpremeditated crime,** due to passion or sudden impulse.] **premeditated**[a].

premise, premiss = a proposition or judgment from which a conclusion is to be drawn. [Cf. **deduction.**] — Ger. *Voraussetzung*.

premonition = 1. the thought or dread of a coming event, aroused by irrelevant experiences or by some very indirect cue or suggestion; 2. (*psych. res.*) a revelation of some future event ascribed to other than normal sources. [(2) a form of **cryptesthesia.** (1) distg. fr. **presentiment,** in which the forethought is attributed to the individual himself.] — Ger. *Vorahnung, Ahnung*.

prenatal = pert. to the organism before birth.

prenubile = 1. pert. to the period of life before puberty; 2. characterizing a condition of non-marriageability due to lack of development.

pre-Oedipal phase, see **pre-Edipal phase.**

preparation = 1. the growth and coordination of functions in an organism during the earliest period of life, regarded as a basis for the comparatively stable behavior of mature life; 2. the initial stages of a complex response, of an experiment, etc. [Cf. (2) **preparatory response.**] — Ger. *Vorübung, Vorbereitung*.

preparatory interval = the duration of time in a response experiment between the (preliminary) warning signal and the moment when the actual stimulus is given.

preparatory response (or **reaction**) = a response which occurs in the initial or intermediate stages of a behavior series, and which makes possible the final consummatory response.

preparatory set = 1. a bodily attitude or posture which is assumed as the initial stage of a complex act of behavior, e.g. the attitude of listening; 2. a neural condition which increases the effectiveness of certain stimuli while decreasing that of others. [Syn. (1) **preparatory response,** which includes both posturing and acting.] — Fr. *ajustement préparatoire*.

preperception = 1. the preparatory attitude (including any ideational experience) which facilitates the integration of a clear or vivid perception; 2. a primary form of perception, or a sensory datum before it becomes perceptual, e.g. a film color which lacks surface and cannot be localized definitely; 3. (*exper. psychol.*) the anticipation of a perception by a thought, idea, or mental image before the sensory stimulus is actually presented to the subject or observer.

prepossession = favorable bias or prejudice toward a theory, etc.

prepotence = the power exhibited by certain reflexes to inhibit other reflex action, in the area in which they manifest themselves. [Distg. fr. **prepotency** in which the idea of inhibition is replaced by the idea of relative frequency.]—Fr. *prévalence*; Ger. *Vorherrschen*.

prepotency = the characteristic of certain specific biological phenomena, such that they tend to prevail as compared with other possible phenomena.

prepotent habit = a habit which is so well established that it tends to prevail over other, less well established habits. [Used by analogy with Sherrington's **prepotent reflex.**]

prepotent reflex = a reflex which takes precedence over another through **prepotence.**

presbyopia = a condition of the eye characterized by ability to see distant objects clearly and inability to obtain a clear picture of near-by objects. [Due to inelasticity of the lens, with consequent restriction of accommodation, which develops with advancing age (whence the name). Syn. **far-sight (edness)** (ambig.). Distg. fr. **hyperopia.**] **presbyope**^{np}, **presbyopic**^{a}. — Fr. *presbytie*; Ger. *Weitsichtigkeit*.

present/psychological = the amount of duration included in a single conscious experience. [Syn. **specious present,** a philosophical phrase.] **present**^{a}. — Ger. *Präsenzzeit* (Stern).

presentation = 1. any experience which is the immediate consequence of sensory (usually exteroceptive) stimulation, i.e. a sense perception; 2. the same as (1) plus revived experiences or images in which an object appears as in sense perception; 3. the mental operation by which such experiences (1 or 2) are brought about. [Fairly equivalent to Ger. *Vorstellung*.] (**pres-**, not **pre-**.) **presentative**^{a} = pert. to presentations, **presentational**^{a} = pert. to the study.

presentationism, see **realism.**

presentiment = an impression or feeling foreshadowing a future event, esp. a foreboding of calamity. [Cf. **cryptesthesia, premonition.**] — Fr. *pressentiment*; Ger. *Vorahnung*.

pressor nerve = an afferent nerve which stimulates a vasomotor center to heighten the blood pressure. [Contr. w. **depressor nerve** (2).]

pressure = 1. (*phys.*) the force exerted upon each unit area of a surface; 2. an impingement on the skin which deforms its outer surface and serves as stimulus for a specific sort of sensation called **pressure sensation;** 3. the specific sensation due to **pressure** (1). [Cf. **pressure sensation.**] **pressury**^{a}. — Ger. *Druck*.

pressure/acoustic = the mean force per unit area exerted upon a surface by a succession of sound waves. [A convenient unit is the dyne per square cm.]

pressure balance = 1. an instrument for exerting measured pressure on the skin, consisting of levers which permit increase or decrease of pressure, instantaneously or gradually, the speed of change being determined by clockwork or by hydrostatic control; 2. an instrument for testing judgments of lifted weights. — Ger. *Druckwage*.

pressure blower = an apparatus for supplying an air stream of uniform pressure to a pipe organ or other wind instrument, in order to insure constancy of pitch and intensity in the resulting sound waves. [The essential feature of the blower is a tank, with adjustable top which rises if the air pressure increases and falls when it decreases, thus regulating the outgoing pressure within the limits of the apparatus.] — Fr. *soufflerie*.

pressure gradient = the grade or inclination which results when adjoining areas of an elastic surface are subjected to unequal pressure. [The transition from a region of greatest, to a state of least pressure may be slow or abrupt, but in any case is continuous rather than saltatory. In psychology it usually refers to the gradient established when pressure is applied to a limited area of the skin.]

pressure-pain pattern = perceptual experiences, such as thirst, which arise from various cutaneous or visceral stimulations. — Fr. *complexus de pression et douleur*.

pressure pattern = a perceptual experience, such as smoothness and roughness, which arises from several simultaneous and successive pressure stimulations. — Fr. *complexus de pression*.

pressure point = a slender blunted point of thermally non-conductive material, which serves as a stimulus for individual pressure spots. — Ger. *Druckpunkt*.

pressure sensation = a touch sensation stimulated by an impression or impact of appreciable intensity. [Distg. fr. **contact sensation,** in which the impact is less intense and involves practically no dermal deformation. Cf. **touch sensation,** a generic term which includes both.] — Ger. *Druckempfindung*.

pressure spot = a locality or small area on the skin which has a lower threshold for pressure sensibility than the adjacent regions. [Syn. **touch spot.**] — Fr. *point de pression*.

prestidigitation, -tor, see **conjure** (1).

prestige = a temporary reputation for social achievement which attaches to a given individual according to the general judgment of the members of the community. [Distg. fr. **fame** = a reputation for achievement which outlasts the individual's life. Cf. **reputation.**] (Accent **-teezh.**)

presumption = 1. a conclusion incompletely proved but indicated as probable by the evidence at hand; 2. an attitude of arrogance. [(1) is properly distg. fr. **assumption,** in which the conclusion is held merely in the absence of proof to the contrary; this distinction is often ignored.] **presume**^{v}, **presumptive**^{a}. — Ger. (1) *Annahme*, (2) *Einbildung*.

presupposition, see **postulate.**

pretend^{v} = to imagine vividly a given situation as actually existing, and to act as though the imagined situation were real. [Syn. **make-believe**^{v}, **simulate, play**^{v}.] **pretence**^{n}, has an ethical implication absent in **make-believe**^{n}.

prevision = (*psych. res.*) supernormal awareness of future events. [Cf. **cryptesthesia.**]

Preyer reflex, see **pinna reflex.**

pride = a sentiment or emotion marked by high esteem for one's own ability or attainments, and characterized by a tendency to emotional elation. [Distg. fr. **vanity,** which implies a marked desire for notice and praise, and **conceit** which implies excessive pride, often ill-founded.] **proud**[a]. — Fr. *fierté, fier*[a]; Ger. *Stolz.*

primacy = the state or fact of being first, or of being in the first rank. **prime**[a] = first in importance; **primal**[a] = first in time; **primary, primordial**[a] = first in logical or hierarchical rank; **primitive**[a] = characterizing the first stages of evolution or development. — Fr. *primauté*; Ger. *Primat, Vorrang.*

primacy/law of = a principle used to explain learning (e.g. memorization, maze-running) according to which earlier items of a series are more readily learned and are favored in recall. [Cf. **recency/law of.**]

primal, see **primacy.** — Ger. *Ur-.*

primal scene = (*psychoan.*) a fragment of recollections or impressions retained from early childhood which constitute the prehistory of a neurosis (not forgotten, but latent and unconscious) and relate to early sexual experiences. [E.g. observing seduction, parental intercourse, etc. Cf. **screen memory, infantile amnesia.**] — Ger. *Urszene.*

primary = fundamental or first in logical or hierarchical rank. [Often used for first in time for which **primal** is prefd. Cf. **primacy.**] — Ger. *primär.*

primary attention, see **attention.**

primary color, see **color/primary.**

primary function = the original nerve process which arouses in the mind an idea without the after-function which determines the course of subsequent associative activity (O. Gross). [Contr. w. **secondary function.**]

primary memory = 1. the manifestation of retention in the lowest organic species; 2. the persistence of impressions for a few seconds after their reception, i.e. the remembering of that which has occurred but a few seconds before. [Syn. (2) **memory after-images** (prefd.).]

primary personality, see **personality/primary.**

primary position = the position which the eyes assume when the head and body are erect and the eyes fixate an infinitely distant point in the median and horizontal planes.

primary process = (*psychoan.*) the underlying, unconscious mental mechanism which produces condensation and displacement. [Contr. w. **secondary process.** Cf. **condensation, displacement.**] — Ger. *Primärvorgang.*

primary qualities = (*hist.*) those properties of an object, such as size and shape, which the object cannot be without, and which give rise to perceptions that directly resemble these (primary) qualities (Locke, 1690). [The primary qualities were supposed to be more fundamental than the **secondary qualities,** which are additional properties of an object that give rise indirectly to perceptions that do not resemble the property, such as warmth or cold, which are unlike physical heat.]

Primates = an order of mammals which includes lemurs, monkeys, apes, and man. [There are two sub-orders: **Lemuroidea** and **Anthropoidea.**]

prime[a] = first in importance. [Used technically as noun for **prime number** = one divisible only by itself or unity; also used to denote a stroke distinguishing symbolic letters: b′ = *b prime.* Cf. **primacy.**] — Ger. *erst.*

prime[n] = the fundamental tone or first partial of a clang.

primiparous = characterizing a female who has borne offspring only once. (Accent **-mip-.**)

primitive = 1. pert. to the first or earliest stages of development or evolution; 2. (*anthrop.*) characterizing peoples and cultures which do not possess true histories. [Cf. **primacy.**]

primitive credulity = the earliest stage in the development of belief in the individual, characterized by uncritical acceptance of traditions, unsupported statements, and casual observations.

primitive sheath, see **neurilemma.**

primordial = first in logical or hierarchical rank. [Frequently used to denote first position in time, etc. Syn. **primary.** Cf. **primacy.**] — Ger. *ursprünglich.*

primordium = the embryonic basis of an organ or part. [Syn. **Anlage.**]

principal[a] = 1. most important, chief, or leading; 2. characteristic of data which constitute the chief points of reference in a system. [E.g. (2) the principal colors red, yellow, green, and blue, when introspectively pure. (1) is frequently confused with **principle**[n].]

principal focus = the point at which light-rays, entering parallel to the axis of a lens or lens-system, will come to a focus. [There are two such points, according as the rays enter the system from one end or from the other.]

principal plane = 1. a plane at right angles to the optical axis of a lens or lens-system, passing through a principal point; 2. in the case of double refraction, the plane which includes both refracted rays.

principal point = the point on the optical axis at which refraction may be considered to take place, in computing the focal distances of a lens or lens-system. [A single refracting surface has one, situated at the surface; a lens or lens-system has two, located according to the design of the system.]

principle[n] = 1. a more or less fundamental uniformity discovered in nature; 2. the formulation of that uniformity (i.e. a law); 3. a guiding maxim for conduct or canon for scientific procedure; 4. (*hist.*) an active agent in nature. [Strictly, **principle** is the uniformity, **law** is its verbal expression, **formulation** is the careful preparation of the statement; a **canon** is a working device, accepted on account of its general application, but not demonstrated in this particular case; e.g. (Lloyd) Morgan's canon.] — Ger. *Prinzip.*

prior entry experiment, see **complication experiment.**

prior entry/law of = a principle of attention formulated by Titchener as follows: "The stimulus for which we are predisposed, requires less time than a like stimulus for which we are unprepared, to produce its full conscious effect"; i.e. the object of attention comes to consciousness more quickly than the objects that we are not attending to. [This law is illustrated in the **complication experiment.**]

priority = a loose term signifying that which is earlier in time, or more important, or logically more fundamental. [Cf. **primacy.**] **prior**[a].

prism = (*opt.*) a wedge-shaped piece of glass or other transparent material which by refraction bends the rays of light or radiant energy passing through it; the short waves being bent more than the long waves, the result in the case of mixed light is that the rays spread out and form a spectrum. [**prisms** of comparatively low deflecting power are used with the trial-frame or worn as a spectacle-glass to offset a deviation of one eye from normal fixation.]

prism degree = (*ophthal.*) a unit of prism strength represented by a prism whose refracting surfaces make an angle of one degree. [With the kind of glass commonly in use, this unit is only slightly different from the **centrad.**]

prism diopter = a term indicating prism strength, measured by 100 times the tangent of the angle through which the prism deflects the light-rays. [At low deflections the strength expressed in **prism diopters** is only slightly greater than that expressed in **centrads.**]

private = 1. pert. to a single individual, as contr. w. the **social group;** 2. personal or unofficial, as contr. w. **public. privacy**[n] = seclusion.

privation = (*psychoan.*) removal of the possibility of satisfaction for the libido. — Ger. *Mangel, Entbehrung.*

probability = 1. (*math.*) the degree to which, under a given hypothesis, an empirical sampling of data may be expected to conform to the total distribution prescribed by that hypothesis; 2. (*psychol.*) the feeling or judgment of credibility attaching to hypotheses or doubtful propositions, for which the supporting data are meager, and the contradictory of which is conceivable. [Distg. (1) fr. **likelihood** = the degree to which the given hypothesis is confirmed by empirical data. Cf. **probability/theory of. probability** (2) represents a rough scale of values, whose zero limit is **impossibility,** and which ascends through **bare possibility, high improbability,** etc. to **certainty.**] **probable**[a]. — Ger. *Wahrscheinlichkeit.*

probability/curve of = a graph representing the numerical distribution of the values of a series of events, measures, or scores, the occurrence of which is (or behaves as though) governed solely by the laws of chance or probability. [According to the **theory of probability** the results group about a central value, this value appearing most frequently; the number of cases decreases for each value as the distance from the central value increases. The relation is expressed by a formula $y = (N/\sigma[2\pi]^{\frac{1}{2}})\ e^{(-x^2/2\sigma^2)}$ (called **probability function** or **normal curve**) which gives a bell-shaped curve when plotted graphically.]

probability integral = the integral of the function whose graph is the **normal curve of distribution.**

probability ratio = the fraction obtained by dividing the number of ways which would result in the occurrence of a given event by the total number of possible ways (assumed equally probable) in which the event may occur. [It is assumed that the number of actual occurrences in a sequence of trials divided by the number of trials approximates this ratio.]

probability/theory of = the mathematical treatment of **probability** based upon certain specific assumptions regarding the uniformity of nature, mutual compensation of incidental factors, etc.

probable error = a measure of reliability (or stability) calculated for some obtained measure (e.g. average, score, coefficient of correlation, etc.) which indicates within what limits the value of the obtained quantity will lie as often as it does not. [The **probable error** measures the amount of fluctuation resulting from sampling; it is 0.6744898 times the **standard error.** Abbrev. **p.e.** or **P.E.** Syn. **probable deviation.**] — Fr. *e. probable*; Ger. *wahrscheinlicher Fehler.*

problem = the formulation of a situation in which certain elements, factors, or conditions are known and others are unknown, the suggestion or implication being to discover the unknown elements, factors, or conditions. [Applied to scientific investigation in any field. Cf. **Aufgabe.** Where the problem involves actual construction of any sort (e.g. drawing lines) rather than discovery, it is more properly called a **task.**]

problem box = a box with a more or less intricate set of fastenings, which the human individual is directed to open, or which the subhuman creature must open in order to obtain food, mate, liberty, etc. [Cf. **puzzle-box experiment.**] — Fr. *boîte avec mécanismes cachés.*

problem-solving = a form of experiment in which a situation of some kind is presented (to an individual or animal) which requires an intricate series of actions or of thought processes for the attainment of a specific goal. [Used in the study of certain forms of learning, insight, and thought. Cf. **problem box.**] — Fr. *épreuve de problèmes à resoudre.*

problematic = of uncertain or doubtful validity. [Hist. used to characterize any sort of open question.] — Ger. *zweifelhaft.*

procedure = the manner of arranging and carrying out a research, esp. in scientific investigation. [In an experiment, **procedure** refers to both experimenter and observer (or subject), and denotes the exact routine or sequence of conditions and tasks throughout. Cf. **method.**] — Fr. *technique expérimental*; Ger. *Verfahren.*

procedure with knowledge = a type of experimental procedure in which the observer is informed beforehand of essential conditions of the problem, i.e. what to expect. [Contr. with **procedure without knowledge,** in which certain significant features are concealed from the observer.] — Fr. *technique comportant connaissance préalable.*

process = 1. a change or a transformation of activity in any object or organism, as contr. w. the constitution or structure of that object or organism; 2. the manner in which a change is effected; 3. any sensation or other content observed as a mere occurrence without reference to its meaning or value (Titchener); 4. (*anat.*) a projecting part of an organ. [(1) and (2) usually imply a progressive action or series of actions, events, motions, or occurrences leading to some specific result. Syn. (2) **function.**] — Fr. *processus*; Ger. (1, 2) *Vorgang, Prozess,* (4) *Fortsatz.*

process attitude = the attitude in which the observer gives attention to the processes (sensations, images, etc.) which the stimulus arouses. [Contr. w. **object attitude.**]

process/mental = a **process** (1, 2 or 3) which occurs among mental phenomena. [Syn. **process of consciousness** = (strictly) the mode of such change. In structural psychology the mental process became the **mental element** and was often used without the implication of change.]

process of consciousness = a directly observable elementary experience with emphasis on its temporal character, its rise, poise, and fall. [One of the existential data revealed in a longitudinal section of consciousness. Syn. **process/mental.**]

procreation = the process of engendering a new organism. [Distg. fr. **fertilization** or **impregnation,** which applies to the effect upon the female.] **procreate**^{v} (syn. **beget).**

prodigy = 1. an individual who manifests supernormal mental ability, either special or general, particularly in early childhood (e.g. infant prodigy); 2. (*hist.*) a monster or monstrosity, i.e. a creature which varies excessively from the anatomical type of the species. — Fr. *prodige*; Ger. (1) *Wunder*, (2) *Monstrum*.

prodigy/mathematical = an individual who possesses in extraordinary degree the ability to perform arithmetical calculations. — Fr. *grand calculateur*.

prodrome = 1. (*med.*) a preliminary symptom or sign of a disease; 2. a conscious event or meaning which is not tied to the ideas that evoke it, and which has not yet issued in definitely recalled concepts. [Contr. w. **aura** (2).] **prodromata**^{pl}.

product moment = (*statist.*) usually the average of the products of paired measures. [Cf. **moment.** If the paired measures are deviations from means it is **covariance.**]

product moment coefficient of correlation = the coefficient of correlation between two variables calculated (from arbitrary origins) by the formula $\left(\frac{\Sigma x'y'}{n} - C_xC_y\right)/\sigma_x\sigma_y$ or (where x and y deviations are taken from means) $\Sigma(xy)/N\sigma_x\sigma_y$. — Fr. *coefficient de corrélation des produits-moments*.

Produktionsvorgang = an intellectual activity or process by which, according to Meinong and his followers, sensations are united to form complex spatial and temporal patterns and relations. [Contr. w. **purely sensational processes.** Ger. signifying **production process**. Cf. **founding process.**]

profane^{v} = 1. to treat with abuse, irreverence, or contempt; 2. to put to a non-approved or unworthy use, esp. as regards objects connected with the worship of a deity. [Cf. **sacred.**] **profane**^{a}. — Ger. (1) *profanieren*, (2) *entweihen*.

profession = 1. an occupation which involves a specialized education, embracing many intellectual elements, as contr. w. manual labor, however skilled; 2. a declaration of one's views. [(2) often used to denote an insincere declaration, a pretense.] (1) **professional**^{a}, (2) **profess**^{v}, (2) **professed**^{a}.

proficiencies = capacities for response of simple or complex type, mental or motor, which have been learned by an individual to the point where they may be carried out by him promptly and accurately. [Syn. **skills.**] — Fr. *habiletés*.

proficiency = degree of acquired knowledge, skill, or ability in industrial operations, school subjects, etc. [Distg. fr. **capacity** or **aptitude,** which is present in advance of specialized practice.] — Fr. *progrès, avancement*; Ger. *Fertigkeit*.

profile/psychic (or **mental,** or **psychological**) = a schematic outline of the characteristic mental traits of an individual, in so far as they can be determined quantitatively and presented in graphic form. [Syn. **psychograph** (1).]

profile test = a kind of test series in which the testee's scores on the individual subtests, though treated independently, are exhibited in relation to one another (usually graphically) so as to produce a **psychic** (or **psychological**) **profile** or **psychograph.** [E.g. **Rossolimo method, Downey will-temperament test, Seashore music test.** Distg. fr. **feature profile test.**] — Fr. *t. de profil mental*.

prognathous = designating a type of human skull in which the upper jaw protrudes beyond the forehead. [Contr. w. **orthognathous.**] (Accent **prog-.**) **prognathism**^{n}.

prognosis = 1. an opinion or judgment concerning the duration, course, and termination of a disease or pathological condition; 2. the foretelling of an event. **prognoses**^{pl}. — Fr. *prévision*; Ger. *Prognose*.

program, programme = a prearranged plan for carrying out an investigation or other task.

progress = 1. motion or movement in a given direction; 2. change in structure or organization (biological, social, etc.) which brings about an increase in fitness, or a general advancement toward some preconceived and melioristic goal. [Contr. w. **regression.**] (Accent **prog-** or **pro-.**) **progressive**^{a}, **progress**^{v} (accent **-gress**). — Ger. *Fortschritt*.

progression = 1. the act of advancing or improving; 2. (*math.*) a sequence of terms each of which bears a constant relation to the one just preceding. [In an **arithmetical progression** each term is derived from the preceding by adding (e.g. greater by 2); in a **geometrical progression** by multiplication (e.g. 3 times greater).]

progression/law of = a formulation devised by J. R. L. Delboeuf as a partial substitute for Weber's law; it states that successive sensation-increments increase by arithmetical progression when the corresponding stimulus-increments increase by geometrical progression. [Cf. **degradation/law of,** and **tension/law of.**] — Fr. *l. de progression*.

progressive relaxation, see **relaxation/progressive.**

project^{n} = a course of study or scientific research within a somewhat vaguely defined field set forth as a prospective undertaking. [The final goal may or may not be definitely foreseen. Cf. **project method.**] (Accent **proj-** or **pro-.**)

project method = 1. (*hist.*) a method which made use of practical activities in the home or on the farm, such as baking bread or raising corn, to supplement the work of the school; 2. more generally, a method which organizes the academic work of the school about complex activities or enterprises, such as planning and organizing a school circus, or making a school garden.

projection = 1. (*general*) the jutting out (or extension) of something beyond a given mass or body; 2. (*psychol.*) the reference or localization of sensations to the source or place of origin of the stimulus (e.g. hunger to the stomach, touch sensation to the skin, sound to a point in space), esp. the localization of perceptions beyond the observer's body; 3. (*soc.*) the ascription by an individual to other persons of experiences similar to his own; 4. (*psychoan.*) the tendency or act of ascribing to the external world repressed mental processes which are not recognized as being of personal origin, as a result of which the content of these processes is experienced as an outer perception (e.g. the mechanism of delusions of persecution); 5. (*math.*) the defining of a figure on a surface according to some rule, from points composing some object in another plane (e.g. the shadow of an object thrown by a single source of light upon a wall). [Syn. (4) **projection mechanism.**] **project**[v] (accent **-ject**).

projection center = an area or region in the cerebral cortex which connects directly with some definite sensory or motor center or tract, in the basal ganglia or cord.

projection/optical = 1. the formation of an image of a given object by means of an optical instrument, esp. when the image falls outside the instrument, as with a stereopticon; 2. localization in space as optically projected from points or areas on the retina by the refractive apparatus of the eye.

projection/visual = the total process by which activities within restricted portions of the nervous apparatus of the visual organs of the observer may, in conscious experience, be correspondingly localized in space. [Distg. fr. **projection/optical.**]

prolegomena = a somewhat lengthy and formal introduction to a scholarly work or to a subject of study. **prolegomenon**[sing] (rare).

proliferation = the multiplication of cells in the body of the organism. [Applied in neurology to the multiplication of nerve cells; in pathology, applied to cysts and other growths.]

promiscuity = practice of copulation with many partners.

prompting/method of = a memory method in which the degree or rate of learning is measured by the number of times the observer must be prompted before the content can be reproduced perfectly (Ebbinghaus). — Ger. *Hilfenmethode.*

pronation = a movement of the hand or forelimb, usually rotary, which tends to bring the palmar surface downward. [It may occur in the act of writing and in fencing. Contr. w. **supination.**]

pronunciation = the act of producing vowels and consonants in formal combinations.

proof = evidence (either facts or generalizations), brought to one's notice by another or by observation and thinking, which is sufficient to produce conviction or belief. [The presentation of proof is called **demonstration. proof** is classed as **deductive** = from premises or judgments already accepted, and **inductive** = from empirical accumulation of new facts, inducing conviction; it is contr. w. **authority,** in which the basis of acceptance is the promulgator's general credibility.] **prove**[v]. — Fr. *épreuve*; Ger. *Beweis, Probe.*

proof-reader's illusion = an illusion of visual perception which consists in the overlooking of a typographical error, due to the vivid memory image of a familiar word which is aroused by the printed form and supplants the perception of the letters as actually seen. [So called because of its frequent occurrence in proof-reading.] — Fr. *illusion du correcteur d'épreuves.*

propaedeutic, propedeutic = a preliminary study which serves as an introduction to some higher branch of learning. **prop(a)edeutic**[a].

propaganda = organized publicity used as a means of influencing attitudes.

propagate = 1. to reproduce; 2. to cause the spread or multiplication of an organism (as when a gardener propagates plants by cuttings).

propagated disturbance, see **nerve impulse,** and **wave of excitation.**

propagation = syn. for transmission or conduction of an impulse along a nerve or neural pathway.

propensity, propension = a strong tendency toward some given action or mode of behavior, whether due to inheritance or to habit.

property = 1. (*psychol.*) an intrinsic character or attribute of a conscious experience; 2. an attribute or quality of an object, which always characterizes it but does not enter into the definition of it. [Syn. (1) **character, attribute** (both preferable).] — Fr. *propriété*; Ger. *Eigenschaft.*

prophecy formula = (*statist.*) any formula (usually a regression equation) employed for estimating the scores to be expected on some future measurement. — Fr. *formule de prédiction.*

prophylaxis = systematic preventive measures against disease. **prophylactic**[a].

proportion = 1. (*math.*) the ratio of one number to another or of the magnitude of one portion of an object to another, ordinarily the ratio of a part to the whole: also the equality of two ratios; 2. (*esth.*) the esthetically pleasing or agreeable relation of parts in a total presentation. [Cf. (1) **percent.**] **proportional**[a] = pert. to proportion; **proportionate**[a] = in a certain proportion, or in proper proportion.

propose = to formulate, verbally or in thought, some specific action or procedure, with a view to actually carrying it out.

proposition = the verbal or other symbolic equivalent of a judgment. **propositional**[a].

propriety = fitness of an act or mode of conduct in a given situation as judged by prevailing standards of morals, social or professional etiquette, or scientific procedure. [Usually limited to minor conventions. Contr. w. **impropriety** = unfitness, implying a minor lapse.] **proper**[a]. — Fr. *convenance, convenable*[a], *appropriation, approprié*[a], *comme il faut*[a]; Ger. *Schicklichkeit, Anstand.*

proprioceptive reflex = a deep or tendon reflex depending on a simple spinal arc stimulated through proprioceptors. [Cf. **monomuscular reflex, myotatic reflex.**]

proprioceptive system = the sensory mechanisms concerned chiefly in the automatic maintenance of muscular adjustments or posture, consisting of receptors in muscles, tendons, joints, and the vestibule of the inner ear, stimulated mechanically by gravity or movements of media in which the receptors are embedded.

proprioceptor = a receptor or sense organ which is (generally) located in muscles, tendons, tendon sheaths, and joints, and whose stimuli result from movement of the body or its parts. [Sometimes extended in meaning to include the receptors in the non-auditory labyrinth of the internal ear. In general, **proprioceptors** are associated with supporting tissues of mesodermal origin. [Distg. fr. **exteroceptor** and **interoceptor.** Cf. **receptor, nociceptor.**] **proprioceptive**[a].

pro-secretin = a term applied by Bayliss and Starling to an inactive substance in the duodenal mucous membrane which becomes an active hormone when acted upon by an acid, the later product being termed **secretin.**

prosencephalon = that part of the vertebrate brain which is embryologically derived from the anterior portion of the primary forebrain vesicle and includes the cerebrum, striata, and olfactory lobes.

prosody = that branch of grammar which deals with the laws of verse and poetry generally, considered in relation to its rhythmical form and characteristics. **prosodic**[a].

prosopopesis = (*psych. res.*) the personation of a discarnate personality by means of a metapsychic collection of the characteristics of that person from the memories of the living. [**spontaneous prosopopesis** implies a degree of **cryptesthesia** and is distg. fr. **induced prosopopesis,** or **mythomania,** which is a recognized normal trance phenomenon.] **prosopopetic(al)**[a].

prospection, prospective reference = the reference of a present thought to some future situation, i.e. the assumption that the thought corresponds to a situation which will arise in future time.

prostitution = the practicing of promiscuous sexual intercourse (generally by a woman) for financial remuneration. [Technically limited to the habitual practice as a profession or means of livelihood.] **prostitute**[np].

prostration = a loose term signifying the onset of extreme exhaustion, due to disease or shock. [It includes 3 types: **muscular, nervous, general.**]

protanomalous = characterizing color vision which differs from the normal chiefly in the diminished effectiveness of low-frequency radiations, as indicated by the altered proportions of red and green in the Rayleigh equation. [An inadequately investigated type, resting on 3-color theory concepts. Cf. **deuteranomalous.**]

protanopia = a type of partial color-blindness, or **dichromatism,** in which the spectrum is darkened at the red end, and the Purkinje phenomenon occurs in daylight. [von Kries's term, signifying the loss of the "first" ("protos") color process of the three-component theory, hence **red blindness.** Now usually identified as a variant of red-green blindness. Distg. fr. **deuteranopia** and **tritanopia.**] **protanopic**[a], **protanope**[np].

protective resemblance, protective coloring = the resemblance of an organism in form or color to some part of its natural environment, resulting in a tendency toward concealment from its enemies or its prey. [Contr. w. **aggressive resemblance,** which enables a creature to attack its prey more readily (a rare term).] — Fr. *ressemblance protectrice*; Ger. *Schutzfärbung.*

protensity = the temporal characteristic or attribute of mental phenomena, i.e. the stretching forward in time, temporality. [Syn. **duration.** Strictly, **protensity** = the characteristic, **duration** = any specific instance; cf. **extensity** and **extent.**] **protensive**[a], **protend**[v].

protista = unicellular organisms, whether plants or animals. [Used by Haeckel to designate an assumed type of low organism consisting of protoplasm without a nucleus.]

protocol = the original record of the results of an experiment or research. [Usually (and properly) limited to a record made during the progress or immediately upon the conclusion of the experiment. Cf. **document.**]

proto-esthesia, protesthesis = the assumed primitive form of sensory experience.

proton = 1. (*biol.*) the primitive rudiment or incipient form of an organ or part, in the evolution of organisms along any direct line; 2. (*phys.*) the elementary unit of positive electricity. [Contr. (2) w. **electron.**]

protopathetic emotion = the earliest type of emotional reaction that appears in the child, assumed to be characterized by bare unpleasantness. [Not to be confused w. **protopathic.**]

protopathic sensibility = a system of sensibility by which only painfully intense stimulations of pressure, cold, and heat are appreciated in the viscera, and on cutaneous surfaces where the more finely discriminating **epicritic sensibility** is lacking (Head). [Contr. w. **epicritic sensibility.**]

protopathy = (rare) primary and direct emotional experience, distg. fr. **sympathy.**

protophyta = unicellular plants.

protoplasm = living substance, consisting of **karyoplasm** (or **nucleoplasm**) and **cytoplasm.** [Sometimes erroneously confused with the substance of a cell outside the nucleus.]

prototype = the primitive or earliest form of organ or organism in a given line of evolution. [Extended, by analogy, to earliest forms of response-pattern, etc.] — Ger. *Urbild.*

protoveratrum = the active principle of *Veratrum viride* and *Veratrum album,* which acts locally as an irritant and, on absorption, as a stimulant of the cardio-inhibitory center in the medulla.

protozoa = the phylum of unicellular animals. [Distg. fr. **protophyta** = unicellular plants, and contr. w. **metazoa** = many-celled animals. The term is plural.] **protozoön**[sing] (rare), **protozoan**[sing], **protozoan**[a].

proverb test = a type of test in which the task is to restate in everyday language the meaning of a proverb. [The response may be given orally or by checking the correct one of several statements given.]

provisional = adopted or accepted temporarily, with expectation of future amendment or refinement. — Fr. *provisoire*; Ger. *vorläufig.*

proximal = nearer (or in the direction of) the point of reference or the point of attachment of a whole member. [Contr. w. **distal** = farther away from such point of reference or attachment.] **proximad**[adv].

proximate = near or nearest to some object, phenomenon, or event which is under discussion.

proximoceptor, see **contiguous receptor.**

prudery, prudishness = the display of an exaggerated or fastidious regard for the moral code. [Usually applied to oversensitiveness of an individual to minor infractions by others, esp. in matters of conventional sexual behavior.] **prudish**[a], **prude**[np].

pseudesthesia, pseudaesthesia = an illusion of sensation, esp. of the localization of the source of cutaneous sensation. [Applied specifically to the localization of pain or irritation in the fingers or some other part of an amputated limb.] **pseudesthesic**[a].

pseudochromesthesia, pseudochrom(a)esthesis = the arousal of a color sensation or impression by a tone. [Syn. **color-hearing, synesthesia** (a generic term).]

pseudoclonus = a response which simulates the typical ankle clonus but in which the rhythmic contractions soon subside. [Noted in exhaustion, toxic states, and hysteria.]

pseudodementia = an extreme condition of general apathy resembling dementia, but without defect of intelligence.

pseudologia fantastica = an obsessive-compulsive

or constitutional tendency to make false statements.

pseudomemory = a false memory of an experience that never actually occurred. [Allied to **déjà vu,** and **pseudo-presentiment;** frequent in dreams. Syn. **paramnesia;** as pathol. type, **pseudomnesia.**] — Fr. *faux souvenir, pseudo-mémoire, paramnésie.*

pseudomnesia = a pathological condition in which the patient seems to remember events which he has not actually experienced. [Cf. **paramnesia, pseudomemory.**]

pseudomyopia = a condition, due to lowered visual acuity, in which the patient holds objects nearer to the eyes than in normal vision, simulating myopia.

pseudonystagmus = a term sometimes applied to nystagmus-like movements of the eyes, possibly voluntary in character. [Cf. **nystagmus.**]

pseudoparalysis = apparent loss of muscular power, similar to paralysis, without actual paralysis.

pseudoparesis = a condition which simulates the symptoms of **paresis** without evidence of the syphilitic nature of the process.

pseudoperception, see **hallucination.**

pseudophone = an instrument for studying sound localization by means of the illusions produced when the natural condition of the ears is changed. [S. P. Thompson's pseudophone consisted of a pair of ear-flaps, or reflectors which could be directed to the front, back, above, below, etc., producing illusions of auditory direction. P. T. Young's pseudophone interchanged acoustically the position of the ears by passing sound-proof tubes over the head to receiving-trumpets located on the opposite sides; it produced a right-left reversal of auditory space. Cf. **pseudoscope.**]

pseudopod, pseudopodium = a projection formed by the temporary flowing of the protoplasm of certain unicellular animals in one direction, thus effecting locomotion of the animal. **pseudopodia**[pl].

pseudopresentiment = an "instantaneous and irresistible hallucination of memory which makes it seem to one that something which now excites or astonishes him has been prefigured in a recent dream, or in the form of some other warning" (Royce), although this supposition is wholly unfounded. [Allied to **déjà vu.** Cf. **pseudomnesia.**]

pseudopsychology = any system, doctrine, or exposition which purports to be psychology or to represent a psychological point of view, but which embodies or involves principles, postulates, or procedures that are in conflict with the best established principles of psychology. [Often carries an emotional tinge.]

pseudoscope = an instrument which, by means of prisms or mirrors, transposes the optical images of an object or stereogram as they are normally brought to the two eyes, thus reversing the relief. [An intaglio appears as a bas-relief and a solid object seems hollow. The effect may be produced by interchanging the separate photographs or diagrams on a stereogram. Wheatstone obtained the effect by introducing a right-angle prism before each eye, with the hypotenuses parallel to the median plane. Cf. **pseudophone.**]

psittacism = argument based on the verbal form of propositions without regard for the relations of the concepts involved. [Lat. *psittacus* = a parrot. Cf. **dialectic.**]

psychanalysis, see **psychoanalysis.**

psychasthenia = a type of neurosis characterized by morbid anxiety, fixed ideas, etc. [Janet's term for the large group of obsessive disorders; syn. **obsessive ruminative tension states** (A. Meyer). Often uncritically used as contr. to **neurasthenia,** or euphemistically for **anxiety psychosis.** Syn. **obsessive doubt.**] **psychasthenic**[a].

psychasthenics, see **psychoasthenics.**

psyche = 1. the principle of life; 2. the principle (specifically) of mental life; 3. mental life itself, including both conscious and unconscious processes. [Used as a substitute for **mind** or the hist. term **soul** by recent psychoanalytic writers.]

psychergograph = an apparatus for measuring serial responses, which provides a fixed number of stimuli that are presented in chance order and are given continuously until the subject becomes fatigued, and which records the time and accuracy of all individual responses; responding correctly to one stimulus causes the next stimulus to appear. [Employed in continuous discrimination reaction experiments. Syn. **serial discrimeter.**]

psychiatrist = a specialist in the investigation and treatment of mental disorders, including the psychopathological and general medical aspects of the conditions. [Syn. **alienist** = a specialist in the determination of legally committable insanity.] (Accent **-ky-.**)

psychiatry = a specialized discipline which deals with mental disorders. (Accent **-ky-.**) **psychiatric**[a] (accent **-at-**). — Ger. *Psychiatrie.*

psychic(al)[a] = 1. syn. for **mental,** emphasizing the higher phases of mind; 2. pert. to the **psyche.** [Often confused with **psychological.** The term **psychic** is generally used in sense (1), e.g. psychic blindness; both **psychic** and **psychical** are used in sense (2), e.g. psychical research, psychic forces.] — Ger. *seelisch.*

psychic[n] = (*pop.*) an individual possessed of extraordinary or mysterious mental powers. [Cf. **medium** (2).]

psychic blindness (deafness, etc.) = inability to see (hear, etc.) due to some impairment of the cerebral cortex, the receptor being normal. [Properly limited to psychogenic (hysterical) inabilities to see (hear, etc.). Distg. fr. **mind blindness** = a condition in which one can see, but cannot understand or interpret (apperceive) what is seen.] — Fr. *cécité psychique, (surdité p.)*; Ger. *Seelenblindheit, (-taubheit).*

psychic determinism = the theory (in psychoanalysis) that mental processes are not only causally related (as in the association theory) but are motivated through factors in the unconscious (complexes, wishes). [E.g., a supposedly fortuitous idea or number, 34718, is not aroused accidentally but is fully determined by latent, dynamically operative motives.]

psychic (or **psychical) distance** = (*esth.*) the degree of detachment assumed by an individual towards the practical appeal of an object, esp. a work of art.

psychic force = (*hist.*) a term applied to the supposed cause of telekinetic phenomena, on the hypothesis that the unknown physical force exerted upon objects in a séance is intelligent (Cox and Wm. Crookes).

psychic profile, see **profile/psychic,** and **psychograph** (1).

psychic science, see **psychical research.**

psychical communism = a similarity in the constitution and processes of human minds, arising from a common nurture and training, which results in agreement among the individual experiences, cognitions, associations, inferences, inductions, sentiments, feelings, conations, etc. in response to the same stimulus or situation. [This phenomenon appears in guessing and in the events of daily life and results in striking coincidences which are (*pop.*) regarded as evidence for **telepathy.** Syn. **associative community** or **community of ideas.**]

psychic(al) research = the systematic investigation of various borderline or debatable phenomena concerning the relation of body and mind. [The topics generally included are **telepathy** and **telekinesis, spiritism** (i.e. communication with the dead), and **veridical premonitions.** Distg. fr. **psychological research** in that its typical phenomena are attributed to unknown causes of a supernormal or a supernatural (occult) nature. Syn. **metapsychics** (prefd.), **parapsychology;** these avoid ambiguity in use of terms **psychic** and **psychical.**] **psychist**[np].

psychical segregation = the disintegration or breaking up of mental processes or mental structure into constituent parts and the separation of these parts from one another. [A reversal of the normal integrative processes.]

psychism, see **metapsychics.**

psychoanalysis, psychanalysis = a dynamic system of psychology originated and developed by S. Freud, which attributes behavior to repressed factors in the unconscious, for the investigation of which it has developed an elaborate technique, utilized esp. in the treatment of nervous and mental disorders or personality flaws, as well as in the interpretation of a variety of cultural phenomena. [Cf. **depth psychology.**] **psychoanalytic**[a], **psychoanalyze**[v] (or **-lyse**[v]), **psychoanalyst**[np].

psychoasthenics = the investigation of feeblemindedness.

psychobiology = 1. the field of biology which deals with the nervous system, receptors, effectors, and other topics germane to psychology; 2. psychology as investigated by biological methods. [Syn. (1) **biopsychology** (prefd.).] **psychobiological**[a].

psychodiagnostics = the study of personality by the aid of external manifestations (physiognomy, gait, voice inflection, gesture, posture, handwriting, etc.).

psychodometer = 1. a response-time measuring device of the mechanical type devised by Obersteiner and Exner, in which a 100 d.v. tuning fork writes upon a moving strip of smoked glass; the sound of the fork constitutes the stimulus, and the observer reacts by raising the fork from the glass; 2. a name recently applied to the **Dunlap chronoscope** and accessories. [Cf. **Dunlap chronoscope.**]

psychodynamics = the branch which investigates the changes and development of mental processes. [Contr. w. **psychostatics** = the investigation of mental elements or content.]

psychogalvanic reflex, P.G.R., see **galvanic skin response.**

psychogalvanometer = a term applied to any electric circuit employed in the measurement of the galvanic skin response.

psychogenesis = 1. the origin and development of mind and mental phenomena; 2. the theory of mental growth; 3. the mental origin and development of any peculiarity of behavior; e.g. the psychogenesis of hysteria. **psychogenetic**[a].

psychogenic disorders = conduct disorders which are not attributed to physiological changes, and in which mental conflicts, suggestions, preoccupations, appear as underlying causes; e.g. hysteria.

psychognosis = 1. the study of mental processes by means of hypnosis or hypnoidal states (Sidis); 2. the reading of character from anatomical signs (Dessoir, 1912). **psychognostic**[a]. — Ger. *Psychognostik.*

psychogram, see **psychograph.**

psychograph = 1. a chart used by personality investigators to indicate an individual's measure in the fundamental personality traits, these traits being placed at equal distances, either in a row along the abscissa, or in a column along the ordinate axis, the values obtained for each being marked at the appropriate point on the other axis; the chart is completed by connecting these points by lines so as to form a **psychic** (or **trait) profile;** 2. a descriptive account of an individual's mental functions (i.e. attention, memory, perception, etc.) treated differentially and functionally (W. Stern); 3. a biographical sketch written from a psychological standpoint (Ostwald); 4. (loosely) a record in literary form of an individual's traits and responsive behavior, as revealed by a series of laboratory experiments and tests (Toulouse, Binet). [Syn. (1) **psychic** (or **mental) profile, psychogram** (rarely used; but prefd. for (1)).] **psychographic**[a].

psychography = 1. (*psych. res.*) writing without the operation of the medium's muscles (e.g. slate-writing); 2. (*psychol.*) the method of charting the traits of individuals by means of the **psychograph.**

psychoid = a special form of entelechy (autonomous, non-mechanical activity), namely that which displays itself in the actions of a human body (Driesch).

psychological[a] = pert. to psychology. [The form **psychologic** is not used. Often confused w. **mental** or **psychical** = pert. to the mind and its phenomena.]

psychological automatism, see **automatism.**

psychological color solid, see **color solid/psychological.**

psychological present, see **present/psychological.**

psychological time, see **time/psychological**

psychological zero, see **zero/physiological.**

psychologism = 1. the view that psychology is the basis of philosophy and of the sciences concerned with mankind (i.e. art, social customs, language, politics, religion, etc.); 2. the view that the principles of the normative sciences (logic, ethics, esthetics) are subjective and empirical in origin; 3. the view that psychology is the basis of all science. [Contr. (2) w. **logicism.** Syn. (3) **subjectivism.**]

psychologist = one versed in the facts, theories, procedures and practical applications of psychology.

psychologist's fallacy = an error of method and

interpretation which consists in attributing to a mental process all the characteristics which seem to the psychologist to be logically necessary from his knowledge of the relations of the process, the psychologist thus confusing his own knowledge about the process with the subject's direct experience during the process. [A common instance is the attributing of a human mental process to an animal.] — Fr. *sophisme des psychologues*.

psychology = 1. the branch of science which investigates mental phenomena or mental operations; 2. the science concerned with the mutual interrelations of organism and environment through transmission of energy (i.e. stimulation, response), as distg. fr. interchange of substance; 3. the systematic investigation of the behavior of organisms; 4. the science of the self or personal individual. [The term has been given many different definitions, representing various views of the field covered by the science and methods employed in investigation. The definitions above typify, in a general way, the different uses, past and present, though in many cases some extension or qualification is needed. — (1) is the earlier use; it covers several different concepts: the activity of mind (mental operations or *functions*) is emphasized by Aristotle and his followers, including the scholastics, and later by the faculty psychologists; while mental phenomena (the *data* of conscious experience) are the subject matter of the association psychology. These two paths have been followed in recent times: the former by act psychology (Brentano), which deals with the activities or operations of consciousness, and the latter by structural psychology (Wundt), which studies mental phenomena. American functional psychology occupies an intermediate position, since it considers the function of mental phenomena for the use of the organism, and both structural and functional psychology have accepted a physiological (more specifically a neurological) basis or correlate of consciousness, a factor which was considered only incidentally in the historic treatment of the field. The teleological or hormic psychology recognizes in addition the principle that mental events have a purposive implication. The Gestalt psychology emphasizes total organizations of both structure and function. — (2) is a different concept, which applies to several contemporary treatments of psychology: the motor psychologists consider that (motor) responses determine the characteristics of consciousness; investigators who emphasize the evolutionary standpoint consider adjustment the significant characteristic of response. — (3) is adopted by the behavior psychologists, either without qualification (i.e. so as to exclude conscious phenomena from the scope of the science), or with some extension which admits the validity of these phenomena. — (4) emphasizes the unitary character of the organism and the substantiality of the self. — The term was first used in lectures by Melanchthon (ca. 1550), and in print by Goclen (ca. 1600). Hist. divided into **rational** = the investigation of mental processes by the use of logic and *a priori* assumptions, and **empirical** = the investigation by observation and experiment. The divisions proposed by contemporary writers into human, animal, pathological, physiological, etc. represent branches rather than methods of investigation. Cf. **abnormal psychology, animal psychology, child psychology, dynamic psychology, genetic psychology, industrial psychology, social psychology.** — The practical applications of psychology are to be distinguished from the investigations of the facts, principles, etc. involved (art vs. science). Cf. **applied psychology, psychoanalysis.** In pop. use the term *psychology* is often confused with *mentality*; e.g. psychology (meaning mentality) of the student, of the business man, of the crowd, etc.] **psychologic (al)**[a] = pert. to the science, **psychologist**[np]. — Fr. *psychologie*; Ger. *Psychologie*.

psychology/abnormal (animal, etc.), see **abnormal (animal,** etc.) **psychology.**

psychology/new = a vague term, used at various epochs to designate a recently introduced method of psychological research. [Applied in the late 19th century to experimental psychology and to hypnotism, more recently to psychoanalysis and to Gestalt psychology.]

psychometric function = a type of mathematical expression or formula which expresses the relation between (*a*) a series of stimuli that differ quantitatively, and (*b*) the reports of an observer upon the corresponding sensory experiences, e.g. the observed relative frequencies of *less* judgments for a series of judgments of comparative stimuli.

psychometrics = the quantitative or mathematical aspects of psychological procedure. [Hist. applied to (1) **reaction-time** experiments, and (2) **psychophysical** experiments. In the latter sense (still in use) it includes (*a*) determination of the math. relation between quantitatively varied stimuli and the frequencies of a given judgment made upon them (= **psychometric function**); determination of (*b*) **thresholds of sensitivity,** and of (*c*) **relative sensory thresholds** (e.g. Weber's law). More recently applied to (3) **mental testing,** and now widely used in this sense.] **psychometric**[a].

psychometrizing = (*psych. res.*) the practice of a **sensitive** in receiving impressions relative to human drama in which an object that she holds in her hands has played a part. [The object is assumed to release personal or historical effluvia through which the **cryptesthesia** of the sensitive is directed: e.g. the sensitive is supposed to be able to reveal events constituting the history of the object (a ring, cuff-link, letter, etc.) and of persons connected with it; a form of **metagnomy.** Syn. (*pop.*) **psychometry** (3).] **psychometrize**[v].

psychometry = 1. the investigation of the temporal factor in mental processes; 2. (sometimes, more broadly) mental measurement in general; 3. (*psych. res.*) the supposed supernormal acquisition of knowledge by a **sensitive** through the influence of an object which she handles for the purpose of putting her in rapport with the history of itself or of a person connected with it. [Not commonly used today. Syn. (1) **mental chronometry,** (3) **psychometrizing.** Cf. **psychometrics.**] (Accent **-kom-.**) **psychometric**[a].

psychomotor = pert. to the motor effects of mental or cerebral processes. [A generic term embracing **sensorimotor** and **ideomotor** phenomena.]

psychoneural parallelism/theory of = the theory that every fact of consciousness is concomitant with some neural change without implication of the reverse relation, namely that all neural conditions are concomitant with conscious process. [Cf. **parallelism/psychophysical,** which is wider in its application.]

psychoneuroses^{pl} = 1. (*hist.*) the group of functional disorders which are less pronounced and less fundamental than psychoses; 2. the entire group of functional disorders of the central nervous system, so far as they involve or are caused by mental factors or functions; 3. (*psychoan.*) a generic term for the transference and narcissistic neuroses as contr. w. the actual neuroses. **psychoneurosis**^{sing}. — Fr. *psychonévroses*.

psychonomic forces = 1. the various active conditions which play a part in mental development; 2. (*soc.*) the active conditions or forces of a mental character which assist in determining social organization.

psychonomics = 1. that branch of psychology which investigates the relation of the individual mind, and its development, to the environment, both physical and social; 2. (*hist.*) the science of mental laws.

psychopath = an individual with pathological instability but no outspoken mental derangement; in particular, one with intellectual functions intact.

psychopathology = the systematic study of mental factors, functions, and processes in pathology or disease. [Distg. fr. **psychiatry** = the practical study and treatment, and fr. **psychopathy** = a mental disorder; syn. **mental pathology.** Cf. **abnormal psychology.**] **psychopathological**^{a}, **psychopathologist**^{np}.

psychopathy = any specific mental disorder. [Often euphemistically used as syn. for **insanity;** in its best use tending to give a dynamic rather than a static setting to psychiatry. Syn. **minor psychoses.**] **psychopathic**^{a}. — Ger. *Psychopathie*.

psychopharmacology = the study of the effect of drugs and poisons on psychological functions.

psychophysical law = any expressed relation between stimuli and sensory experiences, such as the Weber-Fechner law in any of its forms of statement. [Cf. **Weber's law.**]

psychophysical methods = a group of specific procedures used in psychophysical investigation. [Fechner adopted the following list: method of **limits,** method of **average error,** and method of **right and wrong cases (constant stimuli).**] — Fr. *méthodes psychophysiques*.

psychophysical parallelism, see **parallelism/psychophysical.**

psychophysics = 1. the science of the functional relations, or relations of dependency, between the body and mind (Fechner); 2. more especially the study of the quantitative relations between a stimulus and the ensuing sensation or other experience. [W. Wirth defines **psychophysics** as including the whole of quantitative experimental psychology.] **psychophysical**^{a}.

psychophysiology = a term applied indiscriminately to **physiological psychology,** or **psychophysics,** or both.

psychosexual = pert. to sex life in its widest aspect.

psychosexual hermaphroditism = (*psychoan.*) the condition in which a sexual object belongs indefinitely to either of the sexes, thus lacking the character of sexual exclusiveness.

psychosis = 1. any abnormal or pathological mental condition which tends to constitute a disease-entity; 2. (*hist.*) any specific mental state or conscious experience, or the total conscious experience at a given instant. [Distg. (in both uses) fr. **neurosis.**] (Accent **-ko-.**) **psychoses**^{pl}, **psychotic**^{a} (1). — Ger. (1) *Geisteskrankheit*, (2) *Seelenzustand*.

psychosis/deteriorative = mental disorder with tendency to progressive loss of mental functions.

psychosocial = pert. to those social relations which are determined largely by mental factors. [Distg. fr. **biosocial** and **physicosocial.**]

psychosomatic = pert. to bodily symptoms which arise from mental states.

psychostatics = the branch of psychology which investigates the composition or structure of mental states or conscious experiences. [A term proposed to designate the structural treatment of psychology. Distg. fr. **psychodynamics,** proposed to designate the functional treatment. Neither term has been generally adopted. Syn. **structural psychology.**]

psychotechnology = the body of general principles governing the art of applying psychology to practical ends. [Syn. **psychotechnics,** which refers more often to the skills and specific procedures of the art, rather than to the broad general principles. Syn. **technopsychology,** which usually deals with the applications of psychology to industry and business. Cf. **applied psychology.**]

psychotherapy, psychotherapeutics = the treatment of disorders by psychological methods; these methods differ widely, including waking suggestion, hypnotic suggestion, reeducation, persuasion, psychoanalysis, Christian Science, etc. [Occasionally used as syn. for **psychiatry.**] **psychotherapeutic**^{a}.

ptosis = a falling (usually a paralytic drooping) of one or both eyelids. **ptotic**^{a}.

pubertas praecox = a state of abnormal development resulting in premature or unusually early appearance of puberty and of the characteristics associated with puberty.

puberty = the period of life at which the reproductive functions mature, i.e. become operative. [Commonly, but not strictly, confined to the human species. Cf. **adolescence, maturity.**] — Ger. *Geschlechtsreife*.

pubes = the hairy region of the lower abdomen. (Accent **pew-.**) **pubic**^{a}. — Ger. *Schamgegend*.

pubescent = characterizing an individual who is just reaching or has just reached puberty. **pubescence**^{n}.

public^{a} = 1. characterizing an individual's behavior or status in so far as it affects the community at large; 2. pert. to the **public**^{n}. [Contr. w. **private.**] — Ger. *öffentlich*.

public = (*soc.*) an aggregation of persons having common interests or habits, who are affected (usually indirectly) by the conduct or behavior of one or more prominent individuals or leaders. [E.g. the great mass of persons in a state, an author's public.] — Ger. *Publikum*.

public opinion = 1. the average judgment or consensus of the individuals of a community (sometimes actual, but often assumed) regarding a given social, ethical, or political question, or regarding an individual; 2. the normative aspect of collective consciousness, more or less clearly defined, with regard to any object or question.

puericulture = (*hist.*) the art of rearing children.

puerilism = a condition of mental non-development or degeneration, in which the patient's mental processes and behavior seem to return to the immature type characteristic of childhood or early adolescence (Dupré).

puerperal psychosis = mental disorder following childbirth.

pugnacity = an instinct or innate tendency to fight or quarrel with other individuals. [Syn. **combativeness.**] **pugnacious**[a]. — Fr. *combativité, pugnacité*; Ger. *Kampflust*.

pull sensation, see **traction sensation.**

pulmonary = pert. to or located in the lungs. (Accent **pul-.**)

pulsation = an auditory experience of regularly varying intensity, produced by conducting to the ear a train of sound-waves of periodically varying amplitude. [Distg. fr. **auditory flicker,** or **tonal intermittence,** in which the intensity changes are abrupt.] **pulsate**[v]. — Ger. *Pulsieren*.

pulse = the rhythmical wave of tension in the arteries, due to heart action. [Generally applied to the measurement of rate and strength of heart action as indicated by the waves of tension in the radial artery at the wrist.] — Fr. *pouls*; Ger. *Puls*.

pulse metabolism/law of = the principle that the pulse rate tends to vary in the same direction as the metabolic rate or level. — Fr. *l. métabolique du pouls*.

pulvinar[n], **pulvinar body** = the projecting caudal extremity of the dorsolateral portion of the thalamus. [Syn. **posterior tubercle.**] — Fr. *pulvinar*.

punctal lens = a trade name applied to a system of spectacle lenses of similar design to the **toric lens** but with somewhat different specifications. — Fr. *lentille punctale*.

punctiform distribution = characterizing spatially discrete location on the skin of points, spots, or areas of pressure, pain, warmth, and cold sensibility. [Each *point* is believed to be subtended by a separate receptor, the *spots* or *areas* by groups of receptors.]

punishment = 1. the infliction of pain or discomfort upon an organism in consequence of the violation of a regulation, or following a course of action not desired by the inflictor; 2. a negative motivating stimulus, e.g. electric shock. [Applied both to social and legal procedure and to educational methods with human children and criminals, and in animal learning. The term harks back to the traditional notion of retribution, but has been retained in psychology to denote a method of deterrence and of learning. Contr. w. **reward.**] **punish**[v], **punitive**[a]. — Fr. *châtiment, punition, peine*; Ger. *Strafe*.

pupa = the third stage of development in an insect that undergoes a complete metamorphosis, the stage following the larval stage and preceding the imago stage.

pupil = the circular opening in the iris of the eye, which forms the diaphragm of the optical system, regulating the amount of light admitted to the eye by contracting as the light increases, or the reverse. [In the human eye the pupil remains circular as it contracts; in the cat (e.g.) it becomes oblong, then slit-like.] **pupillary**[a]. — Fr. *pupille*; Ger. *Pupille*.

pupillary reflex = (*vis.*) the change in size of the pupil which results from contraction or relaxation of the iris muscle when the visual stimulus varies in intensity. [Syn. **iris reflex,** a more appropriate term, but less used.]

pupillary-skin reflex, see **cutaneous-pupillary reflex.**

pupilloscope = an instrument for testing color-blindness or color weakness by measuring pupillary changes when the wave-length or composition of light stimuli is altered. [Devised and used by von Hess.]

pure = not mixed with anything foreign or extraneous. [Used technically in philosophy (e.g. pure judgment) and in chemistry (e.g. pure oxygen); in psychology generally a non-technical qualification, except as applied to sensory qualities; e.g. pure tone.] **purity**[n]. — Ger. *rein*.

pure color = a color due to stimulation by radiant energy of a single wave-length. [Syn. **spectral color.** Distg. fr. **saturated color,** which includes also purple. Contr. w. **impure** or **unsaturated color,** in which the dominant wave-length is mixed with another wave-length or wave-lengths somewhat remote in the spectrum.]

pure experience = experience from which all evaluation, objective reference, and the like have been abstracted. [Sometimes called **bare sensation** or **pure feeling.** The abstraction may be either logical or experimental.]

pure line = (*biol.*) a series of generations which have similar hereditary characters, usually the result of a special type of inbreeding.

pure scale = (*mus.*) a scale of true or untempered intervals. [See **interval, scale** (2).]

pure tone, see **tone/simple.**

purity = a characteristic of certain sensory qualities denoting their uniformity or the absence of diverse elements. [E.g. **pure color, pure tone.** Cf. **principal** (2).] — Ger. *Reinheit*.

purity/color = a measure, in stimulus terms, of the degree in which a color, or its stimulus, approaches the condition required for maximum saturation. [Various measures have been suggested for estimating purity; the one in commonest use involves the ratio of homogeneous (or spectral) to white stimulus required in a mixture in order to match the given color.]

Purkinje after-image = the second positive visual after-sensation which appears most plainly in the hue complementary to that of the primary sensation. [Syn. **Bidwell's ghost.**] (Accent **Poor-**; last syll. **-yea.**) — Fr. *image consécutive de P.*

Purkinje figures = the shadows cast on the retina by the blood vessels which lie just within the retinal layer of nerve fibers, seen projected outward into the visual field. [They are observed when the interior of the eyeball is illuminated by a strong light concentrated on the sclera or white of the eye; they appear branched and tortuous. Syn. **snake figure.**]

Purkinje images, see **Purkinje-Sanson images.**

Purkinje phenomenon = a phenomenon concerning the relative brilliance of different colors, namely, that as the spectrum is darkened, the long-wave end darkens more rapidly than the short-wave end. [E.g. red appears brighter in an intense general illumination, blue in faint illumination. Concomitant dark adaptation is required, since the effect rests upon the transition from cone to rod vision.]

Purkinje-Sanson images = the images of reflection on the anterior and posterior surfaces of the eye-lens. [Cf. **phakoscope.**]

purple = a series of hues which are distinctive and apparently simple, but which are due to combinations or mixtures of long and short wave-lengths of radiant energy within the visible spectrum and are not produced by stimulation with any single wave-length. [The complement of **green.**] — Fr. *pourpre*; Ger. *Purpur.*

purple/visual, see **visual purple.**

purpose[n] = 1. a situation imagined as the outcome of certain actions to be performed by the thinker himself, which situation he is determined to bring about; 2. the end, real or apparent, toward the attainment of which vital processes are coordinated, such as the maintenance or the perpetuation of life; 3. (*behav.*) an objectively definable determinant of behavior-acts in so far as the organism persists in those acts until it reaches some specific type of environmental situation or inner physiological state, and in so far as it shows a tendency to select the shorter (easier) of these acts for reaching this final situation or state. [Syn. **aim, goal,** and **end,** which emphasize the objective result, while **purpose** (1) refers to the present thought representing this future situation.] **purpose**[v] (1). **purposive**[a]. — Fr. *intention, idée de but, idée de finalité*; Ger. *Zweck, Vorsatz, Absicht.*

purposive idea = 1. an anticipatory idea of action accompanied by an attitude of self-determination; 2. an idea which represents (at least in part) a given action and is ordinarily followed by the performance of that action. [Cf. **purpose** (1).] — Fr. *idée intentionnelle*; Ger. *Zielvorstellung.*

purposivism = any type of psychological system which holds that purposes in some sense are, in addition to stimuli, effective determinants of behavior. [Cf. **purpose** (1, 3).] — Fr. *intentionnisme.*

pursuit coordination = a series of responses in which the subject endeavors to adjust certain of his movements so as to accord with the rate and amount or direction of change exhibited continuously in a moving stimulus; e.g. to maintain visual fixation on a swinging pendulum, to direct a searchlight on a moving airplane. [The error, while essentially temporal, may be measured in spatial or other terms.]

pursuit movement = a coordinated response of appropriate direction and rate made as an attempt to follow a moving stimulus. [Applied esp. to a type of eye movement. Contr. w. **compensatory movement** and w. movement in reference to static objects.]

pursuit pendulum = an apparatus for measuring eye-hand coordination, consisting of a swinging pendulum from the bob-end of which flows a continuous stream of water or sand, and a cup of small diameter with which the subject endeavors to match the pendulum motion and catch the oscillating stream; the score is in terms of volume captured in a given number of pendulum swings.

pursuit response (or **reaction**) = response to a moving stimulus or response by means of an indicator which is itself in motion. [E.g. following a swinging pendulum with the hand; gun-pointing at a fixed target from a rolling ship. A pursuit response is continuous or semi-continuous in character.]

pursuitmeter = an instrument for measuring eye-hand coordination, which combines (1) a stimulus target, whose movements the subject endeavors to match by keeping in step, or to eliminate by complete compensation, and (2) an integrating or totalizing meter or meters which register the amount of coordination-error in terms of amplitude or time or both. — Fr. *perséquomètre.*

putamen = (*neurol.*) the outer portion of the lenticular nucleus. (Accent **-tay-.**)

putrid = a quality of olfactory sensation of which the smells of hydrogen-sulphide and decaying meat are typical examples. [Syn. **nauseous, foul.** Cf. **odor, odor prism.**] — Fr. *fétide*; Ger. *ekelhaft, faul.*

putting through = a mode of training an individual to perform an action, in which the investigator mechanically moves the individual's limbs so as to accomplish the desired action.

puzzle-box experiment = a type of experiment in which an animal is confronted with a box which is opened by some special device, and must discover the means of opening it in order to obtain reward. [In general the animal is placed outside the box with the food (or mate) inside; the reverse procedure is sometimes employed. When the experiment is used with human subjects, the task is to open a box provided with an intricate set of fastenings. Cf. **problem box.**]

puzzle-experiment, see **blank experiment.**

pyknic = a type of bodily build, with short legs, thick neck, and relatively large barrel-shaped trunk, associated with cyclothymic mental disorders (Kretschmer).

pylorus = the opening from the stomach into the duodenum. (Accent **-lor-.**) **pyloric**[a]. — Ger. *Pförtner.*

pyramidal tract = a group of nerve fibers which combine in the anterior portion of the internal capsule to form the efferent path from the pre-central gyrus of the cerebral cortex to the motor ganglia (in the brain stem) and to the cord. (Accent **-ram-.**) — Fr. *voie pyramidale*; Ger. *Pyramidenbahn.*

pyramids = elevated regions on the front of the medulla, lying on either side of the anterior median fissure.

pyromania = a chronic tendency to incendiarism, found in certain cases of insanity and psychopathic states. [Cf. **incendiarism, arson.**]

pyrosis = a burning sensation, referred to the stomach and lower esophagus, due to acid irritation. [Syn. **heartburn.**]

Pythagorean scale, see **scale.**

Q

Q = abbrev. for **quartile deviation.**

quadrate lobe = an area on the mesial surface of the cerebrum lying between the internal parieto-occipital fissure and the upturned end of the calloso-marginal fissure. [Syn. **precuneus.**] — Ger. *Vorzwickel.*

quadrature = an expression of the phase relation between two sinusoidal quantities when the phase difference between them is 90° or $\pi/2$ radians.

quadriceps extensor reflex, see **patellar reflex.**

quadrigemina, corpora quadrigemina = a group of four oval masses or tubercles situate behind the third ventricle of the brain and forming the dorsal part of the mesencephalon. [They consist of the upper or anterior tubercles (= **colliculi superiores**), and the lower or inferior tubercles (= **colliculi inferiores**).] — Fr. *tubercules quadrijumeaux*; Ger. *Vierhügel*.

quale = any sensation or other bit of experience, considered simply with regard to its factual description and without regard to its significance or reference beyond itself. (Pron. **kway-ly.**) **qualia**[pl].

qualities/primary, secondary, see **primary qualities, secondary qualities.**

quality = (*psychol.*) an aspect, attribute, characteristic, or fundamental dimension of experience, which involves variation in kind and not in degree; i.e. a non-quantitative variable of experience. [Distg. fr. **quantity** = a characteristic whose variations admit of numerical expression. Cf. **intensity.**] **qualitative**[a].

quantity = 1. (*math.*) the general character of phenomena according to which they can be measured or counted; 2. (*logic*) the character of a term as being universal or particular or singular.

quantum = a determinate, discrete quantity. [The **quantum theory** is based upon the conception of discrete or discontinuous changes in physical phenomena; contr. w. the **continuity hypothesis.**]

quarter-tone music = a type of music based upon a scale which divides the octave into 24 equal quarter-tone intervals. [The ordinary equally-tempered scale divides the octave into 12 semitones.]

quartile = one of the points by which a serially arranged group is divided into quarters. [Sometimes used as syn. for **quarter,** which denotes the interval. The lowest **quartile** = that point of value below which fall 25% of the cases and above which fall the remaining 75%. Cf. **percentile.**] (Pron. **-till** prefd.)

quartile deviation, Q = a measure of dispersion or scatter, equal to 1/2 the distance between the 3rd and 1st quartiles (75th and 25th percentiles) in a frequency distribution. [Cf. **quartile.**] — Fr. *écart quartile*.

questionary, questionnaire = a set of questions dealing with some topic or related group of topics, sent out or given to a selected group of individuals for the purpose of gathering data on the subject-matter or problem under consideration. [The results so obtained are treated statistically; the total procedure is called the **questionary** (or **questionnaire**) **method** of research.] — Fr. *enquête, questionnaire, dépistage*; Ger. *Fragebogen*.

quiescence = the feeling of restfulness, contr. w. the feeling of **excitement** in the Wundtian tridimensional scheme of feeling. — Ger. *Beruhigung*.

Quincke tubes = 1. a set of small open pipes for producing tones of high pitch; 2. a type of **interference tube.** [(1) is used for the study of difference tones.]

quotient hypothesis = an interpretation of Weber's law according to which the quotients or ratios of any two successive just noticeable differences in a given sensory series are always equal.

R

R = 1. abbrev. for Ger. *Reiz* (stimulus); 2. abbrev. for **response,** as in S–R (stimulus-response) relation. [(1) is used in psychophysics. Prefd. in roman cap. without period. Cf. **S.**]

r = a symbol denoting **coefficient of correlation.**

rabbit-duck figure = a deceptive drawing which can be visually perceived either as the head of a duck facing in one direction or as the head of a rabbit facing in the opposite direction.

rabdomancy, see **rhabdomancy.**

race = a group of organisms that are relatively similar in form and have common ancestry. [A loose term, applied esp. to man and other high species, e.g. negro race, perpetuation of the race, race characters.] **racial**[a], **race**[a]. — Ger. *Rasse*.

race experience = the accumulated experiences, habits, knowledge, traditions, etc. of (the members of) successive generations in a community, transmitted and made generally available by social intercourse.

race psychology = that branch of psychology which investigates the specific mental traits of different races. [Usually limited to the human species; in this sense it is a subdivision of **comparative psychology.**]

radial = 1. in a radiating manner, i.e. branching or spreading out in all directions; 2. towards the **radius bone** of the lower arm. (Accent **ray-.**)

radial reflex = flexion of the forearm, often with concomitant flexion of fingers, upon tapping lower end of radius. [Mediated by 5th to 8th segments of cord.]

radian = that arc of a circle which is equal to the radius; or the central angle measured by such an arc. [A radian equals $180/\pi°$ or $57.2956°$.]

radiant energy = an electromagnetic disturbance, of oscillatory or wave character, which travels through free space at a velocity of approx. 300,000 km. (186,000 miles) per second. [**radiant energy** of wave-lengths 400 to 760 $m\mu$ affects the human retina and is commonly known as **light.** The term **homogeneous** is applied to radiant energy or light which is all substantially of a single wave-length; and **heterogeneous** to radiant energy which includes a considerable variety of wave-lengths.]

radiant flux = the rate of emission of **radiant energy** from a given source, or of its incidence upon a specified surface, evaluated as energy and properly expressed in ergs per second, or in watts. [Distg. fr. **luminous flux.**]

radiation = 1. divergence or emission in all directions from some center; 2. emission or diffusion of energy in form of (rectilinear) rays; applied to light, heat, radio-active materials and the like; 3. (*physiol.*) the spreading of an excitation to adjacent areas in a nerve-center, giving rise to various secondary or induced effects (responses); 4. (*anat.*) the system of fibers which connect the primary with a secondary sense center; 5. syn. for **radiant energy.** [Not to be confused with **irradiation** = a dispersal (of fibers, retinal excitation, etc.) at right angles to the general line of direction.] **radiate**[v]. — Ger. *Strahlung*.

radical[a] = a loose term signifying *thoroughgoing* or *extreme*. [Lit. going to the root, **radix.** **radical**[n] has technical meanings in chemistry, linguistics, and politics; in psychology it is usually applied loosely to the holder of any very unusual views.]

radiometer = an instrument for measuring **radiant energy.**

radiometry = the measurement of radiation in terms of energy. [Distg. fr. **photometry,** based on visual brilliance effects.]

radius = 1. (*math.*) the distance between the center and circumference of a circle, or a line drawn from the center to any point on the circumference; 2. (*anat.*) that one of the two bones of the lower arm which lies on the same side as the thumb. [Contr. (2) w. **ulna,** the other bone.] (Accent **ray-.**) **radial**[a]. — Ger. (1) *Halbmesser.*

radix = a nerve-root, or bundle of nerve fibers, at their point of entry into the central nervous system or of departure therefrom. — Fr. *racine.*

rage = an intense degree of anger, accompanied by violent facial and bodily expressions. [The response is usually marked by movements of attack and a disregard of self-protection.] — Ger. *Wut.*

Ragona Scinà experiment = a demonstration of **simultaneous contrast;** the apparatus consists of two white screens at right angles, and a colored glass at 45° between them; the two fields are seen superimposed, one through the glass, the other reflected in its surface; a black spot on the screen observed through the glass is seen in the color complementary to that of the glass, while a similar spot on the reflected screen appears of the same color as the glass.

ramus = a branch. [Applied generally to nerves, veins, etc. and specifically to certain connections of the sympathetic nervous system with the spinal.] **rami**[pl].

rana = a genus of anurin amphibians, including the frog.

random[a] = 1. occurring without deliberate volition or determination; 2. haphazard, casual, fortuitous. [Applied in statistical work to a **sampling** which is not selected by any criterion, so that the sample drawn presumably does not differ to any marked degree from the entire group (i.e. the **population**) to which it belongs; it is therefore assumed to represent the total group, with an error which decreases proportionately with the increase in the size of the sample drawn. Used as a substitute for **chance** to avoid the popular meaning of the latter (= uncaused); cf. **casual, sampling.**] **randomness**[n], **at random**[a]. — Fr. *au hasard*[a], *hasard*[n]; Ger. *zufällig, aufs Geratewohl.*

random group = (*statist.*) a group of subjects drawn at random (i.e. without selection), from a larger group or population, with the aim of securing a representative sampling of the larger group with respect to some characteristic or ability to be investigated. [As the **random group** increases in size with reference to the larger group the conclusions become more truly representative of the latter. Syn. **random sample;** contr. w. **selected group.**] — Fr. *groupe formé au hasard.*

random movements, random activities = responses which are apparently not organized with reference to biological or experimental ends recognized by the observer. [Usually applied to diffuse activity, as in infants, or to errors made in adaptive behavior. Contr. w. **reflexes, organized behavior, habits, stereotyped movements,** in all of which a definite stimulus or stimulus pattern leads to a definite response.] — Fr. *mouvements au hasard.*

random sample = a limited number of cases in a group, taken for examination in place of the entire group, every precaution being used to prevent the selection of certain specific kinds or values, the aim being to make the sampling representative of the entire group. [Syn. **random group, random sampling** (= also the procedure used). Cf. **random.**] — Fr. *échantillonnage au hasard.*

range = 1. the entire interval between (and including) the highest and lowest values in any series of data; 2. the series of variations within these observed limits. [The term **range of sensation** is applied to the entire field of intensity for any class of sensation, **range of stimulation** denoting the corresponding region of values of the stimuli. **range** is applied to the field of sensation qualities also.] — Fr. *étendue, marge, rangée*; Ger. *Umfang.*

range of attention, see **attention/range of.**

range of audibility (or **hearing**), see **audibility range.**

rank = the position of a given datum of any sort, with relation to all other data which belong to the same group, when the data are arranged in order of value beginning with the lowest or the highest value. **rank**[v]. — Fr. *rang*; Ger. *Rang.*

rank correlation = (*statist.*) the correlation between two series of paired measures, each of which has been ranked in order of magnitude. [In the correlation of ranks, Spearman's rank-difference formula, $\rho = 1 - [6\,\Sigma D^2/N(N^2 - 1)]$ is usually employed; D^2 = the sum of the squared differences in rank of the paired measures and N = the number of ranks.] — Fr. *corrélation par la méthode des rangs.*

rank difference formula (and **method**), see **rank correlation.**

rank order = the arrangement of the entire set of measures which form a statistical group in serial order of magnitude. — Fr. *ordre du rang*; Ger. *Rangordnung.*

rank order method, see **order of merit/method of.**

Ranschburg inhibition = the inhibition of like material by like as demonstrated in Ranschburg's experiments, in which it was found that more numbers could be recognized in a single tachistoscopic exposure when the numbers were all different than when some were the same.

rape = sexual intercourse effected against the will of one of the partners concerned, usually the female. — Fr. *rapt*; Ger. *Notzucht.*

rapport = 1. an apparent but pseudo-insensibility to all stimuli which emanate from persons other than the hypnotizer, sometimes displayed by subjects in the hypnotic state, probably due entirely to suggestion either direct or indirect; 2. a special heightened susceptibility to suggestions emanating from the hypnotizer which may readily be transferred, in large part at least, from the hypnotizer to any other person, by simple verbal suggestion of the former. [French; accent **-por.**]

raps = (*psych. res.*) percussive sounds (such as taps or knocks) which manifest intelligence (as by giving ages of persons or by answering questions addressed to disembodied spirits) and which are commonly ascribed to supernormal causes although they are often known to be produced by mechanical means, as by snapping toe-joints, by slowly moving a shoe-sole or thumb-nail against a smooth or polished surface, etc. [A phenomenon of **objective metapsychics.** The intelligence may inhere in the agent or sitter who calls the alphabet or number and involuntarily gives the cue when the rapping should stop.] — Fr. *coups*; Ger. *Klopflaute*.

ratchet mechanism, see **catch muscle.**

rate[n] = amount of change (in any specified respect) per unit of time. [E.g. rate of growth (in cm. per year), rate of sound-wave transmission (in meters per sec.).] — Fr. *taux*.

rate[v] = (*statist.*) to assign a rank, score, or mark, to a given individual or datum in a group of values. — Fr. *noter, donner une notation*; Ger. *schätzen*.

rate score = the number of problems attempted, of letters written, or of items completed in a specified time. [Syn. **speed score.** Cf. **comprehension score.**] — Fr. *notation de taux*.

rating[n] = 1. the assignment of rank, score, or mark; 2. the position of a given individual or datum in a scale of values. [Cf. **rate, rank.**] — Fr. *appréciation*; Ger. *Schätzung*.

rating scale, see **graphic rating scale; man-to-man rating scale.**

ratio = the quantitative relation between two values. [**ratios** are either **rational** = reducible by division to a definite numerical expression, or **irrational** = not so reducible (e.g. π).] — Fr. *rapport*; Ger. *Verhältnis*.

ratiocination = the act of reasoning or drawing deductive conclusions. [According to J. S. Mill, the term should be limited to the drawing of *necessary* deductive conclusions.] (Pron. **rash-i-oss-.**)

rational[a] = 1. pert. to the reasoning process; 2. having the capacity of reasoning; 3. conducted according to correct reasoning. — Fr. (1) *rationnel*, (2) *raisonnable*, (3) *raisonné*; Ger. *vernünftig*.

rational and integral function = (*math.*) a polynomial or convergent infinite series, in the terms of which the independent variable appears to finite integral powers only. [E.g. $y = ax^{\sqrt{2}}$ is neither rational nor integral, $y = ax^{\frac{1}{2}}$ is rational but not integral, $y = ax^2$ is both rational and integral.]

rational behavior, rational conduct = behavior of organisms which rests upon reasoning or which is interpreted or judged as proceeding in a logical manner. — Fr. *comportement rationnel*.

rational self, rational ego, see **self.**

rationalism = 1. the theory that knowledge is derived from reason rather than from experience. [Contr. w. **empiricism.**] **rationalist**[np].

rationalization = the mental process of devising ostensible reasons, to justify an act or opinion which is actually based on other motives or grounds, although this may not be apparent to the rationalizer; 2. the act or opinion resulting from (1). **rationalize**[v].

rationalization appeal = (*advert.*) a combination of short-circuit and long-circuit appeals. [Cf. **appeal.**]

raw score = a score obtained on a test as determined by the performance itself, to which no correction or modification of any kind has been applied. [Syn. **crude score.**] — Fr. *note brute*.

ray = (*opt.*) a line indicating the presence and direction of travel of light or radiant energy. [A geometrical concept, esp. useful in the study of optical systems.] — Fr. *rayon*; Ger. *Strahl*.

ray of direction = any ray of light which, if produced, passes through the nodal point of the eye or any lens-system, and determines for the observer the direction of any external point on its course.

Rayleigh disk (or **disc**) = an apparatus for determining the intensity of sound, which utilizes the principle that a disk suspended in an alternating air current tends to orient itself at right angles to the direction of the current; the disk (of thin mica or like material) is suspended by a light fiber in a resonator tube, and the torque exerted on the fiber when the resonator is excited by sound is registered by the deflection of a light-beam reflected from a mirror attached to the fiber. [The deflection is proportional to the sound intensity.]

Rayleigh equation = the proportion of spectral red and green required by the normal human eye to match spectral yellow. [So called from Lord Rayleigh, who discovered through its use the existence of **anomalous trichromates,** who will not accept the equation formed by persons with normal color vision.]

reactance = a form of impedance offered by an inductance or capacity to a periodic electric current. [See **impedance.**]

reaction = 1. (*psychol.*) a movement, glandular effect, or other change in an organism resulting from stimulation; 2. (*phys.*) the force which one body (A) exerts upon another (B) when B is itself acting on A; 3. (*chem.*) the change which occurs when two or more substances, brought into effective contact, give rise to other substances of different properties than the originals; 4. (*soc.*) the onset of a social movement in the direction opposite to the prevailing tendency of social evolution or progress. [On account of the varied uses of the term **reaction,** the word **response** is preferable in psychology. In physiology the word is commonly used as syn. for **reflex.**] — Ger. *Reaktion*.

reaction (or **response**) **experiment** = an experiment which measures the time intervening between the onset of a stimulus (e.g. sound of a buzzer) and the subject's motor response (e.g. lifting finger from electric key). [Cf. **chronoscope.**]

reaction-formation = (*psychoan.*) the development of a character trait, usually the exact reverse of the original trait, which keeps in check, and conceals, repressed partial impulses or components of infantile sexuality; e.g. aggression or cruelty held in check by sympathy or modesty. [**sublimation** may proceed along the path of reaction-formations.]

reaction (or **response**) **key** = a type of circuit interrupter resembling a telegraph key, used in reaction-time experiments. [The observer or subject in responding presses or lifts his finger from the key, which makes or breaks an electric circuit and thus marks off the end of the time period between stimulation and response. [Cf. **lip-key.**] — Fr. *presselle, clef de réaction*; Ger. *Fingerschlüssel*.

reaction (or **response**) **time** = the interval of time between the onset of a stimulus and the beginning of the observer's overt intentional response. [The character of the response is usually prearranged through experimental conditions, and instructions given to the observer. The term **reaction time** is historically established; **intentional response time** is a more accurate term. Cf. **compound reaction.**] — Fr. *temps de réaction*; Ger. *Reaktionszeit.*

reaction (or **response**) **type** = a manner of responding which is conditioned by the direction of the subject's attention. [Instructions may determine **reaction type,** but a specific type of reaction may become habitual in the absence of definite directions. Distinguishable types are: **sensory** (or **sensorial**), **motor** (or **muscular**), and **mixed.**]

reactive tendency = an instinctive tendency evoked by the apprehension of some object without, or some situation in which we are placed (Drever). [Contr. w. **appetite.**]

reactor = an individual who reacts, or who performs in a reaction experiment. [Preferable to **reagent,** which applies more properly to chemical activity.] — Fr. *sujet réagissant.*

readiness = the condition of preparation on the part of an organism to respond to a given stimulus or type of stimulus. [Cf. **mental set.**] — Fr. *prédisposition*; Ger. *Bereitschaft.*

readiness/law of = a principle, advanced as explanatory of learning, according to which a response may be facilitated by neural preparation due to such factors as recency, frequency, etc. [**readiness** implies that a connection has already been formed in the nervous system.]

reading = 1. the visual reception and understanding of words or other symbolic sensory data; 2. with a qualifying adjective, extended to include the understanding of tactually received symbols. [Usually limited to the reception of permanently traced symbols; e.g. printed or engraved words; but applied also to interpretation of gestures, lip movements (where no sound is conveyed), etc. The term is never applied to auditory reception, for which no technical English word exists; the term **hearing** is extended to mean sound-reading.]

reading aloud = the mental process of **reading** accompanied by a speaking of the symbols read. — Ger. *laut lesen.*

reading habit = the tendency on the part of the reader to look first (e.g.) at the upper left corner of a page, due to the fact that he has repeatedly done this in the course of reading printed pages. — Fr. *habitude de la lecture.*

reagent = 1. (*chem.*) a substance which causes a chemical change or reaction in another substance; 2. (*psychol.*) an individual who reacts; 3. (*pharmacol.*) a substance which produces a pharmacological or toxicological effect. [Syn. (2) **reactor** (prefd. as applied to the responses of organisms).] — Fr. (1) *réactif*, (2) *sujet réagissant*, (3) *agent*; Ger. (1) *Reagens*, (2) *Versuchsperson.*

real = 1. having actual existence, as contr. w. theoretical or imaginary existence; 2. having physical existence, as contr. w. conscious (experiential) interpretation of physical data. [(1) applies to both things and relations; (2) is used esp. in discussions of illusions, hallucinations, and delusions. Syn. (1) **actual** (more emphatic). Distg. fr. **true,** which applies to propositions and conclusions.] **reality**[n]. — Ger. *wirklich.*

real number = a positive or negative number. [Contr. w. **imaginary number.**]

realism = 1. a term applied to several types of world-view, all of which emphasize the independent reality, or objectivity, of the experienced world, as contr. w. views that emphasize its subjective character; 2. (*esth.*) the theory that the beauty of a work of art depends upon its correspondence with nature. [In scholastic philosophy applies also to the theory that *universals* possess objective reality. In modern use **realism** (1) includes the following types of view, distg. according to the basis for accepting the theory: (*a*) **naive r.** = that knowledge of the objective world arises immediately from direct awareness of objects; (*b*) **critical r.** = that this knowledge arises only through the selective and critical elaboration of the data of consciousness; (*c*) **empirical r.** (Kant) = that the objects which constitute the physical (phenomenal) world can be directly experienced, subject to the a priori conditions of all experience. Syn. **presentationism.** Contr. (1, 2) w. **idealism.**] **realistic**[a], **realist**[np].

reality = 1. existence in general; 2. the totality of existing objects, as distg. fr. the data of **imagination and thought;** 3. syn. for **activity** and **actuality.** — Ger. *Realität.*

reality/adaptation to = the ability of an individual to envisage and respond to the actual situations of life, without falsifying to himself either the environmental conditions or his own relations thereto by imagination, day-dreaming, rationalization, or other forms of self-deception.

reality/feeling of = (*hist.*) a feeling *sui generis* which constitutes the essential factor in belief (James). — Fr. *sentiment de réalité*; Ger. *Bewusstsein der Realität.*

reality-principle = 1. (*psychoan.*) the replacement or control of the demands of the pleasure-principle through social, ethical or other external considerations, for the purpose of adapting the organism to the exigencies of reality; 2. the striving of the ego towards self-preservation. [Contr. w. **pleasure-principle,** to which the reality-principle is related, both having been derived from one primal, undifferentiated source.]

reason[n] = 1. an assigned cause or explanation of some given situation or phenomenon; 2. the totality of the higher intellectual processes; 3. (*hist.*) the mental faculty of acquiring knowledge by thinking or by intuition. [Contr. (3) w. **instinct;** also w. **sensation, perception,** and **imagination.**] **rational**[a]. — Ger. (1) *Grund*, (2) *Vernunft.*

reason[v] = to employ logical thought processes; i.e. to draw deductive or inductive conclusions.

reason/law of sufficient, see **sufficient reason/law of.**

reasonable = the characteristic of a conclusion or hypothesis, such that it is considered to have an adequate logical justification. [In pop. usage, the adequacy in *fact* as well as in *logic* is generally implied. Contr. w. **unreasonable** = without adequate justification.]—Ger. *vernünftig, verständig.*

reasoning = 1. a process of thinking, the end terms of which are tested by their logical necessity rather than by their concurrence with observed fact; 2. the process of solving a problem by means of a concept or general principle; 3. (*hist.* and *pop.*) any mental process whatsoever. [Syn. **ratiocination.**] — Ger. *Denken.*

reasoning/error of = any mistake in thinking, particularly in judging or concluding.

reasoning insanity, see **paranoia** and **psychasthenia.**

reasoning test = a term somewhat loosely applied to mental tests in which the testee is required to draw conclusions from stated conditions or to check the "best reason" among several presented to explain a statement. [The term is applied (strictly) to such tests as Thurstone's syllogism-A test, but also to such tests as Army Alpha 3 (common-sense test) and to complex verbal relations tests such as Army Alpha 7 (analogies).]

rebirth-fantasy = (*psychoan.*) an unconscious fantasy, expressed most frequently in dreams, in which one's birth is symbolically represented. [E.g. of being in water or emerging from an enclosed space.] — Fr. *imagination de renaissance.*

rebound, rebound contraction = 1. a spontaneous contraction sometimes observed in a muscle at the moment of its release from (brief) inhibition; 2. the increased reflex excitability of a muscle (upon stimulation) after it has been for a prolonged period inhibited. [Syn. (1, 2) **successive spinal induction, indirect spinal induction, successive induction** (Sherrington).]

rebus writing = a form of graphic expression, intermediate between picture-ideographs and phonetic characters, which consists of symbols and pictures of objects, the names of which resemble in sound the words or word-elements for which they are substituted. [E.g. a picture of a bee and a leaf, to represent the word belief.] — Fr. *écriture en rébus.*

recall = the operation of arousing or initiating a memory image, or otherwise reporting a previous event. [Syn. **recollection,** best restricted to the *product* of recall.] **recall**[v]. — Fr. *rappel, évocation*; Ger. *Erinnerung, Reproduktion.*

recall method = a method of measuring the degree of retention (or rate of forgetting) by computing the percentage of items once learned that a subject can name or otherwise reproduce after any given interval or intervals from the learning period. — Fr. *m. d'évocation.*

recapitulation = the repetition of the course of earlier race history in individual developments. [Applied to the order in which specific organs arise and develop.] **recapitulate**[v].

recapitulation principle (or **doctrine**) = the theory that organisms pass through stages in which they resemble types which have occurred in the evolution of their respective ancestors; i.e. they **recapitulate** the history of the species.

recency/law of = 1. a principle concerning the course of association, according to which experiences of more recent occurrence are more likely than earlier ones to be associated with a given experience; 2. a principle advanced as explanatory of the (motor) learning process, according to which the arousal of any previously learned response varies in ease or readiness inversely with the length of time since it was learned or practised. — Fr. *l. de récence, influence du contenu récent.*

recept = a mental image formed by the mere repetition of percepts, resulting in the reinforcement of their common characteristics. [Term proposed by Romanes. Syn. **generic** (or **general) image.**] — Fr. *image composée.*

receptivity = a characteristic of organisms, such that they may be stimulated by forces or conditions in the environment or in portions of their own body outside of the nervous system. [The act of receiving impressions is called **reception,** the receiving organ, a **receptor.**]

receptor = the ending of an afferent neuron, or a specialized cell in connection with such neuron, which is so specialized as to have a low threshold for one sort of stimulus and a high threshold for other sorts of stimuli, and which when adequately or inadequately activated initiates an impulse or impulses in the associated afferent nerve. **receptor**[a].

receptor field = the collection of receptive points upon a surface or in other situations, from which a given type of reflex response can be elicited. [E.g. in the spinal dog, the saddle-shaped area of skin from which the scratch reflex may be evoked.] — Fr. *champ récepteur.*

recessive = (*biol.*) suppressed or not manifested. [Applied to Mendelian characters which fail to appear in the presence of the factor for the corresponding dominant character.] — Fr. *récessivité*[n].

recessive character = one member of a pair of Mendelian characters which, when crossed with the other member of the pair, does not appear in any individuals of the first filial generation, but is latent and may appear in subsequent generations. [Contr. w. **dominant,** which appears in all individuals of the first generation.]

recess period = a period of rest or of no practice between periods of practice in learning.

recidivation = relapse of a disease, or of a criminal.

recidivist = a habitual criminal. [Technically, one who has been convicted two or more times.]

reciprocal[n] = (*math.*) in respect to a given number, unity divided by that number. [Two numbers are reciprocals when their product is unity.] — Ger. *reziproke Grösse.*

reciprocal innervation = the principle that the two motor centers (i.e. paired **motor half-centers:** Sherrington) which innervate a pair of mutually antagonistic muscles (e.g. biceps and triceps of the arm) are interrelated in such a way that as one of them comes into action and contracts its muscle, the other center commonly (not invariably) inhibits (i.e. relaxes) the antagonistic muscle. [This interrelation of the paired centers is important for the production of alternating flexion and extension of a joint; e.g. of the hip and knee joints in walking.] — Ger. *reziproke Innervation.*

reciprocity law = the principle that response is determined by the product of the duration and intensity of the stimulus, independently of the magnitude of either one alone. [This principle has been found to hold for various visual and other biological phenomena, but only within rather narrow limits. Syn. **Bunsen-Roscoe law.**] — Fr. *l. de réciprocité*; Ger. *Reziprozitätsgesetz.*

recitation = the repeating aloud of verbal material which has been memorized. **recite**[v].

recitation method = a technique of memorizing in which the subject, instead of exclusively rereading or reviewing the items, attempts to recall the items, reviewing them as often as necessary, until complete recall is effected. [Contr. w. **rereading method.**]

recognition = perception of an object or individual, accompanied by a feeling of familiarity, or the knowledge that the object is familiar or has been perceived at an earlier time. [Cf. **recollection.**] **recognitional**[a] (prefd. to **recognitive** for euphony). **recognize**[v] (pronounce the **g**). — Fr. *reconnaissance, récognition*; Ger. *Erkennen, Wiedererkennung.*

recognition method = an experimental method of measuring memory for a presented series of items, by requiring that they be identified on a later occasion, or discriminated from other items with which they now appear for the first time. — Fr. *m. de reconnaissance.*

recollection = 1. the process of initiating a memory experience; 2. an elaborated memory image or systematic succession of such images. [Syn. (1) **recall.** Cf. **recognition.**] **recollective**[a] pert. to the act; **recollectional**[a] = pert. to the investigation. — Fr. *souvenir*; Ger. *Erinnerung.*

reconditioning = the process of changing a conditioned reflex so as to reinstate an earlier form of response; or, the response so obtained. [Cf. **conditioned reflex.**] **recondition**[v].

reconstruction = (*psychoan.*) the interpretation of the clinical meaning of a neurosis from the assembling of technical psychoanalytic material. — Ger. *Wiederherstellung.*

reconstruction method = a method of testing memory, in which the subject is required to rearrange, in the original order, a disordered series of items that was previously studied in the original order. [Developed by E. A. McC. Gamble (1908). Syn. **reconstruction procedure** (or **test**).]

recording camera, see **photokymograph.**

recovery = the return of an organism or organ to its normal condition after some impairment of function. [Applied clinically to restoration from any disease; in physiol. to the renewed ability of the neuron to conduct impulses after the refractory period, to the restoration of motor ability after fatigue, etc.] **recover**[v]. — Fr. *récupération.*

recreation = any diverting or pleasurable activity which involves relaxation from work. [Applied both to short periods of diversion during the day's occupation, and to an interruption of an individual's regular occupation for several days or months.] — Ger. *Erholung.*

recruitment = 1. (*excitatory*) a phenomenon, particularly of spinal extensor reflexes, in which continued application of a stimulus, unaltered in its intensity, causes more and more muscle fibers to be brought into activity, thus increasing the degree of reflex contraction; 2. (*inhibitory*) an analogous phenomenon when a stimulus produces inhibition, and its prolonged application causes more and more muscle fibers to be inhibited, thus increasing reflex relaxation (Sherrington). — Fr. *recrutement, propagation de mise en jeu*; Ger. *Rekrutierung.*

rectal reflex = the defecation urge caused by accumulation of feces in the rectum. [Mediated by 3d to 5th sacral segments of the cord.]

rectilinear correlation, see **correlation.**

rectum = the posterior division of the intestine. **rectal**[a].

rectus/inferior, /superior, see **eye muscle.**

recurrent[a] = reappearing or repeated after an interval of time. [Usually distg. fr. **periodic** or **rhythmic,** in which the repetition occurs at regular intervals.] **recur**[v]. — Ger. *wiederkehrend.*

recurrent conation = the repeated expression of an instinct or tendency after incomplete satisfaction.

recurrent image = a visual, auditory, or other image which persistently returns. [It is more likely to occur after a strongly emotional or continuous sensory impression.]

recurrent psychoses = mental disorders appearing in attacks which repeat themselves, with emphasis on their constitutional rather than specifically caused nature. — Fr. *psychoses à répétition.*

recurrent vision = the succession of positive and negative after-images or after-sensations. [Cf. **after-image.**] — Fr. *vision récurrente.*

red = 1. a visual sensation typically evoked by stimulation of the normal retina with radiation of wave-lengths within the range of 670 to 760 millimicrons ($m\mu$); 2. any color which manifests a hue predominantly similar to that of the typical red. [The complement of **blue-green** or **cyan. Primal red,** which is tinged neither with purple nor orange, does not occur as a **pure color,** but may be got by adding some blue to spectral red, which is yellowish.] — Fr. *rouge*; Ger. *rot.*

red-green blindness = the common type of partial color-blindness, or **dichromatic vision,** in which the visual system is reduced to yellows, blues, and grays. [Reds and greens are seen as certain saturations or brightnesses of yellow, blue, or gray. Cf. **protanopia** and **deuteranopia.**] — Fr. *cécité au rouge-vert.*

red reflex = a red appearance of the pupil of an observed eye, seen when light is directed into it nearly along the line of sight of the observing eye. [It is due to light emerging from the pupil after reflection from the retina of the eye observed; in using the **ophthalmoscope** it is the first indication that the light is being properly directed.] — Fr. *réflexion rouge.*

red-sighted = displaying a heightened color sensitivity for red, or a tendency to see all objects tinged with red: due to (*a*) some unknown variation in the eye or nervous system, or (*b*) following prolonged exposure to the stimulus for the complementary green, or (*c*) sequent upon over-exposure to intensive light and possibly hemorrhagic. [Syn. (*c*) **erythropsia**[n].] — Fr. *hypersensibile au rouge*; Ger. *rotsichtig.*

redintegration, reintegration = 1. the reinstatement of a total presentation, in the form of a memory or idea, upon the appearance of a partial constituent of such (former) presentation; 2. the arousal of a response by a fraction of the stimuli whose combination originally aroused it. [The shorter form is more euphonic; historic usage from W. Hamilton down favors the spelling **redintegration.** Cf. **relative suggestion.**]

reduce = 1. to lessen; 2. to simplify; 3. (*math., statist.*) to change an algebraic expression or a set of observations from one form to a simpler form. [E.g. (3) one **reduces** data by deriving from the multitude of original observations a few representative values, e.g. the mean and standard deviation.] **reduction**[n]. — Ger. (1) *vermindern,* (2) *vereinfachen,* (3) *reduzieren.*

reduced cue = a principle used to explain the learning process, which states that as learning progresses a smaller and smaller part of the original stimulus situation is able (or is needed) to elicit the desired response. [Syn. **law of partial activity** (Thorndike).] — Fr. *repère réduit.*

reduced eye = a simple schematic system designed to have the same optical properties as the average unaccommodated human eye. [It consists of a single convex spherical refracting surface bounding a medium of refractive index 1.334, the same as that of water; the radius of curvature of the surface is 5.2 mm., and parallel rays entering the system form an image within the medium 15.5 mm. beyond the center of curvature or 20.7 mm. from the pole of the refracting surface; the device is a mnemonic help and serves to facilitate the calculation of the size of the retinal image, etc. Syn. **Listing's reduced** or **schematic eye.**] — Ger. *reduziertes Auge.*

reductio ad absurdum = the disproof of a proposition by demonstrating that it leads logically to some conclusion which is admittedly false. [Lat.]

reduction-division = the division of a cell in which the number of chromosomes is halved.

reduplication = the presence in the same organism of two or more organs or segments of substantially the same form. [E.g. two arms, a series of vertebrae.] — Ger. *Verdoppelung.*

reed = a flexible metallic or wooden tongue, whose vibrations (when actuated by a blast of air or otherwise) generate sound waves of varying pitch according to the length of the tongue. [Used in instruments such as the clarinet, oboe, bassoon, etc. (which are called reed instruments) and in pitch pipes as well as in certain organ pipes. Cf. **lamella.**] — Fr. *roseau*; Ger. *Zunge, Rohr.*

reed organ, see **organ** (2).

re-education = the process of restoring a lost function or ability by an appropriate form of training. [The function may be a specific one (e.g. the loss of some form of manipulation due to a cerebral lesion or an injury to some part of the body), or a much more general one resulting from a mental disease, such as hysteria or paranoia, without any known cerebral lesion.]

reference/objective = that characteristic of certain perceptual experiences whereby they are assigned to the external or objective world.

referred sensation = a sensory experience localized at a point or area different from that stimulated. [Cf. **eccentric projection.**]

reflected color = color as seen reflected from a perceived object (Katz). — Ger. *gespiegelte Farbe.*

reflection = 1. (*psychol.*) attention to imaginal reproductions of past experiences; 2. (*hist.*) the more or less careful observation of one's own mental processes (Locke); 3. (*phys.*) reversal of direction of a wave of any sort, due to a change in the density or elasticity of the medium through which it is passing. [Syn. (1) **introspection.** Cf. (3) **refraction.**] **reflect**[v], **reflective**[a] (1), **reflected**[a] (3). — Ger. (1) *Überlegung,* (2) *Nachdenken,* (3) *Zurückstrahlung.*

reflection coefficient = the ratio of the flux of light (or of radiant energy) leaving a given surface by reflection, to that incident upon the surface.

reflex[n] = 1. any constant, congenital effector response which follows stimulation of a receptor with which the effector is in communication by means of a neural arc; 2. a mechanically determined response. [A **simple reflex** is the response of a single effector unit to the stimulation of a single receptor unit when these are linked together in a **simple reflex arc.** The simple reflex concept is taken as a convenient abstraction; probably a single reflex arc seldom or never functions alone. Syn. **reflex response.**] (Accent **re-.**) **reflex**[a].

reflex after-discharge = the continuation of reflex response after cessation of the stimulus. [A general characteristic of reflex action.] — Fr. *décharge consécutive réflexe.*

reflex arc, reflex circuit = a unit reaction mechanism of the nervous system, consisting of (1) a group of similar receptors (sense organs) to which the stimulus is applied; (2) a conductor nerve path containing afferent nerve fibers which on entering the spinal cord or brain stem enter into synaptic relation with a group of motor cells; (3) a conductor nerve path consisting of efferent (motor) nerve fibers which end in special terminals in the effector tissues (e.g. in muscle fibers or gland cells). [The **simple reflex arc** is usually diagrammatically represented as consisting of a chain or arc of neurons.]

reflex center = any group of nerve cells which act in unison for the performance of a specific reflex activity. [Syn. **center** (2).]

reflex/chain, see **chain reflex.**

reflex conduction = transmission of nerve impulses through a reflex arc. [It involves both neural and synaptic conduction.]

reflex inhibition = the depressed or inhibited state of a reflex, which is generally correlated in some way with (or produced by) the activity of some other (e.g. an antagonistic) reflex.

reflex integration = the combination of simple allied reflexes in the production of a more complex but harmonious (synergic) end-effect.

reflex latency = the delay in reflex arc conduction, as measured by the latent interval between application of a stimulus and the appearance of the end-effect.

reflex response, see **reflex.** — Ger. *Reflexbewegung.*

reflex time = the interval of time between the onset of a stimulus and the beginning of a subject's unavoidable and unintentional response. [Syn. **reflex latency.**] — Fr. *temps de latence réflexe.*

reflexes/allied, /antagonistic, see **allied reflexes,** etc.

reflexogenous zones = areas in the skin and mucous membrane from which definite, often generalized, motor responses may be elicited upon appropriate stimulation. [Cf. **segmental reflex.**]

reformism = a type of aggressive mental attitude, characterized by a striving on the part of the individual toward remedying certain evils in others, as a defense against the detection by others of a propensity toward the same evil in himself. **reformist**[np].

refracting media = those transparent tissues and fluids of the eye which refract the entering light to form an image upon the retina: viz., the cornea, the aqueous humor, the crystalline lens, and the vitreous humor (or body). — Fr. *milieux réfringents*; Ger. *Brechungsmittel.*

refraction = a change in the angle of propagation of a wave (light, sound, etc.) in passing from one medium to another of different density or elasticity. [The change is a function of the angle at which the wave strikes the boundary, of the difference in density or elasticity, and of the wave-length. Distg. fr. **reflection,** in which the wave does not penetrate the second medium.] **refract**[v], **refractive**[a]. — Ger. *Brechung.*

refraction/error of = the failure of the optical image to focus normally upon the retina, due to imperfection of the dioptric system of the eye, or to imperfection in the shape of the eyeball.

refraction/index of, refractive index = (*phys.*) a numerical expression indicating the degree to which the path of light or radiant energy is bent in passing from one transparent medium into another. [The **index of refraction** is relative to the two media concerned; it is the ratio of the sine of the angle of incidence to the sine of the angle of refraction, the two angles being measured between the perpendicular to the bounding surface and the incident and refracted rays respectively; and it is independent of the magnitude of these angles. When stated with reference to a single substance, the other implied substance is usually air. Cf. **refraction.**] — Fr. *indice de réfraction*; Ger. *Brechungsindex.*

refractoriness = a loose term expressing inamenability to discipline or active disregard of social conventions on the part of children, mentally retarded individuals, or criminals. **refractory**[a].

refractory period, refractory phase = a brief period of time following the excitation of a nerve or muscle fiber, during which the nerve or muscle fiber is inexcitable and does not transmit impulses. [The **refractory period** is divided into an *absolute r.p.*, which follows immediately after the excitation and passage of the impulse, and a later *relative r.p.*, during which the neural substance is excitable by strong but not by weak impulses.] — Fr. *phase réfractaire.*

refutation = the destruction of the credibility of a conclusion, either by establishing the contradictory or by showing the logical error which led to its acceptance. — Ger. *Widerlegung.*

regard/field of = the total region of the external world embraced by the moving eye. [Distg. fr. **field of vision** (or **visual field**) = embraced by the unmoving eye.] — Fr. *champ de regard*; Ger. *Blickfeld.*

regard/line of = the straight line which connects the objective fixation point (or **point of regard**) with the center of rotation of the eye. [Distg. fr. **line of sight,** which joins fixation point and fovea.] — Ger. *Blicklinie.*

regard/plane of = a theoretical plane which passes through the center of rotation of the two eyeballs and the fixation point in the objective field. [Cf. **center of rotation, fixation-point.**]

regard/point of = the point in the objective field toward which the center of the eye is directed. [Syn. **fixation-point.**] — Ger. *Blickpunkt.*

regeneration = 1. the restoration or replacement of an injured or lost part of the body; 2. renewal of vigor or vitality. [Syn. (2) **rejuvenescence.**] **regenerate**[v]. — Ger. *Wiederhervorbringung.*

regional reflex, see **segmental reflex.**

regional static reaction, see **segmental static reaction.**

register[n] = 1. the range or compass of sound frequencies which a musical instrument, apparatus, or voice is capable of producing; 2. a portion of the compass of an instrument, etc. within which the sounds are similarly produced or of a particular timbre.

regression = 1. the tendency, on the part of individual organisms, species, or societies, toward checking the effect of progress, by reverting to the mean or typical form; 2. (*statist.*) a general term which refers to the relation between paired variables when such relation is expressed by the equation of a straight line or curve. [Contr. (1) w. the notion of **progress** = the tendency to change (or the process of changing) toward greater adaptiveness. The statistical computation of **regression** (2) is effected by means of certain formulae: cf. **regression equation.** (2) is properly called **regression** because, for a given value of an independent variable, the most probable value of the dependent variable, as shown by the regression line or curve, regresses toward the mean of the dependent variable, as compared with the values when the relations of dependence are reversed. Cf. **filial regression.** The concept of **regression** (2) originated with Galton (1885) and is fundamental to the concept of **correlation** (3). For psychoanalytic use, see **regression (of libido).**] **regress**[v], **regressive**[a]. — Ger. *Rückkehr.*

regression coefficient = a constant in the regression equation, which indicates the slope of the regression line in a correlation diagram. [The equation of the regression of Y on X is $Y = \bar{Y} + r\,(\sigma_y/\sigma_x)\,[X - \bar{X}]$ in which $r\,(\sigma_y/\sigma_x)$ is the regression coefficient.]

regression equation = an equation, generally linear, for estimating the mean value of a dependent variable from given values of one or more independent variables. [Cf. **regression coefficient.** The general regression equation when regression is linear is
$\bar{x}_0 = b_{01.23\ldots n}x_1 + b_{02.13\ldots n}x_2 + \ldots + b_{0n.12\ldots(n-1)}x_n$.
x_0 is the dependent variable, $x_1 \ldots x_n$ the independent variables and the b's are **regression coefficients.**]

regression/law of filial, see **filial regression/law of.** — Ger. *Rückschlagsgesetz.*

regression line = a line whose course represents regression either graphically or by means of an equation.

regression (of libido) = (*psychoan.*) a tendency on the part of the libido to revert to some channel of expression which belongs to an earlier phase of the libido development (e.g. pregenital). [Cf. **libido.**]

regression time = the interval or intervals in the reading process, during which the reader makes a readjustment fixation at the beginning of a new line or visually re-examines words or phrases that he has previously fixated or inadequately perceived within a line. — Fr. *temps de retour.*

regret = an emotional reaction characterized by unpleasant feeling-tone and by an ideational reference to some past experience, with the desire that it might have been otherwise. — Ger. *Reue, Bedauern.*

regular = following a definite law, formula, or principle. [Contr. w. **irregular** = not in accordance with any known law, etc.] — Ger. *regelmässig.*

regulation = (*biol.*) the maintenance of the normal structure or functions in organisms.

Reichenbach phenomenon, see **od, odic force.**

Reil/island of, see **island of Reil.**

reinforced reflex = a reflex whose motor manifestation has been accentuated. [Supposed to be due to overflow of energy from one spinal segment to others.]

reinforcement = 1. (*neurol.*) the action of one neural excitatory process upon a second, such that it increases the intensity or efficiency of the second; 2. (*psychoan.*) a dream mechanism in which the primary motive of the dream is expressed anew for the purpose of emphasis, usually by means of a dream within a dream. [(1) applies esp. to the increased muscular contraction which is produced by a summation of neural processes. Syn. **facilitation** (2).] — Fr. *renforcement*; Ger. (1) *Bahnung*.

reintegration = reinstatement of a complex phenomenon or experience. [Syn. **redintegration,** the more common term.]

Reissner's membrane = (*aud.*) a delicate membrane which extends from near the outer edge of the spiral lamina to the bony wall of the cochlear canal, a little above the attachment of the suspensory ligament. [It separates the scala vestibuli and cochlear duct. Syn. **vestibular membrane.**]

rejection = 1. (*beh.*) a type of response whereby a substance is avoided, or is cast out after being partly taken into the body; 2. an experience or element of experience characterized by a negative or antagonistic attitude with respect to some concept or judgment. [Syn. (2) **disbelief.**] — Ger. *Ablehnung, Zurückweisung, Verwerfung*.

rejuvenation = the process of restoring vitality, esp. the renewal of youthful physiological vigor in a senescent organism. — Fr. *rajeunissement*.

relation = 1. any connection or mutual influence between two or more data; 2. that which can be observed or conceived to hold good as between two data though not in either datum taken alone, e.g. difference, cause-effect. [Some psychologists hold that a specific type of mental process called **relation** (or **relating**) is involved in thinking of relations.] **related**[a] = applied to the data; **relational**[a] = pert. to the connection; **relationship**[n] = the fact of being in relation; **to be related**[v]. — Fr. *relation, rapport, parenté*; Ger. *Beziehung, Verhältnis*.

relation/consciousness of = awareness or the conscious assumption of a relation or connection between certain data of experience. [Cf. **relation.**] — Fr. *conscience de rapport*.

relation/measures of = (*statist.*) coefficients which indicate how closely the changes in one variable are paralleled by changes in another variable. — Fr. *mesures de rapport*.

relational states, see **substantive states.**

relationship system = any system of terminology for designating and classifying kinship, whether these be actual blood relations or socially prescribed relations between individuals. [Usually reckoned in either the mother's or the father's line, often according to generation levels rather than by direct descent, and in social practice governing incest, marriage, inheritance, and sometimes social intercourse as well.] **relative**[np]. — Fr. *système de rapport*.

relative[a] = not intrinsic, but dependent upon comparison with other data. [Contr. w. **absolute.**] — Ger. *bezüglich, relativ*.

relative accommodation = the accommodation of the two eyes when working together in binocular vision. [Cf. **absolute accommodation.**]

relative fatigue = a decrement in the amount of work relative (or proportional) to the intensity of the total stimulus (or incentive).

relative pitch, see **pitch/relative.**

relative sensitivity = awareness of a difference or change between two experiences, the exact determination of which is called the **difference limen.**

relative suggestion = a type of association in which the reinstated material is dependent upon comparatively new connections (Thos. Brown). [Not identical with the traditional formula of association by contiguity and similarity; significant as laying emphasis on mental activity. Cf. **redintegration.**]

relative threshold (or **limen**), see **threshold.**

relative variability = the relation between (*a*) the deviations of the individual observations from the mean, and (*b*) the magnitude of the mean; it is obtained by the formula $r.v. = 100MV/M$, in which MV is the mean variation and M the mean.

relativity/law of = 1. (*psychol.*) the principle that every phase of experience is influenced by every other simultaneous phase of experience; 2. the principle that an experience is understood only in its relation to other experiences, as when the visual localization of an object depends upon the perception of the relation of the object to the frame of reference; 3. (*psychophys.*) the **Weber-Fechner law,** which states that relative and not absolute differences are perceived.

relax = 1. to cease active contraction of a muscle or other motor organ; 2. to relieve oneself of mental strain. [Contr. (1) w. **contract**[v], (2) w. **to be under stress** or **strain.**] **relaxation**[n]. — Fr. *se relâcher*[v], *relâchement*[n]; Ger. (1) *erschlaffen*, (2) *sich zerstreuen*.

relaxation/feeling of, see **tension-relaxation/feeling of.**

relaxation principle = (*psychoan.*) a principle used by the analyst to increase the easy atmosphere of the analytic situation by adjusting his own attitude to the unconscious mood of the patient.

relaxation/progressive = a process of training to relax the skeletal musculature consciously (E. Jacobson). [Used both as a psychological technique and as a psychotherapeutic measure.]

relearning = the process of learning or stereotyping some complex motor act or of establishing some sequence of memory material which has already been mastered by the individual but has been lost (or partly lost) through disuse or through some injury to the central nervous mechanism or the response mechanism. [Syn. **re-education,** a broader term, applied to the general process involved, while relearning applies to a specific act.] — Fr. *réapprentissage, réacquisition*.

reliability = 1. (*psychol.*) the degree of accuracy of a given report (of an event, phenomenon, etc.) or the degree of dependability of the testimony, in general, of a given individual; 2. (*statist.*) the self-consistency of a test or other measuring device; 3. the reciprocal of the variability of a series of measures from some chosen standard. [**coefficient of reliability** = the correlation among a set of measurements or between two similar measures.] — Fr. (1, 2) *fidélité*, (2) *cohérence*, (3) *constance*; Ger. *Zuverlässigkeit*.

relief = 1. (*vis.*) the deviation or projection of parts of an object from the general plane in which it lies, when such deviation is in the direction of the observer; 2. (*affect.*) a feeling characterized by pleasantness, which arises from the removal of tension or strain. [Contr. (1) w. **intaglio** = deviation or projection from the plane in the direction away from the observer.] — Fr. (1) *relief*, (2) *soulagement*; Ger. (1) *Relief*, (2) *Erleichterung*.

religion = 1. beliefs, attitudes, and practices with respect to superhuman personal or personified power or powers which are responsible for some or all of the processes of nature, animate or inanimate, and are conceived as capable of being influenced by human behavior; 2. (in a narrower sense) a specific systematic theory regarding the nature of superhuman power or powers and of its or their relation to man, together with the cult in which this relation expresses itself; 3. (more loosely) belief in an inspiring, directing philosophy of the universe; or devotion to whatever is regarded as most worthwhile in life. [Distg. fr. philosophical **belief** in that it includes a felt, practical relation to superhuman power or powers; distg. fr. **magic** in that *magical* power is so conceived as to make worship ineffective and coercion possible.] **religious**[a].

religion/psychology of = that branch of psychology which investigates the phenomena of religion in the individual or in different groups or races of man. [Includes various fields, e.g. the origin of religion, its development in society and in the individual, etc., also the study of particular aspects of religious consciousness, e.g. the psychology of religious mysticism.]

religious conduct = 1. the behavior of man in so far as influenced or determined by religion; 2. the ritualistic or ceremonial behavior of man prescribed or suggested by religion.

religious consciousness = the experiences of the individual in so far as they concern religion or religious conduct.

religious experience = 1. an experience whose content includes as a prominent factor or constituent the belief in a superhuman being and a conscious interrelation with that being; 2. (more loosely) an experience of momentous consequence in the spiritual life of a person.

religious instinct = a tendency, assumed to be inherited by all men, to be interested in religion and to desire to participate in religious practices. [Cf. **religion.**]

remedial instruction = systematic training of defectives or delinquents which seeks to remove the defect or the cause of delinquency. — Fr. *éducation de redressement*.

remember = to instate a memory image or otherwise to report an earlier experience. [Syn. **recollect.** Cf. **recollection.**] — Fr. *se souvenir de, se rappeler*; Ger. *sich erinnern*.

remembrance = a loose term sometimes used to cover the various processes concerned in memory, such as retention and recollection. — Fr. *mémoire*; Ger. *Erinnerung*.

reminiscence = 1. the tendency of an experience to become more firmly fixed with the passage of time (Ballard); 2. syn. for **recall.** [Contr. w. **obliviscence,** the ordinary tendency to forget. Cf. **memory.**]

remission = 1. temporary abatement or subsidence of a physiological or pathological process; 2. the period of diminution of a paroxysmal action, esp. that of remittent fever. — Ger. *Nachlassen*.

remorse = an emotion of regret, in which the individual's feeling of responsibility for his own past conduct is a leading source of the emotional reaction. [Cf. **regret.**] — Fr. *remords*; Ger. *Gewissensbiss*.

remote[a] = 1. at a great distance in time or space from the location of the speaker, or from the object or individual under consideration; 2. characterizing sensations of bodily movement which originate in receptors not located in the member whose movement is sensed. [Contr. (2) w. **resident** (W. James).] — Fr. *éloigné*; Ger. *entfernt*.

remote association = a connection between an item of a series and any other item not contiguous to it, e.g. in the alphabet, a-c, a-x, c-g, etc.

renal = pert. to or located in the kidneys. (Accent **ree-.**)

renunciation = (*relig.*) the surrender of one's personal (selfish) will to what is regarded as the divine will.

repetition-compulsion = (*psychoan.*) a compulsion on the part of the patient to reproduce, during the analysis, according to the condition of resistance or transference, the process of his (or her) individual development or experience, thus gradually transforming the repressed material into remembered and current experience (Freud). — Fr. *contrainte de répétition, répétition coercitive, compulsion de répétition;* Ger. *Wiederholungszwang*.

repetition/law of, see **frequency/law of.**

report = the account given by either the observer or the experimenter of the occurrences, experiences, impressions, data, or the like, in connection with any investigation, trial, or momentary presentation. **report**[v]. — Ger. *Bericht*.

repose = 1. a condition of comparative inactivity or rest; 2. (*esth.*) a feeling of composure or rest induced in the observer of an esthetic object by the balance of its formal elements. — Ger. (1) *Ruhe*, (2) *Gemütsruhe*.

re-present[v] = to present again. [Distg. fr. **represent** = to resemble or stand for.] (Accent **ree-.**)

represent[v] = to stand for and in some respects take the place of another thing. [Best limited to symbolic substitution; distg. fr. **reproduce,** which implies resemblance.] (Accent **rep-.**)

representation = 1. an experience whose content is a reproduction of some earlier experience which occurs in the absence of the original stimuli (e.g. a memory image or imagination); 2. the operation by which such an experience is brought about. [Syn. (1) **image,** (2) **imagination.**] **representative**[a] = pert. to representations; **representational**[a] = pert. to the study. — Ger. *Vorstellung*.

repressed complex = (*psychoan.*) a complex, or pathological emotion, whose gratification is systematically inhibited by the individual himself by means of repressive forces existent in either the unconscious or the superego. [Cf. **repression.**] — Fr. *complexe refoulé*.

repressed wish = (*psychoan.*) a wish, or desire, whose gratification is systematically inhibited by the individual himself by means of repressing forces existent in either the unconscious or the superego. [Cf. **repressed complex.**] — Fr. *désir refoulé.*

repression = 1. (*psychoan.*) the mental process by which perceptions and ideas which would be painful to consciousness are forced into the unconscious system, while still remaining dynamic; 2. (*psychoan.*) the rejection, by the ego, of impulses emanating from the id (topographic-dynamic conception); 3. (*beh.*) syn. for **self-control.** [Cf. (1) **blocking,** (1, 2) **suppression.**] — Fr. *refoulement*; Ger. *Verdrängung.*

reproduction = 1. (*psychol.*) experiencing again some part of an earlier experience; 2. the execution of a previously learned response, or the duplication of some objective stimulus-pattern by a motor response; 3. (*biol.*) the genesis of a new individual organism from a parent or parents. [The modes of biological **reproduction** (3) are classed as **asexual** (or **non-sexual**), including **fission, budding** (**gemmation**), and **sporulation;** and **sexual** (**gamogenetic**).] **reproduce**[v]. — Ger. (1, 2) *Wiederholung, Reproduktion,* (3) *Wiederhervorbringung.*

reproduction/method of = 1. a method of testing either the subject's retention or his reproductive skill, by directing him to "reproduce," orally or graphically, a given memorial or perceptual experience; 2. (*psychophys.*) syn. for **method of average error.** [Cf. (1) **recall method.**]

reproductive function = 1. the entire series of operations involved in bringing new organisms into existence, in so far as these operations are activities of the parent organism or organisms; 2. any one of the different operations in this series (e.g. ovulation, impregnation, parturition.) [Syn. **generative function, generation** (in common use but less distinctive); **sexual function** should be applied only to the distinctive role of either of the two sexes in reproduction.] — Fr. *fonction reproductrice.*

reproductive imagination = that type of imagination which tends to conform to previously observed patterns, rather than to generate new patterns. [Contr. w. **creative imagination,** which produces new patterns.]

reproductive selection = a subordinate theory of evolution by selection, according to which the most fertile members of a species produce a large proportion of each successive generation, whence it follows that those characters which are correlated with fertility are most likely to be selected. — Fr. *sélection génétique.*

reproductive tendency = a general term which includes **associative tendencies, impressional tendencies, perseverative tendencies,** and other factors which make for reproduction. [Sometimes used as syn. for **associative tendency.**]

reptilia, reptiles = a class of cold-blooded vertebrates characterized by lung-breathing throughout life, and usually by a covering of horny scales. [In the evolutionary series, reptiles rank above fishes and amphibia and below birds and mammals.]

repugnance = an emotional attitude characterized by extreme unpleasantness, and directed (in the form of antagonism or opposition) toward some definite object or class of objects. [Syn. **antipathy, aversion, disgust.**] **repugnant**[a]. — Ger. *Widerwille.*

repulsion = a term applied figuratively to an attitude of avoidance, usually tinged with disgust, taken by one individual toward another. [Contr. w. **attraction.**] — Ger. *Abscheu.*

reputation = the estimate of an individual's character on the part of society at large or of the members of the social group to which he belongs. [Usually applied to a contemporary estimate, irrespective of degree, and distg. fr. **prestige** = a high contemporary estimate, and fr. **fame** = a high posthumous estimate. Syn. **repute.**] **reputable**[a] = having a good reputation.

rereading method = a technique of memorizing. in which the repetitions consist in reading the items, instead of attempting to recall them. [The amount learned is usually tested by recall, recognition, reconstruction, or other methods, after a prescribed number of rereadings, or at a time when the individual signifies belief that he has learned the series. Contr. w. **recitation method.**] — Fr. *m. des lectures répétées*; Ger. *Wiederlesungsmethode.*

research = any systematic attempt to discover the constitution or operation of nature by first-hand observation of phenomena. [Syn. **investigation,** which has a more specific connotation; **investigation** = of definite situations; **research** = upon the general field; **investigate**[v] is used for both and prefd. to **research**[v].] (Accent **-search.**) — Fr. *recherche*; Ger. *Forschung, Erforschung.*

resemblance = an observed similarity or correspondence between two objects, events, or other data. [Emphasizes the *observation* or *judgment* of similarity or correspondence, in contr. w. syns. **similarity, likeness,** which emphasize the *objective* correspondence.] **resemble**[v]. — Ger. *Ähnlichkeit.*

resemblance/law of, see **similarity/law of.**

resentment = an emotional attitude characterized by unpleasantness, and antipathy aroused by the idea of injury to oneself (or to a friend) by some other individual, toward whom the attitude is directed. — Fr. *ressentiment*; Ger. *Umwille, Nachtragen.*

reservation = the concealment or deliberate omission of some presumably significant detail in an introspective report.

reserve = a mental attitude characterized by a natural or a habitual disinclination on the part of the individual to participate in social conversation or intercourse. [Syn. **shyness.** Contr. w. **frankness, expansiveness.**] **reserved**[a]. — Fr. *réserve*; Ger. *Zurückhaltung.*

residual = the numerical or quantitative difference between the observed and the computed value of a result in a given experiment.

residues/method of = a method or canon used in inductive procedure, according to which if one deduct or subtract from any phenomenon such part as is already known to be the effect of certain antecedents, it may be concluded that the residue or remainder of the phenomenon is the effect of the remaining antecedents. [Formulated by J. S. Mill. Cf. **Mill's canons.**]

residuum = 1. a remainder left over in a given complex phenomenon, after certain significant elements or constituents have been accounted for; 2. a trace or engram remaining as an after-effect of an experience. [Syn. **residual.**] **residua**[pl]. — Fr. *résidu.*

resignation = 1. the attitude, usually coupled with some feeling, of not making any positive response to a cognized object, event, or situation; 2. the voluntary act of renouncing something previously possessed or espoused. — Ger. *Entsagung.*

resinous = a quality of olfactory sensation of which gum benzoin is a typical example. [A class of Henning's. Cf. **odor, odor prism, balsamic.**] — Ger. *harzig*.

resistance = 1. (*phys.*) the action of a body against an opposing force; 2. (*psychol.*) the response of an organism to stimulation, in which the direction of the movement or activity is opposite to the direction of the applied force; 3. (*psychoan.*) an instinctive opposition, in the dynamic sense, toward any attempt to bring unconscious material into consciousness, or to lay bare the unconscious, thus excluding from consciousness all repressed material and tendencies which displease it. [The constant ratio of electromotive force to current is called **electrical resistance;** its unit is the ohm. **resistance** (3) is a manifestation of the forces of **repression.**] — Ger. *Widerstand*.

resistance/galvanic, see **ohmic resistance.**

resistance/sensation of = a fusion of kinesthetic and cutaneous sensations evoked by pressure and muscular tension, when the muscle or muscles concerned are contracting against an opposing external force. — Ger. *Widerstandsempfindung*.

resoluteness, resolution = an attitude characterized by firm adherence to some line of conduct previously decided upon. [Syn. **decision, determination;** owing to the ambiguity of these terms (and of **resolution**), **resoluteness** is prefd.] **resolute**[a]. — Fr. *résolution*; Ger. *Entschlossenheit*.

resolution = 1. a decision which involves some general line of conduct; 2. syn. for **resoluteness;** 3. the analysis of a compound into its constituent parts. [Syn. (1) **resolve**[n].] **resolve**[v] (1, 3). — Fr. (1, 2) *résolution*, (3) *analyse*; Ger. *Entschluss*.

resolution/law of = a principle formulated by H. S. Jennings as a partial explanation of the modification of behavior, as follows: "the resolution of one physiological state into another becomes easier and more rapid after it has taken place a number of times."

resonance = the vibratory response of a body to a frequency imposed upon it. [If the resonating body has the same frequency as the inducing sound-wave, the phenomenon is called **tuned resonance,** or **sympathetic vibration;** if the resonating body has a different frequency, it is called **forced resonance** or **forced vibration.**] **resonant**[a].

resonance box = a type of resonator consisting of a wooden box of appropriate dimensions, on which is mounted a tuning fork in order to amplify the intensity of the sound. — Ger. *Resonanzkasten*.

resonance theory, see **hearing/theories of.**

resonator = a device for magnifying the intensity of a tone of some given pitch. [The effect of a resonator depends upon its air capacity, the diameter of the openings, its shape, temperature of the vibrating medium, and other factors. The Helmholtz resonator is spherical in shape, with a tubular projection for connection with the ear. The König resonator is cylindrical.]

respect[n] = a sentiment characterized by appreciation of certain qualities in another individual or (figuratively) by appreciation of laudable aspects of some system, social philosophy, program, or pattern of living, and marked by a certain intellectual deference, if not acceptance. **respectful**[a], **respect**[v]. — Ger. *Achtung*.

respectability = a social judgment concerning an individual or type of conduct, to the effect that the general conduct of the individual, or the type of conduct in question, conforms to accepted social standards. **respectable**[a].

respiration/external = the breathing function, i.e. the operation of the lungs, gills, etc. in alternately expanding and contracting, so as to admit oxygen and remove waste products from the blood. [It includes **inspiration** = drawing in, and **expiration** = an expulsion of the oxygen and waste. Distg. fr. **internal respiration** = exchange of gases between tissues and body fluids.] **respire**[v], **breathe**[v], **respiratory**[a] (accent -pie-.) — Ger. *Atmung*.

response = the muscular contraction, glandular secretion, or any other activity of an organism which results from stimulation. [Syn. **reaction,** a generic term, embracing not merely organic responses but inorganic interplay; in psychol. both terms are used; **response** is prefd. for the motor effects of stimulation, as avoiding ambiguity. Cf. **stimulation.**] **respond**[v], **responsive**[a], **response**[a].

response/direction (or **sense) of** = the spatial orientation of a response with respect to the source of stimulation. [Tropisms are classified as positive (adient) or negative (abient) according as the organism moves toward or away from the source of stimulation; other orientations occur, e.g. the transverse (= horizontal) geotropism of the branches of certain trees.]

response experiment, see **reaction experiment.**

response key, see **reaction key.**

response psychology, reaction psychology = the view and treatment of psychological phenomena which emphasizes the motor or action aspect, the action being considered little or not at all as conation or volition, but principally or exclusively as reaction-to-stimulation.

response time, see **reaction time.**

response type, see **reaction type.**

responsibility/feeling (or **consciousness) of** = awareness on the part of the normal human adult that he is bound to act according to social standards and is amenable to punishment for infraction of social prescriptions. [A fundamental attitude of general conformity to the prescriptions and prohibitions of society.] — Fr. *sentiment de responsabilité*.

responsible = 1. actively concerned in the production of a certain specific event or condition of affairs; 2. characterizing the social and legal status of the normal human adult, in that he is assumed to be so constituted as to be able to conform to the prescriptions of social custom, moral standards, and government, and is judged deserving of and amenable to punishment if he runs counter to these prescriptions. **responsibility**[n]. — Fr. *responsable*; Ger. *verantwortlich*.

rest = 1. (*phys.*) the maintenance, by a physical mass, of the same position in relation to its surroundings; 2. (*psychol.*) cessation of overt movements on the part of an organism; 3. (*physiol.*) the period of recuperation after the completion of some specific work or exercise; 4. (*music*) a definite period of silence, occurring within a composition. [Contr. w. (1) **motion,** (2) **movement,** (3) **activity.** In written music the length of the **rest** (4) is measured by symbols, corresponding to the measure of the composition, e.g. 1/4 rest, 1/8 rest, etc.] — Fr. *repos*; Ger. *Ruhe*.

rest-pause = a pause or intermission, introduced during a period of work with a view to eliminating fatigue. — Fr. *intervalle de repos*.

restlessness = 1. a general state of the organism in certain situations, characterized by a tendency to aimless activity whose direction or pattern is constantly changing; 2. a fundamental type of feeling — "the feeling of that value of our experience which makes it an object of momentary discontent" (Royce). [Contr. w. **quiescence.**] — Fr. *inquiétude, agitation*; Ger. *Rastlosigkeit, Unruhe*.

restoration = (*physiol.*) the replacement of any lost structure, function, or material in an organism. [Syn. **regeneration** (of structure only).] — Fr. *restauration*; Ger. *Wiederherstellung*.

restrain = to actively prevent another living being (or oneself) from performing some act, or from pursuing some course of action. [Contr. w. **constrain** = to compel another to adopt some course of action.] — Fr. *empêcher de, restreindre, retenir*; Ger. *zurückhalten, abhalten*.

restraint[n] = the inhibition of an organism's activity by some other organism or through physical bonds or barriers. — Fr. *frein*; Ger. *Zurückhaltung, Zwang*.

result = 1. a phenomenon or situation viewed in relation to certain preceding conditions, without which it would not have arisen; 2. the data obtained from scientific observation or experimentation. [Syn. (1) **consequence,** (1) **effect.** Distg. (2) fr. **conclusions,** based on the **results.**] — Ger. (1) *Erfolg*, (2) *Ergebnis*.

resultant = the simplest force whose operation is equivalent to the operation of two or more forces working simultaneously.

resultant tone, see **combination tone.**

retained members/method of = a memorizing method in which the measure of memory is the proportion or percentage of the material memorized that is correctly reproduced at the time of the test. [The method economizes time, and is applicable to group testing.] — Ger. *Methode der behaltenen Glieder*.

retardation/mental = the slowing up of mental development, resulting in a condition of mild mental inferiority. [Syn. **backwardness.** Strictly, **retardation** denotes the slowing-up process, **backwardness,** the resulting condition.] **retarded**[a] (applied to individuals or to mental functions). — Fr. *arriération mentale*.

retention = the persisting after-effect of an excitation, experience, or response, on the basis of which modified responses or experiences may occur on subsequent occasions. [Generally assumed as an essential factor in determining **memory** and **habit.**] **retentive**[a], **retain**[v]. — Ger. *Behalten*.

retentiveness, retentivity = capacity for **retention.**

reticular layer, see **granular layer.**

reticular stratum, see **corium.**

retina = the innermost of the three coats of the eyeball, which receives the image formed by refraction at the cornea and lens, and serves as receptor organ for vision. [In the human retina 10 layers are distinguished, of which the layer of **rods and cones,** the second from the exterior, is the specific visual receptor. Cf. **retinal layers.** See Table XI.] **retinal**[a], **retinas** (or **-ae**)[pl]. — Ger. *Netzhaut*.

retina/cortical = (*embryol.*) a modified portion of the cerebral cortex forming the layer at the back of the eye, which is specifically receptive to light stimuli and contains the neurons whose axons form the optic nerve.

retinal elements = the rods and cones, or the nerve-paths leading from them, esp. as having optical reference each to a particular directional element in the visual field.

retinal horizon = the horizontal meridian of the retina, i.e. the one upon which the terrestrial horizon is imaged when the eyes are in the **primary position.**

retinal image, see **image/retinal.**

retinal layers = the strata of the retina which may be distinguished microscopically in sections cut perpendicularly to its surface. [See Table XI.] — Fr. *couches rétiniennes*; Ger. *Netzhautschichten*.

retinal light, see **idioretinal light.**

retinal oscillations = a variation in the state of excitation of the visual neural apparatus following a single momentary stimulation, which is experienced as a brief succession of alternating bright and dark phases, such as **Charpentier's bands** or recurrent after-images.

retinal picture, see **picture/retinal.**

retinal rivalry = alternation of sensations first from one eye and then from the other, when the two eyes are simultaneously stimulated by different colors or figures. [Syn. **binocular rivalry.** Contr. w. **binocular fusion,** in which the two impressions are fused into a single impression.] — Fr. *lutte rétinienne, antagonisme des champs visuels*; Ger. *Wettstreit der Sehfelder*.

retinitis = an inflammation of the retina. [Since the retina contains the nerve-endings upon which vision depends, **retinitis** may cause blind areas (**scotomata**) in the visual field, and blindness.]

retinitis pigmentosa = a pathological condition of the pigmentary layers of the retina, accompanied by diminished color sensitivity (esp. for blue), retracted color fields, and lowered power of dark adaptation.

retinoscope = a small perforated mirror for determining the refractive condition of the eye by observing the motions of light and shadow across the pupil when light is thrown into the eye and upon the retina from the mirror as it is rocked back and forth. [Syn. **skiascope.**] **retinoscopic**[a], **retinoscopy**[n].

retraction = 1. (*beh.*) withdrawal of an appendage by an organism, e.g. pseudopodia in ameba, limb of a vertebrate; 2. (*logic*) acknowledgment of the falsity or error of a proposition previously advanced. — Ger. *Zurückziehen*.

retroaction = the effect of an act or experience upon the retention of a previously acquired act or experience. [If the effect is favorable it is **retroactive facilitation;** if unfavorable, it is **retroactive inhibition.** These are termed also **positive** and **negative retroaction** respectively.]

retroactive = affecting what is past. (Pron. **ret-,** not **re-.**)

retroactive amnesia, see **amnesia/retroactive.**

retroactive association = a connection between an item of a series and any other item which preceded it, e.g. in the alphabet, z-y, y-x, y-g, etc.

retroactive facilitation, see **facilitation/retroactive.**

retroactive inhibition, see **inhibition/retroactive.**

retrobulbar = 1. situate dorsad to the medulla oblongata; 2. behind the eyeball.

retrograde = 1. moving backward; 2. degenerating. [Cf. **anterograde amnesia.**]

retrograde amnesia, see **amnesia/retroactive** (2).

retromalleolar = pert. to or located in small areas lying just behind the ankle. (Double accent, **ret-, -lee-.**)

retroperitoneal = behind the peritoneum (the membrane which lines the abdominal cavity), between it and the abdominal wall. (Double accent **ret-, -nee-.**)

retrospection = 1. the mental act of reviewing past events in a systematic manner; 2. introspection based upon the immediate memory of a past experience. [Distg. fr. **reminiscence,** which may be desultory.] (Pron. **ret-,** not **ree-.**) **retrospect**[v], **retrospective**[a]. — Ger. *Rückblick.*

retrospective falsification = a normal or pathological experience, in which an imagination is regarded as a memory. [The falsification may concern either the entire experience or certain imagined details which are imposed upon an actual memory.]

retrospective reference = that characteristic of a memory experience through which is determined the location of the original experience in the temporal series.

revenge = 1. the act of inflicting injury upon some individual or group, in return for an actual or imagined injury inflicted upon the individual himself; 2. the injury so inflicted. [Syn. (2) **vengeance.**] **revengeful**[a]. — Fr. *vengeance*; Ger. *Rache.*

reverberation = the repeated reflection of sound within an enclosure, or a pent-in area (e.g. a valley), which causes a single sound impulse to give rise to a continued roll or tattoo effect. — Ger. *Widerhall.*

reverence = an attitude of solemn regard for a person or object, marked by a judgment of the superiority (usually moral superiority) of that person or object; e.g. reverence for one's father or mother, for a sanctuary, for God. [Cf. **awe, adoration.**] **revere**[v], **reverent**[a]. — Ger. *Verehrung.*

reverie, revery = indulgence in an aimless train of ideas, with marked insensibility to external stimuli. [Distg. fr. **daydreaming,** in which the course of thought is more or less actively directed toward pleasurable situations which are generally unreal. Usually spelled **reverie; revery** prefd.] — Ger. *Träumerei.*

reverse[n] = the opposite. [Applied esp. to logical opposition or contrast.] — Fr. *inverse.*

reverse[v] = to so alter the direction of motion of an object that the same positions are assumed in the opposite order; or to so rearrange a picture, etc. that every part assumes the opposite position with respect to one axis of reference. **reversal**[n]. — Fr. *inverser*; Ger. *umkehren.*

reversible = capable of being reversed. [Cf. **reverse**[v].] — Fr. *reversible*; Ger. *umkehrbar.*

reversible perspective = a type of illusion in which a given picture is seen (i.e. interpreted) successively in two different perspective relations, those parts which in one case appear near, appearing in the other case as farther from the observer.

reversion = the inheritance from any ancestor of some trait which has not been manifest in the immediately preceding generation or ancestors. [Distg. fr. **atavism** = reappearance of a trait present in a remote ancestor.] **revert**[v]. — Ger. *Rückfall.*

revery, see **reverie.**

revival = the recurrence or repetition of an earlier experience, in the absence of the original stimuli. [Generally attributed to **association.** Syn. **recall.** The revived experience is termed a **memory image.**] — Fr. *réveil, rappel*; Ger. *Wiederbelebung.*

revolution = a complete rotation, i.e. a rotation through 360°.

reward = a positive motivating stimulus presented to the subject upon the successful termination of a complex response in order to arouse activity or assist the fixation or learning of the desired reactions. [Applied to human and animal subjects in maze tests and various sorts of experiments involving choice of movements. The reward may be food, sex stimuli, praise, etc. Contr. w. **punishment** = a negative motivating stimulus, e.g. electric shock.] — Fr. *récompense, appât*; Ger. *Lohn, Belohnung.*

rhabdomancy, rabdomancy = (*magic*) divination by means of rods, or wands. [Cf. **divining rod.**]

rheobase, rheobasis = the minimum potential of an electric current of indefinite duration which will (just barely) excite nerve or muscle tissue; i.e. the fundamental galvanic threshold of nerves or other excitable tissue (L. Lapicque, 1909). [Cf. **chronaxy.**]

rheostat = an instrument for regulating the magnitude of an electric current by varying the resistance to which the current is exposed.

rheotropism, rheotaxis = a simple orienting response to a current of water. [Applied usually to orientation in the direction opposite to the flow, or to locomotion (e.g. of certain fish) upstream. Cf. **tropism.**] (Accent **-ot-, -tax-.**) **rheotropic**[a], **-tactic**[a].

rhinencephalon = a region of the brain situate in the Sylvian fissure and covered by those portions of the temporal, frontal, and parietal lobes which border the fissure. [A portion of the forebrain consisting of the olfactory bulbs, peduncles, lobes (pyriform areas), hippocampal formation and fornix and their interconnections. Connected chiefly with the hypothalamus and epithalamus by the fornix, medullary striae, terminal striae and medial forebrain bundle. Syn. **olfactory brain.**]

rhinophonia = a form of **dysphonia** characterized by nasal voice.

rhodopsin, see **visual purple.**

rhythm = the serial recurrence of a given time interval or group of time intervals, marked off by sounds, organic movements, etc. [E.g. the temporal sequence of tones in music, of accented syllables in poetry, of heart-beats, of alternating movements of the members in locomotion, etc.] **rhythmic(al)**[a].

Ridgway colors = a system of 1115 pigment colors, chosen so as to cover a wide range of variation in hue, saturation, and brilliance in as evenly distributed a manner as possible.

[Designed originally for naming the plumage colors of birds.]

right[a] = conforming to ethical or moral standards. [In scientific work the term means conforming to the conditions or aims of a given experiment.] **rightness**[n], **the right**[n]. — Fr. *correct, juste, convenable, rectitude*[n]; Ger. *recht, richtig.*

right[n] = that side of an animal which, if the animal faces the rising sun, lies to the south. [Contr. w. **left.**] **right**[a], **dextral**[a]. — Fr. *droite*; Ger. *Recht.*

right and wrong cases/method of = a method of psychophysical measurement, developed by G. T. Fechner, in which two stimuli of nearly the same value are compared many times in either order, the observer being asked to distinguish between them in respect to some character (e.g. weight, loudness, size, etc.), the percentage of correct answers being taken as the measure of discrimination. [Syn. **method of positive and negative cases, method of constant stimuli.**] — Fr. *m. des cas vrais et faux*; Ger. *M. der richtigen und falschen Fälle.*

right associates/method of = a memory method, developed by G. E. Müller, for use when materials to be memorized are presented in pairs; after the learning period one member of each pair is presented in turn and the subject is expected to reproduce its associate, i.e. the other member of the pair. [Syn. **method of paired associates.**] — Fr. *m. des couples associés*; Ger. *Treffermethode.*

righteousness = conformity of an individual to ethical or moral standards of conduct which are conceived to be the commands of a deity or the formulation of some divinely established plan or way of living. [Distg. fr. **rightness,** which refers to the conduct (or to behavior in general).] **righteous**[a]. — Fr. *droiture morale*; Ger. *Gerechtigkeit.*

righthandedness, see **dextrality.**

righting response, righting reaction = the movements of certain animals (e.g. starfish) when placed upon their back, which result in a return to the normal position. — Fr. *réaction de redressement.*

rigid = 1. logically precise or exact; 2. tense (as applied to muscles). [Cf. **rigidity/muscular.**] — Ger. *starr.*

rigidity/decerebrate, see **decerebrate rigidity.**

rigidity/hypnotic = a state of muscular contraction sometimes encountered in hypnosis. [It is probably the result of suggestion emanating from the hypnotizer or from the subject, rather than an aspect of hypnosis itself.]

rigidity/muscular = the state of persistent contraction of the skeletal musculature due to disturbance of extrapyramidal pathways of the central nervous system. [Distg. fr. **contractures,** which are peripheral in origin.] **rigid**[a].

ripen = to approach maturity. [Properly limited to plants and applied to the fruit and seed. Cf. **mature.**] — Fr. *mûrir*; Ger. *reifen.*

rite = a solemn service or ceremony, established by law or custom, having usually a religious or magical significance. — Fr. *rite*; Ger. *Ritus.*

ritual = an organized system of rites or ceremonies. [Applied generally to a series in which there is repetition of the same actions or spoken phrases. Cf. **rite.**] **ritualistic**[a]. — Fr. *rituel.*

rivalry = competition between two or more individuals or groups for certain specific objects or distinctions, without direct conflict between the individuals concerned. [Cf. **social facilitation.**] — Fr. *rivalité*; Ger. *Wetteifer.*

rivalry/retinal, see **retinal rivalry.**

RL = stimulus limen. [Cf. **threshold.**]

rms, see **root-mean-square value.**

Roback mentality tests, see **superior adult tests.**

robot = 1. a machine which simulates a human being; 2. an insensitive, unintelligent, mechanical kind of person. (Pron. **roe-bot.**)

rod/retinal = a rod-like type of structure found in the retina of the eye which constitutes a specific receptor for vision. [The rods in the human eye are 0.04 to 0.06 mm. long and about 0.002 mm. in diameter. Distg. fr. **retinal cones,** another visual receptor; the **rods** contain visual purple and are believed to operate for achromatic (gray) visual qualities at low (twilight) stimulation-intensities, the cones for chromatic and achromatic at the higher levels of stimulation; the rods and cones form the 2nd layer of the retina from the outside, lying just within the layer of pigmented cells; it is estimated that there are 130,000,000 rods in the human retina; at the center of the retina there are no rods, farther out they are more numerous than the cones.] — Fr. *bâtonnet rétinien*; Ger. *Stäbchen.*

rod vision = sight or vision in which the cones of the retina are absent or play no part. [Syn. **twilight vision, scotopic vision.**] — Fr. *vision par bâtonnets, v. scotopique, v. crépusculaire*; Ger. *Stäbchensehen.*

rods and cones/layer of = the 2d stratum of the retina from without inward, consisting of the **rods** and **cones,** which are the outer parts of the visual or **neuro-epithelial** cells and constitute the end-organs or receptors for the sense of vision. [Syn. **bacillary layer, Jacob's membrane.** Cf. **rod/retinal, cone/retinal, retinal layers** and Table XI.]

rods of Corti = elongated structures in the organ of Corti of the internal ear, whose bases rest on the basilar membrane, and whose upper ends lie between the inner and outer hair cells. [There are two types, the *inner* and *outer* rods of Corti, which fuse at their upper ends to form the arches of Corti. Syn. **pillars of Corti.** Cf. **Corti/organ of.**] — Fr. *piliers de C.*; Ger. *Cortische Pfeiler.*

Rolandic fissure, fissure of Rolando = a deep cortical sulcus, or furrow, on the lateral aspect of each hemisphere; it arises just above the middle of the Sylvian fissure and passes dorsad and a little caudad to the vertical, ending at the median fissure: it is bounded in front by the gyrus centralis anterior (the cortical locus for muscle movements) and caudad by the g. centralis posterior, the locus for skin sensations. [Syn. **sulcus centralis.**] — Fr. *scissure rolandique, sillon de R*; Ger. *Rolandoscher Spalt, Zentralfurche.*

rolling, see **torsional rotation.**

Romberg sign = the tendency of the individual to sway when standing with feet together and eyes closed, common in locomotor ataxia.

Röntgen rays, see **x-rays.**

root = 1. (*philol.*) the common basis of a given group of similar words after removal of all grammatical inflections and allowing for the consequent modifications; 2. (*math.*) in respect to an algebraic equation, a specific value of the variable which satisfies the equation; 3. (*neurol.*)

a collection of fibers connected with a part of the central nervous system such as spinal cord or brain, and related to the periphery. [Syn. (1) **radical**[n], which has a much broader connotation.] — Fr. *racine*; Ger. (1) *Stamm*, (2, 3) *Wurzel*.

root-mean-square = (*statist.*) the square root of the mean of the squares of the magnitudes in question. [When these magnitudes are deviations from the **mean**, it equals the **standard deviation.**]

Rorschach test = a form of **ink-blot test** which features colored blots.

Rosanoff association test, see **Kent-Rosanoff test.**

Roscoe-Bunsen law, see **reciprocity law.**

Rossolimo method = a collection of tests comprising 38 subtests of 10 items each, classified under 9 rubrics (e.g. attention, memory), designed to provide a psychological profile, or psychograph, of the testee's general mental capacity. [Syn. **Rossolimo profile method, psychograph of Rossolimo.** Hist. significant as an attempt to develop profile tests for analyzing general mental capacity. Cf. **profile tests.**]

rotation = angular movement or motion about a center or axis. **rotate**[v]; **rotary**[a] = characterized by rotation; **rotational**[a] = pert. to the process. — Ger. *Achsendrehung*.

rotation/center of, see **center of rotation.**

rotation chair = a chair of special design, mounted to rotate around a vertical axis, and used to stimulate receptors of bodily motion. [The Bárány chair is propelled by hand; the Dunlap chair by an electric motor and magnetic clutch; the Dodge chair by an electric fan mounted as an air propeller, or oscillated in harmonic motion by crank and pulley.] — Fr. *chaise tournante*.

rotation perception = a quality of static-sense experience induced by positive or negative rotary acceleration of the individual's body about any axis, such that one of the semicircular canals or a combination of these is stimulated. — Fr. *perception (sens) de rotation*.

rotation table = a horizontal board poised upon a vertical pivot so as to rotate freely in the horizontal plane; the observer being placed in any desired position on the board, the instrument is used to investigate his perception of rotation. [Cf. **tilting board.**] — Fr. *planche rotative*.

rote learning = the repeated utterance or observation of a phrase, sentence, stanza, or long passage in prose or poetry, until the subject is able to recite it without error or prompting, regardless of the meaning. [Contr. w. **logical learning,** in which the meaning of the passage is used associatively to facilitate the learning process.] — * Fr. *mémoire brute*; Ger. *auswendig lernen*.

rote memory, see **memory.**

rotoscope = an apparatus for providing very brief exposures in rapid succession, in order to isolate or select a certain temporal part of a complex stimulus; the observer controls the rate of repeated exposure, causing this to correspond to the repetition rate of the movement being studied. [An instrument of observation to aid in investigating rapidly moving machinery.]

roughness = 1. the unevenness arising from several simultaneous or successive pressure stimuli of contrasting intensity; 2. a characteristic of certain tonal sounds which undergo relatively rapid alterations of wave form or amplitude. [**Tonal roughness** (2) is characteristic, e.g. of beats of fairly rapid frequency. Syn. **harshness,** which applies esp. to **roughness** (2) of high degree Contr. (1, 2) w. **smoothness.**] — Fr. *sensation de rugosité*; Ger. *Rauheit*.

round window, see **window/round.**

Rubin's goblet-profile figure = a plain white figure of a goblet on an even background of black, portrayed in such a way as to produce alternatively the perception of two faces in silhouetted profile when the white space becomes the background and the black the principal figure. [Illustrative of a number of reversible figures and diagrammatic presentations of some of the principles underlying *Gestalt* psychology. Cf. **figure-ground.**] — Fr. *figure du vase à profils humains de R.*

rudiment = 1. the incipient form of an organ or member, which later, in the individual or in the evolutionary line of descent, may become a complete organ or member; 2. (*hist.*) a degenerate form of an organ which was at one time more completely developed. [The term **vestige** is prefd. for (2).] (Accent **ru-**.) **rudimentary**[a]. — Fr. *rudiment, ébauche*.

Ruffini corpuscle (or **cylinder**) = a type of branched nerve end-organ, mostly located in subcutaneous tissue. [Believed by some writers to arouse warmth sensations. Distg. fr. **Ruffini's papillary endings.** Dogiel, who discovered them, identified the two, and considered the latter a variant and called them *arboriform terminations*.] — Ger. *Ruffinisches Köperchen*.

Ruffini papillary endings (or **plumes**) = nerve end-organs located in the papillary layer of the skin. [Believed by some writers to arouse pressure sensations.] — Fr. *terminaisons nerveuses papillaires de Ruffini*.

rule = a working principle for regulating behavior or conduct. [In ethical contexts, a **rule** is usually regarded as arbitrarily imposed, contr. w. a **law,** which springs from the nature of things. In practical contexts (including the conduct of scientific or scholarly reasoning or investigation) a **rule** states what is most useful or workable. Distg. fr. **maxim** a more popular and less systematic working principle, and fr. **canon,** a more general working principle. In science contr. w. **law,** a statement of some general uniformity existing in nature. Cf. **principle.**] — Fr. *règle*; Ger. *Regel*.

rumor, rumour = an unverified story or report, purporting to represent actual occurrences, which circulates in a given community, and is often communicated inaccurately.

Russmethode = a procedure in which smoke rings from a small gas jet are deposited on a continuously passing ribbon of paper (Marbe). [The pulsations of the voice cause variations in the supply of gas fed to the flame. A time-line is similarly recorded by means of an electrically driven tuning fork. Ger.]

S

S = abbrev. for **subject** (2). [Prefd. italic without period; plural *S*s, possessive *S*'s, *S*s'.]

S = 1. abbrev. for **stimulus;** 2. abbrev. for **sensation** or sensory intensity, when **R** is abbrev. for stimulus. [Prefd. roman cap., without period. Cf. **R.**]

S.D. = abbrev. for **standard deviation.**

s factor, specific factor = a psychoneural element, or determiner of ability, according to the two-factor doctrine of intelligence, which, in contradistinction to the **general** or **g factor,** varies for the same individual with different abilities (e.g. dancing and juggling), and is independent of the (general) g factor, which is relatively constant for the individual (Spearman). [Cf. **g factor, two-factor theory of intelligence.**]

sac = any bag-like structure in the body of an organism.

saccadic movement = sudden movement of the eyes from one fixation point to another. [Contr. w. **pursuit movement.**]

saccadic speed = the rate of angle-velocity of the simple eye movements which separate successive visual fixations, e.g. in ordinary reading. — Fr. *vitesse de saccade.*

saccadic time = the sum of the time intervals during which the eye is in motion when reading, as contr. w. the fixation time. — Fr. *temps de saccade.*

saccule, sacculus = one of the two sac-like dilatations of the membranous labyrinth of the vestibule within the inner ear, which communicates with the cochlear duct and with the endolymphatic duct. [Distg. fr. **utricle.**] — Ger. *Säckchen.*

sacral nerve = any of the spinal nerves which join the cord in the sacral region. [There are 5 pairs. Cf. **sacrum.**]

sacral segment = the portion of the spinal cord situate near the caudal extremity, which gives rise to the five sacral nerves. [Applied also to the corresponding portion of the autonomic system.]

sacred = characterizing a state or quality belonging to a divine being or power, and (by association) to persons or objects connected with a divinity or its worship. [Syn. **hallowed.** Contr. w. **profane, secular.** Cf. **taboo.**] — Ger. *heilig, geheiligt.*

sacrospinal reflex = a contraction of part of the sacrospinal muscle, elicited by scratching the skin along its lateral border. [Mediated by the thoracic region of the cord. Syn. **dorsal r., erector spinal r., lumbar r.**]

sacrum = a triangular bone situate near the base of the spinal column above the coccyx, and forming the dorsal part of the pelvis. (Accent **say-.**) **sacral**^{a}, **sacrad**^{adv}. — Ger. *Kreuzbein.*

sadism = a type of sexual perversion, characterized by pleasure, or sexual gratification, in whipping or otherwise maltreating individuals of the same or opposite sex. [Syn. **active algolagnia.** Contr. w. **masochism,** in which the individual takes pleasure in being maltreated.] **sadistic**^{a}.

sadness = an emotional attitude characterized by unpleasant feeling tone and expressing itself in sighing, weeping, and passivity and diminished tone of the voluntary muscles. [Syn. **sorrow, grief, despair** = more intense; contr. w. **joy.**] — Fr. *tristesse*; Ger. *Traurigkeit.*

sagittal axis = 1. in man, any line passing through the body in a dorsoventral direction; 2. the line of direction in the eye and in the visual function, which connects the center of the retina with the center of the lens and pupil, together with the projection of this line in the field of vision beyond the eye. (Accent **saj-.**)

sagittal plane = any plane of the body parallel to the mesial (or medial) plane. (Accent **saj-.**)

Saint Vitus' dance, see **chorea.**

salesmanship/institutional = effort designed to promote a favorable attitude toward an entire industry, commodity, or service, irrespective of any particular firm or brand. [E.g. institutional advertising of life insurance, or of electric power.] — Fr. *propagande.*

saline, salty = a quality of gustatory sensation of which the taste of common salt (sodium chloride) is a typical example. [Cf. **gustatory qualities.**] — Fr. *salé*; Ger. *salzig.*

saliva = the watery, viscous, and somewhat opalescent fluid containing many constituents including mucin and the amylolytic enzyme, ptyalin, which is secreted by the salivary glands and discharged into the buccal cavity. [The composition of saliva may vary from gland to gland and from time to time. Saliva has the function of assisting in mastication and swallowing and in the digestion of starch.] **salivate**^{v} = to produce a flow (usually excessive) of saliva; **salivary**^{a} = pert. to **saliva.** — Ger. *Speichel.*

salivary apparatus/Pavlov's, see **Pavlov's experiment.**

salivary glands = a system or group of glands with ducts opening into the mouth cavity whereby they discharge saliva, which assists in mastication and swallowing and contributes an enzyme, ptyalin, concerned in the digestion of starch. [In man the principal salivary glands are the paired parotid, sublingual, and submaxillary or mandibular glands; other smaller glands of the mouth and pharynx also produce saliva.] — Ger. *Speicheldrüsen.*

salivary reflex = a process involving any increase, decrease, or change in the specific secretory activity of one or more salivary glands, due to excitation or inhibition of their efferent nerves resulting from stimulation of an afferent nerve. [Mediated by lingual nerve to secretory centers of VII and IX cranial nerves. Cf. **Pavlov's experiment.**] — Ger. *Speichelreflex.*

Salpêtrière school = the systematic views on abnormal psychology and hypnosis held by J. M. Charcot (1878 ff.) in his neurological clinic at the Salpêtrière in Paris. [This school emphasized the importance of hysteria, and it regarded hypnosis as an abnormal hysterical phenomenon; contr. w. the **Nancy school** (Bernheim) which regarded hypnosis as a normal phenomenon of suggestibility.]

salpinx = the oviduct. [Syn. **fallopian tube.**] **salpinges**^{pl}. — Fr. *trompe.*

saltation, see **mutation.**

sameness = absence of essential change in a sense datum, situation, or any complex unity at two different times. [Contr. w. **difference.** Distg. fr. **similarity,** which characterizes two separate data, etc., between which there is no essential difference.] — Fr. (*impression d'*) *identité*; Ger. *Gleichheit.*

same-opposite test, see **synonym-antonym test.**

sample, see **sampling** (2). — Fr. *échantillon.*

sampling^{n} = 1. the selection (for statistical treatment) of a limited number of cases taken at random out of an entire group or population, i.e. taken without preference or regard to any characteristic, the assumption being that these randomly taken cases are representative of the entire group; 2. the small representative group employed in sampling (1). [Syn. (2) **sample, sample group, unselected group.**] **sample**[v]. — Fr. (1) *échantillonnage*, (2) *groupe-type*.

sampling/errors of = deviations of the values yielded by a sample, from the values yielded by the entire population. [They are due to the fact that this random group or sample is not exactly representative of the whole. Cf. **sampling.**] — Fr. *erreurs d'échantillonnage*.

sanction = 1. (*psychol.*) the ground or reason for an individual's action whether consciously formulated or not; 2. (*sociol.*) any means by which officials or other agents of a social group induce or compel the individual to act in conformity with the standards commonly accepted in the group, e.g. legal, moral, religious. — Ger. (1) *Bestätigung*, (2) *Sanktion*.

Sanford envelopes = a set of envelopes, similar in visual appearance but weighted so as to form a progressive series, used to test the discrimination of lifted weights. [Devised by E. C. Sanford.]

sanguine = a type of temperament which combines active expression with a pleasant feeling-tone, and is characterized by enthusiasm, changeableness, and freedom from load. [Hist. attributed to the predominance of the blood in the body as against the other humors. Cf. **temperament** (1).]

sanity = the normal mental condition of the human individual. [Contr. w. **insanity.**] **sane**[a]. — Fr. *santé mentale*.

Sanson images, see **Purkinje-Sanson images.**

santonin = the active principle of *Santonica*, or Levant wormseed, a crystalline drug, odorless and colorless, insoluble in cold water. [It is an efficacious vermifuge for *Ascaris lumbricoides*, or round-worm. In large doses it produces yellow vision, headache, vertigo, and convulsions. Lat. Santoninum.]

Santorini's cartilages, see **corniculate cartilages.**

Sapphism = erotic attachment of women to one another. [Cf. **Lesbian, cunnilingus.**]

sarcasm = (*esth.*) a form of wit concerned with ridiculing vice, folly, etc. [Distg. fr. **humor,** which is subjective in reference, and fr. **irony** in being more severe and less dramatic.]

sarcode = the jelly-like substance which constitutes the living matter of a protozoan (Dujardin).

satire = (*esth.*) sustained sarcasm in finished oral or literary form. — Ger. *Spott, Spottgedicht*.

satisfaction = an attitude characterized by a feeling of pleasantness and motor quiescence, usually due to the onset of a situation which has been previously pictured and the idea of which has aroused motor activity. [Contr. w. **dissatisfaction** = characterized by unpleasantness and unrest.] — Ger. *Befriedigung*.

satisfier = any stimulus or situation which fulfills or extinguishes the fundamental wants or desires of the individual. [Contr. w. **annoyer;** these terms are emphasized by Thorndike.]

Sattler's elastic layer = a thin layer of elastic connective-tissue fibers situate in the choroid coat of the eye, between the layer of large blood-vessels and the inner layer of capillaries. — Fr. *couche élastique de S.*

saturation = 1. the degree to which any color possessing a hue differs from a gray of the same brilliance; 2. that condition of a liquid which marks the degree to which a chemical substance (e.g. a salt) has been dissolved in it. [Syn. (1) **chroma, tint.** A **pure color** (or **hue**), in which only a single wave length is effective, is said to be **completely saturated;** a mixture in which no single wave-length predominates, or which is complementary to no single wave-length, is **completely unsaturated.** Contr. (1) w. **hue** and **brilliance.** Cf. (1) **color.**] — Ger. *Sättigung*.

saturation scale = a scale of numbers applied to a series of color-stimuli that are held to be alike in hue and brilliance but different in saturation, parallel to a corresponding scale of desaturation in terms of stimulus, and such that adjacent numbers represent stimuli which are just noticeably different. [Such a scale usually involves a spectral or highly saturated stimulus progressively desaturated by the suitable substitution of white light or a gray component; the number of steps in the scale depends somewhat upon the method of experimentation, and also upon the hue, e.g. the normally most saturated extreme spectral colors, red and blue, yield a maximum of 24, while a minimum of 17 is found for the intermediate yellow of wave-length 575 $m\mu$.]

satyriasis = 1. an exaggerated degree of sexual desire in the human male; 2. erotic insanity. [Analogous to **nymphomania** = in the female. Cf. **erotomania.**]

Savart wheel = a disk bearing around its entire circumference a set of teeth placed at uniform distances; when the wheel is rotated, the teeth strike a tongue, producing a succession of clicks which in rapid rotation merge into a tone, the pitch varying with the speed of rotation. [Used to investigate tonal pitch in relation to vibration frequency.] — Fr. *disque de S.*

saving method = a method of determining the degree of retention of learning, by measuring the time required to learn a given amount of material and the time required to relearn the same material after some standard time-interval, and computing the percentage of the latter as compared with the former. [Used by Ebbinghaus in his pioneer work on forgetting, 1885.] — Fr. *m. d'économie*; Ger. *Ersparnismethode*.

scala media (cochlearis) = the smallest of the three tubes into which the cochlea is divided; it contains the **organ of Corti.** [Cf. **cochlea, cochlear duct.**] — Ger. *Schneckenkanal*.

scala tympani = one of the two large spiral tubes into which the cochlear canal is divided by the **spiral lamina** and **cochlear duct.** [It extends from the round window at the base of the cochlea to the apex, where it communicates with the second large tube, the **scala vestibuli,** through an opening called the **helicotrema.**] — Fr. *rampe tympanique*; Ger. *Paukentreppe*.

scala vestibuli = one of the two large spiral canals into which the cochlea is divided, separated from the **scala tympani** by the **spiral lamina** and **cochlear duct,** and extending from the oval window at the base of the cochlea (where it receives the auditory stimuli from the stapes) to the apex, where it connects with the **scala tympani** through the **helicotrema.** [Like the **scala tympani,** it is filled with a fluid, the **perilymph.**] — Fr. *rampe vestibulaire*; Ger. *Vorhofstreppe*.

scale = 1. (*math.*) a progressive system of values, each of which constitutes a standard, used in measuring data of some specific sort. — Fr. (1) *échelle*.

scale = 2. (*mus.*) a graduated series of pitches arranged in a conventional scheme of steps or intervals. [Most scales, including all modern European forms, are founded on the octave, and the scheme of division is repeated for each octave of the musical range. The **Pythagorean scale,** from which modern scales were derived, was formed by combining two Greek tetrachords, and was made up of two kinds of intervals, the tone and the hemitone, in a variety of arrangements, two of which, the Lydian and the Hypo-Dorian, divided the octave in the manner indicated in Diagrams 1 and 4, where the size of the intervals is indicated in tempered semitones = a vibration ratio of $1:2^{1/12}$. (The size of the intervals in all the diagrams may be indicated in the conventional unit of the **cent** by multiplying each number by 100.) **The major diatonic scale** (used in modern music) was derived from the Lydian form by the adjustment of certain tones to increase the harmonic possibilities of the scale; see Diagram 2 (a). The **minor diatonic scale** was derived from the Hypo-Dorian form, but has been considerably modified by assimilation to the major diatonic scale; it has three modern forms: (*a*) the *pure* or *ascending form,* which corresponds to the Hypo-Dorian except for the alteration of minor tone and semitone intervals; this type is still used in descending melodies; (*b*) the *harmonic form,* in which the terminating intervals have been altered to make it possible to close a musical sequence with a *perfect cadence,* i.e. a major third (E–G sharp) followed by a perfect fourth (E–A′); (*c*) the *ascending melodic form,* in which the large interval of an augmented second of the harmonic form has been avoided by changing the F to F-sharp, thereby affording a smoother melodic effect; this form is common in ascending melodies. See Diagram 5. The **chromatic scale** consists of the diatonic scale, together with a varying number of additional tones which serve the purposes of embellishment and of permitting passage from one key to another. One form of chromatic scale is shown in Diagram 2 (b). The **equal-tempered scale** consists of twelve equal semitones to the octave, as shown in Diagram 3; the notes approximate those of the major, minor, and chromatic scales and make it possible on keyed instruments to execute music written for any of these scales, and to pass readily from one key to another; this scale has the outstanding disadvantage that all the intervals, except the octave, are slightly mistuned. There are numerous other scales, both historical and modern, consisting of varying numbers of steps or divisions of the octave or of some other arbitrary compass; of these the most notable are **tetrachords** = four-tone scales used by the ancient Greeks, **pentatonic scales** = five-tone scales common in Oriental and other music, and **heptatonic scales** = seven-tone scales, developed from the Greek tetrachords. See Table VII.] — Fr. (2) *gamme*; Ger. *Tonleiter*.

scale/mental = a series of standard values of mental development or mental age, based upon the individual's ability to answer or solve a set of graded tests. [Often confused with the tests themselves; but the Binet-Simon *tests* (e.g.) may be evaluated according to either the **Binet-Simon scale** or the **point scale;** and the evaluating principle of the Binet *scale* may be applied to other series of tests.] — Fr. *échelle mentale*.

scale/tonal = 1. the extent of vibration-frequencies perceptible to the average human ear as sound; i.e. the tones from about 20 to 20,000 cycles per second; 2. any arbitrary set of tones selected from the above range. [Cf. **scale** (2).] — Fr. *échelle tonale*.

scale value = the numerical value attaching to a test item, which places it in its proper position in relation to other test items as regards difficulty, attitude, interest, or other characteristics measured by the items. — Fr. *valeur numérique en échelle*.

scaphocephalic = having a keel-shaped head.

scapula = the shoulder-blade. (Accent **skap-.**) **scapular**[a].

scapular reflex = contraction of the scapular muscle elicited by scratching the skin over the scapula, or between the scapulae. [Mediated by 5th cervical to 4th thoracic segments of the cord. Syn. **interscapular r.**]

scatter = the spread, variability, or dispersion of the items which compose a statistical series. — Fr. *dispersion*; Ger. *Streuung*.

scatter diagram, scatter plot = a double entry or two-way table, showing the relation between two series of paired measures. — Fr. *tableau de distribution, pointage de régression*.

scent = gaseous particles given off by a substance, which act as stimuli to the olfactory receptors; 2. syn. for **odor.** [The technical use of the term is preferably limited to (1) to avoid ambiguity. Cf. **olfaction, odor.**] — Fr. *odeur*; Ger. *Duft*.

Schafhäntl phonometer, see **audiometer.**

Scheiner's experiment = a demonstration of visual accommodation, in which the eye is covered with a card, provided with two pinholes that are separated by a distance less than the pupillary diameter; objects at a distance either less or greater than that of the focus of accommodation are seen double. [The other eye should be closed.]

schema = 1. a formula, model, outline, or plan, by the application of which a body of data may be systematically arranged for scientific purposes, i.e. a framework for the systematic presentation of data; 2. the standard resulting from previous postures and movements of the body, against which all postural changes are measured or to which immediate reference is made when a fresh position is recognized (Head). [According to Head, this standard lies outside consciousness; every recognizable change in posture enters consciousness already charged with its relation to something which has gone before, and the final product is directly perceived as a measured postural change. And similarly with recognition of the locality of stimulated spots on the body. Distg. (1) fr. **scheme,** which has a more active meaning.] **schemata**[pl], **schematism**[n] = the use or working out of schemata, or the quality of being schematic; **schematic**[a] (more generally coupled with scheme).

schematic eye, see **reduced eye.**

scheme = a plan, device, outline, or systematic project. [In science the term emphasizes the orderly nature of the plan, or program.] **schematic**[a] (also = in outline, **diagrammatic**). — Fr. *plan, projet*; Ger. *Entwurf, Plan*.

schizoid = 1. a personality type in which the interest or libido is directed more to the inner life than to the external world (Bleuler); 2. a shut-in or introverted personality, unsocial, given to fantasy, whose emotional life is more or less dissociated from his ideational content,

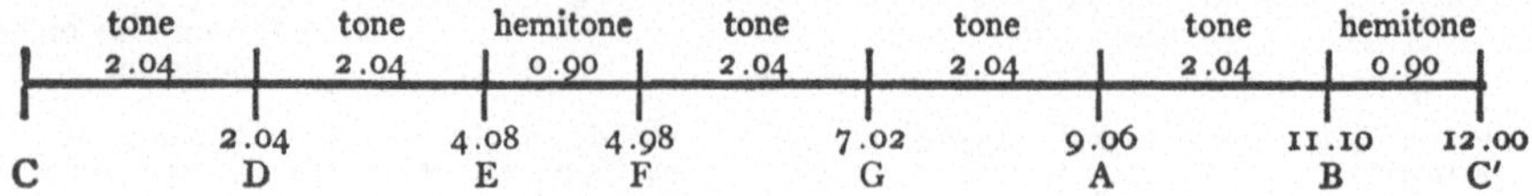

PYTHAGOREAN SCALE

(Lydian Form)

Diagram 1

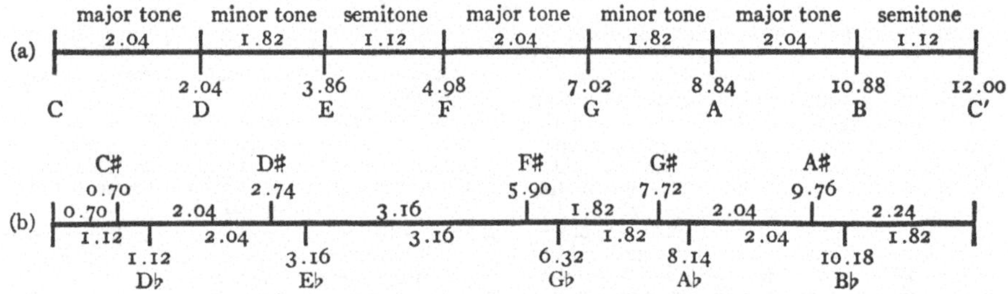

MAJOR DIATONIC AND CHROMATIC SCALES

Diagram 2

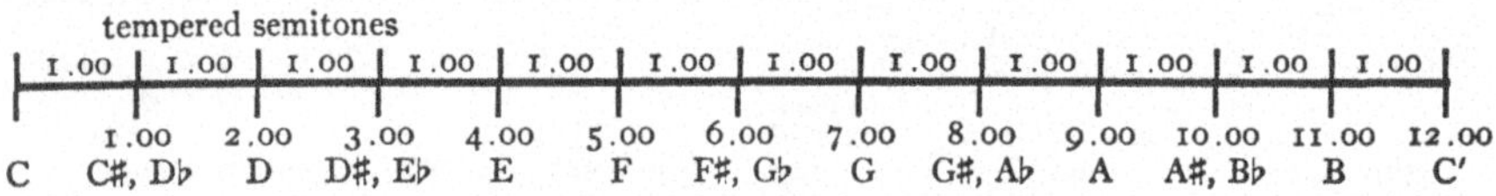

EQUAL-TEMPERED SCALE

Diagram 3

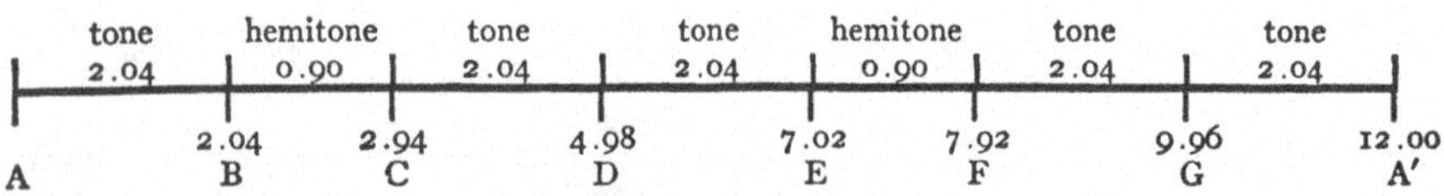

PYTHAGOREAN SCALE

(Hypo-Dorian Form)

Diagram 4

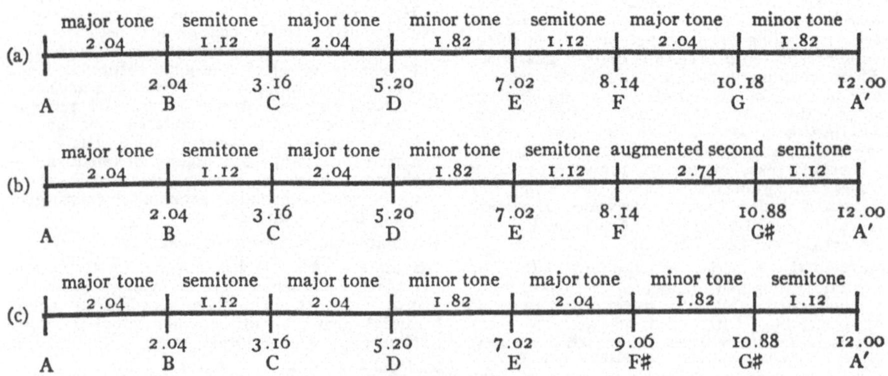

MINOR DIATONIC SCALES

(a) Pure or Descending Form. (b) Harmonic Form. (c) Ascending Melodic Form.

Diagram 5

due to abnormal mental development (Kretschmer); 3. resembling or pert. to **schizophrenia,** to which individuals of this type are subject. [Contr. w. **syntonic.**]

schizophrenia = syn. for **dementia praecox** (Bleuler). [Literally "splitting of the mind." **schizophrenia** has largely replaced **dementia praecox** in scientific usage. It avoids the implications regarding age of onset and outlook for deterioration, and emphasizes the dissociative phenomena, e.g. hallucinations, fantastic delusions, and disorganized emotional life, in the presence of relative intellectual preservation. Somewhat broader than **dementia praecox,** since it includes, on the basis of dissociative symptoms, cases that would scarcely have received the earlier designation.] (Pron. **skiz-.**) **schizophrenic**[a].

schizothymia = manifestation of schizoid traits within normal limits (Kretschmer).

Schlaftiefenmesser = an apparatus intended to measure the depth of sleep (Kraepelin); at fixed temporal intervals it automatically releases a series of balls of constant weight, from increasing heights, which fall upon sound-boards and disturb the sleeper, who is instructed to stop the apparatus at the instant of awaking. [The height from which the last ball fell is arbitrarily taken as a measure of the depth of sleep. Ger.]

Schlemm's canal = a small ring-shaped channel in the sclera of the eye, close to its junction with the cornea, forming the outlet through which the aqueous fluid finds its way back into the general circulation.

scholastic = 1. pert. to a school; 2. pert. to medieval philosophy. **scholasticism**[n] (2).

school = 1. an institution of instruction and learning of any grade; 2. the body of adherents to some specific theory, doctrine, method, or leader. [When used without qualification (1) generally denotes in America an institution of primary or secondary level.] — Fr. *école*; Ger. *Schule*.

schooling = systematic instruction. — Fr. *instruction, écolage, enseignement*; Ger. *Unterricht, Schulerziehung*.

sciatic nerve = the large peripheral nerve which connects the receptor and effector organs in the leg with the spinal cord. — Ger. *Hüftnerv*.

science = organized or systematic knowledge. [**science** denotes the systematic investigation of some specific field or coherent group of phenomena. Distg. fr. **art, technology,** and **desultory knowledge.**] **scientific**[a]. — Ger. *Wissenschaft*.

scientific management = a term (first used in 1910) to denote the system of doctrines and broad general principles derived from industrial experiments by F. W. Taylor and his associates beginning in 1881; it emphasizes the primary importance of scientific attitude in the accomplishment of predetermined objectives, and implies the detachment or impartiality which arises from factual and objective thinking, and the philosophy of control, in contrast to drift. [Syn. **Taylorism,** which is also applied to the special system devised by Taylor.]

scientific method = a systematic program for the acquisition of exact knowledge. [Cf. **method, methodology.**]

sciosophy = any system of thought or belief, the grounds of which are at variance with contemporary scientific knowledge, e.g. modern **astrology, theosophy,** and **phrenology.** [Contr. w. **science.** Cf. **superstition.**] **sciosophist**[np].

sclera, see **sclerotic.**

sclerosis = hardening of the neural or other tissues of the body.

sclerotic, sclerotic coat = the white outer fibrous coat of the eyeball, primarily a supporting or skeletal structure. [Syn. **sclera.** Cf. **cornea.**] — Fr. *sclérotique*.

scope = the entire group of phenomena, events, or general data which properly fall within the limits of a given inquiry. — Fr. *étendue, portée*; Ger. *Bereich*.

scopic method = that method of observing quantitative results in which the values are seen and recorded by the experimenter. [Contr. w. **graphic method,** in which the values are recorded often by the apparatus itself.]

scopophilia = sexual pleasure derived from looking at the human form, articles of apparel, etc. or from observing sexual acts. [Syn. **inspectionism.** The passive counterpart of **exhibitionism.** Sometimes improperly written **scotophilia** or **scoptophilia.**] **peeper**[np] (*pop.*). — Fr. *voyeurisme*; Ger. *Schaulust*.

score = 1. a credit or weighted value assigned to a specific response made to a test item; 2. the sum or other composite result obtained from compiling the responses of an individual to all the items of a single test, or battery of tests. **scoring**[n] = the process or method of obtaining a score. **score**[v]. — Fr. *note, notation, dépouillement*[n].

score/raw, /standard, etc., see **raw score, standard score,** etc.

scorn = an emotional attitude toward another person, class or group, norm, or plan of action characterized by dislike tinged with disgust, and by a feeling of superiority to the person, class, or plan in question. **scorn**[v]. — Fr. *dédain*; Ger. *Verachtung, Spott*.

scoterythrous = characterizing a type of color vision in which long wave-length stimuli are lessened in effectiveness or darkened. [A peculiarity of **protanopia,** and of certain forms of **anomalous trichromasy.** Suggested by Rivers to replace the non-descriptive term **protanopic.** Contr. w. **photerythrous.**]

scotoma = a blind or partially blind area of the retina, usually due to a pathological condition. [Classed according to location as **central, paracentral** (near the macula), and **peripheral;** according to character as **positive** (seen as a black spot), **negative** (not ordinarily noticed), **absolute** (excluding even light-perception), **relative** (function not wholly lost), **ring** (surrounding the macula), **scintillating** (giving sparks or flashes of light), **physiological** (syn. for **blind spot**).] **scotomata**[pl].

scotometer = (*ophthal.*) an instrument, similar in principle to the **perimeter,** used for determining the location and the limits of **scotomata** in the visual field. [Cf. **scotoma.**]

scotomization = (*psychoan.*) a process of psychic depreciation, by means of which the individual attempts to deny everything which conflicts with his ego (Laforgue).

scotophilia, see **scopophilia.**

scotopic adaptation = syn. for **dark-adaptation,** but with more explicit reference to the part played by the rod-system of the retina. [Cf. **adaptation** (2).]

scotopic vision, scotopia = vision which occurs in faint light, or after dark adaptation. [It is attributed to the operation of the retinal rods. Syn. **twilight vision.** Distg. fr. **daylight** (or **photopic) vision.**]

scratch reflex = scratching movements of hind leg of an animal, elicited by sticking or pricking the flank, back, or neck. — Fr. *réflexe de grattage*; Ger. *Kratzreflex*.

screen memory = (*psychoan.*) fragments of recollection which break through the childhood amnesia but are represented through processes of condensation and displacement by something trivial. [More accurately descriptive than syn. **cover memory,** which implies a process of concealment.] — Fr. *souvenir-écran*; Ger. *Deckerinnerung*.

script = the characters which constitute handwriting, or type which imitates them. — Fr. (*écriture*) *anglaise*; Ger. *Schrift*.

Scripture weights = a set of small elder-pith disks, 3 mm. in diameter, suspended by a fine cocoon-fiber, each from a separate handle; they form a graded series of weights, 1 mg., 2 mg., 3 mg.,... to 10 mg. or to any desired magnitude; the stimulus-limen for pressure is determined by finding the lightest disk which, when applied carefully to a given area, evokes a perceptible pressure sensation. [Named for E. W. Scripture; similar weights were used by Aubert and Kammler (1858).]

scruple = a minor ground of hesitation, involving ethical considerations, in respect to some proposed course of action. [Usually implies that the person feeling or exhibiting it is sensitive to ethical considerations even of slight importance.] — Ger. *Bedenklichkeit*.

scrying = (*psych. res.*) the process of inducing visual hallucination or projected visual imagery by gazing into a crystal sphere, or other translucent or reflecting body or substance. [Forms of objects, faces, or figures are seen or events are witnessed in the crystal. Syn. **crystal-gazing.** Cf. **automatism, cryptesthesia.**] — Fr. *cristalloscopie, vision au cristal*.

sculpture = the art or act of producing solid or three-dimensional representations of a more or less permanent character.

sea-anemone = an animal of the phylum Coelenterata and class Actinozoa, which is devoid of an external skeleton and commonly attached to rocks or other support. [It possesses a primitive nervous system but no central nervous system.] — Fr. *actinie*.

séance = (*psych. res.*) a sitting, usually in a darkened room, for the purpose of obtaining metapsychic phenomena. [The duration of a sitting is commonly from three to five hours; conditions are favorable for **malobservation, illusion** and **hallucination**; the medium and the "spirits" retain control of the phenomena.]

Seashore audiometer, see **audiometer.**

Seashore measures of musical talent, Seashore test of musical ability = a series of phonographic records, with manual of instructions and norms and blanks for recording results, used in measuring specific and relatively elemental musical capacities, such as tonal memory and the sensory discrimination of pitch, intensity, time, rhythm, timbre, and consonance. [They form part of a battery of other measures of musical ability not yet phonographically recorded but standardized in terms of laboratory techniques.]

seat of mind, seat of consciousness = a region of the brain assumed to be the location or central controlling area for mind, or consciousness. [(Hist.); originally the **seat of the soul** and not considered as necessarily localized in the brain.] — Fr. *siège de l'esprit*; Ger. *Sitz der Seele, — des Geistes*.

sebaceous gland = a type of gland, scattered over almost the entire surface of the skin except the palms and soles, which secretes an oily liquid.

seclusiveness = a tendency, frequently pathological, of an individual to cut himself off from social intercourse. — Fr. *isolement*.

second (*mus.*), see **interval** and Table VII.

second sight, see **clairvoyance.**

secondary attention, see **attention.**

secondary automatic = characterizing certain types of response, which have become automatic only after repetition or practice.

secondary elaboration, see **elaboration/secondary.**

secondary function = the tendency for every nervous process which arouses in the mind an idea, to persevere for some time after its proper function has been fulfilled, as an after-function, which, however, no longer has anything in consciousness to correspond with it. [It is this activity which determines, according to its exponent Otto Gross, the determined, persevering, intensive and concentrated type of individual.]

secondary function type = an individual who is dominated by the secondary function, showing signs of a narrow but deep consciousness, and possessing the characteristics of persistence, stubbornness, introversion, intensiveness, inflexibility, etc.

secondary personality, see **personality/secondary.**

secondary position = (*vis.*) any position of binocular fixation other than the **primary position.**

secondary process = (*psychoan.*) the psychical process which inhibits primary processes and directs the energy into more complex paths. [Contr. w. **primary process.**]

secondary qualities = 1. (*hist.*) the properties of stimulus objects which enable them to arouse sensory qualities that do not resemble the properties of the stimulus, e.g. the arousal of a tone by a sound wave; 2. less technically, the sensory qualities thus aroused. [Contr. w. **primary qualities,** which are assumed to be more fundamental. The two terms originated with Locke.]

secondary sensation = a concomitant sensory experience which is aroused by a stimulus in addition to the appropriate experience, e.g. the visual sensations in colored hearing. [Cf. **synesthesia.**]

secondary sex (or **sexual**) **character** = any structural, physiological, or mental character which serves to differentiate the two sexes, but which apparently plays no direct role in the functions of reproduction. [E.g. the horns of male deer; brilliant plumage of male birds, facial hair in human males. Contr. w. **primary sex character.** Cf. **sex character.**]

secondary tympanic membrane = a thin membrane, which covers the round or cochlear window of the vestibule. [It oscillates in and out in accordance with the alternating pressures exerted on the perilymph by movements of the stapes at the oval, or vestibular window. Cf. **window/round.**]

secretin = a term applied by Bayliss and Starling to an active substance yielded by the epithelial cells of the duodenum; when this substance is in the blood stream, digestive glands, more particularly the pancreas, at a distance are excited to action independently of the nervous system. [Syn. **autacoid of duodenum.**]

secretion = 1. the specific chemical substances (usually in solution) or cells in suspension, or both, produced by the activity of a gland or other tissue, and physiologically serviceable; 2. the process by which gland cells, by expending energy, form and discharge a **secretion** (1). [Distg. (1) fr. **excretion** = waste products in solution or suspension, and (2) fr. the production of material by diffusion or filtration through cells without the active intervention of the cells.] **secretory**[a] = pert. to secretion (1, 2). **secrete**[v] (2). — Ger. (1) *Absonderungsstoff, Sekret,* (2) *Absonderung, Sekretion.*

sect = a group or party of persons who adhere to certain opinions or practices or both, or follow a certain leader. [In religion, applied to those holding to a common creed or cult, or following a certain leader.]

section = 1. (*anat.*) a thin slice cut, usually transversely, from the brain or cord; 2. the cutting or destruction of a nerve, muscle, etc. at some point. — Ger. (1) *Schnitt,* (2) *Sezierung.*

section/golden, see **golden section.**

sectional sensitivity = a value of sensitivity which is measured by "equating and differentiating two supraliminal sense distances" or sections cut from the whole sense continuum (Titchener).

secular = 1. (*soc.*) characterizing cultural change which takes place continuously and always in one direction; 2. (*pop.*) pert. to things, persons, or activities which are not religious. [Distg. (1) fr. **cyclical change**, in which culture is regarded as proceeding in cycles. In science, the progress has been *secular*, i.e. toward the accumulation and retention of the same type of culture. In government, changes have been *cyclical*.] — Ger. (1) *säcular,* (2) *weltlich.*

security = (*indiv. psychol.*) a state in which conquest is guaranteed without struggle.

seed = 1. (*bot.*) a fertilized ovule with an embryo formed within it; 2. (*zool.*) the male fertilizing element; 3. (*pop.*) syn. for offspring. — Fr. *semence*; Ger. *Same.*

segment/behavior, see **behavior segment.**

segmental reflex = a reflex mediated by a single region of the cord. [Strictly, the term is incorrect, since more than one cord segment may be involved. **regional reflex** prefd.]

segmental static reaction = a static reflex which involves one region of the body on both sides, e.g. both hind limbs, both front limbs, trunk, or neck. [**regional static reaction** prefd.]

segmental theory of the nervous system = the doctrine that each segment of the nervous system, in segmented animals, regulates and controls primarily (or exclusively) the activities of the corresponding segment of the body.

segmentation = 1. progressive division of the original germ cell into many cells; 2. the division (usually in embryonic stages) of the body of higher animals into a series of segments or **metameres. segmented**[a] (2).

segregation = 1. the reappearance, in the second or a subsequent filial generation, of characters which were not evident in the first filial generation (i.e. recessive characters) but which were evident in one of the parents; 2. syn. for **isolation**; 3. (*Gestalt*) a product of dynamic self-distribution, which results in the phenomenal appearance of certain wholes detached from their surroundings without recourse to previous knowledge (Köhler).

segregation/law of = the principle that characters in which parents differ come to be segregated out in the second generation of their progeny in a definite numerical ratio. [Where only one character difference is involved, this ratio is typically three of the dominant to one of the recessive trait.] — Fr. *l. de ségrégation.*

segregation/psychical, see **psychical segregation.**

seizure = a sudden onset or recurrence of a disorder; e.g. a convulsive seizure in epilepsy. — Fr. *crise.*

sejunction = an interruption of the continuity of associative processes, which leads to the breaking up of the unitary personality of an individual (Wernicke).

selected group = a group of individuals among whom there is more than random similarity in respect to the particular characteristic or characteristics in question. [**selected groups** sometimes occur by accident and are sometimes assembled deliberately. A selected group may be representative of a larger selected group of the same sort, but not of a **random group.** A given group of individuals may be at once **selected** as regards one characteristic and **random** as regards another. Syn. **selected sample, biased sample.** Contr. w. **random group.**] — Fr. *groupe sélectionné.*

selection = the picking out or emergence of a character, an object, or a phenomenon, from a group of alternatives in accordance with some standard or principle. [Syn. **choice,** which implies voluntary activity; **selection** includes also the emergence of one member of the group in other ways. Cf. **natural selection.**] **select**[v]; **selective**[a]. — Fr. *choix, sélection*; Ger. *Auslese, Wahl.*

selection/method of = a procedure used in certain experiments, in which the observer picks out from a series that object, figure, etc., which he judges as equal to a previously presented standard object, etc.

selection/natural, see **natural selection.**

selection/social, see **social selection.**

selection/vocational = the process of choosing from a group of applicants for a vocation those most likely to succeed in that vocation. [Distg. fr. **guidance/vocational,** which aims to assist the individual in choosing from among many possible vocations.] — Fr. *sélection professionnelle.*

selectionist = one who holds the doctrine of natural selection, as an explanation of the process of organic evolution.

selective action = an action which is multiply determined, and not singly as in impulsive action. [Cf. **impulsive action.**]

selective agent (or **agency**) = any factor or combination of factors in the environment, through whose operation the process of natural selection is brought about.

selective response (or **reaction**), see **discrimination response.**

selective synthesis = the connection or association between successive thoughts in a train. [Cf. **selective thinking.**]

selective thinking = the succession of thoughts in a train, regarded as determined, each in turn, through a process of selective association, or synthesis. — Fr. *pensée sélective.*

selective value = the relative importance of any given factor or combination of factors in determining the progress or rate of change in the evolution of organs, or of species, through natural selection. — Fr. *valeur sélective.*

selenium cell = a device used to detect changes in the quantity of light, by means of the chemical element selenium, whose electrical resistance changes with the amount of light falling upon it.

selenium dog = a device used by J. H. Hammond and B. F. Miessner to illustrate the role of stimuli in determining the direction of responses; it consists of a pair of selenium cells, representing eyes, placed on the front end of a wheeled contrivance, representing an artificial dog; the cells are separated by an opaque, projecting partition like a nose, which cuts off the light from one side or the other; the cells operate the wheels in such fashion that the dog follows a moving light at night in whatever direction the light is moved.

self = an individual regarded as conscious of his own continuing identity and of his relation to the environment. [Syn. **ego,** used in contr. w. **alter** (other being) or **non-ego** (environment). Hist. divided into **rational self** and **empirical self.** Cf. **mind** (impersonal).] **self**[a]. — Fr. *le soi*; Ger. *Selbst.*

self-abasement = social behavior accompanied by a feeling of inferiority and characterized by humility and by extreme submission to the will or dictates of others. — Fr. *abaissement de soi-même*; Ger. *Selbsterniedrigung.*

self-absorption = an extreme manifestation by an individual of abstraction from external stimuli and outer events. — Fr. *absorption.*

self-accusation = false or exaggerated and morbid self-incrimination. [Common in depression and occasionally in hysteria.] — Fr. *auto-accusation*; Ger. *Selbstanklange.*

self-activity = changes within the conscious individual which are determined by himself, for the most part, without other conditioning factors. — Fr. *activité propre*; Ger. *Selbsttätigkeit.*

self-assertion = a tendency to emphasize one's own importance in the presence of other individuals or in dealing with others. [Used also (*pop.*) to designate a characteristic endeavor on the part of an individual to avoid submitting to another. In animals the tendency appears in the form of **self-display.** Cf. **ascendence.**] — Fr. *affirmation de soi*; Ger. *Selbstbehauptung.*

self-consciousness = 1. awareness of one's own existence and activities, usually in relation to other individuals or objects; 2. (*pop.*) embarrassment. **self-conscious**[a]. — Fr. *conscience de soi*; Ger. *Selbstbewusstsein.*

self-consistency = the character of a theory, etc., such that the various phases, items, etc., of the situation which it describes are all mutually compatible. [Cf. **consistency.** Contr. w. **self-contradictory**[a].] **self-consistent**[a]. — Fr. *cohérence*; Ger. *Widerspruchsfreiheit.*

self-control = 1. the ability of an individual to repress emotional expression and to guide his own behavior appropriately in social situations; 2. the exercise of this ability. **self-controlled**[a]. — Fr. *empire sur (maîtrise de) soi-même*; Ger. *Selbstbeherrschung.*

self-deception = the fact of drawing a false conclusion, owing to some bias or strong motivation. [Syn. **rationalization,** a broader term. Cf. **deception.**] **self-deceived**[a]. — Fr. *autoduperie*; Ger. *Selbstbetrug.*

self-denial = the attitude of refusing to satisfy one's own wants, desires, and ambitions. — Ger. *Selbstverleugnung.*

self-determination = the determination or guidance by an individual of his own conduct and behavior through inner or personal initiative, as distg. fr. determination by social norms or by the general environment. [The doctrine of self-determination is closely related to that of **free-will.** Contr. w. **cultural determinism** = the theory that the culture or pattern of society molds the behavior of the individual and prescribes the limits and often the character of his actions.] — Fr. *détermination par soi-même*; Ger. *Selbstbestimmung.*

self-display, self-exhibition = the tendency on the part of certain individuals to make unduly conspicuous in social intercourse their own personal, physical, intellectual, or moral excellences. [The term **self-exhibition,** used in the older literature, is liable to confusion with **exhibitionism,** an abnormal tendency to expose the genitals; **self-display** is prefd. Contr. w. **shyness.**] — Fr. *parade, étalage de soi*; Ger. *Prahlerei, Prunken.*

self-evident = characterizing certain fundamental truths which are held to be indisputable, and to be worthy of acceptance as soon as they are stated, without other evidence or proof. **self-evidence**[n]. — Fr. *évident par soi-même*; Ger. *selbstverständlich.*

self-expression = such acts of the human organism as serve to reveal and (often) to develop the forms of behavior which are most characteristic of the individual in question; they employ his natural capacities, distinguish him from others, and involve a large portion or the whole of his organized personality rather than a limited segment. [Used esp. in social psychology, in the study of social intercourse.] — Fr. *expression de sa personnalité.*

selfishness = an exaggerated regard for one's own advantage, accompanied by a disregard for the welfare or happiness of others. [Syn. **egoism,** a slightly broader term; contr. w. **unselfishness, altruism.**] **selfish**[a]. — Fr. *egoïsme*; Ger. *Selbstsucht.*

self-knowledge = a loose term denoting an individual's ability to appraise his own mental qualities and deficiencies. [Probably based on the Socratic maxim, γνῶθι σαυτόν.] — Fr. *connaissance de soi*; Ger. *Selbsterkenntnis.*

self-love = the emotional element in the attitude of **egotism.** — Fr. *amour de soi*; Ger. *Eigenliebe.*

self-observation = 1. a translation of the German term *Selbstbeobachtung,* which usually has either of the two meanings of **introspection;** 2. the study of one's consciousness and behavior by both subjective and objective methods; 3. the objective study of one's own behavior. [The term lays less emphasis upon memory and other internal (central) data than the syn. **introspection,** and is less open to misunderstanding. Syn. **self-study.**] — Fr. *observation de soi.*

self-preservation = any type of behavior which tends to prolong the life of an organism, particularly by warding off some acute peril. [Used (loosely) in phrases such as **instinct of, tendency** to, **attitude** of **self-preservation.**] — Fr. *conservation personnelle*; Ger. *Selbsterhaltung*.

self-psychology = that system of psychology which holds the self to be the point of reference, given in introspection, to which every psychological phenomenon must be referred. [Founded by Calkins. Similar to **personalistic psychology,** but with an introspective rather than a biological emphasis.]

self-punishment mechanism = (*psychoan.*) a psychic process which gives rise to moral and ethical overseverity of the superego in its conflict with the primitive impulses of the id and results in neurotic symptoms. — Fr. *mécanisme du punition de soi-même*.

self-rating = the attempt by an individual to evaluate his own personality or any class of characteristics, in comparison with the personality or characteristics of other members of a given social group. [Cf. **rating.**] — Fr. *appréciations (estimations) personnelles*.

semantic aphasia, see **aphasia.**

semantics[sing] = the systematic investigation of the history and evolution of the meanings of words. [Cf. **semeiology** (2).]

semblance = the characteristic of an idea, mental image, response (simple or complex), or emotional expression, such that it appears to indicate a certain object, movement, or emotional disposition, whereas it has actually some other reference. [The term covers a wide field, e.g. conscious self-deception, undetected illusion, mimicry and make-believe, artificial emotion.] — Ger. *Schein*.

semeiology, semeiotics, semiology, semiotics = 1. the scientific investigation of sign language; 2. the systematic investigation of the symptoms or signs of specific diseases. **semeiotic**[a].

semen = the spermatozoa and liquid products of the testes, plus the secretions of the excretory ducts and associated glands, which are discharged as a viscid, homogeneous mass in orgasm. — Ger. *Same*.

semicircular canals, semicirculars = three bony canals which emerge and terminate at the posterior end of the vestibule of the internal ear of higher vertebrates, and serve as receptors for the static sense. [They lie at right angles to one another in three planes which do not correspond to the conventional reference planes of the body. They are termed the **superior** (anterior), **posterior** (vertical), and **horizontal** (lateral) canals. Each presents an expanded portion called an **ampulla,** just after it leaves the vestibule. Each canal consists of an outer, bony structure, called the **osseous canal,** and an inner structure called the **membranous canal.** The superior and posterior canals fuse in a common crus before leaving the vestibule. Cf. **labyrinthine sense, nystagmus, dizziness.**] — Fr. *canaux semi-circulaires osseux*; Ger. *Bogengänge*.

semicircular ducts = membranous tubes contained within the semicircular canals. [They are three in number: the **superior** (anterior); the **posterior** (vertical), and the **horizontal** (lateral) semicircular ducts, corresponding to the bony canals of like designation. Each duct presents a dilation at one end, called the **ampulla.**] — Fr. *canaux semi-circulaires membraneux*.

semiconscious, half conscious = a loose term applied either to an extremely low degree of attention or to subconscious or subliminal experiences. — Ger. *halbbewusst*.

semi-interquartile range = one-half the difference between the 75th and the 25th percentiles (or 3rd and 1st quartiles). [Syn. **quartile deviation,** or **Q.** Cf. **quartile.**]

semitone = a half step on a musical scale. [The diatonic semitone has the ratio 15:16; the chromatic semitone has the ratio 24:25, and the tempered semitone the ratio $1:2^{1/12}$. Cf. **interval.** See Table VII.] — Ger. *Halbton*.

senescence = 1. the period of old age during which mental decay sets in; 2. the degenerative changes which take place in this period. **senescent**[a]. — Ger. *Greisenalter*.

senile dementia = dementia which results from a specific shrinking of the brain in advancing age, with marked memory defect and narrowing of outlook.

senilism = presence of senile signs with or without actual old age.

senility = mental and physiological impairment incident to old age. [Cf. **senescence.**] **senile**[a] (last syll. **-il** or **-ile**). — Ger. *Greisenhaftigkeit*.

senium praecox, see **senilism.**

sensa[pl], see **sensum.**

sensal = 1. pert. to sense or sensation; i.e. sensory; 2. pert. to the meaning of a word as distg. fr. its sound or visual form. [Rarely used.]

sensation = 1. (*psychol.*) an experience aroused from outside the nervous system, which is not further analyzable by introspection; i.e. an element of consciousness; 2. (*physiol.*) an afferent neural process which commences in a receptor and extends to the cerebrum; 3. (*psychophysiol.*) a conscious sensory process which is correlated with a physiological process; 4. (*psychophys.*) any one of the total number of discriminable experiences which may exist within a given modality as determined by the formula $(TR - RL)/DL$, in which TR denotes the upper limen, RL the lower limen, and DL the difference limen; 5. (*epistemol.*) the ultimate item of awareness or knowledge (James); 6. (*logic*) a systematic and classificatory term, the sum of the observable attributes or dimensions of experience (Titchener, Bentley); 7. (*general*) the process of sensing or sense-perceiving, abstractly considered; distg. fr. **perception, thought, affection,** etc. **sensational**[a], **sensory**[a] (more properly = pert. to sense). — Ger. *Empfindung*.

sensation increments = added degrees of intensive change in a given sensory quantum in connection with a psychophysical procedure (Fechner, Meinong, *et al.*). — Ger. *Empfindungszuwüchse*.

sensation level/auditory = the number of decibels (db) (expressed in units of energy), above a chosen reference level, usually the threshold of the sound in question. [If two sounds S_1 and S_2 have loudness L_1 and L_2 and S_2 is the louder, the sensation level of S_2 is N decibels above that of S_1 when $N = 10 \log_{10} L_2/L_1$. This is the **relative sensation level.** If S_1 is chosen at the threshold, N expresses the **absolute sensation level** of S_2.] — Fr. *niveau de sensation auditive*.

sensation unit/auditory = a logarithmic unit of loudness, corresponding to the physical intensity unit, the **decibel.** [It has been supposed to be a just perceptible (or just noticeable) difference of loudness, but is so only under certain limited conditions. Abbrev. **SU.**]

sensation(al)ism = 1. (*hist.*) that form of empirical psychology which asserts that all mental contents are originally given as sensations, that all the so-called higher faculties are developments from sensation, and that all ideas are produced by composition of sense-data; 2. the view that sensations are the ultimate elements in the psychological analysis of cognitions. [The theory (1) received most complete statement in the work of Condillac (1758) after which a reaction favored emphasis on the power of the mind to do more than merely compound data. In the latter form of the doctrine (2) the elements are not *ideas of sensation*, but *psychophysical events* or processes. Cf. **associationism, rationalism.**] **sensationistic**[a], **sensation(al)ist**[np].

sense = 1. the sphere of sensation as distg. fr. **ideational** and **affective** experiences; 2. meaning; 3. (*pop.*) good judgment. **sensory**[a] (1), **sensuous**[a] (1), **sense**[a] (2), **sensible**[a] (3). — Ger. (2) *Sinn.*

sense/a = a specific class of experiences, dependent upon a special type of receptor, or upon a specific manner of application of stimuli. [Syn. **modality, a mode.** The classification of the **senses** depends on empirical evidence, and various schemes have been proposed; the two most widely adopted are (*a*) into external and internal, and (*b*) into external, systemic, and motor.] **sense**[v]. — Ger. *Sinnesgebiet.*

sense-datum = 1. a specific sensation; 2. a discriminable detail or group of related details in the organism or in the external world, capable of being experienced through sense, but considered in abstraction from the process of sensing. **sense data**[pl].

sense discrimination, see **sensory discrimination.**

sense-distance = the interval which separates two given sensations as judged or perceived by the observer. — Fr. *intervalle sensible.*

sense-feeling = a sensory pattern or complex group of sensations, usually organic or kinesthetic, highly colored with feelings of pleasantness or unpleasantness. [E.g. hunger, nausea, headache, etc.] — Ger. *sinnliches Gefühl.*

sense (or **sensory**) **illusion** = a mistaken perception due primarily to some characteristic of the sensory mechanism, or to conditions that are inherent in the objective relations presented. [E.g. the Müller-Lyer illusion.]

sense impression = 1. a sensation; 2. a sense datum. [This term is used to denote the action of the *sensorium*, by those who wish to avoid the implication of *consciousness*.]

sense intuition = (*hist.*) the final synthesis of sensory data in the act of perception, which results in the apprehension of external objects. [Cf. **intuition** (3).]

sense (or **sensory**) **limen,** see **sense threshold.**

sense/motor, see **motor sense.**

sense organ = an organ consisting in the ending of an afferent nerve, or in a specialized cell or cells associated with the ending of such nerve, which is differentially affected by some specific type of stimulus. [The term is often considered to include **accessory apparatus,** e.g. convergence mechanism of eye. Syn. **receptor,** but **sense organ** is sometimes used more narrowly, to include only mechanisms which arouse activities that are correlated with sensory experience.] — Ger. *Sinnesorgan.*

sense perception = 1. the knowing of facts directly from the stimuli received by the senses; 2. the process by which this knowledge is obtained; 3. the power or function of gaining such knowledge.

sense process, sensory process = the psychophysical operation involved in **sensation.**

sense quality = 1. the characteristic of a particular sensation, or of a particular sense datum, which persists through all quantitative changes; 2. a specific item of sensory experience.

sense/systemic, see **systemic sense.**

sense threshold, sensory threshold = (*psychophys.*) that value of the comparison stimulus which is judged different from the standard stimulus with a probability arbitrarily chosen (usually 0.5 in psychophysical experimentation) and statistically determined from a set of observations. [Syn. **sense limen, sensory limen.**] — Fr. *seuil sensoriel;* Ger. *Unterschiedsschwelle.*

sensed differences = differences of sensation which are actually noticed or observed. [Titchener distinguishes **sensed differences** from **sensation differences** (i.e. differences in sensation) in that the latter may be in different minds or in the same mind but separated in consciousness (i.e. in experiences) by a long period of time.] — Fr. *différences sensibles.*

sensibile = any object, or any part or aspect of an object, which may be apprehended directly through sensory receptors. **sensibilia**[pl].

sensibility = 1. the capacity of an organism to receive stimulation; 2. sensory capacity measured in terms of the attributes of quality, intensity, extensity, and duration; esp. capacity to experience certain distinct groups of sensations (e.g. protopathic sensibility, etc.); 3. marked susceptibility for affective and emotional experiences; 4. (*pop.*) possession of good judgment or common sense. [Syn. (1) **receptivity.** Distg. fr. **sensitivity,** which usually has a narrower meaning.] **sensible**[a]. — Ger. (1) *Empfindungsvermögen,* (2) *Empfindlichkeit,* (3) *Empfänglichkeit,* (4) *Vernünftigkeit.*

sensibility/common, see **common sensibility.**

sensibility/deep, /epicritic, /protopathic, see **deep sensibility,** etc.

sensibilometer = a form of touch-key, in which the application of pressure makes the circuit. [Distg. fr. the usual touch-key, in which the pressure breaks the circuit.]

sensible, see **sensibility.**

sensible discrimination, see **sensory discrimination.**

sensitive[a], see **sensitiveness, sensitivity.** — Ger. *empfindlich, empfindend.*

sensitive[np] = (*psych. res.*) a person who is subject to sensory hallucinations, mental impressions, or motor automatisms, which are assumed to be the means for the acquisition of supernormal knowledge. [Syn. **psychic**[np], **seer.** Cf. **medium** (2).] — Fr. *sensitif.*

sensitive zones = certain regions of the (human) body which are markedly susceptible to cutaneous stimulation. [Applied particularly to the development of cutaneous sensitivity in the child.]

sensitiveness = a psychophysical disposition

marked by a low threshold for various stimuli or situations, including those which give sensations, pleasure, or unpleasantness, or which elicit certain emotions. [Distg. fr. **sensitivity** = capacity to respond to sensory stimuli; and fr. **irritability** = 1. capacity to respond to sensory or motor stimuli; 2. a tendency to respond with anger reactions when the stimulus is not particularly provocative.] **sensitive**[a]. — Fr. *sensibilité*; Ger. *Empfindlichkeit.*

sensitivity = 1. susceptibility of an organism to stimulation; 2. capacity to be affected by stimuli of relatively slight intensity and to receive sensations therefrom or respond thereto; 3. (*phys.*) the ratio of the change in a measuring instrument to the change in the phenomena which it measures; 4. (*pop.*) marked susceptibility to feel aggrieved. [Distg. fr. **sensibility,** which usually denotes a general capacity, whereas **sensitivity** refers to a specific state. **sensitivity** is best used in quantitative and technical work (1, 2, 3); rather than syns. (1) **receptivity;** (1, 2) **irritability** (which carries no implication as to sensation). Syn. (4) **affectivity** (rather than **sensitiveness**) prefd.] **sensitive**[a]. — Fr. *sensibilité*; Ger. *Empfindlichkeit.*

sensitivity/visceral = susceptibility of the internal organs to stimulation. [Parts of the alimentary canal are sensitive to pressure and pain, the esophagus and stomach to variations in temperature.] — Fr. *sensibilité viscérale.*

sensitization = 1. the process by which a receptor becomes excitable to a definite stimulus; 2. a condition of increased sensitivity, irritability, or responsiveness. [E.g. visual receptors are sensitized in dark adaptation and the brightness limen is thereby reduced.] **sensitize**[v]. — Fr. *sensibilisation.*

sensitization period = the interval of time required for an end-organ to become sensitive to a given stimulus.

sensorial reaction, see **sensory reaction.**

sensorimotor[a] = pert. to neural activity in which both the afferent and efferent segments of the neural arc are involved, or pert. to the structure concerned in such activity.

sensorimotor activity = responses which follow directly upon sensory stimulation. [Contr. w. **ideomotor activity,** which follows upon thought processes.]

sensorimotor arc = the path or paths which function in the conduction of neural impulses from receptor to effector. [A more comprehensive term than **reflex arc;** it includes paths at all levels of organization. Syn. **neural arc, nervous arc.**]

sensorium = 1. the gray matter of the cerebral cortex, in so far as it is concerned with the reception of nerve impulses from the receptors, or sense organs; 2. the entire sensory mechanism of the organism. [Contr. w. **motorium.**]

sensory = 1. pert. to the activity of the receptors and afferent nerve mechanism; 2. pert. to a sense; 3. pert. to sensation; 4. pert. to a directly observable or palpable experience. [Preferably limited to (1) and (4). Contr. (1) w. **motor.**] — Ger. *sinnlich, Sinnes-.*

sensory acuity = 1. the degree to which an individual may distinguish stimuli of small quality, intensity, or duration; 2. the degree to which an individual can distinguish between stimuli which differ in intensity, extent, position, temporal onset, or quality, as measured by the stimulus or the differential limen; 3. the degree to which details in a sensory pattern may be distinguished or resolved.

sensory amusia, aphasia, see **amusia, aphasia.**

sensory areas = those regions of the cerebral cortex in which the afferent paths from the sense-organs terminate, and which are therefore regarded as the specific centers of the several senses. — Fr. *aires sensorielles.*

sensory circle, see **tactile circle.**

sensory discrimination = the ability to distinguish between stimuli which differ either quantitatively or qualitatively, and the degree in which small differences can be distinguished. [Syn. **sensible** (or **sense**) **discrimination,** both of which are ambig.]

sensory habit = a learned discrimination between stimuli which takes the form of a differential response to one only, or one type, the motor act itself being often already in the repertory of the subject. [Syn. **discrimination habit;** contr. w. **motor habit.**]

sensory nerve = any nerve which conducts impulses from a receptor or peripheral terminal to the cord or central nervous system. [Syn. **afferent nerve.** Contr. w. **motor (efferent) nerve.**]

sensory organization = (*Gestalt*) that organization in which the stimulus pattern on the sense surface supplies the forces to start and maintain the nervous excitations, and which therefore depends upon the properties of the stimulus pattern.

sensory process = 1. syn. for **sensation;** 2. a neural process externally aroused; 3. the result of the action of a receptor, or sensory end-organ.

sensory reaction (or **response**) = a response in which the subject's attention during the foreperiod is directed to the stimulus rather than to the response. [Syn. **sensory reaction, sensorial reaction** (or **response**). Distg. fr. **motor** and **natural response** (or **reaction**). Used esp. in reaction time experiments. Cf. **compound reaction.**]

sensory reaction (or **response**) **type,** see **reaction type.**

sensory stimuli = stimuli which produce responses directly without the mediation of aroused ideas.

sensory system = the afferent nervous system with its appended organs of sense.

sensual = characterizing exaggerated preference for and response to organic stimuli, esp. those of food and sex. [Distg. fr. **sensuous,** which characterizes overindulgence in pleasurable stimuli of any sort; and fr. **sensory** and **sensational** = pert. to sensation in general.] — Fr. *sensuel*; Ger. *sinnlich.*

sensual pleasure = pleasure, or affective experiences of a pleasant tone, due directly to sensory stimuli. [Distg. fr. **ideational** (or **ideal**) **pleasure** = due to ideas or thoughts and only indirectly to sensory stimuli.] — Fr. *plaisir sensoriel*; Ger. *sinnliche Lust.*

sensum = any sensory datum. **sensa**[pl].

sensuous = 1. pert. to or markedly displaying the sensory aspects of experience, e.g. sensuous poetry; 2. liable to be affected emotionally by the sensory aspects of experience. [Distg. fr. **sensual,** which pertains, rather, to certain organic desires, as for food or sex; and fr.

voluptuous, which implies a luxurious indulgence in sensuous or sensual pleasures.] **sensuousness**[n]. — Fr. *sensible.*

sentience = 1. the property of the nervous system (or its earlier prototype) to receive stimuli; 2. the lowest grade of consciousness; 3. syn. for **sensibility** (1). **sentient**[a]. — Fr. *excitabilité.*

sentiendum = any elementary or analytically unresolvable qualitative feature of perceptible objects, considered exclusively as something observable, i.e. without reference to the sensory process of observing (Dunlap). **sentienda**[pl].

sentiment = 1. an emotional disposition which has reference to an object, person, or abstract idea, and lacks the characteristic of a true emotion; 2. an acquired disposition to certain types of emotional experience and action, in relation to some one object or to any object of some one kind (Shand); 3. an experience made up chiefly of ideas and systemic sensations. [**sentimental**[a] is used only with **sentimentality.**]

sentiment/esthetic = emotional expression resulting from esthetic appreciation.

sentimentality = overindulgence in sentiment, esp. in emotional display connected with love or pity. [Rarely used as a technical term.] **sentimental**[a], **sentimentalist**[np], **sentimentalize**[v].

septum = (*biol.*) a partition or wall. — Ger. *Scheidewand.*

septum lucidum = a thin double-walled partition below the callosum, which separates the anterior parts of the two lateral ventricles. [The cleft between the two walls (called **cavum septi pellucidi**) is sometimes designated the 5th ventricle, but has no relation to the ventricles proper.]

septum transversum = the ridge in the wall of the ampullae of the semicircular canals, which contains the nerve endings.

sequela = any morbid condition which results from an attack of disease. [Commonly used in plural, **sequelae.**]

sequence = 1. the occurrence or presentation of one event or phenomenon immediately after another in point of time; 2. a temporal series of events or phenomena; 3. (*math.*) a succession of quantities or algebraic elements, each term of which is derived from the one just preceding it by the same operation as that by which all the others are derived. **sequential**[a]. — Fr. (1, 2, 3) *suite,* (1) *ordre,* (2) *série*; Ger. (1) *folgen*[v], *nachfolgen*[v], (2) *zeitliche Reihe,* (3) *Reihe, Folge.*

serial, see **series.**

serial behavior = an integrated sequence of responses, as in maze running, typewriting, or other acts of skill. — Fr. *comportement en serie.*

serial discrimeter, see **psychergograph.**

serial method = in experimental research, the method of presenting stimuli successively, as distg. fr. simultaneous presentation, e.g. as in learning nonsense syllables.

serial reaction, see **continuous discrimination response.**

series = 1. a group of objects, phenomena, events, terms, etc. which are given (or admit of arrangement) in a definite array or succession; 2. (*math.*) a succession of terms deducible from a single principle, or a succession of items which embody some common characteristic. [(1) applies either to the successive **presentation** of objects, etc. regardless of their relations, or to the **arrangement** of data in some given respect. **series** (2) are classed as **continuous** (or **quantitative**), which vary by infinitely fine gradations, and **discontinuous** (or **discrete**), in which the items differ qualitatively or by discrete quantitative amounts.] **series**[pl], **serial**[a]. — Ger. *Reihe.*

sessile = characterizing organisms which are fixed in location, i.e. which lack active or adequate locomotor organs. [Applied to plants and certain animals and contr. w. **motile** = capable of locomotion, applied to most animals.]

set = 1. a temporary condition of the organism which facilitates a certain specific type of activity; 2. a group or series. [Syn. (1) **adjustment, Einstellung, determining tendency, preparation, disposition.**] — Fr. *ajustement, prédisposition.*

set/culture, see **culture set.**

set/mental = a condition of readiness for some specific type of mental performance. — Ger. *Einstellung.*

set/neural = a (temporary) state of subexcitation of a reflex path; such a path offers a lowered resistance to nerve impulses which can reach it, and appears to *attract* such impulses. [This temporary state is also called **Bahnung** (S. Exner), and the corresponding permanent state is called **canalization.** A permanently canalized path is a **neurogram** or **engram.**] — Fr. *prédisposition nerveuse.*

set/organic = the disposal of any given bodily organ into a definite and relatively permanent form. — Fr. *prédisposition organique.*

setting = the arrangement of the environment of a given object, or the disposal of the elements accompanying a given experience, in relation to the object or experience in question. — Fr. *mise en place.*

set-up = a configuration of instruments or apparatus as arranged and adjusted for the investigation of a given experimental problem.

seventh (*mus.*), see **interval.**

sex = 1. a fundamental distinction of the organisms within a given species into those which produce ova or egg-cells (female) and those which produce sperm cells (male); 2. (*psychoan.*) any form of organ pleasure or gratification, which may or may not enter into the service of reproduction. **sex**[a] = pert. to sex or to a sex; **sexual**[a] = pert. to the generative functions. — Ger. *Geschlecht.*

sex character = any one of the structural, physiological, or mental characters which differentiate the two sexes. [They include (1) **primary,** which are directly concerned with the reproductive functions, and (2) **secondary,** which differentiate individuals of the two sexes but apparently play no direct role in the functions of reproduction.]

sex chromosomes, see **chromosomes X and Y.**

sex differences = (*psychol.*) any significant deviations in mental traits which characterize members of the two sexes generally. [A term used in mental testing, in connection with individual, age, racial differences, etc. Cf. **group differences.**] — Fr. *différences entre les sexes*; Ger. *Geschlechtsunterschiede.*

sex feeling = any distinctive feeling, emotion, or sentiment experienced by members of one sex toward members or a member of the other, attributable to their difference in sex. [Cf. **sex sensation.**]—Fr. *sentiment sexuel*; Ger. *Geschlechtsgefühl*.

sex intergrade, see **intersex.**

sex (or **sexual**) **sensations** = a species or group of organic or systemic sensations which are initiated through receptors that lie in or about the reproductive organs and in other **erogenous zones** and which constitute the sensory phase of the reproductive act or the associated stimulation of the genitalia. [Distg. fr. **sex feeling,** a complex or integrated experience.]

sexual infantilism = 1. prepuberal condition of the gonads, the secondary sex characters, and sex behavior in persons or animals past the age of puberty; 2. (*psychoan.*) an arrest at one of the early stages of pregenital development.

sexual instinct, psychosexual instinct = (*psychoan.*) a broad, dynamic, instinctual tendency, whose aim is a striving for the attainment of organ-pleasure, and which only at puberty enters into the service of the function of reproduction. [Contr. w. **ego instinct.**]

sexual intercourse, see **coition.**

sexual latency period = (*psychoan.*) the period in childhood from about the fifth or sixth year to puberty, in which there is a pause of sexual development, and in which this latent development may at a later time assume a high cultural standard through sublimation. [During this period the previous mental experiences and excitations succumb to the infantile amnesia. Cf. **latency period.**]

sexual object = whatever serves to stimulate sexual attraction, whether a person or a thing.

sexual reflex = the events which precede orgasm upon stimulation of the genitalia, together with the orgasm itself. [Mediated by the nervus erigens and 3rd and 4th sacral segments.]

sexual reproduction = that mode of generation or reproduction of new organisms which involves and follows the union of two sex cells. [Syn. **gamogenesis.** Distg. fr. **fission** and **sporulation,** which are unisexual.]

sexual selection = the selection, by organisms belonging to one sex, of certain individuals of the other sex for mating, on the basis of certain structural or functional characters, resulting in the gradual preponderance of these characters in the population.

sexual trauma = the emotional shock, usually of a sexual nature, experienced in early childhood, which in earlier psychoanalytic theory (now abandoned) was regarded as the cause of hysteria.

sexuality = the totality of primary and secondary sex characters, regarded as a major phase of the individual's make-up. [In psychol. generally limited to mental traits; in pathol. often used to denote hypertrophy of the sexual traits.]

sexuality/latent, see **latency period.**

shade = 1. any color darker (i.e. of a lower **brilliance**) than median gray; 2. (*pop.*) the specific brilliance of any gray. [Contr. (1) w. **tint.**] — Fr. *teinte foncée, valeur élevée.*

shadow/acoustic, see **acoustic shadow.**

shadow experiment/Fechner's, see **Fechner's shadow experiment.** — Fr. *expérience des ombres de F.*

shadow-strokes = upstrokes, downstrokes, or lateral strokes which are written with considerable pressure. [Contr. w. **hair-strokes.**]

sham feeding = experimental abstraction of the gustatory from the gastric effects of eating by feeding animals which have oesophageal fistulas, so that the food swallowed does not enter the stomach.

shaman = 1. (*originally*) a person in primitive Siberia who engaged in magic, regarded as able, by trances or other procedures, to communicate with supernatural beings; 2. (*anthrop.*) any primitive person who professes magic or who deals with the supernatural. [Sometimes syn. (2) w. **medicine man.**]

shame = an emotional attitude which arises in connection with real or fancied defects of body or behavior, lack of proper clothing, etc., and is characterized by shrinking or avoidance, and sometimes by some autonomic expression, such as blushing, digestive disorders, etc. [Distg. fr. **modesty** (2) which lacks the emotional element.] — Fr. *honte, pudeur*; Ger. *Scham.*

shamming = an attitude, posture, or activity manifested by a human or subhuman organism, which simulates or resembles the responsive posture or attitude ordinarily due to some quite different stimuli or situations. [Used generically for the trait, often without specification, while the syn. **feigning** is generally accompanied by a specific characterization, e.g. feigning death or lameness.] — Fr. *feinte, faux semblant.*

sharp[a] = 1. characterizing an intense, painful, acid taste, or a pungent smell, or a well-localized intense pain; 2. characterizing a sudden sound of relatively high pitch; 3. applied to a tone of pitch higher than the true interval sequence (contr. w. **flat**); 4. characterizing intense cold; 5. mentally acute. [Not recommended for technical use, except (3).] **sharpness**[n]. — Fr. (1) *piquant*, (2) *aigu*, (3) *dièse*, (4) *vif, perçant*, (5) *éveillé, intelligent*; Ger. (1, 2, 5) *scharf*, (3) *erhöht.*

sharp[n] = 1. (*mus.*) a tone whose pitch is slightly higher than a given standard; 2. a tone which is a semitone higher than some natural tone; 3. the sign (♯) used to indicate a half-step rise in pitch. [(2) contr. w. **flat.**] **sharp**[a]. — Fr. *dièse*; Ger. (1) *erhöhter Ton*, (3) *Kreuz.*

sheath of Schwann, see **neurilemma.** — Fr. *gaine de S.*

shell-shock = a loose term for the transitory or more protracted reactions to actual shell explosions or mere fear or fright. [First considered as structural damage (Mott), later recognized as having a large fear and self-protective component.]

shift/binaural, see **beat/binaural.**

shock = 1. a sudden depression of the nervous system produced by accident, operation, or strong emotion; 2. a condition of lowered excitability in nerve centers following section of their connections with other centers; 3. the direct physical effects of the impact of one mass upon another; 4. (*hist.*) the elementary nerve impulse (G. H. Lewes). — Ger. *Nervenanfall.*

shock/spinal = the (functional) depression of spinal reflex centers after spinal transection.

short-circuit appeal = a method of salesmanship which involves the use of suggestion or the arousal of an instinctive tendency. [Distg. fr. **long-circuit appeal,** which gives reasons or information.]

short-circuit theory = a provisional hypothesis proposed by Wertheimer, according to which phenomenal movement (the phi-phenomenon) is due to a short-circuit (*Kurzschluss*) between the regions of the brain excited by each stimulus, thereby giving rise to a new, structured unity. — Fr. *t. du court-circuit*; Ger. *Kurzschluss-theorie*.

short-circuiting = 1. (*neurol.*) the passage of a nerve impulse through a shorter path upon repetition; 2. (*psychol.*) the gradual simplification of the processes involved in an acquired act of behavior as the latter becomes habitual; it is attributed to the **short-circuiting** (1) of the nerve impulse. — Fr. *mise en court-circuit*.

shrill, see **high.**

shut-in personality = a reclusive and often self-centered personality type, particularly liable to schizophrenic breakdown. — Fr. *personnalité retirée, introvertie*.

shyness = an attitude characterized by discomfort when in the presence of others and by the partial inhibition of the usual social responses. [Syn. **bashfulness, timidity.**] **shy**[a]. — Fr. *réserve, timidité*.

sib = 1. (*anthrop.*) a social group, larger than the family, which reckons descent through either the father or the mother; 2. (*biol.*) syn. for **sibling.**

sibling, sib = one of two or more offspring, either of the same or of different sexes, produced by the same parents.

sibyl, see **oracle** (1).

side-window experiment = an experimental demonstration of **binocular contrast,** in which the individual stands in profile to a window so that the near eye is exposed to bright illumination while the other eye is shielded by the nose; if a piece of white paper be held near the face, the double picture will be seen in two different shades, that of the shielded eye being brighter and more yellow than the other.

sigh = a prolonged, generally audible, inspiration followed by short exhalation. **sigh**[v]. — Fr. *soupir*; Ger. *Seufzer*.

sight = the sense whose receptive organ is the eye and whose proper stimulus is radiant energy of wave-lengths approximately 400 to 760 millimicrons. [Syn. **vision** (more common, but slightly ambiguous). Cf. **sense.**] **see**[v], **visual**[a]. — Fr. *vision*; Ger. *Gesicht, Gesichtssinn, Sehen*.

sight/line of, sighting line, see **visual axis** and **direction/line of.** — Fr. *rayon visuel, ligne de regard*; Ger. *Visierlinie*.

sigma = 1. (*psychophys.*) one thousandth (i.e. 1/1000) of a second; 2. (*statist.*) the **standard deviation.** [(1) is used in reaction-time and tachistoscopic experiments, e.g. 150^{σ}; (2) is a measure of dispersion in a distribution, e.g. $\sigma = 2.5$.]

sign = an object, impression, symbol, response, etc. which is substituted for another object, etc., or which suggests the other. [E.g. the written word *cat* is a **sign** for this animal or for the mental picture of the animal. Cf. **signal, symbol.**] — Ger. *Zeichen*.

sign language, see **gesture language.**

sign manual = 1. an autograph signature; 2. an official or royal signature or monogram affixed to a document written by another person.

signal = a sign which is communicated by one individual or creature to another and may become a sign for him. [Cf. **sign.**]

signal experiment = an experiment, often with animals, in which the subject after repeated motivated trials regularly makes the required response, as between several possible responses, to a specific stimulus or signal. [The experiment usually includes some test or control of the effectiveness of the signal, such as reversal of spatial relations confronting the animal, intensive change in the signal, or variation of the time between signal and response. Cf. the special cases, **choice experiment, discrimination experiment, delayed response experiment.**]

signature = 1. syn. for **local sign;** 2. in music, the symbolic notation at the beginning of the staff indicating the key and the measure.

significance, signification = the meaning or value of phenomena or events. [**significance** usually calls attention to some important meaning or value, while **signification** is more general. Contr. w. **factuality.** In reporting conscious experiences, distinction is made between **description** (Ger. *Beschreibung*) = report of facts, and **appreciation** or **evaluation** (Ger. *Kundgabe*) = report of **signification.**] **signify**[v], **significant**[a] = meaningful.

signify = 1. to be an indication of the existence of something; 2. to mean or to have meaning. **significant**[a] (2). — Ger. *bezeichen*.

similarity = 1. a correspondence in some given respect between two data or among several data; 2. (*beh.*) the characteristic of stimuli, situations, objects, occurrences, etc., such that they bring about identical responses. [Syn. **likeness, resemblance** (= observed similarity). Contr. w. **dissimilarity, unlikeness.**] **similar**[a]. — Fr. *ressemblance*; Ger. *Ähnlichkeit*.

similarity/law of = a principle of mental association, according to which one thought or present experience recalls another thought which resembles it in some respect. [More properly, **law of resemblance.**]

simple = 1. elementary, i.e. without parts or complication; 2. easily understood or performed. [Contr. (1) w. **complex,** (2) w. **subtle** or **difficult.**] **simplicity**[n]. — Ger. *einfach*.

simple eye = an eye which contains only one focusing system. [It is characteristic of vertebrates and certain invertebrates. Contr. w. **compound eye,** which contains more than one focusing system.]

simplex inheritance = inheritance of a given character through a single gamete, i.e. from one parent only. [Contr. w. **duplex inheritance** through both parental gametes.]

simplicity, see **simple.**

simplicity/canon of, see **economy/principle of.**

simulation = 1. the act of feigning on the part of an animal; 2. the voluntary production of factitious lesions resembling those produced by disease, for the purpose of escaping military duties or collecting insurance, and as a manifestation of neurosis, e.g. dermatitis factitia. [Syn. (2) **malingering,** which is more inclusive.] **simulate**[v], **simulative**[a], **simulated**[a]. — Ger. *Verstellung*.

simultaneity = the occurrence of two or more phenomena at the same time. (Pron. **sy-** or **sim-,** accent **-nee-.**) **simultaneous**[a].

simultaneous contrast, see **contrast.**

simultaneous light-induction, see **light-induction/simultaneous.**

sin = conduct which violates the established moral code. [Used only where the moral code is conceived to be the law of a deity or a divine plan of life, the violation being regarded as an offense against God. In certain mental disorders, consciousness of sin (or sinfulness) is a recognized symptom.] — Fr. *péché*; Ger. *Sünde*.

singing = the vocal expression of music, i.e. the act of producing, with the larynx, tones in which a musical scale is an essential part. **song**[n] = the product; **sing**[v].

single stimuli/method of = any psychophysical method in which a report follows the presentation of one stimulus only.

singular = 1. applying or pert. to one individual or instance only; 2. (*pop.*) unusual, strange, remarkable. **singularity**[n]. — Ger. (1) *einzeln*, (2) *sonderbar*.

singularism = the theory that the entire universe may be explained in terms of a single principle. [Contr. w. **pluralism.**]

sinister = the left side. [Contr. w. **dexter, right.**] (Accent **sin-**.) **sinistral**[a]. — Fr. *gauche*; Ger. *links*.

sinistrad writing = writing in which the line of progress is from right to left. [Individual letters are usually formed by movements in harmony with the general direction of writing. Distg. fr. **dextrad writing**, which progresses from left to right.] — Fr. *écriture sénestre*.

sinistral = pert. to or located on the left side of the body. [Contr. w. **dextral.**] (Accent **sin-**.) **sinistrad**[adv] = towards the left. — Ger. *links liegend*.

sinistrality = the preference on the part of certain individuals for using the left hand (or side) rather than the right in motor activity, and the tendency to use the left for guiding and directing bimanual operations. [Syn. **left-handedness** (less general). Contr. w. **dextrality**, and w. **ambidextrality.**] **sinistral**[a], **left-handed**[a]. — Fr. *gaucherie*.

sinus = a cavity, diverticulum, or sac in an organism. — Ger. *Höhle*.

siren = a sound-producing device consisting of a rotating disk with perforations through which blasts of air, steam, etc., are forced from a nozzle. [The pitch of the sound is determined by the number of blasts per second, which is a function of the number of perforations in the disk and the speed of its rotation.]

sitophobia = morbid fear of eating or of food.

situation = 1. the stimulus-pattern which affects an individual at a given moment or during the receptive period; 2. the environment and the organism in that environment at a given moment; 3. the place or locality in which a given object exists. [**situation** (1) is broader than **environment**, including internal as well as external stimuli.] — Ger. (1) *gesamte Reizlage*, (2) *Situation*, (3) *Umgebung*.

situational analysis = an analysis of the forms of behavior characteristically associated with *natural* situations as distg. fr. laboratory or artificially arranged situations.

sixth (*mus.*), see **interval** and Table VII. — Fr. *sixte*.

size-weight illusion = a normal misinterpretation of comparative weights, due to the influence of visual perception of size. [Objects of greater volume are judged lighter (in weight) than smaller objects of the same weight.] — Fr. *illusion de soupèsement*.

skeletal muscle, see **musculature/skeletal.**

skeletal reflex = a reflex response whose path terminates in the striate skeletal muscles. [Distg. fr. **autonomic reflex**, which terminates in the smooth muscles or glands, and whose response is concerned with the autonomic functions.] — Fr. *réflexe squelettique*.

skewness = (*statist.*) the departure, or deviation, of a frequency distribution from the bilaterally symmetrical form. [**skewed distribution** = one wherein there is a bunching of measures on one side of the average and a stretching out of measures on the other. Symmetrical distribution gives **zero skewness. coefficient of skewness** = a figure or ratio which indicates the degree of departure from symmetry.] **skewed**[a]. — Fr. *asymétrie*.

skiascope = an instrument for the objective determination of ocular refraction. [Syn. **retinoscope.**] **skiascopic**[a], **skiascopy**[n] (accent **-as-**).

skill = ease and precision in the performance of acts. **skillful**[a] = using skill; **skilled**[a] = possessing skill. — Fr. *habileté*; Ger. *Geschicklichkeit*.

skin = the external integument of an animal, which serves as a protective investment, a temperature regulator, an excretory structure, and a sensory medium for the body. [Syn. **cutis.** The **skin** consists of two distinct portions: (*a*) the outer epithelial layer = **epidermis**, or **cuticle**; (*b*) the deeper connective tissue stratum = **derma, dermis, true skin**, or **cutis vera.** The upper part of the derma is the **corium** (sometimes syn. with **derma**); the deeper part is the **tela subcutanea.** The cutaneous receptors are located in the lower layers of the epidermis and throughout the rest of the derma.] **skin**[a], **cutaneous**[a], **dermal**[a]. — Fr. *peau*; Ger. *Haut*.

skin erotism = (*psychoan.*) a condition in which the skin is an erogenous zone, and in which pleasure is produced by scratching or rubbing. [Syn. **dermal erotism.**] — Fr. *érotisme de la peau*.

skin reflex, see **superficial reflex. — Fr.** *réflexe de la peau*.

skin sensation, see **dermal sensation.**

skioptic response (or **reaction**) = a response to shadows or changes in shading. [A primitive type of visual response, noted (e.g.) in echinoderms.]

slate-writing, see **psychography** (1).

sleep = a special state of the organism, due to certain as yet undetermined physiological conditions, which is characterized by relative immotility and failure of effective response to external stimuli, and (generally) by absence of observable signs of consciousness. [Contr. w. **waking state**; distg. fr. **hypnosis**, in which there are effective responses to the words and gestures of another individual; fr. **swooning**, which is characterized by general relaxation of the skeletal musculature; and fr. **coma**, which involves a more complete failure of the response mechanism. Cf. **drowsiness, stupor.**] **sleep**[v], **asleep**[a, adv], **sleeping**[a]. — Fr. *sommeil, endormi*[a]; Ger. *Schlaf*.

sleeplessness, see **insomnia.**

sleep-walking, see **somnambulism.**

slip comparison = in experiments involving comparison of members of pairs, presented in succession, a comparison of the second datum of a pair, not with the first, but with some earlier presentation, i.e. with a member of some preceding pair. — Fr. *comparaison décalée.*

slip of speech (or **of the tongue**) = an irrelevant word or words inserted in a spoken sentence, due not to ignorance or mispronunciation but to some confusion of association. [Regarded by psychoanalysts as symptomatic of repressed ideas or complexes, which act as wish-fulfillments, due to strong counter tendencies.] — Fr. *lapsus*; Ger. *Versprechen.*

slow motion = a term used in cinematography to describe a motion picture film which was originally exposed at the rate of 128 frames per second but which is projected at a speed of about 16 frames per second, thereby lengthening the duration of a given motion or action to approximately 8 times the normal. [Applied loosely to any projection of a motion picture film at a slower rate than that of the original exposure, e.g. for studying coordination in acts of skill.] — Fr. *mouvement ralenti*; Ger. *Zeitlupe.*

smell = 1. a quality of **olfactory sensation;** 2. syn. for (the sense of) **olfaction.** — Ger. *Geruch.*

smell compensation = a term applied by Zwaardemaker to obliteration of two odors, each by the other. [Henning and many others have failed to verify this phenomenon.] — Fr. *neutralisation d'odeurs.*

smile = a facial expression chiefly characterized by drawing the corners of the mouth upward and backward, by elevation of the cheeks with or without parting of the lips, and by reduction of the palpebral space with wrinkling of the skin under the eyes; expressive of a variety of sensations, feelings, and emotions. [Distg. fr. **laughter**, which involves greater muscular activity and phonation.] **smile**[v]. — Fr. *sourire*; Ger. *Lächeln.*

smoked drum = a recording device which consists of a cylinder overlaid with glazed paper, the latter being blackened with smoke so as to receive tracings from a stylus, which moves to and fro at right angles to the direction of the drum's rotation. [It is generally used in conjunction with some form of **kymograph.**] — Fr. *cylindre enregistreur (avec feuille noircie).*

smoky, see **empyreumatic.**

smooth curve = (*statist.*) a curve so drawn as to eliminate the minor fluctuations shown by the (raw) data. [The **moving average** is one method of smoothing.] — Fr. *courbe polie*; Ger. *glatte Kurve.*

smooth muscle = the contractile tissues of the body which are innervated by the autonomic nervous system and are responsible for the internal adjustments of the body. [So termed because the individual fibers have a characteristic appearance without striation and hence are termed **smooth;** contr. w. **striate muscle,** in general activated by the central nervous system.] — Ger. *glatter Muskel.*

smoothness = 1. the characteristic of certain complex tactile stimuli, in that they give a continuous and uniform impression; 2. a character of certain sapid substances in that they fail to give any distinctive gustatory quality; 3. a characteristic of certain tonal combinations which fuse or blend evenly. [Contr. w. **roughness** and w. **sharpness.** Cf. **sharp**[a](1).] **smooth**[a]. — Fr. *sensation de lisse*; Ger. *Glätte, Glattheit.*

snake figure, see **Purkinje figures.**

Snellen letters = (*ophth.*) printed letters of a special design, which are arranged on a test-card or test-chart in groups of different sizes, and used for testing the acuteness of vision.

snow-blindness = a temporary abnormality of the color sense, in which all objects are tinged with red. [Caused by long-continued exposure to very bright light, as in Arctic exploration, on glaciers, in telescopic observation of the sun, watching welding operations, etc. Cf. **erythropsia.**] — Fr. *cécité des glaciers*; Ger. *Schneeblindheit.*

sociability = the characteristic of being agreeable and friendly with other individuals; 2. the inclination to seek the company of others. [Syn. (2) **sociality** (1).] **sociable**[a]. — Ger. *Geselligkeit.*

social = pert. to the specific relationship of individuals to other members of the species, or to habits, characteristics, etc. which have been acquired through experience with other individuals. [Distg. fr. **sociable** = characterizing a socially adapted individual.] **sociality**[n].

social adaptation = the adjustment or modification of individual behavior necessary to harmonious interaction with other individuals; esp., conformity to custom and taboos. [Syn. **social accommodation.** Cf. **social adjustment.**] **social adaptability**[n] = ability to make such modifications.

social adjustment = the changes in habitual conduct and behavior which an individual must make in order to fit into the community in which he lives. [The term generally implies a notable divergence, or a conflict which must be overcome. Distg. fr. **social adaptation, which** does not imply conflict.]

social attitudes = those attitudes of an individual which are specifically directed toward other members of the species, or which have been developed by social interaction. [Cf. **attitude/social.**]

social behavior = behavior in which the responses are either directed toward other organisms, usually of the same species, or serve as social stimuli to other individuals. — Fr. *comportement social.*

social censorship, see **censorship** (1). — Fr. *censure sociale.*

social consciousness = the awareness (or capacity in any individual for experience) which concerns other members of the species as distinct from the general environment. [Occasionally used as syn. for **social mind, collective consciousness, group consciousness,** or **consciousness of kind.**]

social contract = (*hist.*) an early theory, advanced to explain the origin of social relations, according to which mankind at first lived in isolated families or as isolated individuals, and upon recognizing the advantages of cooperation, met together and voluntarily agreed to forego certain individual privileges in order to secure the benefits of united action.

social control = 1. the influence, whether direct or indirect, exerted by individuals through the medium of organized society upon the behavior and conduct of other individuals; 2. any form or means of stimulation used by one or more individuals to evoke desired responses from other individuals, or the exercise of such stimulation. [Language, propaganda, government, custom, and fad are means or instruments of **social control,** differing only in degree of organization.]

social decrement = 1. the amount of loss in the average quantity of work done in a group as compared with that accomplished by the component individuals when working alone; 2. the decrease in output of an individual working in a group, as compared with his performance when alone. [Contr. w. **social increment,** which is regarded as the more usual phenomenon. Distg. fr. **social subvalent,** which refers to *quality* of performance.]

social degeneracy = a term loosely used to denote (*a*) the supposed degeneration of a society conceived as a super-individual person; (*b*) the condition of a social group which contains a large number of individual degenerates; (*c*) the condition of a group whose members are characteristically degenerates when measured by the standard of the speaker; (*d*) a social condition in which the circumstances and habits of individuals have become so ill-adapted to healthy living that the members of the group can no longer function together and tend to regress to more primitive institutions and customs.

social disapproval = an unfavorable overt or indirect judgment passed by a significant portion of a given social group upon certain members, based upon their conduct, general behavior, or physical makeup. — Fr. *désapprobation sociale.*

social distance = 1. the degree of prejudice or antipathy which the members of one group exhibit toward the members of another group, usually expressed in terms of the relations to which the members of one group will admit members of the other group; 2. the degree of difference in the development of culture between two social groups.

social dynamics = 1. that branch of sociology which investigates the progressive changes in the constitution of (human) society in the course of time; 2. the historical approach to the study of human attitudes and habits, esp. those which constitute institutions. [Often, though not necessarily, limited to the study of radical and revolutionary epochs and of catastrophic social movements.]

social elimination = selective action, by social means, which results in the destruction or removal from society of individuals who are constitutionally inferior, unadjusted to the prevailing type of social organization, or subject to social disapproval. [Contr. w. **social selection,** the preferment of certain individuals.]

social evolution = the series of progressive changes in the organization of society which take place in the course of time. [Usually syn. w. **social progress,** and contr. w. **social retrogression.**]

social facilitation = the enhancement of a response by contributory social stimuli, such as the sight and sound of other persons engaged in the same activity. [Distg. fr. **rivalry** = an emotional reinforcement of movement, accompanied by a desire to win in competition with others.] — Fr. *frayage social.*

social factor = any component of the forces that act upon the individual and influence his responses, which is attributable to the social relation (i.e. to stimuli coming from other members of the species as distinct from the general environment) and which tends to induce social responses or to modify his behavior, attitudes, or habits. [Cf. **social force.**]

social feeling = (*indiv. psychol.*) the recognition of the needs of others as contr. w. the original and fundamental will to power.

social force = 1. any type of stimulus (or organized group of stimuli) acting upon an individual, which is generated directly by other members of the species as distg. fr. general environment, and which usually tends to induce social responses in the individual; 2. any power, energy, or stimulating value which is supposedly inherent in the group, as distg. fr. the powers, etc. of individuals; 3. any habit formed by social training. [E.g. custom, imitation, suggestion, authority, etc. Cf. **social stimulus.**]

social group = a collection of organisms (usually human beings) which live for the most part in proximity to one another, or respond to one another or to a common stimulus. [**social groups** are classified as **primary** or **face-to-face** (e.g. the family) and **secondary, derivative,** or **co-acting** (e.g. a church, a "radio public").]

social habit = any acquired mode of behavior which involves cooperation with other members of the species, or which has developed through social interaction. [Cf. **custom.**]

social heredity = an inaccurate syn. for **social transmission.**

social increment = 1. the amount of gain in the average quantity of work done by individuals in a group over that accomplished by individuals working alone; 2. the increase in output of an individual working in a group, as compared with his solitary performance. [Contr. w. **social decrement,** which measures the loss. Distg. fr. **social supervalent,** which refers to **quality** of performance.]

social instinct = any inherited type of complex behavior which involves cooperation of the individual with other members of the species. [Cf. **instinct, gregariousness.**]

social intelligence = 1. the effective dealing by an individual with novel situations involving the mutual relations of members of a group; 2. such intelligence as is measured by tests which require an understanding of the mutual relation of individuals. [Cf. **intelligence.**]

social maladjustment = the condition of any individual, in which his characteristic modes of behavior or subjective experiences are such that he fails notably to meet the ordinary needs and relations of life by interaction with the individuals about him. — Fr. *mésadaptation sociale.*

social mind = 1. a shorthand term to denote the average or characteristic intellectual data of a given community. 2. (*hist.*) the conception of an organic system of ideas, which persists apart from the minds of individuals and constitutes the general psychic aspect of a nation or an epoch. [Syn. (1) **collective mind;** cf. **crowd mind, public opinion.**] — Fr. *esprit social.*

social organism = the **social organization** regarded as a type of organization similar or analogous to the biological organism. [Cf. **biological analogy, group fallacy.**]

social organization = 1. the general system of social relations, esp. as regards specialization of functions and cooperative behavior; 2. society in general; 3. a relatively permanent group of persons whose purpose is mutual interstimulation, generally of a pleasant nature, e.g. a fraternity.

social progress = any change in social habits, culture, and institutions, or in social organization, regarded as evidence of improvement, esp. of moral betterment. [Distg. fr. **social evolution,** which denotes change, but not necessarily improvement.]

social psychology = 1. that branch of psychology which investigates the behavior of the individual in so far as his behavior stimulates other individuals, or is itself a reaction to their behavior, and which describes the consciousness of the individual in so far as it is consciousness of social objects and social reactions; 2. the study of the behavior characteristic of individuals in multi-individual situations; 3. the study of personality as it develops in relation to social environment; 4. the study of the distinctive mental phenomena which come into existence among men in consequence of their association; 5. the study of the behavior and consciousness of groups. [Cf. **social mind, social force, collective psychology.**] — Ger. *Sozialpsychologie, Völkerpsychologie.*

social retrogression = the phase of social change which is characterized by deterioration, i.e. by less effective organization. [Contr. w. **social progress.**]

social science = a generic term which covers all sciences dealing with human relations and including sociology, economics, political science, ethnology, history, and other related disciplines.

social selection = selective action by social means, which results in the preferment of certain individuals and gives them greater opportunities in the struggle for existence. [Contr. w. **social elimination** and w. **social suppression.**]

social self = 1. the consciousness of one's self or personality as determined by the attitudes of others toward him; 2. that part of the individual's behavior or personality which has social significance. [(1) frequently referred to as the **looking-glass self.**] — Fr. *le soi social.*

social situation = the totality or pattern of stimuli presented to a given individual at a given time, in so far as these stimuli are concerned with other members of the species.

social statics = that branch of sociology which investigates the social forces as they effect the organization of society at any given time; i.e. the study of social forces in equilibrium. [Cf. **social dynamics.**]

social status = the position or special function of a given individual in a social group, as defined by the attitudes toward him of the other individuals composing the group.

social stimulus = any activity or characteristic of an organism which gives rise to a conscious experience or a response on the part of another organism. [E.g. movement, sound, color, odor emanation, or mere presence. Usually denotes interstimulation among members of a high organic species, esp. man.]

social subvalent [**supervalent**] = loss [gain] in quality of work done by an individual working in a group, as compared with the performance of the same individual working alone. [Frequently used to denote the *average* loss [gain] when solitary performances are compared with those in the group situation. Distg. fr. **social decrement** [**increment**] which refers to decrease [increase] in *amount* of work done.]

social suppression = a drastic form of **social elimination,** in which the individual is ignored, punished, exiled, or put to death.

social theory = any systematic attempt to account for **social organization.**

social transmission = the passing on of language, customs, traditions, inventions, and other data or habits from generation to generation through their general use or prevalence in the community, as distg. fr. transmission by biological inheritance. [Often called **social inheritance,** which is misleading, as it suggests a biological process, which is not present.]

social will = the average or dominating desire and decision of the members of a social group, regarded figuratively as an individual phenomenon. [Syn. **general will.** Cf. **social mind.**] — Fr. *volonté sociale*; Ger. *Gemeinwille, gesellschaftlicher Wille.*

sociality = 1. a characteristic of certain species or individuals, such that they cooperate, individual with individual, in various activities; 2. a supposed instinct or tendency which forms the basis of social organization. [Syn. (1) **sociability,** (2) **gregariousness.**] **social**[a]. — Ger. *Gesellschaftstrieb.*

socialization = 1. (*psychol.*) the process by which individuals acquire socially desirable habits and become able to live as members of a social group; 2. (*econ.*) the control of industries by the community. [Cf. (1) **assimilation** (4).] **socialized**[a], **socialize**[v].

society = 1. a group of individuals of any species who live in mutual intercourse and cooperate in various activities; 2. a group of persons, usually co-acting in behavior, who are associated for a common purpose or because of a common interest; 3. (*pop., fig.*) the mass of individuals, as distg. fr. a single individual; 4. (*soc.*) the practices, traditions, sentiments, and more formal organization of the aims and interests that define the relations of human beings to one another. **social**[a] (applied to individuals); **societal**[a] (applied to the group). — Ger. *Gesellschaft.*

sociology = the branch of science which investigates the phenomena of social relations and the history and principles or laws of social organization. [The objects or data investigated in sociology are principally *groups* or individuals in their relation to group behavior, while in psychology the object of study is the *individual* organism.]

socionomic force = a force which, though not itself social in character, modifies the action of **social forces** and is therefore a factor in determining social organization and progress.

socionomics[sing] = the branch which investigates the relation of social groups to the factors in their environment. **socionomic**[a].

socius = the person, regarded as a social unit, having characteristics in common with his fellows. [Contr. w. **personality,** which represents personal distinctiveness.]

Socratic method = an inductive dialectic procedure, which consists in leading a pupil or disciple to accept or admit the desired conclusion by means of a progressive series of leading questions which he answers in turn. [Devised or popularized by the Greek philosopher Socrates.]

sodomy = sexual intercourse between males by the anus. [Pop. used as syn. for **bestiality.**]

soft palate, see **palate.**

softness = 1. characteristic of complex tactile experiences which occur when the moving member can readily depress the object touched; 2. characterizing an auditory sensation of slight intensity. [Syn. (2) **faintness** (prefd.).] **soft**[a]. — Fr. (1) *mollesse*, (2) *douceur*; Ger. (1) *Weichheit*.

sole reflex, see **plantar reflex.**

solidity = the characteristic of having three dimensions. [In visual space, perception of **solidity** depends upon retinal disparity of double images and upon shadows, perspective, etc.; in tactual space it depends upon the cutaneous and muscular experiences received as a member moves over the object investigated. Contr. w. **surface** and **linearity.**] **solid**[a]. — Ger. *Körperlichkeit*.

solipsism = a world-view of the extreme idealistic type, according to which the universe consists solely of the individual in question and his own experiences. [Cf. **idealism.**] **solipsistic**[a]. (Accent **sol-.**)

solution = 1. the obtaining of a satisfactory answer or explanation of a problem which at the outset presented difficulties, or the answer so obtained; 2. (*math.*) the determination of the specific value or values of the variables of an equation which fulfill the conditions imposed by the equation; 3. (*chem.*) the absorption of a gaseous liquid, or solid substance in a liquid, thus forming a homogeneous mixture. **solve**[v]. — Ger. *Lösung*.

soma = all the cells in an organism except the germ cells. **somatic**[a].

somaplasm, somatoplasm = the protoplasm which constitutes the body, exclusive of the germ cells. [Contr. w. **germ-plasm.**] **somatoplasmic**[a].

somatic = 1. pert. to the body substance in general, as distg. fr. the germ cells; 2. pert. to the framework of the body, as distg. fr. the viscera, or internal organs. — Ger. *körperlich*.

somatic disorders = disorders of the body exclusive of the nervous system.

somatic functions = those functions of sensation and muscular contraction in which the somatic nerves are concerned. [Contr. w. **visceral functions** = the functions controlled by the autonomic nervous system.]

somatic hermaphroditism = the anatomical union, in the genitals, of both male and female characteristics, either well developed or stunted. [Syn. **bisexuality.** Cf. **hermaphroditism.**]

somatic induction = the production of germinal variations through the influence of the soma, or body, on the germ plasm.

somatic nerves = the nerves which supply the exteroceptors and proprioceptors and the striate muscles. [Cf. **exteroceptors, proprioceptors.** Contr. w. **visceral nerves.**]

somatic postures = postures or attitudes of the body and its members, as contr. w. visceral expressions.

somatology = the investigation of the general bodily constitution and physiology of man. [Syn. **physical anthropology.**]

somatoplasm, see **somaplasm.**

somatopsychosis = a type of mental disorder in which the leading symptom is some delusion regarding the constitution or condition of the patient's body. (Accent **so-** and **-ko-.**)

somesthesia, somaesthesia, som(a)esthesis, som(a)esthetic sense = 1. the tactile sense, external and internal; 2. an indefinite sensation due to various faint stimuli of touch, temperature, etc., acting on the surface of the body. [Syn. **somatic sensitivity.** Often used in contr. w. the special senses of sight, hearing, etc.] **som(a)esthetic**[a].

somite = a serial segment of the body, characteristic of such organisms as vertebrates, arthropods, and annelid worms.

Sommer tridimensional movement-analyzer = an instrument by means of which the free movements of the forearm and two fingers are analyzed into vertical, lateral, and sagittal components, these being traced (by recording levers) in a single plane on a smoked drum. [Devised by R. Sommer in 1898, and used chiefly to analyze involuntary responses to various sensory stimuli, e.g. odors.]

somnambulism = a condition (usually regarded as a hysterical symptom), in which the individual may walk about and execute various complex movements for which there is an amnesia upon returning to the normal condition. [Syn. **sleep-walking.**] **somnambulist**[np], **somnambulistic**[a]. — Ger. *Schlafwandeln, Nachtwandeln*.

somnambulism/artificial = (*hist.*) a term formerly applied to certain phases of hypnosis, because hypnotic subjects sometimes manifest behavior resembling that of a sleep-walker.

somniferous[a], see **soporific.**

somnolence = abnormal drowsiness. [Used pop. to denote sleepiness.] **somnolent**[a]. — Ger. *Schlafsucht*.

somnology, see **hypnology.**

sonance = a fusion of successive pitches. [Distg. fr. **timbre,** which involves simultaneous fusion.]

song, see **singing.**

sonometer = an instrument for auditory research, consisting ordinarily of two or three strings, variable in length and tension, stretched over a resonance box. [Cf. **monochord.**]

sophism = a false argument (usually propounded intentionally), so devised that the nature of the fallacy is difficult to detect or demonstrate. [Cf. **sophistry, psittacism, paralogism.**] **sophistic**[a].

sophistry = the intentional use of fallacious or ambiguous arguments. [Cf. **sophism.**] (Accent **soff-.**) **sophist**[np]. — Ger. *Sophisterei*.

soporific[n] = a sleep-inducing agent, esp. a drug. [Syn. **hypnotic**[n] (ambig.).] **soporific**[a], **somniferous**[a].

sorcery[n] = 1. (*hist.*) divination from the casting of lots; 2. (*pop.*) the use of supernatural knowledge or power gained in any manner, esp. through the connivance of evil spirits. [Syn. **magic, necromancy, witchcraft, enchantment.**] **sorcerer**[np], **sorceress**[np] (fem.). — Fr. *sorcellerie;* Ger. *Zauberei*.

sorrow = syn. for **grief** and for **regret.** — Fr. *chagrin*; Ger. *Sorge, Trubsal*.

soul = 1. (*hist.*) the mind or specific substance manifested in mental phenomena; 2. (*pop.*) a human being; 3. (*pop.*) a disembodied spirit; 4. the characteristic qualities of an individual's nature, esp. the emotional qualities of sympathy. [Cf. **soul theory.**] — Fr. (1) *âme*, (2) *être*, (1, 3) *esprit*; Ger. *Seele*.

soul theory = the theory which holds that mental phenomena are the manifestations of a specific substance, usually assumed to be distinct from material substance. — Fr. *t. de l'âme*; Ger. *Seelentheorie*.

sound[n] = 1. (*phys.*) a mechanical disturbance in the air or other medium propagated away from the source; 2. (*psychol.*) a mode of sensation dependent upon (1) and also upon the ear with its associated neural mechanism. [Syn. (1) **sound-waves;** they are classed as **periodic** and **aperiodic;** syn. (2) **sound sensations;** they are generally classed as **tones** and **noises;** some recognize a third class, **vocal sounds.**] **sound**[a]. — Fr. *son;* Ger. *Schall.*

sound-absorption = the dissipation through friction of all or a portion of the sound energy transmitted to a body or surface. [Contr. w. **sound-reflection.** The degree to which a body or surface absorbs (and hence does not reflect or transmit) the sound-energy conveyed to it, is called its sound-absorbing power.]

sound cage = an apparatus for determining the precision of localization of the source of an auditory stimulus and for measuring the degree and direction of errors. [In its earliest form the device consisted of a spherical network of wires in three systems, each system passing through the poles of one of the chief axes of space, the observer being seated within, with the center of his head at the center of the hollow sphere. The stimulus was supplied by the click of a telephone receiver placed at some point of intersection of two wires. The observer points to (or calls off in degrees) the supposed source of the sound, and the error is measured in angular degrees on the axes of reference. In later models the wires are replaced by a single semicircular tube or rod which can be rotated freely in two axial directions, the receiver sliding freely along the rod; by rotating the rod and shifting the receiver the sound can be given at any directional position except immediately beneath the observer's body.]

sound energy flux = the average over one period, in ergs per second, of the rate of flow of acoustic energy through a given area.

sound hammer = an electrical make-stimulator commonly used, in connection with other apparatus, for measuring auditory response time; it consists of a pivoted lever which when released or activated strikes a metal block, thereby simultaneously closing the reaction circuit and producing the auditory stimulus. — Fr. *marteau sonore;* Ger. *Schallhammer.*

sound image, see **phantom sound.**

sound intensity = 1. (*phys.*) the sound energy flux per unit area perpendicular to the direction of propagation; 2. (*psychol.*) the quantitative attribute of sound. [The unit of (1) is erg per sec. per sq. cm. Cf. (2) **loudness.**] — Fr. *intensité sonore;* Ger. *Schallstärke.*

sound key, see **voice-key.** — Ger. *Schallschlüssel.*

sound-pattern theory, see **hearing/theories of.**

sound pendulum/Wundt, see **Wundt sound pendulum.**

sound perimetry = the measurement and mapping of a subject's field of auditory space with reference to the precision of localization in direction and distance. [Cf. **localization of sound.**]

soundproof room = a room so constructed as to be (relatively) impervious to sound.

sound-ranging = a method of locating the position of a sound source by determining the time of arrival of the sound-wave at various adjacent points. — Fr. *localisation sonore par ordination.*

sound/velocity of = the rate of progression of sound vibrations in a given medium. [The velocity in air at 20°C. is 344 meters per second.] — Fr. *vitesse du son;* Ger. *Schallgeschwindigkeit.*

sound-wave = a periodic alteration in the density of molecules or particles of air or other medium acted upon by some oscillatory pressure. [Usually restricted to density changes of such frequency as to cause auditory sensations when conducted to the ear. In free air sound-waves are propagated in concentric spheres away from the source. Audible sound-waves fall within the frequencies of approximately 20 to 20,000 cycles per second.] — Fr. *onde sonore;* Ger. *Schallwelle.*

sound-wave/complex = a sound-wave which is not of sine form, and hence may be regarded as the sum of two or more simple periodicities. [Syn. **compound sound-wave.** According to **Fourier's law** a complex sound-wave can be analyzed into a series of pendular vibrations.]

sounding board, sound board = a sheet of wood or other material in a musical instrument or sound apparatus which is set into forced resonance and thus reinforces the tones produced by the instrument. [Cf. **resonator.**] — Ger. *Schallbrett.*

sour = a quality of gustatory sensation of which the taste of tartaric acid is a typical example. [Syn. **acid** (preferably applied to stimulus rather than sensation). Cf. **gustatory qualities, taste.**] — Fr. *acide, sur;* Ger. *sauer.*

space = 1. the system of simultaneous positions, directions, and magnitudes, considered apart from material content (physics) and from sensory qualities and intensities (psychology); 2. the interval between objects or points at a given instant of time. [Syn. (1) **extension** (*physics*), **extensity** (*psychol.*), (2) **gap, distance.**] **space**[a], **spatial (spacial)**[a]. — Fr. *espace;* Ger. *Raum.*

space error = the error or deviation which occurs in psychophysical experimentation as the result of presenting two stimuli (either simultaneously or successively) in different **spatial relations** to the observer. [According to Fechner's convention, the **space-error** (designated by q) is *positive* when it operates to make the left of two equal stimuli appear greater than the right one, and *negative* when the left one appears less than the right. Cf. **time-error** (p).] — Fr. *erreur spatiale;* Ger. *Raumfehler.*

space orientation = 1. position in space; 2. adjustment of the position of the body (or some part of it) to the position of objects or forces in space, as in a tropism; 3. awareness of one's position in space. — Fr. *orientation spatiale;* Ger. *Raumstellung.*

space perception = the experience of space or extensity, either as a character or attribute of phenomena, or as a distinct element of experience, whose relations may be investigated apart from the specific sensory data perceived. [A generic term applied to investigation by any or all sense modalities, or to any explanatory theory; specific terms (visual, tactual or cutaneous, kinesthetic, auditory space perception) are applied to investigations limited to one type of modality. The factors involved are position, direction, size, form, distance.] — Fr. *perception d'espace;* Ger. *Raumwahrnehmung.*

space relations, spatial relations = the direction and extensity differences of objects from one another or from the observer.

spaced repetition = a procedure employed in

learning, in which the material to be memorized is repeated at intervals with a period of rest after each period of learning. [Syn. **distributed repetition** (or **practice**). Contr. w. **unspaced repetition,** in which the material is repeated again and again without respite till it is completely memorized.] — Fr. *répartition des présentations dans le temps.*

span/law of = "every mind tends to keep its total simultaneous cognitive output constant in quantity, however varying in quality" (Spearman).

span of apprehension, see **attention/range** (or **span**) **of.**

span of attention, see **attention/range** (or **span**) **of.**

span of consciousness = the number of separate objects simultaneously perceived. [Distg. fr. **span** (or **range**) **of attention** in that it includes all objects perceived, whatever their degree of clearness.]

spark chronoscope = a heavy pendulum which swings along a calibrated scale and demarcates the beginning of the duration to be measured by tripping an electrical contact when it passes the zero point of the scale; the end of the duration is recorded by a jump spark from a point on the pendulum to a paper-covered metal plate paralleling the scale, the paper being perforated or dotted by the spark. — Fr. *chr. à étincelle.*

spark method = a method of recording response times and other temporal data in which a time line is registered by a vibrating fork on a smoked drum, the beginning and end of the period in question being registered by means of an electric spark which perforates the paper at the corresponding points on the time line. [Spark recording has been applied to the **pendulum chronograph.** Cf. **spark chronoscope.**] — Fr. *m. de l'étincelle.*

spasm = a convulsive involuntary contraction of a muscle or set of muscles. — Ger. *Krampf.*

spasmophemia = a disturbance in the rhythm of speech, an intermittent blocking, or the convulsive repetition of a sound. [A form of **dysphemia.** Syn. **stuttering, stammering.** Cf. **aphemia.**]

spatial, see **space.**

spatial threshold (or **limen**) = the threshold which marks the point in a series of stimuli, where two objects or impressions are sensed as just spatially separate, or, more precisely, where the spatial separation is just as often sensed as it is not. — Ger. *Raumschwelle.*

spatialization, spacialization = the perceptual spatial reference of objects to positions beyond the body. [A rare term, contr. w. **localization,** which is then limited to the reference of stimuli to positions on the surface of the observer's body or, as in sound localization, to positions externally related in space to the observer's body. Syn. **projection** (2).]

spayed = the condition in the female of having the reproductive organs removed or rendered incapable of functioning.

speaking = the act of producing vocal sounds in conventional symbolic combinations, in which a specific musical scale is not an essential part. [Distg. fr. **singing.**] **speech**[n] = the product; **speak**[v].

Spearman footrule = a formula devised by C. S Spearman for computing correlation by the equation $R = 1 - [6\,\Sigma G/(N^2 - 1)]$.

special abilities = a vague expression suggesting a set of non-overlapping abilities, each of which may vary more or less independently of any general ability or average level of ability; e.g. ability to construct wooden models of ships, ability to draw, etc. [Cf. **specific ability.**] — Fr. *capacités spéciales.*

special ability tests = tests designed to measure some special ability or restricted group of capacities, as distg. fr. general ability tests. [E.g. the Seashore musical ability tests and numerous vocational and educational tests, such as the Thurstone tests of clerical ability, the Stenquist tests of mechanical ability, tests of spelling ability, arithmetical ability, etc.]

special aptitude test, see **aptitude test.**

special creation theory = the theory that all species of organisms were separately created by divine agency, and that they are immutable.

special senses = the four cranial senses, vision, audition, gustation, and olfaction.

species = 1. (*logic*) a subdivision of a larger group (a genus) marked off from other subdivisions by one or more qualitative differences; 2. the subdivision of organic life immediately subordinate to **genus** and superordinate to **variety.** [Since the advent of the evolution doctrine the concept and the demarcation of species (2) have been less rigid. Cf. **classification/zoological.**] — Fr. *espèce*; Ger. (2) *Art.*

specific = 1. characterizing a datum of any sort as distinctive; 2. pert. to a species.

specific ability = 1. an ability regarded in its totality and as distinct from all other abilities; 2. a factor which determines the degree of excellence in some particular test performance but does not affect any other really different performance. [According to Spearman's **two-factor theory, specific abilities** (symbolized by s) are uncorrelated with one another, and always operate in conjunction with a general factor (g), which affects many performances.] — Fr. *capacité spécifique.*

specific energy of nerves = (the theory that) each sensory nerve or neuron, however stimulated, gives rise to only one type of sensory process and a single quality of sensation (Ch. Bell, 1811; Joh. Müller, 1826). [A later modification of this theory holds that the specificity resides in the central brain areas rather than in the afferent nerves.] — Ger. *spezifische Sinnesenergien.*

specific factor, see **s factor.**

specific gravity = the ratio of the mass of a body or substance to an equal volume of water at 4° C. — Ger. *spezifisches Gewicht.*

specification = 1. the act of making a full, detailed, and definite statement or classification; 2. the citation of definite examples to illustrate a classification or argument. **specify**[v], **specified**[a] (not **specific**[a], which has another meaning).

specificity = the characteristic of a given quality, datum, etc. such that it is manifested in connection with a certain phenomenon or type of phenomenon and not with others. **specific**[a].

specificity doctrine of traits = the view that human behavior consists of *specific* acts and habits, contr. w. the view that it can be categorized into *general* traits such as honesty, dishonesty, cleanliness, suggestibility, etc. [Cf. **w factor, factor theory.**]

specify, see **specification.**

specious present, see **present/psychological.**

spectators = those present at a spectacle or visually presented performance. [Syn. **onlookers.** Distg. fr. **audience,** present at an auditory presentation. Technically, **spectators** is used to denote those present but not participating in a given social or individual activity.]

specter, spectre = (*pop.*) a fantasm which assumes the form of a human corpse, a disembodied spirit, or of some fear-inspiring being.

spectral chroma scale, spectral scale = a scale or series of colors formed by arranging the spectrum as a series of equal units according to just-noticeable chromatic differences, while differences in brilliance are eliminated. [About 130 just noticeably different colors are found. Since the spectral colors differ in saturation as well as in hue, the scale cannot properly be regarded as one of pure hue.] — Fr. *échelle spectrale chromatique.*

spectral energy = the radiant energy in a given small interval of the spectrum (esp.) as compared with another similar interval taken as a standard.

spectral line = any one of the narrow lines, each representing light of a definite wave-length, which are observed in the solar and other spectra, certain groups of lines being characteristic of specific chemical elements. [These lines are characteristic of substances in the gaseous state, and appear bright when due to emission from these, or dark when due to absorption by them. Cf. **Fraunhofer's lines, spectrum,** and see Table XIII.]

spectre, see **specter.**

spectrocolorimeter = an instrument designed to measure colors in order to designate them numerically; the sample is matched by partial reflection with a mixture of spectral light of a single wave-length and a standard white; the color of the sample is then stated in terms of the dominant wave-length and the percentage of desaturation with white as found in the matching mixture.

spectrometer = (*phys.*) an instrument essentially similar to a **spectroscope,** but designed especially for the accurate measurement of the wave-lengths of lines or of regions in the spectrum. [It is frequently adapted for use in visual work to obtain a beam or beams of pure spectral light of known wave-length. Cf. **spectroscope.**]

spectrophotometer = an instrument, combining the properties of a **spectrometer** and a **photometer,** which permits the measurement of relative intensities of light at substantially single wave-lengths, selected at will from those comprising the given sample. **spectrophotometric**[a].

spectroscope = an instrument for making a spectrum visible and locating therein the position of spectral lines and of light of the various wave-lengths; the spectrum is produced usually by a prism, sometimes by a diffraction grating, and a linear scale is projected so as to be seen superimposed upon it. [Used chiefly for the qualitative detection of chemical substances.]

spectrum = 1. (*opt.*) a band of radiant energy in which, after passing through a prism or being otherwise dispersed, energy of each wave-length is segregated and all components lie spread out in regular order; 2. (*vis.*) the series of colors evoked by stimulation of the retina with radiant energy of continuously differing single wave-lengths from approximately 400 to 760 millimicrons value. [The spectral series shows no purples, and fails to include the psychologically primary red, since these colors are evoked only by mixed wave-lengths. Cf. **spectroscope** and Table XIII.] **spectral**[a].

spectrum/acoustic = the range of sound frequencies audible to the human ear, approx. from 20 to 20,000 cycles per second.

speculation = the act of propounding theories and making generalizations which are only slightly suggested by the available facts. [Often applied derogatively to what is asserted to be purely *a priori* thinking. If the insecure basis of the speculation is recognized, it becomes a **hypothesis** or preliminary to a hypothesis.] **speculative**[a].

speech = (a system of) communication through conventional vocal symbols. [Distg. fr. **gesture, graphic language, writing,** etc. Cf. **language.**] **speak**[v] **or talk**[v]; **speech**[a], **oral**[a], **or vocal**[a] — Ger. *Sprache.*

speech-reading, see **lip-reading.**

speech/subvocal (or **inarticulate**) = initiated contractions of the vocal musculature which do not result in audible sounds.

speed = 1. time-rate of motion, change, or progress; 2. the inverse measure of the time required to perform a given act. [In learning, speed is one of the measures of progress. Cf. (1) **velocity,** (2) **accuracy.**] — Fr. (1, 2) *vitesse,* (2) *rapidité*; Ger. *Schnelligkeit, Geschwindigkeit.*

speed counter, speedometer, see **tachometer.**

speed score, see **rate score.**

speeding up = the exerting of pressure on workers, either through wage incentives or by other means, in order to increase the quantity of output or to reduce labor costs. **speeding-up**[a]. — Fr. *presse, activité.*

spell = (*magic*) a stanza, verse, phrase, or series of nonsense syllables supposed to be capable, when spoken in certain ways or under certain conditions, of controlling the actions of men, deities, or forces of nature. [Applied also to the result so produced.] — Fr. *charme.*

sperm = 1. the semen or seminal fluid; 2. one of the mature male sex-cells or spermatozoa.

sperm-cell = a male germ-cell. [Cf. **spermatozoon.**]

spermatogenesis = the development of a spermatozoon or male sex-cell from a primitive sex-cell. [Cf. **gametogenesis** = the development of mature sex-cells, both spermatozoa and ova. Contr. w. **oögenesis** = the development of an ovum from a primitive sex-cell.]

spermatogonium = the primordial germ cell which gives rise to the male germ cell or spermatozoon. **spermatogonia**[pl].

spermatozoon = a mature sperm-cell or male germ-cell, which has undergone the reduction division and is in condition to fertilize an ovum or female germ-cell. **spermatozoa**[pl].

sphenoid sinuses = a paired cavity in the body of the sphenoid bone, each sinus communicating with the nasal cavity by a narrow channel.

spherical aberration, spherical error = (*opt.*) failure of the rays of light from a given point to come to an identical focus, owing to the fact that the rays traversing the outer zones of the refracting (or reflecting) surfaces are bent farther and meet earlier than those traversing the inner zones. [So called because most curved optical surfaces are spherical, and the error is inherent in this form.] — Fr. *aberration de sphéricité*.

spherical lens = a lens whose surfaces are either spherical, or spherical and plane, and which consequently refracts equally in all meridians. [Cf. **cylindrical lens.**] — Fr. *lentille sphérique*; Ger. *sphärische Linse, Kugellinse*.

sphincter = a ring-shaped muscle which, on contracting, partly or wholly closes a natural orifice. [E.g. iris muscle of the eye.] — Ger. *Schliessmuskel*.

sphygmograph = an instrument for recording the form, rate, and force of pulse movements; it consists typically of a button, applied to the wrist over the radial artery; the pulse movement is communicated to the button, which actuates a light lever system terminating in a stylus, which traces upon a moving strip of smoked paper a magnified record of the pulse. [Cf. **tonograph.**] **sphymogram** = the record obtained.

sphygmomanometer, sphygmometer = an instrument for measuring the pressure in the arterial system by the effect of an applied external pressure; its essential features are: an air-tight cuff to be fastened around the upper arm, a pump for increasing air pressure within the cuff, and a device (either a mercury column or a spring scale) for measuring pressure when the pulse ceases. [The usual method employed is to first increase the pressure until the artery is completely closed, then with the pressure slowly declining to note the point on the sphygmomanometer scale when the first pulse wave is observable distal to the cuff.]

spicy = a quality of olfactory sensation of which nutmeg is a typical example. [A class of Henning's. Cf. **odor, aromatic.**] — Fr. *épicé*; Ger. *würzig*.

spinal = 1. pert. to the backbone or spine; 2. pert. to the spinal cord, i.e. that part of the nervous system enclosed within the backbone or spine. — Ger. *Rückgrats-, Rückenmark-*.

spinal accessory nerve, see **accessory nerve/spinal.**

spinal animal = an animal in which the entire cephalic nervous system has been isolated from functional influence upon the spinal cord. [Generally a more specific term is used; e.g. spinal dog, spinal frog, etc.]

spinal cord = a cord-like structure consisting mainly of neurons and tracts of neurons situate within the spine or backbone. [Often abbrev. to **cord.** Syn. **myelon.**] — Fr. *moelle épinière*; Ger. *Rückenmark*.

spinal ganglia = groups of cells which form an enlargement on the dorsal root of each spinal nerve. [These cells give rise to the afferent spinal-root fibers.]

spinal induction, see **induction/immediate spinal, rebound.**

spinal nerve = any one of the peripheral nerves (sensory and motor) which issue from the cord below the medulla oblongata. [There are 31 pairs. Distg. fr. **cranial nerves,** which pass within the cranium and connect with the brain. Cf. **peripheral nerve.**] — Fr. *nerf spinal, n. rachidien*.

spinal reflex = a reflex response whose paths lie entirely caudad to the medulla oblongata. [E.g. **patellar reflex.** Distg. fr. **cranial reflex,** whose paths lie wholly within the cranium, and **cerebrospinal reflex,** which involves both the brain and cord.]

spinal tonus = muscular tonus which is mediated by the spinal nerves and spinal cord only. [Exhibited by a **spinal animal** (e.g. spinal dog or turtle) after the cord has been cut.]

spindle = 1. (*neuromuscular*) a type of proprioceptive fusiform receptor, widely distributed among the muscles of the body; 2. a long, slender cytoplasmic body, produced during mitotic cell division, and situate between the asters. [Cf. (1) **muscle spindle.**] — Fr. *fuseau*; Ger. *Spindel*.

spindle/color, see **color solid.**

spindle/olfactory, see **olfactory cell.**

spine = 1. a column of ring-like bones which extends from the head to the tail in the dorsal region of vertebrates; 2. a hard pointed projection, usually on the outer covering of the body of a plant or animal, or on the internal skeleton, e.g. the spine of the ilium. [Syn. (1) **vertebral column, backbone.**] **spinal**[a] (1), **spiny**[a] (2). — Fr. *colonne vertébrale, épine dorsale*; Ger. (1) *Rückgrat*.

spiral lamina = a delicate osseous shelf, wound spirally about the modiolus of the cochlea in the internal ear, which forms the inner support of the basilar membrane. [It contains numerous foramina or openings for the passage of fibers of the cochlear nerve.]

spiral ligament = a broad ligament attached externally to the outer wall of the cochlear canal in the internal ear and internally to the basilar membrane, which it maintains in tension.

spireme = (*biol.*) a coiled thread of chromatin, which commonly appears in the nucleus before mitotic cell division.

spirit = 1. the total mental organization of man, regarded as distinct from the atomic structure and material organization of the body; 2. (*hist.*) a distinctive type of substance of which this organization (1) is composed; 3. (*pop.*) the disembodied personality of a dead human being; or a supernatural incorporeal being; 4. vigor and energy of behavior. [Rarely used technically in contemporary psychology.] **spiritual**[a] (1, 2); **spiritistic**[a] (3); **spirited**[a] (4). — Fr. *esprit*; Ger. *Geist*.

spirit photography = (*psych. res.*) the production of photographs of persons, upon which appear superposed images, assumed to be of spirits and to be produced by supernormal means.

spiritism = belief in communication with discarnate personalities or spirits. [Commonly (but improperly) designated **spiritualism.**] **spiritistic**[a].

spiritualism = 1. (*philos.*) the doctrine that the nature of ultimate reality is typified by the subjective purposive world of mind or by mind, spirit, soul; 2. (*pop.*) a religious cult whose chief tenet is the belief in communication with the spirits of the dead. [(1) contr. w. **materialism.** (2) is properly termed **spiritism.**]

spirituality = a quality of personality which leads an individual to preoccupy himself with moral and religious issues, especially in deed, rather than with affairs of the world or even merely intellectual pursuits.

spirograph = an instrument used to register respiratory movements.

spirometer = 1. an instrument used to measure the air-capacity of the lungs; after the lungs are filled, the contents are expelled through a tube into an inverted chamber submerged in a water bath; the chamber rises in the water as the air enters, the limiting value being reached when the lungs are completely emptied; the cubic contents are indicated on a scale; a spring scale is sometimes substituted for the air chamber; 2. an air or oxygen measuring chamber used in connection with metabolism apparatus.

spite = an emotional attitude which is aroused by the idea of some real or imagined injury inflicted upon the individual by another (or others) and which expresses itself in some trivial injury or annoyance directed toward the latter. **spiteful**[a]. — Fr. *dépit, rancune*; Ger. *Trotz, Groll, Übelwollen.*

splanchnic = pert. to the viscera. [Syn. **visceral.**]

splanchnopleure = the inner layer of the mesoblast, together with the associated entoderm in the embryo.

spleen = a ductless gland, situate at the left side of the cardiac end of the stomach. **splenic**[a] (accent **splen-**). — Fr. *rate*; Ger. *Milz.*

splenic, see **spleen.**

split-field method = the procedure adopted in examining the subject-matter of a field of search, whereby the subject-matter is bifurcated and dealt with as **differents** (Bott).

split-off consciousness (or **experience**) = a partly organized set of experiences in an individual, which are independent of his organized consciousness. [Used by James, to designate the subordinate phases of dual and multiple personality. Cf. **co-consciousness, sejunction, dissociation.**] — Fr. *conscience dissociée.*

spontaneity = activity which is initiated by an organism or object without immediate external stimulation. (Accent **-ee-.**) **spontaneous**[a] = self-initiated.

spontaneous deflections = galvanic skin reflexes which occur without known stimulation or cause.

spontaneous generation = the formation of organisms from inanimate substance apart from the mediation of other organisms. [Syn. **abiogenesis.** Contr. w. **biogenesis.**] — Ger. *Urzeugung.*

spontaneous movements = those movements of an organism which arise from internal (i.e. organic) stimuli or conditions. [Applied esp. to the autonomic movements of growth and variation in plants and to movements arising from physiological states in animals. Contr. w. **externally aroused movements.**]

spontaneous variation = a variation, or heritable alteration in type of the organism, which is due to factors within the germ cell itself and not to crossing or to environmental factors.

spore = a cell which is capable of giving rise to a new individual without fertilization. [Usually applied to specialized reproductive cells of plants or to small reproductive cells produced by the divisions of some protozoa. A **spore** differs from a **seed** in that the latter contains a multicellular embryo. Cf. **sporulation.**] — Ger. *Spore.*

sport = 1. an organism, either animal or plant, which is markedly different from its parents and from the general type of the species; 2. a contest engaged in for pleasure. [Syn. (1) **freak** (*pop.*). [Cf. (1) **mutation.**] — Ger. (1) *Abart,* (2) *Sport.*

sporulation = the process of spore formation. [Cf. **spore.**]

spot-pattern test = a type of test in which the task is to reproduce, after brief exposure, a pattern or design consisting of spots or dots. — Fr. *t. du groupe de points.*

spurious = deceptively similar to a given object or datum, but not genuinely belonging to the same class or category. — Fr. *illégitime*; Ger. *unecht, falsch.*

spurious correlation = correlation obtained between two sets of measures, which is due in whole or part to factors other than those to which it is ascribed. — Fr. *corrélation illégitime.*

spurt = 1. a quickening or intensification (or both) of a response which has been in progress for some time; 2. renewed or accentuated effort. [Cf. **end spurt.**] — Fr. *élan.*

square contingency, see **contingency method.**

squint, see **strabismus.**

stability = 1. (*phys.*) absence of motion in a physical mass or organic body which is regarded as a whole in relation to its surroundings; 2. (*biol.*) the characteristic of certain species or of specific characters in a given species, such that they do not vary from generation to generation; 3. (*psychol.*) a type of temperament or personality characterized by an absence of unusual variations in emotional reactions or traits. **stable**[a]. — Ger. (1) *Stabilität,* (2) *Dauerhaftigkeit,* (3) *Beständigkeit.*

stability/occupational = a measure of the proportion of employees in a given group who have held the same post for one, two, three, or more years. [The inverse of **labor mobility.** Cf. **turnover/labor.**]

stage = any one of the natural divisions of a progressive series of events, evolutionary changes, etc. [Distg. fr. **class, category,** etc., which apply to static groups.] — Fr. *stade*; Ger. *Stufe.*

staircase illusion = a visual illusion of the reversible type, in which a line drawing of a staircase is interpreted either as a stairway seen from above or as cellar stairs seen from beneath (or the under side of an overhanging cornice), the perception usually alternating between the two interpretations. — Fr. *illusion de la figure en escalier*; Ger. *Treppentäuschung.*

staircase phenomenon = the response of muscle to single induction shocks of equal strength, by progressively greater contractions up to a maximum (H. P. Bowditch, 1871). — Fr. *phénomène de l'escalier*; Ger. *Treppe.*

stammering, see **stuttering, spasmophemia.** — Ger. *Stammeln*; *Stottern.*

stance/reflex = reflex maintenance of pose or posture on the feet in which the relative positions of head, trunk, and limbs are held in a fixed position by a closely integrated reflex mechanism. [Cf. **postural reflex.**] — Fr. *réflexes de posture.*

standard = 1. that which constitutes a model or guide with reference to procedures, levels to be attained, etc.; 2. a fixed and durable unit of any sort used for comparison and quantitative evaluation of data of the same sort. [Cf. **scale** (1).] **standard**[a] = pert. or conforming to a given standard. — Fr. *étalon*; Ger. *Massstab.*

standard deviation, standard error = the square root of the mean (i.e. arithmetic average) of the squares of all the deviations of the measures comprising a series from their mean. [Abbrev. to *S.D.* or σ (sigma).] — Fr. *écart étalon, erreur type, erreur quadratique.*

standard error of estimate = the standard deviation of the differences between a series of true values and the estimates of them; i.e. the standard deviation of the errors of estimate. — Fr. *erreur type d'estimation.*

standard score = the deviation of a score from the average score of the group, expressed in units of the standard deviation of the distribution. [If X represents the score of individual A in a given test, $\bar{X}$ the average, and σ_x the standard deviation, then A's **standard score** is $(X-\bar{X})/\sigma_x$.] — Fr. *note étalonnée.*

standard stimulus = in psychophysical research, that one of a pair or group of stimuli which is treated as the basis of comparison with the others. [Syn. **normal stimulus** (ambig.).]

standard tests = materials used in testing, (1) in which the component items have been selected and checked empirically, (2) in which the method of administration and scoring are prescribed with exactitude, and (3) for which norms of performance are supplied to indicate the dependence of the score upon sex, age, school grade, or similar factors. [A well-standardized test should also (4) be accompanied by data concerning its reliability and its validity. Sometimes contr. w. **informal tests.**] — Fr. *tests (épreuves) étalonné.*

standardization of tests = the establishment of a fixed or standard procedure in the giving and scoring of tests, as well as the establishment of adequate age, grade, race, sex, or other norms. — Fr. *étalonnage des tests.*

standardize[v] = 1. to bring a group of data into relation with a given standard; 2. to devise a standard for treatment of certain data. [Cf. **standard, calibration.**] — Fr. *étalonner*; Ger. *normieren.*

Stanford Achievement Test = a battery of tests, devised by T. L. Kelley, G. M. Ruch, and L. M. Terman, for measuring the achievement of children in the basic school subjects. [The Primary Examination, for Grades 2 and 3, includes reading, arithmetic, and spelling. The Advanced Examination, for Grades 4 to 9, includes arithmetic computation, arithmetic reasoning, reading, spelling, language usage, literature, history and civics, geography, and physiology and hygiene.]

Stanford-Binet scale = a revision of the Binet-Simon scale of mental tests worked out by Terman and his associates for use in measuring the general level of intellectual development attained by an individual. [It covers a wider range than the original Binet-Simon scale and contains many additional tests. Distg. fr. **Stanford achievement tests** and **Terman group test.** Syn. **Stanford revision, Stanford-Binet tests.**] — Fr. *échelle de S.-B.*

stapes = one of the **auditory ossicles,** which is articulated with the **incus** and is attached to the oval window of the vestibule. [Syn. **stirrup, stirrup-bone.**] (2 syll.) — Ger. *Steigbügel.*

starfish = popular name for Asteroides, a class belonging to the phylum of Echinodermata, which is characterized by a central disk and usually five arms, the whole body being enclosed in a tough skin containing calcareous plates. — Fr. *astérie*; Ger. *Seestern.*

starting (or **startle**) **reflex** = a reflex observed in the newborn infant (and later), stimulated by loud sounds, withdrawal of support, etc., and manifested in jerking movements, changes in respiration, etc. [Mediated by brain stem and spinal cord. **starting** here means a sudden jerking movement and is related to the phrase "being startled."] — Fr. *réflexe de sursaut.*

startle[v] = (to cause) a violent or sudden motor response, largely reflex, and resembling a momentary fear; as by an unexpected noise or flash of light. [Syn. **start**[v] (ambig.).] **startling**[a] (active), **startled**[a] (passive).

state = 1. a condition which shows no progressive change for the time and in the respect considered; e.g. a state of health, a state of anxiety; 2. (*hist.*) any momentary experience or mental process, e.g. state of consciousness. — Fr. *état*; Ger. *Beschaffenheit, Zustand.*

state of consciousness = the totality of experience at any given moment, with emphasis on the actual contents and their interrelation. [Syn. **conscious state, mental state.**] — Fr. *état de conscience.*

static reaction/local = a **static reflex** which is confined to one limb or part of body.

static reflex = a postural response of the body as a whole, orientated in reference to gravity or other forces. [The two types are: **stance reflexes** and **righting reflexes.** Contr. w. **statokinetic reflexes.**]

static sense = the sense whose receptors are usually the semicircular canals (or the statocysts in invertebrates) and whose stimuli are changes in position of the head. [The resulting data are called **static sensations,** which term is sometimes extended to include data from the muscle sense, touch, etc., which furnish indications of the position in space of the individual's body or its members. Cf. **equilibrium/perception of.**] — Ger. *statischer Sinn.*

statistic = any item of a statistical series, including any derived item such as a value calculated from an observed sample with a view to characterizing the population, e.g. as the **mean, standard deviation,** or **coefficient of correlation.**

statistical errors = inaccuracies either of measurement, of sampling, or of treatment which tend to vitiate statistical results. [They are mainly of 2 sorts, **chance** (or **variable**) **errors,** and **systematic** (or **constant**) **errors.** Both kinds may occur either in the measurement of the data (**errors of observation**), in the sample selected (**sampling errors**), in the methods employed (**errors in technique**), or in arithmetic accuracy (**computational errors**).]

statistical series = a set of values, quantitative or qualitative, which vary more or less among themselves, but which have some common characteristic or origin. [E.g. ages (variable feature) of pupils in a given fifth school grade (common characteristic).]

statistics = 1. the plural of statistic; 2. the branch of general mathematics which evaluates or arranges groups of data on the basis of the number (or relative number) of cases falling into each different category; 3. classified facts or data. [(2) is sing.; (1 and 3) are pl.] **statistical**[a].

statocyst = a receptor organ, present in some invertebrates, which consists of a membranous sac filled with liquid, lined with cilia and containing one or more particles called **statoliths.**

[The particles, being heavier, lie at the base of the sac and are displaced as the head is moved, impinging upon the cilia and giving rise to labyrinthine stimulation. Syn. **otocyst.**]

statokinetic reflexes = postural responses and adjustments of the body during movement, which serve to maintain the normal position of the body against disturbing forces such as velocity, gravity, etc. [Contr. w. **static reflex.**]

statoliths = solid particles which are present in the invertebrate **statocysts.** [Changes of position on the part of the organism cause them to impinge on the cilia of the statocysts, and give rise to stimulation important in equilibrium. Syn. **otoliths.**]

statue of Condillac = an illustration used by Condillac to portray the development of mental life from sensation; he assumed a statue in likeness of a man but with no sensation at first; one sense after another was assumed to be opened to stimuli, beginning with smell, and the resulting growth of consciousness was traced. [The idea of the statue is found in Cicero and others; it was common to many writers in France who supported sensationism or the doctrine that mind is the aggregate of sense-experiences.]

steadiness apparatus = a device used to measure the amount of involuntary movement which is made when the finger or arm is held as nearly motionless as possible; it commonly consists in a metal plate containing holes of graduated size into which the subject attempts to insert a metal stylus without contact; touching the side of a hole closes an electric circuit and registers the contact. [Certain modified forms are called **ataxiagraph, tremograph, digitalgraph.** Cf. **ataxiameter.**] — Fr. *appareil pour mesurer la stabilité motrice.*

stem, see **brain stem.**

stentor = a trumpet-shaped ciliate protozoan, alternately free-swimming and attached to some solid body by its foot or stem.

step interval, see **class interval.**

stepwise phenomenon = a structure which exhibits a directional tendency among its members, e.g. an ascending or descending series of pitches or brilliance; response to the differential aspects of a stimulus-complex. [According to the Gestalt psychology, step-wise phenomena are special cases of configurational patterns and responses.] — Fr. *phénomène de l'échelon.*

steradian = the unit of solid angle, equal to that subtended by a surface on a sphere equivalent to the square of the radius. [A point in space is surrounded by 4π **steradians.**]

stereo-agnosis, see **astereognosis.**

stereognosis = perception of the solidity of external objects. **stereognostic**[a]**.**

stereogram = a pair of pictures (usually though not necessarily photographic), or a single picture, so arranged that on being viewed binocularly, the effect is that of a solid object seen in relief. [The two pictures are nearly but not exactly alike, so that when seen through a **stereoscope** each offers the view of the solid object as seen by the corresponding eye in a free field. In the single picture effect, the two pictures may be superimposed in different colors, such as red and green; each eye is covered with a glass of one of these colors; the two pictures shown by the two colors are slightly different as in the other case and combine stereoscopically. Cf. **stereoscope.**]

stereoreceptor = any receptor of an organism by means of which responses to solid substances are initiated. [Cf. **thigmotropism, stereotropism.**]

stereoscope = an instrument for combining two flat pictures, viewed by right and left eyes, into an impression of a solid object in relief; it usually consists of a pair of prisms, one before each eye, such that each prism displaces the picture behind it in the nasal direction and the two images combine into one. [A projecting piece hides the left picture from the right eye, and vice versa; the picture holder is usually mounted on a slide for altering the distance of the pictures from the eyes. In other forms mirrors are used to displace the visual angle in such a way as to combine the two separate images into one apparent object or scene. Cf. **stereogram.**] **stereoscopic**[a]**, stereoscopy**[n]**.**

stereoscopic motion pictures = motion pictures which give the impression of third dimension or depth; they are taken with two cameras and projected so that the right eye sees the pictures taken with the right camera and the left eye those taken with the left camera. [Used in motion study and in showing a beginner how an expert performs an industrial operation.] — Fr. *cinématographie stéréoscopique.*

stereoscopic vision = 1. the binocular perception of solidity and relief; 2. perception of solidity and distance (third dimension) in flat pictures by means of a **stereoscope.**

stereotropism, stereotaxis = a simple orienting response to contact with solid objects usually positive, resulting in a tendency to crawl into corners or holes. [Cf. **tropism.**] (Accent **-ot-, -tax-.**) **stereotropic**[a]**, -tactic**[a]**.**

stereotyped (responses) = characterizing certain responses which are always performed in substantially the same manner. **stereotype**[n] = a stereotyped segment of behavior. [Contr. w. **varied response.**] **stereotype**[v] (rarely used).

stereotypy = a pathological phenomenon consisting in the endless repetition of fragmentary or apparently senseless words, apparently useless movements, or of certain postures.

sterility = inability to reproduce. [Applied to both sexes. Syn. **infecundity.**] **sterile**[a]. — Ger. *Unfruchtbarkeit.*

sterilization = the process of rendering an organism incapable of reproduction. [A generic term applicable to both sexes. Cf. **castration, sterility.**] **sterilize**[v]**, sterilized**[a]**.**

Stern variator, see **tone variator.**

sternal = pert. to or located on the sternum or breastbone.

sternocleidomastoid, sternomastoid = pert. to the region at either side of the neck.

sthenic = (*rare*) characterizing an individual possessed of vigor and strength. [Contr. w. **asthenic** = weak, feeble.]

sthenic feelings = feelings of heightened energy, activity, or excessive excitement such as anger or pronounced joy. [Contr. w. **asthenic feelings.**]

stigma = 1. any natural peculiarity of the body of a given individual which is considered a sign of degeneracy; 2. (usually in pl.) marks which resemble the wounds of the crucifixion, or other marking, said to have been supernaturally impressed on the bodies of certain saints. **stigmata**[pl]**, stigmatization**[n]**.** — Fr. *stigmate;* Ger. (1) *Stigma,* (2) *Wundmal.*

Stilling test = a device for testing color blindness; it consists of a set of plates, each bearing many round colored spots, of various sizes, shades, and hues, scattered about; the spots of one color are so grouped as to form some numeral, which is obvious to the normal eye, but is not observed by color-blind individuals.

stimulant = a drug or other chemical which, when introduced into the body, tends to produce heightened neural activity, or heightened activity of some other physiological function. — Ger. *Reizmittel*.

stimulate = 1. to apply a **stimulus** to a receptor; 2. to start a nerve impulse; 3. to arouse a high degree of organic activity, e.g. by a stimulant or by suggestion. [(1) is properly distg. fr. **excite,** although currently employed to include both the act of stimulating and the consequent exciting. Cf. **stimulation.**] — Ger. (1, 2) *reizen,* (3) *aufregen, antreiben.*

stimulation = 1. any observable change (typical or atypical, and including inhibition) in the metabolism or other function of a living tissue, which is produced by applying some external agency; 2. the act of applying such an external agency (i.e. a stimulus). [Distg. fr. **excitation.**] **stimulate**[v]. — Ger. *Reizung*.

stimulation/bipolar = a method of electrical stimulation in which a current is passed through the tissue between two closely approximated electrodes.

stimulation time = the interval between the application of a stimulus and the arousal of the afferent nerve impulse, i.e. the time taken to overcome the inertia of a receptor by a given stimulus.

stimulation/unipolar = a method of electrical stimulation which involves the passage of current through tissue between a large and a small electrode placed some distance apart. [The greater current density at the small area of contact results in stimulation at this area only.]

stimulator = any apparatus or instrument employed to generate or apply a stimulus.

stimulogeneous fibrillation = the observed fact that nerve axons grow (galvanotropically) *away* from other active neurons, i.e. away from a cathode pole (S. T. Bok).

stimulus = 1. an energy external to a receptor, which excites the receptor; 2. loosely, an external or internal object or event, or an aspect of such an object, or a change in an aspect of the object, which arouses or alters an experience, or which alters activity in the living organism; 3. a presented stimulus (1) which releases a prepared response. [(2) is general usage, (1) applies to the psychophysical laboratory and is often symbolized by *R* (= Ger. *Reiz*); a stimulus is termed **adequate** when it evokes response through the normal action of a receptor; it is termed **inadequate** if it arouses the typical modal experience by its direct action on the *nerve* or if it acts abnormally upon a receptor, and also, in reflexology, if it is **conditioned** to a response which it does not natively evoke; it is **supraliminal** if it is well above the **threshold,** a condition in which it is usually distinctly perceived; it is **liminal** when it is in the region of the **threshold,** where perception may or may not occur; it is **subliminal** when it is below the **threshold,** where it may have an indirect effect upon the response although no direct effect; the transition value of the stimulus from no stimulation to stimulation is the **stimulus threshold** (limen) designated by *RL,* and the corresponding transition value limiting the upper end of a modal series is a **terminal stimulus,** *TR*.] — Ger. *Reiz*.

stimulus attitude = an attitude in which the observer gives attention to the stimulus as object. [Cf. **object attitude.**]

stimulus error = a criticized procedure in psychology, in which reference to the *source of stimulation* is substituted for description of *actual experience*.

stimulus-response view = that conception of psychological phenomena which holds them all to be describable in terms of stimuli and responses, both terms being taken inclusively. [Not essentially an objective or behavioristic treatment, experiential phenomena being also describable in these terms. Not to be confused with **reflexology,** a simplified special form of the stimulus-response view. It does not exclude the consideration of neural or other intraorganic processes.]

stirp = the sum-total of the genes or determiners present in a given fertilized ovum. [Syn. **stock.**] — Fr. *lignée*.

stirpiculture = (*hist.*) the culture or artificial improvement of the breed, or **stirp.** [Syn. **eugenics.**]

stirrup-bone, see **stapes.**

stock, see **stirp.**

stomach = a sac-like enlargement of the alimentary tract, following the esophagus, in which the preliminary process of digestion takes place. — Ger. *Magen*.

strabismometer, strabometer = an instrument for measuring the deviation of the eyes in **strabismus.**

strabismus = the failure of one of the two eyes to take its proper position of binocular fixation with reference to the other, due to defect or lack of control of the extrinsic ocular muscles. [Distg. fr. **heterophoria** or **muscular imbalance,** in which the eye does not so deviate unless covered. Syn. **heterotropia, squint.**] **strabismal, strabismic**[a] (prefd.). — Ger. *Schielen*.

strain = 1. (*phys.*) the degree of deformation (bending, elongation, etc.) produced in a body by a given stress; 2. extreme muscular tension resulting from voluntary effort; 3. injury due to overuse; 4. a quality of certain kinesthetic sensations, which are stimulated by muscular tension; 5. (*biol.*) syn. for breed or stock. [Syn. (4) **sensation of tension.**] — Fr. *tension*; Ger. (2) *Spannung*, (4) *Spannungsempfindung*.

Stratton's experiment = an experiment on visual inversion performed by G. M. Stratton, which consisted in wearing over the eyes for several days a set of lenses which turned the entire visual field through 180°, and noting the gradual growth of coordination between this reversed field and the tactuomuscular space relations.

stream of consciousness, stream of thought = the conscious experience of an individual, likened to a stream in order to emphasize its continuity, in opposition to the conception of it as a series of discrete states. [A term introduced by James.] — Fr. *courant de la conscience, cours de la pensée*.

strength = degree of capacity for exertion of muscular force. [Distg. fr. **endurance** = the temporal duration of exerted muscular force.] **strong**[a]. — Fr. *force*; Ger. *Stärke*.

strength-duration curve = 1. (*psychol.*) the record of the progressive decrease in muscular work over a long period of time or until complete exhaustion of the muscle is reached; 2. a graph relating intensity of a constant current (ordinates) to the duration of flow (abscissae) necessary to excite a tissue. — Fr. *courbe de force-durée.*

strephosymbolia = the perceiving of objects reversed as though in a mirror.

stress = 1. (*phys.*) the force per unit area tending to produce deformation in a body; 2. (*vocal*) the relatively greater force of breath in the utterance of certain syllables as compared with others; 3. (*physiol.*) application of tension to a muscle up to or beyond the point of strain; 4. (*pathol.*) a condition of extreme mental tension. [Syn. (2) **ictus.**]

stretch reflex, see **myotatic reflex.**

striae acusticae, striae medullares (or **acusticae**) = a band of transverse nerve fibers passing across the floor of the 4th ventricle, which connect with the cochlear division of the auditory nerve. [They mark the transverse limit between the pontine and medullary parts of the 4th ventricle.]

striate body, see **corpus striatum.**

striate (or **striped**) **muscle** = muscle whose fibers are divided histologically into striations by transverse bands. [The class includes the skeletal muscles generally, attached at one end to a fixed part of the body and at the other to a movable member; also the heart; contr. w. **smooth** or **non-striate muscles,** which are in general activated by the autonomic nervous system.] — Ger. *gestreifter Muskel.*

string galvanometer, see **galvanometer.** — Fr. *galvanomètre à corde*; Ger. *Saitengalvanometer.*

striped muscle, see **striate muscle.**

strive = to exert intense muscular or psychomotor effort toward a goal. — Fr. *s'efforcer*; Ger. *streben.*

strobophotograph = a device for the photographic recording of sound waves; it resembles the tonoscope, with the added feature of a moving film for recording changes in frequency. [Cf. **tonoscope.**]

stroboscope = a device for presenting a rapid series of exposures of a related sequence of visual stimuli; two illusions produced are of importance: (*a*) if the scenes presented are related and differ but little from each other, an illusion of continuous motion is produced, as is the case in the cinema and with animated cartoons; (*b*) if the stimulus itself is moving continuously and periodically, it may be made to appear to slow down, stand still, or reverse its direction of motion, as is often the case in cinematographic pictures of revolving wheels or stroboscopic disks. [Cf. **stroboscopic disk.** Syn. **zoetrope, vitascope, thaumatrope, dadeleum, praximoscope.**] **stroboscopic**[a].

stroboscopic disk = a device, usually consisting of a cardboard disk upon which is a series of regularly spaced dots or radial lines; when this disk is rotated about its center and viewed by intermittent light (usually a 60 cycle A.C. lamp), the series of dots or lines may be made to appear to slow down, stop, or reverse its direction of rotation by changing the speed of the disk or the frequency of the exposures; if either of these latter functions is known the other may be calculated.

stroboscopic illusion = the apparent motion of an object or event, presented visually or tactually by means of a series of discrete impressions, each one of which indicates an advance in the progressive motion of the object or event. [In vision a series of momentary exposures of successive positions is presented at the optimal rate of 16 per sec., alternating with an occlusion of light during which period the positive after-image continues the previously exposed figure or scene. Motion pictures embody this illusion. Tactual stroboscopic illusions are possible through successive and discrete stimulation of neighboring points under favorable conditions on the skin.]

stroke (or **shock**) = (*pop.*) an apoplectic attack, due generally to rupture of a blood vessel in the internal capsule of the brain. [Syn. **hemiplegia.**] — Fr. *ictus, attaque*; Ger. *Schlag.*

strong, see **strength.** — Fr. *fort*[a]; Ger. *stark.*

structural psychology = a method or systematic treatment of psychology which investigates and describes the composition and the integration of the various mental states and conscious experiences. [Syn. **content psychology, existential psychology, psychostatics.**]

structure = 1. (*biol.*) the composition, spatial interrelations, and character of material parts in an organism; 2. (*general*) the arrangement of materials or of parts in any complex aggregate, e.g. in a sentence, a house, consciousness, etc. [Contr. (1) w. **function** = activity of an organ.] **structural**[a]. — Ger. *Struktur, Organisation, Bau.*

structure = 3. (*Gestalt*) a characteristic of an organized whole or unit with special reference to the positional interdependence of its parts. [Usually applied to phenomenal data or their physiological correlates, but may refer also to physical organization, since there are, according to Köhler, physical Gestalten or structures. Contr. w. **constellation** = a group of units having no functional relations. Cf. **configuration, Gestalt.**]

structure-function = a relation, property, or response activity which results from a totality regarded as a unit rather than from its parts as such or their interconnections; i.e. a configurational pattern or response. [Cf. **configuration, step-wise phenomenon.**]

struggle for existence = a phrase formulated by Darwin to designate biological competition, which emphasizes the fact that the securing of nutriment and mates, and the avoidance of climatic dangers and of enemies, involve a competitive contest between members of the same or allied species. [Cf. **natural selection, survival of the fittest.**] — Fr. *concurrence vitale, lutte pour la vie*; Ger. *Kampf ums Dasein.*

struggle reflex, struggling = a type of response consisting of violent, usually uncoordinated movements. [Exhibited by the newborn child when his limbs or head are confined so that the usual random movements are prevented. Mediated by brain stem and spinal cord.] — Fr. *réflexe de lutte.*

strychnin = a powerful alkaloid found in the fruit of *Strychnos nux-vomica* and in St. Ignatius Bean, which possesses an extremely bitter taste and acts promptly on the spinal cord, producing convulsions. [By its action on the anterior-horn cells of the cord, it destroys reciprocal innervation of antagonistic muscle groups.

Sensory stimulation causes convulsive seizures of both extensor and flexor muscles. Lat. *Strychninum.*]

study[n] = 1. a loose term signifying relatively protracted attention to a topic or subject, for the purpose of acquiring information about it, or of solving problems arising in it, or of memorizing it; 2. (esp. in pl.) particular branches of learning or objects of attentive consideration; 3. a report of results of **investigation. study**[v], **studious**[a] = inclined to study; pursuing study. — Fr. *étude*; Ger. *Arbeit, Studium.*

stupor = a state of non-responsiveness and partial unconsciousness, differing from sleep and also from coma, which usually involves almost complete intellectual insensibility. **stuporous**[a]. — Ger. *Betäubung.*

stuttering = a disturbance in the rhythm of speech, either an intermittent blocking, or the convulsive repetition of a sound. [A form of **dysphemia.** Syn. **spasmophemia, stammering. stuttering** and **stammering** are sometimes distg. in that the former is convulsive repetition, whereas the latter is blocking.] — Fr. *begaiement*; Ger. *Stottern.*

style = a distinctive type or mode of artistic presentation, dress, literary composition, etc. [A loose term, which includes types of architecture, music, painting, etc.] — Fr. *mode, style*; Ger. *Stil, Manier.*

style of life = (*indiv. psychol.*) the individual's technique for achieving superiority. [Differences in childhood experience are responsible for the individual differences in **styles of life** which are the central interest of individual psychology.]

stylus = 1. a pointed or pen-shaped instrument used for recording on smoked drums, etc.; 2. a pencil-like device, with or without a metal tip, for maze tracing, tapping, or coordination test.

SU = abbrev. for **sensation unit.** — Ger. *Stift.*

subclavian = below the clavicle or collar-bone. (Accent **-clay-.**)

subconscious = 1. pert. to processes of which the individual is not aware, but which appear to be otherwise akin to the processes of (conscious) experience; 2. dimly or marginally conscious. [Distg. fr. **subliminal** = lacking in intensity; **subordinate (consciousness)** = belonging to lower centers and not connected with one's personal experiences; **unconscious** (3).] **subconsciousness**[n], **the subconscious**[n]. — Fr. *subconscient*; Ger. *Unbewusstsein.*

subcutaneous sensibility = the sensory capacity, allied to the touch senses, which exists in the deeper portion of the true skin (the **tela subcutanea**), and of which the Pacinian corpuscles are assumed to be a representative receptor. [Sometimes applied also to muscle, bone, joint, and organic sensitivity.] — Fr. *sensibilité souscutanée.*

subdural = beneath or within the dura, or outer covering of the brain.

subhuman = pert. to organisms or organic phenomena below the human level of organization. [Usually applied to characteristics of animal rather than of plant life.]

subinguinal = pert. to or located on small regions lying just below the groin on either side of the front of the human body.

subject = 1. the self or experiencing individual; 2. an individual or animal used for psychological experimentation; 3. any topic. [Syn. (2) **observer;** applied to human subjects who report their experiences under given experimental conditions; abbrev. *S.*] **subject**[a] (1), **subjective**[a] (1) — Ger. (2) *Versuchsperson* (*Vp.*).

subject of consciousness, subject-consciousness = the self considered as undergoing experiences. [Distg. fr. **object of consciousness** = the experiences which the self undergoes.]

subject organization = the constitution of the personality-function at the given moment or as the self for protracted continuity.

subjective = 1. dependent upon the individual organism; 2. not admitting of record by physical instruments; 3. not open to verification by other investigators; 4. localized in psychological space within the observer's body (e.g. feelings, as contr. w. most visual data, etc.). [In psychol. the term **subjective data** and other phrases are used by different writers in senses (2), (3), and (4), often without precise discrimination. Contr. w. **objective data,** etc. Cf. **objective.**]

subjective accent = rhythm read into a series of impressions that objectively are alike and equally spaced. [Syn. **subjective rhythm, subjective accentuation.**]

subjective psychology = the investigation of mental phenomena introspectively observed. [Syn. **introspective psychology.** Contr. w. **objective psychology.**]

subjective selection = (*biol.*) any type of selection which involves consciousness.

subjective sensations = sensations arising in connection with the external senses, where the sources of the stimuli are not external to the organism itself. [E.g. entoptic phenomena; ringing in the ears.]

subjective trait = a trait which is not accessible to measurement in terms of any standard performance; e.g. cheerfulness. [Contr. w. **objective trait.**]

sublimation = (*psychoan.*) the unconscious process of deflecting the energy of the sexual impulse (i.e. libido) to new objects or aims of a non-sexual and socially useful goal. [**sublimation** results in a desexualized sexual impulse. Syn. **diversion of sex energy.** Cf. **libido.**] **sublimated**[a]. — Ger. *Sublimierung.*

sublime/the = an object or situation which impresses the observer with the feeling of power, magnitude, loftiness, or moral greatness in that object or situation. **sublime**[a] = characterizing the object or the feeling which it arouses.

subliminal = below the threshold. [Applies to (*a*) stimuli which are not sufficiently intense to arouse definite sensations, but which nevertheless have some effect upon the responses or mental life of the individual; or to (*b*) the effects of such stimuli, or to (*c*) differences between stimuli which are not sufficiently great for the differences to be perceived. Not to be confused with **sublimated.**] — Fr. *infraliminaire.*

subliminal consciousness, see **consciousness/subliminal.** — Fr. *conscience subliminale.*

subliminal learning = acquisitions in the form of neurograms or habit equipment, which cannot be directly recalled. — Fr. *apprentissage (acquisition) infraliminaire.*

subliminal stimulus = a stimulus of such slight intensity, saturation, etc. that it fails to produce any conscious effect. — Fr. *stimulus infraliminaire.*

sublingual = located below the tongue.

submaxillary = located below the jaw. (Accent **-max-**.)

submental = pert. to or located in the region just below the chin.

submission, submissiveness = a mode of behavior in an individual's face-to-face relations with others, characterized by the tendency to yield to others, or to adjust one's behavior to the domination of others. [Contr. w. **ascendance,** or **dominance** = characterized by effort to rule or control others.] **submissive**[a]. — Ger. *Unterwerfung*.

submissive reflex, see **catalepsy.**

subnormal = below normal; i.e. varying from the normal in the direction of the less, or of inferiority.

subordination = in classification, the placing of a given species, or class of data, as a lower group within or under a certain higher class or category. [Contr. w. **coordination.**] **subordinate**[a]. — Ger. *Unterordnung*.

subordination/social = (*soc.*) a term used by Georg Simmel to describe the type of social accommodation in which behavior (individual or group) is dominated by the actions of others or by impersonal principles or laws. [**superordination** and **subordination** in part constitute the sociological analogy to **ascendence** and **submission,** respectively.] **subordinate**[v].

subpotency = a lesser degree of potency in the inheritance of certain characters, as compared with others. [Cf. **potency, prepotency.**] **subpotent**[a].

subscapular = pert. to or located in the regions of the middle back below the scapula and above the lumbar regions.

subservience, subserviency = willingness to subordinate one's behavior to the purpose or interests of another person. [Contr. w. **mastery.** Cf. **submission.**] **subservient**[a]. — Ger. *Unterwürfigkeit*.

subsistence = the presence or inclusion of an object or other datum, whether existent or not, in the field or universe of discourse. [A logical and philosophical conception used to avoid the issue of the reality or present existence of the classes, etc. under discussion. Cf. **form** (1).] **subsist**[v], **subsistent**[a].

substantia nigra, see **nigra/substantia.**

substantive states = parts of an experience which have sufficient definiteness and sufficient duration to be observed and denoted by nouns, verbs, and adjectives. [Contr. (by James) w. **transitive** (or **relational**) states, which elude distinct observation but are indicated by prepositions, conjunctions, etc.] — Fr. *états substantifs*.

substitute[a] = syn. for **conditioned,** in the expressions *substitute stimulus, substitute response*. — Ger. *Ersatz-*.

substitution = (*math.*) the replacing of a variable quantity by some specific value of it, in order to determine the corresponding value of a related variable or variables.

substitution test = a type of test in which the task is to substitute the elements of one system of characters (e.g. numbers) for those of another (e.g. letters), the elements being paired according to a prearranged plan or key. [In a typical example, the **symbol-digit test,** ten or fewer digits are paired with simple geometric forms.]

subsume = to assign an object, datum, class of phenomena, or law to its logical position under a more general class or law. **subsumption**[n].

subtraction method = a method of treating the results of **compound reaction** (or **response**) **time,** which consists in determining the simple sensory or muscular reaction time and subtracting this from the total time of the complex reaction (e.g. of recognizing a word or letter), the remainder being regarded as the time required for the special mental process (e.g. of recognition). [The validity of this method is challenged by contemporary psychologists, because the **higher mental processes** are now regarded as **Gestalten** and not as formed by the addition of certain fixed increments to simpler mental processes. Külpe effectively criticized the **subtraction method** in 1893. Cf. **compound reaction.**]

subtractive principle = in color mixture, a principle depending upon the fact that the apparent color of a pigment, or any body which selectively absorbs light of different wave-lengths, is complementary to the color of the light which is absorbed. [This means that when two transparent colored screens are superimposed, the resulting color will differ from that which would be obtained by the mixture of all the wave-lengths of light yielded by both screens independently. The latter type of mixture is strictly **additive,** in contr. w. the nominally **subtractive** result obtained by the combination of the screens. The mixture of pigments also involves the **subtractive principle.**] — Fr. *principe soustractif*.

successful act = 1. a response or a series of responses in trial and error learning which lead directly or advantageously toward the goal or objective; 2. a reaction to a portion of some situation, which is part of the most economical response to the total situation. [Contr. w. **unsuccessful act.**] — Fr. *action réussie*.

succession = 1. the serial replacement of one experience by another; 2. a temporal series of experiences. [Distg. fr. **duration,** which characterizes an experience that occupies without change a period or extent of time. Contr. w. **simultaneity.**] **succeed**[v], **successive**[a].

successive = (*psychol.*) characterizing two or more experiences which are present in contiguous segments of time. [Contr. w. **simultaneous.**]

sucking = 1. an early postnatal reflex, aroused by grasping the nipple with lips and tongue, whereby the mammalian infant draws milk through the lips into the mouth; 2. the entire chain of reflexes involved in the infant's feeding, including the swallowing reflex. [(1) is mediated by the V (sensory, motor) cranial nerve. To avoid ambiguity (1) is prefd., using the term **suckling** for the chain of reflexes, or food-getting instinct.] — Fr. *succion*; Ger. *saugen, lutschen*.

suckling = 1. the entire chain of reflexes in the infant involved in feeding; 2. the maternal act of giving breast to the infant; 3. a nursing infant. [Cf. **sucking.**] **suckle**[v] (2). — Fr. (1) *acte de teter*, (2) *allaitement*, (3) *nourrisson* (*-ne*); Ger. (3) *Säugling*.

sudomotor nerves = nerves which control sweat secretion.

sudoriferous glands = glands in the skin which secrete a saline substance, called sweat.

sudorific = pert. to the secretion of the sweat glands.

suffer = 1. (*pop.*) to experience intense pain;

2. (*hist.*) to permit; to accept without resistance. **sufferer**[n], **suffering**[n] (1). — Ger. (1) *leiden*, (2) *zulassen*.

sufficient reason/law of = a formula devised by Leibnitz according to which, given sufficient knowledge, one might discover why any specific occurrence is such as it is, and not otherwise. [Contr. w. **insufficient reason.**] — Fr. *principe de raison suffisante*; Ger. *Gesetz des zureichenden Grundes*.

suggestibility = a more or less permanent susceptibility to suggestion. **suggestible**[a].

suggestion = 1. the inducing or the attempt at inducing of an idea, belief, decision, action, etc. by one individual in another through stimulation, whether verbal or otherwise, but exclusive of argument or command; 2. the stimulus, usually verbal in nature, by which one individual seeks to arouse action in another by circumventing the critical, integrative functions. [In hypnosis the suggestion may take the form of a command. Syn. **heterosuggestion.** Distg. fr. **autosuggestion** = the inducing of a belief, etc., by the individual in himself.] **suggest**[v].

suggestion/negative = a suggestion which is designed to inhibit some other mental or motor process already under way or otherwise likely to become so. [Cf. **counter-suggestion, contra-suggestion.**]

sui generis = unique in its class, single (or singular). [Used to designate an individual datum of any sort which is the sole instance in the class to which it belongs. Lat.]

sulcus, see **fissure.**

sulkiness = a mood or disposition characterized by undue resentment, without marked motor expression, when one is rebuked, overruled, or ignored. **sulky**[a]. — Fr. *bouderie*; Ger. *Schmollen, Trotzen*.

sum = (*math.*) the amount obtained when two or more members are added.

sum-total = an emphatic syn. for **sum.**

summation effect = the enhanced result of the rapid repetition of stimuli or excitations. [The phenomenon occurs in the sensory process, through repetition of stimulations; in muscle contractions, through repetition of excitations.]

summation of stimuli = the process of superimposing or adding other stimuli or other processes to an originally given stimulus or induced process. [Sometimes used as syn. for **summation effect.**] **summate**[v].

summation/reflex = the fusion and mutual reinforcement of two or more afferent nerve impulses in the production of a reflex response.

summation time = the longest interval between the presentation of two similar stimuli whose joint action produces a response.

summation tone = a tone which is produced by the simultaneous sounding of two different tones, and whose pitch is equal to the sum of their vibration rates. [Contr. w. **difference tone,** whose pitch is equal to the difference of the two vibration rates. Cf. **combination tone.**] — Fr. *son résultant additionnel, son de sommation*.

superego = (*psychoan.*) that part of the mental apparatus which criticizes the ego, and which produces distress, anxiety, or punishment whenever the ego tends to accept impulses emanating from the reservoir of primitive instinctual impulses (the **id**). [Conceived of as an inner monitor, syn. w. **unconscious conscience;** a deposit left by the earliest parental **object-choices** of the id, an energetic **reaction-formation** against these choices. Cf. **ego, id, ego-ideal.**] — Fr. *le surmoi, le super-ego*; Ger. *Überich*.

superficial = 1. (*anat.*) pert. to or located on the surface of the body or of an organ; 2. (*logic*) treating or dealing with only the obvious or apparent aspects of a problem, and failing to examine the underlying factors and fundamental principles involved. [Contr. w. **deep.**] **superficies**[n] (1), **surface**[n] (1), **superficiality**[n] (2). — Ger. *oberflächlich, äusserlich*.

superficial reflex = contraction of muscles elicited by scratching or pinching the skin immediately over or near them. [Syn. **skin r.**]

superhuman = 1. beyond human knowledge or ability; 2. pert. to a hypothetical *superman*. — Fr. *surhumain*; Ger. *übermenschlich*.

superior adult = 1. loosely, an adult possessed of **superior intelligence;** 2. more technically, a person, of any age, possessed of the level of intelligence requisite to pass the **superior adult tests.**

superior adult tests = 1. a group of six tests in the Stanford Revision of the Binet-Simon Scale lying in difficulty next above the group known as Year XVI, Average Adult, and assumed to represent a level of intelligence equivalent to a (theoretical) mental age of 18; 2. a set of unusually difficult and steeply graded tests known as the **Roback Mentality Tests for Superior Adults.** [Among the subtests included in (2) are **analogies, abstraction, subsumption,** and **cryptogram.**]

superior child = 1. a child of high intelligence, i.e. with high **intelligence quotient;** 2. a child who possesses desirable traits to an unusual degree. — Fr. *enfant bien doué (d'élite)*.

superior intelligence = the degree of general mental ability possessed by the best 20 or 25 per cent of persons tested by a reliable intelligence test; equivalent approx. to an IQ of 110 or better on the Stanford Revision of the Binet-Simon Scale. [This range of ability is often subdivided into three sections: *superior* (in the narrow sense), IQ 110–120; *very superior,* IQ 120–140; *near genius,* IQ 140+.]

superior oblique, rectus, see **eye-muscles.**

superiority feeling = the subjective experience of exaggerated self-worth; i.e. the tendency to look upon one's own qualities, achievements, or possessions as superior to those of others. [Contr. w. **inferiority feeling,** and sometimes regarded as an overcompensation for the latter.] — Fr. *sentiment de supériorité*.

superman = a hypothetical being, superior to the human type, who is assumed to possess all the intellectual and other mental characters of man, without human limitations. **superhuman**[a] (used more frequently to characterize that which is beyond human knowledge or power). — Fr. *surhomme*; Ger. *Übermensch*.

supernatural = belonging to a higher order or system than that of nature, or transcending the ordinary course of nature. [Distg. fr. **supernormal** = belonging to an unknown but natural order or system.] — Fr. *surnaturel*; Ger. *übernatürlich*.

supernormal[a] = 1. characterizing certain occurrences which are not open to explanation in terms of any known principles of science, but which are believed to be consistent with natural law, and destined with the advance of science to be reduced to natural law; 2. distinctly above the norm or median, e.g. in intelligence or other ability. [Used in *psychical research* to designate certain supposed phenomena, or the mental processes which produce them. Distg. fr. **supernatural** = beyond the domain of science.] — Fr. *surnormal*.

supernormal recovery phase = a phase (following the total and partial refractory periods) in the recovery of conductivity in nerve fiber after the transmission of a nerve impulse, during which excitability and the intensity of the nerve impulse are increased above the normal.

superstition = 1. a disposition or tendency to ascribe phenomena which admit of a natural explanation to occult or supernatural causes; 2. a belief or practice which manifests this tendency; 3. an accepted belief whose falsity has been scientifically demonstrated. [Strictly, it is incorrect to apply the term to primitive attempts at scientific knowledge, or the adjective to individuals who lived before the falsity of these primitive beliefs was demonstrated. Cf. **magic, sciosophy.**] **superstitious**[a]. — Ger. *Aberglaube*.

supination = a movement of the hand or forelimb, usually rotary, which tends to bring the palmar surface upward. [It sometimes occurs in the act of writing and fencing. Contr. w. **pronation.**] **supinatory**[a].

supinator longus reflex = flexion of the forearm, elicited by tapping the tendon of the brachioradial muscle. [Mediated by 5th cervical segment of spinal cord.]

support/sense of = sensory processes connected with the muscle, pressure, and static senses, which furnish data whereby an animal maintains an erect or other normal posture against gravity. [Cf. **tonus.**]

supposal = a mental attitude in which the subject is aware that the choice of an alternative is arbitrary. [Syn. **make-believe;** contr. w. **belief,** in which the alternative chosen is regarded as determined objectively.]

supposition = a loose term denoting a casual assumption, and emphasizing its doubtful character. [Syn. **hypothesis.**] **suppose**[v].

suppression = the tendency on the part of individuals to dismiss from consciousness the memory of unpleasant experiences, or thoughts, desires, etc., which are under social taboo. [The psychoanalytic school interprets suppression as a conscious activity of inhibition, in contr. w. **repression,** which is an unconscious process; with W. H. R. Rivers these meanings of the two terms are interchanged.] — Ger. *Unterdrückung*.

suppression/social, see **social suppression.**

supraclavicular = pert. to or located in the triangular regions just above the clavicular regions. (Accent **-vick-**.)

supraliminal = above the threshold of sensation, or above the threshold of difference. (Accent **-lim-**.) — Fr. *supraliminaire*; Ger. *übermerklich*.

supraliminal differences/method of, see **mean gradations/method of.** — Ger. *M. der übermerklichen Unterschiede*.

supraorbital = pert. to or located in the region above the orbit, or eye-socket.

supraorbital reflex = contraction of the orbicularis oculi (eyelid muscle) elicited by a tap over the supraorbital foramen. [Mediated by trigeminofacial arc. Syn. **McCarthy's r., ophthalmic r.**]

suprarenal = located above the kidneys. [Syn. **adrenal.**] (Accent **-ree-**.) — Fr. *surrénal*.

suprarenal capsule, glands, see **adrenal glands.**

suprarenal cortex = the outer portion of the suprarenal glands. — Fr. *écorce surrénale*.

suprarenal medulla = the mass of chromaffin cells, together with the blood vessels, connective tissue cells, and nerve tissue, which constitute the histologically distinct central mass of a suprarenal body. [Distg. fr. **suprarenal cortex** = the histologically distinct outer portion of a suprarenal body.]

suprarenalin, see **epinephrin.**

suprarenin, see **epinephrin.**

suprascapular = pert. to or located on the regions at the top of the back, above the scapular regions.

sural = pert. to or located on the calf of the leg.

surdimutism, see **deaf-mute.**

surdity, see **deafness.**

surface = 1. (*math.*) a continuum having two dimensions; 2. (*psychol.*) visual or tactual perception of objects in terms of a plane of two dimensions, i.e. without reference to depth. — Ger. *Fläche, Oberfläche*.

surface color = a color which appears as definitely occupying the surface of a perceived object. [Contr. w. **film color.**] — Ger. *Oberflächenfarbe*.

surplus energy theory = the theory which explains the play activities of human and subhuman young as due to the superabundance of energy in growing organisms, this extra energy manifesting itself in inherited modes of behavior which are typical of the species.

surprise = an attitude aroused by some unexpected situation which manifests itself in certain characteristic gestures, facial expression, etc. [Applied to less violent demonstrations than those characterized by the terms **astonishment** and **alarm.**] — Fr. *étonnement, surprise*; Ger. *Überraschung*.

surreptitious = characterizing an unwarranted insertion of data, premise, or argument in a report or discussion, usually intentionally and always in an obscure way, which is designed or which tends to deceive the reader or listener. **surreptitiously**[adv]. — Fr. *subreptice*; Ger. *erschlichen*.

surrogate = (*psychoan.*) a representation of a person which conceals from conscious recognition the identity of that person. [E.g. in a dream, a king or an unrecognized man may represent the dreamer's father; or an animal phobia may be a substitute for the fear of a certain member of the family.]

sursumvergence = 1. a deviation of one eye upward, with respect to the other, from its position of fixation, in the absence of any artificial interference; 2. the measurement of the power of the eye to so deviate in overcoming the effect of a prism placed before it. [Cf. **convergence.**]

survey tests = a type of test, esp. of educational test, designed to afford reasonably exact information concerning the general level of attainment of a school class or other group of persons.

[Distg. fr. **diagnostic tests** and from tests designed to give precise information concerning the abilities or needs of single individuals as contr. w. a group.]

survivalⁿ = a mode of behavior which was distinctly useful to the organisms of a given species at an earlier stage of evolution, but which has become useless or without significance through changes in structure or modes of life. [E.g. certain facial expressions, such as the snarling attitude, are said to be **survivals** of the predatory stage of man's ancestors. A functional term, which corresponds to **vestige** in the structure of organisms.] — Ger. *Überleben, Überrest.*

survival of the fittest = a phrase devised by Herbert Spencer to describe the results of biological competition or struggle for existence. [Equivalent to "survival of the best adapted organisms." Cf. **natural selection, struggle for existence.**] — Fr. *survivance des plus aptes.*

survival value = the degree in which a given organic structure or mode of behavior is fitted to prolong the life of those individuals which possess it and the continuity of their line of descent. [Applied esp. to new variations in the structure of organs or in modes of behavior, i.e. the greater their usefulness (in the given environment) the greater their **survival value.**]

survive = to escape destruction as an organism. **survival**ⁿ.

suspense = an attitude which results from the balance of conflicting motives, or from the absence of certain data requisite to the formation of a decision or judgment, and which is characterized by the inhibition of responsive activity. — Ger. *Unschlüssigkeit.*

suspicion = 1. a social attitude characterized by doubt of the sincerity of another, or of the friendliness of his attitude; 2. a trait which predisposes an individual to such doubt in his general social relations. [Syn. (2) **suspiciousness.**] **suspicious**ᵃ. — Fr. *soupçon*; Ger. *Argwohn, Verdacht.*

sustained = prolonged or continued. [E.g. sustained attention; a sustained tone.] — Fr. *soutenu.*

suture of nerve = an artificial union of the cut ends of a severed nerve trunk, which permits regeneration by the outgrowth of nerve fibers along the course of the degenerated portion of the trunk.

swallowing reflex = the simultaneous and chained activity of certain deglutition muscles in the mouth and throat, whereby liquid or solid food is passed from the mouth into the esophagus. Mediated by V to XI cranial nerves and oblongata. [Syn. **deglutition.**] — Fr. *réflexe de déglutition*; Ger. *Schluckreflex.*

sweet = a quality of gustatory sensation of which the taste of cane-sugar is a typical example. [Cf. **gustatory qualities.**] — Fr. *sucré*; Ger. *süss.*

Swindle's ghost = an excessively long positive after-sensation.

swoon, see **syncope.** — Fr. *évanouissement*; Ger. *Ohnmacht.*

syllabism = the use of syllabic characters instead of letters as adopted in certain written languages, e.g. the Japanese.

syllable-span test = a mental test similar to the digit-span test except that syllables are used instead of digits. [Cf. **digit-span test.**] — Fr. *t. de mémoire immédiate des syllabes.*

syllogism = a form of reasoning or argument in which a general statement is given, followed by some more particular statement, the two together leading to a third or dependent statement, according to the accepted principles of logic. [The preliminary statements are termed the **major** and **minor premise,** respectively; the final statement is called the **conclusion.**] **syllogistic**ᵃ, **syllogize**ᵛ (rare).

Sylvian aqueduct, see **aqueduct of Sylvius.**

Sylvian fissure, fissure of Sylvius = a deep groove or fissure on the lateral surface of each cerebral hemisphere, which extends horizontally from the gyrus frontalis inferior to the gyrus supramarginalis and demarcates the temporal from the frontal and parietal lobes. — Fr. *scissure de S.*; Ger. *Sylvische Spalte.*

symbiosis = the social relationship of one species with another. [A generic term which includes all types of subordination, equality, and superiority; generally limited to subhuman species. Cf. **parasite, commensalism, myrmecophily.**] **symbiotic**ᵃ.

symbol = 1. (*psychol.*) an object, expression, or responsive activity which replaces and becomes a representative substitute for another; 2. (*math.*) a conventional mark used consistently to represent a class of things, or a type of relation; 3. (*psychoan.*) a disguised representation of unconscious sexual material, which has a constant meaning and is not consciously associated with sexual activity. [In psychol., words are symbols for objects, ideas, etc., and verbal or other responsive activities are symbols for more general acts of behavior. The terms *symbolic act, s. behavior, s. experience, s. expression, s. reaction, s. response,* etc., are used in this sense. In math. a symbol may stand for an operation (e.g. +, =), or for any of the succession of values which a variable may take. See Table XV.] — Ger. *Sinnbild, Symbol.*

symbol-digit test, see **substitution test.**

symbolic act, etc., see **symbol.**

symbolic function = the mental process whereby one idea, response, experience, etc. becomes the representation or substitute of another. [Cf. **symbol.**]

symbolism = 1. the systematic use of symbols, or the theory of symbols; 2. (*psychoan.*) the expression of unconscious thinking, usually sexual, when the real meaning of an idea is so transformed as to become unrecognized by consciousness; 3. (*esth.*) that form of art which makes a systematic use of symbols its chief method. [(2) is considered by psychoanalysts to be the basis of myths, dreams, and wit, and a characteristic of neurotic symptoms. Cf. **symbol.**] **symbolize**ᵛ, **symbolic**ᵃ.

symbolization = (*psychoan.*) a mental process occurring in dreams, wit, myths, neurotic manifestations, etc., in which a situation or idea assumes an indirect, condensed or elaborated, but always figurative form. [Cf. **symbolism.**]

symmetry = 1. (*biol.*) the arrangement of the parts or constituents of a complex whole with reference to one another, such as to produce a balance, either of one side with the other, or of radiating sectors with one another, or of the members of a linear series; 2. (*esth.*) regularity in the arrangement of the formal elements of an art object so that it may be divided into similar parts. [In (1) these three types are called **bilateral, radial,** and **linear symmetry** respectively; in each case the symmetry may be either 2- or 3- dimensional.] **symmetric(al)**[a].

sympathetic ganglion = any one of the ganglia or nerve centers in the sympathetic nervous system. [Applied also more generally to the entire set of ganglia belonging to the autonomic system.] — Fr. *ganglion sympathique.*

sympathetic induction, see **induction/sympathetic.**

sympathetic nervous system = 1. the system of ganglia lying outside the spinal cord in the thoracic and lumbar regions, together with the peripheral nerves connected therewith, which serve the organs of digestion, secretion, etc.; 2. syn. for **autonomic system** (1). [The narrower meaning (1) is prefd. Distg. (1) fr. **parasympathetic n. s.**]

sympathetic vibration, see **resonance.**

sympathy = 1. an emotion or emotional attitude aroused in an individual by the perception or idea of suffering in others, and characterized by a feeling of unpleasantness and usually by actions which tend to relieve this suffering; 2. the supposed tendency to repeat in oneself any emotion observed in another. **sympathize**[v], **sympathetic**[a]. — Ger. *Mitgefühl, Sympathie.*

symptom = 1. (*pathol.*) any structural change or functional peculiarity which indicates the presence of a disease or disorder in a given individual; 2. (*general*) any phenomenon which points to the presence, otherwise unsuspected, of an underlying condition or incipient change, esp. in the maturing of individual behavior or in the progress of social development; 3. (*psychoan.*) a distortion or displacement of unconscious libidinal wish-fulfillments, whereby a genuine but disguised satisfaction for the libido is secured. [Cf. **index, symbol.**] **symptomatic**[a]. — Fr. (1, 2, 3) *symptôme*; Ger. (1) *Symptom,* (2) *Kennzeichen.*

synapse, synapsis = the region of contact between the end of one neuron and the beginning of the next in a neural chain. [It is characterized by a splitting of each nerve-terminal into minute fibrils, which intermesh with the fibrils of the other terminal, or are applied directly to or within the body of the neuron. Syn. **synaptic junction.**] (Accent (1) **syn-**, 2 syll.; accent (2) **-aps-**.) **synapses**[pl], **synaptic**[a].

synapse time = that part of the latent period of a reflex which is supposed to be consumed by transmission of the nerve impulse across synapses. — Fr. *temps synaptique.*

synaptic junction, see **synapse.**

syncope = a temporary suspension of consciousness due to cerebral anemia. [Syn. **swoon, swooning, faint, fainting,** all of which emphasize the onset rather than the condition itself.] (3 syll.)

syncretism = 1. a term (usually derogatory) employed to characterize an indiscriminate attempt to combine mutually incompatible doctrines into a system; 2. a type of thinking, characteristic of young children, in which analysis based upon objective relations, as conceived by adults, plays little or no part; in the mind of the child, everything is connected with everything else but not in terms of adult conceptions of time, space, or cause (Piaget). [Distg. (1) fr. **eclecticism.**] **syncretic**[a].

syncryptic = pert. to protective resemblances between diverse species.

syncytium = an aggregation of cells between which there is some direct continuity of cytoplasm without separating membranes.

syndactylism = the condition of having two or more fingers or toes partly or completely grown together or joined together by a webbed structure.

syndrome = a term denoting the aggregate symptoms of a disease, i.e. a symptom complex; e.g. Parkinson's syndrome. **syndromes**[pl].

synergic = exerting force together. [Applied to groups of muscles all of which act together to produce extension (or flexion) of a joint or limb, or to produce a definite (purposive) action of the whole organism. Contr. w. **antergic.**]

synergic reflex, see **allied reflexes.**

synergy = the union or combining together of partial or elementary motor processes or movements into a complex motor process or coordinate movement. [Cf. **coordination/muscular.**] **synergic**[a]. — Ger. *Zusammenwirken, Synergie.*

synergy theory = the theory that mental synthesis consists in a unitary response, whether perceptual or motor, aroused by the aggregate of sensory or other elements, which are conceived as stimuli converging upon a single response mechanism (Woodworth).

synesthesia, synaesthesia, syn(a)esthesis = a phenomenon characterizing the experiences of certain individuals, in which certain sensations belonging to one sense or mode attach to certain sensations of another group and appear regularly whenever a stimulus of the latter type occurs. [There are various types, of which **colored hearing (synopsia)** is the most common; e.g. the vocal sound *o* may appear red.] **synesthetic**[a], **synesthete**[np].

synonym-antonym test = a type of test in which pairs of synonymous words and pairs of antonyms (opposites) are presented in random order, the task being to indicate which pairs of words are synonyms and which antonyms. [E.g. test 4 of Army Alpha. Syn. **same-opposite test.**]

synopsia = a type of **synesthesia** in which visual sensations are closely associated with auditory sensations and appear regularly whenever the latter are stimulated. [Usually a given quality of visual sensation is associated with some specific quality of audition.] Cf. **colored hearing, synesthesia.**

syntactical aphasia, see **aphasia.**

syntechnic = characterizing an incidental resemblance of any sort between two unallied organic species.

synthesis = the joining together, either actually or in thought, of two or more data of any sort whatever, so as to form a complex unit. [Distg. fr. **association,** in which the mutual interaction of the data joined together is minimized or neglected (though by some writers association as a mental operation is regarded as the *basis* of all mental synthesis); fr. **fusion,** in which the data lose their individual identity; and fr. **integration,** which emphasizes the formation out of the elements of a *compact* whole; **association** and **fusion** are applied in psychology chiefly to **mental contents; synthesis** and **integration** to any data. Cf. **creative synthesis** and **mental chemistry.** Contr. w. **analysis** = the separation of a complex unit into its constituents.] **synthesize**[v], **synthetic**[a]. — Ger. *Verknüpfung.*

synthesis/chemical, see **chemical synthesis.**

synthesis/mental, see **mental synthesis.**

syntonic = characterizing a type of personality which is emotionally responsive to the environment so as to give reactions suited to each momentary situation. [Regarded by Bleuler as the normal type from which manic-depressive insanity arises by exaggeration.] **syntone**[n].

syringomyelia = (*pathol.*) an extensive longitudinal cavity formation in the spinal cord and medulla, often with abolition (dissociation) only of the pain and temperature senses. (7 syll., accent 5th, **-ee-**.)

system = 1. a group of entities or data which are related to one another by interaction or interdependence; 2. a group of concepts or principles which serve as a framework for holding in orderly arrangement the data of any branch of science; 3. (*Gestalt*) a totality, phenomenal or actual, all the parts or aspects of which are interrelated members of the whole. **systematic**[a], **systematize**[v] (2).

system/mental = the mental life of an individual, regarded as a progressive organization of experiences and functions into a **system,** or unitary whole.

systematic determination = the serial flow or progress of thought in an individual, which proceeds according to the principles of association.

systematic error = an error due to the manner of collecting the data or of their subsequent treatment, which results in a tendency to diverge from the truth continually in the same direction. [Contr. w. **incidental error.**]

systematic errors of observation = alterations in the values under investigation which occur persistently and are due to some general bias of the observer or to the method of conducting the investigation. [A special case of this is **constant error,** in which the alterations are all in one direction. Contr. w. **accidental errors.** Cf. **personal equation.**]

systematized amnesia, see **amnesia/localized.**

systemic sense = a generic name for those senses whose receptors are distributed in the internal organs (i.e. interoceptors), in contradistinction to the senses whose receptors are distributed more superficially (e.g. the cutaneous and special senses). [Syn. **visceral sense.** Cf. **organic sense, sensitivity/visceral.**] — Ger. *Gemeinsinn.*

systole = 1. the duration of a single contraction of the heart; 2. the phase of contraction of the heart's activity. [Contr. w. **diastole.**] (3 syll.) **systolic**[a].

T

T-scale = a scale used in interpreting scores obtained on a test; it ordinarily ranges from 0 to 100 (or from -5σ to $+5\sigma$), the unit of measurement being one-tenth of the standard deviation of unselected 12-year old children, whose mean score is 50 on the scale. [The scores on this scale are called **T-scores.**] — Fr. *échelle T.*

T-type = in eidetic theory, a type of individual who manifests certain tetanoid symptoms and a disposition to eidetic imagery that is obsessive, inflexible, photographic. [According to W. Jaensch, the imagery is diminished by calcium treatment. Cf. **B-type.**]

tabes, tabes dorsalis = a disease of the posterior columns of the spinal cord, marked by loss of muscular sensation and by inability to make coordinated movements with those parts of the body corresponding to the affected segments of the cord. [Sometimes called **locomotor ataxia.**] **tabetic**[a]. — Ger. *Rückenmarksschwindsucht.*

table-turning, table-tipping, see **autoscope.**

taboo, tabu = 1. (*anthrop.*) a conventional ban placed by tradition or custom upon certain acts, modes of dress, topics, or words in conversation, etc., the infringement of such convention being a matter not of legal prosecution but of social reproval and persecution; 2. (*relig.*) an interdiction of intercourse with, approach to, or handling of given persons, places, or objects, except by privileged persons (e.g. priests) or in prescribed ways; religious taboo is based upon the assumed sacredness and consequent dangerousness of the persons, places, or objects in question; 3. (*psychoan.*) a prohibition enforced from without, concerning actions which are strongly wished or desired. [Syn. **negative magic.** While the subject matter of taboo varies tremendously with culture-stage, community, and area, the social attitudes toward infringement are very dissimilar.]

tabula rasa = a blank tablet or clean slate. [Lat. A figure of speech employed by 17th and 18th century writers to express the idea that the mind of the new-born babe is prepared to receive impressions, but at the outset has no innate impression or content. The phrase came into use through the popular Stoic manuals written in Latin in the 17th century. The Greek equivalent is found in a fragment of Chrysippus, but the modern use of it as the typical formula of the empirical school does not accurately represent its original meaning; nor should the term be confused with the wax-tablet simile introduced by Plato, which had reference only to images and memory. Locke (1690) at the beginning of British empiricism, compared the babe's mind to a piece of white paper.]

tabulation = the arrangement of a collection of data or results in tabular form, i.e. in two or more columns (or rows), the corresponding rows (or lines) in each column (or row) presenting comparable data. **tabulate**[v], **tabular**[a]. — Ger. *Tabellierung.*

tachistoscope = an instrument for the presentation of visual stimuli such as a picture, a word, or a group of symbols, or for successive presentation of a series of any such data, the duration of each single stimulus being extremely short; exposure time varies according to the aim of the experiment; the onset and disappearance of the whole field is practically instantaneous. [The exposure may be controlled by a falling screen (gravity tachistoscope), by a moving pendulum (as in Whipple tachistoscope), by a spring-actuated shutter (focal plane shutter type), or by use of a transparent mirror (Dodge exposure apparatus).]

tachometer = a variety of devices for measuring linear or angular velocity or change in velocity; most commonly applied to a manual instrument which, through the operation of centrifugal force and a hand on a dial, is used to measure the revolutions per minute of shafting. [Syn. **hematachometer, speedometer, speed counter.**] — Ger. *Tourenzähler.*

tachycardia = excessive (often paroxysmal) rapidity in the action of the heart. [Term usually limited in the human heart to a rate of over 130 beats per second.]

tachyphemia, tachylogia = a form of dysphemia characterized by morbid rapidity or volubility of speech. [Observed in nervous patients.]

tacit = assumed or agreed upon implicitly, i.e. without being actually stated in words, and often without being recognized; e.g. a tacit assumption. — Ger. *schweigend.*

tact = the ability displayed by certain individuals to adjust themselves socially to others, esp. in conversation, so as to promote friendly relations and to avoid remarks, topics, or situations, likely to engender an antagonistic attitude. [Contr. w. **tactlessness** = the propensity of certain individuals to arouse antagonism somewhat needlessly.] **tactful**[a]. — Ger. *Taktgefühl.*

tactile, see **tactual.**

tactile circle = a cutaneous area within which two points of pressure are perceived as a single point. [Syn. **sensory circle** (E. H. Weber, 1846), **tactile field.**]

tactual, tactile = pert. to the sense of touch. [Either form is correct. **tactual** is prefd. as corresponding to **visual.**] — Ger. *Tast-.*

tactual (or **tactile**) **illusions** = illusions in the field of tactual or cutaneous sensation. [Cf. **illusion,** and Table XII.] — Ger. *Tasttäuschungen.*

tactual (or **tactile**) **sensation,** see **touch sensation.**

Talbot-Plateau law = the principle that periodically variable or intermittent light-stimuli of any sort, when presented at a frequency sufficiently high to eliminate flicker, have an effect upon the organ of vision indistinguishable from that due to the same total flux of energy continuously and uniformly applied.

talent = a natural aptitude which renders the possessor susceptible to a high degree of training in some special field of endeavor, such as music, diplomacy, etc. — Ger. *Talent, Anlage.*

talisman = a figure, inscription, or object of any sort which is believed to possess magical properties favorable to the possessor.

tambour = a drum-shaped vessel (usually quite shallow) covered on one side with an elastic membrane to which a writing lever is attached so as to record changes communicated to it through an enclosed column of air. [Cf. **Marey tambour.**]

taming = the process of teaching an animal to obey the experimenter's commands and to inhibit fierce or sudden natural responses. **tame**[v]. — Fr. *apprivoisement*; Ger. *Zähmung.*

tantrum = a violent display of ill-temper aroused without adequate cause so far as the external situation is concerned, for the most part manifested by children or adolescents. [Syn. **temper tantrum.**] — Fr. *accès de colère*; Ger. *Wutanfall.*

tanyphonia = a form of **dysphonia** characterized by a thin voice.

taphophobia = morbid fear of being buried alive.

tapping board = an apparatus for measuring manual tapping performance; it usually consists of a metal plate on which the subject taps with a metal stylus, the taps being registered either by a mechanical or by an electromagnetic counter. — Fr. *planche de tapping.*

tapping test = a test in which the testee is directed to make (usually with a pencil or metal stylus) as many taps as possible within a given time limit. [The test puts a premium upon speed rather than precision of voluntary movement, and has been regarded as an index of motor capacity.]

Tarchanoff phenomenon, see **galvanic skin reflex.**

target test, see **aiming test.**

Tartini's tone, see **difference tone.**

task, see **Aufgabe.** — Fr. *tâche.*

taste = 1. a quality of **gustatory sensation;** 2. syn. for (the sense of) **gustation;** 3. capacity for making valid esthetic judgments. [Contemporary investigators usually limit gustatory qualities, i.e. **tastes** (1), to four: saline, sweet, sour, and bitter. Henning lists these as primary tastes (like primary colors), with simple intermediate tastes connecting them. Cf. **taste tetrahedron, alkaline.**] — Fr. *goût*; Ger. *Geschmack.*

taste bud = a bottle-shaped epithelial structure which contains receptor cells of gustation. [These structures are found in all mucous membrane which is sensitive to taste, esp. in the circumvallate, fungiform, and foliate papillae of the tongue. Syn. **taste-bulb, taste-beaker.** Cf. **papilla/lingual.**] — Fr. *bourgeon gustatif*; Ger. *Geschmacksknospe, Schmeckbecher.*

taste tetrahedron = a figure devised by Henning to show in schematic fashion the mutual relations of the four principal tastes, and the transitional tastes between them. [Cf. **gustation,** and **gustatory qualities.**]

tau effect = an illusion in which judgment of spatial intervals is influenced by the temporal intervals involved.

tautology = repetition of the same word or phrase, or of a literal equivalent in the same sentence. [Applied most frequently to the inclusion of a word or its equivalent in the definition of that word.] **tautological**[a].

taxinomy, taxonomy = the investigation of the principles of classification. **taxinomic**[a], **taxonomic**[a] (etymol. incorrect, but more usual form).

taxis = a generic type of simple response whereby motile organisms orient themselves as a whole to the source of external stimulation. [Syn. **tropism;** this term (applied originally to sessile organisms) has superseded **taxis.** The principal **taxes** are *chemotaxis, galvanotaxis, geotaxis, hydrotaxis, phototaxis, rheotaxis, stereotaxis, thermotaxis, thigmotaxis.*] **taxes**[pl], **tactic**[a] (rare, except in compounds). — Fr. *tactisme.*

Taylorism, Taylor system, see **scientific management.**

tears = the saline secretion of the lacrimal glands. **weep**[v]. — Fr. *larmes*; Ger. *Tränen.*

teasing = a form of social behavior by which an individual, though adopting a playful attitude himself, intentionally induces in another a feeling and attitude of annoyance. [Applied to comparatively trivial stimuli and minor annoyances.] **tease**[v]. — Fr. *taquinerie*; Ger. *Neckerei.*

technical = pert. to some branch of science or art esp. to the practical details rather than to principle or theory.

technical term = a word or phrase used in any science in a specialized way, to denote some datum, method, or other subject-matter comprised within the given field. [Generally used to distinguish the scientific from the common or popular meaning of a given term.]

technique, technic = 1. (*pop.*) a characteristic way of achieving a given end by specially skilled manual or other bodily activity as distg. fr. mere verbalization; 2. (*exper.*) the specific way or means of securing data or of working upon an experimental problem. [**technique** may involve method, procedure, apparatus, and (in psychol.) the individuality of the experimenter or the observer. It is limited to the conduct of research as distinct from the treatment of results.] **technical**[a] (a broader term).

technopsychology, see **psychotechnology.**

tectorial membrane, tectorium = a spiral body, made up of clear fibers in a soft matrix, which lies over the internal spiral sulcus and organ of Corti within the cochlear duct of the ear, with its inner edge attached to the limbus of the spiral lamina. [Its lower surface is believed to lie normally in close contact with the hairs of the sense-cells of the organ of Corti, serving as a bearing surface against which the hairs are pushed with the movements of the basilar membrane in response to sound.]

tegmentum = 1. the outer covering of organisms; 2. (*neurol.*) the dorsal layer which covers the crura cerebri and the pons as viewed in transverse sections. — Fr. (1) *tégument*, (2) *étage supérieur du pédoncule.*

tela subcutanea = the deeper layer of the connective tissue stratum of the skin. [Cf. **skin.**]

telegnosis = (*psych. res.*) knowledge of distant events assumed to be obtained by other than sensory means. [A generic term including **clairvoyance** and **clairaudience;** a form of **cryptesthesia.** Cf. **metagnomy.**]

telegony = the supposed influence of an earlier impregnation upon the character of the same mother's later offspring by another male.

telekinesis = (*psych. res.*) levitation or movement of objects in the presence of a medium, without contact, attributed to unknown or occult forces. **telekinetic**[a].

telencephalon = the anterior end of the brain considered from the developmental standpoint, consisting chiefly of the cerebral hemispheres. [Syn. **end-brain.** Cf. **neëncephalon, prosencephalon.**]

tele(o)ceptor, see **distant receptor.**

teleology = 1. the investigation of such acts of behavior and events as are carried out with reference to some future situation; 2. the characteristic of certain acts of behavior in that they relate to future situations; 3. the doctrine that certain trains of events are directed toward goals or ends; i.e. that the nature of the end in some sense and degree plays a part in determining or governing the course of those events; 4. the theory that organic processes depend upon a formative agency directed toward some end. [Syn. **purpose;** strictly, **teleology** is the scientific investigation, **purposiveness** is the characteristic, and **purpose, aim, end,** etc. denote the future situation as a factor in determining the present behavior.] (1) **teleological**[a]; **telic**[a] (2–4).

teleostereoscope = an instrument which causes an object or scene, either actually or pictorially presented, to be seen in exaggerated relief, or solidity, and to seem also closer at hand. [In the usual form the effect is produced through a series of mirrors which cause the images to be seen as if the eyes were much farther apart from each other (greater interocular distance) than normally.]

telepathy = (*psych. res.*) the communication of feelings, impulses, ideas, or more complex experiences, from one mind to another, which is assumed to be effected without sense organs. [Distg. fr. **mind-reading,** which makes conscious or unconscious use of the special senses in reading signals, signs, or cues, and fr. **muscle-reading,** which makes use of muscular twitches or ideomotor cues through physical contact; syn. **thought transference.**] **telepathic**[a]. — Ger. *Gedankenübertragung.*

telephone theory of hearing, see **hearing/theories of.**

telephone transmitter, see **microphone.**

teleplasm = (*psych. res.*) a hypothetical emanation from the body of a medium, which is supposed to pass through vaporous and viscous states to that of flesh and bone indistinguishable from a proper member of a human body, and occasionally to attain the proportions of a complete and independently active person (a materialized séance personality). [It is said to be responsible for **telekinesis,** i.e. the movement of objects at a distance. Syn. **ectoplasm** (discarded because of its established place in biology). A more neutral term (e.g. **metaplasm**) would be preferable.]

telergy = (*psych. res.*) the supposed direct influence of the mind of a person or spirit upon the brain of another person. [A process resulting in **telepathy** (Myers).]

telesis = the realization, or accomplishment, of an end, or purpose.

telesthesia = (*psych. res.*) 1. sensibility for events at a supernormal distance; 2. sensitivity for simple stimuli at a source beyond the normal range. [(1) is a form of **cryptesthesia;** prefd. to syn. **clairvoyance** when modality of sense is not defined.] **telesthetic**[a].

telesthetic taste = the chemical or food sense in aquatic animals. [A term proposed by Lloyd Morgan, on the ground that it corresponds to the taste sense but includes distant reception of stimuli.] — Fr. *goût télesthétique.*

teletactor = an instrument used to transmit the vibrations caused by sound waves to the skin; used experimentally and practically in the instruction of the deaf in speech, in speech reading, and in musical appreciation.

telic[a] = characterizing a final end or purpose, i.e. with intention. [Contr. w. **ecbatic,** which is mere result or consequence without aim or intention.]

telodendron = the branching terminal of the axon of a neuron. [Syn. **endbrush.**]

temper[n] = 1. (*pop.*) a display of anger, or an undue readiness to become angry; 2. (*hist.*) syn. for temperament (1); 3. the expression of the way in which the conative impulses work within an individual, i.e. the strength or urgency of an individual's impulses (McDougall). — Ger. *Laune.*

temper[v] (*mus.*), see **temperament** (2).

temperament = 1. (*psychol.*) the general affective nature of an individual as determined by his inheritance and life history; 2. the sum of the effects upon one's mental life of the metabolism or chemical changes that are constantly going on in all the tissues of one's body (Mc-

Dougall). [Various types and degrees are differentiated according as these factors modify the character, intensity and direction of the individual's responses to specific stimuli and situations. Attributed by Hippocrates and Galen to predominance of some one of the humors in the body. The ancients recognized 4 classes; **sanguine, melancholic, choleric, phlegmatic.** The temperaments are now attributed to the functions of endocrine glands. **nervous temperament,** high excitability of the nerves, physiological in origin (Hadfield).] **temperamental**[a] (usually implying alternation of moods and intensity of responsive reactions).

temperament = 3. (*mus.*) the system of tuning a pianoforte or other fixed-tone instrument. [In **just temperament** the theoretically correct tone intervals are maintained for a certain key, but when modulation is attempted the intervals are not correct for other keys. **Mean tone temperament** is based upon an interval halfway between the great and the small major second; modulation is possible but only to certain keys. The **equal temperament** generally used today was advocated by J. S. Bach and divides the octave into 12 equal semitones; in **equal temperament** the only correct interval is the octave, but the practical gain is that modulation is equally possible in all keys.] **tempered**[a]. [Cf. **scale** (2).]

temperature = the average amount of heat in a given substance or region, measured in physical units. **thermal**[a].

temperature illusion = the overestimation of a warm or cold environment when one's body or some member has been stimulated just before by a less warm or a less cold environment, respectively. [Locke describes an experiment in which the two hands are held for a time, one in warm water, the other in cold. When both are transferred to luke-warm water the former feels cold, the latter warm.]

temperature sensation = a generic term applied to both **cold** and **warmth sensations.**

temperature senses = the senses of **warmth** and **cold.**

temperature sensitivity = the ability of an organism to distinguish degrees of warmth (or cold) by means of specific receptors.

temperature spot = a generic term applied to both **cold spots** and **warm spots** on the skin. — Fr. *point de sensibilité thermique.*

tempered scale, see **scale** (2), **temperament** (2).

temporal = 1. pert. to time or to time relations. — Ger. *zeitlich.*

temporal = 2. pert. to or located at the temples, i.e. the sides of the forehead.

temporal bone = a bone at the side and base of the skull, which contains the mechanisms of hearing. [The external auditory meatus is in the tympanic and squamous portions, and the internal ear in the petrous portion.] — Fr. *os temporal*; Ger. *Schläfenbein.*

temporal lobe = a major division of either cerebral hemisphere, comprising (in man) that portion which lies on the under surface and side of the brain ventrad to the Sylvian fissure, and is bounded caudally by the bifurcation of the sulcus temporalis superior. — Ger. *Schläfenlappen.*

temporal maze = a maze where the subject must pass through the same alleys and same parts of the extra-maze environment more than once, so that a temporal succession of movements without different localization in space is learned. [In the **double alternation** form, used to study symbolic processes.]

temporal perspective, see **perspective/temporal.**

temporal sign = any characteristic of a memory experience which serves as a cue to locate the original experience at a certain point in the time series.

temporality = the time-attribute or characteristic of sensation or other experiences. [Syn. **protensity, duration.**] **temporal**[a].

temptation = a stimulus or motive which tends to change the direction of an individual's attention and activity from a well-considered or dominant course of behavior to some incidental action. **tempt**[v]. — Ger. *Versuchung.*

tendency = 1. the characteristic of certain movements, changes, courses of events, or masses of data of any sort, such that they indicate a definite line or direction of progression or an approach to some point or goal which the observed phenomena or data may not actually attain; 2. the characteristic or quality of an organism which furnishes the basis for the persistence of a given type of behavior despite fairly wide variety in stimulating conditions. [(1) is used generally in connection with a specification of the point or goal which the data appear to approach. Syn. **trend,** applied to a series of events.] **tend**[v]. — Fr. *tendance*; Ger. *Tendenz.*

tendency/acquired = an impulse to respond or behave, which is essentially the product of education or training. [Generally contr. w. **inherited tendency** = an impulse which is native and need not be learned.]

tendency/central (*math.*), see **central tendency.**

tendency/determining, see **determining tendency** and **directive tendency.**

tendency/inherited = an impulse to respond or behave which is native, i.e. which need not be learned. [Contr. w. **acquired tendency.**] — Fr. *tendance innée.*

tendency/perseverative, see **perseveration.**

tendo calcaneus (or **Achilles**) **reflex,** see **Achilles' tendon reflex.**

tendon = the fibrous cord of inelastic connective tissue in which the muscle fibers end, and by means of which they are attached to a bone or other structure. **tendinous**[a]. — Ger. *Sehne.*

tendon reflex = contraction of a muscle produced by percussing (i.e. smartly tapping) its tendon; e.g. the knee-jerk.

tendon (or **tendinous**) **sensation** = a type of kinesthetic sensation aroused by stimulation of receptors situated in the tendons. [Generally used in connection with the term **joint sensation,** since the location of these two sorts of reception is not clearly differentiated. Cf. **articular sensation.**] — Ger. *Sehnenempfindung.*

tendon spindle = a nerve-ending which consists of an elongated elliptical mass pierced by medullated nerve fibers, situate near the junction of tendon and muscle. [Syn. **neurotendinous spindle; Golgi** (or **Golgi-Mazzoni**) **corpuscles.**] — Fr. *fuseau tendineux.*

Tenon's capsule = a fibrous sheath which envelops the back of the eyeball, the tendons of its extrinsic muscles, and to a certain extent the muscles themselves; it constitutes the socket within which the eyeball turns.

tenotomy = the surgical operation of cutting a tendon to correct a fault due to contracture or overaction of the muscle. [Practiced in ophthalmology to correct **heterophoria,** esp. **strabismus.**]

tense[a] = 1. stretched taut; 2. characterizing an individual attitude or social situation of strain. [Cf. **tension.**] — Fr. *tendu*; Ger. (1) *straff*, (2) *gespannt*.

tension = 1. a feeling of strain or suspense; 2. the condition of muscle when it is acting against considerable resistance; 3. a state of inequilibrium produced in an organism, which leads to a change in behavior tending to restore equilibrium. — Ger. *Spannung*.

tension/law of = a principle formulated by J. R. L. Delboeuf as a partial substitute for Weber's law; starting with the postulate that an organism is normally accommodated to a certain optimal level of external stimuli (temperature, atmospheric pressure, illumination, sound), the law states that any change (increase or decrease) in these stimuli produces a condition of disequilibrium or **tension** in the organism; this tension constitutes the excitation whose conscious accompaniment is the sensation; these tensions and sensations thus have an upper (positive) and a lower (negative) limit, where they pass into some kind of distress or fatigue. [Cf. **degradation/law of, progression/law of.**]

tension-relaxation/feeling of = one of the three dimensions or attributes of affective experience (Wundt). [Introspective evidence indicates that judgments of tension are referable to kinesthetic sensation rather than to affection.] — Ger. *Spannungs-Losungsgefühl*.

tension/sensation of, see **strain** (3).

tentative = characterizing a preliminary or trial hypothesis or evaluation or procedure. [Contr. w. **definitive.**]

teratology = the branch of biology which deals with structural malformations of organisms. [E.g. acephalic monsters, hermaphrodites, supernumerary limbs, deficiencies of members, double monsters, etc.] **teratological**[a].

term = 1. the verbal expression of a concept or definite idea; 2. one of the simple items between which relations subsist; 3. (*hist.*) a natural boundary of a thing or event. [In science and technology the word **term** (1) is applied to any word or phrase which designates any datum, instrument, method, etc. within the scope of the given branch; the meaning (and definition) of such terms is (in theory at least) precise and unambiguous, and may be distg. in that respect fr. the pop. use of the same terms.] — Ger. (1) *Ausdruck*, (2) *Glied*, (3) *Grenze*.

Terman group test of mental ability = a battery of ten verbal tests devised by L. M. Terman as a measure of the general mental ability of testees in grades 7 to 12. [The component tests are information, best answer, word meaning, logical selection, arithmetic, sentence meaning, analogies, mixed sentences, classification, and number series.]

terminal inhibition = the checking or stopping of the activity of a muscle by the action of an antagonistic muscle.

terminal organ = (*psychol.*) the special organ connected with either of the two terminals of the neural arc, called **receptor** and **effector** respectively.

terminal sensitivity = the greatest degree of intensity of sensation that the organism is capable of experiencing. [Contr. w. **liminal** or **minimal sensitivity** = the faintest degree of sensation as the intensity of the stimulus approaches zero.] — Ger. *Reizhöhe, Grenze*.

terminology = the systematic treatment of terms in any branch of science. [Cf. **nomenclature, term.**] **terminological**[a].

terror = an extreme emotional manifestation of fear. [Applied to both normal and pathological phenomena.] **terrified**[a]; **terror-stricken**[a]. — Ger. *Schrecken, Grausen*.

tesselated = (*biol.*) characterizing inherited structural patterns in which two different colors or textures alternate in checker-board fashion on the body covering of the creature. [Syn. **checkered.**] — Fr. *en mosaïque*.

test = 1. (*logic*) any criterion or procedure used to determine the truth or falsity of a hypothesis, either by empirical evidence or by reasoning; 2. (*psychol.*) a routine examination administered to individuals belonging to the same group, in order to determine the relative position of a given individual in the group with respect to one or more mental traits, motor abilities, etc. or in order to compare one group with another in these characteristics. [In practice a series or battery of psychological tests (2) is generally used, and the scores are arranged or plotted on a definite scale; cf. **mental test, scale** (1).] **tester**[np] (contr. rarely w. **testee,** the individual tested). — Fr. (1) *épreuve*, (2) *test*; Ger. (1) *Prüfung*, (2) *Test, Probe*.

test age = the standing, or rating, obtained by a testee in any test, which is scored in terms of age, or in which a point score is transmuted into terms of age, e.g. mental age, arithmetical age, etc.

test chart, test card = (*vis.*) a series of letters, numerals, arbitrary characters, lines, or pictures, used to determine visual acuity and the range of distinct vision. [They are usually arranged in rows, each row consisting of smaller letters, etc. than the one immediately above. **visual acuity** varies inversely with the size of the letters, etc.] — Fr. *optotypes, caractères pour l'examen de l'acuité visuelle*.

test/mental, see **mental test.**

test scaling = the process of arranging or grading the material of a test, and the scoring of it in such a way as to secure a series of quantitative values in which (ideally) each unit shall be equal to every other unit, and in which (ideally) each quantitative value shall denote a proportionate amount, above zero, of the ability being measured. [Tests are commonly scaled in terms of points (**point scale**), or in terms of ages (**age scale**).] — Fr. *dépouillement des tests*.

test score = the measure of performance, usually numerical, on some given **test.** — Fr. *notation de l'épreuve*.

test standardization, see **standardization of tests.**

test value = a tentative result, obtained with a relatively few observations, designed primarily to determine the limits of the stimuli to be employed in psychophysical experimentation (Titchener).

testimony = 1. the oral or written statements of a witness used as evidence of certain facts and events; 2. (figuratively) any evidence produced to substantiate a hypothesis. [(1) applies to court trials and to the reports given by subjects in the **Aussage tests.**] **testify**[v]. — Fr. *témoignage*; Ger. *Zeugnis, Aussage.*

testis, testicle = a gland which produces male sex-cells. [Contr. w. **ovary,** a gland which produces female sex-cells. **gonad** is a generic name for any gland which produces sex-cells.] **testes**[pl]. — Ger. *Hode, Testikel.*

tetanus = a state of continued contraction of a muscle due to a rapid succession of nerve impulses. [In the skeletal muscles of warm-blooded animals, the range is from 10 to 100 per second. Characterized by absence of twitching.] **tetanic**[a]. — Ger. *Starrkrampf, Muskelzusammenziehung.*

tetrachromatism = 1. color vision characterized by ability to discriminate all four of the Hering primaries; 2. a color theory based on the assumption of four primaries, red, green, yellow, and blue.

tetrad = 1. (*mus.*) a chord composed of four tones, e.g. c-a-g-c′; 2. see **tetrad equation.**

tetrad equation = the equation $t_{1234} = r_{12}r_{34} - r_{13}r_{24}$, where x_1, x_2, x_3, x_4 represent four tests, and r a product moment coefficient of correlation (Spearman). [The right-hand member of this equation is called the **tetrad.** The equality of the **tetrad** to zero is the important criterion in Spearman's theory of two factors. The difference between $r_{12}r_{34}$ and $r_{13}r_{24}$ is called the **tetrad difference,** or simply the **tetrad.**]

tetraploid = (*biol.*) having four sets of chromosomes. [Cf. **diploid, triploid.**]

text-blindness, see **alexia.** — Fr. *cécité verbale.*

thalamencephalon, see **diencephalon.**

thalamus, optic thalamus = a central mass of gray matter situate at the base of the cerebrum, bounding and projecting into the third ventricle. [It is developed from the walls of the first primary cerebral vesicle and comprises a number of cell groups forming recognizable nuclei. It contains the central terminals of afferent neurons.] (Accent **thal-.**) **thalami**[pl], **thalamic**[a]. — Fr. *couches optiques*; Ger. *Sehhügel.*

thanatomania = suicidal or homicidal mania.

thanatophobia = morbid fear of death.

thaumatrope, see **stroboscope.**

theme = 1. a topic presented for discussion; 2. the systematic discussion of a given topic; 3. (*mus.*) a simple melody which serves as the basis for varied development. — Ger. (1) *Aufgabe,* (2) *Aufsatz,* (3) *Thema.*

theorem = 1. (*logic*) a proposition which is capable of being proved by a relatively restricted series of steps; 2. (*math.*) a statement of relation (or of a set of conditions) for which rigorous proof can be adduced. — Ger. *Lehrsatz.*

theory = 1. a general principle or formula propounded for the purpose of explaining some given group of phenomena; 2. (*pop.*) a principle based on reasoning but apparently impracticable in immediate application. [Distg. fr. **hypothesis,** in that a body of evidence more substantial is available than in the case of a hypothesis.] **theoretic(al)**[a] (emphasizes the possible divergence of the principle or formula from actual facts).

theory of knowledge, see **epistemology.** — Fr. *t. de la connaissance*; Ger. *Erkenntnistheorie.*

therapeutics, therapy = the branch of medical science which deals with the treatment or application of remedies to the cure, alleviation, or prevention of disease. **therapeutic**[a].

therapeutics/mental, see **psychotherapy.**

therblig = a name for an identifiable part of a repeated work-act (such as *search, find, select, grasp, transport,* etc.) devised by F. B. Gilbreth as an aid in recording and studying the motions of the worker, in the interest of economy of movement. [An inversion of the originator's name.]

theriomorphism, see **anthropomorphism.**

thermal sense, see **temperature senses.**

thermal stimulation = the application or withdrawal of physical heat, by either convection or radiation, to excite a receptor.

thermalgesia, thermoalgesia = a condition of the organism in which a warmth stimulus causes a pain sensation. **thermalgesic**[a].

thermalgia = 1. a sensation of burning pain; 2. (*med.*) pain produced by heat. [Syn. **causalgia.**] **thermalgic**[a].

thermanalgesia, thermoanalgesia, see **thermanesthesia.**

thermanesthesia, thermanaesthesia = insensitivity to warmth and cold stimuli. [Syn. **thermanalgesia, thermoanalgesia.**] **thermanesthetic**[a].

thermesthesia, thermaesthesia = sensitivity to warmth and cold; i.e. the ability to feel changes in temperature. [Syn. **temperature sense(s).**] **thermesthetic**[a].

thermesthesiometer, thermo(a)esthesiometer = an apparatus devised to furnish continuous warm or cold stimulation to the skin at controlled temperatures, usually by means of mixed hot and cold water flowing through a pointed tube.

thermogenic nerves = nerves which control heat production.

thermohyperesthesia, thermohyperaesthesia = excessive sensitivity to warmth and cold.

thermohypesthesia, thermohypaesthesia = diminished sensitivity to warmth and cold.

thermophone = a device which translates an alternating electric current into sound waves by means of the heating effect of the current when passed through a thin metal foil or wire. [The sound output is low, but the intensity can be calculated from the constants of the device and the current used, an advantage favoring its employment in the calibration of sound-producing apparatus.]

thermophor = a device for applying thermal, or temperature stimulation to the skin and registering the time of application; a rounded metal cap is applied to the skin, the contact making an electric circuit; water of the required temperature flows through this metal stimulus-cap.

thermoreceptor = a receptor or sense organ which may be adequately activated by appropriate temperature stimuli.

thermotropism, thermotaxis = a simple positive or negative response to external thermal stimulation. [Cf. **tropism.**] (Accent **-mot-, -tax-.**) **thermotropic**[a], **-tactic**[a].

thesis = 1. a principle formally stated as basis for argumentation and proof; 2. the systematic discussion of a principle or specific problem,

[(2) is applied to formal and elaborate discussions put forward by a candidate for academic honors. Cf. **theme,** which is less elaborate.] **theses**[pl].

thigmesthesia, see **touch.**

thigmotropism, thigmotaxis = a simple orienting response, either positive or negative, to external contact. (Accent **-mot-, -tax-.**) **thigmotropic**[a], **-tactic**[a].

thing = a loose term applied to unitary objects, generally exclusive of living organisms. — Fr. *chose*; Ger. *Ding*.

thinking = 1. a train of thought; 2. the process of arousing a single thought; 3. a determined course of ideas, symbolic in character, initiated by a problem or task, and leading to a conclusion. [Cf. **thought.**] **think**[v]. — Fr. *pensée*; Ger. *Denken*.

thinking aloud = a type of **thinking** in which the symbolic terms are audibly spoken words. — Fr. *pensée à haute voix*.

thinking/stream of = a succession of ideational experiences uninterrupted by significant experiences of any other type. [Syn. **stream of thought.**] — Fr. *cours de la pensée*; Ger. *Gedankenstrom*.

third (*mus.*), see **interval** and Table VII. — Fr. *tierce*; Ger. *Terz*.

third dimension = projection (or distance away) from the body of an organism, esp. man. [Syn. **depth.** Distg. fr. the two spatial dimensions occupied by the surface of the creature's body, or of the retina. Used esp. in investigations of visual perception, and responses to distant objects.] **third-dimensional**[a].

thirst = 1. desire for water; 2. (figuratively) strong desire for anything. [The sensation of thirst includes the perception of **dryness** of the mouth.] **thirsty**[a]. — Fr. *soif*; Ger. *Durst*.

thobbing = thinking misdirected by emotion, prejudice, will to believe, or other non-rational states or processes of the mind. [The verb **thob** is an artificial word devised by Henshaw Ward, composed of the initial sounds of the words *thinking, opinion, belief*. Related to **Bacon's idols;** contr. w. **logical thinking.**] **thob**[v], **thobbery**[n], **thobber**[np], **thobbic**[a], **thobistic(al)**[a].

thoracic nerves = the nerves which enter the spinal cord in the thoracic region, i.e. between the neck and the abdomen. [There are 12 (double) pairs in man.]

thorax = that portion of the body situate between the neck and the abdomen. [Syn. **chest.**] **thoracic**[a] (accent **-rass-**). — Ger. *Brust*.

thought = 1. a type of ideational experience which is symbolic; 2. (*beh.*) subvocal movements; 3. a succession or train of symbolic processes; 4. (*hist.*) cognitive experience in general, as distg. fr. **feeling** and **action;** 5. a single one of the several ideas in a course of thinking. [Cf. **thinking.**] — Fr. *pensée*; Ger. *Gedanke*.

thought/laws of = 1. the uniform principles according to which thinking proceeds; 2. (*hist.*) the principles of rational or logical thinking. [The two meanings are often confused; (2) is prefd.] — Fr. *l. de cognition*; Ger. *Denkgesetze*.

thought-reading, see **mind-reading.**

thought-transference, see **telepathy.**

three-component theory = (*vis.*) any doctrine to the effect that color vision can be explained on the basis of three elementary chromatic processes which combine in varying degrees of activity to yield the various colors, including grays. [E.g. Young-Helmholtz theory.]

threshold = 1. (*psychol.*) a statistically determined point on the stimulus scale, at which occurs a transition in a series of sensations or judgments; 2. (*physiol.*) the stimulus intensity required to initiate a nerve impulse or muscle contraction. [Syn. (1) **limen** (the two terms are used interchangeably). **thresholds** (1) are of three kinds: (*a*) the *threshold of sensation* or *stimulus threshold*, designated as *RL* = that magnitude of stimulus at which a transition occurs from no sensation to sensation; (*b*) the *terminal stimulus* or *terminal threshold*, designated as *TR* = the greatest magnitude of stimulus that will produce sensation of a given type; (*c*) the difference threshold = the least amount of change of a given stimulus necessary to produce a noticeable change in sensation. It is designated as the *DL*, or *j.n.d.* (just noticeable difference). In some psychophysical procedures judgments are made upon stimuli both above and below a given standard stimulus; the stimulus distance from the standard to the point of transition from *equal* to *less* is called the *lower DL*, while the corresponding distance to the transition from *equal* to *greater* is called the *upper DL*. The average of the two values is the *absolute DL*. The ratio between the standard stimulus and the above values gives rise respectively to three types of *relative DL*'s. **threshold** is sometimes confused with **sensitivity,** which is actually its inverse; i.e. as sensitivity increases, the threshold becomes lower.] — Fr. *seuil*; Ger. *Schwelle*, (*a*) *Reizschwelle* (= *RL*), (*c*) *Unterschiedsschwelle* (= *DL*).

threshold for bodily motion = the minimum rate of rotation, or the minimum rate of positive and negative acceleration in rotary and rectilinear motion, necessary to stimulate the end organs (labyrinthine and kinesthetic receptors, and receptors for organic sensibility) for the perception of bodily motion. — Fr. *seuil de mouvement corporel*.

threshold for rotation = 1. the minimum rate of acceleration required to stimulate the labyrinthine end-organs; 2. the minimum rate of rotation necessary to elicit perception of bodily movement. — Fr. *seuil de rotation*.

threshold of consciousness = the psychic level at which the non-conscious becomes conscious experience. — Fr. *seuil de conscience*; Ger. *Bewusstseinsschwelle*.

thrill[n] = a sudden, intense emotional condition which may be either pleasant or unpleasant, as the thrill of joy or of horror, and in which there are often confused dermal sensations, as of tingling and temperature, these sensations changing rapidly in location and intensity. — Fr. *tressaillement*; Ger. *Schauer*.

thymus = a multilobate ductless gland of lymphoid structure, situate medially in the lower neck region, and largely in the thorax beneath the upper part of the sternum; it is composed of two lateral halves attached to a medial cord. [It is developed from the 3d pair of pharyngeal pouches, reaches its greatest size about the time of puberty, and then slowly atrophies. It has no established endocrine function.] **thymic**[a].

thyroid[a], **thyreoid**[a] = pert. to or located in a small area over the thyroid gland and just below the laryngeal region.

thyroid gland, thyreoid gland, thyroid[n] = an endocrine gland, which in the mammalia consists of two lobes situate on either side of the larynx and upper trachea, united in some species by an isthmus passing over the ventral aspect of the trachea. [The mammalian thyroid normally elaborates an amount of internal secretion which maintains the basal metabolic rate, is necessary for normal growth, and has other less well-defined influences upon the bodily economy.] **thyroid**[a], **thyreoid**[a]. — Ger. *Schilddrüse.*

thyroid cartilage = the large cartilage of the larynx which forms the prominence known as the pomum adami, or Adam's apple.

tibia = the inner and larger of the two bones of the lower leg. **tibial**[a] (accent **tib-**). — Ger. *Schienbein.*

tic = 1. a psychoneurosis characterized by quick, sudden spasms similar in form to voluntary movements; 2. spasmodic twitching of the face or a spasmodic movement of any sort, repeated at frequent intervals, which bears no significant relation to the situation. — Ger. *krampfhaftes Zucken.*

tickle = 1. a sensory experience involving a complication of contact sensations and a strong feeling tone; 2. an emotional experience involving strong feeling tone and marked by convulsive movements of escape and laughter. [Two sorts of **tickle** (1) are distinguished: **light tickle,** aroused by light pressure in certain regions, e.g. lips; **deep tickle,** aroused by heavier pressure in other regions, e.g. ribs.] **ticklish**[a] = susceptible to tickle stimulation. — Fr. *chatouillement;* Ger. *Kitzel.*

tied relations = relations cognized, yet fused in the object known so that they are not explicitly observed. [Contr. w. **free relations.**]

tilting board, tilt-board = an apparatus used for vestibular stimulation; it consists essentially of a flat board about 6 ft. by 2 ft. which swings freely about a horizontal axis; the subject lies upon the board. [Cf. **rotation table.**] — Fr. *planche de rotation.*

timbre = the specific qualitative aspect of a complex sound, which depends upon the number and relative intensities of partial tones present. [Musical instruments sounding the same fundamental tone are distinguished in terms of their **timbre,** i.e. by differences in overtones and incidental noises (e.g. scraping of the bow in the violin). Syn. **clang-color, clang-tint, clang quality, tone-color, tone-tint, tone-** (or **tonal**) **character.**] (Pron. **timber** or **tambr.**) — Ger. *Klangfarbe.*

time = 1. (*psychol.*) the measurable aspect of duration; 2. the objective basis of the characteristic or attribute of duration; 3. that which distinguishes events with reference to their occurring now, before, or after, and their beginning and end; 4. (*mus.*) grouping of successive rhythmic beats or pulses into equal measures. [**time** (1, 2) is measured by any device in which a pointer or other part moves uniformly in reference to a scale (chronoscope; time clock), or a recorder registers on a uniformly moving chart (chronograph).] **temporal**[a]. — Fr. *temps;* Ger. *Zeit.*

time error = the error produced in psychophysical experimentation due to presenting two stimuli successively. [According to Fechner's convention, the **time error** (designated by p) is *positive* when it operates to make the first of two equal stimuli appear greater than the second, and *negative* when the second appears greater than the first.] — Fr. *erreur de temps;* Ger. *Zeitfehler.*

time-limit method = a method of arranging test material and instructions such that each testee shall work for the same length of time, and efficiency be measured by the amount (or amount and quality) of work done in this constant time. [Contr. w. **work-limit method.** Group tests commonly use the **time-limit** method.]

time order = the sequence in which stimuli are presented in psychophysical experiment. [**first time order** = standard (or normal) stimulus followed by the comparison stimulus; **second time order** = comparison stimulus followed by the standard stimulus.] — Ger. *Zeitlage.*

time perception = 1. apprehension of the amount of duration, rate of change, placement in time, order of occurrence, beginning and end, etc. of experiences; 2. (*mus.*) apprehension of rhythm in a melody. [Syn. (1) **time apprehension** (prefd.).] — Fr. *perception du temps;* Ger. *Zeitanschauung, Zeitwahrnehmung.*

time perspective, see **perspective/temporal.**

time/psychological = the subjective impression of the temporal duration of an experience or of the duration elapsing between experiences. [Contr. w. **physiological time.**]

time sense = a loose term, denoting apprehension of duration, change, order of occurrence, and in general of the duration aspect or attribute of experience. [Generally applied to *capacity* of apprehending, while **time perception** refers to specific occurrences.] — Fr. *sens du temps;* Ger. *Zeitsinn.*

time-sense apparatus = an instrument for determining the accuracy of time estimation; it consists essentially of a uniformly rotating metal arm, which during rotation comes into contact with two (or more) sets of terminals or contacts, producing similar sounds, or other forms of stimulation, separated by a time interval which depends on the rate of rotation and the distance between the contacts. [In some forms a swinging pendulum is used to make the contacts.]

timidity = an emotional attitude marked by hesitation, and by a tendency to experience fear in situations which do not justify the fear attitude. [Distg. fr. **shyness,** a special form of timidity confined to social situations.] **timid**[a]. — Ger. *Furchtsamkeit, Schüchternheit.*

tingling = an experience characterized by short, intermittent, tactual sensations which are localized at some point or region of the periphery. **tingle**[v]. — Fr. *picotement;* Ger. *Kribbeln, Prickeln, Stechen.*

tinnitus = an auditory disorder characterized by a ringing, buzzing, or rushing sound in the ear in the absence of any external stimulus. (Accent **-nigh-.**) — Fr. *tintement;* Ger. *Ohrenklingen.*

tint = 1. any color lighter (i.e. of higher brilliance) than median gray; 2. sometimes used as syn. for degree of **saturation.** [Contr. (1) w. **shade** (1).] — Fr. (1) *teinte claire;* Ger. (1) *Tinte,* (2) *Schattierung.*

tissue = any structure in organisms which is composed of similar cells or other elements joined together and performing a common function. — Ger. *Gewebe.*

tonal, see **tone**, (1, 2).

tonal bell = a bell-shaped wire model designed to illustrate the interrelations of the qualitative tonal attributes; viz. pitch-brightness, volume, tonality (Ruckmick). [Cf. **tonal pencil.**] — Fr. *cloche des tons*.

tonal gap = a region of the tonal continuum within which, for a given individual, auditory sensitivity is lacking or is greatly reduced, bounded on either side by regions in which sensitivity is wholly or practically normal. [Syn. **tonal lacuna.** Contr. w. **tonal island.** Cf. **deafness, audiogram.**] — Ger. *Tonlücke*.

tonal island = a region of the tonal continuum within which, for a given individual, auditory sensitivity is normal, bounded on either side by regions of complete or relatively great insensitivity. [Contr. w. **tonal gap.** Cf. **audiogram.**] — Ger. *Toninsel*.

tonal pencil = a pencil-shaped figure designed to illustrate the relation between pitch and volume within the tonal scale (Titchener). [Cf. **tonal bell.**] — Fr. *crayon des tons*.

tonal standard = an instrument giving a tone whose pitch is fixed and definitely known. [The most common standards are calibrated tuning forks. Other useful standards are electrical tone-producing instruments, such as audio-oscillators. Cf. **pitch/standard.**] — Fr. *étalon tonal*.

tonality = a characteristic of musical tones, arising from their relationships with other tones, esp. with the key note or tonic. [Since any tone and its octave are regarded as equivalent, or of the same **tonality,** this characteristic of sounds is a periodic function of frequency, repeating itself in every octave. Sometimes regarded as an attribute of all sounds, whether musical or not. Syn. **octave quality.**] — Ger. *Toncharakter*.

tone = 1. auditory sensation aroused by the periodic vibration of an elastic medium; 2. an interval between two musical sounds (e.g. whole tone, semitone); 3. visual quality, w. esp. reference to minor differences of hue, saturation, and brilliance; 4. (*photog.*) the relative brilliance (brightness) of any given portion of a scene or picture; 5. general level of emotional reactivity, mood, or feeling; e.g. pleasant tone, depressed tone; 6. state of muscular reactivity, or general bodily condition; e.g. the tone (or tonicity) of the biceps. [Syn. (6) **tonus** (prefd.).] **tonal**[a] (1); **tonic**[a] (2, 6). — Fr. (1) *son*, (2) *ton*; Ger. *Ton*.

tone/beat, tone/combination, etc., see **beat tone, combination tone,** etc. — Fr. *ton de battement, ton résultant*.

tone (or **tonal**) **character,** see **timbre.**

tone-color, see **timbre.** — Fr. *coloration tonale*; Ger. *Tonfarbe*.

tone/compound = 1. (*psychol.*) any tonal experience which can be analyzed into component tones by direct observation or with the aid of instruments; 2. (*phys.*) a complex periodic sound-wave which can be analyzed into component waves of the sinusoidal type. [Contr. w. **simple** (or pure) **tone.**] — Fr. *son composé*; Ger. *Klang*.

tone-deafness = inability on the part of an individual to discriminate differences in pitch, and hence to distinguish one tune from another. [Syn. **asonia.**] — Fr. *surdité musicale*; Ger. *Tontaubheit*.

tone/feeling, see **feeling tone, hedonic tone.**

tone/muscle, see **muscle tonus.**

tone (or **tonal**) **sensation** = an experience produced by stimulation of the ear by relatively simple periodic sound-waves. [As the stimulus approaches sine-wave form, the experience increases in simplicity and becomes (theoretically) a **pure tone sensation.** Contr. w. **noise** (**noise sensation**) and **vocality.** Cf. **sound** (2).] — Ger. *Tonempfindung*.

tone/simple (or **pure**) = 1. (*psychol.*) any tonal experience which cannot be analyzed by direct observation or with the aid of instruments; 2. (*phys.*) periodic sound-waves of the sinusoidal type; 3. (*psychophys.*) the experience correlated with such waves. [Contr. w. **compound tone.**]

tone/subjective = a perceived tone whose primary basis is in the auditory mechanism of an observer and not in the sound-waves outside the ear. [Cf. **tinnitus.**]

tone-tint, see **timbre.**

tone variator = an adjustable resonator excited by blowing across the mouth, used as a source of moderately pure tone. [The desired frequency is obtained by raising or lowering a piston within the resonator by means of a graduated cam. The variations of pitch are continuous within the limits of each particular variator, which is about two octaves. There are several models, covering the ordinary musical range. Cf. **Stern variator.**]

tongue = 1. (*anat.*) a muscular organ situate on the floor of the mouth, which assists in deglutition and in articulate speech; the mucous lining contains papillae, in some of which are embedded the taste-buds, the receptors for taste; 2. a loose term denoting a differentiated language system (e.g. English, Latin, etc.). **lingual**[a]. — Fr. *langue*; Ger. *Zunge*.

tonic[a] = pert. to **tonus,** i.e. the postural contraction of muscle.

tonic[n] = 1. (*mus.*) the first tone or keynote of any given scale, or a chord having this tone for its root; 2. a medicine which promotes nutrition and gives tone to the system. [Syn. (2) **invigorative.**] — Ger. (1) *Tonika*.

tonic immobility = the condition of total quiescence set up in animals of some species by stimuli naturally or artificially presented. [Syn. **animal hypnosis, death feigning** (or **feint**). It seems to be of an all-or-none character and to have camouflage value.]

tonic labyrinth reflexes = extensor tonus of limbs when an animal is placed on its back, elicited by a stimulation of the vestibular organ. [They are mediated by the vestibular nerve and nuclei, and by the vestibulospinal tracts.]

tonic labyrinth-eye reflexes = reflex eye-movements whereby the same object is instantly fixated in spite of movements of the animal as a whole in any plane except the horizontal. [The external and internal recti muscles take no part in these reflexes. They are mediated by the vestibular nerve, nuclei, vestibulo-mesencephalic tracts, and nerves of eye movement.] — Fr. *réflexes toniques oculaires d'origine labyrinthique*.

tonic neck reflexes = modifications of the extensor tonus of the limbs when the head is moved into various relations with the trunk. [They originate in the proprioceptors in the neck, and are mediated by the VIII cranial to

4th cervical nerves.] — Fr. *réflexes toniques du cou.*

tonic neck-eye reflexes = compensatory eye movements in response to changes of position of the head with reference to any plane, including the horizontal. [They are mediated by the VIII cranial to 4th cervical and oculomotor nerves.] — Fr. *réflexes oculaires toniques d'origine posturale céphalique.*

tonic reflex = 1. abnormal prolongation of tension after a reflex; 2. any reflex which deals with muscular tonicity. [Cf. **static reflex.**]

tonicity = the degree of muscle tonus or postural contraction. [Syn. **muscle tonus.**]

tonograph = a form of **sphygmograph** used for measurement of blood pressure and the radial pulse (Jacquet).

tonometer = an instrument for producing tones of known frequency or for determining the approximate pitch of a tone. [**Appunn's tonometer** consists of a wind-chest with many reeds tuned through two or three octaves by small steps, e.g., 129 reeds ranging from 512 to 1024 cycles by steps of 4 cycles.] — Ger. *Tonmesser.*

tonoscope = an instrument for the visual analysis of complex sounds by the principle of the **stroboscope.** [A moving drum contains many series of perforations which are intermittently lighted from within by a flame, a neon tube, etc. which is regulated by the sound to be analyzed; the rows of perforations, which appear stationary, indicate the frequency components of the sound. Cf. **strobophotograph.**]

tonsil = (*anat.*) a small, almond-shaped mass, composed mainly of lymphoid tissue, situate between the fauces. **tonsillar**[a] (accent **ton-**). — Fr. *amygdale*; Ger. *Mandel.*

tonus, tone/muscle, see **muscle tonus.**

tonus/plastic = a tonic state of skeletal muscles, such that a limb whose muscles are so innervated will remain fixed in the position in which a manipulator places it. [Sometimes called "lead pipe plasticity."]

topographic = (*psychoan.*) characterizing mental processes interpreted from the standpoint of their localization in the mental apparatus.

topography = the mapping out of localities. [See Tables XVI, XVII and XVIII.]

topography/mental = (*psychoan.*) the schema of the mind used for purposes of description and interpretation. [According to this view the mental apparatus is divided into the **id,** the **ego,** and the **superego.** Syn. **topography of the mind, topographical psychology.**]

toric lens = (one of) a system of spectacle lenses having a highly concave surface toward the eye of the wearer, thereby affording a larger field of vision than otherwise. [In order to get the effect of a cylindrical lens, the anterior face of the lens is ground to the form of a **torus** having unequal circular curvatures in two perpendicular meridians. For a purely spherical effect such a lens, although usually so called, is not properly a **toric lens,** but a **meniscus.**] — Fr. *lentille en tore.*

torpor = temporary lack of response to stimuli of normal intensity. [Syn. **torpidity.** Distg. fr. **sleep.**] **torpid**[a]. — Ger. *Betäubung.*

torsion = the twisting of one end of a cord, flexible metal rod, or pair of cords or rods about the axis, the other end remaining fixed, so that when the twisted end is released it tends to rotate in the contrary direction. **torsional**[a].

torsional movement, torsion, torsional rotation = rotation of the eyeballs about their sagittal or antero-posterior axes. [It occurs as a component in the normal coordinated movements of the eyeballs, as a deviation from Listing's law. Syn. **wheel-movement, rolling.** Cf. **rotation.**] — Ger. *Raddrehung, Rollung.*

total color blindness, see **achromatism.**

totem = a species of animal or plant, or some organic object, held in peculiar veneration by members of a given sib, community, or sex, or by an individual or member, as symbolic of their group, or regarded as the protective deity of their sib, or sex, or of those having the same individual totem or guardian spirit. **totemic**[a].

totemism = the system of totems and the customs attached thereto, considered as a social or religious institution.

touch = 1. contact of an individual with an object or body of any sort, by movement of his members; 2. contact of an object with some portion of the body surface; 3. the experience aroused by such contact. [Syn. (1) **palpation,** (2) **touch sensation** (prefd.), (3) **thigmesthesia, feeling** (ambig.).] **tactual**[a], **tactile**[a]. — Fr. *tact, toucher, sensation de contact*; Ger. *Berührung.*

touch/field of = 1. the totality of tactual stimulations which occur at any given moment; 2. a generic term embracing all aspects of tactual sensibility.

touch pyramid = a geometrical representation of the relations between the principal pressure-pain sensations (Titchener). — Fr. *pyramide du tact.*

touch sensation = 1. a sensation aroused by stimulation of certain receptors in the skin, through contact with some object, regardless of the temperature of the stimulus of body surface; i.e. either a pressure or a contact sensation; 2. (more narrowly) **contact sensation,** as distg. fr. **pressure.** — Fr. *sensation tactile*; Ger. *Tastempfindung* (distg. fr. *Druckempfindung* = pressure).

touch spot = a point on the skin which is peculiarly sensitive to faint punctiform pressure stimuli; i.e. a spot which has a much lower limen for contact stimuli than the adjacent regions. [The points in the skin directly over the roots of the hairs are usually touch spots.] — Fr. *point de pression, p. de tact*; Ger. *Tastpunkt.*

toxic = pert. to poison, poisons, or poisoning. — Ger. *giftig.*

toxic psychosis = mental disorder due to poisons, including also the absorption of bacterial products or toxins formed at a local source of infection.

toxin = 1. any poisonous albumen produced by bacterial action; 2. (*pop.*) a poisonous substance. [**toxins** (1) are distinguished by their capacity to excite the production of **antitoxins,** are soluble, thermolabile secretory products of bacteria. Toxin-like substances are present in snake venom and in some vegetable tissues.] **toxinic**[a].

toxophobia = morbid fear of being poisoned.

TR = abbrev. for terminal stimulus, the maximal value of a stimulus scale or the upper absolute threshold. [Cf. **R, threshold.**]

trace = (*neurol.*) an altered physical state of conductive tissue, postulated as the product of learning and as the physical basis of memory. [Syn. **engram, bond.**] — Fr. *empreinte*; Ger. *Spur*.

trachea = the cartilaginous and membranous tube which descends from the larynx to the bronchi. [Syn. **windpipe.**] (3 syll., accent **trake-**) **tracheal**[a]. — Ger. *Luftröhre*.

trachoma = a contagious disease, primarily of the conjunctiva of the eyelids, characterized by the formation of small elevations or granules, and later by the formation of scar-tissue which may lead to deformities of the lids. [It may also affect the eyeball and lead to permanent impairment of vision.] (Accent **-kome-**.)

trachyphonia = a form of **dysphonia** characterized by hoarseness or roughness of the voice.

tract = a collection or bundle of nerve-fibers having the same origin, termination, or function. [E.g. spinothalamic tract, having same origin and termination, but possibly a number of functions (sensory).] — Fr. *faisceau, voie*; Ger. *Leitungsbahn, Nervenstrang*.

tractable, see **docility.**

traction sensation = a cutaneous sensation aroused by pulling the skin away from the member. [Syn. **pull sensation.**]

trade test = a test of proficiency in a trade or other skilled occupation, designed to measure an applicant's information about the trade, or his skill in performance of standard tasks. [The **trade tests** developed in the U.S. Army for measuring proficiency in 84 occupations such as welder, truck-driver, typist, are of three types: oral, picture, and performance. Distg. fr. **aptitude** (or **capacity**) **test.**] — Fr. *test commercial*.

tradition = any body of social customs or history handed down orally or by direct training of individuals, as contr. w. transmission through graphic records. [Cf. **custom.**] **traditional**[a].

tragedy = (*esth.*) a serious drama ending with a catastrophe (usually the death of the hero or heroine) brought about by inevitable conflict of the hero or heroine with the environment, to which he or she is not adjusted. — Ger. *Trauerspiel*.

tragic = 1. pert. to tragedy in art; 2. arousing emotional reactions of horror similar to those aroused by tragedy in the dramatic art; 3. (*pop.*) fatal or calamitous.

train = to guide or direct the learning process in a human being, or in an animal, so as to induce certain habitual responses, complex habits, or attitudes which are desired by the trainer. — Fr. *guider, diriger*; Ger. *erziehen, dressieren*.

training = 1. a systematic series of activities designed to bring about the development of some specific habit, ability, or attitude in a human being or animal; 2. the care and education of human offspring during the years of immaturity, e.g. child training. **trained**[a], **train**[v]. — Fr. *entraînement, dressage*; Ger. *Dressur, Erziehung*.

training analysis = (*psychoan.*) analysis, by a trained analyst, of an individual who plans to do therapeutic analyses.

train of thought (or **of ideas**) = a sequence or succession of associated ideational processes or functions. — Ger. *Gedankengang*.

trait = 1. any biological or psychological character or inherited mark; 2. a distinctive mode of behavior, of a more or less permanent nature, arising from the individual's native endowments as modified by his experience. (Amer. pron. **trait,** Brit., **tray.**) — Ger. (2) *Charakterzug*.

trance = a condition of dissociated consciousness characterized by suspension of voluntary movements and by the presence of automatic activity and stereotypy of thought. [Applied loosely to certain conditions of hysteria, hypnosis, ecstasy, and the state of mediumship.] — Fr. *extase*, "*transe*," *sommeil*; Ger. *Verzückung, Ekstase*.

transcendental, see **metempirical.**

transfer of training = the improvement of a mental or motor function without direct training, through the practice of some kindred function. [Applied to the formation of motor coordinations, to the improvement of sensory discrimination and perception, to the formation of attitudes, and to thinking or reasoning; **transfer of training** is sometimes attributed to the existence of identical elements in the two functions or to the process of generalization. Cf. **cross-education.**] — Fr. *transfert d'entraînement*.

transference = (*psychoan.*) 1. the development of an emotional attitude on the part of a patient toward the analyst, in the form of either an affectionate reaction (positive) or of a hostile reaction (negative), the attitude in either case being derived from earlier relations of the patient with one or both of his parents and not from the actual analytic situation; 2. displacement of affect, either positive or negative. — Ger. *Übertragung*.

transformation = 1. (*logic*) the operation by which one formula or proposition is substituted for another, or by which the several items in a complex system are exchanged for the equivalent items of another system; 2. (*math.*) the substitution of a second variable y for a first variable x, of which it is a function; 3. (*vis.*) a process, believed to be subjective or cerebral, owing to which visual objects are represented in conscious experience in sense-qualities that are relatively independent of the conditions of illumination (or of the absolute values of the corresponding retinal stimuli), and that correspond to the reflection characteristics of the objects; 4. (*phys.*) change of an entity or process from one form into another, e.g. of mechanical energy into thermal energy. [The **transformation** (2) is called a **linear transformation** if y is a linear function of x, i.e. if $y = a + bx$. Cf. **transformation theory.**] **transform**[v].

transformation theory, transformism = the theory that one biological species becomes changed in the course of time into another radically different species. [Syn. **evolution, evolutionism.** Contr. w. **special creation theory.**]

transilient variation = (*hist.*) syn. for **mutation.**

transitive states, see **substantive states.**

transmission = 1. (*biol.*) the passing on of biological characters from parent to child; 2. the passing on of any effect from one individual or generation to another, whether by inheritance or by other means. [Cf. **social transmission.**] **transmit**[v]. — Ger. *Übertragung*.

transmission/neural, see **neural conduction.**

transmission unit, TU = (*aud.*) a logarithmic unit of sound intensity. [The units in common use are the **decibel** and the **napier** (or **neper**).]

transparent plane color = a two-dimensional color which presents a clear, unclouded *mode of appearance* and permits objects to be seen beyond and behind it in visual space, e.g. colors seen in clear glass panes. — Ger. *durchsichtige Flächenfarbe.*

transposition = 1. the interchange of position as between two units in any complex system; 2. (*mus.*) the transference of an entire musical composition from one key to another; 3. any change of parts which does not involve a change of structure. [E.g. (1) interchange of terms in a proposition.] **transpose**^{v}. — Ger. (1) *Versetzung,* (2) *Transposition.*

transverse = lying or moving across, athwart, or crosswise. [**transverse vibrations** are movements perpendicular to the direction of transmission; e.g. light-waves. **transverse axis** = an axis lying athwart the principal axis of reference (usually the longitudinal or major axis). Contr. w. **longitudinal.**] — Ger. *querlaufend.*

transverse plane = (*anat.*) any plane in the body at right angles to the cephalocaudal axis. [In man, syn. **horizontal plane.**]

transvestism, transvestition = the propensity of certain individuals to dress in the mode of clothing prescribed for the opposite sex. **transvestite**^{np}, **transvestitism**^{n}.

trapezoid body = (*neurol.*) a strand of transverse fibers in the lower part of the pons, which arise from the cells of the cochlear nucleus. [Syn. **trapezium.**] — Fr. *corps trapezoïde.*

Traube-Hering waves = relatively long-period changes in the pulse curve alleged to be related to psychological changes.

trauma = any wound or injury, esp. a structural injury. [Syn. **traumatism.**] **traumata**^{pl}, **traumatic**^{a}.

trauma/psychic = an emotional shock which may cause a lasting disturbance to mental functions.

traumatic neurosis = a psychoneurosis (e.g. hysteria, anxiety states) which is precipitated by the effects of a **trauma** and in which the symptoms are attached to the original traumatic experience. — Ger. *Unfallsneurose.*

treatment = the systematic working over by an investigator or technician of the data at hand. [Applied also to operation by a physician upon a given disease, etc.] **treat**^{v}. — Ger. *Behandlung.*

tree structure (*neurol.*), see **dendrite.**

trembling = a moderate or slight, involuntary, and phasic contraction of some group of muscles, continued indefinitely. [Cf. **convulsion.**] — Fr. *tremblement*; Ger. *Zittern.*

tremograph, see **steadiness apparatus.**

tremolo = periodic variations in the loudness or pitch (or both) of a tone which is produced on a musical instrument. [On the violin, e.g., the effect is gained by altering regularly the pressure of the finger against a string, in wind instruments by varying the air supply or pressure of the instrument against the lips. Syn. **vibrato,** prefd. when applied to corresponding changes produced by the singing voice.] (Accent **trem-.**)

tremor = a continuous muscular spasm of limited range, which is associated with emotion and fatigue or with pathological states such as cerebellar lesions (*intention tremor*), or lesions of the basal ganglia of the brain (*resting tremor*). [E.g. Parkinsonism. Cf. **spasm.**] — Fr. *tremblement*; Ger. *Zittern.*

trend = 1. the line or direction of progression of a series of events, forms, types, etc.; 2. inclination in a specific direction or towards a particular mode of behavior; 3. delusional or autistic ideas. [As describing behavior, the term is metaphorical and seldom used with great precision, though it has been put forward as a synonym for normal homologues of the Freudian complex.] — Fr. (1, 2) *tendance*; Ger. *Tendenz, Richtung.*

trepan, see **trephine.**

trephine^{n} = a hollow cylindrical or conical cutter used in brain surgery to remove a circular disk from the skull. [Syn. **trepan,** an obsolete form of this instrument.] **trephine**^{v}, **trepan**^{v} = to operate with the trephine.

Treppe, see **staircase phenomenon.**

triad = a chord composed of three tones; e.g. c-e-g. — Fr. *accord à trois sons, triade*; Ger. *Dreiklang.*

trial and error method = the name applied to a mode of learning, in which the learner tries various movements in his repertory, apparently in a somewhat random manner and without explicit recognition of the connection between the movement and the desired result; tentative movements which succeed (i.e. which lead to habit formation) are more frequently repeated in subsequent trials, and those which fail gradually disappear. [The movements, though termed *random,* are generally characteristic of the behavior of the animal or human individual in somewhat analogous situations. The term was first used by Lloyd Morgan in 1894. The procedure was (more properly) named by Thorndike the method of 'trial, error, and accidental success.] — Fr. *m. des essais et erreurs.*

tribal self = 1. the psychical factors which are assumed to be involved in the organization of a social group or tribe, in so far as that group is analogous to an organism or personality; 2. the consciousness which an individual has of himself as a member of a tribe, partaking of the views, sentiments, etc. common to all members; or the behavior which reveals an individual to others as partaking of such tribal consciousness or characteristics. — Fr. *conscience sociale, moi tribal.*

tribe = a partly organized social group of individuals, which consists of loosely connected communities or sibs, usually speaking a common language, with a common territory and name, and having, in many cases, a common military organization, but usually lacking in the cultural and judicial systems which characterize a **state.** **tribal**^{a}. — Fr. *tribu*; Ger. *Volkstamm.*

triceps reflex = contraction of the triceps brachii, following a sharp tap on the tendon near the olecranon while the forearm is supported at right angles to the arm. [Mediated by 6th to 7th cervical segments. Syn. **elbow r., elbow jerk.**]

trichromatic theory = a color theory based upon the facts of color mixture, namely that all hues may be derived from the mixture of two or more of three primaries, usually given as red, green, and violet.

trichromatism = normal color-vision, so named under the influence of the Young-Helmholtz three-color theory. [Distg. fr. **dichromatism** = ability to distinguish only two primary hues and their variants, and fr. **achromatism,** the ability to distinguish only differences of grays.] **trichromatic**[a], **trichromate**[np].

trick = (*indiv. psychol.*) a psychic mechanism by which an individual conceals from himself a knowledge of his weaknesses.

tridimensional theory of feeling = the theory that there are three attributes or dimensions of affection: (*a*) pleasantness-unpleasantness; (*b*) excitement-quiescence; and (*c*) tension-relaxation (Wundt).

trigeminal nerve = the V cranial nerve, which has three main branches: (*a*) afferent from face and scalp; (*b*) efferent to the lacrimal gland; and (*c*) afferent from mucosa of nose and tongue. — Fr. *nerf trijumeau*.

trigger action = the case in which one train of energy serves to release another train of (latent) energy; e.g. application of a spark to gunpowder, where the energy of the spark is not transmitted beyond the point where the gunpowder is ignited. [A term applied to the mode of excitation of receptors, nerves, and muscles.] — Fr. *déclanchement*.

triploid` = having three sets of chromosomes. [Cf. **diploid, tetraploid.**]

trireceptor theory = a type of theory, such as that of Young and Helmholtz, which assumes that color vision depends upon the operation of three kinds of receptors in the retina; each of these, with its nerve connections, being assumed to mediate a fixed fundamental or primary hue-quality, all gradations of color being dependent upon the proportions of activity of the three. [Cf. **Young-Helmholtz theory.**]

trisomic = (*biol.*) possessing an extra chromosome, so that in an ordinary diploid organism there are three chromosomes in place of one of the usual pairs.

tritanopia = a rare type of partial color-blindness, or dichromatic vision, in which the spectrum is apparently shortened at the violet end (von Kries). [The term signifies loss of the *third* color process of the three-component theory. Syn. **blue** (or **violet**) **blindness.** Probably identical with **blue-yellow blindness**. Usually acquired, but sometimes apparently congenital. Distg. fr. **protanopia** and **deuteranopia.**] **tritanopic**[a], **tritanope**[np].

tritone = a musical interval which is equal, or nearly equal, to half an octave. [The major diatonic tritone, or augmented fourth, has a frequency ratio of 32:45, and is slightly less than half an octave. The equal tritone has a ratio of 1:2$^{1/2}$ (or 99:140) and is exactly half an octave. The Pythagorean tritone, ratio 512:729, is somewhat larger than half an octave.]

trochanteric = pert. to or located in a small region on the outer and uppermost part of the human thigh. (Accent **-ter-**.)

trochlear nerve = the IV cranial nerve, which controls the superior oblique muscle of the eyeball. [Syn. **patheticus.**] — Fr. *nerf pathétique*.

tromophonia = a form of **dysphonia** characterized by tremulous voice.

trophic = pert. to nutrition and the nutritive functions.

trophic nerve = a nerve which aids or regulates the nutrition of a tissue. [Evidence opposes the view that there are specialized **trophic nerves** having no other function than control of the metabolism of tissue, and indicates that all nerves exercise a trophic influence on the tissue which they supply.]

trophism = direct nutritive or trophic influence; more specifically, the control of the nutritive functions by the nervous system.

trophoplasm, see **idioplasm.**

tropism = response in a cell, an organ, or an organism, which results in the assumption of a definite axial position in reference to the direction of an external stimulating agent. [Syn. **orientation; taxis,** applied to motile types of organisms. The principal tropisms are **chemotropism, thermotropism, thigmotropism (stereotropism), phototropism (heliotropism), galvanotropism, geotropism, rheotropism;** others investigated are **anemotropism, hydrotropism, magnetotropism, chromotropism, barotropism, chromatotropism;** all accented **-ot-.**] **tropistic**[a] (**-tropic**[a], the only form in compounds).

tropostereoscope = an instrument employed to demonstrate the influence of double images in the perception of depth; it consists of two metal tubes, hinged together at one end, so that the other ends may be adjusted to the distance between the eyes; circular bits of colored glass are fitted into the ends away from the eye; on the glass in each tube is a large circle concentric with the tube, and on each a smaller circle symmetrically placed at one side of the center in each tube. [The tubes may be turned in opposite directions, so that while one looks through the tubes, the large circles are constantly superimposed, while the small circles may fall upon the vertical meridian in each eye, or they may be made to produce on the retina either crossed or uncrossed double images. As one looks through the tube with the eyes converged upon a distant object, the small circles fuse into one, which seems to move back and forth through the large circle.]

trough, see **cycle.**

true = corresponding to reality, conforming to fact, coherent, or consistent with logical relations. [Syn. **correct.** Contr. w. **false** = not so conforming, or w. **erroneous,** which emphasizes the role of the individual in making the judgment.] **truth**[n]. — Fr. *vrai*; Ger. *wahr*.

true-false test = a form of mental test, employed most often in checking the testee's possession of general information, wherein a series of statements is made (or questions asked), each one of which is to be designated as right or wrong (or answered "yes" or "no"). [Since by chance alone one-half of the responses would tend to be correct, the test is often scored Rights minus Wrongs.]

true resistance, see **ohmic resistance.**

true score = the measure which would be obtained by taking the average of an indefinitely large number of measurements of a given individual on similar tests taken under similar conditions. [A **true score** is not possible of determination experimentally.] — Fr. *notation valable*.

true vocal cords, see **vocal cords.**

truism = a statement or proposition whose **truth** is so obvious to both speaker and audience that it need not be formulated or need not be supported by argument or fact. — Fr. *vérité évidente, truisme*; Ger. *Gemeinplatz*.

truth = the correspondence of a judgment or thought with an actual occurrence, or with actual processes of nature, or (in the case of mathematical generalization) with its own implications. [Pragmatists explain correspondence with actual occurrences as meaning that the judgment guides one safely among facts; i.e. it works. Others explain it as coherence with other judgments which in their totality symbolize reality itself. Contr. w. **falsity** and w. **error;** the former emphasizes objective disparity, the latter an incoherent mental procedure.] **true**[a]; **the true**[n] (abstract and general). — Fr. *vérité*; Ger. *Wahrheit*.

TU, see **transmission unit.**

tuber cinereum = a gray area on the ventral aspect of the forebrain and caudad to the optic tracts, from which the infundibulum extends to the pituitary body. — Fr. *tubercule cendré*.

tumid = enlarged, swollen. **tumescence**[n], **tumidity**[n], **tumescent**[a]. — Fr. *enflé*; Ger. *geschwollen*.

tune[n] = a series of musical sounds which form a rhythmical, melodic pattern. — Fr. *air*; Ger. *Weise, Melodie*.

tune[v] = to adjust the natural frequency of a sounding body or resonator to agree with some standard. — Fr. *accorder*; Ger. *stimmen*.

tuned resonance, see **resonance.**

tuning = (*cutan.*) the definite maximum of sensory intensity that can be aroused in each specific pressure, warm, and cold spot, and that cannot be increased by any excessive degree of stimulation. [The tuning of each spot is believed to be independent of every other. First reported by Goldscheider.]

tuning fork = a two-pronged (two-tined) instrument of highly tempered metal, adjusted so as to generate sound-waves of constant frequency. [Abbrev. to **fork.** Used in determining pitch standards. In a variable **tuning fork** the pitch may be altered within a limited range by sliding small weights along the tines.] — Ger. *Stimmgabel*.

tunnel of Corti = a triangular space enclosed within the **arch of Corti** of the internal ear.

turnover/labor = the proportion of shifts and replacements necessary for the maintenance of the work force; i.e. the ratio of the number of labor changes to the number of full-year workers. [Often computed as the ratio of the number of accessions to the average number on the payroll.] — Fr. *taux de fluctuation de la main d'oeuvre*.

twelfth = in the musical scale, a tone whose vibration rate is 3 times that of the tonic or key-tone.

twilight sleep = a condition of dim awareness, which is usually induced by drugs. [Generally restricted to the stupor induced by a combination of morphine and scopolamine.]

twilight states/hysterical = mental attacks in hysteria in which the patients imagine themselves in an entirely different environment or are the subjects of remarkable adventures. [In this condition they often repeat scenes they have actually experienced in the past, fulfill wishes which have remained unfulfilled, or exclude unpleasant episodes they have experienced in the past.] — Fr. *états crépusculaires hystériques*; Ger. *Dämmerzustände*.

twilight vision, see **scotopic vision.** — Fr. *vision crépusculaire*; Ger. *Dämmerungssehen*.

twin = a member of a pair of offspring produced at one birth. [In man, classified as (1) **fraternal** (or **dizygotic**) **twins,** which may be of the same or of different sexes, and are usually no more alike than other siblings of the same family, and (2) **identical** (or **monozygotic** or **monochorionic**) **twins** = of the same sex and usually very similar in their characteristics; the latter are believed to arise from the same fertilized egg and hence to have the same heredity.] — Fr. *jumeau*[m], *jumelle*[f], (1) *j. dizygote*, (2) *j. vrai, j. monozygote*; Ger. *Zwilling*.

twinge = a sharp, sudden pain of short duration. — Fr. *douleur aiguë, élancement*; Ger. *Zwicken*.

twitching = a sudden, local, convulsive movement, or a series of such movements. **twitch,**[v, n]. — Fr. *contraction spasmodique, spasme musculaire*; Ger. *Zuckung*.

two-aspect theory, see **double-aspect theory.**

two-factor theory of intelligence = the doctrine, expounded by Spearman, that all modes of cognitive activity have in common one fundamental factor or group of factors (g), while the specific elements (s) are different in the same individual for different abilities. [Cf. **g factor, s factor;** contr. w. **multimodal theory** (Thorndike).]

two-point discrimination = determination of the distance which must separate two points in order that they may be perceived as two by skin or eye. [This distance is an accepted measure of the delicacy of spatial perception in the cutaneous senses.]

tympanic canal, see **scala tympani.**

tympanic cavity = an irregular space within the temporal bone, filled with air, which communicates with the pharynx by means of the Eustachian tube. [It is bounded laterally by the tympanic membrane, and contains the auditory ossicles, a chain of bones which serve to convey to the internal ear the vibrations transmitted by the tympanic membrane. Syn. **middle ear cavity.** Cf. **ear.**] — Fr. *cavité* (*creux*) *tympanique*; Ger. *Trommelhöhle, Paukenhöhle*.

tympanic membrane = a thin, fibrous, semitransparent membrane, slightly conical in shape, which separates the inner termination of the external auditory meatus from the tympanic cavity within the ear. [It vibrates in response to sound, and communicates the vibrations to the first of the auditory ossicles (the malleus), one arm of which is attached near its center. Syn. **ear-drum membrane** (incorrectly called **ear-drum**).] — Ger. *Trommelfell, Paukenfell*.

tympanum = the middle ear. [Often applied (ambig.) to the tympanic or ear-drum membrane. Cf. **ear/middle.**] (Accent **tym-.**) **tympanic**[a]. — Ger. *Pauken, Trommel*.

type = 1. a set or pattern of characteristics which more or less closely resemble those possessed by certain individual beings, objects, etc.; 2. a class of individuals who have a set or pattern of distinguishing characteristics in common; 3. a specimen selected from (2) as representative of the class as a whole; 4. (*anal. psychol.*) a group defined in terms of its fundamental way of directing its psychic energy. [The two major types (4) are introvert and extravert, each being subdivided according to the specific mental acts through which the psychic energy expresses itself. Cf. **type/mental.**] **typical**[a] = embodying or representing a given type; **type**[a]. — Ger. *Typus*.

type/mental = a distinctive mode of behavior, which differentiates one group of individuals from another in some important respect. [There are various bases for distinguishing types; e.g.

sensory (auditory, visual, motile, etc.), attitudinal (introvert, extravert), temperamental (phlegmatic, etc.), general character (emotional, logical, etc.).]

type/physical = one of three physical types distinguished and correlated with certain mental states (Kretschmer). [**pyknic** = tendency to distribution of fat around the trunk; **asthenic** = poor muscular development; **athletic** = well-developed muscles.]

typical dreams = (*psychoan.*) certain dreams, of general occurrence (although varying with different individuals in the character of the manifest content), which point to a common groundwork of unconscious material. [E.g. of flying, of being partly naked, of emergence from a dark chamber containing water, or of the death of a beloved person.] — Fr. *rêves typiques*.

U

ugly = characterizing that which is esthetically unpleasant. [Contr. w. **beautiful.**] **ugliness**[n]. — Fr. *laid*; Ger. *hässlich*.

ulna = the larger bone of the forearm, situate on the side opposite to the thumb. **ulnar**[a]. — Fr. *cubitus*; Ger. *Elle*.

ulnar nerve = the sensory and motor nerve which supplies the shoulder, wrist, palm, and little finger. — Fr. *nerf cubital*; Ger. *Ellenbogennerv*.

ultimate value = (*math., statist.*) that value toward which a series tends as more and more terms are included. [Cf. **limit, true score.**]

ultra-violet = radiant energy of wave-lengths shorter than the extreme violet and lying beyond the visible spectrum. [Usually assigned to vibrations below 400 or 390 millimicrons ($m\mu$).]

umbilicus = the navel. (Accent **-lie-**.) **umbilical**[a] (accent **-bil-**).

unanschaulich = 1. abstract, conceptual; i.e. not given perceptually or imaginally; 2. impalpable. [Ger.]

uncertainty = absence of belief, due to insufficient data. [Distg. fr. **doubt**, which implies the presence of conflicting evidence; contr. w. **certainty** = high degree of belief based on supporting evidence.] **uncertain**[a]. — Fr. *incertitude*; Ger. *Ungewissheit*.

uncertainty/interval of, see **interval of uncertainty.**

uncinate gyrus, see **fornix.** — Fr. *circonvolution de l'hippocampe*.

unconditioned reflex = an original, or innate, as contr. w. an **acquired** or **conditioned reflex.**

unconscious = 1. characterizing an activity which occurs with no awareness of it on the part of the organism that executes the activity; 2. characterizing an individual who is unaware of the activities that he is executing at the moment; 3. (*psychoan.*) in the strictly Freudian sense, characterizing certain dynamic processes (not merely latent thoughts) which do not reach consciousness in spite of their effectiveness and intensity, and which cannot be brought into conscious experience by any effort of the will or act of memory. [Contr. w. **conscious;** distg. fr. **non-conscious** (applied to lifeless beings or substances). Cf. (3) **id.** Jung postulates a *collective* or *racial unconscious* (3) and Rank a *primary, embryonal state*, existing unchanged in the adult.] **unconsciousness**[n]. — Fr. *inconscient*; Ger. *unbewusst*.

uncontrolled = characterizing factors whose variations the experimenter has not regulated or measured.

unconventional = characterizing actions which depart from the correct or traditional patterns of behavior common to the members of a given group. [Cf. **convention, folkways, unmoral.**] **unconventionality**[n].

uncritical, see **critical.**

underestimate[n] = the adoption (in the statistical treatment of experimental work) of a value below, or of a quantity less than that which the data warrant. [The value which is the underestimate is generally used deliberately in order to avoid the possibility of the quantitative conclusions being invalidated by unnoted factors, etc.] **underestimate**[v]. — Fr. *dépréciation, dévalorisation*; Ger. *Unterschätzung*.

undersensitivity, see **hypesthesia.**

understanding = 1. (*hist.*) the mental power, faculty, or function whereby the meaning of phenomena or propositions is apprehended by the individual, as distg. (by Locke and others) fr. **intuitive** or **pure reason;** 2. a loose syn. for **apprehension of meaning.** [Syn. (2) **comprehension,** which applies to apprehension of specific situations, whereas **understanding** emphasizes the type of mental process involved. Contr. (1) w. **sensation** and w. **reason.**] **understand**[v]. — Fr. *compréhension*; Ger. *Verstand*.

understatement = a report concerning some value obtained partly from empirical data and partly by estimate, in which report liberal allowance is made for possible error, so that the value reported is reasonably assumed to be considerably less than the true value. [Cf. **underestimate.** Contr. w. **overstatement.**] **understate**[v], **understated**[a]. — Fr. *jugement subordonné, proposition subalterne*.

undoing mechanism = (*psychoan.*) a ceremonial symptom in the compulsion neuroses, whereby a second action is intended to abolish the first action, as if it had not happened. — Fr. *mécanisme d'annulation rétroactive*.

undulation = 1. a wave; 2. the propagation of a series of waves in a given medium, and the condition induced in that medium thereby. [Syn. **vibration,** applied usually to single or separate waves.] **undulate**[v], **undulatory**[a]. — Fr. *ondulation*; Ger. *Wellenbewegung*.

unequivocal = admitting only a single interpretation. [Syn. **univocal.** Contr. w. **equivocal** = admitting of two or more conflicting interpretations.] **unequivocality**[n]. — Ger. *eindeutig*.

unfitness = (*biol.*) inferiority of an organism in structure or behavior, which results in its inability to cope successfully with environmental conditions. [Cf. **fitness.**] **unfit**[a]. — Fr. *inadaptation, inapte*[a]; Ger. *Ungeeignetheit, Untüchtigkeit, Untauglichkeit*.

ungual = pert. to or located in the regions around the finger-nails and toe-nails. (Pron. **un-gwal.**)

uniaural = pert. to one ear alone. [Syn. **monaural** (etymologically incorrect). Contr. w. **binaural** = pert. to the two ears acting conjointly.] — Fr. *monauriculaire*; Ger. *einohrig*.

unicellular organism = an animal or plant which consists of a single cell. [Includes **protozoa** = one-celled animal organisms, and **protophyta** = one-celled plants; contr. w. **multicellular organism.**]

uniceptors = (*immunol.*) hypothetical bodies which fix and inactivate toxins independently of complement. [Cf. **amboceptor.**]

uniformity = the similarity of two or more events or processes, such that their essential characteristics (or components) and relations can be named and described in a single statement or law, which applies to any and all instances of the given data. — Ger. *Gleichförmigkeit.*

uniformity of nature = a final or highest summarization of all the laws formulated regarding the operations observed in physics, chemistry, and other branches of natural phenomena, which states that, given the same or exactly similar antecedents, the same or exactly similar consequents will in every instance follow.

unilateral = pert. to one side of the body.

unimodal = characterizing a frequency curve which possesses only one peak or high point. [Cf. **mode** (2), **frequency polygon.**]

unintentional = characterizing acts and their results, in cases where the outcome is not the end foreseen and desired by the agent.

uniocular, monocular = pert. to the single eye. [Contr. w. **binocular** = pert. to the two eyes acting conjointly. The form **monocular** is more frequently used, but is etymologically incorrect.] — Ger. *einäugig.*

union = (*relig.*) the state of one who thinks and feels himself joined to God, i.e. one with God. [The highest degree of mystical ecstasy.] — Ger. *Vereinigung.*

unipolar cell, see **multipolar cell.**

unique = characterizing that which is the only example or member of a class; that which occurs but once; or that which differs notably from all other individual characters or items with which it might seem to be comparable. [Syn. **sui generis.**] — Ger. *einzigartig, ausgezeichnet.*

unison = (*mus.*) a chord consisting of two tones which are the same in pitch. [Syn. **prime.** Cf. **interval,** and Table VII.] — Ger. *Einklang.*

unit = 1. (*math.*) a magnitude used as a common denominator in measurement; 2. any datum considered without regard to its internal differences. **unit**[a] (1); **unitary**[a] (2). — Ger. *Einheit.*

unit character = (*biol.*) a character or character-group of any organism which is transmitted in its entirety to the offspring, so that if it appears in any given descendant it manifests itself as a whole and not partially. [According to Mendel's views, **unit characters** exist in pairs, which are opposite and mutually exclusive.]

unit normal distribution = (*statist.*) a normal distribution of measures or magnitudes whose standard deviation is equal to one (unity), and whose total area is equal to one.

unit-task tests, see **work-limit method.**

unitary function, see **functional unity.**

unitary type = according to eidetic theory, the type of individual whose after-images, eidetic images, and memory images show marked similarity. [The existence of such cases suggested to E. R. Jaensch the genetic theory that the origin of various levels of imagery and of experience lies in an original, undifferentiated, eidetic unity.] — Ger. *Einheitstypus.*

unity = 1. the characteristic of a datum such that it is (inherently or for purposes of investigation) regarded as being without parts or internal distinctions (= functional oneness or simplicity); 2. the characteristic of numerically distinct data of being so essentially similar that they may be regarded as forming a single class (= logical unity); 3. the characteristic of being a numerically distinct individual, though differentiated into a manifold of parts (= organic unity or **singleness**); 4. (*esth.*) the characteristic of a work of art in that the parts are closely related. [Cf. **unit** (1); contr. w. **plurality** = the presence or distinguishing of more than one datum or part.] **unitary**[a]. — Ger. *Einheit.*

universal complex = (*psychoan.*) an emotional experience, or complex, based upon one of the fundamental instincts. [Contr. w. **particular complex** = based upon incidental circumstances in the individual's life history.]

universality = 1. the validity which is assumed for certain propositions, in that they are accepted by mankind as true, although the grounds of their validity may not be known and may be purely emotional; 2. (*biol.*) the presence or occurrence of a certain trait or function in all organisms of a given species. [(2) is frequently used as a criterion of instinct.] **universal**[a]. — Ger. *Allgemeinheit.*

universality/impression of = (*soc.*) the belief that numerous other persons are responding similarly to oneself in a given situation, thereby justifying one's acceptance of an idea or facilitating one's behavior or course of action.

universe = 1. the totality of existing things or phenomena, considered as constituting a single system; 2. syn. for **universe of discourse.**

universe of discourse = the field in which is situated the subject under discussion or investigation, and to which the treatment is limited. [The concept is used esp. to rule out possible exceptions to formulated laws, when such exceptions pertain to a different field from that under consideration.]

univocal = having but one meaning. [Syn. **unequivocal.** Contr. w. **equivocal.**] **univocality**[n]. — Fr. *univoque*; Ger. *eindeutig.*

unknowable[n,a] = (that which is) beyond the power of man to discover. [Used by philosophers to denote a critical or dogmatic generalization. Distg. fr. **undiscoverable,** or **unascertainable,** which usually imply contemporary inability to attain certain data or solutions, and fr. **unknown** = not yet discovered.] — Fr. *inconnaissable*; Ger. *unerkennbar.*

unmusical = characterizing certain individuals who are unable to distinguish relatively large differences of pitch or to identify tunes; i.e. who are low in musical aptitude or are lacking in musical ability. — Fr. *amusical.*

unpleasantness = a quality of hedonic tone or feeling whose motor correlate is movement away from the source of stimulation. [Contr. w. **pleasantness,** correlated w. movement toward the stimulus. The German terms *Unlust* and *Lust* carry the meaning and the contrast better. Distg. fr. **pain** (1), an acute sensation usually accompanied by hedonic unpleasantness.] **unpleasant**[a]. — Fr. *déplaisir*; Ger. *Unlust.*

unreality/feeling of = a feeling attached to a perceptual experience, esp. in pathological conditions, such that the experience appears to lack objectivity or reality. [Cf. **reality feeling.**] — Fr. *sentiment d'irréalité*; Ger. *Gefühl der Unwirklichkeit.*

unreasonable = 1. (*logic*) characterizing a conclusion or hypothesis which is reached in violation of the canons of logic; 2. (*soc.*) characterizing an individual who makes demands upon his associates which cannot be justified, or characterizing these demands. [Contr. w. **reasonable.**]—Fr. *illogique*; Ger. *unlogisch, unvernünftig.*

unreasoning = 1. characterizing an individual who tends to act without use of the logical processes; 2. characterizing behavior which is not influenced or controlled by reasoning. — Fr. *alogique.*

unreflective = without use of thought processes.

unsociable = inclined to shun the company of other persons. **unsociability**[n]. — Ger. *ungesellig.*

unsocial = 1. characterizing an individual who does not fit into the current social system, or an act which is at variance with contemporary social usage; 2. not inclined to seek the company of other individuals. [Syn. (2) **unsociable.** Cf. **antisocial,** which denotes active opposition to social intercourse or to social organization.] — Fr. *asocial*; Ger. *ungesellig.*

unsocialized = lacking in social training or habits, or in qualities of sympathy and social cooperation.

unspaced repetition = a procedure in the learning of a verbal series, or of a complicated motor act that is performed at first only with errors and malcoordinations, by which repetitions or trials are made to succeed one another without interruption or intervening rest periods till the learning is completed. [Contr. w. **spaced repetition** = repetitions with intervening rest periods. Cf. **massed learning.**] — Fr. *répétition sans intervalles de repos.*

unstimulable = characterizing an organ or region of the body which is not susceptible to stimulation of a given sort or intensity.

unsuccessful act = 1. a response or series of responses in trial and error learning which, taken by itself, does not lead towards the goal, and is thus apparently futile; 2. a response to a portion of some situation, which is not part of the most economical response to the total situation. [Contr. w. **successful act.**] — Fr. *acte malheureux.*

unthinkable = characterizing a proposition or generalization which, upon attempted analysis, reveals such intrinsic inconsistency that it cannot be either affirmed or denied. [Syn. **inconceivable.**] — Fr. *inconcevable, impensable*; Ger. *undenkbar.*

upper category = (in the method of single stimuli) those reports which will surpass the other reports in frequency if the stimulus-magnitude is sufficiently increased.

upset[n] = 1. a condition of the organism brought about by a series of stimuli which cannot be responded to adequately, resulting in dissociation of neural function and of various, usually integrated behavior patterns; 2. a marked emotional disturbance. (Accent **up-**.) — Fr. *bouleversement*; Ger. *Aufregung.*

uraniscolalia = speech hindered by a cleft palate. [A form of **dyslalia.**]

uranism = homosexuality accompanied by aversion for persons of the opposite sex.

Urban's tables = a set of tables for use with F. M. Urban's modification of the constant process (phi-function of gamma). [Published in *Arch. f. d. ges. Psychol.*, 1912, **24,** 240 f., reprinted w. corrections in Brown and Thomson, Essentials of Mental Measurements, 3d. ed., 202 f.]

urethra = the duct by which urine is discharged from the bladder. **urethral**[a] (Accent **-ree-**.) — Ger. *Harnröhre.*

urethral character, see **character trait.**

urethral erotism = (*psychoan.*) the centralization of libidinal feelings in the urethral zone.

urge = a strong tendency to perform a certain act; i.e. a strong motive, usually not definitely conscious. [Syn. **drive** (prefd.).] — Fr. *impulsion, appétence*; Ger. *Drang.*

urinary reflex, see **vesical reflex.**

urine = the excretion of the kidneys, stored in the bladder and discharged through the urethra. **urinate**[v], **urination**[n]. — Ger. *Urin, Harn.*

urning, urningism = a male who consciously feels like a woman towards men (Ulrichs, 1864-5). [Cf. **homosexuality.**]

urogenital = pert. to the combined urinary and genital systems. [Syn. **urinogenital.**]

use[n] = 1. the function or type of operation for which a given structure or organic mechanism is fitted; 2. the actual operation of a given structure or mechanism. [Cf. **utility.**] **use**[v] (2) (pron. **uze**). — Fr. (1) *emploi*; (2) *usage*; Ger. *Gebrauch.*

use and disuse theory, use-inheritance = the theory, advanced by J. B. Lamarck, according to which the structural or functional changes in organs, brought about by their use or their disuse, are passed on to the progeny. — Fr. *t. de l'usage et de la désuétude, hérédité par l'usage.*

use/law of = a law of learning which states that the more a neural connection between a given stimulus and a given response is exercised, the more readily will the stimulus bring about this response. [Syn. **law of exercise.**]

useful (serviceable) duration = that temporal portion of the initial passage of electric current which is instrumental in producing a response in nerve or muscle, further stimulus duration having no additional effect (Lapicque). — Fr. *temps utile*; Ger. *Nutzzeit.*

useless movements = those movements in a complex response which in no wise assist in attaining an adaptive result, and which (usually) impede its attainment. [The **learning** process consists, in part, in the elimination of many such movements.] — Fr. *mouvements inutiles.*

uterine life = the period of life of a mammal before birth. — Fr. *vie uterine.*

uterus = a sac-like structure, present in mammals, in which the embryo develops. [Syn. **womb.**] **uterine**[a]. — Fr. *matrice, utérus*; Ger. *Gebärmutter.*

utilitarianism = the social or economic theory which regards the practical usefulness of any object or plan as the proper criterion for judging its value. [Hist. linked with **hedonism,** but contr. w. it by some recent writers, **utilitarian** behavior being regarded as characterized by social (moral) sanctions.] **utilitarian**[a]. — Fr. *utilitarisme.*

utility = the fitness of a character, organ, mechanism, function, or type of operation, to preserve the life of a given organism, to continue the species, or to bring to completion some biological process. [Syn. **usefulness** (abstract).] **useful**[a]. — Ger. *Nützlichkeit.*

utricle, utriculus = a membranous sac of oblong form, contained within the posterior portion of the vestibule of the internal ear. [It opens posteriorly by five orifices, which communicate with the semicircular ducts, and anteriorly by the utriculosaccular duct, which connects with the endolymphatic duct. The anterior-dorsal wall of the utricle is thickened to form an epithelial structure called the *macula of the utricle,* to which are distributed filaments of the VIIIth nerve. Distg. fr. **saccule.**]

uvea = the iris, ciliary body, and choroid coat of the eye, considered as a unit and constituting the pigmentary layers of the eyeball.

uvula = the conical appendage which hangs from the free edge of the soft palate. — Fr. *luette (du palais)*; Ger. *Gaumenzäpfchen.*

V

v.d. (**double vibration**), see **vibration.**

v.s. (**single** or **simple vibration**), see **vibration.**

vagina = the passage leading from the exterior of the body to the uterus. (Accent **-jye-**.) **vaginal**[a] (accent **vaj-**). — Ger. *Scheide.*

vaginismus = spasmodic involuntary contraction of the sphincter vaginae or associated muscles, resulting in prevention of intromission (or retention) of the penis; usually psychogenic. — Ger. *Scheidenkrampf.*

vagus nerve, see **pneumogastric nerve.**

valence = (*Gestalt*) a term used by analogy to signify the attracting or repelling value of objects or activities (Lewin). [It may be positive (toward) or negative (away from) the object or activity.] Ger. *Aufforderungscharakter.*

valence/chromatic = a measure of the color-producing power of a visual stimulus, as contr. w. its capacity to evoke brilliance. [**chromatic valence** is a relative measure as between stimuli of different hues; when the stimuli yield *white* by mixture, the chromatic valences are ordinarily taken as equal; under such conditions, their brilliance-producing powers are usually very different. Cf. **chroma-brilliance coefficient.**]

valence/light = the effectiveness of a given light stimulus, which varies with its frequency and intensity as well as with the constitution of the retina, in evoking a given light or color quality. [In **color-blindness,** the *yellow* valence of certain long or medium wave-length stimuli may be retained, while their *red* or *green* valence is lost.]

validity = 1. the characteristic of an argument or inference, such that it is set forth in correct logical form, and that it leads to a reliable conclusion provided the premises or bases are correct; 2. (*statist.*) the agreement between a test score or other measure and the thing which it reputedly measures. [(1) usually denotes formal *correctness*, not objective **truth.**] **valid**[a]. — Ger. *Gültigkeit.*

validity coefficient = (*statist.*) the product moment coefficient of correlation between the measure of a test and that which it reputedly measures (usually indicated by the title of the test), when quantitative scores of both are available.

value = 1. the quantitative or numerical measure of any datum in a general scale or in terms of a standard; 2. the subjective appreciation or measure of the importance of a given datum or factor in relation to other data or factors of the same class; 3. (*vis.*) syn. for **brilliance.** [Syn. (2) **worth,** avoids confusion with **value** (1). (3) is used in art and esthetics, rarely in visual treatises.] — Fr. *valeur*; Ger. *Wert.* **evaluate**[v] (1, 2); **value**[v] (2); **valued**[a] (2); **valuable**[a] (2).

vandalism = malicious or careless destruction of property, esp. property characterized by beauty or historical association. — Ger. *Zerstörungswut.*

vanity = excessive self-appreciation, and often a marked desire for the notice and praise (by others) of one's own appearance, attainments, etc. [Cf. **conceit, pride.**] **vain**[a]. — Ger. *Eitelkeit.*

variable[n] = 1. (*math.*) a quantity which may take different values; 2. the symbol which stands for this quantity. [When two or more variables are interrelated as indicated by an algebraic equation, and values are assigned to all the variables except one, that one is called the **dependent variable;** the other variable or variables are the **independent variables.** Contr. w. **constant.**] **variable**[a]. — Ger. *veränderliche Grösse.*

variable error = a deviation of experimental results from the true value or from an established standard, due to (random) factors which affect each observation separately. [Distg. fr. **constant error** = due to a factor which remains unchanged during the entire series.] — Ger. *veränderlicher Fehler.*

variability = 1. (*biol., psychol.*) the characteristic of being subject to change in value, quality, form, etc., from time to time. [Applied to biological characters and species, to modes of behavior and experience, to temperament, etc. In biology, classed as (*a*) **continuous** (e.g. variations in height of human beings), and (*b*) **discontinuous** (e.g. production of discrete types with no intermediate forms).] **vary**[v], **variable**[a]. — Ger. *Variabilität, Veränderlichkeit.*

variability = 2. (*statist.*) the dispersion of the measures which constitute a frequency distribution. [The most common measure of variability is the **standard deviation;** other measures used are the **variance, average deviation, quartile deviation, probable error,** and **range.**]

variance = (*statist.*) the standard deviation squared.

variation = 1. (*biol.*) a generic term used to characterize any difference between organisms, whether due to environment (somatic variation, modification) or to a change in the germ plasm (germinal variation, mutation); 2. a change or alteration of any datum in some specific respect. [(2) includes changes in behavior, temperament, mathematical terms, etc.] **vary**[v]. — Ger. (1) *Variation,* (2) *Veränderung, Änderung.*

variational psychology, see **differential psychology.**

variations/concomitant, see **concomitant variations/method of.**

variator, see **tone variator** and **Stern variator.**

varied response = behavior of an organism (usually in a condition of maladjustment, or goal-seeking) characterized by a succession of acts or trials which change in direction, in motor organs involved, or otherwise. [Contr. w. **stereotyped response.**]

variety = a subdivision of a species, based upon differential characteristics less important than those which distinguish species. [Cf. **classification/zoological.**] — Ger. *Verschiedenheit.*

vas deferens = the duct which leads from the testis to the ejaculatory duct. — Fr. *canal déférent.*

vascular = pert. to or rich in vessels, more esp. blood vessels.

vascular sensation = a complex of sensations (temperature, and a mingled tension, tickling and mixed pain) which attends abrupt and extreme vascular changes in the skin, as in blushing.

vascular system = the system of blood vessels in the body. — Ger. *Gefässsystem.*

vasoconstrictor, vasodilator, see **vasomotor nerve.**

vasomotor centers = regions in the tuber cinereum, medulla oblongata, and spinal cord, which formerly were supposed to govern the normal tonus of the blood-vessels and control variations of this tonus.

vasomotor nerve = a variety of sympathetic or autonomic nerves which control the expansion or the contraction of the blood vessels. [They are called **vasodilator** and **vasoconstrictor** respectively.] — Ger. *Gefässnerv.*

Vater-Pacinian corpuscles, see **Pacinian corpuscles.**

vector = (*phys.*) a directed magnitude, e.g. a force or a velocity.

vegetable = (*pop.*) an edible plant. — Fr. *légume.*

vegetate = 1. to fulfill the functions of a plant, i.e. the nutritive and growth functions; 2. (*pop.*) to live like a plant without noticeable performance of the higher human functions.

vegetative = pert. to nutrition and growth in organisms. — Fr. *végétatif.*

vegetative function = any one of the biological processes which are concerned with nutrition and growth in organisms. [Contr. w. **mental function,** or **response function,** concerned with the adjustment of relations between the organism and its environment.]

vegetative nervous system, see **autonomic nervous system, sympathetic nervous system.**

vein = a duct or tube which conveys the blood toward the heart. [Distg. fr. **artery,** which conveys blood away from the heart.] **venous**[a] (accent **vee-**). — Ger. *Ader, Vene.*

velleity = 1. incomplete volition; 2. the lowest degree of desire. (4 syll. Accent **-lee-**.) — Fr. *velléité*; Ger. *tatloser Wille.*

velocity = rate of motion in a given direction. [Cf. speed = rate of motion without regard to direction.] — Fr. *vélocité, vitesse*; Ger. *Geschwindigkeit.*

venereal = 1. pert. to coitus; 2. pert. to infectious diseases which may be transmitted by coitus. (Accent **-nee-**.)

vengeance = an act which is motivated by the desire or aim to inflict injury upon another individual as compensation for some injury inflicted, or believed to have been inflicted, by that individual or his associates. [Cf. **revenge.**] — Fr. *vengeance*; Ger. *Rache.*

ventral = pert. to or located on the belly. [Contr. w. **dorsal.** These terms are now generally substituted for **anterior** and **posterior,** used hist. in human anatomy.] **ventrad**[adv].

ventricle = 1. one of the cavities within the brain, developed out of the embryonic medullary cavity; 2. one of the chambers of the heart; 3. any cavity or hollow organ of the body. [In man there are four ventricles in the brain, the first two lying laterally — one in each hemisphere; between them in the midline is the third ventricle, connected with the lateral on each side by the foramen of Monro, and with the fourth ventricle by the aqueduct of Sylvius.] **ventricular**[a]. — Ger. *Höhle* (= brain ventricle), *Kammer* (= heart ventricle).

ventriloquism = a mode of speaking employed by certain individuals in which the lips are kept closed, so that the listener mislocates the source of sound and is often subject to the illusion that inanimate objects are talking. **ventriloquize**[v]; **ventriloquist**[np]. — Ger. *Bauchreden.*

veratrin = a name applied to a mixture of alkaloids extracted from cevadilla seeds. [Not to be confused with **veratrum,** a heart drug. **veratrin** produces a characteristic effect on muscle and nerve endings. Medicinally, it is used as a counter-irritant in neurologic conditions.]

verbal = pert. to words, or to the wording of definitions. [Embraces both **oral** and **written,** but sometimes confused with **oral.** Distg. fr. **factual,** pert. to actual phenomena.] — Ger. *Wort-.*

verbal aphasia, see **aphasia.**

verbal behavior = the making of responses which, when overt, produce vocal, gestural, or written language symbols. [Contr. w. **general skeletal behavior,** w. **visceral behavior** and often w. **non-verbal behavior.**] — Fr. *comportement verbal.*

verbalism = 1. the reliance, in one's thinking, upon associations between words instead of upon relations between things; 2. uncritical acceptance of definitions as if they were explanations, or statements of causal relations.

verbiage = the use of a superabundance of words in sentences. [A vocomotor attitude in certain normal individuals, and a characteristic of certain mental disorders.] — Ger. *Wortschwall.*

verbigeration = a condition in which the individual repeats words and sentences without reference to their meaning. [A form of **dyslogia.** Syn. **cataphasia, catalogia.**] — Ger. *Wortsalat.*

verbogestural coordination = the simultaneous use of speech and gesture language.

vergence = (*ophthal.*) a mutilated word, which conveys the undifferentiated meaning implied in the terms **convergence, divergence,** and **sursumvergence,** esp. the extent to which these ocular movements may be forced by placing prisms before the eye.

veridical = corresponding to truth or objective fact. [Applied (rarely) to testimony, more commonly (in psychic research) to the correspondence of dream content or of the products of motor or sensory automatisms to otherwise unrelated objective events.] — Ger. *wahrhaftig.*

verification = the collecting of empirical evidence which proves a stated hypothesis; in particular, the discovery of phenomena or events which agree with predictions based upon the hypothesis in question. **verify**[v], **verifiable**[a]. — Ger. *Bestätigung.*

vermis = the median portion of the cerebellum, between the cerebellar hemispheres. — Ger. *Wurm.*

vernier = a subsidiary scale annexed to a scale of larger units of measurement, so as to permit an experimenter to read off directly fractions of the latter. [There are several forms: (*a*) the **vernier scale,** in which 9 or 11 units are equivalent to 10 units of the actual scale; (*b*) the **screw vernier,** in which the circumference is divided into 10 units; (*c*) the **pendular vernier,** for time measurements, which is 1/10 longer or shorter than the measuring pendulum. These all measure to tenths of the coarser scale. Syn. **nonius.**]

vertebra = one of the series of bones or cartilages which form the vertebral or spinal column. **vertebrae**[pl], **vertebral**[a] (accent **ver-**). — Ger. *Rückenwirbel, Wirbelknochen.*

vertebral column, see **spine.**

vertebral theory of the skull = the theory, advanced by Oken and Goethe, and now generally accepted, that the skull consists of a series of modified vertebrae. — Fr. *t. vertébrale du crâne.*

vertebrata, vertebrates = a major division of the animal kingdom, which comprises all animals having a segmented bony or cartilaginous spinal column on the dorsal side. [**vertebrate**[sing] is applied to any animal belonging to this division. Syn. **craniata, craniates.**] — Ger. *Wirbeltiere.*

vertex = 1. the uppermost point of a geometrical figure; 2. the meeting point of lines (e.g. the vertex of an angle), or of a curve and its axis; 3. the top of the human head. — Ger. (1, 3) *Scheitel,* (2) *Scheitelpunkt.*

vertical = pert. to the axial direction of the force of gravity, or characterizing an object or other datum oriented in that direction.

vertical axis = 1. the axis of the human body from head to feet; 2. the axis of the eyeball which corresponds to the direction of gravity. [Syn. (1) **cephalocaudal axis,** which applies also to subhuman anatomy.]

vertigo = a sensation of whirling and dizziness, attributable usually to over-stimulation of the semicircular canal receptors. **vertiginous**[a]. [Cf. **dizziness.**] — Ger. *Drehschwindel, Schwindel.*

vesical = pert. to or located in the bladder.

vesical reflex = reflex micturition or urination, stimulated by filling of the bladder. [Mediated by 3d to 5th sacral segments of cord. Syn. **bladder r., urinary r.**]

vesicle = (*anat.*) a small sac which contains liquid. **vesicular**[a]. — Ger. *Blase, Bläschen.*

vesicle/auditory = the embryonic expansion of the epiblast, which later becomes the membranous labyrinth. Syn. **acoustic v., otic v.**] — Ger. *Hörbläschen.*

vesicular layer, see **ganglion cells/layer of.** — Fr. *couche ganglionnaire.*

vestibular aqueduct = (*aud.*) a canal in the petrous portion of the temporal bone, through which the endolymphatic duct runs inward to the cranial cavity.

vestibular canal, see **scala vestibuli.**

vestibular membrane, see **Reissner's membrane.**

vestibular nystagmus, see **nystagmus.**

vestibular stimulation = stimulation of the end-organs of the vestibular branch of the VIII cranial nerve, normally by rotation of the head. [**galvanic v.s.** = passage of sufficient electric current through the labyrinthine region of the head to elicit vestibular response; **mechanical v.s.** = direct application of mechanical pressure in region of the VIII cranial nerve endings, by inflation of the vestibule through a fistula in man, by surgically opening the vestibule in animals, by substitution of iron filings for otoliths in fishes (i.e. pressure produced by magnetically moving the filings); **thermal** or **caloric v.s.** = irrigation of the ear with cold or warm liquid. Cf. **nystagmus.**]

vestibular system = the neural mechanism for reception and integration of sensory data from the static sense and for the resulting responsive adjustment of the organism's postures and movements with respect to gravity. [Cf. **labyrinthine perception, rotation perception, nystagmus, equilibrium/perception of, labyrinthine righting reflexes.**]

vestibule = a portion of the osseous labyrinth of the internal ear, situate between the cochlea and the semicircular canals. [In its lateral and median walls are two openings to the tympanic cavity, the oval and round windows; it contains two membranous sacs, the utricle and the saccule.] **vestibular**[a]. — Ger. *Vorhof.*

vestibule school = a factory school for teaching beginners in a separate room rather than in the regular workshop. [The emphasis is on learning rather than production.] — Fr. *école d'apprentissage.*

vestibulospinal tracts = the efferent nerve-columns at the sides of the spinal cord towards the front, which lead from the vestibular nuclei of the auditory nerve into the cord. — Fr. *faisceaux vestibulospinaux.*

vestige = a structure in an organism, which was more highly developed in its ancestors. [Contr. w. **rudiment** (1) or **Anlage** = a primitive structure which later may evolve or develop into a functioning organ.] **vestigial**[a]. — Ger. *Überbleibsel.*

viable[a] = capable of living. [Used esp. to characterize the capacity of a normal organism in its earliest stages to survive.] — Ger. *lebensfähig.*

vibration = a periodic to-and-fro motion of any body or particle. [A pendulum executes a complete **cycle** or **double vibration** (v.d., D.V.) when it swings (e.g.) from the extreme right to the extreme left and back again. In the older literature the term **simple vibration** or **single vibration** (v.s.) was applied to a single swing (e.g. from right to left), but was often confused with v.d. The term cycle (~) avoids this ambiguity. The form of the **pendular vibration** may be expressed mathematically by a simple sine (or cosine) equation, and is called a **sine wave.** The sound waves from tuning forks, lightly blown bottles, etc., are of this form. Cf. **sound, sound-wave, cycle.**] **vibrate**[v], **vibratory**[a]. — Ger. *Schwingung.*

vibration rate = the number of times in a given interval that a body passes through successive cycles of change of position. [Syn. **frequency.**] — Ger. *Schwingungszahl.*

vibration/sympathetic, /forced, see **resonance.**

vibrato, see **tremolo.**

vibratory sensation, vibration sensation = a sensory experience characterized by quick pulsations, normally aroused by contact with a vibrating body. [Syn. **pallesthesia.**]

vice = a significant or minor habitual mode of behavior at variance with social standards. [Pop. limited to sex indulgence, alcohol, drugs, and gambling. Contr. w. **virtue** = adherence to the higher social norms of behavior.] **vicious**[a]. — Ger. *Laster, Untugend.*

Vierordt's law = the principle that the more moveable a part is, the lower is the two-point limen of the skin over it; i.e. the two-point limen decreases from the acromion to the tips of the fingers.

Vincent learning curve = a learning curve, first suggested by S. B. Vincent, which makes comparable the learning curves of different subjects by basing each curve upon the same number of units, each of which consists of a given part of the time or number of trials required to achieve mastery of the given problem. — Fr. *courbe d'apprentissage de V.*

violet = the short-wave radiations of the visible spectrum, from about wave-length 433 mμ to the limit of visibility; or the specific color-quality excited by these rays.

violet blindness, see **tritanopia.**

viraginity = a form of homosexuality in which the sexual feelings and mental characteristics of a woman resemble those of a normal man. **virago**[np].

virile reflex = 1. contraction of the bulbocavernous muscle of the urethra, elicited by tapping the back of the penis near the scrotum, the sheath having been made tense; 2. erection of the penis elicited by visual, remote tactual, olfactory or other stimuli. [(1) is a normal reflex, mediated by 3d to 5th sacral segments of the cord. Syn. (1) **bulbocavernous r., penile r., penis r.** Syn. (2) **virile response** (prefd.), **erection.**]

virtual = in almost exact agreement with. **virtually**[adv].

virtual image = (*opt.*) an image apparently formed by a lens or a mirror at a place not actually traversed by the light rays, but capable of geometrical reconstruction by retracing the rays in straight lines. [E.g. the so-called *reflection* of an object as seen apparently behind an ordinary mirror.]

virtue = 1. the act of adhering (or the quality through which one adheres) to those social ideas and standards in general which involve the notion of moral conduct; i.e. the choice of the right and avoidance of the wrong; 2. a specific type of conduct (e.g. honesty), through which one adheres to a social standard to which moral significance is attributed. [Contr. w. **vice** = departure from these standards.] **virtuous**[a]. — Fr. *vertu*; Ger. *Tugend.*

virulent = a quality of olfactory sensation of which morphine is a typical example. [A class of Zwaardemaker's. Cf. **odor, odor prism.**] — Fr. *repoussant.*

viscera[pl] = the large internal organs of the body. **visceral**[a]. — Ger. *Eingeweide.*

visceral reflex = any reflex caused by excitation of one of the viscera.

visceral sense, see **organic sense.**

visceromotor reflex = contraction of a parietal muscle of the abdomen or thorax elicited by a stimulus arising in one of the contained viscera. [Mediated by 1st to 12th thoracic segments of the cord.]

viscosity = the resistance of a substance to change of form. — Ger. *Zähigkeit.*

visibility = a property assigned to radiant energy within a certain range of wave-lengths by reason of its power to excite a visual receptor process, or to evoke the introspective phenomenon of brilliance. [Cf. **visibility coefficient.**] **visible.**[a] — Ger. *Sichtbarkeit.*

visibility coefficient = the numerical designation of the visibility of radiant energy, particularly that of a single spectral wave-length. [The relative visibility coefficient of a given sample of radiant energy is the reciprocal of the energy required to evoke a brilliance equal to that of a standard field; spectral energy of maximum visibility and of wave-length about 554 mμ being taken as unity. A visibility coefficient may also be assigned to any mixture of wave-lengths.]

visibility curve = a graphic representation of the manner in which brilliance varies as a function of wave-length. [The curve is drawn by plotting the visibility coefficients of spectral radiant energy of various wave-lengths, each against its respective wave-length as abscissa. The standard visibility curve represents photopic or daylight vision for the average normal human eye. Cf. **visibility coefficient.**]

visible = capable of being seen, or represented in consciousness by the operation of the organs of vision. — Ger. *sichtbar.*

visile, visual type = a class of individuals who use mainly the sense of sight, or whose imagery is mainly visual. [Cf. **type/mental.**]

vision = 1. the sense whose receptor organ is the eye and whose proper stimulus is radiant energy of wave-lengths approximately 400 to 760 millimicrons; 2. a visual hallucination or apparition. — Ger. (1) *Gesicht.*

vision/binocular, /uniocular, see **binocular vision,** etc.

vision/field of, see **visual field.**

vision/foveal = visual experiences due to stimulation of the fovea centralis, or center of the retina. [Contr. w. **peripheral vision.**]

vision/line of, see **visual axis** and **direction/line of.**

vision/peripheral = visual experiences due to stimulation of the outlying portions of the retina. [Contr. w. **foveal vision.**]

vision/persistence of = the tendency of visual excitation to outlast the stimulus, or (more generally) the tendency of changes in visual excitation to lag behind changes in the stimulus.

vision/theory of = a systematic attempt to account for the various phenomena of visual perception in relation to the known structure and functions of the visual organs. [Included by extension are the study of photo-receptors, the action of nerve-endings and of related nervous structures in general, responses to light in lower organisms, the higher psychological implications of light, color, form, and their spatial and temporal relations, etc. The anatomical and physiological basis may be, to a considerable extent, hypothetical, as is the case with the current **theories of color vision.** The leading theories are known as (1) **Young-Helmholtz** (three-component); (2) **Hering** (antagonistic process); (3) **Ladd-Franklin** (genetic); (4) **von Kries** (duplicity); (5) **Edridge-Green.**]

visual acuity = the capacity of the visual organ for recognition of small space-intervals in the discrimination of form. [The threshold separation of two points is the simplest illustration; cf. **two-point discrimination.** Numerous variations in test-object are possible. Cf. **test chart. visual acuity** varies inversely with the angle subtended by the letter, etc., in the chart.] — Ger. *Sehschärfe.*

visual angle = the angle subtended by any object of vision at the nodal point of the eye. [The magnitude of this angle determines the size of the corresponding retinal image, independently of the size or of the distance of the object alone.] — Ger. *Gesichtswinkel.*

visual axis = a straight line passing through the external point of fixation and the nodal point of the eye, to the point of clearest vision on the retina. [It does not usually coincide with the **optical axis** of the eye. Syn. **sighting line;** also in loose usage **line of sight, line of vision, visual line.** Distg. fr. **line of direction.**] — Ger. *Gesichtsachse, Gesichtslinie.*

visual cells, see **neuro-epithelial layer.**

visual field = the totality of visual stimuli which act upon the unmoving eye at a given moment, esp. when considered as projected upon a spherical surface from the eye as center, or upon a plane surface at right angles to the visual axis. [Syn. **field of vision.** Cf. **perimeter, campimeter.**] — Fr. *champ visuel;* Ger. *Gesichtsfeld, Sehfeld.*

visual field/subjective = that spatial aspect of conscious experience which is derived from the relative locational references existing between visual presentations. [This field is a three-dimensional manifold or space-field, and has a natural center of coordinates at the *empirical eye,* or subjective point of view. Cf. **visual space.**]

visual line, see **visual axis** and **direction/line of.**

visual process = any change or operation which occurs in vision, or (in certain contexts) the operation of vision in general.

visual purple = a substance found in the rods of the vertebrate retina, esp. of the dark-adapted eye, which bleaches rapidly on exposure to light, and is believed to be the substance underlying scotopic or twilight vision. [Syn. **rhodopsin.**] — Fr. *pourpre visuel, p. rétinien;* Ger. *Sehpurpur.*

visual righting reflexes = orientation of the head depending upon the fixation of an object in the visual field. [Mediated by the optic tracts and tectospinal and descending corticospinal tracts to neck muscles.] — Fr. *réflexes de redressement visuel.*

visual space = the extended world as perceived by means of the eye. [In practice it is the generic term for the discussion of perception of position and length by the retina, of depth or distance away from the retina, and of form or figure in one and two dimensions. Cf. **visual field/subjective.**] — Ger. *Sehraum.*

visual yellow = a yellow substance formed in the retina under certain circumstances when **visual purple** is bleached by the action of light. — Fr. *jaune visuel;* Ger. *Sehgelb.*

visualization = the experiencing of visual imagery. **visualize**[v], **visualizer**[np].

vital = 1. pert. to life; 2. of essential importance.

vitalism = a biological theory which assumes the existence and operation of a non-material entity or causal agent as an essential factor in the regulation of form, behavior, and evolution of organisms. [Contr. w. **mechanism.**] **vitalistic**[a], **vitalist**[np].

vitality = 1. the property or characteristic of being alive or of exercising the organic functions; 2. ability of an organism to maintain its organic existence; 3. syn. for **vigor, power of endurance.** — Ger. *Lebenskraft.*

vitascope, see **stroboscope.**

vitreous, vitreous body, vitreous humor, vitreum = the transparent, jelly-like mass which fills the eyeball from the concave surface of the retina as far forward as the lens. — Ger. *Glaskörper.*

vividness, see **clearness.** — Fr. *vivacité;* Ger. *Lebhaftigkeit.*

vocabulary test = a type of test in which a standard list of words is presented to the testee, who is asked to define them (or check those whose meaning he knows); when the list is a random sampling from a complete general dictionary, the score earned is taken as an index of the testee's total vocabulary. [A typical example is found in the Stanford Revision of the Binet-Simon Scale.]

vocal cords = the ligaments of the larynx which are concerned in vocalization. [They include (1) **true vocal cords** or **vocal bands** = two inferior thyro-arytenoid ligaments, and (2) **false vocal cords** = two superior thyro-arytenoid ligaments.] — Ger. *Stimmbänder, Stimmlippen.*

vocal language, see **speech.**

vocal muscles = the extrinsic and intrinsic muscles of the larynx. — Ger. *Stimmmuskeln.*

vocal organs = the entire group of organs concerned in the production of (vocal) sounds.

vocal register = the tonal range or compass of the voice. — Ger. *Stimmregion.*

vocal (or **speech**) **response** (or **reaction**) **time** = the period from the presentation of a stimulus to the beginning of a vocalized response. [Cf. **word-reaction time.**]

vocal tone recorder = an apparatus designed to record the pitch of sung tones by means of smoke rings (Marbe) or by other methods. — Ger. *Kehltonschreiber.*

vocality = a vowel-like characteristic or attribute of sound. [**vocality** varies with the pitch of the pure tone.] — Ger. *Vokalität.*

vocation = that form of productive activity in which an individual engages as a means of subsistence. — Ger. *Gewerbe, Beruf.*

vocational aptitude test = a type of test which aims to disclose the fitness of the testee to succeed in a given vocation. — Ger. *Eignungsprüfung.*

vocational guidance, selection, see **guidance/v., selection/v.**

voice = the sounds produced by the vocal organs, in which any succession of sounds primarily involves the use of the larynx. **vocal**[a], **vocalization**[n] = the process; **vocalize**[v], **utter**[v], **speak**[v] (more restricted). — Ger. *Stimme.*

voice-key = a response key operated by sound waves of the human voice. [Scripture's voice-key makes use of a mica plate which covers the wide end of a funnel; the reactor speaks into the smaller end of the funnel, causing the mica plate to vibrate and break an electric contact;

Dunlap's voice-key employs a small swinging hammer, which, at rest, makes contact with a round metal diaphragm supported vertically before the mouth. Syn. **sound-key.**] — Fr. *clef vocale*; Ger. *Schallschlüssel.*

voices = (*pop.*) a hallucination of talk, esp. of derogatory or accusatory or other remarks concerning the individual himself.

volar = pert. to or located in the palm of the hand or the sole of the foot.

volition = 1. the act of deciding upon a course of action and initiating it; 2. a complex experience in which kinesthetic sensations and the idea of end (or goal) are prominent. [Syn. **will.**] **voluntary**[a] = pert. to the will or initiated by the individual himself; **volitional**[a] = pert. to the study. — Ger. *Willenshandlung, Willensvorgang.*

volley, volley fire = 1. (*neurol.*) synchronous discharge, esp. the case in which rhythmic series of pulsations of like frequency and in phase with one another are transmitted simultaneously along the different fibers of a nerve; 2. a brief succession of nerve pulsations, of muscular twitches, etc. [Contr. (1) w. **platoon fire,** where the pulsations on different fibers are not in phase with one another.] — Fr. *salve.*

volt = the electromotive force necessary to produce a current of one ampere through a resistance of one ohm.

voltmeter = an instrument for measuring electromotive force in volts.

volume = size in three dimensions. [Distg. fr. **mass** = amount of content in a given volume.] — Ger. *Rauminhalt.*

volume/auditory = 1. the spatial characteristic of auditory experience, described in terms of size or diffusion; e.g. low tones are large, massive, and all-pervasive, whereas high tones are small, thin, and concentrated; 2. (*mus.*) the loudness, quantity, or fullness of tone. [Some psychologists regard **volume** (1) as an attribute of pure tones; it is not to be confused with **loudness.**

volume hypothesis = the hypothesis that auditory experiences possess an attribute called **volume,** which varies from large to small. [**volume** is said to vary with pitch and intensity, and with localization. Its attributive status is at present uncertain.]

voluminousness = the extensity attribute or dimension of experience. [Applied esp. to the auditory and olfactory fields. Cf. **extensity.**] — Fr. *voluminosité.*

voluntarism = 1. (*psychol.*) the theory that will or a will-unit is the typical and fundamental psychic element or aspect; 2. (*philos.*) the theory that ultimate reality is will.

voluntary = pert. to the will or its activity. **will**[n], **volition**[n]. — Ger. *freiwillig, willkürlich.*

voluntary activity = 1. activity which is preceded by the idea and desire of accomplishing a certain result; 2. delayed conscious response; 3. (*beh.*) a conditioned response aroused by self-excited stimulation and having a longer latent time and duration than the corresponding unconditioned response. [Cf. **will.**] — Ger. *Willkürhandlung.*

voluntary reaction, see **intentional response.**

Volvox = a flagellate found only in spherical colonies of interconnected individuals. [Its colonial habit suggests an intermediate position between Protozoa and Metazoa; the fact that it manufactures its food out of inorganic substances causes botanists to claim it as a plant. The pigment- or eye-spot of every member of the colony is turned toward the outside of the sphere.]

vomiting = the forcible expulsion of substance from the stomach through the mouth, elicited by intestinal, gastric, cardiac, or pharyngeal irritation. [Mediated by X cranial to 12th thoracic nerves, and vomiting center in lower oblongata.] — Fr. *vomissement*; Ger. *Erbrechen.*

vomiting center = the lower central region in the medulla oblongata which mediates the vomiting reflex.

von Baer's law, see **Baer's law.**

von Frey esthesiometer (or **aesthesiometer**), see **hair esthesiometer.**

von Frey hairs = standard hairs (horse hair or human hair) used in the **hair esthesiometer.** — Fr. *crins de von F.*

von Frey limen gauge, see **limen gauge.** — Fr. *appareil de von F. pour mesurer le seuil de pression.*

von Kries theory of vision, see **duplicity theory.**

voodooism = a system of beliefs and practices in sorcery and magic prevalent among the natives of West Africa, and among negroes of the West Indies and southern United States. **voodoo**[a, np]. — Fr. *vaudou.*

Vorstellung = 1. that mental process or function whereby an object is presented to consciousness or is experienced; 2. that mental process or function whereby an object is presented by way of memory or imagination. [Ger. In sense (1) the term includes both **perception** and **idea,** and corresponds to the historic use of idea in associationism; in sense (2) the word is limited to *reproduced* contents and consequently may be translated as **idea** in contradistinction to **perception,** corresponding in general to *representation* as contr. w. *presentation* in English usage. In the **act psychologies** the term frequently includes both the act (*Vorstellen*) and its content (*Vorstellungsinhalt*).] **vorstellen**[v].

Vorticella = a genus of ciliate Protozoa which resemble Stentor but are distinguished from it by more concentration of cilia about the mouth and by oval rather than trumpet shape.

vowel = 1. a conventional vocal sound produced by certain positions of the vocal organs, which offer little obstruction to the breath, and form a double resonating system above the larynx; 2. the letter which represents such a sound. [Distg. fr. **consonant.**] — Ger. *Vokal, Selbstlaut.*

voyeur = (*psychoan.*) a person who obtains sexual gratification from watching sexual stimuli. [Syn. **inspectionism, scopophilia.** Contr. w. **exhibitionism.**]

W

w factor, will factor = a determiner of success in certain lines of activity, postulated by Webb and adopted by Spearman as accounting for purposive consistency or the persistence of motives. [It represents the will element in intelligence, and is independent of the **c factor.** Cf. **g factor, c factor.**] — Fr. *facteur de volonté.*

wakanda = a term in Siouan languages signifying (literally) the mysterious one, and denoting an impersonal all-pervading supreme power in the universe. [Cf. **manitou.**]

wake^n = 1. (*anthrop.*) the practice of remaining awake during the normal time for sleep, esp. for solemn festive purposes; 2. the sitting up of persons at night, esp. w. a dead body before its burial, often attended with a degree of festivity.

wake^v = to remain in a normal condition of consciousness, as contr. w. **sleep.** [Distg. fr. **awake**^{v} = to pass from sleep to the waking state, and fr. **awaken**^{v} = to cause another to awake.] **waking**^{a}. — Fr. *veiller*; Ger. *wachen*.

wakefulness = insomnia of short duration. — Fr. *veille*; Ger. *Wachsamkeit, Schlaflosigkeit*.

walking = the function of locomotion by means of feet or similar members, which are successively lifted and planted again in a new position, usually cephalad or ventrad to the old. [Distg. fr. swimming, flying, revolving, and other modes of locomotion. Sometimes used generically to include running, hopping, etc.; sometimes distg. fr. these.] — Fr. *marche*; Ger. *Gehen*.

Wallerian degeneration = fatty degeneration of that portion of a transected neuron which does not include the latter's trophic center, (the cell-body). [The degeneration starts at the point of section and progresses toward the termini (of dendrite or axon).]

Waller's law = the law that if posterior roots of the spinal cord are cut on the central side of the ganglia, those portions of the (cut) nerves which lie within the spinal cord degenerate, while the peripheral portions of the same nerves (not being severed from the ganglia) do not degenerate (A. Waller, 1850).

Wanderlust = a propensity to leave home or to move frequently from one locality to another. [Ger. Often observed in children, and characterizing a type of adults. Cf. **nomadism.**] — Fr. *manie ambulatoire*.

want = 1. a condition, factor, or element absent from the present situation of a creature, the presence of which would promote his comfort or ameliorate his relations to the environment; 2. a mental attitude with more or less definite awareness of some lack, accompanied by an unpleasant feeling tone. [Syn. **need.**] — Fr. *besoin*; Ger. (1) *Mangel*, (2) *Bedürfnis*.

warm (or **warmth**) **sensation** = a quality of sensation due normally to stimulation by some object whose temperature is higher than the temperature of the skin or other part stimulated. [Contr. w. **cold sensation.**] — Fr. *s. de chaleur*; Ger. *Wärmeempfindung*.

warm spot, warmth spot = a point or minute area on the skin which is peculiarly sensitive to stimuli above the body temperatures. [Cf. **paradoxical warmth.** Contr. w. **cold spot** = sensitive to cold stimuli.] — Fr. *point de chaud*; Ger. *Wärmepunkt*.

warm stimulus = a stimulus, normally one of a range of temperatures, which gives rise to a warm sensation. [Besides the proper or adequate **warm stimulus,** certain substances, such as mustard plasters, give rise to warm sensations regardless of their temperature.]

warming up = a characteristic of the beginning of certain series of experiments on human subjects, in that these earlier attempts are irregular, slow, or inexact, even with practiced individuals, but lead at length to a succession of fairly uniform results. [The preliminary trials are termed the **warming-up period** or process.] — Fr. *mise en train, échauffement*.

warning signal = a preliminary stimulus or signal commonly used in response experiments to prepare the subject for prompt intentional response. [Syn. **ready signal.**] — Fr. *signal avertisseur*; Ger. *Wahrnungszeichen*.

Wassermann test = a serological test for syphilis which depends upon the fixation of complements in the blood and spinal fluid.

watch test = a rough procedure for determining acuity of hearing; it consists in moving a watch gradually toward the observer's ear till he hears the ticking, and moving it away till the sound vanishes. — Fr. *t. de la montre*.

waterfall illusion = an illusion of motion, in which a steady visual fixation on any portion of a waterfall, when shifted to the surrounding scenery, causes this scenery to appear to move in the opposite (upward) direction. [The term is applied to any laboratory device which produces a similar effect; e.g. model described by James (1890). The apparent motion of the road after one's car has stopped is an analogous phenomenon. Cf. **antirrheoscope.**] — Fr. *illusion de la chûte d'eau*.

watt = a unit for measuring energy expended or work done per second, one watt being the power employed in doing one joule (10^7 ergs) of work in one second. [This unit is most commonly used in the measurement of electrical work. One watt equals one volt times one ampere. In many measurements the **kilowatt** (=1000 watts) is the standard.]

wave = a regular motion of particles to and fro, which is communicated to adjacent particles, so that the to-and-fro motion advances continuously. [The advance may be either in the same direction as the first phase of the to-and-fro motion (e.g. sound waves) or at right angles thereto (e.g. light waves); the wave-breadth or amplitude is measured by the extent of to-and-fro motion, the wave-length by the distance at any given instant of one crest to the next in the forward propagation.] — Fr. *onde*; Ger. *Welle*.

wave-length = the distance, at any instant, between two adjacent crests (or identical phases) of a series of waves which are advancing through a uniform medium. [The **wave-length** varies inversely with the **vibration rate,** or number of waves passing any given point in one second or other standard period of time. Cf. **wave.**] — Fr. *longueur d'onde*; Ger. *Wellenlänge*.

wave of excitation = a wave of chemical or electrochemical change propagated through living tissue and capable of arousing responses from effectors. [Syn. **propagated disturbance; nerve impulse.**] — Fr. *onde d'excitation*.

weak = 1. having a low degree of intensity; 2. characterizing lack of bodily strength or instability of character. [(1) is applied to sensations and stimuli of any sort, and to motor responses; preferably limited to stimuli, the sensations being termed **faint,** the movement **slight.** Contr. (1, 2) w. **strong.**] — Fr. *faible*; Ger. *schwach*.

weakness sensation = a type of experience characterized by an abnormal intensity of the kinesthetic sensations accompanying slight muscular exertion. — Fr. *s. de faiblesse*.

weaning = (*psychoan.*) a breaking up or dissolving of the transference situation, applied esp. to the end phases of analysis. [Cf. **transference.**] — Fr. *sevrage*; Ger. *Entwöhnung*.

weariness, see **fatigue** (2).

Weber's law = a formulation of the relation between changes in stimulus-intensity and perception, devised by E. H. Weber, and expressed as follows: The just perceptible difference of sensation occurs when the stimulus is increased (or decreased) by a certain proportion of itself, that proportion being constant for any given sense. [If ΔR is the change in the stimulus corresponding to a just perceptible difference of intensity, and R is the value of the stimulus, then **Weber's law** may be written: $\Delta R/R$ = constant. The name was suggested by Fechner, who extended the law to include imperceptible increases of sensation as well. Sometimes called **Weber-Fechner law.** Cf. **Fechner's law, psychophysical law.**]

Wedensky inhibition, Wedensky effect = the principle that with a nerve-muscle preparation a critical frequency for stimulating the nerve can be found, at which rate the muscle responds with a very rapid series of twitches (e.g. 200 per second), whereas if the rate of stimulation be somewhat *increased* the muscle responds with a single contraction followed by complete relaxation. [This phenomenon is of interest in connection with the theory of neuromuscular inhibition by interference or *overcrowding* of nerve pulsations.]

weight = 1. (*phys.*) the force with which a given mass is attracted toward the center of the earth; 2. a body of determined mass, used in experiments on the pressure sense, kinesthetic sense, or lifting; 3. the relative importance of a given datum or result, as compared with others in the same set of experiments or category of data. [Cf. **weighting.**] — Fr. *poids*; Ger. *Gewicht*.

weight experiment = a psychophysical experiment in which the observer judges small differences between freely lifted weights (Titchener). — Fr. *expérience de pesanteur*.

weight holders/Fechner, see **Fechner weight holders.**

weight sensation = the sensation stimulated by the active supporting or lifting of a weight. — Fr. *s. de poids*.

weight sense, see **kinesthesia.** — Fr. *sens de la pesanteur*.

weighted score = (*statist.*) a score to which special value or weight is given because of its significance or relative importance as compared with the other items scored. — Fr. *note pondérée*.

weighting = the assignment of definite proportional values to the various data, results, etc., in a set of experiments, tests, or statistics, in accordance with their assumed or determined value in relation to the other data, etc., in the set or group. — Fr. *attribuer des poids*.

weights/lifting = a type of apparatus developed for the determination of liminal differences in kinesthetic appreciation of weight; they vary greatly in form, but generally embody the following principles: (*a*) convenient size for grasping, (*b*) tactual indistinguishability, (*c*) material relatively unaffected by moisture, and (*d*) resistance of material to temperature changes. [Frequently called **lifted weights.** Cf. **cartridge weights, Jastrow cylinders.**] — Fr. *souleveur de poids*.

weights/Scripture, see **Scripture weights.**

Weismannism = the theory of evolution, advocated by August Weismann as a result of his experiments, which denies the heritability of acquired characters, and assumes the continuity of the germ-plasm through successive generations.

welfare work = supervision of employees' health, safety, recreation, education, training, employment, pensions, cafeterias, relations with shop committees, etc. — Fr. *oeuvres de bien-être*.

well-being = a condition of general good health and prosperity experienced by an individual, or the conscious state (marked by a pleasant feeling tone) which accompanies this condition. — Fr. *bien-être*; Gr. *Wohlsein*.

Wernicke/area of = 1. an area of fibers forming the extreme posterior segment of the internal capsule; 2. a cerebral area comprising parts of the supramarginal angular and first and second temporal gyri, on the left side in a right-handed person. [Identified by Wernicke as the cortical center for understanding language heard.]

wetness sensation = a quality of tactual experiences, normally aroused by the application of some moist surface to the individual's skin, or by the application of cold pressure. — Fr. *s. d'humidité*; Ger. *Nassempfindung*.

Wharton's duct = the duct of the submaxillary gland.

Wheatstone bridge = an electrical circuit (often built as a special instrument) for the equating of resistance; it is essentially a direct or proportional division of the electrical flow with a connection between the two arms of this division; in this connection or bridge is inserted a galvanometer; when the resistance of both arms is so adjusted as to be equal, there is no flow of electricity across the bridge; this equating of resistance in either arm gives a direct or proportional reading of ohmic resistance. [Used in investigations of the **galvanic skin response** or any other measurement of electrical resistance. This circuit was invented by Christie (1833).] — Fr. *pont de Wh*.

wheel-movement, see **torsional movement, torsion.**

whirl sensation, whirling = an experience characterized by a sense of circular movement of the head, or of rotation of the entire objective world about the head, due to persistent stimulation of the semicirculars by stimulants, by rotation of the head, etc. and at times by stimulation from nystagmic movements of the eyes. — Fr. *s. de rotation*.

whispering, see **hypophonia.** — Fr. *chuchotement*; Ger. *Flüstern*.

whistle/Galton, see **Galton whistle.** — Fr. *sifflet de G*.

white = a visual sensation evoked by stimulation of the retina by a mixture of radiant energies of different wave-lengths (usually of high intensity), approximating in physiological action that which is characteristic of normal daylight, or of the black-body radiation at a color temperature of about 5400 degrees, Kelvin. [It constitutes the upper limit of the gray or achromatic series of colors. The complement, or antagonist, of **black.**] **white**[a]. — Fr. *blanc*; Ger. *weiss*.

white matter = the parts of the brain and spinal cord which show whitish or very light gray color due to the presence of myelinated nerve fibers; it consists of nerve fibers without their cell-bodies. [Distg. fr. **gray matter,** composed chiefly of cell-bodies massed together with their attached fibers.] — Fr. *substance blanche*.

whole[n] = that which, though possessed of parts or members or distinguishable aspects, yet possesses such character as a unit that it may be treated without reference to the parts, members, or aspects. [Syn. **totality, entirety.** Contr. w. **part** = a constituent or subgroup of such a complex unit, which has properties or characters not referable to the whole; and w. **member** = a constituent of such a complex unit, none of whose characters are independent of their relation to the whole.] **whole**[a], **entire**[a]. — Fr. *l'ensemble*; Ger. *Ganzes, Ganzheit.*

whole and part learning = a generic term comprising the two alternative methods of memorizing material or acquiring habits, either by repetition of the entire material or performance, or by repetition of some portion till it is learned and then proceeding to the next portion, etc. [The term is applied to the problem as to which method is the more efficient. In recent experimental work several intermediary forms of practice have been employed. Syn. **part and whole learning.**] — Fr. *apprentissage (acquisition) global (fractionné), acquisition du tout et des parties*; Ger. *Ganz- und Teil-Lernmethode.*

whole-part test, see **part-whole test.**

whole tone = one of the larger steps in a musical scale, roughly equivalent to two semitones. [In the diatonic scale, the whole tones are of two kinds, major and minor: the major tone has a ratio of 8:9, the minor tone a ratio of 9:10. In the tempered scale a whole tone is exactly equal to two semitones, and has a ratio of $1:2^{1/6}$. Cf. **scale,** and Table VII.] — Ger. *Ganzton.*

wild = characterizing an animal in its native habitat and condition, uninfluenced by the effects of human training or domination. [Contr. w. **domesticated, tame,** or **trained.**] — Fr. *sauvage*; Ger. *wild.*

will = 1. the function or group of functions concerned in delayed conscious response; 2. conscious decision to act or undertake a course of action; 3. the self in action; 4. (*hist.*) as employed by Schopenhauer and many others, the totality of irrational and emotional impulses, usually regarded as having primacy over intellect. [Syn. **volition.**] **will**[v], **will**[a], **volitional**[a], **voluntary**[a]. — Fr. *volonté, vouloir*[v]; Ger. *Wille.*

will/free, see **free-will doctrine.**

will profile = a psychograph or diagram showing the scores made by an individual in a considerable number of tests purporting to measure will and temperament. — Fr. *profil de volonté.*

will-temperament test = a series of tests devised by June E. Downey for the purpose of bringing to light qualitative differences in certain aspects of volition and temperament. [The Downey tests are based chiefly upon handwriting, which is executed under various instructions to write fast, slow, disguised, with eyes closed, etc. The traits to be brought to light are such as speed of reaction, decisiveness and forcefulness, carefulness, resistance to opposition.] — Fr. *t. de volonté-tempérament.*

Willis/circle of = a ring of arteries at the base of the brain.

window/oval = an oval opening in the wall of the bony labyrinth in the vestibular region; it abuts upon the middle ear, and is closed by the base of the stapes, which is attached by an annular ligament. [The vibratory movements of the stapes are communicated to the perilymph of the scala vestibuli, and thereupon affect the sensory endings within the cochlear duct. Syn. **fenestra ovalis, fenestra vestibuli.**] — Fr. *fenêtre ovale*; Ger. *ovales Fenster.*

window/round = a round opening, situated somewhat below and behind the oval window, in the vestibular wall of the bony labyrinth. [It is closed by a flexible membrane, the secondary tympanic membrane, which separates the scala tympani from the middle ear and takes up the alternating pressures communicated to the perilymph by the movements of the stapes. Syn. **fenestra rotunda, fenestra cochleae.**] — Fr. *fenêtre ronde*; Ger. *rundes Fenster.*

windpipe, see **trachea.**

winking, wink reflex = 1. closure of the eyelid, stimulated by drying of the cornea; 2. syn. for **corneal reflex.** [(1) is a normal reflex, mediated by V (sensory) to VII (motor) cranial nerves. Syn. (1) **eyelid closure, eye-wink.**] — Ger. *Blinzeln, Blinzelreflex.*

wisdom = reflective knowledge, esp. concerning the practical conduct of life. — Fr. *sagesse*; Ger. *Weisheit, Klugheit.*

wish = 1. a pictured or otherwise represented situation which is tinged with feeling and accompanied by the belief that the situation, if attained, would satisfy a present want; 2. (*psychoan.*) the motive force which determines the flow of dynamic mental processes to seek discharge of their tension, without necessarily implying awareness of the motivation. **wish**[v]. — Fr. *désir*; Ger. *Wunsch.*

wish fulfillment = (*psychoan.*) a fundamental striving of mental processes for relief from psychic tension. [A definite consummation appears in the form of a fulfilled wish.] — Fr. *réalisation du désir.*

wit = 1. an unexpected and ingenious association of ideas, presented usually in spoken language, which causes surprise and pleasant excitement in the hearer unless he is the one against whom it is directed; 2. ready appreciation of any novel complex situation. [Syn. (1) **witticism.** Distg. (1) fr. **humor,** a more subjective type.] **witty**[a] (1). — Fr. *esprit*; Ger. *Witz.*

witchcraft = a magical power attributed to certain individuals; or their exercise of this power. [Usually traced, in folklore, to possession or control of the individual by evil spirits. Cf. **sorcery.**] **witch**[np] (female), **wizard**[np] (male). — Fr. *sorcellerie*; Ger. *Hexerei.*

withdrawing response = a response which retracts a bodily member or the entire organism from the stimulus or situation that induced it. [Syn. **negative** (or **abient**) **response, nociceptive reflex, defense reaction, avoiding response.** Contr. w. **approaching** (or **positive**), **or adient response.**] — Fr. *réaction de recul.*

witness[v] = to observe an occurrence of any sort. [Usually, but not necessarily, limited to visual observation.] **witness**[np] (**eye-witness**[np]). — Fr. *attester, rendre témoignage, témoin*[np]; Ger. *bezeugen, zeugen, beobachten.*

womb, see **uterus.**

wonder = an emotional condition elicited usually by objects which are novel, seemingly important, and intellectually baffling. [Distg. fr. **astonishment,** which is stronger, and fr. **amazement,** much stronger.] **wonder**[v] (also = to experience doubt). — Fr. *étonnement*; Ger. *Staunen.*

word = the smallest unit in vocal, graphic, or gestural language, signifying a single idea.

word-blindness, see **alexia**. — Fr. *cécité verbale*.

word-building test = a form of mental test in which the testee is presented with a number of letters, as *a, e, o, b, m, t*, and asked to form from them as many different words as possible within a time limit of (e.g.) five minutes. —Fr. *t. de construction des mots*.

word-deafness = a form of aphasia characterized by inability to understand spoken words. [Cf. **aphasia**.] — Fr. *surdité verbale*; Ger. *Worttaubheit*.

word-reaction (or **-response**) **time** = the interval between the presentation of a stimulus word and the moment of beginning the utterance of the response word.

word salad = a jumble of words apt to be characteristic of the verbigeration of catatonics. [A translation of Forel's (Ger.) term, *Wortsalat*.] — Fr. *salade de mots*.

word-span test = a mental test essentially similar to the **digit-span test**, save that words are used instead of digits. — Fr. *t. de mémoire immédiate des mots*.

work = 1. (*phys.*) the production of motion in a body by the action of a force against a resistance; 2. (*physiol.*) the expenditure of energy in muscular or mental performance; 3. (*psychol.*) production through muscular or psychological activity of physical or psychological results; e.g. a weight lifted, a poem written. [The erg is the **work** (1) performed by a force of one dyne in moving the body through one centimeter. The **joule** is 10^7 ergs, and the watt-hour is 3.6×10^{10} ergs. The physiological effects of prolonged **work** (2) are indicated by **fatigue**.] — Fr. *travail*; Ger. *Arbeit*.

work curve = a plotted record of the amount of muscular or mental performance in successive time periods of uniform length. — Fr. *courbe de travail*; Ger. *Arbeitskurve*.

work decrement, see **decrement/work**.

work-limit method = a method of arranging material and instructions, such that every testee shall perform the same task, i.e. cover the same material. [Syn. **unit-task tests.** Contr. w. **time-limit method**, in which the time is constant, but the material covered varies with the testee.]

world/external, see **external world**.

world-view = any theory regarding the nature of the universe, or of phenomena in general and their interrelations. — Ger. *Weltanschauung*.

worry = an emotional attitude characterized by unpleasantness, either depressing or exciting. [This attitude is set up by some situation whose solution or outcome causes indecision or conflict; e.g. worry over debts.] **worry**^{v}, **worried**^{a}. — Fr. *souci*; Ger. *Sorge*.

worship = 1. (*relig.*) the act of offering honor and adoration to a deity; 2. (*relig.*) the system of practices which constitute a person's relation with his god or gods. [(2) includes not only adoration but also prayer, sacrifice, etc.] — Fr. (1) *adoration*, (2) *culte*; Ger. (1) *Anbetung*, (2) *Kultus*.

worth = the subjective appreciation, or measure, of the importance of a given datum or factor of any sort, in relation to other data or factors of the same class. [Syn. **value**, a broader term, including also objective importance, as measured on a quantitative or numerical scale.] — Fr. *valeur*; Ger. *Wert*.

wrath, see **anger**.

Wrisberg/cartilages of, see **cuneiform cartilages**.

Wrisberg/nerve of = the glossopalatine nerve, usually considered to be part of the facial nerve.

writer's cramp = a functional spasm which affects the writing process by causing an abnormal contraction or paralysis of some of the muscles employed in writing. [Syn. **graphospasm**.] — Fr. *crampe des écrivains*; Ger. *Schreibkrampf*.

writing = the act of recording ideas in symbolic form, esp. by tracing letters and words on paper, etc., in more or less permanent form with a pen or other recording device. **write**^{v}. — Fr. *écriture*; Ger. *Schrift*.

writing accent = the peculiar characteristics of an individual's handwriting which also appear in the handwriting of other persons of the same nationality. [By analogy with **accent** in speech, which denotes a characteristic manner of pronunciation.] — Fr. *accent caractéristique de l'écriture*.

writing angle, angle of writing = the angle between the downstroke and the base-line of writing. [Very slanting writing = under 45°; normal slanting writing = about 60°; vertical writing = about 90°; backhand writing = over 90°.]

writing tremor = quivering, shaky movements in writing, which arise from a variety of causes such as lapse of muscular control in old age, alcoholic intoxication, or writer's cramp. [Occurs also in paralysis agitans, paresis, multiple sclerosis, etc.; it is not possible as yet to use varieties of tremor in differential diagnosis.] — Fr. *tremblement scriptural*.

Wundt gravity phonometer = an apparatus for determining the difference limens for intensity of sound; it consists of a steel ball, held in an electromagnetic device which can be fixed at any desired height above a plate of hard wood (ebony); when released, the ball produces a sound whose objective intensity (*Schallstärke*) is roughly proportional to (height of fall) × (weight of ball).

Wundt illusion = an illusion, of distorted perception of visual form, observed when a number of lines radiating from two points on the margins above and below are crossed by two parallel lines on opposite sides of the junction of the radiating lines and equidistant from it, the parallel lines appearing closer together in the neighborhood of the center of the figure. [Distg. fr. **Hering illusion**, in which lines radiate *from* the center and the parallel lines between them appear to bow *outward* at the center.]

Wundt sound pendulum = an apparatus devised by W. Wundt for determining the difference threshold for sound; it consists of two pendulums which are so supported that their bobs, when at rest, just touch the opposite faces of an ebony block; when raised through any desired arc and released, each bob strikes the block with a force proportional to its height of fall. [By varying the height, two intensities of sound-stimuli can be produced successively and compared. In some models only one pendulum is used.] — Ger. *Wundtsches Schallpendel*.

Wundt's principles of emotional expression = three principles formulated by Wundt (1900) as a reformulation of **Darwin's principles**: (1) the principle of *direct innervation*; (2) the principle of association of *analogous sensations*; (3) the principle of *relation of movements to images*.

Würzburg school = the school of **imageless thought,** directed by O. Külpe at Würzburg in 1901–9.

X

X-O tests = a series of tests for investigating emotional traits and attitudes, in which the testee responds by crossing items that are deemed wrong, or are worried about, or are liked, and circling those that are deemed most wrong, or are most worried about, or are most liked (S. L. Pressey, 1919). [Later (1933) developed into a series of 4 **interest-attitude** tests (including crossing out items that the testee is interested in) to determine emotional age.]

X-rays = transverse electromagnetic vibrations produced by impact of cathode rays on some kind of matter; they are propagated in straight lines at the speed of light, have an average wave-length of 1×10^{-8} cm., and possess many properties similar to ordinary light, but are far more penetrating. [Syn. **Röntgen rays.]**

xanthic[a] = syn. for **yellowish.**

xanthogenic radiations = light stimuli which normally give rise to the experience of yellow.

xanthopsia = a condition in which objects looked at appear abnormally yellow. [It sometimes accompanies jaundice, and occurs after the ingestion of certain drugs, notably santonin.]

xenoglossis = (*psych. res.*) the understanding, reading, writing, and pronunciation by a sensitive of a *real* language which it is alleged she has never learned. [A form of **cryptesthesia.** Distg. fr. **glossolalia** = a pseudolanguage fabricated by sensitives or automatists, or observed in certain pathological types.]

xenophobia = morbid fear of strangers.

Y

yawning = a reflex, usually induced by bodily fatigue, consisting of an automatic opening of the lower jaw and deep inspiration. — Fr. *bâillement*; Ger. *Gähnen.*

yellow = 1. a visual sensation typically evoked by stimulation of the normal retina with radiation of wave-length approximately 575.5 millimicrons (mμ); 2. any color manifesting a hue predominantly similar to that of the typical yellow. [The complement of **blue.]** **xanthic**[a], **yellow**[a]. — Fr. *jaune*; Ger. *gelb.*

yellow spot, see **macula lutea.** — Fr. *tache jaune*; *gelber Fleck.*

yellow-sighted = characterizing a heightened color sensitivity for yellow, or a tendency to see all objects tinged with yellow. [The phenomenon occurs (1) in individuals who possess a peculiar pigmentation of certain tissues of the eye; (2) in normal individuals following blue-adaptation, or (3) following the use of certain drugs.] — Fr. *hypersensibilité au jaune.*

Yerkes-Bridges scale = a series of twenty tests, nineteen of them from the Binet scale, made available in 1915 by R. M. Yerkes, J. W. Bridges, and Rose Hardwick. [It differs from the Binet scale in being scored in points instead of ages, though these points are afterwards assigned age standards.] — Fr. *échelle de Y.-B.*

Yoga = a Hindu system of ascetic philosophy and practice which involves meditation and contemplation, and culminates in a trance regarded as union with the Supreme Being. **Yogi**[np].

Young-Helmholtz theory = a theory which seeks to explain the phenomena of color vision on the assumption of three independent component mechanisms (or processes) in the retina or its attached nervous apparatus, these mechanisms, when separately aroused (chiefly by radiant energy of corresponding regions in the spectrum) giving rise to the colors red, green, and blue, respectively, all other colors, including yellow, purple, and white or gray, being due to various combinations of the three component activities. [Cf. **three-component theory.]**

youth = the period of adolescence in the human being, i.e. the period between puberty and maturity. [Sometimes extended to include late childhood, or the prepubertal period.] **youthful**[a] = characteristic of the period or the individual; **juvenile**[a] = pert. to the period. — Fr. *jeunesse*; Ger. *Jugend, Jugendzeit.*

Z

zee (or **z**) **chart** = (*statist.*) a time chart consisting of three curves: (1) the original amount, i.e. sales or production of other data, per each successive unit of time; (2) a cumulative curve which gives an amount at each point, i.e. the sum of the ordinates of the preceding curve; and (3) a total curve each point of which gives the total amount for a preceding interval of time, which is the same interval as that covered by the original curve, e.g. 52 weeks, 24 hours, or other natural period. [The curves usually so cross as to yield a Z-shaped picture. The ordinate for the cumulative and total curves is the same, but is different from that for the original data curve.] — Fr. *graphique de z.*

Zeising's principle, see **golden section.**

zenith = 1. the point or location directly above the observer's head; 2. the highest point in a given system of phenomena. [Contr. w. **nadir.]** — Ger. *Scheitelpunkt.*

Zeno's arrow = an argument against the possibility of motion if the units of space and time are discrete: anything in one and the same place is at rest; therefore an arrow is at rest every moment, and hence throughout its whole flight. — Fr. *flèche de Z.*

zero/developmental, see **developmental zero.** — Ger. *Nullpunkt* = zero.

zero/physiological (or **psychological**) = the temperature of the skin at which thermal experiences are not aroused. [It usually lies for the exposed areas of the skin at about 33° C., but it varies considerably for different parts of the body, e.g. inside mouth, 37° C., ear lobe, 28° C.]

Zielvorstellung = idea of end, goal, or purpose (Ach). [Ger.]

zoetrope, zootrope, see stroboscope.

Zöllner illusion = an illusion of visual space perception, in which a series of parallel lines appear to slant alternately in opposite directions, when the alternate lines in the series are crossed by a number of short lines at an (acute) angle, the cross-line in one row slanting one way, in the next the other way, etc. [One theory explains the effect as an exaggeration of the apparent size of the acute angles and a pronounced distortion in the direction of the parallel lines.] — Ger. *Zöllnersche Täuschung*.

zone = 1. a belt or strip of surface; 2. (*neurol.*) a region of the brain, body, or retina. — Ger. *Zone, Gürtel*.

zone/reflexogenous, /aphasia, /apraxia, see **reflexogenous zones,** etc.

zones/chromatic (or **color**) = regions of the **visual field** which have different characteristics as to chromatic response. [For most individuals, the central portion of the field shows full chromatic response, while red and green responses disappear at a moderately peripheral position, and blue and yellow fail in the extreme periphery. The exact boundaries of any zone depend upon the extent, intensity, and chromatic power of the stimuli used; they vary also with the individual, and with the technique employed. Cf. **perimetry.**]

zones/erogenous, see **erogenous zones.**

zones/retinal = zones of the retina, optically corresponding to those of the visual field, and similarly differentiated according to chromatic or other function. [Cf. **zones/chromatic.**]

zonule of Zinn = the set of radial fibrous bands which extend from the ciliary body to the equator of the lens of the eye, constituting its suspensory ligament.

Zoöid = 1. a component member of a colonial aggregate of connected animal forms, as in Hydroids and Bryozoa; 2. a motile stage in those species which have alternation of generations (a Medusa or Medusoid); 3. a motile stage in the early development of an animal; 4. a **spermatozoon.**

zoology = the branch of biology which deals with animals. [Distg. fr. **botany** = the study of plants.] (Pron. **zo-**, not **zoo-**; 4 syll.) **zoological**[a].

zoophilism, zoophily = 1. love of animals; 2. (*psychoan.*) an abnormal devotion to animals.

zoophobia = morbid fear of animals.

zoophyte = an animal which superficially resembles a plant, e.g. hydroid, sponge, coral.

zoopsia = hallucinations in which the patient imagines that he sees animals.

zygomatic area = pert. to or located in the area on the upper part of either cheek near the prominent cheek bone. — Ger. *Jochbein-*.

zygomatic reflex = lateral movements of the jaw, elicited by tapping the **zygomatic area.** — Ger. *Jochreflex*. [Mediated by V (sensory) to V (motor) cranial nerves.]

zygote = a cell formed by the union of two gametes. [Cf. **gamete.**]

APPENDIX

APPENDIX

TABLES

Table I

COLOR-VISION TESTS

1. **Matching Tests**
   Holmgren wool-sorting
   Jennings self-recording
   Westcott lantern slide for group testing
   Nela tests

2. **Confusion Tests**
   Stilling Pseudo-isochromatische Tafeln
   Ishihara color-perception test
   Podesta Wandtafeln
   Edridge-Green cards
   Nagel Tafeln

3. **Practical Tests**
   Edridge-Green lantern
   Williams lantern
   Thomson lantern
   Scripture color sense teste

4. **Laboratory Research**
   Nagel Anomaloskop
   von Hess Farbensinnprüfer
   von Hess Differential-Pupilloskop

Table II

COMPLEXES

A LIST OF THE FUNDAMENTAL TYPES

castration complex
Edipus (Œdipus) complex (syn. mother-fixating, mother-complex)
Electra complex (syn. father-fixation, father-complex, female Edipus complex)
inferiority complex
Jehovah complex (syn. God-complex)
nuclear complex

Table III

DEXTRALITY, OR ONE-SIDED DOMINANCE

(Including some terms not in use, but formed according to correct etymology and by analogy with accepted conventions.)

A. GENERAL

Noun	Adj. and Personal Noun	Meaning: Dominance of
dextrality	**dextral**	motor or sensory function on one side

B. SIDE OF MEMBER

sidedness	**(sided)**	one side
unidextrality	**unidextral**	one side, or hand, etc., over the other
(one-sidedness)	**(one-sided)**	one side (ambig.)
dextrodextrality	**dextrodextral**	right side, or hand, etc., over left
right-sidedness	**right-sided**	right side over left
sinistrodextrality	**sinistrodextral**	left side, or hand, etc., over right
sinistrality	**sinistral**	left side, or hand, etc., over right
left-sidedness	**left-sided**	left side over right
ambidextrality	**ambidextral, -ous**	neither side, hand, etc. over the other
(both-sidedness)	**(both-sided)**	neither side over the other

C. HANDS

handedness	**one-handed** (ambig.)	one hand (generic term)
manudextrality	**manudextral**	one hand (generic term)

Noun	Adj. and Personal Noun	Meaning: Dominance of
unimanuality	**unimanual**	one hand over the other

[**unimanual** and **bimanual** generally mean "(operations) performed by one hand alone," and "by two hands together" respectively.]

right-handedness	**right-handed**	right hand over left
dextromanuality	**dextromanual**	right hand over left
left-handedness	**left-handed**	left hand over right
sinistromanuality	**sinistromanual**	left hand over right
ambimanuality	**ambimanual**	neither hand over the other
(both-handedness)	**(both-handed)**	neither hand over the other (ambig.)

D. FOOT

pedidextrality	**pedidextral**	one foot over the other
(footedness)	**(footed)**	one foot over the other (ambig.)
unipedality	**unipedal**	one foot over the other
dextropedality	**dextropedal**	right foot over left
right-footedness	**right-footed**	right foot over left

— and other terms, formed like the **-manual** and **-handed** compounds

E. EYE

oculodextrality	**oculodextral**	one eye over the other
eyedness	**eyed** (ambig.)	one eye over the other
(uniocularity)	**(uniocular)**	one eye over the other (ambig.)
right-eyedness	**right-eyed**	right eye over left
oculodextrality	**oculodextral**	right eye over left
ambocularity	**ambocular**	neither eye over the other

— and other terms, formed like the **-manual** and **-handed** compounds

F. EAR

auridextrality	**auridextral**	one ear over the other
earedness	**eared** (ambig.)	one ear over the other
(uniaurality)	**(uniaural)**	one ear over the other (ambig.)

— **right-earedness, dextraurality, ambaurality,** and other terms, formed like the **-manual** and **-handed** compounds

Refer to:

Downey, J. E., *Amer. J. Psychol.*, 1927, **38**, 317–367.
Jones, E., *Psychol. Bull.*, 1909, **6**, 130–132.
Rife, J. M., *Psychol. Rev.*, 1922, **29**, 474–480.

Table IV

ERRORS

OCCURRING IN EXPERIMENTAL INVESTIGATION

1. **Errors in technique**
   - Errors of planning
   - Errors of instrumental set-up
   - Systematic errors of operation
     (sampling errors, faulty instructions to observers, incomplete performance, etc.)
   - Incidental errors of observation
     (disarrangement or failure of apparatus, secondary cues, etc.)
2. **Instrumental errors**
   - Constant error
   - Variable error
3. **Observational errors** (in psychophysics)
   - Temporal error
   - Spatial error
   - Errors of recognition
   - Errors of expectation
   - Errors of reference
   - Stimulus error
4. **Errors in treatment of data**
   - Errors of perception (reading) or recording
   - Errors of computation, etc.
   - Motivated errors (= errors of bias)
   - Errors of contravention

Table V

GLANDS FREQUENTLY TREATED IN PSYCHOLOGICAL LITERATURE

(For complete list of several hundred glands found in the human body, see *Anatomical Names*, by A. C. Eycleshymer.)

Name	Location (*in or near*)	Duct or Endocrine [1]
adrenal (= suprarenal)	retroperitoneal region	E
apical	tongue	D
areolar	nipple (f.)	D
bulbocavernous	penis (m.)	D
cutaneous	skin	D
duodenal	duodenum	D
gastric	stomach	D
Harder's	eye	D
intestinal	intestines	D, E
lacrimal, lachrymal (tear)	eye region	D
lingual (= apical)		
mammary (milk)	breast (f.)	D
mucous (= muciparous)	mucous membrane	D
ovary	pelvis (f.)	D, E
pancreas	near intestine	D, E
parathyroid	embedded in thyroid	E
parotid (saliva)	in front of ear	D
pineal (= epiphysis cerebri)	caudal roof of diencephalon	E
pituitary (= hypophysis cerebri)	under cerebral hemispheres	E
prostate	bladder (m.)	D
salivary	mouth	D
sebaceous	skin	D
sex (= testes, ovary)	genitals	D, E
sublingual (saliva)	under tongue	D
submaxillary (saliva)	lower jaw	D
sudoriparous (= sudoriferous, sweat)	skin	D
suprarenal (= adrenal)		
tarsoconjunctival	eyelids	D
testes (semen)	scrotum (m.)	D, E
thymus	cervical region, thorax	
thyroid	cervical region	E
vulvovaginal (= vestibular)	genitals (f.)	D

Proper Name; Alternatives	Equivalent
Bartholin's (Tiedemann's)	vulvovaginal
Blandin's (Nuhn's)	apical
Boerhaave's	sudoriferous
Bowman's	in olfactory region
Bruch's	tarsoconjunctival
Brunner's	duodenal
Cowper's	bulbocavernous
Duverney's	vulvovaginal
Gley's (Sandstroem's)	parathyroid
Henle's (= meibomian)	conjunctiva of eyelids

[1] Typical classification. Endocrinal function may be present, even when not indicated.

TABLE VI

LOGICAL FALLACIES IN REASONING AND INTERPRETATION

(Any classification of fallacies is more or less arbitrary. The following list, based on Creighton, presents a convenient scheme. Historical names often apply to overlapping sorts.)

A. MISTAKES IN REASONING

I. FORMAL

1. Four terms
2. Undistributed middle
3. Illicit major
4. Illicit minor
5. Negative premises
6. Denying the antecedent
7. Affirming the consequent
8. Imperfect disjunction

II. MATERIAL

(*a*) Equivocation

1. Ambiguous middle
2. Composition
3. Division
4. Accident
5. Dilemmatic fallacy
6. False analogy, or Figure of speech

(*b*) Presumption

1. Begging the question and Question-begging epithets
2. Complex question
3. Irrelevant conclusion
   - i. Argumentum ad hominem, ad populum, ad ignorantiam, ad verecundiam, ad misericordiam
   - ii. Fallacy of objections
4. Non sequitur, or Post hoc ergo propter hoc, or False cause
5. Hasty generalization
6. Consequent
7. Many questions, or Complex questions

B. MISTAKES IN INTERPRETING DATA

1. Improper observation, or conversion
2. Ambiguous sentence structure, or Amphiboly
3. Accent, or Emphasis

TABLE VII

MUSICAL INTERVALS

NAME [1]	MUSICAL NOTATION [1]	FREQUENCY RATIO	MAGNITUDE [2]		
Unison; prime	**C -C**	1:1	0.00		
Cent	......	1730:1731	0.01		
Comma, comma of Didymus	......	80:81	0.22		
Pythagorean comma	......	73:74	0.24		
Enharmonic or great diesis	......	125:128	0.42		
Chromatic or small semitone, augmented unison	**C -C#**	24:25	0.70	minor	seconds
Pythagorean limma; hemitone	Ẹ -F	243:256	0.90	minor	seconds
Tempered semitone; tempered minor second	Ċ -*C#*	$1:2^{1/12}$	1.00	minor	seconds
Diatonic semitone; true minor second	**E -F**	15:16	1.12	minor	seconds
True minor tone; grave major second	**D -E**	9:10	1.82	major	seconds
Tempered major second	**C** -*D*	$1:2^{2/12}$	2.00	major	seconds
True major tone or major second; Pythagorean tone or second	**C -D**	8:9	2.04	major	seconds
Diminished minor third	**A#-C′**	225:256	2.24	major	seconds

[1] Names and tonal letters in bold-face indicate tones in the Diatonic and Chromatic scales; those in italic, tones in the Tempered scale; tonal letters in light-face with a period beneath indicate tones in the Pythagorean scale. See **scale.**

[2] Measured in tempered semitones and hundredth parts (i.e. musical *Cents*); e.g. comma of Didymus is 22/100 of a tempered semitone.

Name	Musical Notation	Frequency Ratio	Magnitude	Group
Augmented second	C -D♯	64:75	2.74	minor thirds
Pythagorean minor third	D -F	27:32	2.94	minor thirds
Tempered minor third	C -*D♯*	$1:2^{3/12}$	3.00	minor thirds
True minor third	E -G	5:6	3.16	minor thirds
True major third	C -E	4:5	3.86	major thirds
Tempered major third	C -*E*	$1:2^{4/12}$	4.00	major thirds
Pythagorean major third	C -Ė	64:81	4.08	major thirds
Diminished fourth	C♯-Ḟ	25:32	4.28	major thirds
Perfect fourth; Pythagorean fourth	C -F	3:4	4.98	fourths
Tempered fourth	C -*F*	$1:2^{5/12}$	5.00	fourths
Acute fourth	C♯-F♯	20:27	5.20	fourths
Augmented fourth; tritone	C -F♯	32:45	5.90	tritone group
Tempered tritone	C -*F♯*	$1:2^{6/12}$	6.00	tritone group
Diminished fifth	D -A♭	45:64	6.10	tritone group
Grave fifth	D -A	27:40	6.80	fifths
Tempered fifth	C -*G*	$1:2^{7/12}$	7.00	fifths
Perfect fifth; Pythagorean fifth	C -G	2:3	7.02	fifths
Augmented fifth	C -G♯	16:25	7.72	minor sixths
Pythagorean minor sixth	Ẹ -C′	81:128	7.92	minor sixths
Tempered minor sixth	Ċ -*A♭*	$1:2^{8/12}$	8.00	minor sixths
True minor sixth	C -A♭	5:8	8.14	minor sixths
True major sixth	C -A	3:5	8.84	major sixths
Tempered major sixth	C -*A*	$1:2^{9/12}$	9.00	major sixths
Pythagorean major sixth	C -Ȧ	16:27	9.06	major sixths
Diminished seventh	D♯-Ċ′	75:128	9.26	major sixths
Augmented sixth	C -A♯	128:225	9.76	minor sevenths
True minor seventh; Pythagorean minor seventh	D -C′	9:16	9.96	minor sevenths
Tempered minor seventh	C -*B♭*	$1:2^{10/12}$	10.00	minor sevenths
Acute minor seventh	C -B♭	5:9	10.18	minor sevenths
True major seventh	C -B	8:15	10.88	major sevenths
Tempered major seventh	C -*B*	$1:2^{11/12}$	11.00	major sevenths
Pythagorean major seventh	C -Ḃ	128:243	11.10	major sevenths
Diminished octave	C♯-Ċ′	25:48	11.29	major sevenths
Octave; perfect octave	C -C′	1:2	12.00	

Table VIII

PHOBIAS

A LIST OF THE MOST COMMON TYPES

-phobia	Dread of	-phobia	Dread of
acro-	high places	**nycto-**	darkness, night
agora-	open places	**patho- (noso-)**	disease, suffering
algo-	pain	**peccato-**	sinning
astra- (astrapo-)	thunder and lightning	**phono-**	speaking aloud
claustro-	closed (confined) places	**photo-**	strong light [1]
copro-	excreta	**sito-**	eating
hemato-	sight of blood	**tapho-**	being buried alive
hydro-	water	**thanato-**	death
lalo- (glosso-)	speaking	**toxo-**	being poisoned
myso-	dirt, contamination	**xeno-**	strangers
necro-	dead bodies	**zoo-**	animals

[1] Distinguished from hyperphoto-esthesia (normal).

A list of 135 phobias is given by G. Stanley Hall, in *Amer. J. Psychol.*, 1914, **25**, 171–172.

TABLE IX

PREFIXES AND SUFFIXES

COMMONLY USED IN SCIENTIFIC TERMS

[N. B. prefixes ending in *o-* generally drop the *o* before vowels and *h*. In forming new scientific terms the *o-* is often retained.]

	LANGUAGE	MEANING	EXAMPLE	OPPOSITE
a-	Grk.	without; deprived of	achromatic	....
		= **an-** before vowel or **h**	anhedonic	....
ab-	Lat.	away from	aberration	**ad-**
		= **abs-** before **c, q, t**	abstract	....
acro-	Grk.	high; exaggerated; extremities (anat.)	acro-esthesia	....
ad-	Lat.	toward; to; = **ac-, af-, ag-, al-, ap-, as-,** before these consonants	adient	**ab-**
-ad	Lat.	toward	dorsad	....
-al	Lat.	pertaining to; accent antepenult	dorsal	....
		if any	sagittal	....
ambi-	Lat.	both; either	ambidextral, -ous	....
amphi-	Grk.	around; all about	amphibia	....
ana-	Grk.	up; forward; constructive	anabolism	**cata-**
ante-	Lat. (A.S.)	before (in time)	antemeridian	**post-**
antero-	Lat.	in front of	anterograde	**postero-**
anti-	Grk., Lat. (A.S.)	opposed to or opposite to	antibody	**pro-**
		= **ant-** before vowel or **h**	antagonist	....
apo-	Grk.	separation, derivation from	apoplexy	....
auto-	Grk.	self	autonomic	**allo-**
bi-	Lat.	two, two-fold	bisexual	**uni-, multi-**
		= **bin-** before vowel	binocular	....
brachy-	Grk.	short	brachycephalic	**dolicho-**
cata- (kata-)	Grk.	downward; destructive	catabolism	**ana-**
centi-	Lat.	hundred; usually 1/100	centigram	....
circum-	Lat.	around	circumvallate	....
con-	Lat.	with; affiliated; = **col-** before **l**, **cor-** before **r**, **com-** before **m, p**; **co-** before vowel, **h**, and A.S. compounds	congenital	....
contra-	Lat.	against	contrasuggestion	....
		often becomes **counter-**	counteract	....
de-	Lat.	from; reversal of a process	decompose	....
di- (*or* **dis-**)	Grk.	two; two-foldness	dichromatic	**mono-**
dia-	Grk.	through	diameter	....
dis- (*or* **di-**)	Lat. (A.S.)	apart; separation	disruption, dilation	....
dolicho-	Grk.	long	dolichocephalic	**brachy-**
dynamo-	Grk.	strength; force	dynamometer	....
dys-	Grk.	imperfect; faulty	dysarthria	**eu-**
ec-	Grk.	out; out from	ecphoria	**en-**
		= **ex-** before a vowel	exorcise	....
ecto-	Grk.	external; outside	ectoderm	**endo-**
-ectomy	Grk.	surgical removal	thyroidectomy	....
en-	Grk.	in	encephalon	....
endo-	Grk.	internal; inside	endoderm	**ecto-**
epi-	Grk.	upon (position); = **ep-** before vowel or **h**	epithelium	....
eso-	Grk.	within; inner	esoteric	**exo-**
-esia, -esis	Grk.	-tion; -ship	synthesis, anesthesia	....

There is no etymological rule or uniform practice for distinguishing these two forms; generally **-esis** in abstract nouns, **-esia** for concrete things

eu-	Grk.	good; healthy; agreeable	eugenics	**dys-**
ex-	Lat.	from; out from; = **ef-** before **f**, **e-** before **b, d, l, m, n, v**	excite	....
extero-	Lat.	from outside	exteroceptor	**intero-**
extra-	Lat.	outside; outward	extravert	**intro-**

	Language	Meaning	Example	Opposite
extro- (rare)	Lat.	directed outward		
-genetic	Grk.	pert. to origins	ontogenetic	....
-genic	Grk.	denoting a genus or kind	psychogenic	....
-gram	Grk.	a written record	neurogram	....
-graph	Grk.	writing or recording	chronograph	**-scope**
hemi-	Grk.	half (Lat. = semi)	hemiopia, hemicy	....
hemero-	Grk.	day	hemeralopia	**nyct-**
hetero-	Grk.	different; unlike	heterogeneous	**homo-; ortho-**
histo-	Grk.	tissue	histology	....
homo-	Grk.	similar; not related to Lat. **homo-** = man	homogeneous	**hetero-**
hyper-	Grk.	excess; superiority	hyperesthesia	**hypo-**
hypno-	Grk.	sleep; hypnosis; confusion avoided by using Lat. **somno-** for sleep	hypnotic	....
hypo-	Grk.	to a low degree; inferior	hypodermic, hypoglossal	**hyper-**
-ia	Grk., Lat.	denotes a quality or characteristic; often becomes **-y**	aphasia	....
-iatry, -iatric	Grk.	medicine; physicians	psychiatry	....
-ic	Grk.	of; pertaining to	basic	....
-ical	Lat., Grk.	of; pertaining to	radical	....

There is a growing tendency to substitute **-ic** for **-ical,** but note (e.g.) electric current, electrical device. Accent all **-ic** words on penult, exc. arithmetic [n] and lunatic and certain proper names; **-ical** words on antepenult

ideo-	Grk.	idea; thought	ideomotor	....
idio-	Grk.	personal; private	idiosyncrasy	....
in-	Lat.	not; antagonism	inability, indeterminate	....
		= **il-** before **l, im-** before **b, m.**	immoral, imbecile	....
		Often replaced by A.S. **un-** esp. in adj. forms. Distg. fr. **non-** which denotes absence	unable, undetermined non-moral	....
infra-	Lat.	(position) below; beneath	infraclavicular	**supra-, ultra-**
inter-	Lat.	between; distg. fr. **infra-** = within	interaction	....
intero-	Lat.	from inside	interoceptor	**extero-**
intra- (rare)	Lat.	lying within		**extra-**
intro-	Lat.	directed inward	introspection	**extra-**
iso-	Grk.	equal	isometric	....
-itis	Grk.	inflammation	encephalitis	....
-ize, -ise	Grk.	to make or cause to be	organize	....
juxta-	Lat.	close to	juxtapose	....
kata-	Grk.	(see **cata-**)		
kilo-	Grk.	thousand (times)	kilometer	....
kine-, kineto-	Grk.	movement	kinetogenesis	....
-lalia	Grk.	speech process	echolalia	....
lalo-	Grk.	speech process	lalopathy	....
logo-	Grk.	reasoning; words	logorrhea	....
macro-	Grk.	large; great	macrocephalic	**micro-**
mal-	Lat.	defect (of)	malformation, maladjustment	**bene-**
medio-	Lat.	mid-position	mediocrity	....
meso-	Grk.	mid-position; median size	mesoderm	....
meta-	Grk.	change; after	metabolism	....
		= **met-** before vowel or aspirate **h**	method	....
-meter	Grk.	measure; measuring device. Accent **-ometer** on antepenult	algometer	....
micro-	Grk.	small	microcosm	**macro-**
mid-	A.S.	middle; median, etc.	midbrain	....
milli-	Lat.	thousand; usually 1/1000	millimicron, milligram	....
mis-	A.S.	wrong (less emphatic than **mal-**); used also with Lat. terms	mislead, misapprehend	....
mono-	Grk.	single; unitary; not properly used with Lat. terms	monosyllabic	**di-, poly-**

	Language	Meaning	Example	Opposite
multi-	Lat.	many; manifold	multicellular	**uni-**
myo-	Grk.	muscle	myograph	....
neo-	Grk.	new; later version	neo-Lamarckism	....
non-	Lat.	absence; used also with Grk. and A.S. terms; distg. fr. **in-** = contrast, antagonism	non-rational	....
nyct-	Grk.	night	nyctalopia	**hemero-**
ob-	Lat.	toward; opposite to; etc.; = **oc-**, **of-**, **og-**, **op-**, before these consonants	object	....
-oma	Grk.	tumor; growth	sarcoma	....
omni-	Lat.	all	omnivorous	....
onto-	Grk.	being; individual	ontogenesis	**phylo-**
-opia	Grk.	-eyed; vision	myopia	....
ortho-	Grk.	straight; correct; direct	orthogenesis	**hetero-**
-osis, -otic	Grk.	diseased condition	neurosis	....
oto-	Grk.	ear	otological	....
over-	A.S.	excessive, used also w. Lat. terms	overlearning overvaluation	**under-**
pan-	Grk.	all	panpsychism	....
para-	Grk.	distortion; perversion	paramnesia, parageusic	....
per-	Lat.	through; excess of	perceive	....
peri-	Grk.	around	perimeter	....
philo-	Grk.	love; lover	philosophy	**-phobia**
-phobia	Grk.	dread (pathological)	agoraphobia	**philo-**
phylo-	Grk.	race; species	phylogenesis	**onto-**
pneumato-	Grk.	air	pneumatic	....
pneumo- (pneumono-)	Grk.	the lungs	pneumograph	....
poly-	Grk.	many; manifold	polygamy	**mono-**
post-	Lat.	later; behind	post-natal	**ante-, pre-**
pre-, prae-	Lat.	before (place or time); prehistoric	praecox	**post-**
pro-	Grk., Lat.	favorable; in place of; in front	project	**(anti-)**
pros-	Grk.	before; in front of	prosencephalon	....
proto-	Grk.	earliest (types, etc.)	protoplasm	....
pseudo-	Grk.	false; erroneous; used also w. A.S. and Lat. terms	pseudoscope	....
psycho-	Grk.	mind	psychology	....
re-	Lat.	again	reiterate	....
retro-	Lat.	behind; backward	retrograde	**pro-**
-scope	Grk.	visual observation device	chronoscope	....
scoto-	Grk.	darkness	scotopia	**hemero-**
se-	Lat.	separation; apart	segregation	....
semi-	Lat.	half; not properly used w. Grk. or A.S. terms	semiconscious	....
skia-	Grk.	light-and-shape (no color)	skiascope	....
somno-	Lat.	sleep	somnolence	....
sphygmo-	Grk.	pulse	sphygmometer	....
stereo-	Grk.	solid	stereoscope stereotropism	....
sub-	Lat.	beneath; a lower order	subhuman, subnormal	**super-**
super-	Lat.	above; a higher order; both **sub-** and **super-** used w. A.S. terms, not properly w. Grk.	supernatural	**sub-**
supra-	Lat.	lying above or upon	suprascapular	**infra-**
syn-	Grk.	together; accompanying	synthesis	**ana-**
thermo-	Grk.	heat; warmth	thermometer	....
-tomy	Grk.	cutting	anatomy	....
trans-	Lat.	across; from one to another	transmission	....
ultra-	Lat.	beyond; extreme	ultra-violet	**infra-**
un-	A.S.	lack; absence; used also w. Lat. terms	unjust undetermine	....
under-	A.S.	nearer zero; center of gravity; etc.	underestimate	**over-**
uni-	Lat.	single; unitary	uniocular	**bi-, multi-**
ur-	Ger.	primitive	Urrot (primitive red)	....

TABLES

Table X

HUMAN REFLEXES FREQUENTLY TREATED IN PSYCHOLOGICAL LITERATURE

Reflex	Stimulus	Pathway	Response
abdominal	stroking skin laterad to rectus abdominus	8th to 12th thoracic	contraction of ventral abdominal wall
abdominocardiac	irritation of abdominal aortic plexus	1st to 10th thoracic	inhibition of heart
Achilles' tendon	tapping calcaneal tendon or percussing anterior tibial muscles	4th lumbar to 2d sacral	plantar flexion at ankle
acromial	tapping acromial process in shoulder	4th cervical to 1st thoracic	pronation and flexion of forearm
anal	stim. of skin and mucosa of anus	3d to 5th sacral	contraction of sphincter ani
ankle, see **Achilles' tendon**			
audito-oculogyric	sudden sound	auditory and oculomotor arcs	turning eyes toward source of sound
Babinski (abnormal)	stroking sole of foot	5th lumbar to 2d sacral	extension (i.e. dorsiflexion) of great toe with similar extension and lateral deviation of outer toes
biceps	tapping anticulital tendon	5th to 7th cervical	contraction of biceps brachii
bladder, see **vesical**			
bone, see **periosteal**			
bulbocavernous, see **virile**			
chin, see **mandibular**			
ciliospinal, see **cutaneous-pupillary**			
conjunctival, see **corneal**			
corneal	touching cornea or conjunctiva	trigemino-facial arc	closure of eyelids
cremasteric	stroking skin over femoral triangle or inner side of thigh	1st and 2d lumbar	contraction of dartos tunic and of cremaster muscle
cutaneous-pupillary	scratching of skin of jaw or cheek	sensory V to 1st thoracic, sympathetic, to eye	dilation of pupil
cutaneous secretory	galvanic stim. on skin	cutaneous sensory and sympathetic fibers	activity of sweat glands
dorsal, see **sacrospinal**			
elbow, elbow-jerk, see **triceps**			
epigastric	stroking skin from nipple downward	7th and 8th thoracic	drawing in of abdominal wall
erector spinae, see **sacrospinal**			
extensor thrust	pressure on sole of foot	2d lumbar to 3d sacral	reflex extension of leg
eyelid closure, see **corneal** and **eye-wink**			
eye-wink, see **winking**			
faucial	irritation of passage from mouth to pharynx	IX and X cranial	contraction of faucial muscle, elevation of hyoid, gagging, vomiting
fixation	light on an extra-foveal point of retina	optic tracts to oculomotor; midbrain	turning eye toward source of stim

Reflex	Stimulus	Pathway	Response
flexion (lower extremity)	nociceptive stim.	2d lumbar to 3d sacral	withdrawal of lower limb
front tap	striking skin above muscle on anterior part of leg, with leg and foot extended	3d lumbar to 2d sacral	contraction of gastrocnemius
galvanic, galvanic skin	physiological activity controlled by autonomic system	cutaneous to sympathetic	decreased galvanic resistance of skin
gastrocolic	introduction of food into empty stomach	arcs through thoracic cord	peristaltic wave in colon
gastro-iliac	pressure of food in stomach	autonomic arcs through thoracic cord	relaxation of iliocecal valve
gluteal	irritation of skin over gluteal muscles	4th to 5th lumbar	contraction of gluteal muscles
grasping (involuntary)	cutaneous stim. of palms or fingers	7th to 8th cervical (observed after lesions of premotor area of cortex)	flexion of fingers
Haab's pupil	attention to bright object in darkened room	optic tracts to oculomotor; midbrain	iris contraction of both eyes
head retraction	irritation of nares	V sensory and upper cervical	withdrawal of head
hunger contraction	hormone acting on empty stomach	musculature and nerve plexuses of stomach	contraction of stomach
hypochondriacal	pressure below inferior border of ribs	8th thoracic to 4th cervical	quick intake of breath
hypothenar	pressure on pisiform bone of wrist	8th cervical to 1st thoracic	flexion of little finger
infraspinatus	tapping shoulder-blade near its inner margin	5th to 7th cervical	outward rotation of arm and straightening of elbow
interscapular, see **scapular**			
iris	increase or decrease of light intensity	retina, optic tracts, oculomotor (constriction); 1st thoracic and cervical sympathetic (dilation)	contraction or relaxation of iris muscles
jaw, see **mandibular**			
knee-jerk, see **patellar**			
labyrinthine righting	stim. of labyrinth (vestibular) origin	vestibular, vestibulo-spinal tracts, motor to neck and limbs	rotating head to upright position or righting the body to normal antigravity position
lacrimal, lachrymal	irritation of nasal mucous membrane	V (sensory) and VII cranial and great petrosal and sphenopalatine ganglion	increased secretion of tears
laryngeal	irritation of larynx or fauces	X cranial to 4th cervical and thoracic	coughing
lid-closure, see **corneal**			
lumbar, see **sacrospinal**			
mandibular	a blow on chin or teeth	V (sensory), V (motor) cranial; pons	contraction of masseter muscles, elevation of lower jaw
mandibuloconjunctival	touching corneal conjunctiva	trigeminal and masticator nucleus and n.	drawing lower jaw toward side of stimulus

Reflex	Stimulus	Pathway	Response
mass (abnormal)	stim. of skin below level of spinal injury	below level of injury	movement extending over entire area innervated, usually lower limb
masseteric, see **mandibular**			
McCarthy's, see **supraorbital**			
myenteric	stim. of some portion of intestine	autonomic	contraction above, and relaxation below
myotatic	stretching of any muscle	reflex arc	increase of tonus in muscle
nasal	irritation of mucous membrane of nose	V cranial (sensory) 4th cervical	sneezing
nasomental	a blow on side of nose	trigemino-facial arc; oblongata	contraction of mentalis muscle and elevation of chin
oblique (also syn. for **cremasteric**)	irritation of skin below inguinal ligament	1st and 2d lumbar	contraction of obliquus externus muscle
oculocardiac	pressing one or both eyeballs	V (sensory), X (motor cranial); oblongata	slowing of heart-beat
ophthalmic, see **supraorbital**			
orthocardiac	assumption of upright position of body	autonomic	dilation of right side of heart
palatal	touching the palate	V sensory, IX and X cranial, oblongata	contraction of palatal and pharyngeal muscles; swallowing
palmar	irritation of palm of hand	8th cervical to 1st thoracic	flexion of fingers
paradoxical patellar	tapping the patellar tendon	3d lumbar	contraction of adductoı muscle, but not of quadriceps femoris
paradoxical pupillary	stim. of retina by light	optic tract; oculomotor	dilation of pupil
patellar, patellar tendon	tapping patellar tendon	2d to 4th lumbar	contraction of quadriceps femoris
penile, penis, see **virile**			
periosteal	tapping of a bone of forearm or leg	5th to 8th cervical (or) 2d lumbar to 3d sacral	contraction of muscle tapped
peristaltic	stim. by food in alimentary canal	autonomic	wave-like contractions in alimentary canal and intestines
peroneal	stroking peroneal muscles of fibula	5th lumbar to 1st sacral	movement of those muscles
pharyngeal	touching back of pharynx	glossopharyngeal and vagal arcs	contraction of pharyngeal constrictors
plantar	stroking sole of foot	1st and 2d sacral	flexion of toes
platysma, see **cutaneous-pupillary**			
positive supporting, postural	disturbance of equilibrium	proprioceptive arcs in cord	bringing (and holding) leg in position to support body
psychogalvanic, see **galvanic**			
pupillary, see **iris**			
pupillary-skin, see **cutaneous-pupillary**			
quadriceps extensor, see **patellar**			
radial	tapping lower end of radius	5th to 8th cervical	flexion of forearm (and often of fingers)
rectal	accumulation of feces in rectum	3d to 5th sacral	defecation

Reflex	Stimulus	Pathway	Response
sacrospinal	scratching skin on lateral border of spinal muscle	thoracic region	contraction of sacrospinal muscle
salivary	stim. of afferent nerve	lingual V to secretory centers of VII and IX cranial	change in secretory activity of one or more salivary glands
scapular	scratching skin over scapula or between the scapulae	5th cervical to 4th thoracic	movement of shoulders
sexual	stimulation of genitalia	3d and 4th sacral	activities which precede orgasm and orgasm itself
skin, see **superficial**			
sole, see **plantar**			
starting, startled	loud sound, withdrawal of support, etc.	brain stem and cord	jerking movements, change in respiration, etc.
stretch, see **myotatic**			
struggle	confinement of limbs or head	brain stem and cord	violent (usually unco-ordinated) movements
sucking	grasping of nipple with lips and tongue	V (sensory) to V (motor)	drawing of liquid into mouth
superficial	pinching skin over a muscle	V cranial to 1st thoracic	contraction of that muscle
supinator longus	tapping tendon of brachioradialis	5th cervical	flexion of forearm
supraorbital	tapping supraorbital foramen	trigemino-facial arc	contraction of eyelid muscle
swallowing	food in mouth	V to XI cranial, oblongata	activity of deglutition muscles
tendo Achillis, tendon of Achilles, tendo calcaneus, see **Achilles' tendon**			
tonic neck	movement of head in relation to trunk	VIII cranial to 4th cervical	modification of posture of limbs
tonic neck-eye	changes of position of head in relation to any plane	VIII cranial to 4th cervical and oculomotor	compensatory eye-movements
triceps	tapping tendon near olecranon	6th to 7th cervical	contraction of triceps brachii
urinary, see **vesical**			
vesical	filling of bladder	3d to 5th sacral	micturition
virile	tapping back of penis near scrotum	4th and 5th sacral	contraction of bulbocavernous muscle of urethra
visceromotor	stim. of one of viscera in abdomen or thorax	1st to 12th thoracic	contraction of a parietal muscle in abdomen or thorax
visual righting	fixation of an object in visual field	optic tracts, tectospinal and descending corticospinal tracts to neck muscles	orientation of head
vomiting	intestinal, gastric, cardiac or pharyngeal irritation	X cranial to 12th thoracic, vomiting centers in lower oblongata	expulsion of substance through the mouth or nose or both
winking, wink	dryness of cornea	V (sensory) to VII (motor)	closure of eye
zygomatic	tapping the zygoma (cheek-bone)	V (sensory) to V (motor)	lateral movements of jaw

TABLES

Table XI

RETINAL LAYERS IN THE HUMAN EYE

(From outer surface to center of eyeball)

1. **Pigment layer:**	a single layer of epithelial cells containing pigment
2. **Layer of rods and cones:**	syn. bacillary layer or Jacob's membrane
3. **External limiting membrane:**	a part of the supporting tissue of the retina
4. **Outer nuclear layer:**	it contains the nuclei of the neurons, of which the rods and cones are a part
5. **Outer granular, molecular, plexiform,** or **reticular layer:**	a complex network of fine processes of the neurons of layer 6, as they come into functional relation with the processes of the visual cells in layer 4
6. **Inner nuclear layer,** or **layer of bipolar nerve-cells:**	it serves as a connecting neural link between the visual cells of layer 4, and the ganglion cells of layer 8
7. **Inner granular, molecular, plexiform,** or **reticular layer:**	it consists chiefly of processes from the cells of layer 6, coming into relation with those of layer 8
8. **Layer of ganglion cells:**	vesicular layer
9. **Fibrous layer,** or **layer of nerve fibers:**	it consists of the axis-cylinder processes of the ganglion cells, passing across the surface of the retina to collect and form the optic nerve
10. **Internal limiting membrane:**	it is derived from the supporting tissue of the retina and lies in contact with the vitreous.

[Layers 2 and 4 are grouped together as the **neuro-epithelial layer**; layers 5 to 9, as the **cerebral layer.**

Table XII

SENSORY ILLUSIONS

A. VISUAL

I. Geometrical (or geometric-optical) illusions
   a. reversible perspective; e.g. staircase
   b. extent
      1. variable; e.g. Müller-Lyer
      2. constant; e.g. vertical-horizontal
   c. direction
      1. variable; e.g. parallel lines (Zöllner, Wundt, Hering)
      2. constant; e.g. chess-board (Helmholtz)
   d. assimilative (associative); e.g. Müller-Lyer rectangles
   e. miscellaneous; e.g. Poggendorff
II. Physical distortions
   a. mirage
   b. *wetness* on pavements
   c. effects of mirrors, lenses, prisms, pseudoscopy, stereoscopy, teleostereoscopy, etc.
III. Physiological phenomena
   a. after-images
   b. contrast
   c. recurrent images
   . eidetic images
   e. hypnagogic images
   f. autokinetic images
IV. Movement; e.g. stroboscopic, moon and clouds, stationary and moving train, *trip to the moon.*
V. Distance; e.g. mountains on clear day vs. foggy conditions, sun or moon on horizon.

B. TACTUAL

I. Juxtaposition; e.g. Aristotle's illusion
II. Parallelism; e.g. lines across face, along arm, etc.
III. Movement; e.g. stroboscopic, objects crawling
IV. Temperature; e.g. Locke's cold and warm illusion

C. KINESTHETIC-VISUAL

E.g. size-weight; Stratton's reversal of visual field

D. AUDITORY-VISUAL

E.g. Young's binaural reversal

Table XIII

SPECTRAL LINES AND RANGE OF COLORS

Spectral Line	Wave Length mμ	No. of Vibrations (*trillion per second*)	Color Hue	Range mμ
A	759	395		
B	687	437	Red	760–647
C	656	457		
D	589	509	Orange	647–588
Primal Yellow	574	520	Yellow	588–550
E	527	569	Green	550–492
Primal Green	505	599		
F	486	617	Blue	492–433
Primal Blue	478	629		
G_1	432	695	Violet	433–390
H	397	756		

Visible Range: 760–390 mμ at ordinary intensities, 395–769 trillion.

Limits of Color Change: 655–430 mμ.

Primal Red does not appear in the spectrum, but is evoked by a mixture of lights from the extreme ends of the spectrum (red and blue).

Table XIV

STATISTICAL FORMULAE

USEFUL IN PSYCHOLOGY AND EDUCATION

Note: The use of certain symbols in the formulae marked with an asterisk (*) is indicated at the end of the table.

$$M = \frac{\Sigma X}{N}$$ Arithmetic mean calculated from raw scores — ungrouped data.

$$\sigma_M = \frac{\sigma}{\sqrt{N}}$$ Standard error of the mean.

$$*Mdn = l + i\left(\frac{\frac{N}{2} - F}{f_p}\right)$$ Median calculated from below up — grouped data.

$$\sigma = \sqrt{\frac{\Sigma x^2}{N}}$$ Standard deviation (root-mean-square error), dispersion, calculated from the mean — ungrouped data.

$$*\sigma = i\sqrt{\frac{\Sigma f(x')^2}{N} - c^2}$$ Standard deviation calculated from an arbitrary origin — grouped data.

$$\sigma_\sigma = \frac{\sigma}{\sqrt{2N}}$$ Standard error of the standard deviation.

$$*\sigma_p = \sqrt{\frac{pq}{N}}$$ Standard deviation of the proportion in one category of a Bernoullian distribution.

$$Q = \frac{Q_3 - Q_1}{2}$$ Quartile deviation computed from upper and lower quartiles (semi-interquartile range).

$$AD \text{ from } M = \frac{\Sigma|x|}{N}$$ Average deviation from the mean calculated from the mean — ungrouped data, mean deviation, mean error.

$\beta_1 = \frac{\mu_3^2}{\mu_2^3}$	One measure of skewness, a criterion of curve type.
$\beta_2 = \frac{\mu_4}{\mu_2^2}$	One measure of kurtosis, a criterion of curve type.
$Sk = \frac{3(M - Mdn)}{\sigma}$	One measure of skewness.
$y = \frac{N}{\sigma\sqrt{2\pi}} e^{\frac{-x^2}{2\sigma^2}}$	Normal probability curve (Gaussian error curve, curve of the normal law of error, normal curve, normal error curve, normal distribution curve, bell-shaped curve).
$y_0 = \frac{N}{\sigma\sqrt{2\pi}} = \frac{N}{2.5066\,\sigma}$	Maximum ordinate of the normal probability curve.
$V = 100\frac{\sigma}{M}$	A coefficient of variation (measure of relative dispersion, coefficient of variability).
$\sigma_{(x_1 - x_2)} = \sqrt{\sigma_1^2 + \sigma_2^2 - 2r_{12}\sigma_1\sigma_2}$	Standard deviation of the difference of two raw scores when they are correlated.
$\sigma_{(x_1 \pm x_2)} = \sqrt{\sigma_1^2 + \sigma_2^2}$	Standard deviation of the sum or difference of two raw scores when they are uncorrelated.
$r_{12} = \frac{\Sigma x_1 x_2}{N\sigma_1\sigma_2}$	Pearson product moment coefficient of correlation (product moment method, product moment coefficient of correlation, correlation coefficient, Pearsonian coefficient of correlation), calculated from the means.
$r_{12} = \frac{\Sigma x_1 x_2}{\sqrt{\Sigma x_1^2}\sqrt{\Sigma x_2^2}}$	Pearson product moment coefficient of correlation, calculated from the means.
$r_{12} = \frac{\frac{\Sigma x_1' x_2'}{N} - c_1 c_2}{\sigma_1\sigma_2}$	Pearson product moment coefficient of correlation, calculated from arbitrary origins.
$\sigma_{r_{12}} = \frac{1 - r_{12}^2}{\sqrt{N}}$	Standard error of the Pearson product moment coefficient of correlation.
$\bar{x}_1 = r_{12}\frac{\sigma_1}{\sigma_2}x_2$ $\bar{x}_2 = r_{12}\frac{\sigma_2}{\sigma_1}x_1$	Regression equation in terms of deviations from the means — two variables.
$\sigma_{1\cdot2} = \sigma_1\sqrt{1 - r_{12}^2}$ $\sigma_{2\cdot1} = \sigma_2\sqrt{1 - r_{12}^2}$	Standard error of estimate (partial σ, standard deviation of an array, standard deviation of errors of estimate) — two variables.
$*\rho = \frac{6\,\Sigma d^2}{N(N^2 - 1)}$	Rank correlation coefficient (rho, Spearman's method, method of rank correlation, method of rank differences, coefficient of correlation calculated from ranks).
$r_{\infty\omega} = \frac{r_{12}}{\sqrt{r_{1\mathrm{I}}}\sqrt{r_{2\mathrm{II}}}}$	Spearman's formula for correction for attenuation (estimated true correlation between 1 and 2, estimated correlation between perfect measures of 1 and 2).

$r_{AA} = \dfrac{A\, r_{11}}{1 + (A - 1) r_{11}}$	Spearman-Brown formula for correlation between A forms of a test and A other similar forms.
$r_{12\cdot 34\cdots n} = \dfrac{r_{12\cdot 345\cdots(n-1)} - r_{1n\cdot 345\cdots(n-1)} r_{2n\cdot 345\cdots(n-1)}}{\sqrt{1 - r^2_{1n\cdot 345\cdots(n-1)}}\,\sqrt{1 - r^2_{2n\cdot 345\cdots(n-1)}}}$	$(n-2)^{th}$ order partial correlation coefficient in terms of coefficients of lower order — n variables.
$r_{1\cdot 23} = \sqrt{\dfrac{r^2_{12} + r^2_{13} - 2\, r_{12} r_{13} r_{23}}{1 - r^2_{23}}}$	Multiple correlation coefficient in terms of zero order coefficients — three variables.
$\overline{X}_1 = b_{12\cdot 34\cdots n} X_2 + b_{13\cdot 2456\cdots n} X_3 + \ldots b_{1n\cdot 234\cdots(n-1)} X_n + C$	Regression equation in terms of raw scores — n variables.
$\dfrac{D}{\sigma_D}$	The reliability of the difference between two calculated quantities measured in terms of the standard error of the difference (critical ratio).

* The use of certain symbols in these formulae is as follows:

l... lower limit of the class in which the measure considered lies.
i... interval.
F... sum of frequencies of all classes below this class.
f_p... frequency of class in which the measure considered lies.
f... frequency in a class.
c... correction.... $M-M'$.
p... probability of success.
q... $1 - p$.
d... a difference in rank of an individual on two measures.

Table XV

SYMBOLS AND TECHNICAL ABBREVIATIONS

(For roman letters used as symbols see part F.)

A. MATHEMATICS

Symbol	Verbal Equivalent	Meaning (*or* Operation)
$+$	plus	addition
$-$	minus	subtraction
$\pm$	plus or minus	either add or subtract
$\times$	times	multiplication: $a \times b$; also $a \cdot b$, or ab
$\div$ /	divided by	division: $a \div b$, a/b; also $\frac{a}{b}$
$=$	equals	equality
$\neq$	is not equal to	inequality
$>$	is greater than	
$\not>$	is not greater than	
$\leqq$	is less than or (at most) equal to	
$<$	is less than	
$\not<$	is not less than	
$\geqq$	is more than or (at least) equal to	
$\equiv$	is identical with	identity
$\fallingdotseq$ $\div$	is approximately equal to	
$\perp$	perpendicular	
$\doteq$	approaches equality as a limit	
$\Leftrightarrow$	is equivalent to, in terms of some modulus. [See Note 1.]	
$\mid\ \mid$	absolute value of the quantity enclosed	e.g. $\lvert a \rvert$ signifies the quantity a regardless of algebraic sign

Symbol	Verbal Equivalent	Meaning (*or* Operation)
⌊ !	factorial	continued product of integers up to the number indicated: ⌊9 9!
$\sim$	tilde	varies in a fixed relation with the difference between
$\rightarrow$	arrow	(variable at left) approaches as limit (variable at right)
$\surd$	(square) root o	with superscript numeral: extract that root: $\sqrt[3]{x}=$ cube root; without superscript: square root
$\int$	integral of	integration, in calculus
Σ	sigma (large)	summation of (the expression which follows)
Π	pi (large)	the continued product of. [See Note 2.]
π	pi	ratio of circumference to diameter of circle: 3.141592+
∞	infinity	
δ	delta	a small variation (with or without a following symbol)
Δ	delta (large)	(alternative for δ). [Cf. C.]
ϕ, ψ, f, F	phi, psi, f, F	(commonly used to indicate a function)
—	bar (over a symbol)	the mean of: $\overline{X}$
( )	parentheses	subjects terms enclosed to the same operation
[ ]	brackets; sum of	subjects terms enclosed to the same operation
——	vinculum	brace uniting several algebraic terms to show that all are subject to the same operation

Note 1. — The modulus is the rule or principle which defines the relation.

Note 2. — With superscript and subscript Π indicates the limiting values which the variables in the function take: e.g. in $\prod_{1}^{4}(x+\frac{1}{x})$ the continued product is to include all possible values of x between 1 and 4: $(1+1/1)(2+1/2)(3+1/3)(4+1/4)$.

B. PHYSICS

σ	sigma	thousandth of a second. [Cf. C.]
μ	mu; micron	millionth of a meter, i.e. thousandth of a millimeter. [Cf. C.]
$m\mu$	millimicron	thousandth of a micron
μf	microfarad	millionth of a farad; unit of electrical capacity
$\mu\mu$	mu-mu; micromicron	millionth of a micron
$\sim$	cycle	a complete wave vibration
$^{\circ}$	degree(s)	e.g. $15^{\circ}=15$ degrees
$'$	minutes	e.g. $15'=15$ minutes (angular measure or time)
$''$	seconds	e.g. $15''=15$ seconds (angular measure or time)
λ	lambda	wave-length
Ω, ω	ohm	unit of electrical resistance

C. STATISTICS; PSYCHOPHYSICS

σ	sigma	standard deviation. [See Note 3.]
Σ	sigma (large)	the sum of. [See Note 4.]
Δ	delta (large)	in interpolation, denotes a finite difference. [See Note 5.]
γ	gamma	argument of normal distribution [of errors]
$\phi\gamma$	phi-function of gamma	values of the ordinate of the cumulative (ogive) form of the normal distribution

SYMBOL	VERBAL EQUIVALENT	MEANING (*or*) OPERATION
$\rightarrow$	arrow	(1) direction (forward) on a scale of measurement; (2) variable on left approaches as limit the one on right
∞, ω	infinity, omega	as subscript, indicates a true score
ρ	rho	the coefficient of correlation based upon squares of differences in rank
ϕ, ω, η	(phi, omega, eta)	and other symbols are used to designate various other kinds of correlation coefficients
β	beta	product-moment regression coefficient when standard scores are employed. [See Note 6.]
β_1	beta sub-one	Pearson's measure of skewness ($= \mu_3^2/\mu_2^3$)
β_2	beta sub-two	Pearson's measure of kurtosis ($= \mu_4/\mu_2^2$)
κ	kappa	Pearson's criterion of curve type
$\mu_1, \mu_2 \cdots \mu_n$	mu	the moments, first (= 0), second, (. . . n^{th}) of a distribution from the mean
χ^2	chi square	the square contingency (in tests of goodness of fit)
ϕ^2	phi square	mean square contingency

Note 3. — $\sigma_{1 \cdot 2}$ denotes the standard deviation measured from the regression line of the first variable for constant values of the second.

Note 4. — With no symbol above or below the Σ, $\Sigma\, x$ means that all possible values of x are summed. $\sum_{1}^{10} x$ indicates that the x's in the series, from x number one (or value 1) to x number ten (or value 10), are summed. $\Sigma\, xy$ indicates the sum of all the products of the x's and the corresponding y's. $\sum_{\substack{j=1\\i=1}}^{\substack{j=b\\i=a}} r_{ij}$ indicates the sum of all the r's, when i takes all values from 1 to a, and j all values from 1 to b, inclusive.

Note 5. — Δ also stands for a major determinant when written without subscript, and for minor determinants when written with subscripts; e.g. Δ_{12} represents the minor determinant obtained from the major by crossing out the first row and the second column.

Note 6. — The subscripts are of two sorts: b_{12} (or β_{12}), and $b_{12 \cdot 34}$ (or $\beta_{12 \cdot 34}$).

D. BIOLOGY

♂	male	used in describing a male specimen
♀	female	used in describing a female specimen
☿	hermaphrodite	used in describing a hermaphrodite

E. ELECTRICAL CIRCUIT DIAGRAMS

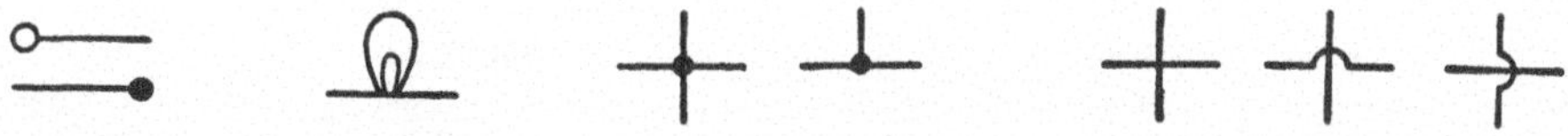

Terminal — Light — Wires, Joined — Wires, Crossed (not joined)

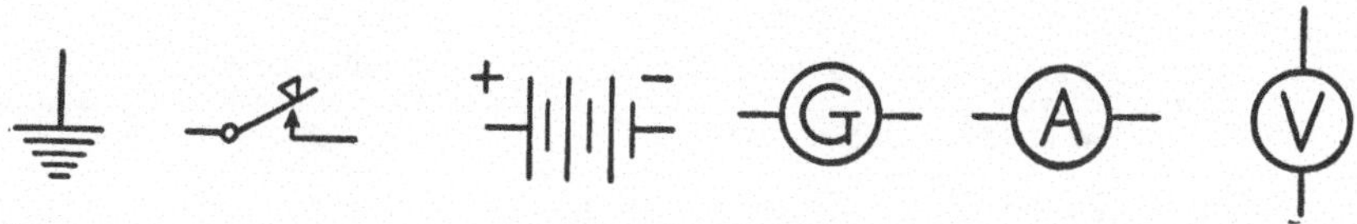

Ground — Key — Battery — Galvanometer — Ammeter — Volt meter

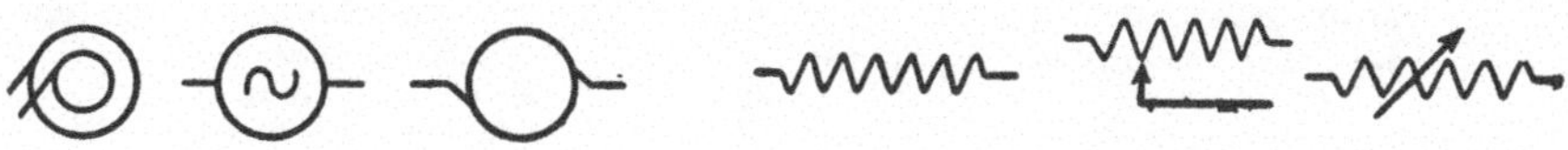

ac — dc — Fixed — Adjustable — Variable

Generators — Resistors

Fixed — Adjustable — Variable — Tapped

Inductors, Air Core

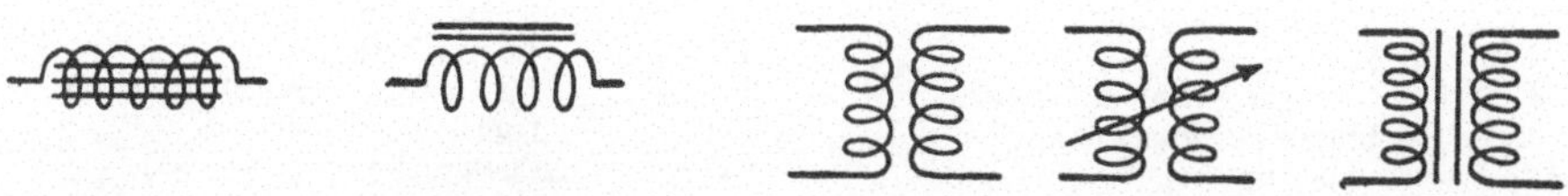

Iron-Core — Inductors — Transformers, Air and Iron Core

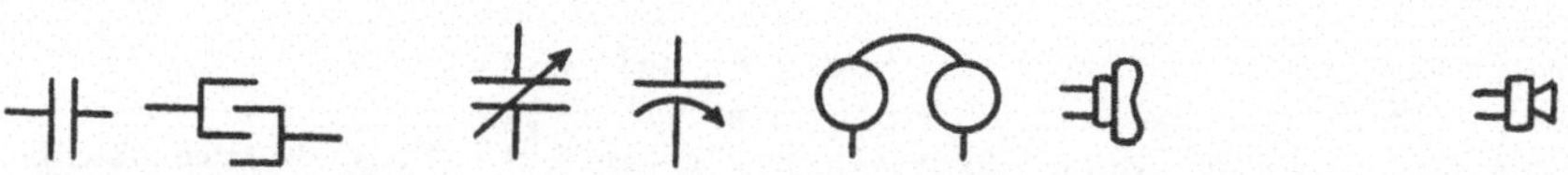

Fixed — Variable

Condensers — Receivers — Transmitter

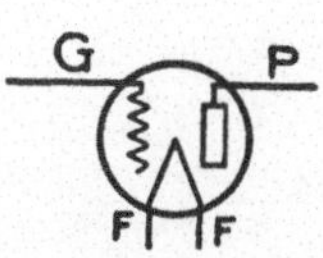

G = grid, or control electrode
F, F = filament, or cathode
P = plate, or anode

Three-Electrode Vacuum Tube

F. TECHNICAL ABBREVIATIONS

Abbreviation	Meaning
A.D.	average deviation
AQ	achievement (accomplishment) quotient
Å, ÅU	Angström unit (one ten-thousandth of a micron)
b	product-moment regression coefficient. [See Note 6.]
CA	chronological age
c.g.s.	centimeter-gram-second system
CI	central interval
d	differential of, differentiation (calculus)
x	difference or deviation, esp. from an average (statistics)
db	decibel
DL	difference limen
DS	difference sensation
D.V., d.v.	double vibration (cycles)
E	experimenter. [See Note 7.]
e	base of natural series or logarithms =2.71828183
f	frequency of a category or class-interval
F_1, F_2	(first, second) filial generations
F.T.U., F.U.	Freeman time unit
GSR	galvanic skin reflex
g	general factor
h	index of precision, value 0.4769/P.E. or $1/\sigma\sqrt{2}$
i	square root of minus 1
i	intensity
IQ	intelligence quotient
IU	interval of uncertainty; cf. CI
j.n.d.	just noticeable difference
k	a constant
k	a product-moment alienation coefficient. [See Note 8.]
L	limen or threshold
L_L	lower limen
l.p.d.	least perceptible difference
LS	liminal (or least) sensation
L_U	upper limen
M	the mean, or arithmetic average
MA	mental age
Mdn	the median
Mo	the mode
MS	modal sensation
ms	millisecond
N	the number of cases in the sample studied
n	(commonly) the number of variables involved
O	observer. [See Note 7.]
p	time error (Fechner)
p	practical intelligence
p	probability ratio
p	the proportion in the class in question. [See Note 9.]
P.E., p.e.	probable error
P.G.R.	psychogalvanic reflex
PSE	point of subjective equality; cf. PS
PS	point of symmetry
Q	coefficient of association (Yule)
Q	the semi-interquartile range or quartile deviation
q	the proportion not in the class in question. [See Note 9.]
q	space error (Fechner)
R	stimulus (Ger. *Reiz*)
r	product moment coefficient of correlation. [See Note 10.]
r_t	tetrachoric coefficient of correlation
R.D.	reaction of degeneration
RL	stimulus limen
S	errors of reference (Calles or Ferree)
S	limen or threshold (Urban); cf. L
S	sensation (as opposed to R, stimulus)
S	subject. [See Note 7.]
s	specific factor
S.D.	standard deviation
SU	sensation units
S.V., s.v.	single vibrations (half cycles)
t	time
TL	terminal limen
TR	terminal stimulus
TS	terminal (or greater) sensation
TU	transmission unit
v.d.	double vibrations (cycles)
v.s.	single vibrations (half cycles)
z	the ordinate in a unit normal distribution; with subscript, indicates a standard measure

Note 6. — The subscripts are of two sorts: b_{12} (or β 12), and $b_{12.34}$ (or β 12.34).

Note 7. — Pl. *Es*, *Os*, *Ss*; possessive *E*'s, etc., possessive pl. *Es*', etc.

Note 8. — *k* with any subscript is defined as equal to $[1 - r^2]^{1/2}$, the *r* having the same subscript as the *k*. The positive sign of the radical is necessary.

Note 9. — In other words, $p + q = 1$.

Note 10. — Sometimes (not with best warrant) *r* is used for other sorts of correlation coefficients. Subscripts are of three sorts: r_{12}, the total correlation; $r_{12.3\ldots n}$ the partial correlation; $r_{1.23}, r_{1.234}, \ldots_n$ the multiple correlation.

TABLES

TABLE XVI

TOPOGRAPHICAL REFERENCE TERMS

1. AXES OF REFERENCE

cephalocaudal	head-tail (syn. in man: vertical; in sessile animals: apicobasal)
dorsoventral	back-belly (syn. in man: anterior-posterior)
dextrosinistral	right-left (syn. lateral)

2. PLANES OF REFERENCE

transverse	at right angles to cephalocaudal axis (syn. in man: horizontal)
frontal	at right angles to dorsoventral axis
mesial, medial	at right angles to dextrosinistral axis, dividing body into halves
sagittal	any plane parallel to the mesial
coronal	any plane in head at right angles to cephalocaudal axis

3. GENERAL LOCATIONS AND DIRECTIONS

PERTAINING TO	LOCATION IN (*adj.*)	DIRECTION (*adv.*)	CONTRASTED WITH
aboral	end opp. mouth (protozoa)	....	oral
anterior	front	....	posterior
appendicular	the appendages of body	....	axial
axial	the frame of body	....	appendicular
caudal	tail	caudad = tailward	cephalic, cephalad
central	center	centrad = toward center	peripheral, peripherad
cephalic	head	cephalad = toward head	caudal, caudad
coronal	top of head	coronad = toward top of head	....
dextral	right side	dextrad = to the right	sinistral, sinistrad
distal	farther from point of origin	distad = away from point of origin	proximal, proximad
dorsal	back	dorsad = toward back	ventral, ventrad
exterior	outside	....	interior
external	outer (applied to walls of cavities, one of a pair of bodies, etc.)	....	internal
frontal	forehead	....	....
horizontal	parallel to horizon	....	....
interior	inside	....	exterior
internal	inner (applied to walls of cavities, one of a pair of bodies, etc.)	....	external
lateral	side	laterad = toward side	vertical [horizontal]
mesial			
medial			
meson	neither right nor left	....	....
occipital	back of head	....	....
oral	mouth end (protozoa)	....	aboral
peripheral	outer surface or boundary	peripherad = toward outside	central, centrad
proximal	nearer to point of origin	proximad = toward point of origin	distal, distad
sinistral	left side	sinistrad = to the left	dextral, dextrad
transverse	across the body	....	....
ventral	belly	ventrad = toward the belly	dorsal, dorsad
vertical	up-and-down	....	horizontal [lateral]

TABLES

Table XVII

TOPOGRAPHICAL TERMS RELATING TO THE HUMAN BODY

A. Head and Neck	Pertaining to; Located in
auricular	ear
buccal	cheeks at either side of mouth
ciliary	eyelashes
facial	face
hyoid	upper part of front of throat
labial	lips
mastoid	just behind ears
mental	chin
nasal	nose
nuchal	nape of neck
occipital	back of head
oral	mouth
orbital	eye-socket
palpebral	eyelid
parietal	sides of head at top
peristomial	around mouth
sternocleidomastoid	sides of throat in front
submaxillary	jaw-bone
submental	below chin at sides
supraorbital	above eye
temporal	temples above ears
thyroid, thyreoid	lowest part of throat in front
zygomatic	over cheek bones

B. Trunk	
aboral	end furthest from mouth
anal	anus
caudal	tail
dorsal	back
epigastric	stomach
hypochondriac	right and left of epigastric region
inguinal	groins
infraclavicular	below collar-bones on either side
inframammary	below nipples on either side
infrascapular	below shoulder-blades
intercostal	between ribs
interscapular	between shoulder-blades
lumbar	back, above buttocks
mammary	breasts
mesogastric	middle of abdomen
pectoral	chest
perineal	surrounding openings of excretory and reproductive organs
pubic	above perineal region
pudendal	sex organs, external
scapular	shoulder-blades either side
sternal	above breast bone
subinguinal	front of leg below groin
subscapular or **infrascapular**	below shoulder-blades
supraclavicular	above collar-bone
suprascapular	above shoulder-blades
umbilical	navel
ventral	abdominal

C. Limbs	Pertaining to; Located in
acromial	tip of shoulder
antibrachial	inner surface of forearm
axillary	armpits
brachial	inner surface of upper arm
calcaneal	heel
carpal	wrist
coxal	tip of thigh
crural	lower legs
cubital	inside of elbow
deltoid	upper arm, over shoulder joint
digital	fingers and toes
femoral	thigh
gluteal	buttock
malleolar	ankle
olecranal	tip of elbow
patellar	knee
plantar	sole
popliteal	rear knee
radial	side of forearm near thumb
retromalleolar	behind ankle
sural	back of calf
trochanteric	side portion of hips, below coxal regions
ulnar	forearm, same side as little finger
ungual	finger and toe nails
volar	palm and palmar surface of forearm

D. Deep and Visceral Regions	
abdominal	abdomen
adrenal	kidneys, usually referring to glands
alveolar	gums
bronchial	tubes connecting lungs to windpipe
caecal	middle part of large intestine
cardiac	heart
cephalic	head
colonic	large intestine
cortical	surface of brain and glands
duodenal	upper intestines, opening from stomach
endocardiac	in heart
esophageal, oesophageal	tube connecting mouth and stomach
gastric	stomach
glossal	tongue
guttural	in throat
hepatic	liver
intestinal	intestines
jugular	throat
lacrimal, lachrymal	tear glands and ducts
laryngeal	larynx, containing vocal cords
maxillary	jaws

D. Deep and Visceral Regions	Pertaining to; Located in
meningeal	meninges, membranes wrapping brain
mesenteric	intestinal fold
ophthalmic	eye
ovarian	ovaries
pericardial	around the heart
peritoneal	peritoneum, membrane wrapping intestines
pharyngeal	mouth cavity near beginning of esophagus
pleural	in lungs
pulmonary	lungs
pyloric	opening from stomach to duodenum
rectal	rectum
renal	kidneys
retroperitoneal	behind the peritoneum
splenic	spleen
sublingual	under the tongue
suprarenal	above the kidneys
testicular	testicles, testes
thoracic	chest
tonsillar	tonsils
tracheal	windpipe
tympanic	ear drum
uretal	tubes connecting kidneys with bladder
urethral	canal through which urine is discharged from the bladder
urogenital	organs of urine secretion and excretion and organs of reproduction
vaginal	vagina
uterine	womb, uterus
vesical	bladder
visceral	internal organs

E. Skeletal Regions	
appendicular	bones of limbs
articular	joints
axial	skull and spine
carpal	wrist bones
coccygeal	prolongation at lower end of spine
costal	ribs
cranial	skull
ethmoidal	behind nose
fibular	fibia bone in leg
humeral	bone from shoulder to elbow
iliac	ilium
metacarpal	bones of body of hand
metatarsal	bones of front part of foot
pelvic	pelvis
sacral	base of spine
sphenoidal	base of skull
tarsal	bones of rear part of foot
tibial	shin-bone
vertebral	bones of spine

Table XVIII

TOPOGRAPHY OF THE HUMAN CENTRAL NERVOUS SYSTEM

I. FOREBRAIN

A. STRUCTURES AND LOCALITIES

angular gyrus	small area behind upper end of temporal (parallel) fissure of cerebral hemisphere
anterior central gyrus	ascending frontal (or precentral) gyrus
Broca's gyrus	posterior third of inferior frontal gyrus in the hemisphere on the side opposite to the more usable hand; regarded by Broca as the cortical emissive speech center
callosal gyrus	cingulate gyrus (or gyrus fornicatus)
central lobe	island of Reil
central sulcus	fissure of Rolando between precentral and postcentral gyri
cingulate gyrus	gyrus on mesial surface of cerebral hemisphere above and parallel to edge of corpus callosum
claustrum	thin layer of grey matter in white matter between lentiform nucleus and island of Reil
collateral eminence	elongated swelling lying along lateral side of hippocampus major in lateral ventricle, under and corresponding to collateral fissure
corpus albicantia	mammillary bodies
corpus striatum	portion of forebrain lying in front of thalamus and, like it, under cerebral hemispheres; so called because the mingling of white fibers with grey matter gives it a striped appearance
cuneus	triangular lobe on mesial surface of cerebral hemisphere (at extreme back of brain) behind parieto-occipital and above calcarine fissure

dentate gyrus	narrow corrugated band of receptive cortex running downward and forward above hippocampal gyrus, separated from it by hippocampal fissure
epithalamus	region including habenular nuclei, pineal body, and habenular commissure
fascia dentata hippocampi	dentate gyrus
frontal gyrus/ascending	parallel to and in front of fissure of Rolando
frontal gyrus/inferior	lying just below middle frontal gyrus
frontal gyrus/middle	nearly horizontal gyrus lying just below superior frontal gyrus
frontal gyrus/superior	running along top of frontal lobe and occupying space on both outer and medial (or mesial) surfaces of cerebral hemisphere
frontal lobe	large lobe of cerebral hemisphere in front of central (or Rolandic) fissure and above the Sylvian fissure
frontal pole	front end of cerebral hemisphere
fusiform gyrus	gyrus on mesial surface of cerebral hemisphere near bottom between collateral fissure and inferior temporal gyrus
geniculate body/external	lateral geniculate body
geniculate body/internal	medial geniculate body
geniculate body/lateral	swelling on rear end of thalamus toward outer (left or right) side
geniculate body/medial	swelling on rear end of thalamus between lateral geniculate and pulvinar bodies
genu of corpus callosum	front bent portion of corpus callosum
genu of internal capsule	curve of internal capsule, passing in front of lentiform nucleus and projecting into lateral ventricle between caudate nucleus and toward thalamus
globus pallidus major	middle segment of lentiform nucleus
globus pallidus minor	inner (mesial) segment of lentiform nucleus
hippocampal gyrus	gyrus on mesial surface of cerebral hemisphere, below and behind callosum
hippocampus major	curved eminence extending the length of floor of inferior horn of lateral ventricle
hypophysis cerebri	pituitary body
hypothalamus	region including mammillary bodies, tuber cinereum, infundibulum, hypophysis, pre-optic region, and optic chiasm
infundibulum	stalk by which pituitary body is attached to tuber cinereum arising from the forebrain under cerebral hemispheres
insula	island of Reil
isthmus	constriction between pons and midbrain
isthmus (gyri fornicati)	small region on inner surface of cerebral hemisphere at rear end of hippocampal gyrus, between calcarine fissure and corpus callosum
interpeduncular fossa	triangular area between the crura cerebri with its apex at the dorsal border of the pons and its base at the level of the corpora mammillaria
limbic lobe	cingulate and hippocampal gyri
lingual gyrus	tongue-shaped gyrus on inner surface of cerebral hemisphere, at rear, below calcarine fissure and above collateral fissure
mammillary bodies, corpora mammillaria	two small round bodies in floor of third ventricle, between the cerebral peduncles and behind tuber cinereum
marginal gyrus	superior frontal gyrus
massa intermedia	band of gray matter connecting the lateral walls of third ventricle
metathalamus	geniculate bodies, posterior nucleus of the thalamus and posterior commissure
occipital gyrus/inferior	lower end of the two horizontal gyri on lateral surface of occipital lobe of cerebral hemisphere
occipital gyrus/superior	upper of the two horizontal gyri composing lateral surface of occipital lobe of cerebral hemisphere
occipital lobe	lobe of cerebral hemisphere in extreme rear
occipital pole	extreme rear end of cerebral hemisphere
occipitotemporal gyrus	fusiform gyrus
olfactory bulb	oval mass, front end of olfactory tract, lying under frontal lobe, and receiving olfactory nerves from nasal cavity
olfactory lobe	region under frontal lobe, including olfactory bulb, tracts, and trigone, parolfactory area, and anterior perforated substance to which the olfactory peduncle is attached
olfactory trigone	small triangular area in front of anterior perforated substance
opercula	edges of convolutions which surround fissure of Sylvius and conceal island of Reil

orbital gyrus	any one of the four gyri, anterior, lateral, medial, and posterior orbital, on the bottom surface of frontal lobe of cerebral hemisphere
orbital surface of cerebral hemispheres	lower surface
parietal gyrus/ascending	gyrus lying directly behind the fissure of Rolando, continued from central gyrus
parietal gyrus/posterior	area of cerebral hemisphere lying just above and behind the angular gyrus and intraparietal sulcus
parietal gyrus/superior	superior parietal lobule, along top of cerebral hemisphere, back of the central sulcus, above horizontal portion of intraparietal fissure
parietal lobe	lobe of cerebral hemisphere behind fissure of Rolando and in front of parieto-occipital fissure, extending down to level of fissure of Sylvius, thus occupying roughly the upper half of the region of the hemisphere behind the sulcus centralis; consists of precuneus, superior and inferior parietal gyri or lobules
parolfactory area	small triangular area on mesial surface of cerebral hemisphere in front of subcallosal gyrus, continuous below with olfactory trigone and above and in front with cingulate gyrus
pars basilaris	small area on outer surface of cerebral hemisphere, just back of pars triangularis and above fissure of Sylvius
pars orbitalis	small lobe of cerebral hemisphere on outer surface, extending down from inferior frontal gyrus above front end of fissure of Sylvius
pars triangularis	small lobe of cerebral hemisphere lying between pars orbitalis front and pars basilaris behind, above fissure of Sylvius
perforated substance/anterior	area in front of the optic tract and behind the olfactory trigone perforated with blood vessels; surface of olfactory tubercle
pituitary body	small body, largely glandular, connected with hypothalamus under cerebral hemispheres and projecting forward toward olfactory tracts
posterior central (or **postcentral**) **gyrus**	ascending parietal (or frontal) gyrus
precentral gyrus	ascending frontal gyrus
precuneus	quadrate lobe
prosencephalon	forebrain
psalterium	lyre-shaped layer of fibers connecting rear parts of the fornix lying on either side of medial (or mesial) line; contains hippocampal commissure
pulvinar body	swelling on rear end of thalamus toward lateral side
putamen	outer (side) portion of lentiform nucleus striatum
quadrate lobe	region on inner surface of cerebral hemisphere, toward rear, between parieto-occipital fissure and mesial end of central sulcus
Reil/island of	region lying at the bottom of fissure of Sylvius and covered by portions of temporal, frontal, and parietal lobes; it covers the corpus striatum
rhinencephalon	olfactory lobes, hippocampi, and structures surrounding corpus callosum on mesial surface of cerebral hemisphere; olfactory brain
rostrum	thin, pointed, backward curved end of genu of corpus callosum
septum pellucidum	semi-transparent membrane continuous with and below corpus callosum toward rear between callosum and fornices, separating the two lateral ventricles of cerebral hemispheres
splenium	rear end of corpus callosum
stratum zonale	layer of white substance on upper surface of thalamus
subcallosal gyrus	narrow region on mesial surface of cerebral hemisphere, behind parolfactory area and below rostrum of corpus callosum; continuous with diagonal band of Broca
subcallosal fasciculus	longitudinal bundle of fibers between caudate nucleus and callosum
subfrontal gyrus	inferior frontal gyrus
substantia innominata (Meynert)	layer of gray and white substance below front part of thalamus and lentiform nucleus, lying in relation to optic tracts
subthalamic tegmental region (or **subthalamus**)	continuation of tegmentum of the midbrain upward between thalamus and internal capsule
supracallosal gyrus	thin layer on upper surface of corpus callosum extending out from the side of cingulate gyrus
supramarginal gyrus	gyrus encircling rear end of fissure of Sylvius
telencephalon	cerebral hemispheres, pre-optic regions of hypothalamus, and front portion of third ventricle

temporal gyrus/inferior	gyrus on outer surface of cerebral hemisphere at lowest part of side of head, under middle temporal gyrus
temporal gyrus/middle	gyrus at lower part of side of head between superior and inferior temporal gyri and parallel to them
temporal gyrus/superior; parallel gyrus	gyrus just below and parallel to fissure of Sylvius
temporal gyri, transverse	short gyri starting at bottom of fissure of Sylvius and running obliquely forward and outward on rear part of upper surface of superior temporal gyrus
temporal pole	front end of temporal lobe of cerebral hemisphere
temporal lobe	lobe forming lowest side portion of cerebral hemisphere, bounded above in its anterior portion by fissure of Sylvius
thalamus	portion of brain stem lying on either side of third ventricle, under cerebral hemispheres, in front of corpora quadrigemina; consists of metathalamus, dorsal thalamus, subthalamus, hypothalamus, and epithalamus
trigonum collaterale	triangular area in floor of lateral ventricle between posterior and inferior horns
trigonum habenulae	small triangular depressed area in front of superior colliculus
trigonum/olfactory	*see* olfactory trigone
tuber cinereum	conical swelling on the hypothalamus, under cerebral hemispheres, from which infundibulum arises
uncus	small hook-like region on inner surface of cerebral hemisphere at front end of hippocampal gyrus

B. FISSURES AND CAVITIES

calcarine fissure	fissure on mesial surface of cerebral hemisphere running forward from extreme rear, below cuneus, to join parieto-occipital fissure
callosal fissure	fissure on mesial surface of cerebral hemisphere separating top of corpus callosum from cingulate gyrus
callosomarginal fissure	fissure on mesial surface of cerebral hemisphere running from front near bottom successively forward, upward, and backward, forming upper boundary of cingulate gyrus and ending at top of hemisphere back of middle point
central sulcus	fissure of Rolando
cingulate sulcus	callosomarginal fissure
circular fissure	surrounding island of Reil
collateral fissure	on mesial surface of cerebral hemisphere at lower part of extreme rear, under gyrus lingualis and hippocampal gyrus
cornu, cornua*pl*	horn (of lateral ventricle)
dentate fissure	short horizontal fissure on mesial surface of cerebral hemisphere above hippocampal gyrus
fimbriodentate fissure	separating dentate gyrus from fimbria of hippocampus
frontal sulcus/medial	fissure dividing middle frontal convolution into upper and lower portions
foramen of Monro	opening through which lateral ventricles communicate with third ventricle and each other, interventricular foramen
hippocampal fissure	on mesial surface of cerebral hemisphere starting behind rear end (splenium) of corpus callosum and running forward between hippocampal and dentate gyri to end in uncus
horn of lateral ventricle/anterior	portion entering frontal lobe
horn of lateral ventricle/descending	inferior horn
horn of lateral ventricle/inferior	largest portion of ventricle, entering temporal lobe
horn of lateral ventricle/posterior	portion entering occipital lobe
interpeduncular fossa	depression bounded in front by corpora mammillaria, behind by pons, and at sides by optic tracts and cerebral peduncles
interventricular foramen	foramen of Monro
intraparietal fissure	on outer surface of cerebral hemisphere, composed of postcentral sulcus, occipital ramus, and transverse occipital sulcus
lateral cerebral fissure	fissure of Sylvius; in reality a fossa
longitudinal cerebral fissure	deep cleft separating cerebral hemispheres
Monro/sulcus of	fissure from foramen of Monro to cerebral aqueduct, in side walls of the third ventricle
occipital fissure/lateral	short horizontal fissure on exterior surface of cerebral hemisphere at extreme rear and near the bottom

occipital fissure/transverse	short horizontal fissure at extreme rear of cerebral hemisphere, running around from outer to mesial surface, continuous and at right angles with intraparietal
occipital ramus	fissure branching horizontally backward from postcentral fissure to occipital lobe
occipitotemporal fissure	on bottom surface of cerebral hemisphere extending from occipital to temporal regions
orbital sulcus	an H-shaped fissure on the bottom surface of a frontal lobe of the cerebral hemisphere, dividing the four orbital gyri from one another
parallel fissure	superior temporal fissure
paramesial sulcus	interrupted fissure on mesial surface dividing superior frontal gyrus into an upper and a lower portion
parieto-occipital fissure/horizontal	at extreme rear of cerebral hemisphere outer surface above level of transverse occipital fissure, extending on mesial surface of hemisphere as internal parieto-occipital fissure and joining calcarine fissure; these fissures forming two boundaries of cuneus
parieto-occipital fissure/internal	fissure on mesial surface of cerebral hemisphere continuous with external parieto-occipital fissure, running downward and forward to join calcarine fissure
postcentral sulcus	fissure just back of the posterior central gyrus, parallel to the fissure of Rolando
Rolando/fissure of (**central sulcus**)	deep fissure extending on outer surface of cerebral hemisphere from top of head just back of middle, downward and forward to a point near middle of fissure of Sylvius
Sylvius/fissure of	deep nearly horizontal cleft in cerebral hemisphere, separating frontal and parietal lobes from temporal lobe
temporal fissure/inferior	middle fissure on under (inferior) surface of cerebral hemisphere, traversing the temporal lobe from near the occipital pole to near the temporal pole
temporal fissure/middle	horizontal fissure on exterior surface of cerebral hemisphere below and parallel to superior temporal fissure and dividing middle from inferior temporal gyrus
temporal fissure/superior	two oblique fissures below and parallel to fissure of Sylvius
ventricle/fifth	space between two layers of septum lucidum, the partition separating the two lateral ventricles; not communicating with any other ventricle
ventricle/lateral	cavity in each cerebral hemisphere, continuous with cavities in thalamus, midbrain, hindbrain, and spinal cord
ventricle/third	vertical median slit in hinder portion of forebrain, between right and left thalami, communicating behind through aqueduct with fourth ventricle and in front with lateral ventricles, one in each cerebral hemisphere

C. NUCLEI

caudate nucleus	inner pair of the two large nuclei of corpus striatum, lying against front of thalamus and projecting into lateral ventricles
claustrum	layer of nerve cells on lateral surface of external capsule
corpus subthalamicum	nucleus of nerve cells on dorsal side of base of cerebral peduncle
interpeduncular ganglion	nerve centers in extreme caudal end of interpeduncular fossa
lateral nucleus	area of nerve centers in outer side of thalamus
lenticular nucleus	lentiform nucleus
lentiform nucleus	outer pair of two large nuclei of corpus striatum, surrounded by white matter of cerebral hemisphere, covered by claustrum and insula
nucleus amygdalae	ovoid mass of nerve cells at lower end of roof of inferior horn of lateral ventricle in pyriform lobe
nucleus of posterior commissure	nerve cells at upper end of cerebral aqueduct dorsad to oculomotor nucleus; posterior nucleus of thalamus

D. NERVE TRACTS

ansa lenticularis	strand of white fibers in substantia innominata, connecting corpus striatum with subthalamus and tegmental region
anterior stalk (or **peduncle**)	nerve fibers from thalamus through frontal part of internal capsule to frontal lobe

capsula extrema	layer of nerve fibers separating claustrum from cortex of island of Reil
capsule/external	layer of white substance on lateral side of lentiform nucleus between it and claustrum, continuous with internal capsule below and behind lentiform nucleus
capsule/internal	band of white fibers separating inner portion of lentiform nucleus from caudate nucleus in front and thalamus in rear
cerebrospinal fibers	fibers in internal capsule, running from motor region of cortex through pyramids of medulla to spinal cord
cingulum	bundle of association fibers contained within cingulate gyrus
commissure/middle	band (nerve tissue) connecting the two thalami
commissure of Gudden	fibers connecting medial (or mesial) geniculate bodies and lying in rear part of optic commissure
commissure/optic	optic chiasm
commissure/posterior	band of nerve fibers connecting posterior nuclei of thalamus with interstitial nuclei and lying over upper (anterior) end of aqueduct
corona radiata	fibers of internal capsule radiating to and from cerebral cortex
corpus callosum	great band of fibers connecting the two cerebral hemispheres
corticopontine fibers	nerve fibers connecting cortex with pons
fasciculus retroflexus	fibers connecting the trigonum habenulae with the interpeduncular ganglion
fimbria hippocampi	white fibers from crura of fornix forming a narrow band in hippocampal region, prolonged into uncus
forceps/anterior	fibers of corpus callosum curving forward from the genu into the frontal lobe
forceps/posterior	fibers of corpus callosum curving backward into occipital lobe
fornix	bundle of fibers below corpus callosum connecting hippocampus with mammillary bodies and habenula
fornix/columns of	bands of white fibers forming front portion of fornix, passing down in front of foramen of Monro and behind anterior commissure through lateral wall of third ventricle to mammillary bodies
fornix/crura of	flat bands of white fibers forming rear portion of fornix, curving round rear end of thalamus, and passing downward and forward into hippocampal region in inferior horn of lateral ventricle
geniculate fibers	fibers in genu of internal capsule, running from motor region of cortex to motor nuclei of cranial nerves on opposite side
habenular commissure	nerve fibers connecting nuclei in one trigonum habenulae with that on opposite side
hippocampal commissure	fibers connecting right hippocampus with left
longitudinal fasciculus/inferior	association fibers connecting temporal and occipital lobes, along lateral walls of inferior and posterior horns of lateral ventricle
longitudinal fasciculus/superior	long association fibers connecting frontal lobe with occipital and temporal lobes, passing above lentiform nucleus and island of Reil
lyra	hippocampal commissure
occipitofrontal fasciculus	association fibers connecting frontal lobe with occipital and temporal lobes, passing along lateral border of caudate nucleus and mesial side of corona radiata
optic chiasma	band of fibers at junction of floor and front wall of third ventricle, in which fibers from the nasal halves of the retinas cross to opposite optic tract, while those from temporal halves continue into that on the same side
optic commissure	optic chiasm
optic radiations	fibers passing from lateral geniculate body, pulvinar, and superior colliculus through occipital part of internal capsule to cortex of occipital lobe
optic tracts	fibers passing from optic chiasm to lateral geniculate body, pulvinar, and superior colliculus
perpendicular fasciculus	association fibers running vertically through front part of occipital lobe, connecting inferior parietal lobule with fusiform gyrus
stalk/inferior	fibers from under and medial surface of thalamus, passing under lentiform nucleus to temporal lobe and insula
stalk/parietal	fibers from lateral nucleus of thalamus to parietal lobe
stalk/posterior	nerve fibers from pulvinar through occipital part of internal capsule to occipital lobe; optic radiations; radiations of Gratiolet
stria terminalis	white fibers lying between caudate nucleus and thalamus, connecting nucleus amygdalae with pre-optic region (tuber cinereum)

tapetum	fibers of corpus callosum extending sidewards into temporal lobe, covering central part of lateral ventricle
thalamomammillary fasciculus	fibers from mammillary bodies to thalamus; bundle of Vicq d'Azyr
uncinate fasciculus	association fibers connecting frontal lobe with front end of temporal lobe, passing across front end of lateral fissure

II. MIDBRAIN

A. STRUCTURES AND LOCALITIES

brachium/inferior	white band extending from side of inferior colliculus, passing forward and upward under medial geniculate body
brachium/superior	white band extending from side of superior colliculus, passing forward and upward between pulvinar and medial geniculate body, arising partly in lateral geniculate body and partly in optic tract, and occipital cortex
colliculi/superior and inferior	the four corpora quadrigemina
corpora quadrigemina	four rounded prominences constituting dorsal part of midbrain, above and in front of superior peduncle, below and behind third ventricle and posterior commissure
crura cerebri	cerebral peduncles
crusta	base of cerebral peduncle; basis pedunculi
cerebral peduncles	lower portion of midbrain, consisting of two cylindrical masses emerging from upper surface of pons and passing into cerebral hemispheres
pineal body	cone-shaped body, largely glandular, projecting backward from habenular region over corpora quadrigemina
posterior perforated substance	layer of gray substance in interpeduncular fossa containing habenulopeduncular tracts and mammillary peduncle, perforated by blood vessels
stratum cinereum	layer of nerve cells and fibers in superior colliculus just under stratum zonale
stratum lemnisci	layer of fibers and nerve cells in superior colliculus immediately under stratum opticum, the fibers derived partly from stratum opticum and partly from mesial lemniscus
stratum opticum	layer of large nerve cells and fibers in superior colliculus just under stratum cinereum
stratum zonale	outer layer of white fibers, mostly from optic tract, in superior colliculus
substantia nigra	pigmented layer of gray substance separating dorsal and ventral portions of cerebral peduncle, containing many nerve cells, extending from upper surface of pons to subthalamic region
tegmentum	dorsal portion of cerebral peduncle

B. FISSURES AND CAVITIES

aqueduct (of Sylvius)	narrow prolongation of third ventricle under corpora quadrigemina, leading to fourth ventricle
interpeduncular fossa	depression between crura cerebri
lateral sulcus	longitudinal furrow on lateral surface of cerebral peduncle
oculomotor sulcus	longitudinal furrow along median surface of cerebral peduncle, from which roots of oculomotor nerve emerge
ventricle/third	space in thalamus under pineal gland, over hypophysis and mammillary body, and between the right and left lobes of thalamus; continuous with aqueduct in rear and lateral ventricles of cerebral hemispheres forward by the foramen of Monro at each side

C. NUCLEI

interpeduncular ganglion	nerve cells in interpeduncular fossa at level of inferior quadrigemina
oculomotor nucleus	nerve cells extending under superior colliculus and into gray substance of third ventricle, giving origin to oculomotor nerve
red nucleus	nerve cells in front part of tegmentum, extending up to posterior part of subthalamic region, giving origin to rubrospinal tract

trigeminal nucleus	nerve cells extending alongside of pons and oblongata
trochlear nerve nucleus	nerve cells in ventral part of gray matter surrounding aqueduct, giving origin to trochlear nerve

D. NERVE TRACTS

cerebrospinal fibers	fibers from motor area of cerebral cortex, passing through middle region of cerebral peduncle
fillet	lemniscus
frontopontine fibers	fibers from frontal lobe of cortex to nuclei of pons, passing through medial (or mesial) region of cerebral peduncle
lemniscus/lateral	afferent fibers starting in terminal cochlear and superior olivary, passing to inferior colliculus; some are prolonged through lateral geniculate body of thalamus and occipital part of internal capsule to middle and superior temporal gyri of cerebral cortex
lemniscus/medial (or **mesial**)	afferent nerve tracts starting in gracile and cuneate nuclei, crossing at sensory decussation, ascending in interolivary tract through medulla; occupying in pons the ventral part of reticular formation and tegmentum and further up dorso-lateral part of tegmentum between red nucleus and substantia nigra; mostly in the ventral lateral sensory nuclei of thalamus; upward continuation of posterior funiculus of spinal cord
medial (or **mesial**) **longitudinal fasciculus**	fibers in midbrain and oblongata lying on ventral side of aqueduct, below nuclei of oculomotor and trochlear nerves; continued below by anterior and lateral proper fasciculi of spinal cord
rubrospinal tract	efferent nerve tracts starting in red nucleus and passing down in lateral funiculus of spinal cord ventral to crossed pyramidal tract
tectospinal tract	efferent nerve tracts starting in superior colliculus, crossing and descending in tegmentum, mingling with those of median longitudinal bundle and vestibulospinal tract in spinal cord
temporopontine fibers	fibers from temporal lobe of cortex to nuclei of pons, passing along side of cerebrospinal fibers through crusta

III. HINDBRAIN: CEREBELLUM

A. STRUCTURES AND LOCALITIES

anterior medullary velum	thin layer of white substance between superior cerebellar peduncles
cerebellum	largest portion of hindbrain and of brain with the exception of cerebral hemispheres; situate in lower part of back of skull
clivus	rear part of monticulus
culmen	front part of monticulus
epencephalon	generic term, syn. for hindbrain
flocculus	part of cerebellar hemisphere furthest forward on under side, lying on either side of nodule of vermis
folium vermis	short band at rear end of vermis, connecting superior semilunar lobules of cerebral hemispheres
hemispheres/cerebellar	expanded portions of cerebellum at either side
lingula	front end of superior vermis lying on anterior medullary velum
lobes/crescentic, anterior, and **posterior**	lobes forming upper portion of cerebellum
lobe/semilunar	superior semilunar lobule and folium vermis taken together
lobules/biventral	lobes on under surface of cerebellum between tonsillar and inferior semilunar lobule
lobules/quadrangular, anterior, and **posterior**	largest lobules of upper surface of cerebellum
lobule/superior semilunar	lobules forming rear third of upper surface of cerebellar hemisphere
lobulus centralis	region in vermis just back of lingula
lobus noduli	region on under side of cerebellum including flocculi, posterior medullary velum, and nodule of vermis
lobus pyramidis	region on under side of cerebellum including pyramid and biventral lobules
monticulus	largest part of vermis, back of lobulus centralis and in front of folium vermis
nodule, nodulus	front end of inferior vermis, close to roof of fourth ventricle

peduncles/inferior cerebellar	fiber bands connecting cerebellum with back of medulla and spinal cord, restiform body
peduncles/middle cerebellar	band connecting pons with cerebellum, brachium pontis
peduncles/superior cerebellar	band connecting cerebellum with red nuclei and subthalamic region
posterior medullary velum	thin layer of white substance on either side of nodule of vermis; roof of fourth ventricle
pyramid, pyramis	conical projection on inferior vermis
restiform bodies	inferior cerebellar peduncles
tonsilla cerebelli	part of under side of cerebellar hemisphere on either side of uvula of vermis
tuber vermis	rear end of inferior vermis
uvula	largest portion of inferior vermis, behind nodule
vermis	median portion of cerebellum, between cerebellar hemispheres
vermis/inferior	part of vermis on under surface of cerebellum

B. FISSURES AND CAVITIES

aperture/medial (or **mesial**)	opening in middle of roof of fourth ventricle through posterior medullary velum, foramen of Magendie
apertures/lateral	openings in roof of fourth ventricle at either side of medial aperture, foramina of Luschka
cerebellar notch/anterior	notch separating cerebellar hemispheres in front
cerebellar notch/posterior	notch separating cerebellar hemispheres in rear
horizontal sulcus	fissure across back of cerebellum dividing it into an upper and a lower portion
postcentral fissure	fissure in cerebellum between monticulus and lobus centralis
postnodular fissure	fissure across inferior vermis separating nodule from vermis
postpyramidal fissure	fissure across inferior vermis, separating pyramid from tuber vermis, continuing between tonsil and biventral, lobes of cerebellar hemispheres, along side border of inferior semilunar lobule
preclival fissure	fissure running across upper surface of cerebellar hemispheres, separating anterior from posterior quadrangular lobules, and crossing monticulus into culmen and clivus
prepyramidal fissure	fissure across inferior vermis, separating uvula from pyramid, curving forward between tonsil and biventral lobule, and joining postnodular fissure
sulcus valleculae	groove separating inferior vermis from cerebellar hemisphere on under surface
vallecula cerebelli	deep median groove on under surface of cerebellum, in which medulla rests

C. NUCLEI

dentate nucleus	large group of nerve cells in interior of lateral lobes
nucleus emboliformis	group of nerve cells medial to dentate nucleus toward the median line
nucleus fastigii	group of nerve cells at front end of superior vermis and over the roof of the fourth ventricle
nucleus globosus	elongated group of nerve cells beside nucleus emboliformis toward the median line

D. NERVE TRACTS

arcuate fibers	association fibers, connecting medulla with cerebellum
direct cerebellar tract	dorsal spinocerebellar fasciculus, Flechsig's tract
peduncles/inferior cerebellar	fibers from various regions of medulla, pons, and spinal cord; restiform body
peduncles/middle cerebellar	afferent fibers from cells of nuclei pontis to cerebellar cortex
peduncles/superior cerebellar	fibers from cells of dentate nucleus, passing under corpora quadrigemina, crossing to opposite side under aqueduct: the efferent fibers go to red nucleus and subthalamus
spinocerebellar tract/dorsal	afferent fibers from spinal cord passing through inferior peduncle to upper vermis
spinocerebellar tract/ventral	afferent fibers from spinal cord over superior peduncle to lower vermis

IV. HINDBRAIN: MEDULLA AND PONS

A. STRUCTURES AND LOCALITIES

ala cinerea	small area in floor of rhomboid of fossa just lateral to trigonum hypoglossi, over sensory nuclei of vagus and glossopharyngeal nerves
anterior columns	continuation of anterior columns of spinal cord
area acustica	swelling in rhomboid fossa at side, vestibular area containing vestibular nuclei
bulb	medulla oblongata
clava	swelling on fasciculus gracilis containing nucleus gracilis
calamus scriptorius	angle on floor of fourth ventricle where columns of Goll diverge at lower end of rhomboid fossa
cuneate tubercle	swelling on fasciculus cuneatus containing nucleus cuneatus
decussation of pyramids	oblique crossing of cerebrospinal or corticospinal fibers from each side of medulla to the other, over anterior median fissure
decussation/sensory	region in medulla where fibers from nucleus gracilis and nucleus cuneatus on each side cross and interlace with those from opposite side
eminentia acustica	large prominences on floor of fourth ventricle over nucleus of abducens nerve
eminentia teres	prominence on floor of fourth ventricle over nucleus of abducens nerve
formatio reticularis	network of fibers and nerve cells in central regions of medulla oblongata
inferior cerebellar peduncles	restiform bodies
medulla oblongata	thickened floor or anterior part of hindbrain, directly continuous with upper portion of spinal cord containing centers for lower seven cranial nerves
middle cerebellar peduncle	fibers from pons Varolii to cerebellar cortex; syn. brachium pontis
olives, olivary bodies/superior	elevated regions on upper end of medulla oblongata, lying one on either side of pyramids
pons, pons Varolii	portion of hindbrain directly in front of cerebellum, its ventral part consisting of transverse fibers arching across medulla, or middle cerebellar peduncle, its dorsal part enclosing upper part of rhomboid fossa and continuing the reticular formation of the medulla
posterior columns	continuation of posterior columns of spinal cord, i.e., fasciculus gracilis and fasciculus cuneatus
pyramids	elevated regions on front of medulla lying one on either side of anterior median fissure, formed by cerebrospinal tracts
restiform bodies	rope-like elevations behind olives on rear surface of medulla, passing upwards and outwards to cerebellum: inferior peduncles
taeniae of fourth ventricle	bands of white matter crossing the auditory eminence of fourth ventricle; lines of attachment of choroid plexus and posterior medullary velum
trigonum hypoglossi	elevation on floor of fourth ventricle over nucleus of hypoglossal nerve
trigonum vagi	elevation on the floor of fourth ventricle over nuclei of vagus and glossopharyngeal nerves

B. FISSURES AND CAVITIES

dorsal intermediate fissures	fissures on rear surface of medulla parallel to and on either side of fasciculus gracilis
dorsal median fissure	fissure running along the length of spinal cord on its rear part ending at obex, or calamus scriptorius
dorso-lateral fissures	fissures on front of medulla parallel to antero-lateral fissures but further toward the sides
foramen cecum	enlargement of anterior median fissure of medulla at lower border of pons
median fissure of rhomboid fossa	longitudinal fissure dividing fossa into right and left halves
rhomboid fossa	floor of fourth ventricle (so called from its shape)
sulcus limitans	fissure parallel to and on either side of median sulcus of rhomboid fossa

ventral median fissure	running along length of spinal cord and medulla in front
ventricle/fourth	cavity between cerebellum and pons and upper half of medulla; continuous below with central canal of medulla and spinal cord and above with aqueduct and third ventricle
ventro-lateral fissures	fissures on front of medulla on either side of and parallel to pyramids

C. NUCLEI

abducens nerve nucleus	nerve cells in floor of fourth ventricle, giving origin to abducens nerve
cochlear nucleus/lateral	nucleus on dorsal side of inferior cerebellar peduncle, ventral or accessory, on ventral lateral side of inferior peduncle
cuneate tubercle	swelling on fasciculus cuneatus on posterior surface of medulla, containing nucleus cuneatus
Deiters/nucleus of	lateral vestibular nucleus
dorsal motor nucleus of vagus	nerve centers lying parallel to hypoglossal nucleus toward the back and side and extending from lowest part of medulla to level of olive; its fibers belong to sympathetic part of vagus
facial nerve nucleus	nerve cells in reticular formation of pons, on back of the superior olivary nucleus; origin of facial nerve
gracile tubercle	nucleus of gray matter on column of Goll on posterior surface of medulla
hypoglossal nucleus	nerve centers lying on under side of central canal in lower part of medulla; in upper part ending near rhomboid fossa in middle line; origin of hypoglossal nerve
inferior central nucleus	small nucleus near inferior olivary nucleus, in formatio reticularis
lateral nucleus, nucleus lateralis	cell groups in lateral side of oblongata below inferior olives, giving origin to latero-cerebellar fibers (external arcuate)
medial (or **mesial**) **nucleus, cuneatus**	larger part of nucleus cuneatus
nucleus ambiguus	nerve centers on front surface of medulla extending from sensory decussation to upper end of medulla; origin of accessory nerve and motor fibers in vagus and glossopharyngeal nerves
nucleus arcuatus	nerve cells in anterior external arcuate fibers over pyramid, continued forward in nucleus pontis
nucleus cuneatus	nerve centers on fasciculus cuneatus on rear of medulla
nucleus gracilis	nerve centers on fasciculus gracilis on rear of medulla; origin of mesial lemniscus
nucleus intercalatus	nerve cells at side of hypoglossal nucleus
nuclei pontis	nerve centers of pons; origin of middle cerebellar peduncles
olivary nuclei/inferior	nerve centers within olive; medial accessory, between inferior olivary nuclei and pyramid; dorsal accessory, behind inferior olivary nuclei; superior, on dorsal surface of side of trapezoid body
tractus solitarius/nucleus of	long slender nucleus running length of medulla, parallel in upper portion to and on outer side of dorsal motor nucleus
trapezoid nucleus	nerve cells in trapezoid body
trigeminal nerve nucleus (**motor**)	nerve cells in upper part of pons near rear surface and along lateral margin of medulla oblongata; end of trigeminal nerve
tubercles of Rolando	sensory nuclei in medulla above sensory decussation
vestibular nucleus/lateral	nerve cells in lateral angle of rhomboid fossa
vestibular nucleus/mesial	nerve cells in mesial part of acoustic (vestibular) area
vestibular nucleus/superior	nerve cells in upper part of area acustica (vestibularis) in rhomboid fossa

D. NERVE TRACTS

arcuate fibers/anterior external	afferent fibers near surface of pyramid and olive, from reticular formation, crossing to opposite side on external surface and entering cerebellum through inferior peduncle
arcuate fibers/internal	fibers from gracile and cuneate nuclei forming larger part of mesial lemniscus
arcuate fibers/posterior external	afferent fibers from nucleus lateralis and probably cuneate nuclei passing into inferior peduncle on same side
cerebrospinal fasciculi (or **tracts**)/ **anterior and lateral**	efferent tracts originating in motor area of cortex and passing downward through internal capsule, cerebral peduncle, and pons,

crossing to opposite side in pyramidal decussation to descend and end in entire length of cord

fasciculus cuneatus — tract of afferent nerve fibers on rear of medulla lying parallel to and further toward the side than fasciculus gracilis; separated from it by posterior intermediate fissure; ending in nucleus cuneatus

fasciculus gracilis — tract of afferent nerve fibers on rear of medulla along the side of posterior median fissure, ending in nucleus gracilis

fillet — band of afferent fibers arising in cuneate and gracilis nuclei, running up in medulla just behind pyramidal tracts and crossing in sensory decussation

lemniscus — fillet

medial (or **mesial**) **longitudinal fasciculus** — longitudinal fibers near floor of fourth ventricle on each side of median fissure

olivocerebellar fibers — afferent fibers from inferior olivary nuclei, passing around and through opposite olives and entering cerebellum by inferior peduncle

proper fasciculi — fibers in formatio reticularis and medial longitudinal fasciculus

spinocerebellar tract/dorsal — afferent tracts from spinal cord passing to vermis through inferior peduncle; some through lemniscus and superior peduncle

spinocerebellar tract/ventral — afferent fibers from spinal cord near level of inferior colliculus, reaching vermis

spinotectal tract — fibers from dorsal horn of spinal cord, joining portion of mesial lemniscus, passing to tectum or superior colliculus of midbrain

spinothalamic tract/lateral — sensory tracts through formatio reticularis to ventro-lateral region of thalamus

striae medullares (**acusticae**) — secondary acoustic fibers from dorsal cochlear nucleus crossing inferior peduncles near their entrance into cerebellum, and leading to median sulcus of rhomboid fossa

superficial antero-lateral fasciculus — ventral spinocerebellar, lateral spinothalamic, spinotectal, and ventral spinothalamic fasciculi

trapezoid body — strand of transverse fibers in lower part of pons, arising from cells of cochlear nucleus; beginning and decussation of lateral lemniscus

V. CRANIAL NERVES

abducens nerve (VI) — sixth cranial nerve efferent to external rectus eye muscles, leaving brain from furrow between lower border of pons and upper end of pyramid of medulla

accessory nerve/cranial (XI) — portion of eleventh cranial nerve, efferent to pharyngeal, leaving side of medulla below vagus nerve

accessory nerve/spinal (XI) — portion of eleventh cranial nerve; spinal portion supplies sternomastoid and trapezius muscle, accessory portion joins vagus and enters into formation of pharyngeal plexus

auditory nerve (VIII) — eighth cranial nerve, afferent from cochlea and labyrinth, entering medulla in floor of fourth ventricle under middle cerebellar peduncle just below facial nerve

facial nerve (VII) — seventh cranial nerve, efferent to facial muscles and afferent from taste organs, leaving brain at lower border of pons between olive and inferior cerebellar peduncle

glossopharyngeal nerve (IX) — ninth cranial nerve, afferent from back of tongue and throat, entering brain in groove between olive and inferior cerebellar peduncle just below auditory nerve

hypoglossal nerve (XII) — twelfth cranial nerve, efferent to tongue, leaving brain from anterolateral sulcus between pyramid and olive, below cranial accessory nerve

oculomotor nerve (III) — third cranial nerve, efferent to accommodation, internal rectus, superior rectus, inferior rectus, and inferior oblique muscles of the eye; leaving brain from oculomotor sulcus on medial (or mesial) side of cerebral peduncle

olfactory nerve (I) — first, i.e., most anterior, cranial nerve, afferent from smell sense organ, entering brain through under surface of olfactory bulb

optic nerve (II) — second cranial nerve, afferent from retina, entering brain through optic chiasm and optic tracts

patheticus nerve (IV) — syn. for trochlear nerve

pneumogastric nerve (X) — syn. for vagus nerve

trigeminal nerve (V)	fifth cranial nerve, mostly afferent from face, entering brain near upper border of side of pons
trochlear nerve (IV)	fourth cranial nerve, efferent to superior oblique eye muscles, leaving brain from anterior medullary velum just behind inferior colliculus
vagus nerve (X)	tenth cranial nerve, efferent and afferent fibers to pharynx, larynx, windpipe, lungs, esophagus, stomach, pancreas, upper part of intestine, and heart; attached to brain in groove between olive and inferior cerebellar peduncle immediately behind glossopharyngeal nerve; it has afferent and two efferent components

VI. SPINAL CORD

A. STRUCTURES AND LOCALITIES

cervical enlargement	enlargement of spinal cord at level of arms, where nerves to arms are given off
conus medullaris	conical lower extremity of spinal cord
crossed commissural fibers	axons crossing to opposite side of cord through anterior commissure
dorsal gray columns	dorsal columns of gray matter in spinal cord; syn. dorsal horns
dorsal funiculus	portion of spinal cord lying between posterior median fissure and dorsolateral fissure, fasciculus gracilis, and cuneatus
dorsal gray commissure	gray substance in cord mainly behind central canal
dorsal horns	dorsal enlargement of the column of gray matter in the spinal cord
dorsal nerve root	afferent nerve fibers of each spinal nerve, entering cord in posterior column
dorsomedial column	column of nerve cells in anterior column behind anteromedial column
filum terminale	filament of pia mater passing down from conus medullaris and attached to first segment of the coccyx
formatio reticularis	network of gray substance in the lateral funiculus between anterior and posterior gray columns
lateral column	side projection from anterior column in thoracic region of spinal cord, containing spinal sympathetic nucleus
lateral cornu or horn	lateral column
lateral funiculus	part of anterolateral region nearest the posterolateral sulcus; the anterior and lateral funiculi are separated by the line of exit of the anterior spinal nerve roots
Lissauer/tract of	thin layer of white substance separating dorsal column from dorsolateral fissure; fine myelinated and non-myelinated fibers from dorsal nerve roots
lumbar enlargement	enlargement of spinal cord at lower level of cord where nerves to legs are given off
root zone	lateral part of posterior column formed by entering posterior nerve roots
substantia gelatinosa centralis	neuroglia around central canal
substantia gelatinosa of Rolando	neuroglia and small nerve cells around dorsal margin of the dorsal horn
ventral gray columns	front enlargements, on either side of the anterior median fissure, of the column of gray matter of which the gray commissure is the central portion
ventral cornu or horn	anterior gray column
ventral funiculus	part of anterolateral funiculi region nearest anterior median fissure
ventral gray commissure	gray substance in cord directly in front of central canal
ventral nerve root	region where efferent nerve fibers of each spinal nerve leave cord from anterior gray column
ventrolateral region	portion of spinal cord lying in front of posterolateral sulcus
ventromedial column	column of nerve cells in medial (or mesial) part of anterior column

B. FISSURES AND CAVITIES

canal of spinal cord/central	very slender canal running inside the cord for its whole length
dorsal median fissure	shallow and narrow groove along middle of back of spinal cord
dorso-intermediate sulcus	longitudinal furrow in cervical and upper thoracic regions of posterior funiculus, marking position of a septum dividing fasciculus gracilis from fasciculus cuneatus

dorsolateral sulcus	furrow on either side of dorsal column, along which posterior nerve roots are attached
terminal ventricle	dilated portion of central canal in lower part of conus medullaris
ventral median fissure	groove along middle of front of spinal cord

C. NUCLEI

cervical nucleus	nerve cells in spinal cord opposite third cervical nerve
Clarke/column of	dorsal nucleus
dorsal nucleus	nerve cells in base of dorsal column of spinal cord, running from levels of second or third lumbar to last cervical or first thoracic nerve; origin of dorsal spinocerebellar tract
sacral nucleus	nerve cells in middle and lower part of sacral region of spinal cord
spinal ganglion	oval swelling, one on posterial root of each spinal nerve, containing nerve cells

D. NERVE TRACTS

Burdach/columns (or tracts) of	spinobulbar tracts lying between columns of Goll and dorsal cerebellar tracts; fasciculus cuneatus
direct cerebellar tract	dorsal spinocerebellar fasciculus
fasciculus cuneatus	portion of dorsal funiculus lying between fasciculus gracilis and posterior column of gray matter; its longest columns end in nucleus cuneatus of medulla
fasciculus gracilis	portion of dorsal funiculus lying nearest dorsal median septum; its fibers end in nucleus gracilis of medulla
Goll/columns (or tracts) of	spinobulbar tracts on either side of dorsal median fissure in spinal cord; fasciculis gracilis
Gowers/tract of	superficial anterolateral fasciculus; ventral spinocerebellar tract
lateral cerebrospinal tract	tract of efferent fibers extending the whole length of lateral funiculus of spinal cord, inside of spinocerebellar fasciculi; originating in cortical motor area, crossing to opposite side in medulla, and ending in anterior gray column of cord. (Voluntary motor impulses)
lateral fasciculus proprius	innermost side tracts of afferent fibers in spinal cord
Lissauer/fasciculus of	tract of small afferent fibers lateral to entrance of posterior nerve roots
olivospinal fasciculus	tract of fibers passing beside inferior olivary nucleus in medulla and found in cervical region of spinal cord
posterior proper fasciculus	tract of intersegmental fibers lying behind posterior gray columns
prepyramidal tract	syn. for rubrospinal tract
pyramidal tracts	the principal cerebrospinal tracts
pyramidal tracts/crossed	lateral cerebrospinal fasciculus, lying at either side toward rear of cord between ventral horns and dorsal spinocerebellar tracts
pyramidal tracts/direct	lying on either side of the anterior median fissure
reticulospinal tracts	fibers from tegmental region and reticular nuclei in midbrain, pons, and medulla to spinal cord
rubrospinal tract	tract of efferent fibers on ventral side of lateral cerebrospinal fasciculus, originating in red nucleus of midbrain and ending in anterior column of cord. (Cerebellar striatal reflexes)
spinobulbar tracts	columns of Goll and Burdach, leading to gracile and cuneate tubercles on medulla
spinocerebellar tract/dorsal	tract of afferent fibers at extreme outside of lateral funiculus
spinocerebellar tract/ventral	tract of afferent fibers running in front of dorsal spinocerebellar fasciculus from level of third lumbar nerve to cerebellum
spinotectal tract	tract of afferent fibers in front of lateral spinothalamic fasciculus, ending in corpora quadrigemina
spinothalamic tract/lateral	tract of afferent fibers on inner side of ventral spinocerebellar fasciculus, running to ventrolateral region of thalamus
spinothalamic tracts	(afferent) nerve-tracts on front of spinal cord leading to thalamus
spinothalamic tract/ventral	tract of afferent fibers in marginal part of anterior funiculus of spinal cord, probably ending in thalamus (cutaneous sensibility)
superficial anterolateral fasciculus	tract of afferent fibers including ventral spinocerebellar, lateral spinothalamic, spinotectal, and ventral spinothalamic
tectospinal fasciculus, tectospinal tracts	efferent nerve-tracts at sides of spinal cord toward front, leading from superior corpora quadrigemina into cord

ventral cerebrospinal fasciculus	tract of efferent nerve fibers from motor area of cerebral hemispheres crossing to opposite side in medulla and ending in anterior column of spinal cord
ventral proper fasciculus	tract of fibers surrounding gray matter beginning and ending within cord
vestibulospinal tracts/direct	efferent fibers chiefly from cells of lateral vestibular nucleus in rhomboid fossa, passing down through marginal part of anterior funiculus of the spinal cord and ending among motor cells of anterior column
vestibulospinal tracts/crossed	efferent nerve-tracts at sides of spinal cord toward front, leading from nuclei of vestibular nerve into cord

TECHNICAL DICTIONARIES AND VOCABULARIES

A. PSYCHOLOGICAL DICTIONARIES, GLOSSARIES, ETC. — ENGLISH LANGUAGE

A.P.A. Committee: Definitions and Delimitations of Psychological Terms. — Psychol. Bull., 1918, 15, No. 3; 1922, 19, No. 4; 1925, 22, No. 6. [79 fundamental terms.]

[Anon.] Word List of Psychological Terms. — Child Study, 1928 (Oct.), pp. 18, 20. [53 terms; mental testing, psychoanalysis.]

Baldwin, J. M. (ed.): Dictionary of Philosophy and Psychology. — New York: Macmillan, 1901. [2 vols. of text, 2 vols. of bibliography. Complete and authoritative at that date. About 2600 of the terms were included in our lists.]

Baldwin, J. M.: Report on Terminology. — VIme Congrès International de Psychologie; Genève, Kundig, 1909, 480–481.

Dunlap, K.: Results of a Questionary on Psychological Terminology. — J. Hopkins Circ., No. 285, 1916 (May). [Discussion of fundamental terms; consciousness, experience, sensation, etc.]

English, H. B.: A Student's Dictionary of Psychological Terms (4th ed.). — New York, Harpers, 1934. [Over 2000 terms.]

Goodenough, F., and Anderson, J. E.: Experimental Child Study. — New York: Century Co., 1931. [Glossary of Child Study.]

Hutchings, R. H.: A Psychiatric Word Book: a lexicon of terms employed in psychiatry and psychoanalysis. — Utica, N.Y., The State Hospitals Press, 1930, pp. 162.

Kitson, H. D.: Definitions in Industrial Psychology, Person, J., 1933, 12, 164–165.

Robbins, S. D., and Stinchfield, S. M.: A Dictionary of Terms dealing with Disorders of Speech. —Amer. Soc. for Study of Disorders of Speech, 1931. [400 terms.]

Warren, H. C. and Carmichael, L.: Elements of Human Psychology (rev. ed.). — Houghton Mifflin, 1930. [Subject Index includes numerous definitions.]

B. PSYCHOLOGICAL AND PHILOSOPHICAL DICTIONARIES — FOREIGN LANGUAGES

Birnbaum, K.: Handwörterbuch der medizinischen Psychologie. — Leipzig: Thieme, 1930. [672 pp.]

Claparède, E.: L'unification et la fixation de la terminologie psychologique. — VIme Congrès International de Psychologie; Genève, Kundig, 1909, 467–479.

Commission linguistique pour l'unification du vocabulaire psychanalytique français. — Rev. franç. de Psychanalyse, 1927, 1, 403–408, 582–583. [German-French equivalents for 44 terms.]

Coriat, I. H. [Abstract of above.] — Psychol. Abstracts, 1928, 2, titles 949, 2475. [Includes English equivalents for these terms.]

Duncker, K., and Watt, D. B.: German-English Dictionary of Psychological Terms. — Ann Arbor (Mich.): Edwards Bros., 1930. [About 7000 terms.]

Eisler, R.: Handwörterbuch der Philosophie (2nd ed.). — Berlin: Mittler, 1922. [About 4500 terms.]

Freud, S.: Handwörterbuch f. Sexualwissenschaft, Bonn, 1923. Reprinted in Gesammelte Schriften, 1928, Bd. XI, pp. 201–223. [40 psychoanalytical terms defined at length.]

Giese, F.: Psychologisches Wörterbuch. — Leipzig: Teubner, 1920. [About 2000 terms, including personal names; 60 cuts.]

Goblot, E.: Le vocabulaire philosophique. — Paris: Alcan, 1901. [About 1500 terms.]

Hamilton, J. A.: Englisch-Deutsch für Psychologen. — Frankfurt: Gaul and Bartelmann, 1931. [2000 terms.]

Jones, E. (ed.): Glossary for the Use of Translators of Psycho-Analytical Terms. — Internat. J. Psychoanal., Suppl. No. 1, 1924. [443 terms.]

Lalande, A. (ed.): Vocabulaire technique et critique de la philosophie (rev. ed.) — Paris: Alcan, 1928. [2 vols. Long articles on numerous terms. Appendix with lists of German, English, and Italian terms giving their French equivalents.]

Ruckmick, C. A.: German-English Dictionary of Psychological Terms. — Iowa City: Athens Press, 1928. [About 1300 terms.]

Titchener, E. B.: A Psychophysical Vocabulary. — Amer. J. Psychol., 1895–96, 7, 78–85. [290 German terms.]

Webel, A.: A German-English Technical and Scientific Dictionary. — New York: Dutton, 1930. [35,000 terms.]

Wundt, W.: Outline of Psychology. Eng. trans. by C. H. Judd (3d ed.). — Leipzig, Engelmann, 1907, pp. 392. [With Ger.-Eng. Glossary of about 225 terms.]

Ziegler, H. E.: Zoologisches Wörterbuch (3rd ed.). — Jena: Fischer, 1927. [786 pp.]

[Anon.] Unification du vocabulaire psychotechnique. — Année Psychol., 1931, 32, 931–933. [19 terms, mostly statistical.]

C. DICTIONARIES OF COGNATE BRANCHES

Acoustics. — Frederick, H. A. (ed.): Report of Committee on Acoustical Standardization. — J. of Acoust. Soc. of America, 1931, 2, 311–324. [160 terms.]

Art. — The Federal Council on Art Education. Report of the Committee on Terminology. Boston, Berkeley Press, 1929, pp. 79.

Bacteriology. — Partridge, W.: Dictionary of Bacteriological Equivalents (Ger.-Eng.; Fr.-Eng.; Ital.-Eng.; Sp.-Eng.). — Baltimore, Williams and Wilkins.

Biology. — Artschwager, E.: Dictionary of Biological Equivalents (Ger.-Eng.). — Baltimore, Williams and Wilkins, 1930.

— Henderson, E. F., and W. D.: A Dictionary of Scientific Terms: in Biology [etc.]. — Edinburgh: Oliver and Boyd, 1920. [About 9500 terms.]

Chemistry. — Hackh, I. W. D.: A Chemical Dictionary. — Phila.: Blakiston, 1929. [About 24,000 terms.]

— Patterson, A. M.: A German-English Dictionary for Chemists. — New York: Wiley.

— Turner, F. M. (ed.): Condensed Chemical Dictionary (rev. ed.). — New York: Chemical Catalogue Co., 1930. [About 12,000 terms.]

Education. — Bollinger, E. W.: A Contemporary Study of Professional Terms in Industrial Arts and Vocational Education. — Master's Thesis, Columbus, Ohio State Univ. Library, 1931, pp. 141.

— Odell, C. W.: A Glossary of 300 Terms Used in Educational Measurement. — Urbana, Univ. of Illinois Bulletin, 1928.

Electricity. — Report on Proposed American Standard Definitions of Electrical Terms. — New York, Amer. Institute of Electrical Engineers, no date. [About 3000 terms.]

— Manly, H. P. (ed.): Drake's Cyclopedia of Radio and Electrotonics. — Chicago, Drake and Co., 1932.

Illumination and Photometry. — American Engineering Standards Committee: Illuminating Engineering Nomenclature and Photometric Standards. — New York, Illuminating Engineering Society, 1925.

Medicine. — Comrie, J. D. (ed.): Black's Medical Dictionary (10th ed.). — London: Black, 1931. [998 pp.]

— Dorland, W. A. N.: The American Illustrated Medical Dictionary (16th ed.). — Phila.: Saunders, 1932. [About 100,000 terms.]

— Meyers, M. K. (ed.): Lang's German-English Dictionary (of terms used in medicine and the allied sciences) (4th ed.). — Phila.: Blakiston, 1932.

— Robinson, Wm. J.: Medical and Sex Dictionary. — New York: The Eugenics Publishing Co., 1933 (?). [187 pp.]

— Scott, R. J. E. (ed.): Gould's Medical Dictionary (3rd ed.). — Phila.: Blakiston, 1931. [1538 pp.]

Mental Hygiene. — Bumke, O. (ed.): Handwörterbuch der psychischen Hygiene u. psychiatrischen Fürsorge. — Berlin: De Gruyter, 1931. [400 pp.]

Music. — Grove's Dictionary of Music and Musicians. — New York: Macmillan, 1927. [5 vols. Amer. Suppl. 1928, 1 vol.]

Optics (Colorimetry). — Troland, L. T. (ed.): Report of the Colorimetry Committee. — J. of Optical Soc. of America, 1922, 6, 527–596.

Physics. — Glazebrook, R.: Dictionary of Applied Physics. — Macmillan, 1922. [5 vols.]

Social Science. — Seligman, E. R. C., and Johnson, A.: Encyclopaedia of the Social Sciences. (A-Ser, 13 vols.) — New York, Macmillan, 1930 et seq.

GLOSSARY OF FRENCH TERMS

Note: Where there are given in the body of the Dictionary two or more definitions of any one of the following English equivalents, the figure in parentheses after the equivalent indicates which of these dictionary definitions applies to the foreign word.

A

abaissement de soi-même, self-abasement.

abattement, grief.

abcès cérébral, abscess of the brain.

aberration de la lumière, aberration of light.

aberration de sphéricité, spherical aberration, s. error.

abréaction, abreaction.

abréviation de réaction, abridgment of response.

absorption, self-absorption.

accent caractéristique de l'écriture, writing accent.

accès de colère, tantrum.

accès épileptiforme, epileptiform seizure.

accomplissement, performance.

accord, chord (1).

accord à trois sons, triad.

accord consonant, concord.

accorder, tune[v].

accouplement, pairing.

accoutumance, habituation.

acide, sour.

acquisition associative, associative learning.

acquisition du tout et des parties, whole and part learning.

acquisition, learning (3, mental).

acquisition/finale, acquisition initiale, attainment/final, /initial.

acquisition mentale, ideational learning.

acte de téter, suckling (1).

acte malheureux, unsuccessful act.

actinie, sea-anemone.

action globale, mass action.

action réussie, successful act.

activité, speeding up.

activité propre, self-activity.

adaptation à l'obscurité, dark adaptation, darkness adaptation.

adaptation d'apprentissage, adaptation in learning.

adaptation lumineuse, bright adaptation.

adoration, worship (1).

affaiblissement, deterioration.

affect, affect.

affection, attachment (2), feeling (1).

affirmer, posit.

affirmation de soi, self-assertion.

âge critique, climacteric, climacterium.

âge de procréation, child-bearing age.

âge de rendement, achievement age.

agent, reagent (3).

agir, act[v], behave.

agitation, restlessness.

agrandissement, growth (2).

agrément, agreeableness.

agressivité, aggressiveness.

aigu, acute, sharp (2).

aimant, liking.

aimer, like[v].

air, tune[n].

aire, area.

aire analgésique de la joue, (Kiesow's) painless cheek-area.

aire de Broca, Broca/area of.

aire motrice, motor area.

aire olfactive, olfactory area.

aires sensorielles, sensory areas.

ajustement, set.

ajustement mental, mental set.

ajustement préparatoire, preparatory set.

alcoolisme aigu, alcoholism/acute.

aliénation mentale, insanity.

alignement, array.

aliment, nutriment.

allaitement, suckling (2).

alogique, unreasoning.

ambiance, environment.

âme, soul (1).

amer, bitter.

amitié, friendship.

amortissement, damping.

amour, love.

amour de soi, self-love.

amour platonique, platonic friendship.

ampèremètre, ammeter.

amusical, unmusical.

amygdale, tonsil.

analyze, resolution (3).

analyze de la profession, job analysis.

anesthésie en gant, anesthetic glove.

anglaise, script.

angoisse, anxiety.

antagonisme des champs visuels, retinal rivalry.

anthropoïdes, apes.

anticorps, antibody.

antipathie, dislike.

anxiété, anxiety.

appareil, apparatus.

appareil de von Frey pour mesurer le seuil de pression, von Frey limen gauge.

appareil mental, apparatus/mental,

appareil pour mesurer le seuil, limen gauge.

appareil pour mesurer la stabilité motrice, steadiness apparatus.

appareil sensoriel accessoire, accessory sense-apparatus.

appareil terminal, end-organ.

apparence, appearance.

appât, reward.

appétence, urge.

appréciation, judgment (2), rating[n].

appréciations (estimations) personnelles, self-rating.

apprendre par cœur, memorize.

apprentissage, learning (1, 2, motor).

apprentissage (acquisition) global (fractionné), whole and part learning.

apprentissage (acquisition) infraliminaire, subliminal learning.

apprentissage (acquisition) massé, massed learning.

apprentissage mental, ideational learning.

apprentissage moteur, motor learning.

apprentissage (acquisition) occasionnel, incidental learning.

apprivoisement, taming.

appropriation, propriety.

approprié[a], propriety.

apte[a], fit.

arrêt, inhibition, blocking (1).

arrêter, check[v] (1).

arrièration, backwardness.

arrièration mentale, retardation/mental.

arrière-cerveau, hind-brain.

arriéré simple, moron.

ascendant, ascendence, ascendance.
asensorial, non-sensory.
asile, asylum.
asocial, non-social, unsocial.
assentiment, consent.
association dirigée, controlled association.
association héréditaire, linkage.
association libre, free association.
associations rétrogrades (à rebours), backward associations.
assoupissement, drowsiness.
astérie, starfish.
asymétrie, skewness.
attaque, fit, stroke (or shock).
atteinte, injury (1).
attente, expectation.
attention à niveau unique, one-level attention.
attester, witness.
attribuer des poids, weighting.
audition, audition.
audition (ouïe) binaurale, binaural hearing.
audition colorée, colored hearing.
audition monauriculaire, monaural (or uniaural) hearing.
au hasard, random[a].
auréole, halo.
auto-accusation, self-accusation.
auto-duperie, self-deception.
autorité, ascendence, ascendance.
l'autrui, other/the.
avancement, proficiency.
avantageux, beneficial.
aveuglement, blindness.
avis, opinion.
avoir l'intention de, intend[v].
axone, axon.

B

baguette de Maddox, Maddox rod.
baguette divinatoire, divining rod.
bâillement, yawning.
bande, gang.
barème de fréquence, frequency table.
bâtonnet rétinien, rod/retinal.
battement, beat.
battement binaural, beat/binaural.
batterie de tests, battery.
beauté, beauty.
begaiement, stuttering.
bémol, flat (2).
besoin, need, want.
biais, bias.
bien doué, gifted.
bien-être, well-being.
bienveillance, kindness.
binauriculaire (binaural), binaural.
blanc, white.
blessure, injury (1).
bleu cyanique, peacock (blue).
blocage, blocking (1).
blocage du nerf, nerve block.
bobine d'induction, induction coil.
boîte avec mécanismes cachés, problem box.
bon, good.
bonheur, happiness.
bonté, kindness.
bouderie, sulkiness.
bougie, candle.
bouleversement, upset[n].
bourgeon gustatif, taste bud.
brilliance, brightness.
bruit, noise.
brûlant, hot.
bulbe, medulla oblongata.
but, aim, goal.

C

caché, cryptic.
canal de l'épendyme, canal/central, canalis centralis.
canal déférent, vas deferens.
canaux semi-circulaires membraneux, semicircular ducts.
canaux semi-circulaires osseux, semicircular canals, semicirculars.
canon d'accord, agreement/canon (or method) of.
capacité, ability.
capacité d'acquisition (d'apprentissage), learning capacity.
capacité d'appréhension, memory span.
capacité spécifique, specific ability.
capacités differenciées, differentiable abilities.
capacités spéciales, special abilities.
caprice, fad.
capsules surrénales, adrenal glands.
caractère acquis, acquired character.
caractères enchaînés, linked characters.
caractères pour l'examen de l'acuité visuelle, test chart, test card.
carré de lettres, letter square.
carrière, career.
cartouches de soupèsement, cartridge weights.
caryoplasure, karyoplasm.
cas marginaux, borderline cases.
catégorie inférieure, lower category.
cauchemar, nightmare.
cauchemar éveillé, daymare.
cause efficace, efficient cause.
cause formelle, formal cause.
cavité de la conque, concha.
cavité (creux) tympanique, tympanic cavity.
cécité, blindness.
cécité au bleu, blue-blindness.
cécité au bleu-jaune, blue-yellow blindness.
cécité au rouge-vert, red-green blindness.
cécité aux couleurs, color-blindness.
cécité chromatique, color-blindness.
cécité corticale, mind-blindness.
cécité crépusculaire, moon-blindness, night-blindness.
cécité des glaciers, snow-blindness.
cécité diurne, day-blindness.
cécité fonctionnelle, blindness/functional.
cécité mentale, mind-blindness.
cécité nocturne, night-blindness.
cécité psychique, object-blindness, psychic blindness.
cécité verbale, text-blindness, word-blindness.
ceinture de Hitzig, Hitzig girdle.
cellule, cell.
cellule apolaire, apolar cell.
cellule bipolaire, bipolar cell.
cellule germinale, germ-cell.
cellule photo-électrique, photo-electric cell.
cellules ciliées, hair cells.
cellules de Betz, Betz cells.
cellules de Deiters, Deiters' cells.
censure de rêve, dream censorship.
censure sociale, social censorship.
centile, percentile.
céphalée, headache.
cercle chromatique, color circle.
cerveau, brain, cerebrum.
cerveau antérieur, forebrain.
cerveau moyen, midbrain.
cerveau postérieur, hindbrain.
cervelet, cerebellum.
chagrin, grief, sorrow.
chaîne d'actes réflexes, chain reflex.
chaise tournante, rotation chair.
chaleur, heat (1).
chaleur paradoxale, paradoxical warmth.
champ auditif, audibility range.
champ d'attention, attention/range (or span) of.
champ de conscience, consciousness/field of.
champ de mémoire immédiate, memory span.
champ des tons audibles, audibility range.
champ phénomenal, phenomenal field.
champ récepteur, receptor field.
champ tactile, field of touch.

champ tubulaire, field/tubular.

champ visuel, field of vision, visual field

chanvre indien, Cannabis indica.

charme, spell.

chasse, hunting, hunting behavior.

châssis de rotation de Mach, Mach rotation frame.

châtiment, punishment.

chatouillement, tickle.

chevaux d'Elberfeld, Elberfeld horses.

choc, collapse.

choix, choice, selection.

choix objectal, object-choice.

chorée, chorea.

chorium, corium.

chose, thing.

chronomètre de chute, fall chronometer.

chronoscope à étincelle, spark chronoscope.

chuchotement, whispering.

cinéma, motion picture.

cinématographie stéréoscopique, stereoscopic motion pictures.

circonvolution, convolution, gyre, gyrus.

circonvolution de l'hippocampe, uncinate gyrus.

clair, light (1).

clarté, brilliance, clearness.

clef de réaction, reaction (or response), key.

clef labiale, lip-key.

clef vocale, voice-key.

clignement, blinking.

cloaque, cloaca.

cloche des tons, tonal bell.

cloison, membrane.

clonus de la cheville, ankle clonus.

clou hystérique, clavus hystericus.

co-conscience, co-consciousness.

coefficient d'acquisition (d'apprentissage), learning coefficient.

coefficient de corrélation des produits-moments, product moment coefficient of correlation.

coefficient du rapport chroma-brilliance, chroma-brilliance coefficient.

cœur, heart.

cohérence, reliability (2), self-consistency.

coït, coition, coitus.

colère, anger.

collapsus, collapse.

colonne vertébrale, spine.

coloration tonale, tone-color.

combativité, pugnacity.

comique, ludicrous[n].

comme il faut[a], propriety.

commençant, incipient.

communautés fourmis, ant communities.

comparaison décalée, slip comparison.

complexe refoulé, repressed complex.

complexus, pattern (2).

complexus de pression, pressure pattern.

complexus de pression et douleur, pressure-pain pattern.

complexus de réaction, pattern reaction.

complexus émotionnel, emotional pattern.

complexus nerveux, neural pattern.

comportement, behavior, behaviour.

comportement d'accouplement, mating behavior.

comportement animal, animal behavior.

comportement apopathétique, apopathetic behavior.

comportement collectif, group behavior.

comportement en série, serial behavior.

comportement envers l'aliment, food-response, food-getting behavior.

comportement instinctif, instinctive behavior.

comportement maternel, maternal behavior.

comportement parental, parental behavior.

comportement pluraliste, pluralistic behavior.

comportement rationnel, rational behavior, rational conduct.

comportement social, social behavior.

comportement verbal, verbal behavior.

composé, compound.

composé mental, compound/mental.

compréhension, understanding.

compulsion de répétition, repetition-compulsion.

concurrence vitale, struggle for existence.

condition, condition[n] (1, 2).

condition physiologique, physiological state.

conditions ambiants, environment.

conduction aérienne, air conduction.

conduction avec decrément, conduction with decrement.

conduire, conduct[v].

conduit auditif externe, meatus/external auditory.

conduit auditif interne, meatus/internal auditory.

conduit endolymphatique, endolymphatic duct.

conduite, behavior, conduct[n].

confusion mentale, clouding of consciousness.

congenital, connate.

congru, congruous.

congruent, congruent.

conjugaison, conjugation.

connaissance, cognition, knowledge.

connaissance de soi, self-knowledge.

connaissance du monde extérieur, external world.

connaissance intuitive, insight.

connaissance profonde dans l'acquisition, learning/insight in.

connaître, knowledge.

consanguinité, kinship.

conscience, consciousness.

conscience collective, group consciousness.

conscience de classe, consciousness of kind.

conscience de liberté, freedom/consciousness of.

conscience de rapport, relation/consciousness of.

conscience de similitude, consciousness of kind.

conscience de soi, self-consciousness.

conscience dissociée, split-off consciousness.

conscience sociale, tribal self.

consentement, assent.

conservation personnelle, self-preservation.

constance, reliability (3).

constant d'amortissement du son, damping constant.

contenu, content[n].

contenu de la conscience, content of consciousness.

contenu de rêve, dream-content.

contraction, contraction.

contraction de faim, hunger contraction.

contraction isométrique, isometric twitch.

contraction musculaire spasmodique, muscular twitching.

contraction spasmodique, twitching.

contraindre, constrain.

contrainte, compulsion.

contrainte de répétition, repetition compulsion.

contraste lumineux, brilliance contrast.

contravention, misdemeanor.

contrôle de la procréation, birth control.

contrôler, check[v] (2).

convaincre, convince.

convenable[a], propriety.

convenable, right[a].

convenance, propriety, decency.

convoitise, lust.
coquetterie, coyness.
corde dorsale, notochord.
corne d'Ammon, horn of Ammon.
corporel, corporal[a], corporeal.
corps, body.
corps astral, astral body.
corps calleux, callosum, corpus callosum.
corps cellulaire, cell-body.
corps de métier, craft.
corps genouillé latéral, geniculate body/lateral.
corps genouillé médial, geniculate body/medial.
corps olivaires, olives, olivary bodies.
corps polaire, polar body.
corps trapézoïde, trapezoid body.
correct, right[a].
corrélation illégitime, spurious correlation.
corrélation par la méthode des rangs, rank correlation.
cortex, cortex.
couche bacillaire, bacillary layer.
couche cérébrale, cerebral layer.
couche choroïde, choroid (or chorioid), choroid coat.
couche de cellules ganglionnaires, ganglion cells/layer of.
couche des bâtonnets et des cônes, layer of rods and cones.
couche élastique de Sattler, Sattler's elastic layer.
couche fibreuse, fibrous layer.
couche ganglionnaire, vesicular layer.
couche germinale, germ layer.
couche granulaire externe, granular layer/outer.
couche granulaire interne, granular layer/inner.
couches de la paupière, coats of eyeball.
couches optiques, thalamus, optic thalamus.
couches rétiniennes, retinal layers.
couleur de température, color temperature.
couleur du son, clang-color, clang-quality, clang-tint.
couleur inductive, inducing color.
couleur induite, induced color.
couleur pelliculaire, film color.
couleur volumineuse, bulky color.
coups, raps.
courant, current.
courant de la conscience, stream of consciousness, stream of thought.
courant de lésion, injury/current of.
courant de repos, current of rest.
courbe, curve.
courbe cumulative de progrès, band-chart.
courbe d'apprentissage (**d'acquisition**), learning curve.
courbe d'apprentissage de Vincent, Vincent learning curve.
courbe d'entraînement, practice curve.
courbe de force-durée, strength-duration curve.
courbe de repos, curve of rest.
courbe de travail, work curve.
courbe polie, smooth curve.
courbure, flexure.
cours de la pensée, stream of thought, thinking/stream of.
courtiser, philander.
coutume, custom.
crainte, dread.
crainte révérencieuse, awe.
crampe des écrivains, writer's cramp.
crayon des tons, tonal pencil.
crèche clinique, clinical crib.
crête, crest.
crête neurale, neural crest.
crêtes ciliés des ampoules, hair cells of ampullæ.
crins de von Frey, von Frey hairs.
crise, seizure.
crise émotionnelle, brain-storm.
crises hystériformes, hysteriform seizures.
cristallin, lens, crystalline lens.
cristalloscopie, scrying.
critique, criticism.
crochet-support rotatif, carrier bracket.
croissance, growth (1).
croyance, belief.
cruauté, cruelty.
cubitus, ulna.
culte, worship (2).
culte des ancêtres, ancestor worship.
culte du feu, fire-worship.
culte phallique, phallus worship.
cycle, cycle.
cylindraxe, axon, axone, neurite.
cylindre enregistreur (avec feuille noircie), smoked drum.

D

danse de St. Guy, chorea.
débile simple, moron.
débutant, incipient.
décence, decency.
décharge consécutive, after-discharge.
décharge consécutive reflexe, reflex after-discharge.
décharge d'influx nerveux, neural discharge, nervous discharge.
déclanchement, trigger action.
déclic, click.
décomposition, decay.
découvrir, discover.
dédain, scorn.
dédoublement de la personnalité, personality/dual.
défaillance affective, affective failure.
défaut, defect, deficiency.
défaut optique, defect/optical.
déficience, deficiency, disability.
déficience (**insuffisance**) **mentale,** deficiency/mental.
déficient, defective.
defumée, empyreumatic.
dégoût, disgust.
dégradation, deterioration.
degré, grade.
déjà vu, *see* definition.
déjà vu, error of recognition (1), *also see under* **pseudopresentiment.**
délire du toucher, *see* definition.
délit, misdemeanor.
démangeaison, itch.
démence, dementia.
dépistage, questionary.
dépit, spite.
déplaisir, unpleasantness.
dépouillement[n], score.
dépouillement des tests, test scaling.
dépréciation, underestimate.
déranger[v], disturbance.
derme, derma, dermis.
désagrégation, decay.
désagrément, disagreeableness.
désapprobation sociale, social disapproval.
description, picture (2).
déséquilibre de convergence, imbalance/muscular.
désespoir, despair.
désincarné, discarnate.
désir, wish.
désir ardant, craving, longing.
désir refoulé, repressed wish.
dessein, design/purposive.
dessin, drawing, design/pictorial.
dessin automatique, automatic drawing.
dessin en miroir, mirror-drawing.
dessiner, drawing.
dessin mnémonique, memory drawing.
détermination par soi-même, self-determination.
dévalorisation, underestimate.
déviations des méridiens verticaux apparents, deviations of the retinal meridians.

devoir, duty.
dextralité, dextrality.
diagramme, diagram.
diapason étalon, pitch fork.
diapasons désaccordés, mistuned forks.
diése, sharp (3), **sharp**[n].
diéte, diet.
dieu, god.
diffamer, malign.
différence juste perceptible, just noticeable difference, difference/least noticeable.
différences entre les sexes, sex differences.
différences sensibles, sensed differences.
direction, leadership.
diriger, train.
discernable, discernible.
dispersion, scatter.
dispositif, apparatus.
disque de Savart, Savart wheel.
disque rotatif, color wheel.
dissemblance, dissimilarity.
dissentiment, dissent.
dissonance, discord.
distance, depth.
distension papillaire, choked disk.
distortion en barillet, distortion/barrel.
distortion en croissant, distortion/pincushion.
distraction, absent-mindedness, detraction.
distribution de capacité, ability distribution.
doctrine de l'action causal, causal theory.
doctrine de la volonté libre, free-will doctrine.
doctrine de l'influence naturelle, causal theory.
don, endowment.
don inné, native endowment.
donnée, given.
données, data[pl].
donner une notation, rate[v].
douceur, softness (2).
douleur, pain.
douleur aiguë, twinge.
douleur en ceinture, girdle sensation.
dressage, training.
droite, right[n].
droitier, dextrality.
droiture morale, righteousness.
duperie, deception.
durée de l'attention, attention/duration of.
durée minimale perceptible, duration/least perceptible.

E

ébauche, rudiment.
ébranlement, concussion.
écart étalon, deviation/standard, standard deviation, standard error.
écart interquartile, interquartile range.
écart médian, median deviation.
écart moyen, average deviation, deviation/mean.
écart quartile, deviation/quartile, quartile deviation.
échange, intercourse.
échantillon, sample.
échantillonnage, sampling[n] (1).
échantillonnage au hasard, random sampling.
échauffement, warming up.
échec, failure (1).
échelle d'âge, age-scale.
échelle de Binet-Simon, Binet-Simon scale.
échelle de correspondence d'individu à individu, man-to-man rating scale.
échelle de dessin, drawing scale.
échelle d'écriture, handwriting scale.
échelle d'intelligence, intelligence scale.
échelle de Kelvin, Kelvin scale.
échelle de saturation, saturation scale.
échelle de Stanford-Binet, Stanford-Binet scale.
échelle de Yerkes-Bridges, Yerkes-Bridges scale.
échelle en points, point scale.
échelle mentale, scale/mental.
échelle spectrale chromatique, spectral chroma scale, spectral scale.
échelle T, T-scale.
échelle tonale, scale/tonal.
échelon d'épreuves de sévérité croissante, difficulty scale.
échelon graphique d'appréciation, graphic rating scale.
échelons égaux, equal steps.
éclairage du champ sombre, dark-field illumination.
éclairement, illumination.
éclat, brightness, luminosity.
écolage, schooling.
école, school.
école d'apprentissage, vestibule school.
économie dans l'effort, economy of effort.
écorce, cortex.
écorce calcarine, calcarine cortex.
écorce cérébelleuse, cortex cerebelli.
écorce cérébrale, cortex cerebri.
écorce surrénale, suprarenal cortex.
écran pour la vision dans une seule direction, one-way vision screen.
écriture, handwriting, script, writing.
écriture ataxique, ataxic writing.
écriture au pied, foot-writing (foot-drawing).
écriture automatique, automatic writing.
écriture buccale, mouth-writing.
écriture courante, cursive writing.
écriture cursive, cursive writing.
écriture d'aveugle, blind writing.
écriture dextre, dextrad writing.
écriture directe sur ardoise, slate-writing.
écriture en miroir, mirror writing.
écriture en rébus, rebus writing.
écriture hiéroglyphique, hieroglyphic writing.
écriture manuscrite, manuscript writing.
écriture renversée, back-hand, backhand writing.
écriture sénestre, sinistrad writing.
éducation de redressement, remedial instruction.
effet consécutif, after-effect.
effet d'affaiblissement lumineux, dimming effect.
effet d'auréole, halo effect.
effet d'entraînement, practice effect.
effluence, leakage.
effort initial, initial spurt.
effort terminal, end spurt.
égalité, equality.
egoïsme, selfishness.
élan, spurt.
élancement, twinge.
élargissement de la tache aveugle, choked disk.
élément hédonique, hedonic tone.
élevage de la progeniture, bringing up.
élevé, high.
élimination de mouvements, dropping out of movements.
éloigné, remote[a].
embarras, embarrassment.
embarras de parole, impediment/speech.
émoussé, dull (1).
empêcher de, restrain.
empiètement des groupes, overlapping of groups.
empiètement des réponses, overlapping of responses.
empire sur (maîtrise de) soi-même, self-control.
emploi, use[n] (1).

emploi d'une surpression, overblowing.
empreinte, trace.
enceinte[a], pregnancy.
enchaînement, linkage (1).
enchaînement causal, causal chain.
endormi[a], sleep.
enfance, infancy (1, 2).
enfant, child.
enfant bien doué (d'élite), superior child.
enflé, tumid.
engagement, commitment (2).
engendrer, breed[v].
engouement, craze.
enjambement, crossing over.
ennui, boredom.
enquête, questionary.
enseignement, schooling.
ensemble structurel, pattern (2).
entendant-muet, hearing mute.
entourage, environment.
entraînement, training, practice[n].
entraîner, practice[v].
entre mise, mediation.
épellation (langage) digitale, finger spelling.
épicé, spicy.
épiphénomène, epiphenomenon.
épouvante, fright.
épreuve, proof, test (1).
épreuve cruciale, crucial test, crucial experiment.
épreuve de complètement de dessins (phrases) inachevés, completion test.
épreuve de problèmes à resoudre, problem-solving.
épreuve (test) de rendement, achievement test.
épuisement, exhaustion.
équilibre, balance.
équilibre mental, balance of mind, mental balance.
érotisme de la peau, skin erotism.
érotisme labial, lip-eroticism.
erreurs d'échantillonnage, sampling/errors of.
erreur de préjugé, bias/error of.
erreur de temps, time error.
erreur moyenne, average error.
erreur probable, probable error.
erreur quadratique, standard deviation, standard error.
erreur spatiale, space error.
erreur type, standard deviation, standard error.
erreur type d'estimation, standard error of estimate.
espace, space.
espèce, species.
espérance, hope.
esprit, mind, soul (1, 3), spirit, wit.
esprit collectif, collective mind.
esprit social, social mind.
essai, experiment.
esthésiomètre à crin, hair esthesiometer (or æsthesiometer).
étage niveau, level (3).
étage supérieur du pédoncule, tegmentum (2).
étalage de soi, self-display, self-exhibition.
étalement, extent.
étalon, standard.
étalon tonal, tonal standard.
étalonnage des tests, standardization of tests.
étalonner, standardize.
état, condition[n] (3), state.
état affectif, affect.
état de conscience, state of consciousness.
états crépusculaires hystériques, twilight states/hysterical.
états substantifs, substantive states.
étendue, extent, range, scope.
éthique, ethics.
étonnement, surprise, wonder.
étourdissement, bewilderment, dizziness.
être, being/a, soul (2).
étude, study[n].
évanouissement, faint[n], swoon.
éveillé, awake[a], sharp[a] (5).
événement, event.
événement fortuit, chance occurrence.
évident par soi-même, self-evident.
évocation, recall.
examen des lieux, locality survey.
excès de compensation, overcompensate.
excitabilité, sentience.
excitation, elation.
excitation maniaque, mania.
exemplaire, exponent (2).
exemple, instance, exponent (2).
exercer, drill.
exhibitionnisme, exhibitionism.
expectation, expectation.
expérience, experiment.
expérience d'Aristote, Aristotle's experiment.
expérience de choix, choice experiment.
expérience de contrôle, blank experiment.
expérience de l'ombre colorée, colored shadow experiment.
expérience de pesanteur, weight experiment.
expérience des nuages de F., cloud experiment/Fechner's.
expérience des ombres de F., shadow experiment/Fechner's.
expérience du picotement des poulets, pecking experiment.
exposant, exponent (1).
expression de sa personnalité, self-expression.
extase, ecstacy, trance.
extériorisation des sensations, eccentric projection.
externe, outer.

F

face, face.
facteur de volonté, w factor, will factor.
facteur d'habileté, c factor, cleverness factor.
facteurs ambiants, environmental factors.
facteurs communs, overlapping elements (or factors).
facultés actives, active powers.
faible, faint, low (2), weak.
faiblesse, faintness, helplessness.
faiblesse chromatique, color-weakness.
faiblesse mentale, amentia, feeblemindedness.
faim, hunger.
faire des investigations, investigate.
faisceau, tract.
faisceaux vestibulospinaux, vestibulospinal tracts.
fait, fact.
fantaisie, fancy (1).
fantôme, ghost.
fatigue cérébrale, brain fag.
fausseté, falsity.
faux, falsity.
faux semblant, make-believe, shamming.
faux souvenir, pseudomemory.
feinte, feigning, make-believe, shamming.
femelle, female.
féminin[a], female.
fenêtre de Hering, Hering window.
fenêtre ovale, window/oval.
fenêtre ronde, window/round.
fétiche, fetish.
fétide, putrid.
feuillet moyen, mesoblast, mesoderm.
fibre nerveuse, nerve fiber.
fibrilles terminales, endbrush.
fidélité, reliability (1, 2).
fierté, pride.
figure de points, dot figure.
figure du vase à profils humains de Rubin, Rubin's goblet-profile figure.

figure et fond, figure-ground.
fin, end.
fixation de l'enfant à ses parents, child-parent fixation.
flèche de Zeno, Zeno's arrow.
flexion, flexion.
flirt, flirtation.
floral, flowery.
flou, blur.
flou hypéropique, hyperopic blur.
fluctuations d'échantillonnage, fluctuations of sampling.
foi, faith.
folie, *see* definition.
folie, lunacy.
folie à deux, *see under* **folie.**
folie à double forme, alternating psychosis.
folie (idées délirantes) de la persécution, persecution/delusion of.
folie du doute, *see under* **folie.**
folie lucide, paranoia.
folie morale, moral insanity.
folie périodique, manic-depressive psychosis.
folies de développement, developmental insanities.
follicule pileux, hair-follicle.
fonction reproductrice, reproductive function.
fond, ground (2).
fond de l'œil, eyeground.
fondement, basis, ground (1).
force, strength.
force magnétique (d'aimantation), magnetic force, magnetism.
forme, Gestalt, pattern (2).
formula de prédiction, prophecy formula.
fort[a]**,** strong.
fortuit, causal.
foule, crowd, mass (2), mob.
foyer, focus.
foyer d'attention, attention/focus of.
franchise, frankness.
frange, fringe.
frayage, facilitation.
frayage social, social facilitation.
frayeur, fear.
frein, restraint.
fréquence critique de papillotement, critical flicker frequency.
froid paradoxal, paradoxical cold.
fuite, flight.
fuite des couleurs, flight of colors.
fuite des idées, flight of ideas.
furieux, amuck, amok.
fuseau, spindle.
fuseau tendineux, tendon spindle.
fuseaux musculaires, muscle spindles.
fuseaux neuro-musculaires, neuromuscular spindles.
fusion, blend, blending.

G

gaine de Schwann, sheath of Schwann.
gaine médullaire, myelin, myelin sheath.
gaine myélinique, myelin, myelin sheath.
galvanomètre à corde, string galvanometer.
gamme, scale (2).
gamme chromatique, chromatic scale.
gamme diatonique, diatonic scale.
gamme mineure, minor scale.
gamme pentatonique, pentatonic scale.
gamme tempérée, equal-tempered scale.
ganglion sympathique, sympathetic ganglion.
gauche, left, sinister.
gaucherie, sinistrality.
gemmation, budding.
gêne, embarrassment.
génie, genius.
genre, genus.
genre humain, man, mankind.
gestion, management.
glande pinéale, pineal body.
glandes endocrines, ductless glands.
globe de l'œil, eyeball.
glomérule (bâtonnet) olfactif, olfactory cell.
goût, flavor, test.
goût télesthétique, telesthetic taste.
gouttière neurale, neural groove.
gradient, gradient[n].
gradient physiologique, physiological gradient.
grand calculateur, prodigy/mathematical.
grandeur, magnitude.
graphique, chart.
graphique de z, zee (or z) chart.
gratitude, gratitude.
grave, deep, low (1).
gris, gray, grey.
gris cortical, cortical gray.
grossesse, pregnancy.
groupe de vis-à-vis, group/face-to-face.
groupe formé au hasard, random group.
groupe sélectionné, selected group.
groupe-type, sampling[n] (2).
groupes sanguins, blood groups.
guérison (cure) mentale, mental healing.
guérison par la foi, faith cure.
guider, train.

H

habileté, ability, craft (1), skill.
habileté (capacité) générale, general ability.
habiletés, proficiencies.
habitude, habit.
habitude de la lecture, reading habit.
habitude motrice, motor habit.
haine, hate, hatred.
hallucination induite, induced hallucination.
hallucinose aiguë, acute hallucinosis.
halo, halo.
hanter, haunting.
hasard[n]**,** randomness (*see under* **random**[a]).
hasard, chance.
hauteur, pitch (2).
hauteur absolue, pitch/absolute.
hauteur des lettres dans l'écriture, graphic size.
hauteur tonale, pitch (1).
héméralopie, day-blindness.
hérédité, inheritance (1).
hérédité par l'usage, use and disuse theory, use-inheritance.
héritage, inheritance (2).
héritage] nulliplexe, nulliplex inheritance.
hérité, inherited[a].
hériter, inherit.
hétérophorie, imbalance/muscular.
hiérarchie professionnelle, occupational hierarchy.
heureux[a]**,** happy (*see under* **happiness**).
homme de Crô-magnon, Crô-magnon man.
homme de Java, Java man.
honnêteté, honesty.
honte, shame.
horde, herd.
humeur, mood.
hypersensible au bleu, blue-sighted.
hypersensible au jaune, yellow-sighted.
hypersensible au rouge, red-sighted.
hypothèse de la tache cérébrale, brain-spot hypothesis.
hypothèse du drainage, drainage hypothesis.

I

idéal du moi, ego-ideal.
idée, idea.
idée de but, purpose.

idée de finalité, purpose.

idée directrice, guiding idea.

idée fixe, monoideism.

idée force, *see* definition.

idée intentionnelle, purposive (or purpose) idea.

idiot-savant, *see* definition

illégitime, spurious.

illogique, unreasonable.

illusion, delusion.

illusion de l'âme collective, group fallacy.

illusion de l'échiquier, chess-board illusion.

illusion de la balançoire, haunted swing illusion.

illusion de la chûte d'eau, waterfall illusion.

illusion de la figure en escalier, staircase illusion.

illusion de la lune à l'horizon, moon illusion.

illusion de soupèsement, size-weight illusion.

illusion des cœurs flottants, fluttering hearts (illusion).

illusion du correcteur d'épreuves, proof-reader's illusion.

îlot tonal, island/tonal.

image, drawing, picture (1).

image composée, generic image, recept.

image consécutive, after-image.

image consécutive de Purkinje, Purkinje after-image.

image rétinienne, picture/retinal.

images congruentes, congruent figures.

imagination de renaissance, rebirth-phantasy.

impensable, unthinkable.

(impression d') identité, sameness.

impression neuve, novel impression.

impulsion, impulse, urge.

impulsiveté, impulsiveness.

inadaptation, unfitness.

inapplicable, irrelevant.

inapte[a], *see under* **unfitness.**

incandescence, glow.

incendie par malveillance, arson.

incertitude, uncertainty.

inconcevable, unthinkable.

inconnaissable, unknowable.

inconscient, unconscious.

inconsistance, discrepancy.

incrédulité, disbelief.

indice de réfraction, refraction/index of, refractive index.

indolent, listless.

induction simultanée de lumière, light-induction/simultaneous.

inexactitude, inaccuracy.

influence du contenu récent, recency/law of.

influx nerveux, nerve impulse, nervous impulse.

infraliminaire, subliminal.

inhibition, inhibition.

inné, connate, inborn, native

innervation, innervation.

inquiétude, restlessness.

instinct, instinct (3).

instinct artistique, art impulse.

instinct de mort, death instinct.

instinct de vie, life instinct.

instinct différé, delayed instinct.

instinct du moi, ego-instinct.

instinct grégaire, gregariousness.

instruction, schooling.

insula de Reil, island of Reil.

intellect, intellect.

intelligent, sharp (5).

intensité sonore, sound intensity.

intensionnel, intentional.

intention, purpose.

intentionnisme, purposivism.

interne, inner.

interposé, mediate.

interprétation des rêves, dream interpretation.

intervalle de repos, rest pause.

intervalle sensible, sense distance.

introvertie, shut-in personality.

inverser, reverse[v].

investigation relative au milieu, field investigation.

investissement, cathexis.

investissement objectal, object-cathexis.

irritant, annoyer.

isolement, seclusiveness.

ivrogne, drunkard.

J

jalousie, jealousy.

jaune, yellow.

jaune visuel, visual yellow.

jeu, game, play.

jeunesse, youth.

joie de vivre, *see* definition.

journalier, journeyman.

jugement, judgment (1).

jugement subordonné, understatement.

jumeau[m], jumelle[f], twin.

jumeau dizygote, twin (1).

jumeau monozygote, twin (2).

jumeau vrai, twin (2).

juste, right[a].

L

labyrinthe, maze.

la connaissance, acquaintance with.

lacune tonale, gap/tonal.

laid, ugly.

langage (parole) automatique, automatic speaking.

langue, language, tongue.

langueur, languor, languour.

languissant[a], *see under* **faint[a].**

la plus petite différence perceptible, difference/least noticeable.

lapsus, slip of speech.

larmes, tears.

la sensible, leading tone.

le beau, beautiful/the.

le ça, id (2).

le moi, ego.

l'ensemble, whole[n].

le soi, self.

le soi social, social self.

le super-ego, le surmoi, superego.

lecture de la pensée, mind-reading.

lecture de la pensée par les muscles, muscle-reading.

lecture sur les lèvres, lip-reading.

léger, light[a].

légume, vegetable.

lentille cylindrique, cylindrical lens.

lentille en tore, toric lens.

lentille punctale, punctal lens.

lentille sphérique, spherical lens.

les hommes, man, mankind.

lésion, injury (2).

l'humanité, mankind.

liberté morale, freedom/ethical.

lien, bond, linkage (2).

lien causal, causal nexus.

ligne de moindre résistance, least resistance/line of.

ligne de regard, sight/line of, sighting line.

lignée, stirp.

limaçon, cochlea.

limite auditive inférieure, lowest audible tone.

limite auditive supérieure, highest audible tone.

limite d'entraînement, practice limit.

limites d'audibilité, audibility limits.

liquide céphalo-rachidien, cerebrospinal fluid, fluid/cerebrospinal.

lisibilité, legibility.

localisation sonore par ordination, sound ranging.

loi, law.

loi biogénétique, biogenetic law.

loi d'association par contiguité, contiguity/law of.

loi d'associations opposées, conflicting associations/law of.

loi d'avantage, advantage/law of.

loi d'héritage ancestral, inheritance/law of.

loi de combination, combination/law of.

loi de contraste, contrast/law of.

loi de cosinus, cosine law.

loi de dégradation, degradation/law of.

loi de diminution du progrés, diminishing returns/law of.

loi de fréquence, frequency/law of.

loi de progression, progression/law of.

loi de récence, recency/law of.

loi de réciprocité, reciprocity law.

loi de régression filiale, filial regression/law of.

loi de répétition, frequency/law of.

loi de ségrégation, segregation/law of.

loi de tension, tension/law of.

loi de l'activité fragmentaire, piecemeal activity/law of.

loi de l'effet, effect/law of.

loi de l'exercise, exercise/law of.

loi de l'inverse du carré, inverse square law.

loi de la biogenèse, biogenesis/law of.

loi de la désuétude, disuse/law of.

loi de la nature, nature/law of.

loi de la précision, precision/law of.

loi des moindres carrés, least squares/law of.

loi du parallélisme, parallel law.

loi du tout et rien, all-or-none law.

loi métabolique du pouls, pulse metabolism/law of.

loi naturelle, natural law.

lois d'acquisition (de l'apprentissage), learning/laws of.

lois de cognition, thought/laws of.

longueur d'onde, wave-length.

longueur d'onde dominante, dominant wave-length.

longueur focale, focal length.

luette (du palais), uvula.

luisance, lustre, luster.

lumière, light[n].

lumière rétinienne, idioretinal light.

lumineux, bright.

luminosité, brilliance, luminosity.

lutte binoculaire, binocular rivalry.

lutte pour la vie, struggle for existence.

lutte rétinienne, retinal rivalry.

M

machine à arracher des aveux, lie detector.

magie noire, black art.

main, hand.

maîtrise, mastery.

mal, evil.

maladie d'Alzheimer, Alzheimer's disease.

maladie de Marie, Marie's disease.

maladie mentale, mental disease.

maladie nerveuse, nervous disease, nervous disorder, neuropathy.

mal à la tête, headache.

malentendu[n], misunderstand.

malhonnêteté, dishonesty.

malveillance, malevolence.

mammifères, mammilia, mammals.

mandat de dépôt, commitment (1).

manie ambulatoire, Wanderlust.

manque, failure (2).

marche, walking.

marge, range.

marque de naissance, birth-mark.

marteau sonore, sound hammer.

masse, mass (1).

matière de rêve, dream material.

matrice, uterus.

mauvais, bad, evil.

mauvais œil, evil eye.

mécanisme d'annulation rétroactive, undoing mechanism.

mécanisme du punition de soi-même, self-punishment mechanism.

médiat, mediate.

médiation, mediation.

méduse, jellyfish.

méfiance, distrust.

mélancolie anxieuse, anxiety-melancholia.

mélange binoculaire des couleurs, color mixture/binocular.

mélange de couleurs, color mixture.

mélangeur de couleurs, color mixer.

membrane, membrane.

mémoire, remembrance, memory (1).

mémoire brute, rote learning.

mémoire occasionnelle, incidental memory.

mémoriser, memorize.

mensonge[n], *see under* **lying.**

mentalité de la foule, crowd mind.

menteur constitutionnel[np], *see under* **pathological lying.**

mentir, lying.

méprise, misunderstand.

mésadaptation, maladjustment.

mésadaptation professionnelle, maladjustment/vocational.

mésadaptation sociale, social maladjustment.

mésencéphale, midbrain.

mésoblaste, mesoblast.

mésoderm, mesoderm.

mesure, measure, measurement.

mesures de rapport, relation/measures of.

méthode d'acquisition complète, complete learning (or memorizing) method.

méthode de cas égaux et inégaux, equal and unequal cases/method of.

méthode de contrôle sur des jumeaux, co-twin control/method of.

méthode d'économie, saving method.

méthode d'évocation, recall method.

méthode de gradations moyennes, mean gradations/method of.

méthode de l'étincelle, spark method.

méthode de limites, disappearing differences/method of.

méthode de polissage, moving average method.

méthode de reconnaissance, recognition method.

méthode des cas vrais et faux, right and wrong cases/method of.

méthode des couples associés, right associates/method of.

méthode des différences juste perceptibles, difference/method of least (or just) noticeable.

méthode des équidistances sensorielles, equal sense distances/method of.

méthode des erreurs moyennes, average error/method of.

méthode des essais et erreurs, trial and error method.

méthode des intervalles jugés égaux, equal-appearing intervals/method of.

méthode des lectures répétées, rereading method.

méthode des moindres changements, minimal change (or changes)/method of.

méthode des moindres carrés, least squares/method of.

méthode des variations concomitantes, concomitant variations/method (or canon) of.

méthodes globales, mass methods.

méthodes psychophysiques, psychophysical methods.

métier, craft (2).

milieu, environment.

milieux réfringents, refracting media.

mineur, infancy (3).

minimum indispensable, minimal (or minimum) essentials.

mise en court-circuit, short-circuiting.

mise en place, setting.

mise en train, warming up.
mitose, mitosis.
mode, fashion, style.
modèle, pattern (1).
moelle, cord, medulla.
moelle épinière, spinal cord.
moi tribal, tribal self.
mollesse, softness (1).
moment, momentum.
monauriculaire, uniaural.
monde externe, external world (1).
monde physique, physical world.
monoidéisme, monoideism.
morale, ethics.
mort, death.
mort simulée, death feint.
en mosaïque, tesselated.
motif, motive.
mouches volantes, muscæ volitantes.
mouvement, motion.
mouvement associé, accompanying movement.
mouvement relenti, slow motion.
mouvements au hasard, random movements, random activities.
mouvements de manége, circus movements.
mouvements forcés, forced movements.
mouvements inutiles, useless movements.
mouvements oculaires, eye-movements.
moyenne, average, mean.
moyenne géométrique, geometrical mean.
moyenne harmonique, harmonic mean.
moyens, means.
muet, dumb.
mûrir, mature, ripen.
muscle fléchisseur, flexor muscle, flexor.
muscles extrinsèques oculaires, extrinsic eye-muscles.
muscles intrinsèques de l'œil, intrinsic eye-muscles.
muscle-verrou, catch muscle.
mutation, mutation.
myélencéphale, medulla oblongata.

N

naissant, incipient, nascent.
narines, nostrils.
nerf cubital, ulnar nerve.
nerf dépresseur, depressor nerve.
nerf pathétique, trochlear nerve.
nerf rachidien, spinal nerve.
nerf spinal, spinal nerve.
nerf trijumeau, trigeminal nerve.
neutralisation d'odeurs, smell compensation.
névrite, neuritis.
névropathie, neuropathy.
névrose, neurosis.
névrose actuel, actual neurosis.
névrose d'angoisse, anxiety neurosis.
névrose de compulsion, névrose d'obsession, obsessional neurosis.
névrose de transfert, neurosis/transference.
névrose narcissique, neurosis/narcissistic.
névrose orale, oral neurosis.
névrosique, neurotic.
nez, nose.
nidification, nesting.
niveau, level (1, 2).
niveau d'attention, attention-level, level of attention.
niveau de sensation, sensation level/auditory.
niveau de soutien (d'entretien), maintenance level.
niveaux d'adjustement, adjustment levels.
niveaux mnémoniques, memory levels.
noeud, node.
noir, black.
nom, name.
non-moi, non-ego.
norme d'age, age-norm.
norme de valeur scolaire, grade norm.
notable, noticeable.
notation, score.
notation de l'épreuve, test score.
notation de taux, rate score.
notation objective, objective score.
notation valable, true score.
note, score.
note brute, raw score.
note centrale, midscore.
note d'âge, age score.
note de compréhension, comprehension score.
note de précision, accuracy score.
note étalonnée, standard score.
note médiane, midscore.
note (notation) moyenne, average score.
note pondérée, weighted score.
note sensible, leading tone.
noter, rate[v].
notochorde, notochord.
nourrisson, (-ne), suckling (3).
noyau, nucleus.
noyau caudé, caudate nucleus.
noyau dentelé, dentate nucleus.
nuance, hue.
nuance extra-spectrale, extra-spectral hue.
nystagmus céphalique, head nystagmus.

O

obéissance, obedience.
obligation, duty.
observation de soi, observation of self, self-observation.
observations éthologiques, field observations, field studies.
observer, notice.
obstacle à l'inceste, incest barrier.
occasionnel, incidental.
odeur, odor, scent.
odorat, olfaction.
œil, eye.
œil adapté à l'obscurité, dark-adapted eye.
œil composé, compound eye.
œil cyclopéen, cyclopean eye.
œil emmétrope, emmetropic eye.
œil en mosaïque, mosaic eye.
œuf, egg, ovum.
œuvres de bien-être, welfare work.
ombre acoustique, acoustic shadow.
onde, wave.
onde d'excitation, wave of excitation.
onde sonore, sound-wave.
ondes lumineuses, light waves.
ondulation, undulation.
opinion, opinion.
optotypes, test chart, test card.
ordre, order (1, 2), sequence (1).
ordre du rang, rank order.
oreille, ear.
oreille moyenne, middle ear.
oreillette du cœur, auricle (2).
organisation du personnel, personnel management.
orgue, organ (2).
orgueil, conceit.
orientation lointaine dans le retour au gite, homing.
orientation pédagogique, guidance/educational.
orientation professionnelle, guidance/vocational.
orientation spatiale, space orientation.
os auriculaires, ear bones.
os hyoïde, hyoid bone.
os temporal, temporal bone.
oscillations de l'attention, attention/fluctuation of.
osselet du marteau, malleus.
osselets auriculaires, ossicles/auditory.
ouïe, audition.
ovum, egg.

P

palais, palate.
pâleur, pallor.
palper, feel[vt].
pangène, pangen.
papiers gris de Hering, Hering grays.
papille optique, optic disk (or disc).
papillotement, flicker, flicker phenomenon.
papillotement binoculaire, binocular flicker.
parade, self-display, self-exhibition.
paralysie générale, paresis.
paramnésia, pseudomemory.
parenté, kinship, relation.
parent moyen, midparent.
pariade, mating[n], mating behavior.
pathonévrose, pathoneurosis.
pavillon, auricle (1), pinna.
peau, skin.
péché, sin.
pédoncule, peduncle.
peine, grief, punishment.
pénalité, penalty.
penchant, bias.
pénible[a], pain.
pensée, thinking, thought.
pensée abstraite, abstract thought, abstract thinking.
pensée à haute voix, thinking aloud.
pensée analogique, analogical thinking.
pensée autistique, autistic thinking.
pensée constructive, constructive thinking.
pensée dirigée, directed thinking.
pensée sans images, imageless thought.
pensée sélective, selective thinking.
perçant, sharp[a] (4).
perceptible, noticeable.
perception d'espace, space perception.
perception (visuelle) de la profondeur, depth perception.
perception (sens) de rotation, rotation perception.
perception du temps, time perception.
période, cycle.
période d'entraînement, practice period.
période moyenne, midperiod.
période préliminaire, foreperiod.
péristaltisme, peristalsis.
perséquomètre, pursuitmeter.
personnalité insuffisante (incomplète), inadequacy, inadequate personality.
personnalité retirée, shut-in personality.
pesanteur, gravity.
petit mal, *see* definition.
peur, fear.
phase réfractaire, refractory period, refractory phase.
phénomène d'affaiblissement chromatique, chromatic dimming phenomenon.
phénomène de l'échelon, step-wise phenomenon.
phénomène de l'escalier, staircase phenomenon.
phénomène de l'ombre colorée, colored shadow experiment.
phénomène des raccourcisseurs, flexion reflex.
photométrie de papillotement, flicker photometry.
physionomie, physiognomy (1).
picotement, tingling.
pie-mère, pia mater, pia.
piliers de Corti, rods of Corti.
piquant, sharp[a] (1).
pitié, pity.
plaisir, agreeableness, pleasantness.
plaisir-douleur, pleasure-pain.
plaisir sensoriel, sensual pleasure.
plaisir terminal sexual, end-pleasure/sexual.
plan, scheme.
planche de rotation, tilting board, tilt-board.
planche de tapping, tapping board.
planche rotative, rotation table.
planchette d'ouija, ouija board.
plaque motrice, end-plate.
plexus, plexus.
poids, weight.
poids du cerveau, brain weight.
poil, hair.
pointage consécutif, past pointing.
pointage de régression, scatter plot.
point central, midscore.
point crucial, crux.
point de chaud, warm spot, warmth spot.
point de douleur, pain spot.
point de froid, cold spot.
point de pression, pressure spot, touch spot.
point de repère, cue.
point de sensibilité thermique, temperature spot.
point de tact, touch spot.
point médian, midscore.
points de repère, landmarks.
points de repères occasionnels, incidental cues.
polygone de fréquence, frequency polygon.
pont de Wheatstone, Wheatstone bridge.
populace, mob.
portée, import, scope.
poser, posit.
potentialité, potency.
pouls, pulse.
pourpre, purple.
pourpre rétinien, pourpre visuel, visual purple.
pouvoir, power.
pouvoir de conduction, conductivity.
pratique, practice[n], practise[n].
précision, accuracy.
prédisposition, readiness, set.
prédisposition mentale, mental set.
prédisposition nerveuse, set/neural.
prédisposition organique, set/organic.
pré-exercise, fore exercise.
prégnance, closure.
préjugé émotionnel, emotional bias.
présage, omen.
presbytie, presbyopia.
prescience, forethought.
presse, speeding up.
presselle, reaction (or response) key.
pressentiment, presentiment.
prétendre, intend[v].
preuve tirée des circonstances par induction, circumstantial evidence.
prévalence, prepotence.
prévision, forethought, prognosis.
prévoyance, foresight.
prière, prayer.
primauté, primacy.
primauté génitale, genital primacy.
principe de l'agréable, pleasure-principle.
principe de raison suffisante, sufficient reason/law of.
principe soustractif, subtractive principle.
problème de l'esprit et du corps, mind-body problem.
processus, process.
processus constitutif, founding process.
processus mentaux supérieurs, higher mental processes.
prodige, prodigy.
productivité, efficiency.
productivité industrielle, efficiency/industrial.
profil de volonté, will-profile.
profond, deep.
profondeur, depth.
progrès, improvement, proficiency.
projet, scheme.
propagation de mise en jeu, recruitment.
propager, breed[v].

se proposer, intend[v].
proposition subalterne, understatement.
propriété, property.
provisoire, provisional.
pseudomémoire, pseudomemory.
psychologie, psychology.
psychologie de la conduite, behavior psychology.
psychologie de l'enfant, child psychology.
psychologie de la foule, crowd psychology.
psychologie des peuples, folk psychology.
psychologie du comportement, behavior psychology.
psychologie éducative, educational psychology.
psychologue consultant, consulting psychologist
psychonévroses, psychoneuroses[pl].
psychophysique interne, inner psychophysics.
psychose circulaire, alternating psychosis.
psychose maniaque-dépressive, manic-depressive psychosis.
psychoses à répétition, recurrent psychoses.
pudeur, shame.
pugnacité, pugnacity.
puissance, power.
pulsion, instinct (1, 2).
pulvinar, pulvinar[n], pulvinar body.
punition, punishment.
punition capitale, capital punishment.
pupille, pupil.
pyramide du tact, touch pyramid.

Q

qualité de chef, leadership.
quart, fourth.
questionnaire, questionary, questionnaire.

R

race, breed[n].
racine, radix, root.
racine médullaire, nerve root.
radiation du corps noir, black body radiation.
raison, ground (1).
raisonnable, rational[a] (2).
raisonné, rational[a] (3).
raisonnement abstrait, abstract reasoning.
rajeunissement, rejuvenation.
rampe tympanique, scala tympani.
rampe vestibulaire, scala vestibuli.
rancune, spite.
rang, grade, rank.
rangée, array, range.
rapidité, speed (2).
rapidité de l'évanouissement du souvenir, rapidité de l'oubli, forgetting rate.
rappel, recall, revival.
se rappeler, remember.
rapport, relation, attachment, ratio.
rapport, *see* definition.
rapport entre parent et enfant, parent-child relation.
rapprochement par degrés, graded approach.
rapt, rape.
rate, spleen.
rationnel, rational[a] (1).
rayon, ray.
rayon visuel, sight/line of, sighting line.
réacquisition, relearning.
réactif, reagent (1).
réaction de recul, withdrawing response.
réaction d'équilibre, balancing response.
réaction de l'œil, eye reaction (or response).
réaction de rapprochement, approaching response.
réaction de redressement, righting response.
réaction de soutien, positive supporting reaction (or reflex).
réaction différée, delayed reaction.
réaction galvanique de la peau, galvanic skin response (or reflex).
réalisation du désir, wish fulfillment.
réapprentissage, relearning.
récessivité[n], recessive.
recherche, research.
rechercher, investigate.
réclame, advertising.
récognition, recognition.
récompense, reward.
reconnaissance, recognition, gratitude.
recrutement, recruitment.
rectitude[n], *see under* **right[a].**
récupération, recovery.
réflexe auriculaire, pinna reflex.
réflexe composé, compound reflex.
réflexe conditionné, réflexe conditionnel, conditioned reflex.
réflexe coordonné d'attitude, positive supporting reaction (or reflex).
réflexe croisé, crossed reflex.
réflexe d'agrippement, grasping reflex.
réflexe d'extension en poussée, extensor thrust reflex.
réflexe de déglutition, swallowing reflex.
réflexe de grattage, scratch reflex.
réflexe de la peau, skin reflex.
réflexe de lutte, struggle reflex, struggling.
réflexe de masse, mass reflex.
réflexe de sursaut, starting (or startled) reflex.
réflexe différé, delayed reflex.
réflexe du choc sur la face antérieure de la jambe, front tap reflex.
réflexe du clignement palpébral, eye-wink reflex.
réflex du coude, elbow-jerk reflex.
réflexe mandibulaire, jaw reflex.
réflexe massétérin, jaw reflex.
réflexe osseux, bone reflex.
réflexe patellaire, patellar (or patellar-tendon) reflex.
réflexe périosté, periosteal reflex.
réflexe profond, deep reflex.
réflexe psychogalvanique, galvanic skin response (or reflex).
réflexe rotulien, patellar (or patellar-tendon) reflex.
réflexe squelettique, skeletal reflex.
réflexes de posture, stance reflex.
réflexes de redressement visuel, visual righting reflexes.
réflexes oculaires toniques d'origine posturale céphalique, tonic neck-eye reflexes.
réflexes toniques du cou, tonic neck reflexes.
réflexes toniques oculaires d'origine labyrinthique, tonic labyrinth-eye reflexes.
réflexion rouge, red reflex.
refoulement, repression, blocking (2).
régime, diet.
règle, rule.
règle de Kundt, Kundt's rule.
relâchement[n], se relâcher, relax.
relation, relation.
relation de dominance-soumission, ascendent- (or ascendant-) submissive relation.
relief, relief (1).
remarquer, notice[v].
remords, remorse.
rendement, achievement.
rendre témoignage, witness[v].
renforcement, reinforcement.
renom, fame.
renversement de l'orientation, orientation/illusion of.
répartition des présentations dans le temps, spaced repetition.
répétition corrective, repetition-compulsion.
répétition sans intervalles de repos, unspaced repetition.
repos, rest.
repoussant, virulent.

représentation, imaging.
représentation graphique, picture (1).
reproduction, copy[n].
répugnance, disgust.
réseau, plexus.
réseau de diffraction, diffraction grating.
réserve, reserve, shyness.
résidu, residuum.
résidus de jour, day residues.
résolution, resoluteness, resolution (1, 2).
responsable, responsible.
ressemblance, similarity.
ressemblance protectrice, protective resemblance, protective coloring.
ressentiment, resentment.
restauration, restoration.
restreindre, retenir, restrain.
rêve, dream.
rêve clairvoyant, dream/clairvoyant.
rêve d'inceste, incest dream.
rêve de jour, day-dreaming.
réveil, revival.
revendication masculine, masculine protest.
rêverie, mind wandering.
reversible, reversible.
rêves hermaphroditiques, hermaphroditic dreams.
rêves typiques, typical dreams.
rire, laughter.
risible, ludicrous[n].
rite, rite.
rituel, ritual.
rivalité, rivalry.
roseau, reed.
rouge, red.
rougeur, blush, blushing.
rudiment, rudiment.

S

sagesse, wisdom.
salade de mots, word salad.
salé, saline, salty.
salve, volley, volley fire.
sans rapport à, irrelevant.
santé mentale, sanity.
satisfaction, complacence.
saut, mutation.
sauvage, wild.
saveur, flavor.
savoir *vs.* **connaître,** *see under* **comprehension.**
schéma, pattern (2).
schème (diagramme) numérique, number form.
scissiparité, fission.
scissure, fissure.
scissure calcarine, calcarine fissure.
scissure centrale, central fissure.
scissure de Sylvius, Sylvian fissure, fissure of Sylvius.
scissure rolandique, Rolandic fissure, fissure of Rolando.
sclérose en plaques, multiple sclerosis.
sclérotique, sclerotic, sclerotic coat.
secousse, concussion, contraction.
section dorée, golden section.
s'efforcer, strive.
segmentation, cleavage.
sélection, selection.
sélection entre individus, individual selection.
sélection génétique, reproductive selection.
sélection professionnelle, selection/vocational.
semence, seed.
sens, meaning (1, 3).
sensation ardente, heat (2).
sensation associée, concomitant sensation.
sensation consécutive, after-sensation.
sensation d'effort, effort experience.
sensation d'humidité, wetness sensation.
sensation de chaleur, warm (or warmth) sensation.
sensation de contact, touch.
sensation de faiblesse, weakness sensation.
sensation de froid, cold sensation.
sensation de lisse, smoothness.
sensation de poids, weight sensation.
sensation dermique, dermal sensation.
sensation de rotation, whirl sensation, whirling.
sensation de rugosité, roughness.
sensation de verre, glass sensation.
sensation du goût, gustation.
sensation générale, common sensation.
sensation lumineuse, light sensation.
sensation tactile, touch sensation.
sens de la douleur, pain sense.
sens de la pesanteur, weight sense.
sens du corps, common sensation.
sens du froid, cold sense.
sens du temps, time sense.
sensibilisation, sensitization.
sensibilité, sensitiveness, sensitivity.
sensibilité de pression profonde, deep pressure sensibility.
sensibilité entopériphérique, entoperipheral feelings.
sensibilité épipériphérique, epiperipheral feeling.
sensibilité liminaire, liminal sensitivity.
sensibilité pilaire, hair sensibility.
sensibilité profonde, deep sensibility.
sensibilité sous-cutanée, subcutaneous sensibility.
sensibilité viscérale, sensitivity/visceral.
sensible, sensuous.
sens interne, organic sense.
sensitif, sensitive.
sensuel, sensual.
sentiment, feeling.
sentiment d'infériorité, inferiority feeling.
sentiment d'irréalité, unreality/feeling of.
sentiment d'obstruction mentale, blocking (3).
sentiment de culpabilité, guilt/sense of.
sentiment de familiarité, familiarity feeling.
sentiment de la congruence, fitness/feeling of.
sentiment de l'effort mental, effort/mental.
sentiment de réalité, feeling of reality, reality/feeling of.
sentiment de responsabilité, responsibility/feeling (or consciousness) of.
sentiment de supériorité, superiority feeling.
sentiment du moi primitif (organique), consentience.
sentiment esthétique, feeling/esthetic.
sentiment négatif de soi, negative self-feeling.
sentiment positif de soi, positive self-feeling.
sentiment sexuel, sex feeling.
sentiments de passivité, passivity feelings.
sentir la pesanteur, heft[v] (2).
se relâcher, relax.
se réveiller, awake[v].
série, sequence (2).
se souvenir de, remember.
seuil, threshold.
seuil absolu, absolute threshold.
seuil absolu lumineux, brilliance threshold (or limen)/absolute.
seuil auditif absolu, auditory absolute threshold.
seuil de conscience, threshold of consciousness.
seuil de mouvement corporel, threshold for bodily motion.
seuil de rotation, threshold of rotation.

seuil différentiel, difference limen, difference threshold, differential threshold (or limen).

seuil différentiel d'intensité, intensity difference limen (or threshold).

seuil sensoriel, sense threshold, sensory threshold.

sevrage, weaning.

siège de l'esprit, seat of mind, seat of consciousness.

sifflet de Galton, Galton whistle.

signal avertisseur, warning signal.

signal duplex, duplex marker.

signes locaux, local sign, locality sign.

signification, import, meaning (2, 3).

sillon, fissure.

sillon de Rolando, Rolandic fissure, fissure of Rolando.

simulation, feigning.

simuler (une maladie), maligner.

singe, monkey.

sixte, sixth.

soif, thirst.

soins de convalescence, after-care.

sombre, dark.

sommeil, sleep, trance.

son, clang, sound, tone (1).

son composé, tone/compound.

son de sommation, summation tone.

son étalon, pitch/standard.

sonorité du son, loudness.

son résultant additionnel, summation tone.

son résultant différentiel, difference tone.

sophisme, fallacy.

sophisme biologique, biological fallacy.

sophisme des psychologues, psychologist's fallacy.

sophisme historique, historical fallacy.

sorcellerie, sorcery, witchcraft.

souci, worry.

soufflerie, pressure blower.

soulagement, relief (2).

soulever, heft[v].

souleveur de poids, weights/lifting.

soupçon, suspicion.

soupir, sigh.

sourd-muet, deaf-mute.

sourire, smile.

soutenu, sustained.

soutiens de poids de Fechner, Fechner weight holders.

souvenir, memory (2, 3), recollection.

souvenir-écran, screen memory.

se souvenir de, remember.

spasme musculaire, twitching.

spectre, ghost.

stade, stage.

stade agricole, agricultural stage.

stade éjectif, ejective stage.

stade oral, oral stage, oral libido.

stade pastoral, pastoral stage.

stigmate, stigma.

stimulus froid, cold-stimulus.

stimulus adéquat, adequate stimulus.

stimulus infraliminaire, subliminal stimulus.

structure, Gestalt.

style, style.

subconscient, subconscious.

subreptice, surreptitious.

substance blanche, white matter.

substance grise, gray matter.

succion, sucking.

sucré, sweet.

suite, order (1), sequence (1, 2, 3).

sujet réagissant, reagent (2), reactor.

supraliminaire, supraliminal.

sur, sour.

surapprentissage, overlearning.

surdétermination, overdetermination.

surdité, deafness.

surdité corticale, deafness/cortical.

surdité de transmission, conduction deafness.

surdité musicale, tone-deafness.

surdité nerveuse, nerve deafness.

surdité psychique, *see under* **psychic blindness (deafness,** etc.).

surdité verbale, word-deafness.

surhomme, superman.

surnaturel, supernatural.

surprise, surprise.

surproduction, overproduction.

surrénal, suprarenal.

survivance des plus aptes, survival of the fittest.

syllabe privée de sens, nonsense syllable.

symptôme, symptom (1, 2, 3).

syndrome anxieuse, hysteria/anxiety.

système cérébro-spinal, cerebrospinal system.

système de comportement, behavior pattern.

système d'écriture, handwriting system.

système de rapport, relationship system.

T

table des couleurs, color circle.

tableau, chart.

tableau de distribution, scatter diagram.

tâche, task.

tache aveugle, blind spot.

tache jaune, yellow spot.

taches d'empreinte respiratoire, breathing spots.

tact, touch.

tactisme, taxis.

taquinerie, teasing.

tâter, feel[vt].

taux, rate[n].

taux de déficience auditive, hearing loss.

taux de fluctuation de la main d'œuvre, turnover/labor.

technique comportant connaissance préalable, procedure with knowledge.

technique expérimental, procedure.

tégument, tegmentum (1).

teinte foncée, shade.

teinte claire, tint (1).

teintes, color shades.

témoignage, testimony.

témoin[np], witness.

temps, time.

temps d'accommodation, accommodation time.

temps d'adaptation, adaptation time.

temps d'association, association time.

temps de conduction, conduction time.

temps de discernement, discrimination time.

temps de latence réflexe, reflex time.

temps de latence physiologique, physiological time.

temps de perception, perception time.

temps de réaction, reaction (or response) time.

temps de réaction de fixation de l'œil, fixation response time.

temps de retour, regression time.

temps de saccade, saccadic time.

temps synaptique, synapse time.

temps utile, useful (serviceable) duration.

tendance, tendency, trend (1, 2).

tendance à s'échapper, escape tendency.

tendence innée, tendency/inherited.

tendu, tense[a].

tension, strain.

terminaison nerveuse, nerve ending.

terminaisons nerveuses libres intraépidermiques, free nerve endings.

terminaisons nerveuses papillaires de Ruffini, Ruffini capillary endings (or plumes).

terreur, fright.

terreurs nocturnes, night terrors.

test, test (2).

test collectif, group test.

test commercial, trade test.

test d'association de partie à tout, part-whole test.

test d'exécution, performance test.

test d'interprétation d'image, picture interpretation test.

test de capacité d'appréhension de chiffres, digit-span test.

test de comparaisons paires, paired associates.

test de complètement de chiffres, number-completion test.

test de complètement de dessins, picture-completion test.

test de construction des mots, word-building test.

test de cubes colorés, test de dessins de Kohs, block-design test.

test de la balle et du champ, ball-and-field test.

test de la capacité limite d'appréhension, apprehension-span test.

test de la montre, watch test.

test de mémoire immédiate des chiffres, digit-span test.

test de mémoire immédiate des mots, word-span test.

test de mémoire immédiate des syllabes, syllable-span test.

test de phrases en désordre, disarranged-sentence test.

test de profil mental, profile test.

test de rapidité du classement de cartes, card sorting, card-sorting test.

test de séquences de chiffres, number-completion test.

test des taches d'encre, ink-blot test.

test de "tapping" à points, dotting test.

test de volonté-tempérament, will-temperament test.

test du groupe de points, spot-pattern test.

test (épreuve) du champ d'attention, attention-span, attention-span test.

tests (épreuves) étalonnés, standard tests.

tests sanguins, blood tests.

théorie animiste, ghost theory.

théorie d'émotion induite, induced emotion/theory of.

théorie d'entraînement, practice theory.

théorie de conduction membraneuse, conduction/membrane theory of.

théorie de la connaissance, theory of knowledge.

théorie de la forme, Gestalt theory.

théorie de la matière mentale, mind-stuff theory.

théorie de l'âme, soul theory.

théorie de la sensibilité, hedonics.

théorie de l'atomisme mental, mind-dust theory.

théorie de l'unité à double face, double-aspect theory.

théorie de l'usage et de la désuétude, use and disuse theory, use-inheritance.

théorie des fantômes (t. animiste), ghost theory.

théorie du court-circuit, short-circuit theory.

théorie du moi et d'autrui, ego-alter theory.

théorie égoiste du rêve, egoistic theory of dreams.

théorie vertébrale du crâne, vertebral theory of the skull.

théories de l'acquisition (de l'apprentissage), learning/theories of.

théories de l'audition, hearing/theories of.

théories enfantines de naissance, infantile birth theories.

tierce, third (*mus.*).

timbre, clang-color, clang-quality, clang-tint.

timidité, shyness.

timidité instinctive, timidité spontanée, bashfulness.

tintement, tinnitus.

ton, tone (2).

ton affectif, feeling tone.

tonalité affective, affective tone.

tonalité chromatique, hue.

tonalité de plaisir ou peine, hedonic tone.

ton de battement, beat-tone.

ton de combinaison, combination tone.

ton grave (bas), flat[n].

ton partial (harmonique) supérieur, overtone.

ton résultant, combination tone.

toucher, touch.

toux, cough.

toxicomane, addict.

trait inné, native trait.

transe, trance.

transfert d'apprentissage, cross-education, cross-training.

transfert d'entraînement, transfer of training.

transmission antidromique, conduction/antidromic.

transmission osseuse, bone-conduction.

trauma de la naissance, birth trauma.

travail, work.

travail de rêve, dream work.

tremblement, trembling, tremor.

tremblement scriptural, writing tremor.

tressaillement, thrill.

triade, triad.

tribu, tribe.

tristesse, sadness.

trompe, salpinx.

trompe d'Eustache, Eustachian tube.

tronc cérébral, brain stem.

tronc nerveux, nerve root.

trouble, disturbance.

trouble propagé, disturbance/propagated.

truisme, truism.

tubercule cendré, tuber cinereum.

tubercules quadrijumeaux, corpora quadrigemina.

tumulte, disturbance.

tuyau d'interférence, interference tube.

tuyau d'orgue étalon, pitch pipe.

tuyau sonore, pipe.

type coercitif, compulsive type.

types individuels dans la capacité d'apprendre, learning types.

U

unité temporelle de Freeman Freeman time-unit.

univoque, univocal.

usage, custom, use[n] (2).

utérus, uterus.

utilitarisme, utilitarianism.

V

valeur, value, worth.

valeur numérique en échelle, scale value.

valeur sélective, selective value.

vanité, conceit.

vantardise, boasting.

variation fortuite, chance variation.

variation graduelle, gradient (1).

vaudou, voodooism.

végétatif, vegetative.

veille, wakefulness.

veiller, wake[v].

velléité, velleity.

vélocité, velocity.

vengeance, revenge.

vérité, truth.

vérité évidente, truism.

ver plat, flatworm.

vert, green.

vertige, dizziness.

vertu, virtue.

vie, life.

vie mentale, mental life.

vie utérine, uterine life.

vif, sharp^{a} (4).
visage, face.
vision, sight.
vision au cristal, crystal gazing, scrying.
vision crépusculaire, rod vision, twilight vision.
vision cristalloscopie, crystal gazing.
vision monoculaire, monocular (or uniocular) vision.
vision par bâtonnets, rod vision.
vision récurrente, recurrent vision.
vision scotopique, rod vision.
vitesse, speed (1, 2).
vitesse de saccade, saccadic speed.
vitesse du son, sound/velocity of.
vivacité, clearness, vividness.
vivre^{v}, live.
vogue, fashion.
voie, path, pathway, tract.
voie d'élan, delay-path.
voie pyramidale, pyramidal tract.
voie supplémentaire, delay-path.
voie terminale, end-path.
voie terminale commune, final common path.
voies optiques, optic tracts.
voies volitionnelles, conative channels.
volonté, will.
volonté générale, general will.
volonté sociale, social will.
voluminosité, voluminousness.
vomissement, vomiting.
vouloir^{v}, will.
voussure, kurtosis.
voyeurisme, scopophilia.
vrai, true.
vraisemblance, likelihood.

Z

zéro de productivité, efficiency/zero.
zéro de progrès, improvement/zero.
zone marginale de la conscience, consciousness/marginal.

GLOSSARY OF GERMAN TERMS

Note: Where there are given in the body of the Dictionary two or more definitions of any one of the following English equivalents, the figure in parentheses after the equivalent indicates which of these dictionary definitions applies to the foreign word.

A

Abart, sport (1).
abbildend, imaging.
Aberglaube, superstition.
abhalten, restrain.
Abhängigkeit, dependence, dependency.
Abklingen, *see* definition.
Ablehnung, rejection.
Ablenkung, distraction (1), diversion (1).
Abnahme, decrement.
Abneigung, antipathy, aversion, dislike.
Abreagierung, abreaction.
Abscheu, repulsion.
Absicht, design/purposive, intent, purpose.
Absicht, *see* definition.
absoluter Eindruck, absolute impression.
absolutes Gehör, pitch/absolute.
Absonderung, detachment, secretion (2).
Absonderungsstoff, secretion (1).
Abstand, distance (2).
Abstossung, repulsion.
Abstraktion, abstraction (2).
Abtragung, extirpation.
Abulie, abulia, aboulia.
Abweichung, deviation, dissent.
Abweichung des Lichtes, aberration of light.
Achillessehnenreflex, Achilles' tendon reflex.
Achsendrehung, rotation.
Achsenfortsatz, Achsenzylinder, axon, axone.
Achtung, respect^{n}.
Adaptationszeit, adaptation time.
adäquater Reiz, adequate stimulus.
Ader, vein.
Aderhaut, choroid, choroid coat.
Affekt, affect, emotion.
Affe-n^{pl}, monkey(s), ape(s).
After, anus.
Ähnlichkeit, resemblance, similarity.
Ahnung, premonition.
Akkord, chord (1).
Akt, act^{n}.
Aktionsstrom, action current.
Aktivität, activity.
Aktpsychologie, act psychology.
Akustik, acoustics (1).
akut, acute (3).
alles oder nichts Gesetz, all-or-none law.
allgemein, general.
Allgemeinbegriff, general concept, general idea.
Allgemeinheit, universality.
Allgemeinvorstellung, general idea.
Allmacht der Gedanken, omnipotence of thought.
Allyl-Cacodylgerüche, alliaceous.
Alpdrücken, nightmare.
Amber-Moschusgerüche, ambrosiac.
Amboss, incus.
Ammonswindung, hippocampus.
Amperemeter, ammeter.
Amplitude, amplitude.
Analerotik, anal erotism.
Analphabetismus, illiteracy.
Analyse, analysis.
Anbetung, adoration, worship (1).
Änderung, variation (2).
Aneignung, acquisition.
Anfall, attack.
Anfänger, novice.
Angaben, data.
angeboren, congenital, connate, inborn, inherited, innate, native.
angewandte Psychologie, applied psychology.
Angleichung, assimilation.
Angriffslust, aggressiveness.
Angst, anxiety.
Angsthysterie, hysteria/anxiety.
Ängstlichkeit, apprehensiveness.
Angstneurose, anxiety neurosis.
Anhaltspunkt, cue.
Anhänglichkeit, attachment (2).
Anklingen, *see* definition.
Anlage, disposition (2, 3, 5), predisposition (2), talent, *see also under* **primordium.**
Anlage, *see* definition.
Anlehnungstypus, anaclitic object-choice.
Anmut, grace (1).
Annahme, assumption, presumption (1).
Annehmlichkeit, agreeableness, pleasantness.
Anordnung, form, disposition (1), pattern (2).
Anpassung, adaptation, adjustment.
Anpassungsfähigkeit, adaptability.
Anregung, *see* definition.
Anregung, incentive (2).
anschaulich, palpable.
Anschauung, intuition (1).
Anschauung, *see* definition.
Anschauungsbild, eidetic image.
Anschein, appearance (2).
Ansicht, opinion.
Anstand, decency.
Ansteckung, infection.
Anstoss, impulse.
Anstrengung, effort (2).
antreiben, stimulate (3).
Antrieb, *see* definition.
Anziehung, attraction.
Apparat, apparatus.
Apperzeption, apperception.
Äquivalenz, equivalence.
Arbeit, study, work.
Arbeitskurve, work curve.
Ärger, anger.
Argwohn, suspicion.
aromatisch, aromatic.
Art, species (2).
Assimilation, assimilation.
Assoziationsfasern, association fibers.
Assoziationstäuschung, associative illusion.
Assoziationszeit, association time.
assoziative Hemmung, associative inhibition.
ätherisch, ethereal.
Atmung, respiration/external.
Attribut, attribute.
Auffassung, apperception.
Aufforderungscharakter, appeal, valence.
Aufgabe, instruction (2), theme (1), *see also under* **mental set.**
Aufgabe, *see* definition.
Aufgaben, *see under* **Ausfragemethode.**
Aufmerksamkeit, attention.
Aufmerksamkeitsschwankung, attention/fluctuation of.

Aufmerksamkeitsumfang, attention /range (or span of).
aufregen, stimulate (3).
Aufregung, excitement (1), upset.
Aufrichtigkeit, frankness.
Aufsatz, theme (2).
aufs Geratewohl, (at) random.
Aufzählung, enumeration.
Augapfel, eyeball.
Auge, eye.
Augenachse, optical axis.
Augenbewegungen, eye-movements.
Augenblick, instant, moment (2).
Ausarbeitung, elaboration.
Ausdauer, endurance.
Ausdehnung, extent, extension (1).
Ausdruck, expression, term (1).
ausdrücklich, explicit.
Ausdrucksbewegung, expression.
Ausfragemethode, *see* definition.
Ausgeprägtheit, distinctness.
ausgezeichnet, unique.
Auslese, selection.
Aussage, testimony.
Aussage test, *see* definition.
Aussenwelt, external world.
äusserer, outer.
äusserer Gehörgang, meatus/external auditory.
äusserer Kniehöcker, geniculate body/lateral.
äusserlich, external, superficial.
Äusserung, expression.
auswendig lernen, memorize, rote learning.
Auswertung, evaluation.
Autorität, authority.

B

Bahn, path, pathway.
Bahnung, facilitation, reinforcement, *see also under* **cross-conditioning.**
Balken, callosum, corpus callosum.
Bande, gang.
Basilarmembran, basilar membrane.
Bastard, hybrid.
Bau, structure.
Bauch, abdomen.
Bauchfell, peritoneum.
Bauchreden, ventriloquism.
Bauchspeicheldrüse, pancreas.
Bausinn, constructiveness.
beabsichtigen, intend.
Beben, thrill[n].
Bedauern, regret.
Bedenklichkeit, scruple.
Bedeutung, meaning (2).
bedingter Reflex, conditioned reflex.
Bedingung, condition[n] (1, 2).
Bedürfnis, need, want (2).
Befriedigung, gratification, satisfaction.
begabt, gifted.
Begabung, ability, aptitude, endowment.
Begehren, desire.
Begleitsumstände, circumstances.
Begriff, concept.
Behalten, retention.
Behandlung, treatment.
Beharren, persistence (1).
Beharrlichkeit, persistence (3).
Behauptung, assertion.
Beispiel, instance, example.
Bekanntheitsgefühl, familiarity feeling.
Bekanntschaft, acquaintance with.
Bekanntsqualität, *see* definition.
Bekehrung, conversion (3).
belanglos, irrelevant.
Beleuchtung, illumination.
Belohnung, reward.
bemerken, notice.
beobachten, witness[v].
Beobachtung, observation.
Beobachtungsfehler, errors of observation.
berechtigt, legitimate (1).
Bereich, scope.
Bereitschaft, readiness, *see also under* **Aufgabe, mental set.**
Bereitschaft, *see* definition.
Bericht, report.
Beruf, vocation.
Berufsberatung, guidance/vocational.
Beruhigung, quiescence.
Berührung, touch.
Berührungsempfindung, contact sensation.
Beschaffenheit, state.
Bescheidenheit, modesty.
Beschleunigung, acceleration.
Beschreibung, description, *see also under* **information.**
Beschwörung, exorcism.
Besessenheit, obsession.
Besetzung, cathexis.
Besonnenheit, discretion.
Besorgnis, anxiety.
Beständigkeit, stability (3).
Bestätigung, sanction (1), verification.
bestimmen, determine.
bestimmt, definite.
Bestimmung, determination.
Bestürzung, bewilderment.
Betäubung, stupor, torpor.
Betragen, conduct[n] (1).
Betrug, deception.
Beugung, diffraction.
Beuteltiere, marsupialia, marsupials.
Bevölkerung, population.
Bewegung, motion.
Beweis, evidence, proof.
Beweisführung, demonstration.
Bewunderung, admiration.
Bewusstheit, awareness (3), *see also under* **Bewusstseinslage.**
Bewusstheit, *see* definition.
Bewusstsein, consciousness.
Bewusstsein der Freiheit, freedom/consciousness of.
Bewusstsein der Realität, reality/feeling of.
Bewusstseinsfeld, consciousness/field of.
Bewusstseinsinhalt, content of consciousness.
Bewusstseinslage, attitude, mental attitude (2), mental set, *see also under* **Bewusstheit.**
Bewusstseinslage, *see* definition.
Bewusstseinsschwelle, threshold of consciousness.
bezeichnen, signify.
Bezeichnung, denotation.
bezeugen, witness[v].
Beziehung, relation.
bezüglich, relative[a].
Bezugsvorstellung, *see* definition.
Bezugsvorstellung, *see under* **Absicht.**
Bild, picture.
Bilderschrift, hieroglyphic writing, pictograph, pictogram.
Bildung, culture.
Bisam, musk.
Bläschen, vesicle.
Blase, vesicle.
Blässe, pallor.
Blaublindheit, blue-blindness.
Blaugelbblindheit, blue-yellow blindness.
Blickfeld, regard/field of.
Blickfeld des Bewusstseins, consciousness/field of.
Blicklinie, regard/line of.
Blickpunkt, fixation-point, point of fixation (1, 2), regard/point of.
blinder Fleck, blind spot.
Blindheit, blindness.
Blinzeln, blinking, winking.
Blinzelreflex, wink reflex.
blumig, flowery, *see also under* **balsamic.**
Blutgefäss, blood vessel.
Blutung, hemorrhage.
Bogengänge, semicircular canals, semicirculars.
böser Blick, evil eye.
Bosheit, malice, maliciousness.
Böswilligkeit, malevolence.

Brandstiftung, arson.

Brechmittel, emetic.

Brechung, refraction.

Brechungsindex, refraction/index of, refractive index.

Brechungsmittel, refracting media.

Brennpunkt, focus.

Brennpunkt der Aufmerksamkeit, attention/focus of.

Brennweite, focal length.

brenzlich, empyreumatic.

Bruch, disruption.

Brücke, pons Varolii.

Brust-, pectoral.

Brust, thorax.

Busse, penitence.

C

Charakterzug, trait (2).

Chiasma, chiasm, optic chiasm.

Cortische Bogen, arches of Corti.

Cortische Pfeiler, rods of Corti.

Cortisches Organ, Corti/organ of.

D

Dämmerungssehen, twilight vision.

Dämmerzustände, twilight states/hysterical.

Dankbarkeit, gratitude.

Darm, intestine.

Darstellung, dramatization.

Dasein, existence.

Dauer, duration.

Dauerhaftigkeit, stability (2).

Deckerinnerung, screen memory.

Deckpunkte (Hering), identical points.

Demut, humility.

Denken, reasoning, thinking.

Denkgesetze, thought/laws of.

Denkvermögen, elaborative faculty.

determinierende Tendenz, directive tendency, determining tendency.

Deutlichkeit, distinctness.

Dichtigkeit, density.

Differenzierung, differentiation.

Differenzton, difference tone.

Differenzurteil, difference judgment.

Ding, thing.

Diskretion, discretion.

Doppelbewusstsein, personality/dual.

Doppelhändigkeit, ambidextrality.

Doppelich, personality/dual.

Doppelsehen, diplopia.

doppelte Persönlichkeit, personality/dual.

Drang, impulsion, urge.

Drehpunkt, center of rotation.

Drehschwindel, vertigo.

Dreiklang, triad, *see also under* **chord.**

dressieren, train.

Dressur, training.

Droge, drug.

Druck, pressure.

Druckempfindung, pressure-sensation, *see also under* **touch sensation.**

Druckpunkt, pressure point.

Druckwage, pressure balance.

Drüse, gland.

Drüsen der inneren Sekretion, ductless glands.

Duft, scent.

duftig, fragrant.

dunkel, dark.

Dunkeladaptation, dark adaptation, darkness a.

Dunkelauge, dark-adapted eye.

Dunkelfeldbeleuchtung, dark-field illumination.

Durchmesser, diameter.

Durchschnitt, average.

durchsichtige Flächenfarbe, transparent plane color.

Durst, thirst.

Durtonleiter, major scale.

E

ebenmerklicher Unterschied, difference/least noticeable, just noticeable difference.

Ehe, marriage.

ehelich, legitimate (2).

Ehre, honor.

Ehrfurcht, awe.

Ehrlichkeit, honesty.

Ei, egg, ovum.

Eidetiker, *see* definition.

eidetisch, eidetic.

eidetische Anlage, eidetic disposition.

Eierstock, ovary.

Eifersucht, jealousy.

Eigenlicht der Netzhaut, idioretinal light.

Eigenliebe, egotism, self-love.

Eigenschaft, attribute, property.

Eignung, ability.

Eignungsprüfung, vocational aptitude test.

einäugig, uniocular, monocular.

einäugiges Sehen, monocular (or uniocular) vision.

Einbildung, conceit, presumption (2).

Einbildungskraft, imagination.

eindeutig, unequivocal, univocal.

Eindringlichkeit, insistence.

Eindruck, impression.

Eindrucksmethode, impression/method of.

einfach, simple.

Einfallswinkel, angle of incidence.

Einfühlung, empathy.

Eingeweide, viscera.

Einheit, unit, unity.

Einheitstypus, unitary type.

Einklang, unison.

einohrig, uniaural.

einohriges Hören, monaural (or uniaural) hearing.

Einrichtung, device.

Einsicht, insight.

Einstellung, *see* definition.

Einstellung, attitude, mental attitude (3), mental set, *see also under* **Aufgabe, Bereitschaft, directive tendency, set.**

Einwilligung, assent, consent.

einzeln, singular (1).

einzigartig, unique.

Eitelkeit, conceit, vanity.

Ekel, disgust.

ekelhaft, putrid.

Ekstase, ecstasy, trance.

Elle, ulna.

Ellenbogennerv, ulnar nerve.

Empfänglichkeit, sensibility (3).

Empfängnis, conception (2).

empfindend, empfindlich, sensitive[a].

Empfindlichkeit, sensibility (2), sensitiveness, sensitivity.

Empfindung, sensation.

Empfindungsvermögen, sensibility (1).

Empfindungszuwüchse, sensation increments.

empyreumatisch, empyreumatic.

endokrine Drüse, endocrine, endocrine gland, ductless gland.

Energie, energy (2).

Entartung, degeneracy, degeneration.

Entbehrung, privation.

entdecken, discover.

entfernt, remote[a].

Entfernung, distance (1).

entnerven, enervate.

Entsagung, resignation.

Entscheidung, decision.

Entschlossenheit, resoluteness.

Entschluss, decision, resolution.

Entstehung, genesis.

Enttäuschung, disappointment.

entweihen, profane[v] (2).

Entwicklung, development, evolution.

Entwicklungshemmung, development/arrest of.

Entwicklungslehre, evolutionism.

Entwicklungspsychologie, genetic psychology.

Entwöhnung, weaning.

Entwurf, scheme.

erben, inherit.

Erblichkeit, heredity (2).

Erbrechen, vomiting.

Erbschaft, heritage, inheritance (1).

Erdichtung, fiction (1).

Ereignis, event.

Erfahrung, experience (1, 2).

Erfassung, apprehension.

Erfindung, invention.

Erfolg, result (1).

erforschen, investigate.

Erforschung, research.

Ergebnis, result (2).

Ergreifen, prehension.

Erhaltung der Energie, conservation of energy.

erhöht, sharp[a] (3).

erhöhter Ton, sharp[n] (1).

Erholung, recreation.

sich erinnern, remember.

Erinnerung, memory (3), recall, recollection, remembrance.

Erkennen, recognition.

Erkenntnis, cognition.

Erkenntnistheorie, epistemology, theory of knowledge.

Erklärung, explanation.

Erlebnis, experience (3).

Erleichterung, relief (2).

Erlernungsmethode, complete learning (or memorizing) method.

Ermüdbarkeit, fatiguability.

Ermüdung, fatigue.

Ernährung, nutrition.

Ernst, gravity (1).

Erörterung, argument.

Erregbarkeit, excitability.

Erregung, excitement (2), excitation.

Erregungs-Beruhigungsgefühl, excitement-inhibition/feeling of.

Erregungszustand, exaltation.

Ersatz-, substitute.

Erschaffung, creation.

Erscheinung, apparition, appearance (1), phenomenon.

Erscheinungsweise, mode of appearance.

erschlaffen, relax (1).

erschlichen, surreptitious.

Erschöpfung, exhaustion.

Erschütterung, concussion.

Ersparnismethode, saving method.

erst, prime.

Erwachsener, adult.

Erwartung, anticipation, expectation.

erworbene Eigenschaft, acquired character.

erziehen, train.

Erziehung, education (1), training.

Es, id (2).

Etikette, etiquette.

Eustachische Röhre, Eustachian tube.

Examen, examination (1).

Existenz, existence.

Experiment, experiment.

Exponent, exponent (1).

F

Fachmann, expert.

Fähigkeit, ability, capacity.

falsch, spurious, false.

Falschheit, falsity.

Farbe, color.

Farbenblindheit, color-blindness.

Farbendreieck, color triangle.

Farbenempfindung, color sensation.

Farbenhören, colored hearing.

Farbenkreis, color circle (1).

Farbenkreisel, color wheel.

Farbenlehre, chromatics.

Farbenmischung, color mixture.

Farbenschwäche, color-weakness.

Farbentafel, color circle (2).

Farbenton, Farbton, hue.

farblos, achromatic (1).

Faser, fiber.

Faserkreuzung, decussation.

Faserschicht, fibrous layer.

faul, putrid.

Faxensyndrom, *see* definition.

Fehler, error (1), fault.

Fehlermethoden, error methods.

Fehlhandlung, error (2), error/motivated.

Fehlleistung, parapraxis.

Feindschaft, hostility.

Fernpunkt, distant point.

Fernsinn, distant (or distance) sense.

Fertigkeit, proficiency.

feststellen, determine.

Feueranbetung, Feuerverehrung, fire-worship.

Figur, diagram.

Fingerschlüssel, response key, reaction key.

Fingersprache, finger spelling.

Fixationslinie, fixation-line, line of fixation.

Fixationspunkt, fixation-point, point of fixation.

Fläche, area (1, 2), surface.

Flächenfarbe, film color.

Flimmergrenze, critical flicker frequency.

Flimmern, flicker, flicker phenomenon.

Flimmerphotometrie, flicker photometry.

Flucht, flight.

Flüstern, whispering.

Folge, sequence (3).

folgen[v], sequence (1).

Folgerung, conclusion, inference.

Form, form.

Formel, formula.

Forschung, research.

Fortsatz, process (4).

Fortschritt, progress.

Fragebogen, questionary, questionnaire.

Franse, fringe.

freiwillig, voluntary.

Freude, joy.

Freundschaft, friendship.

Fruchtbarkeit, fertility.

fruchtig, fruity.

früher, anterior (1).

Frühreife, precocity.

Fühler, Fühlhorn, antenna.

Führerschaft, leadership.

Fundamentalformel, fundamental formula.

fundierter Inhalt, content/founded.

fundierende Inhalte, *see under* **complex** (3).

Furche, fissure.

Furcht, dread, fear.

Furchtsamkeit, timidity.

G

Gähnen, yawning.

Galtonpfeife, Galton whistle.

galvanischer Strom, galvanic current.

Gang, duct.

Ganzes, Ganzheit, whole[n].

Ganzton, whole tone.

Ganz- und Teil-Lernmethode, whole and part learning.

Gattung, genus (2).

Gaumen, palate.

Gaumenzäpfchen, uvula.

Gebärde, gesture.

Gebärdensprache, gesture language.

Gebärmutter, uterus.

Gebet, prayer.

Gebrauch, use[n].

gebundene Assoziation, association/controlled.

Gedächtnis, memory (1).

Gedächtnisfarbe, memory color.

Gedächtnisstufen, memory levels.

Gedanke, thought.

Gedankengang, train of thought (or of ideas).

Gedankenlesen, mind-reading.
Gedankenstrom, thinking/stream of.
Gedankenübertragung, telepathy.
Gedränge, crowd.
Gefässnerv, vasomotor nerve.
Gefässsystem, vascular system.
Geflecht, plexus.
Gefühl, feeling.
Gefühl der Unwirklichkeit, unreality/feeling of.
Gefühlston, feeling tone.
(das) **Gegebene,** given.
Gegebenheiten, data.
Gegebenheitsgeruch, *see under* **object-odor.**
Gegenfarben, antagonistic colors.
Gegensatz, opposition.
Gegenstand, object.
gegenständlich, objective.
Gegenstandsgeruch, object-odor, object-smell.
Gegenstandstheorie, *see* definition.
geheiligt, sacred.
geheimnisvoll, mysterious.
Gehen, walking.
Gehirn, brain.
Gehör, audition.
Gehörknöchelchen, ossicles/auditory.
Gehorsam, obedience.
Gehörsempfindung, auditory sensation.
Geisselung, flagellation.
Geist, mind, spirit.
Geistesabwesenheit, abstraction (1), absent-mindedness.
Geisteskrankheit, derangement/mental, psychosis (1).
Geistesstörung, aberration/mental.
geistig, mental.
gelb, yellow.
gelber Fleck, macula, macula lutea, yellow spot.
Gelegenheit, occasion.
Gelehrigkeit, docility.
Gemeinempfindung, common sensation.
Gemeinempfindungen, Gemeingefühl, common sensibility.
Gemeinplatz, truism.
Gemeinschaft, community.
Gemeinsinn, systemic sense.
Gemüt, Gemütsbewegung, *see* definition.
Gemütsbewegung, affect, emotion.
Gemütsruhe, repose.
Gemütsstimmung, disposition (4).
Genauigkeit, accuracy, precision.
Genie, genius (1).
Genitalprimat, genital primacy.
geometrisches Mittel, geometric(al) mean.
Geräusch, noise.
Gerechtigkeit, justice (1, 2, 3), righteousness.
Geruch, odor, olfaction, smell.
Geruchsinn, olfaction.
Gesamtbewusstsein, general consciousness.
gesamte Reizlage, situation (1).
Geschäftigkeit, industry (1).
Geschehen, event.
Geschichte, history.
Geschicklichkeit, dexterity, skill.
Geschlecht, sex.
Geschlechtsgefühl, sex feeling.
geschlechtslose Zeugung, asexual reproduction.
Geschlechtsreife, puberty.
Geschlechtsunterschiede, sex differences.
Geschlossenheit, closure.
Geschmack, taste.
Geschmacksempfindung, gustation.
Geschmacksknospe, taste bud.
Geschmackslähmung, ageusia.
Geschmacksqualitäten, gustatory qualities.
Geschwindigkeit, speed, velocity.
geschwollen, tumid.
Geselle, journeyman.
Geselligkeit, sociability.
Gesellschaft, society.
gesellschaftlicher Wille, social will.
Gesellschaftstrieb, sociality.
Gesetz, law.
Gesetz der Berührungsassoziation, contiguity/law of.
Gesetz der Prägnanz, precision/law of.
Gesetz des zureichenden Grundes, sufficient reason/law of.
Gesetzeskunde, nomology.
Gesicht, face, sight, vision (1).
Gesichtsachse, visual axis.
Gesichtsfeld, visual field.
Gesichtslinie, visual axis.
Gesichtssinn, sight.
Gesichtswinkel, facial angle, visual angle.
gespannt, tense[a] (2).
gespiegelte Farbe, reflected color.
Gespräch, conversation.
Gestalt, *see* definition.
Gestalt, form.
Gestaltqualität, form quality.
Gestalt(s)qualität, *see* definition.
gestreifter Muskel, striate (or striped) muscle.
Gewebe, tissue.
Gewerbe, vocation.
Gewicht, weight.
Gewimmel, crowd.
Gewissen, conscience.
Gewissensbiss, remorse.
Gewissheit, certainty.
Gewohnheit, habit.
Gewöhnung, habituation.
Gewölbe, fornix.
giftig, toxic.
Gitter, diffraction grating.
Glanz, luster.
Glasempfindung, glass sensation.
Glaskörper, vitreous, vitreous body, vitreous humor, vitreum.
Glätte, smoothness.
glatte Kurve, smooth curve.
glatter Muskel, smooth muscle.
Glattheit, smoothness.
Glaube, belief, faith.
Glaubwürdigkeit, credibility.
Gleichartigkeit, homogeneity.
gleichbedeutend, identical (3).
gleichförmigkeit, homogeneity, uniformity.
Gleichgewicht, equilibrium.
Gleichheit, equality, sameness.
gleichmässige Stufen, equal steps.
Gleichung, equation.
Glied, term (2).
Glück, happiness.
Glühen, glow.
Gnade, grace (2).
goldener Schnitt, golden section.
Gott, god.
Grad, degree.
Gradient, gradient.
graphische Darstellung, graph.
grau, gray, grey.
graue Substanz, gray matter.
Grausamkeit, cruelty.
Grausen, terror.
Greif-, greifend, prehensile.
Greisenalter, senescence.
Greisenhaftigkeit, senility.
Grenze, limit (1), terminal sensitivity, term (3).
Grenzmethode, limits/method of.
Grenzwert, limit (2).
Grimasse, grimace.
Groll, spite.
Grösse, magnitude.
Grössenwahn, grandeur/delusions (or ideas) of, megalomania.
Grosshirn, cerebrum.
Grosshirnrinde, cortex cerebri.
grün, green.
Grund, ground (1, 2), reason[n] (1).
Grundfarbe (Mach), color/fundamental.
Grundfarbe, color/primary.
Grundstoff, element.
Grundton, fundamental tone, fundamental.
Gültigkeit, validity.

Gürtel, zone.
gut, good.

H

Haargefäss, capillary.
Haarzellen, hair cells.
halbbewusst, semiconscious, half-conscious.
Halbmesser, radius (1).
Halbton, semitone.
Haltung, attitude (1), mental attitude, posture.
Handhabung, management (1).
Handlung, action.
Handschrift, handwriting.
Handschriftendeutung, graphological portrait.
Harmonium, organ (3).
Harn, urine.
Harnröhre, urethra.
harzig, resinous.
Hass, hate.
hässlich, ugly.
Häufigkeitskurve, frequency curve.
Hauptfarbe, color/primary.
Hauptwert, central tendency.
Haut, derma, dermis, skin.
Hautempfindung, cutaneous sense, dermal sensation.
Hautsinn, cutaneous sense.
heben, heft.
Hefnerkerze, Hefner candle (*see under* **candle**).
heftig, acute (2).
heilig, sacred.
Heimkehrvermögen, homing.
Held, hero.
Heldensage, myth.
hell, bright, light[a] (1).
Helligkeit, brightness, brilliance, luminosity.
Helligkeitskontrast, brilliance contrast.
Hellsichtigkeit, clairvoyance.
Hemmung, inhibition.
Herde, herd.
Herdeninstinkt, gregariousness.
Herrschaft, dominance, mastery.
Herz, heart.
Herzvorhof, auricle (2).
Hetzjagd, hunting.
Heuchelei, hypocrisy.
Hexerei, witchcraft.
Hilfenmethode, prompting/method of.
Hilflosigkeit, helplessness.
Hilfsapparat, accessory sense-apparatus.
Hinterhaupt, occiput.
Hinterhauptslappen, occipital lobe.
Hinterhirn, hindbrain.
Hirn, brain.
Hirnhaut, meninges.
Hirnrinde, cortex.
Hirnschädel, cranium.
Hirnschenkel, pedunculi cerebri.
Hirntrichter, infundibulum.
Hirnwindung, gyrus, gyre.
Hitze, heat.
hoch, high.
Hode, testis, testicle.
Hof, halo.
Hoffnung, hope.
Höhle, sinus, (brain)ventricle, *see under* **ventricle.**
Hörbläschen, vesicle/auditory.
Hören, hearing.
Hornhaut, cornea.
Hörschärfe, auditory acuity.
Hörschärfe(n)messer, audiometer.
Hüftnerv, sciatic nerve.
Hühnerblindheit, night-blindness.
Humor, humor.
Husten, cough.
Hypothese, hypothesis.

I

Ich, ego.
Ichtrieb, ego-instinct.
Ideenflucht, flight of ideas.
identisch, identical.
Impuls, impulse.
Inbegriff, *see* definition.
Indifferenzpunkt, indifference point.
Inhalt, content[n].
innerer Gehörgang, meatus/internal auditory.
innerer Kniehöcker, geniculate body/medial.
innere Wahrnehmung, introspection (1).
Insel, island (of Reil).
Instinkt, instinct.
Instruktion, instruction (1).
Intelligenz, intelligence.
Intelligenzprüfung, intelligence test.
Intensität, intensity.
Intermittenzton, intermittence tone.
Intervall, interval (3).
Ironie, irony.
Irradiationskreise, *see under* **diffusion circle.**
Irrenarzt, alienist.
Irrgarten, maze.
irrgläubig, heterodox.
Irrsinn, insanity.
Isolierung, isolation.
Isomorphismus, isomorphism.

J

Jagd, hunting, hunting behavior.
Jochbein-, zygomatic.
Jochreflex, zygomatic reflex.
Jucken, itch.
Jugend, youth.
jugendlich, juvenile.
Jugend (zeit), adolescence, youth.
Jünglingsalter, adolescence.

K

Kälteempfindung, cold sensation.
Kältepunkt, cold spot.
Kamm, crest.
Kammer, (heart) ventricle, *see under* **ventricle.**
Kammerwasser, aqueous, aqueous humor.
Kampflust, pugnacity.
Kampf ums Dasein, struggle for existence.
Kaprylgeruch, hircine.
Karriere, career.
Kausalität, causality (2).
Kehldeckel, epiglottis.
Kehlkopf, larynx.
Kehltonschreiber, vocal tone recorder.
Keim, germ.
Keimzelle, germ cell.
Kenntnis, knowledge.
Kennzeichen, symptom (2).
Kern, nucleus.
Kernkomplex, nuclear complex.
Kerze, candle.
Kind, child.
Kinderpsychologie, child psychology.
Kindesalter, infancy.
Kinematograph, cinematograph, motion picture.
Kitzel, tickle.
Klang, clang, tone/compound.
Klangfarbe, clang-color, clang-quality, clang-tint, timbre.
Klarheit, clearness, distinctness, lucidity.
Kleinhirn, cerebellum.
Kleinhirnrinde, cortex cerebelli.
Klopflaute, raps.
Klugheit, wisdom, intelligence.
Kniesehnenreflex, patellar (or patellar-tendon) reflex.
Knochenleitung, bone conduction.
Knotenpunkt, nodal point.
Koinzidenzpunkt, coincidence point.
Koller, tantrum.
Kombinationsmethode, *see under* **combination test.**
Kombinationston, combination tone.

Komplementärfarben, complements, complementaries, complementary colors.

Komplikation, complication.

Kompromissbildung, compromise-formation.

konstanter Fehler, constant error.

Konstanzannahme, constancy hypothesis.

Kontiguität, contiguity.

Kontraktion, contraction.

Kontrast, contrast.

Kontrollversuch, control experiment.

Koordination, coordination.

Kopfschmerz, Kopfweh, headache.

Kopie, copy[n] (1).

Körper, body.

Körperbau, physique.

Körperchen, corpuscle.

körperlich, corporal, somatic.

Körperlichkeit, solidity.

korrespondierende Netzhautpunkte, identical points.

Kraft, energy (1), force, power (2).

Kraftidee, idée-force.

Krampf, cramp, spasm.

krampfartiger Anfall, paroxysm

krampfhaftes Zucken, tic.

krankhaft, morbid.

Krankheit, disease, disorder (2)

Kratzreflex, scratch reflex.

Kreuz, sharp[n] (3).

Kreuzbein, sacrum.

Kreuzung, crossing over, decussation.

Kribbeln, tingling.

Kristallsehen, crystal gazing.

Kriterium, criterion.

kritische Beurteilung, criticism.

Kugellinse, spherical lens.

Kultur, culture.

Kultus, worship (2).

Kummer, grief.

Kundgabe, *see* definition.

Kundgabe, *see under* **description, information, significance.**

Kunst, art.

Kunstgenuss, artistic appreciation.

Kurzschlusstheorie, short-circuit theory.

Kurzsichtigkeit, myopia, near-sight, near-sightedness.

L

Lächeln, smile.

Lachen, laughter.

Lage, level (1), position, situation (3).

Lähmung, paralysis, paresis.

Längen-, längs-, longitudinal.

Langeweile, ennui.

Langlebigkeit, longevity.

Lappen, lobe.

Laster, vice.

Latenz, latency.

Latenzzeit, latent period.

laugig, alkaline.

Laune, humor, temper.

Lautgesetz, phonetic law.

Lautheit, loudness.

laut lesen, reading aloud.

Leben, life.

Lebensalter, age, chronological age.

lebensfähig, viable.

Lebenskraft, vitality.

Lebhaftigkeit, vividness.

Lederhaut, corium.

Lehre, doctrine.

Lehrsatz, theorem.

Leib, body.

leicht, light[a] (2).

Leichtgläubigkeit, credulity.

leiden, suffer (1).

Leidenschaft, passion.

leise[a], low (2).

Leistung, achievement, power, performance.

leiten, conduct[v].

Leitfähigkeit, conductivity.

Leitton, leading tone.

Leitung, conduct[n].

Leitungsbahn, path, pathway, tract.

Lenden-, lumbar.

Lernen, learning.

Lernkurve, learning curve.

Lernfähigkeit, learning capacity.

Lernstoff, learning material.

Lesbarkeit, legibility.

Lesen von den Lippen, lip-reading.

Leuchtfarbe, glowing color.

Libidoentwicklung, libido development.

Libidostauung, libido damming.

Licht, light.

Lichtempfindung, light sensation.

Lichtschwelle, brilliance threshold (or limen)/absolute.

Lichtwellen, light waves.

Liebe, love.

Liebelei, flirtation.

Liebhaberei, fad.

links, left.

links liegend, sinister, sinistral.

Linse, lens, crystalline lens.

Lippenschlüssel, lip-key.

Lohn, reward.

Lokalzeichen, local sign, locality sign.

Lösung, solution.

Lücke, discontinuity.

Lückenergänzungstest, completion test.

Luftleitung, air conduction.

Luftröhre, trachea.

Lüge[n], lie.

lügen, lying.

Lungenmagennerv, pneumogastric nerve.

Lust, pleasantness.

Lustprinzip, pleasure-principle.

Lust-Unlust, pleasure-pain.

lutschen, sucking.

M

Magen, stomach.

magnetische Kraft, magnetic force, magnetism.

Mandel, tonsil.

Mangel, defect, privation, want (1).

mangelhaft, defective.

Manier, style.

Manieriertheit, mannerism.

Männchen, male.

Mannigfaltigkeit, manifold.

Mark, medulla, cord.

Markscheide, myelin, myelin sheath.

Mass, measure (2, 3).

Masse, mass.

Massenpsychologie, crowd psychology.

Massformel, metric formula.

Massmethode, measurement method.

Massstab, standard.

Mattigkeit, languor, languour.

Medullarohr, neural tube.

mehrdeutig, ambiguous, equivocal.

Mehrklang, chord.

Mehrstimmigkeit, polyphony.

Meinung, opinion.

Meissnersche Körperchen, Meissner corpuscles.

Meisterschaft, mastery.

Melodie, tune[n], melody.

Menge, mass, crowd.

Menschenaffen, anthropoidea, anthropoids.

Menschengeschlecht, man, mankind.

Menschheit, man, mankind.

merklich, noticeable.

Merkmal, characteristic.

Messung, measurement.

Methode der Äquivalente, equivalents/method of.

Methode der behaltenen Glieder, retained members/method of.

Methode der Minimaländerungen, minimal change (or changes)/ method of.

Methode der mittleren Abstufungen, mean gradations/method of.

Methode der mittleren Fehler, average error/method of.

Methode der paarweisen Vergleichung, comparison/method of paired.

Methode der richtigen und falschen Fälle, right and wrong cases/ method of.

Methode der übermerklichen Unterschiede, supraliminal differences/method of.

Milz, spleen.

Minderwertigkeit von Organen, *see under* **organ** (or **organic**) **inferiority.**

Minderwertigkeitsgefühl, inferiority complex.

Mischung, mixture.

Missbildung, malformation.

Misserfolg, failure.

Missklang, discord.

Misstrauen, distrust.

missverstehen, misunderstand.

Mitempfindung, concomitant sensation.

Mitgefühl, sympathy.

Mitleid, pity.

mittelbar, mediate.

Mittelhandknochen, metacarpal.

Mittelhirn, midbrain.

Mittelohr, middle ear.

Mitwirkung, cooperation.

Mode, fashion.

Modell, copy[n] (2).

möglich, possible.

Molltonleiter, minor scale.

Monstrum, prodigy (2).

Moschus, musk.

Motiv, incentive (1), motiv.

motorisches Zentrum, motor area.

mündlich, oral.

Muskel, muscle.

Muskelsinn, muscle (or muscular) sensation.

Muskelzusammenziehung, tetanus.

Muster, pattern (1).

Mut, courage.

mütterliches Verhalten, maternal behavior.

Mythos, myth.

N

Nachahmung, imitation.

Nachbild, after-image.

Nachdauer, lag.

Nachdenken, reflection (2).

Nachempfindung, after-sensation.

nachfolgen, sequence (1).

Nachhirn, myelencephalon.

Nachlassen, remission.

Nachtblindheit, night-blindness.

Nachtragen, resentment.

Nachtwandeln, somnambulism.

Nachwirkung, after-effect.

Nahrungsstoff, nutriment.

Narkose, narcosis.

Nase, nose.

Nasenlöcher, nares, nostrils.

Nassempfindung, wetness sensation.

Nasskälte, clamminess.

Naturforschung, natural sciences.

Naturgesetz, natural law.

natürliche Auslese, natural selection.

Naturwissenschaften, natural sciences.

Nebennieren, adrenal glands.

Nebenordnung, coordination.

Neckerei, teasing.

Neid, envy.

Nerven-, nervous (1).

Nervenanfall, shock.

Nervenendigung, nerve ending.

Nervenendplatte, endbrush.

Nervenfaser, nerve fiber.

Nervenhügel, nerve ganglion.

Nervenknoten, ganglion.

Nervenkrankheit, neurosis.

Nervenleiden, neuropathy.

Nervenstrang, tract.

Nervenwurzel, nerve root.

nervös, nervous (3).

Netzhaut, retina.

Netzhautbild, image.

Netzhautgrube, fovea, fovea centralis.

Netzhautschichten, retinal layers.

neuer Eindruck, novel impression.

Neugier, curiosity.

Nicht-Ich, non-ego.

Niedergeschlagenheit, dejection, depression.

Nisten, nesting.

Niveau, level (1).

Nivellierung, *see under* **precision/ law of.**

Normalreiz, normal stimulus.

Normalstimmung, pitch/standard.

normieren, standardize.

Notwendigkeit, necessity.

Notzucht, rape.

Nullpunkt, zero, *see under* **zero/ developmental.**

Nummer, number.

Nützlichkeit, utility.

Nutzzeit, useful (serviceable) duration.

O

Oberarmknochen, humerus.

Oberfläche, surface.

Oberflächenfarbe, surface color.

oberflächlich, superficial.

Oberton, overtone.

Objekt, *see under* **Gegenstand.**

Objektbesetzung, object-cathexis.

Objektwahl, object choice.

offenbar, evident.

Offenheit, frankness.

öffentlich, public[a].

Ohnmacht, faint[n], swoon.

Ohr, ear.

Ohrenklingen, tinnitus.

Ohrmuschel, auricle (1), concha, pinna.

Ohrschnecke, helix.

Ohrspeicheldrüse, parotid gland.

Ohrtrompete, Eustachian tube.

Oliven des verlängerten Mark, olives, olivary bodies.

optische Täuschung, optical illusion.

optische Unvollkommenheit, *see under* **defect/optical.**

Ordnung, order (2).

Organempfindung, common sensation, organic sensation.

Organisation, structure, organization.

Orgel, organ (2).

Orientierung, orientation.

Ort, situation (3).

Ortsgedächtnis, locality memory.

Ortsveränderung, locomotion.

ovales Fenster, window/oval.

P

Paarung, mating, pairing.

paradoxe Kälte, paradoxical cold.

paradoxe Wärme, paradoxical warmth.

pathologische Psychologie, abnormal psychology.

Pauke, tympanum.

Paukenfell, tympanic membrane.

Paukenhöhle, middle ear, tympanic cavity.

Paukentreppe, scala tympani.

Pendel, pendulum.

Penisneid, penis envy.

Personalismus, Personalistik, personalism.

persönliche Gleichung, personal equation.

Pfeife, pipe.

Pflicht, duty.

Pförtner, pylorus.

Phänomen, phenomenon.

Phantasie, fancy, imagination.

Phantasieren, mind wandering.

Phonopsie, colored hearing.

Plan, scheme.

Platzangst, agoraphobia.

Pöbelhaufen, mob.

Poltergeist, *see* definition.

Prahlerei, self-display, self-exhibition, boasting.

Präsenzzeit (Stern), present/psychological.

Präzisierung, *see under* **precision/law of.**

Präzision, precision.

Prickeln, tingling.

primär, primary.

Primärvorgang, primary process.

Primat, primacy.

Prinzip, principle.

Prinzipalfarbe (Aubert), color/fundamental, color/primary.

Probe, proof, test.

Produktionsvorgang (Benussi), founding process.

Produktionsvorgang, *see* definition.

profanieren, profane[v] (1).

Prognose, prognosis.

Prozess, process (1, 2).

Prüfung, examination (1), test (1).

Prunken, self-display, self-exhibition.

Psyche, mind.

Psychiatrie, psychiatry.

Psychognostik, psychognosis.

Psychologie, psychology.

Psychopathie, psychopathy.

Publikum, public.

Puls, pulse.

Pulsader, artery.

Pulsieren, pulsation.

Punkt, point.

Punktfigur, dot figure.

Punktschrift, Braille.

Pupille, pupil.

purpur, purple.

Pyramidenbahn, decussation of pyramids, pyramidal tract.

Q

Qualle, jellyfish.

Quart, fourth (*mus.*).

querlaufend, transverse.

R

Rache, revenge, vengeance.

Raddrehung, torsional movement, torsion, torsional rotation.

Randkontrast, marginal contrast.

Rang, rank.

Rangordnung, rank order.

Rappel, tantrum.

Raserei, frenzy.

Rasse, race.

Rastlosigkeit, restlessness.

Rauheit, roughness.

Rauhigkeit, harshness.

Raum, space.

Raumfarbe, bulky color.

Raumfehler, space error.

Rauminhalt, volume.

Raumschwelle, spatial threshold (or limen).

Raumstellung, space orientation.

Raumwahrnehmung, space perception.

Reagens, reagent (1).

Reaktion, reaction.

Reaktionszeit, reaction (or response) time.

Realität, reality.

Recht, right[n].

recht, right[a].

reduzieren, reduce (3).

reduziertes Auge, reduced eye.

Reflexbewegung, reflex response.

Regel, rule.

regelmässig, regular.

Regenbogenhaut, iris.

Regung, impulse.

reifen, mature, ripen.

Reifung, maturation.

Reihe, sequence (3), series.

Reihenfolge, order (1).

rein, pure.

Reinheit, purity.

Reiz, stimulus, *see under* **R.**

Reizbarkeit, excitability, irritability.

reizen, stimulate (1, 2).

Reizhöhe, terminal sensitivity.

Reizmittel, stimulant.

Reizschwelle, threshold (1, *a* = RL).

Reizung, stimulation.

Reklame, advertisement, *see under* **advertising.**

Rekrutierung, recruitment.

relativ, relative[a].

Relief, relief (1).

Reproduktion, recall, reproduction (1).

Resonanzkasten, resonance box.

Reue, penitence, regret.

reziproke Grösse, reciprocal[n].

reziproke Innervation, reciprocal innervation.

Reziprositätsgesetz, reciprocity law.

richtig, right[a].

Richtung, direction, trend.

Riechkolben, olfactory cell.

Riechlappen, olfactory lobe.

Riechsphäre, olfactory area.

Rinde, cortex.

Rindengrau, cortical gray.

Ritus, rite.

Rohr, reed (or tube).

Rolandoscher Spalt, Rolandic fissure, fissure of Rolando.

Rollung, torsional movement, torsion, torsional rotation.

rot, red.

rotsichtig, red-sighted.

Rückblick, retrospection.

Rückenmark, cord, spinal cord.

Rückenmark-, spinal.

Rückenmarksschwindsucht, tabes, tabes dorsalis.

Rückenstrang, notochord.

Rückenwirbel, vertebra.

Rückfall, reversion.

Rückgrats-, spinal.

Rückgrat, spine (1).

Rückkehr, regression.

Rückschlagsgesetz, filial regression/law of.

Ruffinisches Körperchen, Ruffini corpuscle (or cylinder).

Ruhe, repose, rest.

Ruhm, fame.

rundes Fenster, window/round.

S

Sachverständiger, expert.

Säckchen, saccule, sacculus.

säcular, secular (1).

Saitengalvanometer, string galvanometer.

salzig, saline, salty.

Same, seed, semen.

Sanktion, sanction (2).

Sättigung, saturation.

sauer, sour.

Säufer, drunkard.

saugen, sucking.

Säugetiere, mammalia, mammals.

Säugling, suckling (3).

Schall, sound.

Schallbrett, sounding board, sound board.

Schallgeschwindigkeit, sound/velocity of.

Schallhammer, sound hammer.

Schallschlüssel, sound key, voice key.

Schallstärke, sound intensity.

Schallverstärkung, amplification/sound.

Schallwelle, sound-wave.

Scham, modesty, shame.

Schamgegend, pubes.

scharf, sharp[a] (1, 2, 5).

Scharfsinn, perspicacity.

scharfsinnig, acute (1).

Schattierung, tint (2).

schätzen, rate[v].

Schätzung, rating[n].

Schätzungsdifferenz, Schätzungsfehler, estimation difference.

Schauer, thrill[n].

Schaulust, scopophilia.

Scheibe, disk, disc.

Scheide, vagina.

Scheidenkrampf, vaginismus.

Scheidewand, septum, diaphragm.

Schein, appearance (3), semblance.

scheinbar, apparent.

scheinbare Grösse, apparent magnitude.

Scheinbewegung, apparent (motion or) movement.

Scheintod, death-feigning (or feint).

Scheitel-, parietal (1).

Scheitel, vertex (1, 3).

Scheitellappen, parietal lobe.

Scheitelpunkt, zenith, vertex (2).

Schenkel, femur.

Schicklichkeit, decency, propriety.

Schielen, strabismus.

Schienbein, tibia.

Schilddrüse, thyroid gland, thyreoid gland, thyroid[n].

Schlaf, sleep.

Schläfenbein, temporal bone.

Schläfenlappen, temporal lobe.

Schlaflosigkeit, insomnia, wakefulness.

Schlafsucht, somnolence.

Schlaftiefenmesser, *see* definition.

Schlafwandeln, somnambulism.

Schlag, stroke (or shock).

Schlaganfall, apoplexy.

Schlagrute, divining rod.

Schleife, fillet.

Schleimhaut, mucous membrane.

Schliessmuskel, sphincter.

Schliessung, closure.

Schlucken, hiccup, hiccough.

Schluckreflex, swallowing reflex.

Schluss, inference, conclusion.

Schlussfolgerung, deduction.

Schmeckbecher, taste bud.

Schmerz, pain (1).

Schmerzempfindlichkeit, algesia.

Schmerzlosigkeit, analgesia, analgia, analgesthesia.

Schmerzpunkt, pain spot.

Schmerzsinn, pain sense.

Schmollen, sulkiness.

Schnecke, cochlea.

Schneckenkanal, scala media (cochlearis).

Schneeblindheit, snow-blindness.

Schnelligkeit, speed.

Schnitt, section (1).

Schönheit, beauty.

schöpferische Synthese, creative synthesis.

Schöpfung, creation.

Schreck, fright.

Schrecken, terror.

Schreibkrampf, writer's cramp.

Schrift, script, writing.

Schüchternheit, bashfulness, timidity.

Schuldgefühl, guilt/sense of.

Schule, school.

Schulerziehung, schooling.

Schutzfärbung, protective coloring, protective resemblance.

schwach, faint[a], weak.

Schwäche, debility, faintness.

Schwachsinn, dementia, feeblemindedness.

Schwangerschaft, pregnancy.

Schwankungen, fluctuations.

schwarz, black.

Schwatzhaftigkeit, loquacity, loquaciousness.

Schwebung, beat.

schweigend, tacit.

Schwelgerei, debauchery.

Schwelle, limen, threshold.

Schwerkraft, gravity (3).

Schwindel, vertigo.

Schwingung, vibration.

Schwingungsknoten, node.

Schwingungsweite, amplitude.

Schwingungszahl, vibration rate.

Seele, mind, soul.

Seelenblindheit, mind-blindness.

Seelenblindheit, (-taubheit), psychic blindness (-deafness).

Seelenleben, mental life.

Seelentheorie, soul theory.

Seelenvermögen, faculty.

Seelenzustand, psychosis (2).

seelisch, mental, psychic(al).

Seestern, starfish.

Sehen, sight.

Sehfeld, visual field.

Sehgelb, visual yellow.

Sehgrösse, apparent magnitude.

Sehhügel, thalamus, optic thalamus.

Sehne, tendon.

Sehnenempfindung, tendon (or tendinous) sensation.

Sehnerv, optic nerve.

Sehnervenkreuzung, chiasm, optic chiasm.

Sehnervenscheibe, optic disk (or disc).

Sehnsucht, longing.

Sehpurpur, visual purple.

Sehraum, visual space.

Sehschärfe, visual acuity.

sekundäre Bearbeitung, elaboration/secondary.

Selbst, self.

Selbstanklage, self-accusation.

Selbstbehauptung, self-assertion.

Selbstbeherrschung, self-control.

Selbstbeobachtung, introspection (2), observation of self.

Selbstbestimmung, self-determination.

Selbstbetrug, self-deception.

Selbstbewusstsein, self-consciousness.

Selbsterhaltung, self-preservation.

Selbsterkenntnis, self-knowledge.

Selbsterniedrigung, self-abasement.

Selbstlaut, vowel.

Selbstsucht, selfishness, egoism.

Selbsttätigkeit, self-activity.

Selbstverleugnung, self-denial.

selbstverständlich, self-evident.

Selbstvertrauen, assurance (1).

Seufzer, sigh.

Sezierung, section (2).

sichtbar, visible.

Sichtbarkeit, visibility.

simulieren, malinger.

simultane Lichtinduktion, light induction/simultaneous.

Sinn, meaning (1), sense (2).

Sinnbild, symbol.

Sinnes-, sensory.

Sinnesgebiet, sense/a.

Sinnesorgan, sense organ.

Sinnesschärfe, acuity.

Sinnestäuschung, illusion.

sinnlich, sensory, sensual.

sinnliche Lust, sensual pleasure.

sinnliches Gefühl, sense-feeling.

sinnlose Silbe, nonsense syllable.

sinnvoll[a], meaningful.

Sinnwidrigkeit, absurdity.

Sitte, custom.

Sittenlehre, ethics.

Situation, situation (2).

Sitz der Seele — des Geistes, seat of mind, seat of consciousness.

sonderbar, singular.

Sophisterei, sophistry.

Sorge, sorrow, worry.

Sozialpsychologie, social psychology.

Spalt, fissure.

Spannung, strain (2), tension.

Spannungsempfindung, strain (4).

Spannungs-Lösungsgefühl, tension-relaxation/feeling of.

Speichel, saliva.

Speicheldrüsen, salivary glands.

Speichelreflex, salivary reflex.

Sperrung, interference/psychic.

spezifisches Gewicht, specific gravity.
spezifische Sinnesenergien, specific energy of nerves.
Sphäre, area (2).
sphärische Linse, spherical lens.
Spiegelschrift, mirror-writing.
Spiegelzeichnung, mirror-drawing.
Spiel, game, play.
Spindel, spindle.
spiralförmig, helicoid.
spitz, acute (4).
Spore, spore.
Sport, sport (2).
Spott, satire, scorn.
Spottgedicht, satire.
Sprache, language, speech.
Sprachverwirrtheit, glossosynthesis.
Sprödigkeit, coyness.
spuken, haunt.
Spur, trace.
Stäbchen, rod/retinal.
Stäbchensehen, rod vision.
Stäbchen- und Zapfenschicht, layer of rods and cones.
Stabilität, stability (1).
Stamm, root (1).
Stammbaum, arbor vitae.
Stammeln, stammering.
stark, strong.
Stärke, intensity, loudness, strength.
starr, rigid.
Starrkrampf, tetanus.
statischer Sinn, static sense.
Staunen, wonder.
Stechen, tingling.
Steckenpferd, hobby, *see under* **fad.**
Steigbügel, stapes.
Steigung, gradient (2).
Stellung, posture, position.
Stift, stylus.
Stigma, stigma (1).
Stil, style.
Stimmbänder, vocal cords.
Stimme, voice.
stimmen, tune[v].
Stimmgabel, tuning fork.
Stimmlippen, vocal cords.
Stimmmuskeln, vocal muscles.
Stimmregion, vocal register.
Stimmritze, glottis.
Stimmung, mood.
Stirnlappen, frontal lobe.
Stoffwechsel, metabolism.
Stolz, pride.
Störung, disturbance.
Stosston, beat-tone.
Stottern, stammering, stuttering.
Strafbarkeit, culpability.
Strafe, punishment.
straff, tense (1).
Strahl, ray.
Strahlung, radiation.
Streben, conation.
streben, strive.
Streuung, scatter.
Streuungsgesetz, distributive law.
Strom, current.
Struktur, form, structure.
Studium, study.
Stufe, grade, level (3), stage.
stumm, dumb.
Stummheit, mutism, mutitas.
stutzen, startle.
Sublimierung, sublimation.
Sünde, sin.
süss, sweet.
Sylvische Spalte, Sylvian fissure, fissure of Sylvius.
Symbol, symbol.
Sympathie, sympathy.
Symptom, symptom (1).
Synergie, synergy.

T

Tabellierung, tabulation.
Tagblindheit, day-blindness.
Tagesreste, day-residues.
Takt, beat (3), measure (1).
Taktgefühl, tact.
Talent, talent.
Tanz-, dancing.
Tanzmaus, dancing mouse.
Tast-, tactual, tactile.
Tastempfindung, touch sensation.
Tast(er)zirkel, esthesiometer, æsthesiometer.
Tastkörperchen, *see under* Meissner corpuscles.
Tastpunkt, touch spot.
Tasttäuschungen, tactual (or tactile) illusions.
Tätigkeit, action, activity.
Tätigkeitsgefühl, activity/feeling of.
tatloser Wille, velleity.
Tatsache, fact.
Taubheit, deafness.
Taubstumm, deaf-mute.
Täuschung, illusion.
Teil, part.
Teilbarkeit, divisibility.
teilnahmlos, listless.
Teilton, partial tone, partial.
Tendenz, tendency, trend.
Terz, third (*mus.*).
Test, test (2).
Testikel, testis, testicle.
Thema, theme (3).
Theorie der bewussten Selbsttäuschung, conscious illusion theory.
Theorie der Gehörsempfindungen, hearing/theories of.
tief, deep (2), low (1).
Tiefe, depth.
Tiefenpsychologie, depth-psychology.
Tiefenwahrnehmung, depth perception.
Tier, animal.
Tierpsychologie, animal psychology.
Tinte, tint.
Tod, death.
Todestrieb, death instinct.
Ton, tone.
Tonabstand, interval (3).
Toncharakter, tonality.
Tonempfindung, tone (or tonal) sensation.
Tonfarbe, tone-color.
tonfrei, achromatic (1).
Tonhöhe, pitch.
Tonika, tonic.
Toninsel, tonal island.
tonisch, tonic[a].
Tonleiter, scale.
Tonlücke, tonal gap.
Tonmesser, tonometer.
Tontaubheit, tone-deafness.
Tourenzähler, tachometer.
Tränen, tears.
Transposition, transposition (2).
Trauerspiel, tragedy.
Traum, dream.
Traumarbeit, dream work.
Traumdeutung, dream interpretation.
Träumerei, reverie, revery.
Traumerreger, dream instigator.
Trauminhalt, dream content.
Traumstoff, dream material.
Traurigkeit, sadness.
Treffermethode, paired associates, right associates/method of.
Trennung, detachment.
Treppentäuschung, staircase illusion.
Trieb, drive, instinct.
Triebfeder, motive.
Triebhandlung, impulsive action.
Trinker, drunkard.
Trockenheit, aridity.
Trommel, tympanum.
Trommelfell, tympanic membrane.
Trommelhöhle, tympanic cavity.
Trotz, spite.
Trotzen, sulkiness.
Trübsal, sorrow.
Trugschluss, fallacy.
Tugend, virtue.
Typus, type.

GERMAN GLOSSARY

U

übel, evil[a].

Übelkeit, nausea.

Übelwollen, spite, malice.

üben, practise, practice[v].

Überbleibsel, vestige.

Überich, superego.

Überleben, survival[n].

Überlegung, deliberation, reflection (1).

Übermensch, superman.

übermenschlich, superhuman.

übermerklich, supraliminal.

Übermut, elation.

übernaturlich, supernatural.

Überproduktion, overproduction.

Überraschung, surprise.

Überredung, persuasion.

Überrest, survival[n].

Übertragung, cross-education, cross training, **transference,** transmission.

überzeugen, convince.

Überzeugung, conviction.

Übung, exercise, practice.

Übungsgrenze, practice limit.

Übungskurve, practice curve.

Übungswirkung, practice effect.

Übungtheorie, practice theory.

Umfang, periphery, range.

Umgebung, environment, situation (3).

umkehrbar, reversible.

umkehren, reverse[v].

Umkehrung, inversion.

Umkreis, periphery.

Umstand, condition[n] (3).

Umstellung, inversion.

Unabhängigkeit, independence.

unanschaulich, *see* definition.

unanschauliches Denken, imageless thought.

Unanständigkeit, indecency.

unbestimmt, indefinite.

unbewusst, unconscious.

undenkbar, unthinkable.

unecht, spurious.

unerkennbar, unknowable.

unfähig, incapable.

Unfähigkeit, disability.

Unfallsneurose, traumatic neurosis.

Unfruchtbarkeit, sterility.

Ungeeignetheit, unfitness.

Ungenauigkeit, inaccuracy.

ungesellig, unsociable, unsocial.

Ungestaltheit, deformity.

ungesund, morbid.

Ungewissheit, uncertainty.

Unglaube, disbelief.

Ungleichheit, dissimilarity.

ungültig, invalid.

unlogisch, unreasonable.

Unlust, disagreeableness, unpleasantness.

Unmännlichkeit, effeminacy.

unmerklicher Unterschied, imperceptible difference.

unmittelbar, direct, immediate.

unmöglich, impossible.

Unordnung, disorder (1).

Unredlichkeit, dishonesty.

Unrichtigkeit, falsity.

Unruhe, restlessness.

Unschlüssigkeit, suspense.

Unsinn, nonsense.

Unsterblichkeit, immortality.

Untauglichkeit, unfitness.

Unterbewusstsein, subconscious.

Unterdrückung, suppression.

Unterleib, abdomen.

Unterordnung, subordination.

Unterricht, education (2), instruction (1), schooling.

Unterschätzung, underestimate.

Unterscheidung, discrimination.

Unterscheidungsreaktion, discrimination response (or reaction).

Unterscheidungsversuch, discrimination experiment.

Unterscheidungszeit, discrimination time.

Unterschiedsempfindlichkeit, differential sensiblity.

Unterschiedsschwelle, difference limen, difference threshold, differential threshold (or limen), threshold (1, c = DL), sense threshold, sensory threshold.

untersuchen, investigate.

Untersuchung, examination (2).

Unterwerfung, submission, submissiveness.

Unterwürfigkeit, subservience, subserviency.

Untüchtigkeit, unfitness.

Untugend, vice.

unvernünftig, irrational, unreasonable.

unverständlich, incomprehensible.

Unvollständigkeit, deficiency.

Unwille, resentment.

unwillkürlich, involuntary.

Unzufriedenheit, dissatisfaction.

Ur-, primal.

Urbild, prototype, type.

Urfarbe, color/primal.

Urin, urine.

Ursache, cause.

ursprünglich, primordial.

Urszene, primal scene.

Urteil, judgment.

Urzeugung, spontaneous generation.

V

Variabilität, variability.

Variation, variation (1).

Veitstanz, chorea.

Vene, vein.

Verachtung, scorn.

veränderliche Grösse, variable.

veränderlicher Fehler, variable error.

Veränderlichkeit, variability.

Veränderung, variation (2), change.

Veranlagung, disposition/neural.

verantwortlich, responsible.

Verbesserung, improvement.

Verbindung, connection (1).

verborgen, cryptic.

Verbrechen, crime.

Verdacht, distrust, suspicion.

Verdauung, digestion.

Verdichtung, condensation.

Verdoppelung, reduplication.

Verdrängung, repression.

Verehrung, reverence.

vereinfachen, reduce (2).

Vereinigung, combination, union.

vererbt, inherited.

Vererbung, heredity (1), inheritance.

Vererbungswissenschaft, genetics.

Verfahren, procedure.

Verfall, decadence.

Verfolgungswahn, persecution/delusion of.

Vergehen, misdemeanor.

Vergesslichkeit, forgetfulness.

Vergleich, comparison.

vergleichende Methode, comparative method.

vergleichende Psychologie, comparative psychology.

Vergleichsreiz, comparison stimulus.

Verhalten, behavior, behaviour, conduct[n].

Verhältnis, ratio, relation.

Verkehr, intercourse.

Verkehrtheit, perversion (2).

Verkettung, linkage.

Verknüpfung, attachment (1), colligation, synthesis.

Verlagerung, displacement.

verlängertes Mark, medulla oblongata.

Verlegenheit, embarrassment.

Verletzung, injury, lesion.

verleumden, malign.

Vermeidungsreaktion, avoiding response.

vermindern, reduce (1).

Vermittelung, mediation.

Vermögen, faculty, power (3).

Vernunft, reason[n] (2).
vernünftig, rational, reasonable.
Vernünftigkeit, sensibility (4).
Verpflichtung, obligation.
Verrücktheit, amentia.
Verschiebung, displacement.
Verschiedenartigkeit, heterogeneity.
Verschiedenheit, variety.
Verschlechterung, perversion (1).
Verschlimmerung, deterioration.
Verschmelzung, blending, fusion.
Verschwendung, dissipation.
Versetzung, transposition (1).
Versicherung, assurance (2).
Versprechen, slip of speech (or of the tongue).
Verstand, intellect, understanding.
verständig, reasonable.
Verständnis, comprehension (1).
Verstehen, intuition (2).
Verstellung, dissimulation, simulation, perversion (3).
Verstümmelung, mutilation.
Versuch, experiment.
Versuch der farbigen Schatten, colored shadow experiment.
Versuchsleiter (Vl), experimenter.
Versuchsperson (Vp), observer, reagent (2), subject (2).
Versuchung, temptation.
Verteilung, distribution.
Vertiefung (Herbart), absorption.
Vertreter, exponent (2).
Verwaltung, management (2).
Verwandtenehe, endogamy.
Verwandtschaft, kinship.
Verwechselung, confusion (1).
Verwerfung, rejection.
Verworrenheit, confusion (3).
Verzierung, decoration.
Verzückung, trance.
Verzweiflung, despair.
Vexierversuch, blank experiment.
Vierhügel, quadrigemina, corpora quadrigemina.
Visierlinie, sight/line of, sighting line.
Vokal, vowel.
Vokalität, vocality.
Völkerpsychologie, folk psychology, social psychology.
Volkskunde, folklore.
Volksstamm, tribe.
Vorahnung, premonition, presentiment.
Voraussetzung, premise, premiss.
Voraussicht, foresight.
Vorbeizeigen, past pointing.
Vorbereitung, preparation.
(das) Vorbewusste, preconscious.
Vorder-, anterior (2).
Vorderhirn, forebrain.
Vorgang, process (1, 2).
Vorhersagung, prediction.
Vorherrschen, prepotence.
Vorhof, vestibule.
Vorhofstreppe, scala vestibuli.
vorläufig, provisional.
Vorlust, forepleasure.
vormachen[v], make-believe.
Vorperiode, foreperiod.
Vorrang, primacy.
Vorrichtung, apparatus.
Vorsatz, purpose.
vorstellen, *see under* **Vorstellung.**
Vorstellung, idea, presentation, representation, *see also* definition.
Vorstellungsinhalt, *see under* **Vorstellung.**
Vorübung, preparation.
Vorurteil, prejudice.
Vorzeichen, omen.
Vorzwickel, quadrate lobe.

W

wachen, wake.
Wachsamkeit, wakefulness.
Wachsen, growth (1).
Wachstum, growth (2).
Wahl, choice, selection.
Wahnidee, delusion.
Wahnsinn, insanity, mania.
Wahnvorstellung, delusion.
wahr, true.
wahrhaftig, veridical.
Wahrheit, truth.
Wahrnehmung, perception.
Wahrnehmungsinhalt, percept.
wahrscheinlicher Fehler, probable error.
Wahrscheinlichkeit, likelihood, probability.
Wanderlust, *see* definition.
Wärmeempfindung, warm (or warmth) sensation.
Wärmepunkt, warm spot, warmth spot.
Warnungszeichen, warning signal.
Wasserkopf, hydrocephalus, hydrocephaly.
Wechselwirkung, interaction.
Weibchen, female.
Weichheit, softness (1).
Weise, tune[n].
Weisheit, wisdom.
weiss, white.
Weitsichtigkeit, far-sight, presbyopia.
Welle, wave.
Wellenbewegung, undulation.
Wellenlänge, wave-length.
Weltanschauung, world view, *see also under* **ideology.**
weltlich, secular (2).
Wert, worth, value.
Wesen, being/a.
Wesenheit, entity.
Wetteifer, emulation, rivalry.
Wettstreit der Sehfelder, retinal rivalry.
Widerhall, echo, reverberation.
Widerlegung, refutation.
Widerspruch, contradiction.
Widerspruchsfreiheit, self-consistency.
Widerstand, resistance.
Widerstandsempfindung, resistance /sensation of.
Widerwille, repugnance.
Wiederbelebung, revival.
Wiedererkennung, recognition.
Wiederherstellung, reconstruction, restoration.
Wiederhervorbringung, regeneration, reproduction (3).
Wiederholung, reproduction (1, 2).
Wiederholungszwang, repetition-compulsion.
wiederkehrend, recurrent.
Wiederlesungsmethode, rereading method.
wild, wild.
Wille, will.
Willenschwäche, abulia, aboulia.
Willensfreiheitslehre, free will doctrine.
Willenshandlung, volition.
Willenslosigkeit, abulia, aboulia.
Willensvorgang, volition.
Willkürhandlung, voluntary activity.
willkürlich, voluntary.
Windung, convolution.
Winterschlaf, hibernation.
Wirbelknochen, vertebra.
Wirbellose, invertebrata, invertebrates.
Wirbeltiere, vertebrata, vertebrates.
wirklich, actual, real.
Wirkung, action, effect.
Wirkungsgrad, efficiency.
Wirkungsvermögen, potency.
Wirtschaft, industry (2).
Wirtschaftspsychologie, industrial psychology.
Wissen, knowledge.
wissen *vs.* **kennen,** *see under* **comprehension.**
Wissenschaft, science.
Witz, wit.
Wohlanständigkeit, decorum.
Wohlsein, well-being.
Wollust, lust.

Wortsalat, verbigeration, *see also under* **word salad.**
Wortschwall, verbiage.
Worttaubheit, word-deafness.
Wunder, miracle, prodigy (1).
Wundmal, stigma (2).
Wundtsches Schallpendel, Wundt sound pendulum.
Wunsch, desire, wish.
Wünschelrute, divining rod.
Wurm, vermis.
Wurzel, root (2, 3).
würzig, spicy.
Wut, anger, rage.
Wutanfall, furor, tantrum.

Z

Zähigkeit, viscosity.
Zähmung, taming.
Zapfen, cone/retinal.
Zauberei, sorcery.
Zeichen, sign.
Zeichnung, drawing, design/pictorial.
Zeigefinger, index (4).
Zeigelust, exhibitionism.
Zeit, time.
Zeitanschauung, time perception.
Zeitfehler, time error.
Zeitlage, time order.
zeitlich, temporal
zeitliche Reihe, sequence (2).
Zeitlupe, slow motion (picture).
Zeitmesskunst, chronometry.
Zeitsinn, time sense.
Zeitvertreib, diversion (2).
Zeitwahrnehmung, time perception.
Zelle, cell.
Zensur, censorship.
Zentralfurche, Rolandic fissure fissure of Rolando.
Zentralwert, median.
Zentralwindung, central fissure.
zentrifugal, efferent.
zentripetal, afferent.
Zerbrechung, disruption.
Zerkauen, mastication.
Zerstörungswut, vandalism.
sich zerstreuen, relax.
Zerstreutheit, distraction (2).
Zerstreuung, dispersion.
Zerstreuungskreis, diffusion circle (2).
zeugen, witness*.
Zeugnis, testimony.
Zeugung, generation.
Ziel, aim, end (2), goal.
Zielvorstellung, *see* definition.
Zielvorstellung, end, purposive idea, *see also under* **Absicht.**
Zirbeldrüse, pineal body.
zirkuläres Irresein, alternating psychosis.
Zittern, trembling, tremor.
Zöllnersche Täuschung, Zöllner illusion.
Zone, zone.
Zorn, anger.
Zucht, discipline.
Zuckung, convulsion, twitching.
Zufall, chance, hazard.
zufällig, accidental, casual, incidental, random.
zulassen, suffer (2).
Zuneigung, liking.
Zunge, reed, tongue.
Zungenbein, hyoid bone.
Zurechnungsfähigkeit, competency, competence (2).
zurückhalten, restrain.
Zurückhaltung, reserve, restraint.
Zurückstrahlung, reflection (3).
Zurückweisung, rejection.
Zurückziehen, retraction.
zusammengesetzt, composite.
Zusammenhang, connection (2).
Zusammenklang, concord.
Zusammenwirken, synergy.
Zusammenziehung, contraction.
Zustand, level (2), state.
Zustimmung, assent, consent.
Zuverlässigkeit, reliability.
Zwang, compulsion, restraint.
Zwangsneurose, obsessional neurosis.
Zweck, purpose.
zweideutig, equivocal.
Zweifel, doubt.
zweifelhaft, problematic.
Zweiklang, *see under* **chord.**
Zweiteilung, dichotomy.
Zwerchfell, diaphragm.
Zwicken, twinge.
Zwilling, twin.
zwingen, constrain.
Zwischenhirn, diencephalon.
Zwischenraum, interval (2).
Zwischenton, intertone.
Zwischenzeit, interval (1).
Zwitterbildung, hermaphroditism.
Zwölffingerdarm, duodenum.
Zyklopenauge, cyclopean eye.
Zylinderlinse, cylindrical lens.